TEACHER'S EDITION OVERVIEW

AUTHORS

The contributing authors guided the direction and philosophy of *Prentice Hall Writing Coach*. Working with the development team, they helped to build the pedagogical integrity of the program and to ensure its relevance for today's teachers and students.

Program Authors

Jeff Anderson

Jeff Anderson has worked with struggling writers and readers for almost 20 years. His works integrate grammar and editing instruction into the processes of reading and writing. Anderson has written articles in NCTE's ***Voices from the Middle, English Journal***, and ***Educational Leadership.*** Anderson won the NCTE Paul and Kate Farmer Award for his ***English Journal*** article on teaching grammar in context. He has published two books, ***Mechanically Inclined: Building Grammar, Usage, and Style into Writer's Workshop*** and ***Everyday Editing: Inviting Students to Develop Skill and Craft in Writer's Workshop*** as well as a DVD, ***The Craft of Grammar.***

Grammar gives me a powerful lens through which to look at my writing. It gives me the freedom to say things exactly the way I want to say them.

Kelly Gallagher

Kelly Gallagher is a full-time English teacher at Magnolia High School in Anaheim, California. He is the former co-director of the South Basin Writing Project at California State University, Long Beach. Gallagher is the author of ***Reading Reasons: Motivational Mini-Lessons for the Middle and High School, Deeper Reading: Comprehending Challenging Texts 4–12, Teaching Adolescent Writers,*** and ***Readicide.*** He is also featured in the video series, ***Building Adolescent Readers.*** With a focus on adolescent literacy, Gallagher provides training to educators on a local, national and international level. Gallagher was awarded the Secondary Award of Classroom Excellence from the California Association of Teachers of English—the state's top English teacher honor.

The best swimmers swim the most; the best writers write the most. There's only one way to become a good writer: write!

Thanks to the wisdom and classroom experience of Jeff Anderson and Kelly Gallagher, *Writing Coach* is a program that is approachable for students and teachers.

Jeff Anderson's commitment to finding ways to make grammar instruction a positive experience for students was key in the development of *Writing Coach.* He authored instruction for *Mentor Texts*, the *What Do You Notice?* feature, the *Grammar Game Plan Find It/Fix It* guide to the 20 most common student errors, and the *Grammar Mini-Lessons.*

Kelly Gallagher's commitment to the need for daily practice in writing was key to the development of *Writing Coach.* Kelly authored instruction for *Mentor Texts*, the *Reader's Eye* and *Writer's Eye, Revision RADaR*, the *ABCDs of On-Demand Writing*, and *Coach's Corner.*

At www.phwritingcoach.com, videos featuring both Anderson and Gallagher provide you and your students with powerful strategies for revising and editing.

Contributing Authors

Evelyn Arroyo

Evelyn Arroyo is the author of **A+RISE,** Research-based Instructional Strategies for ELLs (English Language Learners). Her work focuses on closing the achievement gap for minority students and English language learners. Through her publications and presentations, Arroyo provides advice, encouragement, and practical success strategies to help teachers reach their ELL students.

Your rich, colorful cultural life experiences are unique and can easily be painted through words. These experiences define who you are today, and writing is one way to begin capturing your history. Become a risk-taker and fall in love with yourself through your own words.

When you're learning a new language, writing in that language takes effort. The effort pays off big time, though. Writing helps us generate ideas, solve problems, figure out how the language works, and, above all, allows us to express ourselves.

Jim Cummins, Ph.D.

Jim Cummins is a Professor in the Modern Language Centre at the University of Toronto. A well-known educator, lecturer, and author, Cummins focuses his research on bilingual education and the academic achievement of culturally diverse students. He is the author of numerous publications, including ***Negotiating Identities: Education for Empowerment in a Diverse Society.***

Grant Wiggins, Ed.D.

Grant Wiggins is the President of Authentic Education. He earned his Ed.D. from Harvard University. Grant consults with schools, districts, and state education departments; organizes conferences and workshops; and develops resources on curricular change. He is the co-author, with Jay McTighe, of ***Understanding By Design,*** the award-winning text published by ASCD.

I hated writing as a student—and my grades showed it. I grew up to be a writer, though. What changed? I began to think I had something to say. That's ultimately why you write: to find out what you are really thinking, really feeling, really believing.

Concepts of grammar can sharpen your reading, communication, and even your reasoning, so I have championed its practice in my classes and in my businesses. Even adults are quick to recognize that a refresher in grammar makes them keener—and more marketable.

Gary Forlini

Gary Forlini is managing partner of the School Growth initiative ***Brinkman—Forlini—Williams,*** which trains school administrators and teachers in Classroom Instruction and Management. His recent works include the book ***Help Teachers Engage Students*** and the data system ***ObserverTab*** for district administrators, ***Class Acts: Every Teacher's Guide To Activate Learning***, and the initiative's workshop ***Grammar for Teachers***.

A well-rounded team of authors means a strong, cohesive program.

Evelyn Arroyo works to ensure that students at all levels find instructional materials accessible. She contributed strategies for reaching English Language Learners.

Jim Cummins is committed to empowering culturally diverse learners. He authored strategies for teaching English Language Learners and reaching students from all cultures.

Grant Wiggins champions instruction focused on essential and thought-provoking ideas that ensure knowledge transfer and application. He authored the Big Questions for each chapter, including the *Why write?* strand, which addresses essential ideas about writing.

Gary Forlini, a nationally known education consultant, is a grammar expert. He was a key contributor to the grammar scope, sequence, and pedagogy presented in Prentice Hall *Writing Coach.*

Print and Online Components

***Writing Coach* offers a full writing and grammar program in formats that fit your teaching style, whether you choose print, digital, or a combination of both. All print materials are available online as eTexts. The centerpiece of the online program is the Interactive Writing Coach™ which provides personalized writing support and feedback for students at all ability levels.**

Student Edition

- In-depth 5-stage writing process lessons
- Professional Mentor Texts and Student Models
- 21st Century Skills and writing for multimedia
- Comprehensive grammar, usage, and mechanics instruction and practice
- Test prep review and practice

Teacher's Edition

- Annotated lessons for writing and grammar
- Flexible lesson planning and pacing
- Differentiated instruction for students at all levels
- Support for integration of writing and grammar into the language arts curriculum

www.phwritingcoach.com

For the Student

- Student Edition eText
- Video Library
- Graphic Organizers
- Grammar Tutorials
- Spanish Resources
- Sentence Diagraming

WRITING

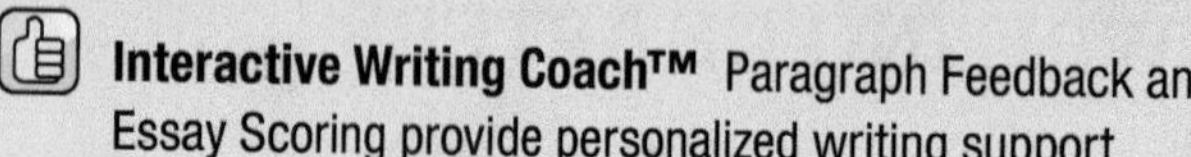

Interactive Writing Coach™ Paragraph Feedback and Essay Scoring provide personalized writing support.

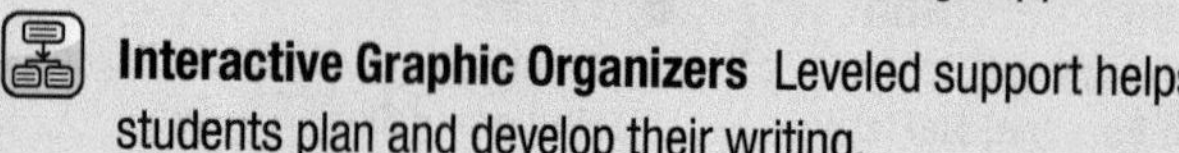

Interactive Graphic Organizers Leveled support helps students plan and develop their writing.

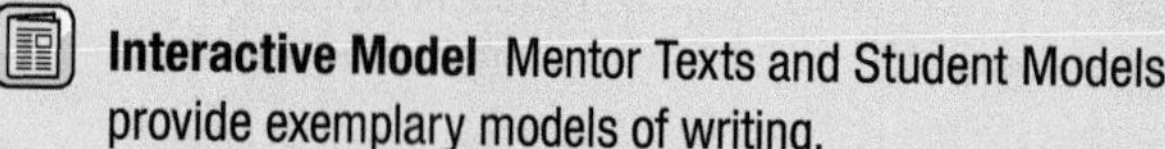

Interactive Model Mentor Texts and Student Models provide exemplary models of writing.

Interactive Online Journal Students record and save all their assignments and writing.

Resources Links to online resources help students research and plan multimedia projects.

Videos Program authors provide point-of-use revising and editing tips.

GRAMMAR

Diagnostic and Practice Diagnostic tests assess skills and automatically assign instruction and practice.

Grammar Tutorials Point-of-use videos reinforce key grammar skills.

ExamView Assessment Suite (diagnostic and assessment) Electronic test generator allows teachers to customize assessment.

Tabula Digitā: DimensionL
www.pearsonschool.com/dimensionL Students hone their grammar skills with this fast-paced, multiplayer video game.

For the Teacher

- Student Edition eText
- Teacher Edition eText
- Lesson Planner
- Video Library
- Graphic Organizers
- Grammar Tutorials
- Sentence Diagraming

CONTENTS IN BRIEF

WRITING

The ***Writing Game Plan*** sets the stage for students to get into the "game" of writing.

WRITING GAME PLAN

Writing without grammar only goes so far. Grammar and writing work together. To write well, grammar skills give me great tools.

The ***Core Writing Chapters*** provide opportunities for using the writing process while focusing on specific genres in featured assignments.

CORE WRITING CHAPTERS

Interactive Writing Coach™

Interactive Graphic Organizer

Interactive Model

Online Journal

Resources

Video

vi

Writing Coach Online provides tools and resources for personalizing instruction. Students and teachers know what to use, and when, via these six easily recognizable icons found throughout the program.

GRAMMAR

GRAMMAR GAME PLAN

Major Grammatical Errors and How to Fix Them

Grammar without writing is only a collection of rules, but when these rules are put into action as I write, the puzzle comes together.

The ***Grammar Game Plan*** focuses on the 20 most common grammatical errors.

CORE GRAMMAR CHAPTERS

Core Grammar Chapters provide in-depth instruction in grammar, usage, and mechanics.

- Grammar Tutorials
- Grammar Practice
- Grammar Games

vii

Students can easily access ***Writing Coach Online*** support as they apply and practice their grammar skills.

The why's, what's, and how's of writing get students comfortable with the idea that "there's a writer in all of us."

An introduction to the various types of writing helps set the stage for the chapters to come, each of which focuses on a particular genre.

CONTENTS

WRITING

WRITING GAME PLAN

CHAPTER 1 You, The Writer 2

CHAPTER 2 Types of Writing 8

An overview of the five-stage **Writing Process** provides the foundation for the core writing chapters.

An overview of the basics of writing sentences and paragraphs also provides an introduction to the ***Interactive Writing Coach*** and how it is integrated into the program.

All content available online

- Interactive Writing Coach™
- Interactive Graphic Organizer
- Interactive Models
- Online Journal
- Resources
- Video

Each writing chapter focuses on a ***Feature Assignment***—a particular form within the genre.

The ***Connect to the Big Questions*** feature encourages students to make connections among ideas and to apply their thoughts to their understanding of writing.

WRITING

Connect to the Big Questions

- **What do you think?**
  What do our accomplishments say about us?
- **Why write?**
  What should we put in and leave out to be accurate and honest?

CHAPTER 6 Fiction Narration 90

Instruction in the five key stages of the **writing process** provides a predictable routine for students' writing. Steps are color-coded for ease of use.

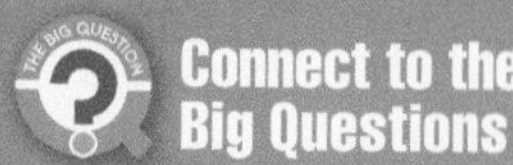

- **What do you think?**
  How do challenges help us grow?
- **Why write?**
  What can fiction do better than nonfiction?

All content available online

- Interactive Writing Coach™
- Interactive Graphic Organizer
- Interactive Models
- Online Journal
- Resources
- Video

Writing Coach Online offers a full digital program that stands alone or supports the print-based approach.

The ***Interactive Writing Coach™*** provides personalized feedback and support to students as they write.

WRITING

Connect to the Big Questions

- **What do you think?** When is a picture better than words?
- **Why write?** How does one best convey feelings through words on a page?

Make Your Writing Count assignments provide opportunities to write with 21st Century learning in mind. Rubrics help you assess students' learning.

CHAPTER 8 Exposition 144

Mentor Texts provide exemplary professional models for writing.

Student Models show students writing done by peers.

Writing for Media assignments provide opportunities for short writing assignments that use 21st Century Skills.

Revision RADaR techniques in ***Revising*** provide students with a simple, effective way to improve their drafts.

Connect to the Big Questions

- **What do you think?** Is newer always better?
- **Why write?** What should we tell and what should we describe to make information clear?

WRITING COACH Online
www.phwritingcoach.com

All content available online

- Interactive Writing Coach™
- Interactive Graphic Organizer
- Interactive Models
- Online Journal
- Resources
- Video

WRITING

CHAPTER 9 Persuasion 170

Connect to the Big Questions

- **What do you think?**
  Which do you think is more important and why—the community's right to ensure that students are not distracted by cell phones or the individual student's right to use a cell phone?
- **Why write?**
  What is your point of view? How will you know if you've convinced others?

CHAPTER 10 Response to Literature 196

Connect to the Big Questions

- **What do you think?**
  What do readers bring to a text that writers may not?
- **Why write?**
  What should you write about to make others interested in a text?

WRITING COACH Online
www.phwritingcoach.com

All content available online

- Interactive Writing Coach™
- Interactive Graphic Organizer
- Interactive Models
- Online Journal
- Resources
- Video

Grammar Mini-Lessons and ***What Do You Notice?*** features let you integrate grammar instruction into writing.

Rubrics in ***Editing*** provide tailored criteria for the featured assignment.

Research Writing includes in-depth coverage of the special processes required to gather, analyze, and synthesize information from a variety of sources.

WRITING

CHAPTER 11 Research Writing 222

Connect to the Big Questions

- **What do you think?**
  What kinds of scientific discoveries affect our lives the most?
- **Why write?**
  Do you understand your subject well enough to write about it? How will you find out what all the facts are?

CHAPTER 12 Workplace Writing 256

Workplace Writing includes non-academic forms that students will need to succeed in their lives and careers.

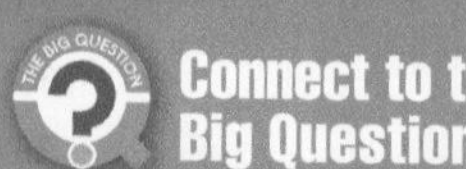

- **What do you think?**
  What is the best way to share information?
- **Why write?**
  What do daily workplace communications require of format, content, and style?

All content available online

- Interactive Writing Coach™
- Interactive Graphic Organizer
- Interactive Models
- Online Journal
- Resources
- Video

ABCDs of On-Demand Writing in ***Writing for Assessment*** offer a helpful memory aid to success with timed writing assignments.

The **_Grammar Game Plan_** guides students to find and fix the 20 most common grammatical errors as they revise and edit.

GRAMMAR GAME PLAN

Find It/Fix It The 20 Errors

GRAMMAR

Chapters focus on specific and manageable topics in grammar, usage and mechanics.

CHAPTER 15 Adjectives and Adverbs 325

CHAPTER 16 Prepositions 345

What Do You Notice? features introduce students to an element of grammar in a real-life context.

All content available online

- Grammar Tutorials
- Grammar Practice
- Grammar Games

Comprehensive instruction and practice activities along with speaking and writing applications ensure mastery of grammar concepts.

GRAMMAR

CHAPTER 17 Conjunctions and Interjections 355

CHAPTER 18 Basic Sentence Parts 367

CHAPTER 19 Phrases and Clauses 397

CHAPTER 20 Effective Sentences 431

All content available online

- Grammar Tutorials
- Grammar Practice
- Grammar Games

Test Warm-Ups give students practice in the format of the Revising and Editing portion of the English Language Arts exam.

GRAMMAR

USAGE

A ***Cumulative Review*** ends each major section of the grammar materials—grammar, usage, and mechanics. Use it to assess your students' progress and tailor remediation.

MECHANICS

All content available online
- Grammar Tutorials
- Grammar Practice
- Grammar Games

Additional grammar instruction and practice in ***Writing Coach Online*** engages students and personalizes instruction.

WRITING COACH
Online
www.phwritingcoach.com
All content available online
• Grammar Tutorials
• Grammar Practice
• Grammar Games

GRAMMAR

Student Resources include important information on writing for media and the workplace, graphic organizers, glossaries—and more!

STUDENT RESOURCES

TEACHING WITH *Writing Coach*

PRENTICE HALL WRITING COACH

1 How Do I Differentiate Instruction?

Prentice Hall *Writing Coach* offers many opportunities for differentiated instruction.

Student Edition

Use **Student Edition** features like **Word Bank** and **Partner Talk** to reach struggling students. **Extension** opportunities in **Mentor Texts** and **Writing for Media** help you meet the needs of advanced students.

Teacher's Edition

Differentiated Instruction features in the **Teacher's Edition** include strategies for providing targeted instruction and enrichment to reach all students.

Differentiated Instruction

Differentiated Instruction Boxes in this Teacher's Edition address these student populations:

- **Below-Level Students**
- **Above-Level Students**
- **Gifted and Talented Students**
- **Special Needs Students**
- **English Language Learners**
- **Spanish Speaking Students**

In addition, for further enrichment, see the Extension features.

Writing Coach Online

WRITING COACH
Online
www.phwritingcoach.com
Interactive Writing Coach™
Interactive Graphic Organizers
Grammar Instruction

Interactive Writing Coach™: Use Paragraph Feedback and Essay Scorer to provide personalized and targeted support and feedback to individual students.

Interactive Graphic Organizers: Scaffolded graphic organizers help tailor the prewriting experience to your students' ability levels.

Grammar Instruction: Based on the results of online diagnostics, students are automatically assigned targeted instruction and practice.

2 How Do I Meet the Individual Needs of ELL Students?

Prentice Hall *Writing Coach* provides the tools and strategies you need to support and challenge English Language Learners in your classroom.

Student Edition

Scaffolded opportunities for language production and reception appear throughout the **Student Edition**. To facilitate language production, use these features: ▶

- **Word Bank**
- **Listening and Speaking**
- **Partner Talk**
- **Speaking Application**

Teacher's Edition

The **Working with ELLs** notes offer strategies tailored for four proficiency levels. Centering on a common skill and topic, the notes make it easy to adapt and differentiate instruction across levels, however diverse your class. At the same time, each note is built around a single core concept, skill, text, or topic, allowing students to share in common learning experiences and helping you build coherent, efficient differentiated lessons.

Working with ELLs ELL Sheltered Instruction: Cognitive

Have students listen to, derive meaning from, and respond orally to information presented in a wide variety of print, electronic, and audiovisual media to build and reinforce language attainment. Find a recording of a rhyming poem or make one yourself of the poem on page 123.

Beginning Play the recording, providing support by acting out ideas. Build and reinforce language attainment by having students respond orally to simple questions, such as: *Which words rhyme?*

Intermediate Play the recording, helping students understand the imagery. Have them respond orally, discussing the poem's topic and images. Have them build language attainment by orally completing sentence frames, like: *The poem has rhyming words like* ________.

Advanced Play the recording and discuss the topic of the poem. To build language attainment, have partners define unfamiliar words and compare lists with another pair.

Advanced High Have partners complete the Advanced activity, then have students orally respond to the *Try It!* questions on page 123.

3 How Can I Reach Spanish-Speaking Students?

To help Spanish-speaking students, use program resources that provide teaching suggestions.

Teacher's Edition

To help Spanish speakers master key ideas in writing and grammar, use differentiated instruction notes that provide targeted support for language transfer issues.

For an overview of the language transfer issues that Spanish speakers may encounter, see the section on Spanish speakers in this frontmatter (pp. W 34–W 35), which includes a linguistic contrastive analysis chart to help you target pronunciation practice.

Differentiated Instruction

RTI **Strategy for Special Needs Students** Remind students that ballads are usually meant to be sung. Play recordings of musical ballads for students. Have them listen carefully and then summarize the story one ballad tells and identify the words in the refrain. Help students identify the use of figurative language and sound devices in the ballad. Then, encourage students who choose to write a ballad to create or borrow a tune to which it could be sung.

Strategy for Spanish Speakers Students whose home language is Spanish may encounter difficulties using assonance due to the phonetic spelling of vowel sounds in Spanish. Remind students that vowel sounds may have multiple spellings in English. Review spellings of different vowel sounds. For example, elicit spellings for the long ē sound such as *e, ea, ee,* and *y.* Then have students give examples for each, such as *even, speak, tree*, and *icy*.

4 What Digital Resources Can Help Me Personalize Instruction?

Prentice Hall *Writing Coach* has an online program—*Writing Coach Online*—that is integrally linked to the print text. References to *Writing Coach Online* appear throughout the Student Edition.

Writing Coach Online

The key component of *Writing Coach Online* is **Interactive Writing Coach™**, which functions like a personal writing tutor for students, giving them personalized feedback on their work. It not only helps you with grading papers but also gives you information to tailor instruction and assignments for your students individually. The **Interactive Writing Coach™** has two parts:

Paragraph Feedback Only Prentice Hall *Writing Coach* provides this tool, which analyzes student work at the paragraph level. It assesses the ideas and topic support for work submitted one paragraph at a time.

Essay Scorer Essay Scorer gives specific feedback on the traits of writing in a composition. It also features model essays at each score point to show students examples of how to improve their writing. Suggestions are focused on these traits of good writing:

- Ideas
- Organization
- Voice
- Conventions
- Word Choice
- Sentence Fluency

www.phwritingcoach.com

WRITING	GRAMMAR
 **Interactive Graphic Organizers** Leveled support helps students plan and develop their writing.  **Interactive Model** Audio recordings let students listen to **Mentor Texts** and **Student Models** at their own pace.  **Interactive Online Journal** Point-of-use format lets students record responses, ideas, and drafts.  **Resources** A variety of resources provide tools including support for 21st Century learning and an audio glossary in English and Spanish.  **Video** Program authors Jeff Anderson and Kelly Gallagher teach strategies for effective writing.	• **Grammar Diagnostic** Online diagnostics automatically assign targeted instruction and practice. • **Grammar Tutorials** For reinforcement, motivation, or engagement, animated videos teach key grammar concepts. • **Grammar Practice** Additional grammar activities help students develop mastery. • **DimensionL** Fast-paced interactive video games test grammar skills.

5 How Do I Monitor Student Progress?

Prentice Hall *Writing Coach* makes progress monitoring easy with frequent opportunities to evaluate student progress and to reteach material.

Monitoring Writing Progress

To provide support for writing and to monitor students' progress, use:

- **Interactive Writing Coach™**, including Paragraph Feedback and Essay Scorer
- Rubrics in the **Student Edition**
- Teacher feedback and conferencing notes in the **Teacher's Edition**

Personalized Assessment

	Ongoing Assessment	Formal Assessment of Feature Assignment	Progress Monitoring at End-of-Chapter
Interactive Writing Coach™	Use Paragraph Feedback and Essay Scorer as a revision tool.	Use Essay Scorer to score students' Feature Assignment papers.	Use Essay Scorer to score students' papers. Students' learner profiles can be adjusted based on their scores.
FEEDBACK Teacher Conferencing	Use rubrics in the Student Edition as a revision tool. Conference with students to review their work and provide personalized support.	Use rubrics in the Student Edition to score students' Feature Assignment papers.	Review each student's work to plan targeted resources for the next writing assignment.

Monitoring Grammar Progress

***Writing Coach* provides a number of resources to monitor student progress in grammar, including diagnostic tests, end-of-chapter tests, and Cumulative Reviews.**

Grammar Assessment

Grammar Coach:	Diagnostic Assessment	End-of-Chapter Assessment	Progress Monitoring
Personalized Instruction	Students take grammar diagnostic test online and are automatically assigned instruction and practice in areas where they need support.	Teacher uses **ExamView** to administer end-of-chapter assessment and remediation. Teachers may customize **ExamView** tests or use the ones provided.	Teachers may use the **Test Warm-Ups** and the **Cumulative Reviews** in the student book or eText to check students' mastery of grammar skills. Students may also play **DimensionL** grammar video games to test their grammar skills.
Teacher-Directed Instruction	Teacher administers the diagnostic test and determines focus of instruction and practice.		

Preparing Students for Tests

To help get your students ready for high-stakes tests, use these built-in test-prep features:

- **Writing for Assessment** in the writing section
- **Test Warm-Up** in the grammar section

6 How Does the Program Address 21st Century Learning Skills?

Prentice Hall *Writing Coach* fosters 21st Century Learning skills. Activities in several features are flexible enough to meet any technology capabilities—they can be completed with or without technology.

Make Your Writing Count

Assign your students these real-world activities that have impact beyond the classroom. Projects include multimedia presentations, debates, movie trailers, and news broadcasts. Features let you:

- Extend the mode of writing.
- Provide practice in collaboration, communication, planning, and presenting.

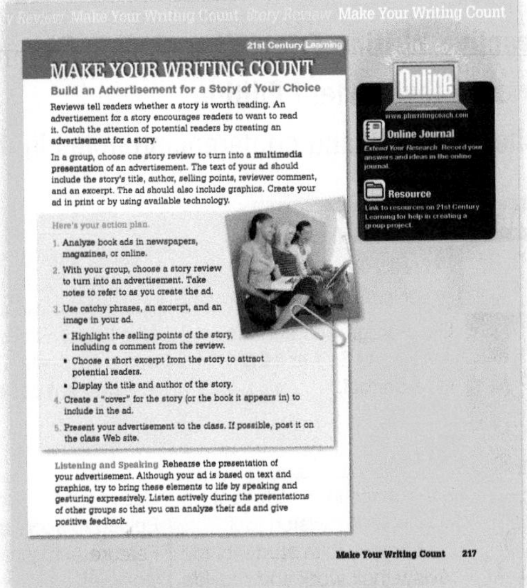

Make Your Writing Count

21st Century Learning

MAKE YOUR WRITING COUNT

Build an Advertisement for a Story of Your Choice

Reviews tell readers whether a story is worth reading. An advertisement for a story encourages readers to want to read it. Catch the attention of potential readers by creating an **advertisement for a story.**

In a group, choose one story review to turn into a **multimedia presentation** of an advertisement. The text of your ad should include the story's title, author, selling points, reviewer comment, and an excerpt. The ad should also include graphics. Create your ad in print or by using available technology.

Here's your action plan.

1. **Analyze** book ads in newspapers, magazines, or online.
2. With your group, choose a story review to turn into an advertisement. Take notes to refer to as you create the ad.
3. Use catchy phrases, an excerpt, and an image in your ad.
   - Highlight the selling points of the story, including a comment from the review.
   - Choose a short excerpt from the story to attract potential readers.
   - Display the title and author of the story.
4. Create a "cover" for the story (or the book it appears in) to include in the ad.
5. Present your advertisement to the class. If possible, post it on the class Web site.

Listening and Speaking Rehearse the presentation of your advertisement. Although your ad is based on text and graphics, try to bring these elements to life by speaking and gesturing expressively. Listen actively during the presentations of other groups so that you can analyze their ads and give positive feedback.

Online
www.phwritingcoach.com
Online Journal
Extend Your Research Record your answers and ideas in the online journal.
Resource
Link to resources on 21st Century Learning for help in creating a group project.

Make Your Writing Count 217

Writing for Media

Expose your students to new forms of content delivery. These individual short writing assignments incorporate non-print media and technology. Projects include webpages, scripts, consumer reports, and travel blogs. Features let you:

- Explore mentor examples.
- Reinforce writing process stages.

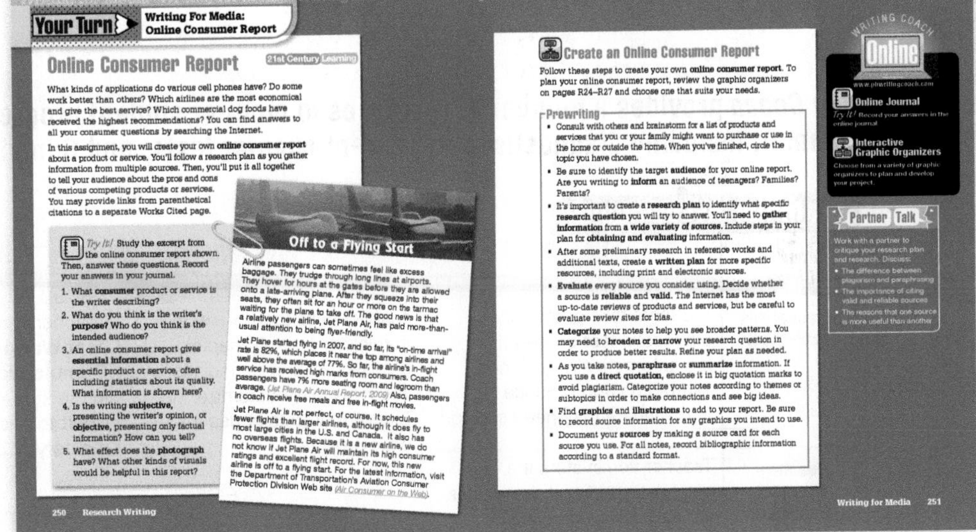

Your Turn **Writing For Media: Online Consumer Report**

Online Consumer Report

21st Century Learning

What kinds of applications do various cell phones have? Do some work better than others? Which airlines are the most economical and give the best service? Which commercial dog foods have received the highest recommendations? You can find answers to all your consumer questions by searching the Internet.

In this assignment, you will create your own **online consumer report** about a product or service. You'll follow a research plan as you gather information from multiple sources. Then, you'll put it all together to tell your audience about the pros and cons of various competing products or services. You may provide links from parenthetical citations to a separate Works Cited page.

Try It! Study the excerpt from the online consumer report shown. Then, answer these questions. Record your answers in your journal.

1. What **consumer** product or service is the writer describing?
2. What do you think is the writer's **purpose?** Who do you think is the intended audience?
3. An online consumer report gives **essential information** about a specific product or service, often including statistics about its quality. What information is shown here?
4. Is the writing **subjective,** presenting the writer's opinion, or **objective,** presenting only factual information? How can you tell?
5. What effect does the **photograph** have? What other kinds of visuals would be helpful in this report?

Off to a Flying Start

Airline passengers can sometimes feel like excess baggage. They trudge through long lines at airports. They hover for hours at the gates before they are allowed onto a late-arriving plane. After they squeeze into their seats, they often sit for an hour or more on the tarmac waiting for the plane to take off. The good news is that a relatively new airline, Jet Plane Air, has paid more-than-usual attention to being flyer-friendly.

Jet Plane started flying in 2007, and so far, its "on-time arrival" rate is 82%, which places it near the top among airlines and well above the average of 77%. So far, the airline's in-flight service has received high marks from consumers. Coach passengers have 7% more seating room and legroom than average. (Jet Plane Air Annual Report, 2009) Also, passengers in coach receive free meals and free in-flight movies.

Jet Plane Air is not perfect, of course. It schedules fewer flights than larger airlines, although it does fly to most large cities in the U.S. and Canada. It also has no overseas flights. Because it is a new airline, we do not know if Jet Plane Air will maintain its high consumer ratings and excellent flight record. For now, this new airline is off to a flying start. For the latest information, visit the Department of Transportation's Aviation Consumer Protection Division Web site (Air Consumer on the Web).

250 Research Writing

Writing for Media

Create an Online Consumer Report

Follow these steps to create your own **online consumer report.** To plan your online consumer report, review the graphic organizers on pages R24–R27 and choose one that suits your needs.

Prewriting

- Consult with others and brainstorm for a list of products and services that you or your family might want to purchase or use in the home or outside the home. When you've finished, circle the topic you have chosen.
- Be sure to identify the target **audience** for your online report. Are you writing to **inform** an audience of teenagers? Families? Parents?
- It's important to create a **research plan** to identify what specific **research question** you will try to answer. You'll need to **gather information** from **a wide variety of sources.** Include steps in your plan for **obtaining and evaluating** information.
- After some preliminary research in reference works and additional texts, create a **written plan** for more specific resources, including print and electronic sources.
- **Evaluate** every source you consider using. Decide whether a source is **reliable** and **valid.** The Internet has the most up-to-date reviews of products and services, but be careful to evaluate review sites for bias.
- **Categorize** your notes to help you see broader patterns. You may need to **broaden or narrow** your research question in order to produce better results. Refine your plan as needed.
- As you take notes, **paraphrase** or **summarize** information. If you use a **direct quotation,** enclose it in big quotation marks to avoid plagiarism. Categorize your notes according to themes or subtopics in order to make connections and see big ideas.
- Find **graphics** and **illustrations** to add to your report. Be sure to record source information for any graphics you intend to use.
- Document your **sources** by making a source card for each source you use. For all notes, record bibliographic information according to a standard format.

Writing Coach Online
www.phwritingcoach.com
Online Journal
Try It! Record your answers in the online journal.
Interactive Graphic Organizers
Choose from a variety of graphic organizers to plan and develop your project.

Partner Talk
Work with a partner to critique your research plan and research. Discuss:
- The difference between plagiarism and paraphrasing
- The importance of citing valid and reliable sources
- The reasons that one source is more useful than another

Writing for Media 251

Rubrics for 21st Century Skills

Teachers Edition support includes rubrics to help you evaluate students' performance against 21st Century Learning criteria.

21st Century Learning

Skills Rubric	Rating
Analyze Media: Look at how media can influence beliefs and behaviors.	1 2 3
Create Media Products: Use the most appropriate expressions in diverse environments.	1 2 3
Think Creatively: Elaborate, refine, analyze, and evaluate ideas in order to improve and maximize creative efforts.	1 2 3
Work Creatively With Others: Be original and inventive and understand limits to idea adoption.	1 2 3

7 How Does the Program Help Me Develop as a Teacher?

The Teacher's Edition of Prentice Hall *Writing Coach* provides built-in professional development features.

Step-by-Step Teaching Guidance

Margin notes provide strategies, tips, and examples for teaching skills. Instructional support includes special features such as:

- **Think Aloud** Specific, scripted guidance for you to walk students through content and activate their metacognitive and critical thinking skills
- **Teacher Tip** Point-of-use notes to help you focus on a particular aspect of a lesson or extend the lesson
- **Personalized Support: Teacher or Peer Feedback** Targeted suggestions and specific questions to use in Teacher or Peer Conferencing on students' writing assignments
- **Personalized Support: Interactive Writing Coach™** Guidance for using **Interactive Writing Coach™** with all levels of students
- **Coach's Corner** Suggestions to help you model the writing process alongside your students

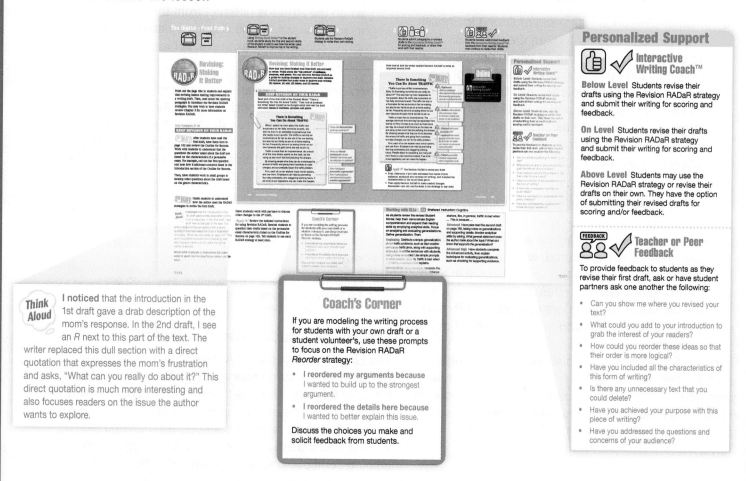

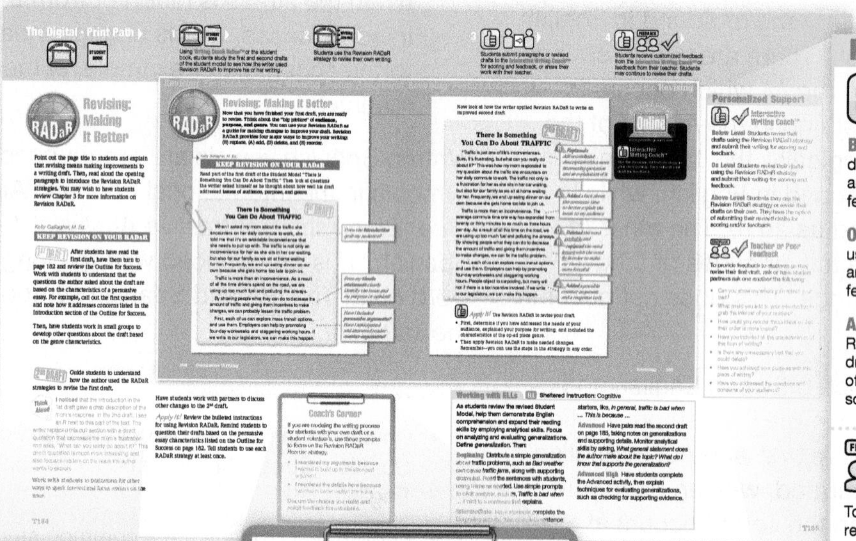

Think Aloud

I noticed that the introduction in the 1st draft gave a drab description of the mom's response. In the 2nd draft, I see an *R* next to this part of the text. The writer replaced this dull section with a direct quotation that expresses the mom's frustration and asks, "What can you really do about it?" This direct quotation is much more interesting and also focuses readers on the issue the author wants to explore.

Coach's Corner

If you are modeling the writing process for students with your own draft or a student volunteer's, use these prompts to focus on the Revision RADaR *Reorder* strategy:

- **I reordered my arguments because** I wanted to build up to the strongest argument.
- **I reordered the details here because** I wanted to better explain this issue.

Discuss the choices you make and solicit feedback from students.

Personalized Support

Interactive Writing Coach™

Below Level Students revise their drafts using the Revision RADaR strategy and submit their writing for scoring and feedback.

On Level Students revise their drafts using the Revision RADaR strategy and submit their writing for scoring and feedback.

Above Level Students may use the Revision RADaR strategy or revise their drafts on their own. They have the option of submitting their revised drafts for scoring and/or feedback.

Teacher or Peer Feedback

To provide feedback to students as they revise their first draft, ask or have student partners ask one another the following:

- Can you show me where you revised your text?
- What could you add to your introduction to grab the interest of your readers?
- How could you reorder these ideas so that their order is more logical?
- Have you included all the characteristics of this form of writing?
- Is there any unnecessary text that you could delete?
- Have you achieved your purpose with this piece of writing?
- Have you addressed the questions and concerns of your audience?

In-Depth Professional Development

Online support including Professional Development from our authors helps you learn more about teaching writing and grammar.

Spanish Speakers

Reaching Spanish Speakers with *Writing Coach*

Spanish is the second most widely spoken language in the world. There are more than 400 million native Spanish speakers in more than 20 countries on three continents. Spanish vocabulary and pronunciation differ from country to country. While most dialect differences in English are in vowel sounds, Spanish dialects differ in their consonants.

Spoken Language

Spanish sounds are similar to those found in English, so there is a strong foundation for the native Spanish speaker learning English. However, there are three key differences between English and Spanish consonants:

1. Most of the alveolar sounds in English, such as /t/, /d/, and /n/, are produced farther forward in the mouth in Spanish. Instead of the tongue touching the alveolar ridge as in English, in Spanish it touches the back of the teeth.
2. Another difference is that the /r/ sound in English is not found in Spanish. There are two /r/ sounds in Spanish. One is the tap /r/, which occurs in English as the quick sound in the middle of the name *Betty.* Psychologically, this tap sound is a kind of /t/ or /d/ sound in English, while in Spanish it is perceived as an /r/. The other /r/ sound in Spanish is a trill, or series of tongue taps on the alveolar ridge. This does not occur in English.
3. The third key difference between English and Spanish can be found in the English production of the voiceless stops /p/, /t/, and /k/. In English these sounds are aspirated, with an extra puff of air at the end, when the sound occurs at the beginning of a word or stressed syllable. So, /p/ is aspirated in *pit.* Learners can add a puff of air to such sounds to sound more like native English speakers.

There are five vowels in Spanish, which are a subset of the English vowels. Spanish vowels include tense vowel sounds /a/, /e/, /i/, /o/, and /u/. Lax vowel sounds in English are the problematic ones for native Spanish speakers.

Culture Clues

The Spanish language covers many countries, dialects, and cultures. Always encourage students to share special things about their culture, such as foods, festivals, or social customs.

Written Language

Like English, written Spanish uses the Roman alphabet, so both writing systems are similar. There are a few orthographic differences to note, however:

- The letter *h* in Spanish is silent, but the sound /h/ is written as *j* or *g*.
- A single letter *r* in Spanish represents a tap, while the double *rr* represents a trill.
- Accents are used to show the stress on a syllable when the stress is different from the usual rules. In some cases, words change meaning according to the accents. For example, *el* means *the* while *él* means *he*.

Written Spanish vowels are pronounced like the symbols in the International Phonetic Alphabet (IPA). (*See "Linguistic Contrastive Analysis" below.*) So, the Spanish "i" is pronounced with the long $\bar{e}$ as in the word *beat.* The IPA and Spanish symbol for this letter is the same: /i/.

Grammar Hot Spots

- Double negatives are part of standard grammar in Spanish. Stress the single negative construction in English.
- English prepositions are a common stumbling point for Spanish speakers.

Linguistic Contrastive Analysis

The Linguistic Contrastive Analysis Chart provides a quick reference for comparing English sounds with those of Spanish. The chart allows you to check which English sounds have equivalents in Spanish. For those sounds that don't have equivalents, you can find the closest sound used as a substitute and suggestions for helping someone gain a native English articulation.

In these charts, the sounds are notated using the International Phonetic Alphabet (IPA), most widely used standard for representing speech sounds in any language. Each sound is represented by one symbol, and each symbol represents only one sound.

Linguistic Contrastive Analysis Chart

THE CONSONANTS OF ENGLISH				
IPA	**English**		**Spanish**	
p	*pit*	Aspirated at the start of a word or stressed syllable	*pato* (duck)	Never aspirated
b	*bit*		*barco* (boat)	Substitute voiced bilabial fricative/ɞ/ in between vowels
m	*man*		*mundo* (world)	
w	*win*		*agua* (water)	
f	*fun*		*flor* (flower)	
v	*very*		**NO EQUIVALENT**	Learners can use correct sound.
θ	*thing*	The tongue should stick out between the teeth.	**NO EQUIVALENT**	Learners can use correct sound.
ð	*there*	When done correctly, the tongue will stick out between the teeth.	*cada* (every)	Sound exists in Spanish only between vowels; sometimes substitute voiceless /θ/.
t	*time*	English tongue-touch is a little farther back in the mouth than in other languages.	*tocar* (touch)	Never aspirated
d	*dime*	English tongue-touch is a little farther back in the mouth than in other languages.	*dos* (two)	
n	*name*	English tongue-touch is a little farther back in the mouth than in other languages.	*nube* (cloud)	
s	*soy*		*seco* (dry)	
z	*zeal*		**NO EQUIVALENT**	Learners can use correct sound.
ɾ	*butter*	Written 't' and 'd' are pronounced with a quick tongue-tip tap.	*rana* (toad)	Written as single *r* and thought of as an /r/ sound.
l	*loop*	At the ends of syllables, the /l/ bunches up the back of the tongue, becoming velarized /ɫ/ or dark-l as in the word *ball.*	*libro* (book)	
ɹ	*red*	Rare sound in world languages. Includes lip-rounding.	**NO EQUIVALENT**	Substitute /r/ sound such as the tap /ɾ/ or the trilled /r/
ʃ	*shallow*	Often said with lip-rounding	**NO EQUIVALENT**	Substitute /s/ or /ʧ/
ʒ	*vision*	Rare sound in English	**NO EQUIVALENT**	Substitute /z/ or /ʤ/
ʧ	*chirp*		*chico* (boy)	
ʤ	*joy*		**NO EQUIVALENT**	Sometimes substituted with /ʃ/ sound. Some dialects have this sound for the *ll* spelling, as in *llamar.*
j	*you*		*cielo* (sky)	Often substitute /ʤ/
k	*kite*	Aspirated at the start of a word or stressed syllable	*casa* (house)	Never aspirated
g	*goat*		*gato* (cat)	
ŋ	*king*		*mango* (mango)	
h	*hope*		*gente* (people)	Sometimes substitute sound with friction higher in the vocal tract as velar /x/ or uvular /χ/

THE VOWELS OF ENGLISH				
IPA	**English**		**Spanish**	
i	*beat*		*hijo* (son)	
ɪ	*bit*	Usually confused with /i/ (*meat* vs. *mit*)	**NO EQUIVALENT**	Substitute /i/
e	*bait*	End of vowel diphthongized—tongue moves up to /i/ or /ɪ/ position	*eco* (echo)	
ɛ	*bet*	Learners may have difficulty distinguishing /e/ and /ɛ/: pain vs. pen.	**NO EQUIVALENT**	Substitute /e/
æ	*bat*	Learners may have trouble getting the tongue farther forward in the mouth.	**NO EQUIVALENT**	Substitute mid central /ʌ/ or low front tense /a/
u	*boot*		*uva* (grape)	
ʊ	*could*	Learners may have difficulty distinguishing /u/ and /ʊ/; *wooed* vs. *wood.*	**NO EQUIVALENT**	Substitute /ù/
o	*boat*	End of vowel diphthongized – tongue moves up to /u/ or /ʊ/ position	*ojo* (eye)	
ɔ	*law*		**NO EQUIVALENT**	Substitute /o/ or /ɑ/. Substituting /o/ will cause confusion (*low* vs. *law*); substituting /ɑ/ will not.
ɑ	*hot*		*mal* (bad)	
ɑ ʊ	*house*	Diphthong starts /ɑ/ and moves to /ʊ/.	*pauta*	
ɔ ɪ	*boy*	Diphthong starts at /ɔ/ and moves to /ɪ/.	*hoy* (today)	
ɑ ɪ	*bite*	Diphthong starts at /ɑ/ and moves to /ɪ/.	*baile* (dance)	
ə	*about*	Most common vowel in English; only in unstressed syllables. Learners may have difficulty keeping it very short.	**NO EQUIVALENT**	Substitute /ʌ/ or the full vowel from the word's spelling
ʌ	*cut*	Very similar to schwa /ə/	**NO EQUIVALENT**	Substitute /a/
ɝ	*bird*	English Learners must bunch the tongue and constrict the throat.	**NO EQUIVALENT**	Substitute /ʌ/ or /er/ with trill

Writing COACH How to Use This Program

This program is organized into two distinct sections: one for WRITING and one for GRAMMAR.

In the **WRITING** section, you'll learn strategies, traits, and skills that will help you become a better writer.

In the **GRAMMAR** section, you'll learn the rules and conventions of grammar, usage, and mechanics.

What DIGITAL writing and grammar resources are available?

The Writing Coach Online boxes will indicate opportunities to use online tools.

In **Writing,** use the **Interactive Writing Coach™** in two ways to get personalized guidance and support for your writing.

- Paragraph Feedback and
- Essay Scorer

Interactive Writing Coach™

- Choosing from the Topic Bank gives you access to the Interactive Writing Coach™.
- Submit your writing and receive instant personalized feedback and guidance as you draft, revise, and edit your writing.

Grammar Tutorials

Brush up on your grammar skills with these animated videos.

Grammar Practice

Practice your grammar skills with Writing Coach Online.

Grammar Games

Test your knowledge of grammar in this fast-paced interactive video game.

In **Grammar,** view grammar tutorials, practice your grammar skills, and play grammar video games.

What will you find in the WRITING section?

Writing Genre

Each chapter introduces a different **writing genre.**

Learn about the key characteristics of the **genre** before you start writing.

Focus on a single form of the genre with the **Feature Assignment**.

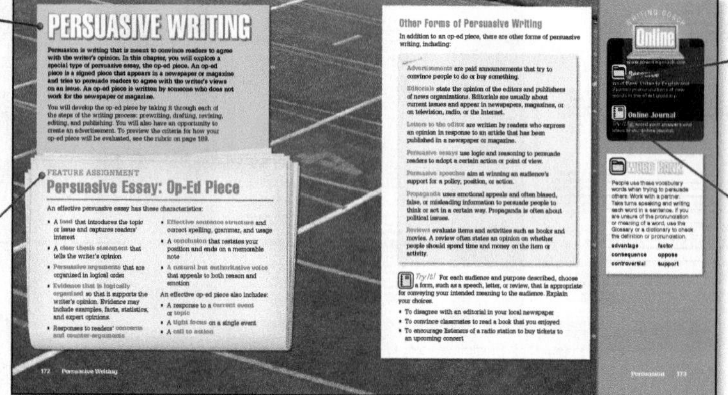

Writing Coach Online

- View the **Word Bank** words in the eText glossary, and hear them pronounced in both English and Spanish.
- Use your **Online Journal** to record your answers and ideas as you respond to ***Try It!*** activities.

Mentor Text and Student Model

The **Mentor Text** and **Student Model** provide examples of the genre featured in each chapter.

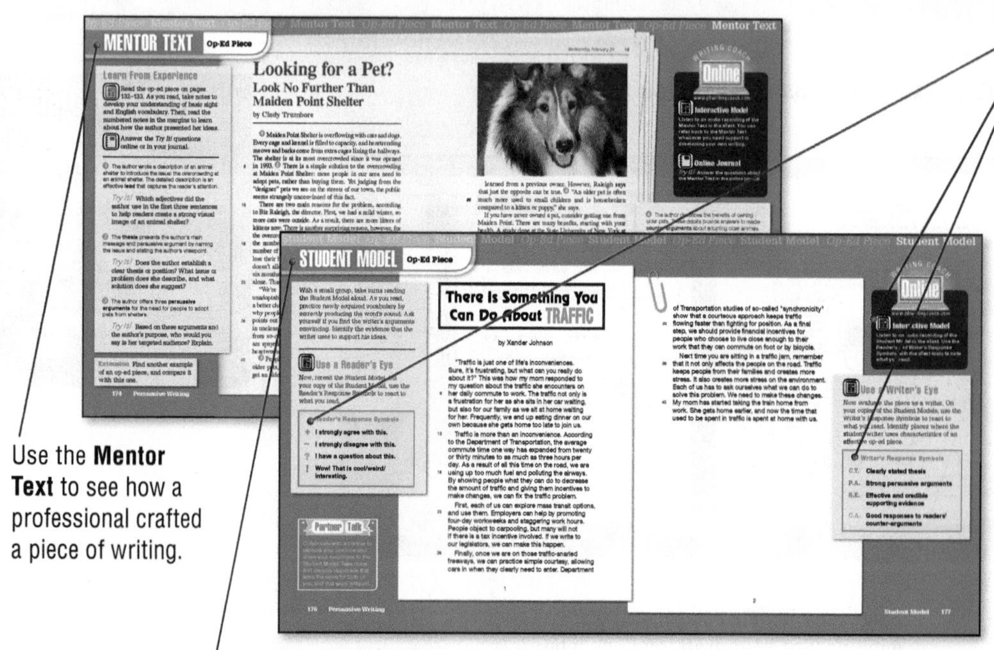

Writing Coach Online

- Use the **Interactive Model** to mark the text with Reader's and Writer's Response Symbols.
- Listen to an audio recording of the **Mentor Text** or **Student Model.**

Use the **Mentor Text** to see how a professional crafted a piece of writing.

Review the **Student Model** as a guide for composing your own piece.

Topic Bank

PREWRITING

The **Topic Bank** provides prompts for the **Feature Assignment.**

Choose from a bank of topics, or follow steps to find an idea of your own.

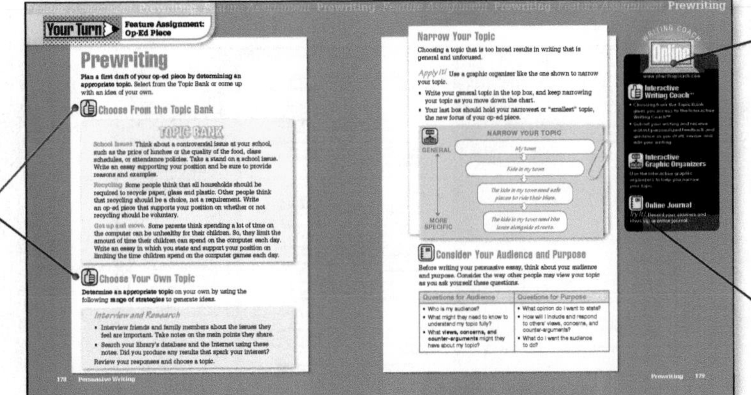

Writing Coach Online

- As you narrow your topic, get the right type of support! You'll find three different forms of graphic organizers—one model, one with step-by-step guidance, and one that is blank for you to complete.
- Use ***Try It!*** ideas to practice new skills. Use ***Apply It!*** activities as you work on your own writing.

Outline for Success

DRAFTING

Whether you are working on your essay drafts online or with a pen and paper, an **Outline for Success** can get you started.

Consult this **outline** for a quick visual specific to the writing task assigned in each chapter.

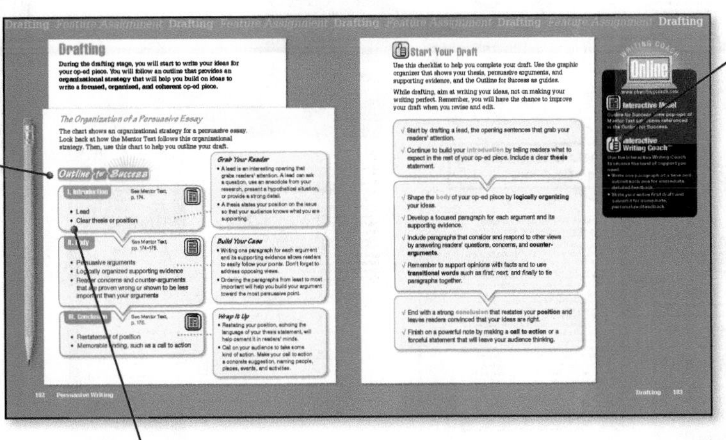

Follow the bulleted suggestions for each part of your draft, and you'll be on your way to success.

Writing Coach Online

- Start with just a paragraph and build up to your essay draft, or if you are ready, go straight to submitting your essay. The choice is yours!

Revision RADaR

REVISING

You can use the **Revision RADaR** strategy as a guide for making changes to improve your draft.

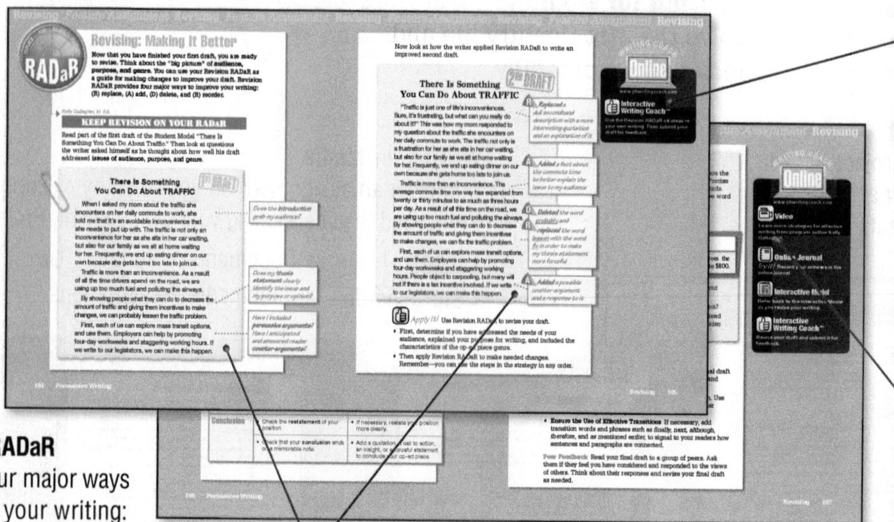

Writing Coach Online

- With **Interactive Writing Coach™**, submit your paragraphs and essays multiple times. View your progress in your online writing portfolio. Feel confident that your work is ready to be shared in peer review or teacher conferencing.
- View **videos** with strategies for writing from program author **Kelly Gallagher.**

Revision RADaR provides four major ways to improve your writing:

- **R**eplace
- **A**dd
- **D**elete
- **R**eorder

Check out these example drafts to see how to apply **Revision RADaR.**

What Do You Notice?

EDITING PUBLISHING

In the editing stage, **What Do You Notice?** and **Mentor Text** help you zoom in on powerful sentences.

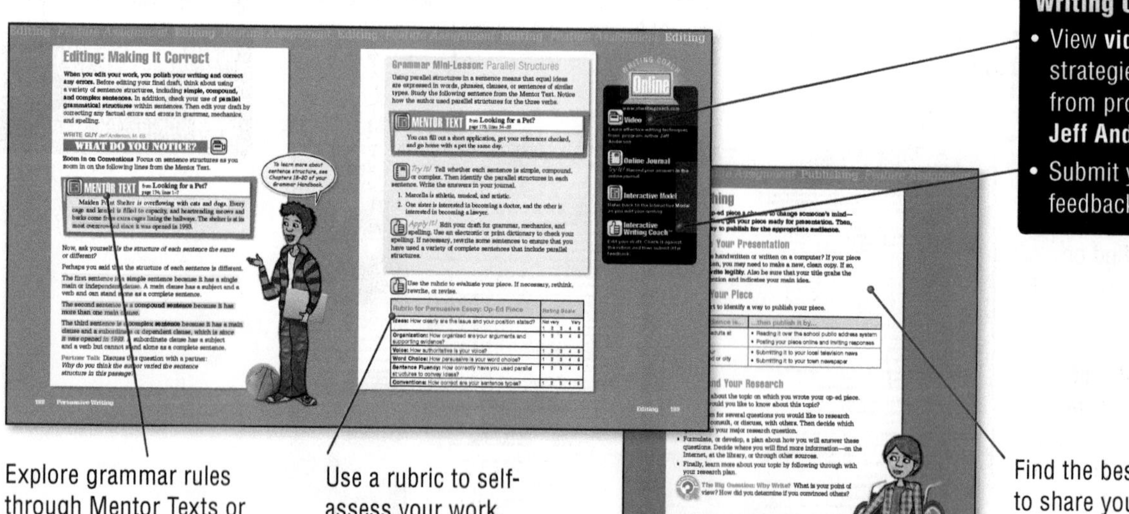

Writing Coach Online

- View **videos** with strategies for writing from program author **Jeff Anderson.**
- Submit your essay for feedback and a score.

Explore grammar rules through Mentor Texts or Student Models.

Use a rubric to self-assess your work.

Find the best way to share your writing with others.

How do end-of-chapter features help you apply what you've learned?

21st Century Learning

In **Make Your Writing Count** and **Writing for Media** you will work on innovative assignments that involve the 21st Century life and career skills you'll need for communicating successfully.

Make Your Writing Count

Work collaboratively on project-based assignments and share what you have learned with others. Projects include:

- Debates
- TV Talk Shows
- News Reports

Writing for Media

Complete an assignment on your own by exploring media forms, and then developing your own content. Projects include:

- Blogs
- Storyboards
- Documentary Scripts
- Multimedia Presentations

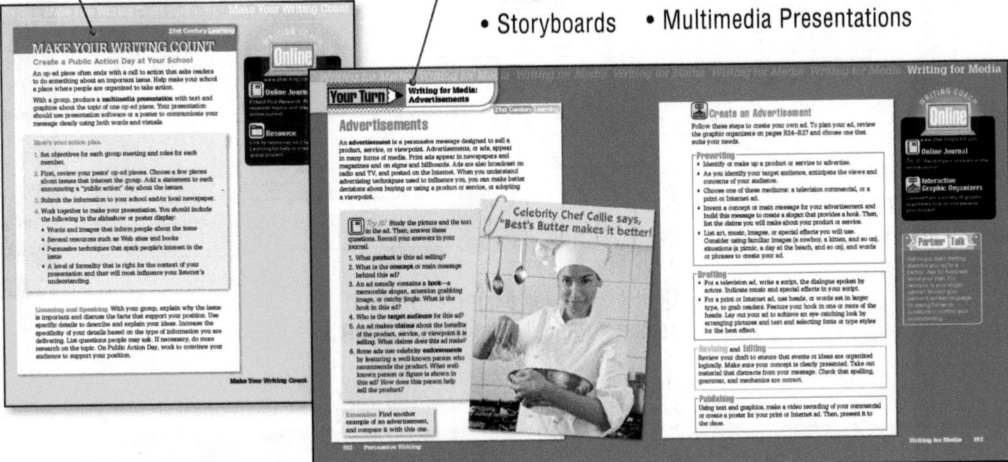

Test Prep

The **Writing for Assessment** pages help you prepare for important standardized tests.

Writing Coach Online

Submit your essay for feedback and a score.

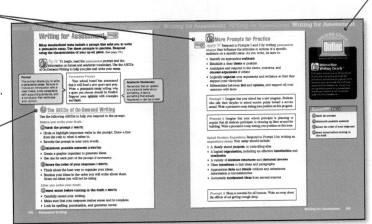

SAT®/PSAT PREP ACT Notice these icons that emphasize the types of writing you'll find on high-stakes tests.

Use **The ABCDs of On-Demand Writing** for a quick, memorable strategy for success.

What will you find in the GRAMMAR section?

Grammar Game Plan

The **Find It/Fix It** reference guide helps you fix the **20** most common errors in student writing.

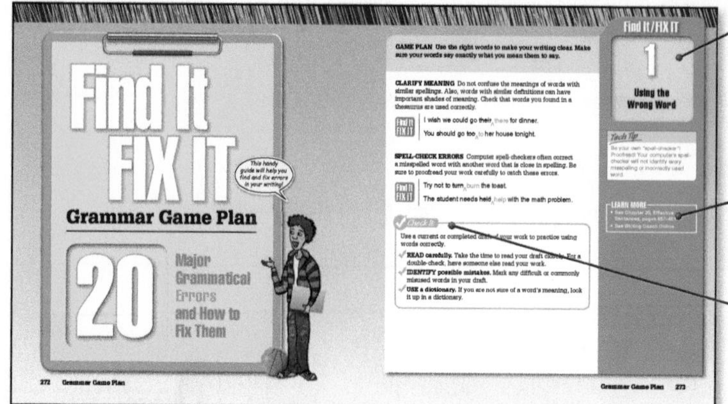

Study each of the 20 common errors and their corrections, which are clearly explained on each page.

Follow cross-references to more instruction in the grammar chapters.

Review the **Check It** features for strategies to help you avoid these errors.

Grammar Chapters

Each grammar chapter begins with a **What Do You Notice?** feature and **Mentor Text.**

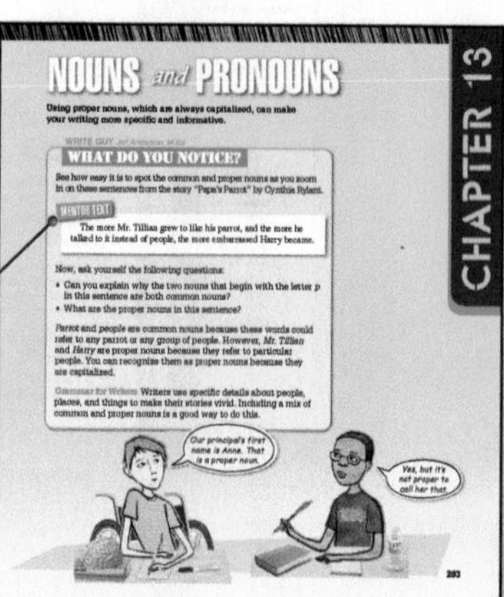

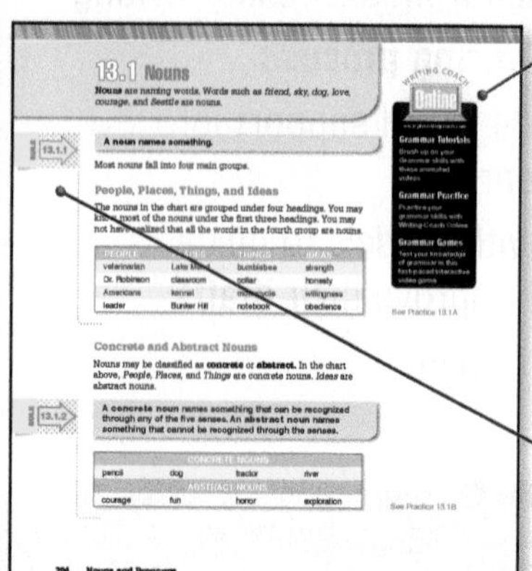

Writing Coach Online

The **Writing Coach Online** digital experience for Grammar helps you focus on just the lessons and practice you need.

Use the **Mentor Text** to help you zoom in on powerful sentences. It showcases the correct use of written language conventions.

Use the grammar section as a quick reference handbook. Each **grammar rule** is highlighted and numbered.

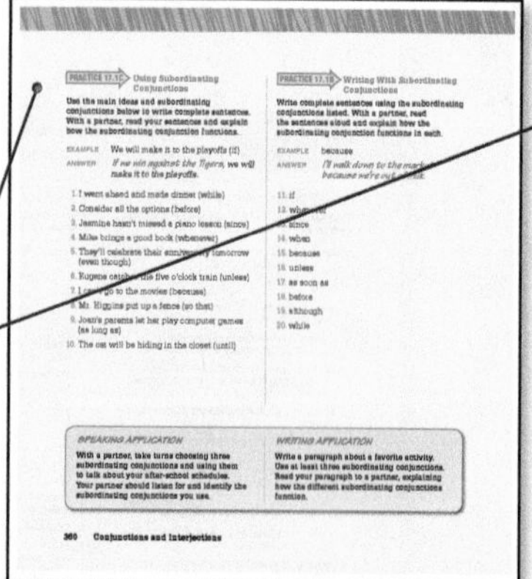

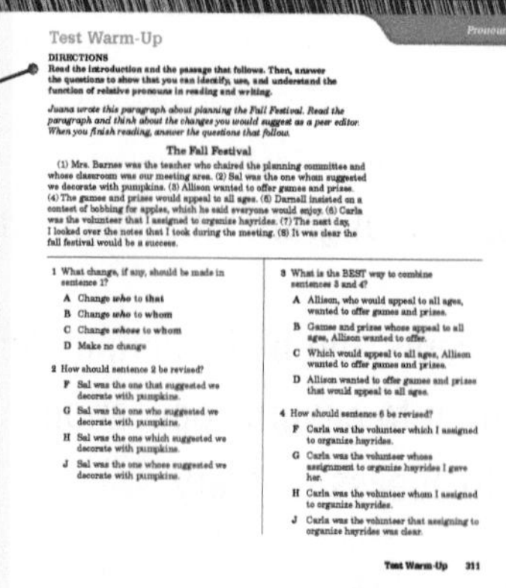

Try **Practice** pages and **Test Warm-Ups** to help you check your progress.

Prentice Hall *Writing Coach* is perfect as a writing and grammar companion to a literature anthology or a novel-based curriculum. Reach for it to help you meet these goals:

- ✔ **Reinforce instruction**
- ✔ **Extend key points**
- ✔ **Remediate**
- ✔ **Provide more practice**
- ✔ **Reteach**
- ✔ **Provide more writing prompts**

Using *Writing Coach* with Your Integrated English Language Arts Curriculum

Use *Writing Coach* to support writing assignments linked to literature. Writing chapters include:

- **In-depth coverage** to introduce the key elements of genres
- **Mentor Texts** to help you teach from exemplary writing
- Step-by-step support of the **writing process**
- **Outline for Success** to provide visual support for organizing drafts in all key genres
- **Revision RADaR** strategies with models to guide students as they analyze and improve their drafts
- **Rubrics** to support self-assessment

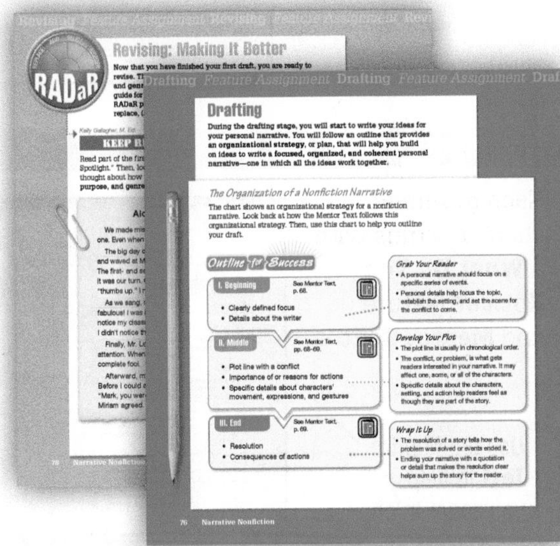

www.phwritingcoach.com

Use online tools to personalize instruction, including paragraph scoring, essay scoring, interactive graphic organizers, and instructional videos.

Use *Writing Coach* to strengthen instruction in conventions. Grammar chapters provide:

- **Thorough instruction** on all aspects of grammar, usage, and mechanics to teach key ideas
- **Practice items** to reinforce concepts and build competence
- **Speaking and Listening activities** to ensure application
- **Diagnostic** and **Chapter tests** to assess mastery

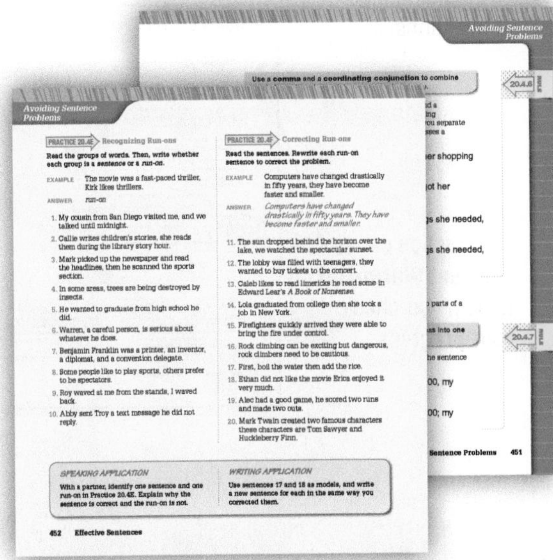

www.phwritingcoach.com

Use online resources to target instruction for each student.

Using *Writing Coach* with Prentice Hall *Literature*

Opportunities to Extend Integrated Language Skills

Leveled Selection choices include integrated language arts skills lessons:

- From **Grammar** lessons in *Literature*, use the *Writing Coach* grammar chapters to further develop concepts.
- From **Writing** lessons in *Literature*, consult the *Writing Coach* writing chapters to expand coverage of prewriting, drafting, revising, and editing.
- From **Listening and Speaking** and **Research and Technology** activities, see *Writing Coach* unit features to support student extension.
- **Make Your Writing Count** provides step-by-step direction for projects.
- **Writing for Media** offers extended instruction in new forms of content delivery.

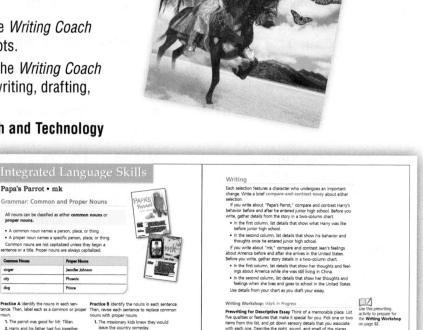

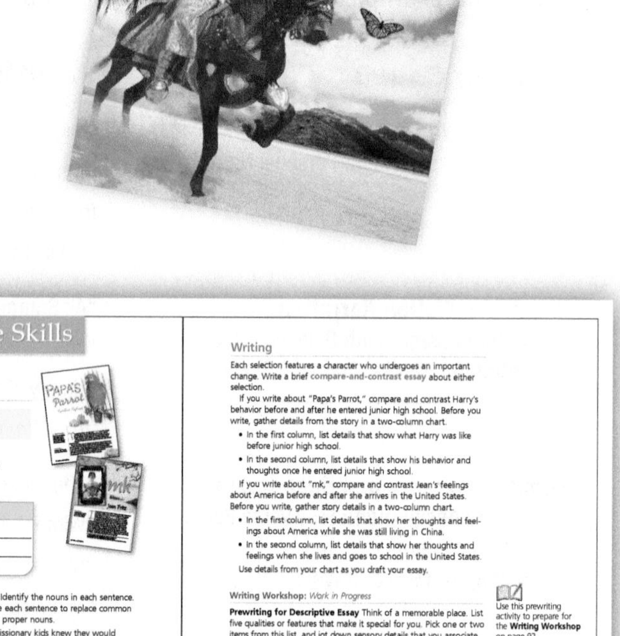

Integrated Language Skills

Papa's Parrot • mk

Grammar: Common and Proper Nouns

All nouns can be classified as either **common nouns** or **proper nouns.**

- A common noun names a person, place, or thing.
- A proper noun names a specific person, place, or thing.

Common nouns are not capitalized unless they begin a sentence or a title. Proper nouns are always capitalized.

Common Nouns	Proper Nouns
singer	Jennifer Johnson
city	Phoenix
dog	Prince

Practice A Identify the nouns in each sentence. Then, label each as a common or proper noun.

1. The parrot was good for Mr. Tillian.
2. Harry and his father had fun together.
3. Mr. Tillian fell onto the candy boxes.
4. Harry helped in the store.
5. That parrot talked to Harry.
6. Harry learned a lesson from Rocky.

Challenge In "Papa's Parrot," find two sentences with common nouns and two sentences with proper nouns.

Practice B Identify the nouns in each sentence. Then, revise each sentence to replace common nouns with proper nouns.

1. The missionary kids knew they would leave the country someday.
2. Jean's favorite book was about the first settlers.
3. Children from around the world attended that school.
4. Many students in her new country asked her silly questions.

Challenge Write two sentences describing what it might be like to go to school in another country. Use at least one common noun and one proper noun in your description.

Writing and Grammar Connection: Chapter 14, Section 1

46 Fiction and Nonfiction

Writing

Each selection features a character who undergoes an important change. Write a brief compare-and-contrast essay about either selection.

If you write about "Papa's Parrot," compare and contrast Harry's behavior before and after he entered junior high school. Before you write, gather details from the story in a two-column chart.

- In the first column, list details that show what Harry was like before junior high school.
- In the second column, list details that show his behavior and thoughts once he entered junior high school.

If you write about "mk," compare and contrast Jean's feelings about America before and after she arrives in the United States. Before you write, gather story details in a two-column chart.

- In the first column, list details that show her thoughts and feelings about America while she was still living in China.
- In the second column, list details that show her thoughts and feelings when she lives and goes to school in the United States.

Use details from your chart as you draft your essay.

Writing Workshop: *Work in Progress*

Prewriting for Descriptive Essay Think of a memorable place. List five qualities or features that make it special for you. Pick one or two items from this list, and jot down sensory details that you associate with each one. Describe the sight, sound, and smell of the places and events. Save this Place List in your writing portfolio.

Use this prewriting activity to prepare for the **Writing Workshop** on page 92.

Listening and Speaking

With a partner, perform a dramatic reading of either "Papa's Parrot" or "mk." Read the story and choose a section that is especially moving, emotional, or funny. Divide the text so that each partner can present a portion. As you rehearse, focus on these points:

- **Speak clearly** so that each word can be heard.
- **Raise and lower your voice** to **express emotion.**
- **Slow down** and **stress certain words for effect.**
- **Make eye contact** with your listeners as you read.

PHLit Online! www.PHLitOnline.com
- Interactive graphic organizers
- Grammar tutorial
- Interactive journals

Integrated Language Skills 47

Springboards to Support Writing Workshops

Two Writing Workshops in each *Literature* unit provide detailed instruction in major writing forms.

From **Writing Workshops** in *Literature*, use these features in *Writing Coach*:

- The **Mentor Text** and **Student Models** support deeper exploration of the mode.
- More instruction in prewriting, drafting, revising, and editing helps students strengthen their writing skills.

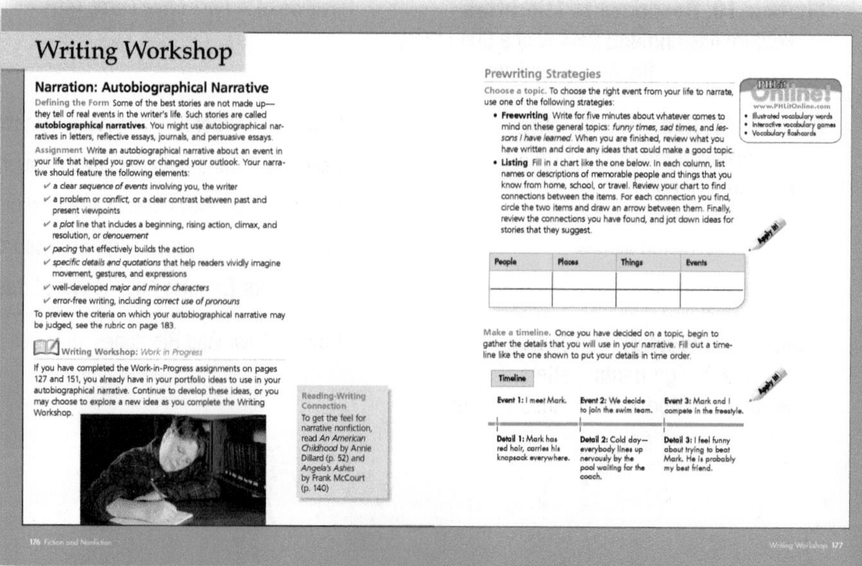

Writing Workshop

Narration: Autobiographical Narrative

Defining the Form Some of the best stories are not made up—they tell of real events in the writer's life. Such stories are called **autobiographical narratives**. You might use autobiographical narratives in letters, reflective essays, journals, and persuasive essays.

Assignment Write an autobiographical narrative about an event in your life that helped you grow or changed your outlook. Your narrative should feature the following elements:

- ✓ a clear *sequence of events* involving you, the writer
- ✓ a problem or *conflict*, or a clear contrast between past and present viewpoints
- ✓ a *plot* line that includes a beginning, rising action, climax, and resolution, or *denouement*
- ✓ *pacing* that effectively builds the action
- ✓ *specific details and quotations* that help readers vividly imagine movement, gestures, and expressions
- ✓ well-developed *major and minor characters*
- ✓ error-free writing, including *correct use of pronouns*

To preview the criteria on which your autobiographical narrative may be judged, see the rubric on page 183.

Writing Workshop: *Work in Progress*

If you have completed the Work-in-Progress assignments on pages 127 and 151, you already have in your portfolio ideas to use in your autobiographical narrative. Continue to develop these ideas, or you may choose to explore a new idea as you complete the Writing Workshop.

Reading-Writing Connection
To get the feel for narrative nonfiction, read *An American Childhood* by Annie Dillard (p. 52) and *Angela's Ashes* by Frank McCourt (p. 140)

176 Fiction and Nonfiction

Prewriting Strategies

Choose a topic. To choose the right event from your life to narrate, use one of the following strategies:

- **Freewriting** Write for five minutes about whatever comes to mind on these general topics: *funny times, sad times*, and *lessons I have learned*. When you are finished, review what you have written and circle any ideas that could make a good topic.
- **Listing** Fill in a chart like the one below. In each column, list names or descriptions of memorable people and things that you know from home, school, or travel. Review your chart to find connections between the items. For each connection you find, circle the two items and draw an arrow between them. Finally, review the connections you have found, and jot down ideas for stories that they suggest.

People	Places	Things	Events

Make a timeline. Once you have decided on a topic, begin to gather the details that you will use in your narrative. Fill out a timeline like the one shown to put your details in time order.

Timeline

Event 1: I meet Mark.	**Event 2:** We decide to join the swim team.	**Event 3:** Mark and I compete in the freestyle.
Detail 1: Mark has red hair, carries his knapsack everywhere.	**Detail 2:** Cold day—everybody lines up nervously by the pool waiting for the coach.	**Detail 3:** I feel funny about trying to beat Mark. He is probably my best friend.

PHLit Online! www.PHLitOnline.com
- Illustrated vocabulary words
- Interactive vocabulary games
- Vocabulary flashcards

Writing Workshop 177

Prentice Hall *Writing Coach*/ Prentice Hall *Literature* Alignment

Use models in Prentice Hall *Literature* to support the teaching of writing.

Prentice Hall *Literature* supports *Writing Coach* with works from noted authors, Mentor Texts, Student Models, and examples of research sources, as shown in the following chart.

Writing Coach	**Prentice Hall *Literature***
Chapter 5, Nonfiction Narration **Feature Assignment:** Personal Narrative	"mk," Jean Fritz (personal narrative), page 34 from *An American Childhood,* Annie Dillard (personal narrative), page 52 from *Barrio Boy,* Ernesto Galarza (personal narrative), page 80 "Volar: To Fly," Judith Ortiz Cofer (personal narrative), page 452
Chapter 6, Fiction Narration **Feature Assignment:** Science Fiction **Writing for Media:** Dramatic Scene	"All Summer in a Day," Ray Bradbury (science fiction short story), page 102 "Zoo," Edward Hoch (science fiction short story), page 340 "He—y, Come on Ou—t," Shinichi Hoshi (science fiction short story), page 378 from *Dragonwings,* Laurence Yep (dramatic scene), page 729
Chapter 7, Poetry and Description **Feature Assignment:** Free Verse Poem and Lyric Poem **Writing for Media:** Travel Blog	"The Rider," Naomi Shihab Nye (lyric poem), page 586 "Winter," Nikki Giovanni (lyric poem), page 594 "Stopping by Woods on a Snowy Evening," Robert Frost (lyric poem), page 678 "Miracles," Walt Whitman (free verse poem), page 694 "To the Top of Everest," Samantha Larson (blog), page 972
Chapter 8, Exposition **Feature Assignment:** Compare-and-Contrast Essay **Writing for Media:** Technical Newsletter	"Conversational Ballgames," Nancy Masterson Sakamoto (compare-and-contrast writing), page 432 "How to Recognize Venomous Snakes in North America" (instruction manual featuring comparisons), page 531
Chapter 9, Persuasion **Feature Assignment:** Op-Ed Piece **Writing for Media:** Advertisement	"All Together Now," Barbara Jordan (persuasion), page 494 "Veteran Returns, Becomes Symbol," *Minneapolis Star and Tribune* (editorial), page 863 "The Wrong Orbit," *The Kansas City Star* (editorial), page 864 "Zoos: Joys or Jails?," *Teen Ink* (op-ed piece), page 1029
Chapter 10, Response to Literature **Feature Assignment:** Review of a Short Story **Writing for Media:** Movie Review	Reviews of *A Christmas Carol,* Terry Kelleher, John Sousanis (drama reviews), pages 813, 814
Chapter 11, Research Writing **Feature Assignment:** Informational Research Report	"Hatching Chirpers," Laura Agajanian (Writing Workshop Student Model: research report), page 1046 "East Asia," Dorling Kindersley (research source: atlas entry), page 73 "Mongoose on the Loose," Larry Luxner (research source: magazine article), page 283 "Indian Grey Mongoose" (research source: encyclopedia entry), page 285 "Walking for Exercise and Pleasure" (research source: government publication), page 365
Chapter 12, Workplace Writing **Feature Assignments:** Letters **Writing for Media:** Set of Instructions	"How to Download Ringtones for a Cell Phone" (technical directions), page 623

Prentice Hall *Literature* Writing Workshops/*Writing Coach* Alignment

When you teach the writing workshops in Prentice Hall Litera*ture* look to Prentice Hall *Writing Coach* for more in-depth instruction.

Users of Prentice Hall *Literature* Writing Workshops can find additional support in *Writing Coach*, including Mentor Texts, Student Models, writing process strategies, grammar applications, and connected assignments, as shown in the following chart.

Prentice Hall *Literature*	*Writing Coach*
Unit 1, Mid-Unit Workshop **Description: Descriptive Essay,** page 92	**Chapter 7, Poetry and Description,** page 118 Forms of Poetry and Description, page 121
Unit 1, End-of-Unit Workshop **Narration: Autobiographical Narrative,** page 176	**Chapter 5, Nonfiction Narration,** page 64 Feature Assignment: Personal Narrative
Unit 2, Mid-Unit Workshop **Response to Literature: Review of a Short Story,** page 302	**Chapter 10, Response to Literature,** page 196 Feature Assignment: Review of a Short Story
Unit 2, End-of-Unit Workshop **Narration: Short Story,** page 384	**Chapter 6, Fiction Narration,** page 90 Feature Assignment: Science Fiction Other Forms of Short Stories, page 93
Unit 3, Mid-Unit Workshop **Exposition: How-to Essay,** page 484	**Chapter 12, Workplace Writing,** page 256 Writing for Media: Set of Instructions, page 266
Unit 3, End-of-Unit Workshop **Exposition: Comparison-and-Contrast Essay,** page 548	**Chapter 8, Exposition,** page 144 Feature Assignment: Compare-and-Contrast Essay Writing for Media: Technical Newsletter, page 166
Unit 4, Mid-Unit Workshop **Exposition: Problem-and-Solution Essay,** page 640	**Chapter 8, Exposition,** page 144 Other Forms of Expository Essays, page 147
Unit 4, End-of-Unit Workshop **Exposition: Persuasive Essay,** page 698	**Chapter 9, Persuasion,** page 170 Other Forms of Persuasive Writing, page 173
Unit 5, Mid-Unit Workshop **Research: Multimedia Report,** page 824	**Chapter 11, Research Writing,** page 222 Feature Assignment: Informational Research Report
Unit 5, End-of-Unit Workshop **Exposition: Cause-and-Effect Essay,** page 878	**Chapter 8, Exposition,** page 144 Other Forms of Expository Essays, page 147
Unit 6, Mid-Unit Workshop **Workplace Writing: Business Letter,** page 982	**Chapter 12, Workplace Writing,** page 256 Feature Assignment: Letter of Request
Unit 6, End-of-Unit Workshop **Research: Research Report,** page 1040	**Chapter 11, Research Writing,** page 222 Feature Assignment: Informational Research Report

Your Writing Coach . . .

Jeff Anderson

MENTOR TEXTS

What can we do about students' declining editing and writing skills? Should we just do more of the same practices? Fight error with more error? Fight lack of correctness with even more correction? For today's students, this focus on the negative isn't working. Yet, simply ignoring errors and hoping they will repair themselves isn't a solution either.

Doing What Works

The recent research report Writing Next (2007) calls for teachers to search out "alternate methods" to teach grammar and editing skills. This research report, focused on improving writing instruction for adolescent writers, recommends we teach using many methods to improve student writing, including:

- Study of models
- Sentence combining
- Inquiry activities

Prentice Hall *Writing Coach* provides Mentor Texts throughout both the writing and grammar sections. These texts model effective and interesting writing, using the conventions of language—punctuation, usage, and grammar—to communicate their messages and entertain readers.

Invite Students to Read Like Writers

In addition to integrating the traits of writing into the writing lessons in this book to help improve student writing, **Prentice Hall *Writing Coach*** also provides multiple opportunities to zoom in on powerful sentences and burn correctness and beauty into students' minds. You can use these models to encourage students to try new structures and patterns. Once students get in the habit of reading like writers, the style of their own writing can truly benefit.

> *"For today's students, this focus on the negative isn't working."*
>
> Jeff Anderson

Jeff Anderson has worked with struggling writers and readers for almost 20 years. He is known for his work with integrating reading, writing, and grammar instruction through the use of mentor texts. He has written two books, *Mechanically Inclined: Building Grammar, Usage, and Style into Writer's Workshop* and *Everyday Editing: Inviting Students to Develop Skill and Craft in Writer's Workshop.* His work has appeared in *The English Journal*, and he won the NCTE Paul and Kate Farmer Award for his *English Journal* article on teaching grammar in context.

See Jeff Anderson's professional development videos at www.phwritingcoach.com.

Your Writing Coach . . .

Kelly Gallagher

KEYS TO TEACHING WRITING

Anyone can write a first draft, but revision is the place where good papers emerge. Revision is the "make or break" moment for the paper. *Re* means "again" and *vision* means "to see"; we want our students to see their first drafts again in a new light. If a first draft has any chance to become strong, it must be "moved" to a better place. This is where good writing emerges.

Revision Is Not Editing

During the revision stage, students should work to make their papers better. This should not be confused with editing—working to make their papers correct. The "stuff" of the paper must be improved before editing comes into play. Who cares if a paper is edited properly if the first draft is so bad no one wants to read it? For a young writer, revising the paper should come before editing the paper. In **Prentice Hall *Writing Coach*,** four concrete *RADaR revision* strategies help students manage this critical stage of the writing process:

Replace
Add
Delete
and
Reorder

The Importance of Modeling

Students benefit immensely from having real-world models in front of them. If you want your students to write an effective persuasive essay, give them an effective persuasive essay to dissect beforehand. We must move students beyond recognizing what the author says, and start having them focus on how it is said. Using professional writing as road maps is beneficial to almost all young writers. **Prentice Hall *Writing Coach*** provides Mentor Texts and Student Models to support this key stage of writing study.

Practice, Practice, Practice

Writing, like swimming, is a skill. The only way to noticeably improve is to practice a lot. If you only swim once in a while, you will not become a better swimmer. The same holds true with writing. To produce competent writers, our students need to write a lot—in many cases much more than they are currently writing. Students should write way more than the teacher can grade. Otherwise, they are not writing enough.

Strong writing happens when the writer has a clear sense of audience and purpose. Who you write for and why you are writing it determines how it will be written.

Kelly Gallagher is a full-time English teacher at Magnolia High School in Anaheim, California, where he has taught for 23 years. He is the author of several books:

- *Reading Reasons: Motivational Mini-Lessons for The Middle and High School*
- *Deeper Reading: Comprehending Challenging Texts*
- *Teaching Adolescent Writers*
- *Readicide*

See Kelly Gallagher's professional development videos at www.phwritingcoach.com.

> *"Writing is a threshold skill for both employment and promotion, particularly for salaried employees."*
>
> **Kelly Gallagher**

NFICTION NARRATION *Personal Narrative* FICTION NARRATION *Scie*

POSITION *Compare-and-Contrast Essay* PERSUASION *Op-Ed Piece* RESPO

RKPLACE WRITING *Friendly Letter, Letter of Opinion, Letter of Request* NON

rt Story POETRY and DESCRIPTION *Free Verse Poem and Lyric Poem* EX

ERATURE *Review of a Short Story* RESEARCH *Informational Research Report*

ON NARRATION *Personal Narrative* FICTION NARRATION *Science Fictio*

ON *Compare-and-Contrast Essay* PERSUASION *Op-Ed Piece* RESPONSE TO

ACE WRITING *Friendly Letter, Letter of Opinion, Letter of Request* NONFICTI

ry POETRY and DESCRIPTION *Free Verse Poem and Lyric Poem* EXPOSIT

Writing

Use the Online Lesson Planner at www.phwritingcoach.com to customize your instructional plan for an integrated Language Arts curriculum.

DAY 1

ONLINE

CHAPTER 1: YOU, THE WRITER

- Why and What Do You Write?
- How Can You Find and Keep Track of Ideas?
- How Can You Get Started?
- How Do You Work with Others?
- Where Can You Keep Your Finished Work?
- Reflect on Your Writing

DAY 2

ONLINE

CHAPTER 2: TYPES OF WRITING

- Genres and Forms
- Nonfiction Narration
- Fiction Narration
- Poetry and Description
- Exposition
- Persuasion

DAY 3

ONLINE

CHAPTER 2: TYPES OF WRITING *(cont'd)*

- Responses to Literature
- Research Writing
- Workplace Writing
- Writing for Media
- Creating Multimedia Projects
- Reflect on Your Writing

DAY 6

CHAPTER 3: THE WRITING PROCESS *(cont'd)*

- Revising: Making It Better

DAY 7

CHAPTER 3: THE WRITING PROCESS *(cont'd)*

- Editing: Making It Correct
- Publishing
- Reflect on Your Writing

DAY 8

ONLINE

CHAPTER 4: SENTENCES, PARAGRAPHS, AND COMPOSITIONS

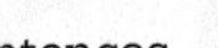

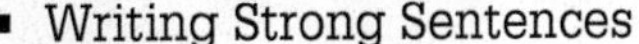

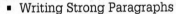

- Writing Strong Sentences
- Writing Strong Paragraphs
- Composing Your Piece

Links to Prentice Hall *LITERATURE*

Featured Authors on Writing Genres and Writing Process

Richard Peck

- What Are Fiction and Nonfiction?, p. 4
- "The Three-Century Woman" (fiction), Richard Peck, p. 9
- "The Fall of the *Hindenburg*" (informative article), Michael Morrison, p. 19

Walter Dean Myers

- What Is a Short Story?, p. 200
- "The Treasure of Lemon Brown" (short story), p. 205
- On Revising to Heighten Tension (Writing Workshop), p. 387

Richard Mühlberger

- What Is an Essay?, p. 408
- "What Makes a Rembrandt a Rembrandt?" (analytical article), p. 413
- On Getting Readers Involved (Writing Workshop), p. 551

Pat Mora

- What Is Poetry?, p. 572
- "Maestro" (poem), p. 577
- "The Desert Is My Mother" (poem), p. 578
- "El desierto es mi madre" (poem), p. 579
- "Bailando" (poem), p. 580
- On Supporting a Point (Writing Workshop), p. 701

Laurence Yep

- What Is Drama?, p. 722
- from the novel *Dragonwings* (novel excerpt), p. 727
- from the dramatization *Dragonwings* (dramatic scene), p. 729
- On Showing Causes and Effects (Writing Workshop), p. 881

Jon Scieszka

- What Is Storytelling?, p. 902
- "Grasshopper Logic" (fable), p. 907
- "The Other Frog Prince" (fairy tale), p. 908
- "Duckbilled Platypus vs. BeefSnakStik®" (fable), p. 910
- *From the Author's Desk* Videos: Featured authors discuss writing.

Differentiated Instruction

Differentiated Instruction Boxes in this Teacher's Edition address these student populations:

- Below-Level Students
- Above-Level Students
- Gifted and Talented Students
- Special Needs Students
- English Language Learners
- Spanish Speaking Students

In addition, for further enrichment, see the **Extension** features.

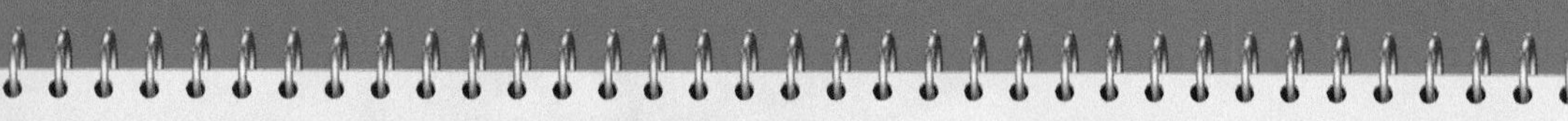

DAY 4

ONLINE

CHAPTER 3: THE WRITING PROCESS

- Writing Traits
  Rubrics and How to Use Them
- What Is the Writing Process?
- Why Use the Writing Process?

DAY 5

ONLINE

CHAPTER 3: THE WRITING PROCESS *(cont'd)*

- Prewriting
- Drafting

DAY 9

ONLINE

CHAPTER 4: SENTENCES, PARAGRAPHS, AND COMPOSITIONS *(cont'd)*

- Rhetorical and Literary Devices
- Using Writing Traits To Develop an Effective Composition

DAY 10

ONLINE

CHAPTER 4: SENTENCES, PARAGRAPHS, AND COMPOSITIONS *(cont'd)*

- Using Interactive Writing Coach
- Interactive Writing Coach and the Writing Process
- Paragraph Feedback With Interactive Writing Coach
- Essay Scoring With Interactive Writing Coach

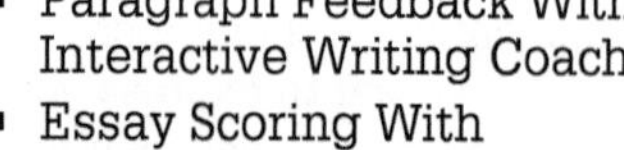

Alternate Pacing Suggestions

- **Block Scheduling** Each day on the Lesson Planner represents a 40–50 minute block. Teachers using block scheduling may combine days to revise pacing to meet their classroom needs.
- **Accelerated Lesson Planning** Combine instructional days, focusing on strategies for revising and for building effective sentences, paragraphs, and compositions.
- **Integrated Language Arts Curriculum** For targeted instruction that covers the essential components of the lesson use either a 3- or a 5-day plan.

3 day plan

DAY 1: Chapters 1 and 2
DAY 2: Chapter 3
DAY 3: Chapter 4

5 day plan

DAY 1: Chapters 1 and 2
DAYS 2/3: Chapter 3
DAYS 4/5: Chapter 4

LESSON OBJECTIVES

- To reflect on reasons for writing.
- To learn the genres and forms of writing.
- To review strategies for generating and recording ideas, preparing to write, working with others, and maintaining a portfolio.
- To review the traits of effective writing and to review how to use a rubric.
- To review the stages of the writing process and consider why it is important to follow the process.
- To review strategies for developing strong sentences, paragraphs, and compositions.
- To learn how to use Interactive Writing Coach online for guidance.

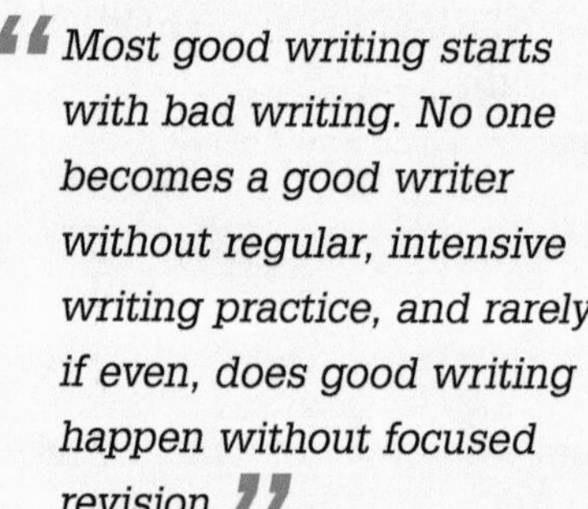

"Most good writing starts with bad writing. No one becomes a good writer without regular, intensive writing practice, and rarely, if even, does good writing happen without focused revision."

—Kelly Gallagher

"Inviting students to write is where the rubber meets the road. We want to inspire their words to flow. Words can also preserve the things we may forget."

—Jeff Anderson

CHAPTER 1

YOU, THE WRITER

Why Do You Write?

Writing well is one of the most important life skills you can develop. Being a good writer can help you achieve success in school and beyond. Most likely, you write for many reasons. You write:

To Share

You probably often write to **share** your experiences with others. Writing can be an easy way to **reach out** to people and connect with them.

To Persuade People

Writing can also be an effective way to **persuade** people to consider your opinions. For example, you may find it's easier to convince someone of your point of view when you've effectively organized your thoughts in an essay or a letter.

To Inform

Another reason to write is to **inform.** Perhaps you want to tell an audience how you built your computer network or how you finally got your e-mail to function properly.

To Enjoy

Personal fullfillment is another important motivation for writing, since writing enables you **to express** your thoughts and feelings. In addition, writing can also help you recall an event, or let you escape from everyday life.

Fortunately, writing well is a skill you can learn and one that you can continue to improve and polish. This program will help you improve your writing skills and give you useful information about the many types of writing.

MOTIVATE AND ENGAGE

As a warm-up activity, have students quickwrite for one minute about the reasons people write. Remind them that during a quickwrite, they should keep writing continuously for one minute even if they repeat words or ideas.

Write these headings on the board: *to share, to persuade people, to inform, to enjoy.* Then, have students share their ideas and list them under the correct heading.

What Do You Write?

Writing is already an important part of your everyday life. Each day is full of opportunities to write, allowing you to capture, express, think through and share your thoughts and feelings, and demonstrate what you know. Here are some ways you might write.

- Recording thoughts in a journal
- Texting friends or posting on social networking sites
- E-mailing thank-you notes to relatives
- Creating lists of things to do or things you like
- Writing research reports, nonfiction accounts, fiction stories, and essays in school

How Can You Find Ideas?

The good news is that ideas are all around you. You just need to be aware of the rich resources that are available.

By Observing

Observing is a good way to start to find ideas. Did you see anything interesting on your way to school? Was there something unusual about the video game you played last night?

By Reading

Reading is another useful option—look through newspaper articles and editorials, magazines, blogs, and Web sites. Perhaps you read something that surprised you or really made you feel concerned. Those are exactly the subjects that can lead to the ideas you want to write about.

By Watching

Watching is another way to get ideas—watch online videos or television programs, for example.

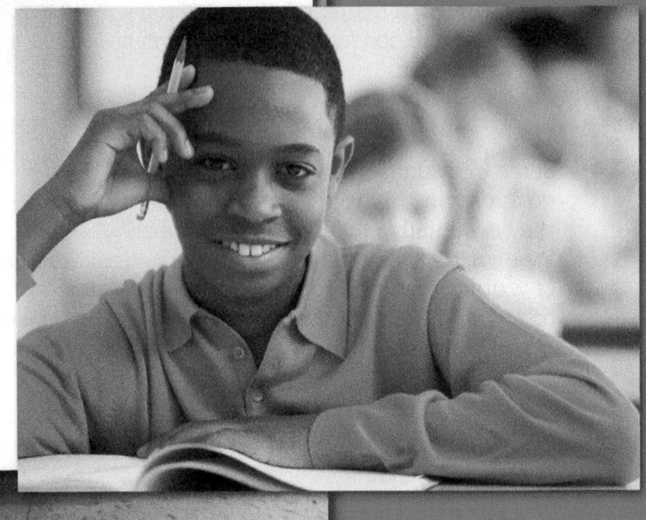

www.phwritingcoach.com

Online Journal

Try It! Record your notes, answers, and ideas in the online journal. You can also record and save your answers and ideas on pop-up sticky notes in the eText.

Writer to Writer

I write when I want to be heard or connect. Writing lets me be a vital part of my community and reach outside it as well. All the while, I get to be me—my unique self.

—Jeff Anderson

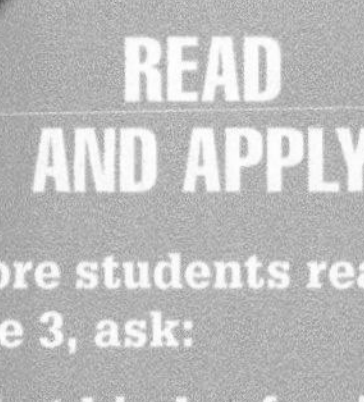

READ AND APPLY

Before students read page 3, ask:

- What kinds of writing do you do in school? At home? In your leisure time?
- Do you ever write lists, notes, or letters? Do you write or text your friends? Do you write on a social networking site?
- How do you find ideas about which to write?

Write all student responses on the board.

Then, have students read the text. Hold a class discussion about the similarities and differences between student responses and the information provided.

Differentiated Instruction

RTI Strategy for Below-Level Students
Students may benefit from previewing the heads on pages 2 and 3 after engaging in the Motivate and Engage activity on page 2 and the Read and Apply activity on page 3. Remind students that previewing the heads in a textbook is a helpful way to figure out the content that lies ahead. Ask students to summarize what they think will be covered on the two pages of text.

Enrichment for Gifted/Talented Students
For students who enjoy creative writing, assign the freewriting strategy to elaborate on where or how they find their best writing ideas and what makes an idea "a good idea" in their minds. Give students a fixed amount of time—five or ten minutes—to write whatever comes to mind. Then, when students have finished the freewrite, suggest that they read their work to determine how they get their best ideas.

How Can You Keep Track of Ideas?

You may sometimes think of great writing ideas in the middle of the night or on the way to math class. These strategies can help you remember those ideas.

Start an Idea Notebook or a Digital Idea File

Reserving a small **notebook** to record ideas can be very valuable. Just writing the essence of an idea, as it comes to you, can later help you develop a topic or essay. A **digital idea file** is exactly the same thing—but it's recorded on your computer, cell phone, or other electronic device.

Keep a Personal Journal

Many people find that keeping a **journal** of their thoughts is helpful. Then, when it's time to select an idea, they can flip through their journal and pick up on the best gems they wrote—sometimes from long ago.

Maintain a Learning Log

A **learning log** is just what it sounds like—a place to record information you have learned, which could be anything from methods of solving equations to computer shortcuts. Writing about something in a learning log might later inspire you to conduct further research on the same topic.

Free Write

Some individuals find that if they just let go and write whatever comes to mind, they eventually produce excellent ideas. **Free writing** requires being relaxed and unstructured. This kind of writing does not require complete sentences, correct spelling, or proper grammar. Whatever ends up on the paper or on the computer screen is fine. Later, the writer can go back and tease out the best ideas.

MOTIVATE AND ENGAGE

Ask students to brainstorm for ways to keep track of their ideas for writing assignments. You may wish to pair students for the activity. Give students one minute to think of as many ways as possible. Remind them not to judge each other's ideas during the brainstorming session.

When the minute is up, ask volunteers to share their responses. Then, compare student responses to the text on page 4.

Working with ELLs — ELL Sheltered Instruction: Cognitive

As students read page 5, help them use the linguistic support of a dictionary to enhance and confirm their understanding of increasingly complex and elaborated spoken language.

Beginning In simple sentences, orally describe the steps to follow in the writing calendar on page 5. To enhance and confirm students' understanding, guide them in looking up *research* and *draft* in a dictionary. Read the definitions aloud, monitoring comprehension with yes/no questions. Then, have them complete sentence frames about the calendar, such as *On (Tuesday, October 1), I (start research).*

How Can You Get Started?

Every writer is different, so it makes sense that all writers should try out techniques that might work well for them. Regardless of your writing style, these suggestions should help you get started.

Get Comfortable

It's important to find and create an environment that encourages your writing process. Choose a spot where you'll find it easy to concentrate. Some writers prefer quiet. Others prefer to work in a room with music playing softly.

Have Your Materials Ready

Before starting to write, gather all the background materials you need to get started, including your notes, free writing, reader's journal, and portfolio. Make sure you also have writing tools, such as a pen and paper or a computer.

Spend Time Wisely

Budgeting your available writing time is a wise strategy. Depending on your writing goal, you may want to sketch out your time on a calendar, estimating how long to devote to each stage of the writing process. Then, you can assign deadlines to each part. If you find a particular stage takes longer than you estimated, simply adjust your schedule to ensure that you finish on time.

October

SUNDAY	MONDAY	TUESDAY	WEDNESDAY	THURSDAY	FRIDAY	SATURDAY
		1 Start Research	2 Finish Research	3 Write Outline	4	5
6	7	8 Finish First Draft	9 Finish Revising	10 Finish Proof-reading	11	12
13	14 DUE DATE	15	16	17	18	19
20	21	22	23	24	25	26
27	28	29	30	31		

READ AND APPLY

Have students read page 5. Then, ask students, on a one-to-one basis if necessary, whether they have a place where they can write and do their homework. If not, ask them how to find or create one.

Pair students to create a plan for writing a research report that will be due in one month. Have them list the different materials they will need and determine deadlines for research, drafting, and revising.

Intermediate Pair students with fluent readers. Read aloud the calendar text on page 5. To enhance and confirm understanding, have partners take notes on unfamiliar words and look them up in a dictionary.

Advanced Group students, and read the Spend Time Wisely section. To enhance and confirm students' understanding, direct them to look up unfamiliar words in a dictionary. Then, have them create a model calendar of their own, based on their past writing experience.

Advanced High Have students complete the Advanced activity and report additional information they found in the dictionary, such as other forms of the words.

How Do You Work With Others?

If you think of writing as a solitary activity, think again. Working with others can be a key part of the writing process.

Brainstorming

Brainstorming works when everyone in a group feels free to suggest ideas, whether they seem commonplace or brilliant.

Cooperative Writing

Cooperative writing is a process in which each member of a group concentrates on a different part of an assignment. Then, the group members come together to discuss their ideas and write drafts.

Peer Feedback

Peer feedback comes from classmates who have read your writing and offered suggestions for improvements. When commenting, it's important to provide constructive, or helpful, criticism.

21st Century Learning

Collaborate and Discuss

In **collaborative writing,** each group member takes a role on a writing project. The goal is to work and rework the writing until all members feel they have produced the best result.

Possible Roles in a Collaborative Writing Project

LEADER Initiates the discussion by clearly expressing group goals and moderates discussions

FACILITATOR Works to move the discussion forward and clarify ideas

COMPROMISER Works to find practical solutions to differences of opinion

LISTENER Actively listens and serves to recall details that were discussed

MOTIVATE AND ENGAGE

Activate prior knowledge by asking students a variety of questions connected to the text on pages 6 and 7. Jot their responses on the board. Then, compare these responses to the text. Ask:

Which methods for working with others have you found helpful? Why?

Which methods have you found difficult or challenging? Why?

Do you save your work?

What has been your best piece of writing? Why was it the best?

Using Technology

Technology allows collaboration to occur in ways that were previously unthinkable.

- By working together on the Internet, students around the world have infinite opportunities to collaborate online on a wide range of projects.
- Collaboration can range from projects that foster community cooperation, such as how to improve debates during local elections, to those that increase global awareness, such as focusing on how to encourage more recycling.
- Being able to log in and to contribute to media, such as journals, blogs, and social networks, allows you to connect globally, express your views in writing, and join a world-wide conversation.

Where Can You Keep Your Finished Work?

A **portfolio,** or growing collection of your work, is valuable for many reasons. It can serve as a research bank of ideas and as a record of how your writing is improving. You can create a portfolio on a computer or in a folder or notebook. You'll learn more about managing a portfolio in chapter 3.

A **Reader's Journal,** in which you record quotes and ideas from your reading, can also be used to store original ideas. Your journal can be housed on a computer or in a notebook.

Reflect on Your Writing

Analyzing, making inferences, and drawing conclusions about how you find ideas can help you become a better, more effective writer. Find out more about how you write by asking yourself questions like these:

- Which strategies have I found most effective for finding good ideas for writing?
- What pieces of writing represent my best work and my weakest work? What do the pieces in each group have in common?

Partner Talk

With a partner, talk about your collaborative writing experiences. Be sure to share your responses to such questions as these: What project did you work on as a collaborative effort? What did you learn that you might not have discovered if you were developing a writing project by yourself?

COLLABORATE AND DISCUSS

Have students read the Collaborate and Discuss feature on page 6. Ask students to quickwrite about collaborative writing groups. Tell students to write about either (1) their prior experiences with collaborative writing, including successes and challenges, or (2) their preferred roles in a group and why. Invite volunteers to share their quickwrites and hold a class discussion about the pros and cons of working in groups.

Differentiated Instruction

RTI Strategy for Special Needs Students Work with students to create flashcards for each method of collaboration. On one side, write the method: brainstorming, cooperative writing, peer feedback, technology. On the other side, write a brief description of the ways students work together to accomplish the goal. Use the flashcards to reinforce the concepts, and suggest that students keep the cards for future reference.

Strategy for Spanish Speakers Students whose home language is Spanish may reflect on their writing by asking themselves what language difficulties they may have when writing. For example, some students may forget to use subject pronouns or use the wrong word order. Encourage them to improve by asking them to make a personal checklist of these areas and refer to it when editing and revising their writing.

CHAPTER 2

TYPES *of* WRITING

Genres and Forms

Genres are types, or categories, of writing.

- Each genre has a specific **purpose,** or goal. For example, the purpose of persuasive writing is to convince readers to agree with the writer's point of view.
- Each genre has specific **characteristics.** Short stories, for example, have characters, a setting, and a plot.

In this chapter, you will be introduced to several genres: nonfiction narratives, fiction narratives, poetry and descriptive writing, expository writing, persuasive writing, responses to literature, and workplace writing.

Forms are subcategories of genres that contain all the characteristics of the genre plus some unique characteristics of their own. For example, a mystery is a form of short story. In addition to plot, characters, and setting, it has a mystery to be solved.

Selecting Genres

In some writing situations, you may need to select the correct genre for conveying your intended meaning.

- To **entertain,** you may choose to write a short story or a humorous essay.
- To **describe** an emotion, writing a poem may be best.
- To **persuade** someone to your point of view, you may want to write a persuasive essay or editorial.

Each genre has unique strengths and weaknesses, and your specific goals will help you decide which is best.

8

MOTIVATE AND ENGAGE

Write the word *genre* on the board. Have students freewrite for one minute about literary genres. Ask them to list as many genres as they can and what the purpose is of each. Then, invite volunteers to write a genre and its purpose on the board.

After they read page 8, have students compare their freewrites to the text. Then, challenge them to list a *form* of each of the genres listed there.

Working with ELLs — ELL Sheltered Instruction: Cognitive

As students study types of nonfiction narration, guide them to demonstrate English comprehension by employing basic reading skills, including summarizing and comparing and contrasting. Have them use graphic organizers to expand these skills.

Beginning Write simple sentences that might appear in a personal narrative. Read them aloud as students follow along, and lead students in recording key words in a cluster diagram. Guide them in using the diagram to summarize what they read.

Intermediate Pair students with fluent speakers and have them read an excerpt from a biography, taking notes in a main idea

Nonfiction Narration

Nonfiction narratives are any kind of literary text that tells a story about real people, events, and ideas. This genre of writing can take a number of different forms but includes well-developed conflict and resolution, interesting and believable characters, and a range of literary strategies, such as dialogue and suspense. Examples include Jean Fritz's "mk" and Annie Dillard's "An American Childhood."

Personal Narratives

Personal narratives tell true stories about events in a writer's life. These types of writing are also called **autobiographical essays.** The stories may tell about an experience or relationship that is important to the writer, who is the main character. They have a clearly defined focus and communicate the reasons for actions and consequences.

Biographical Narratives

In a **biographical narrative,** the writer shares facts about someone else's life. The writer may describe an important period, experience, or relationship in that other person's life, but presents the information from his or her own perspective.

Blogs

Blogs are online journals that may include autobiographical narratives, reflections, opinions, and other types of comments. They may also reflect genres other than nonfiction such as expository writing, and they may include other media, such as photos, music, or video.

WRITING COACH **Online**

www.phwritingcoach.com

Online Journal

Try It! Record your notes, answers, and ideas in the online journal. You can also record and save your answers and ideas on pop-up sticky notes in the eText.

MOTIVATE AND ENGAGE

Before students read page 9 and 10, ask:

- **What is nonfiction writing?**
- **What are some forms of nonfiction?**

Have students work in pairs to answer the questions. Then, have pairs read the text and revise their answers as necessary. Invite volunteers to share their responses.

and details chart. Then, have partners write a summary based on their charts.

Advanced Have students preview page 9, filling in a K-W-L chart with what they know about nonfiction narration and what they want to learn. Have them read page 9 and complete the chart with what they learned. Have them use the chart to write a paragraph describing the similarities and differences among personal narratives, biographical narratives, and blogs.

Advanced High Have students complete the Advanced activity. Then, have them exchange paragraphs with partners and summarize each other's work.

Diary and Journal Entries

Writers record their personal thoughts, feelings, and experiences in **diaries** or **journals.** Writers sometimes keep diaries and journals for many years and then analyze how they reacted to various events over time.

Eyewitness Accounts

Eyewitness accounts are nonfiction writing that focus on historical or other important events. The writer is the narrator and shares his or her thoughts about the event. However, the writer is not the main focus of the writing.

Memoirs

Memoirs usually focus on meaningful scenes from writers' lives. These scenes often reflect on moments of a significant decision or personal discovery. For example, many modern U.S. presidents have written memoirs after they have left office. These memoirs help the public gain a better understanding of the decisions they made while in office.

Reflective Essays

Reflective essays present personal experiences, either events that happened to the writers themselves or that they learned about from others. They generally focus on sharing observations and insights they had while thinking about those experiences. Reflective essays often appear as features in magazines and newspapers.

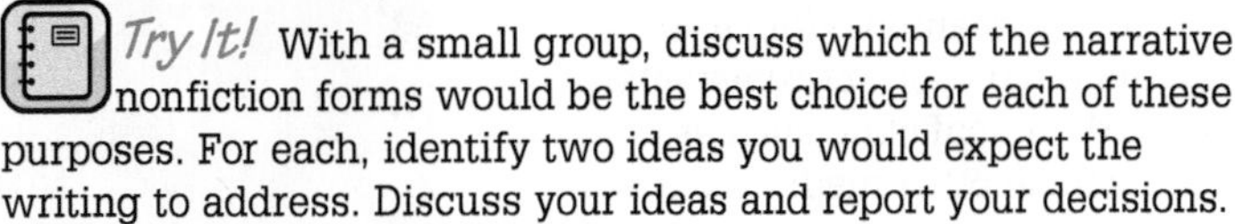

Try It! With a small group, discuss which of the narrative nonfiction forms would be the best choice for each of these purposes. For each, identify two ideas you would expect the writing to address. Discuss your ideas and report your decisions.

- To tell about seeing a championship kite-flying tournament
- To write about one of the first astronauts to walk in space
- To record personal thoughts about a favorite teacher

COLLABORATE AND DISCUSS

Extend the *Try It!* activity by having small groups come up with one writing topic and two ideas about the topic for each form of nonfiction listed on pages 9 and 10. Remind students to assign roles to group members, such as facilitator, scribe or secretary, timekeeper, and presenter. Then, have each group present its examples for the class.

Working with ELLs — ELL Sheltered Instruction: Cognitive

As students read about fictional narratives, help them narrate events, describe places, people, or things, and explain situations with increasing specificity and detail in writing.

Beginning Meet with students and provide simple prompts to facilitate writing. Help students supply words and phrases in response to the following prompt, and write them on the board: *the day school closed*. Then, help students create a story by using the phrases to narrate events, describe characters and setting, and explain a situation with specificity and detail. Finally, read the finished story aloud as students copy it down.

Fiction Narration

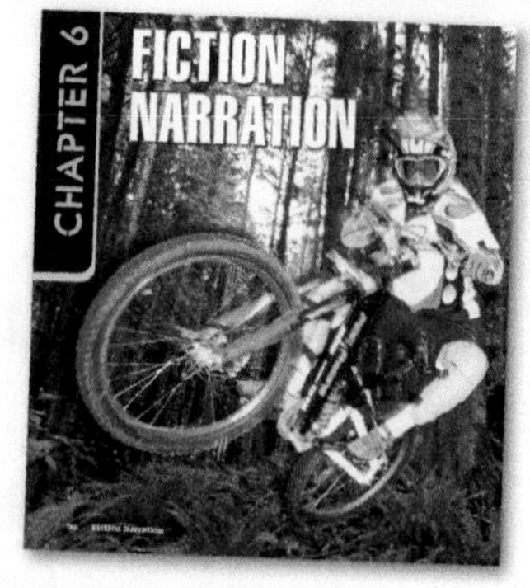

Fiction narratives are literary texts that tell a story about imagined people, events, and ideas. They contain elements such as characters, a setting, a sequence of events, and often, a theme. As with nonfiction narratives, this genre can take many different forms, but most forms include well-developed **conflict** and **resolution.** They also include **interesting and believable elements** and a range of **literary strategies,** such as dialogue and suspense. Examples include Cynthia Rylant's "Papa's Parrot" and Lucille Clifton's "The Luckiest Time of All."

Realistic Fiction

Realistic fiction portrays invented characters and events in everyday situations. Because the focus is on everyday life, realistic fiction often presents problems that many people face and solutions they devise to solve them.

Fantasy Stories

Fantasy stories stretch the imagination and take readers to unreal worlds. Animals may talk, people may fly, or characters may have superhuman powers. Good fantasy stories manage to keep the fantastic elements believable.

Historical Fiction

Historical fiction is about imaginary people living in real places and times in history. Usually, the main characters are fictional people who know and interact with famous people and participate in important historical events.

Mystery Stories

Mystery stories present unexplained or strange events that characters try to solve. These stories are often packed full of suspense and surprises. Some characters in mystery stories, such as Sherlock Holmes, have become so famous that many people think of them as real people.

MOTIVATE AND ENGAGE

Before students read pages 11 and 12, ask:

- **What is fiction?**
- **What are some elements of fiction?**

Pair students to answer the questions. Then, have students read pages 11 and 12, and revise their answers as necessary. As a class, discuss the various forms of fiction and make a list of elements the forms might share, such as characters, setting, and conflict.

Intermediate Distribute story maps to groups of students. Have them use the maps to plan and write a story. As they draft, ask questions to encourage them to narrate events, describe places, people, or things, and explain situations with greater specificity and detail. Call on groups to read their stories.

Advanced Have partners write a short story about a day at school, narrating events, describing places, people, or things, and explaining situations with specificity and detail.

Advanced High Have students complete the Advanced activity. Then, have them revise their stories, incorporating peer feedback.

Myths and Legends

Myths and **legends** are traditional stories, told in cultures around the world. They were created to explain natural events that people could not otherwise explain or understand. They may, for example, tell about the origin of fire or thunder. Many myths and legends include gods, goddesses, and heroes who perform superhuman actions.

Science Fiction

Science fiction stories tell about real and imagined developments in science and technology and their effects on the way people think and live. Space travel, robots, and life in the future are popular topics in science fiction.

Tall Tales

You can tell a **tall tale** from other story types because it tells about larger-than-life characters in realistic settings. These characters can perform amazing acts of strength and bravery. One very famous hero of tall tales is Pecos Bill, who could ride just about anything—even a tornado!

Try It! Think about what you've read about narrative fiction and narrative nonfiction genres. Then, discuss in a group which **genre** would be best if you were planning a first draft and had these purposes in mind. Select the correct genre for conveying your intended meaning to your audiences. Then, identify two or three ideas that you would expect to include in a first draft. Be sure to explain your choices.

- To tell about a Texas rancher who can lasso lightning
- To share a true story about a famous person
- To tell the story of your most exciting day at school

COLLABORATE AND DISCUSS

Review the meaning of the term *audience*. Then, after small groups complete the *Try It!* activity, extend the activity by having the groups identify a specific audience for each topic. Remind groups to review the genre and the purpose as well as the ideas they generated about each. Then, have groups determine whether the purpose, genre, and story ideas would address the needs of that audience. If not, what changes would be necessary?

Poetry and Description

Poetry and other kinds of descriptive literature express ideas and feelings about real or imagined people, events, and ideas. They use rhythm, rhyme, precise language, and sensory details—words that appeal to the senses—to create vivid images. In addition, they use figurative language—writing that means something beyond what the words actually say—to express ideas in new, fresh, and interesting ways.

Structural elements, such as line length and stanzas, also help the poet express ideas and set a mood. Some examples of poetry include Naomi Shihab Nye's "The Rider" and Nikki Giovanni's "Winter."

Ballad

A **ballad** is a form of lyric poetry that expresses the poet's emotions toward someone or something. Ballads rhyme, and some have refrains that repeat after each stanza, which makes them easy to translate into songs.

In many places, traditional folk ballads were passed down as oral poems or songs and then later written. Some ballads tell about cultural heroes. Other ballads tell sad stories or make fun of certain events.

Free Verse

Free verse is poetry that has no regular rhyme, rhythm, or form. Instead, a free verse poem captures the patterns of natural speech. The poet writes in whatever form seems to fit the ideas best. A free verse poem can have almost anything as its subject.

Writer to Writer

Writing fiction and poetry sharpens your creativity—a skill valued by universities and employers.

—Kelly Gallagher

Think about an example of fiction that you've especially enjoyed reading. Then, choose a partner and report your choices to each other. Be sure to explain what made the fiction piece so enjoyable, interesting, or exciting.

MOTIVATE AND ENGAGE

Write these questions on the board: *What forms of poetry are familiar to you? What forms of poetry have you written in the past?* Tell students to use these questions to spark a quickwrite about poetry. Encourage volunteers to share their responses.

After students have read the text on pages 13 and 14, have a class discussion about what they learned from the text and what kind of poetry they would like to write.

Differentiated Instruction

RTI Strategy for Below-Level Students Students may benefit from listening to or reading poetry. Examples of some of the forms on pages 13 and 14 can be found on pages 122 and 123. Give students copies of the latter pages. Go through the examples and help students identify the differences between the different forms.

Strategy for Spanish Speakers Students whose home language is Spanish may have difficulty distinguishing between ballads and free verse because they need help identifying rhyming words in English. Give pairs examples of ballads and free verse poems and have them identify the ballads. Then, have them identify the rhyming words in the ballads. Review the spellings variations in rhyming words, as these often differ in Spanish.

Prose Poem

A **prose poem** shares many of the features of other poetry, but it takes the form of prose, or non-verse writing. Therefore, a prose poem may look like a short story on a page.

Sonnet

The **sonnet** is a form of rhyming lyric poetry with set rules. It is 14 lines long and usually follows a rhythm scheme called iambic pentameter. Each line has ten syllables and every other syllable is accented.

Haiku

Haiku is a form of non-rhyming poetry that was first developed in Japan hundreds of years ago. Typically, the first line has seven syllables, the second line has five syllables, and the third line has seven syllables. Haiku poets often write about nature and use vivid visual images.

Other Descriptive Writing

Descriptive writing includes descriptive essays, travel writing, and definition essays.

- **Descriptive essays** often use words that involve the senses to create a clear picture of a subject.
- A **travel essay** uses sensory words to describe a place.
- A **definition essay** can draw on a writer's emotional experience to describe something abstract, like friendship or happiness.

  Description can be used in other types of writing. For example, a short story may include strong description.

Try It! Now that you've learned more about poetry and description, discuss which specific **genre** would be best for each of these purposes. Select the correct genre for conveying your intended meaning to your audiences. Then, identify two or three types of information that you would want to include in a first draft. Be ready to explain your thinking.

- To tell about a trip to a beach in Mexico
- To describe a drop of rain
- To tell the story of a character who lives in the wilderness

READ AND APPLY

After students have read pages 13 and 14, have pairs complete the *Try It!* activity. Emphasize that descriptive words will be important in all of the genres students might choose. Ask:

- **What specific things do you think you would be describing in each topic?**
- **What words might you use in your descriptions?**

Encourage volunteers to share their responses. Have a discussion on ways to enhance descriptive details.

Working with ELLs — ELL Sheltered Instruction: Cognitive

As students learn about descriptive writing, help them orally narrate events, describe places, people, or things, and explain situations with increasing specificity and detail.

Beginning Display a word bank of basic words that might be used to narrate a shopping trip. Review the words, miming as appropriate. Provide sentence starters about shopping, such as *At the store I saw a* _______ . Have students complete them orally to narrate events, describe people or things, and explain situations.

Intermediate Pair students with fluent partners, and distribute cluster diagrams. Have pairs fill in the diagrams with ideas for a story, including descriptions of characters and settings, narration of events, and

Exposition

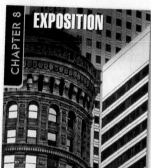

Exposition is writing that seeks to communicate ideas and information. It relies on facts to inform or explain.

- Effective expository writing includes effective introductory paragraphs, body paragraphs, and concluding paragraphs.
- In addition, good expository writing uses a variety of sentence structures and rhetorical devices—deliberate uses of language for specific effects.

Examples of expository writing include Ruwanthi Vigilant's "Houston's Chinatown" and Larry Lunxer's "Mongoose on the Loose."

Analytical Essay

An **analytical essay** explores a topic by supplying relevant information in the form of facts, examples, reasons, and valid inferences to support the writer's claims.

- An **introductory paragraph** presents a thesis statement, the main point to be developed.
- The **body of the essay** provides facts about the topic, using a variety of sentence structures and transitions.
- The **concluding paragraph** sums up ideas.

Compare-and-Contrast Essay

A **compare-and-contrast** essay explores similarities and differences between two or more things for a specific purpose. As with other expository essays, the compare-and-contrast essay offers clear, factual details about the subject.

Cause-and-Effect Essay

A **cause-and-effect essay** traces the results of an event or describes the reasons an event happened. It is clearly organized and gives precise examples that support the relationship between the cause and effect.

Writer to Writer

Expository forms can shape my thinking and help my writing gel. I find the expository patterns clarifying my thoughts and filling in gaps that I may have otherwise missed.

—Jeff Anderson

Choose a different partner this time. Discuss a poem that you've read in class. Share your thoughts about the poem and describe what made the piece successful.

MOTIVATE AND ENGAGE

Before students read pages 15-17, have a discussion about their perceptions of expository writing. Elicit from students that expository writing explains or informs.

Have students quickwrite about different forms of exposition. Provide one or two examples, such as cause-and-effect and compare-and-contrast essays, to get students started. Ask students to write about expository writing they have done, explaining successes and challenges as well as purpose and audience. Then, discuss student responses.

explanations of situations. Then, have partners practice telling their stories. Call on pairs to tell their stories to the class.

Advanced Have students brainstorm and record ideas for a story. Then, have them use their notes to relate the story to a partner. As they practice storytelling, ensure they narrate events, describe places, people, or things, and explain situations with increasing specificity and detail.

Advanced High Have students complete the Advanced activity. To challenge students, have them orally summarize their partners' stories.

Classification Essay

In a **classification essay,** a writer organizes a subject into categories and explains the category into which an item falls.

- An effective classification essay **sorts** its subjects—things or ideas—into several categories.
- It then offers **examples** that fall into each category. For example, a classification essay about video games might discuss three types of video games—action, adventure, and arcade.
- The essay might conclude with a statement about how the items classified are different or about how they are similar.

Problem-Solution Essay

A **problem-solution essay** presents a problem and then offers solutions to that problem. This type of essay may contain opinions, like a persuasive essay, but it is meant to explain rather than persuade.

- An effective problem-solution essay presents a clear statement of the problem, including a summary of its causes and effects.
- Then, it proposes at least one realistic solution and uses facts, statistics, or expert testimony to support the solution.
- The essay should be clearly organized, so that the relationship between the problem and the solution is obvious.

Pro-Con Essay

A **pro-con essay** examines arguments for and against an idea or topic.

- It has a topic that has two sides or points of view. For example, you might choose the following as a topic: Is it right to keep animals in zoos?
- Then, you would develop an essay that tells why it's good to keep animals in zoos, as well as why it's harmful to keep animals in zoos.
- It's important to be sure to give a clear analysis of the topic.

COLLABORATE AND DISCUSS

After students have read pages 15–17, make a class chart of the forms of exposition. Each column head should be the name of a form. Invite volunteers to the board to add purposes and audiences for each form.

Discuss the information in the chart, answering questions and clarifying information. Then, encourage students to copy the chart in their notebooks or writing journals to keep for future reference.

Newspaper and Magazine Articles

Newspaper and **magazine articles** offer information about news and events. They are typically factual and do not include the writer's opinions. They often provide an analysis of events and give readers background information on a topic. Some articles may also reflect genres other than the analytical essay, such as an editorial that aims to persuade.

Internet Articles

Articles on the **Internet** can supply relevant information about a topic.

- They are often like newspaper or magazine articles but may include shorter sentences and paragraphs. In addition, they include more visuals, such as charts and bulleted lists. They may also reflect genres other than analytical essays.
- It's always wise to consider the source when reading Internet articles because only the most reputable sources should be trusted to present correct facts.

On-Demand Writing

Because essay questions often appear on school tests, knowing how to write to **test prompts**, especially under time limits, is an important skill.

Test prompts provide a clear topic with directions about what should be addressed. The effective response to an essay demonstrates not only an understanding of academic content but also good writing skills.

Try It! Think about what you've learned about expository writing and consider the other genres you've discussed. Then, discuss in a group which **genre** would be best if you were planning a first draft with these purposes in mind. Select the correct genre for conveying your intended meaning to your audiences. Then, identify two or three key ideas that you would want to include in a first draft. Be sure to explain your choices.

- To weigh the benefits of two kinds of pets
- To imagine what life would be like on the moon

Partner Talk

Share your experiences with writing expository essays with a partner. Talk about strategies that worked well for you, as well as those that weren't as successful. Be sure to include your analysis of why certain strategies worked better than others.

READ AND APPLY

Before students attempt the *Try It!*, review some of the characteristics of expository writing. Ask:

- **Which is more important in expository writing, clarity or imaginative description?**
- **Is expository writing better for comparing things and ideas or for developing a character?**

Explain that asking these questions will help them to effectively focus their writing.

Differentiated Instruction

RTI Strategy for Below-Level Students Preteach these vocabulary words: *exposition, analytical, classification, on-demand writing*. Have students make flashcards, writing the term and the definition on either side. Then, show them the term and ask them to give you the definition. Finally, brainstorm with students for examples of expository essays. Ask *Can you give me an example of a book report, which is an analytical essay?*

PRE-AP Enrichment for Above-Level Students Provide students with this test prompt: Write an essay in which you discuss the similarities and differences between your daily routine during the school year and during your summer vacation. Then, challenge students to identify the form of exposition, the purpose, and intended audience and write an introduction to this essay, with a thesis statement.

Persuasion

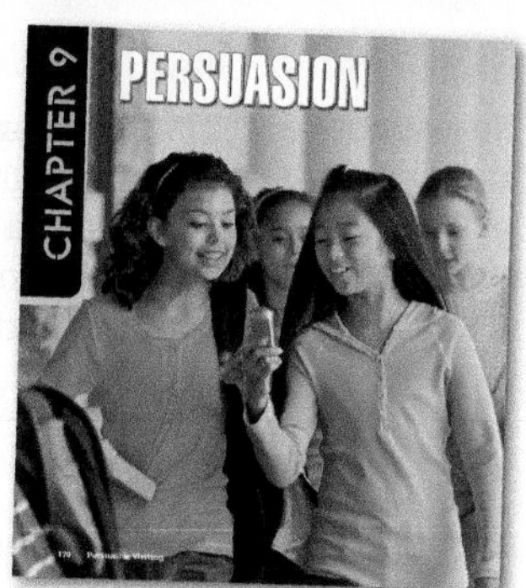

Persuasive writing aims to influence the attitudes or actions of a specific audience on specific issues. A strong persuasive text is logically organized and clearly describes the issue. It also provides precise and relevant evidence that supports a clear thesis statement. Persuasive writing may contain diagrams, graphs, or charts. These visuals can help to convince the reader. Examples include Barbara Jordan's "All Together Now" and Louis L'Amour's "The Eternal Frontier."

Persuasive Essays or Argumentative Essays

A **persuasive essay** or **argumentative essay** uses logic and reasoning to persuade readers to adopt a certain point of view or to take action. A strong persuasive essay starts with a clear thesis statement and provides supporting arguments based on evidence. It also anticipates readers' counter-arguments and responds to them as well.

Motivate and Engage

To activate prior knowledge of persuasion, ask students to write about a time they had to convince someone to agree with them or to do what they asked. Then, have a class discussion based on students' responses. Talk about which strategies worked. Also discuss what tactics are likely NOT to work in persuasion.

Persuasive Speeches

Persuasive speeches are presented aloud and aim to win an audience's support for a policy, position, or action. These speeches often appeal to emotion and reason to convince an audience. Speakers sometimes change their script in order to address each specific audience's concerns.

Editorials

Editorials state the opinion of the editors and publishers of news organizations. Editorials usually present an opinion about a current issue, starting with a clear thesis statement and then offering strong supporting evidence.

Op-Ed Pieces

An **op-ed, or opposite-editorial, piece** is an essay that tries to convince readers to agree with the writer's views on an issue. The writer may not work for the publication and is often an expert on the issue or has an interesting point of view.

Letters to the Editor

Readers write **letters to editors** at print and Internet publications to express opinions in response to previously published articles. A good letter to the editor gives an accurate and honest representation of the writer's views.

Reviews

Reviews evaluate items and activities, such as books, movies, plays, and music, from the writer's point of view. A review often states opinions on the quality of an item or activity and supports those opinions with examples, facts, and other evidence.

Advertisements

Advertisements in all media—from print to online sites to highway billboards—are paid announcements that try to convince people to buy something or do something. Good advertisements use a hook to grab your attention and support their claims. They contain vivid, persuasive language and multimedia techniques, such as music, to appeal to a specific audience.

Propaganda

Propaganda uses emotional appeals and often biased, false, or misleading information to persuade people to think or act in a certain way. Propaganda may tap into people's strongest emotions by generating fear or attacking their ideas of loyalty or patriotism. Because propaganda appears to be objective, it is wise to be aware of the ways it can manipulate people's opinions and actions.

Try It! Think about what you have learned about exposition, description, and persuasion. Form a group to discuss and draw conclusions about which **genres** would be best if you were planning a first draft with each of these intentions in mind. Select the correct genre for conveying your intended meaning to your audiences. Then, identify two or three types of information that you would want to include in a first draft.

- To explain how an event happened
- To describe a beautiful landscape
- To encourage teens to buy teeth-whitening toothpaste

Partner Talk

Share your experiences with various types of persuasive texts with a partner. Talk about the types of persuasive text that you think are most effective, honest, and fair. Be sure to explain your thinking.

READ AND APPLY

After students have read the text on pages 18 and 19, ask:

- **What are the common elements of persuasive writing? What elements are unique to each form?**
- **What types of information would be used in different types of writing?**
- **Would you use facts in an expository essay, metaphors in poem, and statistics in a persuasive essay?**

Tell students to complete the *Try It!* activity on page 19.

Differentiated Instruction

RTI Strategy for Special Needs Students Have students preview the heads on pages 18 and 19 with you. Ask students to identify words that are unfamiliar or challenging. Work with students to define each word. Have students look through a newspaper and find as many examples of the different forms of persuasive writing as they can.

Enrichment for Gifted/Talented Students Have students choose one of the forms of persuasive writing listed on pages 18 and 19 and write a brief persuasive piece, in which they make their argument and persuade their audience to agree or to act. Invite volunteers to read their persuasive piece to the class, and to identify their purpose and intended audience.

Responses to Literature

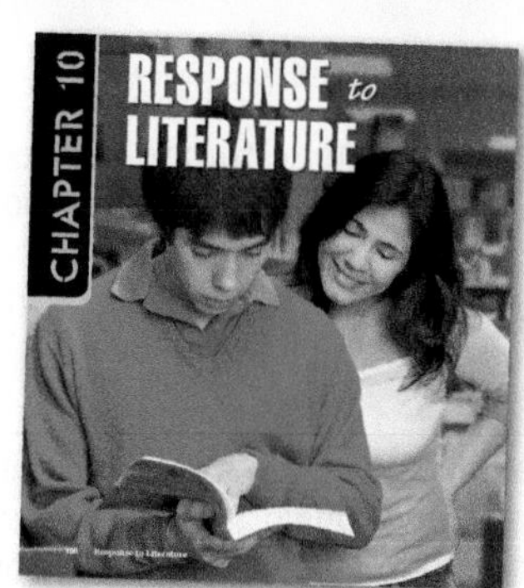

Responses to literature analyze and interpret an author's work. They use clear **thesis statements** and **evidence from the text using embedded quotations to support the writer's ideas.** They also evaluate how well authors have accomplished their goals. Effective responses to literature extend beyond literal analysis to evaluate and discuss how and why the text is effective or not effective.

Critical Reviews

Critical reviews evaluate books, plays, poetry, and other literary works. Reviews present the writer's opinions and support them with specific examples. The responses may analyze the aesthetic effects of an author's use of language in addition to responding to the content of the writing.

Compare-and-Contrast Essays

Compare-and-contrast essays explore similarities and differences between two or more works of literature. These essays provide relevant evidence to support the writer's opinions.

Letters to Authors

Readers write **letters to authors** to share their feelings and thoughts about a work of literature directly.

Blog Comments

Blog comments on an author's Web site or book retailer pages let readers share their ideas about a work. Readers express their opinions and give interpretations of what an author's work means.

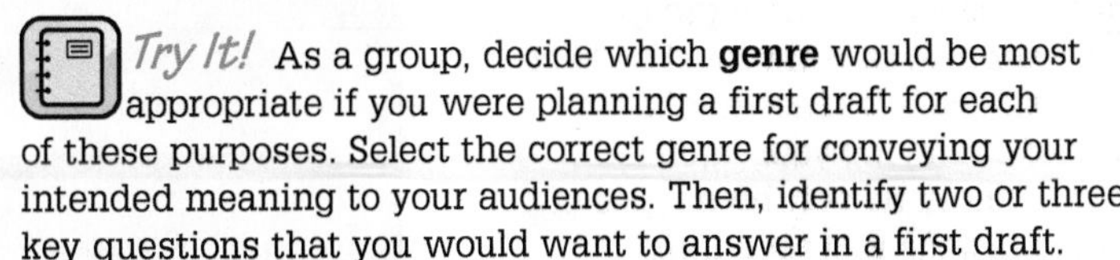

Try It! As a group, decide which **genre** would be most appropriate if you were planning a first draft for each of these purposes. Select the correct genre for conveying your intended meaning to your audiences. Then, identify two or three key questions that you would want to answer in a first draft.

- To tell an author why you think her book is excellent
- To write an opinion about a newspaper article
- To imagine how a certain landform came to be

Partner Talk

Interview your partner about his or her experiences writing interpretative responses. Be sure to ask questions such as these:

- How did you support your opinion of the author's work?
- How did you choose evidence, such as quotes, to support your analysis or opinion?

MOTIVATE AND ENGAGE

Activate students' prior knowledge of the forms listed on page 20. Ask students to quickwrite about what they know and what they would like to learn about these forms of responses to literature: critical reviews, compare-and-contrast essays, letters to authors, and blog comments.

Invite volunteers to share their responses, and ask the class to answer any questions a volunteer may have had about a form.

Research Writing

Research writing is based on factual information from outside sources. Research reports organize and present ideas and information. They present evidence in support of a clear thesis statement.

Research Reports and Documented Essays

Research reports and **documented essays** present information and analysis about a topic that the writer has studied. Start with a clear thesis statement. Research reports often include graphics and illustrations. Documented essays are less formal research writing that show the source of every fact, quote, or borrowed idea in parentheses.

Experiment Journals and Lab Reports

Experiment journals and **lab reports** focus on the purposes, procedures, and results of a lab experiment. They often follow a strict format that includes dates and specific observation notes.

Statistical Analysis Reports

A **statistical analysis report** presents numerical data. Writers of this type of report must explain how they gathered their information, analyze their data, tell what significance the findings may have, and explain how these findings support their thesis.

Annotated Bibliographies

An **annotated bibliography** lists the research sources a writer used. It includes the title, author, publication date, publisher, and brief notes that describe and evaluate the source.

Try It! Discuss which kinds of reports you might write if you were planning a first draft for these purposes. **Select the correct form** for conveying your intended meaning to your audiences. Then, identify two or three key questions that you would want to answer in a first draft. Explain your choices.

- To accompany a project you plan to enter in a science fair
- To write about a poll taken to predict the results of an election

Share with a partner the kinds of research writing you've done in school. Explain which projects you've enjoyed and why.

MOTIVATE AND ENGAGE

Before students read the text on page 21, ask students to write responses to these questions that you write on the board:

- **Have you ever done research writing?**
- **Where did you find information about your topic?**
- **What challenges did you encounter?**
- **What did you like/dislike about research writing?**

Invite volunteers to share their responses, and have a class discussion on the forms of research writing.

Differentiated Instruction

RTI Strategy for Below-Level Students Have students work with a partner or with you to make flashcards for the response-to-literature writing and research-writing forms. To ensure comprehension, have student pairs test each other using the cards.

PRE-AP Enrichment for Above-Level Students Have students choose one form of response-to-literature writing. Ask students to write a brief response to a work of literature they have read recently using the form of their choice. You may wish to provide the work of literature, such as a poem or a short story. Invite volunteers to share their writing with the class and to identify the form and the unique elements of the form they used.

Workplace Writing

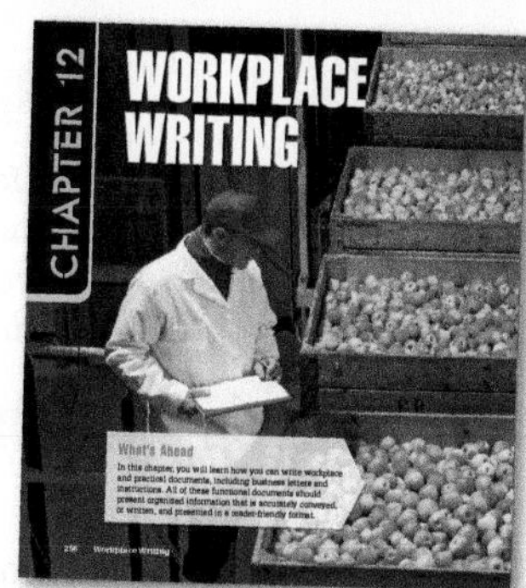

Workplace writing is writing done on the job or as part of a job, often in an office setting. It usually communicates details about a particular job or work project. This type of writing features organized and accurately conveyed information and should include reader-friendly formatting techniques, such as clearly defined sections and enough blank space for easy reading.

Business Letters and Friendly Letters

A **business letter** is a formal letter written to, from, or within a business. It can be written to make requests or to express concerns or approval. For example, you might write to a company to ask about job opportunities. Business letters follow a specific format that includes an address, date, formal greeting, and closing.

In contrast, a **friendly letter** is a form of correspondence written to communicate between family, friends, or acquaintances. For example, you might write a thank-you note for a gift.

Memos

Memos are short documents usually written from one member of an organization to another or to a group. They are an important means of communicating information within an organization.

E-mails

E-mail is an abbreviation for "electronic mail" and is a form of electronic memo. Because it can be transmitted quickly allowing for instant long-distance communication, e-mail is a very common form of communication that uses a computer and software to send messages.

Forms

Forms are types of workplace writing that ask for specific information to be completed in a particular format. Examples include applications, emergency contact information forms, and tax forms.

MOTIVATE AND ENGAGE

Initiate a class discussion about the terms *workplace* and *workplace writing.* Ask:

- What are some examples of workplaces?
- Can you get a job without using any writing skills?
- What types of writing do you think are used at work?
- What is the purpose of each type of workplace writing we have discussed?

Explain to students that workplace writing is often more formal than other types of writing.

Working with ELLs — ELL Sheltered Instruction: Cognitive

To help students internalize and build proficiency with new grade-level academic vocabulary, have them use and reuse the vocabulary in a speaking activity. Focus on these academic words from Partner Talk: *partner, procedural, challenge.*

Beginning Explain the academic words *partner* and *challenge*, using visuals and mime. Help students create a **Concept Illustration** for each word, drawing a humorous caricature with words or symbols. Help students orally present their cards, using and reusing the vocabulary to complete sentence starters such as *Running twenty miles is . . . .*

Intermediate Have students work with fluent partners to complete **Concept Illustration** cards for the academic words, as described in the Beginning

Instructions

Instructions are used to explain how to complete a task or procedure. They provide clear, step-by-step guidelines. For example, recipes and user manuals are forms of instructions.

Project Plans

Project plans are short documents usually written from one member of an organization to another. They outline a project's goals and objectives and may include specific details about how certain steps of a project should be achieved.

Résumés

A **résumé** is an overview of a person's experience and qualifications for a job. This document lists a person's job skills and work history. Résumés can also feature information about a person's education.

College Applications

College applications are documents that ask for personal information and details about someone's educational background. College administrators use this information to decide whether or not to accept a student.

Job Applications

Job applications are similar to résumés in that they require a person to list work experience and educational background. Most employers will require a completed job application as part of the hiring process.

Try It! As a group, discuss which form of workplace writing would be best for each of these purposes. Select the correct form for conveying your intended meaning to your audiences. Identify two or three types of information you would expect to include in a first draft.

- To inform the company that made your cell phone that it does not work properly
- To prepare information about your qualifications for a job search
- To create a plan for your group assignment in science class

Partner Talk

Share with a partner your experience with workplace and procedural writing. For example, have you ever written instructions, created a résumé, or completed a job application? What do you find are particular challenges with this type of writing?

COLLABORATE AND DISCUSS

After students read pages 22 and 23, have them work in small groups to discuss scenarios where they might use the different forms of workplace writing.

Have groups assign roles, such as facilitator, timekeeper, and scribe. Tell groups each scenario should be as detailed as possible (e.g., an architect creates a project plan to build a new school; a car dealer writes an email to her employees about the new model coming out.)

activity. Have them use the words in oral sentences describing their cards and then reuse the words in answers to questions you ask about their illustrations.

Advanced To help students build vocabulary proficiency, use the **Cloze Method** by writing sentences on the board with the academic words omitted. Have volunteers orally state the missing words. Have students then reuse the words in oral sentences of their own.

Advanced High After students complete the Partner Talk, have them orally summarize the activity, using the academic words in context. Have them reuse the words as they meet with Intermediate students to create **Concept Illustration** cards.

Writing for Media

The world of communication has changed significantly in recent years. In addition to writing for print media such as magazines and books, writers also write for a variety of other **media,** in forms such as:

- Scripts for screenplays, video games, and documentaries
- Storyboards for graphic novels and advertisements
- Packaging for every kind of product
- Web sites and blogs

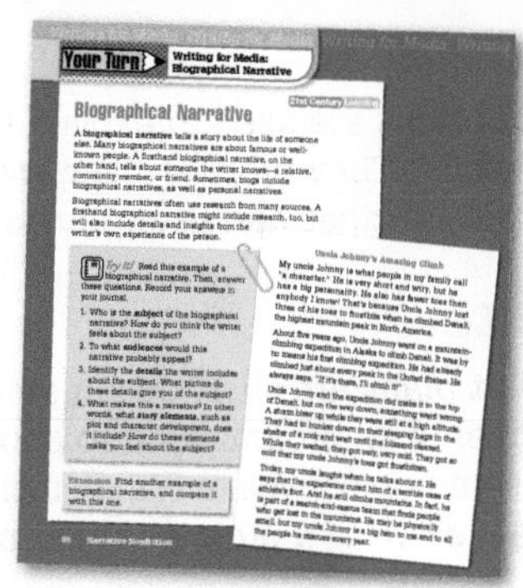

Scripts

Scripts are written for various media, such as documentaries, theater productions, speeches, and audio programs. Movies, television shows, and video games also have scripts.

- A good script focuses on a clearly expressed or implied **theme** and has a specific **purpose.**
- It also contains interesting details, which contribute to a definite **mood or tone.**
- A good script also includes a clear **setting**, **dialogue**, and well-developed **action**.

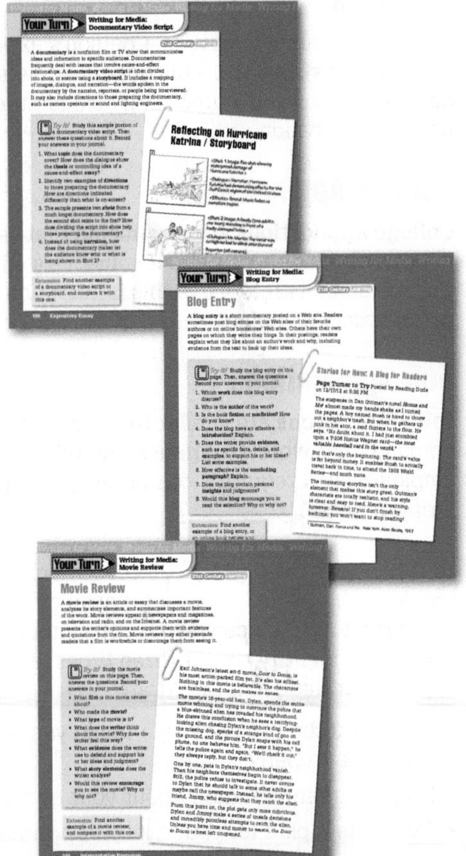

Blogs

Blogs address just about every purpose and interest. For example, there are blogs about local issues, pets, or food.

Advertisements

Advertisements are designed to persuade someone to buy a product or service. Advertisements use images, words, and music to support their message. Writers write the content of advertisements. In addition, they may help create music and design the sound and the images in the ad.

MOTIVATE AND ENGAGE

Activate prior knowledge by asking students to quickwrite about the media and writing for media. Tell students to consider the types of media they use each day and the forms of writing that are specifically for the media.

Invite volunteers to read their responses, and have a class discussion about writing that is specifically for the media.

Working with ELLs — ELL Sheltered Instruction: Social/Affective

Have students ask for and give information in situations ranging from basic communication to extended speaking assignments. Help them to monitor their oral language production and employ the self-corrective technique of watching listeners' reactions to see if they detect confusion and restating their ideas as necessary.

Guide students as they use both high-frequency, concrete vocabulary and content-based words.

Beginning Review the content-based vocabulary term *Web site*. Guide students in asking for and giving information using questions and sentence frames featuring the term, such as *What is your favorite Web site? My favorite site is ______.*

Creating Multimedia Projects

A **multimedia project** or presentation uses sound, video, and other media to convey a point or entertain an audience. No matter what type of project you choose as your own multimedia project, it is important to follow these steps:

- Decide on the project's **purpose** and your target **audience.**
- Choose **media** that will effectively convey your **message.**
- **Plan** your presentation. Will you work alone or with a partner or group? If you work with others, how you will assign the tasks?
- What **equipment** will you need? Will you produce artwork, record audio, and take photographs? Should you produce a storyboard to show the sequence of details in your presentation? Be sure to allow enough time to produce the text and all the other elements in your project.
- Keep the **writing process** in mind. There should be working and reworking along the way.
- **Assess** the progress of the project as you work. Ask questions, such as: Does my project incorporate appropriate writing genres? Will the presentation interest my audience? Have I kept my purpose in mind?
- **Rehearse!** Before presenting your project, be sure to do several "practice runs" to weed out and correct any errors.
- Keep an electronic record of your presentation for future reference.
- After your presentation, have others assess the project. Their critique will help you to do an even better job next time!

Reflect on Your Writing

Learning more about the different types of writing can help you focus on the characteristics of each type so you can keep improving your own writing. Think about what you've learned in Chapter 2 as you answer these questions:

- What type of writing most interests you?
- What type of writing do you think is most useful? Why?

Partner Talk

Share with a partner your experience with writing for media or multimedia projects. Have you created a Web site or contributed to one? Have you had to complete multimedia projects for a class assignment or for a personal project on which you worked? Talk about how writing for media presents different challenges from more traditional writing and how you have dealt with those challenges.

COLLABORATE AND DISCUSS

Before students read the text on page 25, ask them to define the term *multimedia presentation* and give an example of when they have created one (e.g., a science fair or English project).

After students have read the text discuss these questions:

- **How are multimedia presentations different from other forms of writing?**
- **How are they similar?**
- **How can your peers help you to improve a presentation?**

Remind students to use the self-corrective technique.

Intermediate After you review the content-based vocabulary words *Web site* and *media*, have students complete the Partner Talk with fluent students, using the words to ask for and give information. Remind students to use the self-corrective technique while speaking.

Advanced Have partners ask for and give information by completing the Partner Talk. Remind them to use the self-corrective technique while speaking.

Advanced High Have partners complete the Advanced activity. Then, have them orally summarize their discussions in small groups.

CHAPTER 3

THE WRITING PROCESS

Writing Traits

Good writing has specific qualities, or traits. In this chapter you will learn about these traits and how to use rubrics to evaluate them. You will also learn how to apply traits during the stages of the writing process.

Ideas

Good writing sends a strong message or presents a clear "angle" or point of view on a subject. It is also informative. The ideas are well developed, or explained with examples and other details.

Organization

A well-organized paper has an obvious plan. You will want to make sure that your ideas move from sentence to sentence and paragraph to paragraph in a logical way. For example, events in a story often appear in the order in which they occurred.

Voice

Voice is the combination of word choice and personal writing style that makes your writing unique. Voice connects a reader to the writer. It can show your personality or "take" on a story.

MOTIVATE AND ENGAGE

As a warm-up activity, have students quickwrite for one minute about the qualities of good writing. Remind them that during a quickwrite, they should keep writing continuously for one minute even if they repeat words or ideas.

Once students are finished, elicit feedback about what they wrote or experienced during the quickwrite.

26

Word Choice

Your choice of words can help you achieve your purpose. Precise word choice means choosing the word that says exactly what you mean to say. Vivid word choice involves choosing words that create pictures for readers, describing how a subject looks, sounds, smells, and so on.

Sentence Fluency

Good writing is like a song—it has fluency, or a rhythm and a flow. By varying sentence patterns, writers ensure that the rhythm of their writing stays interesting.

Conventions

By following the rules of spelling, capitalization, punctuation, grammar, and usage, you help readers understand your ideas.

Overview of Writing Traits	
Ideas	• Significant ideas and informative details • Thorough development of ideas • Unique perspective or strong message
Organization	• Obvious plan • Clear sequence • Strong transitions
Voice	• Effective word choice • Attention to style
Word Choice	• Precise, not vague, words • Vivid, not dull, words • Word choices suited to audience and purpose
Sentence Fluency	• Varied sentence beginnings, lengths, and structures • Smooth sentence rhythms
Conventions	• Proper spelling and capitalization • Correct punctuation, grammar, usage, and sentence structure

Online Journal

Try It! Record your answers and ideas in the online journal. You can also record and save your answers and ideas on pop-up sticky notes in the eText.

Writer to Writer

Good writing is a symphony of traits—all coming together to make the paper sing.

—Kelly Gallagher

COLLABORATE AND DISCUSS

Ask:

- What qualities does good writing have?

Write all student responses on the board.

Then, have students study the chart on page 27. Explain to students that the items in the first column are qualities of good writing. Have a class discussion on the similarities and differences between student responses and the qualities listed in the chart.

Differentiated Instruction

RTI Strategy for Below-Level Students Before reading the Organization section on page 26, students may benefit from a brief review of the different types of writing: descriptive, expository, persuasive, and narrative. First, ask students to describe each type to establish prior knowledge. For example, *expository writing* is writing to explain and *narrative writing* is writing that tells a story. Help students generate descriptors for each type of writing as needed.

PRE-AP Enrichment for Above-Level Students Challenge students to explore ways to create a strong voice in their writing. Have students write a brief paragraph on a topic of their choice. Then, ask them to examine their word choice and use of active voice to create a livelier tone. Also, suggest that they use a hook to grab their readers' attention and make them want to read further. Invite students to share their paragraphs with a partner or with the class.

Rubrics and How To Use Them

You can use rubrics to evaluate the traits of your writing. A rubric allows you to score your writing on a scale in different categories. You will use a six-point rubric like this to help evaluate your writing in chapters 5–12.

Writing Traits	Rating Scale
Ideas: How interesting, significant, or original are the ideas you present? How well do you develop ideas?	Not very … Very 1 2 3 4 5 6
Organization: How logically is your piece organized? Do your transitions, or movements from idea to idea, make sense?	1 2 3 4 5 6
Voice: How authentic and original is your voice?	1 2 3 4 5 6
Word Choice: How precise and vivid are the words you use? To what extent does your word choice help achieve your purpose?	1 2 3 4 5 6
Sentence Fluency: How well do your sentences flow? How strong and varied is the rhythm they create?	1 2 3 4 5 6
Conventions: How correct is your punctuation? Your capitalization? Your spelling?	1 2 3 4 5 6

MOTIVATE AND ENGAGE

To activate students' prior knowledge of rubrics, ask students if they have ever taken a survey about a product they bought or a service they used. Explain that many surveys, like the rubrics on pages 28 and 29, use a scale to rate items. Ask: What is an advantage to using a rubric to evaluate your own writing? How can asking your peers to rate your writing help you to revise your work?

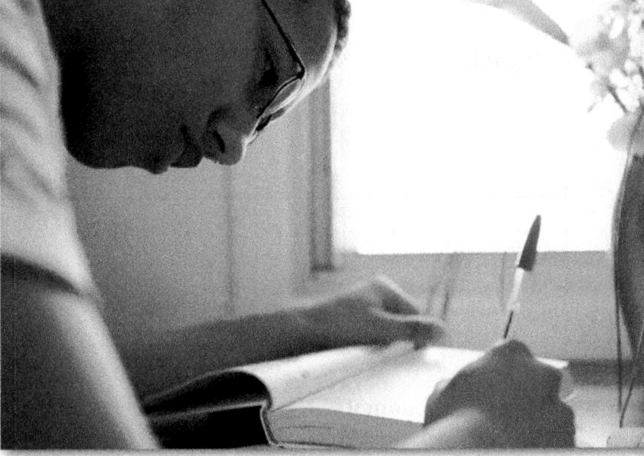

Each trait appears in the first column. The rating scale appears in the second column. The higher your score for a trait, the better your writing exhibits that trait.

Using a Rubric on Your Own

A rubric can be a big help in assessing your writing while it is still in process. Imagine you've just started writing a piece of narrative fiction. You know that narrative fiction should have characters, a setting, and a conflict and resolution. You can check the rubric as you write to make sure you are on track. For example, you may use the rubric and decide that you have not developed the conflict well. You can revise to improve your writing and get a better score.

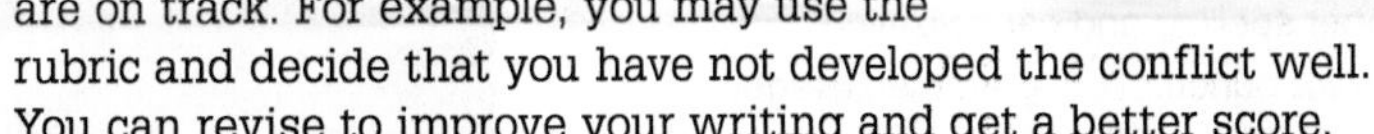

Narrative Fiction Elements	Rating Scale
	Not very Very
Interesting characters	1 2 3 4 5 6
Believable setting	1 2 3 4 5 6
Literary strategies	1 2 3 4 5 6
Well-developed conflict	1 2 3 4 5 6
Well-developed resolution	1 2 3 4 5 6

Try It! If you checked your story against the rubric and rated yourself mostly 1s and 2s, what actions might you want to take next?

Using a Rubric With a Partner

In some cases, building your own rubric can help you ensure that your writing will meet your expectations. For example, if your class has an assignment to write a poem, you and a partner might decide to construct a rubric to check one another's work. A rubric like the one shown here can help point out whether you should make any changes. Extra lines allow room for you to add other criteria.

Poetry Elements	Rating Scale
	Not very Very
Good sensory details	1 2 3 4 5 6
Colorful adjectives	1 2 3 4 5 6
	1 2 3 4 5 6
	1 2 3 4 5 6
	1 2 3 4 5 6

Try It! What other elements might you add to the rubric?

Using a Rubric in a Group

It is also helpful to use a rubric in a group. That way you can get input on your writing from many people at the same time. If the group members' ratings of your piece are similar, you will probably have an easy time deciding whether to make changes. If the responses vary significantly, you might want to discuss the results with the group. Then, analyze what led to the differing opinions and make careful judgments about what changes you will make.

Online Journal

Try It! Record your answers and ideas in the online journal. You can also record and save your answers and ideas on pop-up sticky notes in the eText.

COLLABORATE AND DISCUSS

Discuss with students the benefits and drawbacks of peer evaluations. Students may say that a writer's popularity with group members might lead to a positive (or negative) review regardless of the quality of the writing. Suggest to students that the names of writers should not be disclosed to ensure a more objective review. Have students make other suggestions for ensuring objective reviews.

Differentiated Instruction

RTI Strategy for Below-Level Students Students may benefit from working with a partner or with you to create rubric items. Explain to students that many school writing assignments explain what is expected of students, and are therefore good guides for creating a rubric. Provide students with a writing assignment, and work with them to change the instructions into questions for a rubric.

PRE-AP Enrichment for Above-Level Students Have students create rubrics for a persuasive essay and for an expository essay. Allow students to work in pairs or small groups. Tell students to use the writing traits rubric on page 28 as a starting point, but to add specific items for each type of writing. Invite students to present their rubrics to the class and to discuss why some items in the persuasive rubric differ from those in the expository rubric.

What Is the Writing Process?

The five steps in the writing process are prewriting, drafting, revising, editing, and publishing. Writing is a process because your idea goes through a series of changes or stages before the product is finished.

Study the diagram to see how moving through the writing process can work. Remember, you can go back to a stage in the process. It does not always have to occur in order.

Prewriting
In prewriting, you will:
• Explore ideas
• Choose a purpose and an audience
• Gather details
• Sequence ideas
Drafting
In drafting, you will:
• Put ideas down
• Develop a thesis or controlling idea
• Structure ideas in a sustained way
Revising
In revising, you will:
• Re-read draft to see what works and what does not
• Use a rubric to evaluate
• Analyze what you want to change or improve
• Make changes
Editing
In the editing phase, you will:
• Check the accuracy of facts
• Correct errors in spelling, grammar, usage, and mechanics
Publishing
In publishing, you will:
• Produce a final polished copy of your writing
• Share your writing

MOTIVATE AND ENGAGE

Activate prior knowledge by asking students what processes or steps they go through when they write. Jot their responses on the board. Have students talk about the details involved in each step. Write all responses under the corresponding step.

Compare student responses with the items in the graphic organizer on page 30. Discuss whether and how the organizer is different from the ways that students approach writing. Add and change items on the board as needed.

Why Use the Writing Process?

Writing involves careful thinking, which means you will make changes as you write. Even professional writers don't just write their thoughts and call it a finished work of art. They use a process. For example, some writers keep going back to the revising stage many times, while others feel they can do the revision in just one step. It is up to each writer to develop the style that works best to produce the best results.

You might find that the writing process works best for you when you keep these tips in mind:

- Remember that the five steps in the writing process are equally important.
- Think about your audience as you plan your paper and develop your writing.
- Make sure you remember your topic and stick to your specific purpose as you write.
- Give your writing some time to "rest." Sometimes it can be good to work on a piece, walk away, and look at it later, with a fresh eye and mind.

The following pages will describe in more detail how to use each stage of the writing process to improve your writing.

WRITING COACH Online

www.phwritingcoach.com

Online Journal

Try It! Record your answers and ideas in the online journal. You can also record and save your answers and ideas on pop-up sticky notes in the eText.

"Writer to Writer"

Writing process gives us the freedom to write like mad, tinker like an engineer, evaluate like a judge—playing different roles at different stages. Most importantly it gives us the freedom to get our words out of our heads and into the world.

—Jeff Anderson

READ AND APPLY

Have students read the text on page 31 silently. Tell students to answer these questions in their writing journals or notebooks.

- Which bulleted point on the page did you find most helpful. Why?
- Reflect on your own writing process. What process has worked best for you in the past? Why?
- What process has not worked? Why?

Invite volunteers to share their responses with the class.

Differentiated Instruction

RTI Strategy for Below-Level Students Work with students to create flashcards for each stage of the writing process. On one side, write the name of the stage (prewriting, drafting, and so on). On the other side, write one bulleted step in the stage. Have students organize the cards according to the stages. Use the flashcards to review the writing process with students. When students are ready, shuffle the cards. Read a step, and ask students to identify the stage.

RTI Enrichment for Above-Level Students To reinforce the writing process terminology for students, have them come up with a familiar cue word for each stage. For example, for prewriting, they may use the word *planning*. For drafting, they may use the word *writing*; for revising *fixing* or *rewriting*; for editing *correcting*; and for publishing *sharing*. This strategy may help students remember the purpose of each stage.

Prewriting

Prewriting
Drafting
Revising
Editing
Publishing

No matter what kind of writing you do, planning during the prewriting stage is crucial. During prewriting, you determine the topic of your writing, its purpose, and its specific audience. Then, you narrow the topic and gather details.

Determining the Purpose and Audience

What Is Your Purpose?

To be sure your writing communicates your ideas clearly, it is important to clarify why you are writing. Consider what you want your audience to take away from your writing. You may want to entertain them, or you may want to warn them about something. Even when you write an entry in a private journal, you're writing for an audience—you!

Who Is Your Audience?

Think about the people who will read your work and consider what they may already know about your topic. Being able to identify this group and their needs will let you be sure you are providing the right level of information.

Choosing a Topic

Here are just a few of the many techniques you can use to determine an appropriate topic.

- **Brainstorm**
  You can brainstorm by yourself, with a partner, or with a group. Just jot down ideas as they arise, and don't rule out anything. When brainstorming in a group, one person's idea often "piggy-backs" on another.
- **Make a Mind Map**
  A mind map is a quick drawing you sketch as ideas come to you. The mind map can take any form. The important thing is to write quick notes as they come to you and then to draw lines to connect relationships among the ideas.

MOTIVATE AND ENGAGE

To help students identify audience and purpose, write this topic on the board: *Texting*.

Have students brainstorm for possible audiences for the topic. Write responses on the board and circle one audience. Then, have students work in pairs to generate two purposes for writing about that topic for the audience you've identified. Ask volunteers to offer one purpose they identified and to explain how it addresses the audience.

- **Interview**
  A fun way to find a writing topic is to conduct an interview. You might start by writing interview questions for yourself or someone else. Questions that start with *what, when, why, how,* and *who* are most effective. For example, you might ask, "When was the last time you laughed really hard?" "What made you laugh?" Then, conduct the interview and discover the answers.

- **Review Resources and Discuss Ideas**
  You can review resources, such as books, magazines, newspapers, and digital articles, to get ideas. Discussing your initial ideas with a partner can spark even more ideas.

Narrowing Your Topic

Once you have settled on a topic idea you really like, it may seem too broad to tackle. How can you narrow your topic?

- **Use Graphic Organizers**
  A graphic organizer can help narrow a topic that's too broad. For example, you might choose "Animals" as a topic. You might make your topics smaller and smaller until you narrow the topic to "The Habitat of Emperor Penguins."

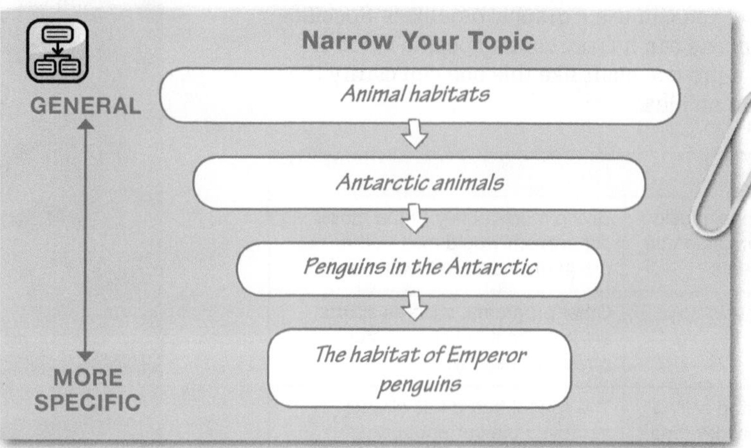

WRITING COACH Online
www.phwritingcoach.com

Online Journal

Try It! Record your answers and ideas in the online journal. You can also record and save your answers and ideas on pop-up sticky notes in the eText.

"Writer to Writer"

Put something down. Anything. Then, magic will happen.

—Jeff Anderson

READ AND APPLY

You may wish to model narrowing a topic by using the graphic organizer on page 33. Then, narrow the topic from *Texting* to *Is Texting Hurting the English Language?* using the chart.

As you complete the chart, engage students in the process. Ask:

- What do I want to focus on in my report?
- How can my topic be narrowed further?
- Is my final topic appropriate for a research report? Why or why not?
- Can I find enough information on the topic?

Differentiated Instruction

RTI Strategy for Special Needs Students Work with students to read and apply the different strategies for choosing a topic. Brainstorm for ideas with the students, jotting down all of their ideas on a topic. Model how to make a mind map, allowing students to draw lines to connect related ideas. Have students interview you briefly. Show students examples of resources, such as newspapers, magazines, and digital articles.

Strategy for Spanish Speakers Students whose home language is Spanish may reverse the subject-verb order when writing questions with the *wh-* words (*When you are going?* versus *When are you going?*). Write or say different *Wh-* questions with correct and incorrect subject-verb order. Have students indicate correct or incorrect usage with a "thumbs up" or "thumbs down" sign. Have volunteers write new questions using the *wh-* words.

Prewriting (continued)

Prewriting
Drafting
Revising
Editing
Publishing

- **Use Resource Materials**
  The resource materials you use to find information can also help you narrow a broad topic. Look up your subject online in an encyclopedia or newspaper archive. Scan the resources as you look for specific subtopics to pursue.

Gather Details

After you decide on a topic, you will want to explore and develop your ideas. You might start by looking through online resources again, talking with people who are knowledgeable about your topic, and writing everything you already know about the topic. It will be helpful to gather a variety of details. Look at these types:

- Facts
- Statistics
- Personal observations
- Expert opinions
- Examples
- Descriptions
- Quotations
- Opposing viewpoints

After you have narrowed your topic and gathered details, you will begin to plan your piece. During this part of prewriting, you will develop your essay's thesis or controlling idea—its main point.

As you plan your piece, you can use a graphic organizer. Specific kinds of graphic organizers can help structure specific kinds of writing. For example, a pro-con chart like this one can clarify the reasons for and against an idea.

Pro	Con
Adding funds to the school music budget would allow more students to learn to play instruments.	Giving more money to the music department would mean other programs would get less money.
Research shows that music helps the brain become more flexible.	Other programs, such as sports, are important in keeping students physically healthy.
Band members could stop selling gift-wrap materials at holiday time.	The school board has already approved the current budget allocations.

READ AND APPLY

Model creating a pro-con chart for the topic explored in Motivate and Engage on page 32. Some possible examples of the pros and cons of texting might be:

- Pros: texting means more people are writing
- Cons: texting is changing the way people spell

Discuss your choices and elicit other suggestions from students. Write student suggestions in the appropriate column in the chart.

Working with ELLs — ELL Sheltered Instruction: Cognitive

As students study the drafting process, help them narrate events, describe places, people, or things, and explain situations in writing with increasing specificity and detail.

Beginning Facilitate writing by using prompts to elicit words from students and scribing them on the board. For example, write the prompts *I found a large box. It was . . . The next thing I did was . . .* Guide students in responding, and then lead them to narrate the events, describe the people, and explain the situation of the story. Have students write the story as you generate it.

Intermediate Have students complete the Beginning activity. Then, have them revise

Drafting

In the drafting stage, you get your ideas down. You may consult an outline or your prewriting notes as you build your first draft.

Prewriting
Drafting
Revising
Editing
Publishing

Online Journal

Try It! Record your answers and ideas in the online journal. You can also record and save your answers and ideas on pop-up sticky notes in the eText.

The Introduction

Most genres should have a strong introduction that immediately grabs the reader's attention and includes the thesis. Even stories and poems need a "hook" to grab interest.

Try It! Which of these first sentences are strong openers? Read these examples of first sentences. Decide which ones are most interesting to you. Explain why they grab your attention. Then, explain why the others are weak.

- Have you ever wondered what it would be like to wake up one morning to find you're someone else?
- There are many ways to paint a room.
- Autumn is a beautiful season.
- On Sunday, we went to the store.
- When I woke up that morning, I had no idea that it would be the best day of my life.

The Body

The body of a paper develops the main idea and details that elaborate on and support the thesis. These details may include interesting facts, examples, statistics, anecdotes or stories, quotations, personal feelings, and sensory descriptions.

The Conclusion

The conclusion typically restates the thesis and summarizes the most important concepts of a paper.

COLLABORATE AND DISCUSS

After students have completed the *Try It!* activity, have them choose one weak opener and rewrite it to create a strong one. Invite volunteers to share their new openers with the class.

Then, as a class, choose one of the new openers and develop two or three main ideas for the body of an essay or story. Finally, discuss the points that might be made in the conclusion.

the written story with fluent partners, narrating, describing, and explaining with increasing specificity and detail.

Advanced Have partners choose an opening sentence from page 35 and use it to write the first paragraph of a short story, narrating events, describing people and places, and explaining situations in detail. Have them meet in small groups to share their paragraphs.

Advanced High Have individuals complete the Advanced activity. Challenge them to revise their paragraphs with increasing specificity and detail and then to share them aloud.

Revising: Making It Better

Prewriting
Drafting
Revising
Editing
Publishing

No one gets every single thing right in a first draft. In fact, most people require more than two drafts to achieve their best writing and thinking. When you have finished your first draft, you're ready to revise.

Revising means "re-seeing." In revising, you look again to see if you can find ways to improve style, word choice, figurative language, sentence variety, and subtlety of meaning. As always, check how well you've addressed the issues of purpose, audience, and genre. Carefully analyze what you'd want to change and then go ahead and do it. Here are some helpful hints on starting the revision stage of the writing process.

Take a Break

Do not begin to revise immediately after you finish a draft. Take some time away from your paper. Get a glass of water, take a walk, or listen to some music. You may even want to wait a day to look at what you've written. When you come back, you will be better able to assess the strengths and weaknesses of your work.

Put Yourself in the Place of the Reader

Take off your writer's hat and put on your reader's hat. Do your best to pretend that you're reading someone else's work and see how it looks to that other person. Look for ideas that might be confusing and consider the questions that a reader might have. By reading the piece with an objective eye, you may find items you'd want to fix and improve.

Read Aloud to Yourself

It may feel strange to read aloud to yourself, but it can be an effective technique. It allows you to hear the flow of words, find errors, and hear where you might improve the work by smoothing out transitions between paragraphs or sections. Of course, if you're more comfortable reading your work aloud to someone else, that works, too.

READ AND APPLY

Take a poll and find out how many students in the class revise their work. Have students that do revise explain their revision processes. Write them on the board.

Compare and contrast students' revision strategies to the strategies on pages 36 and 37. Have students change the chart on page 27 into a checklist or rubric. Model by changing the first bullet into the question: *Is my topic focused?*

Working with ELLs — ELL Sheltered Instruction: Cognitive

As students learn about revising, help them distinguish intonation patterns of English with increasing ease. On the board, write three columns, with examples underneath: (1) *Yes/No Questions:* (2) *Declarative Statements;* (3) *Exclamatory Sentences Showing Surprise.* Read the examples, modeling appropriate intonation: (1) raise your voice at the end; (2) use a falling voice at the end; and (3) use a rising pitch.

Beginning Pair students with English-proficient speakers. Have proficient speakers read the example sentences as students distinguish sentence types based on intonation.

Intermediate Have proficient speakers read aloud the example sentences as students distinguish sentence types based on intonation. Then, have partners complete a **Partner Fluency Check:**

Share Your Work to Get Feedback

Your friends or family members can help you by reading and reacting to your writing. Ask them whether you've clearly expressed your ideas. Encourage them to tell you which parts were most and least interesting and why. Try to find out if they have any questions about your topic that were not answered. Then, evaluate their input and decide what will make your writing better.

Use a Rubric

A rubric might be just what you need to pinpoint weaknesses in your work. You may want to think about the core parts of the work and rate them on a scale. If you come up short, you'll have a better idea about the kinds of things to improve. You might also use a rubric to invite peer review and input.

Online Journal

Try It! Record your answers and ideas in the online journal. You can also record and save your answers and ideas on pop-up sticky notes in the eText.

After a group revision session, talk with a partner to analyze each other's feelings on how the session went. Discuss such issues as these: Did the group adhere to the ground rules? What suggestions could you and your partner make to improve the next session?

21st Century Learning

Collaborate and Discuss

When presenting and sharing drafts in the revision stage with a small group, it may be wise to set some ground rules. That way, the group is more likely to help each other analyze their work and make thoughtful changes that result in true improvements.

Here are some suggestions for reviewing drafts as a group:

- Cover the names on papers the group will review to keep the work anonymous.
- Print out copies for everyone in the group.
- Show respect for all group members and their writing.
- Be sure all critiques include positive comments.
- While it is fine to suggest ways to improve the work, present comments in a positive, helpful way. No insults are allowed!
- Plan for a second reading with additional input after the writer has followed selected suggestions.

COLLABORATE AND DISCUSS

Before students share and present their drafts ask them to assign specific roles to group members to help the group stay focused. Some important roles include:

- ***moderator*, who keeps the conversation on topic and ensures equal participation**
- ***note-taker*, who captures the ideas of the meeting**

Students may come up with their own roles as they learn more about the process of receiving and providing feedback.

Provide a chart with columns labeled *Reading 1, Reading 2*, and so on and a single row labeled *Number Correct;* have partners complete the chart, monitoring speakers' increasing ease in distinguishing intonation patterns after repeated readings.

Advanced Have students write another sentence of each type. Have partners read their work aloud, using correct intonation, as the listener distinguishes sentence types based on intonation.

Advanced High Assign a grade-level text for students to read aloud as partners conduct a **Partner Fluency Check** for correct intonation.

Prewriting
Drafting
Revising
Editing
Publishing

Revision RADaR

The Revision RADaR strategy, which you will use throughout this book, is an effective tool in helping you conduct a focused revision of your work.

You can use your Revision RADaR to revise your writing. The letters **R**, **A**, **D**, and **R** will help you remember to **r**eplace, **a**dd, **d**elete, and **r**eorder.

To understand more about the Revision RADaR strategy, study the following chart.

R	A	D and	R
Replace . . . • Words that are not specific • Words that are overused • Sentences that are unclear	**Add . . .** • New information • Descriptive adjectives and adverbs • Rhetorical or literary devices	**Delete . . .** • Unrelated ideas • Sentences that sound good, but do not make sense • Repeated words or phrases • Unnecessary details	**Reorder . . .** • So most important points are last • To make better sense or to flow better • So details support main ideas

R Replace

You can strengthen a text by replacing words that are not specific, words that are overused, and sentences that are unclear. Take a look at this before and after model.

BEFORE
I kicked the soccer ball hard into the goal.
AFTER
With amazing power, I slammed the soccer ball into the goal.

Apply It! **How did the writer replace the overused word *kicked*? What other replacement do you see? How did it improve the text?**

MOTIVATE AND ENGAGE

To help students understand the RADaR acronym, ask: What does it mean to keep something on your "radar"?

Students may say that it means you are paying extra attention to or are on the lookout for something. Ask students why they think the acronym is used here. Write their responses on the board and explain that the RADaR strategy helps writers remember the purpose and goals of revising.

Add

You can add new information, descriptive adjectives and adverbs, and rhetorical or literary devices to make your piece more powerful. Study this before and after model.

BEFORE
I was happy when I won the award.
AFTER
I was beyond thrilled when I won the Science Fair award.

Apply It! **How did the second sentence make you feel, compared with the first? Explain. What information was added to the second sentence?**

Delete

Sometimes taking words out of a text can improve clarity. Analyze this before and after model.

BEFORE
I knew the test would be difficult, so I should have studied harder for the test before the test day.
AFTER
I knew the test would be difficult, so I should have studied harder for it.

Apply It! **Describe the revision you see. How did taking out unnecessary repetition of the word *test* help the sentences flow more naturally?**

Reorder

When you reorder, you can make sentences flow more logically.

BEFORE
Today, I have band practice, but yesterday I didn't.
AFTER
I didn't have band practice yesterday, but today I do.

Apply It! **Which of the models flows more logically? Why?**

www.phwritingcoach.com

Online Journal

Try It! Record your answers and ideas in the online journal. You can also record and save your answers and ideas on pop-up sticky notes in the eText.

USING TECHNOLOGY

Most word processing programs have a built-in thesaurus tool. You can use the thesaurus to find descriptive words that can often substitute for weaker, overused words.

READ AND APPLY

Have students apply the RADaR strategy to their own writing. With a partner, have students write two or three sentences and then work together to revise them according to each step in the RADaR strategy. Invite students to share their work with the class and explain how they employed the specific strategy in the revision.

Differentiated Instruction

RTI Strategy for Below-Level Students Students may benefit from working with you or with a partner to complete the *Apply It!* questions. Have students write the Before and After sentences on a sheet of paper. Then, encourage them to highlight the words of each sentence that have changed before answering the *Apply It!* question. If necessary, read the question aloud as students study the sentences they have copied and highlighted.

Strategy for Spanish Speakers Students whose home language is Spanish may place adjectives after nouns and add an *–s* to adjectives if the noun is plural, due to Spanish rules of adjective placement and agreement. Elicit nouns with adjectives and write them in two separate columns. Have pairs write a sentence using both words. Have partners check each other's sentences for grammar and meaning.

Revision RADaR (continued)

Prewriting
Drafting
Revising
Editing
Publishing

Read the first draft of the Student Model—a review of the novel *End Game*. Think about how you might use your Revision RADaR to improve the text in a second draft.

Kelly Gallagher, M. Ed.

KEEP REVISION ON YOUR RADAR

End Game Fails to Thrill

I like detective stories. So when my favorite writer, Mary O'Reilly, published a new detective novel, I bought it. Unfortunately, the novel, *End Game,* was incredibly disappointing.

In the story, an online video gamer disappears. A detective, Katherine, tries to track down the missing man through gaming Web sites. But here's where O'Reilly really messed up. It's clear that she didn't research the technology involved in online gaming. For example: "Katherine waited while her dial-up modem connected her to the virtual world."

The cheesy and ridiculous dialogue made my reading experience even worse. The errors in the book were bad enough! For example, the suspect says to Katherine, "I'm gonna get you, copper!" Now, this is the year 2010. A modern-day criminal would never use such outdated, silly lines. Instead of making the story exciting, the dialogue made it laughably bad.

O'Reilly has written many great books. My favorites were *On the High Seas* and *Danger in Denver.* They were great. I loved them! But I think it's time for O'Reilly to put down her pen. She clearly doesn't have what it takes any more to be a great writer. And as for *End Game*...don't waste your money!

Is my introduction interesting? Does it grab my readers' attention?

Have I fully analyzed and explained my examples from the text?

Is my information logically ordered?

Is my information relevant to the thesis? Have I included only necessary information?

After writing a draft, the student asked questions like these:

- What could I **replace**?
- What could I **add**?
- What words might I **delete**?
- Should I **reorder** anything?

READ AND APPLY

You may wish to model for students how to evaluate the first draft of the book review, "End Game Fails to Thrill," by answering the first two bulleted questions on page 40. Write your responses on the board. Then, elicit answers to the last two questions from volunteers. Write all responses on the board. Then, have students read the second draft with the suggested revisions in mind.

The student writer created this second draft.

End Game Fails to Thrill

The suspense and high-paced action in detective stories are so thrilling! I simply can't get enough of these books. So when my favorite writer, Mary O'Reilly, published a new detective novel, I ran to the store to buy my copy. Unfortunately, the novel, *End Game,* was incredibly disappointing.

R *Replaced dull first line with a more engaging opening.*

In the story, an online video gamer disappears. A detective, Katherine, tries to track down the missing man through gaming Web sites. But here's where O'Reilly really messed up. It's clear that she didn't research the technology involved in online gaming. For example: "Katherine waited while her dial-up modem connected her to the virtual world." Dial-up modems aren't fast enough to do serious online gaming!

A *Added a sentence to better explain to my audience why the information from the text was incorrect.*

Although the errors in the book were bad enough, the cheesy and ridiculous dialogue made my reading experience even worse. For example, the suspect says to Katherine, "I'm gonna get you, copper!" Now, this is the year 2010. A modern-day criminal would never use such outdated, silly lines. Instead of making the story exciting, the dialogue made it laughably bad.

R *Reordered text so that the information about the errors connected the ideas in the second and third paragraphs.*

I think it's time for O'Reilly to put down her pen. She clearly doesn't have what it takes any more to be a great writer. And as for *End Game*...don't waste your money!

D *Deleted unnecessary information.*

Try It! What other words did the writer replace? Add? Delete? Reorder?

Online Journal

Try It! Record your answers and ideas in the online journal. You can also record and save your answers and ideas on pop-up sticky notes in the eText.

Partner Talk

Work with a partner to come up with a list of words that describe detective stories. For example, you might use "high-paced action" or "thrilling." Then discuss the value of using more specific words in your writing.

COLLABORATE AND DISCUSS

Have students read both drafts silently, noting the changes the writer made in the revision. Then, have students work in small groups to discuss the changes. Ask each group to answer these questions:

- How did the RADaR strategy help this writer improve the book review?
- What could still be improved?
- How would these changes make the review better?

Invite groups to share their responses with the class.

Differentiated Instruction

RTI Strategy for Below-Level Students Students may benefit from working with a partner to complete the *Try It!* activity. Make a copy of each draft for the students to mark up as they read. Suggest they use a highlighter to note words that have been replaced, added, or deleted and to place brackets around sentences that have been reordered. Remind them to use the same techniques when they evaluate their own writing.

PRE-AP Enrichment for Above-Level Students Challenge students to write a critique of the revised review. Ask students to describe three ways in which the second draft improved the ideas in the first draft. Also have them suggest three more ways to further improve the review. Finally, have them write a final draft, using the RADaR strategy and incorporating the suggestions they made.

Editing: Making It Correct

Prewriting
Drafting
Revising
Editing
Publishing

Editing is the process of checking the accuracy of facts and correcting errors in spelling, grammar, usage, and mechanics. Using a checklist like the one shown here can help ensure you've done a thorough job of editing.

Editing Checklist

Task	Ask Yourself
Check your facts and spelling	❑ Have I checked that my facts are correct? ❑ Have I used spell check or a dictionary to check any words I'm not sure are spelled correctly?
Check your grammar	❑ Have I written any run-on sentences? ❑ Have I used the correct verbs and verb tenses? ❑ Do my pronouns match their antecedents, or nouns they replace?
Check your usage	❑ Have I used the correct form of irregular verbs? ❑ Have I used object pronouns, such as *me*, *him*, *her*, *us*, and *them* only after verbs or prepositions? ❑ Have I used subject pronouns, such as *I*, *he*, *she*, *we*, and *they* correctly—usually as subjects?
Check for proper use of mechanics	❑ Have I used correct punctuation? ❑ Does each sentence have the correct end mark? ❑ Have I used apostrophes in nouns but not in pronouns to show possession? ❑ Have I used quotation marks around words from another source? ❑ Have I used correct capitalization? ❑ Does each sentence begin with a capital letter? ❑ Do the names of specific people and places begin with a capital letter?

MOTIVATE AND ENGAGE

Activate students' prior knowledge of editing by asking them what the difference is between revising and editing. Tell students that revising is fixing the communication of the ideas while editing is fixing errors in spelling, grammar, usage, mechanics, and facts.

After students have reviewed the checklist, ask:

- Why is it beneficial to wait until you have finished revising to edit your work?
- How is the checklist helpful while editing your writing?

Working with ELLs ELL Sheltered Instruction: Metacognitive

Help students monitor and edit their writing for pronoun-antecedent agreement, using self-corrective techniques. Remind students of rules about pronoun-antecedent agreement. Then:

Beginning Write on the board a sentence with incorrect pronoun-antecedent agreement and have students copy it: for example, *The horse walked to their stable.* Model this self-corrective technique: Circle *their* and underline *horse*. Explain that *horse* is the antecedent. Ask *How many?* of each word (*one, more than one*). Guide students in correcting the sentence, and read it with students.

Intermediate Have students complete the Beginning activity. Then, have them write

Using Proofreading Marks

Professional editors use a set of proofreading marks to indicate changes in a text. Here is a chart of some of the more common proofreading marks.

Proofreader's Marks

(b.f.)	boldface
⌐	break text start new line
(caps)	capital letter
⁀	close up
ℯ	deletes
a/	insert word
,/	insert comma
=/	insert hyphen
t/	insert letter
⊙/	insert period
(ital)	italic type
(stet)	let stand as is
(l.f.)	lightface
(l.c.)	lower case letter
[	move left
]	move right
¶	new paragraph
(rom)	roman type
	run text up
(sp)	spell out whole word
	transpose

Online Journal

Try It! Record your answers and ideas in the online journal. You can also record and save your answers and ideas on pop-up sticky notes in the eText.

USING TECHNOLOGY

Many word processing programs have automatic spelling and grammar checks. While these tools can be helpful, be sure to pay attention to any suggestions they offer. That's because sometimes inappropriate substitutes are inserted automatically!

READ AND APPLY

On the board, write several sentences that contain obvious errors in spelling, punctuation, and mechanics. Then, use the proofreader's marks in the chart to correct the first sentences. Invite volunteers to fix the remaining errors. You may also wish to provide copies of the proofreader's marks for students to keep in their writing journals or notebooks.

two short sentences with a pronoun and antecedent. Have groups edit their work together by employing the self-corrective technique of circling the pronouns and underlining the antecedents, checking for agreement.

Advanced Have partners write a short paragraph using pronouns. Then, have partners employ the self-corrective technique of circling the pronouns and underlining the antecedents, checking for agreement and editing as necessary.

Advanced High Have students complete the Advanced activity. Challenge them to edit their writing for vague and unclear antecedents as well.

Editing: Making It Correct (continued)

Prewriting
Drafting
Revising
Editing
Publishing

WRITE GUY *Jeff Anderson, M. Ed.*

WHAT DO YOU NOTICE?

Using an editing checklist is a great way to check for correct grammar. However, using a checklist is not enough to make your writing grammatically correct. A checklist tells you what to look for, but not how to correct mistakes you find. To do that, you need to develop and apply your knowledge of grammar.

Looking closely at good writing is one way to expand your grammar know-how. The *What Do You Notice?* feature that appears throughout this book will help you zoom in on passages that use grammar correctly and effectively.

As you read this passage, from "Jobs for Kids," zoom in on the sentences in the passage.

> I have a paper route. After school, I deliver newspapers on my bike to my neighbors. I love this job because I get exercise, and I get to be outside.

Now, ask yourself: *What do you notice about the sentences in this passage?*

Maybe you noticed that the writer uses sentences of varying lengths and with different structures.

After asking a question that draws your attention to the grammar in the passage, the *What Do You Notice?* feature provides information on a particular grammar topic. For example, following the passage and question, you might read about simple and complex sentences, which are both used in the passage.

The *What Do You Notice?* feature will show you how grammar works in actual writing. It will help you learn how to make your writing correct.

READ AND APPLY

Have students read the What Do You Notice? feature. Explain to students that they will see this feature throughout the book. Ask: What is the purpose of this feature? How will it help you to edit your work and improve your own grammar? What strategies does the writer of this essay use that you could incorporate in your own writing?

Working with ELLs — ELL Sheltered Instruction: Metacognitive

Help students monitor and edit their writing for appropriate verb tenses, using self-corrective techniques. Review with students the rules of verb tenses. Then:

Beginning Display the sentence *The dog barked when he gets the ball.* Read the sentence, using gestures for clarity, and have students copy it. Help students employ self-corrective techniques by modeling these steps: Circle the verbs *barked* and *gets*. Ask *When?* of each word (*before now / now*). Work with students to replace *gets* with *got*. Read the corrected sentence with students.

Intermediate Have students complete the Beginning activity. Then, distribute additional

Jobs for Kids

I like having my own money. That way, I can buy things I want and can also save money for my future. But here's the problem: How can we, as kids, make money? There are many types of jobs for kids, but each job has pluses and minuses.

I have a paper route. After school, I deliver newspapers on my bike to my neighbors. I love this job because I get exercise, and I get to be outside. This job isn't for everyone, though. Some kids have a lot of after-school activities, so they don't go straight home. Because papers have to be delivered on time, this can be challenging.

A friend of mine babysits because she has fun with and loves taking care of children. To be a babysitter, you have to find out if your state has a law about how old you have to be before you can babysit. You also have to be a patient, responsible person who is good with children. Finally, it helps to know first-aid, just in case a child gets injured.

My brother does yard work for neighbors. He rakes leaves, weeds gardens, and mows lawns. He loves to be outside and doesn't mind getting dirty. However, there are certain safety issues involved. For example, you have to know how to handle a lawnmower properly and wear protective gear.

What type of job is right for you? What are your interests? Get creative, and start making some money!

Try It! Read "Jobs for Kids." Then, zoom in on two more passages. Write a response to each question in your journal.

1. What do you notice about the pronouns (*you, he*) in the fourth paragraph?
2. How does the writer use transitions, such as the word *finally*, to connect ideas in the third paragraph?

Online Journal

Try It! Record your answers and ideas in the online journal. You can also record and save your answers and ideas on pop-up sticky notes in the eText.

Writer to Writer

If I wonder how to write any kind of writing, I look at models—well-written examples of the kind of writing I want to do. Models are the greatest how-to lesson I have ever discovered.

—Jeff Anderson

COLLABORATE AND DISCUSS

Have students read "Jobs for Kids." Then, have students work in pairs to answer the *Try It!* questions. Also, ask pairs to answer these questions:

- What are the strongest elements of this essay? Give two examples.
- What have you learned from reading this essay that you can use in your own writing?

Invite pairs to share their responses with the class.

sentences with incorrect verb tenses for students to edit with fluent partners, using the same self-corrective technique.

Advanced Have partners write short paragraphs about a series of events. Partners should use the self-corrective technique of circling all verbs and identifying the tense of each, editing for consistent tense as necessary.

Advanced High Have students complete the Advanced activity. Challenge them to explain when a shift in tense might be appropriate and when it is not.

Publishing

Prewriting
Drafting
Revising
Editing
Publishing

When you publish, you produce a final copy of your work and present it to an audience. When publishing you'll need to decide which form will best reach your audience, exhibit your ideas, show your creativity, and accomplish your main purpose.

To start assessing the optimal way to publish your work, you might ask yourself these questions:

- What do I hope to accomplish by sharing my work with others?
- Should I publish in print form? Give an oral presentation? Publish in print form and give an oral presentation?
- Should I publish online, in traditional print, or both?
- What specific forms are available to choose from?

The answers to most of these questions will most likely link to your purpose for writing and your audience. Some choices seem obvious. For example, if you've written a piece to contribute to a blog, you'll definitely want to send it electronically.

Each publishing form will present different challenges and opportunities and each will demand different forms of preparation. For example, you may need to prepare presentation slides for a speech, or you may want to select music and images if you will be posting a video podcast online.

MOTIVATE AND ENGAGE

Explain that publishing means completing and presenting a piece of work. Activate prior knowledge of publishing one's writing by asking students to volunteer ways in which they have published or shared their work in the past. Write their responses on the board. Have a class discussion about the types of writing that are best suited to be published in the ways that are listed on the board. Compare these responses to the suggestions in the chart on page 47.

Ways to Publish

There are many ways to publish your writing. This chart shows some of several opportunities you can pursue to publish your work.

Genre	Publishing Opportunities	
Narration: Nonfiction	• Blogs • Book manuscript • Audio recording	• Private diary or journal entries • Electronic slide show
Narration: Fiction	• Book manuscript • Film	• Audio recording • Oral reading to a group
Poetry and Description	• Bound collection • Visual display	• Audio recording • Oral reading to a group
Exposition and Persuasion	• Print or online article • Web site • Slide show • Visual display	• Film • Audio recording • Oral reading or speech
Response to Literature	• Print or online letters • Visual displays	• Blogs • Slide show
Research Writing	• Traditional paper • Print and online experiment journals	• Multimedia presentation

Reflect on Your Writing

Think about what you learned in Chapter 3 as you answer these questions:

- What did you learn about the writing process?
- What steps in the writing process do you already use in your writing?
- Which stage do you think is the most fun? Which one may be most challenging for you? Explain.

Online Journal

Try It! Record your answers and ideas in the online journal. You can also record and save your answers and ideas on pop-up sticky notes in the eText.

Partner Talk

Discuss the chart on this page with a partner. If there are ways to publish that neither of you has ever tried, talk about how you might go about experimenting with those forms.

COLLABORATE AND DISCUSS

Have students work in small groups to share their responses to the Reflect on Your Writing questions. Extend the discussion by having group members help each other think of strategies for the stage of the writing process they find most challenging. (See last question.) Invite groups to share their strategies with the class. You may wish to offer your own strategies as well.

Differentiated Instruction

RTI Strategy for Special Needs Students Students may need reinforcement about the different ways to publish their work. Place the class in small groups and have each group choose a genre and one of the publishing opportunities listed next to it in the chart. Have groups create, act out, or find an example of the chosen publishing opportunity for the class. For example, for poetry, a group could find or create a short poem and read it to the class as an "Oral reading to a group."

PRE-AP Enrichment for Above-Level Students Have students write a brief report or give an oral presentation on one of the media listed in the chart and why it provides publishing options for the type of writing in the genre column. Tell students to discuss how that particular form of media addresses the purpose and needs of a specific audience. Invite students to present their work to the class.

CHAPTER 4 SENTENCES, PARAGRAPHS, and COMPOSITIONS

MOTIVATE AND ENGAGE

As a warm-up activity, have students quickwrite for one minute about sentences and paragraphs. Discuss the different purpose and structure of each.

Remind students that during a quickwrite, they should keep writing continuously for one minute even if they repeat words or ideas. Once students are finished, elicit feedback about what they wrote or experienced during the quickwrite.

Good writers know that strong sentences and paragraphs help to construct effective compositions. Chapter 4 will help you use these building blocks to structure and style excellent writing. It will also present ways to use rhetorical and literary devices and online tools to strengthen your writing.

The Building Blocks: Sentences and Paragraphs

A **sentence** is a group of words with two main parts: a subject and a predicate. Together, these parts express a complete thought.

A **paragraph** is built from a group of sentences that share a common idea and work together to express that idea clearly. The start of a new paragraph has visual clues—either an indent of several spaces in the first line or an extra line of space above it.

In a good piece of writing, each paragraph supports, develops, or explains the main idea of the whole work. Of course, the traits of effective writing—ideas, organization, voice, word choice, sentence fluency, and conventions—appear in each paragraph as well.

Working with ELLs — ELL Sheltered Instruction: Cognitive

Orally present the instruction at the top of page 49, and guide students to demonstrate comprehension of general meaning, main points, and important details in contexts ranging from familiar to unfamiliar. First, relate the material to a familiar context, such as writing a paper for school. Then, relate the material to an unfamiliar context, such as writing a newspaper story.

Beginning Repeat portions of the instruction using accessible language. Aid comprehension with the help of an English-proficient speaker of students' home language. Guide students in restating the general meaning, main points, and important details using sentence frames, such as *You can make a more powerful sentence by ____ two sentences.*

Writing Strong Sentences

To write strong paragraphs, you need strong sentences. While it may be your habit to write using a single style of sentences, adding variety will help make your writing more interesting. Combining sentences, using compound elements, forming compound sentences, and using subordination all may help you make your sentences stronger, clearer, or more varied.

Combine Sentences

Putting information from one sentence into another can make a more powerful sentence.

BEFORE	Basketball is a fun game. It takes a lot of skill and practice.
AFTER	Basketball, which takes a lot of skill and practice, is a fun game.

Use Compound Elements

You can form compound subjects, verbs, or objects to help the flow.

BEFORE	Students enjoy many different hobbies. Some play sports. Some write poetry. Some paint.
AFTER	Students enjoy many different hobbies, such as playing sports, writing poetry, and painting.

Form Compound Sentences

You can combine two sentences into a compound sentence.

BEFORE	Some people enjoy skateboarding. It can be a dangerous hobby.
AFTER	Some people enjoy skateboarding, but it can be a dangerous hobby.

Use Subordination

Combine two related sentences by rewriting the less important one as a subordinate clause.

BEFORE	Horseback riding allows you to be outside in the fresh air. That is good for you.
AFTER	Horseback riding allows you be outside in the fresh air, which is good for you.

WRITING COACH
Online
www.phwritingcoach.com
Online Journal
Try It! Record your answers and ideas in the online journal. You can also record and save your answers on pop-up sticky notes in the eText.

LEARN MORE
For more on sentence combining see Chapter 20.

COLLABORATE AND DISCUSS

- What are the different types of sentences?

Write all student responses on the board.

Then, have volunteers read aloud each Before and After sentence. Ask volunteers to explain how the sentences differ and why the revision is an improvement.

Finally, work with students to create two simple sentences and then combine them into a compound or complex sentence. Discuss the changes.

Intermediate Repeat portions of the instruction using accessible language. Give small groups sentence starters, such as *Strong writing makes reading…* to help them summarize and restate the general meaning, main points, and important details of your presentation.

Advanced Have partners create an outline summarizing the general meaning, main points, and important details of your presentation.

Advanced High Have partners complete the Advanced activity, and then write a brief paragraph explaining how one of the techniques discussed makes writing stronger.

Writing Strong Paragraphs

If all the sentences in a paragraph reflect the main idea and work together to express that idea clearly, the result will be a strong paragraph.

Express Your Main Idea With a Clear Topic Sentence

A **topic sentence** summarizes the main idea of a paragraph. It may appear at the beginning, middle, or end of a paragraph. It may even be unstated. When the topic sentence comes at the beginning of a paragraph, it introduces the main idea and leads the reader naturally to the sentences that follow it. When it appears at the end of a paragraph, it can draw a conclusion or summarize what came before it. If the topic sentence is unstated, the rest of the paragraph must be very clearly developed, so the reader can understand the main idea from the other sentences.

Think about the topic sentence as you read this paragraph.

There is no question that computer skills are necessary to have today. Without these skills, it will be difficult to get a college degree and find a good job. Most assignments in college must be done on a computer. Much research in college is done on the Internet, and many libraries have switched from a paper card catalog to a digital catalog. In addition, many companies won't hire someone who has no computer skills. After all, if you can't send e-mails and create important documents in word processing programs, how will you be able to properly do many jobs?

Try It! Look back at the sample paragraph to answer these questions.

1. What is the topic sentence?
2. Does the topic sentence introduce the main idea or draw a final conclusion? Explain.
3. What makes this topic sentence strong?

MOTIVATE AND ENGAGE

To activate students' prior knowledge of paragraphs and topic sentences, ask them to write one sentence about what they did last weekend. Then, tell students to write two or three more sentences that add details to the information in the first sentence. When students have completed the additional sentences, tell them they have written a paragraph with a topic sentence. Invite volunteers to read their paragraphs and identify the topic sentences.

Working with ELLs — ELL Sheltered Instruction: Cognitive

Read aloud the writing sample on page 51. Then, help students expand and internalize initial English vocabulary by learning and using high-frequency words to identify and describe people, places, and things. Begin a cluster diagram with the high-frequency words *dog owner, feed, bathe,* and *protect*. Brainstorm for additional words in the category and add them to the diagram. Then, have students use and reuse this new basic language in speaking activities.

Beginning Have students answer simple questions using the high-frequency words: for example, *What happens when a dog is hungry?(You feed them).* Then, have students reuse the words aloud in cloze sentences, such as *People who have pet dogs are called . . .*

Write Effective Supporting Sentences

A clear topic sentence is a good start, but it needs to be accompanied by good details that support the paragraph's main idea. Your supporting sentences might tell interesting facts, describe events, or give examples. In addition, the supporting sentences should also provide a smooth transition, so that the paragraph reads clearly and logically.

Think about the topic sentences and supporting details as you read this paragraph.

Owning a dog can be hard work, but it is well worth it! A dog owner must be very responsible and take good care of her pet. She has to feed and walk the dog every day and bathe it regularly. Every dog also needs a lot of play time with its owner! All of this takes a great deal of time and energy. However, a dog can be your best friend. It will love you and protect you, and sometimes make you laugh! Plus, what could be better than snuggling up with a sweet, loving dog?

Try It! Look at the paragraph and answer these questions.

1. What is the topic sentence of the paragraph?
2. Do you think it's an effective topic sentence? Why or why not?
3. What supporting details does the writer provide?
4. If you were the writer, what other supporting details might you add to strengthen the paragraph?

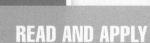

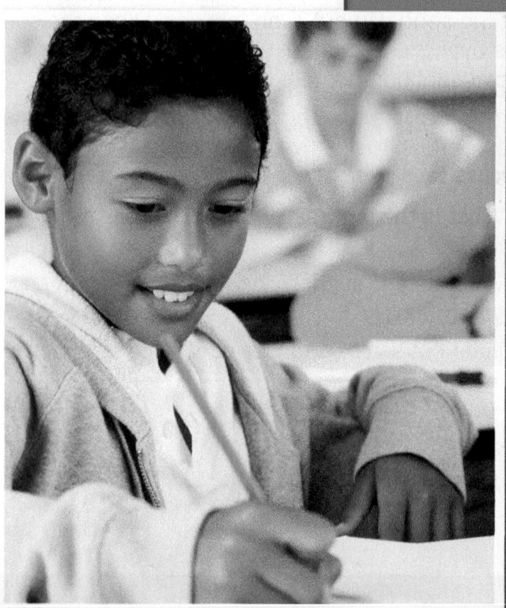

WRITING COACH Online

Online Journal

Try It! Record your answers and ideas in the online journal. You can also record and save your answers on pop-up sticky notes in the eText.

READ AND APPLY

Have students read pages 50 and 51. Then, ask:

- **The example on page 50 is about computer skills, but what is the topic sentence?**
- **What are some details the writer includes in the supporting sentences?**
- **The topic of the second example is pet ownership, but what is the topic sentence?**
- **What are some details the writer includes in the supporting sentences?**

Intermediate Provide students with prompts using the words, such as *What do you feed dogs? How do you feed dogs?* Have partners take turns responding to the prompts, using and reusing the vocabulary words.

Advanced Have partners complete the *Try It!* activity, using and reusing the vocabulary. As one partner answers the questions orally, the other should monitor his or her use of the words.

Advanced High After partners complete the Advanced activity, have students ask Intermediate partners simple interview-style questions reusing the words.

COLLABORATE AND DISCUSS

Extend the Collaborate and Discuss activity by having groups revise the paragraph to improve it further. Groups may consider revising: topic sentence, sentence length, sentence type, and supporting details.

Invite groups to read their revised paragraphs to the class and to explain the revisions the group made. Encourage the class to provide feedback on each revision.

Include a Variety of Sentence Lengths, Structures, and Beginnings

To be interesting, a paragraph should include sentences of different lengths, types, and beginnings. Similarly, if every sentence has the same structure—for example, article, adjective, noun, verb—the paragraph may sound boring or dry.

21st Century Learning

Collaborate and Discuss

With a group, study this writing sample.

On the night of the school concert, I didn't think I'd survive my stage fright. My hands felt cold and clammy, and a lump was stuck in my throat. A trickle of sweat slipped between my shoulder blades and down my back. I was so nervous! As the band began playing the opening notes of the first song and I stepped up to the microphone, the glare of the bright lights blinded me. I closed my eyes, took a deep breath, and belted out the song without even thinking. When the song was over, the audience responded with deafening applause. I had done it!

Discuss these questions about the paragraph.

1. What is the topic sentence? How does it draw in the reader?
2. What details support the topic sentence in each paragraph?
3. Point out some examples of varying sentence lengths and beginnings.
4. What examples can you find of sentences with a variety of sentence structures?

Partner Talk

Work with a partner to take another look at the writing sample on this page. Talk about what you think the writer did well. Then, discuss what might make the paragraph even stronger.

USING TECHNOLOGY

It's often better to use the tab key, rather than the space bar, to indent a paragraph. Using the tab key helps to ensure that the indents in all paragraphs will be uniform.

Working with ELLs — ELL Sheltered Instruction: Cognitive

Help students understand the general meaning, main points, and important details in spoken language ranging from the familiar to the unfamiliar. Describe a baseball championship, using language familiar to students, such as *baseball, home run, teams, pitcher, scoreboard,* and *champion,* as context clues to less familiar vocabulary, such as *decisive, versatile, acclaim, achievement,* and *executed.*

Beginning Ask simple questions to elicit the general meaning, main points, and important details of your description. Encourage students to use illustrations or gestures to demonstrate understanding of the familiar and unfamiliar language.

Composing Your Piece

You've learned that the building blocks of writing are strong sentences and paragraphs. Now it's time to use those building blocks to construct a composition. While the types of writing vary, most types have a definite structure with clearly defined parts.

The Parts of a Composition

Writers put together and arrange sentences and paragraphs to develop ideas in the clearest way possible in a composition. Some types of writing, such as poetry and advertisements, follow unique rules and may not have sentences and paragraphs that follow a standard structure. However, as you learned in Chapter 3, most compositions have three main sections: an introduction, a body, and a conclusion.

I. Introduction

The introduction of a composition introduces the focus of the composition, usually in a thesis statement. The introduction should engage the reader's interest, with such elements as a question, an unusual fact, or a surprising scene.

II. Body

Just as supporting statements develop the ideas of a topic sentence, the body of a composition develops the thesis statement and main idea. It provides details that help expand on the thesis statement. The paragraphs in the body are arranged in a logical order.

III. Conclusion

As the word implies, the conclusion of a composition concludes or ends a piece of writing. A good way to ensure the reader will remember your thesis statement is to restate it or summarize it in the conclusion. When restating the thesis, it's usually most effective to recast it in other words. Quotations and recommendations are other ways to conclude a composition with memorable impact. The conclusion should provide a parting insight or reinforce the importance of the main idea.

“Writer to Writer”

Strong, varied sentences and unified paragraphs are the building blocks of effective writing.

—Kelly Gallagher

MOTIVATE AND ENGAGE

Before students read the text on page 53, have them quickwrite about compositions. Ask students to think about these questions as they write.

- **What kinds of compositions have I written?**
- **What were the easiest and most difficult parts of writing a particular composition?**

When students are finished, invite volunteers to share their responses. Review the parts of a composition: introduction, body, and conclusion.

Intermediate Provide small groups with a main idea web. Instruct them to record your general meaning in the center circle and add main points and important details in the outer circles. Invite groups to discuss their webs, linking familiar to unfamiliar language.

Advanced Provide pairs with a cluster diagram in which to record the general meaning, main points, and important details of your description. Encourage students to use the familiar and unfamiliar language in their diagrams.

Advanced High Have students complete the Advanced activity. Then, have them use language from your presentation in oral context sentences with less-fluent partners.

Rhetorical and Literary Devices

Like any builders, good writers have a set of tools, or devices, at their fingertips to make their writing interesting, engaging, and effective. Writers can use the rhetorical devices of language and their effects to strengthen the power of their style. This section presents some tools you can store in your own writing toolbox to develop effective compositions.

Sound Devices

Sound devices, which create a musical or emotional effect, are most often used in poetry. The most common sound devices include these:

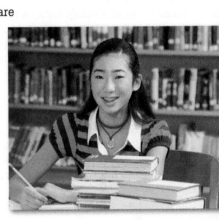

- **Alliteration** is the repetition of consonant sounds at the beginning of words that are close to one another.

  Example: The sweet sound of singing swam in the breeze.

- **Assonance** is the repetition of vowel sounds in words that are close to one another.

  Example: We see shells on the beach, by the sea.

- **Consonance** is the repetition of consonants within or at the end of words.

  Example: The doctor checked the sick patient at three o'clock.

Structural Devices

Structural devices determine the way a piece of writing is organized. Rhyme and meter are most often used to structure poetry, as are stanzas and many other structural devices.

- **Rhyme** is the repetition of sounds at the ends of words. Certain poetry forms have specific rhyme schemes.
- **Meter** is the rhythmical pattern of a poem, determined by the stressed syllables in a line.
- **Visual elements**, such as stanzas, line breaks, line length, fonts, readability, and white space, help determine how a piece of writing is read and interpreted. These elements can also affect the emotional response to a piece.

MOTIVATE AND ENGAGE

Although the terms *rhetorical* and *literary devices* may at first glance be unfamiliar to students, ask them if they have ever heard the terms *alliteration, assonance, consonance,* and *rhyme.* Have students write the meaning of each familiar term, and if possible, provide an example. Then, invite volunteers to share their responses and fill in any gaps. Explain that rhetorical and literary devices strengthen and add interest to writing.

Working with ELLs — ELL Sheltered Instruction: Cognitive

Provide opportunities for students to use and reuse new basic language in speaking activities, and help them expand and internalize initial English vocabulary by retelling basic information supported by pictures. Preteach these basic vocabulary words from the chart on page 55: *compares, nails, chalkboard,* and *flight.* Then:

Beginning Echo read the figurative language entry in the chart. Provide pictures of nails, a chalkboard, a trapeze artist, a bird, and the sun in the sky, and help students use them as support in understanding. Then, guide students in orally retelling the definitions and examples of figurative language, using and reusing the words.

Other Major Devices

You can use these devices in many forms of writing. They help writers express ideas clearly and engage their readers.

Device	Example
Figurative language is writing that means something beyond what the words actually say. Common forms of figurative language include these:	
• A **simile** compares two things using the words *like* or *as.*	*His voice sounded like nails on a chalkboard.*
• A **metaphor** compares two things by mentioning one thing as if it is something else. It does not use *like* or *as.*	*The trapeze artist was a bird in flight.*
• **Personification** gives human characteristics to a non-human object.	*The sun smiled down on us.*
Hyperbole is exaggeration used for effect.	*I felt stronger than a superhero!*
Irony is a contradiction between what happens and what is expected.	In a famous story, a wife cuts her hair to buy her husband a watch fob, and he sells his watch to buy her a brush.
Paradox is a statement that contains elements that seem contradictory, but could be true.	Mother Teresa said, "...if you love until it hurts, there can be no more hurt, only more love."
An **oxymoron** is word or phrase that seems to contradict itself.	The movie was seriously funny!
Symbolism is an object that stands for something else.	The American flag is often considered a symbol of freedom.
An **allegory** is a narrative that has a meaning other than what literally appears.	Some say the story of the sinking ship is an allegory for the effects of pride.
Repetition (or tautology) occurs when content is repeated—sometimes needlessly—for effect.	The band's song was loud, loud and far too long.

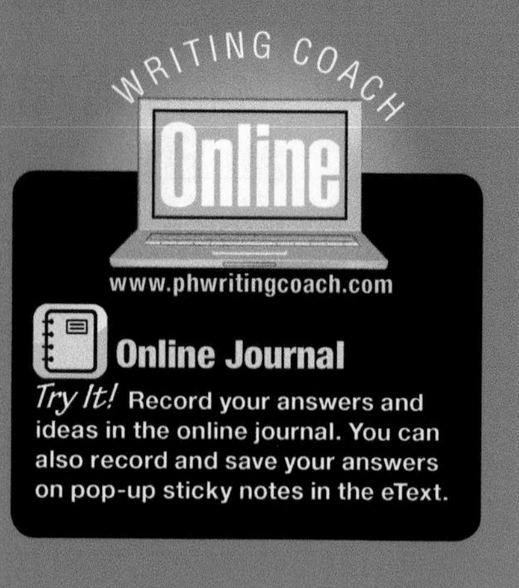

Online Journal

Try It! Record your answers and ideas in the online journal. You can also record and save your answers on pop-up sticky notes in the eText.

USING TECHNOLOGY

Most word processing programs have a built-in thesaurus tool. You can use the thesaurus to find descriptive words that can often substitute for weaker, overused words.

Partner Talk

There are many online tools that can help you strengthen your writing. For example, you can search for examples of figurative language and sound devices. Then you can model your own writing after the samples. Just be sure that you don't plagiarize or copy the written work of others.

READ AND APPLY

Have students read the text on page 54 and review the chart on page 55. Ask:

- What word that begins with *s* could replace *breeze* in the first example on page 54?
- What is one way we personify the moon?

Then, pair students to create examples for as many structural devices as they can. Ask volunteers to share their examples with the class.

Intermediate Echo read the figurative language entry, and provide pictures in support, as in the Beginning activity. Then, have students work in groups to retell the definitions and examples of figurative language, using and reusing the words.

Advanced Have partners read the figurative language entry, and provide pictures in support, as in the Beginning activity. Then, have partners retell the definitions and examples of figurative language, using and reusing the words.

Advanced High After students complete the Advanced activity, have them read and retell the definitions and examples of irony.

Using Writing Traits to Develop an Effective Composition

You read about rubrics and traits in Chapter 3. Now it's time to look at how they function in good writing.

Ideas

A good writer clearly presents and develops important information, a strong message, and original ideas.

As you read the sample, think about the ideas it presents.

Achoo!

Achoo! The common cold can be a major downer. Who wants to be home with a runny nose and sore throat? It happens more often than you might think, though. According to the Mayo Clinic, students can get as many as six to ten colds a year! If you understand the causes of the common cold and take precautions, you can successfully avoid catching a cold.

A common cold is caused by a virus. Many different viruses could be responsible for your runny nose, but all of them have one thing in common: they're very contagious. A common-cold virus can spread in the air when a sick person coughs, sneezes, or even talks.

Once you know how colds spread, you can see that avoiding a cold is fairly easy, if you follow some simple rules. Wash your hands often. Keep doorknobs and countertops clean. Don't share drinking glasses or silverware. Most importantly, avoid being around sick people. If you do happen to catch a cold, sneeze or cough into your elbow to help keep your cold from spreading to others. No one likes to be sick!

Try It! Think about ideas in the writing sample as you answer this question.

What is the writer's message? List three details that clearly convey or give support for this message.

MOTIVATE AND ENGAGE

Remind students of the writing traits introduced in Chapter 3. Ask: What is each trait? How does each trait contribute to an effective composition? Then, have them quickwrite responses to your questions.

When students have finished, invite volunteers to share their responses. Write them on the board, and refer back to them as the class covers pages 56–59. Finally, remind students to look back at the Overview of Writing Traits on page 27.

Organization

A well-organized composition flows easily from sentence to sentence and paragraph to paragraph. It clearly shows relationships between ideas. The paper also avoids needless repetition.

Think about organization as you reread "Achoo!" on page 56.

 *Try It!* Answer the questions about the writing sample on page 56.

1. Which sentence introduces the topic of the piece?
2. Why must the second paragraph appear before the third?
3. List three details in the third paragraph. Explain how each supports the first sentence in the paragraph.

Voice

Voice is the individual "sound" of a writer's writing, reflecting the writer's personality or perspective. A successful paper has a definite voice expressing the writer's individuality.

Read the writing sample. Think about voice as you read.

> I'll never forget the day my parents got home with 4-month-old Liang. I was sitting on the couch, waiting for them. My stomach was doing flip-flops. Then Mom and Dad walked through the door, carrying this little bundle wrapped in a blanket. Mom sat on the couch with me and introduced me to my new brother. I expected him to totally freak out—to scream and cry. Instead, he just looked up at me with his big, brown eyes and smiled. His tiny hand reached out and grabbed my finger. He had a pretty strong grip!
>
> I found out that while babies are sometimes loud, smelly, and drooly, all of that stuff didn't matter. I loved my little brother, and I couldn't wait till he grew up, so I could teach him how to use that strong grip to hold a football!

 *Try It!* Consider the writer's voice as you answer this question.

Which words and phrases give you a clear sense of the writer's personality and perspective? Explain.

Online Journal

Try It! Record your answers and ideas in the online journal. You can also record and save your answers on pop-up sticky notes in the eText.

Partner Talk

Analyze the composition about colds on page 56 with a partner. Discuss how well it might score on the traits of ideas and organization—from ineffective (1), to somewhat effective (2), to fairly effective (3), to effective (4), to highly effective in parts (5), to highly effective throughout (6).

COLLABORATE AND DISCUSS

Have students work in small groups to complete the *Try It!* activities on pages 56 and 57.

Next, have groups use the rubric on page 28 to score "Achoo!" on page 56 for ideas, organization, and voice. As a class, discuss each group's assessment. For each trait, discuss whether improvements could be made to raise the score. If so, what are they? If not, why not?

Differentiated Instruction

RTI Strategy for Below-Level Students
Students may benefit from a review of the Writing Traits (page 27) and scoring rubric (page 28) in Chapter 3. Go over the first three categories in both charts with students before having them complete the Collaborate and Discuss activity on this page. Encourage students to keep copies of each chart in their writing journal or folder for easy reference.

ELL Strategy for Spanish Speakers
Students whose home language is Spanish may have a more limited range of words and phrases for connecting ideas. Help students identify the connections in the sample text and elicit the Spanish equivalent. Encourage students to keep a list of connecting words and phrases in English and Spanish. Remind students to use the list to incorporate the words and phrases in their own writing.

Word Choice

By choosing words with precision, good writers give their writing energy and help readers picture exactly what they are talking about. Think about word choice as you read these two drafts:

Bob got into Ted's car. As he sat down, he realized he was hearing something familiar. "That's right," Ted said. "I finally put our stuff on CD. It sounds so nice on this system!"

2ND DRAFT

Bob climbed over chrome fittings into Ted's customized SUV. As Bob eased into the leather-upholstered seat, he recognized the crunching guitar chords that came crashing through the car stereo's speakers. "That's right," Ted said. "I finally mixed our band's songs down to a CD. They sound so crisp on this system!"

Try It! Answer these questions about the two drafts.

1. List two vague or imprecise words in the first draft.
2. What do the precise words in the second draft help you understand?

Sentence Fluency

In the best writing, sentences have rhythm. They flow smoothly when read aloud, rather than sounding awkward. To control rhythm, good writers use a variety of sentence structures. Think about the rhythm of the writer's sentences as you read this draft:

After six years of weekly lessons, I can say I have done my best to master the cello. I may not have been good enough for the All-County Orchestra last year, but this year will be different. This year, my dedication will pay off!

Try It! Respond to this prompt about the draft.

Describe the rhythm of the sentences in the passage.

COLLABORATE AND DISCUSS

Continue the Collaborate and Discuss activity from page 57. Have groups use the rubric on page 28 to score each sample on page 58 for voice, word choice, and sentence fluency. As a class, discuss the groups' scores and whether improvements could have been made.

Then, have students read the second sample on page 59. Discuss the difference in word choice between the second draft of the story about Bob and Ted and the description of the action movie.

Working with ELLs  Sheltered Instruction: Cognitive

Help students comprehend language structures used routinely in written classroom materials. Compare correctly capitalized geographical names with lowercase common nouns, explaining that common nouns may also be capitalized when used as titles or labels. Provide students with copies of a simple geographical map. Then:

Beginning Review entries on the map. Guide students in identifying nouns spelled with capital letters and nouns not spelled with capital letters. Clarify the meaning of each, identifying the language structure it represents (place name, common noun).

Intermediate Have students work in groups to list nouns on the map that are

Conventions

If a piece of writing reflects a good command of spelling, capitalization, punctuation, grammar, usage, and sentence structure, it is much more likely to communicate clearly to readers.

Pay attention to spelling, capitalization, punctuation, grammar, usage, and sentence structure as you read this first draft.

If your an action-movie fan, you have to run—not walk—to see *Welcome to Mars!* This movie is non-stop action, from start to finish. Me and my friend were blown away by the battle scenes, special effects, and suspense.

The movie has a great message, too: Understanding can lead to peace. In one very tense moment, the lead scientist on Mars is captured by aliens. I was so sure they would kill her! Instead, she stayed with them learning their language and to learn, their ways of life. This led to peace between the humans and the aliens.

Now, read this section of the reviewer's second draft.

If you're an action-movie fan, you have to run—not walk—to see *Welcome to Mars!* This movie is non-stop action, from start to finish. My friend and I were blown away by the battle scenes, special effects, and suspense.

The movie has a great message, too: Understanding can lead to peace. In one very tense moment, the lead scientist on Mars is captured by aliens. I was so sure they would kill her! Instead, she stayed with them, learning their language and their ways of life. This led to peace between the humans and the aliens.

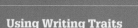

 *Try It!* Answer these questions about both drafts.

1. What errors in convention did the writer correct in the second draft?
2. Why is the next-to-last sentence easier to read in the second draft?

Online Journal

Try It! Record your answers and ideas in the online journal. You can also record and save your answers on pop-up sticky notes in the eText.

READ AND APPLY

Discuss the importance of using conventions correctly in writing. Ask: What might happen if your writing has errors in grammar, spelling, punctuation, or capitalization? Students may say that readers will become distracted or have a difficulty understanding the meaning.

Next, have students rewrite three sentences from the sample first draft. Then, have them exchange papers with a partner and check each other's work for errors in convention.

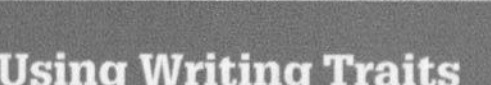

capitalized and nouns that are not and to identify the language structure that each represents (place name, common noun). Then, guide them to write two facts derived from the map, using correct capitalization.

Advanced Have partners list nouns on the map and identify the language structure (place name, common noun) that each represents. Have them write directions from one place on the map to another, using correct capitalization.

Advanced High Have partners complete the Advanced activity. Then, have them use the examples to write rules for capitalizing place names and post their rules in the classroom.

Using Interactive Writing Coach

As you learned in Chapter 3, you can use rubrics and your Revision RADaR to check how well your paragraphs and essays read. With Writing Coach, you also have another tool available to evaluate your work: the Interactive Writing Coach.

The Interactive Writing Coach is a program that you can use anywhere that you have Internet access. Interactive Writing Coach functions like your own personal writing tutor. It gives you personalized feedback on your work.

The Interactive Writing Coach has two parts: **Paragraph Feedback** and **Essay Scorer**.

- Paragraph Feedback gives you feedback on individual paragraphs as you write. It looks at the structure of sentences and paragraphs and gives you information about specific details, such as sentence variety and length.
- Essay Scorer looks at your whole essay and gives you a score and feedback on your entire piece of writing. It will tell you how well your essay reflects the traits of good writing.

This chart shows just a few questions that Paragraph Feedback and Essay Scorer will answer about your writing. The following pages explain Paragraph Feedback and Essay Scorer in more detail.

Sentences	• Are sentences varied in length? • Do sentences have varied beginnings? • Which sentences have too many ideas? • Are adjectives clear and precise? • Is the sentence grammatically correct? • Is all spelling correct in the sentence?
Paragraphs	• Does the paragraph support its topic? • Does the paragraph use transitions? • Does the paragraph contain the right amount of ideas and information?
Compositions	• Does the essay reflect characteristics of the genre? • Does it demonstrate the traits of good writing? • Is the main idea clear? • Is the main idea well supported? • Is the essay cohesive—does it hold together?

MOTIVATE AND ENGAGE

Have students quickwrite about how familiar tools like spell-checkers help them improve their writing. Ask:

- **What other tools would be helpful to writers?**
- **How does feedback from teachers, peers, and family members help you to improve your work?**

After students have finished, explain that the Writing Coach tools—Paragraph Feedback and Essay Scorer—can help writers improve their work. Then, review the features of these tools on pages 60 and 61.

Interactive Writing Coach and the Writing Process

You can begin to use Essay Scorer during the drafting section of the writing process. It is best to complete a full draft of your essay before submitting to Essay Scorer. (While you are drafting individual paragraphs, you may want to use Paragraph Feedback.) Keep in mind, however, that your draft does not need to be perfect or polished before you submit to Essay Scorer. You will be able to use feedback from Essay Scorer to revise your draft many times. This chart shows how you might use the Interactive Writing Coach and incorporate Essay Scorer into your writing process.

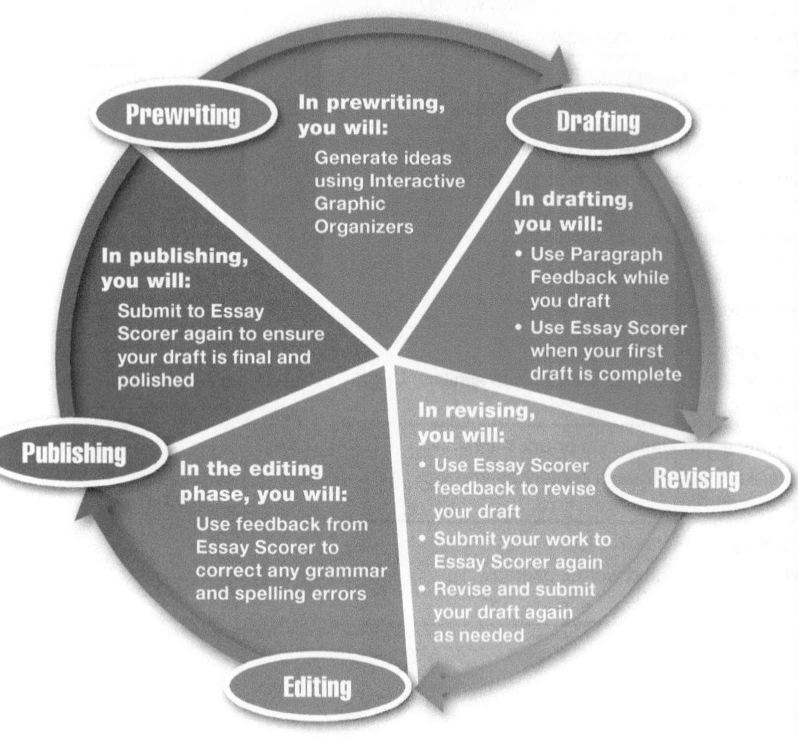

Prewriting
In prewriting, you will:
Generate ideas using Interactive Graphic Organizers
Drafting
In drafting, you will:
• Use Paragraph Feedback while you draft
• Use Essay Scorer when your first draft is complete
Revising
In revising, you will:
• Use Essay Scorer feedback to revise your draft
• Submit your work to Essay Scorer again
• Revise and submit your draft again as needed
Editing
In the editing phase, you will:
Use feedback from Essay Scorer to correct any grammar and spelling errors
Publishing
In publishing, you will:
Submit to Essay Scorer again to ensure your draft is final and polished

MOTIVATE AND ENGAGE

Ask:

- **What types of errors do you struggle with as a writer?**
- **What part of writing do you find the most difficult?**
- **In what ways might the Interactive Writing Coach help you to fix your errors or make writing easier?**

Invite volunteers to share their responses. Answer questions from students about the types of errors the Interactive Writing Coach addresses and problems the program might not address.

Differentiated Instruction

RTI Strategy for Below-Level Students
Students may benefit from working with you to review the information about the Interactive Writing Coach. Go through each item in the chart on page 60. Ask if students have questions about the types of errors the program will address. If possible, have students use Paragraph Feedback to see how it works on their writing. Review the feedback with students and suggest a plan for revision.

RTI Strategy for Special Needs Students
Students may benefit from watching you model how to use Paragraph Feedback on a piece of writing. Sit with students to show them how the tool works on a paragraph you have either written yourself or one that they have chosen from their writing portfolio. Review the feedback with students and suggest a plan for revision.

Paragraph Feedback With Interactive Writing Coach

Paragraph Feedback assesses the ideas and topic support for each paragraph you write. You can enter your work into Paragraph Feedback one paragraph at a time. This makes it easy to work on individual paragraphs and get new feedback as you revise each one. Here are some things that Paragraph Feedback will be able to tell you.

Overall Paragraph Support	• Does the paragraph support the main idea? • Which sentences do not support the main idea?
Transitions	• Which sentences contain transition words? • Which words are transition words?
Ideas	• How well are ideas presented? • Which sentences have too many ideas?
Sentence Length and Variety	• Which sentences are short, medium, and long? • Which sentences could be longer or shorter for better sense or variety? • Are sentences varied?
Sentence Beginnings	• How do sentences begin? • Are sentence beginnings varied?
Sentence Structure	• Are sentence structures varied? • Are there too many sentences with similar structures?
Vague Adjectives	• Are any adjectives vague or unclear? • Where are adjectives in sentences and paragraphs?
Language Variety	• Are words repeated? • Where are repeated words located? • How can word choice be improved?

MOTIVATE AND ENGAGE

Before students have read page 62, have them quickwrite about their favorite writers and what good writing means to them. Ask: How does reading examples of good writing help you to improve your writing?

Have students tell you the components necessary to a good paragraph. Write students responses on the board. Then, compare these responses with the chart on page 62. Discuss what was missing from the board and why it is important.

Essay Scoring With Interactive Writing Coach

Essay Scorer assesses your essay. It looks at the essay as a whole, and it also evaluates individual paragraphs, sentences, and words. Essay Scorer will help you evaluate the following traits.

Ideas	• Are the ideas significant or original? Is a clear message or unique perspective presented? • Is the main idea clearly stated? • Is the main idea supported by informative details?
Organization	• Is the organization logical? • Is the introduction clear? Is the conclusion clear? • What transitions are used, and are they effective?
Voice	• Does the writing have a unique, individual "sound" showing the personality or perspective of the writer? • Does the tone match the audience and purpose?
Word Choice	• Are precise words used? • Are vivid words used? • Do the word choices suit the purpose and audience?
Sentence Fluency	• Are sentence beginnings, lengths, and structures varied? • Do the sentences flow smoothly?
Conventions	• Is spelling correct? • Is capitalization used properly? • Is all punctuation (ending, internal, apostrophes) accurate? • Do subjects and verbs agree? • Are pronouns used correctly? • Are adjectives and adverbs used correctly? • Are plurals formed correctly? • Are commonly confused words used correctly?

Whenever you see the Interactive Writing Coach icon, you can go to Writing Coach Online and submit your writing, either paragraph by paragraph or as a complete draft, for personalized feedback and scoring.

www.phwritingcoach.com

Interactive Writing Coach™

Interactive Writing Coach provides support and guidance to help you improve your writing skills.

- Select a topic to write about from the Topic Bank.
- Use the interactive graphic organizers to narrow your topic.
- Go to Writing Coach Online and submit your work, paragraph by paragraph or as a complete draft.
- Receive immediate, personalized feedback as you write, revise, and edit your work.

MOTIVATE AND ENGAGE

Have a class discussion about the differences between a single paragraph and a full essay. Ask:

- What must an essay convey that a paragraph might not?
- What different kinds of feedback would you need for an essay versus a single paragraph?
- Would you get the same result feeding an essay paragraph by paragraph into Paragraph Feedback as you would using the Essay Scorer? Why, or why not?

Differentiated Instruction

RTI Strategy for Below-Level Students Students may benefit from seeing the Essay Scorer in action. Sit with students and show them how the Essay Scorer works. Use a draft of an essay in this chapter, such as the one on 56, or one that the students have in their writing portfolio. Review the feedback and the score, and discuss a plan for revision.

PRE-AP Enrichment for Above-Level Students Have students use the Essay Scorer to evaluate a piece of writing they have completed. Ask students to critique the tool. **Ask:** What errors did it find? How did the feedback help you to improve your writing? Do you think the score was fair? Next, have students incorporate the feedback in a new draft and use the tool again. **Ask:** Did your score improve? Why or why not?

CHAPTER 5 LESSON PLANNER
Nonfiction Narration

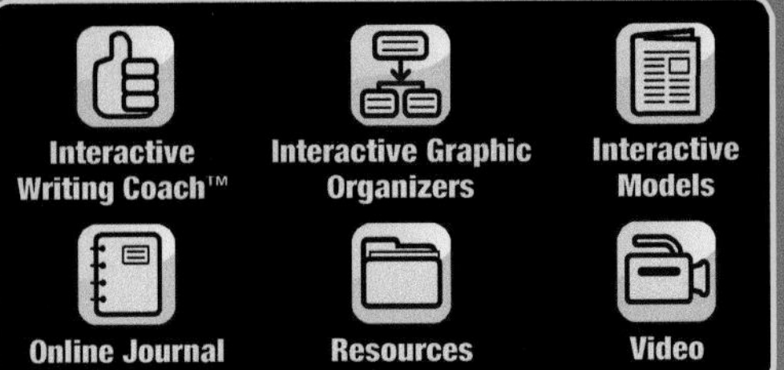

Use the Online Lesson Planner at www.phwritingcoach.com to customize your instructional plan for an integrated Language Arts curriculum.

DAY 1

ONLINE

CHAPTER OPENER/ GENRE INTRODUCTION

- What Do You Remember?
- What's Ahead
- Connect to the Big Questions
- **Feature Assignment: Narrative Nonfiction: Personal Narrative**
- Other Forms of Narrative Nonfiction
- Word Bank

DAY 2

ONLINE

MENTOR TEXT/ STUDENT MODEL

- **Mentor Text: Personal Narrative**
- Learn From Experience
- **Student Model: Personal Narrative**
- Reader's Eye and Writer's Eye

DAY 3

ONLINE

Prewriting

- Choose From the Topic Bank
- Choose Your Own Topic
- Narrow Your Topic
- Consider Your Audience and Purpose

DAY 6

ONLINE

Revising

- Keep Revision on Your RADaR
- Look at the Big Picture
- Focus on Craft
- Fine-Tune Your Draft

DAY 7

For additional grammar support, see Grammar Game Plan, Error 12, p. 284.

ONLINE

Editing

- What Do You Notice/ Grammar Mini-Lesson

Rubric for Nonfiction Narration: Personal Narrative

Publishing

- Publish Your Piece
- Reflect on Your Writing

DAY 8

ONLINE

21st Century Learning

MAKE YOUR WRITING COUNT

- **Bring Your Personal Narrative to Life in a Script**
- Here's Your Action Plan
- Listening and Speaking

Alternate Pacing Suggestions

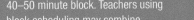

- **Block Scheduling** Each day on the Lesson Planner represents a 40–50 minute block. Teachers using block scheduling may combine days to revise pacing to meet their classroom needs.
- **Accelerated Lesson Planning** Combine instructional days by aiding students in choosing a topic and then focusing on two core stages of the writing process, outlining for success (Day 5) and RADaR revision (Day 6).
- **Integrated Language Arts Curriculum** For targeted instruction that covers the essential components of the lesson use either a 3- or a 5-day plan.

3 day plan

DAY 1: Introduction to the Genre, Mentor Text Student Model

DAY 2: Prewriting/Drafting

DAY 3: Revise/Edit/Publish

5 day plan

Use 3-day plan, and add:

DAY 4: Make Your Writing Count

DAY 5: Writing for Assessment

Links to Prentice Hall *LITERATURE*

Featured Author: Richard Peck

- What Are Fiction and Nonfiction?, p. 4
- "The Three-Century Woman" (fiction), Richard Peck, p. 9
- "The Fall of the *Hindenburg*" (informative article), Michael Morrison, p. 19
- On Conflict in Fiction (Writing Workshop), p. 179
- *From the Author's Desk* Videos: Richard Peck

Additional Mentor Text:

- from *An American Childhood* (autobiography), Annie Dillard, p. 52

Differentiated Instruction

Differentiated Instruction Boxes in this Teacher's Edition address these student populations:

- Below-Level Students
- Gifted and Talented Students
- English Language Learners
- Above-Level Students
- Special Needs Students
- Spanish Speaking Students

In addition, for further enrichment, see the **Extension** features.

DAY 4

Prewriting

- Plan Your Piece
- Gather Details

ONLINE

DAY 5

Drafting

- Outline for Success
- Start Your Draft

ONLINE

DAY 9

WRITING FOR MEDIA

- **Event Letter**
- Create an Event Letter

ONLINE

DAY 10

WRITING FOR ASSESSMENT

- Narrative Prompt
- The ABCDs of On-Demand Writing

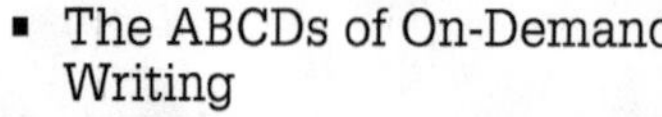

- More Prompts for Practice **Test Prep**

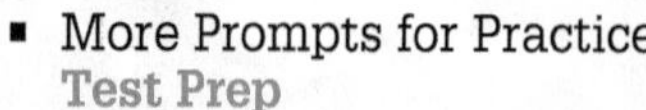

- More Strategies for Writing Assessment

ONLINE

LESSON OBJECTIVES

- To learn the forms and defining characteristics of nonfiction narration.
- To learn the elements of a successful personal narrative, the chapter Feature Assignment.
- To read a Mentor Text in the genre, analyzing its use of the elements of effective nonfiction narration.
- To read a Student Model of a personal narrative, analyzing it from the perspective of a reader and from the perspective of a writer.
- To apply prewriting strategies in developing a personal narrative, including strategies for choosing and narrowing a topic, planning writing, and gathering details, as well as tips for considering audience and purpose.
- To apply drafting strategies in developing a personal narrative.
- To apply RADaR revision strategies to a draft personal narrative.
- To learn about the Focus on Craft topic, simple, compound, and complex sentences, and apply what is learned to a draft personal narrative.
- To edit the draft, zooming in on verb tenses and focusing on maintaining consistent tense.
- To complete the Make Your Writing Count assignment, developing and presenting a script.
- To complete the Writing for Media assignment, developing an event letter.
- To practice writing for assessment.

Personalized Assessment

✓	Ongoing Assessment	Formal Assessment of Feature Assignment	Progress Monitoring at End-of-Chapter
 Interactive Writing Coach	Use Paragraph Feedback and Essay Scorer as a revision tool.	Use Essay Scorer to score students' Feature Assignment papers.	Use Essay Scorer to score students' papers. Students' learner profiles can be adjusted based on their scores.
 FEEDBACK Teacher Conferencing	Use rubrics in the Student Edition as a revision tool. Conference with students to review their work and provide personalized support.	Use rubrics in the Student Edition to score students' Feature Assignment papers. 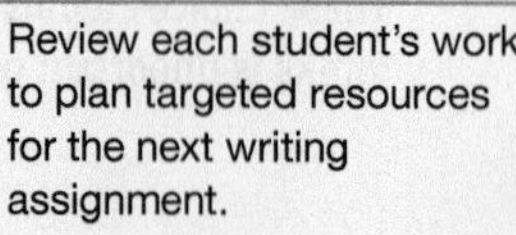	Review each student's work to plan targeted resources for the next writing assignment.

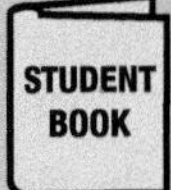

1 Using Writing Coach Online™ or the student book, students discuss the photograph in the chapter opener as it relates to the writing genre.

2 Students record their ideas and responses in their online journals or notebooks. They may also record and save their responses on pop-up sticky notes in Writing Coach Online™.

Chapter Objectives

1. Write a personal narrative by planning, drafting, revising, editing, and publishing individual work.
2. Produce a script.
3. Use the five-step writing process to write an event letter.
4. Write a personal narrative in response to a prompt.

NONFICTION NARRATION

What Do You Remember?

Activate Prior Knowledge Tell students that the purpose of nonfiction narration is to tell a true story about real people's lives, experiences, and thoughts. Explain to students that they will use what they know about accomplishments, or goals we reach, to analyze the photo on page 64. Then, guide students in analyzing the photo.

Think Aloud To analyze means to look at something closely and draw conclusions about its meaning. For example, in the photo **I see** girls in soccer uniforms. I conclude that this is a soccer team. The girls are smiling and holding trophies, so I can conclude that their team has won a soccer championship. Their accomplishment is that they worked hard and won many games to become the top team.

Work with students to brainstorm for other accomplishments that the girls in the photo could achieve together or alone. Record student responses.

Try It! **Have students** work individually to develop responses to the questions. Check that students have included sensory details in their lists.

Possible responses: To see the fish and coral up close at the Great Barrier Reef, I needed to learn to snorkel. I don't like swimming or large bodies of water, yet there I was, out in the ocean, diving and breathing through a tube. I was thrilled to see the vivid, beautiful fish and coral, but more than that, I was proud of myself for overcoming my fears.

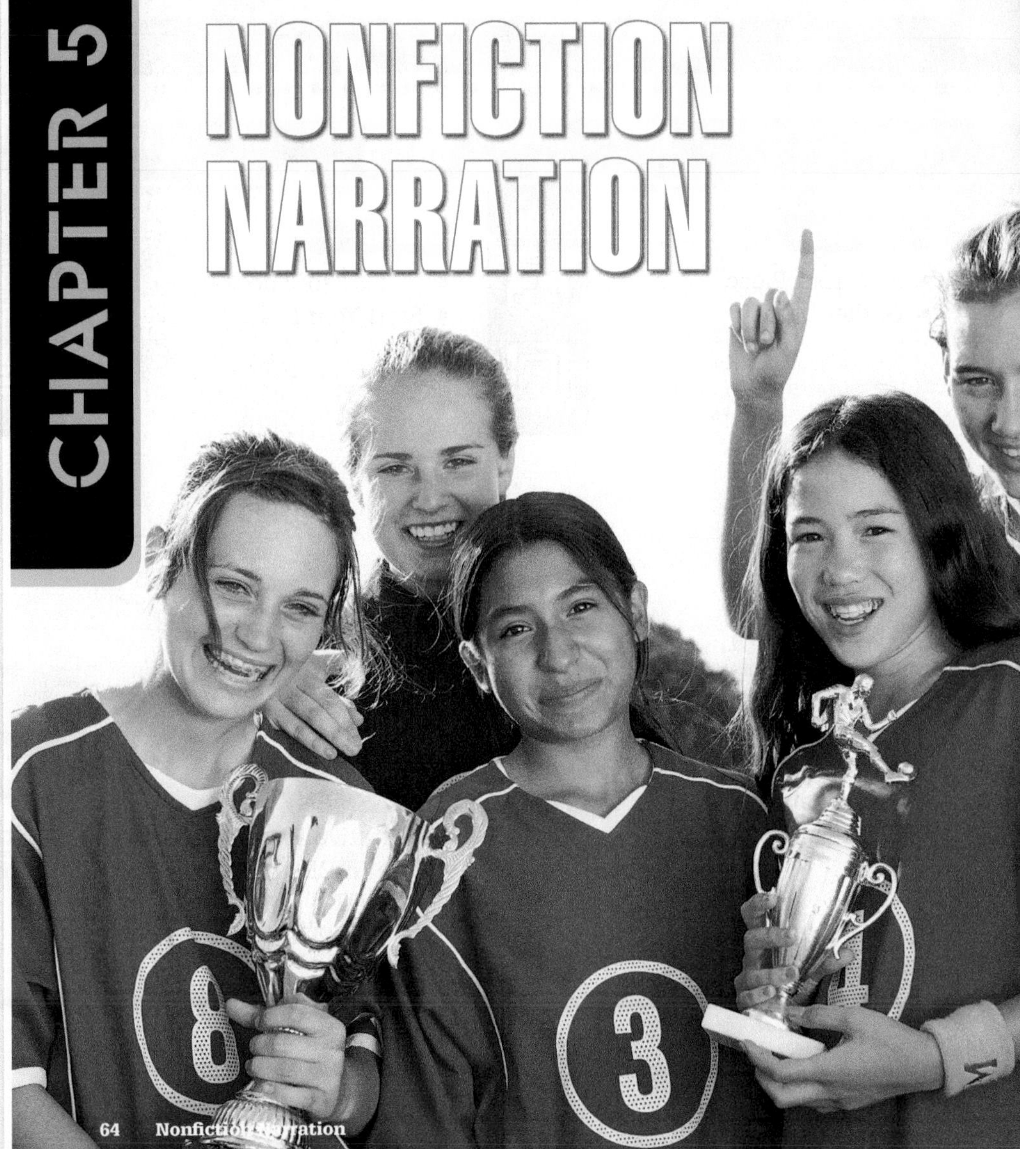

Connect to the Big Questions

Have students use their experience to discuss the Big Questions. Explain that they will revisit **Why write?** at the end of this chapter. Tell students to consider these points during their discussion:

1. In general, a person chooses the accomplishments he or she wants to achieve. These choices tell us about what the person thinks is important or worthwhile.
2. Readers want to read your story about challenges you overcame to accomplish your goal. Any additional facts can be saved for another story.

What's Ahead

Have students preview the Mentor Text and Student Model on pages 68–71. Tell students that they will write their own personal narrative using the five-step writing process: prewriting, drafting, revising, editing, and publishing.

What Do You Remember?

Why are accomplishments important? What might make accomplishments interesting to other people?

To tell a story about an accomplishment, you will need to remember details of the experience. Using vivid details to describe an accomplishment will make the story more interesting to others.

Try It! Think about a recent accomplishment. Consider these questions as you participate in an extended discussion with a partner. Take turns expressing your ideas and feelings.

- What led up to the accomplishment?
- What challenges did you face?
- What did you see, smell, touch, feel, and hear during the experience?

Review the list you made, and then think about how you would include these details when telling someone about your accomplishment.

What's Ahead

In this chapter, you will review two strong examples of a personal narrative: a Mentor Text and a Student Model. Then, using the examples as guidance, you will write a personal narrative of your own.

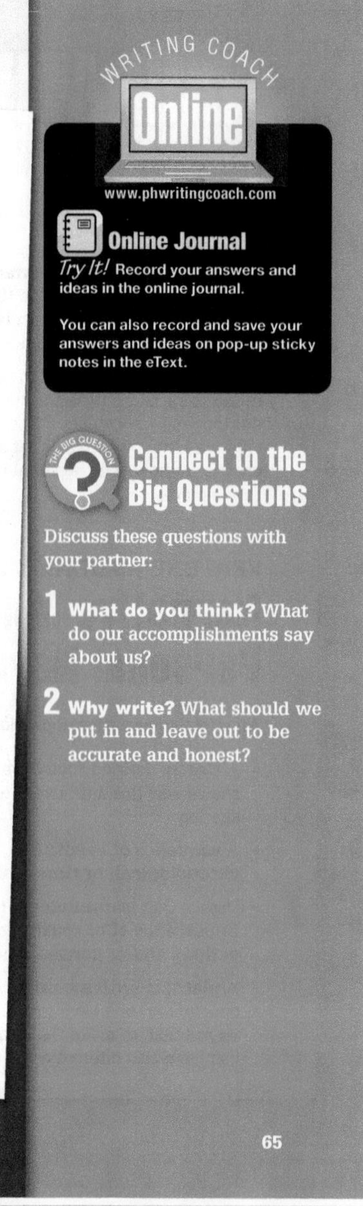

Online Journal

Try It! Record your answers and ideas in the online journal.

You can also record and save your answers and ideas on pop-up sticky notes in the eText.

Connect to the Big Questions

Discuss these questions with your partner:

1 **What do you think?** What do our accomplishments say about us?

2 **Why write?** What should we put in and leave out to be accurate and honest?

65

Personalized Support

Teacher or Peer Feedback

To encourage students in their discussion of the photograph as it relates to the writing genre, ask the following questions:

- What is the first thing you think of when you look at this photo?
- How does it relate to your life?
- How does it relate to things you've learned in other subjects?
- What questions come to mind when you look at this photograph?
- How does your response to the photograph compare to those of your classmates?

Working with ELLs

ELL **Sheltered Instruction:** Metacognitive

Have students demonstrate listening comprehension of increasingly complex spoken English by following the *Try It!* directions after you read them aloud.

Beginning Write the *Try It!* directions as simple statements in a sequence chart. Read them aloud, pointing to the steps in the chart. Ask yes/no questions to help students monitor comprehension, reminding them to seek clarification. Guide them in following directions.

Intermediate Read aloud the *Try It!* directions. Have students listen and write the steps in sequence charts to monitor understanding, seeking clarification as necessary, then follow the directions.

Advanced As you read aloud the *Try It!* directions, have students take notes. Then, have them follow the directions to complete the activity, encouraging them to monitor comprehension and seek clarification as needed.

Advanced High Have one partner read aloud the *Try It!* directions, as the other takes notes; then, have them switch roles. They should review notes to monitor comprehension. Then, have partners follow the directions to complete the activity, seeking clarification as needed.

1 Students learn vocabulary from the Word Bank and listen to English and Spanish pronunciations in the Writing Coach Online™ glossary.

2 Students record answers to questions about forms of writing in their online journals or notebooks.

NARRATIVE NONFICTION

To introduce this chapter's writing form, discuss the opening paragraphs with students. Make sure students understand that a personal narrative is a type of narrative nonfiction. Explain that good writers use a step-by-step process to develop their work. Then, have students preview the rubric on page 83.

Narrative Nonfiction: Personal Narrative

Ask volunteers to read aloud the feature assignment characteristics. Tell students that they will identify these characteristics in a Mentor Text and a Student Model. Then, they will use the characteristics to guide the writing of their own personal narrative.

Other Forms of Narrative Nonfiction

Guide students to understand the main purpose of, or reason for writing, each form of narrative nonfiction.

Say: I notice that there are several forms of narrative nonfiction. If I note the main purpose, or reason for writing each one, I can more easily remember them all. For example, the main purpose of a biographical narrative is to tell a story about someone else's life.

Ask: How are these forms of narrative nonfiction alike? (They all tell a true story.) How are they different? (Each form has a different audience and purpose.)

Have students brainstorm for appropriate topics for each form of narrative nonfiction.

Try It! Remind students that the audience is the people who will read their writing. The purpose is the author's reason for writing. Have students record their responses in their journal.

Possible responses: blog, shares comments online and gets readers' responses; diary entry, reveals personal, private thoughts; reflective essay, tells a story and shares the writer's thoughts about it

NARRATIVE NONFICTION

In this chapter, you will explore a special type of narrative nonfiction: the personal narrative. A personal narrative is a true story in which YOU are the leading character. By writing personal narratives, you can tell readers about yourself and your life. You can entertain them—and maybe make them think, too!

You will develop your personal narrative by taking it through each of the steps of the writing process: prewriting, drafting, revising, editing, and publishing. You will also have an opportunity to create a letter or e-mail about a personal event. To preview the criteria for how your personal narrative will be evaluated, see the rubric on page 83.

FEATURE ASSIGNMENT

Narrative Nonfiction: Personal Narrative

An effective narrative nonfiction essay has these characteristics:

- A **clearly defined focus** that shows why this narrative is worth sharing
- A **sequence of events in chronological, or time, order**
- Details that **communicate the importance of or reason for actions and/or consequences**
- A **plot line with a conflict and resolution**, or a clear problem and its solution, to make the narrative complete and interesting
- **Specific details and quotations**, or dialogue, to help readers imagine characters' actions, gestures, and expressions
- Effective sentence structure and correct **spelling, grammar, and usage**

A personal narrative also includes:

- A focus on yourself, the writer, as the main character
- Vivid images and feelings to help readers experience the setting, characters, and action as you did

66 Narrative Nonfiction

Word Bank

To assist English Language Learners and struggling readers, echo read each word or have students log on to Writing Coach Online to listen to the pronunciations. Then, have partners take turns using each word in a sentence. Ask volunteers to share one of their sentences with the class.

Teacher Tip

Quick Write To extend students' understanding, have them select one of the topics they brainstormed earlier for the different forms of narrative nonfiction and write a brief paragraph explaining why it is a good topic for the form.

Other Forms of Narrative Nonfiction

In addition to a personal narrative, there are other forms of narrative nonfiction, including:

Biographical narratives are stories that share facts about someone else's life.

Blogs are comments that writers share in online forums. They may include personal narratives, opinions, and other types of comments. Blogs often invite other writers to respond online, too. They usually are not thought of as "permanent" writing.

Diary entries, which are highly personal, include experiences, thoughts, and feelings. The audience, however, is private, unless writers choose to share the diary entries.

Narrative essays use personal narratives to illustrate or support a main idea.

Memoirs focus on an important person or event from the writer's own life. Book-length memoirs by famous people are often quite popular.

Reflective essays present personal experiences—events that happened to the writers or that the writers learned about from others. Reflective essays stand out because they do more than tell a story: They also share the writers' thoughts about those experiences. Reflective essays often appear as features in magazines and newspapers.

Try It! For each audience and purpose described, choose a form, such as a blog, diary entry, or reflective essay, that is appropriate for conveying your intended meaning to the audience. Explain your choices.

- To tell online friends a funny story about yourself
- To remind yourself, for the future, about what happened today at your grandmother's birthday party
- To tell and share your feelings about a storm

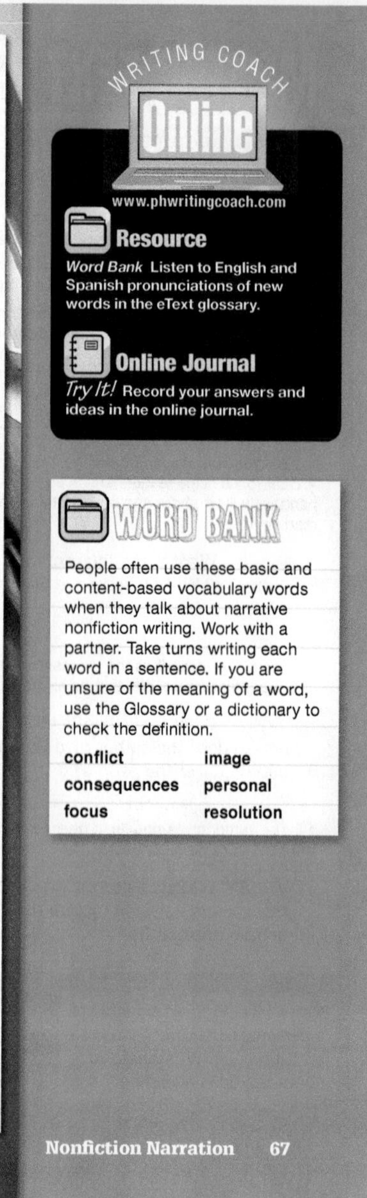

Resource

Word Bank Listen to English and Spanish pronunciations of new words in the eText glossary.

Online Journal

Try It! Record your answers and ideas in the online journal.

WORD BANK

People often use these basic and content-based vocabulary words when they talk about narrative nonfiction writing. Work with a partner. Take turns writing each word in a sentence. If you are unsure of the meaning of a word, use the Glossary or a dictionary to check the definition.

conflict	image
consequences	personal
focus	resolution

Personalized Support

Teacher or Peer Feedback

To help students understand the characteristics of the writing form, ask or have student partners ask one another the following questions:

- What are the main characteristics of narrative nonfiction?
- What makes this form of writing different from other forms?
- Who are the likely readers or audiences for this form of writing?
- What kind of organization could be used for this form of writing?
- What kind of voice would be most effective for this form of writing?

Working with ELLs

ELL **Sheltered Instruction:** Cognitive

Have students use accessible language and strategic learning techniques, like comparing and contrasting, to acquire new essential language, such as basic and grade-level vocabulary. Pair Word Bank words to accessible synonyms, like *conflict/problem.*

Beginning Help students compare and contrast the paired words to acquire new vocabulary and speak each word in a sentence to show comprehension.

Intermediate Have partners write two sentences with the accessible synonyms and swap. Have them read the sentences aloud, then replace the synonyms with the new vocabulary and read again, answering questions, like *How is [focus] different from [point]?*

Advanced Have students write sentences using Word Bank words and accessible synonyms. Have partners swap and ask questions like *What does [conflict] refer to in the sentence? How are [conflict] and [problem] the same/different?*

Advanced High Have students complete the Advanced activity and write a brief paragraph using all six Word Bank words.

1 STUDENT BOOK

Using Writing Coach Online™ or the student book, students read and listen to an audio recording of the Mentor Text. As they complete their writing assignments, they can refer back to the Mentor Text for support whenever they need it.

MENTOR TEXT

About the Selection The selection is a personal narrative in which the author shares a memorable childhood experience. He describes the events and misunderstandings that lead to his hitting a classmate, who then declares revenge on him.

Learn From Experience

After students have read the text, point out that the numbered notes refer to the characteristics of a personal narrative introduced on page 66.

Try It! Guide students to understand how the genre characteristics shape the text.

Say: The first *Try It!* question asks me to write a sentence about the focus of the personal narrative. After **I read** the first four sentences of the narrative, I can write my own sentence about the focus of the story: "The focus of *The Pigman & Me* is to share an awful event that the author does not anticipate, which involves him and a boy named John Quinn."

Ask: What happens in the first four sentences of the story? (The author tells a little about the plot and the characters in the story.) How would you state your ideas about the focus in a sentence? (Responses will vary.)

Have students reply to the *Try It!* questions in their journals. If students have difficulty responding to a particular question, model a response, as with Question 1.

Check the accuracy and completeness of student responses.

1. Responses will vary, but should be based on the information the author gives at the beginning of the narrative.
2. John Quinn insists that the author has to give him the paddle. The author does not hand over the paddle because he is the new kid and thinks that John is trying to take advantage him.
3. *berserk, wound up, frightened, struck out, smacked,* and *instant*
4. Responses will vary, but should note that the dialogue makes readers feel as though they are present at the scene. The dialogue tells about the characters' personalities.
5. John Quinn says he will get even with the author.

Extension Lead a discussion in which students compare and contrast how their additional personal narrative examples use the genre characteristics. Use the *Try It!* questions as a guide.

Personal Narrative Mentor Text Personal Narrative Mentor T

MENTOR TEXT Personal Narrative

Learn From Experience

Read the personal narrative on pages 68–69. As you read, take notes to develop your understanding of basic sight and English vocabulary. Then, read the numbered notes in the margins to learn about how the author presented his ideas.

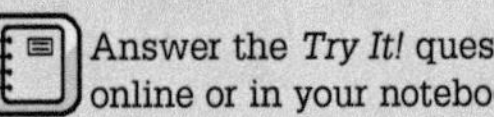

Answer the *Try It!* questions online or in your notebook.

❶ The **focus** is clearly defined from the start. A clear focus helps readers anticipate what the narrative will be about and builds interest in reading it.

Try It! What is the focus of the narrative? Write a sentence telling what you think.

❷ The author describes the events that led up to the **conflict**, or trouble, that he experienced.

Try It! What is the conflict? What reason does the author give for not handing over the paddle?

❸ The author gives **details** to describe how the conflict came to a head.

Try It! Which adjectives and verbs in this section help you picture the high point of the conflict?

Extension Find an example of a personal narrative to compare with this one. What insights about life does each offer?

From

The Pigman & Me

by Paul Zindel

❶ When trouble came to me, it didn't involve anybody I thought it would. It involved the nice, normal, smart boy by the name of John Quinn. Life does that to us a lot. Just when we think something awful's going to happen one way, it throws you a curve and the something awful happens another way. This happened on the first Friday, during gym period, when we were allowed to play games in the school yard. ❷ A boy by the name of Richard Cahill, who lived near an old linoleum factory, asked me if I'd like to play paddle ball with him, and I said, "Yes." Some of the kids played softball, some played warball, and there were a few other games where you could sign out equipment and do what you wanted. What I didn't know was that you were allowed to sign out the paddles for only fifteen minutes per period so more kids could get a chance to use them. I just didn't happen to know that little rule, and Richard Cahill didn't think to tell me about it. Richard was getting a drink from the water fountain when John Quinn came up to me and told me I had to give him my paddle.

"No," I said, being a little paranoid about being the new kid and thinking everyone was going to try to take advantage of me.

"Look, you have to give it to me," John Quinn insisted.

❸ That was when I did something berserk. I was so wound up and frightened that I didn't think, and I struck out at him with my right fist. I had forgotten I was holding the paddle, and it smacked into his face, giving him an instant black eye. John was shocked. I was shocked. Richard Cahill came running back and he was shocked.

Teacher Tip

Ask students to recall a time when a misunderstanding with another person caused a conflict for them. Have them work with a partner to create and present a brief scene in which dialogue and narration reveal the misunderstanding, conflict, and resolution.

2 Writing Journal

Students record their answers to questions about the Mentor Text in their online journals or notebooks.

❹ "What's going on here?" Mr. Trellis, the gym teacher, growled.

"He hit me with the paddle," John moaned, holding his eye. He was red as a beet, as Little Frankfurter, Conehead, Moose, and lots of the others gathered around.

"He tried to take the paddle away from me!" I complained.

"His time was up," John said.

Mr. Trellis set me wise to the rules as he took John over to a supply locker and pulled out a first-aid kit.

"I'm sorry," I said, over and over again.

❺ Then the bell rang, and all John Quinn whispered to me was that he was going to get even. He didn't say it like a nasty rotten kid, just more like an all-American boy who knew he'd have to regain his dignity about having to walk around school with a black eye. Before the end of school, Jennifer came running up to me in the halls and told me John Quinn had announced to everyone he was going to exact revenge on me after school on Monday. That was the note of disaster my first week at school ended on, and I was terrified because I didn't know how to fight. I had never even been in a fight. What had happened was all an accident. It really was.

Interactive Model

Listen to an audio recording of the Mentor Text in the eText. You can refer back to the Mentor Text whenever you need support in developing your own writing.

Online Journal

Try It! Answer the questions about the Mentor Text in the online journal.

❹ The author uses dialogue to explain the **resolution,** or outcome, of the conflict here.

Try It! What is the effect of using dialogue to describe the resolution? What insights into the characters does the dialogue give you?

❺ The author finishes describing the **resolution** here.

Try It! What are the consequences, or results, of the author hitting John Quinn with a paddle?

Personalized Support

Teacher or Peer Feedback

FEEDBACK

To provide feedback to students on their responses to the Mentor Text and their answers to the *Try It!* questions, ask or have student partners ask one another the following:

- What is the thesis or controlling idea of the Mentor Text?
- How does the Mentor Text illustrate the characteristics of narrative nonfiction?
- How did you answer this *Try It!* question? How could you use your answer to help you plan your piece of writing?

Working with ELLs

ELL **Sheltered Instruction:** Cognitive

Have students listen to, derive meaning from, and respond orally to a wide variety of print, electronic, and audiovisual media to build and reinforce concept attainment. Create or provide a recording of dialogue about a conflict. Use it to build and reinforce attainment of the concept of dialogue.

Beginning Pause the recording to clarify as necessary. Review concept-related words like *speaker, conflict,* and *solution.* Have students use them to respond orally to questions about the recording. For example, *What problem is discussed?*

Intermediate During playback, have students seek clarification as needed. Then have them discuss the conversation. To build concept attainment, provide sentence frames to guide responses. For example, *One solution to the conflict could be* ______.

Advanced Have groups discuss the dialogue, identify the conflict, and offer solutions. Have them use sentence frames like *The conflict is* ______. *They might solve it by* ______.

Advanced High Have students complete the Advanced activity. Challenge them to summarize the dialogue.

1 

Using Writing Coach Online™ or the student book, students read and listen to an audio recording of the Student Model.

STUDENT MODEL

Tell students that good writers react to what they read in ways that show their understanding of the text. Explain that students will react to the Student Model by placing two sets of symbols in the text. Then, distribute printed copies of the Student Model or have students log on to Writing Coach Online.

Use a Reader's Eye

Read aloud the instructions for using the Reader's Response Symbols and the meaning of each symbol. Then, guide students through their use.

When **I read** the text, the writer sometimes made me wonder what would happen next. For example, in lines 15–22, he describes the class's rehearsals and says, "If we could keep from crashing into each other, it would look good. Otherwise, it would be a disaster." This section makes me wonder if they really will crash into each other. I'll place a question mark next to this part of the text.

Work with students to identify other places in the text where they wondered what would happen next.

Have students read and respond to the Student Model, using each Reader's Response Symbol at least once.

Narrative Student Model Personal Narrative Student Model

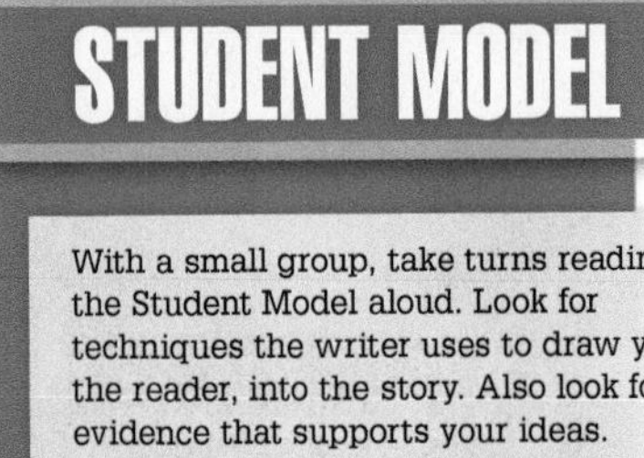

STUDENT MODEL Personal Narrative

With a small group, take turns reading the Student Model aloud. Look for techniques the writer uses to draw you, the reader, into the story. Also look for evidence that supports your ideas.

Use a Reader's Eye

Now, reread the Student Model. On your copy of the Student Model, use the Reader's Response Symbols to react to what you read.

Reader's Response Symbols

- **+ I like where this is going.**
- **− This isn't clear to me.**
- **? What will happen next?**
- **! Wow! That is really cool/weird/interesting!**

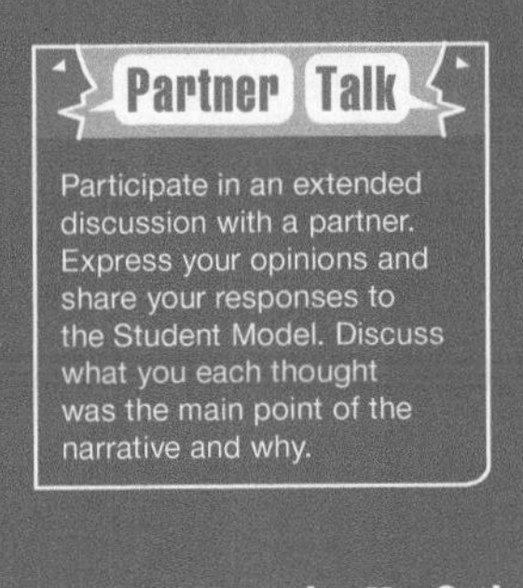

Partner Talk

Participate in an extended discussion with a partner. Express your opinions and share your responses to the Student Model. Discuss what you each thought was the main point of the narrative and why.

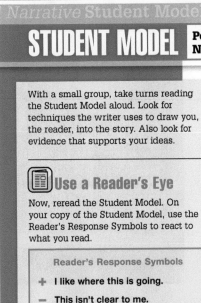

Alone in the SPOTLIGHT

by Mark Walker Williams

Have you ever had that nightmare—the one where everyone is staring at you? That nightmare came true for me!

I was in third grade. My school was preparing a show for Independence Day, and my class was going to sing "This Is My Country." Mr. Lee, the music teacher, helped us learn the song. When I sang it at home, my parents were impressed.

"Wonderful!" cried Mom.

Dad added, "I can't wait to hear you sing on Friday afternoon."

"You won't be able to hear just me," I said, "but my class sounds great."

For the rest of that week, my class rehearsed our song in the auditorium. We practiced marching onto the risers without tripping. And we practiced standing still without fainting. Then we practiced marching off the stage while singing the chorus two final times. A color guard was going to carry flags onto the stage while we did that. If we could keep from crashing into each other, it would look good. Otherwise, it would be a disaster.

We made mistakes at first, and we joked about each one. Even when we got better, though, I scowled. Someone still might mess up!

The big day came. I sat with my class, but I turned and waved at Mom, Dad, Aunt Miriam,

1

70 Narrative Nonfiction

Partner Talk

After partners have shared with each other the main point of the narrative and how the narrative made them feel, have each student pair share their responses with the class.

Use a Writer's Eye

Read aloud the instructions for using the Writer's Response Symbols and the meaning of each symbol. Then, guide students through their use.

Say: **I noticed** that the writer created believable characters. For example, in lines 7–13, after the writer sings for his mom and dad, his mom exclaims, "Wonderful!" His dad adds, "I can't wait to hear you sing on Friday afternoon." And the writer says, "You won't be able to hear just me, but my class sounds great." I can imagine a family speaking exactly that way in that situation. I'll write B.C. there for believable characters.

Ask: Where else does dialogue help create believable characters? (line 43, Grandpa complimenting his grandson; lines 46–48, Mom encouraging the family to sing the song)

Have students read and respond to the Student Model, using each Writer's Response Symbol at least once.

2 

First, students respond to the Student Model as a reader, using symbols to mark the text. They can mark the text using pop-up sticky notes in **Writing Coach Online**™ or they can mark a printed copy of the Student Model.

3 WRITING COACH Online STUDENT BOOK

Then, students respond to the Student Model as a writer, using different symbols to mark the text. They can use either **Writing Coach Online**™ or a printed copy of the Student Model.

www.phwritingcoach.com

Interactive Model

Listen to an audio recording of the Student Model in the eText. Use the Reader's and Writer's Response Symbols with the eText tools to note what you read.

and Grandpa just before the program began. Grandpa grinned and gave me a "thumbs up." I needed that because I was nervous!

The first- and second-graders did a good job. Then it was our turn.

As we sang, my nervousness disappeared. I was inspired—so inspired that I didn't notice my classmates marching off the stage, and I didn't notice the color guard marching onto the stage. I didn't notice the end of the music, either. I just stood there and kept singing!

Finally, Mr. Lee came onto the stage and got my attention. When I walked off with him, I felt like a complete fool.

Afterward, my family met me at my classroom. Before I could apologize, Grandpa exclaimed, "Mark, you were terrific!" Mom, Dad, and Aunt Miriam agreed. They completely ignored my mistake!

"Come on," said Mom as she helped me put on my jacket. "Let's all sing that song while we walk to the bus stop." And we did!

2

Use a Writer's Eye

Now evaluate the narrative as a writer. On your copy of the Student Model, use the Writer's Response Symbols to react to what you read. Identify places where the student writer uses characteristics of an effective personal narrative.

Writer's Response Symbols

E.S.	Engaging story
C.R.	Clear, well-developed conflict and resolution
B.C.	Believable characters
S.D.	Specific and vivid details

Personalized Support

Teacher or Peer Feedback

To provide feedback to students on their responses to the Student Model, ask or have student partners ask one another the following:

- What is the thesis or controlling idea of the Student Model?
- How does the Student Model illustrate the characteristics of a personal narrative?
- Which feature or characteristic of the Student Model might you use in your own piece of writing?
- How could you alter or adapt this feature to make it your own?

Working with ELLs

ELL **Sheltered Instruction:** Cognitive

Help students learn basic vocabulary heard during classroom instruction and interactions. Write the words *author, language, questions,* and *remember* on the board and read them aloud. Help students use prior experiences to understand the words' meanings.

Beginning Say *English is a language I speak,* supporting with mime. Have students complete sentences using the word *language*, drawing on prior experience with English. *_____ is a word in my home language.*

Intermediate Have partners create T-Charts for the words, describing prior experiences related to the meaning of each word. For example: *What do I do when I don't understand? I ask a question.*

Advanced Have students complete the Intermediate activity. Have small groups brainstorm for a story topic. Students should use their prior experiences related to each word to help them use the vocabulary.

Advanced High Have students use the words in an original paragraph describing their prior experiences and share in small groups. Have groups check that each member uses the words properly.

1  STUDENT BOOK

Students select or are assigned a topic for their personal narrative from the Topic Bank, or they may choose a topic of their own.

2 STUDENT BOOK

Students complete online or printed graphic organizers to narrow the topic for their personal narrative.

Prewriting

Explain that the first task students need to complete as they plan their personal narrative is to determine an appropriate topic.

Choose From the Topic Bank

Read aloud each topic and then ask volunteers to describe them in their own words. If you are assigning topics to students, you may wish to do so now. Encourage students to ask questions about their topic.

Choose Your Own Topic

Introduce and discuss the Question and Remember strategies. If students were not assigned writing topics, have them use the strategies to brainstorm for topics for their essays.

Extension Have each student choose one of the strategies. Then, have them write an action plan that outlines the resources and steps they will use to develop their topic.

Narrow Your Topic

Tell students that they will use a Narrow Your Topic graphic organizer to reduce their broad story idea to a narrower story idea. Then, distribute printed copies or have students log on to Writing Coach Online.

Apply It! Guide students through the instructions for completing the graphic organizer. Have students complete the exercise based on their topic.

Consider Your Audience

Guide students to consider the audience and purpose for their personal narrative.

Your Turn Feature Assignment: Personal Narrative

Prewriting

Plan a first draft of your personal narrative by choosing a topic based on your experience. You may select from the Topic Bank or come up with an idea of your own.

Choose From the Topic Bank

TOPIC BANK

I Was There! Think of a memorable event you have attended. It might be a sporting event, a concert, a field trip, a theatrical performance, or even a family reunion. Write a personal narrative in which you describe the event and explain why it was so special.

It's a Group Thing Think about a group you belong to. It could be an informal group of friends or a more formal group, like a sports team or a school club. Write a personal narrative that describes your group and tells about an event that involved you and your group.

First Contact Think of a friend and how you two met. Write a personal narrative that describes how you and your friend met and explains why you became friends.

Choose Your Own Topic

Determine an appropriate topic on your own by using the following **range of strategies** to generate ideas.

Question and Remember

- List some questions that people might ask about you. Which questions could you answer in a personal narrative?
- Ask family members what they remember about your early childhood. Look for story ideas in their answers.
- Remember something that you have done—something that made you happy. How could you show why you took that action and what the results were?

Review your responses and choose a topic.

Say: The questions in the first column of the chart ask about my possible audience, or the people who will read my work. If **I choose** the third topic from the Topic Bank, about a first contact, my audience might be people who are interested in knowing about the special moments in my life, such as my friends and family.

Ask: Based on your topic, who is most likely to read your personal narrative? Whom would you most like to read it? (Responses will vary.)

Have students with similar topics work in small groups to discuss and respond to the remaining questions.

Coach's Corner

You may wish to model prewriting activities for students by brainstorming for your own writing topic. Use these prompts to model your thought process:

- **I am interested in** friendship, so that could be my general topic.
- **I can narrow my topic by** focusing on the day I met my best friend.

Discuss the choices you make and solicit feedback from students.

3 

Students record their answers to questions about audience and purpose in their online journals or notebooks.

Narrow Your Topic

If your topic is too broad, readers might not understand why you are writing. Choose a topic that gives your personal narrative a clearly defined focus.

Apply It! Use a graphic organizer like the one shown to narrow your topic.

- Write the main topic of your story in the top box. Move down the chart, row by row, narrowing your topic.
- Your last box should hold the main focus of your plot.

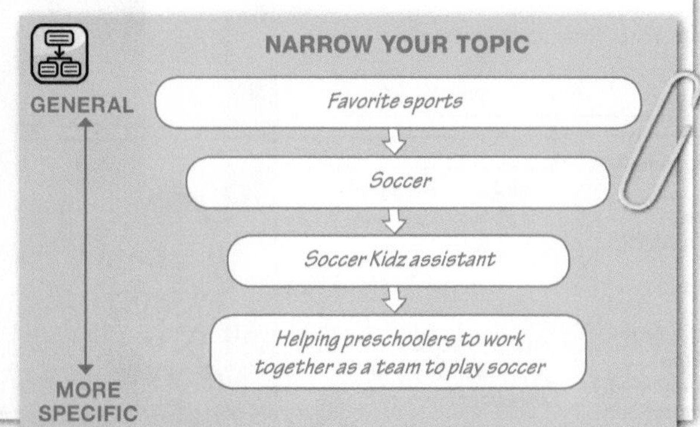

NARROW YOUR TOPIC
GENERAL
Favorite sports
Soccer
Soccer Kidz assistant
Helping preschoolers to work together as a team to play soccer
MORE SPECIFIC

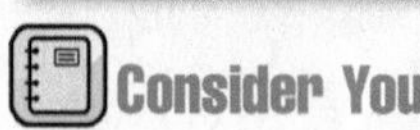

Consider Your Audience

Before writing, think about your audience and purpose. Consider how your writing conveys the intended meaning to this audience. Consider the views of the other as you ask these questions.

Questions for Audience	Questions for Purpose
• Who are the people in my audience? What should I tell them about myself? • What background information will my audience need?	• Why am I writing this personal narrative? What do I want to show, explain, or teach? • What point will this story make?

Record your answers in your writing journal.

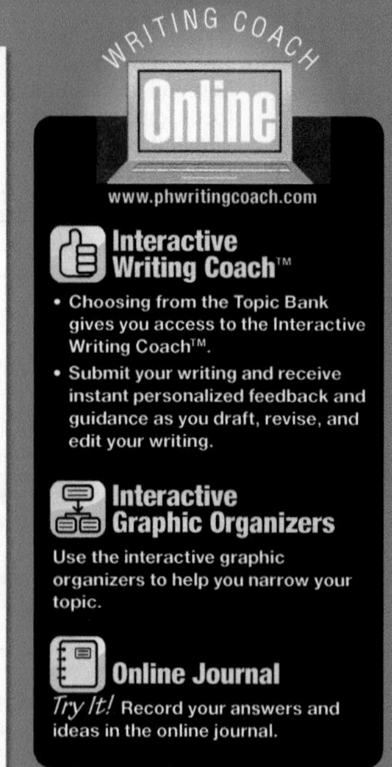

Personalized Support

Interactive Writing Coach™

Below Level Teachers select a topic from the topic bank for below-level students. Students submit their writing to the **Interactive Writing Coach™** for feedback paragraph by paragraph or as a complete draft. It is recommended that below-level students submit their writing one paragraph at a time.

On Level Students may select a topic from the Topic Bank. They may submit their writing for feedback paragraph by paragraph or as a complete draft.

Above Level Students may select from the Topic Bank or come up with their own topic. Above-level students should submit their writing as a complete draft.

Interactive Graphic Organizer

Below Level Students complete three graphic organizers that provide models and scaffolded support.

On Level Students complete one, two, or three graphic organizers, depending on how much support they need.

Above Level Students complete the least scaffolded graphic organizer or narrow their topic without the help of a graphic organizer.

Differentiated Instruction

RTI Strategy for Below-Level Students Tell students that one way to use the graphic organizer is to ask *Who? What? When? Where? Why?* and *How?* to come up with each narrower topic. For example, if they wrote *First contact* in the top row, they could ask, *Who was an important first contact?* They could then answer, *Sandi.* They could then ask, *What was so special about Sandi?* They could then answer, *She became my best friend,* and so on.

PRE-AP Enrichment for Above-Level Students Have students answer the questions about audience and purpose on page 73 for the Student Model on pages 70–71. Ask: *What background information did the writer tell the readers about himself? What else did he tell them?* Based on that information, have students reflect on the characteristics of the people in the audience, the tone of the narrative (serious, humorous, or thoughtful), and why the writer wrote his personal narrative (to explain, teach, share). Then, ask: *What main point does the story make?*

The Digital • Print Path

1  Using Writing Coach Online™ or the student book, students read and discuss the model graphic organizer.

2 Students complete online or printed graphic organizers to develop their ideas and gather details.

Plan Your Piece

Explain that writers use graphic organizers to develop their ideas and show relationships between different parts of the text. Then, point out the Develop Your Personal Narrative graphic organizer on page 74. Tell students that they will use this organizer to outline their personal narrative. Then, distribute printed copies or have students log on to Writing Coach Online.

Introduce the graphic organizer by explaining that the first column lists the different elements, or parts, of a personal narrative. The second column lists specific information for each of those parts.

Define Your Focus Guide students to notice that the topic of the narrative in the example organizer is the narrowed topic from page 73. Then, have students read the information listed in the organizer on page 74 and decide, as a class, on a clearly defined focus for the narrative. (For example: I had to teach kids how to play on a team, and I was successful!) Have students work with a partner to write one sentence that expresses their narrative's focus and record it in the Beginning section of their graphic organizer.

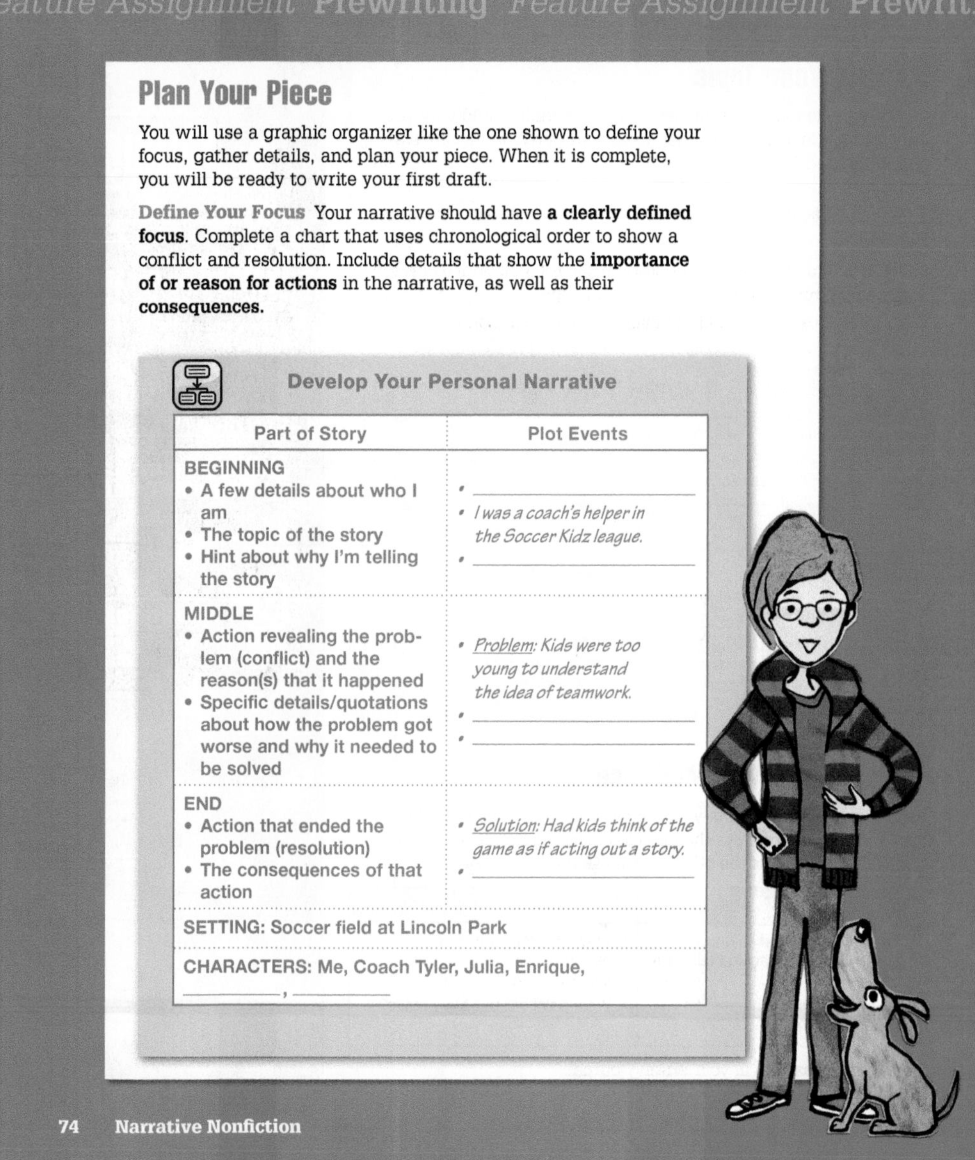

Feature Assignment Prewriting Feature Assignment Prewriting

Plan Your Piece

You will use a graphic organizer like the one shown to define your focus, gather details, and plan your piece. When it is complete, you will be ready to write your first draft.

Define Your Focus Your narrative should have **a clearly defined focus**. Complete a chart that uses chronological order to show a conflict and resolution. Include details that show the **importance of or reason for actions** in the narrative, as well as their **consequences.**

Develop Your Personal Narrative

Part of Story	Plot Events
BEGINNING • A few details about who I am • The topic of the story • Hint about why I'm telling the story	• ______ • *I was a coach's helper in the Soccer Kidz league.* • ______
MIDDLE • Action revealing the problem (conflict) and the reason(s) that it happened • Specific details/quotations about how the problem got worse and why it needed to be solved	• *Problem: Kids were too young to understand the idea of teamwork.* • ______ • ______
END • Action that ended the problem (resolution) • The consequences of that action	• *Solution: Had kids think of the game as if acting out a story.* • ______
SETTING: Soccer field at Lincoln Park	
CHARACTERS: Me, Coach Tyler, Julia, Enrique, ______, ______	

74 Narrative Nonfiction

Gather Details

Ask volunteers to read aloud each narrative element and its example. Then, guide students to place the elements in the example graphic organizer.

I notice that the organizer has space to record information about the story's setting and characters. It also explains what should happen during each part of the plot. Some of that plot information is already recorded in the organizer, but I can add more. For example, the Plot example on page 75, about the kids swarming the ball, reveals the story's problem. I could place that detail in the Middle section of the organizer.

Work with students to develop other details for each section of the example organizer.

Have students work with partners to plan their story on their individual graphic organizers.

Try It! Guide students to understand how the actions of the writer and those of his grandfather help us to understand that the writer is nervous, and that his grandfather notices and is very supportive.

Apply It! Read aloud the bulleted instructions for gathering details. Then, have students develop appropriate details for each of these sections of their graphic organizer. Remind students to use a variety of details to support their ideas.

Writer's Block

IF students can't identify appropriate details for the parts of their personal narrative . . .

THEN have them visualize the events in their narrative and freewrite what they see. Then, have students decide which of these details should be added to their graphic organizer and where.

3 STUDENT BOOK

Students refer back to the Mentor Text or the Student Model as they plan their writing.

Gather Details

To bring their personal narratives to life, writers usually focus on these literary elements.

- **Characters:** *"Josh," Coach Tyler said, "I want you to be my helper for my Soccer Kidz team this summer. Can you handle preschoolers?" "You bet!" I shouted. "I'll be great with them!"*
- **Setting:** *The sun warmed the green field as the kids arrived on Saturday morning. When I waved, they ran across the grass to me.*
- **Plot:** *Despite my instructions, the kids swarmed all over the field. Everyone tried to kick the ball at once. How could we win a game, or even score a goal, if I couldn't get them to understand teamwork?*

Good writers are careful to present **a clearly defined focus**. They also use specific details and vivid images to bring their narratives to life.

Read the Student Model excerpt. Which details help readers understand some of the characters in this personal narrative?

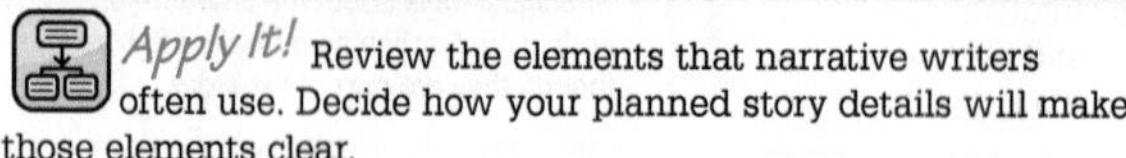

STUDENT MODEL
from Alone in the Spotlight
pages 70–71; lines 26–30

The big day came. I sat with my class, but I turned and waved at Mom, Dad, Aunt Miriam, and Grandpa just before the program began. Grandpa grinned and gave me a "thumbs up." I needed that because I was nervous!

Apply It! Review the elements that narrative writers often use. Decide how your planned story details will make those elements clear.

- Choose details that will help readers zero in on your focus and communicate your purpose for writing.
- Select details that show why events happen, why they are important, and what their outcomes are.
- Add each detail to the correct part of your graphic organizer.

Interactive Graphic Organizers
Use the interactive graphic organizers to help you create a plan for your writing.

Interactive Model
Refer back to the Interactive Model in the eText as you plan your writing.

Personalized Support

Interactive Graphic Organizer

Below Level Students complete three graphic organizers that provide models and scaffolded support.

On Level Students complete one, two, or three graphic organizers, depending on how much support they need.

Above Level Students complete the least scaffolded graphic organizer or narrow their topic without the help of a graphic organizer.

Teacher or Peer Feedback

To provide feedback to students as they plan their first draft, ask or have student partners ask one another the following:

- What do you want your audience to know about the topic?
- What questions or concerns will your audience have about the topic?
- What details have you identified for your piece? How do these details support your thesis or controlling idea?
- Are your details varied? Will they interest your readers? Explain.

Differentiated Instruction

RTI Strategy for Below-Level Students Students may have trouble understanding how all the parts of the organizer work together as a plan for a personal narrative. Have students use the Student Model on pages 70–71 to identify how the student writer organizes his narrative. Then, ask students to point out details the student writer used in each part, for example: actions and their consequences, sensory details, dialogue, and suspense.

PRE-AP Enrichment for Above-Level Students Encourage students to practice writing different engaging introductions for their personal narrative. Encourage them to include their clearly defined focus, or main point, at the end of their introduction. As they write their introduction, be sure they consider their topic, audiences, and purpose. Have students share their introductions with a partner and solicit feedback on the most effective introduction.

The Digital • Print Path

1 

Using Writing Coach Online™ or the student book, students read and discuss the Outline for Success for narrative nonfiction.

2 

Students discuss how the Mentor Text illustrates the characteristics of narrative nonfiction.

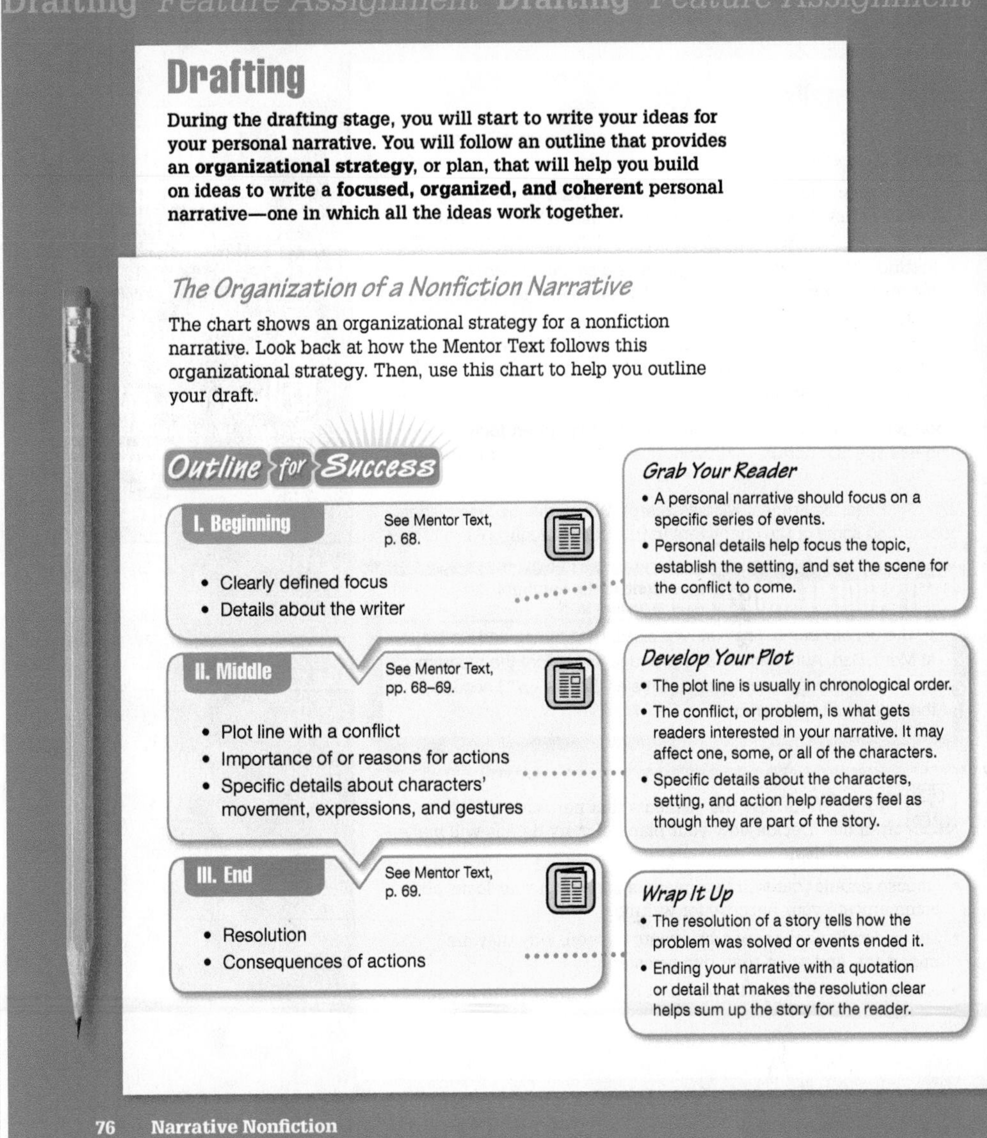

Drafting *Feature Assignment* Drafting *Feature Assignment* Dr

Drafting

During the drafting stage, you will start to write your ideas for your personal narrative. You will follow an outline that provides an organizational strategy, or plan, that will help you build on ideas to write a focused, organized, and coherent personal narrative—one in which all the ideas work together.

The Organization of a Nonfiction Narrative

The chart shows an organizational strategy for a nonfiction narrative. Look back at how the Mentor Text follows this organizational strategy. Then, use this chart to help you outline your draft.

Outline for Success

I. Beginning See Mentor Text, p. 68.

- Clearly defined focus
- Details about the writer

Grab Your Reader

- A personal narrative should focus on a specific series of events.
- Personal details help focus the topic, establish the setting, and set the scene for the conflict to come.

II. Middle See Mentor Text, pp. 68–69.

- Plot line with a conflict
- Importance of or reasons for actions
- Specific details about characters' movement, expressions, and gestures

Develop Your Plot

- The plot line is usually in chronological order.
- The conflict, or problem, is what gets readers interested in your narrative. It may affect one, some, or all of the characters.
- Specific details about the characters, setting, and action help readers feel as though they are part of the story.

III. End See Mentor Text, p. 69.

- Resolution
- Consequences of actions

Wrap It Up

- The resolution of a story tells how the problem was solved or events ended it.
- Ending your narrative with a quotation or detail that makes the resolution clear helps sum up the story for the reader.

76 Narrative Nonfiction

Drafting

Outline for Success

Explain that the Outline for Success shows an organizational strategy for a nonfiction narrative. Students will use the Outline to write a focused, organized, and coherent draft of their personal narrative.

I. Beginning

Link the Outline to a specific personal narrative by having students turn to the Mentor Text on pages 68–69. Ask a volunteer to read aloud the introduction (lines 1–6). Then, guide students to understand how the author clearly defines the focus of his narrative.

Say: **I noticed** that the author tells readers the focus of his narrative very clearly. His first sentence begins, "When trouble came to me..." This tells me that the story is going to be about how the writer gets into trouble. He also says that the trouble comes from "a nice, normal smart boy by the name of John Quinn." These details tell me very clearly the conflict and characters in the story.

Ask: What do we learn about the author when he says that the trouble he encountered "didn't involve anybody I thought it would"? **(Possible response:** The author was already prepared for some kind of trouble.)

Have students work with a partner to draft a focused, detailed beginning for their narrative.

II. Middle

Lead a discussion about how the body of the paragraphs of the Mentor Text reflect the characteristics of a personal narrative.

- Plot with a conflict (lines 13–15, 17–23)
- Reasons for actions (lines 20–22, 40–44)
- Details about characters' movement, expressions, and gestures (lines 17–19, 24–28, 32–34)

III. End

Have small groups discuss how the Mentor Text conclusion reflects the characteristics of a nonfiction narrative (lines 47–51).

Start Your Draft

Have small groups read aloud and discuss the boxed instructions for drafting. Direct students to work individually on their first draft.

Coach's Corner

If you are modeling the writing process for students with your own topic or a student volunteer's, you may wish to use these prompts to guide your drafting and discussion:

- **To capture readers' attention, my introduction will** introduce characters and a conflict.
- **I will organize my body paragraphs** in chronological, or time, order.

Discuss the choices you make and solicit feedback from students.

Students begin writing their personal narrative online or in their notebooks.

Students submit paragraphs or complete drafts to the **Interactive Writing Coach™** for scoring and feedback, or share their work with their teacher.

Students receive customized feedback from the **Interactive Writing Coach™** or feedback from their teacher. Students may continue to work on their drafts.

Start Your Draft

Use this checklist to help you complete your draft. Use the graphic organizer that shows the beginning, middle, and end of your narrative, and the Outline for Success as guides.

While drafting, aim at writing your ideas, not on making your writing perfect. Remember, you will have the chance to improve your draft when you revise and edit.

- √ Start by drafting an attention-getting **opening** sentence.
- √ Continue your **beginning** by focusing on the topic and connecting with readers in a way that makes them want to keep reading. Make sure your narrative has a clearly defined **focus**.

- √ Use chronological order to develop the **middle** of your personal narrative. Present a series of plot events that show **reasons for actions and** the consequences of those actions.
- √ Keep the narrative interesting by including vivid images and specific **details** about the characters, setting, and action.

- √ At the **end** of your narrative, show the **resolution**—how the conflict worked out.
- √ Finish in a way that shows the importance of actions and their **consequences** in the narrative.

WRITING COACH Online

www.phwritingcoach.com

Interactive Model

Outline for Success View pop-ups of Mentor Text selections referenced in the Outline for Success.

Interactive Writing Coach™

Use the Interactive Writing Coach to receive the level of support you need:

- Write one paragraph at a time and submit each one for immediate, detailed feedback.
- Write your entire first draft and submit it for immediate, personalized feedback.

Personalized Support

Interactive Writing Coach™

Below Level Students complete the drafting process in small steps by submitting each paragraph for scoring and feedback.

On Level Depending on the support they need, students submit their writing paragraph by paragraph or as a complete draft for scoring and feedback.

Above Level Students may write their drafts on their own but have the option of submitting them for scoring and/or feedback.

Teacher or Peer Feedback

To provide feedback to students on their first draft, ask or have student partners ask one another the following:

- Can you explain how you organized your ideas in this piece?
- Why did you include this information here?
- Why did you choose this beginning? Does it grab your reader and identify your thesis or controlling idea?
- What supporting details could you add here?
- Why did you choose this conclusion? How does it add to your piece?
- Can you show me a place where I can hear your unique voice?
- Can you show me a place where you used vivid language?

Working with ELLs

ELL Sheltered Instruction: Cognitive

Have students write using and reusing newly acquired basic vocabulary. Encourage them to incorporate the vocabulary in their drafts.

Beginning Introduce the words *but, and, different,* and *same*. Mime a series of actions, such as looking, comparing, and contrasting, providing a verb for each. Guide students as they use and reuse the words to complete sentences such as *Our [socks/shirts] are the same [color/material].*

Intermediate Write *but, and, different, same, such,* and *example* on the board. Help students use the **Frayer Model** for each word by having them fill in four sections of a card, one for a definition, one for characteristics, one for examples, and one for non-examples. Have students use and reuse each word in a written sentence.

Advanced Have pairs create a **Word Bank** of the Intermediate activity words. Help students acquire the vocabulary with examples. Have them use and reuse the words by writing to compare and contrast their interests.

Advanced High Have students complete the Advanced activity, then use and reuse the vocabulary in a paragraph.

1 Using Writing Coach Online™ or the student book, students study the first and second drafts of the student model to see how the writer used Revision RADaR to improve his or her writing.

2 Students use the Revision RADaR strategy to revise their own writing.

Revising: Making It Better

Point out the page title to students and explain that revising means making improvements to a writing draft. Then, read aloud the opening paragraph to introduce the Revision RADaR strategies. You may wish to have students review Chapter 3 for more information on Revision RADaR.

Kelly Gallagher, M. Ed.

KEEP REVISION ON YOUR RADAR

1ST DRAFT After students have read the first draft, have them turn to page 76 and review the Outline for Success. Work with students to understand that the questions the author asked about his draft are based on the characteristics of a nonfiction narrative. For example, call out the first question and note how it addresses the concerns listed in the Middle section of the Outline for Success.

Then, have students work in small groups to develop other questions about the draft based on the genre characteristics.

2ND DRAFT Guide students to understand how the author used the RADaR strategies to revise his draft.

Think Aloud **I noticed** that the first paragraph from the 1st draft didn't explain why the writer had scowled. In the 2nd draft, though, I see an *A* next to this paragraph, meaning that the writer has added new text. The new text explains that the writer had scowled because he was afraid that "someone still might mess up."

Work with students to help brainstorm for other ways the writer could have expressed the reason for his action.

Have students work in small groups to discuss the other changes in the 2nd draft.

Revising Feature Assignment Revising Feature Assignment

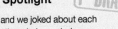

Revising: Making It Better

Now that you have finished your first draft, you are ready to revise. Think about the "big picture" of audience, purpose, and genre. You can use the Revision RADaR strategy as a guide for making changes to improve your draft. Revision RADaR provides four major ways to improve your writing: (R) replace, (A) add, (D) delete, and (R) reorder.

Kelly Gallagher, M. Ed.

KEEP REVISION ON YOUR RADAR

Read part of the first draft of the Student Model "Alone in the Spotlight." Then, look at questions the writer asked himself as he thought about how well his draft **addressed issues of audience, purpose, and genre**.

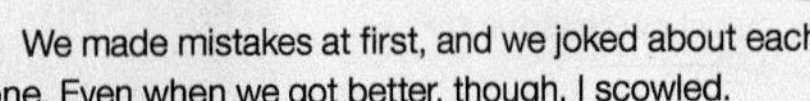

Alone in the Spotlight 1ST DRAFT

We made mistakes at first, and we joked about each one. Even when we got better, though, I scowled.

A narrative should show reasons for actions. Will readers know why I scowled?

The big day came. I sat with my class, but I turned and waved at Mom, Dad, Aunt Miriam, and Grandpa. The first- and second-graders did a good job. Then it was our turn. Grandpa grinned and gave me a "thumbs up." I needed that because I was nervous!

These details aren't quite the way I remember them. Will the sequence be clear to my audience?

As we sang, my nervousness disappeared. I felt fabulous! I was inspired—so inspired that I didn't notice my classmates marching off the stage, and I didn't notice the color guard.

Does "I felt fabulous" help my purpose, or do readers already understand that? Also, my purpose here is to be funny. Do I have enough funny details?

Finally, Mr. Lee came onto the stage and got my attention. When I walked off with him, I felt like a complete fool.

Afterward, my family met me at my classroom. Before I could apologize, Grandpa exclaimed, "Mark, you were terrific!" Mom, Dad, and Aunt Miriam agreed. They actually sounded happy!

A resolution is an important part of writing in this genre. Does my resolution tell about the outcome?

78 Narrative Nonfiction

Apply It! Review the bulleted instructions for using Revision RADaR. Remind students to question their drafts based on the personal narrative characteristics listed on the Outline for Success on page 76. Tell students to use each RADaR strategy at least once.

Coach's Corner

If you are modeling the writing process for students with your own draft or a student volunteer's, use these prompts to focus on the Revision RADaR *Add* strategy:

- **I added sensory details here because** I wanted my readers to experience the setting more fully.
- **I added dialogue here because** I wanted to create believable characters.

Discuss the choices you make and solicit feedback from students.

3 Students submit paragraphs or revised drafts to the **Interactive Writing Coach™** for scoring and feedback, or share their work with their teacher.

4 Students receive customized feedback from the **Interactive Writing Coach™** or feedback from their teacher. Students may continue to revise their drafts.

Feature Assignment **Revising** *Feature Assignment* **Revising**

Now look at how the writer applied Revision RADaR to write an improved second draft.

2ND DRAFT

Alone in the SPOTLIGHT

We made mistakes at first, and we joked about each one. Even when we got better, though, I scowled. Someone still might mess up!

> **A** *Added a sentence to show a reason for an action*

The big day came. I sat with my class, but I turned and waved at Mom, Dad, Aunt Miriam, and Grandpa just before the program began. Grandpa grinned and gave me a "thumbs up." I needed that because I was nervous!

> **R A** *Reordered and added details to make the sequence of events clear*

The first- and second-graders did a good job. Then it was our turn.

As we sang, my nervousness disappeared. I was inspired—so inspired that I didn't notice my classmates marching off the stage, and I didn't notice the color guard marching onto the stage. I didn't notice the end of the music, either. I just stood there and kept singing!

> **D A** *Deleted a sentence that I don't need and added two sentences to make the moment funnier*

Finally, Mr. Lee came onto the stage and got my attention. When I walked off with him, I felt like a complete fool.

Afterward, my family met me at my classroom. Before I could apologize, Grandpa exclaimed, "Mark, you were terrific!" Mom, Dad, and Aunt Miriam agreed. They completely ignored my mistake!

> **R** *Replaced a sentence to make the resolution stronger*

Interactive Writing Coach™

Use the Revision RADaR strategy in your own writing. Then submit your paragraph or draft for feedback.

Apply It! Use your Revision RADaR to revise your draft.

- First, determine if you have included the characteristics of the personal narrative genre.
- Then apply the Revision RADaR strategy to make needed changes. Remember—you can use the steps in the strategy in any order.

Personalized Support

Interactive Writing Coach™

Below Level Students revise their drafts using the Revision RADaR strategy and submit their writing for scoring and feedback.

On Level Students revise their drafts using the Revision RADaR strategy and submit their writing for scoring and feedback.

Above Level Students may use the Revision RADaR strategy or revise their drafts on their own. They have the option of submitting their revised drafts for scoring and/or feedback.

FEEDBACK

Teacher or Peer Feedback

To provide feedback to students as they revise their first draft, ask or have student partners ask one another the following:

- Can you show me where you revised your text?
- What could you add to your beginning to grab the interest of your readers?
- How could you reorder these ideas so that their order is more logical?
- Have you included all the characteristics of this form of writing?
- Is there any unnecessary text that you could delete?
- Have you achieved your purpose with this piece of writing?
- Have you addressed the questions and concerns of your audience?

Working with ELLs

ELL Sheltered Instruction: Cognitive

As you review the revised Student Model with students, have them demonstrate English comprehension and expand their reading skills by employing the analytical skill of evaluating written information.

Beginning Write these words on the board: *First I ate breakfast. Finally it was time for school. After school, I walked home. Next I did my math homework.* Use visuals to ensure that all students understand. Then, guide them to evaluate which order the words belong in to show correct sequence.

Intermediate Distribute the Beginning activity sentences to small groups. Have them read the sentences aloud and place them in sequence. Have them evaluate sequence by completing a sentence starter, such as, *Our sequence is correct because…*

Advanced Have pairs read the second draft on page 79, taking notes on sequence and details. Monitor their their ability to evaluate sequence by asking, *What comes at the beginning of the story? What comes at the middle? What about the end?*

Advanced High Direct students to complete the Advanced activity individually, then compare their evaluations.

The Digital • Print Path

1 

Using **Writing Coach Online™** or the student book, students study and discuss the revision chart.

2 

In a video by program author Kelly Gallagher, students learn more strategies for effective writing.

Revising: Making It Better

Look at the Big Picture

Introduce the revision chart to students. Explain that the Section column identifies the three main parts of a personal narrative. The Evaluate column identifies the characteristics found in each section and explains how to assess them. The Revise column presents specific strategies for revising each characteristic.

Then, have students draw lines between and label the three sections of their drafts. Direct students to work individually to evaluate and revise their draft, using the chart to guide their work.

Focus on Craft: Simple, Compound, and Complex Sentences

Have students read the introductory text. Guide student to understand how using simple, compound, and complex sentences makes writing more interesting.

Say: I notice that the first sentence of the Student Model is a compound sentence. It has two subject-predicate pairs that express equal ideas: "We made mistakes at first," and "we joked about each one." The second sentence has two subject-predicate pairs that express two ideas, one more important than the other: "Even when we got better, though, I scowled." "I scowled" is the independent and, therefore, more important idea.

Ask: What kind of sentence is the third sentence? (a simple sentence) How do you know? (It has one subject and one predicate, which express one idea.)

Have students work with a partner. For each sentence, have them identify the subject(s) and predicate(s).

Revising *Feature Assignment* Revising *Feature Assignment*

Look at the Big Picture

Use the chart to evaluate how well each section of your personal narrative addresses **purpose**, **audience**, and **genre**. When necessary, use the suggestions in the chart to revise your narrative.

Section	Evaluate	Revise
Beginning	• Check the opening sentences of your narrative. Do they get readers' attention?	• Add a question, a quotation, or some other detail that makes readers curious.
	• Consider your **focus**; if it is clearly defined, readers will understand the topic and connect with you as the writer.	• Ask yourself, "Why would I want to read this story?" The answer may help you sharpen your focus.
Middle	• Make sure that the plot of your narrative presents a **conflict**—a problem that readers will understand and care about.	• Add or change details to show why the problem matters to you, the writer and main character. If it matters to you, it should matter to readers.
	• Underline reasons for actions in the narrative. Will readers understand why **characters** do what they do?	• Add a detail that answers the question "Why?" At the same time, keep the plot events moving; don't get off track.
	• Review details about **characters**, setting, and action. Could any images be more vivid, specific, and interesting?	• Add or change details, or images, so that readers can "see," "hear," and so on. Make them feel that they are part of the story!
End	• Make sure that your narrative has a **resolution** that shows how the conflict worked out.	• Add or revise details to show how the problem was solved or how events ended it.
	• Underline **consequences** of actions in the narrative and decide whether readers will understand the **importance** of the actions.	• Add a detail that answers the question "So what?" about the outcome and makes one more connection with your readers.

80 Narrative Nonfiction

Try It! Have students discuss the questions in small groups and record responses in their journals. Follow up with students to check that their responses reflect an understanding of how using a variety of sentence structures enhances the effectiveness of a narrative.

Fine-Tune Your Draft

Apply It! Ask volunteers to read aloud the instructions for fine-tuning their drafts. Then, have students work in pairs to revise their writing to include a variety of sentences and vivid images.

Teacher Feedback Have students identify Mentor Text examples of the characteristics that were marked for improvement. Use the Mentor Text references on page T76 to guide students to appropriate examples.

Teacher Tip

Have students write clauses and phrases from their draft's simple, compound, and complex sentences on separate slips of paper. Ask students to combine the clauses and phrases in new ways to create a variety of sentence structures.

3 Using Writing Coach Online™ or the student book, students refer back to the Mentor Text or Student Model for examples of writer's craft.

4 Students record answers to questions about writer's craft in their online journals or notebooks.

5 Students submit revised drafts to the Interactive Writing Coach™ for scoring and feedback, or share their work with their teacher.

6 Students receive customized feedback from the Interactive Writing Coach™ or feedback from their teacher.

Focus on Craft: Simple, Compound, and Complex Sentences

Subjects and predicates of sentences work together to express ideas. In a **simple sentence**, one subject and one predicate express one idea. In a **compound sentence**, two or more subject-predicate pairs express two or more equal ideas. In a **complex sentence**, two or more subject-predicate pairs express two or more ideas, but one idea is more important than any other. Mixing sentence structures can keep your writing interesting. Think about sentence structures as you read the following sentences from the Student Model.

STUDENT MODEL from **Alone in the Spotlight** page 70; lines 23–25

We made mistakes at first, and we joked about each one. Even when we got better, though, I scowled. Someone still might mess up!

Try It! Now, ask yourself these questions:

- Which sentence is simple? Compound? Complex? Explain.
- Would the first sentence be better if it read "We made mistakes at first. We joked about each one"? Explain.

Fine-Tune Your Draft

Apply It! Use the revision suggestions to prepare your final draft **after thinking how well questions of purpose, audience, and genre have been addressed**.

- **Ensure Simple, Compound, and Complex Sentences** Raise the interest level by using a variety of sentence structures.
- **Ensure Vivid Images** Help readers feel a part of your narrative. Add or revise details so that readers can easily imagine the setting, characters, and action.

Teacher Feedback Read your final draft to your teacher. Ask if your personal narrative has **a clearly defined focus**. Think about your teacher's response and revise your final draft as needed.

www.phwritingcoach.com

Video

Learn more strategies for effective writing from program author Kelly Gallagher.

Online Journal

Try It! Record your answers in the online journal.

Interactive Model

Refer back to the Interactive Model as you revise your writing.

Interactive Writing Coach™

Revise your draft and submit it for feedback.

Personalized Support

Interactive Writing Coach™

Below Level Students complete the revising process by submitting their writing for scoring and feedback.

On Level Students complete the revising process by submitting their writing for scoring and feedback.

Above Level Students finish revising their drafts. They have the option of submitting their revised drafts for scoring and/or feedback.

Teacher or Peer Feedback

To provide feedback to students as they continue to revise their first draft, ask or have student partners ask one another the following:

- What are you trying to say here? What part of the text could you replace to make your meaning clearer?
- Is there a more precise word you could use here?
- How does the rhythm of these sentences sound to you? Could you make the length and structure of these sentences more varied?
- How could you include transitional words and phrases here to help your reader understand these ideas?
- Are there details you could add here to make this part come alive?

Working with ELLs

ELL Sheltered Instruction: Social/Affective

Have students demonstrate listening comprehension of increasingly complex spoken English by collaborating with peers as they share information in cooperative learning interactions. Read the Student Model excerpt aloud as students track. Define key words and discuss. Have them close their books. Then:

Beginning Read the paragraph slowly, using gestures to aid comprehension. Have partners discuss the paragraphs and collaborate, sharing information to answer simple recall questions.

Intermediate Read the paragraph aloud again, reminding students to monitor their comprehension and seek clarification. Have students work in groups to share information about what they heard and collaborate in answering recall questions.

Advanced Read the paragraph aloud again, and have pairs write a short retelling to share information with another pair.

Advanced High Have students complete the Advanced activity. Then, read the first and second drafts on pages 78–79 aloud, then have them collaborate with a peer on a comparison of the two drafts.

1 

In a video by program author Jeff Anderson, students learn effective editing techniques.

2 

Students record answers to questions about writer's craft in their online journals or notebooks.

Editing: Making It Correct

Discuss the opening paragraph with students. Explain that they will edit their drafts for proper grammar, mechanics, and spelling, including use of a consistent verb tense.

WRITE GUY *Jeff Anderson, M.Ed.*

WHAT DO YOU NOTICE?

Introduce students to consistent verb tense by reading aloud the Mentor Text excerpt and discussing responses to the "Ask yourself" question that follows. Then, have students read the explanation of progressive and perfect tense verbs.

Guide students to identify and use verb tenses consistently.

I notice that the first sentence in the Mentor Text excerpt has past progressive and past tense verbs, and that the second sentence has past perfect and past progressive tense verbs. I know that each verb tense is still consistent because each tense tells about actions that happened in the past.

Work with students to identify the verb tenses used in the sentences in lines 26–27, 40–41, and 49–51 of the Mentor Text on pages 68–69.

Have students write several sentences that include progressive and perfect tense verbs, and then check each other's work for consistent verb tense.

Editing Feature Assignment Editing Feature Assignment E

Editing: Making It Correct

To edit your work, read your draft carefully to correct errors in spelling and grammar. It can be helpful to read your draft aloud to listen for where the writing needs correction.

As you edit, make sure that you have used a **consistent verb tense**, and did not shift to another tense without a reason. Then edit your final draft for errors in **grammar, mechanics, and spelling.**

WRITE GUY *Jeff Anderson, M. Ed.*

WHAT DO YOU NOTICE?

Zoom in on Conventions Focus on verb tenses as you zoom in on these lines from the Mentor Text.

To learn more about verb tenses, see Chapter 14 of your Grammar Handbook.

MENTOR TEXT from **The Pigman & Me** pages 68–69; lines 17–19, 46–47

> Richard was getting a drink from the water fountain when John Quinn came up to me and told me I had to give him my paddle....
> John Quinn had announced to everyone he was going to exact revenge on me after school on Monday.

Now, ask yourself: *When did the events in each sentence occur?*

Perhaps you said that both sentences show actions that happened in the past. A **progressive tense** verb shows that an action is or was happening for a period of time. Progressive tense verbs consist of a form of the helping verb *be*, such as *is, are, was,* or *were*, with the present participle of the main verb, which ends in *-ing*. The past progressive tense "was getting" shows the action Richard was completing for a period of time.

A **perfect tense** verb refers to an action that has been completed. Perfect tense verbs consist of a form of the helping verb *have*, such as *had, have,* or *has*, with the past participle of the main verb, which for regular verbs ends in *-ed* or *-d*. The past perfect tense "had announced" refers to an action that John Quinn completed.

82 Narrative Nonfiction

Grammar Mini-Lesson: Consistent Tenses

Discuss the paragraph and the Mentor Text excerpt on page 83 with students. Guide them to understand that by using past tense forms for all four verbs in the sentence, the writer keeps the tense consistent.

Try It! Have students work with a partner to rewrite the sentences.

1. Mom attends/attended every softball game and cheers/cheered us on.
2. Brad left the team in March, but he had played with us for three years.
3. I was practicing soccer when a ball hit me in the head.

Apply It! Remind students to use consistent verb tenses as they edit their drafts.

Use the Rubric Explain to students that they will rate how well their draft addresses the elements of a personal narrative on a scale of 1 to 6, with 6 being the best score.

Then, have students use the rubric to evaluate their drafts. Students should then revise their drafts as necessary.

Writer's Block

IF students have difficulty checking their drafts for consistent verb tense . . .

THEN have them work with a partner who can point out any problems and explain what needs to be changed and why.

3 

Using Writing Coach Online™ or the student book, students refer back to the Mentor Text or Student Model as they edit their writing.

4 

Using Writing Coach Online™ or the studeht book, students evaluate their writing using the rubrics.

5 

Students submit edited drafts to the Interactive Writing Coach™ for scoring and feedback, or share their work with their teacher.

6 

Students receive personalized feedback from the Interactive Writing Coach™ or feedback from their teacher.

Grammar Mini-Lesson: Consistent Tenses

To learn more, see page 284.

Usually, you use one verb tense for consistency. Sometimes, though, you must change tense to show a sequence of events. **Consistent verb tense** is especially important in sentences with more than one action and clause. "He *has been* to Europe, and he *will go* to Asia." Notice how the past tense is used consistently in the Mentor Text.

from **The Pigman & Me**
page 68; lines 24–26

I was so wound up and frightened that I didn't think, and I struck out at him with my right fist.

Try It! Rewrite these simple, compound, and complex sentences so that they use **perfect or progressive tenses** consistently, and shift tenses only to make the sequence clear. Write the answers in your journal.

1. Mom attended every softball game and cheers us on. (simple)
2. Brad left the team in March, but he play with us for three years. (compound)
3. I practice soccer when a ball hit me in the head. (complex)

Apply It! Edit your draft for **grammar, mechanics, capitalization, and spelling**. Check that you have used perfect and progressive verb tenses correctly. Where needed, apply consistent tenses to verbs.

Use the rubric to evaluate your narrative. If necessary, rethink, rewrite, or revise.

Rubric for Nonfiction Narration: Personal Narrative	Rating Scale					
Ideas: How focused is your narrative on a single, important event?	Not very 1	2	3	4	5	Very 6
Organization: How logical is your sequence of events?	1	2	3	4	5	6
Voice: How authentic and engaging is your voice?	1	2	3	4	5	6
Word Choice: How vivid and specific is your word choice?	1	2	3	4	5	6
Sentence Fluency: How varied are your sentence structures?	1	2	3	4	5	6
Conventions: How correct is your verb tense?	1	2	3	4	5	6

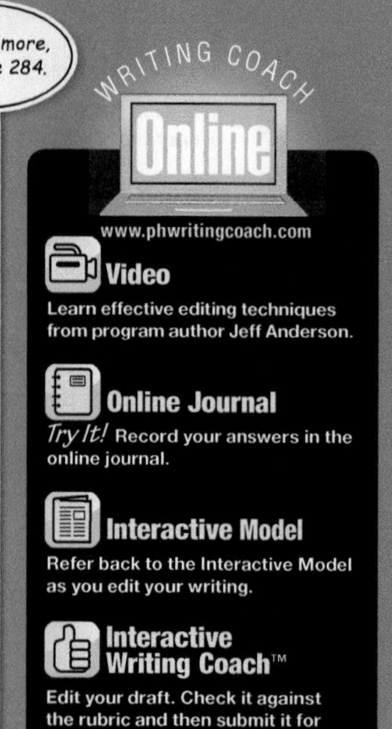

WRITING COACH
Online
www.phwritingcoach.com
Video
Learn effective editing techniques from program author Jeff Anderson.
Online Journal
Try It! Record your answers in the online journal.
Interactive Model
Refer back to the Interactive Model as you edit your writing.
Interactive Writing Coach™
Edit your draft. Check it against the rubric and then submit it for feedback.

Personalized Support

Interactive Writing Coach™

Below Level Students complete the editing process by submitting their writing for scoring and feedback.

On Level Students complete the editing process by submitting their writing for scoring and feedback.

Above Level Students finish editing their drafts. They have the option of submitting their final drafts for scoring and/or feedback.

Teacher or Peer Feedback

To provide feedback to students as they edit their draft, ask or have student partners ask one another the following:

- Can you show me something you changed through editing?
- Did you look for spelling errors?
- Read this sentence aloud. Does the grammar sound correct to you?

Working with ELLs

ELL Sheltered Instruction: Metacognitive

Help students monitor and edit their writing for subject-verb agreement, using self-corrective techniques. Review subject-verb agreement. Then:

Beginning Review the meanings of *plural* and *singular*, using visuals. On the board, write a list of subjects in the Mentor Text excerpt on page 82 (*Richard* and *John Quinn*). Help students determine if they are plural or singular and use the self-corrective technique of highlighting subjects and circling verbs to check agreement in the excerpt and their own work.

Intermediate As students revise their work, have them use the self-corrective technique described in the Beginning activity with an Advanced High student.

Advanced As students revise their work, have them use the self-corrective technique described in the Beginning activity. Have students swap stories with a partner, and double-check subject-verb agreement.

Advanced High Have students complete the Advanced activity, then help an Intermediate student check subject-verb agreement.

The Digital • Print Path

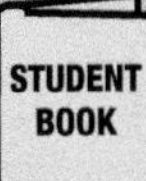

1 

Using Writing Coach Online™ or the student book, students complete the writing process by deciding the best way to publish their writing for their intended audience.

2 Writing Journal

Students record their answers to Reflect on Your Writing in their online journals or notebooks.

Publishing

Wrap Up Your Presentation

Remind students who handwrote their work to use proper margins. For students who wrote their work on a computer, display some easy-to-read computer fonts. Make sure students know how to find them on a computer.

Publish Your Piece

Explain to students that the final step in the writing process is to decide which form of publication will present their work most effectively. Then, tell students that the chart shows how specific audiences can be reached using different media.

Have students whose narratives address similar audiences work in small groups to discuss appropriate ways to publish their work.

Reflect on Your Writing

Have students discuss the questions with a partner, including the Big Question, and record responses in their journal.

Extension Have students develop a research plan for learning more about their topic. Students should identify what they want to learn, which resources they will use, and how this information could be used to improve or embellish their personal narrative.

Manage Your Portfolio You may wish to have students include development materials such as graphic organizers and drafts.

Publishing *Feature Assignment* Publishing *Feature Assignme*

Publishing

Get your personal narrative ready for presentation. Then, choose a way to publish it for the appropriate audience.

Wrap Up Your Presentation

Is your narrative handwritten? If so, you may need to make a new, clean copy. If so, be sure to **write legibly**. Also be sure that your title grabs the reader's attention and indicates the topic of your narrative.

Publish Your Piece

Use the chart to identify a way to publish your personal narrative.

If your audience is...	...then publish it by...
Students or adults at school	• Sharing it in a small-group "read-around" • Presenting it as a humorous reading, if appropriate, in a school talent show
People outside of your school	• Sending it in a letter or e-mail to someone else who played a part in the narrative • Posting it on a blog • Submitting it to an online magazine for young people

Reflect on Your Writing

Now that you are done with your personal narrative, read it over and use your writing journal to answer these questions. Use specific details to describe and explain your reflections. Increase the specificity of your details based on the type of information requested.

- Which part of your narrative do you feel is strongest? Why?
- Is there anything about the narrative that you still want to work on? If so, how will you deal with it?
- Now that you have written this piece of narrative nonfiction, what might you try writing next? Explain.

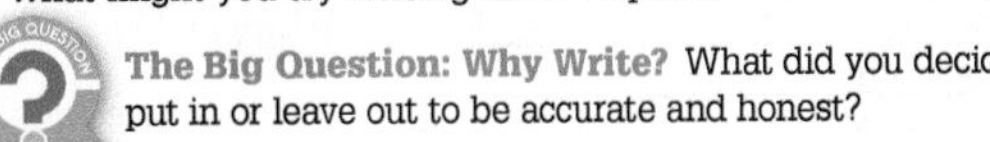

The Big Question: Why Write? What did you decide to put in or leave out to be accurate and honest?

Manage Your Portfolio You may wish to include your published personal narrative in your writing portfolio. If so, consider what this narrative reveals about your writing and your growth as a writer.

84 Narrative Nonfiction

Resources You may wish to have students use these graphic organizers: Meeting Agenda, Meeting Notes, and Flow Chart/ Series of Events. Distribute printed copies or have students log on to Writing Coach Online.

Use the 21st Century Skills Rubric to evaluate each group's process and final product on a scale of 1 to 3, indicating weak, moderate, or strong use of the skill. ▶

Listening and Speaking Monitor students as they use feedback to refine their presentations.

21st Century Learning

Skills Rubric	Rating
Think Creatively: Create new and worthwhile ideas with incremental and radical concepts.	1 2 3
Work Creatively With Others: Be original and inventive in work and understand the limits to adopting new ideas.	1 2 3
Apply Technology Effectively: Use digital technologies to access, manage, and create information.	1 2 3
Collaborate With Others: Work effectively and respectfully with diverse teams.	1 2 3

MAKE YOUR WRITING COUNT

Introduce the biopic activity by discussing the opening paragraphs with students. Make sure students understand that the project may be produced electronically or by hand. Then, guide students through each step in the action plan.

3 STUDENT BOOK

Students use a variety of graphic organizers, either online or in print, to help them work together to create a multimedia group project.

4 STUDENT BOOK

Through Writing Coach Online™ students link to resources on 21st Century Learning for help in creating a multimedia group project.

21st Century Learning

MAKE YOUR WRITING COUNT

Bring Your Personal Narrative to Life in a Script

A **personal narrative** provides a window into a writer's past. Many movies are biopics—filmed stories based on real personal narratives. Write your own biopic by turning a personal narrative into a script to be acted out or filmed.

Work productively in teams to prepare a script called "A Day in the Life" by assigning roles and giving one another feedback as you plan, write, and rehearse your script. Present your script live or as a video.

Here's your action plan.

1. Choose group roles and set objectives.
2. Review your personal narratives. Choose one that tells an interesting story about a day in the writer's life.
3. Look online for model scripts, and follow the model for script format.
4. Create a script based on your narrative by doing the following:
   - Breaking the narrative into separate scenes
   - Including dialogue to convey a clear and distinct perspective
   - Providing stage directions that tell actors how to gesture
5. Assign group members to act out the script in a dramatic reading. Record the reading on video, or present it live to the class. You might also consider using an online movie-making tool.

Listening and Speaking While rehearsing the script, give each other feedback on vocal expression or gestures that would enhance the presentation. Use specific details to describe and explain your ideas. Increase the specificity of your details based on the type of information you are delivering. When presenting the script, remember to incorporate your peers' feedback. Give each audience member a copy of the script to follow along with, and ask for comments on the script and its presentation.

Online Journal

Reflect on Your Writing Record your answers and ideas in the online journal.

Resource

Link to resources on 21st Century Learning for help in creating a group project.

Personalized Support

Teacher or Peer Feedback

FEEDBACK

To provide feedback to students on their published writing, ask or have student partners ask one another the following:

- How did you go about writing this piece? What was your process?
- What did you learn from the writing model that you used in this piece?
- What surprised you the most as you wrote this piece?
- Did you try anything new as you worked on this piece?
- What did you learn from this piece of writing that you would like to remember and reuse?
- What do you think you do best as a writer right now?

Differentiated Instruction

RTI Strategy for Below-Level Students For students who are going to publish their narrative by reading it aloud, have them first practice a few times with a partner. Have them read through their narrative the first time for fluency. On subsequent readings, have them concentrate on expression.

PRE-AP Enrichment for Above-Level Students For students who are going to publish their narrative by submitting it to an online magazine, have them work with a partner to research appropriate magazines and the requirements for submission. Have them write or print the submission requirements and make any necessary adjustments to their narrative, such as for length. Be sure they get permission from their parents or guardians before submitting their narrative.

The Digital • Print Path

1 Students use Writing Coach Online™ or their student books to analyze and discuss the Writing for Media topic.

2 Students learn about the characteristics of a event letter by answering questions about the model. Students record their answers to the Try It! questions in their online journals or notebooks.

Writing for Media: Event Letter

Event Letter

Discuss the opening paragraph with students. As a class, brainstorm for possible topics for an event letter.

Try It! Guide students to understand the structure and content of an event letter.

Say: The first *Try It!* question asks how we know that this event letter is being sent as an e-mail. **I notice** that the header has e-mail addresses in the "From" and "To" lines. It also has a date and time stamp on it. These elements are typical of e-mails.

Ask: Who is the audience and how did the writer engage the reader? (The audience is a friend. The writer engaged the friend by asking him a question that connected both the writer and the reader to the topic—the writer planning to take care of a puppy.)

Have students discuss the remaining questions in small groups and record individual responses in their journals.

Extension Have students bring in other examples of event letters. Lead a media discussion about the examples, using the *Try It!* questions as a guide.

Writing for Media Writing for Media Writing for Media Writi

Your Turn Writing for Media: Event Letter

21st Century Learning

Event Letter

An **event letter** is a letter or e-mail that recounts, or tells a story about, an event that you want to share—an event in which you had a major part. Your writing will tell a story about yourself, so your task will be much like writing a personal narrative. It will not be exactly the same, however. Because the writing takes the form of a letter, its tone will be a little more casual and will sound more like a friendly conversation.

Try It! Read this part of an event letter. Then, answer these questions. Record your answers in your journal.

1. How can you tell that this event letter is being sent as an e-mail?
2. Who is the **audience** for the letter? How did the writer engage the reader?
3. What is the topic or **focus** of the letter? How can you tell that it is a clearly defined focus?
4. What do you think is the **purpose** of the letter?
5. An event letter tells a story, so review what you know about the **plot** of this story. Who are the characters? What is the setting? What conflict does the writer face, and what do you think the resolution might be?
6. Think about the way that the writer expresses himself. How would you describe the **mood** or tone of the letter? Explain.

Extension Find another example of an event letter, and compare it with this one.

From: Marcus <marcfrye@happywriters.com>
Subject: **What a Story!**
Date: April 14, 2011 7:22:03 PM EDT
To: Tomas <texastomas97@friendsring.com>

Hi, Tomas,

Remember how I told you I was going to take care of a puppy? Well I did. Last week I took care of my Aunt Darlene's Chihuahua puppy Goliath. I was pretty excited at first, since I've always wanted a puppy.

Aunt Darlene dropped Goliath off in his crate along with two whole pages of instructions. As soon as she left, Goliath started to whine. He really seemed to miss Aunt Darlene. I was able to quiet him down by playing with him.

Aunt Darlene's list told me exactly what I had to do to take care of Goliath. I had to feed him twice a day, walk him once, and play fetch with him. I also had to let him outside to use the bathroom four times a day. Doing all of these things took up a lot of time, but the hardest thing was making sure he did not chew everything. One day, he got one of my socks and chewed a hole in it. Another day, he pulled my shoelaces out of my shoe.

I mostly enjoyed taking care of Goliath, but it made me wonder if I really want a puppy of my own. It's sure a lot of work!

86 Narrative Nonfiction

Create an Event Letter

Tell students that they will create an event letter using the five-step writing process. Then, preview the writing process instructions on page 87.

Resources You may wish to have students use the Timeline graphic organizer. Distribute printed copies or have students log on to Writing Coach Online.

For each step in the writing process, have partners read aloud and discuss the list of tasks. Then, have them work individually. Once both partners have completed the tasks, have them evaluate each other's work before moving to the next step.

Use the 21st Century Skills Rubric to evaluate each student's process and final product on a scale of 1 to 3, indicating weak, moderate, or strong use of the skill. ▶

Partner Talk

Remind students to point out elements of their partner's narrative that work well and those that need improvement.

21st Century Learning

Skills Rubric	Rating
Think Creatively: Use a wide range of idea creation techniques.	1 2 3
Communicate Clearly: Articulate ideas effectively using oral and written communication skills.	1 2 3
Use and Manage Information: Use information accurately and creatively for the issue at hand.	1 2 3
Work Independently: Monitor, define, prioritize, and complete tasks without direct oversight.	1 2 3

3 STUDENT BOOK

Students follow the five-step writing process to write their own event letter. Students may select online or printed graphic organizers to help them plan and develop their writing.

 Create an Event Letter

Follow these steps to create your own event letter. To plan your event letter, review the graphic organizers on R24–R27 and choose one that suits your needs.

Prewriting

- Identify your target audience. Think about who will read your letter. Will they understand your story?
- Select a topic that you want to share. You might want to share a funny story, or an experience that was out of the ordinary.
- Think about what you want to tell your audience, and make sure that you focus on a single event.
- List or map out the plot of the narrative—its beginning, middle, and end.
- Fill in the details; for example, note things that you or other characters said and how you felt as the action was happening.

Drafting

- Use chronological order to recount the event.
- Write a narrative that tells your personal story and includes details that explain the reasons for actions. You may also want to hint at their importance. Don't forget to reveal consequences.
- Remember to connect to the person who will read the event letter. Think of details or comments that your audience will appreciate.

Revising and Editing

- Review your draft to ensure that your narrative is complete and interesting. Look for specific words and vivid images.
- Review the tone of the letter. If necessary, make changes to give it a more friendly tone.
- Check that spelling, grammar, and mechanics are correct.

Publishing

If you are mailing the letter, create a clean copy and then mail it. If you are sending it as an e-mail, make sure that the recipient's address is correct before you hit SEND. You also may want to attach a photo related to the event.

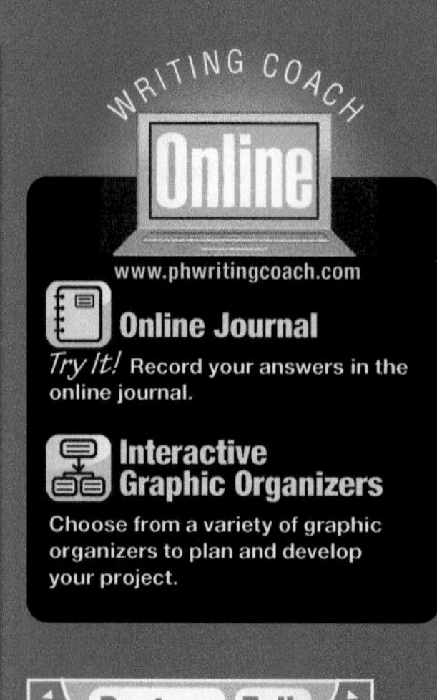

Online Journal

Try It! Record your answers in the online journal.

Interactive Graphic Organizers

Choose from a variety of graphic organizers to plan and develop your project.

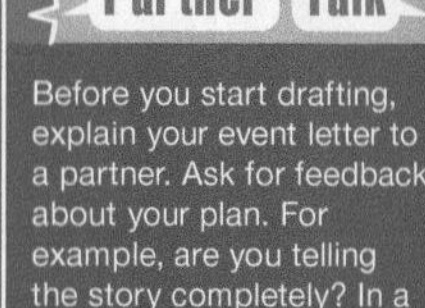

Before you start drafting, explain your event letter to a partner. Ask for feedback about your plan. For example, are you telling the story completely? In a friendly way?

Personalized Support

Teacher or Peer Feedback

To provide feedback to students as they write for media, ask or have student partners ask one another the following:

- What are the main characteristics of this form of writing?
- Have you included most or all of these characteristics in your piece of writing?
- What is your purpose for writing this piece?
- Who is your audience?
- How did you organize your ideas in this piece of writing?
- How did you go about revising the piece? Editing it?
- How do you plan on publishing your piece?
- What other publishing options also might work?

Working with ELLs — ELL Sheltered Instruction: Cognitive

Orally present the event letter on page 86 and help students demonstrate understanding of the general meaning, main points, and important details in spoken language on topics ranging from familiar to unfamiliar. Discuss a familiar topic, babysitting, and use it to aid students' understanding as you read about the unfamiliar topic of pet-sitting.

Beginning Reread the first paragraph aloud, clarifying meaning. Ask questions to elicit the general meaning, main points, and important details of the paragraph. Have students draw to show understanding.

Intermediate Have small groups record the general meaning of the event letter in the center of a **Spider-Web Diagram** and add main points and important details in the outer circles, then discuss their diagrams.

Advanced Provide pairs with a **Spider-Web Diagram** and have them record the general meaning, main points, and important details of the event letter.

Advanced High Have students complete the Advanced activity and describe to partners a recent event in their lives.

1 

Before they write, students use the ABCDs of On-Demand Writing to analyze and plan how to respond to each prompt. They can use either their online journals or notebooks to take notes.

Writing for Assessment

Read aloud or have a student read aloud the introductory text. Then, tell students that they will learn and practice a technique for writing in response to a test prompt.

Try It! Read the Narrative Prompt aloud and then have volunteers read aloud the Format and Academic Vocabulary boxes. Tell students that they will use the ABCD method to respond to the prompt.

The ABCDs of On-Demand Writing

Have students identify the words associated with the ABCD method. (attack, brainstorm, choose, detect) Then, guide students through their use.

I'll attack the prompt by circling the words *share* and *include*. These verbs remind me that I need to write a personal narrative in which I share information about the best trip I ever took. I will include a beginning, middle, and end. I can rewrite the prompt to state that clearly: "Write a personal narrative in which you share information about the best trip you ever took. Include a beginning, middle, and end."

Work with students to brainstorm for an appropriate graphic organizer for a personal narrative, such as a timeline.

Have students write their drafts individually and then work with a partner to detect errors.

Writing to a Prompt *Persuasion* Writing to a Prompt *Persuasion* Writing to a Prompt

Writing for Assessment

Many standardized tests include a prompt that asks you to write a personal narrative. Use these prompts to practice. Your compositions should have the same characteristics as your personal narrative. (See page 66.)

Try It! Read the prompt and the information on format and academic vocabulary. Then, write a **personal narrative** using the ABCDs of On-Demand Writing.

Format
The prompt directs you to write a *personal narrative*. Make sure that you keep a clearly defined focus through your narrative's beginning, middle, and end.

Narrative Prompt
What is the best trip you ever took? Think about what made that trip "best" and then write a personal narrative to share the story. Be sure to include a beginning, a middle, and an end.

Academic Vocabulary
Remember that the *beginning*, *middle*, and *end* make a story. Be sure to include all three parts in your personal narrative.

The ABCDs of On-Demand Writing

Use the following ABCDs to help you respond to the prompt.

Before you write your draft:

A ttack the prompt [1 MINUTE]
- Circle or highlight important verbs in the prompt. Draw a line from the verb to what it refers to.
- Rewrite the prompt in your own words.

B rainstorm possible answers [4 MINUTES]
- Create a graphic organizer to generate ideas.
- Use one for each part of the prompt if necessary.

C hoose the order of your response [1 MINUTE]
- Think about the best way to organize your ideas.
- Number your ideas in the order you will write about them. Cross out ideas you will not be using.

After you write your draft:

D etect errors before turning in the draft [1 MINUTE]
- Carefully reread your writing.
- Make sure that your response makes sense and is complete.
- Look for spelling, punctuation, and grammar errors.

More Prompts for Practice

Apply It! Test Prep Have students apply the ABCD method to the two practice prompts.

Prompt 1 Have partners attack the prompt and brainstorm for possible answers. Then, have each pair swap their information with another group to evaluate whether the teams have developed personal narratives that have a clearly defined focus.

Prompt 2 Have students work individually to attack the prompt and brainstorm for possible answers. Then, have students work in small groups to evaluate their work before writing their drafts.

More Strategies for Writing for Assessment

Review the strategies with students. Then, have students brainstorm for their own strategies for responding to a prompt. Record student responses on the board and discuss which of these strategies the class should adopt for their next prompt-based writing assignment.

2 

Students submit their writing paragraph by paragraph or as a complete draft to the **Interactive Writing Coach™** for feedback, or share their writing with their teacher.

3 

Students receive personalized feedback from the **Interactive Writing Coach™** or feedback from their teacher.

More Prompts for Practice

Apply It! Respond to Prompts 1 and 2 by writing **personal narratives** with **a clearly defined focus.** As you write, be sure to:

- Identify an appropriate audience for your intended purpose
- Use a graphic organizer, such as a beginning-middle-end organizer, to organize and structure your ideas
- Explain **the importance of or reason for your actions and their consequences**

Prompt 1 How far back can you remember? Think about your earliest childhood memory. Then, write a personal narrative to tell the story of what happened to you at that memorable moment.

Prompt 2 Recall a time when you gave a very special gift to someone. In a personal narrative, recount that event. Show why you chose that gift and how the person who received the gift reacted to it.

More Strategies for Writing for Assessment

- Consider several possible topics and quickly list details that you might use in your response. Then, choose the topic for which you have the strongest ideas.
- If you do not understand any words in the prompt, use context clues to determine the meaning of the unknown words.
- Be sure to follow the ABCDs for writing to a prompt. Planning is an important part of writing. Don't just start writing right away.
- Make sure to reread your piece after you have completed it. This will give you time to find and correct errors. If you are in a timed situation, be sure to leave enough time for this step.

www.phwritingcoach.com

Interactive Writing Coach™

Plan your response to the prompt. If you are using the prompt for practice, write one paragraph at a time or your entire draft and then submit it for feedback. If you are using the prompt as a timed test, write your entire draft and then submit it for feedback.

Remember **ABCD**

- **A**ttack the prompt
- **B**rainstorm possible answers
- **C**hoose the order of your response
- **D**etect errors before turning in the draft

Personalized Support

Assessment/Monitor Progress

For timed writing practice, assign students a prompt to be completed in a timed setting. For Prompts 1 and 2, have students submit their writing to **Interactive Writing Coach™** to get immediate feedback.

For a formal writing assessment, assign the Assessment writing prompt for this chapter in **Writing Coach Online™**. Then, have students submit their writing to **Interactive Writing Coach™** to be assessed. Use the results to assess student progress and skill levels. **Interactive Writing Coach™** will update student levels to ensure that students get the appropriate support.

Teacher Feedback

To create an assessment environment, have students use a prompt in a timed setting. Grade papers using the appropriate rubric and use the results to assess student progress and skill levels. In the next writing assignment, ensure that students get the appropriate level of support.

If you conference with students, use these questions to guide your discussion:

- What form of writing did the prompt call for? Does your response include most or all of the characteristics of that form?
- How did you organize your ideas?
- Did you make good use of your time as you planned and wrote your response?
- What did you learn that you can use when responding to a prompt during a timed test?

Differentiated Instruction

RTI Strategy for Special Needs Students Use the Evaluate column in the chart on page 80 and the Student Model on pages 70–71 to review the characteristics of a personal narrative with students. Ask students to name the parts that are the most difficult for them. Have students give more attention to those parts during peer review of their responses to the prompts.

Strategy for Spanish Speakers Students whose home language is Spanish may encounter additional difficulties in understanding words in a writing prompt. Encourage students to look for cognates in the prompt in addition to using context clues to help them determine the meaning. Point out cognates in Prompt 1 on page 89 such as *personal, story, memory,* and *moment,* and have students provide Spanish equivalents.

CHAPTER 6 LESSON PLANNER
Fiction Narration

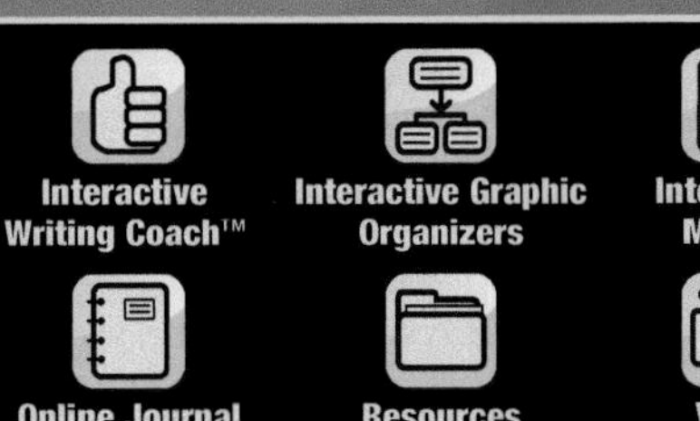

Use the Online Lesson Planner at www.phwritingcoach.com to customize your instructional plan for an integrated Language Arts curriculum.

DAY 1

ONLINE

CHAPTER OPENER/ GENRE INTRODUCTION
- What's the Story?
- What's Ahead
- Connect to the Big Questions
- **Feature Assignment: Short Story: Science Fiction**
- Other Forms of Short Stories
- Word Bank

DAY 2

ONLINE

MENTOR TEXT/ STUDENT MODEL
- **Mentor Text: Science Fiction**
- Learn From Experience
- **Student Model: Science Fiction**
- Reader's Eye and Writer's Eye

DAY 3

ONLINE

Prewriting
- Choose From the Topic Bank
- Choose Your Own Topic
- Narrow Your Topic
- Consider Your Audience and Purpose

DAY 6

ONLINE

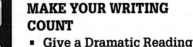

Revising
- Keep Revision on Your RADaR
- Look at the Big Picture
- Focus on Craft
- Fine-Tune Your Draft

DAY 7

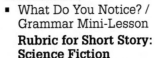

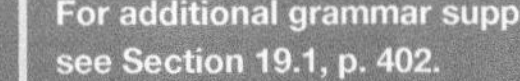
For additional grammar support, see Section 19.1, p. 402.

ONLINE

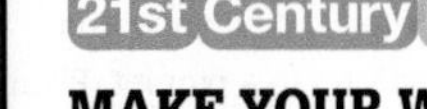

Editing
- What Do You Notice? / Grammar Mini-Lesson

Rubric for Short Story: Science Fiction

Publishing
- Publish Your Piece
- Reflect on Your Writing

DAY 8

ONLINE

21st Century Learning

MAKE YOUR WRITING COUNT
- **Give a Dramatic Reading of a Realistic Story**
- Here's Your Action Plan
- Listening and Speaking

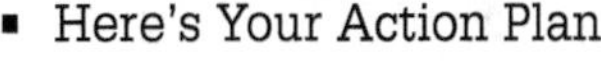
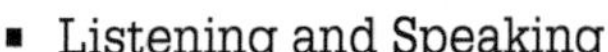

Alternate Pacing Suggestions

- **Block Scheduling** Each day on the Lesson Planner represents a 40–50 minute block. Teachers using block scheduling may combine days to revise pacing to meet their classroom needs.
- **Accelerated Lesson Planning** Combine instructional days by aiding students in choosing a topic and then focusing on two core stages of the writing process, outlining for success (Day 5) and RADaR revision (Day 6).
- **Integrated Language Arts Curriculum** For targeted instruction that covers the essential components of the lesson use either a 3- or a 5-day plan.

3 day plan

DAY 1: Introduction to the Genre, Mentor Text, Student Model

DAY 2: Prewriting/Drafting

DAY 3: Revising/Editing/ Publishing

5 day plan

Use 3-day plan, and add:

DAY 4: Make Your Writing Count

DAY 5: Writing for Assessment

Links to Prentice Hall *LITERATURE*

Featured Author: Walter Dean Myers
- What Is a Short Story?, p. 200
- "The Treasure of Lemon Brown" (short story), p. 205
- On Revising to Heighten Tension (Writing Workshop), p. 387
- *From the Author's Desk* Videos: Walter Dean Myers

Additional Mentor Text:
- "All Summer in a Day" (science fiction short story), Ray Bradbury, p. 102

Differentiated Instruction

Differentiated Instruction Boxes in this Teacher's Edition address these student populations:

- Below-Level Students
- Above-Level Students
- Gifted and Talented Students
- Special Needs Students
- English Language Learners
- Spanish Speaking Students

In addition, for further enrichment, see the **Extension** features.

DAY 4

Prewriting

- Plan Your Piece
- Gather Details

ONLINE

DAY 5

Drafting

- Outline for Success
- Start Your Draft

ONLINE

DAY 9

WRITING FOR MEDIA

- **Dramatic Scene**
- Create a Dramatic Scene

ONLINE

DAY 10

WRITING FOR ASSESSMENT

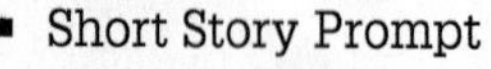

- Short Story Prompt

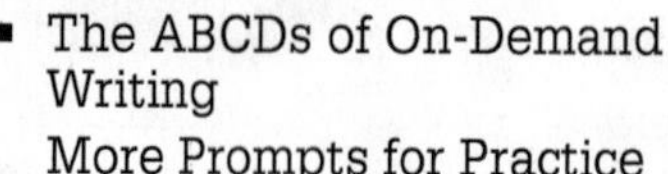

- The ABCDs of On-Demand Writing

More Prompts for Practice
Test Prep

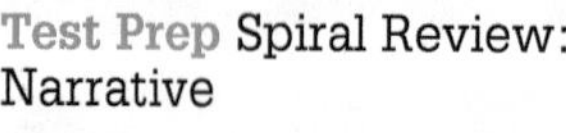

Test Prep Spiral Review: Narrative

ONLINE

LESSON OBJECTIVES

- To learn the forms and defining characteristics of fictional narratives.
- To learn the elements of a successful science fiction story, the chapter Feature Assignment.
- To read a Mentor Text in the genre, analyzing its use of the elements of an effective fictional narrative.
- To read a Student Model of a science fiction story, analyzing it from the perspective of a reader and from the perspective of a writer.
- To apply prewriting strategies in developing a science fiction story, including strategies for choosing and narrowing a topic, planning writing, and gathering details, as well as tips for considering audience and purpose.
- To apply drafting strategies in developing a science fiction story.
- To apply RADaR revision strategies to a draft science fiction story.
- To learn about the Focus on Craft topic, coherence in writing, and apply what is learned to a draft science fiction story.
- To edit the draft, zooming in on pronouns and focusing on clear pronoun reference.
- To complete the Make Your Writing Count assignment, developing and presenting a sci-fi film trailer.
- To complete the Writing for Media assignment, developing a dramatic scene.
- To practice writing for assessment.

Personalized Assessment

Teacher Conferencing

Ongoing Assessment	Formal Assessment of Feature Assignment	Progress Monitoring at End-of-Chapter
Use rubrics in the Student Edition as a revision tool. Conference with students to review their work and provide personalized support.	Use rubrics in the Student Edition to score students' Feature Assignment papers.	Review each student's work to plan targeted resources for the next writing assignment.

1 Using Writing Coach Online™ or the student book, students discuss the photograph in the chapter opener as it relates to the writing genre.

2 Students record their ideas and responses in their online journals or notebooks. They may also record and save their responses on pop-up sticky notes in Writing Coach Online™.

Chapter Objectives

1. Write a short story by planning, drafting, revising, editing, and publishing individual work.
2. Produce a movie trailer storyboard.
3. Use the five-step writing process to write a dramatic scene.
4. Write a short story and a personal narrative in response to a prompt.

FICTION NARRATION

What's the Story?

Activate Prior Knowledge Tell students that the purpose of fiction narration is to describe a series of events in which a main character solves a problem. Explain to students that they will use what they know about mountain biking to analyze the photo on page 90. Then, guide the students in analyzing the photo.

Think Aloud When you write a short story, all the elements, including the setting, the characters, and the plot, come together to create an engaging narrative. In the photo, for example, **I see** an interesting setting—a forest—and a person on a bike whose story is taking place in this setting. I can imagine the events that occurred before and the ones that will occur after this time.

Work with students to brainstorm for some reasons the person is riding a bike through the forest. Record student responses on the board.

Try It! **Have students** work individually to develop responses to the questions. Check that students have imagined specific details about the setting, characters, and events of the story.

Possible responses: The person in the photo is riding through the forest to compete in an all-terrain biking contest. The person's challenge is to ride quickly through the obstacles without getting injured. The person feels focused and excited and relishes the challenge.

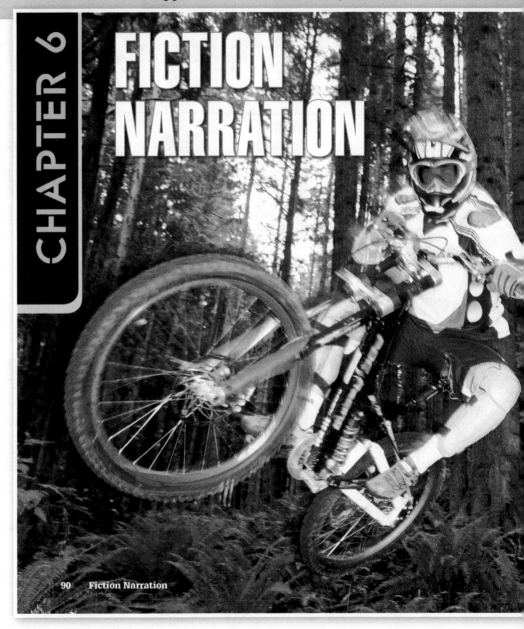

CHAPTER 6 FICTION NARRATION

90 Fiction Narration

Connect to the Big Questions

Have students use their experience to discuss the Big Questions. Explain that they will revisit **Why write?** at the end of this chapter. Tell students to consider these questions during their discussion:

1. What mental and physical skills are required to face a challenge? Is it worthwhile to exercise these skills?
2. How do the characterization, conflict, and plot of a work of nonfiction differ from those of a work of fiction?

What's Ahead

Have students preview the Mentor Text and Student Model on pages 94–99. Tell students that they will write their own science fiction short story using the five-step writing process: prewriting, drafting, revising, editing, and publishing.

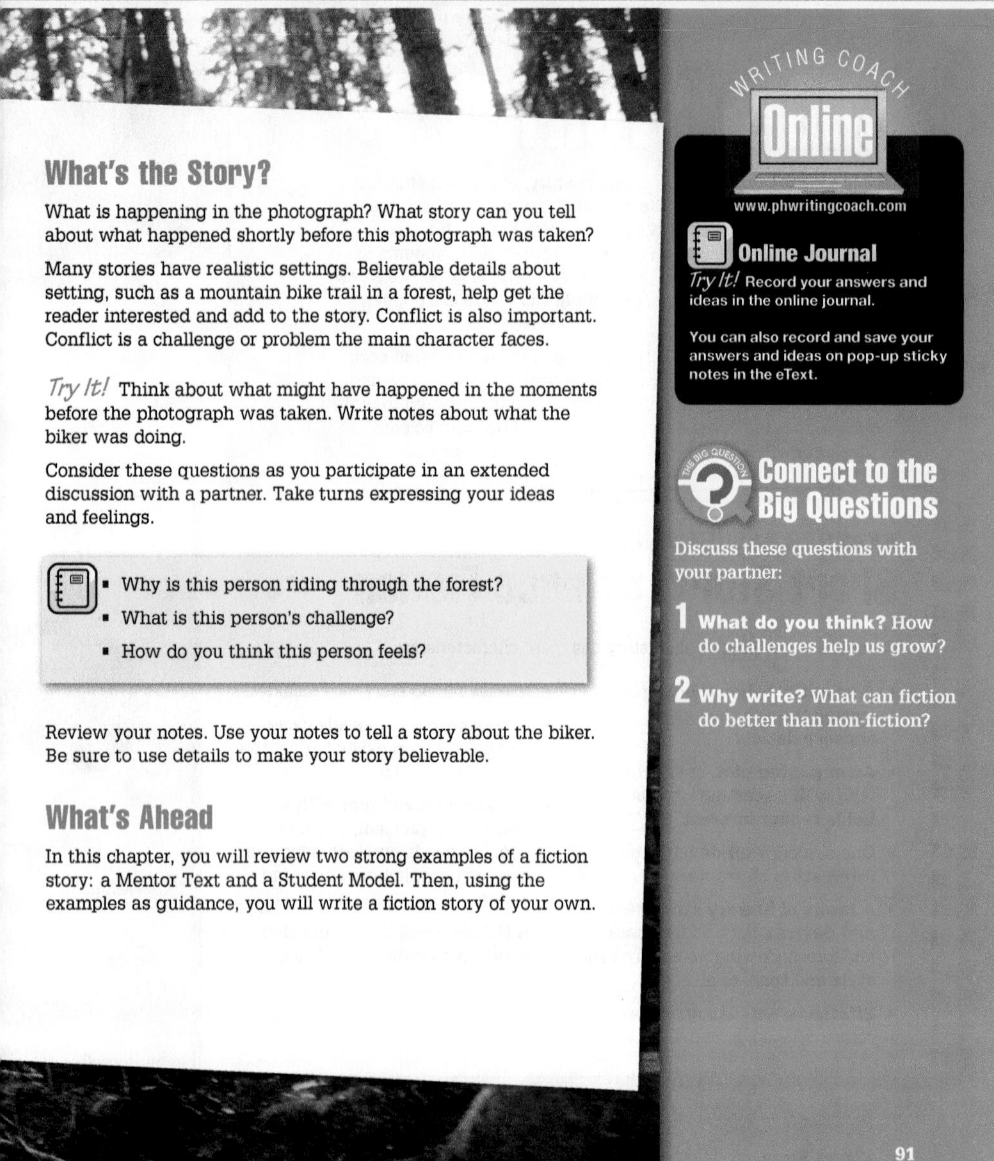

What's the Story?

What is happening in the photograph? What story can you tell about what happened shortly before this photograph was taken?

Many stories have realistic settings. Believable details about setting, such as a mountain bike trail in a forest, help get the reader interested and add to the story. Conflict is also important. Conflict is a challenge or problem the main character faces.

Try It! Think about what might have happened in the moments before the photograph was taken. Write notes about what the biker was doing.

Consider these questions as you participate in an extended discussion with a partner. Take turns expressing your ideas and feelings.

- Why is this person riding through the forest?
- What is this person's challenge?
- How do you think this person feels?

Review your notes. Use your notes to tell a story about the biker. Be sure to use details to make your story believable.

What's Ahead

In this chapter, you will review two strong examples of a fiction story: a Mentor Text and a Student Model. Then, using the examples as guidance, you will write a fiction story of your own.

WRITING COACH **Online**

www.phwritingcoach.com

Online Journal

Try It! Record your answers and ideas in the online journal.

You can also record and save your answers and ideas on pop-up sticky notes in the eText.

Connect to the Big Questions

Discuss these questions with your partner:

1 **What do you think?** How do challenges help us grow?

2 **Why write?** What can fiction do better than non-fiction?

Personalized Support

FEEDBACK

Teacher or Peer Feedback

To encourage students in their discussion of the photograph as it relates to the writing genre, ask the following questions:

- What is the first thing you think of when you look at this photo?
- How does it relate to your life?
- Does it relate to things you've learned in other subjects?
- What questions come to mind when you look at this photograph?
- How does your response to the photograph compare to those of your classmates?

Working with ELLs

ELL **Sheltered Instruction:** Cognitive

Help students learn new expressions heard during classroom instruction and interactions. Discuss the image on page 90 and then tell an anecdote using the following idiomatic expressions: *race against time, rise to the challenge,* and *the sky is the limit.* Then:

Beginning Explain the literal and figurative meanings of the expressions. Have students make **Puzzle Cards,** writing each expression on one half of a card, illustrating it on the other, and cutting the cards in two. Have them raise the correct card as you say each expression.

Intermediate Define each new idiomatic expression for students and use each in a new sentence. Have students form groups and demonstrate understanding by using each expression in their own sentences.

Advanced Have partners find the definition of each new expression in a dictionary and use the expressions in a discussion.

Advanced High Challenge students to use context to infer the meaning of each idiomatic expression. Repeat the anecdote as needed. Have students display understanding in discussion.

1 

Students learn vocabulary from the Word Bank and listen to English and Spanish pronunciations in the Writing Coach Online™ glossary.

2 

Students record answers to questions about forms of writing in their online journals or notebooks.

SHORT STORY

To introduce this chapter's writing form, discuss the opening paragraphs with students. Make sure students understand that a science fiction story is a type of short story. Explain that good writers use a step-by-step process to develop their work. Then, have students preview the rubric on page 111.

Short Story: Science Fiction

Ask volunteers to read aloud the feature assignment characteristics. Tell students that they will identify these characteristics in a Mentor Text and a Student Model. Then, they will use the characteristics to guide the writing of their own science fiction story.

Other Forms of Short Stories

Guide students to understand how the forms of short stories are alike and different.

Say: I notice that different forms of short stories are based on different levels of reality and fantasy. For example, historical fiction and realistic fiction include people and events that are real or seem real. On the other hand, fantasy stories, myths, and legends have many fantastic elements.

Ask: What are some other differences among the types of fiction? (types of characters, setting, plot)

Have students discuss the types of short stories they like most and least and explain why.

Try It! Remind students that the audience is the people who will read their writing. The purpose is the author's reason for writing. Have students record their responses in their journal.

Possible responses: mystery fiction, focuses on an unexplained event the main character tries to solve; realistic fiction, involves characters and events from everyday life; fantasy stories, stretch the imagination and often involve animals

SHORT STORY

In this chapter, you will write a short story, or a series of events that have a beginning, middle, and end. You will also explore a special type of literary text called science fiction. A science fiction short story focuses on real or imagined developments in science and technology and their effects on the way people think and live. Space travel, robots, and life in the future are popular topics for science fiction.

You will develop a science fiction story by taking it through each of the steps of the writing process: prewriting, drafting, revising, editing, and publishing. You will also have an opportunity to write a dramatic scene. To preview the criteria for how your science fiction story will be evaluated, see the rubric on page 111.

FEATURE ASSIGNMENT

Short Story: Science Fiction

An effective imaginative short story has these characteristics:

- **A specific, believable setting** created through the use of **sensory details**
- **An engaging plot**, or storyline, with **well-paced action** that **holds reader interest**
- One or more **well-developed, interesting characters**
- A **range of literary strategies and devices**, such as flashback and foreshadowing, to enhance the **style** and **tone**, or attitude
- **Effective sentence structure** and correct spelling, grammar, and usage

A science fiction story also includes:

- A **setting** with more advanced technology than existed when the story was written
- An action-packed **plot** with a **conflict**, or problem, between people's needs and technology, or between people from Earth and aliens
- A **theme** about the relationship between humans and science

92 **Short Story**

Word Bank

To assist English Language Learners and struggling readers, echo read each word or have students log on to Writing Coach Online to listen to the pronunciations. Then, have partners take turns using each word in a sentence. Ask volunteers to share one of their sentences with the class.

Teacher Tip

Have students extend their understanding by making a class chart that lists examples of each kind of short story described. Encourage students to identify works in other media, such as movies and video games, that correspond to each form of short story.

Other Forms of Short Stories

In addition to science fiction, there are other forms of short stories, including:

Fantasy stories stretch the imagination and take readers to unreal worlds. Animals may talk, people may fly, or characters may have superhuman powers.

Historical fiction tells about imaginary people living in real places and times in history. Usually, the main characters are fictional people who know and interact with famous people in history and participate in important historical events.

Mystery stories focus on unexplained or strange events that one of the characters tries to solve. These stories are often full of suspense and surprises.

Myths and legends are traditional stories that different cultures have told to explain natural events, human nature, or the origins of things. They often include gods and goddesses from ancient times and heroes who do superhuman things.

Realistic fiction portrays invented characters and events in everyday life that most readers would find familiar.

Tall tales are about larger-than-life characters in realistic settings. The main character typically solves a problem or reaches a goal by doing something wild and fantastic that normal people could never do.

Try It! For each audience and purpose described, choose a story form, such as a fantasy story, mystery, or realistic fiction, that is appropriate for conveying your intended meaning to the audience. Explain your choices.

- To describe how a mystery was solved
- To show how a fictional teen deals with a problem
- To catch the imagination of young children

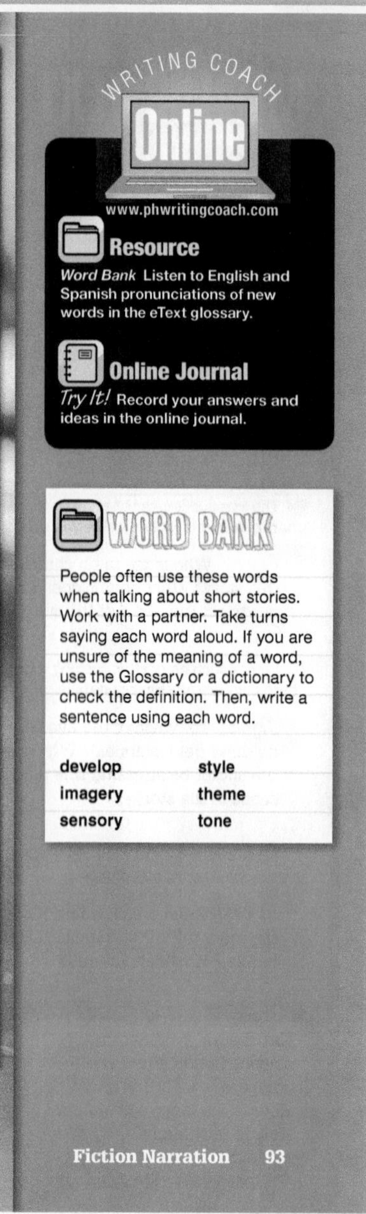
WRITING COACH
Online
www.phwritingcoach.com
Resource
Word Bank Listen to English and Spanish pronunciations of new words in the eText glossary.
Online Journal
Try It! Record your answers and ideas in the online journal.
WORD BANK
People often use these words when talking about short stories. Work with a partner. Take turns saying each word aloud. If you are unsure of the meaning of a word, use the Glossary or a dictionary to check the definition. Then, write a sentence using each word.
develop style
imagery theme
sensory tone

Personalized Support

FEEDBACK

Teacher or Peer Feedback

To help students understand the characteristics of the writing form, ask or have student partners ask one another the following questions:

- What are the main characteristics of a short story?
- What makes this form of writing different from other forms?
- Who are the likely readers or audiences for this form of writing?
- What kind of organization could be used for this form of writing?
- What kind of voice would be most effective for this form of writing?

Working with ELLs

ELL Sheltered Instruction: Cognitive

Help students learn and use basic routine language, such as *understand,* in order to expand and internalize initial English vocabulary. Have them use and reuse the Word Bank vocabulary in a speaking activity.

Beginning Define the word *problem,* using mime to support comprehension. Put a chair in front of the doorway. Say, *This chair is causing a problem*. Have students use and reuse the word by echoing your sentence. Then, have them orally repeat sentences to use and reuse the other Word Bank vocabulary.

Intermediate Help students define each word and repeat a short sentence that uses each. Then, have them reuse the vocabulary words in their own spoken sentences.

Advanced Have students find definitions of the Word Bank words in a dictionary and then use and reuse each word in a question-and-answer session with a partner.

Advanced High Have partners use the words to discuss a story they have read. Have them reuse the vocabulary words in questions about the stories.

The Digital • Print Path

1 

Using Writing Coach Online™ or the student book, students read and listen to an audio recording of the Mentor Text. As they complete their writing assignments, they can refer back to the Mentor Text for support whenever they need it.

2 

Students record their answers to questions about the Mentor Text in their online journals or notebooks.

MENTOR TEXT

About the Selection In this science fiction story, Luis wanders away from his friends at their forest campsite. As he returns, a kid in a tree tells him not to go in that direction. Luis, ignoring him, goes down the path, where he sees strange creatures playing in a waterfall. One creature, the kid, says he is a Traveler from 500 years in the future. He shoves Luis. Luis awakens and returns, shaken, to camp. His friend, Joel, privately guesses that Luis met a Traveler.

Learn From Experience

After students have read the text, point out that the numbered notes refer to the characteristics of a science fiction short story introduced on page 92.

Try It! Guide students to understand how the genre characteristics shape the text.

Say: The first *Try It!* question asks who is the main character of the story. **I notice** that Luis speaks the first lines in the story. Line 2 refers to "his three friends." Since Luis is the only character named at the beginning, I can tell he is the main character.

Ask: Which details help set the scene of the story in a particularly effective way? (One striking detail is "the sun shining off the surface of a small lake.")

Have students reply to the *Try It!* questions in their journals. If students have difficulty responding to a particular question, model a response, as with Question 1.

Check the accuracy and completeness of student responses.

1. Luis; details include the "beautiful, grassy area ringed with tall pines and oaks," "the sun shining off the surface of a small lake," "miles and miles of forest trails," and "a swim in cool water."
2. The details appeal to the sense of hearing. The author stresses this sense because the conflict that occurs comes in the form of a voice.

Mentor Text Science Fiction Mentor Text Science Fiction

MENTOR TEXT

Science Fiction

Learn From Experience

Read the science fiction story on pages 94–97. As you read, take notes to develop your understanding of basic sight and English vocabulary. Then, read the numbered notes in the margins to learn about how the author presented her ideas.

Answer the *Try It!* questions online or in your notebook.

❶ The introduction identifies the main **character** and creates a believable **setting.**

Try It! Who is the main character in this story? What details does the author use to set the scene of the story?

❷ Words such as *chatter, rustling, sighing,* and *sharp calls* are all **sensory details.**

Try It! To which of the five senses do these details appeal? Why might the author be stressing this particular sense in the story?

❸ Here, and throughout the story, the author uses a consistent **point of view.**

Try It! From which point of view is the story told: first person or third person? How can you tell?

Extension Find another science fiction story, and compare it with this one. How is the language similar? How is it different?

Traveler

by Barbara Davis

❶ "Here!" Luis shouted. "We can camp here. It's perfect!" His three friends trudged into the forest clearing. Luis had found a beautiful, grassy area ringed with tall pines and oaks. The boys could see the sun shining off the surface of a small lake not too far from where they stood. After carrying heavy backpacks through miles and miles of forest trails, they relished the idea of a swim in cool water.

Joel groaned as he swung his backpack off his shoulders. He dropped down on the grass and wiped the sweat from his face with the bottom of his T-shirt. "Looks great to me. Plenty of dry wood to start a fire, rocks for a fire ring, a place to swim—I vote we set up camp."

Soon, the four were busy setting up tents and hanging their food in trees to discourage bears. "How about you guys finish up here, and I'll go collect firewood?" Luis suggested. Since finding firewood meant even more walking around in the forest, the other boys readily agreed.

❷ As Luis headed into the forest, the boys' campsite chatter faded from his hearing. Instead, Luis heard the light breeze rustling the leaves in the trees. The tall pines sounded like they were sighing. Every once in awhile, he heard the sharp calls of unseen crows. The bushes rustled with the passage of some kind of small animal. At least Luis *hoped* it was a small animal and not a bear.

❸ Listening to all the forest sounds, Luis lost track of time. Eventually, the increasing weight of the firewood sack he had tied around his shoulder let him know it was time to start making his way back to camp. He had gone much farther into the forest than he had intended. He wasn't worried, though. There wasn't a trail yet that Luis couldn't follow. Shifting the weight of the firewood to a more comfortable position, Luis started to take a step back along the way he had come. Suddenly, a voice said, "Not that way!"

94 Short Story

---

3. The story is told in third person. The protagonist's actions and feelings are reported with third-person pronouns.
4. The dialogue furthers the plot by developing the conflict between Luis and the kid. Luis's lines show that he is brave and stubborn.
5. Suspense makes readers keep reading to find out how the conflict is resolved.

Extension Lead a discussion in which students compare and contrast how their additional science fiction story examples use the genre characteristics. Use the *Try It!* questions as a guide.

Teacher Tip

Quick Write Ask students to think about how the story might unfold on the following pages. Have them jot down an ending they would like to see happen. At the end of the story, discuss students' responses.

Luis was so surprised, he almost dropped the firewood. He whipped his head around to see who had spoken. No one was there. He carefully scanned the area around him. Nothing. Luis wasn't the type of kid to imagine voices but, obviously, he had imagined this one. Shrugging off the mystery, he once again started down the trail.

❹ "You *really* don't want to go that way." Same voice. This time Luis was sure it wasn't just his imagination.

His heart beating just a little bit faster, Luis asked, "Who are you? Where are you?" At first, there was no response. Then, Luis heard the tree leaves just above his head start to rustle. He peered closely into the tree, but still couldn't see anything. He focused his eyes even harder. There! He saw something. It looked like a really skinny kid straddling the lowest branch.

The kid seemed to be wearing some type of camouflage clothing that allowed him to blend in with the surrounding leaves. If Luis took his eyes off the kid for even a second, the kid blended right back into the tree. ❹ "Ah! You can finally see me. Took you long enough."

Now that Luis could see that it was just a kid, he felt foolish for having been slightly scared. "Yeah, I can see you. Why are you telling me not to go this way? This is the way back to my campsite."

The kid in the tree just smiled. He said, "Maybe. But you still don't want to go that way."

The bundle of wood was getting heavier by the minute, and Luis didn't feel like playing a game of riddles. Part of him wanted to know who the kid was and what he was doing there in the middle of the forest. The other part of him wanted to get back to the campsite. The second part won out. Luis said, "Yeah, okay. Whatever." With that, he turned and continued down the path. When he looked over his shoulder, all he could see were the leaves of the tree. No kid. Luis shook his head and kept going.

❺ He wasn't sure when he noticed that the forest had grown still. No breeze, no birds, no sounds at all. It was as if the forest was holding its breath. The sun was still shining in streaks along the path, causing the air to shimmer. In the

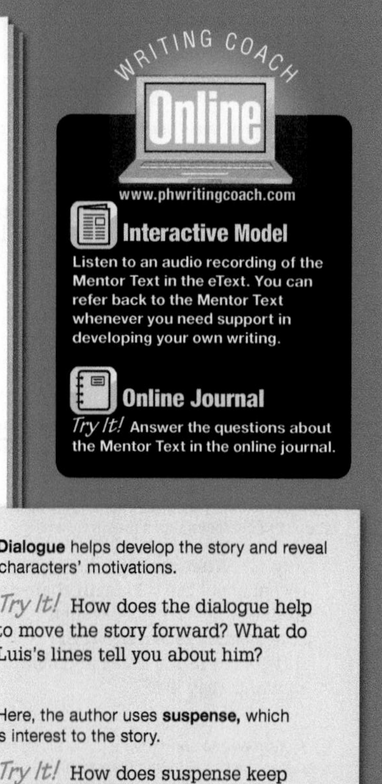

WRITING COACH
Online
www.phwritingcoach.com
Interactive Model
Listen to an audio recording of the Mentor Text in the eText. You can refer back to the Mentor Text whenever you need support in developing your own writing.
Online Journal
Try It! Answer the questions about the Mentor Text in the online journal.

❹ **Dialogue** helps develop the story and reveal the characters' motivations.

Try It! How does the dialogue help to move the story forward? What do Luis's lines tell you about him?

❺ Here, the author uses **suspense,** which adds interest to the story.

Try It! How does suspense keep readers engaged in a story?

Personalized Support

Teacher or Peer Feedback

To provide feedback to students on their responses to the Mentor Text and their answers to the *Try It!* questions, ask or have student partners ask one another the following:

- What is the thesis or controlling idea of the Mentor Text?
- How does the Mentor Text illustrate the characteristics of a science fiction story?
- How did you answer this *Try It!* question? How could you use your answer to help you plan your piece of writing?

Working with ELLs ELL Sheltered Instruction: Cognitive

Help students develop and expand their repertoire of learning strategies by drawing conclusions from a text. Say that to draw conclusions, we use what we've read and know to make educated guesses. Model drawing a conclusion with examples.

Beginning Choral read the first three paragraphs on page 94, supporting comprehension with mime. Model drawing a conclusion about the narrator. Help students reuse the strategy to draw another conclusion: *What conclusion can you draw about Luis?* (He wanted to build a fire.)

Intermediate Have groups read the first three paragraphs and answer the questions in the Beginning activity. Have them reuse the strategy by drawing another conclusion.

Advanced Have pairs apply the strategy by answering question 5 (page 95), drawing a conclusion about why Luis would not want to go in the forest.

Advanced High Challenge students to apply the strategy by drawing two conclusions from the first two pages of the story, identifying details in support. Have them expand their skills by checking the conclusions of a partner.

1 STUDENT BOOK

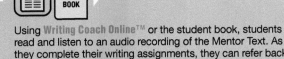

Using Writing Coach Online™ or the student book, students read and listen to an audio recording of the Mentor Text. As they complete their writing assignments, they can refer back to the Mentor Text for support whenever they need it.

MENTOR TEXT

Try It! Continue to guide students to understand how the genre characteristics shape the text.

Check the accuracy and completeness of student responses.

6. These details appeal to the sense of sight. Responses will vary. Details that make the action realistic are the "rushing power" of the waterfall, "the things flying in the air, diving into and out of the frothing water," and "skinny kids with bat-like wings."
7. The author conveys that the creature is fox-like.
8. The dialogue indicates that the creature has more knowledge than Luis; since he comes from the future, he has seen and done things that Luis cannot imagine.
9. Responses will vary. Other words conveying a strong sense of action include *whipped* (page 95); *rushing power, flying,* and *diving* (page 96); and *dumped, ran,* and *tumbled* (page 97).
10. The teaser is Joel's knowledge of Travelers and his guessing that Luis met one.

Teacher Tip

Quick Write Ask students to think about how they would have responded in Luis's situation. Have them write a journal entry telling how their response would have been similar and different.

Mentor Text *Science Fiction* Mentor Text *Science Fiction*

6 The author again uses **sensory details** to describe the scene's setting.

Try It! To which of the five senses do these details appeal? Which details in this passage help you to feel as if you are there, witnessing the action?

7 **Descriptive details** about a character can be a subtle way of saying something about the character's personality.

Try It! What do you think the author is trying to convey about the creature in describing its small, sharp teeth?

8 Further **dialogue** gives more information about the characters and their motives.

Try It! What does the dialogue reveal about the two main characters in this story? What does their conversation reveal about the differences in the times and cultures in which they live?

9 **Action words** can move a story along by changing the pace. In this paragraph, the author uses words such as *burst, panting,* and *skidded* to create a feeling of urgency.

Try It! What other words in the story convey a strong sense of action?

time it took Luis to wonder at how odd the shafts of light looked, he had passed through one of them. When he did, the first thing he realized was that the forest was no longer silent.

It took a moment for him to recognize the sound of water crashing down on rocks. A waterfall? That was impossible. Luis knew for a fact that there were no waterfalls in the forest he and his friends had hiked through. After a few more steps, though, it was clear that he was wrong. 6 There, in all its rushing power was the highest waterfall Luis had ever seen. Even more amazing were the things flying in the air, diving into and out of the frothing water and laughing with the fun of it all. Skinny kids with bat-like wings? Luis's mouth hung open in disbelief. As if that weren't enough, he heard the now-familiar voice: "I told you not to go that way."

This time it was much easier to see the kid because he was standing right next to Luis. Except Luis could now see that it wasn't really a kid at all. With his pointy nose and chin, he almost looked like a cross between a human and a fox. He didn't have fur, though, and his arms and legs were as skinny as twigs. He also had that bizarre quality of looking as if he was constantly blending into and out of his surroundings. Although Luis had a million questions in his brain, none of them were making it to his mouth. For once, "cool as a cucumber in a crisis" Luis was speechless.

7 The creature smiled at Luis. Up close, those teeth were small and sharp. 8 "You're not dreaming. You haven't fallen and conked your head on a stone or anything like that. What you *have* done is pass through one of our portals."

"Portals?" Luis whispered.

"Doorways. Places where we can step between worlds. I'm a Traveler. I travel to other times and other worlds. In Earth years, I'm from about 500 years in the future, and I like this time in your world quite a bit. It's similar to my world. Lots of trees, water. Many of the other places I visit are quite different. Fire, extreme heat, dust. Not so much fun."

The creature smiled again, but it wasn't a pleasant smile. "The thing is, though, we really don't like visitors to *our* world." Luis didn't see what came next, but he felt it—a

Students record their answers to questions about the Mentor Text in their online journals or notebooks.

hard shove against his chest. The next thing he knew, he was sitting on the forest trail looking up at the sunlight. In seconds, he dumped his load of wood and ran as fast as he could back to the campsite.

⑨ He burst out of the forest, wide-eyed and panting. Brad, Tran, and Joel were still pitching the tents and looked up in surprise. Luis skidded into the clearing ready to sputter about what he'd just seen, but he stopped himself. What was he going to say to his friends? They would think he was crazy. His reputation as a practical, not-easily-fooled kind of guy would be ruined. Luis shook his head. He wasn't going to say a word.

"Hey, Luis! What's up? Why are you running? Where's the wood?" Brad and Tran's questions tumbled over each other.

"Nothing. It's nothing. I just thought I heard a bear and got a little spooked." Luis replied. "I must have dropped the load of wood. I'll go back and get it."

⑩ Joel hadn't said anything at all. He gave Luis an odd look and said, "I'll go back with you and give you a hand." Luis was too shaken to protest so he just nodded his head. As the two friends walked back into the forest, Joel said, "So, you met a Traveler, huh?"

www.phwritingcoach.com

Interactive Model

Listen to an audio recording of the Mentor Text in the eText. You can refer back to the Mentor Text whenever you need support in developing your own writing.

Online Journal

Try It! Answer the questions about the Mentor Text in the online journal.

⑩ The story's **resolution** contains a device called a **teaser.** Teasers are sometimes used to suggest there is more to the story than what is specifically written.

Try It! What teaser does the author use? How does it make the story more interesting?

Personalized Support

FEEDBACK

Teacher or Peer Feedback

To provide feedback to students on their responses to the Mentor Text and their answers to the *Try It!* questions, ask or have student partners ask one another the following:

- What is the thesis or controlling idea of the Mentor Text?
- How does the Mentor Text illustrate the characteristics of a science fiction story?
- How did you answer this *Try It!* question? How could you use your answer to help you plan your piece of writing?

Working with ELLs

ELL Sheltered Instruction: Metacognitive

Have students demonstrate listening comprehension of increasingly complex spoken English by retelling or summarizing spoken messages. Read aloud the Mentor Text as students track. Define key words and discuss. Then:

Beginning Read aloud lines 99–130, stopping to have students monitor comprehension and seek clarification. Use images to aid comprehension. Ask simple recall questions to help retell what they heard.

Intermediate Read aloud lines 99–130. Have students monitor comprehension and seek clarification. Have groups retell what they heard.

Advanced Read aloud lines 99–130, and have students work in pairs to write a short retelling to share with another pair. Encourage partners to monitor their comprehension and seek clarification.

Advanced High Read a longer section of the story aloud; encourage students to monitor comprehension and seek clarification as you read. Have them retell the section in their own words.

1 

Using Writing Coach Online™ or the student book, students read and listen to an audio recording of the Student Model.

STUDENT MODEL

Tell students that good writers react to what they read in ways that show their understanding of the text. Explain that students will react to the Student Model by placing two sets of symbols in the text. Then, distribute printed copies of the Student Model or have students log on to Writing Coach Online.

Use a Reader's Eye

Read aloud the instruction for using the Reader's Response Symbols and the meaning of each symbol. Then, guide students through their use.

The student writer does a good job describing settings, or where the action takes place. For example, **I enjoyed** the descriptions in lines 19–22. The vivid sensory details made me see and feel the "freezing," "icy" yard and the "toasty warm" kitchen. I'll place a plus sign next to this part of the text.

Work with students to identify other places in the text where the writer uses strong sensory descriptions.

Have students read and respond to the Student Model, using each Reader's Response Symbol at least once.

Partner Talk

After partners have discussed the things that did and did not work in the story, have each pair suggest ways the less successful elements might be improved.

Use a Writer's Eye

Read aloud the instructions for using the Writer's Response Symbols and the meaning of each symbol. Then, guide students through their use.

Story Student Model Short Story Student Model Short Story St

STUDENT MODEL Science Fiction

With a small group, take turns reading this Student Model aloud. As you read, practice newly acquired vocabulary by correctly producing the word's sound. Also watch for the ways the characters interact with technology. Think about how the culture the characters live in influences that interaction.

Use a Reader's Eye

Now, reread the Student Model. On your copy of the Student Model, use the Reader's Response Symbols to react to what you read.

Reader's Response Symbols

- **+ This is a good description.**
- **– This isn't clear to me.**
- **! This is really cool/weird/ interesting!**
- **? What will happen next?**

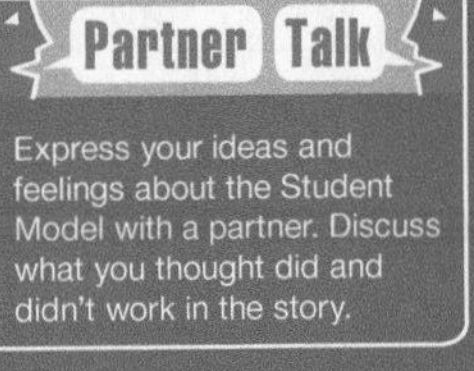

Express your ideas and feelings about the Student Model with a partner. Discuss what you thought did and didn't work in the story.

Be Careful Where You Wish For

by Linda Radner

Sandy's IDP/D woke her up on time, of course. She carefully checked the top of her earlobe. Yes! It was there! Now she was one of the first to have the latest application for her Internal Daily Planner/ Doer (IDP/D). Her IDP/D made sure she was always where she was supposed to be on time. This new app would take her wherever she wished to go!

Sandy found her brother Joe in the kitchen, stirring steamy oatmeal. He was kind of an anti-techno-geek who liked to do things on his own.

"Hey Sis, how's that new app working for you?" Joe asked a little meanly. "Is it living up to the commercials' promises?"

"Haven't tried it yet," Sandy yawned. "But wait: I'd like to have breakfast in the yard." Nothing happened. Then Sandy remembered the new app's default check. She tapped her forehead to confirm her wish.

FLASH! Sandy was freezing in the yard in a storm. Icy rain ran down her neck. She thought about her toasty warm kitchen, tapped her forehead, and FLASH! She was immediately back at the kitchen table.

Joe was laughing. "What happens if you're whisked away in the middle of a class like a crumb off a table?"

"Don't be ridiculous! This app is foolproof. All the commercials say so." Sandy's first class was math. She was already chilled from her soaking

Say: **I found** an example of realistic and believable dialogue in paragraphs 3 and 4. The characters' words sound like the way a real brother and sister might talk to each another. For example, Joe casually says, "Hey Sis," and Sandy responds with a sentence fragment, "Haven't tried it yet." I'll write R.D. next to this part of the text for realistic and believable dialogue.

Ask: What other believable dialogue do you find in the story? (**Possible response:** line 48, "So, how did the new toy work out?" he teased.) What traits does the dialogue communicate about the character who says it? (Joe is a teasing but loving brother.)

Have students read and respond to the Student Model, using each Writer's Response Symbol at least once.

2 

First, students respond to the Student Model as a reader, using symbols to mark the text. They can mark the text using pop-up sticky notes in **Writing Coach Online™** or they can mark a printed copy of the Student Model.

3 

Then, students respond to the Student Model as a writer, using different symbols to mark the the text. They can use either **Writing Coach Online™** or a printed copy of the Student Model.

breakfast. As class started, Sandy looked out the window, wishing she was someplace sunny and warm. But she knew she had to be in school. So she leaned her forehead on her fist and tried to listen.

FLASH! She dropped into a desert of bright sun and hot sand. Dripping with sweat, Sandy thought about the cool lake where they swam each summer. As she wiped the sweat off her face, FLASH! and SPLASH! she landed in the middle of the freezing lake. Shivering and out of breath, Sandy wished herself back in her warm kitchen.

Nothing. The app had failed. Her IDP/D took over and dropped her, like a soaked sponge, back in school where she was supposed to be. There she stayed, cold and dripping, until the last bell.

After school she walked to the accessories store and had the new app removed. Back at home, Joe had already heard all about her adventure. "So, how did the new toy work out?" he teased.

"Just fine!" Sandy answered. "But I'm going to wait for the new and improved version before I try it again!"

2

Writing Coach Online

www.phwritingcoach.com

Interactive Model

Listen to an audio recording of the Student Model in the eText. Use the Reader's and Writer's Response Symbols with the eText tools to note what you read.

Use a Writer's Eye

Now, evaluate the piece as a writer. On your copy of the Student Model, use the Writer's Response Symbols to react to what you read.

Writer's Response Symbols	
R.D.	Realistic and believable dialogue
S.D.	Vivid sensory details that create imagery and suggest mood
W.C.	Well-developed, interesting characters
E.S.	Engaging story

Personalized Support

FEEDBACK

Teacher or Peer Feedback

To provide feedback to students on their responses to the Student Model, ask or have student partners ask one another the following:

- What is the thesis or controlling idea of the Student Model?
- How does the Student Model illustrate the characteristics of a problem-solution essay?
- Which feature or characteristic of the Student Model might you use in your own piece of writing?
- How could you alter or adapt this feature to make it your own?

Working with ELLs  Sheltered Instruction: Cognitive

To provide students with prereading supports to enhance comprehension of written texts, pre-teach key vocabulary. Read the title of the Student Model aloud and discuss predictions about its topic.

Beginning Write, say, and define these words and phrases from the passage: *earlobe, freezing, storm, toasty warm kitchen, shivering,* using gestures as needed. Help students read the model and use their knowledge of the words to enhance comprehension.

Intermediate Have small groups discuss the Beginning activity vocabulary. Then, have them define these words and phrases: *application* (as in *software application* for a computer), *whisked, foolproof, out of breath.* Before reading, have students share their definitions with Beginning students.

Advanced Give students a **Vocabulary Prediction Chart** with the words in the Beginning and Intermediate activities. Have pairs guess the meanings before reading, watch for context clues while reading, and confirm the meanings after reading.

Advanced High Have students complete the Advanced activity independently.

1 

Students select or are assigned a topic for their science fiction story from the Topic Bank, or they may choose a topic of their own.

2 STUDENT BOOK

Students complete online or printed graphic organizers to narrow the topic for their science fiction story.

Prewriting

Explain that the first task students need to complete as they plan their science fiction story is to determine an appropriate topic.

Choose From the Topic Bank

Read aloud each topic and then ask volunteers to describe them in their own words. If you are assigning topics to students, you may wish to do so now. Encourage students to ask questions about their topic.

Choose Your Own Topic

Introduce and discuss the Research and Discuss strategies. If students were not assigned writing topics, have them use the strategies to brainstorm for topics for their stories.

Extension Have each student choose one of the strategies. Then, have them write an action plan that outlines the resources and steps they will use to develop their topic.

Narrow Your Topic

Tell students that they will use a Narrow Your Topic graphic organizer to make their general topic more specific. Then, distribute printed copies or have students log on to Writing Coach Online.

Apply It! Guide students through the instructions for completing the graphic organizer. Have students complete the exercise based on their topic.

Consider Your Audience and Purpose

Guide students to consider the audience and purpose for their short story.

Feature Assignment Prewriting Feature Assignment Prewriti

Your Turn **Feature Assignment: Science Fiction Story**

Prewriting

Plan a first draft of your science fiction story by determining an appropriate topic. You can select from the Topic Bank or come up with an idea of your own.

Choose From the Topic Bank

TOPIC BANK

Living on the Moon Imagine living with other Earthlings in a colony on the moon. Where would you live? What would you eat? Write a science fiction story about your experiences.

New Technology Imagine an amazing technological breakthrough. Write a story about the invention and its effects on a group of characters.

The Alien and the Earthling Two characters—one human and one alien—become friends. Write a short story that explains how they meet and how their friendship grows.

Choose Your Own Topic

Determine an appropriate topic on your own by using the following **range of strategies** to generate ideas.

Research and Discuss

- Skim books or Web sites about the universe to find topics that spark your interest. Take notes on the topics that interest you.
- Research some technology you know well. What's ahead for this technology? How might people use it in the future?
- With a group, discuss some ways science could help, or harm, the world. Brainstorm for a list of possibilities. Monitor spoken language by asking follow-up questions to confirm your understanding.

Review your responses and choose a topic.

100 Short Story

Say: The second question in the first column asks what kinds of story lines my audience will find interesting. **If I choose** the second topic from the Topic Bank, about new technology, I will have to keep my audience in mind. For example, if my audience is students, they might be interested in a plot about advanced forms of familiar technology, such as computers or spacecraft.

Ask: Will your audience find your story line interesting? How can you make it more interesting for your readers? (Responses will vary.)

Have students with similar topics work in small groups to discuss and respond to the remaining questions.

Coach's Corner

You may wish to model prewriting activities for students by brainstorming for your own writing topic. Use these prompts to model your thought process:

- **I am interested in** living on the moon.
- **I can narrow my topic by** focusing on how the conditions on the moon affect the Earthlings' lives.

Discuss the choices you make and solicit feedback from students.

3 Writing Journal

Students record their answers to questions about audience and purpose in their online journals or notebooks.

Narrow Your Topic

Narrowing the topic of your story will help you focus your thinking to write a compelling story.

Apply It! Use a graphic organizer like the one shown to narrow your topic.

- Write the main topic of your story in the top box. Move down the chart, narrowing your topic.
- Your last box should hold the main focus of your plot.

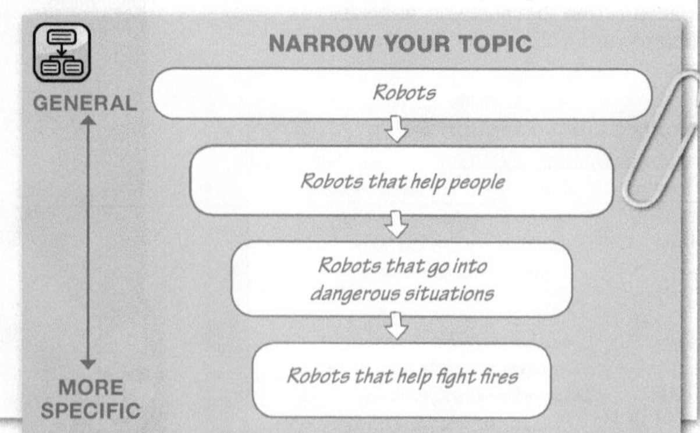

Interactive Graphic Organizers

Use the interactive graphic organizers to help you narrow your topic.

Online Journal

Try It! Record your answers and ideas in the online journal.

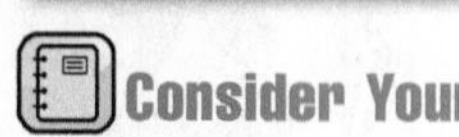

Consider Your Audience and Purpose

Before writing, think about your audience and purpose. Consider how the form you selected conveys the intended meaning to this audience. Consider the views of others as you ask these questions.

Questions for Audience	Questions for Purpose
• Who is my audience? • What kinds of story lines will my audience find interesting? • What will my audience need to know about science or technology to understand my science fiction story?	• Why am I writing the story? Do I want to entertain readers, make them think, or scare them? • What literary strategies and devices can I use to enhance the style and tone?

Record your answers in your writing journal.

Personalized Support

Interactive Graphic Organizer

Below Level Students complete three graphic organizers that provide models and scaffolded support.

On Level Students complete one, two, or three graphic organizers depending on how much support they need.

Above Level Students complete the least scaffolded graphic organizer or narrow their topic without the help of a graphic organizer.

Working with ELLs

ELL **Sheltered Instruction:** Cognitive

To aid students in choosing a topic, help them narrate events, describe people, places, or things, and explain situations with increasing specificity and detail. Write *What Happened?, Who Was There?, What Was It Like?, and Why Did It Happen?* on the board. Then:

Beginning Help students narrate, describe, and explain. Brainstorm for a science fiction event. Answer the questions on the board. Help students write short narrative, explanatory, and descriptive sentences.

Intermediate Have small groups use the questions to write sentences narrating, describing, and explaining an event. Have them share their writing aloud.

Advanced Have pairs write sentences answering the questions by narrating, describing, and explaining an event. Encourage students to be specific and to swap writing with another pair for feedback.

Advanced High Challenge students to write sentences narrating, describing, and explaining an event on their own. Tell students they can use their writing as a springboard for their science fiction story.

The Digital • Print Path

1 Using Writing Coach Online™ or the student book, students read and discuss the model graphic organizer.

2 Students complete online or printed graphic organizers to develop their ideas and gather details.

Plan Your Piece

Explain that writers use graphic organizers to develop their ideas and show relationships between different parts of the text. Then, point out the Develop Your Science Fiction Story graphic organizer on page 102. Tell students that they will use this organizer to outline their science fiction story. Then, distribute printed copies or have students log on to Writing Coach Online.

Introduce the graphic organizer by explaining that the column on the left lists the information to be entered in the column on the right. The first row defines the main character and the story's science fiction focus, while the next three rows identify the three main parts of a story plot.

Develop an Engaging Story Line Guide students to understand that the main character in the example organizer has a clear role in the plot of the story. The setting and main conflict, or problem, are also well defined on the chart. Have students describe a main character, setting, and problem that are specific enough to form the basis of an engaging story and enter them on their graphic organizer.

Organize Your Science Fiction Story Guide students to use the graphic organizer to develop the events that will occur in each part of their story.

Say: I notice that the organizer has helped the writer organize the story's plot. For example, the conflict between the robot and the distrusting firefighters is introduced in the Beginning. The conflict is resolved in the End, after the robot saves a human life.

Ask: What events might happen to these characters in the middle of the story, leading to the main problem being solved? (Responses will vary.) How might you arrange these events to make the action of the story suspenseful and well-paced? (Responses will vary.)

Have students work individually to brainstorm for the events that will occur in the beginning, middle, and end of their story, and then record them on their graphic organizers.

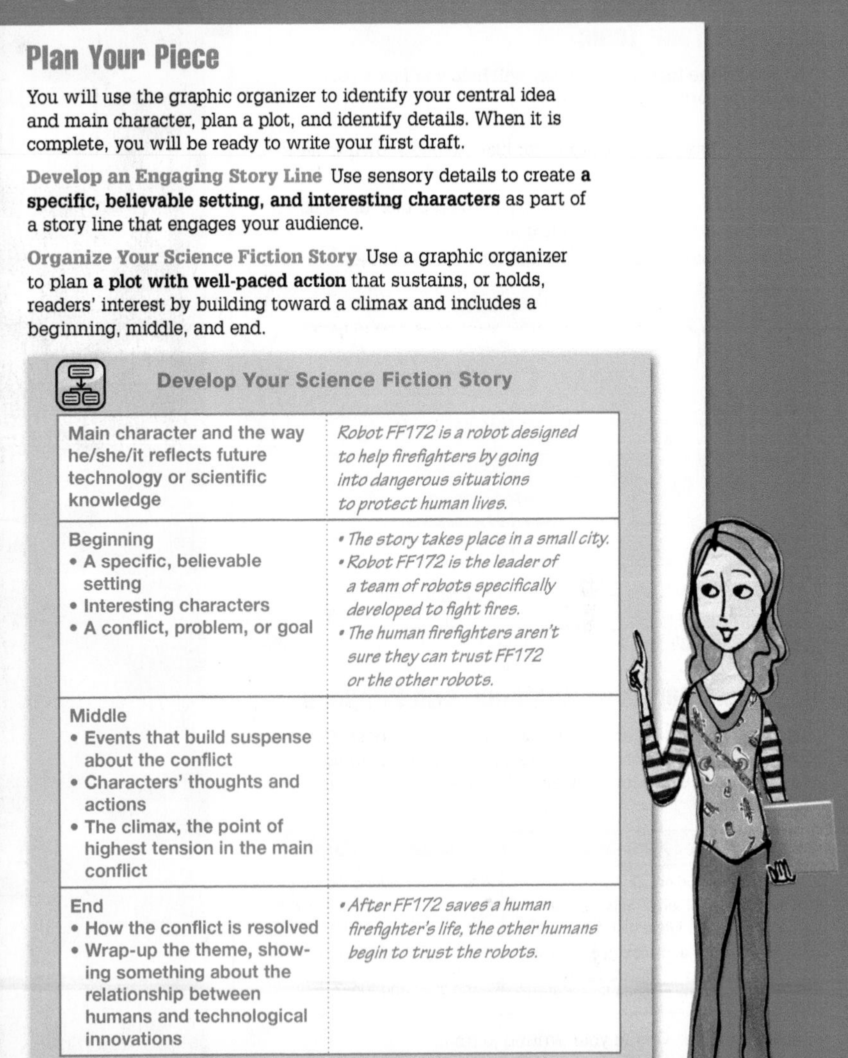

Feature Assignment Prewriting Feature Assignment Prewriting

Plan Your Piece

You will use the graphic organizer to identify your central idea and main character, plan a plot, and identify details. When it is complete, you will be ready to write your first draft.

Develop an Engaging Story Line Use sensory details to create **a specific, believable setting, and interesting characters** as part of a story line that engages your audience.

Organize Your Science Fiction Story Use a graphic organizer to plan **a plot with well-paced action** that sustains, or holds, readers' interest by building toward a climax and includes a beginning, middle, and end.

Develop Your Science Fiction Story

Main character and the way he/she/it reflects future technology or scientific knowledge	*Robot FF172 is a robot designed to help firefighters by going into dangerous situations to protect human lives.*
Beginning • A specific, believable setting • Interesting characters • A conflict, problem, or goal	*• The story takes place in a small city.* *• Robot FF172 is the leader of a team of robots specifically developed to fight fires.* *• The human firefighters aren't sure they can trust FF172 or the other robots.*
Middle • Events that build suspense about the conflict • Characters' thoughts and actions • The climax, the point of highest tension in the main conflict	
End • How the conflict is resolved • Wrap-up the theme, showing something about the relationship between humans and technological innovations	*• After FF172 saves a human firefighter's life, the other humans begin to trust the robots.*

102 Short Story

Gather Details

Remind students that vivid details and strategies such as suspense add interest to a story. Ask volunteers to read aloud each kind of detail and literary device and its example. Then, discuss where in the plot each device is most likely to occur.

Try It! Help students see that the first paragraph includes a flashback and sensory details. The second has foreshadowing.

Apply It! Read aloud the bulleted instructions for using details. Then, have students develop flashback, foreshadowing, and sensory details for their story and enter them on their graphic organizer. Remind students to use a variety of details.

Writer's Block

IF students have difficulty developing events for each part of their story . . .

THEN ask students to identify where the events of a familiar story would be placed on the graphic organizer.

3 STUDENT BOOK

Students refer back to the Mentor Text or the Student Model as they plan their writing.

Gather Details

To make the audience want to keep reading, develop interesting characters and a believable setting through the use of **sensory details.** Use details that appeal to the senses of:

- **Sight:** *Snow-white foam blanketed the fire.*
- **Sound:** *The clanging fire alarm rang in our ears.*
- **Taste:** *I craved the fresh, crisp taste of an apple.*
- **Smell:** *The pungent smell of smoke stuck to her clothes.*
- **Touch:** *Water splashed against his skin, cooling his face.*

Writers also use a **range of literary strategies and devices to enhance the style and tone** of a story.

- **Flashback:** *The chief remembered the time before they had robots: Every firefighter at the station went into the danger zone.*
- **Foreshadowing:** *Tran laughed, "You mean someday you might save my life? Right."*
- **Suspense:** *The beam crashed down and blocked the doorway.*

Try It! Read the Student Model excerpt and identify which kinds of details and devices the author uses.

STUDENT MODEL from **Be Careful Where You Wish For** page 98; lines 19–26

FLASH! Sandy was freezing in the yard in a storm. Icy rain ran down her neck. She thought about her toasty warm kitchen, tapped her forehead, and FLASH! She was immediately back at the kitchen table.

Joe was laughing. "What happens if you're whisked away in the middle of a class like a crumb off a table?"

Apply It! Review the types of details and literary strategies a short story writer can use. Then, include at least one sensory detail and literary strategy or device for each story section.

- Plan to include flashback and foreshadowing **to enhance the style and tone of your story.**
- Be sure to **use sensory details that help create a realistic setting** or help build suspense.

www.phwritingcoach.com

Interactive Graphic Organizers

Use the interactive graphic organizers to help you create a plan for your writing.

Interactive Model

Refer back to the Interactive Model in the eText as you plan your writing.

Personalized Support

Interactive Graphic Organizer

Below Level Students complete three graphic organizers that provide models and scaffolded support.

On Level Students complete one, two, or three graphic organizers depending on how much support they need.

Above Level Students complete the least scaffolded graphic organizer or narrow their topic without the help of a graphic organizer.

Teacher or Peer Feedback

To provide feedback to students as they plan their first draft, ask or have student partners ask one another the following:

- What do you want your audience to know about the topic?
- What questions or concerns will your audience have about the topic?
- What details have you identified for your piece? How do these details support your thesis or controlling idea?
- Are your details varied? Will they interest your readers? Explain.

Differentiated Instruction

RTI Strategy for Below-Level Students Help students understand the role of conflict in a plot. First, explain that a conflict is a problem between people or within a person. Give examples of each. For example, two sisters want to watch different television shows, or a boy wishes he could play basketball better. Then, help students brainstorm for conflicts for each topic in the Topic Bank on page 100. Emphasize that a conflict makes a short story interesting and suspenseful.

Strategy for Spanish Speakers Students whose home language is Spanish may not have a wide range of sensory vocabulary in English. Have students work in small groups to brainstorm Spanish words related to each sense. For example, for smell, they may come up with *aroma* (aroma), *quemado* (burnt), and *perfumado* (perfumed). Then have groups work together to find the English equivalents, using a dictionary if necessary. Encourage students to keep a list of the words for their reference.

1 

Using Writing Coach Online™ or the student book, students read and discuss the Outline for Success for a short story.

2 

Students discuss how the Mentor Text illustrates the characteristics of a short story.

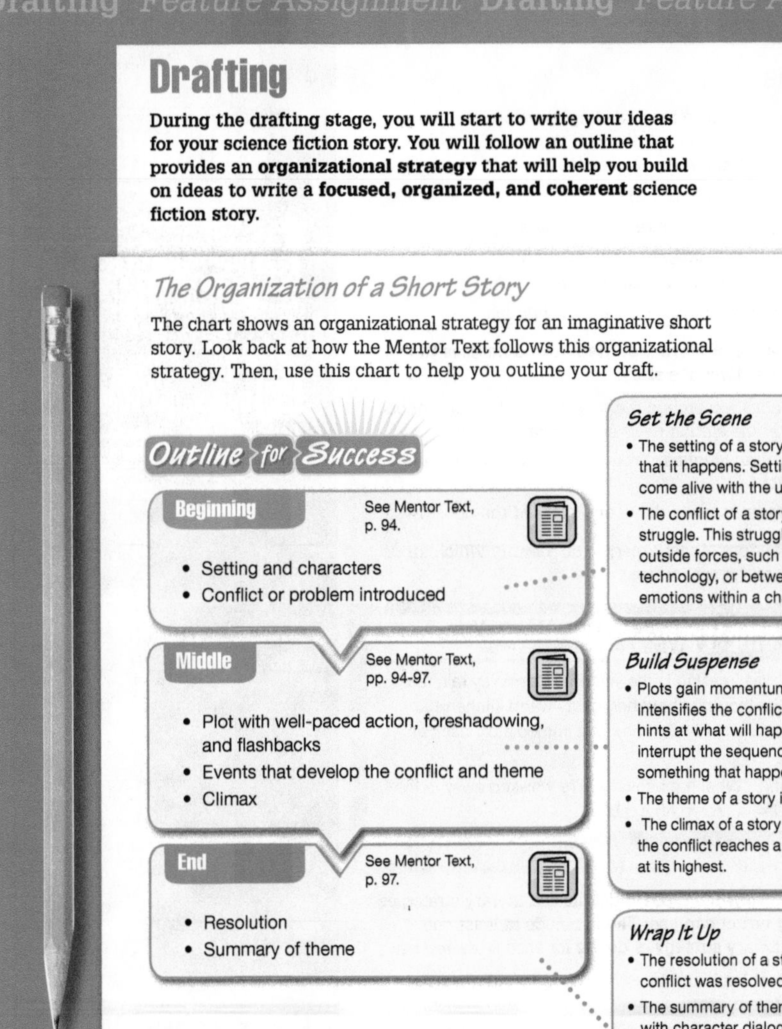

Drafting *Feature Assignment* Drafting *Feature Assignment* Dr

Drafting

During the drafting stage, you will start to write your ideas for your science fiction story. You will follow an outline that provides an organizational strategy that will help you build on ideas to write a focused, organized, and coherent science fiction story.

The Organization of a Short Story

The chart shows an organizational strategy for an imaginative short story. Look back at how the Mentor Text follows this organizational strategy. Then, use this chart to help you outline your draft.

Outline for Success

Beginning See Mentor Text, p. 94.

- Setting and characters
- Conflict or problem introduced

Middle See Mentor Text, pp. 94-97.

- Plot with well-paced action, foreshadowing, and flashbacks
- Events that develop the conflict and theme
- Climax

End See Mentor Text, p. 97.

- Resolution
- Summary of theme

Set the Scene
- The setting of a story is the place and time that it happens. Settings and characters come alive with the use of sensory details.
- The conflict of a story is a problem or struggle. This struggle can be between outside forces, such as humans and technology, or between conflicting emotions within a character.

Build Suspense
- Plots gain momentum as each event intensifies the conflict. Foreshadowing hints at what will happen later. Flashbacks interrupt the sequence of events to show something that happened earlier.
- The theme of a story is its central idea.
- The climax of a story is the point at which the conflict reaches a crisis and suspense is at its highest.

Wrap It Up
- The resolution of a story tells how the conflict was resolved.
- The summary of theme can be shown with character dialogue, an action, or a general statement.

104 Short Story

Drafting

Outline for Success

Explain that the Outline for Success shows an organizational strategy for a short story. Students will use the Outline to write a focused, organized, and coherent draft of their science fiction story.

Beginning

Link the Outline to a specific science fiction story by having students turn to the Mentor Text on pages 94–97. Ask a volunteer to read aloud the first four paragraphs. Then, guide students to understand how the author uses details to introduce the characters.

Say: I see that the author begins the story with details about the setting. For example, lines 2–5 provide details about the "beautiful, grassy area" and "small lake" where the boys make camp. Lines 11–14 provide more details about the items the boys will use to make camp, such as tents and material for a fire pit. From these details, I can tell that the story is set in modern times.

Ask: What other elements of the story are introduced in lines 1–24? (setting, conflict)

Have students work with a partner to evaluate the details they entered next to Beginning on their graphic organizers.

Middle

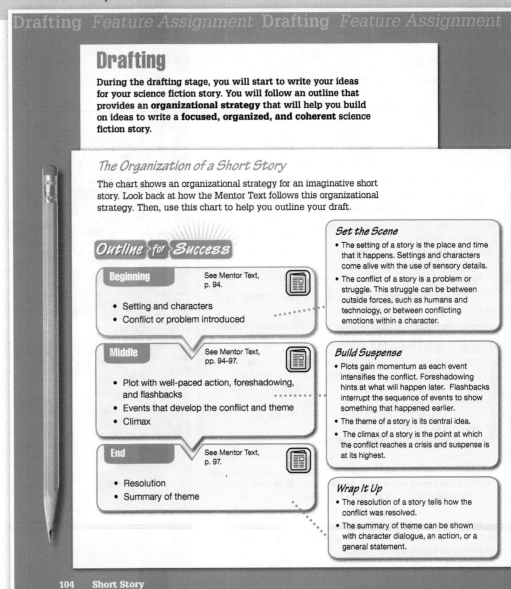

Lead a discussion about how the middle paragraphs of the Mentor Text reflect the characteristics of a science fiction story.

- Plot with well-paced action (lines 6–7, 13–14, 18–19, 32–34, 43–49, 70–71, 80–83, 89–90, 114–117) including foreshadowing (lines 23–24, 33–34, 41, 59–60)
- Events that develop the conflict and theme (lines 22–23, 28–29, 33–34, 41, 48–49, 77–78, 99–115)
- Climax (lines 77–98)

End

Have small groups discuss how the end of the Mentor Text reflects the characteristics of a science fiction story (lines 131–135).

Start Your Draft

Have small groups read aloud and discuss the boxed instructions for drafting. Direct students to work individually on their first draft.

Coach's Corner

If you are modeling the writing process for students with your own topic or a student volunteer's, you may wish to use these prompts to guide your drafting and discussion:

- **To introduce the setting, I will** give details about my story's time and place.
- **I will build suspense by** using foreshadowing.

Discuss the choices you make and solicit feedback from students.

3 

Students begin writing their science fiction story online or in their notebooks.

4

Students share their work with their teacher.

5 FEEDBACK

Students receive feedback from their teacher. Students may continue to work on their drafts.

Start Your Draft

Use this checklist to help you complete your draft. Use the graphic organizer that shows the beginning, middle, and end, as well as the Outline for Success as guides.

While drafting, aim at writing your ideas, not on making your writing perfect. Remember, you will have the chance to improve your draft when you revise and edit.

- √ Start by drafting the opening of your imaginative story. Describe the setting and characters. Include specific details that will **sustain reader interest.**
- √ Set up the **conflict,** or problem, to come.

- √ Create a specific, **believable setting** and an engaging story line by building curiosity or suspense. Use vivid words and **sensory details** to help readers experience what the characters experience.
- √ Create and develop **interesting characters** who respond to each situation based on their individual personalities.
- √ Keep the action moving at a good **pace** and focused on the conflict. Describe events in time order, building to the climax.
- √ Try to use a **range of literary strategies** and devices, such as foreshadowing and flashbacks, to enhance the style and tone of your writing.

- √ Finish by describing how the conflict is resolved or the problem is **solved** and by showing how the character's ideas or feelings have changed as a result of the story events.

Interactive Model

Outline for Success Refer back to Mentor Text in the eText as you write your draft.

Personalized Support

Teacher or Peer Feedback

To provide feedback to students on their first draft, ask or have student partners ask one another the following:

- Can you explain how you organized your ideas in this piece?
- Why did you include this information here?
- Why did you choose this beginning? Does it introduce the conflict?
- What supporting details could you add here?
- Why did you choose this ending? How does it add to your piece?
- Can you show me a place where I can hear your unique voice?
- Can you show me a place where you used vivid language?

Working with ELLs

ELL Sheltered Instruction: Cognitive

Help students in the drafting process by having them narrate events, describe people, and explain situations aloud with increasing specificity and detail. Tell students that including specific details will help them communicate clearly. Then:

Beginning Have students narrate aloud events that took place after school yesterday, describe at least two people or things involved in the events, and explain what the situation was like. Help them complete sentence starters: *After school yesterday, I ______. I saw ______. The events made me feel ______.*

Intermediate Have groups complete the Beginning activity. Encourage listeners to provide constructive feedback about students' use of details.

Advanced Have partners narrate aloud the events of a day they remember, describing the people involved and explaining why it was memorable. Have listeners ask questions about specific details.

Advanced High Have students complete the Advanced activity and incorporate listeners' feedback into a new oral telling.

1 

Using Writing Coach Online™ or the student book, students study the first and second drafts of the student model to see how the writer used Revision RADaR to improve his or her writing.

2 

Students use the Revision RADaR strategy to revise their own writing.

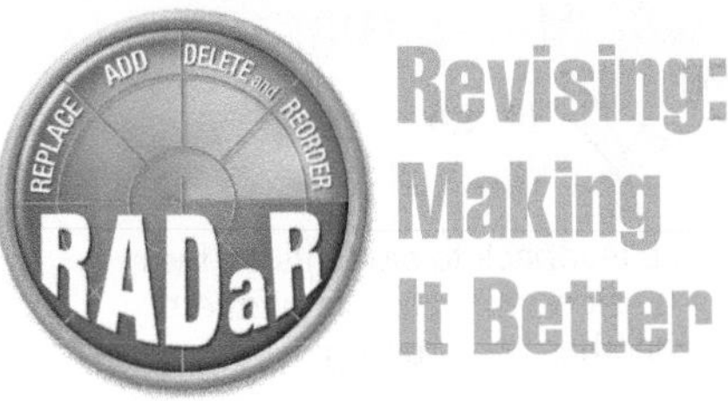

Revising: Making It Better

Point out the page title to students and explain that revising means making improvements to a writing draft. Then, read aloud the opening paragraph to introduce the Revision RADaR strategies. You may wish to have students review Chapter 3 for more information on Revision RADaR.

Kelly Gallagher, M. Ed.

KEEP REVISION ON YOUR RADaR

1ST DRAFT After students have read the first draft, have them turn to page 104 and review the Outline for Success. Work with students to understand that the questions the author asked about the draft are based on the characteristics of a short story. For example, call out the first question and note how it addresses the elements listed in the Beginning section in the Outline for Success.

Then, have students work in small groups to develop other questions about the draft based on the genre characteristics.

2ND DRAFT Guide students to understand how the author used the RADaR strategies to revise the first draft.

I noticed that the first paragraph introduces Sandy, the main character. It doesn't make Sandy sound very interesting, though. In the 2nd draft, however, I see an *A* next to the first paragraph, meaning that the author added details to tell more about Sandy. The new passage "Yes! It was there!" expresses Sandy's enthusiasm. Now the paragraph introduces Sandy in a way that grabs the readers' attention.

Work with students to brainstorm for other ways of introducing the main characters in an interesting way.

Revising: Making It Better

Now that you have finished your first draft, you are ready to revise. Think about the "big picture" of audience, purpose, and genre. You can use the Revision RADaR strategy as a guide for making changes to improve your draft. Revision RADaR provides four major ways to improve your writing: (R) replace, (A) add, (D) delete, and (R) reorder.

Kelly Gallagher, M. Ed.

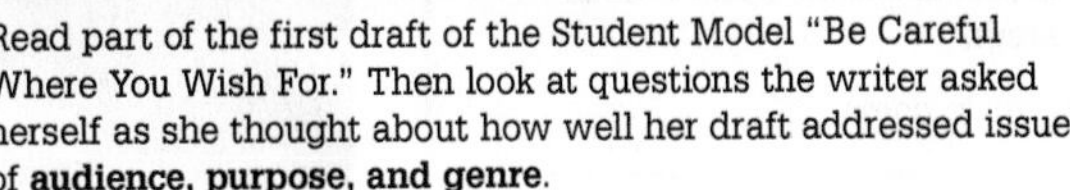

KEEP REVISION ON YOUR RADaR

Read part of the first draft of the Student Model "Be Careful Where You Wish For." Then look at questions the writer asked herself as she thought about how well her draft addressed issues of **audience, purpose, and genre**.

Be Careful Where You Wish For — 1ST DRAFT

Sandy's IDP/D woke her up on time, of course. She carefully checked the top of her earlobe. She felt the new application for her Internal Daily Planner/ Doer (IDP/D). Her IDP/D made sure she was always where she was supposed to be on time. This new app would take her wherever she wished to go!

Does my opening introduce an interesting main character?

Sandy found her brother Joe in the kitchen, stirring steamy oatmeal. He was kind of an anti-techno-geek who liked to do things on his own.

"Good morning, Sandy," Joe said. "How is your new IDP/D application? Is it as great as you hoped?"

Does my dialogue help develop the story and enhance the tone?

"Haven't tried it yet," Sandy yawned. "I'm still too sleepy to think. But wait: I'd like to have breakfast in the yard." Nothing happened. Then Sandy tapped her forehead.

Are my events arranged in chronological order?

FLASH! Sandy was freezing in the yard in a storm. She had remembered the new app's default check. She had to tap her forehead to confirm her wish.

Have students work in small groups to discuss the other changes in the 2nd draft.

Apply It! Review the bulleted instructions for using Revision RADaR. Remind students to question their drafts based on the genre characteristics listed on the Outline for Success on page 104. Tell students to use each RADaR strategy at least once.

Coach's Corner

If you are modeling the writing process with your own draft or a student volunteer's, use these prompts to focus on the Revision RADaR *Replace* strategy:

- **I replaced vague details because** I want to interest my readers.
- **I replaced narration with dialogue that** helps show what the characters are like.

Discuss the choices you make and solicit feedback from students.

3 Students share their work with their teacher.

4 Students receive feedback from their teacher. Students may continue to revise their drafts.

Now look at how the writer applied Revision RADaR to write an improved second draft.

Be Careful Where You Wish For

2ND DRAFT

Sandy's IDP/D woke her up on time, of course. She carefully checked the top of her earlobe. Yes! It was there! Now she was one of the first to have latest application for her Internal Daily Planner/ Doer (IDP/D). Her IDP/D made sure she was always where she was supposed to be on time. This new app would take her wherever she wished to go!

Sandy found her brother Joe in the kitchen, stirring steamy oatmeal. He was kind of an anti-techno-geek who liked to do things on his own.

"Hey Sis, how's that new app working for you?" Joe asked a little meanly. "Is it living up to the commercials' promises?"

"Haven't tried it yet," Sandy yawned. "But wait: I'd like to have breakfast in the yard." Nothing happened. Then Sandy remembered the new app's default check. She tapped her forehead to confirm her wish.

FLASH! Sandy was freezing in the yard in a storm.

A *Added details describing Sandy's attitude toward her new app to better develop her character*

R *Replaced boring dialogue with realistic dialogue that reflects characters' attitudes and tone*

D *Deleted the unnecessary words I'm still too sleepy to think*

R *Reordered sentences to keep events in chronological order*

WRITING COACH Online

www.phwritingcoach.com

Video

Learn more strategies for effective writing from program author Kelly Gallagher.

Apply It! Use your Revision RADaR to revise your draft.

- First, determine if you have engaged your audience, created a specific setting, developed interesting characters, and made the conflict or problem clear.
- Then apply the Revision RADaR strategy to make needed changes. Remember—you can use the steps in the strategy in any order.

Personalized Support

Teacher or Peer Feedback

To provide feedback to students as they revise their first draft, ask or have student partners ask one another the following:

- Can you show me where you revised your text?
- What could you add to your introduction to grab the interest of your readers?
- How could you reorder these ideas so that their order is more logical?
- Have you included all the characteristics of this form of writing?
- Is there any unnecessary text that you could delete?
- Have you achieved your purpose with this piece of writing?
- Have you addressed the questions and concerns of your audience?

Working with ELLs

ELL Sheltered Instruction: Cognitive

Students should show an increasing ability to distinguish between formal and informal English and an increasing knowledge of when to use each. Have them adapt spoken language appropriately for informal purposes. Direct students to identify which situations call for formal and informal language, and put each in a T-chart labeled *Formal* and *Informal:* talking to a friend, giving a speech, etc. Then:

Beginning Say short sentences (*What's up?*) and have students say, *formal* or *informal*. Help students adapt formal sentences for informal purposes.

Intermediate Say formal and informal sentences. Have a volunteer adapt the sentence orally for informal purposes or identify the sentence as *already informal*.

Advanced Have pairs take turns reading the sentences from the Intermediate activity. Listeners should identify sentences as formal or informal and adapt the formal language for informal purposes.

Advanced High Have students complete the Advanced activity, then write their own formal and informal sentences. Have partners check each other's work.

The Digital • Print Path

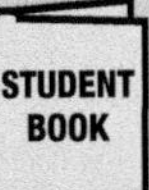

1 

Using Writing Coach Online™ or the student book, students study and discuss the revision chart.

2 

In a video by program author Kelly Gallagher, students learn more strategies for effective writing.

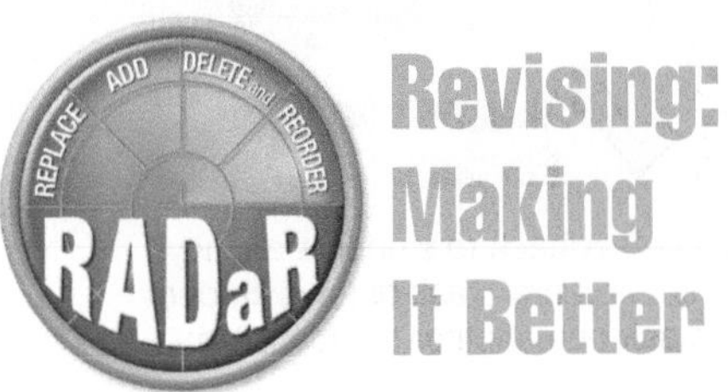

Revising: Making It Better

Look at the Big Picture

Introduce the revision chart to students. Explain that the Section column identifies the three main parts of a short story. The Evaluate column identifies the characteristics found in each section and explains how to assess them. The Revise column presents specific strategies for revising each characteristic.

Then, have students draw lines between and label the three sections of their drafts. Direct students to work individually to evaluate and revise their draft, using the chart to guide their work.

Look at the Big Picture

Use the chart and your analytical skills to evaluate how well each section of your short story addresses **purpose**, **audience**, and **genre**. When necessary, use the suggestions in the chart to revise your story.

Section	Evaluate	Revise
Beginning	• Check the **opening**. Does it introduce an engaging story line? Will it grab readers' attention and make them want to read more?	• Include details about a character, the setting, or the culture that lets readers know this is science fiction. Use precise word choice and vivid images.
	• Make sure that the **conflict** or problem has been introduced.	• Include dialogue, action, and characters' thoughts to help set up the conflict.
	• Check that the **setting** is specific and believable and the characters are realistic and interesting.	• Use sensory and other details to specifically and believably describe the characters, their surroundings, and the technology they use.
Middle	• Check that the **action** is well-paced and the **plot** coherent.	• Present events in time order leading up to the climax.
	• Number in order the **events** that build suspense. Make sure they all build to the **climax**.	• Reorder details as necessary to better build suspense. Take out or replace details that don't contribute to building the story.
	• Use **literary strategies** and **devices** to reinforce the **style** and **tone** of your story.	• Add elements like foreshadowing and flashback to help create suspense.
Conclusion	• Check that **loose ends** of the story are tied up.	• Add details that answer questions such as *What happened then? How did the characters think or act after the climax?*
	• Make sure you sum up the **theme**.	• Add dialogue, events, or a character's thoughts to show how the story illustrates the theme.

Focus on Craft: Internal and External Coherence

Have students read the introductory text. Guide students to understand that internal coherence should exist within each paragraph of a story, while external coherence should exist among all the paragraphs of the story.

Say: I notice that the Student Model paragraph describes two actions taken by the main character, Sandy, and describes her thoughts after each one. The sentences are in logical order; they fit together and make sense as I read them.

Ask: How do the words in capital letters help give the paragraph internal coherence? (The words *FLASH* and *SPLASH* indicate when the character is being transported to a different place.)

Have students work with a partner to discuss how the sensory details help give the paragraph internal coherence.

Try It! Have students discuss the questions and record responses in their journals. Follow up with students to check that their responses reflect an understanding of how each sentence in a paragraph works together to support a central idea.

Fine-Tune Your Draft

Apply It! Ask volunteers to read aloud the instructions for fine-tuning their drafts. Then, have students work in pairs to ensure that their drafts have coherence, imagery, and a consistent point of view.

Peer Feedback Have students identify Mentor Text examples of the characteristics that were marked for improvement. Use the Mentor Text references on page T104 to guide students to appropriate examples.

Teacher Tip

Have students make sketches to storyboard the action in each paragraph or section of their story. They can then work with partners to evaluate the coherence of the story events.

3 

Using Writing Coach Online™ or the student book, students refer back to the Mentor Text or Student Model for examples of writer's craft.

4 

Students record answers to questions about writer's craft in their online journals or notebooks.

5 

Students share their work with their teacher.

6 

Students receive feedback from their teacher.

Focus on Craft: Internal and External Coherence

Coherence in a piece of writing means that all the parts fit together, support the central idea, and make sense. In a paragraph with **internal coherence**, the sentences follow one another in logical order and all support the central idea of that paragraph. In a composition with **external coherence**, the paragraphs all fit together logically and support the central idea of the story as a whole.

Think about internal and external coherence as you read the excerpt from the Student Model.

from **Be Careful Where You Wish For** page 99; lines 34–40

FLASH! She dropped into a desert of bright sun and hot sand. Dripping with sweat, Sandy thought about the cool lake where they swam each summer. As she wiped the sweat off her face, FLASH! and SPLASH! she landed in the middle of the freezing lake. Shivering and out of breath, Sandy wished herself back in her warm kitchen.

Try It! Now, ask yourself these questions. Record your answers in your journal.

- What is the topic—or central idea—of this paragraph?
- How does each sentence support the central idea? Explain.

Online Journal

Try It! Record your answers in the online journal.

Interactive Model

Refer back to the Interactive Model as you revise your writing.

Fine-Tune Your Draft

Apply It! Use the revision suggestions to prepare your final draft.

- **Ensure Internal and External Coherence** Make sure that ideas, sentences, and paragraphs are organized in a logical sequence and that they flow easily.
- **Ensure Vivid Images** Substitute vivid images for vague or boring words and phrases. For example, change *waited nervously* to *drummed her fingers nervously on the table.*
- **Ensure Consistent Point of View** Make sure that the same person, or voice, tells the whole story.

Peer Feedback Read your final draft to a group of peers. Ask if you have **sustained their interest**. Think about their responses and revise your final draft as needed.

Personalized Support

Teacher or Peer Feedback

To provide feedback to students as they continue to revise their first draft, ask or have student partners ask one another the following:

- What are you trying to say here? What part of the text could you replace to make your meaning clearer?
- Is there a more precise word you could use here?
- How does the rhythm of these sentences sound to you? Could you make the length and structure of these sentences more varied?
- How could you include transitional words and phrases here to help your reader understand these ideas?
- Are there details you could add here to make this part come alive?

Differentiated Instruction

RTI Strategy for Special Needs Students

Help students understand the difference between boring descriptions and vivid images. Display a picture, for example of an interesting landscape. Ask students to make up a sentence describing it. Then, discuss ways to improve the description. For example, *The snow looks pretty* could be revised to *The powdery snow glitters like silver in the glaring sunshine.* Continue showing pictures and brainstorming for vivid sensory images. Encourage students to make similar revisions to their stories.

Enrichment for Gifted/Talented Students

Have students work in pairs to find several examples of foreshadowing and flashback in stories they have read. Ask them to read one or two examples aloud to the entire group and explain how these devices increase the interest and suspense of a story. Then, encourage students to add an additional example of one of these devices to their own stories. Have them meet again with their partners to discuss how the devices affect their stories.

1 

In a video by program author Jeff Anderson, students learn effective editing techniques.

2 

Students record answers to questions about writer's craft in their online journals or notebooks.

Editing: Making It Correct

Explain that students will edit their drafts for proper grammar, mechanics, and spelling, including pronoun references.

WRITE GUY *Jeff Anderson, M.Ed.*

WHAT DO YOU NOTICE?

Introduce students to correct pronoun-antecedent usage by reading aloud the Student Model excerpt and discussing responses to the "Ask yourself" question that follows. Then, guide them to identify and use clear antecedents for pronouns.

Say: In the second sentence of the Student Model excerpt, **I notice** the pronoun *they.* When I look for its antecedent I find only singular nouns. The two sentences contain no nouns that could be referred to by the plural pronoun *they.*

Ask: How can the second sentence be revised for clear pronoun reference? ("Dripping with sweat, Sandy thought about the cool lake where she and her family swam...")

Have students write a sentence about Luis and one of the other characters in the Mentor Text story. Write some of the sentences on the board and check for vague pronoun references. You may also wish to have students turn to Chapter 23 of the Grammar Handbook to learn more about clear pronoun references.

Editing *Feature Assignment* Editing *Feature Assignment*

Editing: Making It Correct

Editing your draft means polishing your work and correcting errors. You may want to read through your work several times, looking for different errors and issues each time.

Before editing your draft, review any pronouns you have used in your writing. Each pronoun must have a clear antecedent, or a clearly stated person, place, or thing that the pronoun later replaces. For example, look at these sentences: *Karen and Walter missed the bus. They were late for school.* The pronoun *they* clearly refers to Karen and Walter. Now look at these sentences: *I am going away for the weekend with my family. It should be fun!* The antecedent for *it* is unclear. The second sentence could be corrected this way: *The trip should be fun!*

WRITE GUY *Jeff Anderson, M. Ed.*

WHAT DO YOU NOTICE?

Zoom in on Conventions Focus on the use of pronouns as you read these sentences from the Student Model.

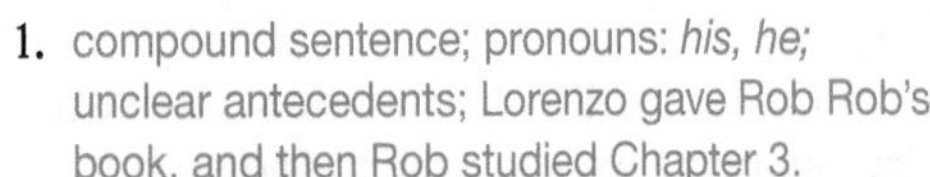

She dropped into a desert of bright sun and hot sand. Dripping with sweat, Sandy thought about the cool lake where they swam each summer.

To learn more about pronouns, see Chapter 23 of your Grammar Handbook.

Now, ask yourself: Which sentence contains a vague pronoun reference?

Perhaps you chose the second sentence, which contains a vague pronoun reference. It is unclear as to whom the pronoun *they* is referring. To correct this vague pronoun reference, the sentence would read: *Dripping with sweat, Sandy thought about the cool lake where she and her family swam each summer.* In this sentence, the antecedent *she* is clear and the vague pronoun *they* is replaced by the specific noun *family.*

It is important to make the antecedents of your pronouns clear when you write. If you have vague pronoun references in your writing, your readers may be confused. Because of this, they will be less likely to want to continue reading your work.

110 Short Story

Grammar Mini-Lesson: Antecedents

Discuss the paragraph and the Student Model excerpt on page 111 with students. Guide them to understand that the use of pronouns and antecedents helps make the writing coherent.

Try It! Have students work with a partner to identify the complex sentence, underline each pronoun, identify its antecedent, and correct unclear pronoun references.

1. compound sentence; pronouns: *his, he;* unclear antecedents; Lorenzo gave Rob Rob's book, and then Rob studied Chapter 3.
2. complex sentence; pronoun: *he;* antecedent: *Rob*

Apply It! Remind students to look closely for correct pronoun-antecedent usage as they edit.

Use the Rubric Explain that students will rate how well their draft addresses the elements of a science fiction story on a scale of 1 to 6, with 6 being the best score.

Then, have students use the rubric to evaluate their drafts. Tell them to support their rankings with concrete examples. Students should then revise their drafts as necessary.

Writer's Block

IF students have difficulty using clear pronoun references in their drafts . . .

THEN have them circle each pronoun, underline its antecedent, and check that the reference is clear.

3 

Using Writing Coach Online™ or the student book, students refer back to the Mentor Text or Student Model as they edit their writing.

4 

Using Writing Coach Online™ or the student book, students evaluate their writing using the rubrics.

5 

Students submit edited drafts to their teacher.

6 

Students receive personalized feedback from their teacher.

Grammar Mini-Lesson: Antecedents

To learn more, see Chapter 13.

A **pronoun** is a word that stands for or replaces a noun or another pronoun. The noun that is being replaced is called the **antecedent.** Often, the antecedent appears in a sentence before the pronoun does. Notice how the use of pronouns and antecedents in the Student Model helps keep the writing coherent.

STUDENT MODEL from **Be Careful Where You Wish For** page 98; lines 1–7

Sandy's IDP/D woke her up on time, of course. She carefully checked the top of her earlobe.... This new app would take her wherever she wished to go!

Try It! Underline each pronoun and identify its antecedent. If the antecedent is unclear, rewrite to clarify the pronoun-antecedent relationship. Write the answers in your journal.

1. Lorenzo gave Rob his book, and then he studied Chapter 3. *(compound sentence)*
2. Rob turned in the report that he completed the night before. *(complex sentence)*

Apply It! Edit your draft for **grammar, mechanics, capitalization, and spelling.** If necessary, rewrite sentences to make sure you have used **pronouns** with clear **antecedents.**

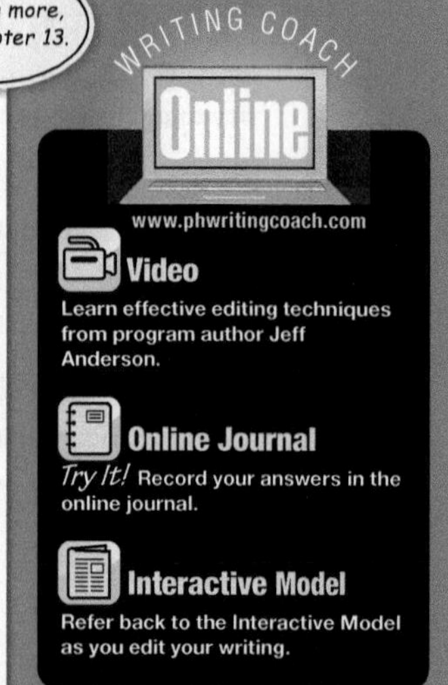

www.phwritingcoach.com

Video

Learn effective editing techniques from program author Jeff Anderson.

Online Journal

Try It! Record your answers in the online journal.

Interactive Model

Refer back to the Interactive Model as you edit your writing.

Use the rubric to evaluate your piece. If necessary, rethink, rewrite, or revise.

Rubric for Short Story: Science Fiction	Rating Scale
Ideas: How well have you developed your characters and plot?	Not very — Very 1 2 3 4 5 6
Organization: How clearly organized is the sequence of events in your story?	1 2 3 4 5 6
Voice: How well does your style engage the reader?	1 2 3 4 5 6
Word Choice: How effective is your word choice in creating setting and characters?	1 2 3 4 5 6
Sentence Fluency: How well have you developed coherence in your writing?	1 2 3 4 5 6
Conventions: How correct are your pronouns and antecedents?	1 2 3 4 5 6

Personalized Support

Teacher or Peer Feedback

To provide feedback to students as they edit their draft, ask or have student partners ask one another the following:

- Have you looked for mistakes that you tend to make?
- Have you read your piece aloud to yourself or to a partner? What kind of errors did you find?
- Can you show me something you changed through editing?
- What resources have you used to look for possible spelling errors?
- Read this sentence aloud. Does the grammar sound correct to you?
- Read this sentence aloud. Does the punctuation accurately convey your meaning?

Working with ELLs ELL Sheltered Instruction: Metacognitive

As students revise, they should monitor and edit writing for pronoun-antecedent agreement, using self-corrective techniques. Review rules about pronoun-antecedent agreement as you revise the sentence *The students went to his desks.* Then:

Beginning Write a list of pronouns on the board. Then, help students use the self-corrective technique of highlighting pronouns and circling antecedents to check agreement in their work.

Intermediate Have students review their writing, using the self-corrective technique described in the Beginning activity with the help of an Advanced High student.

Advanced Have students use the self-corrective technique described in the Beginning activity to check agreement in their drafts. Have them swap stories with a partner, and double-check pronoun-antecedent agreement.

Advanced High Have students complete the Advanced activity, then help an Intermediate student check pronoun-antecedent agreement. Encourage students to provide specific feedback.

The Digital • Print Path

1 

Using Writing Coach Online™ or the student book, students complete the writing process by deciding the best way to publish their writing for their intended audience.

2 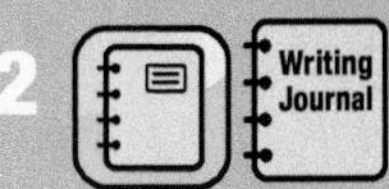

Students record their answers to Reflect on Your Writing in their online journals or notebooks.

Publishing

Wrap Up Your Presentation

Remind students who handwrote their work to use proper margins. For students who wrote their work on a computer, display some easy-to-read computer fonts. Make sure students know how to find them on the computer.

Publish Your Piece

Explain to students that the final step in the writing process is to decide which form of publication will present their work most effectively. Then, tell students that the chart shows how specific audiences can be reached using different media.

Have students whose science fiction stories address similar audiences work in small groups to discuss appropriate ways to publish their work.

Reflect On Your Writing

Have students discuss the questions with a partner, including the Big Question, and record responses in their journal.

Extension Have students develop a research plan for learning more about their topic. Students should identify what they want to learn, which resources they will use, and how this information could be used to improve or embellish their science fiction story.

Manage Your Portfolio You may wish to have students include development materials such as graphic organizers and drafts.

Publishing *Feature Assignment* Publishing *Feature Assignme*

Publishing

Get your science fiction story ready to present. Then choose a way to publish your work for an appropriate audience.

Wrap Up Your Presentation

Is your story handwritten or written on a computer? If you use a computer, be sure to choose a readable font. The purpose of publishing is to share your writing with readers, which means you must choose a plain, easy-to-read font.

Publish Your Piece

Use this chart to identify a way to publish your written work.

If your audience is...	...then publish it by...
A group of science fiction book or movie fans	• Reading it aloud, then holding a question-answer session about the technology in your story's "world" • Posting the story online and inviting comments
Other students in your class	• Submitting it to a class anthology or Web site of science fiction • Producing it as a graphic novel

Reflect on Your Writing

Now that you are done with your science fiction story, read it over and use your writing journal to answer these questions. Use specific details to describe and explain your reflections. Increase the specificity of your details based on the type of information requested.

- What did you enjoy about writing the story? Why?
- Are there any parts of the story with which you struggled? If so, what did you learn from the process?
- Do you think you will try writing fiction again? Explain.

The Big Question: Why Write? What can fiction do better than non-fiction?

Manage Your Portfolio You may wish to include your published science fiction story in your writing portfolio. If so, consider what this piece reveals about your writing and your growth as a writer.

112 Short Story

Resources You may wish to have students use these Graphic Organizers: Meeting Agenda, Meeting Notes, and Time Line. Distribute printed copies or have students log on to Writing Coach Online.

MAKE YOUR WRITING COUNT

Introduce the sci-fi film trailer activity by discussing the opening paragraphs. Make sure students understand that the project may be produced electronically or by hand. Then, guide them through each step in the action plan.

Use the 21st Century Skills Rubric to evaluate each group's process and final product on a scale of 1 to 3, indicating weak, moderate, or strong use of the skill. ▶

Listening and Speaking Monitor students as they use feedback to refine their performances.

21st Century Learning

Skills Rubric	Rating
Work Creatively With Others: Demonstrate originality and inventiveness in work.	1 2 3
Communicate Clearly: Articulate ideas effectively through oral, written, and nonverbal communication skills.	1 2 3
Collaborate With Others: Work flexibly to make compromises in order to achieve a common goal.	1 2 3
Apply Technology Effectively: Use technology as a tool to communicate information.	1 2 3

3 STUDENT BOOK

Students use a variety of graphic organizers, either online or in print, to help them work together to create a multimedia group project.

4 

Through Writing Coach Online™ students link to resources on 21st Century Learning for help in creating a multimedia group project.

21st Century Learning

MAKE YOUR WRITING COUNT

Make a Sci-Fi Film Trailer

Science fiction writing has long been a favorite genre for movie producers. Create a **trailer**—a film advertisement shown in movie theaters—for an imaginary film based on your science fiction story.

With a group, produce your trailer as a **multimedia presentation,** blending text, graphics, sound, and other media. As you work, be open and responsive to all of your group members' opinions and perspectives. Present your trailer in a live performance, or video-record it.

Here's your action plan.

1. Choose roles, such as writer, artist, actor, narrator, and director.
2. Review your group's sci-fi stories. Choose one with great action.
3. Find examples of trailers online. Note what elements are especially strong.
4. Create a storyboard, or a series of sketches showing the visual elements of each scene. Your storyboard should:
   - Introduce the main characters and setting
   - Hint at the main conflict without giving away the ending
   - Build excitement about the movie, perhaps through energetic music or rapidly paced shots
   - Show the title of the movie
5. Rehearse and then present the trailer for your class. Record your efforts on video using available technology, if possible.

Listening and Speaking Work as a team to improvise any dialogue or voice-over narration required in the storyboard. Then, use the storyboard to rehearse the dialogue and action. Give each other feedback during and after rehearsal. Present your trailer in a live performance, or video-record it, keeping the feedback in mind.

Online Journal

Reflect on Your Writing Record your answers and ideas in the online journal.

Resource

Link to resources on 21st Century Learning for help in creating a group project.

Personalized Support

FEEDBACK

Teacher or Peer Feedback

To provide feedback to students on their published writing, ask or have student partners ask one another the following:

- How did you go about writing this piece? What was your process?
- What did you learn from the writing model that you used in this piece?
- What surprised you the most as you wrote this piece?
- Did you try anything new as you worked on this piece?
- What did you learn from this piece of writing that you would like to remember and reuse?
- What do you think you do best as a writer right now?

Working with ELLs  Sheltered Instruction: Cognitive

To help students internalize and build proficiency with new grade-level academic vocabulary, have them use and reuse the vocabulary, in contextual speaking activities. Write and say these academic vocabulary words and have students repeat them after you: *accurate, affect, appreciate, communicate, specify.* Then:

Beginning Provide context sentences for the vocabulary, like *Email helps us communicate with people far away.* Have students repeat, then reuse the vocabulary in cloze sentences like *I _____ when my sister helps me with my homework.*

Intermediate Define each word and check comprehension by having students use them in sentences. Have them reuse the words in a discussion about a movie.

Advanced Have partners look up each word in a dictionary and each say a sentence using the word correctly. Have them reuse each word in a discussion about a movie they have seen.

Advanced High Challenge students to complete the Advanced activity and then use each word as they give feedback on classmates' Sci-Fi Film Trailer.

1 

Students use Writing Coach Online™ or their student books to analyze and discuss the Writing for Media topic.

2 

Students learn about the characteristics of a dramatic scene by answering questions about the model. Students record their answers to the *Try It!* questions in their online journals or notebooks.

Writing for Media: Dramatic Scene

Dramatic Scene

Discuss the opening paragraph with students. As a class, discuss ways in which reading a dramatic scene differs from reading a story.

Try It! Guide students to understand the audience for the sample dramatic scene.

Say: The first *Try It!* question asks about the audience for this dramatic scene. The characters are two friends who say things like "cool down" and "chill." **I think** the audience is most likely young people.

Ask: What other details help you determine the dramatic scene's most likely audience? (The surprise ending in which the friends are revealed to be robots suggests that the scene would appeal to science fiction fans.)

Have students discuss the remaining questions in small groups and record individual responses in their journals.

Extension Have students bring in other examples of dramatic scenes. Lead a media discussion about the examples, using the *Try It!* questions as a guide.

Writing for Media Writing for Media Writing for Media Writin

Your Turn Writing for Media: Dramatic Scene

21st Century Learning

Dramatic Scene

A **dramatic scene** is a story written to be performed by actors on stage or on film. The purpose of a dramatic scene is generally to entertain, but some contain a message, or theme, the writer wants to convey. Dramatic scenes are written as scripts, with lines for each character and stage directions telling actors how to speak and move. Like other stories, they have a setting, characters, plot, and well-paced action.

Try It! Study the example of a dramatic scene. Then, answer these questions. Record your answers in your journal.

1. At what **audience** is this scene most likely aimed?
2. Is the **story line** of "Power Label" engaging? Explain why or why not.
3. What is the **purpose** of "Power Label"?
4. How would you describe the **pace of events**?
5. Which **character** is most interesting to you? Why?

Extension Find another example of a dramatic scene, and compare it with this one.

Power Label

[Two friends standing in a kitchen. Friend 1 is holding a large box, like a cereal box, reading its label and looking dreamy.]

FRIEND 1. [reads excitedly from box label] "Crunchy golden goodness. Power packed in every bite!"

FRIEND 2. [slouching in a chair] Yeah, sounds good.

FRIEND 1. [continues reading, getting more excited] "All the fuel a body needs for a healthy day."

FRIEND 2. [sits up straighter, leans toward Friend 1] Yeah, that could help some, but...

FRIEND 1. [interrupts Friend 2] We have to try this now! Just think how good we'd feel! How strong we'd be! [starts wildly tearing the box to open it, but has trouble getting it open]

FRIEND 2. [stands, walks over to Friend 1] Here, give it to me. Cool down!

FRIEND 1. [hands over the box, but bounces up and down excitedly] Hurry, hurry. I'm so anxious to try it!

FRIEND 2. [gently pushes Friend 1 into a chair; shakes his head] Dude, no food. We're droids, remember? Solar packs, no stomachs? Chill!

FRIEND 1. [head in hands, sadly] But it looks so good....

114 Short Story

Create a Dramatic Scene

Tell students that they will create a dramatic scene using the five-step writing process. Then, preview the writing process instructions on page 115.

> **Resources** You may wish to have students use the Five W's Chart graphic organizer. Distribute printed copies or have students log on to Writing Coach Online.

For each step in the writing process, have partners read aloud and discuss the list of tasks. Then, have them work individually. Once both partners have completed the tasks, have them evaluate each other's work before moving to the next step.

Use the 21st Century Skills Rubric to evaluate each student's process and final product on a scale of 1 to 3, indicating weak, moderate, or strong use of the skill. ▶

Partner Talk

Remind students that a dramatic scene is told mainly through dialogue. Have partners discuss whether their scenes can be told through characters' speech.

21st Century Learning

Skills Rubric	Rating
Think Creatively: Create new and worthwhile ideas.	1 2 3
Communicate Clearly: Articulate thoughts and ideas effectively using oral, written, and nonverbal communication skills.	1 2 3
Work Independently: Monitor, define, prioritize, and complete tasks without direct oversight.	1 2 3
Produce Results: Collaborate and cooperate effectively with teams.	1 2 3

3 STUDENT BOOK

Students follow the five-step writing process to write their own dramatic scene. Students may select online or printed graphic organizers to help them plan and develop their writing.

Create a Dramatic Scene

Follow these steps to create your own dramatic scene. Review the graphic organizers on pages R24–R27 and choose one that suits your needs.

Prewriting

- Identify and narrow a topic, then identify the target audience for your scene. Determine the purpose for writing to this specific audience.
- Create characters and a setting for your scene. When those are in place, outline the story line: the beginning, middle, and end of your scene.

Drafting

- Use a script form to draft your scene. Write an opening that grabs your audience.
- Introduce the characters and create a specific, believable setting.
- Develop an engaging story line with well-paced action through the beginning, middle, and end.
- Write dialogue that gives each of your characters a unique "voice," or way of talking, that characterizes him, her, or it.

Revising and Editing

- Review your draft to make sure events are organized logically. Make sure the conflict, or problem, is clear.
- Use the Revision RADaR strategy to improve your draft.
- Check that spelling, grammar, and mechanics are correct.

Publishing

- Read through your scene with classmates, and then rehearse the scene and perform it for the class with actors and a narrator.
- You may want to record your performance using video. You can also use available technology, such as multimedia software, to add text, graphics, and sound to create a short film from the recording.

Online Journal

Try It! Record your answers in the online journal.

Interactive Graphic Organizers

Choose from a variety of graphic organizers to plan and develop your project.

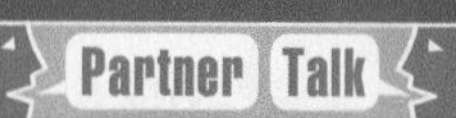

Before you start drafting, explain your dramatic scene to a partner. Use specific details to describe and explain your ideas. Increase the specificity of your details based on the type of information you are delivering. Ask questions about your ideas and plan. For example, will your story hold readers' interest?

Personalized Support

Teacher or Peer Feedback

To provide feedback to students as they write for media, ask or have student partners ask one another the following:

- What are the main characteristics of this form of writing?
- Have you included most or all of these characteristics in your piece of writing?
- What is your purpose for writing this piece?
- Who is your audience?
- How did you organize your ideas in this piece of writing?
- How did you go about revising the piece? Editing it?
- How do you plan on publishing your piece?
- What other publishing options also might work?

Working with ELLs

 Sheltered Instruction: Cognitive

Help students understand the general meaning, main points, and important details in spoken language ranging from the familiar to the unfamiliar. Relate a narrative incident to students, such as a scene in a movie, using language that ranges from the familiar, such as *man*, to the unfamiliar, such as *character*.

Beginning Use movie stills (often available online) to help students understand your summary. Help students identify the general meaning, main points, and important details. Help them use familiar language (*people*) to understand less familiar language (*characters*).

Intermediate Have groups restate the general meaning, main points, and important details of your summary. Help them use familiar language (*story*) to understand less familiar language (*drama*).

Advanced Have partners restate the general meaning, main points, and important details of your summary. Have them identify unfamiliar words to determine the meaning using familiar words as context.

Advanced High Have students complete the Advanced activity, then give a summary of a movie as partners take notes.

1 Writing Journal

Before they write, students use the ABCDs of On-Demand Writing to analyze and plan how to respond to each prompt. They can use either their online journals or notebooks to take notes.

Writing for Assessment

Read aloud or have a student read aloud the introductory text. Then, tell students that they will learn and practice a technique for writing in response to a test prompt.

Try It! Read the Short Story Prompt aloud and then have volunteers read aloud the Format and Academic Vocabulary boxes. Tell students that they will use the ABCD method to respond to the prompt.

The ABCDs of On-Demand Writing

Have students identify the words associated with the ABCD method. (attack, brainstorm, choose, detect) Then, guide students through their use.

I'll attack the prompt by circling the words *dialogue, foreshadowing,* and *literary devices.* These words remind me of ways to make the setting, characters, and plot of the story interesting and believable. I can rewrite the prompt to state that clearly: "Write a story using dialogue, foreshadowing, and literary devices to make the story believable."

Work with students to brainstorm for an appropriate graphic organizer for a short story, such as a story chart.

Have students write their drafts individually and then work with a partner to detect errors.

Writing for Assessment

Some prompts ask you to write an imaginative work. Use these prompts to practice. Respond using the characteristics of your science fiction story. (See page 92.)

Try It! To begin, read the **short story** prompt and the information on format and academic vocabulary. Then use the ABCDs of On-Demand Writing to help you plan and write your short story.

Format
The prompt asks you to write a *short story.* Be sure to start with a beginning that grabs readers' attention and introduces the characters and conflict.

Short Story Prompt
Write a short story about a spaceship crash. Be sure to develop an engaging story line. Use dialogue, foreshadowing and other literary devices in your story.

Academic Vocabulary
Remember, *dialogue* is the conversation between two or more characters in a work of literature. *Foreshadowing* is an author's use of clues about something that will happen later in the story.

 The ABCDs of On-Demand Writing

Use the following ABCDs to help you respond to the prompt.

Before you write your draft:

Attack the prompt [1 MINUTE]

- Circle or highlight important verbs in the prompt. Draw a line from the verb to what it refers to.
- Rewrite the prompt in your own words.

Brainstorm possible answers [4 MINUTES]

- Create a graphic organizer to generate ideas.
- Use one for each part of the prompt if necessary.

Choose the order of your response [1 MINUTE]

- Think about the best way to organize your ideas.
- Number your ideas in the order you will write about them. Cross out ideas you will not be using.

After you write your draft:

Detect errors before turning in the draft [1 MINUTE]

- Carefully reread your writing.
- Make sure that your response makes sense and is complete.
- Look for spelling, punctuation, and grammar errors.

More Prompts for Practice

Apply It! Test Prep Have students apply the ABCD method to the practice prompts.

Prompt 1 Have partners attack the prompt and brainstorm for possible answers. Then, have each pair swap their information with another group to evaluate whether the teams have created an engaging story with a cohesive plot.

Prompt 2 Have students work individually to attack the prompt and brainstorm for possible answers. Then, have students work in small groups to evaluate their work before writing their drafts.

Test Prep Spiral Review: Narrative
Read aloud the instructions and the prompt. Then, have students review the personal narrative characteristics on page 66.

Prompt 3 Remind students to use the ABCD method to write their personal narrative.

2 

Students share their writing with their teacher.

3 

Students receive personalized feedback from their teacher.

More Prompts for Practice

Apply It! Respond to Prompts 1 and 2 by writing **imaginative short stories** with **engaging story lines** that **sustain the reader's interest**.

- Identify an appropriate audience
- Establish a clear plot focus
- Develop logical and well-paced action
- Create a specific, believable setting through the use of sensory details
- Use **literary strategies and devices** to enhance your **style and tone**

Prompt 1 Write a short story about a character who has an unusual job in the year 2500. Develop an engaging story with a cohesive plot through beginning, middle, and end. Include a believable setting and interesting characters.

Prompt 2 Write a short story about a group of aliens who come to Earth to try and save our planet from an asteroid that is hurtling toward Earth. Develop a story line that retains readers' interest throughout the story.

Spiral Review: Narrative Respond to Prompt 3 by writing a **personal narrative**. Make sure your narrative reflects all of the characteristics described on page 66, including **a clearly defined focus** and **explanations of the importance of or reasons for actions and their consquences.**

Prompt 3 Think about a time when you succeeded in doing something that was difficult. Write an appealing narrative that describes what you tried to do and how you succeeded in that attempt. Tell how you felt about your success and describe any other results of your actions.

www.phwritingcoach.com

Interactive Writing Coach™

Plan your response to the prompt. If you are using the prompt for practice, write one paragraph at a time or your entire draft and then submit it for feedback. If you are using the prompt as a timed test, write your entire draft and then submit it for feedback.

Remember **ABCD**

- **A**ttack the prompt
- **B**rainstorm possible answers
- **C**hoose the order of your response
- **D**etect errors before turning in the draft

Personalized Support

Assessment/Monitor Progress

For timed writing practice, assign students a prompt to be completed in a timed setting. For Prompt 3, have students submit their writing to **Interactive Writing Coach™** to get immediate feedback.

For a formal writing assessment, assign the Assessment writing prompt for this chapter in **Writing Coach Online™**. Then, have students submit their writing to **Interactive Writing Coach™** to be assessed. Use the results to assess student progress and skill levels. **Interactive Writing Coach™** will update student levels to ensure that students get the appropriate support.

Teacher Feedback

To create an assessment environment, have students use a prompt in a timed setting. Grade papers using the appropriate rubric and use the results to assess student progress and skill levels. In the next writing assignment, ensure that students get the appropriate level of support.

If you conference with students, use these questions to guide your discussion:

- What form of writing did the prompt call for? Does your response include most or all of the characteristics of that form?
- How did you organize your ideas?
- Did you make good use of your time as you planned and wrote your response?
- What did you learn that you can use when responding to a prompt during a timed test?

Working with ELLs

ELL Sheltered Instruction: Cognitive

Help students respond to creative writing prompts by having them narrate the events, describe the characters, and explain the cause of a fictional event aloud with increasing specificity and detail. Read aloud the Short Story Prompt and ensure comprehension. Have students tell a story about a spaceship crash.

Beginning Give students sentence starters to narrate events (e.g., *The spaceship was flying when* ________), describe characters (e.g., *The aliens were* _______), and explain why the crash happened (e.g., *The spacecraft was old, so* _____).

Intermediate Have groups tell the story aloud, taking turns narrating events, describing characters, and explaining why the crash happened. Provide feedback about their use of specific details.

Advanced Have partners take turns as they tell the story aloud, narrating the events, describing the characters, and explaining why the crash happened. Encourage creativity and the use of specific details.

Advanced High Have students complete the Advanced activity and share their story.

CHAPTER 7 LESSON PLANNER
Poetry and Description

Use the Online Lesson Planner at www.phwritingcoach.com to customize your instructional plan for an integrated Language Arts curriculum.

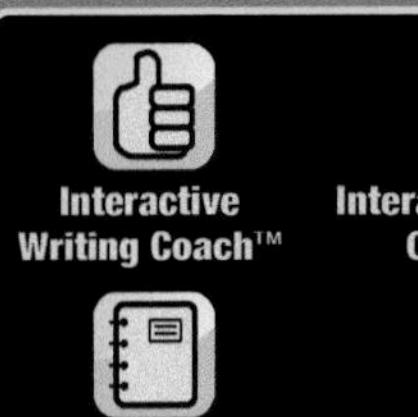

Online Journal

Resources

DAY 1

CHAPTER OPENER/ GENRE INTRODUCTION

- What Do You See?
- What's Ahead
- Connect to the Big Questions
- **Feature Assignment: Poem**
- Other Forms of Poetry and Description
- Word Bank

ONLINE

DAY 2

MENTOR TEXT/ STUDENT MODEL

- **Mentor Text: Free Verse and Lyric Poems**
- Learn From Experience
- **Student Model: Free Verse and Lyric Poems**
- Reader's Eye and Writer's Eye

ONLINE

DAY 3

Prewriting

- Choose From the Topic Bank
- Choose Your Own Topic
- Narrow Your Topic
- Consider Your Audience and Purpose

ONLINE

DAY 6

Revising

- Keep Revision on Your RADaR
- Look at the Big Picture
- Focus on Craft
- Fine-Tune Your Draft

ONLINE

DAY 7

For additional grammar support, see Section 24.1, p. 534.

Editing

- What Do You Notice? / Grammar Mini-Lesson

Rubric for Poetry: Free Verse or Lyric Poem

- Publish Your Piece
- Reflect on Your Writing

ONLINE

DAY 8

21st Century Learning

MAKE YOUR WRITING COUNT

- **Share Poetic Vision Using Graphics and Text**
- Here's Your Action Plan
- Listening and Speaking

ONLINE

Alternate Pacing Suggestions

- **Block Scheduling** Each day on the Lesson Planner represents a 40–50 minute block. Teachers using block scheduling may combine days to revise pacing to meet their classroom needs.
- **Accelerated Lesson Planning** Combine instructional days by aiding students in choosing a topic and then focusing on two core stages of the writing process, outlining for success (Day 5) and RADaR revision (Day 6).
- **Integrated Language Arts Curriculum** For targeted instruction that covers the essential components of the lesson, use either a 3- or a 5-day plan.

3 day plan

DAY 1: Introduction to the Genre, Mentor Text, Student Model

DAY 2: Prewriting/Drafting

DAY 3: Revising/Editing/ Publishing

5 day plan

Use 3-day plan, and add:

DAY 4: Make Your Writing Count

DAY 5: Writing for Assessment

Links to Prentice Hall *LITERATURE*

Featured Author: Pat Mora

- What Is Poetry?, p. 572
- "Maestro" (poem), p. 577
- "The Desert Is My Mother" (poem), p. 578
- "El desierto es mi madre" (poem), p. 579
- "Bailando" (poem), p. 580
- On Supporting a Point (Writing Workshop), p. 701
- *From the Author's Desk* Videos: Pat Mora

Additional Mentor Text:

- "The Rider" (poem), Naomi Shihab Nye, p. 586

Differentiated Instruction

Differentiated Instruction Boxes in this Teacher's Edition address these student populations:

- Below-Level Students
- Above-Level Students
- Gifted and Talented Students
- Special Needs Students
- English Language Learners
- Spanish Speaking Students

In addition, for further enrichment, see the **Extension** features.

DAY 4

Prewriting

- Plan Your Piece
- Poet's Toolbox

ONLINE

DAY 5

Drafting

- Drafting a Free Verse or Lyric Poem
- Start Your Draft

ONLINE

DAY 9

WRITING FOR MEDIA

- **Travel Writing**
- Create a Travel Blog

ONLINE

DAY 10

WRITING FOR ASSESSMENT

- Poetry Prompt
- The ABCDs of On-Demand Writing
- More Prompts for Practice
  Test Prep: Spiral Review: Narrative
- Spiral Review: Imaginative Short Story

ONLINE

LESSON OBJECTIVES

- To learn the forms and defining characteristics of poetry and description.
- To learn the elements of a successful free verse poem and a successful lyric poem, the chapter feature assignments.
- To read mentor texts in the genre, analyzing their use of the elements of effective poetry.
- To read student models of free verse and lyric poems, analyzing them from the perspective of a reader and from the perspective of a writer.
- To apply prewriting strategies in developing a free verse or a lyric poem, including strategies for choosing and narrowing a topic, planning writing, and using poetic devices, as well as tips for considering audience and purpose.
- To apply drafting strategies in developing a free verse or a lyric poem.
- To apply RADaR revision strategies to a draft free verse or lyric poem.
- To learn about the Focus on Craft topic, vivid images, and apply what is learned to a draft free verse or lyric poem.
- To edit the draft, zooming in on modifiers and focusing on phrases used as modifiers.
- To complete the Make Your Writing Count assignment, developing and presenting a collection of images based on a poem.
- To complete the Writing for Media assignment, developing a travel blog entry.
- To practice writing for assessment.

Personalized Assessment

	Ongoing Assessment	Formal Assessment of Feature Assignment	Progress Monitoring at End-of-Chapter
 FEEDBACK Teacher Conferencing	Use rubrics in the Student Edition as a revision tool. Conference with students to review their work and provide personalized support.	Use rubrics in the Student Edition to score students' Feature Assignment papers.	Review each student's work to plan targeted resources for the next writing assignment.

1 Using Writing Coach Online™ or the student book, students discuss the photograph in the chapter opener as it relates to the writing genre.

2 Students record their ideas and responses in their online journals or notebooks. They may also record and save their responses on pop-up sticky notes in Writing Coach Online™.

Chapter Objectives

1. Write a poem by planning, drafting, revising, editing, and publishing individual work.
2. Produce a photo album or slideshow.
3. Use the five-step writing process to write a travel essay.
4. Write a poem and a personal narrative or short story in response to a prompt.

CHAPTER 7

POETRY and DESCRIPTION

POETRY and DESCRIPTION

What Do You See?

Activate Prior Knowledge Tell students that the purpose of poetry is to express ideas and feelings through imaginative language and description. Explain to students that they will use what they know about horses to analyze the photo on page 118. Then, guide students in analyzing the photo.

When you analyze something, you look at it closely and think about what it means. For example, in this photo **I see** a herd of horses galloping quickly. I think about where they are going. The land is dry and dusty, so they could be heading for water. I also think about how the photo makes me feel. I am awed by the horses' size and strength.

Work with students to brainstorm for things they see, think about, or feel as they analyze the photo. Record their responses on the board.

Try It! **Have students** work individually to develop responses to the questions. Check that students have described their feelings about the photo.

Possible responses: I see horses running across dry, dusty land. The close-up view is thrilling. I can almost hear their whinnying and the thunder of their hooves. I can smell the dust in the air and feel the hot sun. If I saw these horses in real life, I would feel excited and impressed. The image of the horses moving at will across the open land means freedom to me.

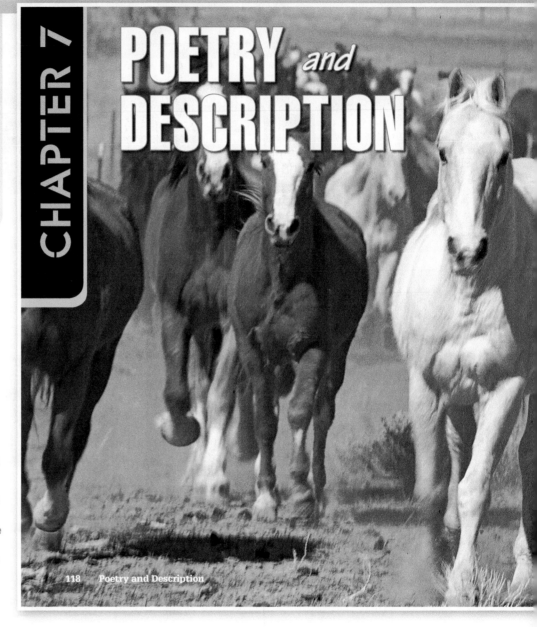

Connect to the Big Questions

Have students use their experience to discuss the Big Questions. Explain that they will revisit **Why write?** at the end of this chapter. Tell students to consider these points during their discussion:

1. It can take many, many words to describe all the details in a single picture.
2. The English language is made up of many words that have similar meanings but that describe different emotions.

What's Ahead

Have students preview the Mentor Text and Student Model on pages 122–125. Tell students that they will write their own poem using the five-step writing process: prewriting, drafting, revising, editing, and publishing.

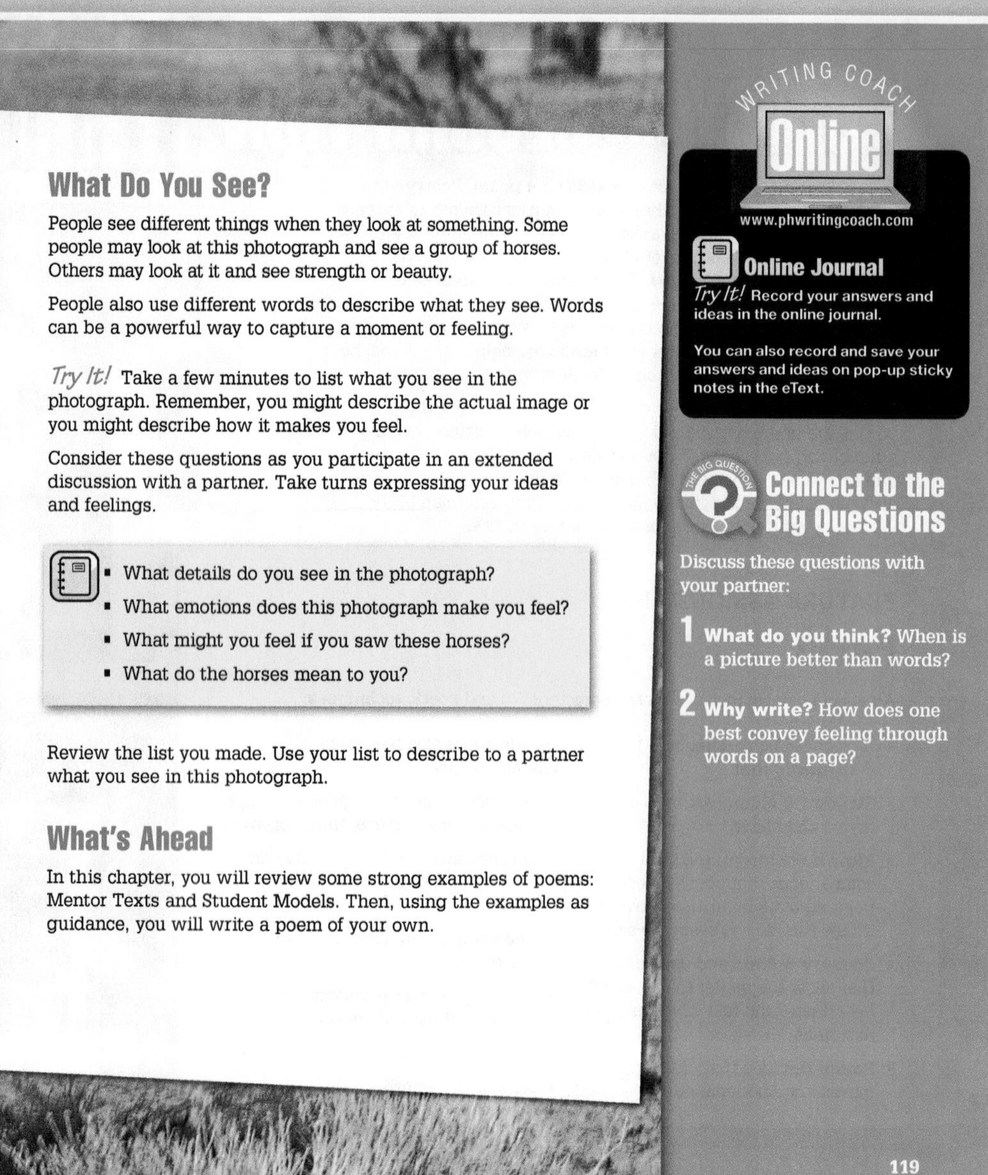

What Do You See?

People see different things when they look at something. Some people may look at this photograph and see a group of horses. Others may look at it and see strength or beauty.

People also use different words to describe what they see. Words can be a powerful way to capture a moment or feeling.

Try It! Take a few minutes to list what you see in the photograph. Remember, you might describe the actual image or you might describe how it makes you feel.

Consider these questions as you participate in an extended discussion with a partner. Take turns expressing your ideas and feelings.

- What details do you see in the photograph?
- What emotions does this photograph make you feel?
- What might you feel if you saw these horses?
- What do the horses mean to you?

Review the list you made. Use your list to describe to a partner what you see in this photograph.

What's Ahead

In this chapter, you will review some strong examples of poems: Mentor Texts and Student Models. Then, using the examples as guidance, you will write a poem of your own.

WRITING COACH Online

www.phwritingcoach.com

Online Journal

Try It! Record your answers and ideas in the online journal.

You can also record and save your answers and ideas on pop-up sticky notes in the eText.

Connect to the Big Questions

Discuss these questions with your partner:

1 **What do you think?** When is a picture better than words?

2 **Why write?** How does one best convey feeling through words on a page?

Personalized Support

FEEDBACK

Teacher or Peer Feedback

To encourage students in their discussion of the photograph as it relates to the writing genre, ask the following questions:

- What is the first thing you think of when you look at this photo?
- How does it relate to your life?
- How does it relate to things you've learned in other subjects?
- What questions come to mind when you look at this photograph?
- How does your response to the photograph compare to those of your classmates?

Working with ELLs

ELL Sheltered Instruction: Metacognitive

Have students demonstrate listening comprehension of increasingly complex English by retelling or summarizing spoken messages. Read a response to the *Try It!* activity. Help students monitor understanding and seek clarification.

Beginning Repeat your response, gesturing to the photo on page 118 for support. Pause often to allow students to monitor comprehension and seek clarification. Help students retell ideas they heard with sentence frames, like: *The horses are* _______. Allow students to gesture or draw as needed.

Intermediate Repeat your response. Ask simple questions to help students monitor comprehension and seek clarification. Then, have groups retell what they heard.

Advanced Have pairs summarize what they heard and monitor comprehension by comparing summaries with another pair. Have students seek clarification as needed.

Advanced High Have individuals complete the Advanced activity, then share their summaries with the class.

The Digital • Print Path

1 

Students learn vocabulary from the Word Bank and listen to English and Spanish pronunciations in the Writing Coach Online™ glossary.

2 

Students record answers to questions about forms of writing in their online journals or notebooks.

POETRY AND DESCRIPTION

To introduce this chapter's writing forms, discuss the opening paragraphs with students. Make sure students understand that a lyric poem and a free verse poem are types of poetry. Explain that poets often use a step-by-step process to develop their work. Then, have students preview the rubric on page 137.

Poem

Ask volunteers to read aloud the feature assignment characteristics. Tell students that they will identify these characteristics in Mentor Texts and Student Models. Then, they will use the characteristics to guide the writing of their own lyric poem or free verse poem.

Forms of Poetry and Description

Guide students to compare and contrast the various forms of poetry and description.

Say: I see that while haiku and sonnets are both kinds of poems, they have very different structures. A haiku has three lines with a specific number of syllables in each line. A sonnet has 14 lines with a specific rhyme pattern.

Ask: How are descriptive essays and prose poems alike? (Both describe a person, place, thing, or event.) How are they different? (Descriptive essays are prose; prose poems look like prose but use poetic techniques.)

Have students compare and contrast other forms on the list.

Try It! Remind students that the audience is the people who will read their poem. The purpose is the poet's reason for writing. Have students record their responses in their journal.

Possible responses: prose poem, uses poetic techniques to describe a person; haiku, talks about nature; ballad, tells a story and is meant to be sung

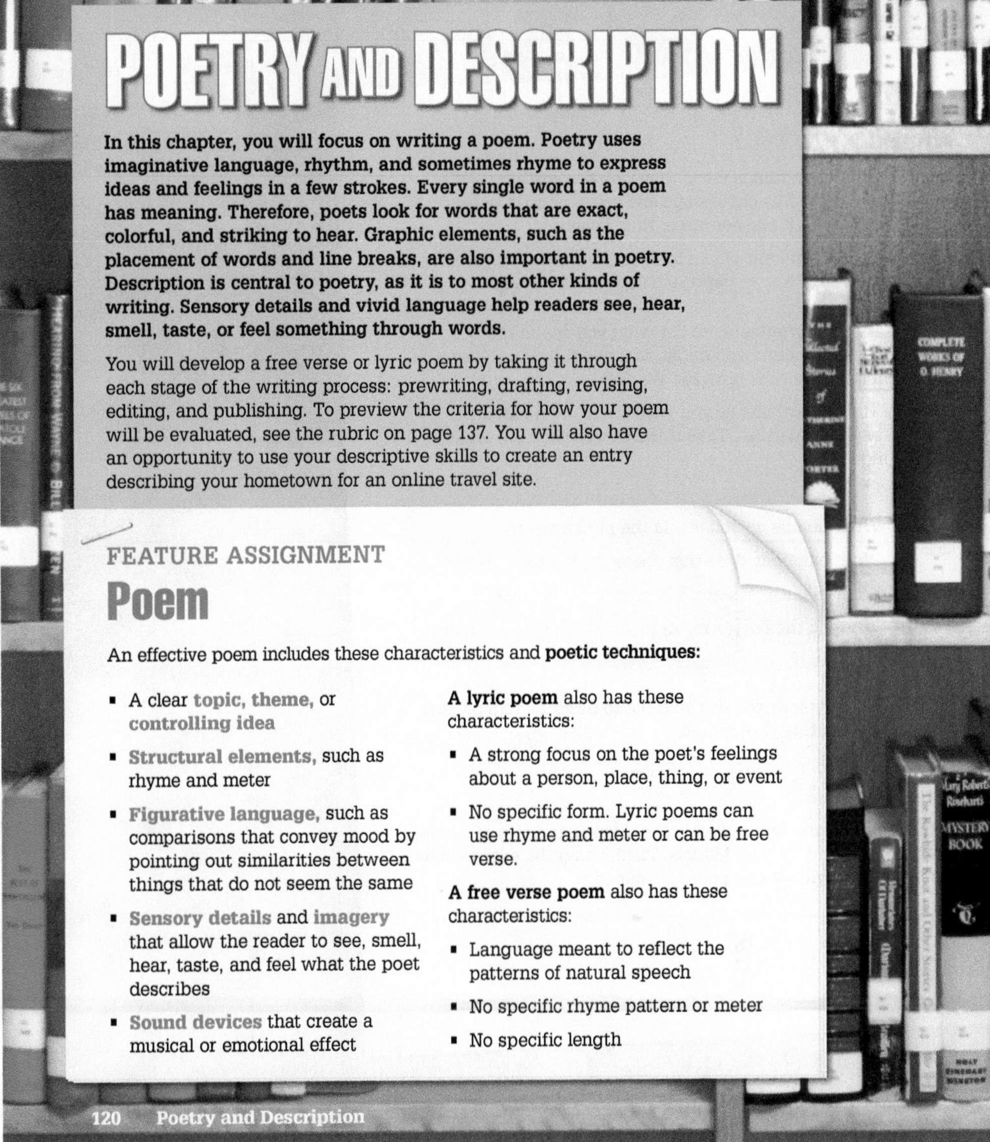

POETRY AND DESCRIPTION

In this chapter, you will focus on writing a poem. Poetry uses imaginative language, rhythm, and sometimes rhyme to express ideas and feelings in a few strokes. Every single word in a poem has meaning. Therefore, poets look for words that are exact, colorful, and striking to hear. Graphic elements, such as the placement of words and line breaks, are also important in poetry. Description is central to poetry, as it is to most other kinds of writing. Sensory details and vivid language help readers see, hear, smell, taste, or feel something through words.

You will develop a free verse or lyric poem by taking it through each stage of the writing process: prewriting, drafting, revising, editing, and publishing. To preview the criteria for how your poem will be evaluated, see the rubric on page 137. You will also have an opportunity to use your descriptive skills to create an entry describing your hometown for an online travel site.

FEATURE ASSIGNMENT

Poem

An effective poem includes these characteristics and **poetic techniques:**

- A clear **topic, theme,** or **controlling idea**
- **Structural elements,** such as rhyme and meter
- **Figurative language,** such as comparisons that convey mood by pointing out similarities between things that do not seem the same
- **Sensory details** and **imagery** that allow the reader to see, smell, hear, taste, and feel what the poet describes
- **Sound devices** that create a musical or emotional effect

A lyric poem also has these characteristics:

- A strong focus on the poet's feelings about a person, place, thing, or event
- No specific form. Lyric poems can use rhyme and meter or can be free verse.

A free verse poem also has these characteristics:

- Language meant to reflect the patterns of natural speech
- No specific rhyme pattern or meter
- No specific length

120 Poetry and Description

Word Bank

To assist English Language Learners and struggling readers, echo read each word or have students log on to Writing Coach Online to listen to the pronunciations. Then, have partners take turns using each word in a sentence. Ask volunteers to share one of their sentences with the class.

Teacher Tip

Give a clue that applies to one or more of the forms of poetry and description and have students identify the form or forms. For example, the clue might be "no specific rhyme pattern or meter." The answer would be "free verse poem, prose poem, and possibly lyric poem."

Forms of Poetry and Description

There are many forms of poetry and description, including:

Ballads are poems that tell a story and are often meant to be sung. Ballads have a regular rhyme pattern and meter, or "beat." Most ballads repeat words or phrases.

Descriptive essays use precise images and details to help readers imagine a person, place, thing, or event. Like all essays, they include an introduction, body, and conclusion.

Free verse is poetry that imitates the rhythms of everyday speech. Freed of set rhythm and rhyme patterns, free verse uses figurative language and sound devices to convey ideas and feelings.

Haiku are three-line poems first developed in Japan. The first and last lines have five syllables, and the middle line has seven syllables. Haiku are usually about nature.

Lyric poems are poems expressing the speaker's feelings about a certain person, place, thing, or event. Lyric poems can use rhyme and meter or can be free verse.

Prose poems look like prose, or regular text you might find in a story or essay, but use poetic techniques to create a memorable description of a person, place, thing, or event.

Sonnets are 14-line poems with a regular meter and rhyme. One type, the English sonnet, is made up of three four-line stanzas and a final couplet, or two rhyming lines. In each stanza, alternating lines rhyme.

Try It! For each audience and purpose described, choose a form, such as a ballad, lyric poem, or prose poem, that is appropriate for conveying your intended meaning to the audience. Explain your choices.

- To tell classmates about the adventures of your elderly great-uncle, a former test pilot
- To share your feelings with the general public about the first leaves in spring
- To honor your school team's championship with a song

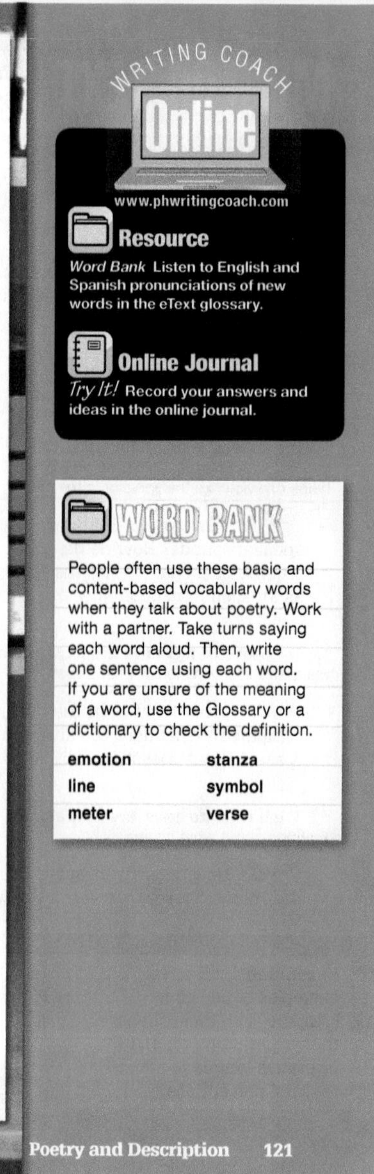

Resource

Word Bank Listen to English and Spanish pronunciations of new words in the eText glossary.

Online Journal

Try It! Record your answers and ideas in the online journal.

WORD BANK

People often use these basic and content-based vocabulary words when they talk about poetry. Work with a partner. Take turns saying each word aloud. Then, write one sentence using each word. If you are unsure of the meaning of a word, use the Glossary or a dictionary to check the definition.

emotion	**stanza**
line	**symbol**
meter	**verse**

Personalized Support

Teacher or Peer Feedback

FEEDBACK

To help students understand the characteristics of the writing form, ask or have student partners ask one another the following questions:

- What are the main characteristics of poetry and description?
- What makes this form of writing different from other forms?
- Who are the likely readers or audiences for this form of writing?
- What kind of organization could be used for this form of writing?
- What kind of voice would be most effective for this form of writing?

Working with ELLs

ELL **Sheltered Instruction:** Cognitive

Have students use strategic learning techniques such as reviewing to acquire basic and grade-level vocabulary, including the words *emotion, stanza,* and *story* in the Word Bank and *poems, lines, verse,* and *rhyme* from the text. Help students use accessible language to learn this new and essential language.

Beginning Define the words with accessible language as students repeat. Have students review by responding to questions, such as: *What is an emotion?*

Intermediate Have partners make **Puzzle Cards** to review the vocabulary. Students should write words on one half and use accessible language to explain them on the other. They should cut the cards, mix them, and match them again.

Advanced Have partners review the vocabulary, using accessible language to explain each and referring to a dictionary as needed. Have them use each word in a sentence about a work they have read.

Advanced High Have partners review the vocabulary, using accessible language to define it. Have them use the vocabulary to discuss the forms on page 121.

The Digital • Print Path

1 

Using Writing Coach Online™ or the student book, students read and listen to an audio recording of the Mentor Texts. As they complete their writing assignments, they can refer back to the Mentor Text for support whenever they need it.

MENTOR TEXT

About the Selections The first selection is a free verse poem in which the poet imagines an alien's interpretation of what it sees on a freeway. The second selection is a lyric poem in which the poet describes a scene in nature, of snow falling on leaves.

Learn From Experience

After students have read the text, point out that the numbered notes refer to the characteristics of free verse and lyric poems introduced on page 120.

Try It! Guide students to understand how the genre characteristics shape the text.

Say: The first *Try It!* question asks about the way the speaker sounds and the effect of the short stanzas on the characterization of the speaker. **I think** the short stanzas make the speaker sound abrupt and mechanical, definitely unnatural, which is just how an alien from outer space might sound when speaking English.

Ask: What else helps characterize the speaker as an alien from outer space? (Responses will vary.)

Have students reply to the *Try It!* questions in their journals. If students have difficulty responding to a particular question, model a response, as with Question 1.

Check the accuracy and completeness of student responses.

1. Responses will vary, but should mention the short, simple sentences and phrases, and the formal tone.
2. a special creature with five eyes instead of four (what the alien thinks it sees) and a police car with a blinking red light on top (what it actually sees)
3. The alien is puzzled by what it sees. It can't decide whether the inside parts are the creatures' guts or brains.
4. Yes. In both stanzas, the second and fifth lines rhyme, and the third and fourth lines rhyme.
5. the fallen leaves on the lawn, which the poet compares to cornflakes in the first stanza

Extension Lead a discussion in which students compare and contrast how their additional poetry examples use the genre characteristics. Use the *Try It!* questions as a guide.

Text Poem Mentor Text Poem Mentor Text Poem Mento

MENTOR TEXT Free Verse and Lyric Poems

Learn From Experience

After reading the free verse and lyric poems on pages 122–123, read the numbered notes in the margins to learn about how the poets presented their ideas.

Answer the *Try It!* questions online or in your notebook.

(1) The poem is written in free verse divided into two-line stanzas. This **graphic element** helps characterize the speaker in the poem.

Try It! How do you think the speaker sounds? How do the short stanzas help characterize the speaker as an alien from outer space?

(2) The poet uses **figurative language** to convey the alien's interpretation of what it sees.

Try It! What two things are being compared? What does the alien think it sees? What does it actually see?

(3) The last stanza helps reveal the alien's **feelings** about what it sees.

Try It! How does the alien feel about the "people" it sees? How can you tell?

Extension Find other examples of poems to compare with these. Evalute the ways that literal and figurative language affect readers' perceptions.

Southbound on the Freeway

by May Swenson

(1) A tourist came in from Orbitville,
parked in the air, and said:

The creatures of this star
are made of metal and glass.

Through the transparent parts
you can see their guts.

Their feet are round and roll
on diagrams or long

measuring tapes, dark
with white lines.

They have four eyes.
The two in back are red.

(2) Sometimes you can see a five-eyed
one, with a red eye turning

on the top of his head.
He must be special—

The others respect him
and go slow

when he passes, winding
among them from behind.

They all hiss as they glide,
like inches, down the marked

(3) tapes. Those soft shapes,
shadowy inside

the hard bodies—are they
their guts or their brains?

Teacher Tip

Ask students to choose one of the poems and draw a picture of what they "see" in their minds when they read the poem. Students who are not comfortable drawing can pair up with a student who draws. Together, they can list possible details and offer ideas for how they each visualize the poem.

2 

Students record their answers to questions about the Mentor Texts in their online journals or notebooks.

December Leaves

by Kaye Starbird

The fallen leaves are cornflakes
(4) That fill the lawn's wide dish,
And night and noon
The wind's a spoon
That stirs them with a swish.

(5) The sky's a silver sifter,
A-sifting white and slow,
That gently shakes
On crisp brown flakes
The sugar known as snow.

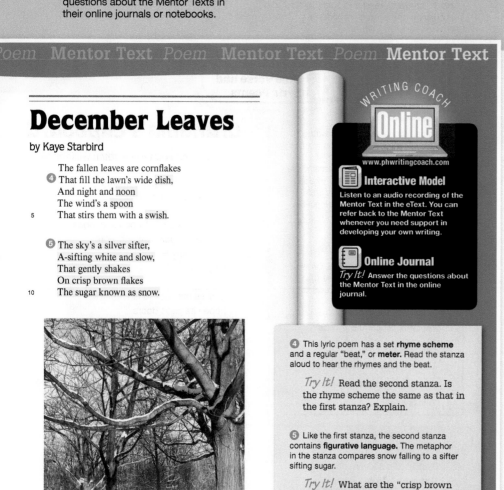

WRITING COACH Online

www.phwritingcoach.com

Interactive Model

Listen to an audio recording of the Mentor Text in the eText. You can refer back to the Mentor Text whenever you need support in developing your own writing.

Online Journal

Try It! Answer the questions about the Mentor Text in the online journal.

(4) This lyric poem has a set **rhyme scheme** and a regular "beat," or **meter.** Read the stanza aloud to hear the rhymes and the beat.

Try It! Read the second stanza. Is the rhyme scheme the same as that in the first stanza? Explain.

(5) Like the first stanza, the second stanza contains **figurative language.** The metaphor in the stanza compares snow falling to a sifter sifting sugar.

Try It! What are the "crisp brown flakes" in the second stanza?

Personalized Support

FEEDBACK

Teacher or Peer Feedback

To provide feedback to students on their responses to the Mentor Texts and their answers to the *Try It!* questions, ask or have student partners ask one another the following:

- What is the thesis or controlling idea of the Mentor Texts?
- How do the Mentor Texts illustrate the characteristics of lyric poems and free verse poems?
- How did you answer this *Try It!* question? How could you use your answer to help you plan your piece of writing?

Working with ELLs

ELL Sheltered Instruction: Cognitive

Have students listen to, derive meaning from, and respond orally to information presented in a wide variety of print, electronic, and audiovisual media to build and reinforce language attainment. Find a recording of a rhyming poem or make one yourself of the poem on page 123.

Beginning Play the recording, providing support by acting out ideas. Build and reinforce language attainment by having students respond orally to simple questions, such as: *Which words rhyme?*

Intermediate Play the recording, helping students understand the imagery. Have them respond orally, discussing the poem's topic and images. Have them build language attainment by orally completing sentence frames, like: *The poem has rhyming words like _____.*

Advanced Play the recording and discuss the topic of the poem. To build language attainment, have partners define unfamiliar words and compare lists with another pair.

Advanced High Have partners complete the Advanced activity, then have students orally respond to the *Try It!* questions on page 123.

1 STUDENT BOOK

Using Writing Coach Online™ or the student book, students read and listen to an audio recording of the Student Models.

STUDENT MODEL

Tell students that good writers react to what they read in ways that show their understanding of the text. Explain that students will react to the Student Models by placing two sets of symbols in each text. Then, distribute printed copies of the Student Models or have students log on to Writing Coach Online.

Use a Reader's Eye

Read aloud the instructions for using the Reader's Response Symbols and the meaning of each symbol. Then, guide students through their use.

In the first poem, the student writer describes his grandma's cupboard. In the second stanza, **I notice** that he says it smells like his grandma's living room, but that doesn't really help me imagine the smell. I need more details. Since I think this image could be stronger, I'll place a dash next to line 9.

Work with students to identify other images in the poem and discuss whether they help the reader imagine what the poet is describing.

Have students read and respond to the Student Models, using each Reader's Response Symbol at least once.

Poem Student Model Poem Student Model Poem Student Mod

STUDENT MODEL Free Verse and Lyric Poems

With a small group, take turns reading the Student Models aloud. As you read, note the structures and elements of poetry. You may want to take a look at the Poet's Toolbox on page 129. Ask yourself how the poetic language informs and shapes your understanding of the poems.

Use a Reader's Eye

Now, reread the Student Models. On your copies of the Student Models, use the Reader's Response Symbols to react to what you read.

Reader's Response Symbols

- **+ I can picture this.**
- **— This image could be stronger.**
- **? I wonder what this means.**
- **! This is cool!**

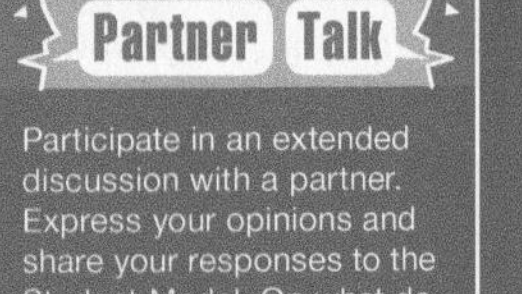

Partner Talk
Participate in an extended discussion with a partner. Express your opinions and share your responses to the Student Model. On what do you agree? How do your feelings about the poems differ?

Grandma's Cupboard

A Free Verse Poem by Jonathan Williamson

Some of Grandma's furniture
lives at our house now.

My favorite is a tall wooden cupboard.
It is golden oak, soft and worn,
and it is very,
very old.

It takes me back to Grandma's.
I open its glass doors,
and it smells like her living room
a thousand miles away,
with someone else living in it now.

Now, at my own house, in my own living room,
I open the old cupboard doors,
I take a deep breath,
and WHOOSH!
I am back in Grandma's house once more.
The cupboard says,
"Welcome back! Good to see you!"

1

124 Poetry and Description

Partner Talk

Before partners share their opinions of and feelings about the poems, have them determine the topics, purposes, and audiences of the poems.

Use a Writer's Eye

Read aloud the instructions for using the Writer's Response Symbols and the meaning of each symbol. Then, guide students through their use.

Say: When **I read** the first stanza of "Sweet Harmony," I hear a regular meter and rhyme pattern, which give the poem a musical quality. These sound devices are especially appropriate for a poem about singing. I'll write S.D. next to the first stanza of the poem.

Ask: Where else are sound devices used in "Sweet Harmony"? (The second stanza has the same meter and rhyme pattern as the first. The poem also has repetition [*and your, it's not*], alliteration [*sad/sing, you/your, such/sweet*], and assonance [*be/deep/breathing, best/friend/melt/blend, sweet/harmony, never/end*].

Have students read and respond to the Student Models, using each Writer's Response Symbol at least once.

2 WRITING COACH Online | STUDENT BOOK

First, students respond to the Student Model as a reader, using symbols to mark the text. They can mark the text using pop-up sticky notes in **Writing Coach Online™** or they can mark a printed copy of the Student Models.

3 WRITING COACH Online | STUDENT BOOK

Then, students respond to the Student Models as a writer, using different symbols to mark the text. They can use either **Writing Coach Online™** or a printed copy of the Student Model.

Sweet Harmony

A Lyric Poem by Clara Montgomery

It's hard to be sad when you sing,
(It might be a deep-breathing thing),
You open your mouth,
And your rib cage goes south,
And your heart feels as grand as a king.

The best is to sing with a friend
And melt your tones to a blend.
It's not "you"—it's not "me"—
It's a glorious "WE!"
Such sweet harmony never should end!

2

WRITING COACH Online

www.phwritingcoach.com

Interactive Model

Listen to an audio recording of the Student Model in the eText. Use the Reader's and Writer's Response Symbols with the eText tools to note what you read.

Use a Writer's Eye

Now, evaluate the poems as a writer. On your copies of the Student Models, use the Writer's Response Symbols to react to what you read. Identify places where the student writers use characteristics of an effective poem.

Writer's Response Symbols	
R.R.	**Rhythm or rhyme fits poem's form**
S.D.	**Effective use of sound devices**
F.L.	**Figurative language conveys a mood**
I.D.	**Images and details appeal to senses**

Personalized Support

FEEDBACK

Teacher or Peer Feedback

To provide feedback to students on their responses to the Student Models, ask or have student partners ask one another the following:

- What is the thesis or controlling idea of the Student Models?
- How do the Student Models illustrate the characteristics of lyric poems and free verse poems?
- Which feature or characteristic of the Student Models might you use in your own piece of writing?
- How could you alter or adapt this feature to make it your own?

Working with ELLs

ELL **Sheltered Instruction:** Cognitive

Provide opportunities for students to use and reuse new basic language in speaking activities, and help them expand and internalize initial English vocabulary by retelling basic information supported by pictures. Bring in a photograph of an antique cupboard similar to the one in "Grandma's Cupboard." Preteach these basic vocabulary words from the poem: *house, wood, favorite, old,* and *smells.* Guide students in reading the poem. Then:

Beginning Have students use the words to complete oral sentences, like: *The cupboard is made of [wood]* and reuse the vocabulary to retell information in the poem.

Intermediate Have groups use the vocabulary to discuss the photograph and reuse it to retell information in the poem.

Advanced Have partners use the vocabulary as they retell the information from the poem, using the picture for support, then reuse the vocabulary by discussing how the picture compares to the cupboard in the poem.

Advanced High Have students complete the Advanced activity. Then, have students share their retellings with the class.

The Digital • Print Path

1 

Students select or are assigned a topic for their poem from the Topic Bank, or they may choose a topic of their own.

2 

Students complete online or printed graphic organizers to narrow the topic for their poem.

Prewriting

Explain that the first task students need to complete as they plan their poem is to determine an appropriate topic.

Choose From the Topic Bank

Read aloud each topic and then ask volunteers to describe the topics in their own words. If you are assigning topics to students, you may wish to do so now. Encourage students to ask questions about their topic.

Choose Your Own Topic

Introduce and discuss the Brainstorm, List, and Read strategies. If students were not assigned writing topics, have them use the strategies to brainstorm for topics for their poems.

Extension Have each student choose one of the strategies. Then, have students write an action plan that outlines the resources and steps they will use to develop their topic.

Narrow Your Topic

Tell students that they will use a Narrow Your Topic graphic organizer to focus their poem's topic. Then, distribute printed copies or have students log on to Writing Coach Online.

Apply It! Guide students through the instructions for completing the graphic organizer. Have students complete the exercise based on their topic.

Consider Your Audience and Purpose

Guide students to consider the audience and purpose for their poem.

Your Turn **Feature Assignment: Free Verse or Lyric Poem**

Prewriting

Plan a first draft of your poem by deciding which form of poem you want to write—a free verse, lyric, or other type of poem—and then determining an appropriate topic. Select a topic from the Topic Bank or come up with an idea of your own.

Choose From the Topic Bank

TOPIC BANK

Amazing Place Write a poem to describe the most exciting, most enjoyable, or weirdest place you have ever visited.

Favorite Thing Write a poem about your most prized possession. Describe the object and tell why it is so important to you.

My Hero Write a poem about a person you consider to be a hero. Describe that person and explain why you admire him or her. Be detailed and specific.

Choose Your Own Topic

Determine an appropriate topic on your own by using the following **range of strategies** to generate ideas.

Brainstorm, List, and Read

- Work with a partner to brainstorm for categories of places, things, and people to write about, such as historical sites, electronic gadgets, famous people, and so on.
- List specific places, things, and people matching those categories. Circle the topics that interest you most.
- Look through a literature book or poetry collection from American, European, and world literature to get ideas from topics published poets chose.

Review your responses and choose a topic.

Say: The first question in the second column asks about my purpose for writing my poem. If **I choose** the first topic from the Topic Bank, an amazing place, then my purpose would likely be to entertain my readers by getting them to experience the amazing place the way I did.

Ask: If you choose the third topic from the Topic Bank, your hero, what would your purpose for writing the poem most likely be? (**Possible responses:** to describe, to inform, to persuade)

Have students with similar topics work in small groups to discuss and respond to the remaining questions.

Coach's Corner

You may wish to model prewriting activities for students by brainstorming for your own writing topic. Use these prompts to model your thought process:

- **I am interested in** family traditions, so that could be my general topic.
- **I can narrow my topic by** focusing on my family's traditions for a specific holiday, such as Thanksgiving.

Discuss the choices you make and solicit feedback from students.

Students record their answers to questions about audience and purpose in their online journals or notebooks.

Narrow Your Topic

Narrowing your topic will help you find vivid details to create a well-crafted poem.

Apply It! Use a graphic organizer like the one shown to narrow your topic.

- Write your general topic in the top box, and keep narrowing your topic as you move down the chart.
- Your last box should hold your narrowest or "smallest" topic, the new focus of your poem.

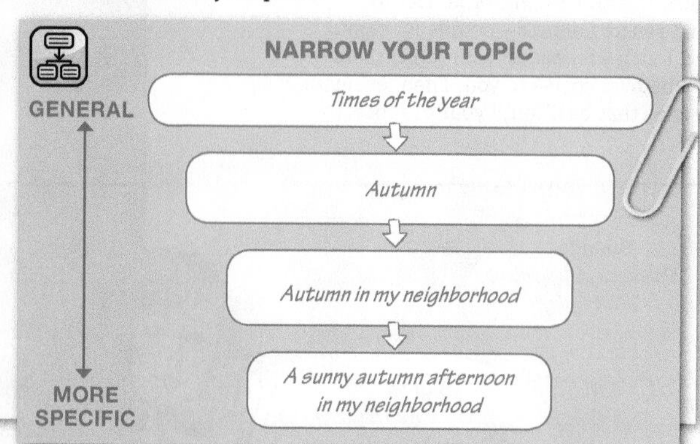

Consider Your Audience and Purpose

Before writing, think about your audience and purpose. Consider how others may see things as you ask yourself these questions.

Questions for Audience	Questions for Purpose
• Who will read my poem? My teacher? My classmates? A family member? Someone else? • What will my readers need to know to understand my poem? • What form of poetry would best convey my meaning to them?	• Why am I writing? Do I want to entertain my readers by making them laugh? Do I want them to see and feel what I saw and felt? • What kinds of **poetic techniques,** such as **figurative language** and **graphic elements,** will help me fulfill my purpose?

Record your answers in your writing journal.

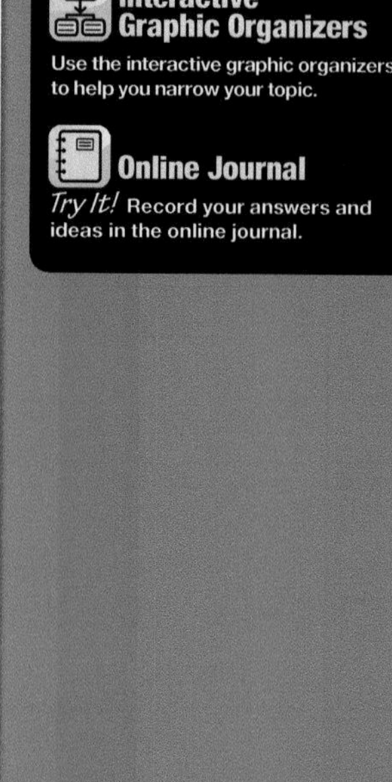

WRITING COACH
Online
www.phwritingcoach.com
Interactive Graphic Organizers
Use the interactive graphic organizers to help you narrow your topic.
Online Journal
Try It! Record your answers and ideas in the online journal.

Personalized Support

Teacher or Peer Feedback

Below Level Students complete three graphic organizers that provide models and scaffolded support.

On Level Students complete one, two, or three graphic organizers, depending on how much support they need.

Above Level Students complete the least scaffolded graphic organizer or narrow their topic without the help of a graphic organizer.

Differentiated Instruction

RTI Strategy for Below-Level Students Students may have trouble understanding how to narrow a topic. Offer additional examples of general topics gradually being refined to specific topics suitable for poems. At each stage in the refinement, ask for students' ideas before giving your response. If students have trouble narrowing their own topic, feedback from you or a partner can help them see possibilities they may not have noticed.

PRE-AP Enrichment for Above-Level Students Have students search for examples of lyric poems and free verse in literature books and poetry collections. Ask them to choose one lyric poem and one free verse poem to present to the class. Students should prepare a short lesson on the poems in which they identify the forms, topics, purposes, and audiences, and point out uses of poetic techniques and structural elements.

1 

Using Writing Coach Online™ or the student book, students read and discuss the model graphic organizer.

2 Students complete online or printed graphic organizers to develop their ideas and gather details.

Plan Your Piece

Explain that writers use graphic organizers to develop their ideas and show relationships between different parts of the text. Then, point out the Develop Your Ideas graphic organizer on page 128. Tell students that they will use this organizer to develop details for their poem. Then, distribute printed copies or have students log on to Writing Coach Online.

Introduce the graphic organizer by explaining that the center oval contains the poem's topic, theme, or controlling idea. The surrounding ovals feature ideas, feelings, and sensory details related to the central idea.

Develop a Topic, Theme, or Controlling Idea Guide students to notice that the controlling idea in the example organizer is based on the narrowed topic from page 127. Have students write a sentence that expresses their topic, theme, or controlling idea and record it on their graphic organizer.

Develop Ideas and Details Ask students to identify the kinds of details recorded in each supporting oval. Remind students that each detail should be related to their topic, theme, or controlling idea. Then, have students work in pairs to discuss and record details for their poems on their graphic organizers.

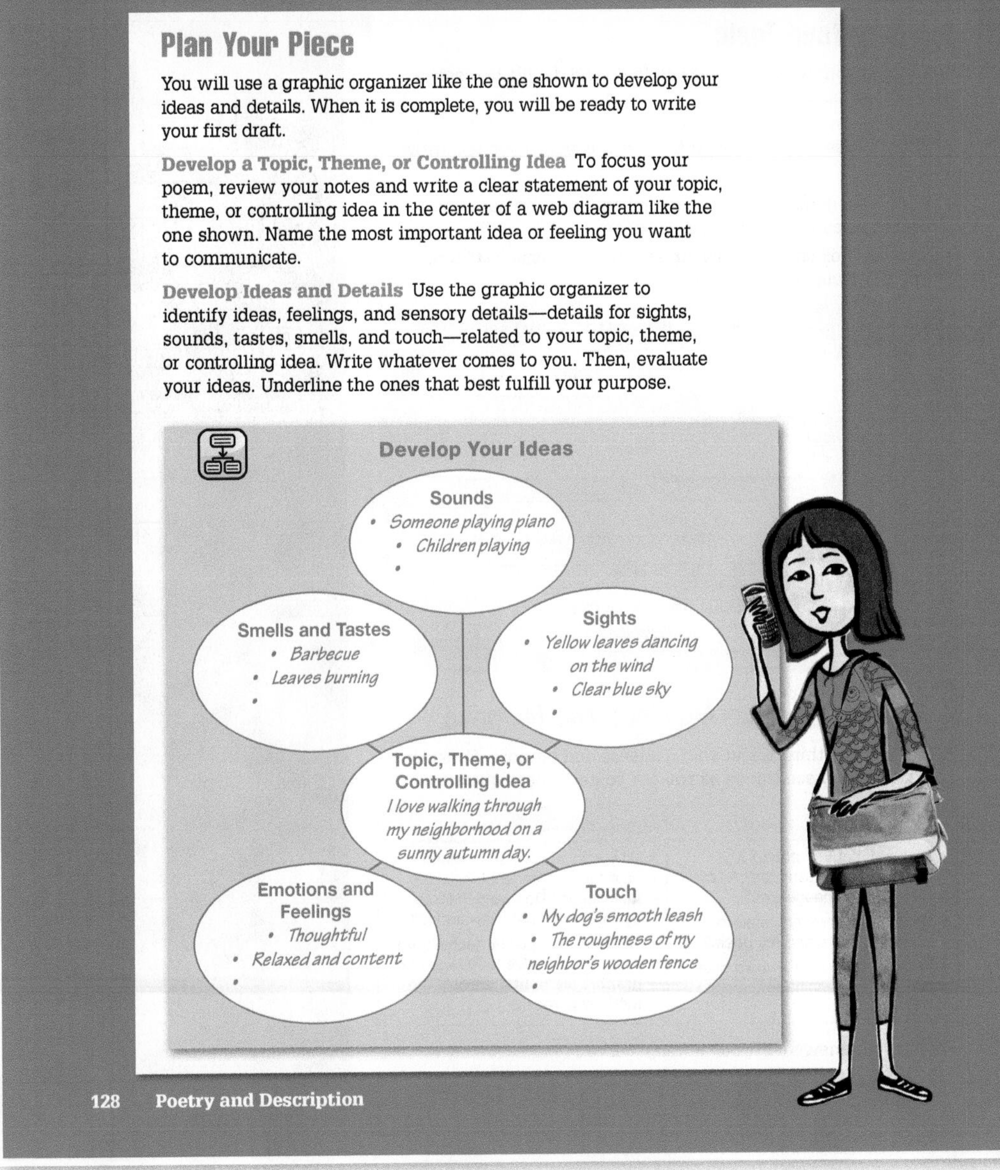
Feature Assignment Prewriting Feature Assignment Prewriting

Plan Your Piece

You will use a graphic organizer like the one shown to develop your ideas and details. When it is complete, you will be ready to write your first draft.

Develop a Topic, Theme, or Controlling Idea To focus your poem, review your notes and write a clear statement of your topic, theme, or controlling idea in the center of a web diagram like the one shown. Name the most important idea or feeling you want to communicate.

Develop Ideas and Details Use the graphic organizer to identify ideas, feelings, and sensory details—details for sights, sounds, tastes, smells, and touch—related to your topic, theme, or controlling idea. Write whatever comes to you. Then, evaluate your ideas. Underline the ones that best fulfill your purpose.

128 Poetry and Description

Poet's Toolbox

Remind students that poets express their ideas in a variety of ways. Then, guide students to use the techniques in the Poet's Toolbox to express the ideas in the example graphic organizer.

Say: I notice that the example organizer's *Sounds* oval contains the detail "Children playing." The alliteration example in the Toolbox shows how this sound device can be used to express this detail: "Children charged into piles of leaves on that chilly afternoon."

Ask: How could you use personification, or human characteristics applied to non-human objects, to express the "Leaves burning" detail from the organizer's *Smells and Tastes* circle? **(Possible response:** "The smell of burning leaves reached out with its long, thin fingers and tickled the inside of my nose.")

Have students work in small groups to apply other poetic techniques to the details in the Develop Your Ideas organizer on page 128.

Try It! Read aloud the instructions for reviewing students' graphic organizers. Then, have students work in small groups to discuss the poetic techniques they would like to use in their poems. Remind students to use a variety of techniques to express their ideas, feelings, and sensory details.

Writer's Block

IF students have difficulty developing details for their topic . . .

THEN suggest that they try freewriting on the topic for several minutes as a way to brainstorm for supporting details.

3 STUDENT BOOK

Students refer back to the Mentor Texts or the Student Models as they plan their writing.

Poet's Toolbox

Poets use a variety of techniques and literary devices to convey ideas, create images, and appeal to readers' emotions. Here are some techniques you might use in your poem.

Figurative Language is writing that means something beyond what the words actually say.	
Simile: comparison using *like* or *as*	*The leaves danced on the wind like birds in flight.*
Metaphor: comparison made by saying that one thing is something else	*The tree's bright red and orange leaves were a fire in the sky.*
Personification: human characteristics applied to non-human objects	*The leaves danced on the wind.*
Symbols add depth and insight to poetry.	
An object that stands for something else	The bright colors of the autumn leaves could symbolize joy.
Sound Devices create a musical or emotional effect.	
Alliteration: repetition of consonant sounds at the beginning of nearby words	***Ch**ildren **ch**arged into piles of leaves on that **ch**illy afternoon.*
Assonance: repetition of vowel sounds in nearby words	*Leaves r**a**ced gracefully **a**way on the wind.*
Consonance: repetition of consonants in the middle or at the end of words	*The bro**wn**, fa**ll**en leaves had a**ll** blo**wn** away.*
Structural Elements help build the framework for poetic language.	
Rhyme: repetition of sounds at the ends of lines of poetry	Jack-o'-lanterns on **porches** Burned brightly, like **torches.**
Meter: rhythmical pattern of a poem. It is determined by stressed syllables in a line. Some forms of poetry have specific patterns of stressed syllables.	*The **brown**, fallen **leaves** had **all** blown **away**.* (Stressed syllables in poetry are marked with a ´, while unstressed syllables are marked with a ˘.)
Graphic Elements position the words on the page.	
Arrangement of words on a page	capital letters, line spacing, and line breaks

Apply It! Review the ideas and details you added to your prewriting graphic organizer.

- Decide what techniques from the Poet's Toolbox you would like to use in your poem.
- Keep in mind that some poetic techniques must be used in specific forms, while other techniques are optional.
- The drafting stage is a good time to try out various techniques.

Interactive Graphic Organizers

Use the interactive graphic organizers to help you create a plan for your writing.

Interactive Model

Refer back to the Interactive Model in the eText as you plan your writing.

Personalized Support

Interactive Graphic Organizer

Below Level Students complete three graphic organizers that provide models and scaffolded support.

On Level Students complete one, two, or three graphic organizers, depending on how much support they need.

Above Level Students complete the least scaffolded graphic organizer or narrow their topic without the help of a graphic organizer.

FEEDBACK

Teacher or Peer Feedback

To provide feedback to students as they plan their first draft, ask or have student partners ask one another the following:

- What do you want your audience to know about the topic?
- What questions or concerns will your audience have about the topic?
- What details have you identified for your piece? How do these details support your thesis or controlling idea?
- Are your details varied? Will they interest your readers? Explain.

Differentiated Instruction

RTI Strategy for Special Needs Students As you discuss page 129 with students, define any difficult or unknown terms that occur in the definitions, such as *consonant, vowel,* and *syllables*. Then, share with the class several examples of poems and descriptive writing. Have students work in groups to find an example of each poetic technique in the Mentor Text and Student Model. Then, have groups share their examples with the other groups and discuss their findings.

Strategy for Spanish Speakers Students whose home language is Spanish may encounter difficulties using assonance due to the phonetic spelling of vowel sounds in Spanish. Remind students that vowel sounds may have multiple spellings. Review spellings of different vowel sounds. For example, elicit spellings for the long *ā* sound, such as a with silent *e, ai, ea, ay, ei,* and *ey,* and have students give examples for each, such as *apron, gate, pain, break, day, reindeer,* and *hey*.

1 

Using Writing Coach Online™ or the student book, students read and discuss the drafting charts for a lyric poem and a free verse poem.

2 Students discuss how the Mentor Texts illustrate the characteristics of lyric poems and free verse poems.

Drafting

Tell students that they will use the charts on page 130 to help them develop drafts of their poems. Explain that the first column of each chart lists the characteristics of a specific poetic form. The second column contains questions that will help guide students' work.

Drafting a Free Verse Poem or Lyric Poem

Link the charts to specific poems by having students turn to the Mentor Texts on pages 122–123. Then, guide students to respond to the chart questions.

Say: I notice that the lyric poem chart asks what other poetic techniques I will use besides sound devices. The lyric poem "December Leaves" on page 123 shows me what I might do. For example, in lines 6–7, the poet uses figurative language to describe the leaves and the lawn, calling the sky a "silver sifter." This metaphor helps me visualize the scene in a new way.

Ask: What other examples of figurative language can you find in the poem? (metaphors: leaves are described as cornflakes in line 1, the lawn as a dish in line 2, the wind as a spoon in line 4, and snow as sugar in line 10)

Have students who are writing the same kind of poem work with a partner to respond to the chart questions. You may wish to direct students writing a free verse poem to these characteristics in the Mentor Text on page 122:

- No meter is used (entire poem)
- Vivid descriptions (lines 3–6, 7–15)

Direct students writing a lyric poem to these characteristics in the Mentor Text on page 123:

- Rhyme scheme (lines 1–5, 6–10)
- Poetic techniques: figurative language (lines 1–2, 3, 6–7, 10)

Drafting *Feature Assignment* Drafting *Feature Assignment* D

Drafting

During the drafting stage, you will start to write your ideas for a free verse, lyric, or other form of poem. You will build on the ideas you developed in prewriting, choosing an organizational strategy appropriate for free verse or lyric poetry.

Drafting a Free Verse Poem or Lyric Poem

Each poetic form has specific characteristics. You will write a **focused, organized, and coherent poem** using these characteristics, the techniques from the Poet's Toolbox, and the ideas, feelings, and sensory details you developed in your graphic organizer.

These charts show the characteristics of the free verse and lyric forms. Review the characteristics. Then, answer the questions in the right column as you draft your poem.

Free Verse Characteristics	Questions to Answer While Drafting
• Number of lines varies • Number of stanzas varies • No meter is used; follows natural patterns of speech • Rhyme is not often used • Poetic techniques used • Feelings or emotions conveyed • Vivid descriptions presented	• How long do I want my poem to be? **Tip:** You don't have to decide an exact number of stanzas and lines. • What sound devices will I use? • What poetic techniques will I use? • What feelings or emotions will I express? • How will I make my descriptions vivid?

Lyric Poem Characteristics	Questions to Answer While Drafting
• Number of lines varies • Stanzas may be used, but they are not required • Rhyme scheme may be used, but it is not required • Meter (regular rhythm) may be used, but it is not required • Poetic techniques used • Feelings or emotions conveyed • Vivid descriptions presented	• How many lines will I write? Will I use stanzas? • Do I want to use rhyme? If so, what words will I rhyme in each stanza? **Tip:** Consult a rhyming dictionary and thesaurus to find the right words. • Do I want to use a regular meter? If so, what rhythm? **Tip:** Read aloud as you write to hear the rhythm. Use a dictionary to see how words are divided into syllables. • What sound devices will I use? • What other poetic techniques will I use? • What feelings or emotions will I express? • How will I make my descriptions vivid?

130 Poetry and Description

Start Your Draft

Have small groups read aloud and discuss the boxed instructions for drafting. Direct students to work individually on their first draft.

Coach's Corner

If you are modeling the writing process for students with your own topic or a student volunteer's, you may wish to use these prompts to guide your drafting and discussion:

- **I will use poetic techniques** to express my ideas.
- **I will use a stanza break** before I discuss a new idea.

Discuss the choices you make and solicit feedback from students.

3 Students begin writing their poem online or in their notebooks.

4 Students share their work with their teacher.

5 Students receive feedback from their teacher. Students may continue to work on their drafts.

Start Your Draft

Writing poetry is different than creating most other genres. It is more open. Use the graphic organizer that shows your topic, ideas, and sensory details, and the Poet's Toolbox as guides, but be open to experimenting with your draft.

Remember, the most important part of drafting is just getting your ideas in writing. You can always go back and refine your writing when you revise and edit.

Before You Write

- √ Choose the **poetic form** you want to use—free verse poem, lyric poem, or another poetic form.
- √ Review the **poetic traditions** of your poetic form that are listed in Drafting a Free Verse Poem or Lyric Poem. Make sure you use these characteristics when you write your draft.
- √ State or imply the **theme, topic,** or **controlling idea.** It does not have to be apparent in each line, but should be clear in the poem as a whole.
- √ Include your ideas from prewriting. If a feeling, emotion, sensory detail, or other idea does not seem to work, you may decide not to keep it in your poem.

While You Write

- √ Use **poetic techniques** to support your ideas. If a technique does not seem to work, try another.
- √ Use **figurative language,** such as similes, metaphors, and personification, in your poem. Figurative language will keep your writing interesting.
- √ Use **sensory details** in your poem, to make your poem come alive to your readers.
- √ Use **graphic elements,** such as line and stanza breaks, to signal changes in ideas.

Interactive Model

Refer back to the Mentor Text in the eText as you write your draft.

Personalized Support

Teacher or Peer Feedback

To provide feedback to students on their first draft, ask or have student partners ask one another the following:

- Can you explain how you organized your ideas in this piece?
- Why did you include this information here?
- Why did you choose this beginning? Does it grab your reader and identify your thesis or controlling idea?
- What supporting details could you add here?
- Why did you choose this ending? How does it add to your piece?
- Can you show me a place where I can hear your unique voice?
- Can you show me a place where you used vivid language?

Working with ELLs

ELL Sheltered Instruction: Cognitive

Help students develop and demonstrate an increasing ability to distinguish formal from informal English and an increasing knowledge of when to use each and adapt spoken language appropriately for informal purposes. Help students identify if these situations call for formal or informal language: a presentation and a friendly conversation. Then:

Beginning Model a situation with formal English, like a response to a presentation: *I enjoyed your work.* Have them repeat, then orally adapt the response for an informal purpose, like telling a friend *Great job!*

Intermediate Say sentences and have partners identify the language as formal or informal and orally adapt the formal language for an informal purpose.

Advanced Have pairs take turns reading aloud written versions of the formal and informal sentences from the Intermediate activity. Listeners should identify language as formal or informal and adapt each formal sentence for an informal purpose.

Advanced High Have students complete the Advanced activity, then say their own formal and informal sentences.

The Digital • Print Path

1 

Using Writing Coach Online™ or the student book, students study the first and second drafts of the student model to see how the writer used Revision RADaR to improve his or her writing.

2 

Students use the Revision RADaR strategy to revise their own writing.

Revising: Making It Better

Point out the page title to students and explain that revising means making improvements to a writing draft. Then, read aloud the opening paragraph to introduce the Revision RADaR strategies. You may wish to have students review Chapter 3 for more information on Revision RADaR.

Kelly Gallagher, M. Ed.

KEEP REVISION ON YOUR RADAR

1ST DRAFT After students have read the first draft, have them turn to page 120 and review the list of poetry characteristics. Guide students to understand that the questions the author asked about the draft are based on these characteristics. For example, call out the third question and note that it asks about patterns of natural speech, which is found on the list.

Then, have students work in small groups to develop other questions about the draft based on the list of poetry characteristics.

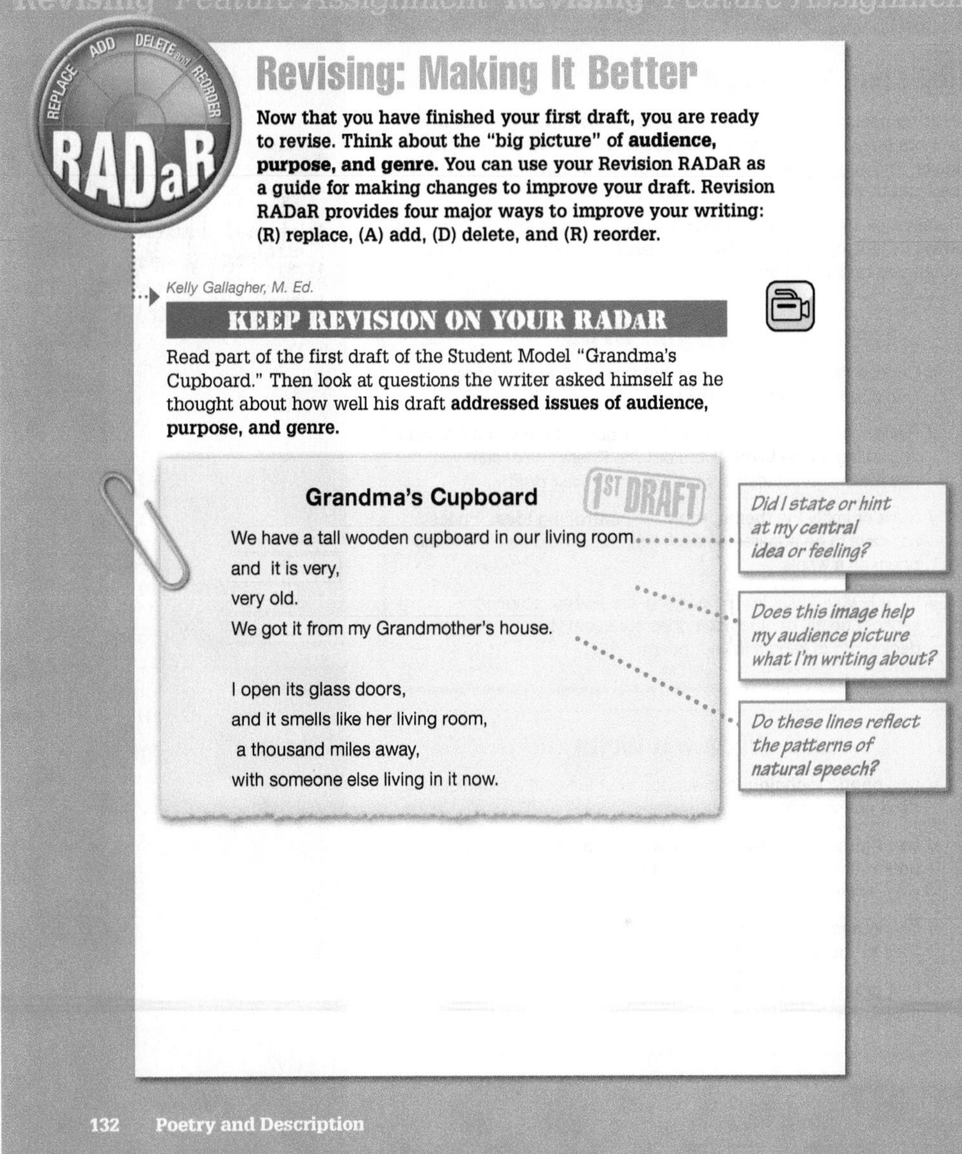

Revising Feature Assignment Revising Feature Assignment

Revising: Making It Better

Now that you have finished your first draft, you are ready to revise. Think about the "big picture" of audience, purpose, and genre. You can use your Revision RADaR as a guide for making changes to improve your draft. Revision RADaR provides four major ways to improve your writing: (R) replace, (A) add, (D) delete, and (R) reorder.

Kelly Gallagher, M. Ed.

KEEP REVISION ON YOUR RADAR

Read part of the first draft of the Student Model "Grandma's Cupboard." Then look at questions the writer asked himself as he thought about how well his draft **addressed issues of audience, purpose, and genre.**

Grandma's Cupboard 1ST DRAFT

We have a tall wooden cupboard in our living room
and it is very,
very old.
We got it from my Grandmother's house.

I open its glass doors,
and it smells like her living room,
a thousand miles away,
with someone else living in it now.

Did I state or hint at my central idea or feeling?

Does this image help my audience picture what I'm writing about?

Do these lines reflect the patterns of natural speech?

132 Poetry and Description

2ND DRAFT Guide students to understand how the author used the RADaR strategies to revise the first draft.

Think Aloud **I thought** that the image of the cupboard in the 1st draft wasn't very clear or vivid. In the 2nd draft, though, I see an *A* next to those lines, which means the writer has added something. The new sensory details such as "golden oak, soft and worn" help me visualize the cupboard, which is the central object of the poem.

Work with students to brainstorm for other sensory details the writer could have added.

Have students work in small groups to discuss the other changes in the 2nd draft.

Apply It! Review the bulleted instructions for using Revision RADaR. Remind students to question their drafts based on the poetry characteristics on page 120. Tell students to use each RADaR strategy at least once.

Coach's Corner

If you are modeling the writing process for students with your own draft or a student volunteer's, use these prompts to focus on the Revision RADaR *Replace* strategy:

- **I replaced a word here because** I wanted to use a stronger, more specific verb.
- **I replaced a phrase here because** I needed a more vivid sensory detail.

Discuss the choices you make and solicit feedback from students.

3 Students share their work with their teacher.

4 Students receive feedback from their teacher. Students may continue to revise their drafts.

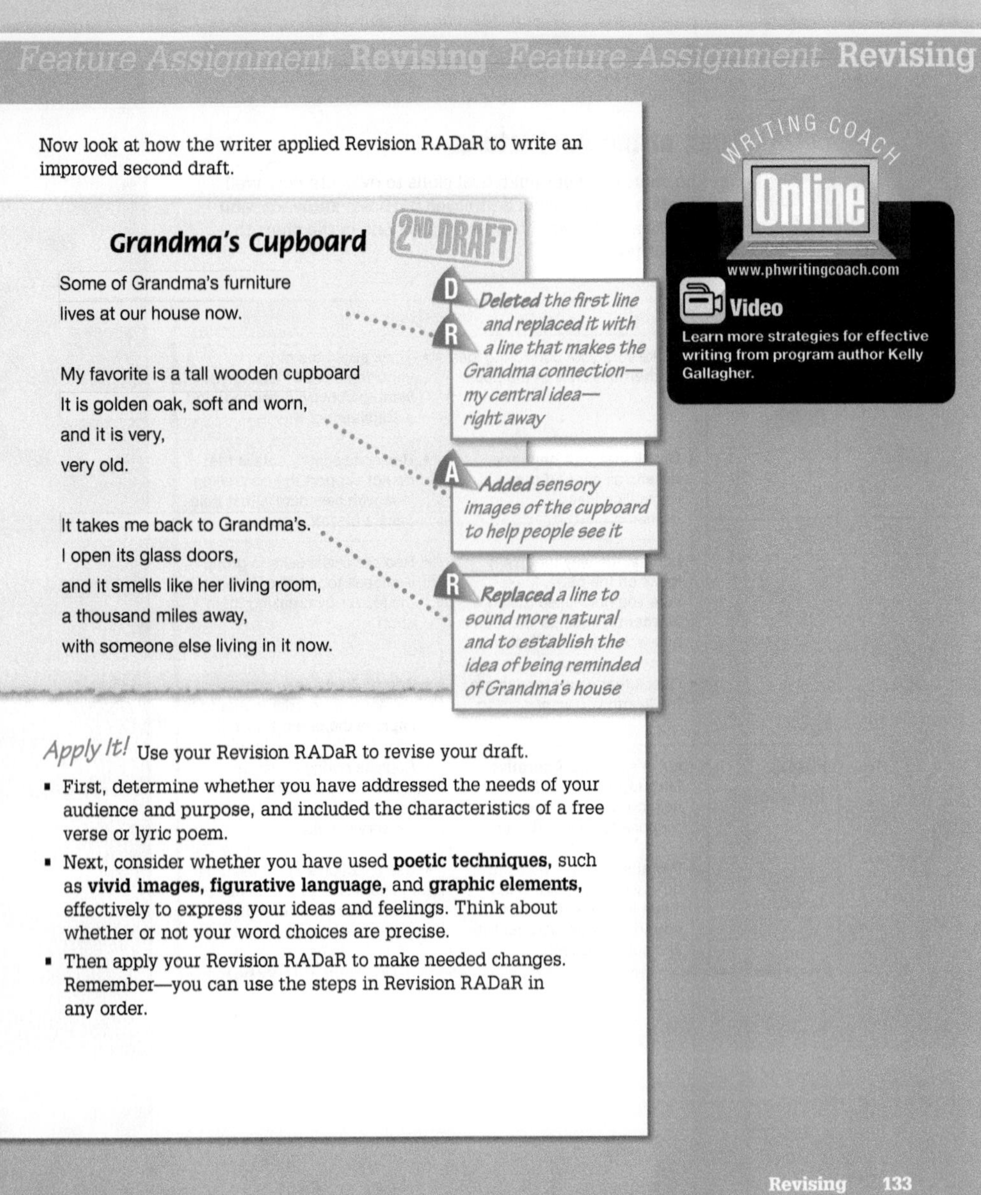

Feature Assignment Revising Feature Assignment Revising

Now look at how the writer applied Revision RADaR to write an improved second draft.

Grandma's Cupboard

2ND DRAFT

Some of Grandma's furniture
lives at our house now.

My favorite is a tall wooden cupboard
It is golden oak, soft and worn,
and it is very,
very old.

It takes me back to Grandma's.
I open its glass doors,
and it smells like her living room,
a thousand miles away,
with someone else living in it now.

D R *Deleted the first line and replaced it with a line that makes the Grandma connection—my central idea—right away*

A *Added sensory images of the cupboard to help people see it*

R *Replaced a line to sound more natural and to establish the idea of being reminded of Grandma's house*

WRITING COACH Online

www.phwritingcoach.com

Video

Learn more strategies for effective writing from program author Kelly Gallagher.

Apply It! Use your Revision RADaR to revise your draft.

- First, determine whether you have addressed the needs of your audience and purpose, and included the characteristics of a free verse or lyric poem.
- Next, consider whether you have used **poetic techniques,** such as **vivid images, figurative language,** and **graphic elements,** effectively to express your ideas and feelings. Think about whether or not your word choices are precise.
- Then apply your Revision RADaR to make needed changes. Remember—you can use the steps in Revision RADaR in any order.

Revising 133

Personalized Support

Teacher or Peer Feedback

To provide feedback to students as they revise their first draft, ask or have student partners ask one another the following:

- Can you show me where you revised your text?
- What could you add to your beginning to grab the interest of your readers?
- How could you reorder these ideas so that their order is more logical?
- Have you included all the characteristics of this form of writing?
- Is there any unnecessary text that you could delete?
- Have you achieved your purpose with this piece of writing?
- Have you addressed the questions and concerns of your audience?

Working with ELLs

ELL Sheltered Instruction: Cognitive

Point out the bulleted list in the *Apply It!* to help students comprehend English language structures, including bulleted directions, used routinely in written classroom materials. Explain how bullets set off items of information.

Beginning Give examples of information often organized using bullets, such as items in a list and steps in directions. Have each student find another bulleted list in a textbook. For each example, help students see how the bullets help the reader.

Intermediate Have groups find at least three other bulleted lists in a textbook and discuss why that format is appropriate in each instance. Then, have them refer to page 133 to write a bulleted list of elements they should check for in their drafts.

Advanced Have pairs find three other bulleted lists in a textbook and discuss why that format is appropriate for each. Then, choose a page of continuous paragraphs, and have pairs adapt the page using bullets.

Advanced High Have students complete the Advanced activity, then compare their bulleted lists with a partner's.

1 

Using Writing Coach Online™ or the student book, students study and discuss the revision chart.

2 

In a video by program author Kelly Gallagher, students learn more strategies for effective writing.

Revising: Making It Better

Look at the Big Picture

Introduce the revision chart to students. Explain that the first column identifies the three main building blocks of poetry. The Evaluate column identifies the characteristics in each block and explains how to assess them. The Revise column presents specific strategies for revising each characteristic.

Then, have students work individually to evaluate and revise their draft, using the chart to guide their work.

Revising *Feature Assignment* Revising *Feature Assignment* R

Look at the Big Picture

Use the chart and your analytical skills to evaluate how well each section of your poem **addresses purpose, audience, and genre.** When necessary, use the suggestions in the chart to revise your poem.

	Evaluate	Revise
Topic and Sensory Details	• Make sure your controlling idea or **theme** is clear in the poem.	• Think about the most important idea or feeling you want to convey. If needed, add a statement of theme.
	• Check that your **sensory details** all support the controlling idea or theme.	• Replace sensory details that do not support the controlling idea with new details that help paint a clearer picture.
Structural Devices	• Look at the way the poem looks on the page. Make sure you have used **graphic elements,** such as line breaks and white space, effectively.	• Reorder line breaks to group like ideas together or to jar the reader by breaking them apart.
	• Check that your **stanzas** are the length you want.	• Add or delete lines and replace and reorder words to improve the poem's flow.
Poetic Techniques	• Make sure your **figurative language** and word choices help convey your meaning and purpose to your audience.	• Replace boring or vague words with figurative language, vivid words, and sensory details.
	• Pay attention to the sound quality of your draft. Read aloud to check that your **sound devices** are effective and sound correct.	• Use a dictionary or thesaurus to find words to create better assonance or alliteration.

134 Poetry and Description

Focus on Craft: Vivid Images

Have students read the introductory text. Guide them to understand how vivid images appeal to readers' senses.

Say: I notice that the Student Model has details that appeal to our sense of sight. We can "see" that the cupboard is made of "golden oak" and that it looks "soft and worn."

Ask: The details in the Student Model appeal to what other senses? How? (They appeal to our sense of touch; the excerpt says the cupboard is "worn" and so we can imagine how it would feel if we touched it.)

Have students work with a partner to think of other details about the cupboard that appeal to the senses.

Try It! Have students discuss the questions and record responses in their journals. Follow up with students to check that their responses reflect an understanding of how vivid images affect the mood in a poem.

Fine-Tune Your Draft

Apply It! Ask volunteers to read aloud the instructions for fine-tuning their drafts. Then, have students work in pairs to improve their drafts' images and graphic elements.

Teacher or Family Feedback Have students identify Mentor Text examples of the characteristics that were marked for improvement. Use the Mentor Text references on page T130 to guide students to appropriate examples.

Teacher Tip

Have students underline each vivid image in the draft of their poem to see how many they included and decide whether they need to add more. They can evaluate the wording of each image to see if it can be improved.

3 Using Writing Coach Online™ or the student book, students refer back to the Mentor Texts or Student Models for examples of writer's craft.

4 Students record answers to questions about writer's craft in their online journals or notebooks.

5 Students share their work with their teacher.

6 Students receive feedback from their teacher.

Focus on Craft: Vivid Images

Vivid images are word pictures that appeal to the senses. They help readers see, hear, smell, taste, and feel what the writer is describing. The best images are fresh and precise—and often unexpected. Carefully chosen images can also create the mood of a description. Consider the difference between "hot, stinging sand" and "soft, drifting sand."

Think about vivid images and precise word choice as you read these lines from the Student Model.

STUDENT MODEL from **Grandma's Cupboard,** page 124, lines 4–6

It is golden oak, soft and worn,
and it is very,
very old.

Try It! Now, ask yourself these questions:

- How do you feel about the cupboard when it is described as "golden oak, soft and worn"?
- How would your feelings about it change if it were described as "brown, old, and scratched" instead?

Fine-Tune Your Draft

Apply It! Use the revision suggestions to prepare your final draft after rethinking how well questions of purpose, audience, and genre have been addressed.

- **Improve Poetic Techniques** Make precise **word choices** and use **figurative language** to create **vivid images** in your poem. Replace words and phrases that do not help convey your meaning or enhance the poem's mood.
- **Fine-tune Graphic Elements** Make sure that the line and stanza breaks keep your meaning clear.

Teacher or Family Feedback Read your poem aloud to your teacher or a family member. Think about the feedback you receive and revise your final draft as needed.

Online Journal
Try It! Record your answers in the online journal.

Interactive Model
Refer back to the Interactive Model as you revise your writing.

Personalized Support

Teacher or Peer Feedback

To provide feedback to students as they continue to revise their first draft, ask or have student partners ask one another the following:

- What are you trying to say here? What part of the text could you replace to make your meaning clearer?
- Is there a more precise word you could use here?
- How does the rhythm of these sentences sound to you? Could you make the length and structure of these sentences more varied?
- How could you include transitional words and phrases here to help your reader understand these ideas?
- Are there details you could add here to make this part come alive?

Working with ELLs

ELL Sheltered Instruction: Social/Affective

Help students read "Grandma's Cupboard," and use peer and teacher support to enhance and confirm understanding and develop background knowledge needed to comprehend increasingly challenging language. Elicit and develop their background knowledge of furniture.

Beginning Show and discuss pictures of cupboards and oak wood to develop background. Preteach *cupboard, oak, soft,* and *worn*. Have students **Echo Read** the Student Model excerpt and clarify meaning.

Intermediate To develop background knowledge, discuss types of furniture. Preteach *wooden, cupboard, oak,* and *worn*. Have pairs read the Student Model on page 124 and discuss how background knowledge aids understanding.

Advanced Have partners discuss types of furniture and read the Student Model on page 124, using a dictionary as necessary, then discuss how background knowledge aids understanding.

Advanced High Have partners complete the Advanced activity, then write a brief description of a piece of furniture.

1 

In a video by program author Jeff Anderson, students learn effective editing techniques.

2 

Students record answers to questions about writer's craft in their online journals or notebooks.

Editing: Making It Correct

Discuss the opening paragraph with students. Explain that they will edit their drafts for proper grammar, mechanics, and spelling, including placement of modifiers.

WRITE GUY *Jeff Anderson, M.Ed.*

WHAT DO YOU NOTICE?

Introduce students to the locations of modifiers by reading aloud the Mentor Text excerpt and discussing responses to the "Ask yourself" question. Then, have students read the explanation of modifier placement.

To monitor students' comprehension, guide them to identify and place modifiers in sentences.

I know the poet could have put the modifiers in other places: "Their round feet," "You sometimes can see," or "You can see sometimes." Writers choose the modifiers they want to use; they also choose where to place the modifiers. They just can't place them too far away from the words they modify.

Work with students to point out the locations of adjectives and adverbs in the Mentor Text poem on page 123 and to identify the words they modify.

Have students work in small groups to add modifiers to simple sentences you provide, such as *The girl called to the horse,* and to try placing the modifiers in different locations.

Editing *Feature Assignment* Editing *Feature Assignment* E

Editing: Making It Correct

Use the editing process to polish your work and correct errors. It is often helpful to work with a partner when editing your drafts.

As you edit your work, think about the **placement of modifiers,** such as adjectives, adverbs, **adjectival phrases, and adverbial phrases**. Then, edit your final draft for any errors in **grammar, mechanics, and spelling.**

WRITE GUY *Jeff Anderson, M. Ed.*

WHAT DO YOU NOTICE?

Zoom in on Conventions Focus on the location of modifiers as you zoom in on these lines from the Mentor Text.

MENTOR TEXT from **Southbound on the Freeway**
page 122; lines 7, 13–14

Their feet are round...
Sometimes you can see a five-eyed
one, with a red eye...

Now, ask yourself: *Which **modifiers** make the description more vivid?*

You may have noticed the adjectives *round, five-eyed,* and *red.* Adjectives are usually placed immediately before or after the noun they modify. In the poem, *red* modifies *eye,* and *five-eyed* modifies *one.* Some adjectives are separated from their noun by a linking verb. For example, the verb *are* separates *feet* from its modifier *round.*

Adverbs often occur immediately before or after the words they modify. However, adverbs can also be placed away from the words they modify. In the poem, the adverb *Sometimes* is placed at the beginning of the sentence, away from *can see,* the verb it modifies.

Partner Talk Discuss this question with a partner: *How does the placement of modifiers affect the rhythm of the poem?*

To learn more about modifiers, see Chapter 15 of your Grammar Handbook.

Grammar Mini-Lesson: Phrases as Modifiers

Discuss the paragraph and the Mentor Text excerpt on page 137 with students. Guide them to understand that one prepositional phrase acts as an adjective and the other acts as an adverb.

Try It! Have students work with a partner to identify the phrases in the sentences.

1. in very dim light (adverbial phrase)
2. by the school (adjectival phrase)

Apply It! Remind students to look closely at their placement of modifiers as they edit their drafts.

Use the Rubric Explain to students that they will rate how well their draft addresses each element on a scale of 1 to 6, with 6 being the best score.

Then, have students use the rubric to evaluate their drafts. Tell them to support their rankings with concrete examples. Students should then revise their drafts as necessary.

Writer's Block

IF students have difficulty determining whether the modifiers in their poems are correctly placed . . .

THEN have them circle the modifiers in their drafts and draw arrows from the modifiers to the words they modify to make sure that the modifiers are located as close to those words as possible.

3 Using Writing Coach Online™ or the student book, students refer back to the Mentor Text or Student Model as they edit their writing.

4 Using Writing Coach Online™ or the student book, students evaluate their writing using the rubrics.

5 Students submit edited drafts to their teacher.

6 Students receive personalized feedback from the teacher.

Grammar Mini-Lesson: Phrases as Modifiers

To learn more, see Chapter 19.

An **adjectival phrase** is a prepositional phrase used as an adjective to modify a noun or a pronoun. An **adverbial phrase** is a prepositional phrase used as an adverb to modify a verb, an adjective, or another adverb. Notice the adjectival and adverbial phrases in the Mentor Text.

MENTOR TEXT from **Southbound on the Freeway** page 122; lines 3–4

The creatures of this star
are made of metal and glass.

Of this star is an adjectival phrase that modifies the noun *creatures*. *Of metal and glass* is an adverbial phrase that modifies the verb *made*.

Try It! Identify the adjectival or adverbial phrase in the **simple sentences** below. Write the answers in your journal.

1. He was reading in very dim light.
2. Sue went to the library by the school.

Apply It! Edit your draft for grammar, punctuation, capitalization, and spelling errors. Be sure to use correctly placed modifiers, including adjectival and adverbial phrases.

Use the rubric to evaluate your poem. If necessary, rethink, rewrite, or revise.

Rubric for Poetry: Free Verse or Lyric Poem	Rating Scale					
Ideas: How well do your ideas develop your poem's subject or controlling idea?	Not very 1	2	3	4	5	Very 6
Organization: How clearly are your ideas organized?	1	2	3	4	5	6
Voice: How effectively do you use figurative language and poetic techniques to create a unique voice?	1	2	3	4	5	6
Word Choice: How well does your word choice create vivid images?	1	2	3	4	5	6
Sentence Fluency: How effective is the rhythm and sound of your poem?	1	2	3	4	5	6
Conventions: How correct is your punctuation, capitalization, and spelling for the form you have chosen?	1	2	3	4	5	6

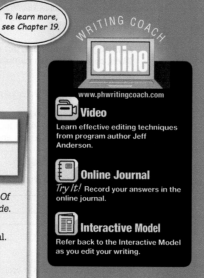

Writing Coach Online

www.phwritingcoach.com

Video
Learn effective editing techniques from program author Jeff Anderson.

Online Journal
Try It! Record your answers in the online journal.

Interactive Model
Refer back to the Interactive Model as you edit your writing.

Personalized Support

Teacher or Peer Feedback

To provide feedback to students as they edit their draft, ask or have student partners ask one another the following:

- Have you looked for mistakes that you tend to make?
- Have you read your piece aloud to yourself or to a partner? What kind of errors did you find?
- Can you show me something you changed through editing?
- What resources have you used to look for possible spelling errors?
- Read this sentence aloud. Does the grammar sound correct to you?
- Read this sentence aloud. Does the punctuation accurately convey your meaning?

Working with ELLs — ELL Sheltered Instruction: Metacognitive

Have students monitor and edit writing for appropriate verb tense. Have them use the self-corrective technique of circling verbs, identifying their tense, and correcting inappropriate tense shifts. Adapt *Try It!* on page 137.

Beginning Write *is, are, was,* and *were* on the board. Write sentence 1 from *Try It!* and a sentence with *was* or *were*. Model the self-corrective technique, asking *When?* about each verb. Help students use the technique to check their work.

Intermediate Have partners complete the Beginning activity, then write their own short paragraphs that begin with the second sentence from *Try It!* using the self-corrective technique to check their work.

Advanced List these irregular verbs: *to go, to have, to come.* Have students write a paragraph using the verbs based on a phrase from *Try It!*, using the self-corrective technique to check their work. Have them apply the technique to their poems.

Advanced High Have students complete the Advanced activity, using adjectival and adverbial phrases in their paragraphs and checking for correct forms.

1 

Using Writing Coach Online™ or the student book, students complete the writing process by deciding the best way to publish their writing for their intended audience.

2 

Students record their answers to Reflect on Your Writing in their online journals or notebooks.

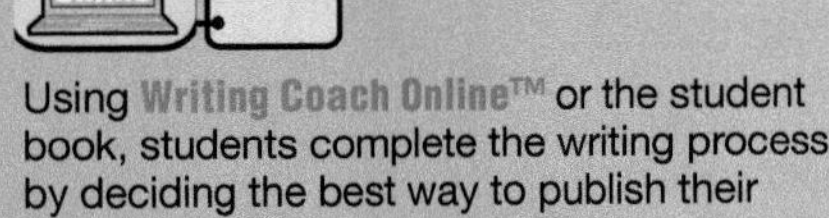

Publishing

Wrap Up Your Presentation

Remind students who handwrote their work to use the proper poetic form for their lines and stanzas. For students who wrote their work on a computer, display some easy-to-read computer fonts.

Publish Your Piece

Explain to students that the final step in the writing process is to decide which form of publication will present their work most effectively. Then, tell students that the chart shows how specific audiences can be reached using different media.

Have students whose poems address similar audiences work in small groups to discuss appropriate ways to publish their work.

Reflect On Your Writing

Have students discuss the questions with a partner, including the Big Question, and record responses in their journal.

Extension Have students develop a research plan for learning more about their topic. Students should identify what they want to learn, which resources they will use, and how this information could be used to improve or embellish their poem.

Manage Your Portfolio You may wish to have students include development materials such as graphic organizers and drafts.

MAKE YOUR WRITING COUNT

Introduce the image collection activity by discussing the opening paragraphs with students. Make sure students understand that the project may be produced electronically or by hand. Then, guide students through each step in the action plan.

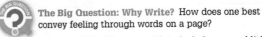

Publishing *Feature Assignment* Publishing *Feature Assignment*

Publishing

Publish your poem! First, get your poem ready for presentation. Then, choose a way to publish your work for appropriate audiences.

Wrap Up Your Presentation

If your poem is handwritten, you may need to make a new, clean copy. If so, be sure to **write legibly.** Also make sure your title grabs the reader's attention and indicates your poem's topic.

Publish Your Piece

Use this chart to help you find a way to publish your poem.

If your audience is...	...then publish it by...
Members of your family	• Printing it with family photos or your own drawings and making keepsake copies • Memorizing it and reciting it on a special occasion
Teachers and classmates at your school	• Submitting it to the school newspaper • Posting it on an arts Web site for other students to see

Reflect on Your Writing

Now that you are done with your poem, read it over and use your writing journal to answer these questions.

- Which parts of your final product are especially strong? Why?
- How does knowing how to write a poem help you appreciate other poets' work? Explain.
- Compare your poem to another piece of writing that expresses a similar theme. As you evaluate what the works have in common, consider ways you might learn from both pieces.

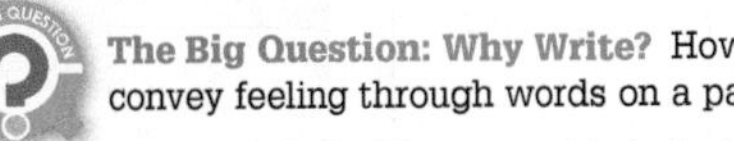

The Big Question: Why Write? How does one best convey feeling through words on a page?

Manage Your Portfolio You may wish to include your published poem in your writing portfolio. If so, consider what this piece reveals about your writing and your growth as a writer.

138 Poetry and Description

Resources You may wish to have students use these organizers: Meeting Agenda, Meeting Notes, and Flow Chart/Chain of Events. Distribute printed copies or have students log on to Writing Coach Online.

Use the 21st Century Skills Rubric to evaluate each group's process and final product on a scale of 1 to 3, indicating weak, moderate, or strong use of the skill. ▶

Listening and Speaking Monitor groups as they deliver and receive feedback.

21st Century Learning

Skills Rubric	Rating
Think Creatively: Elaborate and refine ideas to improve creative efforts.	1 2 3
Work Creatively With Others: Be open and responsive to new and diverse perspectives.	1 2 3
Apply Technology Effectively: Use technology as a tool to organize and communicate information.	1 2 3
Create Media Products: Understand and use the most appropriate media creation tools.	1 2 3

3 STUDENT BOOK

Students use a variety of graphic organizers, either online or in print, to help them work together to create a multimedia group project.

4 STUDENT BOOK

Through Writing Coach Online™ students link to resources on 21st Century Learning for help in creating a multimedia group project.

21st Century Learning

MAKE YOUR WRITING COUNT

Share Poetic Vision Using Graphics and Text

Poetry uses its carefully chosen words to create vivid images in the mind. Help others "see" poetic images by producing a **collection of images** inspired by a classmate's poem.

Work in a group to select a group members' poem and discuss its imagery. Then, brainstorm for ways to illustrate these images using photos, drawings, or other graphic media. Each group member should contribute by preparing or finding appropriate images. The group can then compile text and graphics into a printed photo album or **multimedia presentation.**

Online Journal

Reflect on Your Writing Record your answers and ideas in the online journal.

Resource

Link to resources on 21st Century Learning for help in creating a group project.

Here's your action plan.

1. With your group, read through your peers' poems. Choose one that contains strong "word pictures" or expresses a particular mood or emotion.
2. Work individually to create or find an illustration based on the central image or mood of the poem.
3. Look online for free, downloadable images.
4. Share your illustrations with your group. As a group:
   - Create captions for each image
   - Talk about why different people come up with different illustrations for the same poem
5. Publish the images and poem in a print or electronic multimedia slideshow. Many Web sites offer free photo-album software for creating slide shows.
6. Present your photo album by circulating it among the class groups, by having groups take turns viewing the slideshow on a computer, or by posting it online.

Listening and Speaking After viewing each group's photo album or slideshow, discuss it within your group. Take turns delivering feedback about each of the other groups' work.

Personalized Support

Teacher or Peer Feedback

To provide feedback to students on their published writing, ask or have student partners ask one another the following:

- How did you go about writing this piece? What was your process?
- What did you learn from the writing model that you used in this piece?
- What surprised you the most as you wrote this piece?
- Did you try anything new as you worked on this piece?
- What did you learn from this piece of writing that you would like to remember and reuse?
- What do you think you do best as a writer right now?

Differentiated Instruction

RTI Strategy for Below-Level Students Before students try to create a poem photo album, show them what one might look like. Find and display library books that feature a single poem accompanied by a number of photographs or illustrations. As students look through each book, ask them to describe the images they see and tell why they think those images were chosen to go with that poem. Then, as a class, brainstorm for images for the students' photo album.

PRE-AP Enrichment for Above-Level Students Encourage students to think of a way to organize the process by which their group evaluates their poems and selects one. For example, students might prepare a checklist of criteria, which they fill out for each poem. Comparing the checklists will help them see which poems best meet the criteria. The checklists not only help narrow the choices but also help make the selection process more impartial.

1 

Students use Writing Coach Online™ or their student books to analyze and discuss the Writing for Media topic.

Writing for Media: Travel Writing

Travel Writing

Discuss the opening paragraph with students. As a class, brainstorm for places where people might encounter travel writing, such as in newspapers and magazines and online.

Try It! Guide students to understand the purpose and elements of travel writing.

The third *Try It!* question asks about specific details in the travel writing sample. **I see** these specific details in the first sentence: when the bats fly, where the bats fly, and how many bats fly.

Work with students to identify other specific details in the travel writing sample.

Have students discuss the remaining questions in small groups and record individual responses in their journals.

Extension Have students bring in other examples of travel writing. Then, lead a media discussion about the examples, using the *Try It!* questions as a guide.

Create a Travel Blog

Tell students that they will create a travel blog using the five-step writing process. Then, preview the writing process instructions on page 141.

Resources You may wish to have students use the Cluster Diagram graphic organizer. Distribute printed copies or have students log on to Writing Coach Online.

For each step in the writing process, have partners read aloud and discuss the list of tasks. Then, have them work individually. Once both partners have completed the tasks, have them evaluate each other's work before moving to the next step.

Writing for Media Writing for Media Writing for Media Writi

Writing for Media: Travel Writing

21st Century Learning

Travel Writing

Travel writing is a type of descriptive writing that focuses on a particular place. The aim of a travel writer is to present useful and interesting information about a location for audiences who are thinking of visiting it. Travel writing includes helpful facts about a place—its location and geography, climate, population, transportation, hotels, restaurants, and so on. Travel writing also features colorful details about local attractions so that readers can get a feeling for the place and choose specific spots to tour.

When you understand the purpose and elements of travel writing, you can make good judgments when you read about other places in print media or online.

Try It! Study the text in the travel writing sample. Then, answer these questions. Record your answers in your journal.

1. What particular **place** is the writer describing?
2. What seems to be the writer's overall **feeling** about this place?
3. Good travel writing includes **specific details** in the description of the place. What specific details are included in this sample of travel writing?
4. Travel writing usually includes **reasons** to visit a place. What reasons do you find in this?
5. To what kind of specific **audience** would this example of travel writing appeal?

Extension Find another example of a travel writing, and compare it with this one.

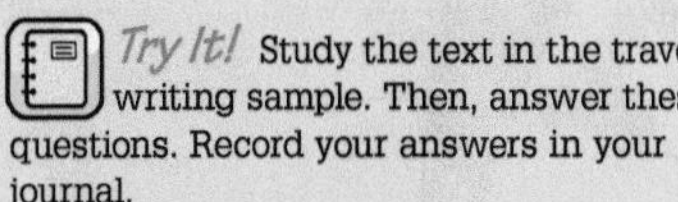

Austin, Texas, "Bats" a Million

Every evening at dusk, nearly two million bats swoop, flutter, and generally darken the skies around Austin's Congress Avenue Bridge. The nocturnal critters took up residence under the bridge after it was rebuilt in 1980, and the spot has since become a wildly popular haunt for bats and tourists alike.

The Congress Avenue bats form the largest urban bat colony on the planet. Thousands of human tourists flock to the bridge every night to watch the bats emerge on their nightly hunt for insects and other goodies.

Several tour boats offer special views of the nightly bat flight from the river. These tours cost only $8–$10. An annual Labor Day festival called Batfest celebrates the colony with live music, crafts, and, of course, a bat costume contest. But whenever you come to town, a visit to Austin would not be complete without spending some time hanging out (so to speak) at the Congress Avenue Bridge.

140 Poetry and Description

Use the 21st Century Skills Rubric to evaluate each student's process and final product on a scale of 1 to 3, indicating weak, moderate, or strong use of the skill. ▶

Partner Talk

Remind students that their feedback to their partner should include specific, constructive comments and suggestions.

21st Century Learning

Skills Rubric	Rating
Communicate Clearly: Articulate ideas using written communication skills.	1 2 3
Analyze Media: Understand how and why media messages are constructed and for what purposes.	1 2 3
Work Independently: Monitor, define, prioritize, and complete tasks without direct oversight.	1 2 3
Produce Results: Demonstrate the ability to manage time and projects effectively.	1 2 3

Students learn about the characteristics of travel writing by answering questions about the model. Students record their answers to the *Try It!* questions in their online journals or notebooks.

Students follow the five-step writing process to write their own travel writing. Students may select online or printed graphic organizers to help them plan and develop their writing.

Create a Travel Blog

Follow these steps to create your own blog entry describing your hometown for an online travel site. To plan your blog entry, review the graphic organizers on pages R24–R27 and choose one that suits your purpose.

Prewriting

- Identify the place to be described, your town.
- Identify a specific audience and consider its needs and interests. Plan questions about the place that will appeal to your readers.
- Write notes on the details you want to include in your travel writing. Answer these questions as you think about details to include: What are the main attractions of the place? Who in your audience would be most likely to visit it? What does your audience need to know in order to plan a visit?

Drafting

- Format the travel writing as a blog entry.
- First, write a title identifying your town. Then, present your travel information, with interesting and helpful details and strong images. Keep your information clear, specific, and accurate.
- As you write, aim for a lively, colorful style to appeal to your audience. Use a conversational tone and humor appropriate to blog writing.
- Select pictures to include with your blog entry.

Revising and Editing

- Review your draft to ensure that the description is logically organized and the details and images are specific.
- Take out details that do not serve your purpose or that might confuse the reader.
- Check that spelling, grammar, and mechanics are correct.

Publishing

Use the information from your travel blog as the basis for a multimedia presentation. Use some of the text from your writing, as well as photos and other graphics you can find or create. Then, present it to the class.

WRITING COACH
Online
www.phwritingcoach.com
Online Journal
Try It! Record your answers in the online journal.
Interactive Graphic Organizers
Choose from a variety of graphic organizers to plan and develop your project.

Partner Talk

Before you start drafting, describe the place to a partner or small group as your blog writer would. Make sure your description is specific and detailed, and ask for feedback about it. For example, does it sound appealing?

Personalized Support

Teacher or Peer Feedback

To provide feedback to students as they write for media, ask or have student partners ask one another the following:

- What are the main characteristics of this form of writing?
- Have you included most or all of these characteristics in your piece of writing?
- What is your purpose for writing this piece?
- Who is your audience?
- How did you organize your ideas in this piece of writing?
- How did you go about revising the piece? Editing it?
- How do you plan on publishing your piece?
- What other publishing options also might work?

Working with ELLs

ELL Sheltered Instruction: Social/Affective

Adapt the Partner Talk to have students ask for and give information in situations ranging from basic communication to extended speaking assignments. Guide students to use both high-frequency and content-based words and monitor their speech using the self-corrective technique of watching the listener's response and restating ideas as needed.

Beginning Review the terms *town* and *place*. Help partners ask for and give information by asking and answering simple questions such as *What is your favorite place in town?* Remind them to use the self-corrective technique.

Intermediate Review the words *town* and *place*, then help partners take turns asking and answering questions using the words. Remind students to use the self-corrective technique.

Advanced Have students complete the Intermediate activity and summarize their partner's ideas.

Advanced High Have students complete Partner Talk, asking for more information and using the self-corrective technique.

1 

Before they write, students use the ABCDs of On-Demand Writing to analyze and plan how to respond to each prompt. They can use either their online journals or notebooks to take notes.

Writing for Assessment

Read aloud or have a student read aloud the introductory text. Then, tell students that they will learn and practice a technique for writing in response to a prompt.

Try It! Read aloud the Poetry Prompt and then have volunteers read aloud the Format and Academic Vocabulary boxes. Tell students that they will use the ABCD method to respond to the prompt.

The ABCDs of On-Demand Writing

Have students identify the words associated with the ABCD method. (attack, brainstorm, choose, detect) Then, guide students through their use.

I'll attack the prompt by circling the key words *describing, choose,* and *use.* These words help me remember what I need to do in my poem. I can rewrite the prompt to state that clearly: "Write a poem describing your feelings about a tree using poetic form and techniques."

Work with students to brainstorm for an appropriate graphic organizer for the poem, such as a Main Idea and Details Web.

Have students write their drafts individually and then trade drafts with a partner to help detect errors in each other's work.

Writing for Assessment Writing for Assessment Writing for Assessment Writin

Writing for Assessment

Writing a good poem can take a lot of practice. You can use these prompts to do just that—practice writing poems. Your responses should include the characteristics on page 120.

Try It! To begin, read the prompt and the information on format and academic vocabulary. Use the ABCDs of On-Demand Writing to help you plan and write your **poem**.

Format
The prompt directs you to write a *poem.* Develop your topic by choosing details that convey your main idea.

Poetry Prompt
Think about a tree you have often seen—perhaps one near your home or school. Write a poem describing that tree and your feelings about it. Choose a poetic form and use poetic techniques.

Academic Vocabulary
Remember that *poetic techniques* are the tools poets use to convey their ideas. Each poem has a specific *poetic form,* such as the lyric or free verse poem.

 The ABCDs of On-Demand Writing

Use the following ABCDs to help you respond to the prompt.

Before you write your draft:

Attack the prompt [1 MINUTE]

- Circle or highlight important verbs in the prompt. Draw a line from the verb to what it refers to.
- Rewrite the prompt in your own words.

Brainstorm possible answers [4 MINUTES]

- Create a graphic organizer to generate ideas.
- Use one for each part of the prompt if necessary.

Choose the order of your response [1 MINUTE]

- Think about the best way to organize your ideas.
- Number your ideas in the order you will write about them. Cross out ideas you will not be using.

After you write your draft:

Detect errors before turning in the draft [1 MINUTE]

- Carefully reread your writing.
- Make sure that your response makes sense and is complete.
- Look for spelling, punctuation, and grammar errors.

142 Poetry and Description

More Prompts for Practice

Apply It! Have students apply the ABCD method to the practice prompts.

Prompt 1 Have partners attack the prompt and brainstorm for possible answers. Then, have each pair swap their information with another group to evaluate whether the teams have chosen a suitable poetic form and included figurative language and vivid images.

Spiral Review: Narrative Read aloud the instructions and the prompt. Then, have students review the narrative nonfiction characteristics on page 66.

Prompt 2 Remind students to use the ABCD method to write their personal narrative.

Spiral Review: Short Story Read aloud the instructions and the prompt. Then, have students review the short story characteristics on page 92.

Prompt 3 Remind students to use the ABCD method to write their short story.

2 Students share their writing with their teacher.

3 Students receive feedback from their teacher.

More Prompts for Practice

Apply It! Respond to Prompt 1 by writing a **poem** that uses poetic techniques, figurative language, and graphic elements. Be sure to:

- Identify your audience and choose from a variety of **poetic forms** and use **graphic elements,** such as line breaks and stanzas appropriate to your chosen form
- Establish a clear topic, theme, or **controlling idea**
- Use **poetic techniques** and **figurative language** to develop ideas

> **Prompt 1** Poets often get inspiration from their surroundings. Look outside your window right now and think about what you see. Write a poem about something you notice outside your window.

Spiral Review: Narrative If you choose to write a **personal narrative** in response to Prompt 2, make sure your story reflects the characteristics described on page 66.

> **Prompt 2** Write a personal narrative about something funny or interesting that happened when you took a trip somewhere. The place could be another state or country, or somewhere close to home.

Spiral Review: Imaginative Short Story If you choose to write a **short story** in response to Prompt 3, be sure that your story reflects the characteristics described on page 92. Your writing should express your ideas and feelings about the real or imagined people, events, and ideas that you describe. In addition, be sure to:

- Sustain **reader interest**
- Develop an **engaging story line** with **interesting characters, well-paced action** and a well-developed conflict that is resolved
- Use **sensory details** to present a specific, believable **setting**
- Use a range of **literary strategies** and **devices** to enhance the **style** and **tone** of the story

> **Prompt 3** Write a serious or humorous short story about a misunderstanding between friends. Make the misunderstanding the main conflict, and be sure that plot events center around it.

Interactive Writing Coach™

Plan your response to the prompt. If you are using the prompt for practice, write one paragraph at a time or your entire draft and then submit it for feedback. If you are using the prompt as a timed test, write your entire draft and then submit it for feedback.

Remember ABCD

- **A**ttack the prompt
- **B**rainstorm possible answers
- **C**hoose the order of your response
- **D**etect errors before turning in the draft

Personalized Support

Assessment/Monitor Progress

For timed writing practice, assign students a prompt to be completed in a timed setting. For Prompt 2, have students submit their writing to **Interactive Writing Coach™** to get immediate feedback.

For a formal writing assessment, assign the Assessment writing prompt for this chapter in **Writing Coach Online™**. Then, have students submit their writing to **Interactive Writing Coach™** to be assessed. Use the results to assess student progress and skill levels. **Interactive Writing Coach™** will update student levels to ensure that students get the appropriate support.

Teacher Feedback

To create an assessment environment, have students use a prompt in a timed setting. Grade papers using the appropriate rubric and use the results to assess student progress and skill levels. In the next writing assignment, ensure that students get the appropriate level of support.

If you conference with students, use these questions to guide your discussion:

- What form of writing did the prompt call for?
- How did you organize your ideas?
- Did you make good use of your time?

Working with ELLs

ELL **Sheltered Instruction:** Cognitive

Students should show an increasing ability to distinguish between formal and informal English and an increasing knowledge of when to use each. Have students determine whether to use formal or informal language and adapt their spoken language appropriately for informal purposes. Act out situations using formal or informal language as appropriate: meeting a student and meeting the principal.

Beginning Guide students to distinguish between the formal and informal English, identify when each is appropriate, and adapt language to the informal situation.

Intermediate Help students determine which type of language should be used in each situation. Have them discuss a trip as if in a formal situation, then adapt their speech for informal purposes.

Advanced Have groups determine whether each situation calls for formal or informal language, then act out a formal situation and adapt their language for informal purposes.

Advanced High Have students complete the Advanced activity and discuss how they chose appropriate language.

CHAPTER 8 LESSON PLANNER
Exposition

Use the Online Lesson Planner at www.phwritingcoach.com to customize your instructional plan for an integrated Language Arts curriculum.

DAY 1

CHAPTER OPENER/ GENRE INTRODUCTION

- How Can You Explain This?
- What's Ahead
- Connect to the Big Questions
- **Feature Assignment: Expository Essay: Compare-and-Contrast Essay**
- Other Forms of Expository Writing
- Word Bank

ONLINE

DAY 2

MENTOR TEXT/ STUDENT MODEL

- **Mentor Text: Expository Essay**
- Learn From Experience
- **Student Model: Compare-and-Contrast Essay**
- Reader's Eye and Writer's Eye

ONLINE

DAY 3

Prewriting

- Choose From the Topic Bank
- Choose Your Own Topic
- Narrow Your Topic
- Consider Your Audience and Purpose

ONLINE

DAY 6

Revising

- Keep Revision on Your RADaR
- Look at the Big Picture
- Focus on Craft
- Fine-Tune Your Draft

ONLINE

DAY 7

For additional grammar support, see Section 25.2, p. 556.

Editing

- What Do You Notice? / Grammar Mini-Lesson

Rubric for Expository Writing: Compare-and-Contrast Essay

Publishing

- Publish Your Essay
- Extend Your Research

ONLINE

DAY 8

21st Century Learning

MAKE YOUR WRITING COUNT

- **Write and Present the Results of a Survey**
- Here's Your Action Plan
- Listening and Speaking

ONLINE

Alternate Pacing Suggestions

- **Block Scheduling** Each day on the Lesson Planner represents a 40–50 minute block. Teachers using block scheduling may combine days to revise pacing to meet their classroom needs.
- **Accelerated Lesson Planning** Combine instructional days by aiding students in choosing a topic and then focusing on two core stages of the writing process, outlining for success (Day 5) and RADaR revision (Day 6).
- **Integrated Language Arts Curriculum** For targeted instruction that covers the essential components of the lesson, use either a 3- or a 5-day plan.

3 day plan

DAY 1: Introduction to the Genre, Mentor Text, Student Model

DAY 2: Prewriting/Drafting

DAY 3: Revising/Editing/ Publishing

5 day plan

Use 3-day plan, and add:

DAY 4: Make Your Writing Count

DAY 5: Writing for Assessment

Links to Prentice Hall *LITERATURE*

Featured Author: Richard Peck

What Are Fiction and Nonfiction?, p. 4

- "The Three-Century Woman" (fiction), Richard Peck, p. 9
- "The Fall of the *Hindenburg*" (informative article), Michael Morrison, p. 19
- On Conflict in Fiction (Writing Workshop), p. 179
- *From the Author's Desk* Videos: Richard Peck

Additional Mentor Text:

- "Conversational Ballgames" (expository essay), Nancy Masterson Sakamoto, p. 432

Differentiated Instruction

Differentiated Instruction Boxes in this Teacher's Edition address these student populations:

- Below-Level Students
- Above-Level Students
- Gifted and Talented Students
- Special Needs Students
- English Language Learners
- Spanish Speaking Students

In addition, for further enrichment, see the **Extension** features.

DAY 4

Prewriting

- Plan Your Piece
- Gather Details

ONLINE

DAY 5

Drafting

- Outline for Success
- Start Your Draft

ONLINE

DAY 9

WRITING FOR MEDIA

- **Technical Newsletter**
- Create a Technical Newsletter

ONLINE

DAY 10

WRITING FOR ASSESSMENT

- Expository Prompt
- The ABCDs of On-Demand Writing
  More Prompts for Practice
  Test Prep
- Spiral Review: Poetry

ONLINE

LESSON OBJECTIVES

- To learn the forms and defining characteristics of exposition.
- To learn the elements of a successful compare-and-contrast essay, the chapter Feature Assignment.
- To read a Mentor Text in the genre, analyzing its use of the elements of an effective expository essay.
- To read a Student Model of a compare-and-contrast essay, analyzing it from the perspective of a reader and from the perspective of a writer.
- To apply prewriting strategies in developing a compare-and-contrast essay, including strategies for choosing and narrowing a topic, planning writing, and gathering details, as well as tips for considering audience and purpose.
- To apply drafting strategies in developing a compare-and-contrast essay.
- To apply RADaR revision strategies to a draft compare-and-contrast essay.
- To learn about the Focus on Craft topic, effective transitions, and apply what is learned to a draft compare-and-contrast essay.
- To edit the draft, zooming in on transitions and focusing on using commas with transitions.
- To complete the Make Your Writing Count assignment, developing and presenting a humorous skit.
- To complete the Writing for Media assignment, developing a technical newletter.
- To practice writing for assessment.

Personalized Assessment

✓	Ongoing Assessment	Formal Assessment of Feature Assignment	Progress Monitoring at End-of-Chapter
 Interactive Writing Coach™	Use Paragraph Feedback and Essay Scorer as a revision tool.	Use Essay Scorer to score students' Feature Assignment papers.	Use Essay Scorer to score students' papers. Students' learner profiles can be adjusted based on their scores.
FEEDBACK Teacher Conferencing	Use rubrics in the Student Edition as a revision tool. Conference with students to review their work and provide personalized support.	Use rubrics in the Student Edition to score students' Feature Assignment papers.	Review each student's work to plan targeted resources for the next writing assignment.

The Digital • Print Path

1 

Using **Writing Coach Online™** or the student book, students discuss the photograph in the chapter opener as it relates to the writing genre.

2 

Students record their ideas and responses in their online journals or notebooks. They may also record and save their responses on pop-up sticky notes in **Writing Coach Online™**.

Chapter Objectives

1. Write an expository essay by planning, drafting, revising, editing, and publishing individual work.
2. Produce a humorous skit.
3. Use the five-step writing process to write a technical newsletter.
4. Write a compare-and-contrast essay and a poem in response to a prompt.

CHAPTER 8

EXPOSITION

144 Exposition

EXPOSITION

How Can You Explain This?

Activate Prior Knowledge Tell students that the purpose of expository writing is to explain an idea or ideas. Tell students that they will use what they know about old and new buildings to explain the photo on page 144. Then, guide the students in analyzing the photo.

To write an expository essay means to explain a topic or idea. Sometimes you may explain a topic by showing how two things are alike and different. For example, in this photo **I see** two buildings. They appear to have many differences. For example, one is round and one has straight lines.

Work with students to brainstorm for other similarities and differences based on their analysis of the photo. Record students' responses.

Try It! **Have students** work individually to develop responses to the questions. Check that students have identified similarities and differences.

Possible responses: The buildings are similar in that they both have walls, a roof, several stories, and windows. They are different in that one has many decorations while the other is plain, one has a round shape while the other has straight lines, and one seems to be old while the other is newer. Details that could be used to describe the buildings include shape, decoration, size, color, and age.

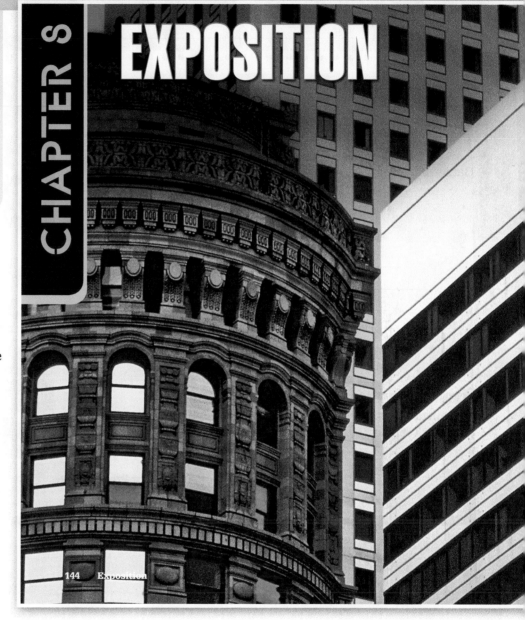

Connect to the Big Questions

Have students use their experience to discuss the Big Questions. Explain that they will revisit **Why write?** at the end of this chapter. Tell students to consider these points during their discussion:

1. Explain that the argument about new versus old is always a matter of opinion. Students should consider style and historical value as well as practicality in their discussion.
2. Descriptions help writers *show* people, places, and things instead of simply *telling* about them. Description is a useful tool in comparing and contrasting.

What's Ahead

Have students preview the Mentor Text and Student Model on pages 148–151. Tell students that they will write their own compare-and-contrast essay using the five-step writing process: prewriting, drafting, revising, editing, and publishing.

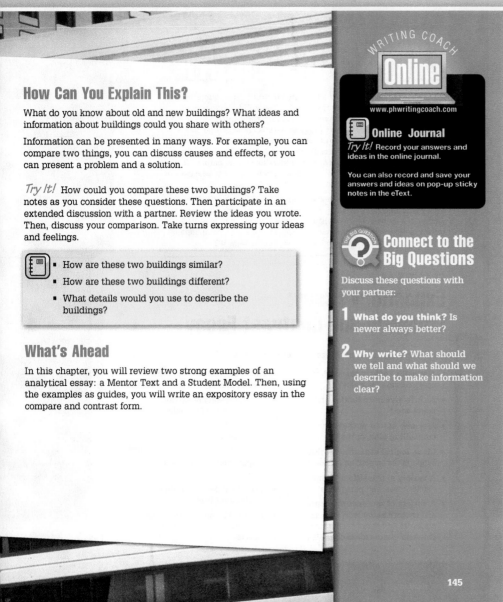

How Can You Explain This?

What do you know about old and new buildings? What ideas and information about buildings could you share with others?

Information can be presented in many ways. For example, you can compare two things, you can discuss causes and effects, or you can present a problem and a solution.

Try It! How could you compare these two buildings? Take notes as you consider these questions. Then participate in an extended discussion with a partner. Review the ideas you wrote. Then, discuss your comparison. Take turns expressing your ideas and feelings.

- How are these two buildings similar?
- How are these two buildings different?
- What details would you use to describe the buildings?

What's Ahead

In this chapter, you will review two strong examples of an analytical essay: a Mentor Text and a Student Model. Then, using the examples as guides, you will write an expository essay in the compare and contrast form.

WRITING COACH

www.phwritingcoach.com

Online Journal

Try It! Record your answers and ideas in the online journal.

You can also record and save your answers and ideas on pop-up sticky notes in the eText.

Connect to the Big Questions

Discuss these questions with your partner:

1. **What do you think?** Is newer always better?
2. **Why write?** What should we tell and what should we describe to make information clear?

Personalized Support

FEEDBACK

Teacher or Peer Feedback

To encourage students in their discussion of the photograph as it relates to the writing genre, ask the following questions:

- What is the first thing you think of when you look at this photo?
- How does it relate to your life?
- How does it relate to things you've learned in other subjects?
- What questions come to mind when you look at this photograph?
- How does your response to the photograph compare to those of your classmates?

Working with ELLs

ELL **Sheltered Instruction:** Cognitive

Help students learn new expressions heard during classroom instruction and interactions. Read the Big Question aloud. Then:

Beginning As students listen, write and say *newer* and *better*, explaining their meanings. Clarify meaning by choosing pairs of objects and orally identifying one of the objects *newer*. Repeat with *better*.

Intermediate As students listen, explain *newer* and *better* (the definitions and that they are adjectives). Discuss how a noun can be described by more than one adjective. Have students practice using two adjectives to describe nouns.

Advanced As students listen, explain: Newer *and* better *are adjectives. The Big Question leaves out the nouns. The question is really asking whether the newest item is always the best item.* Have pairs discuss their initial response to this question.

Advanced High As students listen, explain the idea of describing something as "new and improved" and how it is used in advertising. Then, have individuals write a response to the Big Question and share with the class.

The Digital • Print Path

1 

Students learn vocabulary from the Word Bank and listen to English and Spanish pronunciations in the Writing Coach Online™ glossary.

2 

Students record answers to questions about forms of writing in their online journals or notebooks.

EXPOSITORY ESSAY

To introduce this chapter's writing form, discuss the opening paragraphs with students. Make sure students understand that a compare-and-contrast essay is a type of expository essay. Explain that good writers use a step-by-step process to develop their work. Then, have students preview the rubric on page 163.

Expository Essay: Compare-and-Contrast Essay

Ask volunteers to read aloud the feature assignment characteristics. Tell students that they will identify these characteristics in a Mentor Text and a Student Model. Then, they will use the characteristics to guide the writing of their own compare-and-contrast essay.

Other Forms of Expository Essays

Guide students to understand how the forms of expository essays are alike and different.

Say: I'm familiar with some forms of expository essays. For example, when I read about current issues in a newspaper or magazine, the articles are sometimes cause-and-effect essays or problem-solution essays.

Ask: How are these forms of expository essays alike? (They all explain or give information about a topic.) How are they different? (Each form has a different purpose and may be organized differently.)

Have students brainstorm for appropriate topics for each writing form.

Try It! Remind students that the audience is the people who will read their writing. The purpose is the author's reason for writing. Have students record their responses in their journal.

Possible responses: cause-and-effect essay, tells what causes a volcanic eruption; classification essay, classifies different types of food; pro-con essay, shows reasons for and against using a product

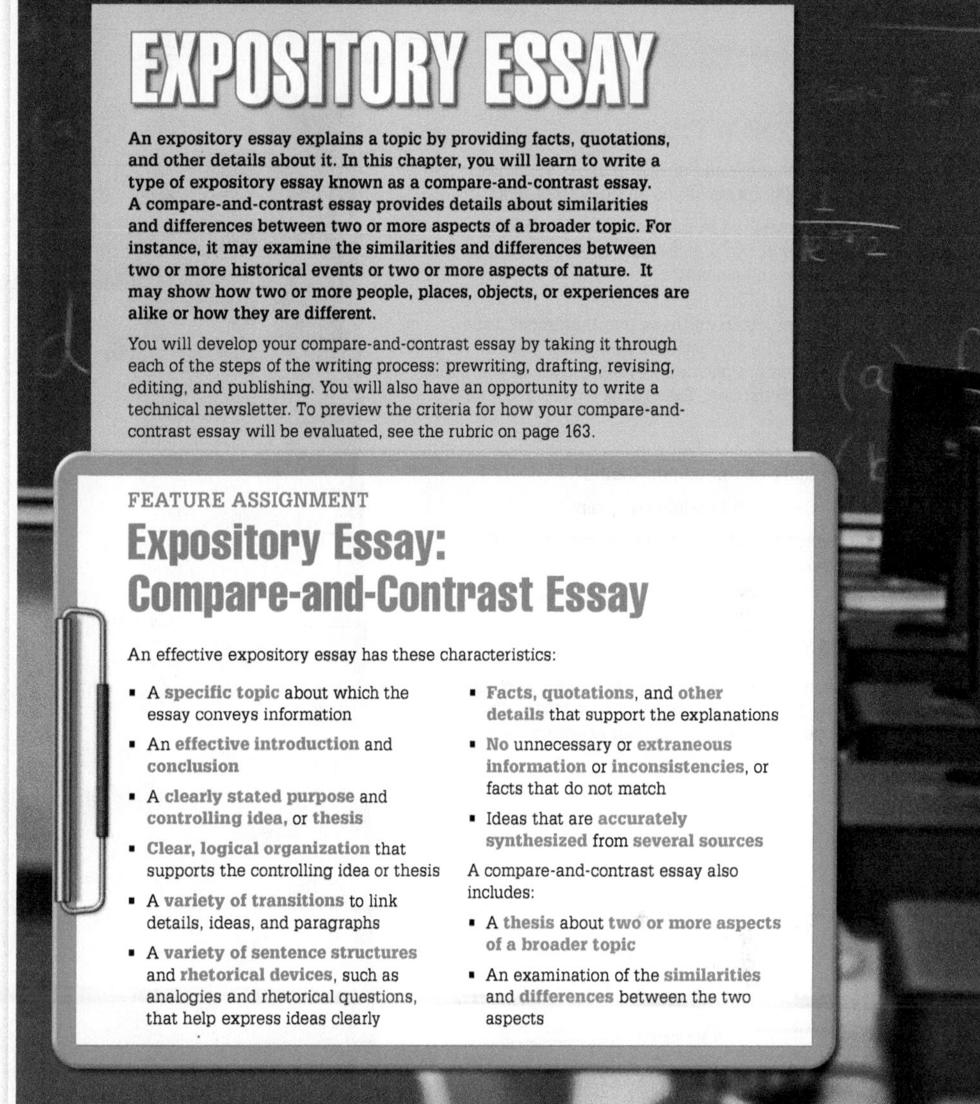

EXPOSITORY ESSAY

An expository essay explains a topic by providing facts, quotations, and other details about it. In this chapter, you will learn to write a type of expository essay known as a compare-and-contrast essay. A compare-and-contrast essay provides details about similarities and differences between two or more aspects of a broader topic. For instance, it may examine the similarities and differences between two or more historical events or two or more aspects of nature. It may show how two or more people, places, objects, or experiences are alike or how they are different.

You will develop your compare-and-contrast essay by taking it through each of the steps of the writing process: prewriting, drafting, revising, editing, and publishing. You will also have an opportunity to write a technical newsletter. To preview the criteria for how your compare-and-contrast essay will be evaluated, see the rubric on page 163.

FEATURE ASSIGNMENT

Expository Essay: Compare-and-Contrast Essay

An effective expository essay has these characteristics:

- A **specific topic** about which the essay conveys information
- An **effective introduction** and **conclusion**
- A **clearly stated purpose** and **controlling idea,** or **thesis**
- **Clear, logical organization** that supports the controlling idea or thesis
- A **variety of transitions** to link details, ideas, and paragraphs
- A **variety of sentence structures** and **rhetorical devices,** such as analogies and rhetorical questions, that help express ideas clearly
- **Facts, quotations,** and **other details** that support the explanations
- **No** unnecessary or **extraneous information** or **inconsistencies,** or facts that do not match
- Ideas that are **accurately synthesized** from **several sources**

A compare-and-contrast essay also includes:

- A **thesis** about **two or more aspects of a broader topic**
- An examination of the **similarities** and **differences** between the two aspects

146 Expository Essay

Word Bank

To assist English Language Learners and struggling readers, echo read each word or have students log on to Writing Coach Online to listen to the pronunciations. Then, have partners take turns using each word in a sentence. Ask volunteers to share one of their sentences with the class.

Teacher Tip

Have students apply their understanding by explaining in what other curricular areas they might use forms of expository writing. For example, they might use a cause-and-effect essay to explain an event in history or a phenomenon in science. They might write a classification essay about genus and species in science or about different media in art.

Other Forms of Expository Essays

In addition to a compare-and-contrast essay, there are other forms of expository essays, including:

Cause-and-effect essays trace the results of an event or the reasons an event happened.

Classification essays organize a subject into categories or explain the category into which an item falls.

Newspaper and magazine articles in print or published on the Internet supply relevant information about a particular topic by analyzing the topic's elements. They may also reflect genres other than expository essays (for example, persuasive writing or narrative nonfiction writing).

Pro-con essays examine the arguments for and against a particular action or decision.

Problem-solution essays identify a problem and explain one or more ways to solve it.

Try It! For each audience and purpose described, choose a form, such as a pro-con essay or a problem-solution essay, that is appropriate for conveying your intended meaning to your audience. Explain your choices.

- To describe the results of a volcanic eruption to students in your science class
- To explain to a friend who is interested in nutrition the categories in which different foods are grouped
- To provide shoppers with an idea of the benefits and drawbacks of a particular product

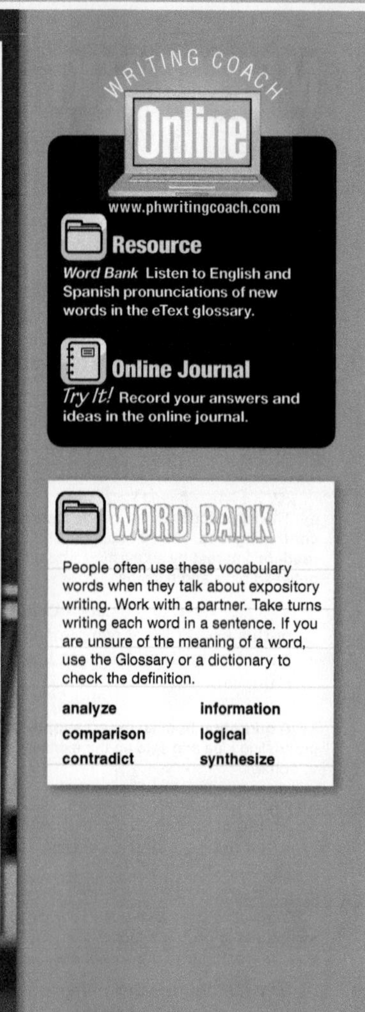

Resource
Word Bank Listen to English and Spanish pronunciations of new words in the eText glossary.

Online Journal
Try It! Record your answers and ideas in the online journal.

WORD BANK

People often use these vocabulary words when they talk about expository writing. Work with a partner. Take turns writing each word in a sentence. If you are unsure of the meaning of a word, use the Glossary or a dictionary to check the definition.

analyze	information
comparison	logical
contradict	synthesize

Personalized Support

Teacher or Peer Feedback

To help students understand the characteristics of the writing form, ask or have student partners ask one another the following questions:

- What are the main characteristics of an expository essay?
- What makes this form of writing different from other forms?
- Who are the likely readers or audiences for this form of writing?
- What kind of organization could be used for this form of writing?
- What kind of voice would be most effective for this form of writing?

Working with ELLs

Sheltered Instruction: Cognitive

Using the first *Try It!* activity, have students expand and internalize initial English vocabulary, learning, using, and reusing basic, high-frequency words to orally identify and describe objects. List these high-frequency words: *whole, together, took, store,* and *center.*

Beginning Use the words in phrases about nutrition. Have students use and reuse the words as they say the phrases aloud.

Intermediate Help students use the vocabulary to orally complete cloze sentences about nutrition and the food groups. Provide corrective feedback, helping students to use and reuse the vocabulary.

Advanced Provide additional high-frequency words, such as *produce, scale, breakfast, farmer,* and *drink.* Tell students to use and reuse each of the words on the expanded list as they talk about nutrition and the food pyramid.

Advanced High Have partners complete the Advanced activity. Extend by having listeners note and discuss any unfamiliar words used by their partners.

The Digital • Print Path

1 STUDENT BOOK

Using Writing Coach Online™ or the student book, students read and listen to an audio recording of the Mentor Text. As they complete their writing assignments, they can refer back to the Mentor Text for support whenever they need it.

MENTOR TEXT

About the Selection The selection is an expository essay about the intelligence of bees. It describes an experiment in which bees were rewarded for "remembering" a pattern of two or three dots. Scientists concluded that bees could tell the difference between two objects and three. The essay subtly compares bees to humans.

Learn From Experience

After students have read the text, point out that the numbered notes refer to the characteristics of an expository essay introduced on page 146.

Try It! Guide students to understand how the genre characteristics shape the text.

Say: The first *Try It!* question asks to tell the controlling idea of the essay. In the first paragraph, **I notice** that the second sentence makes a statement about honeybees: they can recognize patterns composed of different numbers of elements. This is the essay's controlling idea.

Ask: Is the author comparing bees and humans by making this statement? How? (Yes, because humans can also count. In the first sentence the author compares bees to people.)

Have students reply to the *Try It!* questions in their journals. If students have difficulty responding to a particular question, model a response, as with Question 1.

Check the accuracy and completeness of student responses.

1. Honeybees can recognize patterns of different numbers of elements. The author suggests that bees and humans can both count.
2. The author provides the name of the university with which Zhang is associated. Quoting an expert makes the essay trustworthy and convincing.
3. Responses will vary. Students should use simple sentences, such as: "Zhang and his team trained about 20 honeybees." This version is not easy to follow because the cause-and-effect and chronological relationships are more difficult to express in simple sentences.
4. Words such as *then* tell readers what happened first, next, and last.
5. Both bees and humans can only remember a small number of items. This fact may give readers a new respect for bees' intelligence.

Extension Lead a discussion in which students compare and contrast how their additional expository essay examples use the genre characteristics. Use the *Try It!* questions as a guide.

Text Expository Essay Mentor Text Expository Essay Mentor

MENTOR TEXT Expository Essay

Learn From Experience

After reading the expository essay on pages 148–149, read the numbered notes in the margins to learn about how the author presented her ideas. Later you will read a Student Model, which shares these characteristics and also has the characteristics of a compare-and-contrast essay.

Answer the *Try It!* questions online or in your notebook.

1 The introduction has a clearly stated **controlling idea.** The introduction also **grabs readers' interest** by suggesting a comparison between bees and humans.

Try It! What is the **controlling idea** of this essay? What comparison is the author suggesting between bees and humans?

2 A **quotation** from an expert **supports** the controlling idea and sets up the explanations to come.

Try It! How do you know Shaowu Zhang is an expert in bee behavior? What does quoting an expert add to the essay?

3 The author uses a **variety of sentence structures** to explain effectively what Zhang and his team trained the honeybees to do.

Try It! Rewrite this paragraph using only simple sentences. How easy is your version to follow? What other differences do you notice when comparing the two versions?

Brainy Bees Know Two from Three

by Liz Savage

1 One, two, three. . . That's how high you could count if you were a bee. A new study found that honeybees can recognize a pattern based only on the number of elements in it.

If the bees learn to recognize three blue dots, then later they can find three yellow stars, three yellow lemons or three purple blobs. For such tiny creatures, that's a big deal.

Many animals—pigeons, raccoons, dolphins, even salamanders—have shown off their numerical abilities in research experiments. But few studies have ever examined invertebrates, like honeybees.

Honeybees are pretty clever. They can tell which items are similar to each other and which are different. They can even count the landmarks they pass on the way to get their food. 2 "I have been studying honeybees since 1980, and I am often surprised by our experimental results. The bee is smart," says Shaowu Zhang at the Australian National University in Canberra.

3 Zhang and his team trained about 20 honeybees to fly through a tunnel and into a hole that was marked with either two or three blue dots. On the other side, bees found a chamber with two exits. Each exit was marked with a pattern, either two or three blue dots. If the bees remembered the first pattern and picked the matching hole, the one with the right number of dots, they received a sugary treat. By repeating this training, the bees learned that if they matched the pattern, they would get a reward.

The honeybees may not think about counting "one, two, three" the same way we do. But the bees got their sugar snack about 70 percent of the time. This confirmed for the

---

Teacher Tip

Quick Write Ask students to think of another animal that has some type of similarity to humans. Then, have students write a description of the similarity, using vivid language and transitions.

2 Writing Journal

Students record their answers to questions about the Mentor Text in their online journals or notebooks.

researchers that the bees were able to detect "sameness," which earlier studies had suggested.

4 Then the tests got harder. The scientists wanted to see whether the bees could apply that matching rule to new patterns. The bees might have to match two blue dots to two yellow lemons and later on, three green leaves to three yellow stars. Even in these more difficult tests, the bees could tell the difference between two objects and three.

4 When they were trained to learn a pattern with three items, the bees could distinguish between three and four items, but couldn't do the reverse. Given a four-item pattern, the bees could not tell the difference between four and three. Four was too much to keep track of.

5 Before you decide bees are dumb, you should know that memory studies have suggested the number of items a person can consciously remember at any one time is around—four.

WRITING COACH
Online
www.phwritingcoach.com
Interactive Model
Listen to an audio recording of the Mentor Text in the eText. You can refer back to the Mentor Text whenever you need support in developing your own writing.
Online Journal
Try It! Answer the questions about the Mentor Text in the online journal.

4 The author uses **transitions** to link the sentences in **logical order.**

Try It! How do the transitions help you understand the order in which the events occurred?

5 The author concludes by **synthesizing information** from other studies to show an unexpected **similarity** between bees and humans.

Try It! What is the similarity between bees and humans? How does this concluding information affect the way you think about bees?

Extension Find another example of an expository essay, and compare it with this one.

Personalized Support

Teacher or Peer Feedback

FEEDBACK

To provide feedback to students on their responses to the Mentor Text and their answers to the *Try It!* questions, ask or have student partners ask one another the following:

- What is the thesis or controlling idea of the Mentor Text?
- How does the Mentor Text illustrate the characteristics of an expository essay?
- How did you answer this *Try It!* question? How could you use your answer to help you plan your piece of writing?

Working with ELLs

ELL Sheltered Instruction: Cognitive

Help students develop and expand their repertoire of learning strategies by summarizing the Mentor Text, employing the skill of making the text simpler to aid them.

Beginning Read page 149 aloud as students track. Guide students as they draw pictures to depict the different experiments described. Have students use their own words to describe the pictures.

Intermediate Have small groups of students use the **Omit Keep Summarize** strategy by giving them a transparency of the Mentor Text and an erasable marker. Tell students to circle the important ideas in the text and cross out the unimportant details. Help students to read their simplified text and rephrase it to summarize what they read.

Advanced Have pairs complete the Intermediate activity and write summaries of the text, comparing with another pair.

Advanced High Read a sentence from the text and model how to restate the ideas with simpler words or sentences to summarize. Then, have students read the Mentor Text. Tell partners to take turns summarizing one section of the text at a time.

Using Writing Coach Online™ or the student book, students read and listen to an audio recording of the Student Model.

STUDENT MODEL

Tell students that good writers react to what they read in ways that show their understanding of the text. Explain that students will react to the Student Model by placing two sets of symbols in the text. Then, distribute printed copies of the Student Model or have students log on to Writing Coach Online.

Use a Reader's Eye

Read aloud the instruction for using the Reader's Response Symbols and the meaning of each symbol. Then, guide students through their use.

The student writer started his essay with an interesting detail about his sister's confusion of coyotes and wolves. **I was interested** right away, so I'm going to mark lines 3–4 with an exclamation point. He also identified clear similarities between coyotes and wolves in lines 8–12. These similarities explain his sister's confusion. I'm going to put a plus sign next to those lines.

Work with students to identify other moments of understanding when they read the text.

Have students read and respond to the Student Model, using each Reader's Response Symbol at least once.

-Contrast Essay Student Model Compare-and-Contrast Essay

STUDENT MODEL Compare-and-Contrast Essay

With a small group, take turns reading this Student Model aloud. Identify the different characteristics that are being compared or contrasted, and decide if the comparisons and contrasts are clear.

Use a Reader's Eye

Now, reread the Student Model. On your copy of the Student Model, use the Reader's Response Symbols to react to what you read.

Reader's Response Symbols

- \+ **Aha! That makes sense to me.**
- − **This isn't clear to me.**
- ? **I have a question about this.**
- ! **Wow! That is cool/weird/ interesting.**

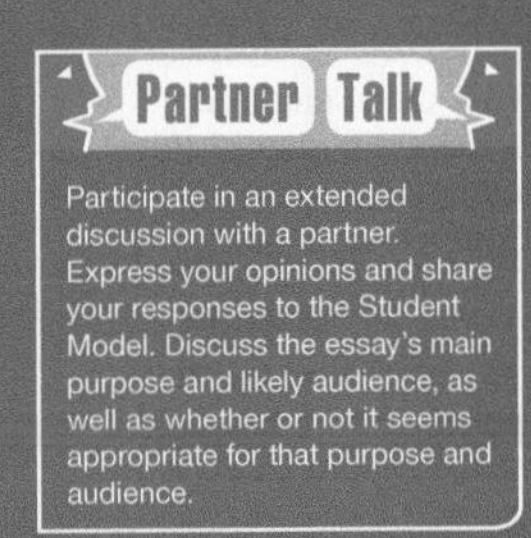

Partner Talk
Participate in an extended discussion with a partner. Express your opinions and share your responses to the Student Model. Discuss the essay's main purpose and likely audience, as well as whether or not it seems appropriate for that purpose and audience.

Canines in the WILD

by Eliot Rayburn

Last summer, my family visited Yellowstone National Park. One morning we saw some animals in the distance. "Look, coyotes!" my sister exclaimed. But a forest ranger told us they weren't coyotes—they were wolves.

My sister's mistake was a common one. Coyotes and wolves have many similarities, even though they are different animals.

Both coyotes and wolves are members of the canine, or dog, family. Their faces are both doglike in appearance and triangular in shape. They are also similar in coloring. Usually their fur is grayish brown, though it can also be rusty, yellowish, white, or black. Wolves have thicker fur than coyotes do, and a coyote's nose and ears are pointier than a wolf's. Still, these differences are rather small.

The biggest difference in appearance is one of size. A full-grown coyote is only about 20 inches tall; a wolf can be nearly twice that tall. A wolf weighs more, too. Some wolves can weigh as much as 80 pounds. In contrast, most coyotes weigh from 20 to 30 pounds. Nevertheless, the size difference won't always help you tell the difference between wolves and coyotes. As the forest ranger at Yellowstone explained, "It's easy to confuse a full-grown coyote with a younger, smaller wolf."

In terms of behavior, wolves and coyotes have many differences. Wolves usually hunt in packs, while coyotes hunt in pairs. Wolves often hunt large animals, like deer and elk. Since coyotes are smaller, they usually go after smaller animals, like mice and

1

150 Expository Essay

Partner Talk

After students have discussed the text, have each student pair share what they think is the writer's purpose and the writer's audience.

Use a Writer's Eye

Read aloud the instructions for using the Writer's Response Symbols and the meaning of each symbol. Then, guide students through their use.

Say: I see that the writer uses a quote from a forest ranger in lines 22–24. This quote supports the idea that, despite their size difference, it isn't always easy to tell a wolf from a coyote. I'll write S.E. next to those lines for effective supporting evidence.

Ask: What other evidence does the writer present in paragraph 4? (statistics about the size and weight of wolves and coyotes)

Have students read and respond to the Student Model, using each Writer's Response Symbol at least once.

2 Writing Coach Online | STUDENT BOOK

First, students respond to the Student Model as a reader, using symbols to mark the text. They can mark the text using pop-up sticky notes in **Writing Coach Online™** or they can mark a printed copy of the Student Model.

3 Writing Coach Online | STUDENT BOOK

Then, students respond to the Student Model as a writer, using different symbols to mark the text. They can use either **Writing Coach Online™** or a printed copy of the Student Model.

rabbits. And coyotes aren't fussy eaters—they will also eat insects, fruits, vegetables, and even garbage!

Wolves have trouble surviving in places where a lot of people live. In the United States, wolves are a protected species, which means they are in danger of becoming extinct. Coyotes, on the other hand, have an incredible talent for adapting. There are coyotes living right in the middle of Los Angeles! Coyotes can be found in the East, too. They began traveling east on the interstate highway system when it was completed in the 1950s. Now they are fairly common in places like rural New England, where wolves once roamed but are no longer found.

Thus, while coyotes and wolves look alike, their behaviors and situations are different. Wolves are growing rarer and rarer. Coyotes, on the other hand, are thriving.

Wolf

Coyote

2

Writing Coach Online

www.phwritingcoach.com

Interactive Model

Listen to an audio recording of the Student Model in the eText. Use the Reader's and Writer's Response Symbols with the eText tools to note what you read.

Use a Writer's Eye

Now evaluate the Student Model as a writer. On your copy of the Student Model, use the Writer's Response Symbols to react to what you read. Identify places where the student writer uses the characteristics of an effective compare-and-contrast essay.

Writer's Response Symbols	
C.T.	Clearly stated thesis
I.C.	Effective introduction and conclusion
R.D.	Good use of rhetorical devices
S.E.	Effective supporting evidence

Personalized Support

FEEDBACK

Teacher or Peer Feedback

To provide feedback to students on their responses to the Student Model, ask or have student partners ask one another the following:

- What is the thesis or controlling idea of the Student Model?
- How does the Student Model illustrate the characteristics of a compare-and-contrast essay?
- Which feature or characteristic of the Student Model might you use in your own piece of writing?
- How could you alter or adapt this feature to make it your own?

Working with ELLs

ELL Sheltered Instruction: Social/Affective

As students read the Student Model on pages 150–151, ensure they use support from peers and from you to enhance and confirm understanding and develop the vocabulary needed to comprehend increasingly challenging language.

Beginning Have students **Echo-Read** the text a few sentences at a time. Pause to explain the vocabulary. Then, make simple statements and have students tell which animal you have described. *(coyote or wolf)*

Intermediate Pre-teach the following phrases: *in terms of [behavior], go after,* and *in danger of;* then, read the text aloud as students follow along. Have students confirm comprehension by answering questions about the text.

Advanced Have students read the pages on their own, writing down any unfamiliar words or usages. Tell partners to help each other determine their meanings, consulting a dictionary and you as needed. Then, have students summarize what they learned about coyotes and wolves.

Advanced High Have students complete the Advanced activity using the new words in their summaries.

1

Students select or are assigned a topic for their compare-and-contrast essay from the Topic Bank, or they may choose a topic of their own.

2 STUDENT BOOK

Students complete online or printed graphic organizers to narrow the topic for their compare-and-contrast essay.

Prewriting

Explain that the first task students need to complete as they plan their compare-and-contrast essay is to determine an appropriate topic.

Choose From the Topic Bank

Read aloud each topic and then ask volunteers to describe them in their own words. If you are assigning topics to students, you may wish to do so now. Encourage students to ask questions about their topic.

Choose Your Own Topic

Introduce and discuss the Associate and Synthesize strategies. If students were not assigned writing topics, have them use the strategies to brainstorm for topics for their essays.

Extension Have each student choose one of the strategies. Then, have them write an action plan that outlines the resources and steps they will use to develop their topic.

Narrow Your Topic

Tell students that they will use a Narrow Your Topic graphic organizer to identify two subjects to compare and contrast. Then, distribute printed copies or have students log on to Writing Coach Online.

Apply It! Guide students through the instructions for completing the graphic organizer. Have students complete the exercise based on their topic.

Consider Your Audience and Purpose

Guide students to consider the audience and purpose for their essay.

Say: The first two questions in the first column ask who my audience is and how familiar they might be with my topic. If **I write** about the first topic from the Topic Bank, film adaptations, my audience would probably be people who are interested in film and know a lot about it. I would have to try to give details that they don't already know.

Ask: Based on your topic, who is most likely to read your compare-and-contrast essay? (Responses will vary.)

Have students with similar topics work in small groups to discuss and respond to the remaining questions.

Feature Assignment Prewriting Feature Assignment Prewriting

Your Turn **Feature Assignment: Compare-and-Contrast Essay**

Prewriting

Plan a first draft of your compare-and-contrast essay. Select from the Topic Bank or come up with an idea of your own.

Choose From the Topic Bank

TOPIC BANK

Film Adaptations It's fascinating to think about how screenwriters make a movie from a book. Think of a book that has been made into a movie. Write a compare-and-contrast essay that explains what is similar and what is different about the two. Be sure to discuss which one you enjoyed more and why.

Methods of Communication People communicate with each other in different ways. Some people just talk to each other face-to-face. Others use "snail mail," e-mail, the telephone, books and magazines, radio, and TV to communicate. Write an essay in which you compare and contrast two ways that people communicate with each other.

Subjects Think about the subjects you are learning in school. You probably have a favorite subject and a subject that you don't like as well or that is more difficult for you. Write an essay in which you compare and contrast your favorite class or subject with another class or subject.

Choose Your Own Topic

Determine a topic on your own by using these ideas.

Associate and Synthesize

- With a partner, play a game of word association in which one of you names something and the other names something that is either the opposite or closely related. After listing your associations, choose one pair to explore in a compare-and-contrast essay.
- List a broad category, such as sports or music. Then, list your favorite type in that category—for example, your favorite type of music might be jazz. Brainstorm for other types in the same category to compare.

Review your responses and choose a topic.

Coach's Corner

You may wish to model prewriting activities for students by brainstorming for your own writing topic. Use these prompts to model your thought process:

- **I am interested in** natural environments, so that could be my general topic.
- **I can narrow my topic by** focusing on the mountains and the seashore.

Discuss the choices you make and solicit feedback from students.

3 Writing Journal

Students record their answers to questions about audience and purpose in their online journals or notebooks.

Narrow Your Topic

Some topics are too broad to cover in a compare-and-contrast essay. By narrowing your topic, you can focus on specific similarities and differences.

Apply It! Use a graphic organizer like the one shown to narrow your topic to a manageable size.

- Write your general topic in the top box, and keep narrowing your topic as you move down the chart.
- Your last box should hold your narrowest topic, which will be the new focus of your compare-and-contrast essay.

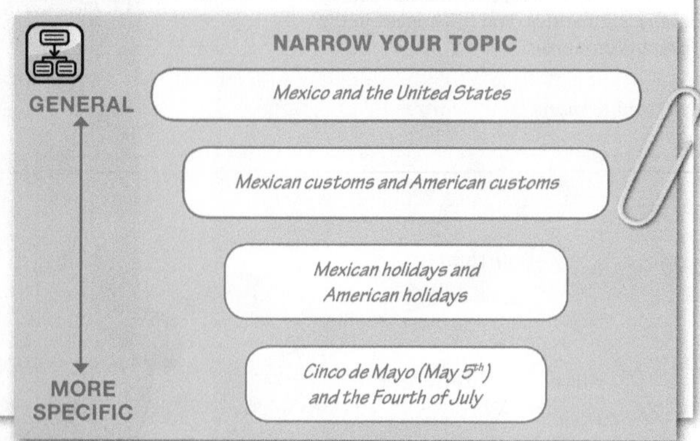
NARROW YOUR TOPIC
GENERAL
Mexico and the United States
Mexican customs and American customs
Mexican holidays and American holidays
Cinco de Mayo (May 5th) and the Fourth of July
MORE SPECIFIC

Consider Your Audience and Purpose

Before writing, think about your audience and purpose. Consider how the form you selected conveys the intended meaning to this audience. Consider the views of others as you ask these questions.

Questions for Audience	Questions for Purpose
• Who is my audience? • Is my audience familiar with my topic? • What questions might my audience have about my topic?	• How might I make the comparisons and contrasts clear to my audience? • What main point about all my comparisons and contrasts do I want to make in my thesis?

Record your answers in your writing journal.

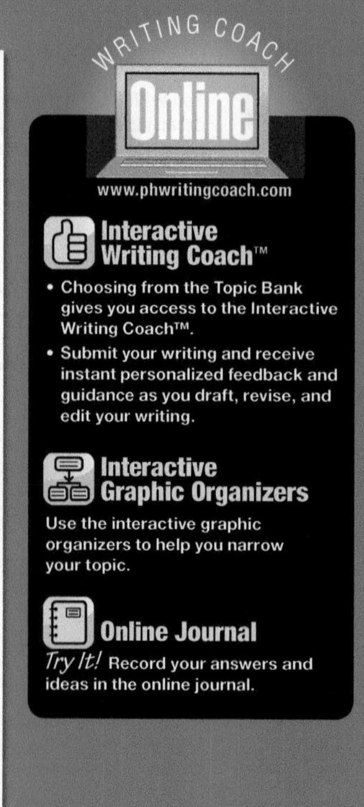
WRITING COACH
Online
www.phwritingcoach.com
Interactive Writing Coach™
• Choosing from the Topic Bank gives you access to the Interactive Writing Coach™.
• Submit your writing and receive instant personalized feedback and guidance as you draft, revise, and edit your writing.
Interactive Graphic Organizers
Use the interactive graphic organizers to help you narrow your topic.
Online Journal
Try It! Record your answers and ideas in the online journal.

Personalized Support

Interactive Writing Coach™

Below Level Teachers select a topic from the topic bank for below-level students. Students submit their writing to the **Interactive Writing Coach™** for feedback paragraph by paragraph or as a complete draft. It is recommended that below-level students submit their writing one paragraph at a time.

On Level Students may select a topic from the Topic Bank. They may submit their writing for feedback paragraph by paragraph or as a complete draft.

Above Level Students may select from the Topic Bank or come up with their own topic. Above-level students should submit their writing as a complete draft.

Interactive Graphic Organizer

Below Level Students complete three graphic organizers that provide models and scaffolded support.

On Level Students complete one, two, or three graphic organizers, depending on how much support they need.

Above Level Students complete the least scaffolded graphic organizer or narrow their topic without the help of a graphic organizer.

Differentiated Instruction

RTI Strategy for Special Needs Students Students may benefit from direct coaching as they select an appropriate topic and narrow it. You might talk them through each step of the process so that they choose suitable topics. Encourage them to identify concrete subjects to compare and contrast, such as two objects that they can observe. Review or provide definitions as necessary of *category, narrow, audience,* and *purpose.*

PRE-AP Enrichment for Above-Level Students Challenge above-level students to choose a topic that requires them to do research and to analyze their research findings in order to compare and contrast. Encourage them to apply higher-level skills, such as research, analysis, inference, evaluation, and drawing conclusions.

1 

Using Writing Coach Online™ or the student book, students read and discuss the model graphic organizer.

2 Students complete online or printed graphic organizers to develop their ideas and gather details.

Plan Your Essay

Explain that writers use graphic organizers to develop their ideas and show relationships between different parts of the text. Then, point out the Develop Your Comparisons and Contrasts graphic organizer on page 154. Tell students that they will use this organizer to outline their compare-and-contrast essay. Then, distribute printed copies or have students log on to Writing Coach Online.

Introduce the graphic organizer by explaining that each circle represents one of the subjects being compared. In the area that overlaps, students will write the ways the two subjects are alike. In the outer part of each circle, students will write corresponding differences.

Develop a Clear Thesis Work with students to record a thesis for the example organizer, which is based on the narrowed topic from page 153. Then, have students write a thesis sentence for their topic and record it on their graphic organizer.

Logically Organize Your Details Point out that the graphic organizer has helped the writer identify many points of similarity and difference between the two holidays. Guide students to pair points of similarity and difference. Suggest they think in terms of compare-and-contrast words and phrases such as *on the other hand, in contrast, like,* and *both.*

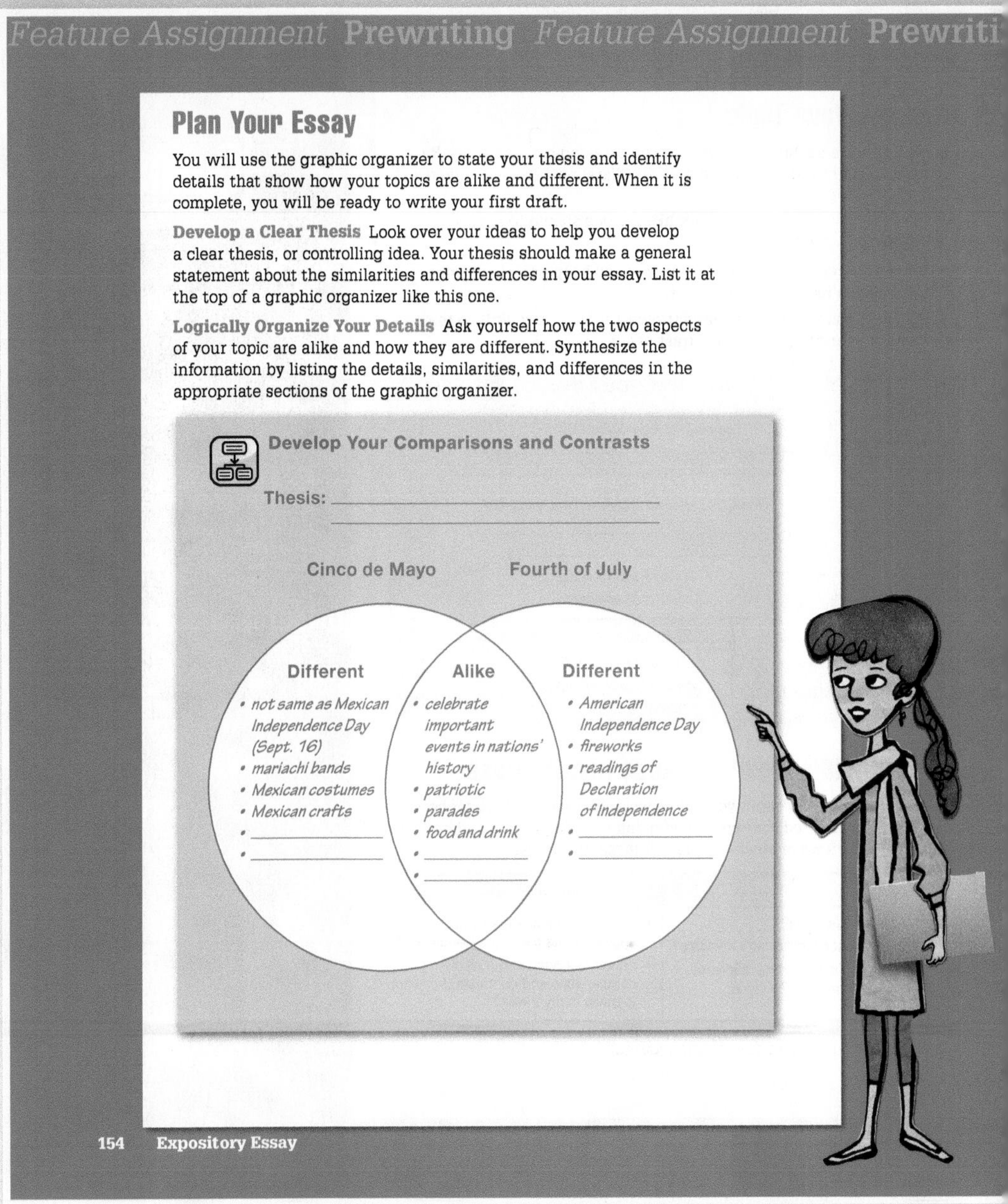

Feature Assignment **Prewriting** *Feature Assignment* **Prewriti**

Plan Your Essay

You will use the graphic organizer to state your thesis and identify details that show how your topics are alike and different. When it is complete, you will be ready to write your first draft.

Develop a Clear Thesis Look over your ideas to help you develop a clear thesis, or controlling idea. Your thesis should make a general statement about the similarities and differences in your essay. List it at the top of a graphic organizer like this one.

Logically Organize Your Details Ask yourself how the two aspects of your topic are alike and how they are different. Synthesize the information by listing the details, similarities, and differences in the appropriate sections of the graphic organizer.

Develop Your Comparisons and Contrasts

Thesis: ______________________

Cinco de Mayo: Different	Alike	Fourth of July: Different
• not same as Mexican Independence Day (Sept. 16) • mariachi bands • Mexican costumes • Mexican crafts • ______ • ______	• celebrate important events in nations' history • patriotic • parades • food and drink • ______ • ______	• American Independence Day • fireworks • readings of Declaration of Independence • ______ • ______

154 Expository Essay

Gather Details

Remind students that compare-and-contrast essays must include details that explain or support points of comparison. Ask volunteers to read aloud each kind of detail and its example. Then, guide students to place the details in the example graphic organizer.

Say: I notice that the example graphic organizer has space for additional similarities and differences. The details on page 155 supply this information. For example, the Example detail says that tacos are served at Cinco de Mayo celebrations. I don't think tacos are typical foods for Fourth of July celebrations, so I'll record that in the *Different* space under *Cinco de Mayo.*

Ask: How might the writer use the Quotation example? (It could be used to show that Cinco de Mayo, like the Fourth of July, celebrates a nation's cultural heritage.) Where might it go on the graphic organizer? (in the *Alike* section)

Have students work in small groups to place the remaining details on the example graphic organizer.

Try It! Lead students to see that the writer's paragraph contains facts ("most coyotes weigh from 20 to 30 pounds") and a quotation from the forest ranger.

Apply It! Read aloud the instructions for gathering and using supporting details. Then, have students gather details for their topic. Remind them to choose details that support their thesis.

Writer's Block

IF students are having difficulty gathering details . . .

THEN have them work with a partner to brainstorm for ideas on a four-column chart with a column for each type of detail listed on page 155.

3 STUDENT BOOK

Students refer back to the Mentor Text or the Student Model as they plan their writing.

Gather Details

When explaining similarities and differences, writers use some or all of these categories of details. Look at these examples.

- **Facts:** *Cinco de Mayo commemorates a Mexican victory against the French in the Battle of Puebla in 1862.*
- **Quotations:** *"Our annual Cinco de Mayo Festival celebrates the Mexican cultural heritage of many area residents."—Sonia Verdugo, Chairwoman, Cinco de Mayo Festival of Martina, Colorado*
- **Examples:** *Tacos are among the Mexican foods served at Cinco de Mayo celebrations.*
- **Personal Experiences:** *In the Cinco de Mayo parade I saw last year, most people on the floats wore traditional Mexican clothing.*

Try It! Read this Student Model excerpt. Then, identify and take notes about which kinds of details the author used to support his ideas.

from **Canines in the Wild**
page 150; lines 19–24

In contrast, most coyotes weigh from 20 to 30 pounds. Nevertheless, the size difference won't always help you tell the difference between wolves and coyotes. As the forest ranger at Yellowstone explained, "It's easy to confuse a full-grown coyote with a younger, smaller wolf."

Apply It! Review the types of support an expository essay can use. Think about the different types you might use in discussing the similarities and differences that support your thesis. Also consider which details might be useful for an **effective introduction or conclusion** to your essay.

- Decide which details best support your purpose as stated in your thesis. Eliminate details that do not seem tightly related or relevant, or change your thesis to take them into account.
- Review your notes to find similarities. Then, **synthesize** your information and identify any **inconsistencies.** Do more research, if necessary, to clear up the inconsistencies.
- Identify one or two details that could help make your **introduction or conclusion more effective.** Sometimes a quotation or a personal experience can help capture reader attention in your introduction or make your conclusion more memorable.

Interactive Graphic Organizers

Use the interactive graphic organizers to help you create a plan for your writing.

Interactive Model

Refer back to the Interactive Model in the eText as you plan your writing.

Personalized Support

Interactive Graphic Organizer

Below Level Students complete three graphic organizers that provide models and scaffolded support.

On Level Students complete one, two, or three graphic organizers, depending on how much support they need.

Above Level Students complete the least scaffolded graphic organizer or narrow their topic without the help of a graphic organizer.

Teacher or Peer Feedback

FEEDBACK

To provide feedback to students as they plan their first draft, ask or have student partners ask one another the following:

- What do you want your audience to know about the topic?
- What questions or concerns will your audience have about the topic?
- What details have you identified for your piece? How do these details support your thesis or controlling idea?
- Are your details varied? Will they interest your readers? Explain.

Differentiated Instruction

RTI Strategy for Below-Level Students Students may have difficulty presenting their comparisons in a logical order. To prepare students to choose either block organization or point-by-point organization, have them create a rough outline or other graphic representation of their notes in both formats. Organizing their points in both ways will help students decide which details work and which organization is better for their topic.

Strategy for Spanish Speakers Students whose home language is Spanish may encounter difficulties forming adjectives with *-er* and *-est* endings, and with the *more + adjective* construction. Identify adjectives in the Student Model on page 155: *easy, younger,* and *smaller.* Elicit different forms of additional one-, two-, and three-syllable adjectives. Have students write the adjectives where they belong in a three-column table labeled *Adjective, Comparative,* and *Superlative*. Have students complete the table with the forms of each adjective.

1 Using Writing Coach Online™ or the student book, students read and discuss the Outline for Success for an expository essay.

2 Students discuss how the Mentor Text illustrates the characteristics of an expository essay.

Drafting

Outline for Success

Explain that the Outline for Success shows an organizational strategy for an expository essay. Students will use the Outline to write a focused, organized, and coherent draft of their compare-and-contrast essay.

I. Introduction

Link the Outline to a specific expository essay by having students turn to the Mentor Text on pages 148–149. Ask a volunteer to read aloud the thesis statement (lines 2–4). Then, guide students to see how the writer engages the reader with a comparison between honeybees and humans.

Say: I notice that the writer states her controlling idea clearly in lines 2–4. However, a good introduction also tells why the controlling idea is important. This gives reader a reason to read on. For example, in line 7, the writer says of honeybees' counting ability, "For such tiny creatures, that's a big deal."

Ask: What else about the writer's introduction helps to engage readers? (She uses concrete details—blue dots, yellow lemons, and purple blobs—to create visual experience.)

Have students work with a partner to brainstorm for an interesting opening for their own compare-and-contrast essays.

Drafting *Feature Assignment* Drafting *Feature Assignment* Dr

Drafting

During the drafting stage, you will start to write your ideas for your essay. You will follow an outline that provides an appropriate **organizational strategy** that will help you build on ideas to write a **focused, organized,** and **coherent** compare-and-contrast essay.

The Organization of a Compare-and-Contrast Essay

The chart provides an organizing structure for a compare-and-contrast essay. As you adapt it for your particular compare-and-contrast essay, be sure to keep in mind your audience and purpose.

Outline for Success

I. Introduction See Mentor Text, p. 148.

- Attention-grabbing opening
- Thesis that states what you are comparing and contrasting

II. Body See Mentor Text, pp. 148–149.

- **Points of comparison and contrast**
  Point-by-Point
  - Point 1: Topic A and B
  - Point 2: Topic A and B
  - Point 3: Topic A and B
- **Logical organization of points**
  Block Organization
  - Topic A: Points 1, 2, and 3
  - Topic B: Points 1, 2, and 3

III. Conclusion See Mentor Text, p. 149.

- Restatement of thesis
- Memorable ending

Grab Your Reader
- An interesting opening captures the reader's attention with a quotation, a personal experience, or another strong detail.
- A thesis is a general statement about the two or more aspects that you are comparing and contrasting.

Compare and Contrast
- Each point of comparison and contrast is supported with evidence that explains your points and informs your reader.
- A clear organizational structure helps readers follow your ideas easily. A point-by-point or block organization structure is a good way to structure your ideas. Block organization works best if you have only one or two points of comparison. Point-by-point is used when you have several points of comparison.

Wrap It Up
- A strong conclusion restates the thesis and briefly summarizes your points of comparison and contrast.
- Analogies or rhetorical questions—questions that make the reader think or emphasize a point—help make your ideas memorable.

II. Body

Lead a discussion about how the body paragraphs of the Mentor Text reflect the characteristics of a compare-and-contrast essay.

- Points of comparison and contrast (lines 8–10, 28–29, 35–38, 39–43)
- Logical organization of points (lines 19–27)

III. Conclusion

Have small groups discuss how the conclusion of the Mentor Text restates the controlling idea and provides a memorable ending (lines 44–47).

Start Your Draft

Have small groups read aloud and discuss the boxed instructions for drafting. Direct students to work individually on their first draft.

Coach's Corner

If you are modeling the writing process for students with your own topic or a student volunteer's, you may wish to use these prompts to guide your drafting and discussion:

- **To capture readers' attention,** my introduction will include a personal story.
- **I will organize my body paragraphs** point by point so that I can explain each point of similarity or difference.

Discuss the choices you make and solicit feedback from students.

3 

Students begin writing their compare-and-contrast essay online or in their notebooks.

4 

Students submit paragraphs or complete drafts to the **Interactive Writing Coach™** for scoring and feedback, or share their work with their teacher.

5 

Students receive customized feedback from the **Interactive Writing Coach™** or feedback from their teacher. Students may continue to work on their drafts.

Start Your Draft

Use this checklist to help you complete your draft. Use the graphic organizer that shows your comparisons and contrasts, and the Outline for Success as guides.

While drafting, aim at writing your ideas, not on making your writing perfect. Remember, you will have the chance to improve your draft when you revise and edit.

- √ Start with **opening** sentences that capture your reader's interest and introduce the topic for comparison and contrast.
- √ Continue building an **effective introduction** by including a thesis that states your controlling idea about the similarities and differences you will be discussing.

- √ Develop the **body** of your compare-and-contrast essay by providing similarities and differences that support your **thesis.**
- √ **Synthesize,** or blend together, ideas and information from several sources.
- √ Logically organize your essay by including specific facts and details that support your main idea. Make sure to avoid **extraneous,** or unnecessary, information and inconsistencies.
- √ Be sure to use **transitions** to link sentences and paragraphs and to make your comparisons and contrasts clear.
- √ Use an appropriate **organizing structure** such as point-by-point organization, discussing each similarity and difference one at a time, or block organization, discussing all the qualities of one thing before moving on to the other.
- √ Use a variety of different **sentence structures,** such as short or long and simple or complex to keep your writing lively and interesting.

- √ End with an effective **conclusion** that restates your thesis in an interesting way and uses a variety of **rhetorical devices** to help your audience see the importance of your topic.

www.phwritingcoach.com

Interactive Model

Outline for Success View pop-ups of Mentor Text selections referenced in the Outline for Success.

Interactive Writing Coach™

Use the Interactive Writing Coach to receive the level of support you need:

- Write one paragraph at a time and submit each one for immediate, detailed feedback.
- Write your entire first draft and submit it for immediate, personalized feedback.

Personalized Support

Interactive Writing Coach™

Below Level Students complete the drafting process in small steps by submitting each paragraph for scoring and feedback.

On Level Depending on the support they need, students submit their writing paragraph by paragraph or as a complete draft for scoring and feedback.

Above Level Students may write their drafts on their own but have the option of submitting them for scoring and/or feedback.

Teacher or Peer Feedback

To provide feedback to students on their first draft, ask or have student partners ask one another the following:

- Can you explain how you organized your ideas in this piece?
- Why did you include this information here?
- Why did you choose this introduction? Does it grab your reader and identify your thesis or controlling idea?
- What supporting details could you add here?
- Why did you choose this conclusion? How does it add to your piece?
- Can you show me a place where I can hear your unique voice?
- Can you show me a place where you used vivid language?

Working with ELLs

ELL Sheltered Instruction: Cognitive

Help students prepare to write their drafts and internalize new basic language by helping them write sentences using and reusing newly acquired basic vocabulary.

Beginning Model the use of *but, and, different, same,* and *not* to compare and contrast classroom objects. Provide sentence frames so that students can use and reuse the words.

Intermediate Write *similarities* and *differences* on the board. Help students use the **Frayer Model** for each word by having them divide a card into four sections, filling in a definition, characteristics, examples, and non-examples. Then guide students in using and reusing the words in written sentences.

Advanced Have students take turns using and reusing basic transition words, such as *but* and *so.* One partner should write a sentence. The other should add a clause that begins with the appropriate transition.

Advanced High Help students create a **word bank** of basic words, such as *difference,* for a compare-and-contrast essay. Have students use and reuse basic vocabulary as they write with the words.

1 

Using Writing Coach Online™ or the student book, students study the first and second drafts of the student model to see how the writer used Revision RADaR to improve his or her writing.

2 

Students use the Revision RADaR strategy to revise their own writing.

Revising: Making It Better

Point out the page title to students and explain that revising means making improvements to a writing draft. Then, read aloud the opening paragraph to introduce the Revision RADaR strategies. You may wish to have students review Chapter 3 for more information on Revision RADaR.

Kelly Gallagher, M. Ed.

KEEP REVISION ON YOUR RADAR

1ST DRAFT After students have read the first draft, have them turn to page 156 and review the Outline for Success. Work with students to understand that the questions the author asked about his draft are based on the characteristics of a compare-and-contrast essay. For example, call out the first question and note how it addresses the point about capturing the reader's attention in the Outline for Success.

Then, have students work in small groups to develop other questions about the draft based on the genre characteristics.

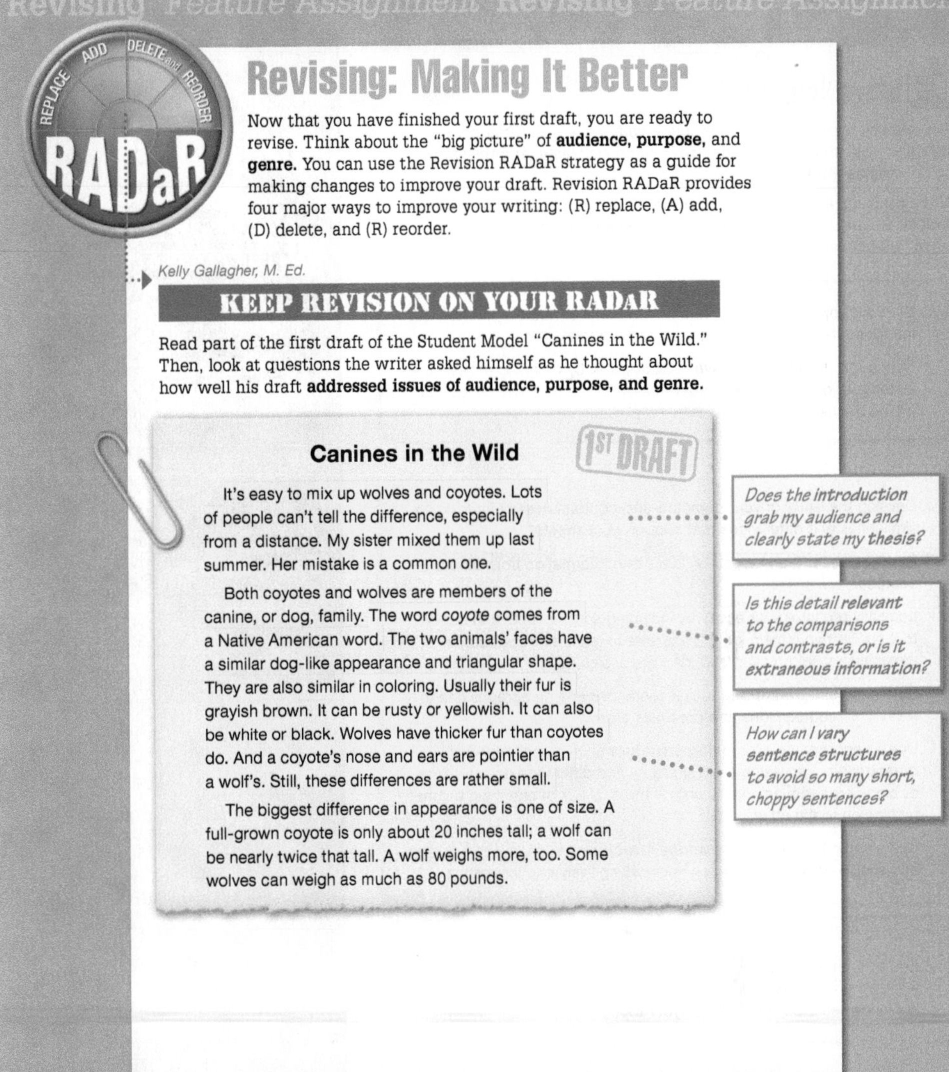

Revising Feature Assignment Revising Feature Assignment R

Revising: Making It Better

Now that you have finished your first draft, you are ready to revise. Think about the "big picture" of **audience, purpose,** and **genre.** You can use the Revision RADaR strategy as a guide for making changes to improve your draft. Revision RADaR provides four major ways to improve your writing: (R) replace, (A) add, (D) delete, and (R) reorder.

Kelly Gallagher, M. Ed.

KEEP REVISION ON YOUR RADAR

Read part of the first draft of the Student Model "Canines in the Wild." Then, look at questions the writer asked himself as he thought about how well his draft **addressed issues of audience, purpose, and genre.**

Canines in the Wild 1ST DRAFT

It's easy to mix up wolves and coyotes. Lots of people can't tell the difference, especially from a distance. My sister mixed them up last summer. Her mistake is a common one.

Does the introduction grab my audience and clearly state my thesis?

Both coyotes and wolves are members of the canine, or dog, family. The word *coyote* comes from a Native American word. The two animals' faces have a similar dog-like appearance and triangular shape. They are also similar in coloring. Usually their fur is grayish brown. It can be rusty or yellowish. It can also be white or black. Wolves have thicker fur than coyotes do. And a coyote's nose and ears are pointier than a wolf's. Still, these differences are rather small.

Is this detail relevant to the comparisons and contrasts, or is it extraneous information?

How can I vary sentence structures to avoid so many short, choppy sentences?

The biggest difference in appearance is one of size. A full-grown coyote is only about 20 inches tall; a wolf can be nearly twice that tall. A wolf weighs more, too. Some wolves can weigh as much as 80 pounds.

158 Expository Essay

2ND DRAFT Guide students to understand how the author used the RADaR strategies to revise the first draft.

Think Aloud **I thought** that the original opening paragraph contained some interesting information, but it didn't really grab me. In the 2nd draft, however, I see an *R* next to that paragraph, meaning that the writer replaced that information with a new, personal example. The new introduction contains exciting dialogue and details about where wolves are found. Now the introduction makes me want to continue reading.

Work with students to brainstorm for other ways of revising the introduction.

Have students work in small groups to discuss other changes in the 2nd draft.

Apply It! Review the bulleted instructions for using Revision RADaR. Remind students to question their drafts based on the genre characteristics listed on the Outline for Success on page 156. Tell students to use each RADaR strategy at least once.

Coach's Corner

If you are modeling the writing process for students with your own draft or a student volunteer's, use these prompts to focus on the Revision RADaR *Replace* strategy:

- **I replaced a general comment with a direct quotation because** the quotation provides support from an expert.
- **I replaced a supporting detail because** it wasn't relevant to my controlling idea.

Discuss the choices you make and solicit feedback from students.

3 

Students submit paragraphs or revised drafts to the **Interactive Writing Coach™** for scoring and feedback, or share their work with their teacher.

4 

Students receive customized feedback from the **Interactive Writing Coach™** or feedback from their teacher. Students may continue to revise their drafts.

Now look at how the writer applied Revision RADaR to write an improved second draft.

Canines in the WILD

2ND DRAFT

Last summer, my family visited Yellowstone National Park. One morning we saw some animals in the distance. "Look, coyotes!" my sister exclaimed. But a forest ranger told us they weren't coyotes—they were wolves.

My sister's mistake was a common one. Coyotes and wolves have many similarities, even though they are different animals.

Both coyotes and wolves are members of the canine, or dog, family. Their faces are both doglike in appearance and triangular in shape. They are also similar in coloring. Usually their fur is grayish brown, though it can also be rusty, yellowish, white, or black. Wolves have thicker fur than coyotes do, and a coyote's nose and ears are pointier than a wolf's. Still, these differences are rather small.

The biggest difference in appearance is one of size. A full-grown coyote is only about 20 inches tall; a wolf can be nearly twice that tall. A wolf weighs more, too. Some wolves can weigh as much as 80 pounds.

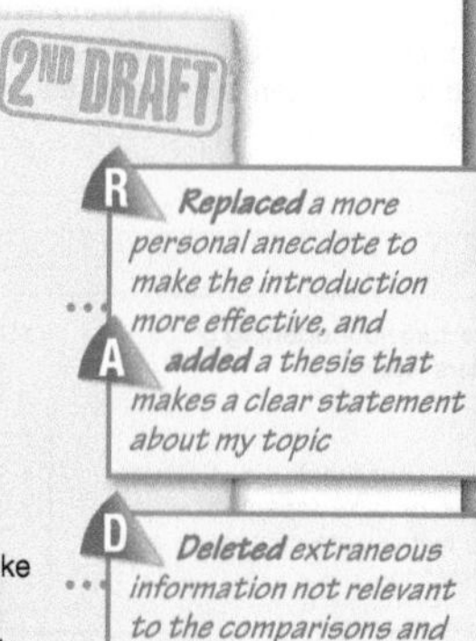

R *Replaced* a more personal anecdote to make the introduction more effective, and
A *added* a thesis that makes a clear statement about my topic
D *Deleted* extraneous information not relevant to the comparisons and contrasts I am making
R *Reordered* sentences by combining them to vary sentence structures

Interactive Writing Coach™

Use the Revision RADaR strategy in your own writing. Then submit your paragraph or draft for feedback.

 *Apply It!* Use your Revision RADaR to revise your draft.

- Include all the appropriate characteristics of the expository essay genre.
- Keep your audience and purpose in mind. Make sure that your introduction is effective, interesting, and presents a clearly stated thesis.
- Exchange drafts with a partner. Listen as your partner provides direction for how to improve your work.
- Then, apply the Revision RADaR strategy to make needed changes. Remember—you can use the steps in the strategy in any order.

Personalized Support

Interactive Writing Coach™

Below Level Students revise their drafts using the Revision RADaR strategy and submit their writing for scoring and feedback.

On Level Students revise their drafts using the Revision RADaR strategy and submit their writing for scoring and feedback.

Above Level Students may use the Revision RADaR strategy or revise their drafts on their own. They have the option of submitting their revised drafts for scoring and/or feedback.

Teacher or Peer Feedback

To provide feedback to students as they revise their first draft, ask or have student partners ask one another the following:

- Can you show me where you revised your text?
- What could you add to your introduction to grab the interest of your readers?
- How could you reorder these ideas so that their order is more logical?
- Have you included all the characteristics of this form of writing?
- Is there any unnecessary text that you could delete?
- Have you achieved your purpose with this piece of writing?
- Have you addressed the questions and concerns of your audience?

Working with ELLs

ELL Sheltered Instruction: Cognitive

As you review the Student Draft with students, have them demonstrate English comprehension and expand reading skills by employing the inferential skill of finding supporting text evidence.

Beginning Have students **Echo-Read** the first paragraph. Explain how you infer that the sister did not know much about wolves. Show students the supporting evidence. *(They weren't coyotes—they were wolves.)* Help students create a simple chart listing the inference and evidence.

Intermediate Model making an inference based on this sentence: "They weren't coyotes—they were wolves." Then, have students read and make an inference based on the sister's response to the wolves (e.g., *She has never seen a coyote or a wolf.*) Have students identify the supporting evidence.

Advanced Have partners read the student draft and make at least two inferences about the sister, identifying the supporting evidence, then review their answers.

Advanced High Expand the Advanced activity to have partners discuss other inferences based on the evidence.

The Digital • Print Path

1 

Using Writing Coach Online™ or the student book, students study and discuss the revision chart.

2 

In a video by program author Kelly Gallagher, students learn more strategies for effective writing.

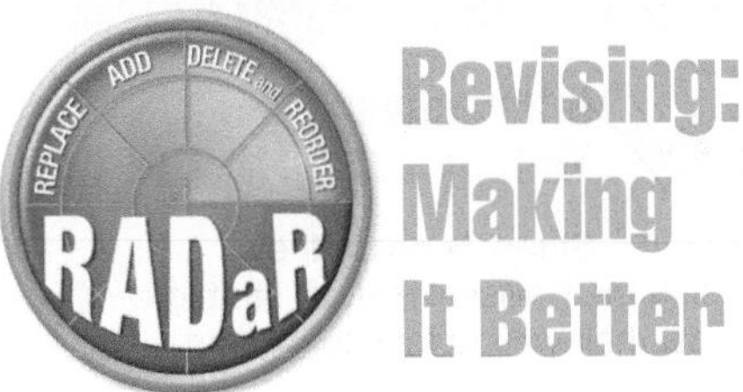

Revising: Making It Better

Look at the Big Picture

Introduce the revision chart to students. Explain that the Section column identifies the three main parts of a compare-and-contrast essay. The Evaluate column identifies the characteristics found in each section and explains how to assess them. The Revise column presents specific strategies for revising each characteristic.

Then, have students draw lines between and label the three sections of their drafts. Direct students to work individually to evaluate and revise their draft, using the chart to guide their work.

Focus on Craft: Effective Transitions

Have students read the introductory text. Guide students to understand that transitions help show the relationship between ideas and lead readers smoothly from one idea to the next.

Say: I notice that the writer includes two facts, one about wolves and one about coyotes. To show the relationship between them, the writer uses the transition *On the other hand,* which shows a contrast between the facts.

Ask: What are some other transitions the writer might have used to show this contrast? *(however, but)*

Have students work with a partner to substitute different transitions in the student model, evaluate the effect of each, and decide which is most effective.

Try It! Have students discuss the questions and record responses in their journals. Follow up with students to ensure that their responses reflect an understanding of the role and effectiveness of transitions in an essay.

Revising Feature Assignment Revising Feature Assignment

Look at the Big Picture

Use the chart and your analytical skills to evaluate how well each section of your compare-and-contrast essay addresses **purpose**, **audience**, and **genre**. When necessary, use the suggestions in the chart to revise your essay.

Section	Evaluate	Revise
Introduction	• Make sure your **opening** grabs readers' attention.	• Use a quotation, a question, or another strong detail to make your introduction effective.
	• Be sure your **thesis** clearly states the two or more aspects of your topic that you are comparing and contrasting.	• Complete and answer these questions to help form a thesis: In general, *how are* ____ *and* ____ *(or* ____, ____, *and* ____*) alike, and how are they different? Why does it matter?*
Body	• Check that you clearly identify **comparisons** and contrasts.	• Add transitions such as *similarly* and *in contrast* to make your ideas clear.
	• Check that your source information is **synthesized** from several sources.	• Combine similar ideas from separate sources to avoid repetition.
	• Check that you have **organized** your comparisons and contrasts in a logical and coherent way.	• Discuss each similarity or difference one at a time, or discuss all the qualities of first one thing and then the other.
	• Check that your **facts** and details are appropriate. Avoid extraneous information or inconsistencies that do not support your thesis.	• Delete details that are not relevant to your thesis or explanations. Confirm that your information is correct and remove any errors or inconsistencies.
	• Check that you have used a variety of **sentence structures.**	• Break or combine sentences to vary their structures.
Conclusion	• Check that you have restated your thesis and summed up **main ideas.**	• Rewrite to sum up all your main points and only your main points.
	• Make sure that your essay ends on a **memorable** note.	• Add rhetorical devices, such as analogies, comparisons, or rhetorical questions, to make your conclusion more effective. Help your audience see why your subject is meaningful.

160 Expository Essay

Fine-Tune Your Draft

Apply It! Ask volunteers to read aloud the instructions for fine-tuning their drafts. Then, have students work in pairs to read each other's drafts and make suggestions for adding transitions, improving coherence, and maintaining a consistent point of view.

Teacher Feedback Have students identify Mentor Text examples of the characteristics that you marked for improvement. Use the Mentor Text references on page T156 to guide students to appropriate examples.

Teacher Tip

Suggest that students read their drafts aloud to a partner, who should listen to the flow of sentences. Have the listener identify places where sentence structure or language may be improved.

3 

Using Writing Coach Online™ or the student book, students refer back to the Mentor Text or Student Model for examples of writer's craft.

4 

Students record answers to questions about writer's craft in their online journals or notebooks.

5 

Students submit revised drafts to the Interactive Writing Coach™ for scoring and feedback, or share their work with their teacher.

6  

Students receive customized feedback from the Interactive Writing Coach™ or feedback from their teacher.

Focus on Craft: Effective Transitions

Your writing will be smoother if you use clear **transitions**, words and phrases that show the connections between ideas. Transitions that indicate a comparison include *similarly, likewise, in the same way,* and *once again*. Transitions that indicate a contrast include *although, in contrast, on the other hand,* and *however*.

Look for a transition as you read these sentences from the Student Model.

STUDENT MODEL from **Canines in the Wild**
page 151; lines 33–36

In the United States, wolves are a protected species, which means they are in danger of becoming extinct. Coyotes, on the other hand, have an incredible talent for adapting.

Try It! Now, ask yourself these questions. Record your answers in your journal.

- What relationship does the transition *on the other hand* signal?
- Would the relationship between ideas in these sentences be different if the transition *similarly* replaced the current transition? Why or why not?

Fine-Tune Your Draft

Apply It! Use these revision suggestions to prepare your final draft after rethinking how well questions of purpose, audience, and genre have been addressed.

- **Choose Effective Transitions to Convey Meaning** To ensure your ideas flow logically, use transitions between sentences and between paragraphs. Use transitions to clarify relationships between points and to be certain that you have a consistent point of view.
- **Ensure Internal and External Coherence** To present a cohesive essay within each section and as a whole, make sure that ideas, sentences, and paragraphs are organized in a logical sequence and that they flow easily.
- **Check Consistent Point of View** Make sure that the entire essay uses the same person, or voice, consistently. For example, avoid switching from first-person "I" to third-person "she."

Teacher Feedback After submitting your final draft for teacher review, **revise it in response to feedback from your teacher.**

www.phwritingcoach.com

Video
Learn more strategies for effective writing from program author Kelly Gallagher.

Online Journal
Try It! Record your answers in the online journal.

Interactive Model
Refer back to the Interactive Model as you revise your writing.

Interactive Writing Coach™
Revise your draft and submit it for feedback.

Personalized Support

Interactive Writing Coach™

Below Level Students complete the revising process by submitting their writing for scoring and feedback.

On Level Students complete the revising process by submitting their writing for scoring and feedback.

Above Level Students finish revising their drafts. They have the option of submitting their revised drafts for scoring and/or feedback.

Teacher or Peer Feedback

To provide feedback to students as they continue to revise their first draft, ask or have student partners ask one another the following:

- What part of the text could you replace to make your meaning clearer?
- Is there a more precise word for this?
- Could you vary the length and structure of these sentences?
- How could you include transitional words and phrases here?
- Are there details you could add here?

Working with ELLs

ELL Sheltered Instruction: Social/Affective

As students read, help them use support from peers and from you to enhance and confirm understanding and to develop their grasp of language structures, such as transitions, needed to comprehend increasingly challenging language. Read the Focus on Craft box with students and create a list of transitions. Then:

Beginning On the board, write, *My friend likes roller coasters. In contrast, I am afraid of heights.* Choral read with students, using gestures. Help students identify *in contrast* as the transition and a transition in the Student Model.

Intermediate Discuss transitions with students, and have them work in groups to identify the transition in the Student Model excerpt and complete the *Try It!* questions.

Advanced Have partners use the **KIM Strategy**, writing a key word, information, and a memory cue about the terms *transition, contrast,* and *similarity.* Have them read the Student Model excerpt, identifying the transition and completing the *Try It!*.

Advanced High Have partners complete the Advanced activity and write another sentence using a transition.

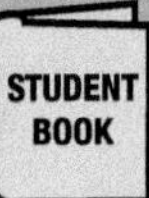

1 

In a video by program author Jeff Anderson, students learn effective editing techniques.

2 

Students record answers to questions about writer's craft in their online journals or notebooks.

Editing: Making It Correct

Discuss the opening paragraph with students. Explain that they will edit their drafts for proper grammar, mechanics, and spelling, including the use of transitions.

WRITE GUY *Jeff Anderson, M.Ed.*

WHAT DO YOU NOTICE?

Introduce students to using transitions by reading aloud the Student Model excerpt and discussing the "Ask yourself" question. Then, guide students to identify and use transitions.

I notice that the Student Model uses the transitions *on the other hand* and *thus* to join ideas. These words and phrases show two different types of relationships between ideas. The Mentor Text also uses transitions: *but* shows contrast: "But few studies have ever examined invertebrates, like honeybees." *Then* shows time order: "Then the tests got harder."

Work with students to list more transitions that express contrast, cause and effect, time order, and similarity (*similarly, like, because of*).

Have students write sentences that use transitions to express these relationships: contrast, similarity, cause and effect, and time order.

Editing Feature Assignment Editing Feature Assignment

Editing: Making It Correct

Use the editing process to polish your work and correct errors. It is often helpful to work with a partner when editing your drafts.

As you edit, think about whether or not you have used **transitions** effectively. A transition is a word or phrase that creates a clear relationship between ideas. Then, edit your final draft for any factual errors and errors in **grammar, mechanics, and spelling**.

WRITE GUY *Jeff Anderson, M. Ed.*

WHAT DO YOU NOTICE?

Zoom in on Conventions Focus on transitions as you zoom in on these sentences from the Student Model.

STUDENT MODEL from **Canines in the Wild**
page 151; lines 33–36, 43–44

In the United States, wolves are a protected species, which means they are in danger of becoming extinct. Coyotes, on the other hand, have an incredible talent for adapting....

Thus, while coyotes and wolves look alike, their behaviors and situations are different.

To learn more about phrases and clauses, see Chapter 19 of your Grammar Handbook.

Now, ask yourself: *Which words and phrases create a relationship between ideas?*

Perhaps you identified the transition *on the other hand,* which makes clear the relationship of contrast between the first two sentences in the passage.

The transition *Thus* makes clear the cause-and-effect relationship between the last paragraph and the paragraphs that came before it.

Partner Talk Discuss this question with a partner: *What other transitions could the Student Model author have used to express the same relationships?*

162 Expository Writing

Grammar Mini-Lesson: Commas With Transitions

Discuss the paragraph and the Student Model excerpt on page 163 with students. Guide them to understand that the writer placed a comma after the transitions *in contrast* and *nevertheless* to set them off from the rest of the sentence.

Try It! Have students work with a partner to identify each transition and tell whether a comma is needed.

1. *In contrast;* comma needed
2. *Accordingly;* comma needed

Apply It! Remind students to look closely for transitions that require commas as they edit.

Use the Rubric Explain that students will rate how well their draft addresses the elements of a compare-contrast essay on a scale of 1 to 6, with 6 being the best score.

Then, have students use the rubric to evaluate their drafts and revise them as necessary.

Writer's Block

IF students have difficulty determining whether commas are needed to set off transitions in their drafts . . .

THEN have them circle all transitions and read each sentence aloud. A natural pause usually indicates a need for a comma after a transition.

3 

Using Writing Coach Online™ or the student book, students refer back to the Mentor Text or Student Model as they edit their writing.

4 

Using Writing Coach Online™ or the student book, students evaluate their writing using the rubrics.

5 

Students submit edited drafts to the Interactive Writing Coach™ for scoring and feedback, or share their work with their teacher.

6 

Students receive personalized feedback from the Interactive Writing Coach™ or feedback from their teacher.

Grammar Mini-Lesson: Commas With Transitions

To learn more, see Chapter 25.

Most **transitions** should be set off from the rest of the sentence by **commas.** The comma may be omitted after a short introductory transition if the sentence is clear without it. Notice how commas set off transitions in the Student Model.

STUDENT MODEL from **Canines in the Wild** page 150; lines 19–22

In contrast, most coyotes weigh from 20 to 30 pounds. Nevertheless, the size difference won't always help you tell the difference between wolves and coyotes.

Try It! Identify two transitions in this passage. Also indicate if any commas need to be added.

The Fourth of July celebrates American independence. In contrast Cinco de Mayo commemorates a Mexican victory in a battle. Accordingly it is a celebration of Mexican culture.

Apply It! **Edit your draft for grammar, punctuation, capitalization, and spelling errors.** Capitalize appropriate words correctly and use an electronic or print dictionary or other resource to check your spelling. Make sure to use transitions for **coherence** between sentences and paragraphs. Use commas correctly.

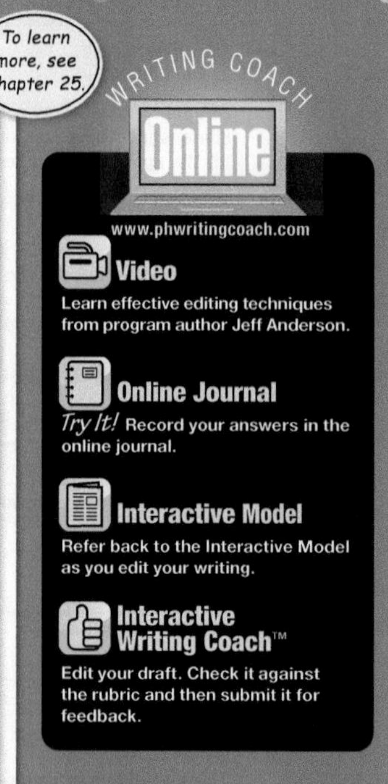

WRITING COACH
Online
www.phwritingcoach.com
Video
Learn effective editing techniques from program author Jeff Anderson.
Online Journal
Try It! Record your answers in the online journal.
Interactive Model
Refer back to the Interactive Model as you edit your writing.
Interactive Writing Coach™
Edit your draft. Check it against the rubric and then submit it for feedback.

Use the rubric to evaluate your essay. If necessary, rethink, rewrite, or revise.

Rubric for Expository Writing: Compare-and-Contrast Essay	Rating Scale
Ideas: How well do you explain the similarities and differences of your topics?	Not very ... Very 1 2 3 4 5 6
Organization: How well do you organize the similarities and differences of your topic?	1 2 3 4 5 6
Voice: How well do you engage the reader?	1 2 3 4 5 6
Word Choice: How clearly do your words convey your specific ideas?	1 2 3 4 5 6
Sentence Fluency: How effectively do you use transitions?	1 2 3 4 5 6
Conventions: How correct is your usage of commas with transitions?	1 2 3 4 5 6

Personalized Support

Interactive Writing Coach™

Below Level Students complete the editing process by submitting their writing for scoring and feedback.

On Level Students complete the editing process by submitting their writing for scoring and feedback.

Above Level Students finish editing their drafts. They have the option of submitting their final drafts for scoring and/or feedback.

Teacher or Peer Feedback

To provide feedback to students as they edit their draft, ask or have student partners ask one another the following:

- Can you show me something you changed through editing?
- What resources have you used to look for possible spelling errors?
- Read this sentence aloud. Does the grammar sound correct to you?

Working with ELLs

ELL Sheltered Instruction: Metacognitive

Use *Apply It!* to help students monitor and edit their writing for subject-verb agreement. Review the rules of subject-verb agreement, and then have students use the following self-corrective techniques:

Beginning Review the forms of a verb students have been studying, writing appropriate singular and plural subjects for each form. Have students write sentences using the verbs and use this self-corrective technique: have them circle the subjects and underline the verbs in their sentences and compare them with those on the board. Guide them in making corrections.

Intermediate Have partners circle four verbs in each other's drafts. Then, have them underline the subject for each verb and check that they have chosen the correct verb form for each subject.

Advanced Have students put a transparency over their drafts and use a marker to circle all the verbs and then check for subject-verb agreement.

Advanced High Have students complete the Advanced activity and exchange papers with a partner to check for agreement.

1 Using Writing Coach Online™ or the student book, students complete the writing process by deciding the best way to publish their writing for their intended audience.

2 Students record their answers and ideas to Extend Your Research in their online journals or notebooks.

Publishing

Wrap Up Your Presentation

Lead a class discussion about the kinds of images that students might use to illustrate their compare-and-contrast essay, such as photographs, maps, and diagrams. Then, have each student find or create at least one image to illustrate his or her essay.

Publish Your Piece

Explain to students that the final step in the writing process is to decide which form of publication will present their work most effectively. Then, tell students that the chart shows how specific audiences can be reached using different media.

Have students whose essays address similar audiences work in small groups to discuss appropriate ways to publish their work.

Extend Your Research

Extension Tell students that their thinking about their topic does not have to end with its final publication. Then, guide students through the instructions for extending their research.

Big Question Have students respond to the question in their journal.

Publishing *Feature Assignment* Publishing *Feature Assignment*

Publishing

Get your compare-and-contrast essay ready for presentation so you can share what you learned with others. Then, choose a way to **publish it for the appropriate audience**.

Wrap Up Your Presentation

To get your essay ready, you may need to make a new, clean copy. Be sure to add images of the items you're comparing to help readers see the similarities and differences. Finally, make sure that your title grabs the reader's attention and indicates your essay's topic.

Publish Your Essay

Use the chart to identify a way to publish your essay.

If your audience is...	...then publish it by...
Classmates and others at your school	• Submitting it to a school newspaper or magazine • Creating a podcast for classmates to hear
Your local community	• Submitting it to a local print or online newspaper • Reading and discussing it on local public-access TV
The larger community	• Posting it online and inviting responses • Entering it in a regional or national essay contest

Extend Your Research

Think more about the topic on which you wrote your compare-and-contrast essay. What else would you like to know about this topic? As you write your ideas, use specific details to describe and explain. Increase the specificity of your details based on the type of information you are recording.

- Brainstorm for several questions you would like to research and then consult, or discuss, with others.
- Formulate, or develop, a plan about how you will answer these questions. Decide where you will find more information—on the Internet, at the library, or through other sources.
- Finally, learn more about your topic by following through with your research plan.

The Big Question: Why Write? What should we tell and what should we describe to make information clear?

164 Expository Essay

MAKE YOUR WRITING COUNT

Introduce the humorous skit activity by discussing the opening paragraphs with students. Then, guide students through each step in the action plan. Make sure students understand that the project may be produced electronically or by hand.

Resources You may wish to have students use these graphic organizers: Meeting Agenda, Meeting Notes, and Venn Diagram. Distribute printed copies or have students log on to Writing Coach Online.

Then, guide students through each step in the action plan.

Use the 21st Century Skills Rubric to evaluate each group's process and final product on a scale of 1 to 3, indicating weak, moderate, or strong use of the skill. ▶

Listening and Speaking Monitor students' oral communication and active listening as they collaborate in groups.

21st Century Learning

Skills Rubric	Rating
Make Judgments and Decisions: Reflect on learning experiences and processes.	1 2 3
Work Creatively With Others: Incorporate group input and feedback into the work.	1 2 3
Collaborate With Others: Be flexible and willing to be helpful in making compromises to reach a common goal.	1 2 3
Apply Technology Effectively: Use technology to research and communicate information.	1 2 3

3 STUDENT BOOK

Students use a variety of graphic organizers, either online or in print, to help them work together to create a multimedia group project.

4 STUDENT BOOK

Through Writing Coach Online™ students link to resources on 21st Century Learning for help in creating a multimedia group project.

21st Century Learning

MAKE YOUR WRITING COUNT

Entertain Audiences With a Humorous Skit

Compare-and-contrast essays identify similarities and differences between two people, things, or issues. In another context, points of contrast can be emphasized for humor. In fact, comedians often use differences as the basis for skits. Use humor to communicate the message of one of your compare-and-contrast essays.

Produce a **humorous skit** inspired by the differences explored in a compare-and-contrast essay. Develop interesting characters representing the two people, items, or issues analyzed in one of your peers' essays. Perform the skit live or video-record it.

Here's your action plan.

1. Choose roles, including writer, director, performer, and prop master.
2. With your group, evaluate your peers' compare-and-contrast essays. Choose one that compares items or ideas that are easily represented—and that might lend themselves to comedy.
3. View comical skits online. Then, write a skit that portrays each item or idea as a character.
   - Write funny dialogue for each character.
   - Make sure that similarities and differences are clear. Exaggeration may help enhance the humor.
   - Assign two group members to play the parts.
   - Work as a team to rehearse the skit, using costumes and props.
   - If possible, perform and record the skit using a video camera.
4. Present the skit to the class or school either live or as a video. Consider posting the video online.

Listening and Speaking Listen actively as your group writes the skit together. Take turns making suggestions for adding humor during the planning and rehearsal stages. During the performance, keep your peers' feedback in mind. Work as a team to entertain and inform your audience. Listen for feedback.

WRITING COACH Online

www.phwritingcoach.com

Online Journal

Extend Your Research Record your answers and ideas in the online journal.

Resource

Link to resources on 21st Century Learning for help in creating a group project.

Personalized Support

FEEDBACK

Teacher or Peer Feedback

To provide feedback to students on their published writing, ask or have student partners ask one another the following:

- How did you go about writing this piece? What was your process?
- What did you learn from the writing model that you used in this piece?
- What surprised you the most as you wrote this piece?
- Did you try anything new as you worked on this piece?
- What did you learn from this piece of writing that you would like to remember and reuse?
- What do you think you do best as a writer right now?

Differentiated Instruction

RTI Strategy for Below-Level Students

As students prepare to create a skit, you might wish to provide instruction by modeling the conventions and format of a script:

- The speaker's name is written at left, followed by a colon and the exact words the speaker says. Each speaker's dialogue is written on a new line.
- Directions for tone, expression, gestures, or movement are written in parentheses.

Enrichment for Gifted/Talented Students

Challenge gifted and talented students to provide their comedy groups with creative leadership. For example, they may name a director, costume, and set designers; a stage manager; and a musical director to write or find appropriate music to accompany the presentation.

1  STUDENT BOOK

Students use Writing Coach Online™ or their student books to analyze and discuss the Writing for Media topic.

 Writing for Media: Technical Newsletter

Technical Newsletter

Discuss the opening paragraph with students. Ask students if they have ever read a technical newsletter. As a class, brainstorm for topics that might be found in technical newsletters.

Try It! Guide students to understand the purpose and content of the sample technical newsletter.

Say: The first *Try It!* question asks about the topic and the controlling idea of the sample newsletter. The topic, MP3 players, is stated at the top of the article. **I see** the controlling idea in the first paragraph: there are two basic kinds of MP3 players.

Tell students that a technical newsletter has a very specific purpose and audience. **Ask:** What is the purpose of a technical newsletter? (to give information about new and updated electronics or other technological products)

Have students discuss the remaining questions in small groups and record individual responses in their journals.

Extension Have students bring in other examples of technical newsletters. Lead a media discussion about the examples, using the *Try It!* questions as a guide.

Writing for Media Writing for Media Writing for Media Writi

 Writing for Media: Technical Newsletter

21st Century Learning

Technical Newsletter

A **technical newsletter** gives information about the latest advances in electronics or other technologies. It often compares and contrasts new developments or products to help readers make informed decisions. Newsletters are often e-mailed or sent as direct-mail, or mail sent to a specific target audience. Many technical newsletters are geared to audiences of subscribers who are already familiar with the technical field. Others are aimed at more general audiences who need to make a purchase or research new developments in the field.

Try It! Study this sample technical newsletter. Then, answer the five questions about it. Record your answers in your journal.

1. What topic does the newsletter address? Restate the **controlling idea** in your own words.
2. Describe the newsletter's **audience**—are they general readers ready to buy, or "techies" familiar with the topic? Cite details to explain your answer.
3. List the main **similarities** and **differences** that the newsletter points out.
4. Does the newsletter **use point-by-point** or **block organization?** Does the organization help make the similarities and differences clear to you? Why or why not?
5. What **transitions** help make the similarities and differences clearer?

Extension Find another example of a technical newsletter, and compare it with this one.

TECHNO-TIPS

MP3 Players

An MP3 player is a pocket-sized electronic device that stores and plays back music or other audio files. There are two basic kinds: hard-drive-based MP3 players and flash-based MP3 players. Each has its benefits and drawbacks.

Hard-drive-based MP3 players, sometimes called hard-disk players, have the most gigabytes. This means they have more storage space for your music collection. In fact, some hard-drive-based players can store as many as 40,000 songs. In terms of cost, you get the most storage space for your money with one of these players. However, you also get the largest and heaviest MP3 player. Micro-hard-drive-based MP3 players are a smaller and lighter version, but they also have less storage space. They also do not solve the biggest problem of all hard-drive-based players: Sudden movements cause them to skip. Thus, hard-drive-based players are impractical to use while jogging, running, or working out.

Flash-based MP3 players, sometimes called flash-memory players, are the original MP3 design. They are smaller and lighter than other players, and they do not skip. Their storage space, however, is fairly small. Depending on the model, it ranges from as few as 10 to as many as 8,000 songs. Also, per unit of storage space, flash-based players cost more than their hard-drive-based cousins. Moreover, they can be harder to operate, especially if they have lots of special features.

166 Expository Essay

Create a Technical Newsletter

Tell students that they will create a technical newsletter using the five-step writing process. Then, preview the writing process instructions on page 167.

Resources You may wish to have students use the Outline graphic organizer. Distribute printed copies or have students log on to Writing Coach Online.

For each step in the writing process, have partners read aloud and discuss the list of tasks. Then, have them work individually. Once both partners have completed the tasks, have them evaluate each other's work before moving to the next step.

Use the 21st Century Skills Rubric to evaluate each student's process and final product on a scale of 1 to 3, indicating weak, moderate, or strong use of the skill. ▶

Partner Talk

Suggest that students think of their partner as a target audience and include information to address their partner's questions.

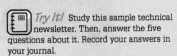

21st Century Learning

Skills Rubric	Rating
Reason Effectively: Use inductive and deductive reasoning as appropriate to the situation.	1 2 3
Communicate Clearly: Use communication to inform, instruct, motivate, and persuade.	1 2 3
Use and Manage Information: Use information accurately and creatively for the issue at hand.	1 2 3
Apply Technology Effectively: Use technology as a tool to research, organize, evaluate, and communicate information.	1 2 3

2 Writing Journal

Students learn about the characteristics of a technical newsletter by answering questions about the model. Students record their answers to the *Try It!* questions in their online journals or notebooks.

3 STUDENT BOOK

Students follow the five-step writing process to write their own technical newsletter. Students may select online or printed graphic organizers to help them plan and develop their writing.

Create a Technical Newsletter

Follow these steps to create a technical newsletter for a specific audience. To plan your newsletter, review the graphic organizers on pages R24–R27 and choose one that suits your needs.

Prewriting

- Choose a technology that you might like to research. For example, you might choose video games, cell phones, or cameras.
- Determine your audience and purpose. Will you be updating an already informed audience or teaching a more general audience?
- After doing research, decide on two aspects of the topic that you will compare and contrast.
- List the similarities and differences that you would like to discuss.
- Develop a controlling idea that makes a general statement about the similarities and differences.

Drafting

- Begin with a paragraph that identifies your topic. Include a thesis about the two aspects of the topic you will discuss.
- Discuss similarities and differences using block or point-by-point organization. Include graphic elements, such as subheadings or boldfaced text, to help organize your ideas.
- Use correct terminology in discussing the topic. If your audience is new to the topic, include definitions or explanations of unfamiliar terms.
- Use clear transitions to show comparisons, contrasts, and other relationships.
- Give your newsletter a catchy title that identifies its content.

Revising and Editing

- Check that your information is accurate and uses correct terminology.
- Make sure that your information is logically organized and will be clear to your particular audience.
- Remove any details that are not relevant to your purpose.

Publishing

Create your own technical Web site and post your newsletter as a multimedia presentation. Use available technology to add text and graphics to the Web site and your newsletter.

WRITING COACH

Online

www.phwritingcoach.com

Online Journal

Try It! Record your answers in the online journal.

Interactive Graphic Organizers

Choose from a variety of graphic organizers to plan and develop your project.

Partner Talk

Discuss your topic with a partner. Ask what questions or concerns he or she might have on the topic of your newsletter, and take notes about his or her responses. Consider your partner's responses in deciding on the information to include in your newsletter.

Personalized Support

FEEDBACK

Teacher or Peer Feedback

To provide feedback to students as they write for media, ask or have student partners ask one another the following:

- What are the main characteristics of this form of writing?
- Have you included most or all of these characteristics in your piece of writing?
- What is your purpose for writing this piece?
- Who is your audience?
- How did you organize your ideas in this piece of writing?
- How did you go about revising the piece? Editing it?
- How do you plan on publishing your piece?
- What other publishing options also might work?

Working with ELLs

ELL Sheltered Instruction: Social/Affective

Use the Partner Talk to help students orally express opinions, ideas, and feelings in contexts ranging from communicating in single words to participating in extended discussions. Help them use learning strategies such as employing nonverbal clues and using synonyms.

Beginning Write: *I feel* ___, *I think* ___, *I like* ___ and help students orally complete the sentences to express their opinions, ideas, and feelings about technology, using nonverbal cues if they lack a word.

Intermediate Help groups brainstorm for ideas about a technology, such as cell phones, and discuss their opinions, ideas, and feelings about it. Have them use gestures and synonyms as needed.

Advanced Have partners discuss the topics they chose to write about, making sure to express their opinions, ideas, and feelings. Have them use synonyms or descriptions of concepts as needed.

Advanced High Have partners complete the Partner Talk and orally express their opinions, ideas, and feelings about their partner's topic using synonyms as needed.

The Digital • Print Path

1 

Before they write, students use the ABCDs of On-Demand Writing to analyze and plan how to respond to each prompt. They can use either their online journals or notebooks to take notes.

2 

Students submit their writing paragraph by paragraph or as a complete draft to the **Interactive Writing Coach™** for feedback, or share their writing with their teacher.

Writing for Assessment

Read aloud or have a student read aloud the introductory text. Then, tell students that they will learn and practice a technique for writing in response to a test prompt.

Try It! Read the Expository Prompt aloud and then have volunteers read aloud the Format and Academic Vocabulary boxes. Tell students that they will use the ABCD method to respond to the prompt.

The ABCDs of On-Demand Writing

Have students identify the words associated with the ABCD method. (attack, brainstorm, choose, detect) Then, guide students through their use.

I'll attack the prompt by circling the verbs *compares, contrasts,* and *discuss.* These words remind me that I must not only point out similarities and differences but support them with details. I can rewrite the prompt to state it clearly: "Compare and contrast the similarities and differences in owning and caring for a cat and a dog."

Work with students to identify an appropriate graphic organizer to help them brainstorm for ideas, such as a Venn diagram. Then, remind them to decide on the organizational structure before they begin to write.

Have students write their drafts individually and then work with a partner to detect errors.

Writing for Assessment *Writing for Assessment* Writing for Assessment

Writing for Assessment

Many standardized tests include a prompt that asks you to write an expository essay. You can use the prompts on these pages to practice. Your responses should include most of the same characteristics as your compare-and-contrast essay. (See page 146.)

 *Try It!* To begin, read the **expository** prompt and the information on format and academic vocabulary. Then write an essay by following the instructions shown in the ABCDs of On-Demand Writing.

Format
The prompt directs you to write a compare-and-contrast *expository essay.* Include an introduction, body paragraphs with similarities and differences, and a conclusion.

Expository Prompt
Write an expository essay that compares and contrasts two different kinds of household pets. Discuss similarities and differences of owning each pet and the work involved in caring for each.

Academic Vocabulary
Remember that *similarities* are elements that are alike; *differences* are elements that are not alike.

The ABCDs of On-Demand Writing

Use the following ABCDs to help you respond to the prompt.

Before you write your draft:

A ttack the prompt [1 MINUTE]

- Circle or highlight important verbs in the prompt. Draw a line from the verb to what it refers to.
- Rewrite the prompt in your own words.

B rainstorm possible answers [4 MINUTES]

- Create a graphic organizer to generate ideas.
- Use one for each part of the prompt if necessary.

C hoose the order of your response [1 MINUTE]

- Think about the best way to organize your ideas.
- Number your ideas in the order you will write about them. Cross out ideas you will not be using.

After you write your draft:

D etect errors before turning in the draft [1 MINUTE]

- Carefully reread your writing.
- Make sure that your response makes sense and is complete.
- Look for spelling, punctuation, and grammar errors.

More Prompts for Practice

Apply It! **Test Prep** Have students apply the ABCD method to the practice prompts.

Prompt 1 Have partners attack the prompt and brainstorm for possible answers. Then, have each pair swap their information with another group to evaluate whether the teams have developed detailed, balanced, and effective comparisons and contrasts.

Prompt 2 Have students work individually to attack the prompt and brainstorm for possible answers. Then, have students work in small groups to evaluate their work before writing their drafts.

Spiral Review: Poetry Read aloud the instruction and the prompt. Then, have students review the poetry characteristics on page 120.

Prompt 3 Remind students to use the ABCD method to write their poem.

3

Students receive personalized feedback from the Interactive Writing Coach™ or feedback from their teacher.

More Prompts for Practice

Apply It! Respond to Prompts 1 and 2 by writing **expository essays**. As you write, be sure to:

- Grab readers' attention with an **effective introductory paragraph** that states a **clear purpose** and end with a memorable **concluding paragraph**
- Use a **variety of sentence structures, rhetorical devices, and transitions** to help make your writing cohesive and interesting
- Use a variety of examples and details to support your ideas. Accurately **synthesize ideas** into a cohesive whole
- For your body, choose a logical **organizing structure appropriate to your facts and details**
- Include **relevant information** with **no inconsistencies**. Remove any extraneous information

Prompt 1 Soccer vs. football? Swimming vs. track? Choose two sports, and write an essay comparing and contrasting them. Be sure that you explain the similarities and differences in a way that would be clear to someone unfamiliar with the sport.

Prompt 2 Write a compare-and-contrast essay in which you discuss the similarities and differences between two foods you enjoy. Focus on their nutritional benefits as well as their taste. You might also consider other qualities, such as the cost or ease of preparation.

Spiral Review: Poetry Respond to Prompt 3 by writing a **poem**. Make sure your poem reflects all of the characteristics described on page 120, including:

- **Poetic techniques**
- **Figurative language**
- **Graphic elements**

Prompt 3 Think about your school. What are your favorite things about your school? What are the best things that have happened there? Write a poem expressing your ideas and feelings about your school.

www.phwritingcoach.com

Interactive Writing Coach™

Plan your response to the prompt. If you are using the prompt for practice, write one paragraph at a time or your entire draft and then submit it for feedback. If you are using the prompt as a timed test, write your entire draft and then submit it for feedback.

Remember **ABCD**

- **A**ttack the prompt
- **B**rainstorm possible answers
- **C**hoose the order of your response
- **D**etect errors before turning in the draft

Personalized Support

Assessment/Monitor Progress

For timed writing practice, assign students a prompt to be completed in a timed setting. For Prompts 1 and 2, have students submit their writing to Interactive Writing Coach™ to get immediate feedback.

For a formal writing assessment, assign the Assessment writing prompt for this chapter in Writing Coach Online™. Then, have students submit their writing to Interactive Writing Coach™ to be assessed. Use the results to assess student progress and skill levels. Interactive Writing Coach™ will update student levels to ensure that students get the appropriate support.

Teacher Feedback

To create an assessment environment, have students use a prompt in a timed setting. Grade papers using the appropriate rubric and use the results to assess student progress and skill levels. In the next writing assignment, ensure that students get the appropriate level of support.

If you conference with students, use these questions to guide your discussion:

- What writing form did the prompt call for?
- How did you organize your ideas?
- Did you make good use of your time?

Differentiated Instruction

RTI Strategy for Below-Level Students

Before students begin, review the use of a Venn diagram for comparing and contrasting. Also, have them review or list transitions to show comparison or contrast. Have them relate the transitions for comparison to the details in the overlapping section of the Venn diagram and the transitions for contrast to the details in the outer circles.

RTI Strategy for Special Needs Students

Emphasize the importance of staying within the ABCD plan to complete the assignment. Tell students not to worry too much about spelling or mechanics while they are drafting. It's better to get their ideas down quickly and logically. They can use their editing time to improve sentence structure and correct spelling and punctuation.

CHAPTER 9 LESSON PLANNER
Persuasion

Interactive Writing Coach™ | Interactive Graphic Organizers | Interactive Models | Online Journal | Resources | Video

Use the Online Lesson Planner at www.phwritingcoach.com to customize your instructional plan for an integrated Language Arts curriculum.

DAY 1

CHAPTER OPENER/ GENRE INTRODUCTION

- What Do You Think?
- What's Ahead
- Connect to the Big Questions
- **Feature Assignment: Op-Ed Piece**
- Other Forms of Persuasive Writing
- Word Bank

ONLINE

DAY 2

MENTOR TEXT/ STUDENT MODEL

- **Mentor Text: Op-Ed Piece**
- Learn From Experience
- **Student Model: Op-Ed Piece**
- Reader's Eye and Writer's Eye

ONLINE

DAY 3

Prewriting

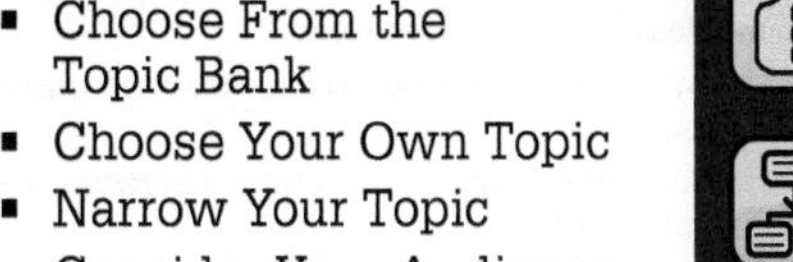

- Choose From the Topic Bank
- Choose Your Own Topic
- Narrow Your Topic
- Consider Your Audience and Purpose

ONLINE

DAY 6

Revising

- Keep Revision on Your RADaR
- Look at the Big Picture
- Focus on Craft
- Fine-Tune Your Draft

ONLINE

DAY 7

For additional grammar support, see Grammar Game Plan, Error 4, p. 276.

Editing

- What Do You Notice?/ Grammar Mini-Lesson

Rubric for Op-Ed Piece

Publishing

- Publish Your Piece
- Extend Your Research

ONLINE

DAY 8

21st Century Learning

MAKE YOUR WRITING COUNT

- **Create a Public Action Day at Your School**
- Here's Your Action Plan
- Listening and Speaking

ONLINE

Alternate Pacing Suggestions

- **Block Scheduling** Each day on the Lesson Planner represents a 40–50 minute block. Teachers using block scheduling may combine days to revise pacing to meet their classroom needs.
- **Accelerated Lesson Planning** Combine instructional days by aiding students in choosing a topic and then focusing on two core stages of the writing process, outlining for success (Day 5) and RADaR revision (Day 6).
- **Integrated Language Arts Curriculum** For targeted instruction that covers the essential components of the lesson, use either a 3- or a 5-day plan.

3 day plan

DAY 1: Introduction to the Genre, Mentor Text, Student Model

DAY 2: Prewriting/Drafting

DAY 3: Revising/Editing/ Publishing

5 day plan

Use 3-day plan, and add:

DAY 4: Make Your Writing Count

DAY 5: Writing for Assessment

Links to Prentice Hall *LITERATURE*

Featured Author: Richard Mühlberger

- What Is an Essay?, p. 408
- "What Makes a Rembrandt a Rembrandt?" (analytical article), p. 413
- On Getting Readers Involved (Writing Workshop), p. 551
- *From the Author's Desk* Videos: Richard Mühlberger

Additional Mentor Text:

- "All Together Now" (persuasion), Barbara Jordan, p. 494

Differentiated Instruction

Differentiated Instruction Boxes in this Teacher's Edition address these student populations:

- Below-Level Students
- Above-Level Students
- Gifted and Talented Students
- Special Needs Students
- English Language Learners
- Spanish Speaking Students

In addition, for further enrichment, see the **Extension** features.

DAY 4

Prewriting

- Plan Your Piece
- Gather Details

ONLINE

DAY 5

Drafting

- Outline for Success
- Start Your Draft

ONLINE

DAY 9

WRITING FOR MEDIA

- **Advertisements**
- Create an Advertisement

ONLINE

DAY 10

WRITING FOR ASSESSMENT

- Persuasive Prompt
- The ABCDs of On-Demand Writing
- More Prompts for Practice

Test Prep: Spiral Review: Expository

ONLINE

LESSON OBJECTIVES

- To learn the forms and defining characteristics of persuasion.
- To learn the elements of a successful op-ed piece, the chapter Feature Assignment.
- To read a Mentor Text in the genre, analyzing its use of the elements of effective persuasion.
- To read a Student Model of an op-ed piece, analyzing it from the perspective of a reader and from the perspective of a writer.
- To apply prewriting strategies in developing an op-ed piece, including strategies for choosing and narrowing a topic, planning writing, and gathering details, as well as tips for considering audience and purpose.
- To apply drafting strategies in developing an op-ed piece.
- To apply RADaR revision strategies to a draft op-ed piece.
- To learn about the Focus on Craft topic, precise word choice, and apply what is learned to a draft op-ed piece.
- To edit the draft, zooming in on sentence structure and focusing on parallel structures.
- To complete the Make Your Writing Count assignment, developing and presenting a multimedia presentation for a Public Action Day.
- To complete the Writing for Media assignment, developing an advertisement.
- To practice writing for assessment.

Personalized Assessment

✓	Ongoing Assessment	Formal Assessment of Feature Assignment	Progress Monitoring at End-of-Chapter
Interactive Writing Coach™	Use Paragraph Feedback and Essay Scorer as a revision tool.	Use Essay Scorer to score students' Feature Assignment papers.	Use Essay Scorer to score students' papers. Students' learner profiles can be adjusted based on their scores.
 FEEDBACK Teacher Conferencing	Use rubrics in the Student Edition as a revision tool. Conference with students to review their work and provide personalized support.	Use rubrics in the Student Edition to score students' Feature Assignment papers.	Review each student's work to plan targeted resources for the next writing assignment.

The Digital • Print Path

1 Using Writing Coach Online™ or the student book, students discuss the photograph in the chapter opener as it relates to the writing genre.

2 Students record their ideas and responses in their online journals or notebooks. They may also record and save their responses on pop-up sticky notes in Writing Coach Online™.

Chapter Objectives

1. Write an op-ed piece by planning, drafting, revising, editing, and publishing individual work.
2. Produce a multimedia presentation.
3. Use the five-step writing process to write an advertisement.
4. Write a persuasive essay and an expository essay in response to a prompt.

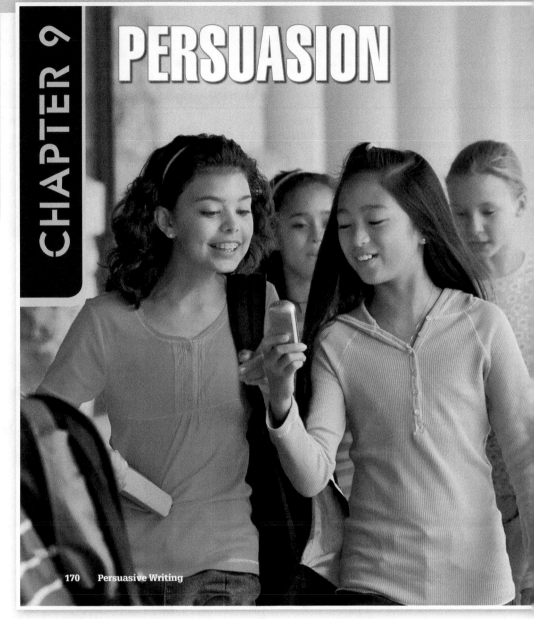

CHAPTER 9

PERSUASION

PERSUASION

What Do You Think?

Activate Prior Knowledge Tell students that the purpose of persuasive writing is to convince readers to think or act as you wish. Explain to students that they will use what they know about student cell phone use to analyze the photo on page 170. Then, guide the students in analyzing the photo.

To persuade is to convince others that your opinion is right. In the photo, **I see** girls using a cell phone at school. To get a cell phone, the girl probably had to persuade her parents that she would use it responsibly. She would have presented as many arguments in her favor as possible to convince them. You probably try to persuade your friends, family, and teachers about similar issues.

Work with students to brainstorm for a list of reasons why students have cell phones at school. Record student responses.

Try It! **Have students** work individually to develop responses to the questions. Check that students have fully explored reasons for and against having cell phones in school.

Possible responses: Students can call family, text friends, and access the Internet. Students might use Internet access for research. Cell phones distract students and decrease learning. Distracted students could fail to see danger coming, but cell phones also allow students to call parents or guardians in case of illness or other emergencies.

Connect to the Big Questions

Have students use their experience to discuss the Big Questions. Explain that they will revisit **Why write?** at the end of this chapter. Tell students to consider these points during their discussion:

1. After partners discuss both sides of the issue, have the class work together to identify the strongest arguments of each side and explain their reasons for thinking so.
2. Explain that sometimes it's difficult to tell if you've been successful in persuading someone. You may be able to determine success by observing changes in behavior.

What's Ahead

Have students preview the Mentor Text and Student Model on pages 174–177. Tell students that they will write their own op-ed piece using the five-step writing process: prewriting, drafting, revising, editing, and publishing.

What Do You Think?

Should students be allowed to use cell phones in school? This is an issue that people debate. Some schools forbid students to carry and use cell phones; other schools allow cell phones.

Maybe you already have an opinion on student cell phone use. Or perhaps you want to learn more about the issue before taking a position. In either case, one day you might want to convince someone to share your opinion. When you use words to convince people to think or act in a certain way, you are using persuasion.

Try It! Take a few minutes to list reasons why students should and should not be allowed to use cell phones in school.

Consider these questions as you work on your list.

- What do students use their cell phones for in school?
- What useful purposes could cell phones serve in the classroom?
- How could cell phone use in school affect learning?
- Is having a cell phone in school a safety issue? Why?

Review the list you made, and then choose a position on the issue. **Plan a draft by developing a clear thesis or controlling idea** that states your position. Then find a partner, and take turns expressing your thesis ideas to one another.

What's Ahead

In this chapter, you will review two strong examples of a persuasive essay: a Mentor Text and a Student Model. Then, using the examples as guidance, you will write a persuasive essay of your own.

Online Journal

Try It! Record your answers and ideas in the online journal.

You can also record and save your answers and ideas on pop-up sticky notes in the eText.

Connect to the Big Questions

Discuss these questions with your partner:

1. **What do you think?** Which do you think is more important and why—the community's right to ensure that students are not distracted by cell phones or the individual student's right to use a cell phone?
2. **Why write?** What is your point of view? How will you know if you have convinced others?

Personalized Support

Teacher or Peer Feedback

To encourage students in their discussion of the photograph as it relates to the writing genre, ask the following questions:

- What is the first thing you think of when you look at this photo?
- How does it relate to your life?
- How does it relate to things you've learned in other subjects?
- What questions come to mind when you look at this photograph?
- How does your response to the photograph compare to those of your classmates?

Working with ELLs

ELL **Sheltered Instruction:** Metacognitive

Have students demonstrate listening comprehension of increasingly complex spoken English by following the *Try It!* directions after you read them aloud.

Beginning Reread aloud the first sentence of the *Try It!* directions. Using mime, clarify the meaning of *reasons, required, recycle,* and *difficulties*. Ask yes/no questions to help students monitor understanding, and seek clarification as needed. Help them follow the direction.

Intermediate As students listen to the directions, have them write the steps in flow charts to monitor understanding and seek clarification as necessary. Help them follow the directions.

Advanced Have students take notes as you read. Encourage them to monitor comprehension and seek clarification as needed as they follow the *Try It!* directions.

Advanced High Have partners take turns reading aloud the *Try It!* directions and taking notes to monitor comprehension, seeking clarification as needed. Then, have them follow the directions.

1 

Students learn vocabulary from the Word Bank and listen to English and Spanish pronunciations in the **Writing Coach Online™** glossary.

2 

Students record answers to questions about forms of writing in their online journals or notebooks.

PERSUASIVE WRITING

To introduce this chapter's writing form, discuss the opening paragraphs with students. Make sure students understand that an op-ed piece is a type of persuasive writing. Explain that good writers use a step-by-step process to develop their work. Then, have students preview the rubric on page 189.

Persuasive Essay: Op-Ed Piece

Ask volunteers to read aloud the feature assignment characteristics. Tell students that they will identify these characteristics in a Mentor Text and a Student Model. Then, they will use the characteristics to guide the writing of their own op-ed piece.

Other Forms of Persuasive Writing

Guide students to understand how the forms of persuasive writing are alike and different.

Say: I notice that there are many forms of persuasive writing. Many forms appear in newspapers, such as advertisements, editorials, and letters to the editor. I have also encountered persuasive messages on television, on the radio, and online.

Ask: How are these forms of persuasive writing alike? (They all try to convince someone to act or believe a certain way.) How do they differ? (They have different kinds of topics. For example, some deal with current issues, while others deal with personal goals.)

Have students work in small groups to brainstorm for appropriate topics for each writing form.

Try It! Remind students that the audience is the people who will read their writing. The purpose is the author's reason for writing. Have students record their responses in their journal.

Possible responses: letter to the editor, responds to an article; review, shares an opinion about an item or activity; advertisement, convinces people to buy something

PERSUASIVE WRITING

Persuasion is writing that is meant to convince readers to agree with the writer's opinion. In this chapter, you will explore a special type of persuasive essay, the op-ed piece. An op-ed piece is a signed piece that appears in a newspaper or magazine and tries to persuade readers to agree with the writer's views on an issue. An op-ed piece is written by someone who does not work for the newspaper or magazine.

You will develop the op-ed piece by taking it through each of the steps of the writing process: prewriting, drafting, revising, editing, and publishing. You will also have an opportunity to create an advertisement. To preview the criteria for how your op-ed piece will be evaluated, see the rubric on page 189.

FEATURE ASSIGNMENT

Persuasive Essay: Op-Ed Piece

An effective persuasive essay has these characteristics:

- A **lead** that introduces the topic or issue and captures readers' interest
- A **clear thesis statement** that tells the writer's opinion
- **Persuasive arguments** that are organized in logical order
- **Evidence that is logically organized** so that it supports the writer's opinion. Evidence may include examples, facts, statistics, and expert opinions.
- Responses to readers' **concerns and counter-arguments**
- **Effective sentence structure** and correct spelling, grammar, and usage
- A **conclusion** that restates your position and ends on a memorable note
- **A natural but authoritative voice** that appeals to both reason and emotion

An effective op-ed piece also includes:

- A response to a **current event** or **topic**
- A **tight focus** on a single event
- A **call to action**

172 Persuasive Writing

Word Bank

To assist English Language Learners and struggling readers, echo read each word or have students log on to Writing Coach Online to listen to the pronunciations. Then, have partners take turns using each word in a sentence. Ask volunteers to share one of their sentences with the class.

Teacher Tip

Display a newspaper and page through it with students, pointing out different forms of persuasive writing. Read excerpts from an editorial, a letter to the editor, a review, and an advertisement. Have students describe the purpose of each piece.

Other Forms of Persuasive Writing

In addition to an op-ed piece, there are other forms of persuasive writing, including:

Advertisements are paid announcements that try to convince people to do or buy something.

Editorials state the opinion of the editors and publishers of news organizations. Editorials are usually about current issues and appear in newspapers, magazines, or on television, radio, or the Internet.

Letters to the editor are written by readers who express an opinion in response to an article that has been published in a newspaper or magazine.

Persuasive essays use logic and reasoning to persuade readers to adopt a certain action or point of view.

Persuasive speeches aim at winning an audience's support for a policy, position, or action.

Propaganda uses emotional appeals and often biased, false, or misleading information to persuade people to think or act in a certain way. Propaganda is often about political issues.

Reviews evaluate items and activities such as books and movies. A review often states an opinion on whether people should spend time and money on the item or activity.

Try It! For each audience and purpose described, choose a form, such as a speech, letter, or review, that is appropriate for conveying your intended meaning to the audience. Explain your choices.

- To disagree with an editorial in your local newspaper
- To convince classmates to read a book that you enjoyed
- To encourage listeners of a radio station to buy tickets to an upcoming concert

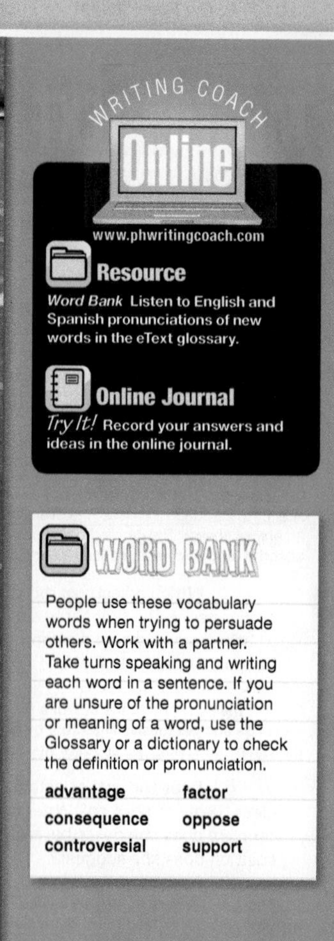
WRITING COACH
Online
www.phwritingcoach.com
Resource
Word Bank Listen to English and Spanish pronunciations of new words in the eText glossary.
Online Journal
Try It! Record your answers and ideas in the online journal.
WORD BANK
People use these vocabulary words when trying to persuade others. Work with a partner. Take turns speaking and writing each word in a sentence. If you are unsure of the pronunciation or meaning of a word, use the Glossary or a dictionary to check the definition or pronunciation.
advantage factor
consequence oppose
controversial support

Personalized Support

FEEDBACK

Teacher or Peer Feedback

To help students understand the characteristics of the writing form, ask or have student partners ask one another the following questions:

- What are the main characteristics of a persuasive essay?
- What makes this form of writing different from other forms?
- Who are the likely readers or audiences for this form of writing?
- What kind of organization could be used for this form of writing?
- What kind of voice would be most effective for this form of writing?

Working with ELLs — ELL Sheltered Instruction: Cognitive

Help students expand and internalize initial English vocabulary by learning and using basic routine language. Have them use and reuse the new basic language in speaking activities that build concept and language attainment.

Beginning Write on the board the basic word *choices* from the *Try It!*. Show two pencils. Say *I pick this one. This is my choice.* Have students repeat and complete oral sentences to reuse the word.

Intermediate Review basic routine words from the *Try It!: choose, try, form, your, each*, and *choice*. For each word, have partners create a **Frayer Model** card, dividing a card into four sections, filling in a definition, characteristics, examples, and non-examples. Have them use and reuse the words to discuss the cards.

Advanced Have students complete the Intermediate activity, then reuse the routine words in oral context sentences.

Advanced High Have students complete the Advanced activity. Then, have them partner with less-fluent students to reuse the words orally in cloze sentences.

The Digital • Print Path

1 

Using Writing Coach Online™ or the student book, students read and listen to an audio recording of the Mentor Text. As they complete their writing assignments, they can refer back to the Mentor Text for support whenever they need it.

MENTOR TEXT

About the Selection The selection describes overcrowding at Maiden Point Shelter and asks readers to adopt a cat or dog from the shelter. The writer points out advantages of owning a mature dog or cat and of pet ownership in general.

Learn From Experience

After students have read the text, point out that the numbered notes refer to the characteristics of an op-ed piece introduced on page 172.

Try It! Guide students to understand how the genre characteristics shape the text.

Say: The first *Try It!* question asks about adjectives used in the lead. The writer uses *overflowing, heartrending,* and *overcrowded* to describe conditions at the shelter. **I like** the writer's use of *heartrending* because the tone of that word helps readers "hear" how upset the animals are and makes readers feel sorry for their helplessness.

Ask: What descriptions or other details in the lead captured your attention? (Responses will vary.)

Have students reply to the *Try It!* questions in their journals. If students have difficulty responding to a particular question, model a response, as with Question 1.

Check the accuracy and completeness of student responses.

1. *Overflowing, heartrending,* and *overcrowded* help readers visualize what it is like at the shelter.
2. Yes, the issue is overcrowding at Maiden Point Shelter; the solution is for more local people to adopt pets instead of buying them.
3. The targeted audience is adult residents of the community. The arguments stress owners having to spend less time training and lowering job stress.
4. Yes, because the quote from an expert gives credibility to the argument for older pets.
5. Those readers who are convinced by the text will be able to act immediately.

Op-Ed Piece Mentor Text Op-Ed Piece Mentor Text Op-Ed Piece

MENTOR TEXT Op-Ed Piece

Learn From Experience

Read the op-ed piece on pages 174–175. As you read, take notes to develop your understanding of basic sight and English vocabulary. Then, read the numbered notes in the margins to learn about how the author presented her ideas.

Answer the *Try It!* questions online or in your journal.

❶ The author wrote a description of an animal shelter to introduce the issue: the overcrowding at an animal shelter. The detailed description is an effective **lead** that captures the reader's attention.

Try It! Which adjectives did the author use in the first three sentences to help readers create a strong visual image of an animal shelter?

❷ The **thesis** presents the author's main message and persuasive argument by naming the issue and stating the author's viewpoint.

Try It! Does the author establish a clear thesis or position? What issue or problem does she describe, and what solution does she suggest?

❸ The author offers three **persuasive arguments** for the need for people to adopt pets from shelters.

Try It! Based on these arguments and the author's purpose, who would you say is her targeted audience? Explain.

Extension Find another example of an op-ed piece, and compare it with this one.

Looking for a Pet?

Look No Further Than Maiden Point Shelter

by Cindy Trumbore

❶ Maiden Point Shelter is overflowing with cats and dogs. Every cage and kennel is filled to capacity, and heartrending meows and barks come from extra cages lining the hallways. The shelter is at its most overcrowded since it was opened in 1993. ❷ There is a simple solution to the overcrowding at Maiden Point Shelter: more people in our area need to adopt pets, rather than buying them. Yet judging from the "designer" pets we see on the streets of our town, the public seems strangely unconvinced of this fact.

There are two main reasons for the problem, according to Biz Raleigh, the director. First, we had a mild winter, so more cats were outside. As a result, there are more litters of kittens now. There is another surprising reason, however, for the overcrowding. Raleigh has noticed a direct link between the number of mortgage foreclosures in our area, and the number of pets that get brought to the shelter. When people lose their homes, they are often forced to find housing that doesn't allow pets. ❸ In fact, Raleigh says that in the past six months, Maiden Point received nearly 200 cats and dogs alone. That's a 100% increase over the previous six months.

"We're at the point where we'll have to start putting unadoptable animals down to make room for the ones with a better chance," Raleigh says, sighing. "I really don't know why people looking for a pet don't come here first." ❸ She points out that pets from pet stores have often been raised in unclean, unhealthy, crowded conditions, especially dogs from so-called "puppy mills." In contrast, the shelter pets are spayed and neutered, and treated for problems such as heartworm and fleas, before they are adopted out.

❸ People especially need to open their minds to adopting older pets, she says. Some people assume that when they get an older pet, they will have to "undo" the bad habits it

174 Persuasive Writing

Extension Lead a discussion in which students compare and contrast how their additional op-ed piece examples use the genre characteristics. Use the *Try It!* questions as a guide.

Teacher Tip

Have students list additional counter-arguments readers may have to the issue of adopting a pet from an animal shelter and work in small groups to brainstorm for convincing responses to each.

2 Writing Journal

Students record their answers to questions about the Mentor Text in their online journals or notebooks.

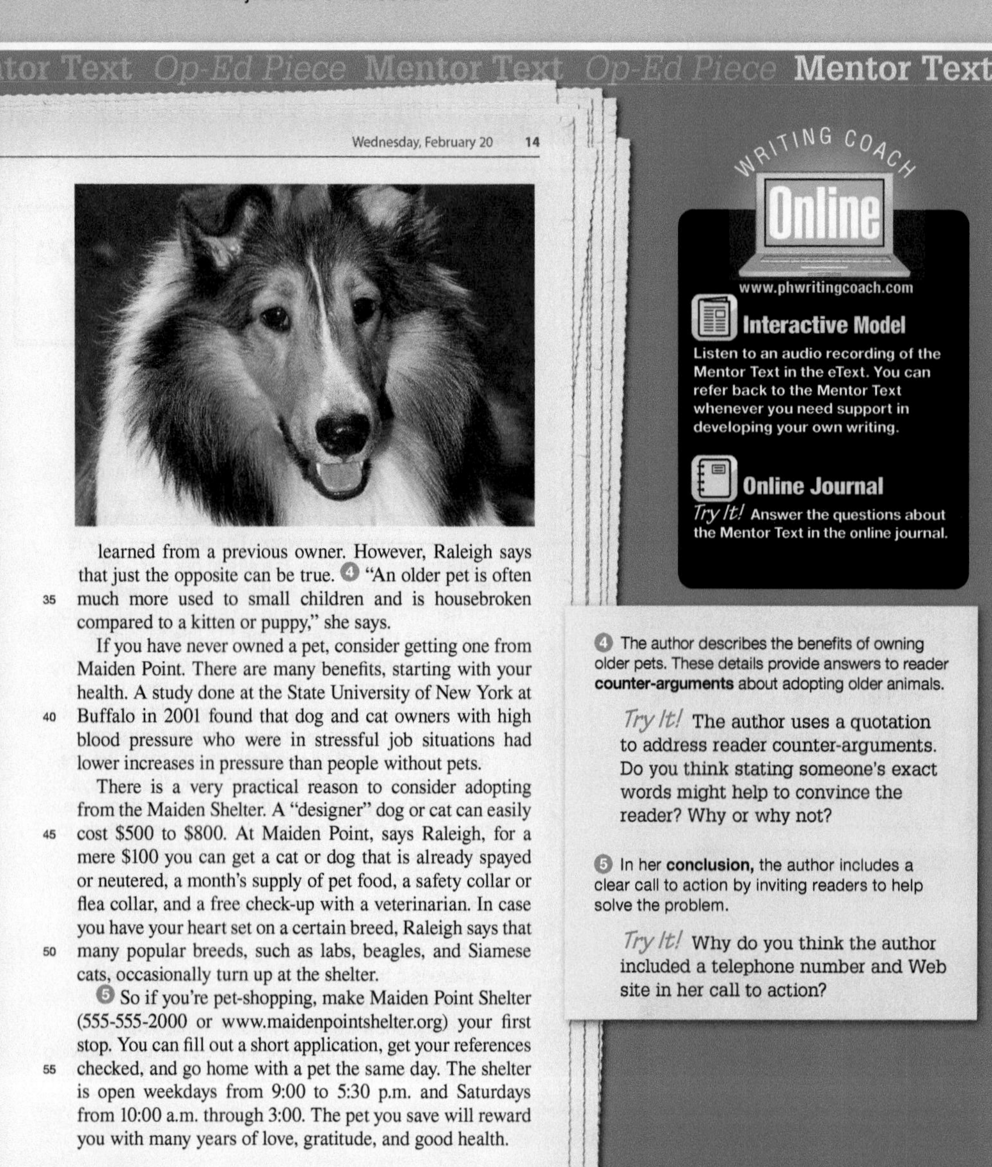

ntor Text *Op-Ed Piece* Mentor Text *Op-Ed Piece* **Mentor Text**

Wednesday, February 20 **14**

learned from a previous owner. However, Raleigh says that just the opposite can be true. ④ "An older pet is often much more used to small children and is housebroken compared to a kitten or puppy," she says.

If you have never owned a pet, consider getting one from Maiden Point. There are many benefits, starting with your health. A study done at the State University of New York at Buffalo in 2001 found that dog and cat owners with high blood pressure who were in stressful job situations had lower increases in pressure than people without pets.

There is a very practical reason to consider adopting from the Maiden Shelter. A "designer" dog or cat can easily cost $500 to $800. At Maiden Point, says Raleigh, for a mere $100 you can get a cat or dog that is already spayed or neutered, a month's supply of pet food, a safety collar or flea collar, and a free check-up with a veterinarian. In case you have your heart set on a certain breed, Raleigh says that many popular breeds, such as labs, beagles, and Siamese cats, occasionally turn up at the shelter.

⑤ So if you're pet-shopping, make Maiden Point Shelter (555-555-2000 or www.maidenpointshelter.org) your first stop. You can fill out a short application, get your references checked, and go home with a pet the same day. The shelter is open weekdays from 9:00 to 5:30 p.m. and Saturdays from 10:00 a.m. through 3:00. The pet you save will reward you with many years of love, gratitude, and good health.

WRITING COACH **Online**

www.phwritingcoach.com

Interactive Model

Listen to an audio recording of the Mentor Text in the eText. You can refer back to the Mentor Text whenever you need support in developing your own writing.

Online Journal

Try It! Answer the questions about the Mentor Text in the online journal.

④ The author describes the benefits of owning older pets. These details provide answers to reader **counter-arguments** about adopting older animals.

Try It! The author uses a quotation to address reader counter-arguments. Do you think stating someone's exact words might help to convince the reader? Why or why not?

⑤ In her **conclusion,** the author includes a clear call to action by inviting readers to help solve the problem.

Try It! Why do you think the author included a telephone number and Web site in her call to action?

Mentor Text 175

Personalized Support

Teacher or Peer Feedback

FEEDBACK

To provide feedback to students on their responses to the Mentor Text and their answers to the *Try It!* questions, ask or have student partners ask one another the following:

- What is the thesis or controlling idea of the Mentor Text?
- How does the Mentor Text illustrate the characteristics of a persuasive essay?
- How did you answer this *Try It!* question? How could you use your answer to help you plan your piece of writing?

Working with ELLs

ELL **Sheltered Instruction:** Cognitive

Help students develop and expand their repertoire of learning strategies by looking for patterns in language and analyzing their effects. Review the language pattern of addressing the audience as "you." Distribute copies of the article.

Beginning Read as students follow along, raising their hands when they hear "you" and circling each instance on their copy. Say that addressing readers as "you" makes the topic more personal. Ask yes/no questions to help students analyze the use of "you" in the text.

Intermediate Have students complete the Beginning activity in small groups and expand the strategy by completing sentences about the language pattern.

Advanced Have pairs read the article looking for references to readers as "you." Then, have them use the examples to explain how addressing readers as "you" can help readers connect to the topic.

Advanced High Have students complete the Advanced activity, then write a paragraph analyzing the effect of the language pattern in the article and compare their work with a partner.

The Digital • Print Path

1 

Using Writing Coach Online™ or the student book, students read and listen to an audio recording of the Student Model.

STUDENT MODEL

Tell students that good writers react to what they read in ways that show their understanding of the text. Explain that students will react to the Student Model by placing two sets of symbols in the text. Then, distribute printed copies of the Student Model or have students log on to Writing Coach Online.

Use a Reader's Eye

Read aloud the instructions for using the Reader's Response Symbols and the meaning of each symbol. Then, guide students through their use.

The student writer did a good job of giving evidence to support his arguments. However, **I have** some questions about some of this evidence. For example, in paragraph 3, lines 22–24, he suggests "a tax incentive" for carpoolers. Readers may not know what a tax incentive is. He should define the term and explain specifically how the incentive might be put in place. I'll place a question mark next to this part of the text.

Work with students to identify other questions they had about the text.

Have students read and respond to the Student Model, using each Reader's Response Symbol at least once.

Partner Talk

After partners work together to share their opinions, have each pair point out the arguments they think are strongest and weakest and explain their reasoning.

Use a Writer's Eye

Read aloud the instructions for using the Writer's Response Symbols and the meaning of each symbol. Then, guide students through their use.

Say: **I think** the thesis statement at the end of paragraph 2, lines 16–18, is very clear and complete. The writer states that the aim is to fix the traffic problem and lists two general actions that will accomplish this aim: show people how to decrease traffic, and give them incentives to change their behavior. I'll write C.T. there for clearly stated thesis.

Ask: According to the details in paragraph 2, what is the "traffic problem"? **(Increased traffic increases commute times, fuel consumption, and pollution.)**

Have students read and respond to the Student Model, using each Writer's Response Symbol at least once.

STUDENT MODEL Op-Ed Piece

With a small group, take turns reading the Student Model aloud. As you read, practice newly acquired vocabulary by correctly producing the word's sound. Ask yourself if you find the writer's arguments convincing. Identify the evidence that the writer uses to support his ideas.

 **Use a Reader's Eye**

Now, reread the Student Model. On your copy of the Student Model, use the Reader's Response Symbols to react to what you read.

Reader's Response Symbols

- **+ I strongly agree with this.**
- **– I strongly disagree with this.**
- **? I have a question about this.**
- **! Wow! That is cool/weird/interesting.**

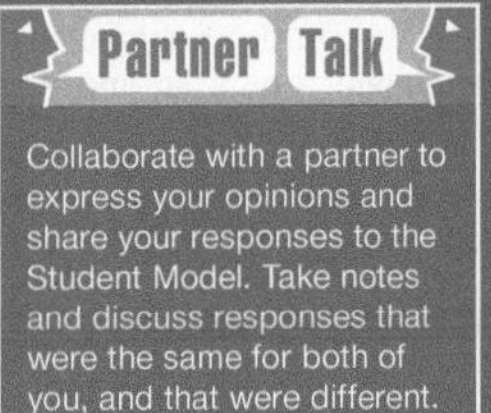

Partner Talk

Collaborate with a partner to express your opinions and share your responses to the Student Model. Take notes and discuss responses that were the same for both of you, and that were different.

There Is Something You Can Do About TRAFFIC

by Xander Johnson

"Traffic is just one of life's inconveniences. Sure, it's frustrating, but what can you really do about it?" This was how my mom responded to my question about the traffic she encounters on her daily commute to work. The traffic not only is a frustration for her as she sits in her car waiting, but also for our family as we sit at home waiting for her. Frequently, we end up eating dinner on our own because she gets home too late to join us.

Traffic is more than an inconvenience. According to the Department of Transportation, the average commute time one way has expanded from twenty or thirty minutes to as much as three hours per day. As a result of all this time on the road, we are using up too much fuel and polluting the airways. By showing people what they can do to decrease the amount of traffic and giving them incentives to make changes, we can fix the traffic problem.

First, each of us can explore mass transit options, and use them. Employers can help by promoting four-day workweeks and staggering work hours. People object to carpooling, but many will not if there is a tax incentive involved. If we write to our legislators, we can make this happen.

Finally, once we are on those traffic-snarled freeways, we can practice simple courtesy, allowing cars in when they clearly need to enter. Department

1

2 Writing Coach Online | Student Book

First, students respond to the Student Model as a reader, using symbols to mark the text. They can mark the text using pop-up sticky notes in **Writing Coach Online™** or they can mark a printed copy of the Student Model.

3 Writing Coach Online | Student Book

Then, students respond to the Student Model as a writer, using different symbols to mark the text. They can use either **Writing Coach Online™** or a printed copy of the Student Model.

of Transportation studies of so-called "synchronicity" show that a courteous approach keeps traffic flowing faster than fighting for position. As a final step, we should provide financial incentives for people who choose to live close enough to their work that they can commute on foot or by bicycle.

Next time you are sitting in a traffic jam, remember that it not only affects the people on the road. Traffic keeps people from their families and creates more stress. It also creates more stress on the environment. Each of us has to ask ourselves what we can do to solve this problem. We need to make these changes. My mom has started taking the train home from work. She gets home earlier, and now the time that used to be spent in traffic is spent at home with us.

2

www.phwritingcoach.com

Interactive Model

Listen to an audio recording of the Student Model in the eText. Use the Reader's and Writer's Response Symbols with the eText tools to note what you read.

Use a Writer's Eye

Now evaluate the piece as a writer. On your copies of the Student Models, use the Writer's Response Symbols to react to what you read. Identify places where the student writer uses characteristics of an effective op-ed piece.

Writer's Response Symbols

C.T.	**Clearly stated thesis**
P.A.	**Strong persuasive arguments**
S.E.	**Effective and credible supporting evidence**
C.A.	**Good responses to readers' counter-arguments**

Personalized Support

FEEDBACK

Teacher or Peer Feedback

To provide feedback to students on their responses to the Student Model, ask or have student partners ask one another the following:

- What is the thesis or controlling idea of the Student Model?
- How does the Student Model illustrate the characteristics of an op-ed piece?
- Which feature or characteristic of the Student Model might you use in your own piece of writing?
- How could you alter or adapt this feature to make it your own?

Working with ELLs

ELL **Sheltered Instruction:** Cognitive

Have students learn basic vocabulary heard during classroom instruction, drawing on prior experiences. Write *work*, *home*, and *people* from the Student Model on the board, as well as *food*, *school*, and *yesterday*. Read the words aloud, then:

Beginning Say *I am a teacher*. *I work when I teach*. Use mime to reinforce meaning. Have students complete sentence starters using *work*, drawing on prior experience of work, like *I work when I* ... Help them brainstorm for words and act them out.

Intermediate Have pairs of students create **Spider-Web Diagrams** for the words, writing phrases describing prior experiences. Call on students to share their diagrams with the class.

Advanced Have small groups use the basic vocabulary in a round-robin story based on their prior experiences relating to each word and monitor for correct use of the words.

Advanced High Have students use the words in a paragraph, describing prior experiences that clarify the meaning of each word. Read it in small groups to monitor use of the words.

1 

Students select or are assigned a topic for their op-ed piece from the Topic Bank, or they may choose a topic of their own.

2 

Students complete online or printed graphic organizers to narrow the topic for their op-ed piece.

Prewriting

Explain that the first task students need to complete as they plan their op-ed piece is to determine an appropriate topic.

Choose From the Topic Bank

Read aloud each topic and then ask volunteers to describe them in their own words. If you are assigning topics to students, you may wish to do so now. Encourage students to ask questions about their topic.

Choose Your Own Topic

Introduce and discuss the Interview and Research strategies. If students were not assigned writing topics, have them use the strategies to brainstorm for topics for their op-ed pieces.

Extension Have each student choose one of the strategies. Then, have them write an action plan that outlines the resources and steps they will use to develop their topic.

Narrow Your Topic

Tell students that they will use a Narrow Your Topic graphic organizer to focus their topic for the op-ed piece. Then, distribute printed copies or have students log on to Writing Coach Online.

Apply It! Guide students through the instructions for completing the graphic organizer. Have students complete the exercise based on their topic.

Consider Your Audience and Purpose

Guide students to consider the audience and purpose for their op-ed piece.

Feature Assignment Prewriting Feature Assignment Prewriting

Your Turn Feature Assignment: Op-Ed Piece

Prewriting

Plan a first draft of your op-ed piece by determining an appropriate topic. Select from the Topic Bank or come up with an idea of your own.

Choose From the Topic Bank

TOPIC BANK

School Issues Think about a controversial issue at your school, such as the price of lunches or the quality of the food, class schedules, or attendance policies. Take a stand on a school issue. Write an essay supporting your position and be sure to provide reasons and examples.

Recycling Some people think that all households should be required to recycle paper, glass and plastic. Other people think that recycling should be a choice, not a requirement. Write an op-ed piece that supports your position on whether or not recycling should be voluntary.

Get up and move. Some parents think spending a lot of time on the computer can be unhealthy for their children. So, they limit the amount of time their children can spend on the computer each day. Write an essay in which you state and support your position on limiting the time children spend playing computer games each day.

Choose Your Own Topic

Determine an appropriate topic on your own by using the following **range of strategies** to generate ideas.

Interview and Research

- Interview friends and family members about the issues they feel are important. Take notes on the main points they share.
- Search your library's database and the Internet using these notes. Did you produce any results that spark your interest?

Review your responses and choose a topic.

178 Persuasive Writing

Say: The first question in the first column of the chart asks about my audience, or the people who will read my work. If **I choose** the first topic from the Topic Bank, about a controversial school issue, my audience could include the teachers, administrators, and students at my school.

Ask: Based on your topic, who will be your most likely audience? Who would you most like to read your op-ed piece? (Responses will vary.)

Have students with the same or similar topics work in small groups to discuss and respond to the remaining questions.

Coach's Corner

You may wish to model prewriting activities for students by brainstorming for your own writing topic. Use these prompts to model your thought process:

- **I am interested in** school lunches, so that could be my general topic.
- **I can narrow my topic by** focusing on the nutritional content of school lunches.

Discuss the choices you make and solicit feedback from students.

3 Writing Journal

Students record their answers to questions about audience and purpose in their online journals or notebooks.

Narrow Your Topic

Choosing a topic that is too broad results in writing that is general and unfocused.

Apply It! Use a graphic organizer like the one shown to narrow your topic.

- Write your general topic in the top box, and keep narrowing your topic as you move down the chart.
- Your last box should hold your narrowest or "smallest" topic, the new focus of your op-ed piece.

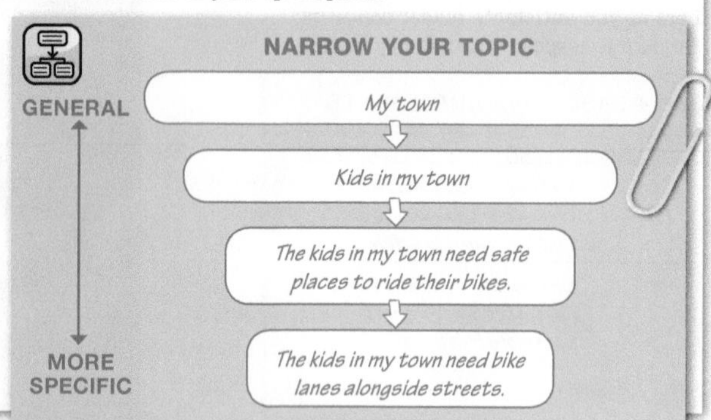

NARROW YOUR TOPIC
GENERAL
My town
Kids in my town
The kids in my town need safe places to ride their bikes.
The kids in my town need bike lanes alongside streets.
MORE SPECIFIC

Consider Your Audience and Purpose

Before writing your persuasive essay, think about your audience and purpose. Consider the way other people may view your topic as you ask yourself these questions.

Questions for Audience	Questions for Purpose
• Who is my audience? • What might they need to know to understand my topic fully? • What **views, concerns, and counter-arguments** might they have about my topic?	• What opinion do I want to state? • How will I include and respond to others' views, concerns, and counter-arguments? • What do I want the audience to do?

Interactive Writing Coach™

- Choosing from the Topic Bank gives you access to the Interactive Writing Coach™.
- Submit your writing and receive instant personalized feedback and guidance as you draft, revise, and edit your writing.

Interactive Graphic Organizers

Use the interactive graphic organizers to help you narrow your topic.

Online Journal

Try It! Record your answers and ideas in the online journal.

Personalized Support

Interactive Writing Coach™

Below Level Teachers select a topic from the topic bank for below-level students. Students submit their writing to the **Interactive Writing Coach™** for feedback paragraph by paragraph or as a complete draft. It is recommended that below-level students submit their writing one paragraph at a time.

On Level Students may select a topic from the Topic Bank. They may submit their writing for feedback paragraph by paragraph or as a complete draft.

Above Level Students may select from the Topic Bank or come up with their own topic. Above-level students should submit their writing as a complete draft.

Interactive Graphic Organizer

Below Level Students complete three graphic organizers that provide models and scaffolded support.

On Level Students complete one, two, or three graphic organizers, depending on how much support they need.

Above Level Students complete the least scaffolded graphic organizer or narrow their topic without the help of a graphic organizer.

Differentiated Instruction

RTI Strategy for Special Needs Students

Explain that an op-ed piece topic is the writer's opinion. Model developing an appropriate topic by writing *I think that . . .* on the board. Have students state opinions based on their experience. Then, explain that an op-ed piece also states what the writer wants readers to do, in the form of a statement that contains the words *should* or *should not*. For example, *Our town should increase the number of parks.* Have students create *should* sentences for their topics.

RTI Strategy for Below-Level Students

Students may have difficulty developing a narrow focus from their broad topic. To help students find a narrow focus for their op-ed piece, have them place their general essay topic in the center oval of a Cluster Diagram graphic organizer. Then, have them write specific facts and ideas they have about the topic in the surrounding ovals. Students should then order these details in the Narrow Your Topic organizer.

1 

Using Writing Coach Online™ or the student book, students read and discuss the model graphic organizer.

2 STUDENT BOOK

Students complete online or printed graphic organizers to develop their ideas and gather details.

Plan Your Piece

Explain that writers use graphic organizers to develop their ideas and show relationships between different parts of the text. Then, point out the Develop Your Persuasive Arguments graphic organizer on page 180. Tell students that they will use this organizer to outline their op-ed piece. Then, distribute printed copies or have students log on to Writing Coach Online.

Introduce the graphic organizer by explaining that the first column identifies the information to be written in the second column. Each row identifies a specific part of an op-ed piece.

Develop a Clear Thesis Point out that the example thesis in the organizer is based on the narrowed topic on page 179. Have students write a thesis statement that clearly states their opinion about a specific issue and record it on their graphic organizer.

Logically Organize Your Arguments Have students identify and read aloud the persuasive arguments in the organizer. Explain that the arguments are organized from least to most important. Then, have students work with partners to develop persuasive arguments in support of their theses and record them on their individual graphic organizers.

Gather Details

Remind students that arguments in persuasive writing are supported by details. Ask volunteers to read aloud the kinds of details and examples. Then, guide students to place the details on the example graphic organizer.

I noticed that the organizer has space to record Supporting Evidence/Details for each persuasive argument. The details on page 181 provide this information. For example, the Statistics example, about bike lanes lowering accident rates in a nearby town, supports the Second Persuasive Argument, which says that kids would have fewer accidents if there were more bike lanes. I'll record that detail in the proper place.

Ask: Which persuasive argument is supported by the Expert Opinion example? (Second Persuasive Argument)

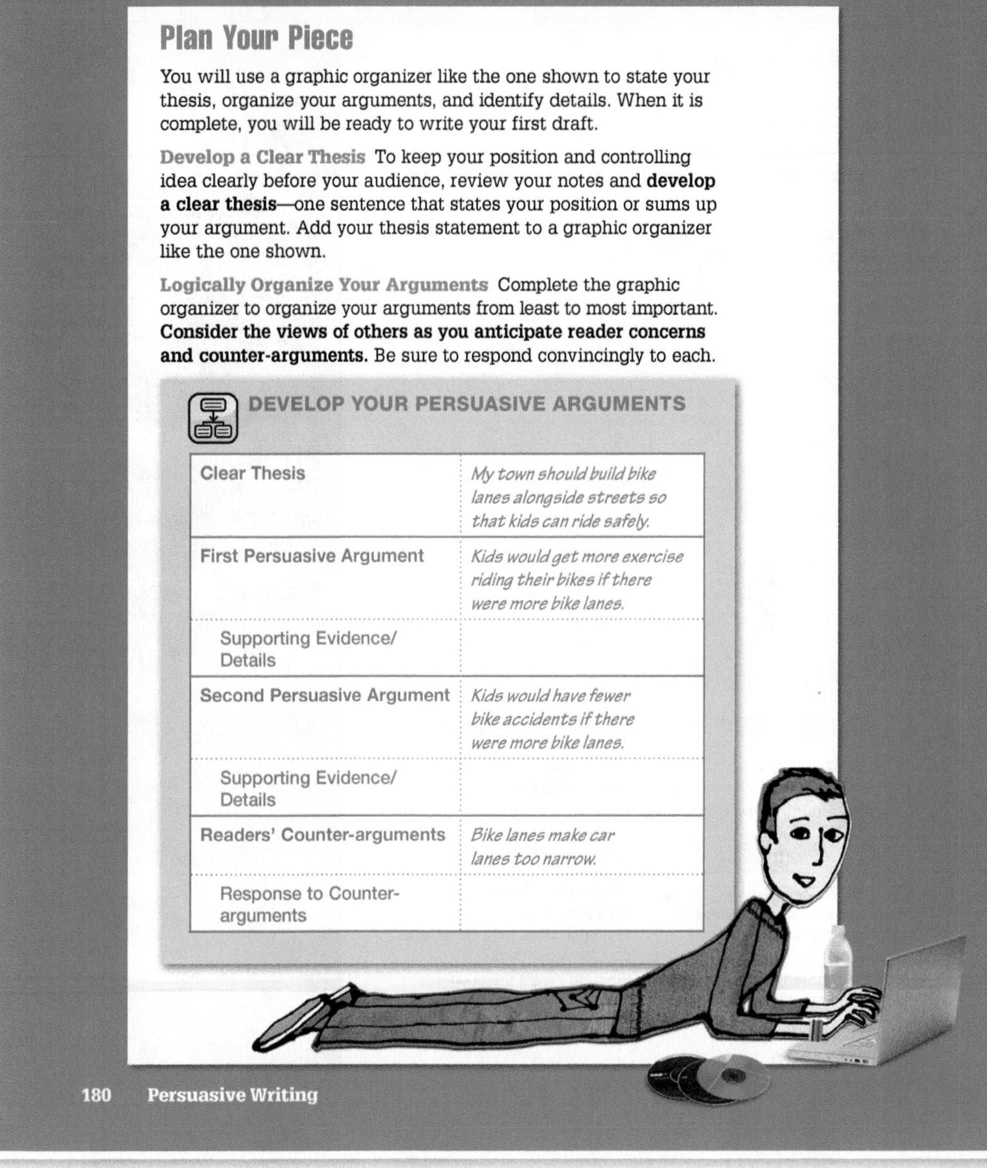

Feature Assignment Prewriting Feature Assignment Prewriti

Plan Your Piece

You will use a graphic organizer like the one shown to state your thesis, organize your arguments, and identify details. When it is complete, you will be ready to write your first draft.

Develop a Clear Thesis To keep your position and controlling idea clearly before your audience, review your notes and **develop a clear thesis**—one sentence that states your position or sums up your argument. Add your thesis statement to a graphic organizer like the one shown.

Logically Organize Your Arguments Complete the graphic organizer to organize your arguments from least to most important. **Consider the views of others as you anticipate reader concerns and counter-arguments.** Be sure to respond convincingly to each.

DEVELOP YOUR PERSUASIVE ARGUMENTS

Clear Thesis	*My town should build bike lanes alongside streets so that kids can ride safely.*
First Persuasive Argument	*Kids would get more exercise riding their bikes if there were more bike lanes.*
Supporting Evidence/ Details	
Second Persuasive Argument	*Kids would have fewer bike accidents if there were more bike lanes.*
Supporting Evidence/ Details	
Readers' Counter-arguments	*Bike lanes make car lanes too narrow.*
Response to Counter-arguments	

180 Persuasive Writing

Have students work in small groups to place the remaining details on the organizer.

Try It! Guide students to understand that the excerpt author cites an expert and uses logic to support the argument.

Apply It! Read aloud the bulleted instructions for gathering details. Then, have students develop relevant support for each of their arguments.

Writer's Block

IF students have difficulty supporting their arguments with appropriate details . . .

THEN have them turn to the Student Model on pages 176–177. Discuss which supporting details exemplify logical reasoning, statistics, expert opinions, and personal observations.

3 STUDENT BOOK

Students refer back to the Mentor Text or the Student Model as they plan their writing.

Gather Details

To provide supporting evidence for their arguments, writers use many kinds of details. Look at these examples:

- **Logical Reasoning:** *There are too many bike accidents in our town. Bike lanes reduce accidents. Therefore, we need more bike lanes.*
- **Statistics:** *After a nearby town built bike lanes, bike accidents were cut in half.*
- **Expert Opinions:** *Public Safety Officer Miller believes that bike lanes will make kids safer.*
- **Personal Observations:** *I feel much safer when I'm biking in a bike lane.*

Good writers are careful to **differentiate between fact and opinion,** supporting their opinions with reliable facts that help prove their points.

- A **fact** is something that actually happened or can be proven.
- An **opinion** is a person's judgment or belief about something.

Try It! Read the Mentor Text excerpt and identify which details the author used to support her argument.

from **Looking for a Pet?**
page 174; lines 24–29

She points out that pets from pet stores have often been raised in unclean, unhealthy, crowded conditions, especially dogs from so-called "puppy mills." In contrast, the shelter pets are spayed and neutered, and treated for problems such as heartworm and fleas, before they are adopted out.

Apply It! Review the types of support a persuasive writer can use. Then identify at least one detail for each of your arguments.

- Review your details to differentiate between fact and opinion. Check that opinions are supported by facts, and record the source of each fact.
- Add these details to your graphic organizer. Be sure to match each detail to the right argument so that your evidence is logically organized to support your viewpoint.

Interactive Graphic Organizers

Use the interactive graphic organizers to help you create a plan for your writing.

Interactive Model

Refer back to the Mentor Text in the eText as you plan your writing.

Personalized Support

Below Level Students complete three graphic organizers that provide models and scaffolded support.

On Level Students complete one, two, or three graphic organizers, depending on how much support they need.

Above Level Students complete the least scaffolded graphic organizer or narrow their topic without the help of a graphic organizer.

FEEDBACK

Teacher or Peer Feedback

To provide feedback to students as they plan their first draft, ask or have student partners ask one another the following:

- What do you want your audience to know about the topic?
- What questions or concerns will your audience have about the topic?
- What details have you identified for your piece? How do these details support your thesis or controlling idea?
- Are your details varied? Will they interest your readers? Explain.

Differentiated Instruction

RTI Strategy for Below-Level Students

Guide students who struggle to distinguish facts from opinions to approach text more analytically. Model asking the following questions about statements in a news story:

- *Can this idea be checked, measured, or shown to be true? If so, how?*
- *Does this statement contain any words or terms whose meaning can differ from person to person, such as favorite, best, or worst?*
- *Which clue words show that this is a personal belief?*

Explain that many writers report facts, but at the same time they interpret those facts, or add their opinions about them. Provide sentences containing mixtures of fact and opinion and ask students to highlight the portion that can be proven. Have students work in groups to tackle another news article, identifying two facts and two opinions.

The Digital • Print Path

1 

Using Writing Coach Online™ or the student book, students read and discuss the *Outline for Success* for an op-ed piece.

2

Students discuss how the Mentor Text illustrates the characteristics of an op-ed piece.

Drafting

Outline for Success

Explain that the Outline for Success shows an organizational strategy for a persuasive essay. Students will use the Outline to write a focused, organized, and coherent draft of their op-ed piece.

I. Introduction

Link the Outline to a specific persuasive essay by having students turn to the Mentor Text on pages 174–175. Have a volunteer read aloud the thesis statement (lines 5–7). Then, guide students to understand how the first paragraph grabs readers' attention and presents a clear position on an issue.

Say: I notice that the author states the issue and explains what he thinks should be done about it in lines 1–7. However, the introduction must also interest readers in the issue. In the first paragraph, the writer grabs readers' attention with vivid details. For example, in line 1 he writes that the shelter is "overflowing with cats and dogs."

Ask: What other details does the writer use to grab the reader? (In lines 2–3 he describes the animals' "heartrending meows and barks.")

Have students work with a partner to discuss the details they will use to grab their readers' attention.

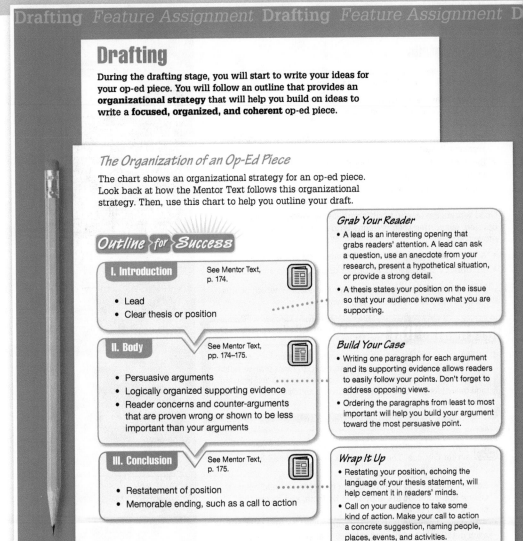

Drafting *Feature Assignment* Drafting *Feature Assignment* D

Drafting

During the drafting stage, you will start to write your ideas for your op-ed piece. You will follow an outline that provides an organizational strategy that will help you build on ideas to write a focused, organized, and coherent op-ed piece.

The Organization of an Op-Ed Piece

The chart shows an organizational strategy for an op-ed piece. Look back at how the Mentor Text follows this organizational strategy. Then, use this chart to help you outline your draft.

Outline for Success

I. Introduction See Mentor Text, p. 174.

- Lead
- Clear thesis or position

Grab Your Reader
- A lead is an interesting opening that grabs readers' attention. A lead can ask a question, use an anecdote from your research, present a hypothetical situation, or provide a strong detail.
- A thesis states your position on the issue so that your audience knows what you are supporting.

II. Body See Mentor Text, pp. 174–175.

- Persuasive arguments
- Logically organized supporting evidence
- Reader concerns and counter-arguments that are proven wrong or shown to be less important than your arguments

Build Your Case
- Writing one paragraph for each argument and its supporting evidence allows readers to easily follow your points. Don't forget to address opposing views.
- Ordering the paragraphs from least to most important will help you build your argument toward the most persuasive point.

III. Conclusion See Mentor Text, p. 175.

- Restatement of position
- Memorable ending, such as a call to action

Wrap It Up
- Restating your position, echoing the language of your thesis statement, will help cement it in readers' minds.
- Call on your audience to take some kind of action. Make your call to action a concrete suggestion, naming people, places, events, and activities.

182 Persuasive Writing

II. Body

Lead a discussion about how the body paragraphs of the Mentor Text reflect the characteristics of a persuasive essay.

- Persuasive arguments (lines 18–20, 38–39, 44–45)
- Support for arguments (lines 10–18, 39–42, 45–51)
- Counter-arguments proven wrong (lines 24–29, 31–36)

III. Conclusion

Have students explain how the Mentor Text conclusion fulfills the requirements of a well-written persuasive essay (lines 52–58).

Start Your Draft

Have small groups read aloud and discuss the boxed instructions for drafting. Direct students to work individually on their first draft.

Coach's Corner

If you are modeling the writing process for students with your own topic or a student volunteer's, you may wish to use these prompts to guide your drafting and discussion:

- **To grab readers' attention, my introduction will** pose a question that makes readers think.
- **I will organize the body by** beginning with the weakest argument.

Discuss the choices you make and solicit feedback from students.

3 

Students begin writing their op-ed piece online or in their notebooks.

4 

Students submit paragraphs or complete drafts to the **Interactive Writing Coach™** for scoring and feedback, or share their work with their teacher.

5 

Students receive customized feedback from the **Interactive Writing Coach™** or feedback from their teacher. Students may continue to work on their drafts.

Start Your Draft

Use this checklist to help you complete your draft. Use the graphic organizer that shows your thesis, persuasive arguments, and supporting evidence, and the Outline for Success as guides.

While drafting, aim at writing your ideas, not on making your writing perfect. Remember, you will have the chance to improve your draft when you revise and edit.

- √ Start by drafting a lead, the opening sentences that grab your readers' attention.
- √ Continue to build your **introduction** by telling readers what to expect in the rest of your op-ed piece. Include a clear **thesis** statement.

- √ Shape the **body** of your op-ed piece by **logically organizing** your ideas.
- √ Develop a focused paragraph for each argument and its supporting evidence.
- √ Include paragraphs that consider and respond to other views by answering readers' questions, concerns, and **counter-arguments**.
- √ Remember to support opinions with facts and to use **transitional words** such as *first, next,* and *finally* to tie paragraphs together.

- √ End with a strong **conclusion** that restates your **position** and leaves readers convinced that your ideas are right.
- √ Finish on a powerful note by making a **call to action** or a forceful statement that will leave your audience thinking.

www.phwritingcoach.com

Interactive Model

Outline for Success View pop-ups of Mentor Text selections referenced in the Outline for Success.

Interactive Writing Coach™

Use the Interactive Writing Coach to receive the level of support you need:

- Write one paragraph at a time and submit each one for immediate, detailed feedback.
- Write your entire first draft and submit it for immediate, personalized feedback.

Personalized Support

Interactive Writing Coach™

Below Level Students complete the drafting process in small steps by submitting each paragraph for scoring and feedback.

On Level Depending on the support they need, students submit their writing paragraph by paragraph or as a complete draft for scoring and feedback.

Above Level Students may write their drafts on their own but have the option of submitting them for scoring and/or feedback.

Teacher or Peer Feedback

To provide feedback to students on their first draft, ask or have student partners ask one another the following:

- Can you explain how you organized your ideas in this piece?
- Why did you include this information here?
- Why did you choose this introduction? Does it grab your reader and identify your thesis or controlling idea?
- What supporting details could you add here?
- Why did you choose this conclusion? How does it add to your piece?
- Can you show me a place where I can hear your unique voice?
- Can you show me a place where you used vivid language?

Working with ELLs — ELL Sheltered Instruction: Cognitive

Point out these content-based academic words from Start Your Draft: *transitional* and *logically*. Help students internalize this new academic language by using and reusing the words in writing activities.

Beginning Write the word *transitional* and simple sentences describing a sequence of events: *I went to school. Then, I came home.* Circle *Then* and say, *This is a transitional word; it shows a passing from one event to another.* Help students write *transitional* on a card and draw to illustrate its meaning.

Intermediate Have students write the two terms on cards. Then, work through examples of each. On the back of each card, have students write two example sentences reusing each word.

Advanced Have students complete the Intermediate activity independently, then write glossary entries for each word.

Advanced High Have students complete the Intermediate activity independently. Then, have them review a writing sample of an essay from their portfolios and reuse the words *transitional* and *logically* in a written evaluation.

The Digital • Print Path

1 

Using **Writing Coach Online**™ or the student book, students study the first and second drafts of the student model to see how the writer used Revision RADaR to improve his or her writing.

2 Writing Journal

Students use the Revision RADaR strategy to revise their own writing.

Revising: Making It Better

Point out the page title to students and explain that revising means making improvements to a writing draft. Then, read aloud the opening paragraph to introduce the Revision RADaR strategies. You may wish to have students review Chapter 3 for more information on Revision RADaR.

Kelly Gallagher, M. Ed.

KEEP REVISION ON YOUR RADAR

1ST DRAFT After students have read the first draft, have them turn to page 182 and review the Outline for Success. Work with students to understand that the questions the author asked about the draft are based on the characteristics of a persuasive essay. For example, call out the first question and note how it addresses concerns listed in the Introduction section of the Outline for Success.

Then, have students work in small groups to develop other questions about the draft based on the genre characteristics.

Revising: Making It Better

Now that you have finished your first draft, you are ready to revise. Think about the "big picture" of audience, purpose, and genre. You can use your Revision RADaR as a guide for making changes to improve your draft. Revision RADaR provides four major ways to improve your writing: (R) replace, (A) add, (D) delete, and (R) reorder.

Kelly Gallagher, M. Ed.

KEEP REVISION ON YOUR RADAR

Read part of the first draft of the Student Model "There Is Something You Can Do About Traffic." Then look at questions the writer asked himself as he thought about how well his draft addressed **issues of audience, purpose, and genre.**

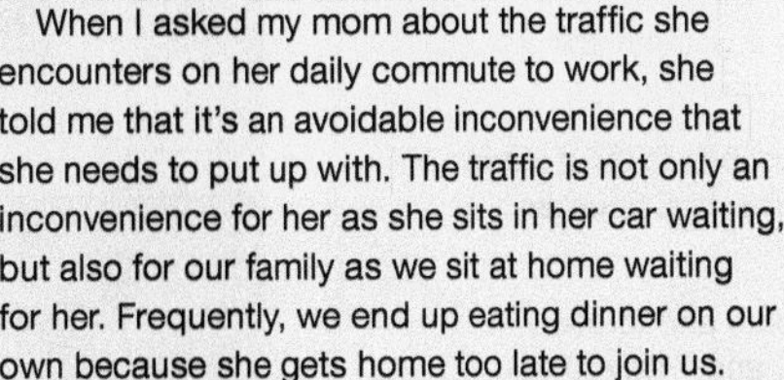

There Is Something You Can Do About TRAFFIC — 1ST DRAFT

When I asked my mom about the traffic she encounters on her daily commute to work, she told me that it's an avoidable inconvenience that she needs to put up with. The traffic is not only an inconvenience for her as she sits in her car waiting, but also for our family as we sit at home waiting for her. Frequently, we end up eating dinner on our own because she gets home too late to join us.

Does the introduction grab my audience?

Traffic is more than an inconvenience. As a result of all the time drivers spend on the road, we are using up too much fuel and polluting the airways.

By showing people what they can do to decrease the amount of traffic and giving them incentives to make changes, we can probably lessen the traffic problem.

Does my thesis statement clearly identify the issue and my purpose or opinion?

First, each of us can explore mass transit options, and use them. Employers can help by promoting four-day workweeks and staggering working hours. If we write to our legislators, we can make this happen.

Have I included persuasive arguments? Have I anticipated and answered reader counter-arguments?

2ND DRAFT Guide students to understand how the author used the RADaR strategies to revise the first draft.

Think Aloud **I noticed** that the introduction in the 1st draft gave a drab description of the mom's response. In the 2nd draft, I see an *R* next to this part of the text. The writer replaced this dull section with a direct quotation that expresses the mom's frustration and asks, "What can you really do about it?" This direct quotation is much more interesting and also focuses readers on the issue the author wants to explore.

Work with students to brainstorm for other ways to spark interest and focus readers on the issue.

Have students work with partners to discuss other changes to the 2nd draft.

Apply It! Review the bulleted instructions for using Revision RADaR. Remind students to question their drafts based on the persuasive essay characteristics listed on the Outline for Success on page 182. Tell students to use each RADaR strategy at least once.

Coach's Corner

If you are modeling the writing process for students with your own draft or a student volunteer's, use these prompts to focus on the Revision RADaR *Reorder* strategy:

- **I reordered my arguments because** I wanted to build up to the strongest argument.
- **I reordered the details here because** I wanted to better explain this issue.

Discuss the choices you make and solicit feedback from students.

3 Students submit paragraphs or revised drafts to the **Interactive Writing Coach™** for scoring and feedback, or share their work with their teacher.

4 Students receive customized feedback from the **Interactive Writing Coach™** or feedback from their teacher. Students may continue to revise their drafts.

Now look at how the writer applied Revision RADaR to write an improved second draft.

2ND DRAFT

There Is Something You Can Do About TRAFFIC

"Traffic is just one of life's inconveniences. Sure, it's frustrating, but what can you really do about it?" This was how my mom responded to my question about the traffic she encounters on her daily commute to work. The traffic not only is a frustration for her as she sits in her car waiting, but also for our family as we sit at home waiting for her. Frequently, we end up eating dinner on our own because she gets home too late to join us.

Traffic is more than an inconvenience. The average commute time one way has expanded from twenty or thirty minutes to as much as three hours per day. As a result of all this time on the road, we are using up too much fuel and polluting the airways. By showing people what they can do to decrease the amount of traffic and giving them incentives to make changes, we can fix the traffic problem.

First, each of us can explore mass transit options, and use them. Employers can help by promoting four-day workweeks and staggering working hours. People object to carpooling, but many will not if there is a tax incentive involved. If we write to our legislators, we can make this happen.

R *Replaced a dull secondhand description with a more interesting quotation and an explanation of it*

A *Added a fact about the commute time to better explain the issue to my audience*

D *Deleted the word probably and* R *replaced the word lessen with the word fix in order to make my thesis statement more forceful*

A *Added a possible counter-argument and a response to it*

WRITING COACH Online

www.phwritingcoach.com

Interactive Writing Coach™

Use the Revision RADaR strategy in your own writing. Then submit your draft for feedback.

Apply It! Use Revision RADaR to revise your draft.

- First, determine if you have addressed the needs of your audience, explained your purpose for writing, and included the characteristics of the op-ed piece genre.
- Then apply Revision RADaR to make needed changes. Remember—you can use the steps in the strategy in any order.

Personalized Support

Interactive Writing Coach™

Below Level Students revise their drafts using the Revision RADaR strategy and submit their writing for scoring and feedback.

On Level Students revise their drafts using the Revision RADaR strategy and submit their writing for scoring and feedback.

Above Level Students may use the Revision RADaR strategy or revise their drafts on their own. They have the option of submitting their revised drafts for scoring and/or feedback.

Teacher or Peer Feedback

To provide feedback to students as they revise their first draft, ask or have student partners ask one another the following:

- Can you show me where you revised your text?
- What could you add to your introduction to grab the interest of your readers?
- How could you reorder these ideas so that their order is more logical?
- Have you included all the characteristics of this form of writing?
- Is there any unnecessary text that you could delete?
- Have you achieved your purpose with this piece of writing?
- Have you addressed the questions and concerns of your audience?

Working with ELLs

ELL Sheltered Instruction: Cognitive

As students review the revised Student Model, help them demonstrate English comprehension and expand their reading skills by employing analytical skills. Focus on analyzing and evaluating generalizations. Define *generalization*. Then:

Beginning Distribute a simple generalization about traffic problems, such as *Bad weather can cause traffic jams*, along with supporting examples. Read the sentences with students, using mime as needed. Use simple prompts to elicit analysis, such as, *Traffic is bad when …* Point to a sentence that explains.

Intermediate Have students complete the Beginning activity, then complete sentence starters, like, *In general, traffic is bad when … This is because …*

Advanced Have pairs read the second draft on page 185, taking notes on generalizations and supporting details. Monitor analytical skills by asking, *What general statement does the author make about the topic? What do I know that supports the generalization?*

Advanced High Have students complete the Advanced activity, then explain techniques for evaluating generalizations, such as checking for supporting evidence.

1 

Using Writing Coach Online™ or the student book, students study and discuss the revision chart.

2 In a video by program author Kelly Gallagher, students learn more strategies for effective writing.

Revising: Making It Better

Look at the Big Picture

Introduce the revision chart to students. Explain that the Section column identifies the three main parts of an op-ed piece. The Evaluate column identifies the characteristics found in each section and explains how to assess them. The Revise column presents specific strategies for revising each characteristic.

Then, have students draw lines between and label the three sections of their drafts. Direct students to work individually to evaluate and revise their draft, using the chart to guide their work.

Revising Feature Assignment Revising Feature Assignment R

Look at the Big Picture

Use the chart and your analytical skills to evaluate how well each section of your op-ed piece addresses **purpose, audience, and genre**. When necessary, use the suggestions in the chart to revise your piece.

Section	Evaluate	Revise
Introduction	• Check the **lead**. Will it grab readers' attention and make them want to read more?	• Make your lead more interesting by adding a question, anecdote, quotation, or strong detail.
	• Make sure the **thesis** clearly identifies the issue and states your opinion of it.	• To clearly identify the issue or state your opinion forcefully, turn the thesis statement into a question and answer the question by stating your opinion.
Body	• Check that you have organized your **persuasive arguments** in a logical way that will be clear to your readers.	• Rearrange arguments so that your second strongest argument is first, the weaker arguments are in the middle, and the strongest argument is last.
	• Underline details that offer **supporting evidence**. Draw a line from each detail to the argument it supports.	• Rearrange any detail that is not in the same paragraph as the argument it supports. When necessary, add or take out details.
	• Check that **supporting evidence** includes facts and differentiates between fact and opinion.	• Add facts where needed to strengthen your arguments and back up your opinion.
	• Review reader concerns and **counter-arguments**. Determine if you have anticipated each one.	• Answer each of your readers' likely concerns and counter-arguments with strong details.
Conclusion	• Check the **restatement** of your position.	• If necessary, restate your position more clearly.
	• Check that your **conclusion** ends on a memorable note.	• Add a quotation, a call to action, an insight, or a forceful statement to conclude your op-ed piece.

186 Persuasive Writing

Focus on Craft: Precise Word Choice

Have students read the introductory text. Guide students to understand how precise word choice influences readers.

Say: I notice that the excerpt from the Mentor Text uses the word *practical* to describe pet adoption. The word *practical* implies that this action is sensible and makes readers favor the idea.

Ask: What other word in the Mentor Text excerpt is precise and might influence readers' attitudes? (designer) What is its effect? (It gives people negative feelings about costly breeds.)

Have students work with a partner to find other examples of precise word choice in the Mentor Text.

Try It! Have students discuss the questions and record responses in their journals. Follow up with students to check that their responses show an understanding of how precise word choices strengthen arguments in persuasive writing.

Fine-Tune Your Draft

Apply It! Ask volunteers to read aloud the instructions for fine-tuning their drafts. Then, have students work in pairs to improve their drafts through precise word choices and use of effective transitions.

Peer Feedback Have students identify Mentor Text examples of the characteristics that were marked for improvement. Use the Mentor Text references on page T182 to guide students to appropriate examples.

Teacher Tip

Have students write supporting details on separate index cards so that they can easily organize the details under the arguments they support.

3 Using Writing Coach Online™ or the student book, students refer back to the Mentor Text or Student Model for examples of writer's craft.

4 Students record answers to questions about writer's craft in their online journals or notebooks.

5 Students submit revised drafts to the Interactive Writing Coach™ for scoring and feedback, or share their work with their teacher.

6 Students receive customized feedback from the Interactive Writing Coach™ or feedback from their teacher.

Focus on Craft: Precise Word Choice

Making **precise word choices** is an effective way to influence the attitudes and actions of your audience on a specific issue. Precise words are more convincing than vague or overly general words. Compare, for example, the vague and precise words in these word pairs: *bad/harmful, hard/backbreaking, nice/gratifying.*

Think about precise word choice as you read the following sentences from the Mentor Text.

MENTOR TEXT from **Looking for a Pet?** page 175; lines 43–45

There is a very practical reason to consider adopting from the Maiden Shelter. A "designer" dog or cat can easily cost $500 to $800.

Try It! Now, ask yourself these questions. Record your answers in your journal.

- Does the first sentence sound convincing? Why or why not?
- Would the first sentence be more or less convincing if it read *There is a good reason to consider adopting from the Maiden Shelter?* Explain.

Fine-Tune Your Draft

Apply It! Use the revision suggestions to prepare your final draft after rethinking how well questions of purpose, audience, and genre have been addressed.

- **Ensure Precise Word Choice** Say exactly what you mean. Use substitutes for words that are vague or imprecise to better describe and explain your points.
- **Ensure the Use of Effective Transitions** If necessary, add transition words and phrases such as *finally, next, although, therefore,* and *as mentioned earlier,* to signal to your readers how sentences and paragraphs are connected.

Peer Feedback Read your final draft to a group of peers. Ask them if they feel you have considered and responded to the views of others. Think about their responses and revise your final draft as needed.

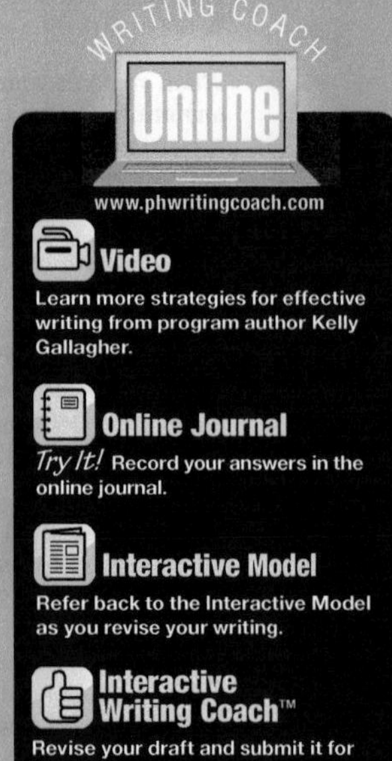

WRITING COACH
Online
www.phwritingcoach.com
Video
Learn more strategies for effective writing from program author Kelly Gallagher.
Online Journal
Try It! Record your answers in the online journal.
Interactive Model
Refer back to the Interactive Model as you revise your writing.
Interactive Writing Coach™
Revise your draft and submit it for feedback.

Personalized Support

Interactive Writing Coach™

Below Level Students complete the revising process by submitting their writing for scoring and feedback.

On Level Students complete the revising process by submitting their writing for scoring and feedback.

Above Level Students finish revising their drafts. They have the option of submitting their revised drafts for scoring and/or feedback.

Teacher or Peer Feedback

To provide feedback to students as they continue to revise their first draft, ask or have student partners ask one another the following:

- What part of the text could you replace to make your meaning clearer?
- Is there a more precise word you could use here?
- How does the rhythm of these sentences sound to you? Could you vary the length and structure of these sentences?
- How could you include transitional words and phrases here to help your reader understand these ideas?
- Are there details you could add here to make this part come alive?

Working with ELLs

Sheltered Instruction: Social/Affective

Help students use support from peers and you to enhance and confirm understanding and to develop their grasp of language structures needed to comprehend increasingly challenging language. Review the definitions of *complex sentence, dependent clause,* and *independent clause.* List words that often begin dependent clauses, like *when*. Then:

Beginning On the board, write, *I like dogs because they are friendly*. Choral read with students. Help students identify *because* as the word that begins the dependent clause. Provide other examples.

Intermediate Discuss complex sentences, guiding partners to read the examples in the Beginning activity and paraphrase each.

Advanced Have partners work together using the **KIM Strategy**, writing a key word, information, and a memory clue about the terms *complex sentence, dependent clause,* and *independent clause.* Then, have them read the Mentor Text excerpt, restating its meaning.

Advanced High Have partners complete the Advanced activity, then combine two sentences from the Mentor Text into a complex sentence and compare versions.

The Digital • Print Path

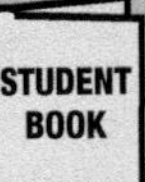

1 

In a video by program author Jeff Anderson, students learn effective editing techniques.

2 

Students record answers to questions about writer's craft in their online journals or notebooks.

Editing: Making It Correct

Discuss the opening paragraph with students. Explain that they will edit their drafts for proper grammar, mechanics, and spelling, including sentence variety and parallel structure.

WRITE GUY *Jeff Anderson, M.Ed.*

WHAT DO YOU NOTICE?

Introduce students to sentence structures by reading aloud the Mentor Text excerpt and discussing responses to the "Ask yourself" question. Then, have students read the explanation of varied sentence structures.

To monitor students' comprehension, guide them to identify and use different kinds of sentences.

I notice that the Mentor Text excerpt contains sentences with different structures and numbers of ideas. The first sentence contains one complete thought with one subject and predicate. The second sentence combines two complete thoughts with two subjects and two predicates, joining them with a comma and the word *and*. This compound sentence makes a strong impression by combining the images of the crowding and types of animals at the shelter.

Work with students to identify and analyze the relationships in other complex sentences from the excerpt, such as in lines 34–37.

Have students work with a partner to combine related sentences in their op-ed piece drafts to create more sentence variety. You may wish to have students turn to Chapters 18–20 of the Grammar Handbook to learn more about sentence structures.

Editing Feature Assignment Editing Feature Assignment E

Editing: Making It Correct

When you edit your work, you polish your writing and correct any errors. Before editing your final draft, think about using a variety of sentence structures, including **simple, compound, and complex sentences.** In addition, check your use of **parallel grammatical structures** within sentences. Then edit your draft by correcting any factual errors and errors in grammar, mechanics, and spelling.

WRITE GUY *Jeff Anderson, M. Ed.*

WHAT DO YOU NOTICE? 

Zoom in on Conventions Focus on sentence structures as you zoom in on the following lines from the Mentor Text.

To learn more about sentence structure, see Chapters 18–20 of your Grammar Handbook.

MENTOR TEXT from **Looking for a Pet?** page 174; lines 1–5

Maiden Point Shelter is overflowing with cats and dogs. Every cage and kennel is filled to capacity, and heartrending meows and barks come from extra cages lining the hallways. The shelter is at its most overcrowded since it was opened in 1993.

Now, ask yourself: *Is the structure of each sentence the same or different?*

Perhaps you said that the structure of each sentence is different.

The first sentence is a **simple** sentence because it has a single main or independent clause. A main clause has a subject and a verb and can stand alone as a complete sentence.

The second sentence is a **compound sentence** because it has more than one main clause.

The third sentence is a **complex sentence** because it has a main clause and a subordinate or dependent clause, which is *since it was opened in 1993.* A subordinate clause has a subject and a verb but cannot stand alone as a complete sentence.

Partner Talk Discuss this question with a partner: *Why do you think the author varied the sentence structure in this passage?*

188 Persuasive Writing

Grammar Mini-Lesson: Parallel Structures

Discuss the paragraph and the Mentor Text excerpt on page 189 with students. Guide them to understand that parallel parts of a sentence must express equal ideas in the same form.

Try It! Have students work with a partner to identify sentence types and parallel structures.

1. simple; parallel words
2. compound; parallel clauses

Apply It! Remind students to look closely at sentences as they edit their drafts to ensure they include a variety of sentence types with parallel structures.

Use the Rubric Explain to students that the rubric lists six important elements of an op-ed piece. Tell students that they will rate how well their draft addresses each element on a scale of 1 to 6, with 6 being the best score.

Then, have students use the rubric to evaluate and revise their drafts as necessary.

Writer's Block

IF students have difficulty identifying and using parallel structures . . .

THEN have partners read aloud sentences with parallel words, phrases, and clauses and highlight subparts of each parallel structure in the same color.

Using Writing Coach Online™ or the student book, students refer back to the Mentor Text or Student Model as they edit their writing.

Using Writing Coach Online™ or the student book, students evaluate their writing using the rubrics.

Students submit edited drafts to the Interactive Writing Coach™ for scoring and feedback, or share their work with their teacher.

Students receive personalized feedback from the Interactive Writing Coach™ or feedback from their teacher.

Feature Assignment Editing Feature Assignment **Editing**

Grammar Mini-Lesson: Parallel Structures

To learn more, see Chapter 20.

Using parallel structures in a sentence means that equal ideas are expressed in words, phrases, clauses, or sentences of similar types. Study the following sentence from the Mentor Text. Notice how the author used parallel structures for the three verbs.

from **Looking for a Pet?**
page 175; lines 54–55

You can fill out a short application, get your references checked, and go home with a pet the same day.

Try It! Tell whether each sentence is simple, compound, or complex. Then identify the parallel structures in each sentence. Write the answers in your journal.

1. Marcella is athletic, musical, and artistic.
2. One sister is interested in becoming a doctor, and the other is interested in becoming a lawyer.

Apply It! Edit your draft for grammar, mechanics, and spelling. Use an electronic or print dictionary to check your spelling. If necessary, rewrite some sentences to ensure that you have used a variety of complete sentences that include parallel structures.

Use the rubric to evaluate your piece. If necessary, rethink, rewrite, or revise.

Rubric for Persuasive Essay: Op-Ed Piece	Rating Scale					
Ideas: How clearly are the issue and your position stated?	Not very 1	2	3	4	5	Very 6
Organization: How organized are your arguments and supporting evidence?	1	2	3	4	5	6
Voice: How authoritative is your voice?	1	2	3	4	5	6
Word Choice: How persuasive is your word choice?	1	2	3	4	5	6
Sentence Fluency: How correctly have you used parallel structures to convey ideas?	1	2	3	4	5	6
Conventions: How correct are your sentence types?	1	2	3	4	5	6

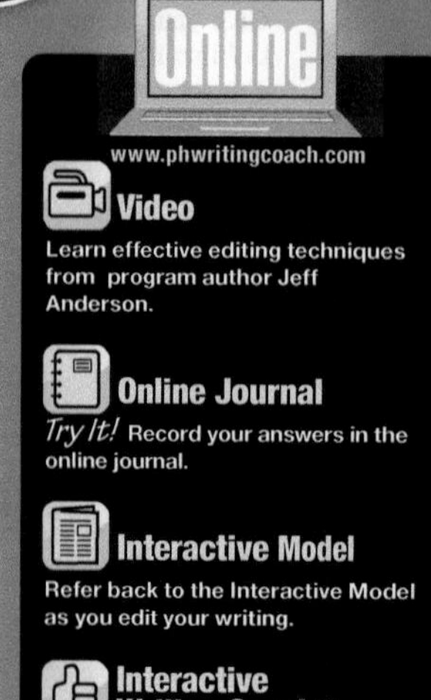

www.phwritingcoach.com

Video
Learn effective editing techniques from program author Jeff Anderson.

Online Journal
Try It! Record your answers in the online journal.

Interactive Model
Refer back to the Interactive Model as you edit your writing.

Interactive Writing Coach™
Edit your draft. Check it against the rubric and then submit it for feedback.

Personalized Support

Interactive Writing Coach™

Below Level Students complete the editing process by submitting their writing for scoring and feedback.

On Level Students complete the editing process by submitting their writing for scoring and feedback.

Above Level Students finish editing their drafts. They have the option of submitting their final drafts for scoring and/or feedback.

Teacher or Peer Feedback

To provide feedback to students as they edit their draft, ask or have student partners ask one another the following:

- Have you looked for mistakes that you tend to make?
- Have you read your piece aloud to yourself or to a partner? What kind of errors did you find?
- Can you show me something you changed through editing?
- What resources have you used to look for possible spelling errors?
- Read this sentence aloud. Does the grammar sound correct to you?
- Read this sentence aloud. Does the punctuation accurately convey your meaning?

Working with ELLs

ELL Sheltered Instruction: Metacognitive

As students study parallel structures, they should also monitor and edit writing for pronoun-antecedent agreement. Have them employ the self-corrective technique of highlighting each pronoun and circling the antecedent to check agreement as they review their writing. Review the meaning of pronoun-antecedent agreement, as needed.

Beginning Provide a word bank of pronouns and help students use it to complete simple sentence frames. For example: *Kwong walks and feeds (his) dog*. Help them employ the self-corrective technique.

Intermediate Have pairs of students complete the examples in the Beginning activity. As they edit their work, model the self-corrective technique and have them apply it as they review their sentences.

Advanced Have pairs of students find sentences with pronouns in their drafts. Have them work together to check for correct pronoun agreement by employing the self-corrective technique.

Advanced High Have partners complete the Advanced activity, then suggest other self-corrective techniques for pronoun use.

1 

Using Writing Coach Online™ or the student book, students complete the writing process by deciding the best way to publish their writing for their intended audience.

2 

Students record their answers and ideas to Extend Your Research in their online journals or notebooks.

Publishing

Wrap Up Your Presentation

Remind students who handwrote their work to use proper margins. For students who wrote their work on a computer, display some easy-to-read computer fonts. Make sure students know how to find them on the computer.

Publish Your Piece

Explain to students that the final step in the writing process is to decide which form of publication will present their work most effectively. Then, introduce students to the chart. Explain that the chart shows how specific audiences can be reached using different kinds of media.

Have students whose op-ed pieces address similar audiences work in small groups to discuss appropriate ways to publish their work.

Extend Your Research

Extension Tell students that their thinking about their topic does not have to end with its final publication. Then, guide students through the bulleted instructions for extending their research.

Big Question Have students respond to the question in their journal.

MAKE YOUR WRITING COUNT

Introduce the Public Action Day activity by discussing the opening paragraphs with students. Make sure students understand that the project may be produced electronically or by hand. Then, guide students through each step in the action plan.

Publishing

Give your op-ed piece a chance to change someone's mind—publish it! First, get your piece ready for presentation. Then, choose a way to publish for the appropriate audience.

Wrap Up Your Presentation

Is your piece handwritten or written on a computer? If your piece is handwritten, you may need to make a new, clean copy. If so, be sure to **write legibly**. Also be sure that your title grabs the reader's attention and indicates your main idea.

Publish Your Piece

Use the chart to identify a way to publish your piece.

If your audience is...	...then publish it by...
Students or adults at school	• Reading it over the school public address system • Posting your piece online and inviting responses
People in your neighborhood or city	• Submitting it to your local television news • Submitting it to your town newspaper

Extend Your Research

Think more about the topic on which you wrote your op-ed piece. What else would you like to know about this topic?

- Brainstorm for several questions you would like to research and then consult, or discuss, with others. Then decide which question is your major research question.
- Formulate, or develop, a plan about how you will answer these questions. Decide where you will find more information—on the Internet, at the library, or through other sources.
- Finally, learn more about your topic by following through with your research plan.

The Big Question: Why Write? What is your point of view? How did you determine if you convinced others?

Resources You may wish to have students use these graphic organizers: Meeting Agenda, Meeting Notes, and Problem-Solution Chart. Distribute printed copies or have students log on to Writing Coach Online.

Use the 21st Century Skills Rubric to evaluate each group's process and final product on a scale of 1 to 3, indicating weak, moderate, or strong use of the skill. ▶

Listening and Speaking Monitor students as they do additional research to answer questions and strengthen their arguments.

21st Century Learning

Skills Rubric	Rating
Communicate Clearly: Utilize multiple media and technologies.	1 2 3
Apply Technology Effectively: Use technology as a tool to research, organize, evaluate, and communicate information.	1 2 3
Work Creatively With Others: Demonstrate originality and inventiveness in work.	1 2 3
Interact Effectively With Others: Know when it is appropriate to listen and when to speak.	1 2 3

3  STUDENT BOOK

Students use a variety of graphic organizers, either online or in print, to help them work together to create a multimedia group project.

4 STUDENT BOOK

Through **Writing Coach Online™** students link to resources on 21st Century Learning for help in creating a multimedia group project.

21st Century Learning

MAKE YOUR WRITING COUNT

Create a Public Action Day at Your School

An op-ed piece often ends with a call to action that asks readers to do something about an important issue. Help make your school a place where people are organized to take action.

With a group, produce a **multimedia presentation** with text and graphics about the topic of one op-ed piece. Your presentation should use presentation software or a poster to communicate your message clearly using both words and visuals.

Here's your action plan.

1. Set objectives for each group meeting and roles for each member.
2. First, review your peers' op-ed pieces. Choose a few pieces about issues that interest the group. Add a statement to each announcing a "public action" day about the issues.
3. Submit the information to your school and/or local newspaper.
4. Work together to make your presentation. You should include the following in the slideshow or poster display:
   - Words and images that inform people about the issue
   - Several resources such as Web sites and books
   - Persuasive techniques that spark people's interest in the issue
   - A level of formality that is right for the context of your presentation and that will most influence your listener's understanding.

Listening and Speaking With your group, explain why the issue is important and discuss the facts that support your position. Use specific details to describe and explain your ideas. Increase the specificity of your details based on the type of information you are delivering. List questions people may ask. If necessary, do more research on the topic. On Public Action Day, work to convince your audience to support your position.

Online Journal

Extend Your Research Record your research topics and ideas in the online journal.

Resource

Link to resources on 21st Century Learning for help in creating a group project.

Personalized Support

Teacher or Peer Feedback

To provide feedback to students on their published writing, ask or have student partners ask one another the following:

- How did you go about writing this piece? What was your process?
- What did you learn from the writing model that you used in this piece?
- What surprised you the most as you wrote this piece?
- Did you try anything new as you worked on this piece?
- What did you learn from this piece of writing that you would like to remember and reuse?
- What do you think you do best as a writer right now?

Differentiated Instruction

RTI Strategy for Below-Level Students Guide students to select an effective call to action. Write a student volunteer's issue on the board and ask students to brainstorm for possible solutions. Record each solution proposed and ask the students questions such as: *How would this work? Is this a realistic action for students, teachers, and administrators to take?* As a group, vote on the solution that would work best for Public Action Day. Direct students to follow the same process in their groups.

Enrichment for Gifted/Talented Students Encourage students to develop and enhance their arguments using original music, writing, acting, dancing, or artwork. For example, students with musical ability could write a theme song for the presentation; those with creative writing ability could write a script to make important points; and artistically talented students could create illustrations and original symbols that enhance important ideas in the presentation.

The Digital • Print Path

1 

Students use Writing Coach Online™ or their student books to analyze and discuss the Writing for Media topic.

2 Writing Journal

Students learn about the characteristics of an advertisement by answering questions about the model. Students record their answers to the *Try It!* questions in their online journals or notebooks.

Writing for Media: Advertisements

Advertisements

Discuss the opening paragraph with students. As a class, look at several print advertisements and suggest ways they attempt to influence readers.

Try It! Guide students to understand the content and the techniques used in the advertisement displayed on the page.

Say: The second *Try It!* question asks about the concept, or main message, of this ad. **I think** the ad is trying to convince consumers that Best's Butter is the best choice of butter because a celebrity chef prefers it.

Ask: What other ads have you seen that use a celebrity to sell a product? (Responses will vary.)

Have students discuss the remaining questions in small groups and record individual responses in their journals.

Extension Have students bring in other examples of advertisements. Lead a media discussion about the examples, using the *Try It!* questions as a guide.

Writing for Media Writing for Media Writing for Media Writi

Writing for Media: Advertisements

21st Century Learning

Advertisements

An **advertisement** is a persuasive message designed to sell a product, service, or viewpoint. Advertisements, or ads, appear in many forms of media. Print ads appear in newspapers and magazines and on signs and billboards. Ads are also broadcast on radio and TV, and posted on the Internet. When you understand advertising techniques used to influence you, you can make better decisions about buying or using a product or service, or adopting a viewpoint.

Try It! Study the picture and the text in the ad. Then, answer these questions. Record your answers in your journal.

1. What **product** is this ad selling?
2. What is the **concept** or main message behind this ad?
3. An ad usually contains a **hook**—a memorable slogan, attention grabbing image, or catchy jingle. What is the hook in this ad?
4. Who is the **target audience** for this ad?
5. An ad makes **claims** about the benefits of the product, service, or viewpoint it is selling. What claims does this ad make?
6. Some ads use celebrity **endorsements** by featuring a well-known person who recommends the product. What well-known person or figure is shown in this ad? How does this person help sell the product?

Celebrity Chef Callie says, "Best's Butter makes it bette

Extension Find another example of an advertisement, and compare it with this one.

192 **Persuasive Writing**

Create an Advertisement

Tell students that they will create an advertisement using the five-step writing process. Then, preview the writing process instructions on page 193.

Resources You may wish to have students use the Cluster Diagram graphic organizer. Distribute printed copies or have students log on to Writing Coach Online.

For each step in the writing process, have partners read aloud and discuss the list of tasks. Then, have them work individually. Once both partners have completed the tasks, have them evaluate each other's work before moving to the next step.

Use the 21st Century Skills Rubric to evaluate each student's process and final product on a scale of 1 to 3, indicating weak, moderate, or strong use of the skill. ▶

Partner Talk

Remind students to use constructive language when offering feedback.

21st Century Learning

Skills Rubric	Rating
Think Creatively: Use a wide range of idea-creation techniques, such as brainstorming.	1 2 3
Use Systems Thinking: Analyze how parts of a whole interact to produce overall effects.	1 2 3
Analyze Media: Understand how and why media messages are constructed.	1 2 3
Be Flexible: Incorporate feedback effectively.	1 2 3

3 STUDENT BOOK

Students follow the five-step writing process to write their own advertisement. Students may select online or printed graphic organizers to help them plan and develop their writing.

Create an Advertisement

Follow these steps to create your own ad. To plan your ad, review the graphic organizers on pages R24–R27 and choose one that suits your needs.

Prewriting

- Identify or make up a product or service to advertise.
- As you identify your target audience, anticipate the views and concerns of your audience.
- Choose one of these mediums: a television commercial, or a print or Internet ad.
- Invent a concept or main message for your advertisement and build this message to create a slogan that provides a hook. Then, list the claims you will make about your product or service.
- List art, music, images, or special effects you will use. Consider using familiar images (a cowboy, a kitten, and so on), situations (a picnic, a day at the beach, and so on), and words or phrases to create your ad.

Drafting

- For a television ad, write a script, the dialogue spoken by actors. Indicate music and special effects in your script.
- For a print or Internet ad, use heads, or words set in larger type, to grab readers. Feature your hook in one or more of the heads. Lay out your ad to achieve an eye-catching look by arranging pictures and text and selecting fonts or type styles for the best effect.

Revising and Editing

Review your draft to ensure that events or ideas are organized logically. Make sure your concept is clearly presented. Take out material that distracts from your message. Check that spelling, grammar, and mechanics are correct.

Publishing

Using text and graphics, make a video recording of your commercial or create a poster for your print or Internet ad. Then, present it to the class.

www.phwritingcoach.com

Online Journal

Try It! Record your answers in the online journal.

Interactive Graphic Organizers

Choose from a variety of graphic organizers to plan and develop your project.

Before you start drafting, describe your ad to a partner. Ask for feedback about your plan. For example, is your slogan catchy? Monitor your partner's spoken language by asking follow-up questions to confirm your understanding.

Personalized Support

Teacher or Peer Feedback

To provide feedback to students as they write for media, ask or have student partners ask one another the following:

- What are the main characteristics of this form of writing?
- Have you included most or all of these characteristics in your piece of writing?
- What is your purpose for writing this piece?
- Who is your audience?
- How did you organize your ideas in this piece of writing?
- How did you go about revising the piece? Editing it?
- How do you plan on publishing your piece?
- What other publishing options also might work?

Working with ELLs

Sheltered Instruction: Cognitive

Have students respond orally to information presented in wide variety of print, electronic, audio, and visual media to build and reinforce language attainment. Provide a word bank of terms pertaining to ads (including words from page 192), such as *product, service, slogan,* and *concept.* Display a print ad and discuss its features.

Beginning Review the ad and the vocabulary. Have students use the words in responding orally to questions, such as *What word names the main message of an ad?*

Intermediate Have students take notes in a cluster diagram. Then, have them respond orally to the ad using sentence frames , like *The main message of the ad is the* ______.

Advanced Distribute magazines to small groups. Have students compare two print ads in a **Venn Diagram.** To build language attainment, have students discuss their Venn diagrams using words and phrases or "terms" such as *product, slogan, viewpoint, and designed to sell.*

Advanced High Have students complete the Advanced activity. Then, have them write a paragraph based on their notes, using the word bank vocabulary.

Before they write, students use the ABCDs of On-Demand Writing to analyze and plan how to respond to each prompt. They can use either their online journals or notebooks to take notes.

Writing for Assessment

Read aloud or have a student read aloud the introductory text. Then, tell students that they will learn and practice a technique for writing in response to a test prompt.

Try It! Read aloud the Persuasive Prompt and then have volunteers read aloud the Format and Academic Vocabulary boxes. Tell students that they will use the ABCD method to respond to the prompt.

The ABCDs of On-Demand Writing

Have students identify the words associated with the ABCD method. (attack, brainstorm, choose, detect) Then, guide students through their use.

I'll attack the prompt by circling the verb *support* and the phrases *telling why* and *examples and facts.* These key words and phrases remind me that my essay needs to state a clear opinion and support it with reasons and facts. I can rewrite the prompt to state that clearly: "Write an essay that gives a clear, specific opinion and supports it with convincing details."

Work with students to brainstorm for an appropriate graphic organizer for a persuasive essay, such as a two-column chart.

Have students write their drafts individually and then work with a partner to detect errors.

Writing for Assessment Writing for Assessment Writing for Assessment

Writing for Assessment

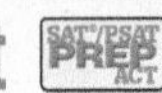

Many standardized tests include a prompt that asks you to write a persuasive essay. Use these prompts to practice. Respond using the characteristics of your op-ed piece. (See page 172.)

Try It! To begin, read the **persuasive** prompt and the information on format and academic vocabulary. Use the ABCDs of On-Demand Writing to help you plan and write your essay.

Format
The prompt directs you to write a *persuasive essay.* Be sure to include an introduction with a clear thesis, body paragraphs with supporting evidence, and a conclusion that reinforces your opinion.

Persuasive Prompt
Your school board has announced that it will fund a new sport next year. Write a persuasive essay telling why a sport you choose should be funded. Support your opinion with examples and facts.

Academic Vocabulary
Remember that an *opinion* is a personal belief about something. A *fact* is something that actually happened or can be proven.

The ABCDs of On-Demand Writing

Use the following ABCDs to help you respond to the prompt.

Before you write your draft:

A ttack the prompt [1 MINUTE]
- Circle or highlight important verbs in the prompt. Draw a line from the verb to what it refers to.
- Rewrite the prompt in your own words.

B rainstorm possible answers [4 MINUTES]
- Create a graphic organizer to generate ideas.
- Use one for each part of the prompt if necessary.

C hoose the order of your response [1 MINUTE]
- Think about the best way to organize your ideas.
- Number your ideas in the order you will write about them. Cross out ideas you will not be using.

After you write your draft:

D etect errors before turning in the draft [1 MINUTE]
- Carefully reread your writing.
- Make sure that your response makes sense and is complete.
- Look for spelling, punctuation, and grammar errors.

194 Persuasive Writing

More Prompts for Practice

Apply It! Have students apply the ABCD method to the practice prompts.

Prompt 1 Have partners attack the prompt and brainstorm for possible answers. Then, have each pair swap their information with another group and evaluate whether the team has stated a focused position and logical, convincing arguments.

Prompt 2 Have students work individually to attack the prompt and brainstorm for possible answers. Then, have students work in small groups to evaluate their work before writing their drafts.

Test Prep Spiral Review: Expository Read aloud the instructions and the prompt. Then, have students review the expository essay characteristics on page 146.

Prompt 3 Remind students to use the ABCD method to write their expository essay.

Students submit their writing paragraph by paragraph or as a complete draft to the **Interactive Writing Coach™** for feedback, or share their writing with their teacher.

Students receive personalized feedback from the **Interactive Writing Coach™** or feedback from their teacher.

More Prompts for Practice

Apply It! Respond to Prompts 1 and 2 by writing **persuasive essays** that influence the attitudes or actions of a specific audience on a specific issue. As you write, be sure to:

- Identify an appropriate **audience**
- Establish a clear **thesis** or position
- Anticipate and respond to the views, concerns, and **counter-arguments** of others
- Logically **organize** your arguments and evidence so that they support your viewpoint
- Differentiate between **fact** and **opinion,** and support all your opinions with facts

Prompt 1 Imagine that your school has a new program. Students who ride their bicycles to school receive points toward a service award. Write a persuasive essay stating your position on this program.

Prompt 2 Imagine that your school principal is planning to require that all students participate in cleaning up litter around the building. Write a persuasive essay stating your position on this issue.

Spiral Review: Expository Respond to Prompt 3 by writing an **expository essay.** Your essay should include:

- A clearly stated **purpose**, or controlling idea
- A logical **organization,** including an effective **introduction** and **conclusion**
- A variety of **sentence structures** and **rhetorical devices**
- Clear **transitions** to link ideas and paragraphs
- Appropriate **facts** and **details** without any extraneous information or inconsistencies
- Accurately **synthesized ideas** from several sources

Prompt 3 Sleep is essential for all humans. Write an essay about the effects of not getting enough sleep.

Interactive Writing Coach™

Plan your response to the prompt. If you are using the prompt for practice, write one paragraph at a time or your entire draft and then submit it for feedback. If you are using the prompt as a timed test, write your entire draft and then submit it for feedback

Remember **ABCD**

- **A**ttack the prompt
- **B**rainstorm possible answers
- **C**hoose the order of your response
- **D**etect errors before turning in the draft

Personalized Support

Assessment/Monitor Progress

For timed writing practice, assign students a prompt to be completed in a timed setting. Have students submit their writing to Interactive Writing Coach™ to get immediate feedback.

For a formal writing assessment, assign the Assessment writing prompt for this chapter in Writing Coach Online™. Then, have students submit their writing to Interactive Writing Coach™ to be assessed. Use the results to assess student progress and skill levels. Interactive Writing Coach™ will update student levels to ensure that students get the appropriate support.

Teacher or Peer Feedback

To create an assessment environment, have students use a prompt in a timed setting. Grade papers using the appropriate rubric and use the results to assess student progress and skill levels. In the next writing assignment, ensure that students get the appropriate level of support.

If you conference with students, use these questions to guide your discussion:

- What form of writing did the prompt call for? Does your response include most or all of the characteristics of that form?
- How did you organize your ideas?
- Did you make good use of your time as you planned and wrote your response?
- What did you learn that you can use when responding to a prompt during a timed test?

Differentiated Instruction

Strategy for Spanish Speakers Students whose home language is Spanish may overuse subordinate clauses when trying to persuade others, due to Spanish subjunctive constructions *(I want that you believe me* versus *I want you to believe me).* Read Prompt 1 on page 195. Elicit different arguments and have students construct complex sentences using the verbs *want, need,* and *tell.* For example, *I want people to ride their bicycle to school because it is a good way to get exercise.*

PRE-AP Enrichment for Above-Level Students Work with students to strengthen and enhance their writing. Have students review their completed expository essays and note in the margins where they could use an additional fact or detail to support an argument or where they could strengthen a section by varying sentence structure or including rhetorical devices such as similes or metaphors. Direct students to work independently to create a second draft incorporating the improvements.

CHAPTER 10 LESSON PLANNER
Response to Literature

Use the Online Lesson Planner at www.phwritingcoach.com to customize your instructional plan for an integrated Language Arts curriculum.

DAY 1

CHAPTER OPENER/ GENRE INTRODUCTION
- What Do You Think?
- What's Ahead
- Connect to the Big Questions
- **Feature Assignment: Interpretative Response: Review of a Short Story**
- Other Forms of Interpretative Response
- Word Bank

ONLINE

DAY 2

MENTOR TEXT/ STUDENT MODEL
- **Mentor Text: Review of a Short Story**
- Learn From Experience
- **Student Model: Review of a Short Story**
- Reader's Eye and Writer's Eye

ONLINE

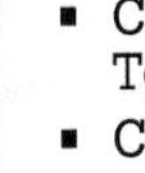

DAY 3

Prewriting
- Choose From the Topic Bank
- Choose Your Own Topic
- Narrow Your Topic
- Consider Your Audience and Purpose

ONLINE

DAY 6

Revising
- Keep Revision on Your RADaR
- Look at the Big Picture
- Focus on Craft
- Fine-Tune Your Draft

ONLINE

DAY 7

For more grammar support, see Sections 25.4 and 25.8, pp. 575 and 601.

Editing

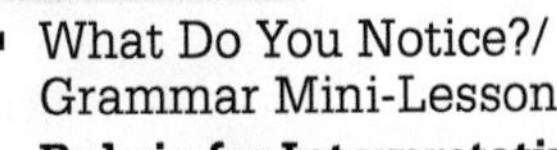

- What Do You Notice?/ Grammar Mini-Lesson

Rubric for Interpretative Response: Letter to an Author

Publishing
- Publish Your Piece
- Extend Your Research

ONLINE

DAY 8

21st Century Learning

MAKE YOUR WRITING COUNT
- **Share Letters With the School Community**
- Here's Your Action Plan
- Listening and Speaking

ONLINE

Alternate Pacing Suggestions

- **Block Scheduling** Each day on the Lesson Planner represents a 40–50 minute block. Teachers using block scheduling may combine days to revise pacing to meet their classroom needs.
- **Accelerated Lesson Planning** Combine instructional days by aiding students in choosing a topic and then focusing on two core stages of the writing process, outlining for success (Day 5) and RADaR revision (Day 6).
- **Integrated Language Arts Curriculum** For targeted instruction that covers the essential components of the lesson, use either a 3- or a 5-day plan.

3 day plan

DAY 1: Introduction to the Genre, Mentor Text, Student Model

DAY 2: Prewriting/Drafting

DAY 3: Revising/Editing/ Publishing

5 day plan

Use 3-day plan, and add:

DAY 4: Make Your Writing Count

DAY 5: Writing for Assessment

Links to Prentice Hall *LITERATURE*

Featured Author: Richard Mühlberger
- What Is an Essay?, p. 408
- "What Makes a Rembrandt a Rembrandt?" (analytical article), p. 413
- On Getting Readers Involved (Writing Workshop), p. 551
- *From the Author's Desk* Videos: Richard Mühlberger

Additional Mentor Text:
- Review of *A Christmas Carol* (review of television drama), Terry Kelleher, p. 813

Differentiated Instruction

Differentiated Instruction Boxes in this Teacher's Edition address these student populations:

- Below-Level Students
- Above-Level Students
- Gifted and Talented Students
- Special Needs Students
- English Language Learners
- Spanish Speaking Students

In addition, for further enrichment, see the **Extension** features.

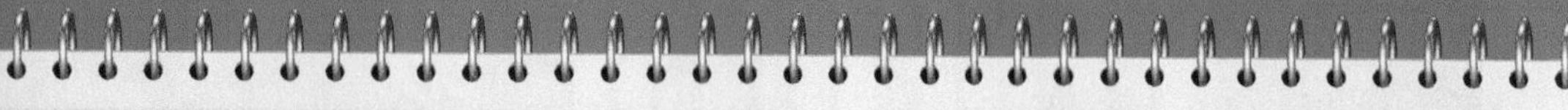

DAY 4

Prewriting

- Plan Your Piece
- Gather Details

ONLINE

DAY 5

Drafting

- Outline for Success
- Start Your Draft

ONLINE

DAY 9

WRITING FOR MEDIA

- **Movie Review**
- Create a Movie Review

ONLINE

DAY 10

WRITING FOR ASSESSMENT

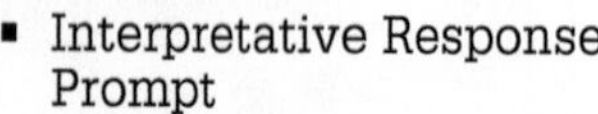

- Interpretative Response Prompt
- The ABCDs of On-Demand Writing

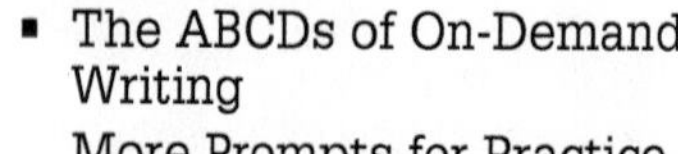

More Prompts for Practice

- Spiral Review: Persuasive

ONLINE

LESSON OBJECTIVES

- To learn the forms and defining characteristics of a response to literature.
- To learn the elements of a successful review of a short story, the chapter Feature Assignment.
- To read a Mentor Text in the genre, analyzing its use of the elements of an effective response to literature.
- To read a Student Model of a review of a short story, analyzing it from the perspective of a reader and from the perspective of a writer.
- To apply prewriting strategies in developing a review of a short story, including strategies for choosing and narrowing a topic, planning writing, and gathering details, as well as tips for considering audience and purpose.
- To apply drafting strategies in developing a review of a short story.
- To apply RADaR revision strategies to a draft review of a short story.
- To learn about the Focus on Craft topic, consistent point of view, and apply what is learned to a draft review of a short story.
- To edit the draft, zooming in on subject-verb agreement and focusing on consistent tenses.
- To complete the Make Your Writing Count assignment, developing and presenting an advertisement for a story.
- To complete the Writing for Media assignment, developing a movie review.
- To practice writing for assessment.

Personalized Assessment

	Ongoing Assessment	Formal Assessment of Feature Assignment	Progress Monitoring at End-of-Chapter
 Interactive Writing Coach™	Use Paragraph Feedback and Essay Scorer as a revision tool.	Use Essay Scorer to score students' Feature Assignment papers.	Use Essay Scorer to score students' papers. Students' learner profiles can be adjusted based on their scores.
 Teacher Conferencing	Use rubrics in the Student Edition as a revision tool. Conference with students to review their work and provide personalized support.	Use rubrics in the Student Edition to score students' Feature Assignment papers.	Review each student's work to plan targeted resources for the next writing assignment.

1 Using Writing Coach Online™ or the student book, students discuss the photograph in the chapter opener as it relates to the writing genre.

2 Students record their ideas and responses in their online journals or notebooks. They may also record and save their responses on pop-up sticky notes in Writing Coach Online™.

Chapter Objectives

1. Write an interpretative response essay by planning, drafting, revising, editing, and publishing individual work.
2. Produce an advertisement.
3. Use the five-step writing process to write a movie review.
4. Write an interpretative response essay and a persuasive essay in response to a prompt.

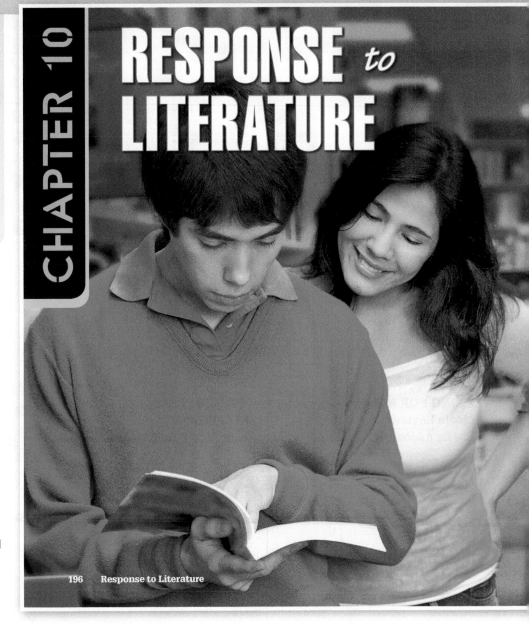

CHAPTER 10

RESPONSE to LITERATURE

196 Response to Literature

RESPONSE to LITERATURE

What Do You Think?

Activate Prior Knowledge Tell students that the purpose of an interpretative response is to analyze an author's work. Explain to students that they will use what they know about choosing books to analyze the photo on page 196. Then, guide students in analyzing the photo.

When **I analyze** something, I look at it, ask questions about it, and draw conclusions from what I see and what I know. For example, in the photo I see two students analyzing a book. They are looking at it. They may be asking questions about it: "Who wrote this book? What is it about?" They are drawing conclusions from what they see and what they know: "I know this author. I like her books. I want to read this book."

Work with students to brainstorm for other things the students might do as they analyze this or another book.

Try It! **Have students** work individually to develop responses to the questions. Check that students have identified the author's purpose.

Possible responses: I was very moved when I read *The Incredible Journey*. The animals in this survival tale were so loyal and courageous. The author made me care about what happened to them. I really wanted them to survive the journey and get home.

Connect to the Big Questions

Have students use their experience to discuss the Big Questions. Explain that they will revisit **Why write?** at the end of this chapter. Tell students to consider these points during their discussion:

1. Each reader brings his or her own opinions, experiences, ideas, and values to the text, which may be different from the writer's intent.
2. Writers cannot control what makes the reader interested in a text. Writers should write what about what they enjoy or their own interests, and hope the readers enjoy reading about it, too.

What's Ahead

Have students preview the Mentor Text and Student Model on pages 200–203. Tell students that they will write their own review of a short story using the five-step writing process: prewriting, drafting, revising, editing, and publishing.

What Do You Think?

Authors have purposes for writing. Some authors write to inform. Some write to entertain. Others write to persuade.

Part of being an active reader is analyzing the author's purpose. You think about the author's purpose and find details that show how the author achieves that purpose.

Try It! Think about your favorite book. What do you think the author was trying to communicate by writing this book?

Consider these questions as you participate in an extended discussion with a partner. Take turns expressing your ideas and feelings.

- How did you feel when reading this book?
- How did the author achieve his or her purpose?
- Do you think the author did a good job achieving his or her purpose? Why or why not?
- What details support your answer?

What's Ahead

In this chapter, you will review two strong examples of an interpretative response essay: a Mentor Text and a Student Model. Then, using the examples as guides, you will write an interpretative response essay of your own.

WRITING COACH

www.phwritingcoach.com

Online Journal

Try It! Record your answers and ideas in the online journal.

You can also record and save your answers and ideas on pop-up sticky notes in the eText.

Connect to the Big Questions

Discuss these questions with your partner:

1 **What do you think?** What do readers bring to a text that writers may not?

2 **Why write?** What should you write about to make others interested in a text?

Personalized Support

Teacher or Peer Feedback

To encourage students in their discussion of the photograph as it relates to the writing genre, ask the following questions:

- What is the first thing you think of when you look at this photo?
- How does it relate to your life?
- How does it relate to things you've learned in other subjects?
- What questions come to mind when you look at this photograph?
- How does your response to the photograph compare to those of your classmates?

Working with ELLs

ELL Sheltered Instruction: Metacognitive

Have students demonstrate listening comprehension of increasingly complex spoken English by following directions for the *Try It!* activity after you read them aloud.

Beginning Read aloud the first paragraph of the *Try It!* and model completing the activity. Then, help students follow your spoken directions to complete the activity. Ask simple questions to help students monitor comprehension and seek clarification, such as *Is this your favorite book?*

Intermediate Read aloud the *Try It!* Have pairs monitor comprehension of your spoken directions by saying back what they have understood you to say. Direct them to seek clarification as needed. Then, guide students as they follow the directions.

Advanced Have partners take notes as you read aloud the *Try It!* directions, directing them to monitor their understanding and seek clarification as needed. Have them follow the directions to complete the activity, seeking clarification as needed.

Advanced High Have students complete the Advanced activity. Then, have them discuss the other works they thought of.

1 

Students learn vocabulary from the Word Bank and listen to English and Spanish pronunciations in the **Writing Coach Online™** glossary.

2 

Students record answers to questions about forms of writing in their online journals or notebooks.

INTERPRETATIVE RESPONSE

To introduce this chapter's writing form, discuss the opening paragraphs with students. Make sure students understand that a short story review is a type of interpretative response. Explain that good writers use a step-by-step process to develop their work. Then, have students preview the rubric on page 215.

Interpretative Response: Review of a Short Story

Ask volunteers to read aloud the feature assignment characteristics. Tell students that they will identify these characteristics in a Mentor Text and a Student Model. Then, they will use the characteristics to guide the writing of their own review of a short story.

Other Forms of Interpretative Response

Guide students to understand the purposes of different forms of interpretative responses.

Say: One of the ways **I can use** the forms of interpretative response is to help me make choices about what to read. For example, I can read blogs that tell me about new books. I can read response to literature essays to find out more about the effect that a book or story has on its readers.

Ask: Which form of interpretative response would you read to learn how two stories are alike and different? (comparison essay)

Have students brainstorm for other purposes that readers might have for reading each form of interpretative response.

Try It! Remind students that the audience is the people who will read their writing. The purpose is the author's reason for writing. Have students record their responses in their journal.

Possible responses: comparison essay, points out similarities in the novels; letter to an author, communicates thoughts and feelings to the author directly; response to literature essay, shows how well an author has accomplished what he or she has set out to do

INTERPRETATIVE RESPONSE

In this chapter, you will explore a special kind of interpretative response, the review of a short story. An interpretative response analyzes an author's work. It often examines story elements, such as theme and plot, as well as features, such as imagery and mood. It discusses what the work communicates to the reader. The reader states his or her opinions about the work and supports those opinions with details from the text.

You will develop your review of a short story by taking it through each of the steps of the writing process: prewriting, drafting, revising, editing, and publishing. You will also have an opportunity to write a movie review. To preview the criteria for how your review of a short story will be evaluated, see the rubric on page 215.

FEATURE ASSIGNMENT

Interpretative Response: Review of a Short Story

An effective interpretative response has these characteristics:

- A strong, interesting **focus or thesis statement**
- **Details** that are focused, organized, and coherent
- A **summary of important features** of the author's work
- **Sustained evidence,** such as examples and quotations from the text to defend and support ideas
- **Ideas and arguments** that demonstrate personal insights, judgments, and understanding of the text
- **Effective sentence structure** and correct spelling, grammar, and usage

A review of a short story also includes:

- an **analysis of story elements,** such as character, plot, setting, and theme
- details about the imagery and mood the author created
- summary of the author's message and overall opinion of the story

198 Interpretative Response

Word Bank

To assist English Language Learners and struggling readers, echo read each word or have students log on to Writing Coach Online to listen to the pronunciations. Then, have partners take turns using each word in a sentence. Ask volunteers to share one of their sentences with the class.

Teacher Tip

Have students extend their understanding by discussing how the forms of interpretative response are like and unlike other forms of interpretative response, such as movie and music reviews.

Other Forms of Interpretative Response

In addition to a review of a short story, there are other forms of interpretative response, including:

Blog comments on an author's Web site share readers' ideas about an author's work. Readers express their opinions and discuss their understanding of what an author's work means.

Comparison essays explore similarities and differences between two or more works of literature. For example, a comparison essay may compare how main characters in two stories handle a similar problem.

Letters to authors analyze an author's work and explain the reader's response to it. The reader shares with the author of the work his or her thoughts and feelings about the content of the work and about the author's writing style.

Response to literature essays analyze and interpret an author's work. These kinds of essays examine what an author states directly and indirectly and what those statements mean. Response to literature essays also judge how well an author has accomplished what he or she has set out to do.

Try It! For each audience and purpose described, choose a form, such as a letter to an author or a comparison essay, that is appropriate for conveying your intended meaning to the audience. Explain your choices.

- To show a teacher how two novels are alike
- To tell an author how much her poetry meant to you
- To persuade classmates to read a particular book

Resource

Word Bank Listen to English and Spanish pronunciations of new words in the eText glossary.

Online Journal

Try It! Record your answers and ideas in the online journal.

Affixes are word parts used to change the meaning of a root word. For example, the word *write* becomes *prewriting* when the prefix *pre-* and the suffix *-ing* are added to the root word *write.* Work with a partner. Take turns using each word in a sentence. If you are unsure of the meaning of a word, identify any roots or affixes that might help you infer its meaning. If you are still unsure, use the Glossary or a dictionary to check the definition.

analysis	**plausible**
consider	**profound**
offensive	**reflect**

Personalized Support

Teacher or Peer Feedback

To help students understand the characteristics of the writing form, ask or have student partners ask one another the following questions:

- What are the main characteristics of an interpretative response?
- What makes this form of writing different from other forms?
- Who are the likely readers or audiences for this form of writing?
- What kind of organization could be used for this form of writing?
- What kind of voice would be most effective for this form of writing?

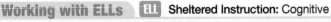

Working with ELLs

ELL **Sheltered Instruction:** Cognitive

Have students use strategic learning techniques such as concept mapping and reviewing to acquire the basic and grade-level vocabulary in the Word Bank. Help students use accessible language to help them learn new and essential language.

Beginning Provide a simple analysis of a text the class has read. Say *This is my analysis of [text]. What is your analysis of [text]?* Encourage students to respond with accessible language. Introduce and review other words using accessible language.

Intermediate Have partners use the **Frayer Model** for concept mapping vocabulary in the Word Bank by dividing index cards into four quadrants with a definition, characteristics, examples, and non-examples and the word in the center. Have pairs discuss the cards using accessible language.

Advanced Have students independently concept map the words in the Intermediate activity. Then, have partners take turns using accessible language to explain each term.

Advanced High Have partners review the Word Bank vocabulary by using accessible language to discuss it, then use it to discuss the forms of interpretative response.

1 STUDENT BOOK

Using Writing Coach Online™ or the student book, students read and listen to an audio recording of the Mentor Text. As they complete their writing assignments, they can refer back to the Mentor Text for support whenever they need it.

MENTOR TEXT

About the Selection The selection is a review of the book *The House on Mango Street* by Sandra Cisneros. The reviewer provides details and evidence to support her thesis that, like the author, the main character yearns for a better life outside the barrio.

Learn From Experience

After students have read the text, point out that the numbered notes refer to the characteristics of a review of a short story introduced on page 198.

Try It! Guide students to understand how the genre characteristics shape the text.

Say: The first *Try It!* question asks me to explain the meaning of a phrase the reviewer uses in the introduction. First **I look for** the phrase in the paragraph. I read the phrase in context and decide that the author means Cisneros was influenced by the cultures of both Mexico and the United States.

Ask: How would you explain the meaning of the phrase? What image does it give you? (Responses will vary.)

Have students reply to the *Try It!* questions in their journals. If students have difficulty responding to a particular question, model a response, as with Question 1.

Check the accuracy and completeness of student responses.

1. Responses will vary but should recognize that the author grew up in two cultures.
2. Each chapter is a story but also part of the whole book, just as a pearl is a jewel on its own but can also be part of a necklace of pearls.
3. Responses should note that the thesis statement reveals that, like Cisneros, the main character finds a way to escape from the barrio.
4. Responses should recognize that the quotation sums up Esperanza's feelings about her life and what she hopes to find outside the barrio.

MENTOR TEXT Review of a Short Story

Learn From Experience

After reading the review on pages 200–201, read the numbered notes in the margins to learn how the author presented her ideas.

Answer the *Try It!* questions online or in your notebook.

❶ The **introduction** provides background about Sandra Cisneros.

Try It! What does the reviewer mean when she says that Cisneros grew up "straddling two countries"?

❷ The reviewer **summarizes** an **important feature** of *The House on Mango Street,* supporting it with a **quotation** from Sandra Cisneros.

Try It! How is each story like a pearl? How is the book as a whole like a necklace?

❸ The **thesis statement** provides a strong focus for the review.

Try It! What does the thesis statement reveal about the plot of *The House on Mango Street?*

Extension Find another example of a review of short story, and compare it with this one.

From Sandra Cisneros: Latina Writer and Activist

by Caryn Mirriam-Goldberg

❶ Sandra Cisneros was born in Chicago, Illinois, but she was actually born into the traditions, histories, and languages of two countries: the United States and Mexico. Her father was Mexican, and her mother was Mexican American. Her family spoke two languages and frequently journeyed to Mexico for long visits with her father's family. Cisneros grew up straddling two countries, each with its own challenges and gifts, each with its own way of defining Mexicans, Americans, and Mexican Americans. . . .

Each of the pieces [in Sandra Cisneros's *The House on Mango Street*] tells of the bittersweet life in a Chicago barrio. ❷ While each chapter works as a story on its own, each is also part of the larger story. This structure, according to Cisneros, was not an accident. She wanted to write a book that a reader could pick up, open to any chapter, and find a story that made its own sense. "You would understand each story like a little pearl, or you could look at the whole thing like a necklace," says Cisneros. "That's what I always knew from the day that I wrote the first one. I said, "I'm going to do a whole series of these, and it's going to be like this, and it's all connected."

❸ She succeeded in creating both pearls and a necklace linking them, but she did more than that. She told a story of a girl similar to herself, named Esperanza, who found herself becoming an artist to escape "the trap of the barrio." Cisneros wanted to show people what life in the barrio was like as well as what it was not like. The book stood in sharp contrast to "those people who want to make our barrios look like Sesame Street or some place really warm and beautiful," Cisneros says. At a time when homes like the one she grew up

200 Interpretative Response

---

5. Responses will vary but should point out that since the resolution occurs at or near the end of the book, the review is ending at the same point as the book.

Extension Lead a discussion in which students compare and contrast how their additional review of a short story example uses the genre characteristics. Use the *Try It!* questions as a guide.

Teacher Tip

Assign small groups of students one chapter each of *The House on Mango Street.* Ask them to look in their chapter for details about Esperanza and evidence supporting the reviewer's thesis. Have them present their findings to the class.

2 

Students record their answers to questions about the Mentor Text in their online journals or notebooks.

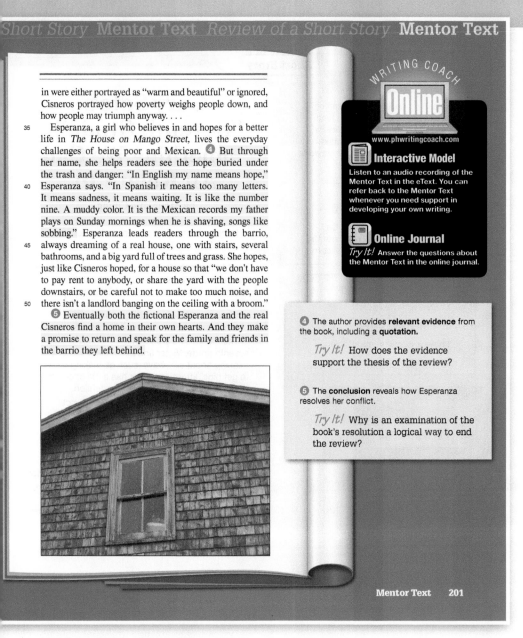

in were either portrayed as "warm and beautiful" or ignored, Cisneros portrayed how poverty weighs people down, and how people may triumph anyway. . . .

Esperanza, a girl who believes in and hopes for a better life in *The House on Mango Street,* lives the everyday challenges of being poor and Mexican. ❹ But through her name, she helps readers see the hope buried under the trash and danger: "In English my name means hope," Esperanza says. "In Spanish it means too many letters. It means sadness, it means waiting. It is like the number nine. A muddy color. It is the Mexican records my father plays on Sunday mornings when he is shaving, songs like sobbing." Esperanza leads readers through the barrio, always dreaming of a real house, one with stairs, several bathrooms, and a big yard full of trees and grass. She hopes, just like Cisneros hoped, for a house so that "we don't have to pay rent to anybody, or share the yard with the people downstairs, or be careful not to make too much noise, and there isn't a landlord banging on the ceiling with a broom."

❺ Eventually both the fictional Esperanza and the real Cisneros find a home in their own hearts. And they make a promise to return and speak for the family and friends in the barrio they left behind.

WRITING COACH **Online**

www.phwritingcoach.com

Interactive Model

Listen to an audio recording of the Mentor Text in the eText. You can refer back to the Mentor Text whenever you need support in developing your own writing.

Online Journal

Try It! Answer the questions about the Mentor Text in the online journal.

❹ The author provides **relevant evidence** from the book, including a **quotation.**

Try It! How does the evidence support the thesis of the review?

❺ The **conclusion** reveals how Esperanza resolves her conflict.

Try It! Why is an examination of the book's resolution a logical way to end the review?

Personalized Support

FEEDBACK

Teacher or Peer Feedback

To provide feedback to students on their responses to the Mentor Text and their answers to the *Try It!* questions, ask or have student partners ask one another the following:

- What is the thesis or controlling idea of the Mentor Text?
- How does the Mentor Text illustrate the characteristics of a review?
- How did you answer this *Try It!* question? How could you use your answer to help you plan your piece of writing?

Working with ELLs

ELL **Sheltered Instruction:** Metacognitive

Have students demonstrate listening comprehension of increasingly complex English by retelling or summarizing spoken messages. Read the Mentor Text, pausing frequently to paraphrase or explain as students monitor their understanding and seek clarification as needed.

Beginning Slowly read lines 35–50 aloud, acting out ideas. Pause often for students to monitor understanding and seek clarification. Have students retell an idea from the article with words or drawings.

Intermediate Review the article as students use a web graphic organizer to monitor their understanding and record ideas. Have partners work together to retell what you said and share in a group.

Advanced Reread the Mentor Text aloud. Have students monitor their understanding by writing questions about the message and have partners respond, seeking clarification as needed. Then, have them summarize the message.

Advanced High Have students complete the Advanced activity and then compare their summaries with partners.

The Digital • Print Path

1 STUDENT BOOK

Using Writing Coach Online™ or the student book, students read and listen to an audio recording of the Student Model.

STUDENT MODEL

Tell students that good writers react to what they read in ways that show their understanding of the text. Explain that students will react to the Student Model by placing two sets of symbols in the text. Then, distribute printed copies of the Student Model or have students log on to Writing Coach Online.

Use a Reader's Eye

Read aloud the instruction for using the Reader's Response Symbols and the meaning of each symbol. Then, guide students through their use.

I think the student writer did a good job interpreting the story. I especially like the way she expressed some of her ideas. For example, lines 7–8 tell me very clearly that she thinks the story is about "what happens when you pretend to be something you are not." These are strong, vivid words. I'm going to put an exclamation point next to this sentence.

Work with students to identify other places in the text where the writer expresses her ideas in a clear, compelling way.

Have students read and respond to the Student Model, using each Reader's Response Symbol at least once.

Partner Talk

Remind students to listen to and respect each other's opinions, even when they differ.

Use a Writer's Eye

Read aloud the instructions for using the Writer's Response Symbols and the meaning of each symbol. Then, guide students through their use.

Say: **I like** that this student used strong evidence to support her interpretations. For example, in lines 15–21 she says that Victor can be awkward, just like other kids his age. Then, in lines 15–21 she gives an example of how he responds strangely to Teresa's greeting by saying "Yeah, that's me." I'll write S.E. next to this for effective supporting evidence. I'm also going to write E.Q. for effective quotation.

Ask: In lines 30–34, what evidence does the writer use to support her idea that Victor is thrilled to have impressed Teresa? (She gives a quotation from the story about Victor's cheeks becoming "bouquets of love.")

Have students read and respond to the Student Model, using each Writer's Response Symbol at least once.

Student Model Review of a Short Story Student Model Review of

STUDENT MODEL Review of a Short Story

With a small group, take turns reading this Student Model aloud. As you read, practice newly acquired vocabulary by correctly producing the word's sound. Look for evidence in the text that supports your understanding of the review.

Use a Reader's Eye

Now, reread the Student Model. On your copy of the Student Model, use the Reader's Response Symbols to react to what you read.

Reader's Response Symbols

- \+ I agree with this point.
- − This isn't clear to me.
- ? I have a question about this.
- ! Well said!

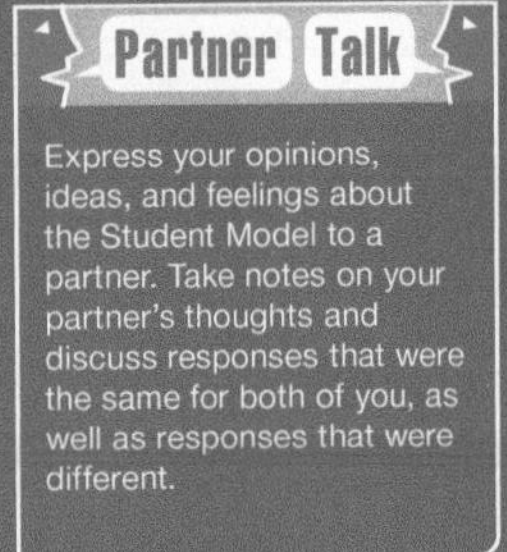

Partner Talk
Express your opinions, ideas, and feelings about the Student Model to a partner. Take notes on your partner's thoughts and discuss responses that were the same for both of you, as well as responses that were different.

Gary Soto's "Seventh Grade": Something We Can All Relate To

by Stephanie Chang

Have you ever liked someone so much that you tried too hard to get that person's attention? I have, and I bet you have, too. That's exactly what happens in Gary Soto's short story "Seventh Grade." You'll laugh as you read about the things Victor does to get a girl named Teresa to notice him. This story is about what happens when you pretend to be something you are not. The characters in this story sound like people you know.

The story takes place on the first day of seventh grade. Victor and his friend Michael are thinking about silly ways, such as making faces, to get girls' attention. Victor has a major crush on Teresa and wants to get her attention.

Victor is like other kids our age. He is not sure how to act or what to say. When Teresa first greets him, saying, "Hi, Victor," his cheeks turn red as he says, "Yeah, that's me." He's embarrassed that he said something so silly and gets frustrated. He wonders why he couldn't just say "something nice." This has happened to me too.

Later that day, in French class, the teacher asks if anyone knows French. Victor sees a chance to show off in front of the girl of his dreams. He raises his hand, even though he doesn't know French. Unfortunately for him, the teacher asks him a

1

2 

First, students respond to the Student Model as a reader, using symbols to mark the text. They can mark the text using pop-up sticky notes in **Writing Coach Online**™ or they can mark a printed copy of the Student Model.

3

Then, students respond to the Student Model as a writer, using different symbols to mark the text. They can use either **Writing Coach Online**™ or a printed copy of the Student Model.

question in French. The author helps the reader imagine Victor's reaction when he writes: "Great rosebushes of red bloomed on Victor's cheeks."

Victor is lucky that Teresa doesn't know French, so he ends up impressing her. The reader knows Victor is thrilled because the "rosebushes" of shame on his cheeks become "bouquets of love"! His cheeks are still red but for another reason.

We've all been embarrassed at one time or another, and the author does a great job of showing how that happens. Not all of our embarrassments end on a happy note, but the happy ending of "Seventh Grade" makes you smile. At the same time, you'll clearly see the author's point: you can save yourself a lot of worry and embarrassment if you just be yourself. You'll enjoy this story because it's easy to understand how the characters feel.

2

www.phwritingcoach.com

Interactive Model

Listen to an audio recording of the Student Model in the eText. Use the Reader's and Writer's Response Symbols with the eText tools to note what you read.

Use a Writer's Eye

Now, evaluate the piece as a writer. On your copy of the Student Model, use the Writer's Response Symbols to react to what you read. Identify places where the student writer uses characteristics of an effective review of a short story.

Writer's Response Symbols	
C.T.	Clearly stated thesis
I.A.	In-depth analysis
S.E.	Effective supporting evidence
E.Q.	Effective quotations

Personalized Support

FEEDBACK

Teacher or Peer Feedback

To provide feedback to students on their responses to the Student Model, ask or have student partners ask one another the following:

- What is the thesis or controlling idea of the Student Model?
- How does the Student Model illustrate the characteristics of a review?
- Which feature or characteristic of the Student Model might you use in your own piece of writing?
- How could you alter or adapt this feature to make it your own?

Working with ELLs

ELL Sheltered Instruction: Cognitive

Have students use and reuse new basic language in speaking activities and expand and internalize initial English vocabulary by retelling basic information supported by pictures. Preteach basic vocabulary words from the Student Model, like *students, school, friend, age,* and *teacher.* Help them read the Student Model. Then:

Beginning Help students use the basic vocabulary to orally complete sentence frames about the photograph, such as *It shows* _____ *and* _____. Then, have them reuse the words to retell information from the first paragraph of the Student Model.

Intermediate Have small groups use the basic vocabulary to discuss the photograph, then reuse it to retell information from the first paragraph of the Student Model.

Advanced Have partners use basic vocabulary to retell what "Seventh Grade" is about, using the picture for support. Have them reuse the vocabulary to describe the relationship between the picture and the story.

Advanced High Have students complete the Advanced activity. Then, have students share their retelling with the class.

The Digital • Print Path

1 

Students select or are assigned a topic for their short story review from the Topic Bank, or they may choose a topic of their own.

2 

Students complete online or printed graphic organizers to narrow the topic for their short story review.

Prewriting

Explain that the first task students need to complete as they plan their review of a short story is to determine an appropriate topic.

Choose From the Topic Bank

Read aloud each topic and then ask volunteers to describe them in their own words. If you are assigning topics to students, you may wish to do so now. Encourage students to ask questions about their topic.

Choose Your Own Topic

Introduce and discuss the Thought and Discussion strategies. If students were not assigned writing topics, have them use the strategies to brainstorm for topics for their essays.

Extension Have each student choose one of the strategies. Then, have them write an action plan that outlines the resources and steps they will use to develop their topic.

Narrow Your Topic

Tell students that they will use a Narrow Your Topic graphic organizer to reduce their topic to a manageable size. Then, distribute printed copies or have students log on to Writing Coach Online.

Apply It! Guide students through the instructions for completing the graphic organizer. Have students complete the exercise based on their topic.

Consider Your Audience and Purpose

Guide students to consider the audience and purpose for their review.

Say: I see that the second question in the first column asks what my audience needs to know to understand my opinions. This question reminds me to use quotations and other evidence from the text to support my interpretation. I might also have to provide some information about the author and his or her other works.

Ask: What information might the audience need to know about the author of your selected work? (name, birth date, accomplishments)

Have students with similar topics work in small groups to discuss and respond to the remaining questions.

Your Turn Feature Assignment: Review of a Short Story

Prewriting

Plan a first draft of your review of a short story **by determining an appropriate topic.** You can select from the Topic Bank or come up with an idea of your own.

Choose From the Topic Bank

Response to Amy Tan's "Two Kinds" Choose one of the memorable characters in "Two Kinds" by Amy Tan. Write a review of the story in which you discuss the traits that make this character stand out.

Response to Plot Think about a story you've read that you enjoyed reading. Write a review of the story in which you summarize the plot and explain why you enjoyed the story.

Response to a Mentor Text Read the excerpt from *The Pigman & Me* by Paul Zindel on page 68. Write a review of the story in which you summarize the conflict between the two characters and discuss the characters' responses.

Choose Your Own Topic

Determine an appropriate topic on your own by using the following **range of strategies** to generate ideas.

Thought and Discussion

- Discuss a favorite story with friends. Take notes about their ideas and feelings. How are their reactions alike? How do they differ?
- Think about a story that surprised you in some way. Consider the reasons why you were surprised. Compare your reaction with that of another student.

Review your responses and choose a topic.

Coach's Corner

You may wish to model prewriting activities for students by brainstorming for your own writing topic. Use these prompts to model your thought process:

- **I am interested in** the writer O. Henry, so that could be my general topic.
- **I can narrow my topic by** focusing on his story "The Last Leaf."

Discuss the choices you make and solicit feedback from students.

3 

Students record their answers to questions about audience and purpose in their online journals or notebooks.

Narrow Your Topic

If you choose a topic that is too broad, your writing will not have a clear focus.

Apply It! Use a graphic organizer like the one shown to narrow your topic.

- Write your general topic in the first box, and narrow your topic as you move down the chart.
- Your last box should hold your narrowest or "smallest" topic, the new focus of your review of a short story.

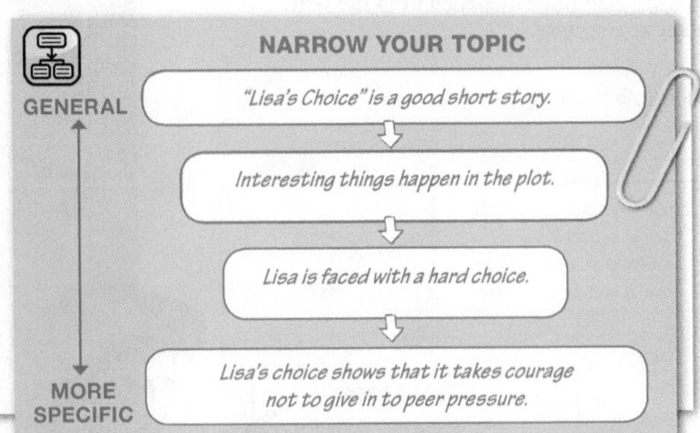

NARROW YOUR TOPIC
GENERAL
"Lisa's Choice" is a good short story.
Interesting things happen in the plot.
Lisa is faced with a hard choice.
Lisa's choice shows that it takes courage not to give in to peer pressure.
MORE SPECIFIC

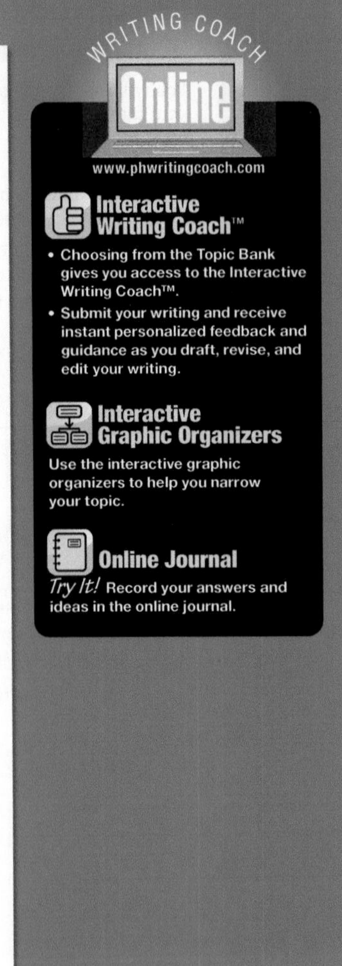

Consider Your Audience and Purpose

Before writing, think about your audience and purpose. Consider the views of others as you ask yourself these questions.

Questions for Audience	Questions for Purpose
• Who will read my review? My teacher? My classmates? • What will my audience need to know to understand my opinions? • Is my audience familiar with the selection I will discuss?	• What do I want my readers to know about the story? • What ideas and feelings do I want to convey in my review? • What approches should I use to show I understand the writer's audience and purpose?

Record your answers in your writing journal.

Personalized Support

Interactive Writing Coach™

Below Level Teachers select a topic from the topic bank for below-level students. Students submit their writing to the **Interactive Writing Coach™** for feedback paragraph by paragraph or as a complete draft. It is recommended that below-level students submit their writing one paragraph at a time.

On Level Students may select a topic from the Topic Bank. They may submit their writing for feedback paragraph by paragraph or as a complete draft.

Above Level Students may select from the Topic Bank or come up with their own topic. Above-level students should submit their writing as a complete draft.

Interactive Graphic Organizer

Below Level Students complete three graphic organizers that provide models and scaffolded support.

On Level Students complete one, two, or three graphic organizers, depending on how much support they need.

Above Level Students complete the least scaffolded graphic organizer or narrow their topic without the help of a graphic organizer.

Differentiated Instruction

RTI Strategy for Below-Level Students Students may find it helpful to talk to a partner about their chosen story. As each student talks, the other can make quick notes such as *good plot, lots of suspense,* and *interesting character.* The students may then use the notes to help organize their thoughts to fill in the Narrow Your Topic organizer on page 205.

PRE-AP Enrichment for Above-Level Students Encourage students to do a deeper analysis of their chosen short stories by thinking about the literary elements in the story. Have them consider the setting of the story and how it affects both plot and character development in the story, for example. Ask them to think about the theme of their story and whether it relates to their own experience and understanding of life.

1 

Using Writing Coach Online™ or the student book, students read and discuss the model graphic organizer.

2 

STUDENT BOOK

Students complete online or printed graphic organizers to develop their ideas and gather details.

Plan Your Piece

Explain that writers use graphic organizers to develop their ideas and show relationships between different parts of the text. Then, point out the Develop Your Response graphic organizer on page 206. Tell students that they will use this organizer to outline their short story review. Then, distribute printed copies or have students log on to Writing Coach Online.

Introduce the graphic organizer by explaining that the top box contains the thesis of their review and the other boxes contain ideas and evidence that support the thesis.

Develop Your Thesis Guide students to notice that the thesis in the example organizer is based on the narrowed topic from page 205. Have them write a thesis statement that clearly states their position and record it in the top square of the graphic organizer.

Logically Organize Your Supporting Evidence Have students identify and read aloud the three ideas listed on the example organizer. Explain that each idea is related to the thesis and that ideas will help them organize their supporting evidence. Then, have students brainstorm for ideas related to their thesis and record them on their graphic organizer.

Gather Details

Remind students that interpretative responses must be supported by details, or evidence. Ask volunteers to read aloud each detail and example. Then, guide students to place the details in the example organizer.

Say: I know that each idea in an interpretative response must be supported by evidence. The details on page 207 provide some of this information. For example, the Quotation example—"I have to do what's right"—supports the third idea, that Lisa decides to speak out despite peer pressure. I'll write that detail in the correct box.

Ask: What detail supports the idea that all the other students keep silent about what they saw? (Detail: "The classroom was suddenly as silent as a graveyard, and the teacher's eyes followed Lisa like a spotlight.")

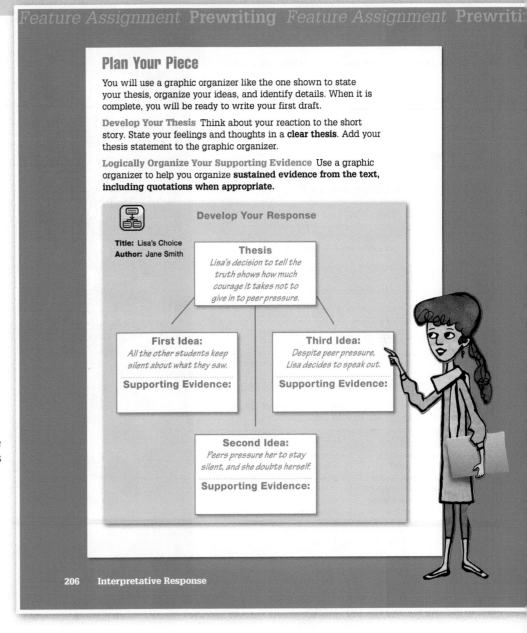

Feature Assignment **Prewriting** *Feature Assignment* **Prewriti**

Plan Your Piece

You will use a graphic organizer like the one shown to state your thesis, organize your ideas, and identify details. When it is complete, you will be ready to write your first draft.

Develop Your Thesis Think about your reaction to the short story. State your feelings and thoughts in a **clear thesis**. Add your thesis statement to the graphic organizer.

Logically Organize Your Supporting Evidence Use a graphic organizer to help you organize **sustained evidence from the text, including quotations when appropriate.**

Develop Your Response

Title: Lisa's Choice
Author: Jane Smith

Thesis
Lisa's decision to tell the truth shows how much courage it takes not to give in to peer pressure.

First Idea:
All the other students keep silent about what they saw.
Supporting Evidence:

Third Idea:
Despite peer pressure, Lisa decides to speak out.
Supporting Evidence:

Second Idea:
Peers pressure her to stay silent, and she doubts herself.
Supporting Evidence:

206 Interpretative Response

Have students work in small groups to place the remaining details on the graphic organizer.

Try It! Help students to see how the quotation from the story supports the writer's statement about how Victor feels.

Apply It! Read aloud the bulleted instructions for gathering details. Then, have students develop relevant details to support their interpretation and enter them on their graphic organizers. Remind students to use a variety of details to support their ideas.

Writer's Block

IF students have difficulty finding supporting evidence ...

THEN have them identify a section of their story that they most enjoyed and look there for a quotation that relates to their thesis.

Students refer back to the Mentor Text or the Student Model as they plan their writing.

Gather Details

To support their ideas, writers **provide sustained evidence** from the text such as the types of details in these examples:

- **Quotations:** *"I have to do what's right," Lisa said.*
- **Details:** *The classroom was suddenly as silent as a graveyard, and the teacher's eyes followed Lisa like a spotlight.*
- **Examples:** *Jason tried to make a joke, but the other kids were too frightened to laugh.*
- **Relevant Information and Judgments:** *Lisa wasn't trying to be a hero. She didn't even like the accused girl.*
- **Personal Insights:** *The situation described could happen to anyone, in school or out of school.*

Try It! Read the Student Model excerpt and identify the evidence that the author uses to support her ideas.

from **Gary Soto's "Seventh Grade": Something We Can All Relate To**
page 203; lines 27–34

The author helps the reader imagine Victor's reaction when he writes: "Great rosebushes of red bloomed on Victor's cheeks."

Victor is lucky that Teresa doesn't know French, so he ends up impressing her. The reader knows Victor is thrilled because the "rosebushes" of shame on his cheeks become "bouquets of love"! His cheeks are still red but for another reason.

Apply It! Review the types of supporting evidence that can be used in a review of a short story. Then identify and write one piece of relevant evidence of each type.

- Review your evidence to make sure it supports your ideas. Be sure to include one or more pieces of each kind of sustained evidence from the text.
- Add your ideas and supporting evidence to your graphic organizer. Remember that your goal is to write a review that is logically organized with appropriate details.
- Be sure to make clear how your evidence supports your thesis.

Interactive Graphic Organizers
Use the interactive graphic organizers to help you create a plan for your writing.

Interactive Model
Refer back to the Interactive Model in the eText as you plan your writing.

Personalized Support

Interactive Graphic Organizer

Below Level Students complete three graphic organizers that provide models and scaffolded support.

On Level Students complete one, two, or three graphic organizers, depending on how much support they need.

Above Level Students complete the least scaffolded graphic organizer or narrow their topic without the help of a graphic organizer.

Teacher or Peer Feedback

To provide feedback to students as they plan their first draft, ask or have student partners ask one another the following:

- What do you want your audience to know about the topic?
- What questions or concerns will your audience have about the topic?
- What details have you identified for your piece? How do these details support your thesis or controlling idea?
- Are your details varied? Will they interest your readers? Explain.

Differentiated Instruction

RTI Strategy for Special Needs Students

Help students grasp the idea of supporting evidence by asking questions, such as *What is your story's main character like? What does the character say? What does he or she do? What is the problem the main character faces? How do you know?* Point out to students that these questions lead them to develop ideas about their story based on specific information found in the text.

RTI Strategy for Below-Level Students

To help students develop their thesis statements, suggest that they try to tell a partner in a sentence or two what the story is about, without telling the plot. Explain that what the story is "about" is the same thing as the most important idea in the story and is probably one of the main reasons they like the story. Have them then develop their thesis statement.

The Digital • Print Path

1 Using Writing Coach Online™ or the student book, students read and discuss the Outline for Success for an interpretative response.

2 Students discuss how the Mentor Text illustrates the characteristics of an interpretative response.

Drafting

Outline for Success

Explain that the Outline for Success shows an organizational strategy for an interpretative response. Students will use the Outline to write a focused, organized, and coherent draft of their review of a short story.

I. Introduction

Link the Outline to a specific review of a short story by having students turn to the Mentor Text on pages 200–201. Ask a volunteer to read aloud the first paragraph. Then, guide students to identify and understand the characteristics of a strong introduction.

Say: I notice that the author begins the review with her thesis statement: "Sandra Cisneros...was born into the traditions, histories, and languages of two countries: the United States and Mexico." This statement tells me the main ideas that I should look for in the rest of the review.

Ask: What details does the author use to support the ideas in her first paragraph?
(lines 4–7: Cisneros had a Mexican father and Mexican-American mother; the family spoke two languages; the family often traveled to Mexico.)

Have students work with a partner to evaluate the details they entered next to Beginning on their graphic organizers.

Drafting *Feature Assignment* Drafting *Feature Assignment* D

Drafting

During the drafting stage, you will start to write your ideas for your review of a short story. You will follow an outline that provides an organizational strategy that will help you build on ideas to write a focused, organized, and coherent review of a short story.

The Organization of an Interpretative Response

The chart shows an organizational strategy for an interpretative response. Look back at how the Mentor Text follows this organizational strategy. Then, use this chart to help you outline your draft.

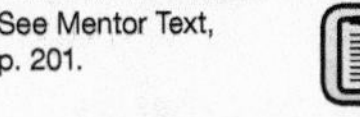

I. Introduction See Mentor Text, p. 200.

- Strong opening paragraph
- Name of the work and the author
- Clear thesis statement

Grab Your Reader
- An interesting opening can make a strong statement, ask a question, or refer to a character or event in the author's work.
- Both the work about which you are writing and its author should be identified.
- The thesis statement focuses on your overall ideas about the text. The rest of your response will support your thesis.

II. Body See Mentor Text, pp. 200–201.

- Introduction to and summary of the work
- Evidence from the text
- Analysis of elements
- Personal insights

Develop Your Ideas
- The important features of the work should be briefly summarized.
- Evidence from the text, including quotations and other examples, should support your ideas about the text.
- An analysis of story elements includes your thoughts of character, plot, setting, and theme.
- Your ideas and arguments should show your personal insights and judgments.

III. Conclusion See Mentor Text, p. 201.

- Restatement of thesis in concluding paragraph
- Explanation of the significance of main points

Wrap It Up
- Briefly restating your thesis in slightly different wording reinforces your point.
- An explanation of the significance of your thesis or main points will leave readers with a clear understanding of your ideas and feelings.

208 Interpretative Response

II. Body

Lead a discussion about how the middle paragraphs of the Mentor Text reflect the characteristics of an interpretative response.

- Introduction to and summary of the work (lines 11–14)
- Evidence from the text (lines 26, 29–30, 36–50)
- Analysis of elements (lines 11–17, 23–28, 35–50)
- Personal insights (lines 23–26, 31–34)

III. Conclusion

Have small groups discuss how the Mentor Text reflects the characteristics of an interpretative response (lines 51–54).

Start Your Draft

Have small groups read aloud and discuss the boxed instructions for drafting. Direct students to work individually on their first draft.

Coach's Corner

If you are modeling the writing process for students with your own topic or a student volunteer's, you may wish to use these prompts to guide your drafting and discussion:

- **To capture readers' attention, my introduction will** ask an interesting question.
- **I will organize my body paragraphs by** showing how the characters answer that question.

Discuss the choices you make and solicit feedback from students.

3 Students begin writing their short story review online or in their notebooks.

4 Students submit paragraphs or complete drafts to the **Interactive Writing Coach™** for scoring and feedback, or share their work with their teacher.

5 Students receive customized feedback from the **Interactive Writing Coach™** or feedback from their teacher. Students may continue to work on their drafts.

Start Your Draft

Use this checklist to help you complete your draft. Use the graphic organizer that shows your thesis and supporting evidence, and the Outline for Success as guides.

While drafting, aim at writing your ideas, not on making your writing perfect. Remember, you will have the chance to improve your draft when you revise and edit.

- √ Start with a strong **opening** that will grab your reader's interest.
- √ Your **introduction** should **identify** the story, poem, or other work about which you're writing, as well as the author of the work.
- √ Present your thesis statement.

- √ The **body** of your review should demonstrate the writing skills for multi-paragraph essays by presenting your **ideas and opinions** in a logical way.
- √ Be sure to also include a brief summary of key features of the work.
- √ Your ideas and opinions should show your understanding of the text and be supported with **sustained evidence** from the text, including quotations.
- √ Include an **analysis** of story elements that relate to your ideas, such as themes or specific plot events.

- √ In your **conclusion**, restate or paraphrase your **thesis.**
- √ End with a strong **final statement** that clearly expresses your thoughts and feelings about the work.

www.phwritingcoach.com

Interactive Model

Outline for Success View pop-ups of Mentor Text referenced in the Outline for Success.

Interactive Writing Coach™

Use the Interactive Writing Coach to receive the level of support you need:

- Write one paragraph at a time and submit each one for immediate, detailed feedback.
- Write your entire first draft and submit it for immediate, personalized feedback.

Personalized Support

Interactive Writing Coach™

Below Level Students complete the drafting process in small steps by submitting each paragraph for scoring and feedback.

On Level Depending on the support they need, students submit their writing paragraph by paragraph or as a complete draft for scoring and feedback.

Above Level Students may write their drafts on their own but have the option of submitting them for scoring and/or feedback.

Teacher or Peer Feedback

To provide feedback to students on their first draft, ask or have student partners ask one another the following:

- Can you explain how you organized your ideas in this piece?
- Why did you include this information here?
- Why did you choose this introduction? Does it grab your reader and identify your thesis or controlling idea?
- What supporting details could you add here?
- Why did you choose this conclusion? How does it add to your piece?
- Can you show me a place where I can hear your unique voice?
- Can you show me a place where you used vivid language?

Working with ELLs — ELL Sheltered Instruction: Cognitive

Teach content-based grade-level academic words from Start Your Draft, including *evidence, thesis,* and *conclusion.* Help students internalize this new academic language by using and reusing it in writing activities.

Beginning On the board, write a short definition of *thesis* and read it aloud. Have students use and reuse the word in writing activities by completing sentence frames, like *A thesis is* _____.

Intermediate Provide pairs with a copy of the Mentor Text and discuss the vocabulary. Have them use and reuse the terms by labeling examples in their copy and writing two sentences using the terms.

Advanced Have students use the **KIM Strategy** to internalize the academic vocabulary. In a three-column chart, they should write *Key Word, Information*, and *Memory Cue* and write the word, a definition, and an example or illustration. Have them use and reuse the words in context sentences.

Advanced High Have students use and reuse the academic vocabulary in written comments about a partner's draft, like *The thesis is stated in the first paragraph.*

1 

Using Writing Coach Online™ or the student book, students study the first and second drafts of the Student Model to see how the writer used Revision RADaR to improve his or her writing.

2 

Students use the Revision RADaR strategy to revise their own writing.

Revising: Making It Better

Point out the page title to students and explain that revising means making improvements to a writing draft. Then, read aloud the opening paragraph to introduce the Revision RADaR strategies. You may wish to have students review Chapter 3 for more information on Revision RADaR.

Kelly Gallagher, M. Ed.

KEEP REVISION ON YOUR RADAR

1ST DRAFT After students have read the first draft, have them turn to page 208 and review the Outline for Success. Work with students to understand that the questions the author asked about her draft are based on the characteristics of a review of a short story. For example, call out the first question and note how it addresses using evidence from the text in the Outline for Success.

Then, have students work in small groups to develop other questions about the draft based on the genre characteristics.

Revising Feature Assignment Revising Feature Assignment R

Revising: Making It Better

Now that you have finished your first draft, you are ready to revise. Think about the "big picture" of audience, purpose, and genre. You can use the Revision RADaR strategy as a guide for making changes to improve your draft. Revision RADaR provides four ways to improve your writing: (R) replace, (A) add, (D) delete, and (R) reorder.

Kelly Gallagher, M. Ed.

KEEP REVISION ON YOUR RADAR

Read part of the first draft of the Student Model, "Gary Soto's 'Seventh Grade': Something We Can All Relate To." Then look at the questions the writer asked herself as she thought about how well her draft **addressed issues of audience, purpose, and genre.**

Gary Soto's "Seventh Grade": Something We Can All Relate To

1ST DRAFT

Victor is not sure how to act or what to say. When Teresa first greets him, he says something silly. He's embarrassed that he said it and gets frustrated. He wonders why he couldn't just say "something nice."

Have I used supporting details, including quotations from the text? Do my ideas demonstrate insights and understanding of the text?

In French class, the teacher asks if anyone knows French. Victor sees a chance to show off in front of the girl of his dreams. He raises his hand, even though he doesn't know French. Unfortunately for him, the teacher asks him a question in French.

Have I included transitions to link paragraphs?

The author shows Victor's embarrassment in this moment by using great imagery. Victor does his best to bluff his way out of the situation, but he fears he has made a fool of himself in front of Teresa. Victor is thrilled. Luckily, Teresa doesn't know French, so she actually *is* impressed.

Have I used supporting details, such as examples from the text? Are my ideas presented in a logical order?

Guide students to understand how the author used the RADaR strategies to revise the first draft.

Think Aloud: In the first paragraph of the 1st draft, **I noticed** that the writer tells me that Victor "says something silly," but she doesn't support that statement with evidence from the story. On the 2nd draft, I see an *A* next to that sentence. The writer has added a quotation that provides strong evidence for her understanding.

Work with students to brainstorm for other ways to revise the introduction.

Have students work in groups to discuss the other changes in the 2nd draft.

Apply It! Review the bulleted instructions for using Revision RADaR. Remind students to question their drafts based on the essay characteristics listed on the Outline for Success on page 208. Tell students to use each RADaR strategy at least once.

Coach's Corner

If you are modeling the writing process for students with your own draft or a student volunteer's, use these prompts to focus on the Revision RADaR *Add* strategy:

- **I added information to my thesis because** I wanted to clearly state my interpretation.
- **I added a quotation from the story here because** I wanted to provide evidence for my ideas.

Discuss the choices you make and solicit feedback from students.

3 

Students submit paragraphs or revised drafts to the **Interactive Writing Coach™** for scoring and feedback, or share their work with their teacher.

4 

Students receive customized feedback from the **Interactive Writing Coach™** or feedback from their teacher. Students may continue to revise their drafts.

Now look at how the writer applied Revision RADaR to write an improved second draft.

Gary Soto's "Seventh Grade": Something We Can All Relate To

2ND DRAFT

Like most people our age, though, Victor is not sure how to act or what to say. When Teresa first greets him, saying, "Hi, Victor," he blushes and says, "Yeah, that's me." He's embarrassed that he said something so silly and gets frustrated. He wonders why he couldn't just say "something nice." I know that this has happened to me and my friends many times!

A Added information to show my understanding of the text

R Replaced vague language with quotations from the text

Later that day, in French class, the teacher asks if anyone knows French. Victor sees a chance to impress the girl of his dreams. He raises his hand, even though he doesn't know French. Unfortunately for him, the teacher asks him a question in French.

A Added a transition to show that time has gone by and to link the ideas in the two paragraphs

The author helps the reader imagine Victor's reaction when he writes: "Great rosebushes of red bloomed on Victor's cheeks."

R Reordered sentences to present information more clearly

Victor is lucky that Teresa doesn't know French, so he ends up impressing her. The reader knows Victor is thrilled because the "rosebushes" of shame on his cheeks become "bouquets of love"! His cheeks are still red but for another reason.

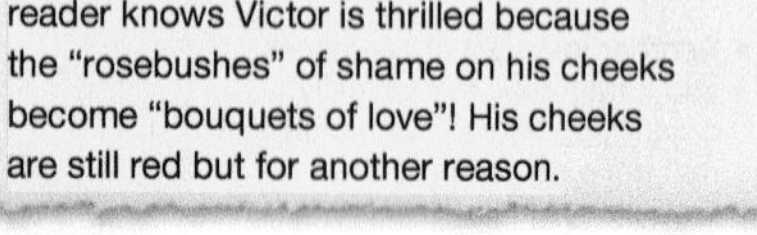

WRITING COACH Online

www.phwritingcoach.com

Interactive Writing Coach™

Use the Revision RADaR strategy in your own writing. Then submit your paragraph or draft for feedback.

Apply It! Use your Revision RADaR to revise your draft.

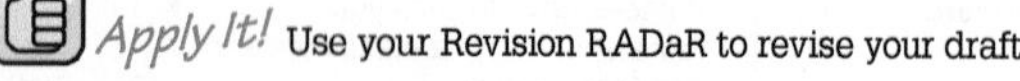

- First, ask yourself: Have I addressed the needs of my audience, made clear my purpose for writing, and included the characteristics of the interpretative response genre?
- Then, apply the Revision RADaR strategy to make needed changes. Remember—you can use the strategy steps in any order.

Personalized Support

Interactive Writing Coach™

Below Level Students revise their drafts using the Revision RADaR strategy and submit their writing for scoring and feedback.

On Level Students revise their drafts using the Revision RADaR strategy and submit their writing for scoring and feedback.

Above Level Students may use the Revision RADaR strategy or revise their drafts on their own. They have the option of submitting their revised drafts for scoring and/or feedback.

Teacher or Peer Feedback

To provide feedback to students as they revise their first draft, ask or have student partners ask one another the following:

- Can you show me where you revised your text?
- What could you add to your introduction to grab the interest of your readers?
- How could you reorder these ideas so that their order is more logical?
- Have you included all the characteristics of this form of writing?
- Is there any unnecessary text that you could delete?
- Have you achieved your purpose with this piece of writing?
- Have you addressed the questions and concerns of your audience?

Working with ELLs ELL Sheltered Instruction: Cognitive

Help students demonstrate comprehension and expand reading skills by employing inferential skills such as drawing inferences from text and finding supporting text evidence. Review the draft on page 211.

Beginning Choral read the first paragraph. Model drawing an inference based on supporting evidence in the text by saying, *The phrase* he blushes *tells me Victor is embarrassed*. Then, draw an inference about the writer's opinion of the story *(She likes it)* and help students identify text evidence *("great imagery")*.

Intermediate Have small groups discuss the draft and then respond to inferential questions such as *Does the writer relate to the boy in the story?* Students should use text evidence as support.

Advanced Have partners review the draft and discuss how the writer feels about the boy in the story, supporting ideas with text evidence. Have them draw other inferences from the text and share with the class.

Advanced High Have students complete the Advanced activity and write a paragraph explaining their inferences and evidence.

1 

Using **Writing Coach Online**™ or the student book, students study and discuss the revision chart.

2 

In a video by program author Kelly Gallagher, students learn more strategies for effective writing.

Revising: Making It Better

Look at the Big Picture

Introduce the revision chart to students. Explain that the Section column identifies the three main parts of a review of a short story. The Evaluate column identifies the characteristics found in each section and explains how to assess them. The Revise column presents specific strategies for revising each characteristic.

Then, have students draw lines between and label the three sections of their drafts. Direct students to work individually to evaluate and revise their draft, using the chart to guide their work.

Focus on Craft: Consistent Point of View

Have students read the introductory text. Guide them to understand how consistent point of view improves written work.

Say: I notice that the writer used the second-person pronoun *you* three times in this passage. The word *you* draws the readers into the text and makes them feel like they are personally involved with the story.

Ask: What other techniques could the writer of an interpretative response use to draw readers into the text? (Responses will vary.)

Have students rewrite the Student Model passage using first-person pronouns.

Try It! Have students discuss the questions and record responses in their journals. Follow up with students to check that their responses reflect an understanding of how point of view influences the effectiveness of an interpretative response.

Revising *Feature Assignment* Revising *Feature Assignment*

Look at the Big Picture

Use the chart and your analytical skills to evaluate how well each section of your review of a short story addresses **purpose, audience, and genre.** When necessary, use the suggestions in the chart to revise your piece.

Section	Evaluate	Revise
Introduction	• Check the **opening.** It should grab readers' interest and make them want to read on.	• Make your opening more interesting by writing a strong first sentence or asking a rhetorical question.
	• Make sure the **thesis** clearly expresses the main idea of your response.	• Does your thesis reflect your thoughts about the story and the controlling idea of your review? If not, rewrite it so that it does.
Body	• Make sure that you have included **sustained evidence** from the text to defend and support ideas.	• Add more supporting evidence as needed. Look for key quotations that support your ideas.
	• Check that you've included ideas and arguments that show personal insights, judgments, and **understanding** of the text.	• Think about the meaning of the story. Add sentences that convey your understanding to readers, if necessary.
	• Make sure you have included an **analysis** of story elements, such as character, plot, setting, and theme.	• Add specific information about story elements to develop and support your main ideas.
	• Check that you have **logically organized** your ideas and supporting evidence. Make sure that you have not included any unnecessary information.	• Reorder text so that sentences and paragraphs are logically organized. Delete information that does not relate to the controlling idea.
Conclusion	• Check the **restatement** of your thesis.	• If necessary, discuss your restatement with a classmate and ask for suggestions.
	• Check that your **conclusion** leaves readers with a clear understanding of your thoughts.	• Add a final statement that sums up how you feel about the work or why it is meaningful to you.

Fine-Tune Your Draft

Apply It! Ask volunteers to read aloud the instructions for fine-tuning their drafts. Then, have students work in pairs to improve the point of view in their drafts.

Peer Feedback Have students identify Mentor Text examples of the characteristics that were marked for improvement. Use the Mentor Text references on page T208 to guide students to appropriate examples.

Teacher Tip

Have students work with a partner to practice using different points of view. Guide students to tell their thesis statements to their partner three times, using a different point of view each time. Ask students to discuss the strengths and weaknesses of each point of view.

3 Using Writing Coach Online™ or the student book, students refer back to the Mentor Text or Student Model for examples of writer's craft.

4 Students record answers to questions about writer's craft in their online journals or notebooks.

5 Students submit revised drafts to the Interactive Writing Coach™ for scoring and feedback, or share their work with their teacher.

6 Students receive customized feedback from the Interactive Writing Coach™ or feedback from their teacher.

Focus on Craft: Consistent Point of View

Your audience will be confused if you don't have a **consistent point of view** in your review of a short story. Many reviews are written in the first-person point of view, using words such as *I* and *we*. Other reviews are written in the second-person point of view, using *you* and *your*, or in third-person point of view, using *he*, *she*, and *it*.

Think about point of view as you read the following example from the Student Model.

from **Gary Soto's "Seventh Grade": Something We Can All Relate To**
page 202; lines 5–8

You'll laugh as you read about the things Victor does to get a girl named Teresa to notice him. This story is about what happens when you pretend to be something you are not.

Try It! Now, ask yourself these questions:

- What point of view does the author of the Student Model use? Why might that be a good choice for a review of a short story?
- Why might a change in point of view confuse the reader?

Fine-Tune Your Draft

Apply It! Use the revision suggestions to prepare your final draft **after rethinking how well questions of purpose, audience, and genre have been addressed.**

- **Use Consistent Point of View** Avoid changing point of view within paragraphs or from one paragraph to the next.
- **Improve Sentence Structure** Break or combine sentences to achieve a variety of sentence structures such as simple, compound, and complex.

Peer Feedback Show your final draft to a group of your peers and ask if your evidence supports your main idea. Listen carefully to their ideas and make revisions as needed.

Video
Learn more strategies for effective writing from program author Kelly Gallagher.

Online Journal
Try It! Record your answers in the online journal.

Interactive Model
Refer back to the Interactive Model as you revise your writing.

Interactive Writing Coach™
Revise your draft and submit it for feedback.

Personalized Support

Interactive Writing Coach™

Below Level Students complete the revising process by submitting their writing for scoring and feedback.

On Level Students complete the revising process by submitting their writing for scoring and feedback.

Above Level Students finish revising their drafts. They have the option of submitting their revised drafts for scoring and/or feedback.

Teacher or Peer Feedback

To provide feedback to students as they continue to revise their first draft, ask or have student partners ask one another the following:

- What are you trying to say here? What part of the text could you replace to make your meaning clearer?
- Is there a more precise word you could use here?
- How does the rhythm of these sentences sound to you? Could you make the length and structure of these sentences more varied?
- How could you include transitional words and phrases here to help your reader understand these ideas?
- Are there details you could add here to make this part come alive?

Differentiated Instruction

RTI Strategy for Below-Level Students
If students need to revise simple retellings in order to include analysis, ask them some of these questions: *What does the character's action tell you about the character? How does that action make you feel? How would the story be different if the character made a different choice here?*

Enrichment for Gifted/Talented Students Challenge students to deepen their reviews by referencing other works that relate to their short story in some way. For example, they might refer to other stories by the same author, stories in the same genre, or stories with similar themes, settings, or plotlines. Have them comment on the strength or weakness of their story by referencing how these other stories use the same elements.

1 

In a video by program author Jeff Anderson, students learn effective editing techniques.

2 

Students record answers to questions about writer's craft in their online journals or notebooks.

Editing: Making It Right

Discuss the opening paragraph with students. Explain that they will edit their drafts for correct subject-verb agreement and consistent verb tenses.

WRITE GUY *Jeff Anderson, M.Ed.*

WHAT DO YOU NOTICE?

Introduce students to subject-verb agreement by reading aloud the Student Model excerpt and discussing responses to the "Ask yourself" question. Then, guide students to identify prepositional phrases and make subjects and verbs agree.

When I need to identify the subject of a sentence, first **I look for** any prepositional phrases. In the Student Model, I underline the prepositions *of* and *on* and then circle their objects, *shame* and *cheeks.* Because those words are part of prepositional phrases, I know that neither word can be the subject of the sentence. I know that *rosebushes* is the subject.

Work with students to identify first the prepositional phrases and then the simple subjects in sentences such as these: *The jacket with the big buttons (is, are) mine. The books on the shelf by the door (is, are) new.*

Have students work with a partner to write two sentences with prepositional phrases in the subjects. Ask pairs to exchange sentences and check one another's subject-verb agreement.

Editing *Feature Assignment* Editing *Feature Assignment*

Editing: Making It Correct

Use the editing process to polish your work and correct errors. It is often helpful to work with a partner when editing your drafts.

Before editing, think about how **prepositions and prepositional phrases** may **influence subject-verb agreement.** Also think about the importance of using **consistent tenses** so that readers can follow the order, or sequence, of events. Then, edit your draft by correcting factual errors and errors in **grammar, mechanics, and spelling.** Use a dictionary to check your spelling.

WHAT DO YOU NOTICE?

Zoom in on Conventions Focus on subject-verb agreement as you zoom in on this sentence from the Student Model.

STUDENT MODEL from **Gary Soto's "Seventh Grade": Something We Can All Relate To** page 203; lines 32–33

The "rosebushes" of shame on his cheeks become "bouquets of love"!

Now, ask yourself: *What role does the word "rosebushes" play in the sentence?*

Perhaps you said that "rosebushes" is the subject of the sentence. The verb is *become.* Two prepositional phrases separate the subject and verb: *of shame* and *on his cheeks.*

A prepositional phrase is a group of words that begins with a preposition and contains a noun or pronoun that is the object of the preposition. Subjects and verbs must agree even when they are separated by prepositional phrases, as in the Student Model.

The subject of a sentence is never part of a prepositional phrase. So, neither *shame* nor *cheeks* can be the subject. The plural subject *rosebushes* agrees with the plural verb *become.* A singular subject agrees with a singular verb, for example: *The* rosebush *of shame on his cheek* becomes *"a bouquet of love"!*

Partner Talk Discuss this question with a partner: *How do perpositions and prepositional phrases affect subject-verb agreement?*

To learn more about subject-verb agreement, see Chapter 23 of your Grammar Handbook.

Grammar Mini-Lesson: Consistent Tenses

Discuss the paragraph and the Student Model excerpt on page 215 with students. Guide them to understand that by using present tense verbs in all three sentences, the writer keeps the tenses consistent.

Try It! Check student responses.

1. A box of candies sits on the table, and I know they are delicious.
2. After we watched the game, we drove into town and ate dinner.

Apply It! Remind students to look closely for correct subject-verb agreement and consistent verb tenses as they edit their drafts.

Use the Rubric Explain that students will rate how well their draft addresses the elements of a short story review on a scale of 1 to 6, with 6 being the best score.

Then, have students use the rubric to evaluate their drafts and revise as necessary.

Writer's Block

IF students have difficulty determining whether they used consistent verb tenses in their drafts . . .

THEN have them circle the verbs and write the words *present, past,* or *future* above them. Each verb tense in the sentence should be the same or the sentence may be incorrect.

3 

Using Writing Coach Online™ or the student book, students refer back to the Mentor Text or Student Model as they edit their writing.

4 

Using Writing Coach Online™ or the student book, students evaluate their writing using the rubrics.

5 

Students submit edited drafts to the Interactive Writing Coach™ for scoring and feedback, or share their work with their teacher.

6 

Students receive personalized feedback from the Interactive Writing Coach™ or feedback from their teacher.

Grammar Mini-Lesson: Consistent Tenses

To learn more, see page 284.

Tenses are verb forms that tell if an action takes place in the past, present, or future. It is important to **use tenses consistently** so readers can follow your writing. Sometimes, though, tenses must vary to show sequence, or the order of events. For example: *Last year, he* studied *Spanish, but this year he* studies *French.* Notice how the Student Model author uses present tense verbs consistently to help readers follow the order of events.

from **Gary Soto's "Seventh Grade": Something We Can All Relate To**
pages 202–203; lines 23–27

Victor sees a chance to show off in front of the girl of his dreams. He raises his hand, even though he doesn't know French. Unfortunately for him, the teacher asks him a question in French.

Try It! Complete each sentence using a consistent verb tense. Write the answers in your journal.

1. A box of candies (sat) on the table, and I (know) they are delicious.
2. After we watched the game, we (drive) into town and (eat) dinner.

Apply It! **Edit your draft for grammar, mechanics, and spelling.** Make sure you have used a **variety of complete sentences** that includes consistent tenses. Make sure that **prepositional phrases** do not interrupt **subject-verb agreement.**

Use the rubric to evaluate your piece. If necessary, rethink, rewrite, or revise.

Rubric for Interpretative Response: Review of a Short Story	Rating Scale
Ideas: How well does your response present a focused statement about the work?	Not very ... Very 1 2 3 4 5 6
Organization: How clearly organized is your analysis?	1 2 3 4 5 6
Voice: How well have you engaged the reader and sustained his or her interest?	1 2 3 4 5 6
Word Choice: How clearly do your words state your views?	1 2 3 4 5 6
Sentence Fluency: How well have you used a consistent point of view in your writing?	1 2 3 4 5 6
Conventions: How correct is your use of consistent verb tenses?	1 2 3 4 5 6

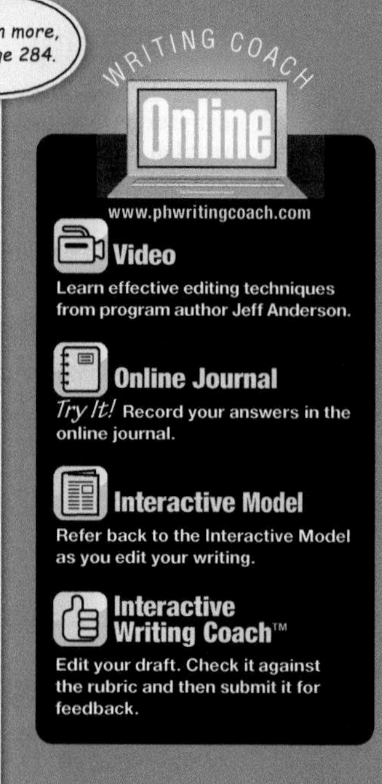

www.phwritingcoach.com

Video
Learn effective editing techniques from program author Jeff Anderson.

Online Journal
Try It! Record your answers in the online journal.

Interactive Model
Refer back to the Interactive Model as you edit your writing.

Interactive Writing Coach™
Edit your draft. Check it against the rubric and then submit it for feedback.

Personalized Support

Interactive Writing Coach™

Below Level Students complete the editing process by submitting their writing for scoring and feedback.

On Level Students complete the editing process by submitting their writing for scoring and feedback.

Above Level Students finish editing their drafts. They have the option of submitting their drafts for scoring and/or feedback.

Teacher or Peer Feedback

To provide feedback to students as they edit their draft, ask or have student partners ask one another the following:

- Can you show me something you changed through editing?
- Have you looked for spelling errors?
- Read this sentence aloud. Does the grammar sound correct to you?

Working with ELLs

ELL Sheltered Instruction: Metacognitive

As students edit in the *Apply It!* activity, help them monitor and edit writing for appropriate verb tense using self-corrective techniques. Review rules for verb tense by thinking aloud as you revise examples on the board. Then:

Beginning Read these sentences aloud as students copy them from the board: *Ana studied until 11. She took her test tomorrow*. As a self-corrective technique, have students underline the verbs and ask themselves *When?* of each *(before now, after now).* Help them see the shift in tenses, and write corrected sentences.

Intermediate Have students complete the Beginning activity and work in small groups to apply the self-corrective technique to more example sentences.

Advanced Have pairs of students work together to apply the self-corrective technique in the Beginning activity to their drafts, editing for appropriate verb tense.

Advanced High Have partners take turns using the self-corrective technique of reading their draft aloud to monitor for appropriate verb tense, editing as needed.

The Digital • Print Path

1 

Using Writing Coach Online™ or the student book, students complete the writing process by deciding the best way to publish their writing for their intended audience.

2 

Students record their answers and ideas to Extend Your Research in their online journals or notebooks.

Publishing

Wrap Up Your Presentation

Remind students who handwrote their work to use proper margins. For students who wrote their work on a computer, display some easy-to-read computer fonts. Make sure students know how to find them on a computer.

Publish Your Piece

Explain to students that the final step in the writing process is to decide which form of publication will present their work most effectively. Then, tell students that the chart shows how specific audiences can be reached using different kinds of media.

Have students whose reviews address similar audiences work in small groups to discuss appropriate ways to publish their work.

Extend Your Research

Extension Tell students that their thinking about their topic does not have to end with its final publication. Then, guide students through the instructions for extending their research.

Manage Your Portfolio Have students prepare a final version of their work for their portfolio. You may wish to have them include development materials such as graphic organizers and drafts.

Big Question Have students respond to the question in their journal.

Publishing *Feature Assignment* **Publishing** *Feature Assignme*

Publishing

Share the ideas expressed in your review—publish it! First, get your review ready for presentation. Then, choose a way to publish it for the appropriate audience.

Wrap Up Your Presentation

Now that you have finished your draft, add the final details. Include page numbers on each page of your final draft.

Publish Your Review

Use the chart to identify a way to publish your review.

If your audience is...	...then publish it by...
People in your community	• Submitting it to a local newspaper • Creating a multimedia presentation for kids at your local library
Students at school	• Reading it aloud in English class • Posting it online and inviting comments

Extend Your Research

Think more about the topic of the story on which you wrote your review. What else would you like to know about this topic?

- Brainstorm for several questions you would like to research and then consult, or discuss, with others. Then, decide which question is your major research question.
- Formulate, or develop, a plan about how you will answer the question. Decide where you will find more information—on the Internet, at the library, or through other sources.
- Finally, learn more about your topic by following through with your research plan.

The Big Question: Why Write? What should you write about to make others interested in a text?

Manage Your Portfolio You may wish to include your published review of a short story in your writing portfolio. If so, consider what this review reveals about your writing and your growth as a writer.

216 Interpretative Response

Resources You may wish to have students use these graphic organizers: Meeting Agenda, Meeting Notes, and Outline. Distribute printed copies or have students log on to Writing Coach Online.

MAKE YOUR WRITING COUNT

Introduce the advertisement activity by discussing the opening paragraphs with students. Make sure students understand that the project may be produced electronically or by hand. Then, guide students through each step in the action plan.

Use the 21st Century Skills Rubric to evaluate each group's process and final product on a scale of 1 to 3, indicating weak, moderate, or strong use of the skill.▶

Listening and Speaking Monitor students as they use feedback to refine their presentations.

21st Century Learning

Skills Rubric	Rating
Analyze Media: Look at how media can influence beliefs and behaviors.	1 2 3
Create Media Products: Use the most appropriate expressions in diverse environments.	1 2 3
Think Creatively: Elaborate, refine, analyze, and evaluate ideas in order to improve and maximize creative efforts.	1 2 3
Work Creatively With Others: Be original and inventive and understand limits to idea adoption.	1 2 3

3 STUDENT BOOK

Students use a variety of graphic organizers, either online or in print, to help them work together to create a multimedia group project.

4 STUDENT BOOK

Through Writing Coach Online™ students link to resources on 21st Century Learning for help in creating a multimedia group project.

21st Century Learning

MAKE YOUR WRITING COUNT

Build an Advertisement for a Story of Your Choice

Reviews tell readers whether a story is worth reading. An advertisement for a story encourages readers to want to read it. Catch the attention of potential readers by creating an **advertisement for a story**.

In a group, choose one story review to turn into a **multimedia presentation** of an advertisement. The text of your ad should include the story's title, author, selling points, reviewer comment, and an excerpt. The ad should also include graphics. Create your ad in print or by using available technology.

Here's your action plan.

1. Analyze book ads in newspapers, magazines, or online.
2. With your group, choose a story review to turn into an advertisement. Take notes to refer to as you create the ad.
3. Use catchy phrases, an excerpt, and an image in your ad.
   - Highlight the selling points of the story, including a comment from the review.
   - Choose a short excerpt from the story to attract potential readers.
   - Display the title and author of the story.
4. Create a "cover" for the story (or the book it appears in) to include in the ad.
5. Present your advertisement to the class. If possible, post it on the class Web site.

Listening and Speaking Rehearse the presentation of your advertisement. Although your ad is based on text and graphics, try to bring these elements to life by speaking and gesturing expressively. Listen actively during the presentations of other groups so that you can analyze their ads and give positive feedback.

WRITING COACH Online

www.phwritingcoach.com

Online Journal

Extend Your Research Record your answers and ideas in the online journal.

Resource

Link to resources on 21st Century Learning for help in creating a group project.

Personalized Support

FEEDBACK

Teacher or Peer Feedback

To provide feedback to students on their published writing, ask or have student partners ask one another the following:

- How did you go about writing this piece? What was your process?
- What did you learn from the writing model that you used in this piece?
- What surprised you the most as you wrote this piece?
- Did you try anything new as you worked on this piece?
- What did you learn from this piece of writing that you would like to remember and reuse?
- What do you think you do best as a writer right now?

Differentiated Instruction

RTI Strategy for Below-Level Students

Help students identify material from their reviews that could be adapted into an advertisement by asking the following questions: *Is there a product or invention that could help your story's main character solve his or her problem? Can you think of a service that the main character might be qualified to provide? Could you create a public service announcement based on the theme of the story?*

RTI Strategy for Special Needs Students

Review with students the purposes of advertisement: to sell products, to get people to change their minds about something, and to lead people to think about an idea in a certain way. Lead them in a discussion about memorable ads they have encountered. Have them describe what made the ads easy to remember. Encourage them to use ads they have seen as models for their ad.

The Digital • Print Path

1 

Students use Writing Coach Online™ or their student books to analyze and discuss the Writing for Media topic.

2 Writing Journal

Students learn about the characteristics of a movie review by answering questions about the model. Students record their answers to the *Try It!* questions in their online journals or notebooks.

Writing for Media: Movie Review

Movie Review

Discuss the opening paragraph with students. As a class, brainstorm for media that frequently publish or present movie reviews.

Try It! Guide students to understand the content and structure of the sample movie review.

Say: The first *Try It!* question asks what movie the review is about. **I see** that the answer is in the first sentence. The movie is titled *Door to Doom*. The second question is answered in the same sentence. The movie was made by Karl Johnson.

Ask: How do you know what kind of movie is being reviewed? (The first sentence says it is a sci-fi movie.)

Have students discuss the remaining questions in small groups and record individual responses in their journals.

Extension Have students bring in other examples of movie reviews. Lead a media discussion about the examples, using the *Try It!* questions as a guide.

Create a Movie Review

Tell students that they will create a movie review using the five-step writing process. Then, preview the writing process instructions on page 219.

> **Resources** You may wish to have students use the Outline graphic organizer. Distribute printed copies or have students log on to Writing Coach Online.

For each step in the writing process, have partners read aloud and discuss the list of tasks. Then, have them work individually. Once both partners have completed the tasks, have them evaluate each other's work before moving to the next step.

Writing for Media Writing for Media Writing for Media Writing

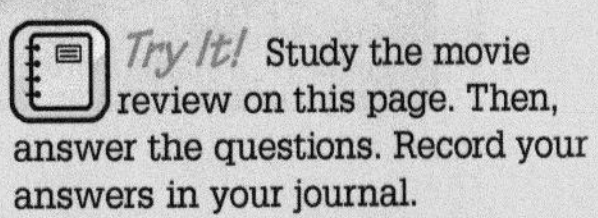

Writing for Media: Movie Review

21st Century Learning

Movie Review

A **movie review** is an article or essay that discusses a movie, analyzes its story elements, and summarizes important features of the work. Movie reviews appear in newspapers and magazines, on television and radio, and on the Internet. A movie review presents the writer's opinions and supports them with evidence and quotations from the film. Movie reviews may either persuade readers that a film is worthwhile or discourage them from seeing it.

Try It! Study the movie review on this page. Then, answer the questions. Record your answers in your journal.

- What **film** is this movie review about?
- Who made the **movie?**
- What **type** of movie is it?
- What does the **writer** think about the movie? Why does the writer feel this way?
- What **evidence** does the writer use to defend and support his or her ideas and judgment?
- What **story elements** does the writer analyze?
- Would this review **encourage** you to see the movie? Why or why not?

Extension Find another example of a movie review, and compare it with this one.

Karl Johnson's latest sci-fi movie, *Door to Doom*, is his most action-packed film yet. It's also his silliest. Nothing in this movie is believable. The characters are brainless, and the plot makes no sense.

The movie's 16-year-old hero, Dylan, spends the entire movie whining and trying to convince the police that a blue-skinned alien has invaded his neighborhood. He draws this conclusion when he sees a terrifying-looking alien chasing Dylan's neighbor's dog. Despite the missing dog, specks of a strange kind of goo on the ground, and the picture Dylan snaps with his cell phone, no one believes him. "But I saw it happen," he tells the police again and again. "We'll check it out," they always reply, but they don't.

One by one, pets in Dylan's neighborhood vanish. Then his neighbors themselves begin to disappear. Still, the police refuse to investigate. It never occurs to Dylan that he should talk to some other adults or maybe call the newspaper. Instead, he tells only his friend, Jimmy, who suggests that they catch the alien.

From this point on, the plot gets only more ridiculous. Dylan and Jimmy make a series of unsafe decisions and incredibly pointless attempts to catch the alien. Unless you have time and money to waste, the *Door to Doom* is best left unopened.

218 Interpretative Response

Use the 21st Century Skills Rubric to evaluate each student's process and final product on a scale of 1 to 3, indicating weak, moderate, or strong use of the skill. ▶

Partner Talk

Remind students to listen carefully and respond politely to their partners.

21st Century Learning

Skills Rubric	Rating
Think Creatively: Use a wide range of idea creation techniques (such as brainstorming).	1 2 3
Make Judgments and Decisions: Effectively analyze and evaluate evidence, arguments, claims, and beliefs.	1 2 3
Communicate Clearly: Use communication for a range of purposes (e.g., to inform, instruct, motivate, and persuade).	1 2 3
Analyze Media: Understand how, why, and for what purposes media messages are constructed.	1 2 3

3 STUDENT BOOK

Students follow the five-step writing process to write their own movie review. Students may select online or printed graphic organizers to help them plan and develop their writing.

Write a Movie Review

Follow these steps to write your own movie review. To plan your movie review, review the graphic organizers on pages R24–R27 and choose one that best suits your needs.

Prewriting

- Choose a movie you have recently seen and have strong feelings about—positive *or* negative. Consider why you feel as you do.
- Think about the kind of movie it is, such as a comedy or an adventure film.
- Identify the audience for the movie. Consider not only which people are sure to go see it but also which people *might* see it.
- Think about how to persuade people to see or avoid the movie.
- Consider what evidence from the movie you will use to support your opinion.

Drafting

- Begin with a strong opening. It should grab your readers' interest and express your main idea.
- Write a brief summary. Include an analysis of story elements, such as character and plot. Analyze how the film may have been influenced by myths or literature from a variety of world cultures.
- Defend and support your ideas and opinions with sustained evidence. Include quotations when appropriate.
- End with a strong statement that sums up your feelings.

Revising and Editing

Make sure that your ideas are logically organized and that you support them with details and examples. Be sure you present evidence in a clear and persuasive way. Also be sure to check that spelling, grammar, and mechanics are correct.

Publishing

Post your movie review on a school Web site, and invite classmates to share their opinions. You might also create a multimedia presentation for your class that combines your review with quotes and images from the film.

www.phwritingcoach.com

Online Journal

Try It! Record your answers in the online journal.

Interactive Graphic Organizers

Choose from a variety of graphic organizers to plan and develop your project.

Before you start drafting, summarize the movie you are reviewing. Then describe and explain your planned movie review to a partner and ask for feedback. For example, you might ask whether you've chosen convincing evidence to support your opinion. Monitor your partner's spoken language by asking follow up questions to confirm your understanding.

Personalized Support

FEEDBACK

Teacher or Peer Feedback

To provide feedback to students as they write for media, ask or have student partners ask one another the following:

- What are the main characteristics of this form of writing?
- Have you included most or all of these characteristics in your piece of writing?
- What is your purpose for writing this piece?
- Who is your audience?
- How did you organize your ideas in this piece of writing?
- How did you go about revising the piece? Editing it?
- How do you plan on publishing your piece?
- What other publishing options also might work?

Working with ELLs ELL Sheltered Instruction: Cognitive

Guide students to demonstrate an understanding of the general meaning, main points, and important details of spoken language in situations where topics range from familiar to unfamiliar. Discuss a familiar topic from the review on page 218, science-fiction movies, and use the discussion to aid students' comprehension of an unfamiliar topic and the role of a director. Then:

Beginning Provide a **Word Bank** of words from your discussion. Use gestures to explain each word. Lead students to identify your general meaning, main points, and important details as they use the words to respond to simple questions.

Intermediate Help groups note key words they hear and use them to summarize the general meaning, main points, and important details of the discussion.

Advanced Have students take notes as you speak. Have partners work together afterward to write short summaries of your general meaning, main points, and important details.

Advanced High Have students take notes and work to summarize your general meaning, main points, and important details.

1  Writing Journal

Before they write, students use the ABCDs of On-Demand Writing to analyze and plan how to respond to each prompt. They can use either their online journals or notebooks to take notes.

Writing for Assessment

Read aloud or have a student read aloud the introductory text. Then, tell students that they will learn and practice a technique for writing in response to a prompt.

Try It! Read the Interpretative Response Prompt aloud and then have volunteers read aloud the Format and Academic Vocabulary boxes. Tell students that they will use the ABCD method to respond to the prompt.

The ABCDs of On-Demand Writing

Have students identify the words associated with the ABCD method. (attack, brainstorm, choose, detect) Then, guide students through their use.

I'll attack the prompt by circling the words *support* and *details*. These words tell me that I will have to give evidence for my interpretation. I can rewrite the prompt to say, "Use evidence to support your ideas about a literary work."

Work with students to brainstorm for an appropriate organizer for an interpretative response, such as a Cluster Diagram.

Have students write their drafts individually and then work with a partner to detect errors.

Writing to a Prompt *Persuasion* Writing to a Prompt *Persuasion*

Writing for Assessment

You may be asked to write to an interpretative response prompt. Use the prompts on these pages to practice. Your responses should include the same characteristics as your review of a short story. (See page 198.)

Try It! To begin, read the prompt and the information on format and academic vocabulary. Use the ABCDs of On-Demand Writing to help you write your essay.

Format
The prompt directs you to write an *interpretative response* to a story, book, or poem. Make sure to create a fully developed introduction, body, and conclusion.

Interpretative Response Prompt
Write a critical review interpretative response of a short story, book, or poem you have read. Analyze and evaluate the work. Support your analysis and judgment with specific details, such as examples and quotations from the work.

Academic Vocabulary
Remember that an *analysis* of a story, book, or poem is a study of its elements and parts. Your *judgment* about the work is your opinion of it. Be sure to use key points from the text to support your analysis and opinion.

The ABCDs of On-Demand Writing

Use the following ABCDs to help you respond to the prompt.

Before you write your draft:

Attack the prompt [1 MINUTE]
- Circle or highlight important verbs in the prompt. Draw a line from the verb to what it refers to.
- Rewrite the prompt in your own words.

Brainstorm possible answers [4 MINUTES]
- Create a graphic organizer to generate ideas.
- Use one for each part of the prompt if necessary.

Choose the order of your response [1 MINUTE]
- Think about the best way to organize your ideas.
- Number your ideas in the order you will write about them. Cross out ideas you will not be using.

After you write your draft:

Detect errors before turning in the draft [1 MINUTE]
- Carefully reread your writing.
- Make sure that your response makes sense and is complete.
- Look for spelling, punctuation, and grammar errors.

220 Interpretative Response

More Prompts for Practice

Apply It! Have students apply the ABCD method to the practice prompts.

Prompt 1 Have partners attack the prompt and brainstorm for possible answers. Then, have each pair swap their information with another group to evaluate whether the teams have supported their comparisons with evidence from the text.

Prompt 2 Have students work individually to attack the prompt and brainstorm for possible answers. Then, have students work in small groups to evaluate their work before writing their drafts.

Spiral Review: Persuasive Read aloud the instructions and the prompt. Then, have students review the persuasive essay characteristics on page 172.

Prompt 3 Remind students to use the ABCD method to write their persuasive essay.

2 Students submit their writing paragraph by paragraph or as a complete draft to the Interactive Writing Coach™ for feedback, or share their writing with their teacher.

3 Students receive personalized feedback from the Interactive Writing Coach™ or feedback from their teacher.

More Prompts for Practice

Apply It! Respond to Prompts 1 and 2 by writing **interpretative responses** that use supporting **evidence from the text.** Be sure to:

- Express the main idea of your response in a clear **thesis statement**
- Summarize **important features of the work**
- Include **sustained evidence from the text to support ideas**
- Use **quotations from the text** when appropriate
- Analyze **story elements,** such as character, plot, and theme

Prompt 1 Many stories have memorable characters. Write an essay that compares and contrasts two characters from two different stories. Support your ideas with details from the texts.

Prompt 2 Most literary works express a theme. For instance, the theme for a work might be "forgiveness is the key to happiness." In an essay, interpret a theme in a short story, book, or poem you have read.

Spiral Review: Persuasive Respond to Prompt 3 by writing a **persuasive essay** with a **clearly stated thesis or position.** Make sure your persuasive essay has all of the characteristics described on page 172, including:

- A goal to **influence** the attitudes or actions of a specific **audience** about the specific **issue**
- Anticipation of and response to the **concerns, views,** and **counter-arguments** of others
- Logically **organized** arguments and evidence that support a viewpoint
- Distinctions between **fact** and **opinion**

Prompt 3 Write a persuasive essay to convince someone that a particular season of the year is the best. Include types of weather and seasonal activities in your supporting evidence.

Interactive Writing Coach™

Plan your response to the prompt. If you are using the prompt for practice, write one paragraph at a time or your entire draft and then submit it for feedback. If you are using the prompt as a timed test, write your entire draft and then submit it for feedback.

Remember **ABCD**

- **A**ttack the prompt
- **B**rainstorm possible answers
- **C**hoose the order of your response
- **D**etect errors before turning in the draft

Personalized Support

Assessment/Monitor Progress

For timed writing practice, assign students a prompt to be completed in a timed setting. Have students submit their writing to Interactive Writing Coach™ to get immediate feedback.

For a formal writing assessment, assign the Assessment writing prompt for this chapter in Writing Coach Online™. Then, have students submit their writing to Interactive Writing Coach™ to be assessed. Use the results to assess student progress and skill levels. Interactive Writing Coach™ will update student levels to ensure that students get the appropriate support.

Teacher Feedback

To create an assessment environment, have students use a prompt in a timed setting. Grade papers using the appropriate rubric and use the results to assess student progress and skill levels. In the next writing assignment, ensure that students get the appropriate level of support.

If you conference with students, use these questions to guide your discussion:

- What form of writing did the prompt call for? Does your response include most or all of the characteristics of that form?
- How did you organize your ideas?
- Did you make good use of your time as you planned and wrote your response?
- What did you learn that you can use when responding to a prompt during a timed test?

Differentiated Instruction

RTI Strategy for Special Needs Students Guide students through the use of the ABCD method for Prompt 1. Discuss together what words in the prompt are most significant and should be attacked. Then, rewrite the prompt until all students agree that they understand what is being asked of them. Do the brainstorming step as a group. Use graphic organizers as necessary. Write possible answers on the chalkboard.

Strategy for Spanish Speakers Students whose home language is Spanish might omit the serial comma in a list of three or more items, as the serial comma is not used in Spanish. Write *and* and *or* on the board. Provide examples of two- and three- item lists and elicit punctuation from students. In their response to Prompt 3, have students write at least one sentence with a list of three reasons. Have partners check each others' punctuation.

CHAPTER 11 LESSON PLANNER
Research Writing

Interactive Writing Coach™

Interactive Graphic Organizers

Interactive Models

Online Journal
Resources

Video

Use the Online Lesson Planner at www.phwritingcoach.com to customize your instructional plan for an integrated Language Arts curriculum.

DAY 1

CHAPTER OPENER/ GENRE INTRODUCTION

- What Do You Want to Know?
- What's Ahead
- Connect to the Big Questions
- **Feature Assignment: Informational Research Report**
- Other Forms of Research Writing
- Word Bank

ONLINE

DAY 2

STUDENT MODEL

- **Student Model: Informational Research Report**
- Learn From Experience
- Reader's Eye and Writer's Eye

ONLINE

DAYS 3–4

Prewriting

- Choose Your Topic
- Formulate Your Research Question
- Consider Your Audience and Purpose
- Make a Research Plan

ONLINE

DAYS 9–10

Revising

- Keep Revision on Your RADaR
- Look at the Big Picture
- Focus on Craft
- Fine-Tune Your Draft

ONLINE

DAY 11

For additional grammar support, see Section 25.4, p. 575.

Editing

- What Do You Notice/ Grammar Mini-Lesson

Rubric for Informational Research Report

Publishing

- Publish Your Piece
- Reflect on Your Writing

ONLINE

DAY 12

21st Century Learning

MAKE YOUR WRITING COUNT

- **Write a Press Conference Script**
- Here's Your Action Plan
- Listening and Speaking

ONLINE

Alternate Pacing Suggestions

- **Block Scheduling** Each day on the Lesson Planner represents a 40–50 minute block. Teachers using block scheduling may combine days to revise pacing to meet their classroom needs.
- **Accelerated Lesson Planning** Combine days by focusing on core stages of the writing process: choosing a topic (Days 3–4), outlining for success (Days 7–8), and RADaR revision (Days 9–10).
- **Integrated Language Arts Curriculum** For targeted instruction that covers the essential components of the lesson use either a 3- or a 5-day plan.

3 day plan

DAY 1: Introduction to the Genre, Student Model
DAY 2: Prewriting/Drafting
DAY 3: Revising/Editing/Publishing

5 day plan

Use 3-day plan, and add:

DAY 4: Make Your Writing Count
DAY 5: Writing for Assessment

Links to Prentice Hall *LITERATURE*

Expand and deepen students' knowledge of research sources using the Informational Texts features, which include excerpts from an atlas, an encyclopedia entry, and other research sources.

Differentiated Instruction

Differentiated Instruction Boxes in this Teacher's Edition address these student populations:

- Below-Level Students
- Gifted and Talented Students
- English Language Learners
- Above-Level Students
- Special Needs Students
- Spanish Speaking Students

In addition, for further enrichment, see the **Extension** features.

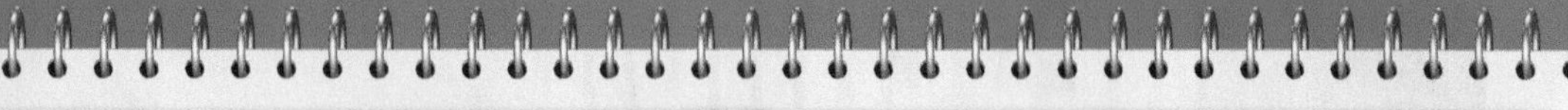

DAYS 5–6

Prewriting *(cont'd)*

- Collect and Organize Your Data
- Avoid Plagiarism
- Document Your Sources

ONLINE

DAYS 7–8

Drafting

- Outline for Success
- Provide and Document Evidence
- Use Graphics and Illustrations

ONLINE

DAYS 13–14

WRITING FOR MEDIA

- **Online Consumer Report**
- Create an Online Consumer Report

ONLINE

DAY 15

WRITING FOR ASSESSMENT

- Research Plan Prompt
- The ABCDs of On-Demand Writing

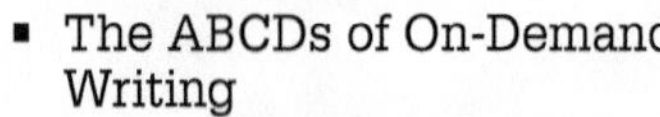

- More Prompts for Practice

Test Prep Spiral Review: Narrative

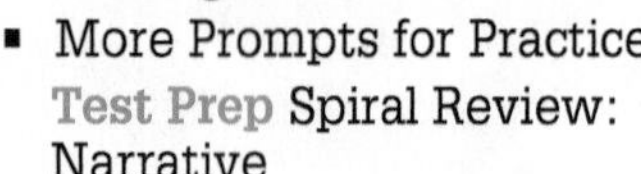

- Spiral Review: Response to Literature

ONLINE

LESSON OBJECTIVES

- To learn the forms and defining characteristics of research writing.
- To learn the elements of a successful informational research report, the chapter Feature Assignment.
- To read a Student Model of an informational research report, analyzing it from the perspective of a reader and from the perspective of a writer.
- To apply prewriting strategies in developing an informational research report, including strategies for choosing a topic, formulating a research question, planning research, gathering details, and documenting sources, as well as tips for considering audience and purpose.
- To apply drafting strategies in developing an informational research report.
- To apply RADaR revision strategies to a draft informational research report.
- To learn about the Focus on Craft topic, sentence variety, and apply what is learned to a draft informational research report.
- To edit the draft, focusing on integrating and punctuating quotations.
- To complete the Make Your Writing Count assignment, developing and presenting a press conference script.
- To complete the Writing for Media assignment, developing an online consumer report.
- To practice writing for assessment.

Personalized Assessment

✓	Ongoing Assessment	Formal Assessment of Feature Assignment	Progress Monitoring at End-of-Chapter
 Interactive Writing Coach™	Use Paragraph Feedback and Essay Scorer as a revision tool.	Use Essay Scorer to score students' Feature Assignment papers.	Use Essay Scorer to score students' papers. Students' learner profiles can be adjusted based on their scores.
FEEDBACK Teacher Conferencing	Use rubrics in the Student Edition as a revision tool. Conference with students to review their work and provide personalized support.	Use rubrics in the Student Edition to score students' Feature Assignment papers.	Review each student's work to plan targeted resources for the next writing assignment.

The Digital • Print Path

1 

Using Writing Coach Online™ or the student book, students discuss the photograph in the chapter opener as it relates to the writing genre.

2 

Students record their ideas and responses in their online journals or notebooks. They may also record and save their responses on pop-up sticky notes in Writing Coach Online™.

Chapter Objectives

1. Write an informational research report by planning, drafting, revising, editing, and publishing individual work.
2. Produce a press conference script.
3. Use the five-step writing process to write an online consumer report.
4. Write a research plan and a personal narrative or a response to literature in response to a prompt.

RESEARCH WRITING

What Do You Want to Know?

Activate Prior Knowledge Tell students that the purpose of a research report is to gather, organize, and present information about a specific topic. Explain to students that they will use what they know about scientists to analyze the photo on page 222. Then, guide students in analyzing the photo.

When you write a research report, you need to have specific questions for which you are looking for answers. For example, in the photo **I see** a scientist looking into a powerful machine. The scientist is not just using the machine to look at something but to find answers to specific questions that he or she wants answered.

Work with students to brainstorm for some research questions the scientists might have. Record student responses on the board.

Try It! **Have students** work individually to respond to the questions. Check that students have developed specific questions about the scientist, the scientist's gear, and the machine.

Possible responses: I want to know, among other things, what kind of scientist this person is, why the scientist is wearing protective clothing, and what kind of information the scientist will obtain from using the machine.

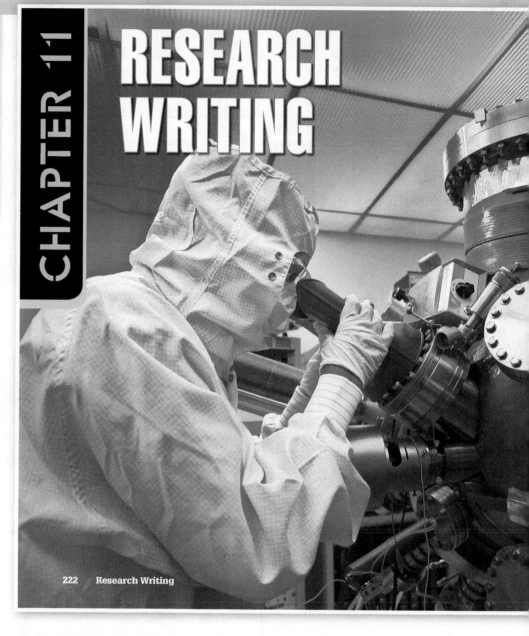

CHAPTER 11 RESEARCH WRITING

222 Research Writing

Connect to the Big Questions

Have students use their experience to discuss the Big Questions. Explain that they will revisit **Why write?** at the end of this chapter. Tell students to consider these points during their discussion.

1. Ask students to evaluate the effect of a wide range of technology, from consumer electronics to medicines.
2. Ask students to assess their knowledge of a familiar topic, such as soccer or the structure of a school day.

What's Ahead

Have students preview the Student Model on pages 226–229. Tell students that they will write their own research report using a five-step writing process: prewriting, drafting, revising, editing, and publishing.

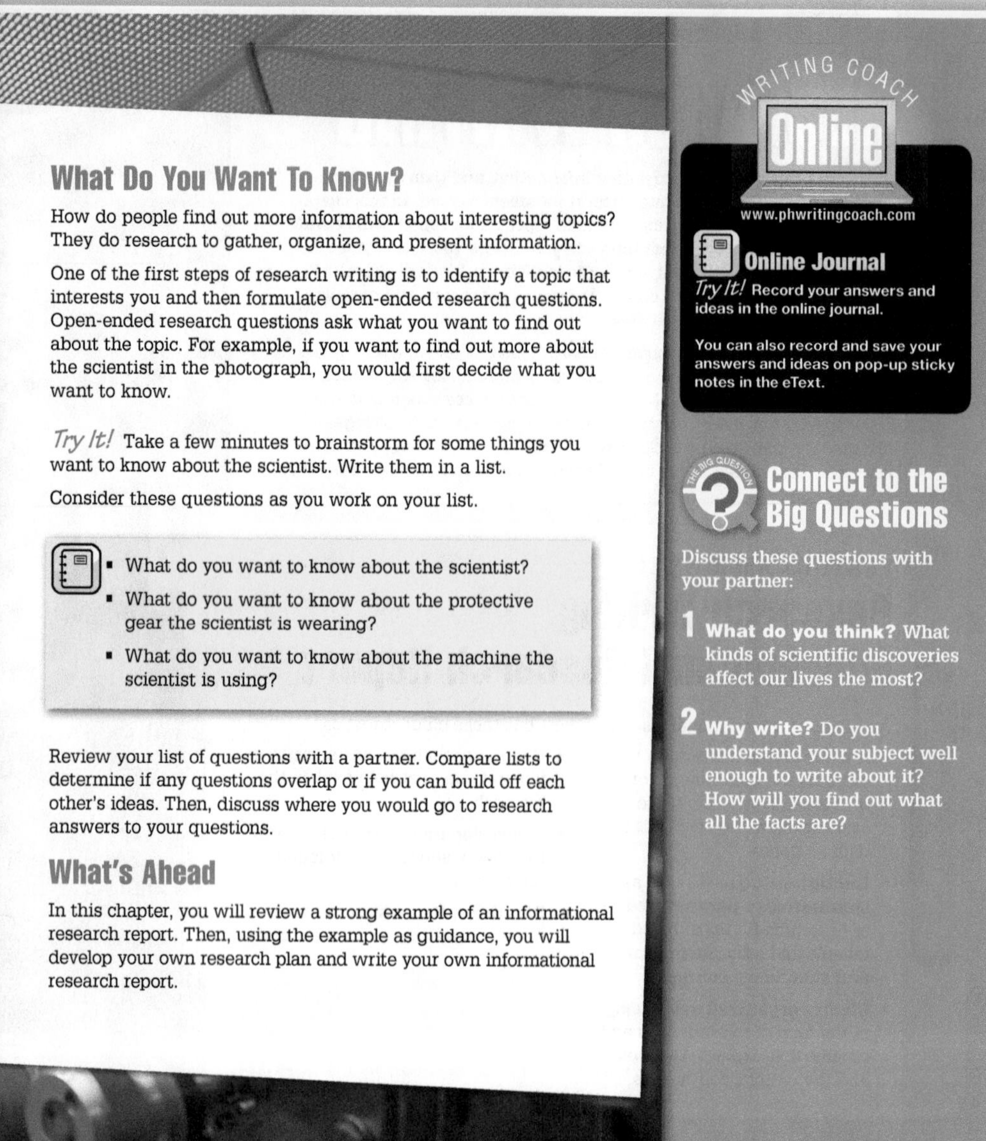

What Do You Want To Know?

How do people find out more information about interesting topics? They do research to gather, organize, and present information.

One of the first steps of research writing is to identify a topic that interests you and then formulate open-ended research questions. Open-ended research questions ask what you want to find out about the topic. For example, if you want to find out more about the scientist in the photograph, you would first decide what you want to know.

Try It! Take a few minutes to brainstorm for some things you want to know about the scientist. Write them in a list.

Consider these questions as you work on your list.

- What do you want to know about the scientist?
- What do you want to know about the protective gear the scientist is wearing?
- What do you want to know about the machine the scientist is using?

Review your list of questions with a partner. Compare lists to determine if any questions overlap or if you can build off each other's ideas. Then, discuss where you would go to research answers to your questions.

What's Ahead

In this chapter, you will review a strong example of an informational research report. Then, using the example as guidance, you will develop your own research plan and write your own informational research report.

WRITING COACH Online

www.phwritingcoach.com

Online Journal

Try It! Record your answers and ideas in the online journal.

You can also record and save your answers and ideas on pop-up sticky notes in the eText.

Connect to the Big Questions

Discuss these questions with your partner:

1. **What do you think?** What kinds of scientific discoveries affect our lives the most?
2. **Why write?** Do you understand your subject well enough to write about it? How will you find out what all the facts are?

Personalized Support

FEEDBACK

Teacher or Peer Feedback

To encourage students in their discussion of the photograph as it relates to the writing genre, ask the following questions:

- What is the first thing you think of when you look at this photo?
- How does it relate to your life?
- How does it relate to things you've learned in other subjects?
- What questions come to mind when you look at this photograph?
- How does your response to the photograph compare to those of your classmates?

Working with ELLs

ELL **Sheltered Instruction:** Cognitive

Support students in learning new expressions heard during classroom instruction and interactions. Use idiomatic expressions while discussing the picture on page 222, such as *sky is the limit, cutting edge, give someone a hand,* and *back to the drawing board.* Then:

Beginning Model *give someone a hand* in a sentence, gesturing for support and providing an explanation. Have students use the expression by completing the sentence *I gave _____ a hand with ____.*

Intermediate Repeat the expressions, explain them, and model using them in sentences. Have partners make **Concept Illustrations** by drawing a picture illustrating the idiomatic meaning of one expression, and then demonstrate their understanding by using it in a sentence.

Advanced Repeat the expressions. Have partners look up the meanings in an idiom dictionary. Have pairs demonstrate that they learned the expressions by using each in a sentence. Partners should share sentences with another pair.

Advanced High Have students complete the Advanced activity, then rewrite each sentence, replacing the idioms.

The Digital • Print Path

1 

Students learn vocabulary from the Word Bank and listen to English and Spanish pronunciations in the **Writing Coach Online™** glossary.

2 

Students record answers to questions about forms of writing in their online journals or notebooks.

RESEARCH WRITING

To introduce this chapter's writing form, discuss the opening paragraphs with students. Make sure students understand that an informational research report is a type of research writing. Explain that good writers use a step-by-step process to develop their work. Then, have students preview the rubric on page 247.

Research Writing: Informational Research Report

Ask volunteers to read aloud the feature assignment characteristics. Tell students that they will identify these characteristics in a Student Model. Then, they will use the characteristics to guide the writing of their own informational research report.

Other Forms of Research Writing

Guide students to understand how the forms of research writing are alike and different.

Say: I notice that there are several types of research writing. Some of them focus on a particular field or subject. For example, historical reports give information about a past event or issue. On the other hand, an informational research report or a documentary is not limited to a specific field.

Ask: In what ways are all the forms of research writing similar? (They involve an in-depth study of facts.)

Have students discuss types of research writing they have done and describe the subjects they researched for them.

Try It! Remind students that the audience is the people who will read their writing. The purpose is the author's reason for writing. Have students record their responses in their journal.

Possible responses: Topic: A local politician; Question: How did a local politician prepare for a life in public service? Topic: The healthiest lunch choices; Question: How can schools serve healthier lunches? Topic: A grandparent's life; Question: What was education like when a grandparent was a child?

Word Bank

To assist English Language Learners and struggling readers, echo read each word or have students log on to Writing Coach Online to listen to the pronunciations. Then, have partners take turns using each word in a sentence. Ask volunteers to share one of their sentences with the class.

Teacher Tip

Quick Write Have students describe an example of one of the types of research writing that they have read and found especially informative or that changed their opinion or attitude toward a topic.

RESEARCH WRITING

Research writing is a way to gather information, and then synthesize, or combine, that information into a report for others to read. In this chapter, you will write an informational research report. Your report will provide information about a topic that interests you. Before you write, you will search for information about your topic in different kinds of sources. You will decide which facts and details to use in your report, and organize your ideas clearly for your audience.

You will develop your informational research report by taking it through each of the steps of the writing process: prewriting, drafting, revising, editing, and publishing. You will also have an opportunity to use your informational research report in an oral report or multimedia presentation involving text and graphics that uses technology available to you. To preview the criteria for how your research report will be evaluated, see the rubric on page 247.

FEATURE ASSIGNMENT

Research Writing: Informational Research Report

An effective informational research report has these characteristics:

- **A clear thesis statement** that explains the **conclusions** of the research and how those conclusions will be supported with evidence
- **Quotations** from—as well as **summaries** or **paraphrases** of—research findings, based on reliable and accurate **primary and secondary sources**
- **Clearly organized evidence,** in the form of relevant facts and details, that explains the topic and the writer's conclusions
- **Graphics,** such as charts, maps, or illustrations, that help explain the research
- Proper **documentation** of sources to show where the writer found information
- Effective sentence structure and **correct spelling, grammar, and usage**

224 Research Writing

Other Forms of Research Writing

In addition to an informational research report, there are other forms of research writing, including these:

Biographical profiles give specific details about the life and work of a real person. The person may be living or dead, someone famous, or someone familiar to the writer.

Documentaries are filmed reports that focus on a specific topic or issue. These multimedia presentations use spoken and written text as well as photographs, videos, music, and other sound effects.

Historical reports give in-depth information about a past event or situation. These kinds of reports focus on a narrow topic and may discuss causes and effects.

Health reports analyze information and data about new research in health and wellness. A health report might explain new findings about the links between nutrition and health, or the latest news on disease research.

I-Search reports blend informational and personal writing. In an I-search report, you tell the story of your research and investigations, including the dead-ends and small victories, in addition to presenting the results of your research.

Lab reports describe scientific experiments, including observations and conclusions.

Try It! For each research report described, brainstorm for possible topics with others. Then, consult with others to decide on and write a major research question for each topic. As you write, keep your audience and purpose in mind.

- A biographical profile of someone in the news
- A health report about school lunches
- A documentary about a family member for a special occasion

WRITING COACH
Online
www.phwritingcoach.com
Resource
Word Bank Listen to English and Spanish pronunciations of new words in the eText glossary.
Online Journal
Try It! Record your answers and ideas in the online journal.

WORD BANK

People use these basic and content-based words when they talk about writing that reports information. Work with a partner. Take turns saying and writing each word in a sentence. If you are unsure of the meaning of a word, use the Glossary or a dictionary to check the definition.

authority	**research**
information	**subject**
note	**support**

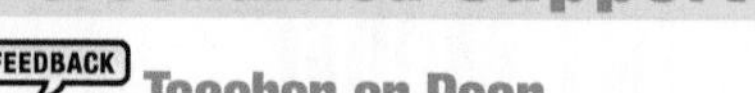

Personalized Support

Teacher or Peer Feedback

To help students understand the characteristics of the writing form, ask or have student partners ask one another the following questions:

- What are the main characteristics of an informational research report?
- What makes this form of writing different from other forms?
- Who are the likely readers or audiences for this form of writing?
- What kind of organization could be used for this form of writing?
- What kind of voice would be most effective for this form of writing?

Working with ELLs

ELL Sheltered Instruction: Cognitive

To help students with the *Try It!*, work with them to expand and internalize initial English vocabulary. Help students learn, use, and reuse basic, high-frequency words in their speaking to identify and describe people related to the research report topics.

Beginning Using a word web, identify and describe family members. Model statements with high-frequency words such as *mother, father, brother,* and *sister,* supporting with pictures. Add the words to the web. Have students repeat your statements and reuse the words orally in sentence frames you provide.

Intermediate Display a newspaper and discuss people in the news using high-frequency words, such as *important, sports, music,* and *election.* Have students use and reuse the words in oral responses to questions, such as *Who won the election?*

Advanced Give students the Intermediate words. Have partners use and reuse them in sentences about people in the news.

Advanced High Give students the Intermediate words. Have groups use and reuse the words in discussion to identify and describe people in the news.

1 

Using Writing Coach Online™ or the student book, students read and listen to an audio recording of the Student Model. As they complete their writing assignments, they can refer back to the Student Model for support whenever they need it.

STUDENT MODEL

Tell students that good writers react to what they read in ways that show their understanding of the text. Explain that students will react to the Student Model by using two sets of symbols in the text and responding to questions about what they have read. Then, distribute printed copies of the Student Model or have students log on to Writing Coach Online.

Use a Reader's Eye

Read aloud the instructions for using the Reader's Response Symbols and the meaning of each symbol. Then, have students read and respond to the Student Model, using each Reader's Response Symbol at least once.

Learn From Experience

Point out that the numbered notes refer to the characteristics of an informational research report introduced on page 224.

Try It! Guide students to understand how the genre characteristics shape the text.

Say: The first *Try It!* question asks about the supporting evidence **I expect** to find based on the information in the thesis sentence. The thesis in lines 12–13 is about the myth versus the reality of the cowboy, so I expect to find evidence such as examples of specific myths about cowboys and facts about how cowboys actually lived.

Ask: Based on the thesis sentence, what other evidence do you expect to find in the research report? **(Responses will vary.)**

Have students respond to the *Try It!* questions in their journals. Then, check the accuracy and completeness of their responses.

2. The main idea is that cowboys' real lives are different from the myths about them. It answers the question "How are real cowboys different from the popular image of cowboys?" The purpose is to explain how the cowboys' image is based on myth, not reality, and to persuade readers that this contention is correct.

5. A man like Buck Taylor would improve the image of the cowboy because instead of being dirty and unruly, he seemed to be a gentle, thoughtful man. He was presented as a person who worked as a cowboy because he enjoyed nature and wide-open spaces.

Informational Research Report Student Model Informational Research Re

STUDENT MODEL Informational Research Report

 Use a Reader's Eye

Read the Student Model on pages 226–229. On your copy of the Student Model, use the Reader's Response Symbols to react to what you read.

Reader's Response Symbols

- √ **OK. I understand this. It's very clearly explained.**
- ? **I don't follow what the writer is saying here.**
- \+ **I think the writer needs more details here.**
- – **This information doesn't seem relevant.**
- ! **Wow! That is cool/weird/interesting.**

Learn From Experience

Read the numbered notes as you reread the Student Model to learn about how the writer presented her ideas.

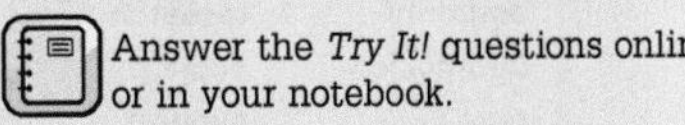
Answer the *Try It!* questions online or in your notebook.

❶ The writer uses **proper formatting** for the first page and pagination of research report.

❷ The writer reveals the **research question;** then she reveals her conclusion about it in the **thesis statement.**

Try It! Read the thesis statement. What is the main idea? What research question does it answer? What is the author's purpose?

❶ Alvarez 1

❶ Emma Alvarez
Mrs. Davidson
History 7A
13 December 2009

❶ The Cowboy: Myth Versus Reality

Everyone can spot a cowboy a mile away. He is a tall, strong man wearing a big hat, high boots, and bandana. He roams the West on horseback, like a knight of old. He spends most of his time alone except for his best friend—his horse. He is brave, self-reliant, and, above all, free. To many, he represents America itself (Savage 6). ❷ How does this image relate to the real cowboys? The popular image has its roots in the real men who herded cattle for a few decades after the Civil War. However, advertising and popular media reshaped the cowboys' image and smoothed away the less appealing parts of their lives (Savage 9). ❷ This report will show that the popular image of the cowboy is more myth than reality.

The era of the real—that is, working—American cowboy lasted only about twenty-five years, from around 1865 to 1890. It began with the first railroads, which connected the large eastern cities with a few western centers like Chicago, Omaha, and Abilene. At this time, the railroads did not go into Texas cattle country. Cattlemen needed to get their herds to eastern markets, where they would earn much higher prices. So the ranchers hired young men—cowboys—to herd the cattle over hundreds of miles to the nearest railhead. There the animals were loaded onto freight trains going east.

As time passed, however, cowboys were less essential to the cattle industry. Railroads had expanded, so that rail depots were much closer to the cattle ranches. Therefore, long cattle drives every spring and fall were no longer needed. Although some cowboys continued to tend cattle on ranches, by the late 1880s, the era of the working cowboy had wound down (Utley 245). At that point, the cowboy myth began to take over.

Teacher Tip

Quick Write Have students describe their impressions of cowboys and give specific examples that tell how they formed the impressions.

2 

Students record their answers to questions about the Student Model in their online journals or notebooks.

3 

First, students respond to the Student Model as a reader, using symbols to mark the text. They can mark the text using pop-up sticky notes in Writing Coach Online™ or they can mark a printed copy of the Student Model.

4 

Then, students respond to the Student Model as a writer, using different symbols to mark the text. They can use either Writing Coach Online™ or a printed copy of the Student Model.

Alvarez 2

Before the cowboy myth was created, the cowboy had not been a very popular figure. One person who had seen "real cowboys" remarked that a cowboy is "just a plain bowlegged human who smelled very horsey at times" (Burns). The public saw cowboys as dirty, unruly men—and they often were just that (figure 1). ③ In 1875, a Wyoming newspaper described a group of "real" cowboys as "rough men with shaggy hair and wild staring eyes in butternut trousers stuffed into great rough boots" (Schultz and Tishler).

In 1884, William F. Cody (known as "Buffalo Bill") began to shine up the cowboy's image:

> ④ Cody took a six-foot, five-inch Texas cowpuncher named William Levi Taylor and in 1884 introduced him to the audiences of Buffalo Bill's Wild West as Buck Taylor, 'the King of the Cowboys.' Buck Taylor thus became the first bona fide cowboy hero. . . . Cody's careful management of Taylor's career as an entertainer did much to alter the public's perception of cowboys. He portrayed the young Texan as a wistful soul who seemed to be longing to return to the bucolic environs of the Great Plains. Promotional literature assured the public that Taylor, despite his size, was a gentle fellow who liked children (Savage).

⑤ In other words, Cody's publicity campaign romanticized and softened the image of the cowboy in order to make his Wild West show more popular. The campaign worked, and the myth

Figure 1. Typical cowboy. Photo taken by D.C.H. Grabill in *Sturgis Dakota Territory* (Washington, DC: Library of Congress; ppmscs 02638; print).

Writing Coach
Online
www.phwritingcoach.com
Interactive Model
Listen to an audio recording of the Student Model in the eText. You can refer back to the Student Model whenever you need support in developing your own writing.
Use the Reader's and Writer's Response Symbols with the eText tools to note what you read.
Online Journal
Try It! Record your answers and ideas in the online journal.

③ This **quotation** gives a firsthand view of nineteenth-century cowboys, **relevant details** provided by an eyewitness who lived among them.

④ Extended quotations of four lines or more are set off from the text, indented, and not set in quotation marks.

⑤ **Evidence** is provided to support the conclusion that the cowboy image was a carefully created myth.

Try It! How does the evidence about Buck Taylor support the writer's thesis statement?

Personalized Support

FEEDBACK

Teacher or Peer Feedback

To provide feedback to students on their responses to the Student Model and their answers to the *Try It!* questions, ask or have student partners ask one another the following:

- What is the thesis or controlling idea of the Student Model?
- How does the Student Model illustrate the characteristics of a research report?
- Which characteristics of the Student Model could you use in your own writing?
- How did you answer this *Try It!* question? How could you use your answer to help you plan your piece of writing?

Working with ELLs

ELL Sheltered Instruction: Cognitive

Help students learn basic vocabulary heard during classroom instruction and interaction. Prepare an oral presentation based on the Student Model that includes these basic vocabulary words: *work, men, horse, cattle,* and *explain.* Help students use their prior experience with ranches or animals to understand the words' meanings.

Beginning Use illustrations and gestures to review the words. Have students use their prior experiences to complete sentences containing the basic vocabulary, such as *Cowboys work with* _____. Allow them to draw or gesture.

Intermediate Have students make **Mental Connections** to the words using their prior experiences. Have students write the words and mental connections on the front of note cards. On the back, have them write a synonym and antonym for the words. Have students share what they wrote.

Advanced Have students complete the Intermediate activity and use each word in a sentence related to prior experiences.

Advanced High Have students use each basic vocabulary word in a paragraph and share their paragraphs with partners.

The Digital • Print Path

1 

Using Writing Coach Online™ or the student book, students read and listen to an audio recording of the Student Model. As they complete their writing assignments, they can refer back to the Student Model for support whenever they need it.

2 Writing Journal

Students record their answers to questions about the Student Model in their online journals or notebooks.

Learn From Experience (continued)

Check the accuracy and completeness of student responses to the *Try It!* questions.

6. The statistics show that cowboys were a diverse group, with a large number of African-American and Hispanic cowboys.
7. The summary helps support the contrast between cowboy myth and reality because it gives specific ways in which reality differed from myth. For example, although the cowboy's life is portrayed as interesting and exciting, the cowboy's job was boring, consisting of riding for 14 hours a day.
8. **Possible response:** The conclusion adds the thought that cowboys still work on ranches today. It changes my idea of cowboys of the past because I know that today cowboys and cowgirls are not romanticized; they are seen as people who do a specific job.
9. It is helpful to list sources in alphabetical order so that a reader can easily locate the source after reading a reference to the source in the report. Readers might want to look up a source for themselves, so it is important to know whether a source came from print, the Web, and so on.

Extension Ask volunteers to share their synopses with the class and explain their source's main idea and most important details.

Use a Writer's Eye

Read aloud the instructions for using the Writer's Response Symbols and the meaning of each symbol. Then, guide students through their use.

I found an example of supporting evidence in lines 64–66. The writer says that real cowboys differed from mythical cowboys in stature. The writer quotes a source that says that most cowboys were short and slight instead of tall "so as not to weigh down their horses." I'll write S.E. next to those lines for supporting evidence.

Informational Research Report Student Model Informational Research Re

STUDENT MODEL Informational Research Report *(continued)*

❻ **Relevant facts,** in the form of statistics, back up the idea that the cowboys came from varied backgrounds.

Try It! What new ideas about cowboys do these statistics help to support?

❼ Here and elsewhere, the writer **summarizes** information she found during her research.

Try It! Do you think this summary helps support the contrast between the cowboy myth and reality? Why or why not?

❽ The final paragraph restates the writer's **reason for her conclusion** about the cowboy image, and adds a new thought.

Try It! What new thought does the conclusion add to the report? How does this new thought change your ideas of cowboys?

❾ The Works Cited list provides proper **documentation** by listing publication information for each source used to write the report. The **formatting** of the list follows the MLA (Modern Language Association) style manual.

Try It! Study the Works Cited list on page 229. Why is it helpful to readers to list sources in alphabetical order? Why might readers want to know what types of resources—print, Web, and so on—were used?

Extension Review the text features and graphics in this report. How do they help you form an overview and locate information?

Alvarez 3

of the cowboy was born. The myth soon grew, fed by novels in the nineteenth century. In the twentieth century, the myth was greatly enlarged by movies and television programs (Savage 9–10).

The real cowboy was different in many ways from his myth, beginning with his stature and background. The mythical cowboy is tall. In contrast, Schultz and Tishler say, most actual cowboys were short and slight (though wiry), so as not to weigh down their horses. Like the "King of the Cowboys," the mythical cowboy is Caucasian and a Westerner. ❻ However, of the 35,000 men who worked as cowboys between 1865 and 1885, about 25% were African-American; about 12% were Hispanic (Schultz and Tishler).

Many cowboys were not Westerners. They were former Confederate soldiers or sons of Southern families whose properties had been lost in the Civil War. They were also young men from Eastern cities and even Europeans who came west (Burns).

The typical cowboy took up cowpunching in his late teens and left it by the time he turned 30. The salary was relatively low: \$30–\$40 a month ("Cowboy"). Due to inflation, \$40 per month in 1880 would be equal to about \$870 in today's money (Officer and Williamson).

The mythical cowboy did not earn much money either, but was seen as a romantic loner who bravely faced down gunslingers. ❼ In contrast, the real cowboy led a hard and very boring life, riding for 14 hours a day. He needed his large hat to protect his neck and eyes from the blistering sun and wore a kerchief so that he could breathe during dust storms. Far from being a romantic loner, his life depended on teaming up with his fellow cowboys (figure 2). They had to keep watchful eyes on the cattle, which would often wander away, or, worse, stampede and kill their herders. The cattle, terrain, and weather were all greater threats to real cowboys than gunslingers were. While the cowboy myth celebrates freedom, the actual cowboy was far from

Work with students to identify other places in the text where the writer supports ideas with effective supporting evidence.

Have students read and respond to the Student Model, using each Writer's Response Symbol at least once.

3 STUDENT BOOK

First, students respond to the Student Model as a reader, using symbols to mark the text. They can mark the text using pop-up sticky notes in Writing Coach Online™ or they can mark a printed copy of the Student Model.

4 

Then, students respond to the Student Model as a writer, using different symbols to mark the text. They can use either Writing Coach Online™ or a printed copy of the Student Model.

Alvarez 4

Figure 2. Cowboys worked together to herd cattle hundreds of miles. Taken by D.C.H. Grabill in *Sturgis Dakota Territory* (Washington, DC: Library of Congress ppmscs 02628; print).

free. He was a hired hand who worked day and night for a rich cattle rancher, and almost every moment of his day was bound over to the animals he herded (Schultz and Tishler).

Like any legendary figure, the mythical cowboy was more heroic and exciting than the reality. 8 So the cowboy myth, eventually repeated by powerful media like movies and television, blotted out the real cowboy in people's minds. However, this is not to say that the working cowboy vanished completely from the American West. Real cowboys (and cowgirls) tend cattle on ranches to this day, much as their nineteenth-century counterparts did. We just have to look behind the towering myth to see them.

9 Works Cited

Burns, Ken. "Episode 5: 'Cowboys'." *The West.* WETA. 2001. Web. 2 Nov. 2009.

"Cowboy." *The New Encyclopedia of the American West.* Ed. Howard R. Lamar. New Haven: Yale UP, 1998. Print.

Officer, Lawrence H. and Samuel H. Williamson. "Six Ways to Compute the Relative Value of a U.S. Dollar Amount, 1774 to Present." *Measuring Worth.* MeasuringWorth, 2009. Web. 2 Nov. 2009.

Savage, William W., Jr. *Cowboy Life: Reconstructing an American Myth.* Norman, Oklahoma: U of Oklahoma P, 1975. Print.

Schultz, Stanley K. and William P. Tishler. "Which 'Old West' and Whose?" *American History 102, Lecture 3.* State Historical Society of Wisconsin, 1997. Web. 2 Nov. 2009.

Utley, Robert M., ed. *The Story of the West.* New York: DK Publishing, Inc., 2003. Print.

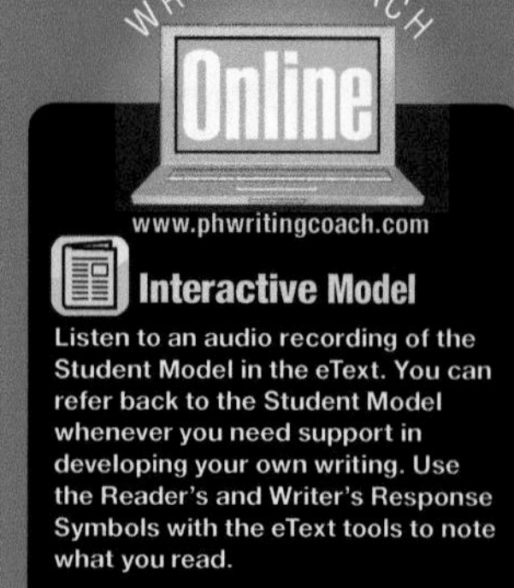

www.phwritingcoach.com

Interactive Model

Listen to an audio recording of the Student Model in the eText. You can refer back to the Student Model whenever you need support in developing your own writing. Use the Reader's and Writer's Response Symbols with the eText tools to note what you read.

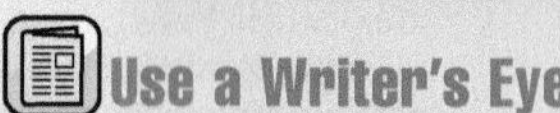

Use a Writer's Eye

Now go back to the beginning of the Student Model and evaluate the piece as a writer. On your copy of the Student Model, use the Writer's Response Symbols to react to what you read. Identify places where the student writer uses characteristics of an effective informational research report.

Writer's Response Symbols	
T.S.	**Thesis statement**
S.E.	**Supporting evidence**
R.G.	**Relevant graphic**
D.S.	**Proper documentation of sources**

Personalized Support

FEEDBACK **Teacher or Peer Feedback**

To provide feedback to students on their responses to the Student Model, ask or have student partners ask one another the following:

- Where did the writer get the information used in the report?
- What kinds of facts and evidence does the writer use to support the research topic?
- Where would you look for information to answer your research question?
- How would you organize your information?

Working with ELLs

ELL **Sheltered Instruction:** Metacognitive

Have students demonstrate listening comprehension of increasingly complex spoken English by responding to oral questions and requests. Have students monitor their comprehension and seek clarification as necessary. Read aloud lines 62–75 of the Student Model. Then:

Beginning Reread the selection, using gestures and mime. Have students monitor comprehension and seek clarification by raising their hands, then respond to questions, like *Were cowboys tall or short?*

Intermediate Provide students with a web graphic organizer, and reread the selection aloud. Help them monitor comprehension by having them fill in the organizer as you read, seeking clarification. Have them respond to questions, such as *How were real cowboys different from the myths?*

Advanced Have students take notes to monitor comprehension of your reading, seeking clarification of unfamiliar words and ideas, and respond to questions such as *What do these paragraphs describe?*

Advanced High Have students complete the Advanced activity, then discuss *Try It!* number 6 with partners.

1 Students select or are assigned a topic for their research report from the Topic Bank, or they may choose a topic of their own.

2 Students complete online or printed graphic organizers to formulate a research question.

Prewriting

Explain that the first task students need to complete as they plan their research report is to determine an appropriate topic.

Choose From the Topic Bank

Read aloud each topic and then ask volunteers to describe it in their own words. If you are assigning topics to students, you may wish to do so now. Encourage students to ask questions about their topic.

Choose Your Own Topic

Introduce and discuss the Brainstorm and Browse strategies. If students were not assigned writing topics, have them use the strategies to brainstorm for topics for their essays.

Extension Have each student choose one of the strategies. Then, have students write an action plan that outlines the resources and steps they will use to develop their topic.

Formulate Your Research Question

Tell students that they will use a Formulate a Research Question graphic organizer to develop their research question. Then, distribute printed copies or have students log on to Writing Coach Online.

Apply It! Guide students through the instructions for completing the graphic organizer. Have students complete the exercise based on their topic.

Consider Your Audiences and Purposes

Guide students to consider the audience and purpose for their research report.

Say: The third question in the first column asks what technical terms **I will need** to explain to my audience. If I explain the origins of lacrosse, which was originally a Native American game, I will need to explain technical terms used in the game, such as *attackers, middies,* and *penalty box.* I must keep this in mind as I plan my report.

Ask: Based on your topic, what technical terms will you need to explain to your audience? (Responses will vary.)

Have students with similar research questions work in small groups to discuss and respond to the remaining questions.

Your Turn Feature Assignment: Informational Research Report

Prewriting

Begin to plan a first draft by choosing an appropriate topic. You can select from the Topic Bank or come up with one of your own.

Choose From the Topic Bank

TOPIC BANK

Balls, Courts, and Hoops People in other times played many games that share traits with today's sports. Learn about a sport developed by Native Americans or another civilization from the Middle Ages to the twentieth century. What were its origins? How was it played?

Making the Headlines Certain dates in history have special meaning to various localities. What date means a great deal to your community or state? What makes the date important?

What's Living in My Backyard? Our communities host many life forms, from microscopic to human size. Research an ecosystem or microhabitat near your home. Describe this habitat and its organisms. How do these organisms co-exist with human beings?

Choose Your Own Topic

Determine an appropriate topic of your own by using the following range of strategies to generate ideas.

Brainstorm and Browse

- **Consult** with a partner to **brainstorm** for and decide upon a list of topics that interest you.
- **Ask research questions** about your topics. Circle key words and phrases in your questions. Use your key words and phrases to browse your library's reference works and other resources.
- Search the Internet, using the same key words. Work with your partner to help you **decide which topics to research.**
- Review your work and choose a topic.

Coach's Corner

You may wish to model prewriting activities for students by brainstorming for your own research question. Use these prompts to model your thought process:

- **I am interested in** writing about a sport developed by Native Americans.
- **I can narrow my topic** to the sport of lacrosse.

Discuss the choices you make and solicit feedback from students.

3 

Students record their answers to questions about audience and purpose in their online journals or notebooks.

Formulate Your Research Question

A broad, general topic is almost impossible to research well and cover thoroughly. Plan to do some preliminary research in order to narrow your topic and then formulate a major research question.

Apply It! Use a printed or online graphic organizer like the one shown to narrow your topic.

- Write your general topic in the top box, and keep narrowing your topic with research questions as you move down the chart.
- Your last box should hold your narrowest or "smallest" research question. This will be the focus of your informational research report.

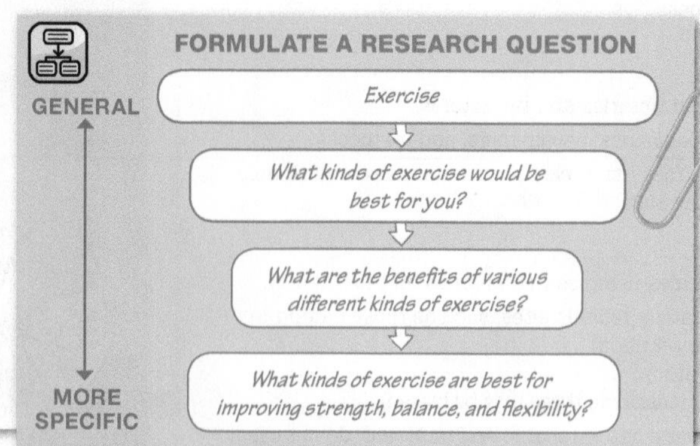

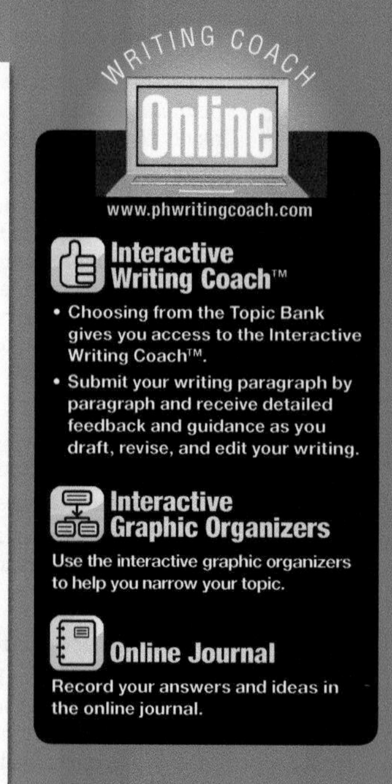

What are the benefits of various different kinds of exercise?
What kinds of exercise are best for improving strength, balance, and flexibility?

WRITING COACH
Online
www.phwritingcoach.com
Interactive Writing Coach™
• Choosing from the Topic Bank gives you access to the Interactive Writing Coach™.
• Submit your writing paragraph by paragraph and receive detailed feedback and guidance as you draft, revise, and edit your writing.
Interactive Graphic Organizers
Use the interactive graphic organizers to help you narrow your topic.
Online Journal
Record your answers and ideas in the online journal.

Consider Your Audiences and Purposes

Before you start researching, think about audiences and purposes. Consider the views of others as you ask yourself these questions.

Questions About Audiences	Questions About Purposes
• Who are my audiences: My teacher? My classmates? Someone else? • What do my audiences need and want to know about the topic for my research report? • What technical terms will I need to explain to my audiences?	• Why am I writing the report: To inform? To make my audiences want to learn more about the topic? • How do I want my audiences to react to my report as they read it? • What is my point of view, or attitude, toward my topic?

Record your answers in your writing journal.

Personalized Support

Interactive Graphic Organizer

Below Level Students complete three graphic organizers that provide models and scaffolded support.

On Level Students complete one, two, or three graphic organizers depending on how much support they need.

Above Level Students complete the least scaffolded graphic organizer or narrow their topic without the help of a graphic organizer.

Differentiated Instruction

RTI Strategy for Below-Level Students With the class, brainstorm for research questions for these topics: desert ecosystems, games in ancient Greece, Fourth of July celebrations, and the Pony Express. Explain that a research question must be specific enough to guide research for a short report but general enough to provide enough research sources. For example, *What games have been played through the ages?* is too general; *How do you play goalie in soccer?* is too specific.

PRE-AP Enrichment for Above-Level Students Encourage students to choose a topic from a subject they have recently studied in another class, such as history, social studies, science, or math. Have students brainstorm for research topics for each of the classes listed above. Then have them develop specific research questions for each topic.

1 Using Writing Coach Online™ or the student book, students use a variety of resources to make a research plan.

2 Students take notes, gather information, and record their ideas in their online journals or notebooks.

Make a Research Plan

Tell students that they will create a research plan for finding and evaluating the sources they need to create an effective informational research report. Explain to students that this is a large, long-term project, but they will have many opportunities to receive your direction, feedback, and other support.

Find Authoritative, Objective Sources Introduce the four kinds of resources listed in the chart. Then, guide students to identify appropriate resources for their topics.

Say: I see that there are several kinds of resources I can use to research a topic. For example, if my topic is about life in the Old West, I could use electronic or online resources such as Web sites on America in the 1800s or the Web sites of historical journals.

Ask: What electronic or online resources could you use to research your topic? (Responses will vary.)

Have students work with a partner to discuss which types of resources will be most useful for their topics.

Evaluate Your Sources Have volunteers read aloud the Checklist for Evaluating Sources. Define unfamiliar or difficult words, or have students look them up in the Glossary. You may wish to refer to works cited on page 229 to model using the checklist to evaluate the relevance and validity of sources.

Distinguish Between Types of Sources Introduce students to primary and secondary sources and discuss the strengths and weaknesses of each. For example, a primary source may be written by an eyewitness, but a secondary source may be written by an expert on the issue or event. Then, have students brainstorm for possible examples of each kind of source for their topics.

Apply It! Guide students through the instructions for creating a research plan and explain that you will provide support for each step. Encourage students to gather the notes and information they need to complete their research plan in a single place, such as a computer folder or a research portfolio.

Feature Assignment **Prewriting** *Feature Assignment* **Prewriting**

Make a Research Plan

Once you have your research question, you are ready to make a research plan. As part of your plan, you will create a time line for finishing your report. You also will find and evaluate sources of information.

Find Authoritative, Objective Sources For your report, you will need to **compile data,** or gather information, from a variety of sources. Make sure the sources you plan to use are **relevant**—they should be related to the topic you are researching and not out of date. Use a variety of **advanced search strategies** including electronic databases, card catalogues, and search engines to locate your resources. For most topics, there are different resources from which to choose. Look at these tips:

Print Resources
- Find print resources in libraries and bookstores.
- Use encyclopedias, magazines, newspapers, and textbooks.
- Search for print resources using electronic databases or with help from the reference librarian.

Electronic Resources
- Find electronic resources using search engines on the Internet.
- Choose only authoritative, reliable sites, such as those ending in:
  .edu (educational institution)
  .gov (government group)
  .org (not-for-profit organization; these may be biased)
- If you are not sure that a site is reliable and unbiased, do not use it.

Interviews with Experts
- Ask questions of an expert on your topic.
- Set up a short in-person, e-mail, or telephone interview.
- Record the interview and take good notes.

Multimedia Resources
- Watch film or TV documentaries about your topic.
- Listen to podcasts related to the topic.
- Search for relevant photos, diagrams, charts, and graphs.

Evaluate Your Sources Do not assume that all sources of information on your topic are useful, good, or trustworthy. Use the checklist on page 233 to evaluate sources of information you find. The more questions that you can answer with a yes, the more likely you should use the source.

232 Research Writing

Modify Your Plan Tell students that a research plan outlines a process that may change over time. Remind them that their research question or sources may change as they discover more information about their topic, but their vigorous approach to gathering and evaluating their sources will not.

> *Teacher Tip*
>
> **Quick Write** Find the text of a brief speech to deliver to the class. After you have given the speech, have students write a summary of what they heard. Then, use the text of the speech and students' summaries to discuss the differences between primary and secondary sources and the validity of each.

3 STUDENT BOOK

Students can refer back to the Student Model as they plan their writing.

Checklist for Evaluating Sources

Does the source of information:

- ❑ Contain **relevant** information that answers your research questions?
- ❑ Provide **facts** and not just unsupported **subjective** opinions?
- ❑ Give facts and details at a level you can understand?
- ❑ Tell all sides of a story, so that it is **unbiased**?
- ❑ Provide **authoritative and accurate** information written or compiled by experts?
- ❑ Have a recent **publication date**, indicating it is up-to-date?

Distinguish Between Types of Sources As you research, you will discover two kinds of sources: primary sources and secondary sources. Your teacher may require that you use both.

- A **primary source** is an original document you use for a firsthand account or investigation of your topic. For example, population data collected by the parks department is a primary source. Letters, diaries, and speeches are other examples.
- A **secondary source** is research that someone else has conducted and published. For example, a book called *The Birds of Central Texas* is a secondary source. When you use a secondary source, you are using another researcher's point of view on a topic.

Apply It! Create a written **research plan** and timeline with steps you can apply to obtain and evaluate information and to finish your report. After you have done some research in reference works and completed some additional text searches, create and follow a written research plan. List at least four relevant sources, including print and electronic resources, of information that you plan to use.

- Work with your teacher to set deadlines for finishing each step: research, thesis statement, drafting, and final report.
- For each source you plan to use, record full **bibliographic** information in a **standard format**. (See page 236.)
- Use the Checklist for Evaluating Sources to explain whether each of your sources is **reliable and valid**.
- Note whether each source is primary or secondary.

Modify Your Plan After you begin to research and investigate a topic, you may need to **narrow, or broaden, your research question**. If you cannot find answers to a research question, you may decide to refocus, or change the emphasis of, your topic.

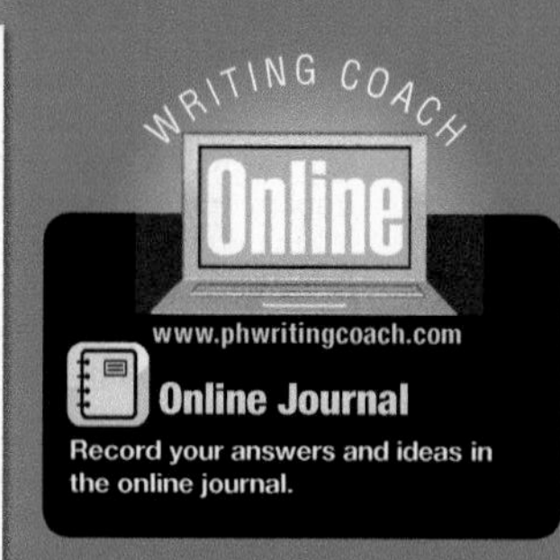

Online Journal

Record your answers and ideas in the online journal.

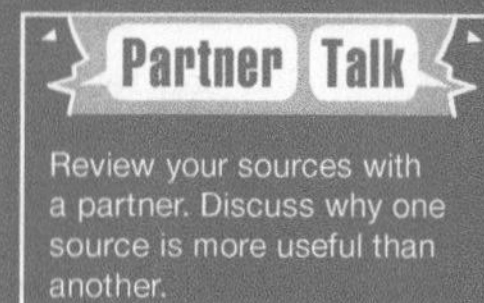

Review your sources with a partner. Discuss why one source is more useful than another.

Personalized Support

FEEDBACK

Teacher or Peer Feedback

To provide feedback to students as they make a research plan, ask or have student partners ask one another the following:

- What do you want your audience to know about your topic?
- Which resources are best for your topic and purpose?
- What sources have you found on your topic? Are they relevant?
- Will you use primary as well as secondary sources?

Working with ELLs

ELL **Sheltered Instruction:** Cognitive

Have students use visual and contextual support as they read to enhance and confirm understanding and develop background knowledge needed to comprehend increasingly challenging language. Show these examples of primary and secondary sources: wildlife population statistics, a diary, a letter, and a book about wildlife. Elicit and develop students' background knowledge of different sources as they read Distinguish Between Types of Sources.

Beginning Read the section, using the examples for support. Hold up a source. Help students complete the sentence *This is a [primary/secondary] source.*

Intermediate Read the section. Show students a source example. Have pairs complete sentences, such as *This diary is a [primary/secondary] source because ____.*

Advanced Support with the example sources. Have pairs read the section and draw a **T-Chart** with *Primary* and *Secondary* columns. List various sources as students categorize them and explain.

Advanced High Have students complete the Advanced activity. Have them identify two sources of each type.

The Digital • Print Path

1 

Using Writing Coach Online™ or the student book, students learn to collect and organize data and the rules regarding plagiarism.

2 Students take notes, gather information, and record their ideas in their online journals or notebooks.

Collect and Organize Your Data

Tell students that they will use a computer or handwritten notes to record information about their topic from multiple sources.

Keep Track of Multiple Sources Have students turn to page 229 and identify the range of sources in the Works Cited section of the Student Model. Tell students that they can learn more about proper citation styles on pages 236 and R16.

Take Notes Guide students through the bulleted instructions for taking notes. Explain that notes should include complete information but do not have to include complete sentences, unless the note is a direct quotation. Conclude by asking students to identify the heading and details on the example note.

Apply It! Have students begin collecting and organizing data for their research reports using proper source tracking and note-taking techniques.

Avoid Plagiarism

Read aloud the introductory paragraph, pointing out the definition of plagiarism. At this time, you may wish to explain to students the consequences of plagiarism in your class.

Careful Note-taking Matters Emphasize to students the importance of careful note-taking during the research process. Then, guide students to identify the plagiarized material in the example note.

Say: I notice that the *Post-Civil War* notes contain many of the same important phrases as the original source. For example, forms of important phrases such as *cradle of the cattle industry* and *depressed conditions* occur in both versions of the source material.

Ask: What other important words are repeated in the source material and the note? (livestock, dominated, economy)

Have students read and discuss the strategies for avoiding plagiarism in the chart. You may wish to present examples of each strategy to the class.

Feature Assignment **Prewriting** *Feature Assignment* **Prewriti**

Collect and Organize Your Data

As you follow your research plan for your informational research report, you will need to use **multiple sources** of information. Notes will help you remember and keep track of your sources and information. Different forms of notes include handwritten notes on note cards, typed notes in an electronic document, and a learning log summarizing what you know and still need to know about your topic.

Keep Track of Multiple Sources You can create a card for each source, and give each its own number. **Note the full bibliographic information,** or publishing details for the source, including the author, title, city of publication, publisher, and copyright date. The example shown is from the Student Model. It matches MLA style used in the Works Cited on page 229.

> *Source 3*
>
> Utley, Robert M., ed. *The Story of the West.* New York: DK Publishing, Inc., 2003. Print.

Take Notes When you take notes from a relevant print or electronic source, follow these guidelines.

- Note only **relevant** information—facts and details that get at your research question.
- Look for longer thematic patterns or constructs in the information you investigate. **Categorize** the notes using headings that sum up the **theme** or main idea of each group of notes.
- Be very careful to use your own words. It's all right to use abbreviations and incomplete sentences in your notes.
- If you want to quote someone, enclose the exact words in large quotation marks. If you are taking notes on a computer, you might also boldface the whole quotation. These techniques will remind you that the words are someone else's and not your own.

> *Notes From Source 3*
>
> Cowboys and railroads
> - Till about 1880, rr lines were far from cattle ranches, so cowboys had to drive cattle to railheads.
> - As rr lines came West, long cattle drives no longer needed.

Apply It! Create numbered source cards for all of your sources. Take notes from each source, creating a different note card for each category of information. Organizing notes by **categories or themes** can help you to make connections between data and to see big ideas. Paraphrase or summarize the information in your own words. If you want to include a direct quotation, carefully copy the original and enclose the quotation in quotation marks.

234 Research Writing

Try It! Have students work with a partner to identify the plagiarized material and write an appropriate paraphrase.

Partner Talk

Remind students to be active listeners when discussing their note-taking procedures.

Writer's Block

IF students have difficulty paraphrasing source material. . .

THEN have partners practice orally paraphrasing passages from the Student Model. One student paraphrases a passage without looking at the text, while the other checks the paraphrase against the original text. Have students discuss how the paraphrase is like and unlike the original passage.

3 STUDENT BOOK

Students can refer back to the Student Model as they plan their writing.

Avoid Plagiarism

Plagiarism is presenting someone else's words or ideas as your own, without documenting, or identifying, the source of the information. Plagiarism is a serious error with severe consequences. Do not plagiarize.

Careful Note-taking Matters You can plagiarize without meaning to do so. The student who wrote this note card made mistakes. She followed the original source too closely. Also, she didn't include a source number that would link the note card to its source's full publication information.

The cradle of the range-cattle industry was post-Civil-War Texas, and there livestock dominated the economy, despite depressed conditions of local markets. Little else was available to returning Confederate veterans who sought employment, or to the adolescent sons of men killed in the war.

Original Source

Post-Civil War

Post-Civil War Texas was the cradle of the cattle industry. Livestock dominated the Texas economy, even though local markets were sometimes depressed. Returning Confederate veterans had little employment available to them. This was also true of sons of men killed in the war.

from Cowboy Life: Reconstructing an American Myth by William W. Savage, Jr.

Plagiarized Notes

Use these strategies to avoid plagiarism.

- **Paraphrase** When you paraphrase information from a source, restate the writer's idea using your own words. Read a passage, and think about what it means. Then, write it as you might explain it to someone else.
- **Summarize** When you summarize a long passage from a source, briefly state its most important ideas in your own words.
- **Direct Quote** If you use a direct quotation, enclose the writer's exact words in quotation marks, and identify who said it.

Try It! Look at the plagiarized notes in the example. Highlight the parts to differentiate the lines that are plagiarizing rather than paraphrasing the original. Now, write a new note based on the original source. Do not plagiarize.

Online Journal

Record your answers and ideas in the online journal.

Review taking notes with a partner. Explain why each of these is important:

- Citing valid and reliable sources
- Using your own words to summarize ideas
- Making large quotation marks for direct quotations

Monitor your partner's spoken language by asking follow-up questions.

Personalized Support

FEEDBACK Teacher or Peer Feedback

To provide feedback to students as they collect and organize data, ask or have student partners ask one another the following:

- Are you relying on several sources, both primary and secondary?
- What questions do you still need answered?
- How are you recording this information?

Differentiated Instruction

RTI Strategy for Special Needs Students

Help students understand how using certain words and phrases from a source can lead to plagiarism. Locate a page from a source, reproduce it, and distribute it to students. Have students make note cards from the source. Work with each student or with pairs to check that their notes do not follow the source too closely. Have them underline passages that are too close and paraphrase or summarize them using different words.

Strategy for Spanish Speakers

Students whose home language is Spanish may use incorrect punctuation for quotes due to the use of angled, double, and single quotation marks in Spanish. Have students read the original source information on page 235 and write a note card with a quoted sentence or phrase. Remind them to use English double quotation marks. Invite volunteers to share their punctuated quotes on the board. Remind students to include complete publication information in notes.

1 

Using Writing Coach Online™ or the student book, students learn to document their sources.

2 

Students practice creating a Works Cited page in their online journals or notebooks.

Document Your Sources

Tell students that the source citations in a research report are like a roadmap; they identify and lead readers to sources for the information presented in the text. Emphasize that the formatting of this information must follow specific guidelines.

Works Cited Have students turn to the Works Cited section of the Student Model on page 229. Guide students to notice that the sources are listed in alphabetical order.

Then, guide students to identify the information cited for each type of source listed on page 236. Tell students that complete information may not be available for some sources; in such cases, leave out the missing information and format the other information as usual. Also, tell students that underlining can be used instead of italics in handwritten work.

At this time, you may wish to have students turn to page R16 to review citation styles for other common sources.

Parenthetical Citations Tell students that parenthetical citations occur at the end of sentences in the main text of a research report. Then, guide students to associate the citation with its corresponding entry on the Works Cited page.

Say: I see that the Student Model passage includes a parenthetical citation. When I turn to the Works Cited on page 229, I see that the information in the passage is from the Web source "The West: Episode 5: Cowboys," by Ken Burns.

Ask: What information is included in the parenthetical citation on page 227, line 40, for a book by two authors? (the last names of both authors)

Try It! **Have students** complete the citation exercise. Then check the accuracy and completeness of their responses.

1. "Rawhide Rodeo Company." *rawhiderodeo.com*. N.p., n.d. Web. 20 Dec. 2009.
2. Bopp, Suzanne. "Calling All Cowboys." *National Geographic TRAVELER* Sept. 2009: 60–64. Print.

Feature Assignment Prewriting Feature Assignment Prewriting

Document Your Sources

When you write a research report, you need to cite all **researched information** that is not common knowledge, and cite it **according to a standard format.**

Works Cited On the Works Cited page at the end of your report, list all the sources that you used. Do not include sources you looked into but did not use. Follow the format shown in a standard style manual, such as that of the Modern Language Association (MLA) or American Psychological Association (APA). Your teacher will tell you which standard format style to use.

Look at the example citations. Use these and the MLA Style for Listing Sources on page R16 as a guide for writing your citations. Pay attention to formatting, including italics, abbreviations, and punctuation.

Book

Author's last name, author's first name followed by the author's middle name or initial (if given). *Full title of book.* City where book was published: Name of publisher, year of publication. Medium of publication.

Slatta, Richard W. *Cowboy: The Illustrated History.* New York: Sterling, 2006. Print.

Magazine Article

Author's last name, author's first name followed by the author's middle name or initial (if given). "Title of article." *Title of magazine* Full date of magazine issue: page numbers or plus sign (+) if the article appears on nonconsecutive pages. Medium of publication.

Draper, Robert. "21st Century Cowboys: Why the Spirit Endures." *National Geographic* Dec. 2007: 114+. Print.

Web Page

Author's last name, author's first name followed by author's middle name or initial (if given) OR compiler, or editor (if given). "Name of page." *Name of Web site.* Name of publisher, institution, or sponsor OR N.p if none given, date of posting OR n.d. if none given. Medium of publication. Date on which you accessed the page.

Officer, Lawrence H. and Samuel H. Williamson. "Six Ways to Compute the Relative Value of a U.S. Dollar Amount, 1774 to Present." *Measuring Worth.* Measuring Worth, 2009. Web. 2 Nov 2009.

236 Research Writing

Critique Your Research Process

Explain to students that their research process might need to change in response to new information. For example, a new source might point their research question in a different direction. Tell students to remain flexible and critical toward their research process in order to make the most of new developments.

Apply It! Read aloud and have students complete the instructions for creating a Works Cited page and writing a thesis statement.

Partner Talk

Remind students to listen and speak in turn as they discuss their research sources.

Students can refer back to the Student Model as they plan their writing.

Parenthetical Citations A parenthetical citation refers to a source listed on the Works Cited page. It helps you to **avoid plagiarizing by integrating,** or including, **source information** right in your report. Because a parenthetical citation gives just the author or title and page number, it does not interrupt **the flow ideas.** Here is a parenthetical citation from the Student Model.

from **"The Cowboy: Myth Versus Reality"** page 227; lines 33–35

One person who had seen "real cowboys" remarked that a cowboy is "just a plain bowlegged human who smelled very horsey at times" (Burns).

If the name of the author is mentioned in the sentence, only the page number is given in parentheses.

In contrast, Schultz and Tishler say, most actual cowboys were short and slight (though wiry), so as not to weigh down their horses (2).

Try It! Use the documentation style shown on page 236 to create a short Works Cited page including these sources:

- A Web page called "Rawhide Rodeo Company." The Web site is called rawhiderodeo.com. No information about the author, publisher, or date is available. The writer looked at the page on December 20, 2009.
- An article titled "Calling All Cowboys" by Suzanne Bopp in *National Geographic TRAVELER* magazine. It was published in September 2008 on pages 60–64.

Critique Your Research Process

At every step in the research process, be prepared to adjust or change your research plan. If you can't find enough information, **try broadening your research question.** If you have too much information, you might need to **narrow your question.** In either case, it's important to stick to your **timetable.** If you've found answers to your research question, you're ready to start drafting.

Apply It! Write an entry on your Works Cited page for every source you used for information in your report. To format your sources correctly, use MLA style or the style your teacher has directed you to use. Confirm that you have researched enough information to begin writing your draft.

www.phwritingcoach.com

Interactive Model

Refer back to the Student Model as you document your sources.

Online Journal

Record your answers and ideas in the online journal.

Partner Talk

Get together with a partner to discuss research sources. Where have you looked for information on your topic? What sources are reliable? How have you been keeping track of the sources you have used? As you speak, practice newly acquired vocabulary by correctly producing the word's sound.

Personalized Support

FEEDBACK **Teacher or Peer Feedback**

To provide feedback to students as they document their sources, ask or have student partners ask one another the following:

- Where can you go to get information on how to cite sources?
- Do you have all the information you need to correctly cite your sources?
- As a result of your research, did you change your research question? How did you change it?

Differentiated Instruction

RTI Strategy for Below-Level Students Have each student record the information, in no particular form or order, for one source being used in the research report. Have students exchange the information and write a correct Works Cited page entry for the source. Ask volunteers to write their entry on the board. Have the class determine whether each entry is written correctly and then correct it if necessary.

PRE-AP Enrichment for Above-Level Students When students are reaching the end of their research process, have them describe their research and their research plan to a partner. Encourage students to discuss issues such as how they have adjusted their plan as necessary, which research techniques have been effective and which have not, and what pitfalls they have encountered. Ask students to write one research tip or lesson they learned from their partner and share it with the class.

The Digital • Print Path

1 

Using **Writing Coach Online**™ or the student book, students read and discuss the Outline for Success for a research report.

2 

Students discuss how the Student Model illustrates the characteristics of a research report.

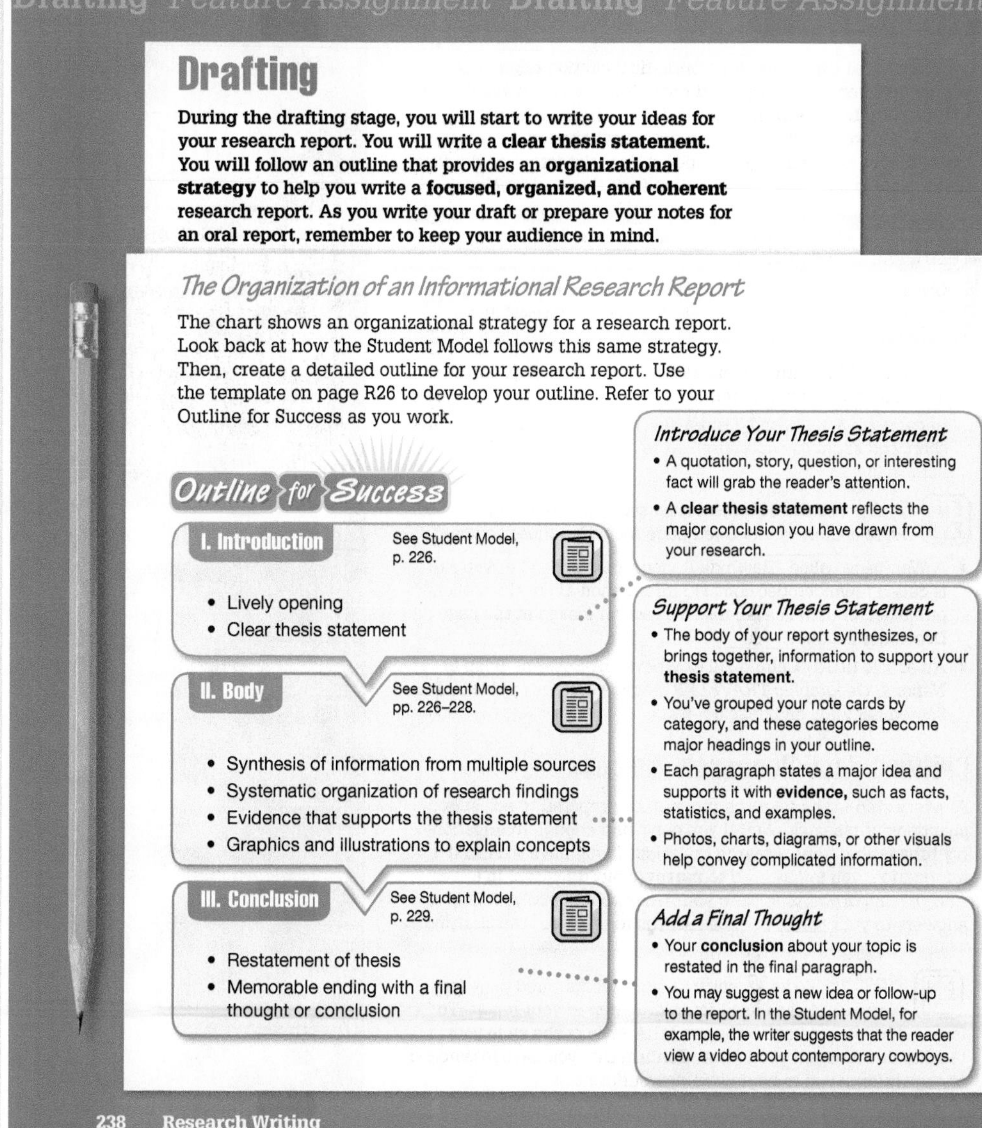

Drafting *Feature Assignment* Drafting *Feature Assignment* D

Drafting

During the drafting stage, you will start to write your ideas for your research report. You will write a clear thesis statement. You will follow an outline that provides an organizational strategy to help you write a focused, organized, and coherent research report. As you write your draft or prepare your notes for an oral report, remember to keep your audience in mind.

The Organization of an Informational Research Report

The chart shows an organizational strategy for a research report. Look back at how the Student Model follows this same strategy. Then, create a detailed outline for your research report. Use the template on page R26 to develop your outline. Refer to your Outline for Success as you work.

Outline for Success

I. Introduction — See Student Model, p. 226.

- Lively opening
- Clear thesis statement

Introduce Your Thesis Statement

- A quotation, story, question, or interesting fact will grab the reader's attention.
- A **clear thesis statement** reflects the major conclusion you have drawn from your research.

II. Body — See Student Model, pp. 226–228.

- Synthesis of information from multiple sources
- Systematic organization of research findings
- Evidence that supports the thesis statement
- Graphics and illustrations to explain concepts

Support Your Thesis Statement

- The body of your report synthesizes, or brings together, information to support your **thesis statement.**
- You've grouped your note cards by category, and these categories become major headings in your outline.
- Each paragraph states a major idea and supports it with **evidence,** such as facts, statistics, and examples.
- Photos, charts, diagrams, or other visuals help convey complicated information.

III. Conclusion — See Student Model, p. 229.

- Restatement of thesis
- Memorable ending with a final thought or conclusion

Add a Final Thought

- Your **conclusion** about your topic is restated in the final paragraph.
- You may suggest a new idea or follow-up to the report. In the Student Model, for example, the writer suggests that the reader view a video about contemporary cowboys.

238 Research Writing

Drafting

Outline for Success

Explain that the Outline for Success shows an organizational strategy for a research report. Students will use the Outline to write a focused, organized, and coherent draft of their research report. Then, distribute printed copies of the outline template or have students log on to Writing Coach Online.

I. Introduction

Link the Outline to a specific research report by having students turn to the Student Model on pages 226–229. Ask a volunteer to read aloud the first paragraph (lines 1–13). Then, guide students to understand how the author uses an interesting description to grab the reader's attention.

Say: I notice that the student writer begins the report with a description of a typical cowboy. She uses vivid details to describe the cowboy's physical appearance, habits, and character traits. The details introduce the report's main topic and immediately grab readers' attention.

Ask: How does the author introduce the idea that the popular image of a cowboy differs from the reality? (She asks the question, "How does this image relate to the real cowboys?")

Have students work with a partner to discuss the techniques they will use to create a lively opening for their research report.

II. Body

Lead a discussion about how the body section of the Student Model reflects the characteristics of a research report.

- Synthesis of information from multiple sources (lines 32–40, 81–96)
- Systematic organization of research findings (lines 14–15, 24–25, 32–33, 41–42, 62–63)
- Evidence that supports the thesis statement (lines 32–40, 41–57, 63–70, 81–88)
- Graphics and illustrations to explain concepts (pages 227, 229)

III. Conclusion

Have small groups discuss how the Student Model conclusion reflects the characteristics of a research report (lines 97–105).

Start Your Draft

Have small groups read aloud and discuss the boxed instructions for drafting. Direct students to work individually on their first draft.

Coach's Corner

If you are modeling the writing process for students with your own topic or a student volunteer's, you may wish to use these prompts to guide your drafting and discussion:

- **I will write a lively opening** to introduce my thesis.
- **I will write a clear thesis statement** that is based on my research.

Discuss the choices you make and solicit feedback from students.

3 Students begin writing their report online or in their notebooks.

4 Students submit their work paragraph by paragraph to the **Interactive Writing Coach™** for scoring and feedback, or share their work with their teacher.

5 Students receive personalized feedback from the **Interactive Writing Coach™** or feedback from their teacher. Students may continue to work on their drafts.

Start Your Draft

To complete your draft, use the checklist. Use your specific thesis statement; your detailed outline that shows your topic sentence and supporting evidence, and your plan for the logical organization of the main ideas; and the Outline for Success as guides.

While drafting, aim at writing your ideas, not on making your writing perfect. Remember, you will have the chance to improve your draft when you revise and edit.

- √ Begin your **introduction** with several sentences that catch your reader's attention.
- √ End with a clearly worded **thesis statement** based on the **conclusion** you've drawn about your research question.

- √ Present your findings in a meaningful format. Develop the **body** of the report one paragraph at a time. Choose only the strongest **supporting evidence** for each **idea**.
- √ For each paragraph, draft a **topic sentence** stating the main idea. Each main idea should support your thesis.
- √ Marshal the evidence you have collected and organized, then synthesize it to support and explain your topic.
- √ Include conclusions you draw from your research. Summarize or paraphrase your research findings in a systematic way that readers can understand. Remember to give relevant, logical reasons for your conclusions.

- √ Draft a **concluding paragraph** that restates your thesis. Try to add a final thought to make the ending more memorable or interesting.

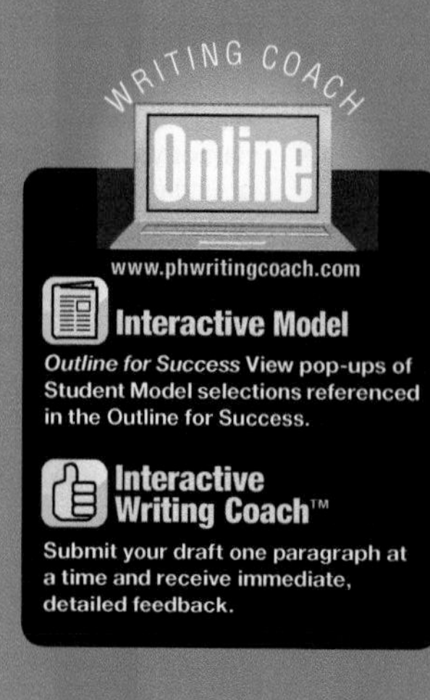

Interactive Model

Outline for Success View pop-ups of Student Model selections referenced in the Outline for Success.

Interactive Writing Coach™

Submit your draft one paragraph at a time and receive immediate, detailed feedback.

Personalized Support

Interactive Writing Coach™

Students submit their research reports paragraph by paragraph for personalized feedback and scores.

Teacher or Peer Feedback

To provide feedback to students on their first draft, ask or have student partners ask one another the following:

- Can you explain how you organized your ideas in this piece?
- Why did you choose this introduction? Does it grab your reader and identify your thesis or controlling idea?
- What supporting evidence have you included?
- How does your conclusion add to your report?

Working with ELLs

ELL Sheltered Instruction: Cognitive

Have students develop and demonstrate an increasing ability to distinguish formal and informal English and an increasing knowledge of when to use each. Have them adapt spoken language appropriately for formal purposes. Present a variety of situations, such as a friendly discussion or a school presentation, and help students determine whether it calls for formal or informal language. Then:

Beginning Model a situation using informal English, such as talking about a movie with a friend: *That movie's awesome!* Have students repeat, then orally adapt the response for a formal purpose: *The movie is impressive.*

Intermediate Speak formal and informal sentences. Have partners identify each as formal or informal and orally adapt the informal language for a formal purpose.

Advanced Have partners read aloud examples of formal and informal sentences. Have listeners identify each as formal or informal and adapt the informal sentences for a formal purpose.

Advanced High Have students complete the Advanced activity, then say their own formal and informal sentences.

1 

Using Writing Coach Online™ or the student book, students identify different forms of supporting evidence.

2 

Students refer back to the Student Model for examples of supporting evidence.

Provide and Document Evidence

Tell students that the evidence they present can take several forms. Then, read and discuss how to use each form of evidence to support their claims, using Student Model examples to guide the discussion:

- **Facts and statistics** (lines 9–11, 14–30, 55–61, 64–70, 71–75, 76–78)
- **Examples** (lines 1–6, 83–96)
- **Quotations** (lines 33–35, 37–40, 43–54)

Apply It! Read aloud the instructions. Then, have students develop responses that show an understanding of how to correctly format quotations and citations.

Use Graphics and Illustrations

Tell students that graphics help readers to understand or visualize complex information. Remind students that they must cite sources both for borrowed graphics and graphics they created from borrowed information.

Then, have students read and discuss the information about each type of graphic. Guide students to understand how the example graph organizes information.

Say: **I noticed** that the graph is a pie chart. It is divided into sections to show the three main ethnic backgrounds of cowboys and what percentage of the whole each ethnicity comprised. The graph helps me understand at a glance the diverse backgrounds of cowboys in the Old West.

Ask: To which ethnic group did the second largest percentage of cowboys in the Old West belong? What was the group's percentage of the whole? (African American; 25%)

Have students work with a partner to discuss where they would place the example graph in the Student Model text on pages 226–229.

Drafting *Feature Assignment* Drafting *Feature Assignment* D

Provide and Document Evidence

While you are drafting, you will provide **evidence** to support your thesis statement and related claims. Your **claims** are an important part of your **analysis** of your topic. They are your **point of view** or understanding of information connected to you. Be careful to differentiate between your opinions and ideas and those of other people. To do so, **document** the words and ideas of other people when you provide evidence.

Give Facts and Statistics Facts are convincing evidence because they can be proven true. Statistics, or facts stated in numbers, are also convincing when they come from authoritative and up-to-date sources. Document facts and statistics that are not common knowledge or that could not be found in most sources about a topic.

Give Examples Use concrete examples to make abstract or complicated ideas easier to understand. You must identify the source of examples that you found in your research, but you do not need to document examples from your personal experience or observations.

Quote Authorities Direct quotations can be convincing evidence. However, you should not use a quotation when **summarizing** or **paraphrasing** would be just as clear. Weave quotations and citations into the flow of your ideas as shown in this example from the Student Model.

STUDENT MODEL from **"The Cowboy: Myth Versus Reality"** page 227; lines 37–40

In 1875, a Wyoming newspaper described a group of "real" cowboys as "rough men with shaggy hair and wild staring eyes in butternut trousers stuffed into great rough boots" (Schultz and Tishler).

Remember these guidelines:

- Use your own words to identify the expert, integrating quotations and citations into your text to maintain the flow of ideas.
- Separate and inset a quote of four lines or more.
- Use correct punctuation and an accepted format. (See pages 246–247.)
- Follow quotes with a proper parenthetical citation.

Apply It! Draft a paragraph for your research report. Your paragraph should include facts, examples, a quotation, and citation. Remember to correctly format your quotations and citations to avoid interrupting the flow of your ideas.

Apply It! Guide students through the instructions for brainstorming for visual elements. Then, have students with similar topics work as partners to discuss and develop appropriate graphics. Have students share their ideas about effective graphics with the class.

Extension Have students bring in examples of each kind of graphic for their topic. Lead a discussion about how each graphic conveys information to the viewer.

Partner Talk

Role play using constructive language when providing feedback on a partner's ideas.

Coach's Corner

If you are modeling the writing process for students with your own draft or a student volunteer's, use these prompts to model using evidence and graphics:

- **I will place a quote here because** I want to provide convincing evidence.
- **I will place a graph here so** my audience can visualize this information.

Discuss the choices you make and solicit feedback from students.

3 Students continue writing their report online or in their notebooks.

4 Students may resubmit their work paragraph by paragraph to the **Interactive Writing Coach™** for scoring and feedback, or share their work with their teacher.

5 Students receive personalized feedback from the **Interactive Writing Coach™** or feedback from their teacher.

Use Graphics and Illustrations

Your report can present evidence in graphics and visuals as well as words. For a report on a scientific topic, diagrams, charts, and other types of graphics can help your audience understand your ideas. In other reports, photographs, maps, and other graphics can add valuable concrete detail. Be sure to refer to the graphic (usually called a "figure") in your text. Then, label your visual with a figure or table number, caption, and source citations for the data. Use caution when copying an existing graphic because you will need permission from the copyright holder if you publish your work for use outside school.

- **Photographs** Use a photograph to help your audience picture how something looks. If you insert a photograph in your report, include a caption, or brief sentence explaining what the photo shows.
- **Maps** By providing geographic information visually, maps give your reader a better idea of locations you mention in your report. Always include a legend and a compass rose.
- **Charts, Tables, and Graphs** Create a chart, table, or graph to provide information in a more visual or organized way. Give each a title that tells what it shows. If you include more than one, number them in numerical order. Include a citation for the source of information you used to create the chart, table, or graph.

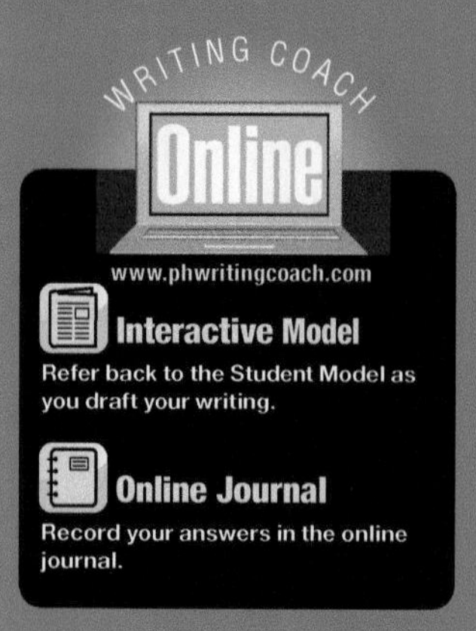

Source: Based on data from Schultz and Tishler

Apply It! Brainstorm for two graphics that you might use to present information in your informational research report in the most meaningful format.

- Be sure to identify the type of information each graphic would explain, find or create the two graphics, and integrate them into your report.
- Remember to give your graphics titles.
- Use a style manual to format graphics and to document your sources.
- Use peer, teacher, or family feedback to check that the quality of your created and researched visuals is appropriate for your report.

WRITING COACH Online

www.phwritingcoach.com

Interactive Model

Refer back to the Student Model as you draft your writing.

Online Journal

Record your answers in the online journal.

Partner Talk

Get together with a partner and participate in an extended discussion to evaluate the graphics that you are considering using. Ask specific questions to enhance your comprehension. Express your opinions and explain to your partner why you have chosen each graphic and how it provides important information for your report.

Personalized Support

Interactive Writing Coach™

Students submit their research reports paragraph by paragraph for personalized feedback and scores.

Teacher or Peer Feedback

To provide feedback to students as they continue drafting, ask or have student partners ask one another the following:

- Have you checked your facts and statistics to make sure they are correct?
- Have you provided all the information you need to cover your topic?
- What kinds of visuals or graphics are you including?
- How do they support your topic?
- What more do you need to do?

Differentiated Instruction

RTI Strategy for Below-Level Students Have several students describe their research topics. Ask other students to describe specific ideas for including each type of graphic described on page 241 in the report. Write the topics and ideas on the board. Then have students discuss which graphics would be most useful, interesting, and practical to include with each report.

Enrichment for Gifted/Talented Students Encourage artistic students to focus on creating interesting graphics for their report. For example, students who are talented photographers or artists can create a variety of illustrations. Encourage students to develop their map-making skills to draw detailed, attractive maps. Point out that graphs, charts, and tables can include artistic elements that make them more interesting and useful. Have students display their completed research reports with the graphics.

The Digital • Print Path

1 

Using **Writing Coach Online™** or the student book, students study the first and second drafts of the Student Model to see how the writer used Revision RADaR to improve his or her writing.

2 Students use the Revision RADaR strategy to revise their own writing.

Revising: Making It Better

Point out the page title to students and explain that revising means making improvements to a writing draft. Then, read aloud the opening paragraph to introduce the Revision RADaR strategies. You may wish to have students review Chapter 3 for more information on Revision RADaR.

Kelly Gallagher, M. Ed.

KEEP REVISION ON YOUR RADAR

1ST DRAFT After students have read the first draft, have them turn to page 238 and review the Outline for Success. Work with students to understand that the questions the author asked about the draft are based on the characteristics of a research report. For example, call out the first question and note how it addresses the concerns listed in the Introduction section in the Outline for Success.

Then, have students work in small groups to develop other questions about the draft based on the genre characteristics.

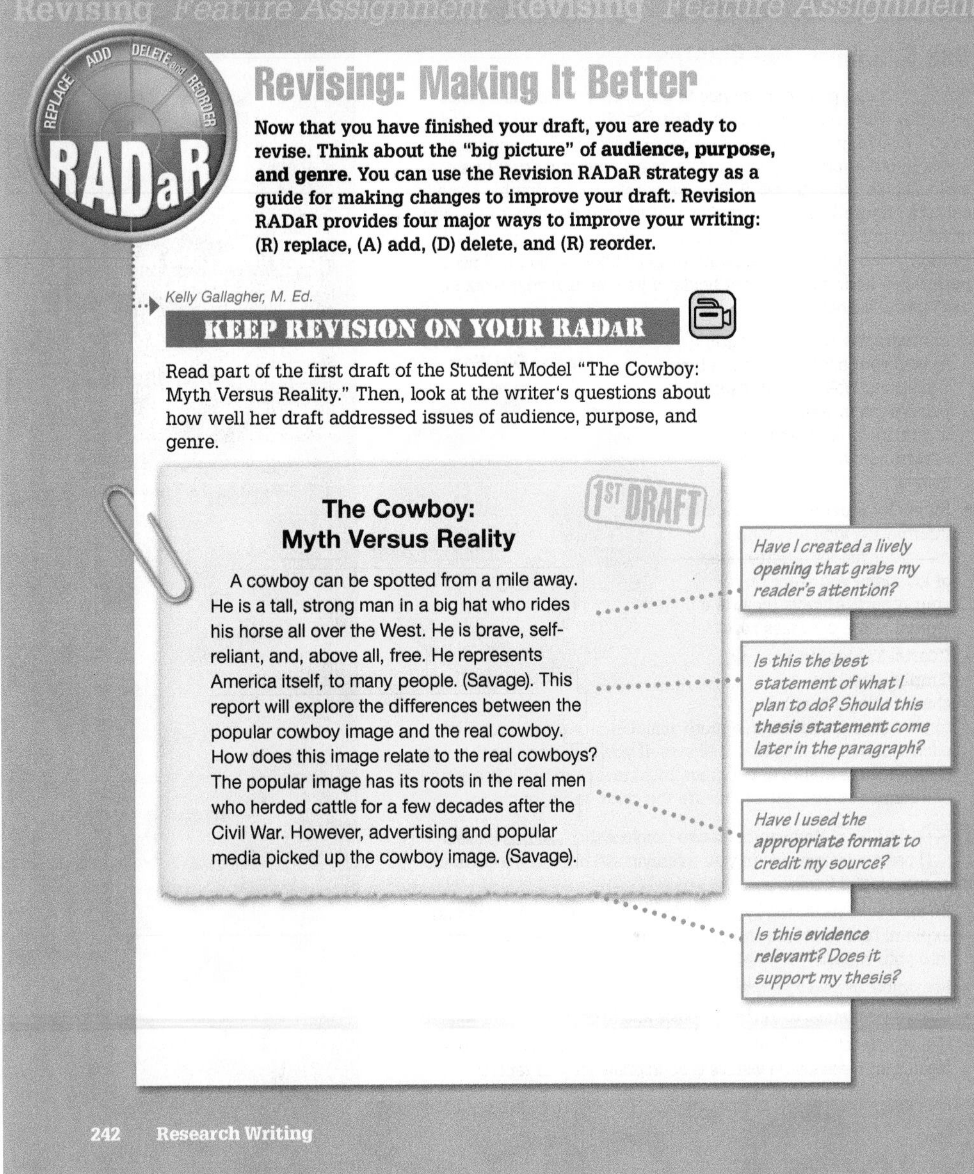

Revising Feature Assignment Revising Feature Assignment

Revising: Making It Better

Now that you have finished your draft, you are ready to revise. Think about the "big picture" of audience, purpose, and genre. You can use the Revision RADaR strategy as a guide for making changes to improve your draft. Revision RADaR provides four major ways to improve your writing: (R) replace, (A) add, (D) delete, and (R) reorder.

Kelly Gallagher, M. Ed.

KEEP REVISION ON YOUR RADAR

Read part of the first draft of the Student Model "The Cowboy: Myth Versus Reality." Then, look at the writer's questions about how well her draft addressed issues of audience, purpose, and genre.

1ST DRAFT

The Cowboy: Myth Versus Reality

A cowboy can be spotted from a mile away. He is a tall, strong man in a big hat who rides his horse all over the West. He is brave, self-reliant, and, above all, free. He represents America itself, to many people. (Savage). This report will explore the differences between the popular cowboy image and the real cowboy. How does this image relate to the real cowboys? The popular image has its roots in the real men who herded cattle for a few decades after the Civil War. However, advertising and popular media picked up the cowboy image. (Savage).

Have I created a lively opening that grabs my reader's attention?

Is this the best statement of what I plan to do? Should this thesis statement come later in the paragraph?

Have I used the appropriate format to credit my source?

Is this evidence relevant? Does it support my thesis?

242 Research Writing

2ND DRAFT Guide students to understand how the author used the RADaR strategies to revise the first draft.

Think Aloud **I noticed** that in the 1st draft the writer uses a description of a typical cowboy to introduce the topic and get readers' attention, but the description isn't as vivid as it might be. In the 2nd draft, though, I see an *A*. This shows that the writer has added sentences containing descriptive language to make the introduction even more vivid.

Work with students to identify words and rhetorical devices such as similes used to create a vivid description in the introduction.

Have students work in small groups to discuss other changes to the draft.

Apply It! Review the bulleted instructions for using Revision RADaR. Remind students to question their drafts based on the genre characteristics listed on the Outline for Success on page 238. Tell students to use each RADaR strategy at least once.

Coach's Corner

If you are modeling the writing process for students with your own draft or a student volunteer's, use these prompts to focus on the Revision RADaR *Replace* strategy and guide discussion:

- **I replaced words that were dull or vague** in order to include more vivid, interesting words.
- **I replaced vague examples with facts** that I summarized from a reliable source.

Discuss the choices you make and solicit feedback from students.

3 Students submit their writing paragraph by paragraph to the **Interactive Writing Coach™** for scoring and feedback, or share their work with their teacher.

4 Students receive customized feedback from the **Interactive Writing Coach™** or feedback from their teacher. Students may continue to revise their drafts.

Now look at how the writer applied Revision RADaR to write an improved second draft.

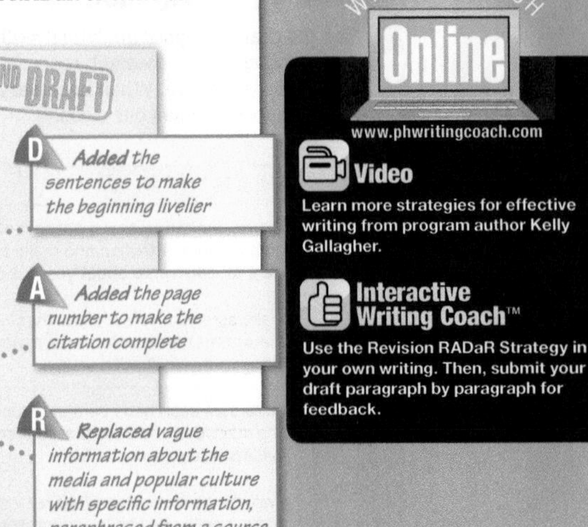

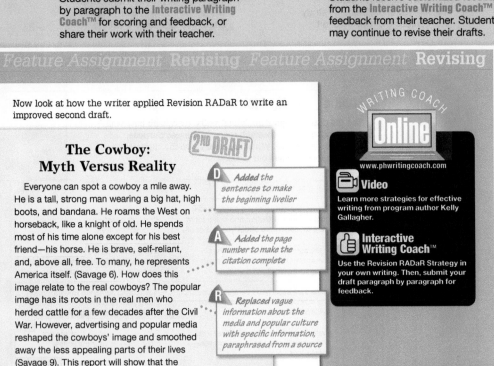

The Cowboy: Myth Versus Reality

2ND DRAFT

Everyone can spot a cowboy a mile away. He is a tall, strong man wearing a big hat, high boots, and bandana. He roams the West on horseback, like a knight of old. He spends most of his time alone except for his best friend—his horse. He is brave, self-reliant, and, above all, free. To many, he represents America itself. (Savage 6). How does this image relate to the real cowboys? The popular image has its roots in the real men who herded cattle for a few decades after the Civil War. However, advertising and popular media reshaped the cowboys' image and smoothed away the less appealing parts of their lives (Savage 9). This report will show that the popular image of the cowboy is more myth than reality.

D *Added the sentences to make the beginning livelier*

A *Added the page number to make the citation complete*

R *Replaced vague information about the media and popular culture with specific information, paraphrased from a source*

R *Reordered the thesis statement, placing it at the end of the introductory paragraph*

WRITING COACH Online

www.phwritingcoach.com

Video

Learn more strategies for effective writing from program author Kelly Gallagher.

Interactive Writing Coach™

Use the Revision RADaR Strategy in your own writing. Then, submit your draft paragraph by paragraph for feedback.

 *Apply It!* Use your Revision RADaR to revise your draft.

- First, determine whether you have addressed the needs of your audience, stated your thesis, and included the characteristics of an effective research report. Then, check that your ideas make sense within each paragraph and sentence, to track whether your text has **internal coherence.** Also check for **external coherence** by making sure the entire report flows logically.
- Then, apply Revision RADaR to make needed changes. Remember—you can use the steps in the strategy in any order.

Personalized Support

Interactive Writing Coach™

Students submit their research reports paragraph by paragraph for personalized feedback and scores.

Teacher or Peer Feedback

To provide feedback to students as they revise their first draft, ask or have student partners ask one another the following:

- Can you show me how you revised your text?
- How could you reorder these ideas so that their order is more logical?
- Is there any unnecessary text that you could delete?
- Have you achieved your purpose with this piece of writing?
- Have you addressed the questions and concerns of your audience?

Working with ELLs

ELL Sheltered Instruction: Cognitive

Help students read the revised Student Model, and use visual and contextual support to enhance and confirm understanding and to develop background knowledge needed to comprehend increasingly challenging language. To develop students' background knowledge about cowboys, show pictures of fictional, historic, and modern cowboys. Discuss the pictures and what they show about both real and mythical cowboys. Then:

Beginning Review the visual support. Refer to it as students read the revised draft. Help them complete frames like *People usually imagine [tall/short] cowboys.*

Intermediate Review the visual support, and have groups read the second draft. Have groups summarize the image of the cowboy discussed in the text.

Advanced Have partners read the second draft. Review the visual support, and have partners summarize the text. Have partners research about the real life of cowboys and present their findings.

Advanced High Have students complete the Advanced activity, then evaluate if the thesis in the second draft is clearly stated.

The Digital • Print Path

1 

Using Writing Coach Online™ or the student book, students study and discuss the revision chart.

2 

In a video by program author Kelly Gallagher, students learn more strategies for effective writing.

Revising: Making It Better

Look at the Big Picture

Introduce the revision chart to students. Explain that the Section column identifies the three main parts of a research report. The Evaluate column identifies the characteristics found in each section and explains how to assess them. The Revise column presents specific strategies for revising each characteristic.

Then, have students draw lines between and label the four sections of their drafts. Direct students to work individually to evaluate and revise their draft, using the chart to guide their work.

Revising Feature Assignment Revising Feature Assignment

Look at the Big Picture

Use the chart and your analytical skills to evaluate how well each section of your research report addresses **purpose, audience, and genre.** When necessary, use the suggestions in the chart to revise your piece.

Section	Evaluate	Revise
Introduction	• Check that the **opening paragraphs** grab readers' attention and make them want to learn more about your topic.	• Add a quotation, anecdote (brief story), or question to make your introduction lively.
	• Make sure you have a **clear thesis statement** that sets forth the major ideas your report will develop.	• Clarify your thesis statement to be sure it identifies the conclusions you have drawn about the topic.
Body	• Make sure each body paragraph develops one main idea and uses **marshalled evidence** to explain the topic.	• Add a topic sentence to each paragraph. Add evidence to support weakly developed paragraphs.
	• Evaluate the **relevance** of the reasons and evidence you use to support your conclusions.	• Take out any details that are not clearly tied to your purposes.
	• Check that information and major ideas are summarized, paraphrased, and organized in a **systematic way.**	• Compare paragraphs to your original outline to make sure similar ideas are categorized by theme or subtopic.
	• Make sure that you have used graphics when a visual can best illustrate the data.	• Convert data into graphics or pick up existing graphics to present your findings in the most meaningful format.
	• Make sure quotations and facts that are not common knowledge are **documented** and **formatted** and do not interrupt the flow of ideas.	• Review your note cards and source cards to confirm the source of each quotation. Add **parenthetical citations** in the correct format and style.
Conclusion	• Check that your final paragraph **restates your thesis.**	• If needed, revise the introduction and conclusion to ensure they agree.
	• Make sure your research report ends with a new **insight.**	• Add a quotation or fact that brings your report to a definite end.
Works Cited/ Bibliography	• Complete your **source list** using the style specified by your teacher.	• Add all documented sources you used in your paper to the Works Cited page.

244 Research Writing

Focus on Craft: Sentence Variety

Have students read the introductory text. Guide students to understand how using different sentence lengths and structures creates variety and helps writing flow better.

Say: I notice that the first sentence of the excerpt is short and uses a simple subject-verb structure. The last sentence, however, uses a different structure for variety.

Ask: How does the structure of the last sentence differ from that of the first sentence? Is this a good choice? Why or why not? (It begins with a prepositional phrase. It is a good choice because it provides variety.)

Have students work with a partner to discuss ways in which the excerpt achieves sentence variety.

Try It! Have students discuss the questions and record responses in their journals. Follow up with students to check that their responses reflect an understanding of how a variety of sentence structures and beginnings makes a paragraph interesting and effective.

Fine-Tune Your Draft

Apply It! Ask volunteers to read aloud the instructions for fine-tuning their drafts. Then have students work in pairs to create variety in sentence length and structure and to use transitions to link ideas.

Teacher and Family Feedback Have students identify Student Model examples of the characteristics that were marked for improvement. Use the Student Model references on page T238 to guide students to appropriate examples.

Teacher Tip

Quick Write Have students focus on one or two paragraphs of their draft and mark each sentence as simple, compound, or complex. Then have them revise the paragraphs to achieve greater variety either in sentence length or in sentence structure.

Using Writing Coach Online™ or the student book, students refer back to the Student Model for examples of writer's craft.

Students record answers to questions about writer's craft in their online journals or notebooks.

Students submit revised drafts to the Interactive Writing Coach™ for scoring and feedback, or share their work with their teacher.

Students receive customized feedback from the Interactive Writing Coach™ or feedback from their teacher.

Focus on Craft: Sentence Variety

Sentences can have different lengths and structures. Some are short and punchy, while others can flow on, connecting several ideas. Sentences can begin in different ways: with a pronoun or noun, with a series of adjectives, or with a prepositional or participial phrase. When you write a research report, try to vary the lengths, structures, and beginnings of your sentences. If you do, your writing will be more interesting to read and will flow more effectively. Look at these sentences from the Student Model.

from **"The Cowboy: Myth Versus Reality"**
page 226; lines 1–7

Everyone can spot a cowboy a mile away. He is a tall, strong man wearing a big hat, high boots, and bandana. He roams the West on horseback, like a knight of old. He spends most of his time alone except for his best friend—his horse. He is brave, self-reliant, and, above all, free. To many, he represents America itself (Savage 6).

Try It! Now, ask yourself these questions. Record your answers in your journal.

1. Compare the first and second drafts (pages 242–243). Why does the student writer change the structure of the first sentence?
2. Do any sentences in this paragraph begin in the same way? Would you advise the writer to change more sentence beginnings, or is repetition effective here?

Fine-Tune Your Draft

Apply It! Use the revision suggestions to prepare your final draft. Make sure you keep your audience and purpose in mind.

- **Focus on Sentence Variety** Ensure a mix of shorter and longer sentences. Follow a simple sentence with a compound or complex sentence.
- **Use Effective Transitions** Use transitional words and phrases such as *also* and *as a result* to link ideas and connect sentences and paragraphs. Because of the length of your work, you may need transitional sentences or paragraphs to help readers follow your thinking.

Teacher and Family Feedback Share your draft with your teacher or a family member. Carefully review the comments you receive and revise your final draft as needed.

Online Journal

Try It! Record your answers in the online journal.

Interactive Model

Refer back to the Student Model as you revise your writing.

Interactive Writing Coach™

Revise your draft and submit it paragraph by paragraph for feedback.

Personalized Support

Interactive Writing Coach™

Students submit their research reports paragraph by paragraph for personalized feedback and scores.

Teacher or Peer Feedback

To provide feedback to students as they continue to revise their first draft, ask or have student partners ask one another the following:

- What are you trying to say here? What part of the text could you replace to make your meaning clearer?
- Is there a more precise word you could use here?
- How does the rhythm of these sentences sound to you? Could you make the length and structure of these sentences more varied?
- How could you include transitional words and phrases here to help your reader understand these ideas?

Differentiated Instruction

PRE-AP Enrichment for Above-Level Students Challenge students to focus on sentence variety when revising their report. Have them create a chart with the headings *Sentence Length* and *Sentence Type* and record the number of sentences for each category in their draft. Encourage students to use the chart to determine which paragraphs need more variety and then to revise accordingly. Remind them to include a variety of sentences, including very short sentences, sentences beginning with phrases, and compound-complex sentences.

Strategy for Spanish Speakers
Students whose home language is Spanish may overuse complex sentences with multiple subordinate clauses, due to sentence structure in Spanish. Write a complex sentence with multiple subordinate clauses about cowboy myths on the board. Have students work in pairs to break the sentence into simple sentences. Invite volunteers to share their sentences with the class. Discuss the different solutions that the pairs came up with.

The Digital • Print Path

1 

In a video by program author Jeff Anderson, students learn effective editing techniques.

2 

Students record answers to questions about writer's craft in their online journals or notebooks.

Editing: Making It Correct

Discuss the opening paragraph with students. Explain that they will edit their drafts for proper grammar, mechanics, and spelling, including integrating quotations.

WRITE GUY *Jeff Anderson, M.Ed.*

WHAT DO YOU NOTICE?

Introduce students to integrating quotations into a paragraph by reading aloud the Student Model excerpt and discussing responses to the "Ask yourself" question that follows. Then, have students read the explanation of working a quotation into a paragraph.

To monitor students' comprehension, guide them to identify the techniques used to surround a quotation.

Say: In the sentence from the Student Model, **I notice** that an introductory phrase helps makes the quotation understandable for readers by telling when the newspaper article was published.

Ask: How does the writer use grammar to help readers understand the quotation? (The introduction and the quote fit together grammatically; even if the quotation marks were not there, the sentence would be grammatically correct.)

Have students give examples of sentences with quotations from their drafts and discuss whether the quotations are integrated properly.

Partner Talk Ask students to consider how punctuation helps distinguish the writer's words from the source material.

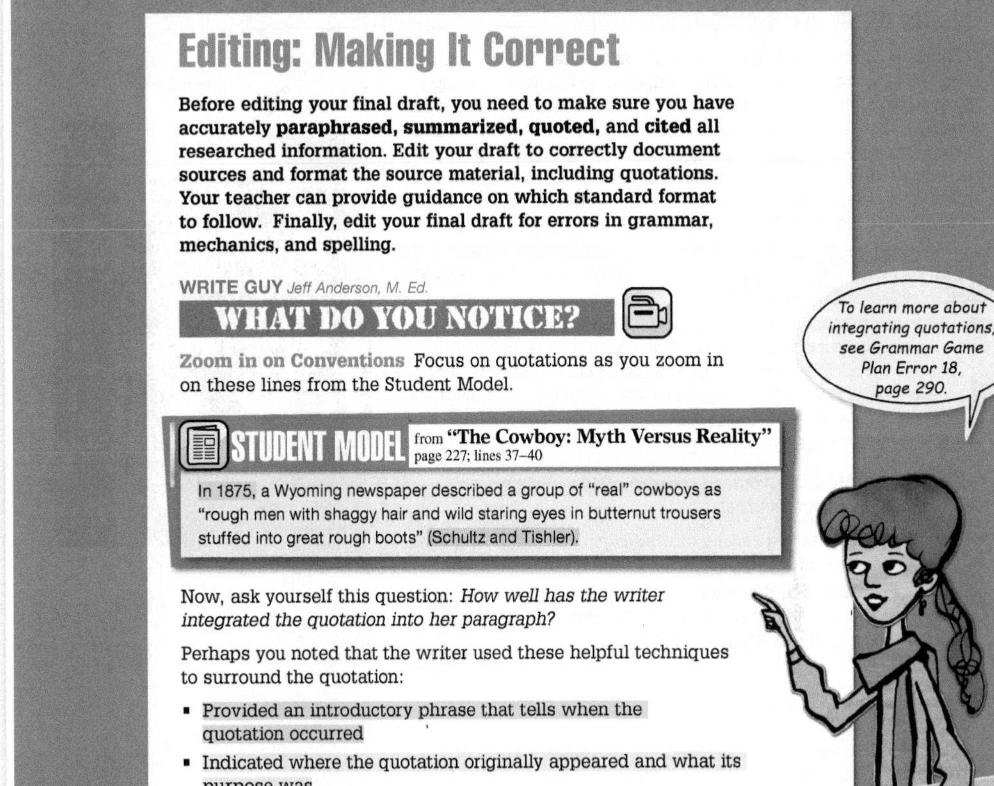

Editing Feature Assignment Editing Feature Assignment E

Editing: Making It Correct

Before editing your final draft, you need to make sure you have accurately paraphrased, summarized, quoted, and cited all researched information. Edit your draft to correctly document sources and format the source material, including quotations. Your teacher can provide guidance on which standard format to follow. Finally, edit your final draft for errors in grammar, mechanics, and spelling.

WRITE GUY *Jeff Anderson, M. Ed.*

WHAT DO YOU NOTICE?

Zoom in on Conventions Focus on quotations as you zoom in on these lines from the Student Model.

STUDENT MODEL from **"The Cowboy: Myth Versus Reality"** page 227; lines 37–40

In 1875, a Wyoming newspaper described a group of "real" cowboys as "rough men with shaggy hair and wild staring eyes in butternut trousers stuffed into great rough boots" (Schultz and Tishler).

Now, ask yourself this question: *How well has the writer integrated the quotation into her paragraph?*

Perhaps you noted that the writer used these helpful techniques to surround the quotation:

- Provided an introductory phrase that tells when the quotation occurred
- Indicated where the quotation originally appeared and what its purpose was
- Told where the quotation was found, using the standard format for parenthetical citations

Partner Talk Discuss this question with a partner: *How easy or hard is it to figure out which words from the Student Model are the student's and which words are not the student's?*

To learn more about integrating quotations, see Grammar Game Plan Error 18, page 290.

246 Research Writing

Grammar Mini-Lesson: Punctuation

Discuss the paragraph and the Student Model excerpt on page 247 with students. Guide them to understand that the excerpt uses quotation marks, parentheses, and end punctuation correctly to integrate the quotation.

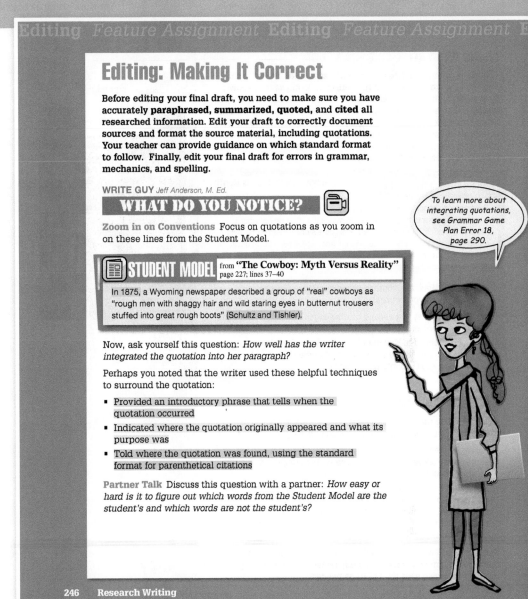

Try It! Have students work with a partner to determine that the second sentence is correctly punctuated; it has a comma after *said* and a period at the end of the sentence.

Apply It! Remind students to look closely at the punctuation of quotations as they edit their drafts.

Use the Rubric Explain to students that the rubric lists six important elements of an informational research report. Tell students that they will rate how well their draft addresses each element on a scale of 1 to 6, with 6 being the best score.

Then, have students use the rubric to evaluate their drafts and revise.

Writer's Block

IF students have difficulty punctuating quotations in their drafts. . .

THEN have them circle each quotation and follow the examples in the Student Model and in the directions on page 247.

3 

Using Writing Coach Online™ or the student book, students refer back to the Student Model as they edit their writing.

4 

Using Writing Coach Online™ or the student book, students evaluate their writing using the rubrics.

5 

Students submit edited drafts to the Interactive Writing Coach™ for scoring and feedback, or share their work with their teacher.

6 

Students receive customized feedback from the Interactive Writing Coach™ or feedback from their teacher.

Grammar Mini-Lesson: Punctuation

To learn more, see Chapter 25.

Punctuating Quotations With Citations Quotations follow some specific rules for punctuation. Study the sentence from the Student Model. Notice how the writer punctuated the quotation with a citation. Notice the period comes after the citation in parentheses.

STUDENT MODEL from **"The Cowboy: Myth Versus Reality"** page 227; lines 33–35

One person who had seen "real cowboys" remarked that a cowboy is "just a plain bowlegged human who smelled very horsey at times" (Burns).

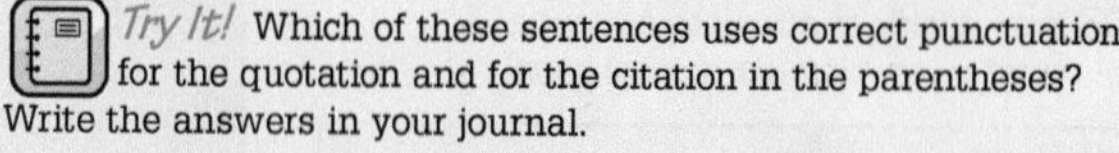

Try It! Which of these sentences uses correct punctuation for the quotation and for the citation in the parentheses? Write the answers in your journal.

1. Ken Burns and Stephen Ives, the filmmakers, have said "America without the West is unthinkable now." (Episode 5.)
2. Ken Burns and Stephen Ives, the filmmakers, have said, "America without the West is unthinkable now" (Episode 5).

Apply It! Edit your draft for grammar, mechanics, and spelling. If necessary, rewrite sentences to integrate quotations more smoothly into your text to maintain the flow of ideas. Punctuate and cite quotations correctly.

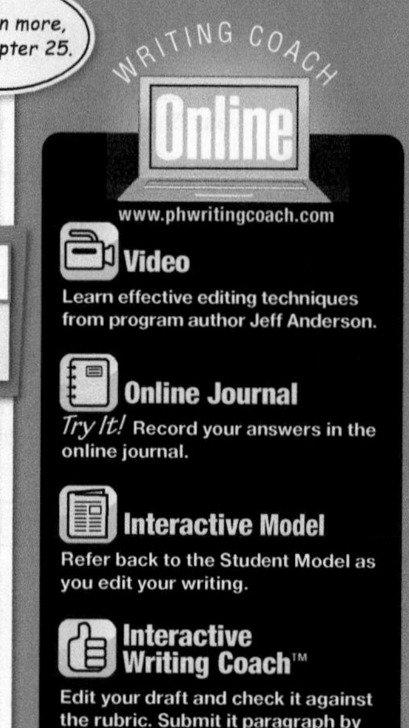

WRITING COACH Online

www.phwritingcoach.com

Video
Learn effective editing techniques from program author Jeff Anderson.

Online Journal
Try It! Record your answers in the online journal.

Interactive Model
Refer back to the Student Model as you edit your writing.

Interactive Writing Coach™
Edit your draft and check it against the rubric. Submit it paragraph by paragraph for feedback.

Use the rubric to evaluate your piece. If necessary, rethink, rewrite, or revise.

Rubric for Informational Research Writing	Rating Scale					
	Not very					Very
Ideas: How focused and clearly supported is your thesis statement?	1	2	3	4	5	6
Organization: How logical is the progression of your ideas?	1	2	3	4	5	6
Voice: How clearly is your point of view expressed?	1	2	3	4	5	6
Word Choice: How effectively does your word choice develop and support your thesis statement?	1	2	3	4	5	6
Sentence Fluency: How well have you varied the sentence types in your report?	1	2	3	4	5	6
Conventions: How correctly are your sources formatted?	1	2	3	4	5	6

Personalized Support

Interactive Writing Coach™

Students complete the editing process by submitting their writing for scoring and feedback.

Teacher or Peer Feedback

To provide feedback to students as they edit their drafts, ask or have student partners ask one another the following:

- Have you read your piece aloud to yourself or to a partner? What kind of errors did you find?
- Have you included correct and complete citations for your sources?
- Have you titled and identified the source for photographs, graphics and other visuals?
- Can you show me something you changed through editing?
- What resources have you used to look for possible spelling errors?
- Read this sentence aloud. Does the grammar sound correct to you?

Working with ELLs

ELL Sheltered Instruction: Metacognitive

Use topics and activities on page 247 to help students monitor and edit their writing for subject-verb agreement, using self-corrective techniques. Remind students of rules about subject-verb agreement by reviewing the meanings of *plural* and *singular*. Then:

Beginning Write: *She say that the cowboys was tall*. Have students copy and correct the sentence using the self-corrective technique of underlining subjects, circling verbs, and asking themselves *How many? (singular or plural)* to check for agreement.

Intermediate Have students complete the Beginning activity. Help them write using irregular verbs and use the self-corrective technique to check agreement.

Advanced Have pairs complete *Apply It!*. As they revise their work, have them use the self-corrective technique of underlining the subjects and circling the verbs, checking for agreement. Have the partners double-check subject-verb agreement in each other's draft.

Advanced High Have students complete the Advanced activity. Have each work with an Intermediate student to check for subject-verb agreement. Have students provide specific, helpful feedback.

1 

Using Writing Coach Online™ or the student book, students complete the writing process by deciding the best way to publish their writing for their intended purpose and audience.

2 Writing Journal

Students record their answers to Reflect on Your Writing in their online journals or notebooks.

Publishing

Wrap Up Your Presentation

To prepare students for more formal academic presentations, you may require students to produce their work using word processing software and a digital printer.

Publish Your Piece

Explain to students that the final step in the writing process is to decide which form of publication will present their work most effectively. Then, introduce to students that the chart shows how specific audiences can be reached using different media.

Have students whose research reports address similar audiences work in small groups to discuss appropriate ways to publish their work.

Extension Have students brainstorm for other publishing opportunities not listed in the chart, such as submitting their report to a magazine dedicated to their topic.

Reflect on Your Writing

Have students discuss the questions with a partner, including rethinking the Big Question, and record responses in their journal.

Manage Your Portfolio You may wish to have students include development materials, such as graphic organizers and drafts.

Publishing *Feature Assignment* Publishing *Feature Assignme*

Publishing

It is time to share your research report. When you've finished your final draft, publish it for an appropriate audience.

Wrap Up Your Presentation

You teacher may require you to turn in a typed report. Follow the guidelines provided. Create a cover sheet, table of contents, and Works Cited list. Also be sure to add a lively title that indicates the topic of the report.

Publish Your Piece

Use a chart to brainstorm for ways to publish your research report to an appropriate audience. You may decide to circulate or post a written report or share an oral report or multimedia presentation.

If your audience is...	...then publish it by...
Students or teachers at school	• Displaying your report in the library, media center, or other public place • Posting your report on a Web site dedicated to student work
A club with a special interest like science, music, or history	• Giving a talk or doing a multimedia presentation at one of the club's meetings • Submitting your report to the club's newsletter or Web site

Reflect on Your Writing

Now that you are done with your informational research report, read it over and use your writing journal to answer these questions.

- Which parts of your research report please you the most? Which parts could be improved?
- What will you do differently for your next research report?
- What useful things have you learned about doing research?

The Big Question: Why Write? Did you understand your subject well enough to write about it? How did you find out what all the facts were?

Manage Your Portfolio You may include your published informational research report in your writing portfolio. If so, consider what this piece reveals about your writing and your growth as a writer.

MAKE YOUR WRITING COUNT

Introduce the press conference script activity by discussing the opening paragraphs with students. Make sure students understand that the project may be produced electronically or by hand. Then, guide students through each step in the action plan.

Use the 21st Century Skills Rubric to evaluate each group's process and final product on a scale of 1 to 3, indicating weak, moderate, or strong use of the skill. ▶

Resources You may wish to have students use these graphic organizers: Meeting Agenda, Meeting Notes, and Main Idea and Details Web. Distribute printed copies or have students log on to Writing Coach Online.

Listening and Speaking Monitor students as they discuss how to present their script.

21st Century Learning

Skills Rubric	Rating
Interact Effectively With Others: Know when it is appropriate to listen and to speak.	1 2 3
Create Media Products: Understand and utilize the most appropriate media creation tools.	1 2 3
Access and Evaluate Information: Evaluate information critically and competently.	1 2 3
Work Creatively With Others: Be open and responsive to new and diverse perspectives.	1 2 3

3  STUDENT BOOK

Students use a variety of graphic organizers, either online or in print, to help them work together to create a multimedia group project.

4  STUDENT BOOK

Through Writing Coach Online™ students link to resources on 21st Century Learning for help in creating a multimedia group project.

21st Century Learning

MAKE YOUR WRITING COUNT

Write a Press Conference Script

Research reports often reveal surprising answers to the questions they pose. Inform your schoolmates about a surprising research report by preparing a **script for a press conference.**

In a press conference, someone with information to share with the press invites journalists to hear that announcement and ask questions. With a group, write a script for a mock press conference about information from a research report. Then, produce a **multimedia presentation.** Your presentation should use text and graphics. Act out your script for classmates, or record it and present it as a podcast.

Here's your action plan.

1. With your group, choose roles such as moderator, one or more experts, and reporters.
2. Select a report from your group that reveals surprising information. Create text, such as a bulleted list of key points, and a supporting graphic to share the news.
3. View a press conference online. Notice how reporters and speakers interact. Pay attention to text and graphics.
4. Plan and write your script.
   - The moderator introduces the experts and topic.
   - The experts give a statement and answer questions, referring to supporting text and graphics.
   - The reporters ask questions and dig for the truth.
5. Practice your presentation. Act out your script for classmates.
6. If presenting a podcast, video-record your press conference and play it for the class.

Listening and Speaking As a group, discuss how to present your script. Memorize the text of the script, and practice your presentation using the graphics. Ask listeners to give feedback on the position and evidence given. Presenters should adjust their content, volume, and pacing accordingly. During the presentation, work to act like participants in a real press conference.

WRITING COACH Online

www.phwritingcoach.com

Online Journal

Reflect on Your Writing Record your answers and ideas in the online journal.

Resource

Link to resources on 21st Century Learning for help in creating a group project.

Personalized Support

FEEDBACK

Teacher or Peer Feedback

To provide feedback to students on their published writing, ask or have student partners ask one another the following:

- How did you go about writing this piece? What was your process?
- What did you learn from the writing model that you used in this piece?
- What surprised you the most as you wrote this piece?
- Did you try anything new as you worked on this piece?
- What did you learn from this piece of writing that you would like to remember and reuse?
- What do you think you do best as a writer right now?

Differentiated Instruction

RTI Strategy for Special Needs Students

Show students a video of a press conference. Together, discuss the purpose, the participants, the topic, and the sequence of events. Help students select a report and topic for a press conference, discussing why it is an appropriate press conference topic. Write a simple script for the press conference on the board as students contribute ideas. Then assign roles, direct a rehearsal, and ask students to perform the script.

Enrichment for Gifted/Talented Students

Challenge students to create a Web site where the research reports can be posted. Ask students talented in computer design to create attention-getting text and graphics. Encourage them to focus on a theme or brainstorm for other ways to make the Web site informative and entertaining.

1 
STUDENT BOOK

Students use Writing Coach Online™ or their student books to analyze and discuss the Writing for Media topic.

2 Writing Journal

Students learn about the characteristics of an online consumer report by answering questions about the model. Students record their answers to the *Try It!* questions in their online journals or notebooks.

Writing for Media: Online Consumer Report

Online Consumer Report

Discuss the opening paragraph with students. As a class, discuss the information students would expect to find in an online consumer report.

Try It! Guide students to understand the purpose and audience of an online consumer report.

Say: The second *Try It!* question asks about the purpose of an online consumer report. The report contains facts and statistics about the effectiveness of Jet Plane Air. **I think** the purpose of the report is to provide information.

Ask: Who is most likely to read this consumer report? (people who might want to use the airline)

Have students discuss the remaining questions in small groups and record individual responses in their journals. Later, address any questions students may have.

Writing for Media Writing for Media Writing for Media Writ

Writing For Media: Online Consumer Report

Online Consumer Report

21st Century Learning

What kinds of applications do various cell phones have? Do some work better than others? Which airlines are the most economical and give the best service? Which commercial dog foods have received the highest recommendations? You can find answers to all your consumer questions by searching the Internet.

In this assignment, you will create your own **online consumer report** about a product or service. You'll follow a research plan as you gather information from multiple sources. Then, you'll put it all together to tell your audience about the pros and cons of various competing products or services. You may provide links from parenthetical citations to a separate Works Cited page.

Try It! Study the excerpt from the online consumer report shown. Then, answer these questions. Record your answers in your journal.

1. What **consumer** product or service is the writer describing?
2. What do you think is the writer's **purpose?** Who do you think is the intended audience?
3. An online consumer report gives **essential information** about a specific product or service, often including statistics about its quality. What information is shown here?
4. Is the writing **subjective,** presenting the writer's opinion, or **objective,** presenting only factual information? How can you tell?
5. What effect does the **photograph** have? What other kinds of visuals would be helpful in this report?

Off to a Flying Start

Airline passengers can sometimes feel like excess baggage. They trudge through long lines at airports. They hover for hours at the gates before they are allowed onto a late-arriving plane. After they squeeze into their seats, they often sit for an hour or more on the tarmac waiting for the plane to take off. The good news is that a relatively new airline, Jet Plane Air, has paid more-than-usual attention to being flyer-friendly.

Jet Plane started flying in 2007, and so far, its "on-time arrival" rate is 82%, which places it near the top among airlines and well above the average of 77%. So far, the airline's in-flight service has received high marks from consumers. Coach passengers have 7% more seating room and legroom than average. (Jet Plane Air Annual Report, 2009) Also, passengers in coach receive free meals and free in-flight movies.

Jet Plane Air is not perfect, of course. It schedules fewer flights than larger airlines, although it does fly to most large cities in the U.S. and Canada. It also has no overseas flights. Because it is a new airline, we do not know if Jet Plane Air will maintain its high consumer ratings and excellent flight record. For now, this new airline is off to a flying start. For the latest information, visit the Department of Transportation's Aviation Consumer Protection Division Web site (Air Consumer on the Web).

250 Research Writing

Create an Online Consumer Report

Tell students that they will create an online consumer report using the five-step writing process. Then, preview the writing process instructions on pages 251–253.

Resources You may wish to have students use the KWL Chart graphic organizer. Distribute printed copies or have students log on to Writing Coach Online.

Introduce students to the Prewriting stage of the online consumer report activity. Have students read aloud and discuss the list of tasks, noting how they addressed the requirements for that task in the chapter's feature assignment, the informational research report.

Then, ask students to predict how these tasks might differ for an online consumer report. For example, students may have to pay special attention to the validity of Internet sources for a consumer-based project.

Following the discussion, have students begin working through each Prewriting task individually. Once they have completed a task, have them work in groups to evaluate their work before moving to the next task.

Partner Talk

Remind students to listen and speak in turn as they discuss their research plan and evaluate sources.

You may wish to have students review this chapter's information about using and evaluating source material:

- Plagiarism and paraphrasing, pages 235 and 240
- Validity and reliability of sources, pages 232–233
- Usefulness of sources, pages 232–233, 241

3  STUDENT BOOK

Students may select online or printed graphic organizers to help them plan their writing.

Create an Online Consumer Report

Follow these steps to create your own **online consumer report**. To plan your online consumer report, review the graphic organizers on pages R24–R27 and choose one that suits your needs.

Prewriting

- Consult with others and brainstorm for a list of products and services that you or your family might want to purchase or use in the home or outside the home. When you've finished, circle the topic you have chosen.
- Be sure to identify the target **audience** for your online report. Are you writing to **inform** an audience of teenagers? Families? Parents?
- It's important to create a **research plan** to identify what specific **research question** you will try to answer. You'll need to **gather information** from **a wide variety of sources.** Include steps in your plan for **obtaining and evaluating** information.
- After some preliminary research in reference works and additional texts, create a **written plan** for more specific resources, including print and electronic sources.
- **Evaluate** every source you consider using. Decide whether a source is **reliable** and **valid.** The Internet has the most up-to-date reviews of products and services, but be careful to evaluate review sites for bias.
- **Categorize** your notes to help you see broader patterns. You may need to **broaden or narrow** your research question in order to produce better results. Refine your plan as needed.
- As you take notes, **paraphrase** or **summarize** information. If you use a **direct quotation,** enclose it in big quotation marks to avoid plagiarism. Categorize your notes according to themes or subtopics in order to make connections and see big ideas.
- Find **graphics** and **illustrations** to add to your report. Be sure to record source information for any graphics you intend to use.
- Document your **sources** by making a source card for each source you use. For all notes, record bibliographic information according to a standard format.

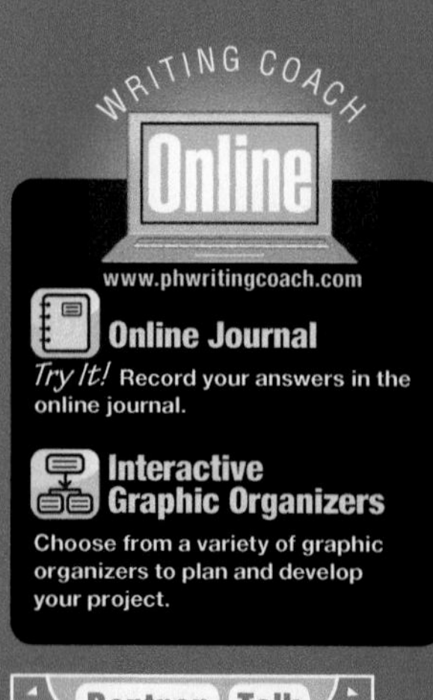

WRITING COACH
Online
www.phwritingcoach.com
Online Journal
Try It! Record your answers in the online journal.

Choose from a variety of graphic organizers to plan and develop your project.

Partner Talk

Work with a partner to critique your research plan and research. Discuss:

- The difference between plagiarism and paraphrasing
- The importance of citing valid and reliable sources
- The reasons that one source is more useful than another

Personalized Support

FEEDBACK

Teacher or Peer Feedback

To provide feedback to students as they write for media, ask or have student partners ask one another the following:

- What are the main characteristics of this form of writing?
- What is your purpose for writing this piece? Who is your audience?
- Have you created a research plan?
- Where will you find information for your topic?
- Will you include photographs, graphics and charts in your report?

Working with ELLs

ELL Sheltered Instruction: Social/Affective

As students prepare to write, help them orally express their opinions, ideas, and feelings in contexts ranging from communicating with single words to participating in extended discussions. Have them speak using learning strategies, such as nonverbal cues or circumlocution, if they lack a word.

Beginning Discuss a product students want to research. Help them orally express their opinions, ideas, and feelings about the product. If students lack a word, have them use the learning strategy of using nonverbal cues, such as gestures.

Intermediate Have partners list products to write about, orally describing their opinions, ideas, and feelings. Have them use circumlocution as needed, using descriptions for nouns they do not know.

Advanced Have partners choose a topic and explain their choice, expressing their opinions, ideas, and feelings about it. Have students use the learning strategy of requesting assistance if they lack a word.

Advanced High Have partners complete the Advanced activity and discuss various audiences for which they may write.

The Digital • Print Path

1 

Students follow the five-step writing process to create an online consumer report.

2 

Students may select online or printed graphic organizers to help them develop their writing.

Writing for Media: Online Consumer Report

Create an Online Consumer Report *(continued)*

Guide students to use their experience writing the chapter feature assignment, an informational research report, to understand the drafting process for the online consumer report activity.

Say: I notice that the third bullet in the Drafting instructions asks you to anticipate the reader's needs and questions about the product or service discussed in your consumer report. We did something similar when we worked on our research reports in this chapter. For example, the writer of the student model, about the myths and realities of cowboy life, had to consider what information her readers would already have about cowboys and what facts she would need to provide.

Ask: What information will your audience already have about the topic of your consumer report? What background information might you have to provide? (Responses will vary.)

Have students begin working through the remaining stages of the writing process. You may wish to direct students who need extra support to the writing process overview in Chapter 3:

- Prewriting, pages 32–34
- Drafting, page 35
- Revising, pages 36–41
- Editing, pages 42–45
- Publishing, page 47

When students have completed their online consumer report, use the 21st Century Skills Rubric to evaluate each student's process and final product on a scale of 1 to 3, indicating weak, moderate, or strong use of the skill.

Extension Have students bring in other examples of online consumer reports. Lead a media discussion about the examples, using the *Try It!* questions as a guide.

Writing for Media Writing for Media Writing for Media Writi

Online Consumer Report *(continued)*

21st Century Learning

Drafting

- **Categorize** your notes by subject heading, such as Product Description, Strong Points, Weak Points, or Overall Recommendation. Create an outline based on your subject headings. Then, start writing sentences and paragraphs.
- Present your findings in a **systematic way,** based on your outline and using summarizing or paraphrasing to share your findings. Lively **subheadings** will organize your report and help readers understand the conclusions you have drawn.
- Do not plagiarize. Use your own words, and enclose any direct quotations in quotation marks.
- A good consumer report anticipates the reader's needs and questions about the product or service. Begin with a lively opening that leads up to a **thesis statement** and clearly reveals the **conclusion** you've drawn from your research.
- Marshal the evidence you have collected and organized to **describe** the product or service. Use **graphics** and **illustrations** to present your findings in a meaningful format. Give readers logical and **relevant reasons** for your conclusions.
- Acknowledge your **sources** as needed in context or in a credits section. Avoid interrupting the flow of the report. Use accepted formats for integrating quotations and citations.

Revising

Use Revision RADaR techniques as you review your draft carefully.

- **Replace** general terms with vivid details and unclear explanations with precise ideas.
- **Add** specific details or missing information to support your argument.
- **Delete** information that does not support your thesis or develop your argument.
- **Reorder** sentences and paragraphs to present ideas clearly and logically.

Read aloud your online report to make sure it reads smoothly. Vary sentence lengths. Tie ideas together with transition words.

252 Research Writing

Partner Talk

Tell students to discuss parts of the project that they found especially difficult, so their partners can look more closely for any errors.

21st Century Learning

Skills Rubric	Rating
Think Creatively: Use a wide range of idea creation techniques, such as brainstorming.	1 2 3
Analyze Media: Understand how and why media messages are constructed.	1 2 3
Work Independently: Monitor, define, prioritize, and complete tasks without direct oversight.	1 2 3
Access and Evaluate Information: Evaluate information critically and competently.	1 2 3

Editing

Now take the time to check your Online Consumer Report carefully before you post it online. Focus on each sentence and then on each word. Look for these common kinds of errors:

- Errors in subject-verb agreement
- Errors in pronoun usage
- Run-on sentences and sentence fragments
- Spelling and capitalization mistakes
- Omitted punctuation marks
- Improper citations and punctuation of quotations

Publishing

- If your school newspaper has an online version, submit your online consumer report to the editor.
- Search for online forums specializing in the type of product or service that you are writing about, and submit your report as a comment. Some sites specialize in communication technology products, while others provide more general consumer information sites.
- Post your consumer report as a blog entry. Search for one of the Web sites that allow users to create a free blog.
- With your classmates, compile your consumer reports into a Student Consumer Guide. Organize the guide by type of product or service. Print it for classroom display or for your school library.

Extension Find another example of an Online Consumer Report, and compare it with the one you are writing.

WRITING COACH Online

www.phwritingcoach.com

Interactive Graphic Organizers

Choose from a variety of graphic organizers to plan and develop your project.

Partner Talk

Exchange drafts with a partner, and give each other feedback. Ask specific questions to help present an effective product. Is your report logically organized and clearly written? Does it give enough information? Consider your partner's suggestions as you revise your draft.

Personalized Support

FEEDBACK

Teacher or Peer Feedback

To provide feedback to students as they write for media, ask or have student partners ask one another the following:

- Have you included most or all of the characteristics of an online consumer report in your piece of writing?
- How did you organize your ideas in this piece of writing?
- Have you correctly and completely cited your sources of information?
- How did you go about revising the piece? Editing it?
- How do you plan on publishing your report?

Differentiated Instruction

RTI Strategy for Below-Level Students Bring to class examples of print and online consumer reports. Pass the reports around and have students skim them. Then, lead a discussion about the products described in the reports and their likely audiences. Ask students to point out types of comments they found most and least useful. Display the reports as students work on their own and encourage them to consult the examples as they complete the assignment.

PRE-AP Enrichment for Above-Level Students Have students locate a consumer report Web site or print publication, analyze it, and write a review of it. Their review should describe the target audience, the types of products included, and the format. They should also evaluate the clarity, interest, and usefulness of the site or publication. Have students share the results of their evaluations orally.

1 Writing Journal

Before they write, students use the ABCDs of On-Demand Writing to analyze and plan how to respond to each prompt. They can use either their online journals or notebooks to take notes.

Writing for Assessment

Read aloud or have a student read aloud the introductory text. Then tell students that they will learn and practice a technique for writing in response to an assessment prompt.

Try It! Read the Research Plan Prompt aloud and then have volunteers read aloud the Format and Academic Vocabulary boxes. Tell students that they will use the ABCD method to respond to the prompt.

The ABCDs of On-Demand Writing

Have students identify the words associated with the ABCD method. (attack, brainstorm, choose, detect) Then, guide students through their use.

I'll attack the prompt by circling the verb phrase *should include*. This phrase reminds me of all the elements my research plan should include. I can rewrite the prompt to state that clearly: "Write a research plan that states the research topic, question, sources, audience, and steps."

Work with students to brainstorm for an appropriate graphic organizer for a research plan, such as a Cluster Diagram.

Have students write their drafts individually and then work with a partner to detect errors.

Writing for Assessment Writing for Assessment Writing for Assessment

Writing for Assessment

Some tests include a prompt that asks you to critique a research plan. Use these prompts to practice. In your response, use the characteristics of your informational research report. (See page 224.)

Try It! Read the prompt carefully, and then create a detailed **research plan**. Use the ABCDs of On-Demand Writing to help you plan and write your research plan.

Format
Write your *research plan* in the form of an outline. List everything you would do in the order you would do it. Use a main heading, such as *Topic*, and subheadings, for example, *Primary Sources*.

Research Plan Prompt
Write a research plan about a person or event related to an American president. Your plan should include a research topic and question, a list of possible sources, the audience, and the steps you'll take following a timeline. [30 minutes]

Academic Vocabulary
A research plan tells what your major research subject is and what *sources* you will use. It also includes a timeline for researching, drafting, and finalizing your report. One of the most important steps is narrowing your research question for a brief research report.

The ABCDs of On-Demand Writing

Use the following ABCDs to help you respond to the prompt.

Before you write your draft:

A ttack the prompt [1 MINUTE]

- Circle or highlight important verbs in the prompt. Draw a line from the verb to what it refers to.
- Rewrite the prompt in your own words.

B rainstorm possible answers [4 MINUTES]

- Create a graphic organizer to generate ideas.
- Use one for each part of the prompt if necessary.

C hoose the order of your response [1 MINUTE]

- Think about the best way to organize your ideas.
- Number your ideas in the order you will write about them. Cross out ideas you will not be using.

After you write your draft:

D etect errors before turning in the draft [1 MINUTE]

- Carefully reread your writing.
- Look for spelling, punctuation, and grammar errors.
- Make sure that your response makes sense and is complete.

More Prompts for Practice

Apply It! Have students apply the ABCD method to the practice prompt.

Prompt 1 Have partners evaluate the prompt and brainstorm for possible answers. Then have each pair swap their information with another group to evaluate whether the teams have included suggestions about graphics and sources.

Test Prep Spiral Review: Narrative Read aloud the instructions and prompt. Then, have students review the nonfiction narrative characteristics on page 66.

Prompt 2 Remind students to use the ABCD method to write their personal narrative.

Spiral Review: Response to Literature Read aloud the instructions and prompt. Then, have students review the response to literature characteristics on page 198.

Prompt 3 Remind students to use the ABCD method to write their interpretative response.

Students submit their writing paragraph by paragraph or as a complete draft to the **Interactive Writing Coach™** for feedback, or share their writing with their teacher.

Students receive personalized feedback from the **Interactive Writing Coach™** or feedback from their teacher.

More Prompts for Practice

Apply It! **Critique** the research plan in Prompt 1. In a written response, report on your ideas and make specific suggestions to improve the research plan.

- Does the writer need to broaden or narrow the **research question**? Is it appropriate for the audience and purpose?
- Is the writer planning to find enough sources? Are they varied?
- Does the writer plan to include graphics?
- Does the research plan say anything about evaluating sources?

Prompt 1 Cheryl wrote this research plan. Evaluate her plan to determine what she did well and what needs improvement.

My Topic: I'm going to research the beginning of World War II. My question is, what started the war?

My Research: I'll look for books and old newspaper articles about what triggered the conflict. I'll also search the Internet.

My Writing: Once I have my notes, I can copy them into a draft and then revise it.

Spiral Review: Narrative If you choose to respond to Prompt 2, write a personal narrative. Make sure your story reflects the characteristics described on page 66.

Prompt 2 Write about a person who has had a major impact on you. This person could be a friend, family member, teacher, or community member. Tell about a significant experience you shared with this person and how it affected you. Use specific details and dialogue.

Spiral Review: Response to Literature If you choose to respond to Prompt 3, write a response to literature. Make sure your response to literature reflects the characteristics on page 198 and includes:

- The writing skills for a **multi-paragraph essay** (See page 146.)
- **Evidence** from the text, including **quotations**
- An analysis of the effects of the author's style or use of literary devices

Prompt 3 Choose an expository or literary text that you feel has an interesting conflict. Write an interpretative response about how the writer created that conflict. Include information about the problem and how it was solved, as well as an analysis of why the conflict was important.

Interactive Writing Coach™

Plan your response to the prompt. If you are using the prompt for practice, write one paragraph at a time or your entire draft and then submit it for feedback. If you are using the prompt as a timed test, write your entire draft and then submit it for feedback.

Remember **ABCD**

- **A**ttack the prompt
- **B**rainstorm possible answers
- **C**hoose the order of your response
- **D**etect errors before turning in the draft

Personalized Support

Assessment/Monitor Progress

For timed writing practice, assign students a prompt to be completed in a timed setting. For Prompts 2 and 3, have students submit their writing to **Interactive Writing Coach™** to get immediate feedback.

For a formal writing assessment, assign the Assessment writing prompt for this chapter in **Writing Coach Online™**. Then, have students submit their writing to **Interactive Writing Coach™** to be assessed. Use the results to assess student progress and skill levels. **Interactive Writing Coach™** will update student levels to ensure that students get the appropriate support.

Teacher or Peer Feedback

To create an assessment environment, have students use a prompt in a timed setting. Grade papers using the appropriate rubric and use the results to assess student progress and skill levels. In the next writing assignment, ensure that students get the appropriate level of support.

If you conference with students, use these questions to guide your discussion:

- What writing form did the prompt call for?
- How did you organize your ideas?
- Did you make good use of your time?

Working with ELLs

ELL Sheltered Instruction: Cognitive

Use Prompt 1 to help students develop and demonstrate an increasing ability to distinguish between formal and informal English and an increasing knowledge of when to use each. Have them adapt spoken language for formal purposes. Describe a variety of situations, such as asking a friend a question, and interviewing an expert, and help students determine which calls for formal or informal language. Then:

Beginning Model a question to a friend: *What was World War II all about?* Have students repeat. Help students orally adapt it for an interview with a historian: *What were the causes of World War II?*

Intermediate Ask questions as partners identify them as formal or informal and adapt the informal language for formal purposes.

Advanced Have partners read aloud versions of the formal and informal questions from the Intermediate activity. Have listeners identify each as formal or informal and adapt informal sentences for a formal interview.

Advanced High Have students complete the Advanced activity. Have them present their own formal interview questions.

CHAPTER 12 LESSON PLANNER
Workplace Writing

Use the Online Lesson Planner at www.phwritingcoach.com to customize your instructional plan for an integrated Language Arts curriculum.

DAY 1

CHAPTER OPENER/ GENRE INTRODUCTION

- What's Ahead
- Characteristics of Writing
- Forms of Writing
- Connect to the Big Questions
- Word Bank

ONLINE

DAY 2

FEATURE ASSIGNMENT: FRIENDLY LETTER

- Student Model
- Learn From Experience
- Choose from the Topic Bank
- Prewriting

ONLINE

DAY 3

FEATURE ASSIGNMENT: FRIENDLY LETTER *(cont'd)*

- Drafting
- Revising
- Editing
- Publishing

ONLINE

DAY 6

21st Century Learning

MAKE YOUR WRITING COUNT

- **Present a Research Report on Activities for Kids**
- Action Plan

ONLINE

DAY 7

21st Century Learning

MAKE YOUR WRITING COUNT *(cont'd)*

- **Present a Research Report on Activities for Kids**
- Action Plan

ONLINE

DAY 8

21st Century Learning

MAKE YOUR WRITING COUNT *(cont'd)*

- **Present a Research Report on Activities for Kids**
- Action Plan

ONLINE

Alternate Pacing Suggestions

- **Block Scheduling** Each day on the Lesson Planner represents a 40–50 minute block. Teachers using block scheduling may combine days to revise pacing to meet their classroom needs.
- **Accelerated Lesson Planning** Combine instructional days, choosing one of the Feature Assignments to focus on.
- **Integrated Language Arts Curriculum** For targeted instruction that covers the essential components of the lesson, use either a 3- or a 5-day plan.

3 day plan

DAY 1: Introduction to the Genre Friendly Letter

DAY 2: Letter of Opinion

DAY 3: Letter of Request

5 day plan

Use 3-day plan, and add:

DAY 4: Make Your Writing Count

DAY 5: Writing for Assessment

Links to Prentice Hall *LITERATURE*

Additional Mentor Text:

"How to Download Ringtones for a Cell Phone" (technical directions), p. 623

Differentiated Instruction

Differentiated Instruction Boxes in this Teacher's Edition address these student populations:

- Below-Level Students
- Above-Level Students
- Gifted and Talented Students
- Special Needs Students
- English Language Learners
- Spanish Speaking Students

In addition, for further enrichment, see the **Extension** features.

DAY 4

FEATURE ASSIGNMENT: LETTER OF OPINION

- Student Model
- Choose from the Topic Bank
- Prewriting – Publishing

ONLINE

DAY 5

FEATURE ASSIGNMENT: LETTER OF REQUEST

- Student Model
- Choose from the Topic Bank
- Prewriting – Publishing

ONLINE

DAY 9

WRITING FOR MEDIA

- **Set of Instructions**
- Create a Set of Instructions

ONLINE

DAY 10

WRITING FOR ASSESSMENT

- Procedural Text Prompt
- The ABCDs of On-Demand Writing
- More Prompts for Practice
  Test Prep Spiral Review: Expository
- Spiral Review: Research Plan

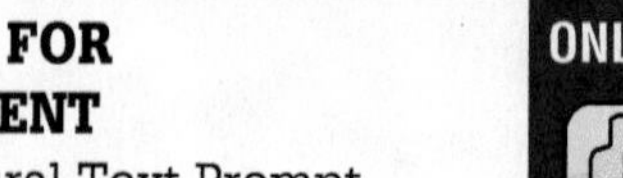

ONLINE

LESSON OBJECTIVES

- To learn the forms and defining characteristics of workplace writing.
- To learn the elements of successful friendly letters, letters of opinion, and letters of request, the chapter Feature Assignments.
- To read Student Models of a friendly letter, a letter of opinion, and a letter of request.
- To apply prewriting strategies in developing a friendly letter, a letter of opinion, and a letter of request, including strategies for gathering details.
- To apply drafting strategies in developing a friendly letter, a letter of opinion, and a letter of request.
- To apply strategies for revising and editing a friendly letter, a letter of opinion, and a letter of request.
- To complete the Make Your Writing Count assignment, developing and presenting a research report on activities for kids.
- To complete the Writing for Media assignment, developing a set of instructions.
- To practice writing for assessment.

Personalized Assessment

✓	Ongoing Assessment	Formal Assessment of Feature Assignment	Progress Monitoring at End-of-Chapter
Interactive Writing Coach™	Use Paragraph Feedback and Essay Scorer as a revision tool.	Use Essay Scorer to score students' Feature Assignment papers.	Use Essay Scorer to score students' papers. Students' learner profiles can be adjusted based on their scores.
 Teacher Conferencing	Use rubrics in the Student Edition as a revision tool. Conference with students to review their work and provide personalized support.	Use rubrics in the Student Edition to score students' Feature Assignment papers.	Review each student's work to plan targeted resources for the next writing assignment.

"This may be the most important chapter for students. If they write well, they will be paid more and generally will have more success in their careers."

—Jeff Anderson

The Digital • Print Path

1 

Using Writing Coach Online™ or the student book, students discuss the photograph in the chapter opener as it relates to the writing genre.

2 

Students record their ideas and responses in their online journals or notebooks. They may also record and save their responses on pop-up sticky notes in Writing Coach Online™.

Chapter Objectives

1. Write a friendly letter, letter of opinion, and letter of request by planning, drafting, revising, editing, and publishing individual work.
2. Produce a research report.
3. Use the five-step writing process to write the set of instructions.
4. Write a procedural text, compare-and-contrast expository essay, and a critique of a research plan in response to a prompt.

WORKPLACE WRITING

What's Ahead

Guide students in understanding what constitutes workplace and procedural documents. Preview the Student Models on pages 258–263. Tell students that they will write their own functional documents using the five-step writing process.

Activate Prior Knowledge Using the photo on page 256, guide students to understand the purposes of workplace writing.

Say: In this photo **I see** a worker looking at bins of apples. The worker could be counting, checking for bad apples, or making sure that all the apples are the same variety. He needs a clear set of instructions in order to accurately perform his task.

Ask: What might happen if the worker didn't have a clear set of instructions to perform his task? **(Possible response:** He might not complete the task properly and have to repeat the work.)

Have students brainstorm for situations where a clear set of instructions is important.

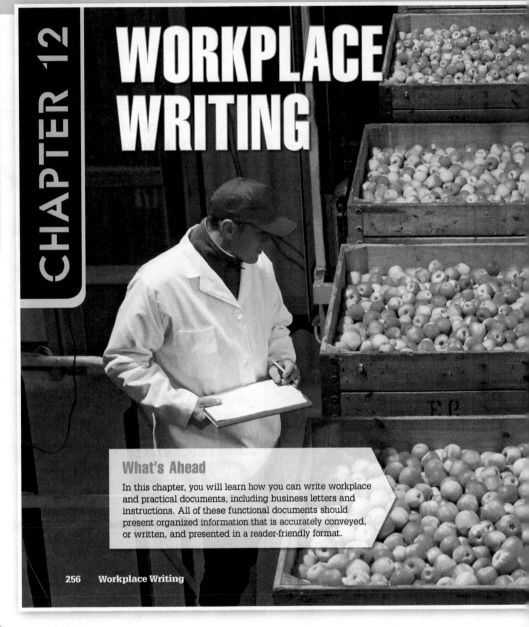

CHAPTER 12

WORKPLACE WRITING

What's Ahead

In this chapter, you will learn how you can write workplace and practical documents, including business letters and instructions. All of these functional documents should present organized information that is accurately conveyed, or written, and presented in a reader-friendly format.

256 Workplace Writing

Characteristics of Writing

Ask volunteers to read aloud the characteristics of workplace and procedural writing. Explain that academic writing forms, such as research papers, also use formal language and standard formats for presenting information. Then, have students identify academic writing forms that share these characteristics.

Forms of Writing

Discuss the forms and purposes of workplace writing.

Try It! Have students record their responses in their journal.

Possible responses: letter of request, asks for information; letter of opinion, expresses an opinion about a topic

Students learn vocabulary from the Word Bank and listen to English and Spanish pronunciations in the Writing Coach Online™ glossary.

Characteristics of Writing

Effective workplace and practical writing has these characteristics:

- **Information** that is clear, concise, and focused
- A clear **purpose** and intended **audience**
- **Formal, polite** language
- **Reader-friendly formatting techniques,** such as sufficient white or blank space and clearly defined sections
- Correct **grammar, punctuation,** and **spelling** appropriate to the form of writing

Forms of Writing

Forms of workplace writing include:

Instructions are used to explain how to complete a task or procedure. They are written in a step-by-step format.

Letters of opinion are formal correspondence written to a newspaper, magazine, or other publication. They are written to express an opinion. Letters to the editor are one example of letters of opinion.

Letters of request are formal correspondence written to a business or outside organization. They are written to request information.

Memos are short documents usually written from one member of a group or organization to another or to another group. They assume some background on the topic.

Other forms of practical writing include:

Friendly letters are informal correspondence written to a friend or acquaintance. They can be written for various reasons, including to ask how someone is doing or just to say hello.

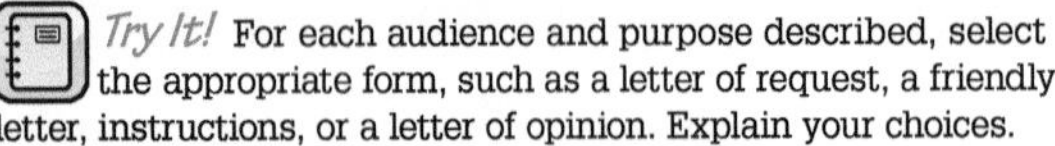

Try It! For each audience and purpose described, select the appropriate form, such as a letter of request, a friendly letter, instructions, or a letter of opinion. Explain your choices.

- To ask for a class schedule from a community center
- To respond to an article in a newspaper

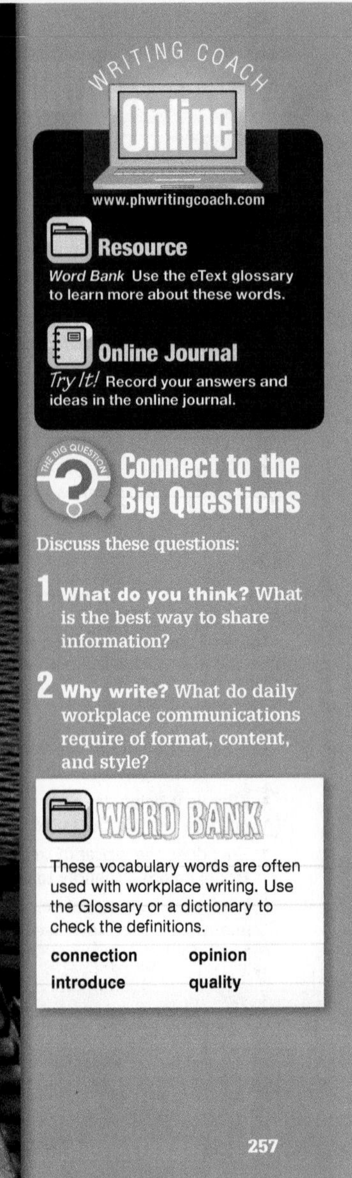

WRITING COACH Online

www.phwritingcoach.com

Resource

Word Bank Use the eText glossary to learn more about these words.

Online Journal

Try It! Record your answers and ideas in the online journal.

Connect to the Big Questions

Discuss these questions:

1 **What do you think?** What is the best way to share information?

2 **Why write?** What do daily workplace communications require of format, content, and style?

WORD BANK

These vocabulary words are often used with workplace writing. Use the Glossary or a dictionary to check the definitions.

connection	opinion
introduce	quality

257

Personalized Support

Teacher or Peer Feedback

To encourage students in their discussion of the photograph and the characteristics of workplace writing, ask the following questions:

- What is the first thing you think of when you look at this photo?
- What kind of communication might be important in this setting?
- How is workplace writing different from other kinds of writing?
- Who is the most likely audience for this form of writing?
- What kind of voice would be most effective for this form of writing?

Connect to the Big Questions

Have students to use their experience to discuss the Big Questions. Explain that they will revisit **Why write?** at the end of this chapter. Tell students to consider these points during their discussion:

1. Ask students to evaluate the best way to communicate a problem to an adult.
2. Ask students to consider how the style of a letter to a supervisor might differ from a letter written in response to a customer complaint.

Word Bank

To assist English Language Learners and struggling readers, echo-read each word or have students log on to Writing Coach Online to listen to the pronunciations. Then, have partners take turns using each word in a sentence. Ask volunteers to share one of their sentences with the class.

Working with ELLs — ELL Sheltered Instruction: Cognitive

Have students use prior knowledge to understand and learn the meanings of English academic vocabulary during classroom instruction and interactions. Distribute an academic vocabulary list with words from page 257: *instruction, procedure, format, topic, schedule.* Discuss each word, modeling the use of prior academic knowledge. For example, *I heard* topic *when we discussed the topic of a grammar lesson.* Topic *must mean "subject."*

Beginning Review the vocabulary, using gestures. Help students use their prior knowledge by completing sentences, like *To do homework, you need ____ to guide you.*

Intermediate Complete the Beginning activity. Have groups use the vocabulary words in context sentences about the page. Help them use prior knowledge to clarify meanings.

Advanced Have partners review the vocabulary, discussing its meaning based on prior assignments. Have them use the words to orally summarize the lesson.

Advanced High Have students complete the Advanced activity. Then have partners use the vocabulary with Word Bank words in oral sentences.

1 

Using Writing Coach Online™ or the student book, students read and listen to an audio recording of the Student Model. As they complete their writing assignments they can refer back to the Student Model for support whenever they need it.

2 

Students record answers to questions about the Student Model in their online journals or notebooks.

STUDENT MODEL

Learn From Experience

After students have read the text, point out that the numbered notes refer to the characteristics of a friendly letter.

Try It! Guide students to understand how the genre characteristics shape the text. For example, use Think Alouds like the one below, which refers to the third *Try It!* question.

The third *Try It!* question asks about the letter's tone. While reading this letter from Janine to Isabel, **I noticed** several words and phrases that show it is a friendly letter, not a more formal business letter or letter of opinion. The letter has an informal tone. In the first paragraph, for example, Janine says, "Last year we had so much fun!"

Work with students to identify other words and phrases that indicate the tone of this letter.

Have students reply to the remaining *Try It!* questions in their journals. If students have difficulty responding to a particular question, model a response, as with the third question.

Check the accuracy and completeness of student responses.

- The purpose of this letter is to communicate personal information and ask personal questions. The letter's audience is Isabel, Janine's friend or family member.
- Stating the purpose early lets the reader know what to expect.
- A friendly tone is created by informal language, or writing as if you are talking.
- Responses for closings will vary but should show familiarity and affection.

STUDENT MODEL Friendly Letter

Learn From Experience

After reading the friendly letter on this page, read the numbered notes in the margin to learn about how the writer presented her ideas. As you read, take notes to develop your understanding of basic sight and English vocabulary.

Try It! Record your answers and ideas in the online journal.

1 The friendly letter includes a **date line** and **salutation.** Notice that a comma is placed after the salutation.

2 The writer **clearly explains the reason for writing.**

3 The writer anticipates questions the reader may have and addresses them.

4 The letter ends with an appropriate **closing.** Notice that when a writer sends a friendly letter on paper, he or she signs it.

Try It!

- What is the purpose of this letter? Who is the intended audience?
- Why is it helpful to state a letter's purpose early in the letter?
- How does the writer of the Student Model create a friendly tone?
- What other appropriate closings might the writer have used to end her letter?

1 May 18, 2010

Dear Isabel,

I'm excited to hear that you are coming to stay with your aunt this summer. Last year we had so much fun! Will you be staying for the whole month of July like last year?

2 I'm wondering if you want to practice with our local swim team while you're here. Remember what a great time we had at the pool? I've joined the swim team, and I thought you might want to participate in summer practices with me.

3 My mom has already talked to Coach Buckley, and she said it would be fine for you to practice with the team. Think about it and let me know. We have plenty of time, and whatever you decide I know we will have lots of fun this summer. I can't wait to see you!

4 Your friend,

Janine

Create a Friendly Letter

Tell students that they will create a friendly letter using the five-step writing process. Then, preview the writing process instructions.

For each step in the writing process, have partners read aloud and discuss the list of tasks. Then, have them work individually. Once both partners have completed the tasks, have them evaluate each other's work before moving to the next step.

Partner Talk

After partners edit each other's letter for a clear purpose and friendly tone, have each student state the purpose of the partner's letter.

Writer's Block

IF the student is not using the characteristics of the genre . . .

THEN discuss how the students can use the model text to plan their piece. Review the plan using the characteristics listed on page 258 as a guide.

3 

Students begin planning their friendly letter by selecting a topic. Then they write their first draft online or in their notebooks.

4 

Students watch videos from program authors Jeff Anderson and Kelly Gallagher to learn effective strategies for revising and editing their writing.

5 

Students submit their letters paragraph by paragraph to the **Interactive Writing Coach™** for scoring and feedback, or share their work with their teacher.

6   

Students receive personalized feedback from the **Interactive Writing Coach™**, or feedback from their teacher.

Feature Assignment: Friendly Letter

Prewriting

- Plan a first draft of your **friendly letter.** You can select from the Topic Bank or come up with an idea of your own.

Reach Out Suppose you have a pen pal who lives in a faraway place. Write a friendly letter to your pen pal, asking what life is like in his or her part of the world.

Good Times Write a friendly letter to a relative, expressing your opinion about a family event you both attended. Include details about the time, place, and purpose of the event.

- Brainstorm for a list of ideas you would like to include in your letter. Consider what **requests for information** you might make.
- Use a telephone directory or online resource to find the accurate contact information for the letter's recipient.

Drafting

- Use reader-friendly formatting techniques, including all the features of an informal letter.
- Use a salutation that matches your relationship with the recipient.
- **Organize the information** so that your purpose is clearly stated.
- Accurately convey information by double-checking your ideas.

Revising and Editing

Before you revise, review your draft to ensure that information is presented accurately and concisely. Ask yourself if the purpose for your letter is clearly identified and addressed.

Publishing

- Print the letter or write it neatly on paper or stationery suitable for the recipient.
- If you plan to e-mail the letter, confirm the correct e-mail address and attach your letter to a message as a Portable Document Format (PDF).

Interactive Model
Listen to an audio recording of the Student Model.

Online Journal
Try It! Record your answers and ideas in the online journal.

Interactive Writing Coach™
Submit your writing and receive personalized feedback and support as you draft, revise, and edit.

Video
Learn strategies for effective revising and editing from program authors Jeff Anderson and Kelly Gallagher.

Work with a partner to edit your letter. Ask for feedback on spelling, punctuation, and vocabulary.

Personalized Support

To provide feedback to students as they plan and write their friendly letters, ask or have student partners ask one another the following questions:

- Which characteristics of a friendly letter have you included? Are you missing any?
- What is your purpose for writing? Is it clearly stated?
- How have you organized your ideas?
- Are your language and tone appropriate for the audience you are addressing?
- What details have you included to make your writing clear?
- How did you revise your draft?
- Have your checked your grammar and spelling?

Working with ELLs — ELL Sheltered Instruction: Cognitive

Provide opportunities to expand and internalize students' initial English vocabulary by learning basic routine language needed for classroom communication. Help them use and reuse this new basic language in speaking activities.

Beginning Write the basic routine word *organize*. Place pencils on a desk and start organizing them. Say *I organize the pencils*. Have students repeat. Help students complete oral sentences, reusing the word.

Intermediate Review basic routine words from page 259: *brainstorm, organize, purpose, clearly,* and *suitable*. For each, have partners create a **Mental Connections Card** by writing a word and a mental connection illustrating the word on one side and a cluster diagram of related words on the other. Have them use and reuse the cards to discuss their words.

Advanced Have partners review the Intermediate activity words then reuse the words in oral sentences about relatives.

Advanced High Have pairs use the Intermediate activity words to discuss a relative, then reuse the words to share what they learned about their partner.

1 

Using Writing Coach Online™ or the student book, students read and listen to an audio recording of the Student Model. As they complete their writing assignments they can refer back to the Student Model for support whenever they need it.

2  

Students record answers to questions about the Student Model in their online journals or notebooks.

STUDENT MODEL

Learn From Experience

After students have read the text, point out that the numbered notes refer to the characteristics of a letter of opinion.

Try It! Guide students to understand how the genre characteristics shape the text. For example, use instruction as shown below, which refers to the first *Try It!* question.

Say: This is an interesting letter because **I see** that it not only states the writer's opinion; it also makes a request. This letter has more than one purpose. In the first sentence, Eddie states that he is unhappy because the kids' section is being dropped. He gives another opinion in the second paragraph about the things he likes in the section. But, the true purpose of his letter is a request that the paper keep Kids' Review.

Work with students to determine whether the details offered in this letter support both the opinion expressed and the action requested.

Have students reply to the *Try It!* questions in their journals. If students have difficulty, model a response using the business letter from the Student Model, as with the first question.

Check the accuracy and completeness of student responses.

- The purpose is to persuade the newspaper to keep the Kids' Review section.
- Responses will vary, but students should expand upon the whole-class discussion, above.

Extension Lead a discussion in which students explore how the tone of the Student Model affected their understanding of the author's opinion and their responses. Use the *Try It!* questions as a guide.

Letter of Opinion Student Model Letter of Opinion Student Mod

STUDENT MODEL Letter of Opinion

Learn From Experience

 After reading the letter of opinion on this page, read the numbered notes in the margin to learn how the writer presented his ideas.

Try It! Record your answers and ideas in the online journal.

1 The writer uses conventional business letter formatting, including:

- Writer's address with street, town, state, and zip code
- Date showing day, month, and year
- Recipient's address with full name
- Formal greeting and closing

2 Notice that a colon is placed after the **salutation** of a business letter.

3 The writer states his **opinion** in this **clear thesis statement.**

4 **Facts and details support the point** that the writer is not the only one who thinks kids should have a voice.

5 The writer includes a closing signature along with his typed name, following proper business formatting.

Try It!

- What is the purpose of the letter?
- In your opinion, does the letter fulfill its purpose? Why or why not?

Extension Use the letter's tone to help you distinguish fact from opinion. Write a response that summarizes the issue and responds to the writer's inferred attitude.

1 Eddie Gates
4307 Windy Circle
Palm Beach Gardens, FL 33418

September 9, 2010

Mr. Maxwell Cooper, Editor
The Downtown Daily
2437 Winston Road
Palm Beach, FL 33480

2 Dear Mr. Cooper:

3 I am very unhappy that the Kids' Review section is being dropped from your newspaper. My parents subscribe to *The Downtown Daily,* and the Kids' Review is the first section I turn to when the newspaper arrives.

The reviews of books, movies, and video games written by kids are interesting to read and give useful information. I think it is important for kids to have a voice in their community, and I know that I am not alone.

4 For example, *Today's News,* in Palm Beach, has a kid's editorial column where young people can give their opinions.

Please do not let kids in our community down. Keep the Kids' Review in *The Downtown Daily.*

Sincerely yours,

5 Eddie Gates

Eddie Gates

Create a Letter of Opinion

Tell students that they will create a letter of opinion using the five-step writing process. Then, preview the writing process instructions.

For each step in the writing process, have partners read aloud and discuss the list of tasks. Then, have them work together to complete each task. Once they have completed the tasks, have them exchange work with another paired team to evaluate each other's work before moving to the next step.

Partner Talk

After students write and revise their letters of opinion, have partners identify facts and details in each other's letters that support the purpose.

Writer's Block

IF the student's writing lacks detail . . .

THEN ask the student to take one idea from the letter and list the supporting facts and evidence that explain it.

3  

Students begin planning their letters of opinion by selecting a topic. Then they write their first draft online or in their notebooks.

4

Students watch videos from program authors Jeff Anderson and Kelly Gallagher to learn effective strategies for revising and editing their writing.

5 

Students submit their letters of opinion paragraph by paragraph to the Interactive Writing Coach™ for scoring and feedback, or share their work with their teacher.

6 

Students receive personalized feedback from the Interactive Writing Coach™, or feedback from their teacher.

Your Turn: Feature Assignment: Letter of Opinion

Prewriting

- Plan a first draft of your **letter of opinion.** You can select from the Topic Bank or come up with an idea of your own.

> **TOPIC BANK**
>
> **Read All About It!** Many students opt to spend their free time playing video games or watching television rather than reading a book for enjoyment. Write a letter to the president of your town's school board about getting students more interested in reading. Offer ideas on how to get students to choose reading over other types of entertainment.
>
> **School Days** Write a letter to the editor of your school paper, either supporting or opposing its coverage of a school sports team or club.

- Brainstorm for a list of things that your letter's recipient will need to know about you and your purpose for writing the letter.
- Find the accurate contact information for the letter's recipient in a telephone directory or online resource.

Drafting

- Use a formal salutation that matches your relationship with the recipient.
- Include organized information that clearly states your opinion.
- Accurately convey information by double-checking your facts.

Revising and Editing

- Review your draft to ensure **precise word choices.** Check to see if you have clearly expressed your opinion or **registered a complaint** in a business context.

Publishing

- If you plan to mail the letter, print the letter on paper suitable for business correspondence.
- If you plan to e-mail the letter, confirm the correct e-mail address and attach your letter to a message as a PDF.

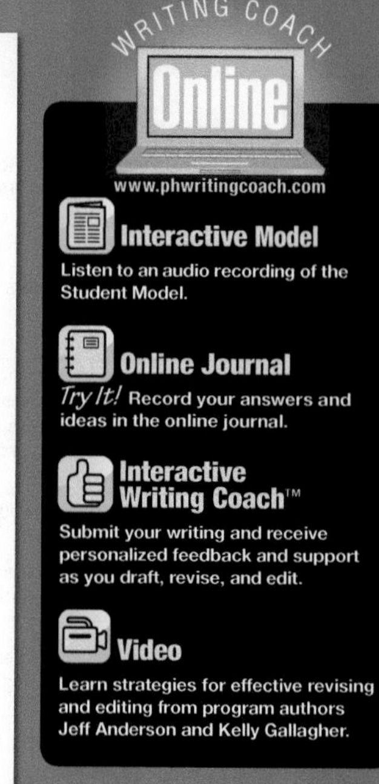

Interactive Model
Listen to an audio recording of the Student Model.

Online Journal
Try It! Record your answers and ideas in the online journal.

Interactive Writing Coach™
Submit your writing and receive personalized feedback and support as you draft, revise, and edit.

Video
Learn strategies for effective revising and editing from program authors Jeff Anderson and Kelly Gallagher.

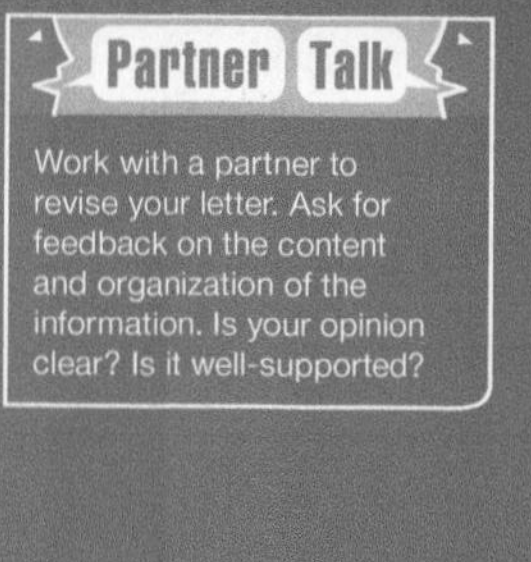

Partner Talk

Work with a partner to revise your letter. Ask for feedback on the content and organization of the information. Is your opinion clear? Is it well-supported?

Personalized Support

Teacher or Peer Feedback

To provide feedback to students as they plan and write their letters of opinion, ask or have student partners ask one another the following questions:

- Which characteristics of a letter of opinion have you included? Are you missing any?
- What is your purpose for writing? Is it clearly stated?
- How have you organized your ideas?
- Are your language and tone appropriate for the audience you are addressing?
- What details have you included to make your writing clear?
- How did you revise your draft?
- Have your checked your grammar and spelling?

Working with ELLs ELL Sheltered Instruction: Cognitive

Have students listen to, derive meaning from, and respond orally to information presented in a wide variety of print, electronic, and audiovisual media to build and reinforce language attainment. Have fluent students hold and record a conversation, about the first Topic Bank prompt, discussing leisure activities. Play the recording.

Beginning Pause often for clarity. Build language attainment with a bank of words, like *reading, books, free time,* and *enjoy.* Review the words using visuals. Have students speak them to answer questions, like, *What is the discussion about?*

Intermediate After playback, have groups respond to the recording. Build language attainment by providing sentence frames for responses: for example, *Reading is a good use of free time because _______.*

Advanced Have partners discuss the recording, offering their views. To build language attainment, have them use sentence frames for oral responses, like, *I agree reading is ____ because ____.*

Advanced High Have students complete the Advanced activity. Have them identify a cause-effect relationship in the recording.

1 

Using Writing Coach Online ™ or the student book, students read and listen to an audio recording of the Student Model. As they complete their writing assignments they can refer back to the Student Model for support whenever they need it.

2 

Students record answers to questions about the Student Model in their online journals or notebooks.

STUDENT MODEL

Learn From Experience

After students have read the text, point out that the numbered notes refer to the characteristics of a letter of request.

Try It! Guide students to understand how the genre characteristics shape the text. For example, use Think Alouds like the one below, which refers to the first question.

Before I even read the words of this letter, **I notice** it is formatted in a very formal way. First, I see that two addresses are given, which is something that is usually only done in formal business letters. Then I see that the greeting is very formal. Instead of writing "Dear David," the writer addresses the recipient of the letter very formally. The closing is also very formal: not only does Amy use the word *sincerely*, she signs the letter with both her first and last names.

Work with students to identify how a businessperson would regard a letter that is written using formal business letter formatting characteristics and one that is handwritten.

Have students reply to the *Try It!* questions in their journals. If students have difficulty responding to a particular question, model a response, as with the question above.

Check the accuracy and completeness of student responses.

- The reader should understand that the letter format shows that the writer has professional intentions.
- Yes. She included a timeline and her return address.
- Yes. Responses may vary but should note that the request is clear and focused.

Friendly Letter Student Model Letter of Request Student Model

STUDENT MODEL Letter of Request

Learn From Experience

After reading the letter of request on this page, read the numbered notes in the margin to learn about how the writer presented her ideas.

Try It! Record your answers and ideas in the online journal.

1 The writer uses conventional **business letter format,** including writer's address, date, recipient's address, formal salutation, and closing.

2 The letter begins with a **clear introduction** that expresses the purpose of the letter.

3 This **request for information** is **clear and focused.** Writers are more likely to get the results they want when their request is clear.

4 In **formal, polite language,** the writer gives a reasonable deadline for receiving the information.

Try It!

- What impression do you think the writer makes on the reader by using proper business letter format?
- Did the writer include all the information the reader would need to fulfill her request? Explain.
- In your opinion, does the letter fulfill its purpose? Why or why not?

1 Amy Parkland
539 Sunset Road
Western Springs, IL 60558

1 March 1, 2010

1 David Nixon, Director
Camp Shady Lanes
2400 Old Oak Lane
Hayward, WI 54843

1 Dear Mr. Nixon,

2 I am writing to ask about Camp Shady Lanes' programs for kids ages thirteen and up. My eight-year-old sister attended the camp last summer, and she had a great time. I think I might like to attend the camp this summer if it has programs for older kids like me.

3 Would you please send me a brochure and any other information about the programs at Camp Shady Lanes? I am in the seventh grade, and I am looking for a camp with a lot of outdoor activities. I especially enjoy swimming and horseback riding. Does the camp offer these?

4 It would be helpful if I could receive the information by April 15. That way, I can make a decision before the April 30 registration deadline. Thank you for your help!

1 Sincerely,

Amy Parkland

Amy Parkland

262 Student Model

For each step in the writing process, have partners read aloud and discuss the list of tasks. Then, have them work individually. Once both partners have completed the tasks, have them evaluate each other's work before moving to the next step.

Writer's Block

IF the student has difficulty expressing meaning clearly . . .

THEN ask the student to speak what he or she wants to say. Use the answer to suggest a place in the text where the meaning can be stated explicitly.

Create a Letter of Request

Tell students that they will create a letter of request using the five-step writing process. Then, preview the writing process instructions.

Partner Talk

After partners revise letters of request, have each student read his or her letter aloud to the other partner. Have the listener state the letter's request when the reader is done.

3 Students begin planning their request letter by selecting a topic. Then they write their first draft online or in their notebooks.

4 Students watch videos from program authors Jeff Anderson and Kelly Gallagher to learn effective strategies for revising and editing their writing.

5 Students submit their request letters paragraph by paragraph to the Interactive Writing Coach™ for scoring and feedback, or share their work with their teacher.

6 Students receive personalized feedback from the Interactive Writing Coach™, or feedback from their teacher.

Feature Assignment Letter of Request Feature Assignment

Your Turn Feature Assignment: Letter of Request

Prewriting

- Plan a first draft of your **letter of request.** You can select from the Topic Bank or come up with an idea of your own.

> **TOPIC BANK**
>
> **How It Works** Imagine that you have just gotten a new video game or electronic device, but it didn't come with any instructions. Write a letter of request to the company asking it to send you the missing instructions.
>
> **Money Back** You have purchased an item and now you have changed your mind. Write a letter requesting a refund from the company. Include details about what the item is and why you no longer want it.

- Brainstorm for a list of things that your letter's recipient will need to know about you and your purpose for writing the letter.
- Find the accurate contact information for the letter's recipient in a telephone directory or online resource.

Drafting

- Use reader-friendly formatting techniques, including all of the features of a business letter.
- Organize the information so that the purpose and the request are clearly stated in the letter. Use formal, business language.
- Accurately convey information by double-checking your facts.

Revising and Editing

Review your draft to ensure that information is presented accurately and concisely. Ask yourself if your letter fulfills the purpose: **to request information in a business context.**

Publishing

- If you plan to mail the letter, print the letter on suitable paper.
- If you plan to e-mail the letter, confirm the correct e-mail address and attach your letter to a message as a PDF.

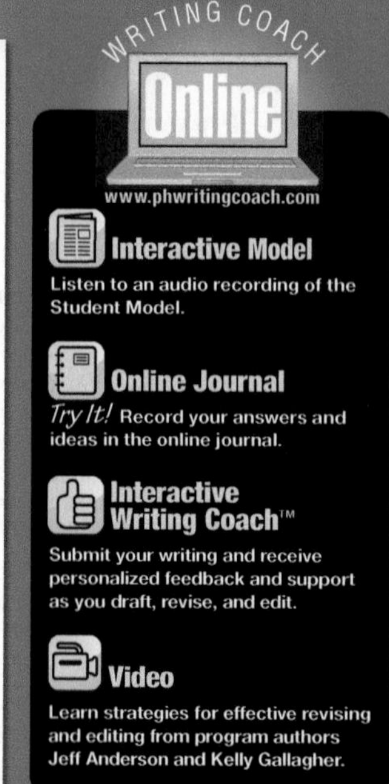

WRITING COACH Online

www.phwritingcoach.com

Interactive Model
Listen to an audio recording of the Student Model.

Online Journal
Try It! Record your answers and ideas in the online journal.

Interactive Writing Coach™
Submit your writing and receive personalized feedback and support as you draft, revise, and edit.

Video
Learn strategies for effective revising and editing from program authors Jeff Anderson and Kelly Gallagher.

Partner Talk

Read your final draft to a partner. Ask him or her if your request is clearly stated. Monitor your partner's spoken language by asking follow-up questions to confirm your understanding.

Personalized Support

Teacher or Peer Feedback

To provide feedback to students as they plan and write their request letters, ask or have student partners ask one another the following questions:

- Which characteristics of a request letter have you included? Are you missing any?
- What is your purpose for writing? Is it clearly stated?
- How have you organized your ideas?
- Are your language and tone appropriate for the audience you are addressing?
- What details have you included to make your writing clear?
- How did you revise your draft?
- Have your checked your grammar and spelling?

Differentiated Instruction

PRE-AP Enrichment for Above-Level Students Before students revise their letters, ask them these questions: *Who will read your letter first? Will that person be authorized, or have the power, to respond to your request? If not, does your letter contain the information necessary to resolve the issue?* Explain that some companies have customer representatives whose only responsibility is to write that they received your request. They may not be able to resolve your problem. Then, have students review their drafts with the answers to these questions in mind.

Strategy for Spanish Speakers Students whose home language is Spanish might use overly formal language in business letters, due to the formality distinction in pronouns and verb forms in Spanish. Elicit and record on the board a list of different titles of people to whom a business letter might be addressed in English. Then provide different English expressions for greetings and closings that match the formality and context of the relationship. Elicit Spanish language equivalents.

1 

Using Writing Coach Online™ or the student book, students create a research plan, collect and organize data, and document sources for an informational research report.

2 Students use a variety of graphic organizers, either online or in print, to help them work together as a group to research and write their report.

Make Your Writing Count

Present a Research Report

Introduce the research report activity by having students read page 264. Make sure students understand that they will work in teams to produce their research report. Then, guide students to formulate a research question for their topic.

Say: I know I want to write a research report on activities for kids. There are many different types of activities. I need to narrow my topic and pick a specific activity. I'll begin by picking an activity that interests me, like writing. This more specific activity helps me narrow my research topic.

Ask: How can I narrow my topic even further? (**Possible response:** Choose one age group.) Why do I need to narrow my topic? (**Possible response:** Kids in different age groups will write about different things and/or will use different writing forms.)

Have students work in their groups to narrow their topics and formulate a focused research question.

Writing Count Research Report Make Your Writing Count Research

21st Century Learning

MAKE YOUR WRITING COUNT

Present a Research Report on Activities for Kids

Letters help people communicate important information to specific audiences. These workplace documents may involve the seeds for activities or ideas that will help classmates learn more. Make a **research report** and presentation to share with your classmates.

With a group, **brainstorm** for several topics from among your work in this chapter. Have a discussion with others and **decide on a topic** that will be helpful to someone thinking about fun activities for kids in and out of school. Work together to **formulate an open-ended research question** that will help you to produce a research report about the topic. Consider topics like joining sports teams, volunteering at local organizations, or planning a family event. Conduct some **preliminary research** in reference works and by searching additional texts to make sure that your question is a good one.

Group members should **consult** one another and **critique the process** as you work, and be prepared to adjust and clarify the research question and process as needed. Remember that a research report should:

- State a specific thesis
- Meet the needs of audience and purpose
- Express a clear point of view
- Provide supporting evidence
- Present ideas in a logical way
- Document sources using correct formatting

Organize a Kids' Fun Day to present your research results to students in your school. Share the information you have gathered in a **multimedia presentation** that uses text and graphics. You may use posters and other displays or an electronic slide show that uses presentation software.

264 **Workplace Writing**

Action Plan

Guide students through each step in the action plan. For additional support, you may wish to direct students to related research report information in Chapter 11:

- Make a Research Plan, page 232
- Collect and Organize Your Data, page 234
- Avoid Plagiarism, page 235
- Document Your Sources, page 236
- Critique Your Research Process, page 237
- Provide and Document Evidence, page 240
- Use Graphics and Illustrations, page 241

Resources You may wish to have students use these graphic organizers: Meeting Agenda, Meeting Notes, and Outline. Distribute printed copies or have students log on to Writing Coach Online.

Use the 21st Century Skills Rubric to evaluate each group's process and final product on a scale of 1 to 3, indicating weak, moderate, or strong use of the skill. ▶

Listening and Speaking Monitor student groups as they consider and incorporate the ideas of all team members.

21st Century Learning

Skills Rubric	Rating
Access and Evaluate Information: Evaluate information critically and competently.	1 2 3
Work Creatively With Others: Incorporate group input and feedback into the work.	1 2 3
Communicate Clearly: Use communication to inform, instruct, motivate, and persuade.	1 2 3
Create Media Products: Understand and use appropriate media creation tools, characteristics, and conventions.	1 2 3

3 STUDENT BOOK

Students take notes, create a research plan, collect and organize data, document sources and write a first draft of a report in their online journals or notebooks.

4 STUDENT BOOK

Through Writing Coach Online students link to resources on 21st Century Learning for help in creating a multi-media group project.

21st Century Learning

Here's your action plan.

1. Research takes time. In a group, make a plan for several group meetings. Set objectives and choose roles for each member.
2. Work together to develop a **written research plan** that includes:
   - Obtaining and evaluating a variety of sources, including a range of **print and electronic sources** as well as data and **quotations from experts**
   - **Categorizing notes by theme** or sub-topic to big ideas
   - Using a standard format to record **bibliographic information** for all notes and sources
   - Checking elements such as publication date and point of view to ensure that your sources are **reliable and valid**
3. Discuss your findings. **Evaluate the sources,** discussing the importance of citing valid and reliable sources. Reject sources that are biased or dated and explain why they aren't useful. Work together to create a **clear thesis statement**.
4. Outline the report. Assign sections of the outline to each group member. You may need to **narrow or broaden your research question** and research further before you draft.
5. Work together to write a draft by **compiling** collected data and using the **marshalled**—collected and organized—evidence to explain the topic. As a group, discuss the difference between **plagiarism** and **paraphrasing.** Use the proper style for acknowledging sources and for **integrating quotations and citations** without interrupting the flow of ideas.
6. Revise and edit to ensure that the thesis statement is **supported by evidence.** Be sure your report **states relevant reasons for conclusions** and **summarizes** your findings in a systematic way.
7. Finally, add appropriate audio and visuals that help explain the topic and present your findings in a **meaningful format**.
8. Present your report to students, counselors, and teachers.

Listening and Speaking Practice the presentation in front of another group or each other. Listen to questions or comments from the audience to help you make improvements. On Kids' Fun Day, speak clearly and confidently to your audience.

Online Journal
Record your answers and ideas in the online journal.

Resource
Link to resources on 21st Century Learning for help in creating a group project.

Personalized Support

FEEDBACK

Teacher or Peer Feedback

To provide feedback to students as they work together to develop a research report, ask or have student partners ask one another the following:

- How is the group organized and how are tasks assigned?
- What is your purpose for writing this piece? Who is your audience? [or What are your audiences?]
- How did you record information and document your sources?
- How did you decide what information to include in your report?
- How did you go about revising the piece? Editing it?
- In what ways did the group work effectively together? What could have been improved?
- What did you learn from the process and the final product that you could use in future writing projects?

Differentiated Instruction

RTI Strategy for Below-Level Students

Students may struggle to stay focused on listening to presentations made by their classmates. Support these students in their efforts to listen effectively by providing them with a set of sentence stems, such as those found here. Challenge students to complete all of the sentence stems after listening to each presentation.

The topic of this report was ________.

The most important point about the topic was ________.

I think this team chose this topic because ________.

For me, the most effective feature of the presentation was ________.

The information that was confusing included ________.

This report would be improved if the team ________.

The Digital • Print Path

1 

Students use **Writing Coach Online™** or their student books to analyze and discuss the Writing for Media topic.

2 

Students learn about the characteristics of a set of instructions by answering questions about the model. Students record their answers to the *Try It!* questions in their online journals or notebooks.

Writing for Media: Set of Instructions

Set of Instructions

Discuss the opening paragraph with students. As a class, brainstorm for examples of how multimedia presentations can be used to present a set of instructions.

Try It! Guide students to understand the content and structure of the sample multimedia presentation.

Say: The first *Try It!* question asks how the title slide communicates the purpose of the presentation. **I know** from the text on the title slide that this presentation will tell me how to get from Miller School to the museum. It is important that the title slide present the purpose of the presentation.

Ask: What would you think the purpose of the title slide would be if no text appeared with the picture? (Responses will vary, but should convey the understanding that the possibilities would be broad.)

Have students discuss the remaining questions in small groups and record individual responses in their journals.

Extension Have students share their examples of other multimedia presentations that provide a set of instructions. Use the *Try It!* questions as a guide to lead a discussion.

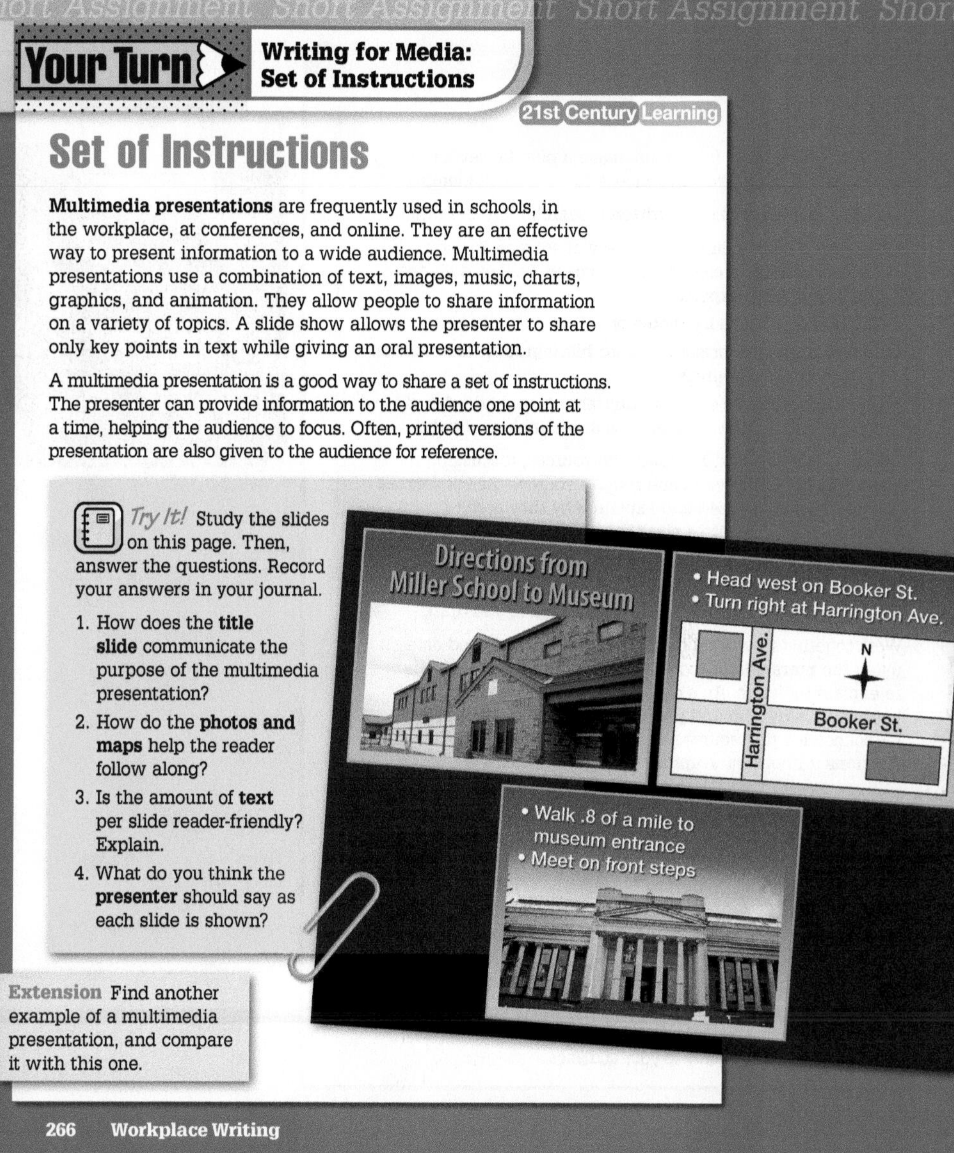

Short Assignment Short Assignment Short Assignment Short
Your Turn
Writing for Media: Set of Instructions
21st Century Learning
Set of Instructions
Multimedia presentations are frequently used in schools, in the workplace, at conferences, and online. They are an effective way to present information to a wide audience. Multimedia presentations use a combination of text, images, music, charts, graphics, and animation. They allow people to share information on a variety of topics. A slide show allows the presenter to share only key points in text while giving an oral presentation.
A multimedia presentation is a good way to share a set of instructions. The presenter can provide information to the audience one point at a time, helping the audience to focus. Often, printed versions of the presentation are also given to the audience for reference.
Try It! Study the slides on this page. Then, answer the questions. Record your answers in your journal.
1. How does the title slide communicate the purpose of the multimedia presentation?
2. How do the photos and maps help the reader follow along?
3. Is the amount of text per slide reader-friendly? Explain.
4. What do you think the presenter should say as each slide is shown?
Directions from Miller School to Museum
• Head west on Booker St.
• Turn right at Harrington Ave.
N
Harrington Ave.
Booker St.
• Walk .8 of a mile to museum entrance
• Meet on front steps
Extension Find another example of a multimedia presentation, and compare it with this one.
266 Workplace Writing

Create a Set of Instructions

Tell students that they will create a set of instructions using the five-step writing process. Then, preview the writing process instructions on page 267.

> **Resources** You may wish to have students use the Series of Events graphic organizer. Distribute printed copies or have students log on to Writing Coach Online.

For each step in the writing process, have partners read aloud and discuss the list of tasks. Then, have them work in small groups to complete the tasks. Once each group has completed the final step, have them evaluate another group's work.

Use the 21st Century Skills Rubric to evaluate each student's process and final product on a scale of 1 to 3, indicating weak, moderate, or strong use of the skill. ▶

Partner Talk

Have students practice their presentation with a partner. Remind students to use new vocabulary words.

21st Century Learning

Skills Rubric	Rating
Access and Evaluate Information: Access information efficiently and effectively.	1 2 3
Communicate Clearly: Articulate thoughts and ideas effectively.	1 2 3
Create Media Products: Understand and utilize the most appropriate media creation tools.	1 2 3
Interact Effectively With Others: Know when it is appropriate to listen and when to speak.	1 2 3

3  

Students use a graphic organizer, either online or printed, to help them plan and develop their writing. Students follow the five-step writing process to write their own set of instructions.

 Create a Set of Instructions

Follow these steps to create your own multimedia slide show that features a **set of instructions.** Review the graphic organizers on R24–R27 and choose one that suits your needs.

Prewriting

- Brainstorm for a list of places to which you could provide directions using a slide show.
- Choose the one place you think is best.
- Make a list of the steps involved in the directions.
- Consider the needs of your specific audience. What does the audience already know? What do they need to know?

Drafting

- Divide your directions into slides. Each slide should contain only a small amount of text. This will allow your audience to focus on your **multimedia presentation.**
- Number the steps and order them according to what is done first, second, next, and so on. Include simple maps to show landmarks and stops along the way.
- Write a script for the oral presentation. Organize the information to support the content of each slide.
- Choose colors, backgrounds, **text fonts, and graphics** that will make it easy for your audience to read each slide.

Revising and Editing

- As you revise, review each slide to be sure that its content correctly matches each section of your oral presentation.
- Be sure the design of your slides makes them easy to read.
- Double-check the accuracy of information on your slides.
- Check spelling and grammar.

Publishing

- Present your slide show to your class or another audience. If you use the slide show for multiple presentations, you may need to adjust it for different **audiences and purposes.**
- Speak clearly and allow time for audience questions.

Online Journal

Try It! Record your answers and ideas in the online journal.

Interactive Graphic Organizers

Use the graphic organizers to plan your multimedia presentation.

Before publishing, practice your presentation with a partner. Practice newly acquired vocabulary by correctly producing the word's sound.

Personalized Support

Teacher or Peer Feedback

To provide feedback to students as they write for media, ask or have student partners ask one another the following:

- What are the main characteristics of this form of writing?
- Have you included most or all of these characteristics in your piece of writing?
- What is your purpose for writing this piece? Who is your audience?
- How did you organize your ideas in this piece of writing?
- How did you go about revising the piece? Editing it?
- How do you plan on publishing your piece? What other publishing options also might work?

Working with ELLs — ELL Sheltered Instruction: Cognitive

Guide students to demonstrate understanding of the general meaning, main points, and important details of spoken language in contexts ranging from familiar to unfamiliar. Orally present the instruction on page 267, and introduce giving informal directions in a familiar context—giving directions to friends. Then, relate the discussion to an unfamiliar context—giving directions at an information desk.

Beginning Clarify your presentation, then help students restate the general meaning, main points, and important details using sentence frames such as *Give (friendly/formal) directions to friends. Give (polite/chatty) directions at an information desk.*

Intermediate Have groups complete sentence frames summarizing your presentation's general meaning, main points, and important details.

Advanced Have partners create a main idea and details chart summarizing your presentation's general meaning, main points, and important details.

Advanced High Have partners complete the Advanced activity and write to compare formal and informal directions.

1 

Before they write, students use the ABCDs of On-Demand Writing to analyze and plan how to respond to each prompt. They can use either their online journals or notebooks to take notes.

2 

Students submit their writing paragraph by paragraph or as a complete draft to the **Interactive Writing Coach™** for feedback, or share their writing with their teacher.

Writing for Assessment

Read aloud or have a student read aloud the introductory text. Then, tell students that they will learn and practice a technique for writing in response to a test prompt.

Try It! Read the Procedural Text Prompt aloud and then have volunteers read aloud the Format and Academic Vocabulary boxes. Tell students that they will use the ABCD method to respond to the prompt.

The ABCDs of On-Demand Writing

Have students identify the words associated with the ABCD method. (attack, brainstorm, choose, detect) Then, guide students through their use.

I'll attack the prompt by circling the key words *stepped-out instructions*. This term tells me that I need to think about the detailed steps that I would take to set up for an experiment. Because this is a procedural text prompt, I will write the steps in a sequential order, and not in an essay format. I will write clearly so that others can read and follow the instruction.

Work with students to brainstorm for an appropriate graphic organizer for a set of instructions, such as a steps-in-a-process chart.

Have students write their drafts individually and then work with a partner to detect errors.

Writing for Assessment Writing for Assessment Writing for Assessment Writi

Writing for Assessment

Many standardized tests include a prompt that asks you to write a procedural text. Use these prompts to practice. Respond using the characteristics of a procedural text. (See pages 266–267.)

Try It! Read the **procedural text prompt** and the information on the format and academic vocabulary. Use the ABCDs of On-Demand Writing to help you plan and write your procedural text.

Format
The prompt directs you to write a *procedural text*. Describe the purpose of the text in the first section. Be sure to include steps with organized information such as a numbered list or materials list.

Procedural Text Prompt
Your new science lab partner wants to know how to set up for an experiment. He wants written instructions to help him. Write a procedural text that includes stepped-out instructions on how to set up your lab table. [30 minutes]

Academic Vocabulary
A procedural text is a kind of text that tells somebody how to perform a task. *Stepped-out instructions* have numbered lists that provide details in the order they are used.

The ABCDs of On-Demand Writing

Use the following ABCDs to help you respond to the prompt.

Before you write your draft:

Attack the prompt [1 MINUTE]
- Circle or highlight important verbs in the prompt. Draw a line from the verb to what it refers to.
- Rewrite the prompt in your own words.

Brainstorm possible answers [4 MINUTES]
- Create a graphic organizer to generate ideas.
- Use one for each part of the prompt if necessary.

Choose the order of your response [1 MINUTE]
- Think about the best way to organize your ideas.
- Number your ideas in the order you will write about them. Cross out ideas you will not be using.

After you write your draft:

Detect errors before turning in the draft [1 MINUTE]
- Carefully reread your writing.
- Make sure that your response makes sense and is complete.
- Look for spelling, punctuation, and grammar errors.

268 Workplace Writing

Test Prep Spiral Review: Expository Read aloud the instructions and prompt. Then, have students review the characteristics for a compare-and-contrast expository essay on page 146.

Prompt 2 Remind students to use the ABCD method to write their expository essay.

Spiral Review: Research Plan Read aloud the instructions and prompt. Then, have students review the research plan characteristics on page 224.

Prompt 3 Remind students to use the ABCD method to write their critique.

More Prompts for Practice

Apply It! Have students apply the ABCD method to the practice prompts.

Prompt 1 Have partners attack the prompt and brainstorm for possible answers. Then, have each pair swap their information with another group to evaluate whether the teams have developed instructions that are clear, concise, and focused.

3

Students receive personalized feedback from the **Interactive Writing Coach™**, or feedback from their teacher.

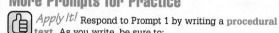

More Prompts for Practice

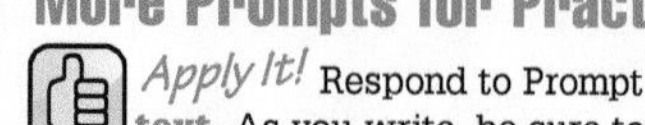

Apply It! Respond to Prompt 1 by writing a **procedural text.** As you write, be sure to:

- Consider what your **audience** knows and needs to know
- **Organize** information into steps or paragraphs
- **Define** any terms that your audience may not know

> **Prompt 1** Your mom needs directions from your house to your friend's house. Write a procedural text that includes stepped-out instructions she can follow when she comes to pick you up.

Spiral Review: Expository If you choose to respond to Prompt 2, write a compare-and-contrast **expository essay.** Make sure your essay reflects the characteristics described on page 146.

> **Prompt 2** Protecting the environment is an important global concern. However, people have different opinions about what must be done on an everyday basis. Write an expository essay that compares and contrasts two different ways you could choose to help protect the environment in your daily life.

Spiral Review: Research Plan If you choose to respond to Prompt 3, write a **critique of the research plan.** Make sure your critique evaluates all of the characteristics described on page 224. Your critique should determine if the research plan:

- Contains a **narrowed topic** and is appropriate for the **audience**
- Includes enough **primary** and **secondary sources,** and says something about **evaluating** sources

> **Prompt 3** Henri wrote this research plan. Explain what he did well and what needs improvement.
> *My Topic:* I'm interested in comparing real cowboys to cowboys in stories.
> *My Research:* I'm going to search the Internet, talk to the reference librarian, and look for print sources. I know that William H. Cody was a real cowboy, so I'll look for and read books and articles about him.
> *My Drafting:* After a month of research, I will copy my notes to write my draft.

Interactive Writing Coach™

Plan your response to the prompt. If you are writing the prompt for practice, write one paragraph at a time or your entire draft and submit it for feedback. If you are using the prompt for a timed test, write your entire draft and submit it for feedback.

Remember **ABCD**

- **A**ttack the prompt
- **B**rainstorm possible answers
- **C**hoose the order of your response
- **D**etect errors before turning in the draft

Personalized Support

Assessment/Monitor Progress

For timed writing practice, assign students a prompt to be completed in a timed setting. For Prompts 1 and 2, have students submit their writing to **Interactive Writing Coach™** to get immediate feedback.

For a formal writing assessment, assign the Assessment writing prompt for this chapter in **Writing Coach Online™**. Then, have students submit their writing to **Interactive Writing Coach™** to be assessed. Use the results to assess student progress and skill levels. **Interactive Writing Coach™** will update student levels to ensure that students get the appropriate support.

Teacher Feedback

To create an assessment environment, have students use a prompt in a timed setting. Grade papers using the appropriate rubric and use the results to assess student progress and skill levels. In the next writing assignment, ensure that students get the appropriate level of support.

If you conference with students, use these questions to guide your discussion:

- What writing form did the prompt call for?
- How did you organize your ideas?
- Did you make good use of your time?

Working with ELLs — ELL Sheltered Instruction: Cognitive

Help students develop and demonstrate an increasing ability to distinguish between formal and informal English and an increasing knowledge of when to use each. Have them adapt spoken language appropriately for formal purposes. Present a variety of situations, such as a family meal or a presentation. Help students identify which call for formal or informal language. Then:

Beginning Say formal and informal statements, such as *Take care of the Earth. Use both sides of the paper.* Help students identify each statement, and adapt the informal statements for a formal purpose.

Intermediate Say formal and informal sentences about the environment and have pairs identify each, then adapt the informal sentences for a formal purpose.

Advanced Provide written sentences from the Intermediate activity. Have partners read them aloud as listeners identify each one as formal or informal and adapt the informal language for formal purposes.

Advanced High After students complete the Advanced activity, have them state rules for when to speak formally.

OUNS AND PRONOUNS *Concrete and Abstract Nouns* VERBS *Transitive Ve*
Adverb? CONJUNCTIONS AND INTERJECTIONS *Subordinating Conjuncti*
sitive Phrases EFFECTIVE SENTENCES *Combining Sentence Parts* PUNCTU
rbs ADJECTIVES AND ADVERBS *Interrogative Adjectives* PREPOSITIONS
nctions BASIC SENTENCE PARTS *Subjects and Predicates* PHRASES AND C
NCTUATION NOUNS AND PRONOUNS *Concrete and Abstract Nouns* VE
ONS *Preposition or Adverb?* CONJUNCTIONS AND INTERJECTIONS *Subo*
ND CLAUSES *Appositive Phrases* EFFECTIVE SENTENCES *Combining Sente*
ERBS *Transitive Verbs* ADJECTIVES AND ADVERBS *Interrogative Adjectiv*

Grammar

The 20 Errors

Find It
FIX IT
Grammar Game Plan
This handy guide will help you find and fix errors in your writing!
20
Major Grammatical Errors and How to Fix Them

272 Grammar Game Plan

ABOUT THE GRAMMAR GAME PLAN

The twenty errors in the Grammar Game Plan represent the most common errors in student writing as determined by a research study conducted by Andrea Lunsford and Karen Lunsford in 2006. Their study of college freshman writers was published by the National Council of Teachers of English in the June 2008 issue of *College Composition and Communication.*

GAME PLAN Use the right words to make your writing clear. Make sure your words say exactly what you mean them to say.

Find It/FIX IT 1

Using the Wrong Word

CLARIFY MEANING Do not confuse the meanings of words with similar spellings. Also, words with similar definitions can have important shades of meaning. Check that words you found in a thesaurus are used correctly.

I wish we could go ~~their~~ ^ there for dinner.

You should go ~~too~~ ^ to her house tonight.

SPELL-CHECK ERRORS Computer spell-checkers often correct a misspelling with a different, similarly spelled word. Be sure to proofread your work carefully to catch these errors. In each of the following examples, the word with a strikethrough represents an inappropriate spell-checker correction.

Try not to ~~turn~~ ^ burn the toast.

The student needs ~~held~~ ^ help with the math problem.

Use a current or completed draft of your work to practice using words correctly.

- **READ carefully.** Take the time to read your draft closely. For a double-check, have someone else read your work.
- **IDENTIFY possible mistakes.** Mark any difficult or commonly misused words in your draft.
- **USE a dictionary.** If you are not sure of a word's meaning, look it up in a dictionary.

Tech Tip

Be your own "spell-checker"! Proofread! Your computer's spell-checker will not identify every misspelling or incorrectly used word.

LEARN MORE

- See Chapter 20, Effective Sentences, pages 457–461
- See Writing Coach Online

HOW TO USE THE GRAMMAR GAME PLAN

This resource will help students identify and correct common errors in writing conventions. Encourage students to refer to the Grammar Game Plan during the editing stage of the writing process. Cross-references to the Grammar Game Plan are provided within the grammar chapters.

Point out that each page of the Grammar Game Plan gives helpful tips to correct a single common error in grammar, spelling, punctuation, or source citation.

Inside TRACK

1. **Tell students to be particularly careful when they use a new word. Remind them that a new word they've heard or read may not mean exactly what they think it means. New words may also be spelled differently than they expect.**
2. **Emphasize the importance of reading word-for-word in the editing and proofreading stage to catch spell-check errors.**

Check It

Encourage students to use the *Check It* strategies when editing. If used consistently, these strategies become good habits. Each *Check It* includes steps to improve students' drafts.

READ, SCAN, REVIEW. Guides students to look over their drafts to find specific errors.

IDENTIFY. Suggests that students highlight or circle errors that they find.

USE, REVISE. Guides students to use a dictionary or another resource to correct their errors or to revise their writing to eliminate the error.

Find It/FIX IT

2 Missing Comma After Introductory Element

Inside TRACK

Students may need the most help simply identifying introductory elements.

1. **Remind students that introductory words are grammatically separate from the rest of the sentence.**
2. **Explain that all prepositional phrases start with a preposition and prepositions are words that usually give information about time, place, or direction.**
3. **Remind students that adverbial clauses have a subject and a verb. Review subordinate conjunctions.**

Tech Tip

Remember to add commas to introductory elements that you cut and paste from different parts of a sentence or paragraph.

LEARN MORE

- See Chapter 25, Punctuation, pages 561, 564
- See Writing Coach Online

GAME PLAN Place a comma after the following introductory elements in your work.

WORDS Place a comma after introductory words.

Hello, I'm here for the party.

Well, it's good to have you.

PHRASES Place a comma after introductory prepositional phrases. If the prepositional phrase has only two words, a comma is not necessary.

Before dinner at 5:00, you can wash the tomatoes.

In the evening, please remember to take out the trash.

After dinner you should wash the dishes.

CLAUSES Introductory adverbial clauses should be followed by a comma.

Find It FIX IT

When the audience clapped, the orchestra stood up to take a bow.

Check It

Use a current or completed draft of your work to practice placing commas after introductory clauses.

- **SCAN your draft.** Look for introductory words, phrases, and clauses.
- **IDENTIFY missing commas.** Mark sentence starters that might need a comma.
- **USE your textbook.** Check the grammar section of your textbook if you are not sure whether or not to use a comma.

Differentiated Instruction

RTI Strategy for Below-Level Students Invite students to create a chart of the types of introductory elements that require commas. Have students create a three-column chart with *Words, Phrases,* and *Clauses* as column headers. Then, have students find sentences in their own drafts with each type of introductory element and add them to their charts. Check students' work for correct use of commas.

PRE-AP Enrichment for Above-Level Students Remind students that strong writing contains a variety of sentence types, including sentences with introductory elements. Have students work in pairs to construct three original sentences for each type of introductory element: word, phrase, and clause. Invite student pairs to exchange papers with others to check for accuracy and correct use of commas.

Find It/FIX IT

3 Incomplete or Missing Documentation

GAME PLAN **Provide complete citations for borrowed words and ideas. Use the citation style (such as MLA) that your teacher recommends.**

MISSING CITATIONS Cite sources of direct quotes and statistics. Remember–when in doubt, cite the source.

The doctor stated, "This is the most interesting case I've seen" (Roberts 12).

Dr. Jones reported that 1 in 10 patients have the disorder (Jones 18).

INCOMPLETE CITATIONS Make sure your citations include complete source information. This information will vary depending on the source and the citation style. It often includes the author's name, the source's title, and the page numbers.

The book has been called "a beautifully written piece" (Lynn 8).

An 18 percent increase in sales was reported (Appleton 72).

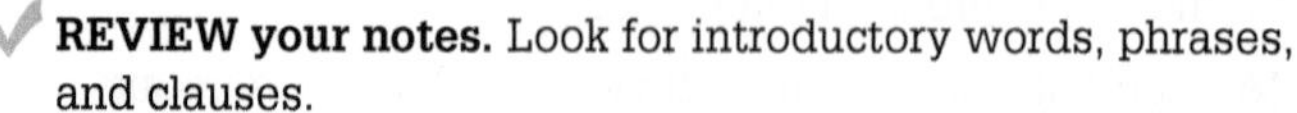

Use a current or completed draft of your work to practice documenting your sources.

- **REVIEW your notes.** Look for introductory words, phrases, and clauses.
- **USE a style guide.** Check the correct format for your citations in the style guide your teacher recommends.

Tech Tip

When researching for an assignment on the Internet, be sure to use only reputable sources that cite their information. Then, use the correct citation style for Internet sources, which often includes the Web site URL and date visited.

LEARN MORE

- See Chapter 11, Research Writing, pages 234–237
- See Writing Coach Online

Inside TRACK

Explain that in certain kinds of writing students will need to prove their points as well as give credit where it is due. That means the reader needs to be able to find *exactly* where students found their information.

1. **Give students tips on how to keep track of their sources as they write a paper, such as maintaining a "Source Sheet" as they research.**
2. **Tell students that when in doubt they should include more information in a citation not less.**

Find It/FIX IT

4 Vague Pronoun Reference

Inside TRACK

Writers sometimes falsely assume that readers will understand intended meanings. Remind students that it is their job as writers to state what they mean as clearly as possible. Tell them that it is better to be clear and simple than unclear and complex.

Have students do a word search in their papers for pronouns and confirm that each pronoun they use has a clear antecedent.

Tech Tip

It is important to proofread your work after you cut and paste text. You may have inserted vague pronoun references while moving text and making new sentences.

LEARN MORE

- See Chapter 6, Fiction Narration, pages 110–111
- See Writing Coach Online

GAME PLAN **Create clear pronoun-antecedent relationships to make your writing more accurate and powerful.**

VAGUE IDEA Pronouns such as *which, this, that,* and *these* should refer to a specific idea. To avoid a vague reference, try changing a pronoun to an adjective that modifies a specific noun.

Abigail bought her younger brother a baseball and a basketball. That ^basketball is the one he has been asking for.

UNCLEAR USE OF *IT, THEY,* AND *YOU* Be sure that the pronouns *it, they,* and *you* have a clearly stated antecedent. Replacing the personal pronoun with a specific noun can make a sentence clearer.

My teacher has taught us about World War I and World War II. ~~It~~ ^World War II will be on the test next week.

The team members asked the coaches ~~if they could~~ ^to practice the play again.

To make the basketball team, ~~you~~ ^potential team members must attend every tryout.

Use a current or completed draft of your work to practice identifying vague pronoun references.

- **READ** carefully. Read your draft slowly to locate pronouns.
- **IDENTIFY** possible errors. Mark any vague pronoun references.
- **REVISE** your draft. Rewrite sentences with vague pronoun-antecedent relationships.

Working with ELLs  **Sheltered Instruction: Metacognitive**

As students work on correcting vague pronoun references, remind them to monitor and edit their writing for pronoun-antecedent agreement, using self-corrective techniques. Remind students of rules of pronoun-antecedent agreement by reviewing the meanings of the words *singular* and *plural.* Then:

Beginning Have two volunteers stand in front of the class. Say *Two students stand.* On the board, write *He stands* and *They stand*. Ask students to copy down the correct sentence and then use the self-corrective strategy of circling the pronoun and comparing it to the antecedent, asking themselves *How many?* about each *(one/more than one).*

Find It/FIX IT

5

Spelling Error

GAME PLAN **Spelling errors can change the meaning of a sentence. Proofread your work after spell-checking to be sure you have used the correct words.**

SPELL-CHECK ERRORS Computer spell-checkers often replace misspelled words with others close in spelling but different in meaning. Proofread your work carefully to correct these errors.

Mrs. Douglas likes ~~line~~ pine trees the best.

After the show, my dad ~~grove~~ drove us home.

HOMOPHONES Words that are pronounced the same but have different spellings and meanings are called homophones. Check that you have used the correct homophones to convey your meaning.

Did you say that a ~~be~~ bee stung you?

When we were in the skyscraper, we were ~~hi~~ high above the ground.

Use a current or completed draft of your work to practice spelling words correctly.

- **READ** carefully. Read your draft word by word looking for spelling errors.
- **IDENTIFY** possible mistakes. Mark any incorrect words or words that are misspelled.
- **USE** a dictionary. If you are not certain how to spell a word or think a homophone has been used incorrectly, check a dictionary.

Tech Tip

Proper nouns are not checked by a computer spell-checker. Proofread to make sure that you have spelled people's names correctly.

LEARN MORE

- See Chapter 20, Effective Sentences, pages 457–461
- See Writing Coach Online

Inside TRACK

Tell students that running spell-check is not a guarantee that all their spelling errors will be fixed. (For example, if they left the *e* off the end of *spine*, the spell-check would not have a problem with *spin*.)

1. **Explain that reading one's work out loud is often the best way to bring spell-check errors to light.**
2. **Encourage students to ask a peer or adult to read their draft for misused homophones.**

Intermediate Have students write two short sentences using pronouns. Then, help them apply the self-corrective technique of writing an ***s*** above singular pronouns and antecedents and a ***p*** above plural pronouns and antecedents and checking that they match.

Advanced Have students write a brief paragraph on a topic of their choice using pronouns. Then, have them apply the self-corrective technique from the Intermediate activity.

Advanced High Challenge students to complete the Advanced activity and then to explain to the class any difficult cases they found and how they resolved them.

Find It/FIX IT

Punctuation Error With a Quotation

GAME PLAN Quotation marks are used to identify direct quotations. Correct punctuation helps to identify quotations and relate them to your work.

DIRECT AND INDIRECT QUOTATIONS A direct quotation is enclosed in quotation marks. Indirect quotations do not need quotation marks.

My mom said, "I'll pick you up from school today."

My mom said that she will pick me up from school.

QUOTATION MARKS WITH OTHER PUNCTUATION When commas or periods end a quotation, the punctuation goes inside the quotation marks. Question marks and exclamation marks go either inside or outside the quotation marks, depending on the sentence structure.

The director said, "Choir tryouts are this Friday."

"I hope I can join the choir!" the girl exclaimed.

Did she say, "I don't think I'll try out for choir"?

Use a current or completed draft of your work to practice punctuating quotations correctly.

- **READ** carefully. If you used indirect quotations, make sure you did not put them in quotation marks.
- **IDENTIFY** direct quotations. Mark each direct quotation in your work. Is each quotation punctuated correctly?
- **REVISE** your sentences. Correct all punctuation errors in your quotations.

Tech Tip

If you cut and paste quotations, remember to copy the taglines to make sure you have included all of the correct punctuation marks with direct quotations.

LEARN MORE

- See Chapter 25, Punctuation, pages 577–583
- See Writing Coach Online

Inside TRACK

1. Remind students that they must use quotation marks when using a source's exact words. Have students explain the difference between a direct quotation and an indirect quotation.
2. Explain that the key to punctuating sentences with quotations is to consider the *entire* sentence. If the sentence (not the quote) asks a question or makes an exclamation, the end mark belongs *outside* the quotation marks.

Differentiated Instruction

PRE-AP Enrichment for Above-Level Students Students may find it helpful to create a quick list of rules for punctuating sentences with quotations to keep in their notebooks. Have students write the rule(s) for commas and periods, question marks and exclamation marks, and colons and semicolons. Then, work with students to create an original example for each rule.

Enrichment for Gifted/Talented Students Gifted/Talented students may do a great deal of informational research writing in their coursework. Have students research a topic of interest and write a paragraph that contains at least two quotations from expert sources. Elicit from students how and why they punctuated sentences with quotations the way they did.

Find It/FIX IT

7

Unnecessary Comma

GAME PLAN **Before you insert a comma, think about how your ideas relate to one another. Make sure the comma is necessary.**

APPOSITIVES If an appositive is essential to the meaning of a sentence, it is *not* set off by commas.

My friend, Jose, was in charge of making sure everyone in class was on the bus.

PARTICIPIAL PHRASES If a participial phrase is essential to the meaning of a sentence, it should *not* be set off by commas.

The student, standing in the bus aisle, was asked to sit in a seat.

ADJECTIVAL CLAUSES Essential adjectival clauses should *not* be set off by commas.

The bus ride, that took us to the museum, was a short trip.

Use a current or completed draft of your work to practice correctly punctuating essential elements.

- **SCAN** Mentor Texts. Notice how professional writers use commas.
- **IDENTIFY** essential elements. Did you incorrectly use commas to indicate these elements?
- **REVISE** your sentences. Delete any commas that set off essential elements.

Tech Tip

Remember to add or delete commas as needed when you cut and paste and move text.

LEARN MORE

- See Chapter 25, Punctuation, pages 562–565
- See Writing Coach Online

Inside TRACK

Students may need the most help identifying the elements.

1. **Remind students that an appositive restates a noun.**
2. **Explain that participles are verbs acting as adjectives that end in *–ing* or *–ed* (e.g., *The girl walking to school is late.*) Point out that if the participle is with a helping verb, it might be acting as the verb in a sentence (e.g., *She was walking to school*).**
3. **Point out that adjectival clauses have a subject and a verb. Review relative pronouns and adverbs.**

Inside TRACK

1. Tell students that one way to find out if a word is a proper noun is to determine whether it *names* something or someone. Have them ask themselves: Is that a word that would apply to many of this thing or is it a special name for just that one?
2. Remind students that all kinds of titles are naming a thing, whether that thing is a book, a movie, a story, a play, a painting or some other work of art.

Find It/FIX IT

8 Unnecessary or Missing Capitalization

GAME PLAN **Follow the rules of capitalization. For example, capitalize proper nouns, the first word of a sentence, and titles of works of art.**

PROPER NOUNS Names, geographical locations, and organizations are examples of nouns that should be capitalized.

My sister Jenna lives in Michigan near Lake Huron.

John Fisher works for the Red Cross.

TITLES OF WORKS OF ART The first word and all other key words in the titles of books, poems, stories, plays, paintings, and other works of art are capitalized.

I like to read *Charlotte's Web* to my younger cousins.

I always liked the story "Beauty and the Beast."

Check It

Use a current or completed draft of your work to practice correctly capitalizing words.

- **SCAN** your draft. Look for words that are capitalized.
- **IDENTIFY** errors in capitalization. Mark words that might be capitalized incorrectly.
- **USE** your textbook. Check the grammar section of your textbook if you are not sure if a word should be capitalized.

Tech Tip

Sometimes word processors will automatically capitalize any word that follows a period, even if the period is part of an abbreviation. Proofread carefully for incorrectly capitalized words.

LEARN MORE

- See Chapter 26, Capitalization, pages 608–628
- See Writing Coach Online

Find It/FIX IT 9

Missing Word

GAME PLAN Make sure there are no missing words in a text so that your ideas flow smoothly and are clear to readers.

ARTICLES To make sure that ideas flow smoothly, you must proofread your work. A missing word, even a missing article (*a, an, the*), can confuse a reader.

My family is going to ^the band concert at school tonight.

KEY IDEAS When copying and pasting text, you might miss moving a word in a sentence. If that word is part of the main idea of the sentence, your meaning could be lost.

After I rode my bike to school, I realized that I ^forgot my bike lock at home!

I asked the principal if I could store my ^bike inside for the day.

Use a current or completed draft of your work to practice proofreading.

- **READ** carefully. Read your draft word by word to make sure that you did not leave out a word.
- **IDENTIFY** unclear sentences. Mark any sentences you find that do not make sense. Are they unclear because of a missing word?
- **REVISE** your sentences. Add words to your sentences to make the meaning clear.

Tech Tip

When cutting and pasting sentences, you may use the same word twice by mistake. Proofread to be sure your sentences read correctly.

LEARN MORE

- See Editing sections in the writing chapters
- See Writing Coach Online

Inside TRACK

1. Tell students that it is easy to mentally insert small words such as articles when we are proofreading our own work, even when the words aren't there. That is why reading out loud, slowly, and word-for-word is such a good way to catch these types of small errors.
2. Point out that anyone can leave out important words when one is writing quickly. Copying and pasting is also a time when words can be lost.

Differentiated Instruction

RTI Strategy for Special Needs Students
Students may find it helpful to review the uses of the articles *a*, *an*, and *the*. Explain that *a* and *an* are used to refer to general nouns, e.g., a dog, an animal, while *the* refers to a specific noun, e.g. *the* dog who ran into the woods. Encourage students to create their own example for each article, and to write the rules and examples in their notebooks for reference.

Strategy for Spanish Speakers
Students whose home language is Spanish may transfer the use of the definite article to English when making generalizations. (*The peace is a universal goal* versus *Peace is a universal goal.*) Write several sentences that use the definite article correctly and incorrectly in generalizations. Have students correct the incorrect sentences by rewriting them.

Find It/FIX IT

10 Faulty Sentence Structure

Inside TRACK

1. Many students have trouble catching their own faulty parallelism. Have them look for commas in their papers and see if those commas are separating a series. Then, have them check to see if the series is parallel.
2. Tell students to look through their papers for coordinating conjunctions. Then, have them determine if the sentence with the conjunction is a comparison. If so, is the comparison parallel?

Tech Tip

Be careful when you cut one part of a sentence and paste it in another. Remember to check that the new sentence structure is correct.

LEARN MORE

- See Chapter 20, Effective Sentences, pages 462–464
- See Writing Coach Online

GAME PLAN Sentences should express complex ideas clearly. Use parallel, or similar, structures to make your writing clear.

WORDS IN A SERIES Check that the words you use in a series have parallel structure.

When I go on vacation, I like to read, to fish, and ~~biking~~ ^to bike.

I like baseball because of the running, catching, and ~~to pitch~~ ^pitching.

COMPARISONS In writing comparisons, be sure to compare a phrase with the same type of phrase. Also, compare a clause with the same type of clause.

She thinks that singing is hard but ^that it is worth the effort.

Billy says the cat is under the bed, but ~~the couch is where his brother thinks he'll find the cat~~ ^his brother thinks the cat is under the couch.

Use a current or corrected draft of your work to practice writing using parallel structures.

- **SCAN** Mentor Texts. Notice how professional writers present complex ideas.
- **IDENTIFY** possible mistakes. Mark any sentences that have faulty parallelism.
- **REVISE** your sentences. Rewrite any sentences that do not have correct sentence structure.

Differentiated Instruction

RTI Strategy for Below-Level Students To reinforce the concepts of faulty parallelism and coordination students may benefit from working with you individually to edit their drafts. Encourage students to use a highlighter to mark sentences that they think contain faulty sentence structures. Work with students to correct a few errors before encouraging them to edit the rest independently or with a partner.

Pre-AP Enrichment for Above-Level Students Remind students that high-level writing often contains complex ideas. Have students work in pairs to construct three original sentences with parallel grammatical structures and three sentences with ideas of unequal importance. Invite student pairs to exchange papers with others to check for faulty parallelism or faulty coordination and to correct errors.

GAME PLAN Use commas to set off nonessential elements of sentences.

APPOSITIVE If an appositive is not essential to the meaning of a sentence, it should be set off by commas.

Mrs. Simon, Bridget's mom, gave me a ride home from school today.

PARTICIPIAL PHRASE A participial phrase not essential to the meaning of a sentence is set off by commas.

Driving a minivan, Mrs. Simon pulled into my driveway.

ADJECTIVAL CLAUSE Use commas to set off an adjectival clause if it is not essential to the meaning of a sentence.

My mom, who had to work late, made meatloaf for dinner.

Use a current or completed draft of your work to practice using commas correctly with nonessential elements.

- **SCAN** Mentor Texts. Notice how professional writers use commas to set off nonessential elements.
- **IDENTIFY** nonessential elements. Did you use commas to indicate these words, phrases, or clauses?
- **REVISE** your sentences. Use commas to set off nonessential elements.

Find It/FIX IT 11

Missing Comma With a Nonessential Element

Tech Tip

When you cut part of a sentence and paste it to another, be sure to include the correct punctuation. Proofread these sentences carefully.

LEARN MORE

- See Chapter 25, Punctuation, pages 562–565
- See Writing Coach Online

Inside TRACK

Tell students that when they are in doubt about whether a word, phrase, or clause is essential or nonessential to a sentence, they should take the words in question out of the sentence. Does the sentence still make sense? If so, then the information is not essential and should be separated by commas.

Another test is to add the words *by the way* before the word, phrase, or clause. If the sentence still makes sense then the phrase or clause is probably nonessential.

Find It/FIX IT

12 Unnecessary Shift in Verb Tense

GAME PLAN **Use consistent verb tenses in your work. Shift tenses only to show that one event comes before or after another.**

ACTIONS OCCURRING AT THE SAME TIME Use consistent tenses to show actions that occur at the same time.

I walked to the movie theater, and I ~~watch~~ ^watched my favorite film.

I dove into the pool, and I ~~swim~~ ^swam to the other end.

ACTIONS OCCURRING AT DIFFERENT TIMES If actions occur at different times, you can switch from one tense to another. You may use a time word or phrase to show the shift in tense.

Yesterday my family hiked in the forest, but today we ~~swam~~ ^are swimming in the lake.

I went to school today, but tomorrow, Saturday, I ~~went~~ ^will go to the mall.

Use a current or completed draft of your work to practice using consistent tenses.

- **SCAN** Mentor Texts. Notice how professional writers use consistent tenses within a sentence.
- **IDENTIFY** possible mistakes. Mark any unnecessary shift in verb tense within a sentence.
- **USE** your textbook. Consult the grammar section of your textbook if you are not sure that have used consistent tenses.

Tech Tip

When you cut text from one section to paste to another, the new sentence may have verbs that are not consistent in tense. Proofread revised sentences to make sure they use consistent tenses.

LEARN MORE

- See Chapter 20, Effective Sentences, pages 466–467
- See Writing Coach Online

Inside TRACK

1. Use a timeline to help students see that actions that happen at the same time should have the same tense.
2. Explain that sentences that contain a shift in time should also have a shift in verb tense (e.g., "The teacher *told* us that we *will have* a test on Friday.") Tell students that time words such as *today, tomorrow, yesterday. first, next*, and *then* can help them indicate a sequence of events.

Working with ELLs — ELL Sheltered Instruction: Metacognitive

Have students monitor and edit their writing to correct unnecessary shifts in verb tense, using self-corrective techniques. Review verb tenses.

Beginning Have students copy these sentences from the board: *I walked to class. Then I sit down.* Read the sentences aloud, miming for support. Then, guide them in using the self-corrective technique of circling the verbs and asking themselves *When?* about each *(before now / now / later)* to help them edit for tense.

Intermediate Have students copy the sentences from the Beginning activity. Have them use a self-corrective technique by writing each verb in the past, present, and future tenses, comparing these forms to the verbs in the sentences, and editing as necessary to avoid a tense shift.

Find It/FIX IT

13 Missing Comma in a Compound Sentence

GAME PLAN Use a comma before a coordinating conjunction to separate two or more main clauses in a compound sentence.

MAIN CLAUSES Place a comma before a coordinating conjunction (e.g. *and, but, or, nor, yet, so, for*) in a compound sentence.

Freddie wants to go to the park, but it is raining.

My aunt is coming to my house for dinner, and she is bringing dessert.

BRIEF CLAUSES The main clauses in some compound sentences are brief and do not need a comma if the meaning is clear.

Mary is 12 years old and Sasha is 14 years old.

SINGLE WORDS Commas should *not* be used to separate single words that are separated by a conjunction.

They brought fruit, and vegetables.

He saw a duck, and goose.

Use a current or completed draft of your work to practice using commas in compound sentences.

- **SCAN** your draft. Look for compound sentences.
- **IDENTIFY** missing commas. Mark any compound sentences that should be punctuated with a comma.
- **REVISE** your sentences. Add commas before coordinating conjunctions to separate main clauses.

Tech Tip

Be careful when you create a compound sentence by cutting and pasting from different parts of a sentence or paragraph. Remember to include a comma to separate the main clauses.

LEARN MORE

- See Chapter 25, Punctuation, pages 556, 559
- See Writing Coach Online

Inside TRACK

Students may confuse compound sentences and compound subjects and verbs.

1. **Remind students that a compound sentence contains two main clauses connected by *and*, *or*, or *but*. Tell them to read each clause by itself to determine if it sounds like a complete thought.**
2. **Explain that "brief main clauses" are usually just a simple subject and predicate.**
3. **Reinforce the fact that commas are not used every time a conjunction is used.**

Advanced Have pairs of students write brief paragraphs on a topic of their choice and then use the self-corrective technique described in the Intermediate activity on page 284. Have students exchange papers and check each other's work.

Advanced High Have students independently complete the Advanced activity. Then, challenge them to write a sentence using a correct shift in tense (for example, *Yesterday, I went to school, but today is Saturday*).

Inside TRACK

Help students identify when a word is possessive.

1. Teach students to check if an *s* is possessive by using the word *of*, as in, *Susan's hat* reworked as *the hat of Susan.*
2. For plural possessives tell students to mentally say the additional *s.*
3. Remind students of the technique of replacing *its* with the phrase *it is* or *it has* in order to determine whether the word needs an apostrophe. If the replacement makes sense, the word should be inserted as *it's*; if the phrase doesn't make sense, insert *its.*

Find It/FIX IT

14 Unnecessary or Missing Apostrophe

Tech Tip

Proofread your draft carefully. Not all computer grammar checkers will point out incorrect uses of apostrophes.

LEARN MORE

- See Chapter 22, Using Pronouns, pages 506–509
- See Chapter 25, Punctuation, pages 595–599
- See Writing Coach Online

GAME PLAN Use apostrophes correctly to show possession.

SINGULAR NOUNS To show the possessive case of most singular nouns, add an apostrophe and *-s.*

The school's talent show was amazing.

PLURAL NOUNS Add an apostrophe to show the possessive case for most plural nouns ending in *-s* or *-es*. For plural nouns that do not end in *-s* or *-es*, add an apostrophe and *-s.*

The students' chatter was distracting the teacher.

The children's clothing store is where my aunt shops for my younger cousin.

POSSESSIVE PRONOUNS Possessive pronouns (e.g. *his, hers, its, our, their*) show possession without the use of an apostrophe. Do not confuse *its* and *it's*. The word *its* shows possession, but the word *it's* means "it is."

~~Hers'~~ Hers is the car on the left; you can see ~~it's~~ its dented hood.

Use a current or completed draft of your work to practice showing possession.

- **SCAN** Mentor Texts. Notice when professional writers use apostrophes to indicate possession.
- **IDENTIFY** possible mistakes. Mark each apostrophe in your draft. Did you use them correctly to show possession?
- **REVISE** your sentences. Make sure to delete any apostrophes you used with possessive pronouns.

Differentiated Instruction

Strategy for Spanish Speakers
Students whose home language is Spanish may have difficulty with possessive pronouns because in Spanish possessive pronouns agree with the gender of the object possessed. Prepare one set of pictures of people and another set of pictures of objects. Hold up a picture from each set and ask students to use the correct possessive pronoun (*their jacket, his book,* and so on).

RTI Strategy for Special Needs Students
Refer students to page 287 and Find It/FIX IT 15. Help students understand the correct punctuation to avoid run-on sentences. Write the following: *The boy's dog ran down the street a man grabbed the leash he brought the dog back.* Have students correct the sentence: *The boy's dog ran down the street. A man grabbed the leash. He brought the dog back.* Ask students to explain why they made their corrections.

Find It/FIX IT

15

Run-on Sentence

GAME PLAN **Use correct punctuation to avoid run-on sentences. A run-on sentence is two or more sentences punctuated as if they were a single sentence.**

FUSED SENTENCE A fused sentence contains two or more sentences joined with no punctuation. To correct a fused sentence, place a period or an end mark between the main clauses.

My aunt bought her wedding ~~dress it~~ ^dress. It was made out of lace.

Why did he want to buy a new ~~jacket his~~ ^jacket? His had hardly been worn.

RUN-ON SENTENCE Place a comma and a coordinating conjunction between main clauses to avoid run-on sentences.

We were going to arrive to the movie on time, ^but my dad got a flat tire on the way to the theater.

Use a current or completed draft of your work to practice correcting run-on sentences.

- **SCAN** your draft. Look for run-on sentences.
- **IDENTIFY** missing punctuation. Mark sentences that might need a period or an end mark to separate main clauses.
- **REVISE** your sentences. When correcting fused sentences, vary your sentence structure.

Tech Tip

Remember to proofread your work. Not all grammar checkers identify run-on sentences.

LEARN MORE

- See Chapter 20, Effective Sentences, pages 449–452
- See Writing Coach Online

Inside TRACK

Students often create fused and run-on sentences by forgetting to link two or more independent clauses with punctuation or connecting words. Remind students to use a comma and a coordinating conjunction to form a compound sentence or a period and proper capitalization to form two separate sentences.

Find It/FIX IT

16

Comma Splice

GAME PLAN **Use correct punctuation to avoid comma splices. A comma splice happens when two or more complete sentences are joined only with a comma.**

PERIOD Replace the comma with a period (and capitalize the following word) to separate two complete thoughts.

The blizzard buried my dad's car under a blanket of snow~~, we~~. We had to shovel the car out before he could drive to work.

SEMICOLON Replace the comma with a semicolon if the ideas are similar.

Charlie built a sand castle~~,~~; the waves knocked it down.

COORDINATING CONJUNCTION A comma splice can be corrected by placing a coordinating conjunction (e.g., *and, or, but, yet, nor*) after the comma.

Clouds started to cover then sun, and it started to rain.

Use a current or completed draft of your work to practice correcting comma splices.

- **READ** carefully. Take time to read your draft carefully. Have someone else read your work for a double-check.
- **IDENTIFY** possible mistakes. Mark any comma splices you find.
- **REVISE** your sentences. Fix comma splices in different ways to vary your sentence structure.

Tech Tip

Some grammar checkers will not catch comma splices. Proofread your work carefully to avoid comma splices.

LEARN MORE

- See Chapter 20, Effective Sentences, pages 449–452
- See Chapter 25, Punctuation, pages 556–557
- See Writing Coach Online

Inside TRACK

Tell students that it is easy but often incorrect to sprinkle one's writing with commas, especially to indicate a pause for breath.

1. **Review periods and remind students that short, clear sentences are not a bad thing.**
2. **Explain to students that independent clauses with similar ideas can be separated by a semicolon.**
3. **Remind students that if they use a comma to separate independent clauses, they must include a coordinating conjunction after it.**

Differentiated Instruction

RTI Strategy for Below-Level Students Students may benefit from working with a partner to review their draft for comma splices. Have partners review each draft and highlight examples of comma splices. Then, work with partners to determine the best strategy for correcting each error: using a comma and coordinating conjunction, using a semicolon, or creating two separate sentences.

PRE-AP Enrichment for Above-Level Students Challenge students to write a paragraph with related independent clauses. Have them avoid comma splices by using each strategy for separating independent clauses: using a comma and coordinating conjunction, using a semicolon, or creating two separate sentences.

Find It/FIX IT

17 Lack of Pronoun-Antecedent Agreement

GAME PLAN Check that pronouns agree with their antecedents in number, person, and gender. When the gender is not specified, the pronoun must still agree in number.

GENDER NEUTRAL ANTECEDENTS When gender is not specific, use *his* or *her* to refer to the singular antecedent.

Each child should be in ~~their~~ ^ his or her bed by 8 p.m.

OR, NOR, AND When two or more singular antecedents are joined by *or* or *nor*, use a singular personal pronoun. Use a plural personal pronoun when two or more antecedents are joined by *and*.

Neither Jerry nor Stu will read the book I gave ~~them~~ ^ him.

Sally and Sue are memorizing ~~her~~ ^ their routine for cheerleading practice.

INDEFINITE PRONOUNS A plural personal pronoun must agree with a plural indefinite pronoun. A singular personal pronoun must agree with a singular indefinite pronoun.

Both of the girls put ~~her~~ ^ their toys away before dinner.

One of the photographers took ~~their~~ ^ his photographs to the studio to get developed.

Use a current or completed draft of your work to practice pronoun-antecedent agreement.

- **READ** carefully. Take time to read your draft carefully. For a double-check, have someone else read your work.
- **IDENTIFY** possible mistakes. Mark any pronouns that do not agree with their antecedents in a sentence.
- **USE** your textbook. Check the grammar section of your textbook if you are not sure whether your pronouns and antecedents agree.

Tech Tip

Be careful when you cut and paste text from one sentence to another. Check that the pronouns agree with the antecedents in the new sentences you create.

LEARN MORE

- See Chapter 23, Making Words Agree, pages 527–531
- See Writing Coach Online

Inside TRACK

1. Remind students that many gender neutral antecedents are singular and require a singular pronoun.
2. Tell students that *or* and *nor* means one or the other, not both. *And*, on the other hand, means "both" which is more than one. Words joined by *and* use a plural pronoun.
3. Have students consider number when using indefinite pronouns.

Find It/FIX IT

18 Poorly Integrated Quotation

GAME PLAN **Quotations should flow smoothly into the sentence that surrounds them. Add information to explain and link quotes to the rest of your work.**

QUOTE IN A SENTENCE Prepare the reader for the information contained in the quote by introducing the quote's idea.

The writer in her book review ^ spoke about the characters in the book: "The main character was brave and loyal" (Jane 2).

Allison says ^ the author should have included more detail: "The writing was not creative."

QUOTE AS A SENTENCE Place an introductory phrase before or after a quotation that stands alone. In most cases, this phrase should identify the quote's author or speaker.

^ According to Mr. Peters, "The volunteer program is starting again in March" (Wolf 3).

Use a current or completed draft of your work to practice integrating quotations.

- **SCAN Mentor Texts.** Notice how professional writers integrate quotations into their work.
- **IDENTIFY quotes.** Mark each quote in your work. Does each quote flow smoothly with the surrounding sentence?
- **REVISE your sentences.** Add information as needed to explain and introduce quotes.

Tech Tip

Sometimes you might cut a quote from one sentence and paste it in another. Remember to revise the surrounding sentence to integrate the quote into the text.

LEARN MORE

- See Chapter 25, Punctuation, pages 577–585
- See Writing Coach Online

Inside TRACK

Students often sprinkle their research reports with quotes without considering how or whether these quotes flow with the rest of their ideas. Tell students that the extra step of framing the quotation can help strengthen the quality of their writing.

Remind students that they must tell readers who said a quote and link the quote to the main points of the report or essay. Explain that an introduction to a quotation can be an independent clause followed by a colon, or a brief phrase following by a comma.

Differentiated Instruction

RTI Strategy for Below-Level Students Have students work with a partner to review their drafts for abrupt uses of quotations. Have partners highlight all quotations. Then, work with partners to determine the best strategy for connecting each quote to the surrounding ideas: using an introductory clause with a colon for a quote in a sentence or using an introductory phrase and a comma for a quote that is a sentence.

PRE-AP Enrichment for Above-Level Students Have students choose a quotation to incorporate into a paragraph. Ask students to introduce the quotation using one of the two strategies presented: using an introductory clause with a colon for a quote in a sentence or using an introductory phrase and a comma for a quote that is a sentence. Invite students to share their paragraphs with classmates.

Find It/FIX IT

19 Unnecessary or Missing Hyphen

GAME PLAN **Use hyphens correctly in your writing, including with compound words and compound adjectives.**

COMPOUND WORDS Hyphens can connect two or more words that are used as one compound word. Some compound words do not require a hyphen. Check a current dictionary if you are not sure about hyphenating a word.

The blue color of my ~~sisterinlaw's~~ ^ sister-in-law's ~~bed-room~~ ^ bedroom is soothing.

My ~~grand-niece~~ ^ grandniece likes to play with a ~~jackinthebox~~ ^ jack-in-the-box.

COMPOUND ADJECTIVES A compound adjective that appears before a noun should be hyphenated. Remember, do not hyphenate a compound proper noun acting as an adjective. Also, do not hyphenate a compound adjective that has a word ending in *-ly*.

The ~~brown eyed~~ ^ brown-eyed girl is my sister.

The ~~friendly-looking~~ ^ friendly looking dog belongs to my neighbor.

My parents enjoy ~~North-Indian~~ ^ North Indian music.

Use a current or completed draft of your work to practice hyphenating words.

- **IDENTIFY** possible errors. Mark any compound adjectives before a noun that are not hyphenated.
- **REVISE** your sentences. Add a hyphen to words that should be hyphenated.
- **USE** a dictionary. Check a dictionary if you are not sure if a word should be hyphenated.

Tech Tip

The automatic hyphenation setting in word processors causes words at the end of a line of text to hyphenate automatically. Be sure that this setting is turned off when you are writing an essay.

LEARN MORE

- See Chapter 25, Punctuation, pages 589–591
- See Writing Coach Online

Inside TRACK

1. **Remind students that the best way to check the use of hyphens in compound words is to use a dictionary.**
2. **Explain to students that a verb with more than one word is *only* hyphenated when it is used as an adjective (i.e., *the filled-up tank*) not when it is acting as the verb (i.e., *they filled up the tank*).**

Find It/FIX IT

20

Sentence Fragment

GAME PLAN Use complete sentences when writing. Make sure you have a subject and a complete verb in each and that each sentence expresses a complete thought.

LACKING A SUBJECT OR VERB A complete sentence must have a subject and a verb.

My grandma is at our house visiting from Arizona. ~~And~~ ^She always has funny stories!

The cat ^started to climb the tree.

SUBORDINATE CLAUSE A subordinate clause cannot stand on its own as a complete sentence because it does not express a complete thought.

Joe ate three helpings of salad~~. After~~ ^after he had already finished an entire serving of pasta!

My dad waited in front of the school~~. While~~ ^while I was finishing a makeup exam.

Tech Tip

Sometimes, when you cut text from a sentence and paste it to another, you may miss cutting the whole sentence. Make sure you have both a subject and a verb in the new sentences.

LEARN MORE

- See Chapter 20, Effective Sentences, pages 444–448
- See Writing Coach Online

Use a current or completed draft of your work to practice writing complete sentences.

- **SCAN** your draft. Look for incomplete sentences.
- **IDENTIFY** missing words. Mark sentences that have missing subjects or verbs.
- **REVISE** your sentences. Rewrite any sentences that are missing subjects or verbs, or are subordinate clauses standing on their own.

Inside TRACK

1. Remind students that the best way to check for use of complete sentences is to read their drafts aloud. Better yet, have a classmate or family member read while the student writer listens for missing words.
2. Students often mistake subordinate clauses, especially lengthy ones, for complete sentences. Again, having someone else read their drafts aloud, pausing after periods, is a good strategy for catching these errors.

Differentiated Instruction

RTI Strategy for Below-Level Students Have students work in pairs and read their drafts aloud to each other. Tell the readers to pause for a long moment at every period, but not unless they actually see a period. Have partners tell each other when they hear a sentence fragment or run-on sentence. Have pairs work together to correct the missing words or sentence fragments in their work.

Enrichment for Gifted/Talented Students Strong writers may think it is acceptable to use sentence fragments in their writing, either to create a certain tone or to express the writer's voice. Explain to students that sentence fragments may distract the reader and create confusion. Invite students to find examples of their written work that contain sentence fragments. Encourage students to defend a decision to keep a fragment or revise the text to correct the fragments.

CHAPTER 13 LESSON PLANNER

Nouns and Pronouns

Use the Online Lesson Planner at www.phwritingcoach.com to customize your instructional plan for an integrated Language Arts curriculum.

DAY 1 13.1 Nouns

"What Do You Notice?" **Objectives:** Identify, use, and understand nouns, including ▪ as people, places, and things ▪ concrete and abstract nouns ▪ collective nouns ▪ count and non-count nouns	**INSTRUCTION AND PRACTICE** **Student Edition** pp. 293–297

DAY 2 13.1 Nouns *(continued)*

Objectives: Identify, use, and understand nouns, including ▪ compound nouns ▪ common and proper nouns	**INSTRUCTION AND PRACTICE** **Student Edition** pp. 298–299

DAY 3 13.2 Pronouns

Objectives: Identify, use, and understand pronouns, including ▪ antecedents of pronouns	**INSTRUCTION AND PRACTICE** **Student Edition** pp. 300–302

DAY 4 13.2 Pronouns *(continued)*

Objectives: Identify, use, and understand pronouns, including ▪ personal pronouns ▪ reflexive and intensive pronouns	**INSTRUCTION AND PRACTICE** **Student Edition** pp. 303–305

Grammar Assessment

Grammar Coach:	Diagnostic Assessment	End-of-Chapter Assessment	Progress Monitoring
Personalized Instruction	Students take grammar diagnostic test online and are automatically assigned instruction and practice in areas where they need support.	Teacher uses **ExamView** to administer end-of-chapter assessment and remediation. Teachers may customize **ExamView** tests or use the ones provided.	Teachers may use the **Test Warm-Ups** and the **Cumulative Reviews** in the student book or eText to check students' mastery of grammar skills. Students may also play **DimensionL** grammar video games to test their grammar skills.
Teacher-Directed Instruction	Teacher administers the diagnostic test and determines focus of instruction and practice.		

Alternate Pacing Plans

- **Block Scheduling** Each day in the Lesson Planner represents a 40–50 minute block. Teachers using block scheduling may combine days to revise pacing to meet their classroom needs.
- **Accelerated Lesson Planning** Combine instructional days, focusing on concepts called out by students' diagnostic test results.
- **Integrated Language Arts Curriculum** Use the instruction and practice in this chapter to provide reinforcement, remediation, or extension of grammar concepts taught in your literature curriculum.

Links to Prentice Hall *LITERATURE*

Unit 1 Common and Proper Nouns, p. 46; Personal Pronouns, p. 126

www.phwritingcoach.com

Grammar Assessment and Practice

Chapter diagnostic tests assess students' skills and assign instruction and practice.

DimensionL Video Games

Fast-paced interactive video games challenge students' mastery of grammar.

Lesson Planner continues on next page

DAY 5 13.2 Pronouns *(continued)*

Objectives: Identify, use, and understand pronouns, including ▪ demonstrative pronouns ▪ relative pronouns ▪ interrogative pronouns ▪ indefinite pronouns	**INSTRUCTION AND PRACTICE** **Student Edition** pp. 306–310, 312 **Test Warm-Up** p. 311

"Having correct pronoun-antecedent agreement is foundational to good writing. Many of my students come to me at the beginning of the year writing sentences similar to the following: 'A person should visit their dentist twice a year.' It is imperative that these students receive practice in straightening out this problem."

—Kelly Gallagher

Differentiated Instruction

Differentiated Instruction Boxes in this Teacher's Edition address these student populations:

- Below-Level Students
- Gifted and Talented Students
- English Language Learners
- Above-Level Students
- Special Needs Students
- Spanish Speaking Students

In addition, for further enrichment, see the **Extension** features.

Grammar Ground Rule: Keep It Clear!

Model with Students

In this chapter, keeping it clear means using pronouns correctly. For example, explain to students that personal pronouns, such as *I, he, she,* and *it,* usually have antecedents. In other words, they stand in for specific nouns or noun phrases.

Say: It's great to use pronouns to keep your writing from being repetitive and boring, but you need to keep clear what each pronoun refers to. Here's an example from someone who didn't. *She told her sister that she was not the neatest person in the world. They decided that her clothes would go only in the dresser and closet near the door and they could be messy if she wanted. Who was not the neatest person in the world? Whose clothes would go in the dresser near the door? What could be messy?* Here's how the sentences sound with clear antecedents. *She told her sister, "You're not the neatest person in the world." They decided that the sister's clothes would go only in the dresser and closet near the door. Then the clothes could be messy if she wanted.*

Small Group Activity – Finding Pronouns and Antecedents

Have students form groups to search articles on the internet or in magazines to find examples of pronouns and their antecedents. Have the groups discuss what they found. Their discussion should answer these questions:

- What is the antecedent of the sentence?
- Is the antecedent clear to the reader?

Have a member of each group present their findings to the class with at least one example, and explain why the group thought the pronoun followed this grammar ground rule: Keep it clear.

Grammar Ground Rules

1. Keep it clear.
2. Make them agree.
3. Make it specific.
4. Dot your *i*'s and cross your *t*'s.
5. Make it active.

NOUNS *and* PRONOUNS

Using proper nouns, which are always capitalized, can make your writing more specific and informative.

WRITE GUY *Jeff Anderson, M.Ed.*

WHAT DO YOU NOTICE?

See how easy it is to spot the common and proper nouns as you zoom in on these sentences from the story "Papa's Parrot" by Cynthia Rylant.

MENTOR TEXT

> The more Mr. Tillian grew to like his parrot, and the more he talked to it instead of people, the more embarrassed Harry became.

Now, ask yourself the following questions:

- Can you explain why the two nouns that begin with the letter *p* in this sentence are both common nouns?
- What are the proper nouns in this sentence?

Parrot and *people* are common nouns because these words could refer to any parrot or any group of people. However, *Mr. Tillian* and *Harry* are proper nouns because they refer to particular people. You can recognize them as proper nouns because they are capitalized.

Grammar for Writers Writers use specific details about people, places, and things to make their stories vivid. Including a mix of common and proper nouns is a good way to do this.

Our principal's first name is Anne. That is a proper noun.
Yes, but it's not proper to call her that.

CHAPTER 13

Grammar for Writers: Syntax

Explain to students that understanding the functions of nouns and pronouns helps writers to use them effectively. The rules and activities on these pages will help students define, identify, and use nouns and pronouns correctly.

NOUNS *and* PRONOUNS

As students progress in their writing skills, it will be important for them to be able to apply the rules of grammar, usage, and mechanics to their own drafts. Use the *What Do You Notice?* feature to help them see effective conventions in the work of professional writers. Encourage students to incorporate proper voice, tense, and syntax as they edit their own writing.

Remind students that common nouns name general types of items and proper nouns name specific people, places, or things. Then, tell them how important it is to distinguish between common and proper nouns in their writing. Point out that proper nouns are capitalized but common nouns are not.

WRITE GUY *Jeff Anderson, M. Ed.*

WHAT DO YOU NOTICE?

When students have read the Mentor Text, **say:** How would this sentence change if the proper nouns were changed to common nouns like *the man* and *the boy*? (**Possible response:** The sentence would not describe what happened specifically to Mr. Tillian and Harry. It would just describe a funny event that happened to some unknown people.)

Explain that proper nouns allow writers to tell about particular people, places, and things. Note that the point of the Mentor Text is to express Harry's embarrassment over Mr. Tillian's new habit of talking to his parrot. **Say:** When it is important to be specific, use proper nouns. When general names or labels are best, use common nouns. **Ask:** Now, what might happen if the common noun *parrot* was replaced with the proper noun *Rocky*? (**Possible response:** We wouldn't really know who or what Rocky was.) **Say:** Common nouns do an excellent job of naming types of people, places, and things. Even if the proper noun, *Rocky,* was the parrot's name, it wouldn't help us understand the sentence. Use common and proper nouns to clearly express meaning.

Lesson Objectives

1. Define, identify, and distinguish among four main noun groups.
2. Use various types of nouns correctly.

RULE 13.1.1 Read aloud the rule and then have students repeat the line with you.

People, Places, Things, and Ideas

Discuss with the class how nouns enable us to communicate about the people we know, the places we visit, the things we see, and the ideas we have.

Concrete and Abstract Nouns

RULE 13.1.2 Read aloud the rule and then have students repeat the lines with you.

Have students use their five senses to determine whether a noun is concrete or abstract. If they come across the word *box* in a sentence, they should ask themselves if they can see, hear, or touch it. Because a box can be touched, it is a concrete noun. In contrast, abstract nouns, like *bravery,* name a quality they might think about or a feeling they might have.

www.phwritingcoach.com

Diagnostic and Instruction
Diagnostic test assesses students' instructional needs. Lessons and practice are assigned based on results.

Additional Practice
- Grammar Tutorials—Animated videos reinforce key grammar skills.
- Grammar Practice—Targeted practice addresses individual needs.
- ExamView—Teachers customize their grammar practice and tests.
- Grammar Games—Interactive video games make grammar fun.

13.1 Nouns

Nouns are naming words. Words such as *friend, sky, dog, love, courage,* and *Seattle* are nouns.

A noun names something.

Most nouns fall into four main groups.

People, Places, Things, and Ideas

The nouns in the chart are grouped under four headings. You may know most of the nouns under the first three headings. You may not have realized that all the words in the fourth group are nouns.

PEOPLE	PLACES	THINGS	IDEAS
veterinarian	Lake Mead	bumblebee	strength
Dr. Robinson	classroom	collar	honesty
Americans	kennel	motorcycle	willingness
leader	Bunker Hill	notebook	obedience

See Practice 13.1A

Concrete and Abstract Nouns

Nouns may be classified as **concrete** or **abstract.** In the chart above, *People, Places,* and *Things* are concrete nouns. *Ideas* are abstract nouns.

A concrete noun names something that can be recognized through any of the five senses. An abstract noun names something that cannot be recognized through the senses.

CONCRETE NOUNS			
pencil	dog	tractor	river
ABSTRACT NOUNS			
courage	fun	honor	exploration

See Practice 13.1B

WRITING COACH Online

www.phwritingcoach.com

Grammar Tutorials
Brush up on your Grammar skills with these animated videos.

Grammar Practice
Practice your grammar skills with Writing Coach Online.

Grammar Games
Test your knowledge of grammar in this fast-paced interactive video game.

Differentiated Instruction

RTI Strategy for Special Needs Students
Students may have difficulty identifying nouns. Take students around the classroom to touch and see a variety of "nouns." You may have students touch windows, doors, desks, and the board. To demonstrate place, you can have students visit the office or cafeteria or use a wall map to point out locations to which they've traveled. Have students record the nouns in a chart labeled *People, Places, Things,* and *Ideas.* (The Ideas column will remain blank until the second half of the activity.)

Once students have completed this activity, remind them that there is still another category of nouns. Explain that ideas are nouns that are feelings, concepts, or things that students can "visit in their minds." Distribute small slips of paper with these nouns written on them: *justice, honesty, courage, patience, friendship.* Talk about how these concepts are named by nouns, and have students come up with several more of their own. Have students write each idea in the *Ideas* column.

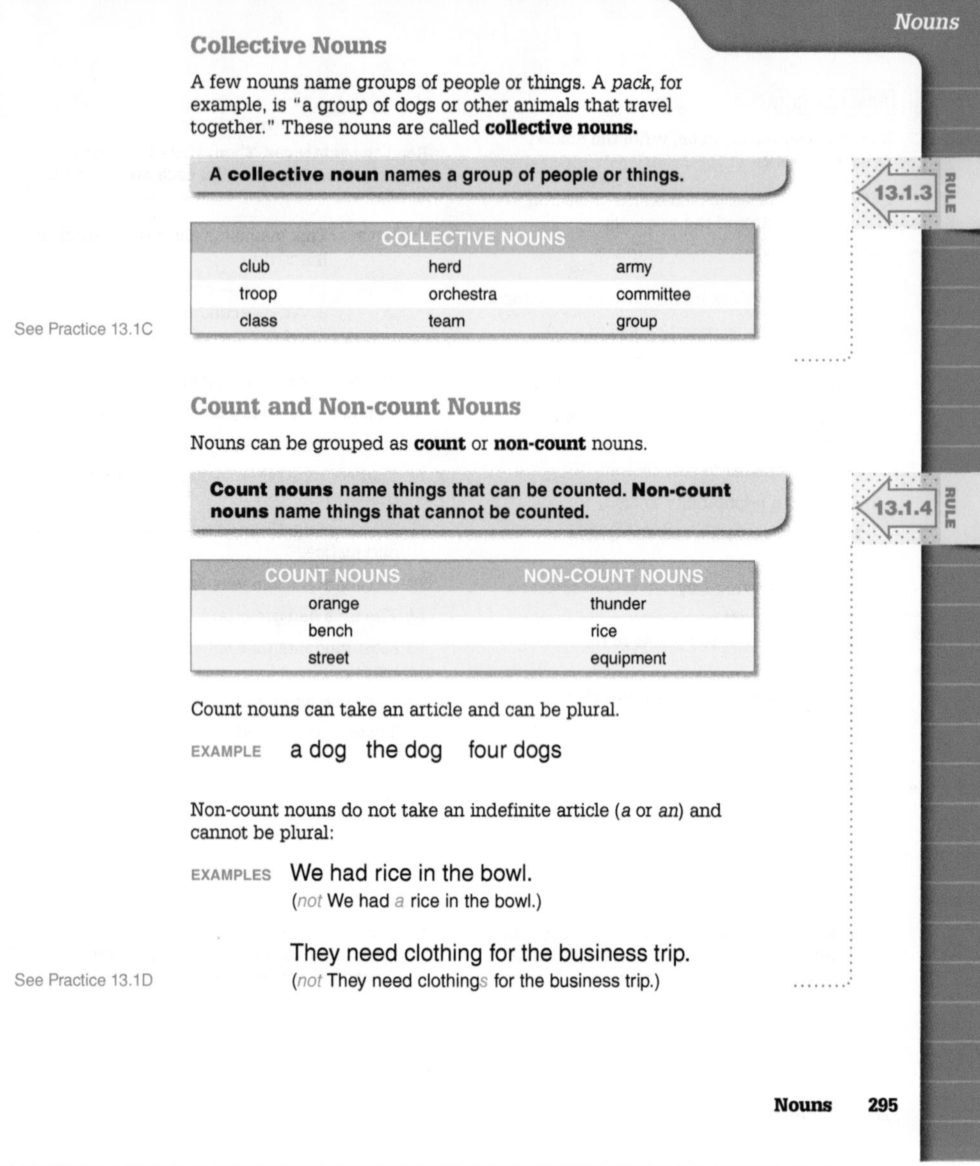

Collective Nouns

A few nouns name groups of people or things. A *pack*, for example, is "a group of dogs or other animals that travel together." These nouns are called **collective nouns.**

A collective noun names a group of people or things.

13.1.3 RULE

COLLECTIVE NOUNS		
club	herd	army
troop	orchestra	committee
class	team	group

See Practice 13.1C

Count and Non-count Nouns

Nouns can be grouped as **count** or **non-count** nouns.

Count nouns name things that can be counted. **Non-count nouns** name things that cannot be counted.

13.1.4 RULE

COUNT NOUNS	NON-COUNT NOUNS
orange	thunder
bench	rice
street	equipment

Count nouns can take an article and can be plural.

EXAMPLE a dog the dog four dogs

Non-count nouns do not take an indefinite article (*a* or *an*) and cannot be plural:

EXAMPLES We had rice in the bowl.
(*not* We had a rice in the bowl.)

They need clothing for the business trip.
(*not* They need clothings for the business trip.)

See Practice 13.1D

Collective Nouns

Explain that collective nouns, such as *staff*, refer to a collection or group of people or things.

RULE 13.1.3 Read aloud the rule and then have students repeat the line with you.

Use a Think Aloud as part of a gradual release progression.

Say: It is sometimes best to give a group of people or things one label. A good example of this would be when **I address all of you**—my students. It wouldn't be wise to call out each of your names when I tell you to open your textbook or take out your homework. Instead, I can just say, "Class, please take out your books." *Class* is a collective noun. It has many members, but it has one name.

Work with students to help them understand collective nouns by having them identify collective nouns that are related. Start with professional sports teams (collective noun: team) or cast members of familiar television programs (collective noun: cast).

Have small groups of students brainstorm for and list several other collective nouns. (**Possible answers:** audience, team, flock, colony, mob)

Count and Non-count Nouns

Direct students' attention to the definitions of count and non-count nouns. Have them discuss the "clues" given by the names *Count* and *Non-count*. Point out to students that an example of a non-count noun is *honey*. You can measure honey, but you can't count it. But *carrots* is a count noun because you can count carrots individually.

RULE 13.1.4 Read aloud the rule and then have students repeat the lines with you.

Have students work in pairs to brainstorm for and list five count and five non-count nouns (without labeling them). Then, have each pair of students exchange lists with another pair. Ask students to categorize each other's words.

Teacher Tip

If identifying nouns is difficult for students, give them an index card with the Noun Test printed on it: 1. Can I hold or touch this word? 2. Can I visit this word? 3. Can I "think" this word or visit it with my mind? Explain that if they answer yes to any of these questions, the word is a noun. Encourage students to continually refer to the Noun Test.

PRACTICE 13.1A

1. Joshua, birthday, October
2. Mr. Grant, miles, work, day
3. sunlight, window
4. Blackstones, vacation, mountains
5. brother, tennis
6. Austin, city
7. Melissa, birds, parakeets
8. Thanksgiving Day, food, homeless shelter
9. team, points, quarter
10. Raneesha, homework, study hall

PRACTICE 13.1B

11. praise—abstract, Jonas—concrete
12. obedience—abstract, quality—abstract, dog—concrete
13. growth—abstract, chart —concrete
14. courage—abstract, danger—abstract, award—concrete
15. people—concrete, United States—concrete, liberty—abstract, justice—abstract
16. Abraham Lincoln—concrete, honesty—abstract
17. fans—concrete, faith—abstract, team—concrete
18. students—concrete, satisfaction—abstract, work—abstract
19. choir—concrete, harmony—abstract
20. children—concrete, childhood—abstract

PRACTICE 13.1A Finding Nouns

Read the sentences. Then, write the nouns in each sentence.

EXAMPLE The leaves fell off the trees and cluttered the sidewalk.

ANSWER *leaves, trees, sidewalk*

1. Joshua will celebrate his birthday in October.
2. Mr. Grant drives twenty miles to work every day.
3. Sunlight streamed through the window.
4. The Blackstones enjoyed their vacation in the mountains.
5. My brother likes to play tennis.
6. Austin is a popular city to visit.
7. Melissa loves birds, and she has two parakeets.
8. On Thanksgiving Day, we served food at a homeless shelter.
9. Our team scored ten points in the first quarter.
10. Raneesha finished her homework in study hall.

PRACTICE 13.1B Identifying Concrete and Abstract Nouns

Read the sentences. Then, write the nouns in each sentence, and label each one *concrete* or *abstract*.

EXAMPLE This magazine has a good article on friendship.

ANSWER *magazine* — concrete
article — concrete
friendship — abstract

11. The teacher's praise pleased Jonas.
12. Obedience is an important quality in a dog.
13. We marked our yearly growth on a chart.
14. Your courage when facing danger merited this award.
15. People in the United States believe in liberty and justice.
16. Abraham Lincoln was known for his honesty.
17. The fans had great faith in their team.
18. Most students take satisfaction in doing good work.
19. The choir sang in harmony.
20. Those children had a happy childhood.

SPEAKING APPLICATION

With a partner, take turns telling about your favorite place. Your partner should listen for and name three nouns that you use.

WRITING APPLICATION

Use sentence 17 as a model to write three sentences that each contain two concrete nouns and one abstract noun.

SPEAKING APPLICATION

Have partners identify each noun that they have used as a collective, count, or non-count noun.

WRITING APPLICATION

Have students identify the abstract nouns and explain how they distinguished them from the concrete nouns.

PRACTICE 13.1C Finding Collective Nouns

Read the pairs of nouns. Each pair includes one collective noun. Write the collective noun.

EXAMPLE teacher, faculty
ANSWER *faculty*

1. senator, Congress
2. bird, flock
3. team, pitcher
4. student, class
5. army, soldier
6. conductor, orchestra
7. uncle, family
8. committee, member
9. crowd, shopper
10. audience, speaker

PRACTICE 13.1D Identifying Count and Non-count Nouns

Read the sentences. Then, list the count and non-count nouns. One sentence has only count nouns.

EXAMPLE The cows shivered in the cold.
ANSWER *count noun — cows*
non-count noun — cold

11. My cup of cocoa spilled.
12. We took pictures of the beautiful scenery.
13. Julie left her cellphone on the bus.
14. I will go to the park with you after I finish my homework.
15. Joey rides his bicycle to school in good weather.
16. The children played for hours in the sand.
17. Heavy rain caused flooding in our city.
18. Jazz has been a popular form of music for many years.
19. Lisa's uniform shrank when she washed it in hot water.
20. Loud thunder frightened the dogs in our neighborhood.

SPEAKING APPLICATION

Choose three of the pairs of nouns above. Make up a sentence using each pair and tell your sentences to a partner.

WRITING APPLICATION

Write three sentences and include one of the following in each: a collective noun, a count noun, and a non-count noun.

Working with ELLs

ELL **Sheltered Instruction:** Cognitive

As students complete Practice 13.1B on page 296, help them use prior knowledge to understand and learn academic vocabulary heard during classroom instruction. Write *noun, concrete,* and *abstract* on the board and orally review their meaning.

Beginning Partner students with more fluent peers to provide home language equivalents for the nouns in sentences 17 and 20, using prior knowledge. Guide them in learning the academic words with simple questions like *Is* chair *a concrete noun?*

Intermediate Have groups of students use prior knowledge to discuss the academic vocabulary and review the nouns in Practice 13.1B. Have them use the words in these cloze sentences: ______ *is a concrete noun. It names a thing.* ______ *is an abstract noun. It names an idea.*

Advanced Direct students to use the **KIM Strategy** as they listen to you explain the academic vocabulary. Have them create a three-column chart labeled *Key Word*, *Information*, and *Memory Cue*, filling in the first column with the vocabulary and using prior knowledge to complete the chart.

Advanced High Have students complete the Advanced activity. Then, have them write a compare-and-contrast paragraph about concrete and abstract nouns, drawing on prior knowledge.

PRACTICE 13.1C

1. Congress
2. flock
3. team
4. class
5. army
6. orchestra
7. family
8. committee
9. crowd
10. audience

PRACTICE 13.1D

11. count noun—cup
non-count noun—cocoa
12. count noun—pictures
non-count noun—scenery
13. count nouns—Julie, cell phone, bus
14. count noun—park
non-count noun—homework
15. count nouns—Joey, bicycle, school
non-count noun—weather
16. count nouns—children, hours
non-count noun—sand
17. count noun—city
non-count nouns—rain, flooding
18. count nouns—form, years
non-count nouns—jazz, music
19. count noun—uniform
non-count noun—water
20. count nouns—dogs, neighborhood
non-count noun—thunder

SPEAKING APPLICATION

Have partners identify the collective nouns and explain how they recognized them.

WRITING APPLICATION

Have students share their sentences with the class, pointing out the collective nouns, count nouns, and non-count nouns.

Recognizing Compound Nouns

Discuss with students the fact that compound words consist of two separate words.

RULE 13.1.5 Read aloud the rule and then have students repeat the lines with you.

Use an index card or sheet of paper to cover up one half of several compound words. Show students how a compound word consists of two separate words. **Say:** Some words are created by combining two or more words. The new word, called a compound word, uses the definitions of two different words to create a new meaning. **Ask:** Can someone explain how the words *tree* and *house* help you understand the compound word *tree house*? **(Accept all correct answers.)**

Separate these compound words into their word parts and list them on the board: *lifetime, elsewhere, upside, grandmother, eyeballs.* Work with students to combine the single words to create compound words.

Have student pairs brainstorm for and write three or more compound words. Ask students to share their words with the class.

Using Common and Proper Nouns

Point out to students that proper nouns name a particular person, place, or thing. For example, the *Pacific Ocean* and *George Washington* are proper nouns. On the other hand, a common noun can bring to mind many different people, places, or things. The word *firefighter* can be used to describe thousands of different people.

RULE 13.1.6 Read aloud the rule and then have students repeat the lines with you.

Say aloud these nouns for students: *mailman, Dorothy, New York, beans, integrity, Mt. Rushmore.* Have students identify the nouns as proper or common. Ask students to explain whether or not each noun should be capitalized.

Teacher Tip

For some students, remembering the many categories of nouns will be a daunting task. Create a worksheet that lists each noun category. Define the noun category and list several examples. Allow students to refer to the sheet when necessary.

Recognizing Compound Nouns

Some nouns are made up of two or more words. *Classroom* is a **compound noun** made up of *class* and *room.*

A compound noun is one noun made by joining two or more words.

Compound nouns are written in three different ways: as single words, as hyphenated words, and as two or more separate words.

COMPOUND NOUNS		
SINGLE WORDS	HYPHENATED WORDS	SEPARATE WORDS
crossbar	by-product	dinner jacket
firefighter	right-hander	pole vault
thunderstorm	middle-distance	pen pal
classroom	mother-in-law	chief justice

See Practice 13.1E

Using Common and Proper Nouns

All nouns can be divided into two large groups: **common nouns** and **proper nouns.**

A common noun names any one of a class of people, places, things, or ideas. A proper noun names a specific person, place, thing, or idea.

Common nouns are not capitalized. Proper nouns are always capitalized.

COMMON NOUNS	PROPER NOUNS
inventor	Alexander Graham Bell
village	Tarrytown
story	"The Tell-Tale Heart"
organization	American Red Cross
idea	Germ Theory of Disease

See Practice 13.1F

Differentiated Instruction

Strategy for Spanish Speakers

Students whose home language is Spanish may transfer Spanish capitalization rules to English nouns, not realizing that the rules are different. On the board, write a list of proper nouns in English. Include days of the week, months of the year, names of languages and personal titles. Call for volunteers to translate the words into Spanish and explain whether the words should be capitalized. (None of the above categories of proper nouns is capitalized in Spanish except for abbreviations of personal titles, such as *Sra.*, or Mrs.) Write the Spanish words next to their English equivalents, and summarize the differences in capitalization rules.

PRACTICE 13.1E **Identifying Compound Nouns**

Read the sentences. Then, write the compound nouns, and draw a line between the words that make up each compound noun.

EXAMPLE I was a lifeguard at the beach last summer.

ANSWER *life\ guard*

1. My dog, Ollie, is a great watchdog.
2. Steven's favorite sports are baseball and basketball.
3. Whenever we have a big snowstorm, we light a fire in the fireplace.
4. The fans cheered from the sidelines.
5. We think our middle school is the best in the state!
6. Serena and Robert joined the Air Force.
7. Hector bought the new commemorative stamps at the post office.
8. Charles is very happy with his new wristwatch.
9. Brenda was the winner and Marty was the runner-up in the essay contest.
10. Simon is taking courses to be a motorboat mechanic.

PRACTICE 13.1F **Using Common and Proper Nouns**

Read the sentences. Then, rewrite them, replacing the underlined words with proper nouns.

EXAMPLE Our math teacher gives a lot of homework.

ANSWER *Mrs. Chen gives a lot of homework.*

11. We watched a movie last weekend.
12. My friend and I like to listen to our favorite band.
13. Our class will be taking a field trip to the state capital.
14. The school nurse will give flu shots next week.
15. My uncle has season tickets to our local basketball team's games.
16. On our summer vacation, we plan to visit two states.
17. We are reading a novel in English class.
18. That doctor works in the emergency room at the hospital.
19. My dad just bought a new car.
20. In two years, we will go to the high school.

SPEAKING APPLICATION

With a partner, take turns stating compound nouns that name occupations. Your partner should notice how the parts create meaning. For example, a *firefighter* is someone who fights fires.

WRITING APPLICATION

Write three sentences describing your town or city. Include at least one proper noun in each sentence.

Working with ELLs

ELL Sheltered Instruction: Cognitive

As students study nouns, guide them to learn the relationships between sounds and letters of the English language. Using the words in the Practice activities, reinforce their ability to decode words by recognizing sound-letter relationships in affixes.

Beginning Write the word *vacation* on the board and use visuals to aid comprehension. Help students decode the first two syllables using sound-letter relationships: /vā/ /kā/. Then, explain they will read the suffix *-tion* at the end of many nouns, and that it is pronounced /shən/. Have them write *vacation* as you sound it out. Repeatedly choral read the word.

Intermediate Say the words *collector, programmer,* and *vacation* and write them on the board. Help students decode each word using sound-letter relationships. Focus on the word parts in each word. Tell them that recognizing familiar suffixes like *-or, -er,* and *-tion* can help them read many nouns.

Advanced Write the Intermediate activity words on the board. Guide students in decoding the words using affixes and sound-letter relationships. Then, have them decode *designer, inspector, condition, education,* and *study*.

Advanced High Have students complete the Advanced activity. Have partners create flash cards to test their reading and spelling of the words.

PRACTICE 13.1E

1. watch | dog
2. base | ball, basket | ball
3. snow | storm, fire | place
4. side | lines
5. middle | school
6. Air | Force
7. post | office
8. wrist | watch
9. runner- | up
10. motor | boat

PRACTICE 13.1F

Answers will vary. Sample answers:

11. We watched *Shrek* last weekend.
12. Marissa and I like to listen to the Jonas Brothers.
13. Our class will be taking a field trip to Austin.
14. Ms. Lu will give flu shots next week.
15. Uncle Willy has season tickets to the Rockets' games.
16. On our summer vacation, we plan to visit Arizona and New Mexico.
17. We are reading *The Giver* in English class.
18. Dr. Chang works in the emergency room at Memorial Hospital.
19. My dad just bought a new Prius.
20. In two years, we will go to Roosevelt High School.

SPEAKING APPLICATION

Have students make up a sentence for each compound noun.

WRITING APPLICATION

Have students explain how they recognized the proper noun.

Lesson Objectives

1. Identify and distinguish between various types of pronouns.
2. Use a variety of complete sentences (simple, compound, complex) that include correctly identified antecedents.
3. Identify, use, and understand the function of relative pronouns such as *whose, that,* and *which*.

Discuss how pronouns eliminate redundancy and contribute to the "flow" of a sentence.

RULE 13.2.1 Read aloud the rule and then have students repeat the lines with you.

Use a Think Aloud as part of a gradual release progression.

Say: Pronouns are far more useful than you might think. **I know** they tend to be short words such as *her* and *it*, but they pack a lot of power. Let's try to have a conversation without using any pronouns.

Work with students to help them understand the function of pronouns. Begin a conversation with a student: *[Student], what is [student]'s favorite sport? Be sure to tell [teacher] why [student] likes [student]'s favorite sport.*

Have small groups of students repeat the same activity. Have them discuss how pronouns helped the flow of the second conversation.

www.phwritingcoach.com

Diagnostic and Instruction

Diagnostic test assesses students' instructional needs. Lessons and practice are assigned based on results.

Additional Practice

- Grammar Tutorials—Animated videos reinforce key grammar skills.
- Grammar Practice—Targeted practice addresses individual needs.
- ExamView—Teachers customize their grammar practice and tests.
- Grammar Games—Interactive video games make grammar fun.

13.2 Pronouns

Pronouns are words that take the place of nouns. They are used rather than repeating a noun again and again. Pronouns make sentences clearer and more interesting.

A pronoun is a word that takes the place of a noun or a group of words acting as a noun.

Imagine, for example, that you are writing about Aunt Bonnie. If you were using only nouns, you might write the following sentence:

WITH NOUNS Aunt Bonnie was late because **Aunt Bonnie** had waited for **Aunt Bonnie's** books to arrive.

WITH PRONOUNS Aunt Bonnie was late because **she** had waited for **her** books to arrive.

Sometimes a pronoun takes the place of a noun in the same sentence.

EXAMPLES My mother ate **her** (pronoun) salad.

Many people say eating well has helped **them** (pronoun).

A pronoun can also take the place of a noun used in an earlier sentence.

EXAMPLES My mother opened her package first. **She** (pronoun) was curious about it.

College students must take a language class. **They** (pronoun) can choose from Spanish or Italian.

A pronoun may take the place of an entire group of words.

EXAMPLE Trying to paint can be very hard work. **It** (pronoun) takes practicing on a daily basis.

www.phwritingcoach.com

Grammar Tutorials
Brush up on your Grammar skills with these animated videos.

Grammar Practice
Practice your grammar skills with Writing Coach Online.

Grammar Games
Test your knowledge of grammar in this fast-paced interactive video game.

Differentiated Instruction

RTI Strategy for Below-Level Students It may be helpful to have struggling students create a reference sheet that lists several common pronouns. This way, they can begin to memorize the most frequent ones while working with them. Have students fold a sheet of paper in half. On one side they should list common pronouns. On the second side they should write sentences using the pronouns. Provide highlighters and have students highlight the pronouns throughout the reference sheet.

PRE-AP Enrichment for Above-Level Students Have students write a short story about a topic of their choice. In the story, students should include these types of sentences:

1. Two sentences in which a pronoun takes the place of a noun in the same sentence
2. Two sentences in which a pronoun takes the place of a noun used in an earlier sentence
3. Two sentences in which a pronoun takes the place of an entire group of words

Antecedents of Pronouns

The word or group of words that a pronoun replaces or refers to is called an **antecedent.**

RULE 13.2.2 An **antecedent** is the noun (or group of words acting as a noun) to which a pronoun refers.

EXAMPLES The **police officers** (antecedent) described how **they** (pronoun) did **their** (pronoun) jobs.

Finally, the **police officer** (antecedent) arrived; **he** (pronoun) took control of the problem.

See Practice 13.2A
See Practice 13.2B

How Amy was saved (antecedent) is incredible. **It** (pronoun) is an event that she'll speak about often.

Although **he** (pronoun) was a pastry chef, **Mike** (antecedent) also enjoyed cooking meals.

Some kinds of pronouns do not have any antecedent.

EXAMPLES **Everyone** (indefinite pronoun) in the room knew the truth.

Who (interrogative pronoun) broke the antique lamp?

The pronouns *everyone* and *who* do not have a specific antecedent because their meaning is clear without one.

Antecedents of Pronouns

Remind students that pronouns will almost always have words to which they refer. The words they reference are called antecedents and are often easy to identify by asking *to whom or what does the pronoun refer?*

RULE 13.2.2 Read aloud the rule and then have students repeat the lines with you.

Write on the board several sentences with pronouns and antecedents. Demonstrate for students the process for identifying the antecedents in each. First, place a box around any pronouns. Then, draw an arrow connecting the pronouns to their antecedents. As you do this, ask questions such as *Who is him?* or *What is it?*

Now, have students create and say aloud several complete sentences that include pronouns and antecedents. Have students identify each pronoun and its antecedent. Then, write the following list of pronouns on the board: *it, his, they, she*. Have students write a short paragraph using these pronouns and clear antecedents. Then, have partners review each other's paragraphs, drawing an arrow from each pronoun to its antecedent.

Extension

To help students synthesize and apply what they have learned about pronouns, have them identify pronouns and their antecedents in a favorite story or book. Direct students to select a passage of at least 100 words, making sure that the passage contains pronouns. Students should copy or scan and print the passage, then underline every pronoun and draw an arrow to its antecedent, if any. When students are finished, they should exchange passages and check each other's work.

Teacher Tip

Anticipate student concern over what constitutes an indefinite pronoun by listing some. Point out indefinite pronouns such as *another, each,* and *either*. Then, have students come up with others. Tell students that words such as *plenty* (*I've had plenty*) and *enough* (*The children have seen enough*) are indefinite pronouns, too.

PRACTICE 13.2A

1. his, Todd
2. their, candidates
3. her, Erica
4. his, Jon; they, dogs
5. their, students; them, essays
6. we, Danielle and I
7. her, Marley; she, Marley; it, wallet
8. her, Rachel; she, Rachel; him, grandfather
9. they, children; it, puppy
10. its, region

PRACTICE 13.2B

11. Even before the ambulance came into sight, we heard its siren.
12. Elizabeth carefully followed the instructions she received.
13. After much discussion, the leaders made their decision.
14. Morgan was late for her first class.
15. Rachel reminded Tyler to bring his video games.
16. The band members took their places on the field.
17. When the president walked in, everyone welcomed him.
18. The dog wagged its tail.
19. Connor and Mark are planning their strategy for the next game.
20. When Laura got home, she turned on the television.

PRACTICE 13.2A Recognizing Pronouns and Antecedents

Read the sentences. Then, write each pronoun and its antecedent.

EXAMPLE Thomas Edison is known for his many inventions.

ANSWER *his, Thomas Edison*

1. Todd left his gym bag on the bus.
2. The candidates rehearsed their speeches.
3. While visiting her cousin at the shore, Erica learned to body surf.
4. Jon has trained his dogs to sit, but they don't always obey.
5. The students took out their essays and passed them forward.
6. Danielle and I wanted to help with the celebration, so we baked cookies.
7. Marley misplaced her wallet, but she found it later.
8. When Rachel saw her grandfather, she gave him a hug.
9. As soon as they saw the puppy, the children wanted it.
10. Every region of the country has its special features.

PRACTICE 13.2B Supplying Pronouns for Antecedents

Read the sentences. Then, write each sentence, filling in the blank with the appropriate pronoun. Correctly identify and underline the antecedent of the pronoun you supply.

EXAMPLE Jake admitted that ____ was wrong.

ANSWER *Jake admitted that he was wrong.*

11. Even before the ambulance came into sight, we heard ____ siren.
12. Elizabeth carefully followed the instructions ____ received.
13. After much discussion, the leaders made ____ decision.
14. Morgan was late for ____ first class.
15. Rachel reminded Tyler to bring ____ video games.
16. The band members took ____ places on the field.
17. When the president walked in, everyone welcomed ____.
18. The dog wagged ____ tail.
19. Connor and Mark are planning ____ strategy for the next game.
20. When Laura got home, ____ turned on the television.

SPEAKING APPLICATION

With a partner, take turns describing the situation of a character in a TV program. Name the character, and use at least two pronouns that refer to the character. Your partner should identify the pronouns and the antecedents.

WRITING APPLICATION

Write three sentences that each contain at least one pronoun and an antecedent. Circle each pronoun and draw an arrow to the antecedent. Use simple, compound, and complex complete sentences.

SPEAKING APPLICATION

Have students explain how they identified the pronouns and antecedents in a variety of complete sentences (*simple, compound, complex*).

WRITING APPLICATION

Have students rewrite one of their sentences to use an indefinite pronoun, showing that they can use a variety of complete sentences (simple, compound, complex) that include correctly identified antecedents.

Recognizing Personal Pronouns

The pronouns used most often are **personal pronouns.**

Personal pronouns refer to (1) the person speaking or writing, (2) the person listening or reading, or (3) the topic (person, place, thing, or idea) being discussed or written about.

The first-person pronouns *I, me, my, mine, we, us, our,* and *ours* refer to the person or persons speaking or writing.

EXAMPLES **I** like the new magazine layout.

Please give **us** a taste.

The second-person pronouns *you, your,* and *yours* refer to the person or persons spoken or written to.

EXAMPLES **You** will see it later.

Your dog is barking at me.

The third-person pronouns *he, him, his, she, her, hers, it, its, they, them, their,* and *theirs* refer to the person, place, thing, or idea being spoken or written about.

EXAMPLES **He** wants to watch the news at 6:00 P.M.

They wrote to the author of the book.

Some personal pronouns show possession. Although they can function as adjectives, they are still identified as personal pronouns because they take the place of possessive nouns.

EXAMPLES **Heather's** (possessive noun) latest novel will be out this February.

Her (possessive pronoun) picture will be on the back cover.

The chart on the next page presents the personal pronouns.

Recognizing Personal Pronouns

Explain that it is important to understand how personal pronouns function so that we can use them correctly when we construct sentences. Read aloud the first examples and explain to whom or what the pronouns refer.

RULE 13.2.3 Read aloud the rule and then have students repeat the lines with you.

Use a Think Aloud as part of a gradual release progression.

Think Aloud **Say:** You and **I use** personal pronouns everyday. They help you refer to people, things, and ideas when you are speaking and writing. My use of the personal pronoun *you* in the previous sentences revealed to whom I am speaking. *You* (point to class) are my listeners. *I* (point to yourself) am the speaker. *We* (gesture to yourself and class) are learning about personal pronouns. Sometimes, personal pronouns show possession.

Work with students to help them understand how possessive nouns show possession. Then, illustrate how possessive pronouns that represent those nouns can also show possession. Ask students a question such as this: *Whose book is that?* **(Possible answer:** This is my book.) **Say:** Which word in your response shows that the object belongs to you? (*my*)

Have student pairs brainstorm for a list of personal pronouns. Have them write their ideas in two columns—*Personal Pronouns* and *Possessive Pronouns.* Work with students to include correct choices and to exclude incorrect choices. Have students put their lists aside. (After students examine the *Personal Pronouns* chart on page 304, have them make adjustments as necessary.)

Differentiated Instruction

RTI Strategy for Below-Level Students
Have students put personal pronouns to work. For those struggling to recognize personal pronouns, provide an index card with five personal pronouns written across the top. Tell students to pretend they're writing a postcard to a relative in a far away place. Explain that their postcard must include each of the listed personal pronouns. Once students are finished, discuss the functions of the personal pronouns in each sentence.

Enrichment for Gifted/Talented Students
Have students go on a creative scavenger hunt for personal and possessive pronouns. Students can listen to a song and write the pronouns they hear or read an excerpt of a play and list as many pronouns as they can find. Once students have collected the personal and possessive pronouns, have them create a crossword puzzle using them. They should design the puzzles and create clues for each pronoun using key words that reveal its definition. Students should share the puzzles with the class.

Reflexive and Intensive Pronouns

Explain that reflexive and intensive pronouns have similar endings—*self* or *selves*—but they do not perform the same function.

RULE 13.2.4 Read aloud the rule and then have students repeat the lines with you.

Draw students' attention to the fact that a reflexive pronoun directs the action of a verb back on the subject of a verb. Point out the importance of being able to identify the subject and verb in a sentence when trying to determine if a pronoun is reflexive. Write this sentence on the board: *Mike laughed himself right out of his chair.* Ask students to name the subject and the verb. (*Mike* and *laughed*) Underline the subject once and the verb twice. Point to the word *himself* and ask if the word *himself* directs the action *laughing* to the subject *Mike*. (Yes.) Tell students that the word *himself* is a reflexive pronoun in this sentence.

Provide several more examples for practice.

RULE 13.2.5 Read aloud the rule and then have students repeat the lines with you.

Tell students that intensive pronouns end similarly to reflexive pronouns but do not direct the verb's action back to the subject. These pronouns add emphasis, but they are not essential to the meaning of the sentence. Write these sentences on the board: *The president himself is an avid basketball fan. The president is an avid basketball fan.* Explain that the intensive pronoun *himself* does not change the meaning of the sentence. Ask students why they think writers and speakers use intensive pronouns. (**Possible answers:** to make a point; for stylistic purposes.)

Teacher Tip

Give students a rectangular slip of paper. Tell them to place the slip over words ending with *-self* or *-selves* when they are unsure if the word is reflexive or intensive. If, when they place the slip over the word, the sentence's meaning does not change, they know they have discovered an intensive pronoun.

PERSONAL PRONOUNS		
	SINGULAR	PLURAL
First person	I, me, my, mine	we, us, our, ours
Second person	you, your, yours	you, your, yours
Third person	he, him, his, she, her, hers, it, its	they, them, their, theirs

See Practice 13.2C

Reflexive and Intensive Pronouns

The ending *-self* or *-selves* can be added to some pronouns to form **reflexive** or **intensive pronouns.** These two types of pronouns look the same, but they function differently within a sentence.

REFLEXIVE AND INTENSIVE PRONOUNS		
	SINGULAR	PLURAL
First person	myself	ourselves
Second person	yourself	yourselves
Third person	himself, herself, itself	themselves

A reflexive pronoun directs the action of the verb toward its subject. Reflexive pronouns point back to a noun or pronoun earlier in the sentence.

A reflexive pronoun is essential to the meaning of a sentence.

REFLEXIVE **Jane** (noun) poured **herself** (reflexive pronoun) a glass of water.

They (pronoun) made **themselves** (reflexive pronoun) some turkey sandwiches.

See Practice 13.2D

An intensive pronoun simply adds emphasis to a noun or pronoun in the same sentence.

An intensive pronoun is not essential to the meaning of the sentence.

INTENSIVE The mayor **herself** attended the carnival.

PRACTICE 13.2C Recognizing Personal Pronouns

Read the sentences. Then, write the personal pronouns in each sentence.

EXAMPLE I would like to tell you about my experience.

ANSWER *I, you, my*

1. He did not hear what I said.
2. Alicia said that she is trying out for the swim team.
3. After you complete this form, give it to the instructor.
4. She practices the piano every day.
5. We thought they wanted to go with us.
6. After Mike helped us, we thanked him.
7. Sarah's mother drove them to the skating rink.
8. Did you remember to tell her what time to come?
9. He doesn't speak to me anymore.
10. They could not find my street, but someone gave them directions from their house to mine.

PRACTICE 13.2D Supplying Reflexive and Intensive Pronouns

Read the sentences. Write the reflexive or intensive pronoun that completes each sentence.

EXAMPLE The principal made the announcement ____.

ANSWER *herself*

11. Will you and Jim do all the work ____?
12. I bought ____ a new jacket.
13. She wondered whether she could lift the huge bundle ____.
14. You should be able to complete this project ____.
15. We did not care for the location, but the house ____ was lovely.
16. The students ____ made all the posters.
17. Jason promised ____ he would exercise more often.
18. We planned the entire event ____.
19. Liz sometimes gives ____ pep talks.
20. We ____ were not interested in seeing that exhibit.

SPEAKING APPLICATION

Tell a partner about something you and a friend did recently. Your partner will listen for and name four personal pronouns you use.

WRITING APPLICATION

Write three sentences, using sentences 12, 14, and 16 as models. Replace the nouns and pronouns in those sentences with your own.

PRACTICE 13.2C

1. he, I
2. she
3. you, it
4. she
5. we, they, us
6. us, we, him
7. them
8. you, her
9. he, me
10. they, my, them, their, mine

PRACTICE 13.2D

11. yourselves
12. myself
13. herself
14. yourself
15. itself
16. themselves
17. himself
18. ourselves
19. herself
20. ourselves

SPEAKING APPLICATION

Have students explain how the effectiveness of their sentences would change if all the pronouns were replaced by nouns.

WRITING APPLICATION

Have students share one of their sentences with the class, pointing out the original and rewritten nouns and pronouns.

Working with ELLs — ELL Sheltered Instruction: Cognitive

As students learn about personal pronouns, help them enhance and confirm their understanding as they read. Help students use visual and contextual support to develop the background knowledge needed to comprehend increasingly challenging language in Practice 13.2C.

Beginning To develop background, write these words on the board and provide pictures illustrating each: *trying out, swim team, form, instructor, practices, piano* (Practice 13.2C, items 2, 3, and 4). Read the words chorally, explaining their meaning. Then, ask simple questions about the pictures, helping students use the words and replace them with pronouns. For example, *Is the instructor tall? Yes, the instructor is tall./ Yes, she is tall.*

Intermediate Review the words and pictures from the Beginning activity. Have students and more fluent partners write sentences about each picture using the words and personal pronouns such as *our(s), your(s),* and *we*. Have partners explain the connection between the sentences and the pictures.

Advanced Have partners complete the Intermediate activity, then review another pair's work, identifying the personal pronouns.

Advanced High Have students complete the Intermediate activity. Have them label each pronoun by case and number, using the pronoun charts on page 304 as additional visual and contextual support.

Demonstrative Pronouns

Discuss with students the fact that demonstrative pronouns help speakers and writers identify or point out specific persons, places, or things. Writers use them to distinguish one noun from another.

RULE 13.2.6 Read aloud the rule and then have students repeat the lines with you.

Refer to items in the classroom to illustrate how demonstrative pronouns function. For example, point to a chair on the other side of the room and call it *that*. Then, point to a chair close to you and call it *this*. Do this several times and include examples of plural demonstrative pronouns as well. Allow students to exhibit their understanding by referring to classroom items of their choosing.

Using Relative Pronouns

RULE 13.2.7 Read aloud the rule and then have students repeat the lines with you.

Draw attention to how short the relative pronoun list is. Encourage students to memorize it so they can focus on how the words function in a sentence.

On the board, write this sentence: *She is the cashier who issued my refund.* **Say:** Who can identify the independent clause in this sentence? If students struggle to identify it, restate the question: *Which part of this sentence can stand alone?* (She is the cashier.) Draw a bridge over the word *who* as if connecting the independent clause to the subordinate clause. Explain that the relative pronoun connects the two.

Teacher Tip

Be prepared to review and define independent clauses and subordinate clauses (see T415–T416). It may be helpful to prepare several examples of each to present to students who may need a refresher.

Demonstrative Pronouns

Demonstrative pronouns point to people, places, and things, much as you point to them with your finger.

A demonstrative pronoun points to a specific person, place, or thing.

There are two singular and two plural demonstrative pronouns.

DEMONSTRATIVE PRONOUNS			
SINGULAR		PLURAL	
this	that	these	those

This and *these* point to what is near the speaker or writer. *That* and *those* point to what is more distant.

NEAR **This** is where I sleep.

These are my favorite movies of the year.

FAR Is **that** the library across the street?

Those are my books.

See Practice 13.2E

Using Relative Pronouns

Relative pronouns are connecting words.

A relative pronoun begins a subordinate clause and connects it to another idea in the same sentence.

There are five relative pronouns.

RELATIVE PRONOUNS				
that	which	who	whom	whose

The chart on the next page gives examples of relative pronouns connecting subordinate clauses to independent clauses. (See Chapter 19 to find out more about relative pronouns and clauses.)

Differentiated Instruction

RTI Strategy for Below-Level Students Because relative pronouns require a firm understanding of independent and subordinate clauses, it may be helpful to have students play a matching game that allows them to use each sentence part. Write a few sentences on sentence strips. Include an independent and a subordinate clause and a relative pronoun in each. Cut the sentence strips so that each sentence part remains intact. Have students arrange the sentences correctly. Point out each sentence part as they do.

PRE-AP Enrichment for Above-Level Students Give students a list of subordinate clauses that begin with relative pronouns. Have students write independent clauses for each. Then, have students mix and match the clauses and relative pronouns to make several new complete sentences. Have students find similar sentence patterns in a magazine.

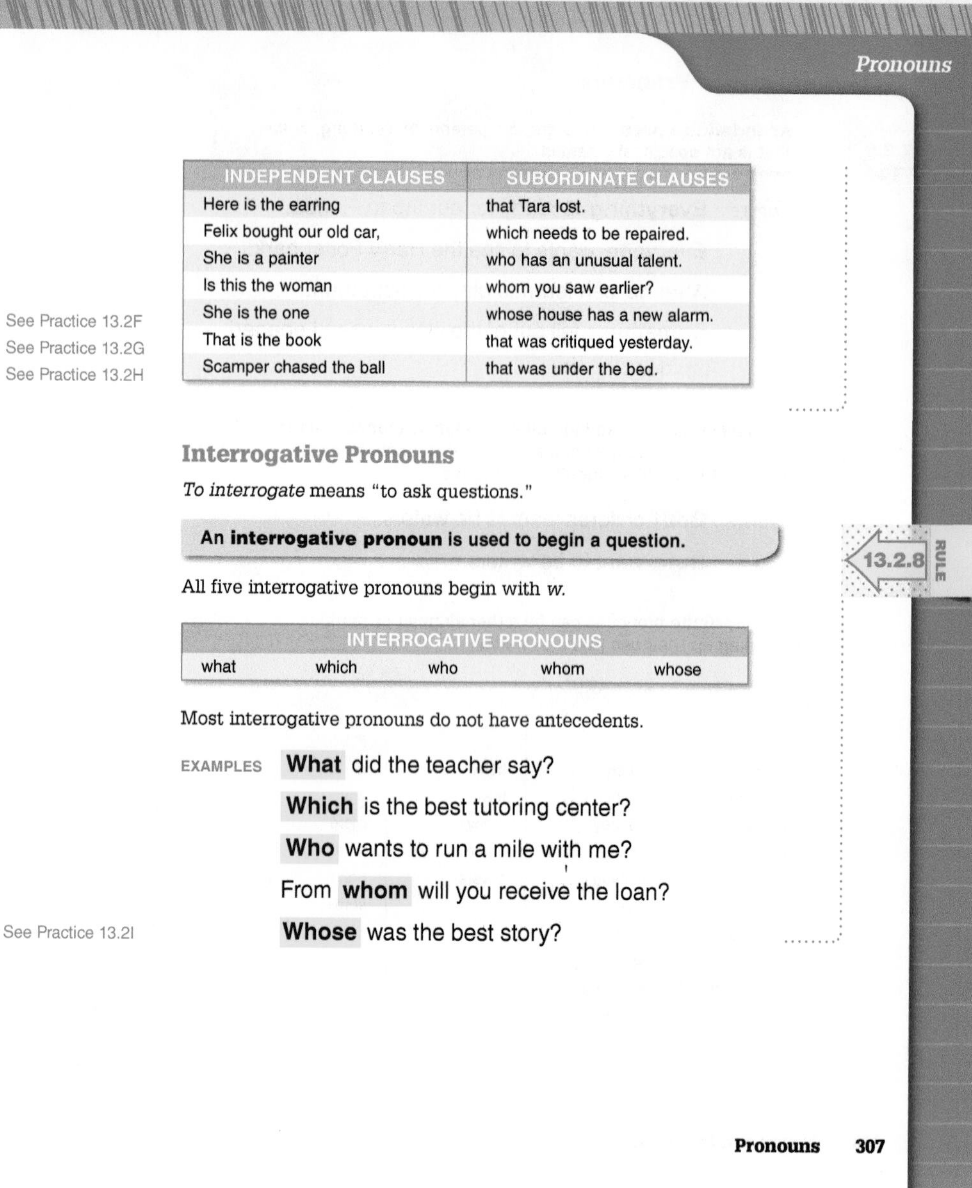

INDEPENDENT CLAUSES	SUBORDINATE CLAUSES
Here is the earring	that Tara lost.
Felix bought our old car,	which needs to be repaired.
She is a painter	who has an unusual talent.
Is this the woman	whom you saw earlier?
She is the one	whose house has a new alarm.
That is the book	that was critiqued yesterday.
Scamper chased the ball	that was under the bed.

See Practice 13.2F
See Practice 13.2G
See Practice 13.2H

Interrogative Pronouns

To interrogate means "to ask questions."

An interrogative pronoun is used to begin a question.

RULE 13.2.8

All five interrogative pronouns begin with *w*.

INTERROGATIVE PRONOUNS				
what	which	who	whom	whose

Most interrogative pronouns do not have antecedents.

EXAMPLES **What** did the teacher say?

Which is the best tutoring center?

Who wants to run a mile with me?

From **whom** will you receive the loan?

Whose was the best story?

See Practice 13.2I

To help students identify and understand relative pronouns, write these sentences on the board. Have students point out each relative pronoun and explain its use in the sentence.

Rose was the one who won the contest. (who)

That book is the one that I lost. (that)

Brion is the boy whose drawing was selected. (whose)

Interrogative Pronouns

Point out that interrogative pronouns can be easily memorized because they each begin with the letter *w* and indicate that a question will be posed.

RULE 13.2.8 Read aloud the rule and then have students repeat the line with you.

Ask for a student volunteer. In front of the class, ask the student several questions using interrogative pronouns; for example, *What did you eat for lunch? Whom do you sit next to?* As you do, display each pronoun on a large sheet of paper.

Explain that interrogative pronouns are used to begin sentences and that they often do not have antecedents.

Have student pairs brainstorm for one question for each interrogative pronoun. Then, ask students to share their questions with the class.

Quick-Write Extension

To help students synthesize and apply what they have learned about interrogative pronouns, have them write poems about themselves or another subject that interests them. Explain that the first line must be a question that begins with an interrogative pronoun; for example, *What do I want?* The second line must answer the question; for example, *I want peace in the world.* Direct students to write five questions and answers, alternating questions and answers throughout the poem. Ask volunteers to read their poems aloud, or post the poems on a class bulletin board or Web page.

Indefinite Pronouns

Explain to students that indefinite pronouns do not refer to any particular person, place, thing, or idea. For example, in the sentence *Everything is ready for our trip to Florida,* the word *Everything* does not refer to any particular thing. It is an indefinite pronoun.

RULE 13.2.9 Read aloud the rule and then have students repeat the lines with you.

Use a Think Aloud as part of a gradual release progression.

Say: One of the many interesting things about the English language is that a single word can serve as several different parts of speech. **I know** that certain words, for example, can function as indefinite pronouns in some sentences and as adjectives in other sentences. Refer to these sentences from page 308: *Both children want to be writers. Both want to be writers.* Explain how the word plays two different roles in the sentences.

Using the *Indefinite Pronouns* chart on page 308, **work with students** to construct three to five sets of sentences in which a single word first serves as an adjective and then as an indefinite pronoun. (**Possible answers:** *Several* people have tried to climb the mountain and failed. *Several* tried to climb the mountain and failed.)

Have pairs of students write their own sentences using a word from the chart on page 308 as an adjective and as an indefinite pronoun.

Indefinite Pronouns

An indefinite pronoun refers to a person, place, thing, or idea that is not specifically named.

EXAMPLES **Everything** is ready for our trip to Florida.

Everyone wants to see the Harry Potter park.

Anyone can learn to play an instrument.

Something fell out of the closet when I opened the door.

Among its other uses, an indefinite pronoun can function as an adjective or as the subject of a sentence. If it functions as an adjective, it is called an indefinite adjective.

ADJECTIVE **Both** children want to be writers.

SUBJECT **Both** want to be writers.

A few indefinite pronouns can be either singular or plural, depending on their use in the sentence.

INDEFINITE PRONOUNS			
SINGULAR		PLURAL	SINGULAR OR PLURAL
another	much	both	all
anybody	neither	few	any
anyone	nobody	many	more
anything	no one	others	most
each	nothing	several	none
either	one		some
everybody	other		
everyone	somebody		
everything	someone		
little	something		

See Practice 13.2J

Working with ELLs — ELL Sheltered Instruction: Cognitive

Help students speak using a variety of grammatical structures with increasing accuracy and ease. Use the chart and examples on page 308 to allow students to practice using indefinite pronouns.

Beginning Read Rule 13.2.9 to students. Then, read the first example sentence. Explain its meaning, using visuals and mime. Then, repeat the sentence aloud, noting the indefinite pronoun in the sentence. Have students respond orally by repeating the sentence after you. Continue with other examples on the page.

Intermediate Write the example sentences on the board. Have partners take turns saying the example sentences to each other. Then, have students identify the indefinite pronoun in each sentence. Allow students to refer to the chart on page 308, as needed.

Advanced Have students write their own sentences with indefinite pronouns using the sentences on page 308 as an example. Then, have partners say their sentences aloud to each other. Partners should identify the indefinite pronoun in each sentence.

Advanced High Have students complete the Advanced activity. Then, challenge students to tell their partners if the indefinite pronoun in each sentence functions as an adjective or as the subject of the sentence.

PRACTICE 13.2E **Identifying Demonstrative Pronouns**

Read the sentences. Then, write the demonstrative pronoun and the noun to which it refers.

EXAMPLE This is the latest version of the computer.

ANSWER *this, computer*

1. These are the most comfortable shoes I have ever worn.
2. Of all the pictures, I like those best.
3. This is a new book, and that is an old one.
4. Is that your brother over there?
5. Those are confident students.
6. Is this your final answer?
7. That seems to be the best way to get to the city.
8. Those were the good old days!
9. This is the camera I would like to have.
10. That may be a difficult choice.

PRACTICE 13.2F **Supplying Relative Pronouns**

Read the sentences. Then, write the correct relative pronoun (e.g., *whose, that, which*) for each sentence.

EXAMPLE I know the person ____ lives here.

ANSWER *who*

11. She planted flowers ____ bloom every spring.
12. It's a popular place ____ kids love.
13. The person ____ answered my questions was very polite.
14. Sondra's outburst, ____ surprised everyone, stopped all conversation.
15. I don't know ____ you're referring to.
16. It was a decision ____ he did not regret.
17. Lee, ____ is very friendly, was the first to greet the new student.
18. We visited the Metropolitan Museum of Art, ____ is on Fifth Avenue in New York.
19. These are the guidelines ____ you must follow.
20. Colin, ____ brother is a star athlete, prefers a quiet life.

SPEAKING APPLICATION

With a partner, take turns identifying and describing items in the classroom. Use relative pronouns (e.g., *whose, that, which*) in your sentences.

WRITING APPLICATION

Write three sentences, and include one of the following relative pronouns in each: *whose, that, which*. Read your sentences aloud to a partner. Have your partner identify each relative pronoun. Then change roles.

PRACTICE 13.2E

1. These, shoes
2. those, pictures
3. This, book; that, one
4. that, brother
5. Those, students
6. this, answer
7. That, way
8. Those, days
9. This, camera
10. That, choice

PRACTICE 13.2F

11. that
12. that
13. who
14. which
15. whom
16. that
17. who
18. which
19. that
20. whose

SPEAKING APPLICATION

Students should show that they can identify and use relative pronouns in speaking by sharing their sentences with partners or the class and pointing out the relative pronouns.

WRITING APPLICATION

Students should show that they can identify and use relative pronouns in writing by determining the subordinate clauses introduced by relative pronouns in each sentence.

PRACTICE 13.2G

Answers will vary. Sample answers:

1. . . . , which were fresh.
2. . . . that had a cavity.
3. . . . that was stolen.
4. . . . which later won a prize.
5. . . . that are for hiking.
6. . . . who sailed the globe?
7. . . . that are due Friday.
8. . . . whom we need to help.
9. . . . that the class uses.
10. . . . that spring begins.

PRACTICE 13.2H

Answers will vary. Sample answers:

11. It was my gym teacher
12. The table held tomatoes,
13. I own the movie
14. Bob sold the car
15. They need to know
16. The judges picked Jim,
17. We shop in New York City,
18. He is the clever person
19. She flunked the student
20. The dog had a big bone

PRACTICE 13.2G Using Relative Pronouns

For each independent clause, supply a subordinate clause using a relative pronoun. Write the new sentence. Then, read your sentences aloud and have your partner identify the relative pronoun.

EXAMPLE He is the chemist

ANSWER *He is the chemist who won the Nobel Prize.*

1. Liz gathered the ingredients
2. The dentist looked at the tooth
3. There is the bike
4. Raphael took the picture
5. Those are the pants
6. Is he the captain
7. Here are the essay topics
8. Bob is the one
9. Wynn wrote the book
10. Tomorrow is the day

PRACTICE 13.2H Writing With Relative Pronouns

For each subordinate clause, supply an independent clause to create a complete sentence. Write the new sentence. With a partner, take turns reading your best sentences and discussing why you wrote what you did.

EXAMPLE which she will bring to the party

ANSWER *Jenna made a casserole, which she will bring to the party.*

11. who taught me how to swim
12. which needed to be washed
13. that Scott borrowed
14. that Mr. Pizzo bought
15. whom you want on your team
16. whose painting took first prize
17. which has all the latest fashions
18. who trained his dog to dance
19. whom I helped in math class
20. that he buried in the yard

SPEAKING APPLICATION

With a partner, take turns talking about your favorite sports, hobbies, or other interests. Use relative pronouns in your questions and answers and identify them.

WRITING APPLICATION

Write three sentences about an interesting person you know or admire. Use a relative pronoun in each sentence.

SPEAKING APPLICATION

Students should show that they can identify and use relative pronouns in reading and speaking by explaining how they determined the function of each pronoun.

WRITING APPLICATION

Students should show that they can identify and use relative pronouns in reading and writing by sharing their paragraphs and pointing out the relative pronouns.

Working with ELLs

ELL Sheltered Instruction: Social/Affective

Scaffold the Speaking Application, and provide opportunities for students to share information in cooperative learning interactions and to demonstrate listening comprehension of increasingly complex spoken English by collaborating with peers and taking notes. Coach students to incorporate relative pronouns in their discussions. Have students monitor their comprehension and seek necessary clarifications.

Beginning Pair students with fluent speakers. Describe an event, incorporating gestures and simple phrases. Have partners ask and answer simple questions to demonstrate listening comprehension, using gestures as needed.

Intermediate Describe an event, using simple vocabulary and pictures. Have small groups take turns sharing information about the event to demonstrate listening comprehension. Provide them with sentence starters, such as *The storm lasted* . . .

Advanced Have partners research an event and take turns describing it to each other. Have them use a main idea and details chart to take notes as they listen. Have them orally summarize the event for the class, using their notes.

Advanced High Have students take notes about an event and then explain the event to a small group. Listeners should complete a *who/what/where/when* chart as they listen. Then, have listeners compare charts and write brief summaries.

Test Warm-Up

DIRECTIONS
Read the introduction and the passage that follows. Then, answer the questions to show that you can identify, use, and understand the function of relative pronouns in reading and writing.

Juana wrote this paragraph about planning the Fall Festival. Read the paragraph and think about the changes you would suggest as a peer editor. When you finish reading, answer the questions that follow.

The Fall Festival

(1) Mrs. Barnes was the teacher who chaired the planning committee and whose classroom was our meeting area. (2) Sal was the one whom suggested we decorate with pumpkins. (3) Allison wanted to offer games and prizes. (4) The games and prizes would appeal to all ages. (5) Darnell insisted on a contest of bobbing for apples, which he said everyone would enjoy. (6) Carla was the volunteer that I assigned to organize hayrides. (7) The next day, I looked over the notes that I took during the meeting. (8) It was clear the fall festival would be a success.

1 What change, if any, should be made in sentence 1?

- **A** Change ***who*** to **that**
- **B** Change ***who*** to **whom**
- **C** Change ***whose*** to **whom**
- **D** Make no change

2 How should sentence 2 be revised?

- **F** Sal was the one that suggested we decorate with pumpkins.
- **G** Sal was the one who suggested we decorate with pumpkins.
- **H** Sal was the one which suggested we decorate with pumpkins.
- **J** Sal was the one whose suggested we decorate with pumpkins.

3 What is the BEST way to combine sentences 3 and 4?

- **A** Allison, who would appeal to all ages, wanted to offer games and prizes.
- **B** Games and prizes whose appeal to all ages, Allison wanted to offer.
- **C** Which would appeal to all ages, Allison wanted to offer games and prizes.
- **D** Allison wanted to offer games and prizes that would appeal to all ages.

4 How should sentence 6 be revised?

- **F** Carla was the volunteer which I assigned to organize hayrides.
- **G** Carla was the volunteer whose assignment to organize hayrides I gave her.
- **H** Carla was the volunteer whom I assigned to organize hayrides.
- **J** Carla was the volunteer that assigning to organize hayrides was clear.

Test Warm-Up

1. **D** Make no change
2. **G** Sal was the one who suggested we decorate with pumpkins.
3. **D** Allison wanted to offer games and prizes that would appeal to all ages.
4. **H** Carla was the volunteer whom I assigned to organize hayrides.

Reteach

If students have not mastered these skills, review the content in Section 13.2.7 Using Relative Pronouns.

Test Tip

Even students who know the correct answer to a multiple-choice question may inadvertently select the wrong answer because they find the distractors confusing. To help students avoid "second-guessing" themselves, suggest that they try to answer questions before they read the answer options. After students have answered a question, they should choose the option that most closely matches their answer.

PRACTICE 13.2I

1. Who
2. What
3. Which
4. Whose
5. What
6. Who
7. whom
8. What
9. Which
10. What

PRACTICE 13.2J

Answers will vary. Sample answers:

11. Everybody
12. Neither
13. Several
14. Most
15. None
16. anyone
17. All
18. Few
19. Many, some
20. Everything

SPEAKING APPLICATION

Students should explain how interrogative pronouns function in their sentences.

WRITING APPLICATION

Have students demonstrate that they can identify, use, and understand relative pronouns by correctly using them in a paragraph and by identifying and explaining them in a partner's paragraph.

PRACTICE 13.2I Identifying Interrogative Pronouns

Read the sentences. Then, write the interrogative pronoun in each sentence.

EXAMPLE What is your favorite television show?
ANSWER *What*

1. Who are those people on the stage?
2. What should I do about my lost wallet?
3. Which is the best route to Tulsa?
4. Whose is the nicest outfit?
5. What is her occupation?
6. Who lives in that big house?
7. With whom are you going to the dance?
8. What will happen if I don't follow the directions exactly?
9. Which is worse: being late or not doing your homework?
10. What should we do when we reach the next intersection?

PRACTICE 13.2J Supplying Indefinite Pronouns

Read the sentences. Then, write an appropriate indefinite pronoun for each sentence.

EXAMPLE ____ was asking about you.
ANSWER *Someone*

11. ____ likes pizza!
12. ____ of the clerks could help me find what I wanted.
13. ____ of these questions have more than one answer.
14. ____ of my friends are conscientious students.
15. ____ of the vocabulary words are familiar to me.
16. I don't know ____ who would say such a thing.
17. ____ of the monuments will be decorated for the holidays.
18. ____ find the reward worth the risk of the investment.
19. ____ of the bystanders watched the rescue, and ____ tried to help.
20. ____ must be put away before you leave.

SPEAKING APPLICATION

Interview a partner, asking five questions that begin with interrogative pronouns. Your partner should name the interrogative pronouns.

WRITING APPLICATION

Write a brief paragraph describing an incident you observed. Use at least three relative pronouns and indefinite pronouns in your paragraph. You may use the sentences in Practice 13.2J as models.

CHAPTER 14 LESSON PLANNER
Verbs

Use the Online Lesson Planner at www.phwritingcoach.com to customize your instructional plan for an integrated Language Arts curriculum.

DAY 1 14.1 Action Verbs

	INSTRUCTION AND PRACTICE
"What Do You Notice?" **Objectives:** Identify, use, and understand verbs and action verbs, including ▪ transitive verbs ▪ intransitive verbs	**Student Edition** pp. 313–316

DAY 2 14.2 Linking Verbs

	INSTRUCTION AND PRACTICE
Objectives: Identify, use, and understand linking verbs, including ▪ forms of *be* ▪ other linking verbs ▪ action or linking verb?	**Student Edition** pp. 317–320 **Test Warm-Up** p. 321

DAY 3 14.3 Helping Verbs

	INSTRUCTION AND PRACTICE
Objectives: Identify, use, and understand helping verbs.	**Student Edition** pp. 322–324

"Look at verbs this way: If a sentence were a car, the verb would be the engine. Strong sentences usually contain strong verbs. Take the following sentence, for example: 'The day was cloudy.' Simply improving the verb elevates the sentence: 'The clouds hung in the sky.' That's the importance of verbs."

—Kelly Gallagher

Grammar Assessment

Grammar Coach:	Diagnostic Assessment	End-of-Chapter Assessment	Progress Monitoring
Personalized Instruction	Students take grammar diagnostic test online and are automatically assigned instruction and practice in areas where they need support.	Teacher uses **ExamView** to administer end-of-chapter assessment and remediation. Teachers may customize **ExamView** tests or use the ones provided.	Teachers may use the **Test Warm-Ups** and the **Cumulative Reviews** in the student book or eText to check students' mastery of grammar skills. Students may also play **DimensionL** grammar video games to test their grammar skills.
Teacher-Directed Instruction	Teacher administers the diagnostic test and determines focus of instruction and practice.		

Alternate Pacing Plans

- **Block Scheduling** Each day in the Lesson Planner represents a 40–50 minute block. Teachers using block scheduling may combine days to revise pacing to meet their classroom needs.
- **Accelerated Lesson Planning** Combine instructional days, focusing on concepts called out by students' diagnostic test results.
- **Integrated Language Arts Curriculum** Use the instruction and practice in this chapter to provide reinforcement, remediation, or extension of grammar concepts taught in your literature curriculum.

Links to Prentice Hall *LITERATURE*

Unit 2 Verbs, p. 246

www.phwritingcoach.com

Grammar Assessment and Practice

Chapter diagnostic tests assess students' skills and assign instruction and practice.

DimensionL Video Games

Fast-paced interactive video games challenge students' mastery of grammar.

Lesson Planner continues on next page

"Verbs sizzle, snap, and move. A verb may just be the most crucial word in a sentence. Without verbs, nothing would ever happen—nothing could even exist. A well-chosen verb can enliven student writing more than any other part of speech."

—Jeff Anderson

Differentiated Instruction

Differentiated Instruction Boxes in this Teacher's Edition address these student populations:

- Below-Level Students
- Above-Level Students
- Gifted and Talented Students
- Special Needs Students
- English Language Learners
- Spanish Speaking Students

In addition, for further enrichment, see the **Extension** features.

Grammar Ground Rule: Make It Active!

Model with Students

In this chapter, making it active means writing most of your sentences in the **active voice,** or **tense**. Explain to students that most sentences in English have a subject that *does* something or that *is* a certain way. It's not wrong to write a sentence in which the subject has something done *to* it, instead, but there should be a good reason for it.

Say: I could tell you what I did this morning this way: *I ate my breakfast. I rode my bike to school. I had a glass of juice.* Or I could tell you this way: *My breakfast was eaten by me. My bike was ridden to school by me. A glass of juice was had by me.* Which one makes me sound more active? Which one is easier to hear and understand?

Explain to students that there will be times when an active verb will just not seem right. They will usually know when that happens. For example, *John F. Kennedy was elected president in 1960* or *That chair was broken before I got here.*

Small Group Activity – Looking at Active and Passive Verbs

Have students form small groups and look at a paragraph from a history book. Have them decide which verbs in the paragraph are active and which are passive. If they find passive verbs, have them see if they can rewrite the sentences in the active voice. Have the groups discuss how the rewrite changes their sense of the event. Their discussion should answer these questions:

- Is it usually important in history to think about who performed an action?
- Does writing a sentence in the active voice help you think about that?

Have a member of each group present their findings to the class, with at least one example, and explain why the group thought the sentence followed this grammar ground rule: Make it active.

Grammar Ground Rules

1. Keep it clear.
2. Make them agree.
3. Make it specific.
4. Dot your *i*'s and cross your *t*'s.
5. Make it active.

VERBS

To bring your writing to life, use verbs that describe actions that can be seen and those that cannot be seen.

WRITE GUY *Jeff Anderson, M.Ed.*

WHAT DO YOU NOTICE?

Pinpoint the action verbs as you zoom in on these sentences from the story "The Bear Boy" by Joseph Bruchac.

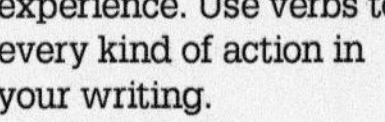

The trackers crept close, hoping to grab the boy and run. But as soon as the mother bear caught their scent, she growled and pushed her cubs and the boy back into the cave.

Now, ask yourself the following questions:

- Which verbs describe actions that you could see or hear?
- How do the verbs *hoping* and *caught* describe a different kind of action?

The verbs *crept, grab, run, growled,* and *pushed* describe actions that could be seen or heard. However, the verbs *hoping* and *caught* describe actions that could not be seen or heard. You could not see the trackers *hoping* because it is something they are feeling. You could not see that the mother bear *caught* the trackers' scent because that action involves her senses.

Grammar for Writers Writers must remember that action is more than just what you do; it is also what you think, feel, and experience. Use verbs to capture every kind of action in your writing.

I want to ace the test on action verbs.
Then you should take action and start studying.

CHAPTER 14

Grammar for Writers: Voice

Help students understand that interesting action verbs make writing come alive. Verbs capture all kinds of action. The rules on these pages will help students use verbs more effectively in their writing and speaking.

VERBS

As students progress in their writing skills, it will be important for them to be able to apply the rules of grammar, usage, and mechanics to their own drafts. Use the *What Do You Notice?* feature to help them see effective conventions in the work of professional writers. Encourage students to incorporate proper voice, tense, and syntax as they edit their own writing.

Read the opening sentence aloud. Discuss how the use of vivid action verbs can bring writing to life. Point out that verbs can describe actions that can be seen (e.g., *smile*) and actions that cannot be seen (e.g., *think*).

WRITE GUY *Jeff Anderson, M. Ed.*

WHAT DO YOU NOTICE?

When students have read the Mentor Text, **say:** What are the trackers doing? (creeping and hoping) What is the bear doing? (catching the trackers' scent, growling, and pushing the boy and the cubs into the cave) The words that describe these actions—*crept, hoping, grab, run, caught, growled, pushed*—are *action verbs.*

Have students finish reading the page. Remind them that verbs describe actions.

Reread the first sentence of the Mentor Text aloud. **Then, say:** *Crept, grab,* and *run* are all verbs that show action. *Hoping* is a verb, too. What kind of action does *hoping* show? **(Possible response:** Hoping is an action you cannot see. *Hoping* describes a feeling someone is having.)

Students should realize that many verbs can describe visible actions or invisible ones. Verbs are vital because they allow writers to express all kinds of actions.

14.1 Action Verbs

Lesson Objectives

1. Recognize and identify action verbs.
2. Distinguish between transitive and intransitive verbs.

Discuss the fact that there is action all around us. People, animals, and the technology around us are always *doing* something. People need to be able to describe the actions they see and the actions they cannot see, like thinking about an idea. Verbs are the words we use to name these actions.

RULE 14.1.1 Read aloud the rule and then have students repeat the lines with you.

Use a Think Aloud as part of a gradual release progression.

Say: It's easy to identify most action verbs. **I simply look** for words that describe actions, or things that can be done. For example, *walk* is an action verb. *I walk around the classroom.* **Demonstrate.** *Walk* describes my action. Some action verbs are harder to identify. *Wonder* is an action verb. Wondering is something I can do. *Wonder* describes thinking. Thinking and feeling are actions, too.

Work with students to identify the action verbs in this group: ***boy, runs, hoping, kick, tree, are, believe.***

Have student pairs brainstorm for examples of different action verbs. Have them sort their examples into two categories: actions they can see and actions they cannot see.

Using Transitive Verbs

Point out the difference between transitive and intransitive verbs.

RULE 14.1.2 Read aloud the rule and then have students repeat the lines with you.

Write this sentence on the board: *Ralph hit the baseball over the fence.* Ask students to identify the verb. Underline *hit.* Then, **ask:** What did Ralph hit? (a baseball) Explain that *baseball* is the receiver of the action. *Hit* is therefore a transitive verb.

14.1 Action Verbs

Verbs such as *walk, sailed, played, migrate, raced, crossed, learn,* and *arrive* all show some kind of action.

WRITING COACH Online
www.phwritingcoach.com

Grammar Tutorials
Brush up on your Grammar skills with these animated videos.

Grammar Practice
Practice your grammar skills with Writing Coach Online.

Grammar Games
Test your knowledge of grammar in this fast-paced interactive video game.

An action verb tells what action someone or something is performing.

EXAMPLES Mother **carries** the platter.

The train **chugged** into the station.

I **believe** it will rain today.

Heather **remembered** to bring her book.

The verb *carries* explains what Mother did with the platter. The verb *chugged* tells what the train did. The verb *believe* explains my action about the weather. The verb *remembered* explains Heather's action with the book.

Some actions, such as *carries* or *chugged,* can be seen. Some actions, such as *believe* or *remembered,* cannot be seen.

See Practice 14.1A

Using Transitive Verbs

An action verb is transitive if the receiver of the action is named in the sentence. The receiver of the action is called the object of the verb.

EXAMPLES Mrs. Brown **opened** (verb) the **door** (object) with great difficulty.

The bus suddenly **hit** (verb) a nearby **tree** (object).

Diagnostic and Instruction
Diagnostic test assesses students' instructional needs. Lessons and practice are assigned based on results.

Additional Practice
- Grammar Tutorials—Animated videos reinforce key grammar skills.
- Grammar Practice—Targeted practice addresses individual needs.
- ExamView—Teachers customize their grammar practice and tests.
- Grammar Games—Interactive video games make grammar fun.

In the first example, *opened* is transitive because the object of the verb—*door*—names what Mrs. Brown opened. In the second example, *hit* is transitive because the object of the verb—*tree*—tells what the bus hit.

Using Intransitive Verbs

RULE 14.1.3 An action verb is **intransitive** if there is no receiver of the action named in the sentence. An intransitive verb does not have an object.

EXAMPLES

The class **began**.

The dog **raced** through the new gate.

The employees **gathered** in the conference room.

The fire alarm **rang** at 1:00 P.M.

Some action verbs can be transitive or intransitive. You need to determine if the verb has an object or not.

TRANSITIVE VERB Kodia **raced** **Terrence** yesterday.

INTRANSITIVE VERB Kodia **raced** across the finish line.

TRANSITIVE VERB The pilot **flew** the **plane**.

INTRANSITIVE VERB The plane **flew** to Cancun, Mexico.

TRANSITIVE VERB The guests **rang** the **doorbell**.

See Practice 14.1B INTRANSITIVE VERB The doorbell **rang** and the dog barked.

Using Intransitive Verbs

Direct students' attention to the text describing intransitive verbs. Review this example sentence with students: *The class began.* Point out that the verb *began* is transitive if you add the words *the book* to the end of the sentence. Explain why.

RULE 14.1.3 Read aloud the rule and then have students repeat the lines with you.

Write this sentence on the board: *The dog barks.* Ask students to identify the verb. Underline *barks*. Point out that *barks* does not take an object. *Barks* is therefore an intransitive verb.

Write this sentence on the board: *The doorbell rang and Julie opened the door.* Have students identify the verbs. Underline *rang* and *opened*. Ask whether *rang* or *opened* takes an object. Circle *the door*. *Opened* is a transitive verb. *Rang* does not take an object, so *rang* is an intransitive verb.

Teacher Tip

If a student has difficulty distinguishing between transitive and intransitive verbs, provide flash cards containing sample sentences such as *The dog barks* and *Wanda kicks the ball*. On the back of the card, label the verb, the object (if there is one), and the category of the verb—transitive or intransitive. Students should read the sentence aloud to a partner and identify the verb and the object (if there is an object). Partners should then discuss whether the verb is transitive or intransitive. Partners can then turn the card over and see if their answer is correct.

Working with ELLs — ELL Sheltered Instruction: Cognitive

Help students employ increasingly complex grammatical structures in writing by having them use correct tenses of action verbs in sentences.

Beginning Pair students with fluent speakers. Have the fluent speaker say a simple sentence that identifies an action in the present. Then, write the sentence one word at a time as Beginning students copy it. Have pairs repeat, changing the verb to past tense. Guide pairs in comparing the sentences.

Intermediate Write the action verbs from page 314 (e.g., *carries, chugged, believe, remembered*) on the board. Have partners write their own sentences using the verbs. Have them discuss how the tense of each verb shows when the action occurs.

Advanced Write *believe, believes, believed,* and *will believe* on the board. Have students write four sentences, each featuring one form of the verb. Then, have partners exchange sentences and identify the tense of the action verb in each.

Advanced High Have students draw a four-column chart and write ten action verbs in the first column. Partners should fill in the rest of the chart with the present, past, and future tense of the verb. Challenge students to write sentences using several action verbs in the correct tense.

PRACTICE 14.1A

1. hiked
2. played
3. thought, knew
4. expressed
5. rolled
6. worries
7. poured
8. cheered, scored
9. top
10. stomped, slammed

PRACTICE 14.1B

11. leaves—intransitive
12. hit—transitive
13. arrives—intransitive
14. gathered—intransitive
15. fell—intransitive
    broke—intransitive
16. smile—intransitive
17. grows—transitive
18. require—transitive
19. likes—transitive
    complain—intransitive
20. provide—transitive

SPEAKING APPLICATION

Have students share their three named action verbs with the class.

WRITING APPLICATION

Have students identify the objects in the sentences that have transitive verbs.

PRACTICE 14.1A Finding Action Verbs

Read the sentences. Then, write each action verb.

EXAMPLE The airplane landed on the ground.
ANSWER *landed*

1. Alex and a friend hiked up the mountain trail.
2. Hannah played the harp in the talent contest.
3. Kaylee thought she knew the answer.
4. Max expressed his concern to the principal.
5. A tornado rolled across the prairie last week.
6. Devon worries about the future.
7. The chef poured the dressing onto the salad.
8. The crowd cheered wildly when the team scored.
9. My grades in science top those in math.
10. Claire stomped out and slammed the door.

PRACTICE 14.1B Identifying Transitive and Intransitive Verbs

Read the sentences. Write each verb and label it *transitive* or *intransitive*.

EXAMPLE Tina wants a summer job.
ANSWER *wants— transitive*

11. The cruise ship leaves tomorrow.
12. A fierce blizzard hit the Northeast.
13. The work crew never arrives on time.
14. Clouds gathered before the storm.
15. My glasses fell and broke.
16. Some people smile all the time.
17. My mother grows vegetables and flowers in her garden.
18. Good jobs usually require a high school diploma.
19. No one likes people who complain all the time.
20. Advanced math courses provide a challenge for some.

SPEAKING APPLICATION

Tell a partner about a movie you saw recently. Your partner should listen for and name three action verbs.

WRITING APPLICATION

Write two sentences with transitive verbs and two sentences with intransitive verbs.

Working with ELLs ELL Sheltered Instruction: Cognitive

As students practice with action verbs, have them demonstrate their comprehension of increasingly complex English by retelling and summarizing.

Beginning Write three simple statements about Texas history on the board. Read them aloud, using pictures and gestures to aid comprehension. Then, have students read the sentences chorally. Help them identify the action verbs and summarize by taking notes in a word web.

Intermediate Provide students with simple written sentences about Texas history. Help them identify the action verbs in the sentences. Provide cloze prompts to help them retell what they read. For example, *At the Johnson Space Center ______.*

Advanced On a transparency, prepare paragraphs about Texas history. Provide partners with a copy of the transparency and an erasable marker. Have them circle all of the action verbs. Then, model crossing out inessential details to summarize a paragraph. Have students mark subsequent paragraphs and write a summary of the passage.

Advanced High Provide each student with a passage about Texas history. Have students complete K-W-L charts to monitor their comprehension. Then, have them write a summary about what they read, using action verbs.

14.2 Linking Verbs

Some widely used verbs do not show action. They are called **linking verbs.**

Grammar Tutorials
Brush up on your Grammar skills with these animated videos.

Grammar Practice
Practice your grammar skills with Writing Coach Online.

Grammar Games
Test your knowledge of grammar in this fast-paced interactive video game.

RULE 14.2.1

> A **linking verb** is a verb that connects a subject with a word that describes or identifies it.

EXAMPLES

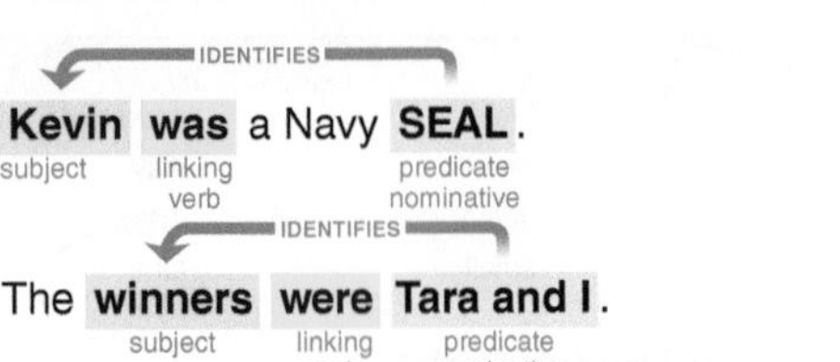

Recognizing Forms of *Be*

In English, the most common linking verb is *be.* This verb has many forms.

FORMS OF *BE*		
am	can be	has been
are	could be	have been
is	may be	had been
was	might be	could have been
were	must be	may have been
am being	shall be	might have been
are being	should be	must have been
is being	will be	shall have been
was being	would be	should have been
were being		will have been
		would have been

WRITING COACH Online
www.phwritingcoach.com

Diagnostic and Instruction
Diagnostic test assesses students' instructional needs. Lessons and practice are assigned based on results.

Additional Practice
- Grammar Tutorials—Animated videos reinforce key grammar skills.
- Grammar Practice—Targeted practice addresses individual needs.
- ExamView—Teachers customize their grammar practice and tests.
- Grammar Games—Interactive video games make grammar fun.

Lesson Objectives

1. Recognize and identify different forms of *be.*
2. Distinguish between linking verbs and action verbs.

Point out to students that not all verbs are action verbs. Some verbs are linking verbs. They *link* a subject to a word that describes or identifies it; for example, *Al is tall.*

RULE 14.2.1 Read aloud the rule and then have students repeat the lines with you.

Use a Think Aloud as part of a gradual release progression.

Say: I know that not all verbs express actions. Some verbs connect a subject with a word that identifies or describes it. These verbs are called linking verbs. Consider these sentences: *I stand in front of the classroom. I walk to the door. Stand* and *walk* are action verbs. They describe my actions. Now, consider this sentence: *I am a teacher.* The word *am* does not describe what I am doing. It links the subject, *I*, to a word that identifies who I am. It is a linking verb.

Work with students to identify the linking verbs in this group: ***is, run, have, being, breaks.*** Help them explain why a verb is a linking verb.

Have student pairs write descriptive sentences about their partner using a form of the linking verb *be.* Invite students to use their sentences to introduce their partner to the group.

Recognizing Forms of *Be*

Explain to students that the most common linking verb is *be. Be* has many different forms.

Have students use different forms of the linking verb *be* in sentences.

Using Other Linking Verbs

Point out that there are other linking verbs besides *be*. These other linking verbs function in the same way as *be*. Like *be,* they connect the subject with a word that describes or identifies it.

Have student pairs brainstorm for example sentences using the verbs listed in the table on page 318.

Action Verb or Linking Verb?

Draw attention to the text that states that some verbs can act as either action verbs or linking verbs. Explain that students can test whether a verb is a linking verb or an action verb by replacing the verb with *is*, *am*, or *are*. If the sentence still makes sense, then the verb is a linking verb.

Write these sentences on the board: *The dog looks angry. The dog looks angrily at the cat.* Ask students to identify the verb. Underline *looks*. Then, erase *looks* and replace *looks* with *is*. Read the revised sentences aloud. *Looks* in the first sentence is a linking verb, but it is an action verb in the second sentence.

Teacher Tip

If students have difficulty distinguishing action verbs from linking verbs, provide them with flash cards containing sentences using verbs such as *look*, *grow*, and *taste*. Have student partners practice substituting *is*, *am*, or *are* in place of the verb to test whether the verb is an action or linking verb in the sentence. Explain that the correct answer is on the back of each flash card.

Using Other Linking Verbs

Several other verbs also function as linking verbs. They connect the parts of a sentence in the same way as the forms of *be*. In the sentence below, *shocked* describes *teacher*.

DESCRIBES

EXAMPLE The **teacher** **looked** **shocked**.
subject / linking verb / predicate adjective

OTHER LINKING VERBS		
appear	look	sound
become	remain	stay
feel	seem	taste
grow	smell	turn

Action Verb or Linking Verb?

Some verbs can be used either as linking verbs or action verbs.

LINKING The glass **looked** dirty.
(*Looked* links *glass* and *dirty*.)

ACTION The host **looked** at the glass.
(The host performed an action.)

LINKING The crowd **grew** impatient.
(*Grew* links *crowd* and *impatient*.)

ACTION The farmer **grew** strawberries.
(The farmer performed an action.)

To test whether a verb is a linking verb or an action verb, replace the verb with *is, am,* or *are*. If the sentence still makes sense, then the verb is a linking verb.

EXAMPLE The crowd **is** impatient.
linking verb

See Practice 14.2A
See Practice 14.2B
See Practice 14.2C
See Practice 14.2D

Working with ELLs — ELL Sheltered Instruction: Cognitive

To help students write using a variety of grade-appropriate sentence lengths in increasingly accurate ways, help them use linking verbs as they review the lesson on page 318.

Beginning Read the example sentences aloud to students, having them repeat after you. Write on the board the verb in each sentence and have students copy. Guide them in writing their own sentences using the verbs.

Intermediate Have students choose *appear, feel,* or *look* from the table on page 318 and use the word as both a linking verb and an action verb in two written sentences. Then, have partners exchange sentences and create longer versions of each sentence by adding words or phrases.

Advanced Write on the board *remain, taste,* and *smell* from the table on page 318. Have students write a sentence with each one as a linking verb and as an action verb. Then, help students combine two sentences into a longer one.

Advanced High Challenge students to create their own sentences with four of the linking verbs in the table on page 318. Then, have students switch papers with a partner and write four longer sentences using their partners' linking verbs as action verbs.

PRACTICE 14.2A **Identifying Action Verbs and Linking Verbs**

Read the sentences. Write the verb in each sentence, and label it either *action* or *linking*.

EXAMPLE We are optimistic about the outcome.

ANSWER *are— linking*

1. The couple attended the opening night of the play.
2. Matt Perez will be the captain of the team.
3. I love Van Gogh's painting *Starry Night.*
4. Your idea seems like a good one.
5. Those two women have been friends for years.
6. Robbie chopped wood for the campfire.
7. May I ask you a question?
8. This chili tastes bland.
9. The bell rang at the end of class.
10. The sky became cloudy very quickly.

PRACTICE 14.2B **Using *Be* and Other Linking Verbs**

Read the pairs of words below. For each pair of words, write a sentence that uses a linking verb to connect them.

EXAMPLE trip adventure

ANSWER *A trip to Alaska could be an adventure.*

11. soccer popular
12. contestants confident
13. Emma hungry
14. Corey energetic
15. Louis Sachar author
16. cellphone lost
17. Yvonne president
18. hurricanes dangerous
19. Oscar handsome
20. You winner

SPEAKING APPLICATION

With a partner, take turns describing someone you admire. Use at least two linking and two action verbs. Your partner should identify and label the verbs.

WRITING APPLICATION

Write a short paragraph about some aspect of the weather. In your paragraph, use three different linking verbs.

Differentiated Instruction

Strategy for Spanish Speakers

Students whose home language is Spanish may have difficulties with subject-verb agreement with the verb *to be*. Practice conjugating the verb *to be* by writing different subjects and subject pronouns on flash cards. Have pairs of students quiz each other on the verb forms by having one partner hold up the flash card and the other partner say the correct form of the verb *to be* that corresponds with the word on the flash card. Then, have students write complete sentences with the word on the flash card and the form of the verb *to be*, pointing out the subject in each sentence that they write. To extend practice, have students complete the activity with different verb tenses.

PRACTICE 14.2A

1. attended—action
2. will be—linking
3. love—action
4. seems—linking
5. have been—linking
6. chopped—action
7. May ask—action
8. tastes—linking
9. rang—action
10. became—linking

PRACTICE 14.2B

Answers will vary. Sample answers:

11. Soccer is becoming more and more popular.
12. The contestants appeared confident.
13. Emma is always hungry by lunchtime.
14. Corey felt energetic after a snack.
15. Louis Sachar remains my favorite author.
16. My cellphone has been lost for some time now.
17. Yvonne is the president of the class.
18. Hurricanes can be very dangerous.
19. Oscar looked handsome in his new suit.
20. You should have been the winner.

SPEAKING APPLICATION

Have students explain to their partners how they identified the linking verbs and action verbs.

WRITING APPLICATION

Have students share their paragraphs, pointing out the linking verbs.

PRACTICE 14.2C

1. coughed—action
2. seemed—linking
3. is—linking; sound—action
4. seems—linking
5. appeared—action; startled—action
6. answered—action; sounded—linking
7. must have been towed—action; is—linking
8. tasted—action; poured—action
9. threw—action; swooshed—action
10. became—linking

PRACTICE 14.2D

Answers will vary. Sample answers:

11. Soon, I will be better at grammar.
12. In the fall, I feel unhappy when it rains.
13. The perfume shop smells good.
14. Some farmers grow tomatoes.
15. Train operators sound the horn at crossings.
16. Bird watchers look in the trees.
17. Bob turned left at the intersection.
18. The new student seems confused.
19. The high score appears on the scoreboard.
20. Experienced forecasters become better at predictions.

SPEAKING APPLICATION

Have students share some of the similarities and differences that they noticed in the sentences.

WRITING APPLICATION

Have students exchange paragraphs and identify the action verbs and linking verbs.

PRACTICE 14.2C Identifying Action Verbs and Linking Verbs

Read the sentences. Then, write the verb or verbs in each sentence, and label them either *action* or *linking*.

EXAMPLE Oliver grew uneasy as he climbed the front steps of the deserted house.

ANSWER *grew*— linking; *climbed*— action

1. The factory coughed puffs of steam out of its smokestacks.
2. Harry seemed excited for the chance to play goalie.
3. When a cat is nearby, the neighborhood birds sound the alarm.
4. With Eleanor at the wheel, a drive to school seems terrifying.
5. Maura appeared out of nowhere, and she startled us.
6. When she answered the phone, Maria sounded sleepy.
7. The car must have been towed because today is street cleaning day.
8. Mom tasted the soup; then, she poured it into bowls.
9. Sean threw the ball, and it swooshed into the basket.
10. The spectators became amazed at the elephant's tricks.

PRACTICE 14.2D Writing With Action and Linking Verbs

Read the verbs below. For each verb, write a sentence using a form of the verb as indicated below.

EXAMPLE turned — linking

ANSWER *At forty years old, his hair turned gray.*

11. be — linking
12. feel — linking
13. smell — linking
14. grow — action
15. sound — action
16. look — action
17. turn — action
18. seem — linking
19. appear — action
20. become — linking

SPEAKING APPLICATION

With a partner, take turns reading the sentences you wrote in Practice 14.2D. Discuss how your sentences are similar and how they are different.

WRITING APPLICATION

Imagine you are exploring another planet. Write a brief paragraph describing this experience. Use four action verbs and four linking verbs in your paragraph.

Extension

To help students synthesize and apply what they have learned about verbs, have students play a verb identification game. Using 12 note cards, a team leader should write six sentences with action verbs and six sentences with linking verbs, one sentence to a card. Direct the leader to shuffle the cards and challenge a group of students to identify the sentences with linking verbs. As the leader slowly reads aloud a sentence, group members listen. The first group member to answer correctly receives a point. The student with the most points wins.

Test Warm-Up

DIRECTIONS
Read the introduction and the passage that follows. Then, answer the questions to show that you can use and understand the function of linking verbs and action verbs in reading and writing.

Denzel wrote this paragraph describing a dream in which he was a famous lion tamer. Read the paragraph and think about the changes you would suggest as a peer editor. When you finish reading, answer the questions that follow.

The Amazing Denzel

(1) I felt a cold breeze as I approached the lion's cage and unlocked it. (2) The lion sounded asleep, but that was about to change. (3) When the door clanged, he opened one golden eye. (4) As he slowly got to his feet, I seemed increasingly nervous. (5) He might have been able to sense my fear. (6) Fortunately, my pockets contained raw meat. (7) As the lion came toward me, I asked him if he wouldn't mind performing a backflip. (8) He was looking like he was hesitant. (9) I think he was about to do the flip when my alarm went off.

1 The meaning of sentence 2 can be clarified by changing the word ***sounded*** to —

- **A** became
- **B** was
- **C** grew
- **D** turned

2 The meaning of sentence 4 can be clarified by changing the word ***seemed*** to —

- **F** appeared
- **G** stayed
- **H** looked
- **J** became

3 What is the BEST way to rewrite sentence 5?

- **A** He was seeming to sense my fear.
- **B** He sensed my fear.
- **C** He had to have been sensing my fear.
- **D** He seemed to sense my fear.

4 What is the BEST way to rewrite sentence 8?

- **F** He felt hesitant.
- **G** He turned hesitant.
- **H** He sounded hesitant.
- **J** He seemed hesitant.

Test Warm-Up

1. **B** was
2. **J** became
3. **B** He sensed my fear.
4. **J** He seemed hesitant.

Reteach

If students have not mastered these skills, review the content in Section 14.2.1 Linking Verbs.

Test Tip

Some incorrect answer choices are very similar to the correct answer choice. When the differences between these choices are very small or subtle, students sometimes choose the first distractor that seems reasonable and move on to the next question without ever reading the remaining answer choices. Remind students that they should read all of the answers carefully before selecting one. If two answer choices sound as if they are the same to a student, then the student has missed something. He or she should carefully reread the question and the answer choices until the difference between the two choices is clear.

Lesson Objectives

1. Recognize, identify, and use different helping verbs.
2. Recognize that helping verbs are part of verb phrases, and that verb phrases are sometimes separated by other words.

Discuss with students the fact that the verb in a sentence may be made up of several words. This type of verb is called a verb phrase.

RULE 14.3.1 Read aloud the rule and then have students repeat the lines with you.

Write these sentences on the board. *Bill opened the door. Bill might have opened the door. Bill should have opened the door.*

Point out the single verb *opened* in the first sentence and the verb phrase *might have opened* in the second sentence. Work with students to identify the helping verbs and main verb that make up the verb phrase in the third sentence (should have opened).

Recognizing Helping Verbs

Point out that forms of *be* are often used as helping verbs. Then, challenge students to make sentences using the different verb phrases in the chart on page 322.

www.phwritingcoach.com

Diagnostic and Instruction
Diagnostic test assesses students' instructional needs. Lessons and practice are assigned based on results.

Additional Practice
- Grammar Practice—Targeted practice addresses individual needs.
- ExamView—Teachers customize their grammar practice and tests.
- Grammar Games—Interactive video games make grammar fun.

14.3 Helping Verbs

Sometimes, a verb in a sentence is just one word. Often, however, a verb will be made up of several words. This type of verb is called a **verb phrase**.

Helping verbs are added before another verb to make a verb phrase.

Notice how these helping verbs change the meaning of the verb *open.*

EXAMPLES open — **might have** opened

had opened — **should have** opened

will have opened — **will be** opened

Recognizing Helping Verbs

Forms of *Be* Forms of *be* are often used as helping verbs.

SOME FORMS OF *BE* USED AS HELPING VERBS	
HELPING VERBS	MAIN VERBS
am	growing
has been	warned
was being	told
will be	reminded
will have been	waiting
is	opening
was being	trained
should be	written
had been	sent
might have been	played

www.phwritingcoach.com

Grammar Practice
Practice your grammar skills with Writing Coach Online.

Grammar Games
Test your knowledge of grammar in this fast-paced interactive video game.

See Practice 14.3A

Differentiated Instruction

RTI Strategy for Below-Level Students
Help students understand that sometimes verbs can be made up of several words.

Distribute five blank index cards to each student. On each card, have students copy one form of *be* from the chart. Then, give each student an index card with a verb written on it (such as *waiting*, *trained*, or *played*). Have students manipulate their index cards to form different verb phrases.

Pair students and have them work together to write an example sentence using one of the verb phrases created with index cards. Invite pairs to share their sentence with the group.

Other Helping Verbs Many different verb phrases can be formed using one or more of these helping verbs. The chart below shows just a few.

HELPING VERBS	MAIN VERBS	VERB PHRASES
do	remember	do remember
has	written	has written
would	hope	would hope
shall	see	shall see
can	believe	can believe
could	finish	could finish
may	attempt	may attempt
must have	thought	must have thought
should have	grown	should have grown
might	win	might win
will	jump	will jump
have	planned	have planned
does	want	does want

Sometimes the words in a verb phrase are separated by other words, such as *not* or *certainly*. The parts of the verb phrase in certain types of questions may also be separated.

WORDS SEPARATED

She **could** certainly **have thought** that was hers.

This **has** not **changed** how we feel.

Jeffrey **has** certainly **hit** the most home runs.

The dentist **had** carefully **examined** my teeth.

Did you ever **expect** to be so scared?

When **may** we **open** the envelope?

Did you ever **expect** to see that kind of experiment?

Sophia **must** not **have taken** the car.

Would you ever **want** to go fishing?

See Practice 14.3B

Other Helping Verbs

Draw attention to the chart that lists other helping verbs. Write these sentences on the board: *I have wanted this book for a long time. I will try to see that movie tonight. I should have finished my work yesterday.* Have students identify the helping verb or verbs in each sentence (*have*, *will*, and *should have*).

Have student pairs make sentences using helping verbs from the chart. Invite pairs to share their sentences with the group.

Point out that sometimes the words in a verb phrase can be separated by other words, such as *not* and *certainly*. Give this example: *I can certainly believe his alibi.* Add that in some questions the subject separates a helping verb from the main verb. Give this example: *Could you have studied harder?* Have students change the question into a statement in order to find the verb phrase more easily: *You could have studied harder.* Point out that to form the questions, the first helping verb is moved to the front of the sentence.

Have student pairs revise the sentences made earlier using helping verbs from the chart. Students should use words such as *not*, *carefully*, *certainly*, and so on to separate the verbs in the verb phrase; for example: *I can definitely believe her excuse.* Invite students to share their revised sentences with the group. Then, call for volunteers to change each statement into a question and identify which words, if any, separate the verbs in the verb phrase.

Working with ELLs — ELL Sheltered Instruction: Cognitive

Help students use visual and contextual support as they read to enhance and confirm understanding and to develop vocabulary needed to comprehend increasingly challenging language.

Beginning Write these words from page 323 on the board and provide pictures illustrating each: *home runs, dentist, envelope,* and *fishing.* Read the words chorally, explaining their meaning. Then, ask simple questions, featuring helping verbs, about the pictures. For example, *Can the dentist help your teeth?* Finally, guide students in reading the example sentences on page 323.

Intermediate Review the words and pictures from the Beginning activity. Have students meet with more fluent partners to write sentences about each picture using the words. Finally, have them read and discuss the meaning of the example sentences on page 323.

Advanced Provide students with visual support for these words from page 323: *examined, expect,* and *experiment.* Then, have them explain what the helping verb adds to the meaning of each example sentence.

Advanced High Have students complete the Intermediate activity. Have them then rewrite each example sentence with a different appropriate helping verb, explaining the difference the new word makes in meaning.

PRACTICE 14.3A

1. main verb
2. helping verb
3. main verb
4. helping verb
5. main verb
6. helping verb
7. helping verb and main verb
8. helping verb
9. helping verb
10. main verb

PRACTICE 14.3B

Answers will vary. Sample answers:

11. Kurt has been going to practice regularly.
12. I have been in the gym all afternoon.
13. Did you get my message?
14. Marla could not remember the name of the actor.
15. Kelly has learned to cook.
16. I might want to try out for the team.
17. Rhode Island is known as the Ocean State.
18. My older sister will have graduated before I get to high school.
19. That play had been produced before.
20. Your essay should be completed by tomorrow.

SPEAKING APPLICATION

Have students explain how they identified the verb phrases and how they distinguished between the main verbs and helping verbs.

WRITING APPLICATION

Assign partners and have students take turns identifying main verbs and helping verbs in each other's underlined verb phrases.

PRACTICE 14.3A **Identifying Helping and Main Verbs**

Read the sentences. Write *main verb* if the underlined verb is a main verb. Write *helping verb* if it is a helping verb.

EXAMPLE Luanne is having a party.

ANSWER *main verb*

1. The city has built a new basketball court in the park.
2. I will be going right home after school.
3. Has your brother returned yet?
4. The puppy has been barking for an hour.
5. I could have done better if I had tried harder.
6. May I be excused now?
7. The group had been in the gym for a long time.
8. Am I bothering you?
9. We had expected a better performance from the group.
10. The witnesses were being questioned by the police.

PRACTICE 14.3B **Using Verb Phrases**

Read the verb phrases. Use each verb phrase in an original sentence.

EXAMPLE have heard

ANSWER *I have heard* the good news.

11. has been going
12. have been
13. did get
14. could remember
15. has learned
16. might want
17. is known
18. will have graduated
19. had been produced
20. should be completed

SPEAKING APPLICATION

With a partner, take turns telling about something that didn't go exactly as planned. Your partner should listen for and identify two verb phrases and name the main and helping verbs in the phrases.

WRITING APPLICATION

Write three sentences with verb phrases. Underline the verb phrases in your sentences.

Quick-Write Extension

To help students synthesize and apply what they have learned about helping verbs, have each student write a memo about an imaginary project being done by an imaginary team of workers. Direct students to describe what the team has already accomplished, what it is doing now, and what it will do in the future. Have students exchange memos and circle all the helping verbs.

CHAPTER 15 LESSON PLANNER
Adjectives and Adverbs

Use the Online Lesson Planner at www.phwritingcoach.com to customize your instructional plan for an integrated Language Arts curriculum.

DAY 1 15.1 Adjectives

"What Do You Notice?" **Objectives:** Identify, use, and understand adjectives, including ▪ articles	**INSTRUCTION AND PRACTICE** **Student Edition** pp. 325–330

DAY 2 15.1 Adjectives *(continued)*

Objectives: Identify, use, and understand adjectives, including ▪ proper adjectives ▪ nouns used as adjectives ▪ compound adjectives	**INSTRUCTION AND PRACTICE** **Student Edition** pp. 331–333

DAY 3 15.1 Adjectives *(continued)*

Objectives: Identify, use, and understand adjectives, including ▪ pronouns used as adjectives ▪ possessive nouns and pronouns as adjectives ▪ demonstrative adjectives ▪ interrogative adjectives ▪ indefinite adjectives	**INSTRUCTION AND PRACTICE** **Student Edition** pp.334–337 **Test Warm-Up** p. 338

DAY 4 15.2 Adverbs

Objectives: Identify, use, and understand adverbs, including ▪ adverbs that modify verbs ▪ adverbs that modify adjectives ▪ adverbs that modify other adverbs ▪ finding adverbs in sentences ▪ adverb or adjective?	**INSTRUCTION AND PRACTICE** **Student Edition** pp. 339–344

Grammar Assessment

Grammar Coach:	Diagnostic Assessment	End-of-Chapter Assessment	Progress Monitoring
Personalized Instruction	Students take grammar diagnostic test online and are automatically assigned instruction and practice in areas where they need support.	Teacher uses **ExamView** to administer end-of-chapter assessment and remediation. Teachers may customize **ExamView** tests or use the ones provided.	Teachers may use the **Test Warm-Ups** and the **Cumulative Reviews** in the student book or eText to check students' mastery of grammar skills. Students may also play **DimensionL** grammar video games to test their grammar skills.
Teacher-Directed Instruction	Teacher administers the diagnostic test and determines focus of instruction and practice.		

Alternate Pacing Plans

- **Block Scheduling** Each day in the Lesson Planner represents a 40–50 minute block. Teachers using block scheduling may combine days to revise pacing to meet their classroom needs.
- **Accelerated Lesson Planning** Combine instructional days, focusing on concepts called out by students' diagnostic test results.
- **Integrated Language Arts Curriculum** Use the instruction and practice in this chapter to provide reinforcement, remediation, or extension of grammar concepts taught in your literature curriculum.

Links to Prentice Hall *LITERATURE*

- **Unit 2** Adjectives, p. 334; Adverbs, p. 360

www.phwritingcoach.com

Grammar Assessment and Practice

Chapter diagnostic tests assess students' skills and assign instruction and practice.

DimensionL Video Games

Fast-paced interactive video games challenge students' mastery of grammar.

Lesson Planner continues on next page

> *"Adverbs do just what they promise—they add to the verb. (She walked briskly), but let's not forget to teach students that adverbs can also modify adjectives (He flexed enormously large muscles) and other adverbs (She spoke quite slowly). Teaching students the various uses of adverbs adds to the sophistication of their writing."*
>
> **—Kelly Gallagher**

Differentiated Instruction

Differentiated Instruction Boxes in this Teacher's Edition address these student populations:

- Below-Level Students
- Above-Level Students
- Gifted and Talented Students
- Special Needs Students
- English Language Learners
- Spanish Speaking Students

In addition, for further enrichment, see the **Extension** features.

Grammar Ground Rule: Make It Specific!

Model with Students

In this chapter, making it specific means choosing **adjectives** and **adverbs** carefully. Explain to students that sometimes they may think of modifiers as decoration for their sentences. But modifiers are really language tools that will allow them to craft sentences that express just about anything they can think.

Say: The difference between giving a piece of information and really communicating often lies with the adjectives and adverbs you choose. I could write, for example, *The cat came into the yard.* This sentence just gives you a piece of information. Or I could write, *The hungry cat came fearfully into my yard.*" The second sentence communicates an image and an emotion, along with the information, because it is specific.

Write this sentence on the board: *The boy ran across the grass.* Have students come up with modifiers that could make that sentence specific and say the new sentence. For example, *The joyful boy walked quickly across the soft, green grass. The sad boy walked slowly across the dry grass.*

Small Group Activity – Finding Adjectives and Adverbs

Have students form groups to find one short story or poem and one newspaper article. Ask the groups to compare the kinds of adjectives and adverbs they find in the two kinds of writing. Their discussion should answer these questions:

- Does this modifier create an image or communicate an emotion?
- Does this modifier add more information to the sentence?
- Does the modifier make the sentence more specific?

Have a member of each group present their conclusions to the class and give one good example of modifier usage that follows this grammar ground rule: Make it specific.

Grammar Ground Rules

1. Keep it clear.
2. Make them agree.
3. Make it specific.
4. Dot your *i*'s and cross your *t*'s.
5. Make it active.

ADJECTIVES *and* ADVERBS

Enrich your descriptions of people, places, and events by using adjectives and adverbs in your writing.

CHAPTER 15

WRITE GUY *Jeff Anderson, M.Ed.*

WHAT DO YOU NOTICE?

Spot the adjectives and adverbs as you zoom in on these sentences from the story "Zoo" by Edward Hoch.

MENTOR TEXT

> The citizens of Earth clustered around as Professor Hugo's crew quickly collected the waiting dollars, and soon the good Professor himself made an appearance, wearing his many-colored rainbow cape and top hat.

Now, ask yourself the following questions:

- Which adverb modifies the verb *collected*?
- Which adjectives does the author use to describe the cape?

The adverb *quickly* modifies the verb *collected*, creating an image of the speed at which the crew gathered the money. The author uses the adjectives *many-colored* and *rainbow* to modify the noun *cape*. Words such as *rainbow*, which are usually used as nouns, can also be used as adjectives.

Grammar for Writers Use adjectives and adverbs to enrich your writing, but vary how you use them. For example, if you place several adjectives in a row before a noun in one sentence, use fewer or no adjectives in the next sentence.

Which adjective would you use to describe my bike? Speedy or quick?
I would go with flat. Look at your tires!

325

ADJECTIVES *and* ADVERBS

As students progress in their writing skills, it will be important for them to be able to apply the rules of grammar, usage, and mechanics to their own drafts. Use the *What Do You Notice?* feature to help them see effective conventions in the work of professional writers. Encourage students to incorporate proper voice, tense, and syntax as they edit their own writing.

Read the opening sentence aloud. Discuss how adjectives and adverbs make descriptions of persons, places, and things more vivid.

WRITE GUY *Jeff Anderson, M. Ed.*

WHAT DO YOU NOTICE?

When students have read the Mentor Text, **say:** As you may already know, adjectives are words that describe nouns and pronouns. Adverbs, on the other hand, can describe verbs, adjectives, or other adverbs. What are some adjectives used in these sentences? What are some adverbs? (Accept all correct responses.)

Have students finish reading the page. **Then, say:** What do you think this sentence would be like without the words, phrases, and clauses that function as adjectives and adverbs? Listen as I reread the sentence. **Reread this:** *The citizens clustered and the professor made an appearance.* How would you describe this sentence now? (**Possible response:** The sentence is not as interesting. It does not provide as much information without adjectives and adverbs.)

Guide students in understanding how adjectives and adverbs provide information.

Grammar for Writers: Voice

Help students understand that adverbs and adjectives enrich their writing by describing and modifying other types of words. They should be careful, however, not to overuse adjectives or adverbs. They should also vary how they use them. The rules on these pages will help students use adjectives and adverbs more effectively in their writing and speaking.

15.1 Adjectives

Lesson Objectives

1. Recognize and identify various types of adjectives.
2. Recognize and identify various types of articles.
3. Demonstrate how to use various types of adjectives and articles in writing and speaking.

Lead a discussion about the ways that people use adjectives to make nouns more specific and detailed. Adjectives make written and spoken statements clearer and more vivid.

RULE 15.1.1 Read aloud the rule and then have students repeat the line with you.

Say: Nouns by themselves are kind of plain. Think of the word *coat.* What words can we use to describe *coat*? **(Possible responses:** blue, long, warm) Write all correct responses on the board. Now, let's use these adjectives together to describe a coat. Use student responses to create different descriptions of a coat. Adjectives describe, or modify, the noun and make it more vivid and specific.

Work with students to identify the adjectives in this group: *shoe, rough, sharp, blue, pony.* Have students tell why each adjective is an adjective.

Write several nouns on the board: *cat, house, school.* Have student pairs choose a noun and brainstorm for examples of different adjectives that describe it. Then, make sentences using different adjectives. Have pairs share their examples with the group.

15.1 Adjectives

Adjectives are words that make language come alive by adding description or information.

www.phwritingcoach.com

Grammar Tutorials
Brush up on your Grammar skills with these animated videos.

Grammar Practice
Practice your grammar skills with Writing Coach Online.

Grammar Games
Test your knowledge of grammar in this fast-paced interactive video game.

Adjectives help make nouns more specific. For example, *car* is a general word, but a *red two-door car* is more specific. Adjectives such as *red* and *two-door* make nouns and pronouns clearer and more vivid.

RULE 15.1.1 An **adjective** is a word that describes a noun or pronoun.

Adjectives are often called *modifiers,* because they modify, or change, the meaning of a noun or pronoun. You can use more than one adjective to modify a noun or pronoun. Notice how *shoes* is modified by each set of adjectives below.

EXAMPLES **old-fashioned** shoes

new red shoes

children's dress shoes

old brown shoes

Adjectives answer several questions about nouns and pronouns. They tell *What kind? Which one? How many?* or *How much?* Numeral adjectives, such as *eleven,* tell exactly how many. In the chart below, notice how adjectives answer these questions.

WHAT KIND?	WHICH ONE?	HOW MANY?	HOW MUCH?
stone house	this judge	two tulips	no time
white paper	each answer	several roses	enough apples
serious argument	those sisters	both brothers	many hobbies
colorful shirts	that student	one car	some birds

WRITING COACH Online

www.phwritingcoach.com

Diagnostic and Instruction
Diagnostic test assesses students' instructional needs. Lessons and practice are assigned based on results.

Additional Practice
- Grammar Tutorials—Animated videos reinforce key grammar skills.
- Grammar Practice—Targeted practice addresses individual needs.
- ExamView—Teachers customize their grammar practice and tests.
- Grammar Games—Interactive video games make grammar fun.

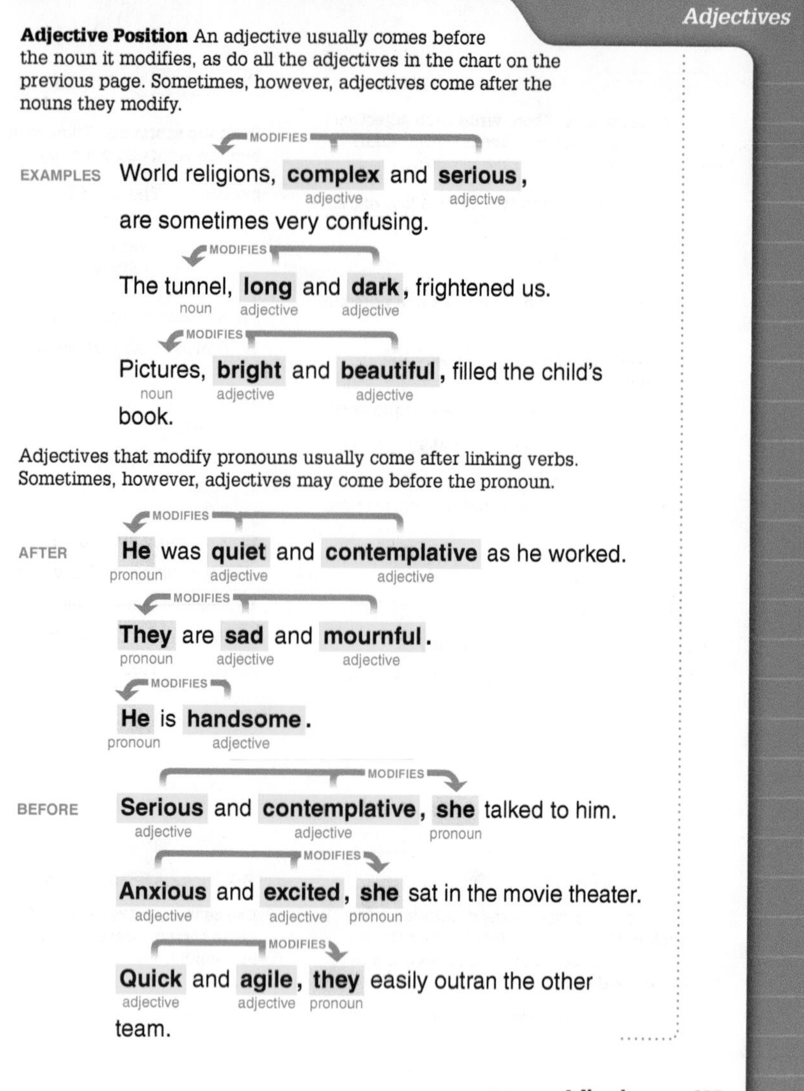

Adjective Position An adjective usually comes before the noun it modifies, as do all the adjectives in the chart on the previous page. Sometimes, however, adjectives come after the nouns they modify.

EXAMPLES World religions, **complex** (adjective) and **serious** (adjective), are sometimes very confusing.

The tunnel (noun), **long** (adjective) and **dark** (adjective), frightened us.

Pictures (noun), **bright** (adjective) and **beautiful** (adjective), filled the child's book.

Adjectives that modify pronouns usually come after linking verbs. Sometimes, however, adjectives may come before the pronoun.

AFTER **He** (pronoun) was **quiet** (adjective) and **contemplative** (adjective) as he worked.

They (pronoun) are **sad** (adjective) and **mournful** (adjective).

He (pronoun) is **handsome** (adjective).

BEFORE **Serious** (adjective) and **contemplative** (adjective), **she** (pronoun) talked to him.

Anxious (adjective) and **excited** (adjective), **she** (pronoun) sat in the movie theater.

Quick (adjective) and **agile** (adjective), **they** (pronoun) easily outran the other team.

See Practice 15.1A
See Practice 15.1B

Write this sentence on the board and read it aloud: *I wore old red tennis shoes.* Ask students to identify the adjectives in the sentence and the word they modify. Then, explain that adjectives usually come before the noun they modify but sometimes come after.

Write this sentence on the board: *Snow, soft and white, covered the ground.* Ask students to identify the adjectives. **Ask:** What word do these adjectives modify? (snow) Explain that adjectives that describe the subject of a sentence often come after linking verbs. Ask students to fill in the blank in these sentences with appropriate adjectives: *Rene is really ______ today. Joe's bike was ______ after he rode it through the mud.*

Point out that adjectives can describe pronouns, too. Adjectives can come before or after pronouns, just as they can with nouns.

Have student pairs use the example sentences on page 327 as models to write sentences using adjectives that modify nouns and pronouns. Some sentences should feature the adjective before the noun or pronoun, and others should feature the adjective after the noun or pronoun. Invite students to read their best sentence aloud.

Teacher Tip

If students have difficulty understanding the placement of adjectives, organize several students into a small group. Assign each group member a word. One student should be a noun or pronoun. The other students should be adjectives. These students can place themselves in front of or behind the other student, depending on which placement makes the most sense. When students are satisfied with their placement, have them brainstorm for a complete sentence.

Working with ELLs ELL Sheltered Instruction: Cognitive

Help students demonstrate comprehension of increasingly complex English by responding to questions about a familiar text they are reading or have read. Guide them in using adjectives in their responses.

Beginning Ask students two simple questions about the selection they read. Before they answer, review adjectives they might use in their responses, such as *funny* and *sad*. Have students respond orally using the adjectives they choose.

Intermediate Write *funny, sad, exciting, several,* and *enough* on the board. Have students say each word aloud. Then, ask students questions about the selection they read and have students respond orally, speaking in complete sentences and using one or more of the words listed on the board.

Advanced Have each student write two questions about the text he or she read using these ideas as a base: *What kind? Which one? How many? How much?* Then, have partners answer the questions using adjectives, supporting their answers with details from the selection.

Advanced High Have students complete the Advanced activity. Then, challenge them to replace the adjectives in their answers with more precise synonyms, consulting a thesaurus and a dictionary.

PRACTICE 15.1A

1. Some—How many?
daily—What kind?
personal—What kind?
2. sudden—What kind?
sleeping—What kind?
3. five—How many?
antique—What kind?
4. Regular—What kind?
good—What kind?
5. This—Which one?
more—How much?
6. two—How many?
unmapped—What kind?
7. enough—How much?
that—Which one?
whole—How much?
8. Several—How many?
electric—What kind?
9. any—How much?
that—Which one?
10. This—Which one?
free—What kind?
legal—What kind?

PRACTICE 15.1B

11. volcanic, eruption
12. tall, model
elegant, model
13. tiny, lizard
thick, undergrowth
14. These, books
heavy, books
15. much, change
16. elderly, man
shady, porch
17. any, rain
two, weeks
18. fire, department
new, truck
ladder, truck
19. Thai, restaurant
first, time
20. two, miles
every, day

PRACTICE 15.1A Identifying Adjectives

Read the sentences. Then, write each adjective and list the question it answers. (*What kind? Which one? How many? How much?*)

EXAMPLE We watched two movies last night.
ANSWER *two— How many?*
last— Which one?

1. Some people write daily entries in a personal journal.
2. A sudden clap of thunder startled the sleeping dogs.
3. I'll give you five dollars for the antique bottle.
4. Regular exercise contributes to good health.
5. This assignment will take more time.
6. The two explorers ventured into unmapped territory.
7. There is not enough space in that room for the whole group.
8. Several electric cars were on display.
9. Is there any water in that cooler?
10. This organization provides free legal help.

PRACTICE 15.1B Identifying Adjectives and Words They Modify

Read the sentences. Then, write the adjectives and the words they modify.

EXAMPLE The timid kitten hid from the noisy visitors.
ANSWER *timid, kitten*
noisy, visitors

11. A volcanic eruption frightened the islanders.
12. A model, tall and elegant, strode along the runway.
13. A tiny lizard scurried through the thick undergrowth.
14. These books are heavy!
15. I don't have much change, but I can give you a dollar.
16. An elderly man sat on the shady porch.
17. We have not had any rain for two weeks.
18. The fire department has a new ladder truck.
19. We ate at a Thai restaurant for the first time.
20. Antonio runs two miles every day.

SPEAKING APPLICATION

With a partner, take turns describing your lunch in the cafeteria. Your partner should listen for and name the adjectives and the questions they answer.

WRITING APPLICATION

Use sentences 12, 14, and 19 as models, and write three sentences with different adjectives and nouns.

SPEAKING APPLICATION

Have partners take turns identifying their adjectives' positions either before or after the nouns or pronouns they modify.

WRITING APPLICATION

Have students write the questions each adjective answers. (What kind? Which one? How many? How much?)

Quick-Write Extension

To help students synthesize and apply what they have learned about adjectives, have them write brief travel brochures for a real or imaginary place. Direct students to use adjectives to help persuade readers to visit the destination. Students may add pictures, but they must also use adjectives to help readers create mental pictures. Have students exchange brochures and identify the adjectives, commenting on their persuasiveness.

Articles

Three frequently used adjectives are the words *a, an,* and *the.* They are called **articles.** Articles can be **definite** or **indefinite.** Both types indicate that a noun will soon follow.

RULE 15.1.2

***The* is a definite article. It points to a specific person, place, thing, or idea. *A* and *an* are indefinite articles. They point to any member of a group of similar people, places, things, or ideas.**

DEFINITE Dr. Kashkin is **the** one to call. (a specific person)
Go into **the** restaurant. (a specific place)
I want to learn **the** song. (a specific thing)

INDEFINITE I want to see **a** movie. (any movie)
Please take **an** application. (any application)
You should ask **a** coach for advice. (any coach)

A is used before consonant sounds. *An* is used before vowel sounds. You choose between *a* and *an* based on sound. Some letters are tricky. The letter *h,* a consonant, may sound like either a consonant or a vowel. The letters *o* and *u* are vowels, but they may sometimes sound like consonants.

USING *A* AND *AN*	
A WITH CONSONANT SOUNDS	*AN* WITH VOWEL SOUNDS
a pink dress	an endangered lion
a happy memory (*h* sound)	an honest president (no *h* sound)
a one-person chair (*w* sound)	an old book (*o* sound)
a union worker (*y* sound)	an uncle (*u* sound)
a truck	an odd shoe
a banana	an apple
a unicorn (*y* sound)	an opponent

See Practice 15.1C

Articles

Explain that the words *a, an,* and *the* are special kinds of adjectives called articles. There are two types of articles: definite and indefinite.

RULE 15.1.2 Read aloud the rule and then have students repeat the lines with you.

Use a Think Aloud as part of a gradual release progression.

Think Aloud

Say: It's easy to remember when to use *a, an,* and *the.* The first thing **I ask myself** is whether the article is pointing to a specific person, place, thing, or idea. If the answer is yes, then I use *the.* Consider this sentence: *I'll meet you at the mall. The* refers to a specific place—a particular mall that I sometimes go to. Now, what happens if the article is not pointing to a specific person, place, thing, or idea? Consider this sentence: *I think I'll sit in a chair. A chair* in this case does not refer to a specific chair. I'll be satisfied with whatever chair is handy.

Why did I use *a* instead of *an*? *Chair* starts with a consonant sound. Use the indefinite article *a* with words beginning with a consonant sound. Use *an* with words beginning with a vowel sound.

Write this sentence on the board: *Would you hand me ____ apple.* **Work with students** to complete the sentence using the correct definite and indefinite articles.

Have student pairs brainstorm for and construct three sentences using *a, an,* and *the.* Invite pairs to share their sentences with the group.

Working with ELLs ELL Sheltered Instruction: Cognitive

As students study adjectives, guide them to demonstrate comprehension of increasingly complex English by taking notes. Provide students with copy of a passage that includes many adjectives. Then:

Beginning Read the passage aloud as students follow along. Take notes in a cluster diagram about the main ideas. Include adjectives that describe events or characters. Students should copy your notes. Then, ask students simple questions about the text as they use their notes to respond.

Intermediate Have partners read the passage aloud and complete a main idea and details chart. Students should include adjectives in their notes. Have students ask each other questions to monitor comprehension: *What is the passage mainly about? What adjectives did you use to describe the events/characters/ideas?*

Advanced Have students read the passage and complete a main ideas and details chart that includes adjectives. Have students exchange charts and discuss similarities and differences in their work.

Advanced High Have students read the passage, taking notes about the adjectives used. Then, have students identify which question—*what kind, which one, how many, how much*—each adjective answers. Challenge students to use the adjectives to write a paragraph summarizing the passage.

PRACTICE 15.1C

1. the—definite
2. a—indefinite
an—indefinite
3. the—definite
4. the—definite
5. The—definite
the—definite
6. an—indefinite
the—definite
7. the—definite
the—definite
8. a—indefinite
the—definite
9. an—indefinite
10. The—definite
a—indefinite

SPEAKING APPLICATION

Have partners explain whether the definite and indefinite articles were correctly used and why.

WRITING APPLICATION

Have students clarify how they determined whether each article was definite or indefinite and explain how they determined the proper use of *a* and *an*.

PRACTICE 15.1C Identifying Definite and Indefinite Articles

Read the sentences. Then, write the articles and label them *definite* or *indefinite*.

EXAMPLE The travelers boarded a plane to Madrid.

ANSWER *the— definite*
a— indefinite

1. I can't wait to meet the new director.
2. A minute can sometimes seem like an hour.
3. Do you have the time?
4. Mr. Chu was elected to the city council.
5. The students dutifully read the novel.
6. There is an old, rundown car in the driveway.
7. We can spend the afternoon at the beach.
8. A mysterious stranger appeared on the scene.
9. This is an interesting dilemma.
10. The storm caused a huge traffic jam.

SPEAKING APPLICATION

With a partner, take turns describing an item without naming it. Your partner should guess what the item is and name at least five definite and indefinite articles you use.

WRITING APPLICATION

Use sentences 2, 8, and 10 as models, and write three sentences in which you use definite and indefinite articles. Circle the articles and label them *definite* or *indefinite*.

Working with ELLs

ELL **Sheltered Instruction:** Metacognitive

Scaffold the Speaking Application, and have students take notes to demonstrate listening comprehension of increasingly complex spoken English by following directions. Have them monitor their comprehension and seek clarification as needed.

Beginning Describe an item using simple phrases and gestures, but do not name it. Pause occasionally to ask students whether they understand and to encourage them to seek clarification. Repeat, guiding students to take notes in a cluster diagram. Finally, lead students in guessing the item.

Intermediate Have students take notes in a prediction chart as you describe an item without naming it. Have them work with a fluent partner to review your clues and guess the item. Guide them to monitor their understanding and to ask their partners to explain unfamiliar words.

Advanced Have partners take turns as one tells about an item without naming it while the other takes notes and then guesses the item. Suggest students monitor understanding by using the self-questioning technique: *Do I understand this clue?* They should seek clarification as needed.

Advanced High Have students complete the Advanced activity. Then, have them write a list of tips on how to clarify understanding of spoken language.

Using Proper Adjectives

A **proper adjective** begins with a capital letter. There are two types of proper adjectives.

A proper adjective is (1) a proper noun used as an adjective or (2) an adjective formed from a proper noun.

A proper noun used as an adjective does *not* change its form. It is merely placed in front of another noun.

PROPER NOUNS	USED AS PROPER ADJECTIVES
Thursday	Thursday afternoon (*Which* afternoon?)
Florida	Florida wetlands (*Which* wetlands?)
December	December weather (*What kind* of weather?)

When an adjective is formed from a proper noun, the proper noun will change its form. Notice that endings such as *-n, -ian,* or *-ese* have been added to the proper nouns in the chart below or the spelling has been changed.

PROPER NOUNS	PROPER ADJECTIVES FORMED FROM PROPER NOUNS
America	American history (*Which kind* of history?)
Japan	Japanese cities (*Which* cities?)
Norway	Norwegian legends (*Which* legends?)
Inca	Incan empire (*Which* empire?)
Florida	Floridian sunset (*Which* sunset?)

See Practice 15.1D

Using Proper Adjectives

Point out that proper adjectives are closely related to proper nouns. Like a proper noun, a proper adjective begins with a capital letter. Explain that there are two types of proper adjectives: proper nouns used directly as adjectives and adjectives formed from proper nouns. For example, in the name *Muir Woods, Woods* uses the proper noun *Muir* as an adjective. *Australian summer* forms an adjective from the proper noun *Australia.*

RULE 15.1.3 Read aloud the rule and then have students repeat the lines with you.

Use a Think Aloud as part of a gradual release progression.

Say: It's pretty easy to identify proper adjectives. **I look just** for adjectives that begin with capital letters. Consider this sentence: *Oh, the August heat is terrible!* I know that there are two adjectives in this sentence: *August* and *terrible. August* is capitalized because it is a proper noun. In this sentence, *August* is a proper noun used as an adjective to describe *heat.* Now consider this sentence: *I am learning how to cook Mexican food.* I know that *Mexican* is a proper adjective. It is capitalized. The ending *-an* has been added to the proper noun *Mexico. Mexican* is an adjective formed from a proper noun.

Guide students into making a list of proper adjectives that come from proper nouns, such as *South American, Dominican,* and *Canadian.*

Have student pairs brainstorm for and construct two sentences using proper adjectives. Have one sentence use a proper noun as an adjective and have the other sentence use an adjective formed from a proper noun. Invite partners to share their sentences with the group.

Differentiated Instruction

Strategy for Spanish Speakers

Students whose home language is Spanish may tend to have a proper adjective follow a noun by using it in a prepositional phrase—*the heat of August* rather than *the August heat.* Remind students that English proper adjectives precede the noun, and like proper nouns, proper adjectives are always capitalized. Elicit different nouns from students and record the nouns on the board. Have students copy them onto pieces of paper. Help students think of proper adjectives and have them write these adjectives on sticky notes. On the board, write a few examples of proper adjectives followed by nouns. Then, have students work in pairs to match the proper adjective with a noun by sticking it next to the noun. Have pairs construct sentences with each proper adjective and noun pair.

Using Nouns as Adjectives

Write these phrases on the board: *a baseball player, the toy store, a car window, a television screen.* Point out to students that nouns can sometimes be used as adjectives. In these examples, *baseball, toy, car,* and *television* are all nouns that are used as adjectives. A noun used as an adjective comes directly before another noun. It answers the question *What kind?* or *Which one?*

Using the phrases you wrote on the board, work with students to ask the questions *What kind?* or *Which one?* to determine how the noun is being used as an adjective.

Using Compound Adjectives

Point out that compound adjectives are often hyphenated words, but sometimes they are combined words.

RULE 15.1.4 Read aloud the rule and then have students repeat the line with you.

Use a Think Aloud as part of a gradual release progression.

Say: I know that most compound adjectives are hyphenated words. A *well-known actress, snow-covered mountains,* and a *full-time job* are a few examples. But some compound adjectives are combined words, such as *heartbreaking news.* If I'm not sure whether a compound adjective is supposed to be hyphenated, I look it up in a dictionary to make sure.

Work with students to generate a list of compound adjectives.

Have student pairs find the words in a dictionary to check whether the words are hyphenated or combined. Invite students to make a sentence using one of the words and share it with the group.

Teacher Tip

Promote student use of the dictionary by having word contests. Say a word aloud and have students compete to be the first one to find it in the dictionary. Try to group students together who are reading at a similar level.

Using Nouns as Adjectives

Nouns can sometimes be used as adjectives. A noun used as an adjective usually comes directly before another noun and answers the question *What kind?* or *Which one?*

NOUNS	USED AS ADJECTIVES
shoe	a shoe salesperson (*What kind* of salesperson?)
waterfowl	the waterfowl refuge (*Which* refuge?)
court	a court date (*What kind* of date?)
morning	a morning appointment (*What kind* of appointment?)

Using Compound Adjectives

Adjectives, like nouns, can be compound.

RULE 15.1.4

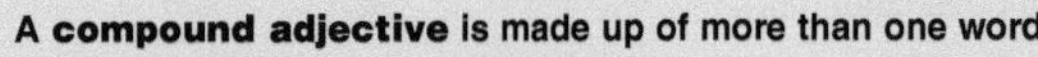

A compound adjective is made up of more than one word.

Most **compound adjectives** are written as hyphenated words. Some are written as combined words, as in "a *runaway* horse." If you are unsure about how to write a compound adjective, look up the word in a dictionary.

HYPHENATED	COMBINED
a well-known actress	a featherweight boxer
a full-time job	a freshwater lake
snow-covered mountains	a sideways glance
one-sided opinions	heartbreaking news
so-called experts	a nearsighted witness

See Practice 15.1E

PRACTICE 15.1D Using Proper Adjectives

Read the sentences. Then, rewrite each sentence to include a proper adjective before the underlined noun.

EXAMPLE My favorite subject is history.

ANSWER *My favorite subject is American history.*

1. Camels are used for travel in the desert.
2. Ana is interested in geography.
3. Rob really enjoys food.
4. The language is easy to learn.
5. We will wear traditional clothing for the play.
6. Bruce wants to study architecture.
7. The Martins visited the ruins on their trip.
8. Ashley dresses in style.
9. When does your class meet?
10. Trina has a pen pal.

PRACTICE 15.1E Recognizing Nouns Used as Adjectives

Read the sentences. Write the noun, proper noun, or compound noun used as an adjective. Then, write the noun that the adjective modifies.

EXAMPLE Do you like my new gym clothes?

ANSWER *gym, clothes*

11. Did you get my text message?
12. Elena doesn't like the July heat.
13. Mr. Preston is an expert on shore birds.
14. You may carry the baseball bats.
15. Spencer would like to be an airplane mechanic.
16. Tomorrow, we will follow our usual Friday schedule.
17. I would like to know what the weekend weather will be.
18. Scott spends his free time playing video games.
19. I'll meet you at the tennis court at 3:00.
20. Will you be going to the Valentine's Day dance?

SPEAKING APPLICATION

With a partner, take turns describing a trip you'd like to take. Your partner should listen for and name the nouns used as adjectives and proper adjectives you use.

WRITING APPLICATION

Write three sentences and include one of the following in each: a noun used as an adjective, a proper noun used as an adjective, or a proper adjective.

PRACTICE 15.1D

Answers will vary. Sample answers:

1. Camels are used for travel in the Arabian desert.
2. Ana is interested in European geography.
3. Rob really enjoys Chinese food.
4. The Spanish language is easy to learn.
5. We will wear traditional Korean clothing for the play.
6. Bruce wants to study Roman architecture.
7. The Martins visited the Grecian ruins on their trip.
8. Ashley dresses in Parisian style.
9. When does your Russian class meet?
10. Trina has a Turkish pen pal.

PRACTICE 15.1E

11. text, message
12. July, heat
13. shore, birds
14. baseball, bats
15. airplane, mechanic
16. Friday, schedule
17. weekend, weather
18. video, games
19. tennis, court
20. Valentine's Day, dance

SPEAKING APPLICATION

Have partners identify which questions the proper adjectives and nouns as adjectives answer. (What kind? Which one?) Discuss whether any compound adjectives were used.

WRITING APPLICATION

Assign partners, and have students circle and identify the proper adjectives and nouns as adjectives in each other's sentences.

Working with ELLs

ELL Sheltered Instruction: Cognitive

Scaffold the Speaking Application, and help students understand information and make inferences about implicit ideas in increasingly complex spoken language.

Beginning Using mime and visuals, describe a trip that you would like to take. Hint at your feelings about the trip without naming them. Then, ask, *Where do I want to go?* and *How do you think I feel about the trip?*

Intermediate Have students working in groups take turns describing a trip they would like to take. Group members should assist each other in expressing ideas. After each member contributes, listeners should answer these questions: *Where does he/she want to go? Based on what he/she has said, why do you think he/she wants to go?*

Advanced Have student pairs take turns describing a trip they would like to take. Instruct them to hint at their reasons for the trip without expressing them directly. Listeners should take notes, identifying proper adjectives, recording information, and making inferences about implied motives.

Advanced High Have student pairs complete the Advanced activity. To extend the activity, have them write about each other's trips as journal entries.

Using Pronouns as Adjectives

Discuss the fact that some words, such as *this, which,* and *that,* can be used as either pronouns or adjectives.

RULE 15.1.5 Read aloud the rule and then have students repeat the line with you.

Say: Consider these sentences: *New students sit on this side of the classroom. Which students are new?* **Ask:** Which words are pronouns? (**Possible responses:** ***this*** **and** ***which***) What word does each pronoun modify? (***This*** **modifies** ***side***; ***which*** **modifies** ***students***.) In both sentences the pronoun becomes an adjective because it modifies a noun.

Using Possessive Nouns and Pronouns as Adjectives

Discuss how possessive personal pronouns function as adjectives. Read aloud the examples and explanations. Then, have students use the examples as models to write their own sentences.

Note About Possessive Nouns

Discuss the examples on page 334. Have student pairs make sentences using possessive nouns and pronouns as adjectives. Students should identify whether each sentence features a possessive pronoun or possessive noun as an adjective. If the sentence uses a possessive pronoun as an adjective, have students circle the word modified by the pronoun and underline the pronoun's antecedent (if it is stated in the sentence). If the sentence uses a possessive noun as an adjective, have students circle the noun the possessive noun modifies. Invite partners to share their sentences with the group.

Using Pronouns as Adjectives

Pronouns, like nouns, can sometimes be used as adjectives.

A pronoun becomes an adjective if it modifies a noun.

EXAMPLES We see the new puppies on **this** side of the porch.

Which puppies are the females?

In the first example, the demonstrative pronoun *this* modifies *side,* and in the second example, the interrogative pronoun *which* modifies *puppies.*

Using Possessive Nouns and Pronouns as Adjectives

The following personal pronouns are often **possessive adjectives:** *my, your, her, his, its, our,* and *their.* They are adjectives because they come before nouns and answer the question *Which one?* They are pronouns because they have antecedents.

EXAMPLES The **puppies** wagged **their** tails.

The **school** wants to improve **its** library.

In the first example, *their* is an adjective because it modifies *tails.* At the same time, it is a pronoun because it refers to the antecedent *puppies.*

In the second example, *its* is an adjective because it modifies *library.* The word *its* is also a pronoun because it refers to the antecedent *school.*

Note About Possessive Nouns Possessive nouns function as adjectives when they modify a noun.

EXAMPLES The field is on the **Wongs'** property.

My **dog's** tail wags when I come home.

See Practice 15.1F
See Practice 15.1G

Differentiated Instruction

RTI Strategy for Below-Level Students Students may find it helpful to create a chart of the ways in which different types of words can be used as adjectives. Have students create a four-column chart and label these headings: *Pronouns as Adjectives, Nouns as Adjectives, Possessive Nouns as Adjectives, Possessive Pronouns as Adjectives*. Then, have students list at least one example of a word used as an adjective for each column. Have students use words from their chart to write example sentences and share them with others. Encourage students to keep their charts handy and refer to them when necessary.

PRE-AP Enrichment for Above-Level Students Remind students that different types of words are frequently used as adjectives. Have students create an adjectives "catalogue" that provides examples of pronouns, nouns, and possessive nouns and pronouns used as adjectives. Examples should be collected from books, magazines, or Web sites. Students can illustrate their examples with photographs clipped from magazines or line drawings. Display student catalogues in the classroom.

Using Demonstrative Adjectives

This, that, these, and *those*—the four demonstrative pronouns—can also be **demonstrative adjectives.**

PRONOUN We heard **that**.

ADJECTIVE **That** hive is home to many bees.

PRONOUN Why do you want **these**?

ADJECTIVE **These** puppies are searching for a chew toy.

Using Interrogative Adjectives

Which, what, and *whose*—three of the interrogative pronouns—can be **interrogative adjectives.**

PRONOUN **Which** do you think she will like?

ADJECTIVE **Which** puppy do you think he will buy?

PRONOUN **Whose** is that?

ADJECTIVE **Whose** cat can that be?

Using Indefinite Adjectives

A number of indefinite pronouns—*both, few, many, each, most,* and *all,* among others—can also be used as **indefinite adjectives.**

PRONOUN I made one of **each**.

ADJECTIVE **Each** member has a vote.

PRONOUN I don't have **any**.

ADJECTIVE Wasn't there **any** soup left?

See Practice 15.1H
See Practice 15.1I

Using Demonstrative Adjectives

Write the four demonstrative pronouns—*this, that, these,* and *those*—on the board. Explain that these words can be used as either demonstrative pronouns or demonstrative adjectives. When one of these words does not modify a noun, it is a demonstrative pronoun, as in *I like that.* Point out that a noun does not follow *that,* so *that* is not a modifier, or adjective, but rather a pronoun. On the other hand, when *this, that, these,* or *those* precedes a noun and modifies it, the word is a demonstrative adjective. Give this example: *I like those kinds of candies.*

Have student pairs use the example sentences on page 335 as models to make two sentences. One sentence should use a demonstrative pronoun, and the other should use a demonstrative adjective. Have partners share their sentences with the group. Challenge other students to identify the sentence using a demonstrative pronoun and the sentence using a demonstrative adjective.

Using Interrogative Adjectives

Write *which, what,* and *whose* on the board. Explain that these interrogative pronouns can also be used as interrogative adjectives. Give this example: *Which assignments are missing?* Explain that *which* is an interrogative adjective because it modifies the noun *assignments.*

Call on individual students and ask them to use an interrogative pronoun or an interrogative adjective in a sentence.

Using Indefinite Adjectives

Draw students' attention to the text that states that a number of indefinite pronouns can be used as indefinite adjectives. Explain that an indefinite adjective modifies a noun. Have students point to the noun modified in the example sentences in the book. Then, have students write sentences using *each* and *any* as indefinite pronouns. Have them repeat the exercise using the words as indefinite adjectives.

PRACTICE 15.1F

1. your
2. doctor's
3. her, cat's
4. Our, its
5. bicycle's
6. his
7. their
8. team's
9. our
10. Maria's

PRACTICE 15.1G

Answers will vary. Sample answers:

11. his
12. Her
13. its
14. his
15. our
16. her
17. their
18. his
19. its
20. his

SPEAKING APPLICATION

Have partners take turns describing a cafeteria lunch (or something else in the school) without using adjectives. Then, students should use adjectives in the description and discuss their effectiveness.

WRITING APPLICATION

Have students underline and identify any possessive nouns and pronouns used as adjectives in their paragraphs.

PRACTICE 15.1F Recognizing Possessive Nouns and Pronouns Used as Adjectives

Read the sentences. Then, write the possessive noun or pronoun used as an adjective in each sentence. Some sentences have more than one answer.

EXAMPLE Ted's canoe almost tipped over.
ANSWER *Ted's*

1. Chelsea would like a piece of your cake.
2. The doctor's waiting room was crowded.
3. Sasha accidentally stepped on her cat's tail.
4. Our class has its own Web page.
5. The bicycle's tires need air.
6. Harry removed his boots when he came inside.
7. The children came in right away when their mother called them.
8. The team's trophies are in the display case.
9. We had our pictures taken for the yearbook.
10. Mrs. Palumbo buys fresh bread at Maria's bakery.

PRACTICE 15.1G Using Possessive Nouns and Pronouns Used as Adjectives

Read the sentences. Then, rewrite each sentence, completing it with a possessive noun or pronoun used as an adjective.

EXAMPLE John's dog has a mind of ____ own.
ANSWER *its*

11. Marco's hard work resulted in ____ success.
12. ____ dress has flowers around its hem.
13. The team's new black and gold uniforms were ____ pride and joy.
14. Ben's grandparents offered to pay for ____ education.
15. After dinner, I took ____ leftovers back to my house.
16. Mrs. Schaffer's computer is ____ link to the rest of the world.
17. My neighbors spend every Saturday in ____ garden.
18. Serena's concentration was broken by ____ bad music.
19. The city's aquarium feeds ____ fish only once a day.
20. On ____ trip, Luis bought a keychain for his brother.

SPEAKING APPLICATION

With a partner, take turns describing something that belongs to another person. Your partner should identify at least one possessive noun and one possessive pronoun used as an adjective.

WRITING APPLICATION

Write a paragraph in which you compare and contrast yourself with a real or imagined brother. Use possessive nouns and pronouns as adjectives to discuss your different tastes and hobbies.

PRACTICE 15.1H Supplying Demonstrative, Interrogative, and Indefinite Adjectives

Read the sentences. Then, write whether the underlined adjective is demonstrative, interrogative, or indefinite.

EXAMPLE Whose hamster is that running around the yard?

ANSWER *interrogative*

1. Which hamster belongs to the Garcia family?
2. These apples are my favorite.
3. Which apples do you prefer?
4. Some baseball players are switch hitters.
5. What kind of music do you like to listen to?
6. I like most types of music.
7. I didn't have any money left after I bought the book.
8. Is this book the best one in the series?
9. Casey and Samantha are friends with those girls.
10. Whose car should we take to the game?

PRACTICE 15.1I Identifying Demonstrative, Interrogative, and Indefinite Adjectives

Read the sentences. Then, write the adjective in each sentence and label it *demonstrative*, *interrogative*, or *indefinite*.

EXAMPLE Whose keys are these?

ANSWER *Whose— interrogative*

11. Several students lingered after the game.
12. What difference will five more minutes make?
13. I will turn fourteen this month.
14. Which movie are you going to see?
15. Here are some magazines for you to read.
16. That building is more than two hundred years old.
17. Most children have a natural curiosity.
18. Do you want that CD?
19. These chairs are so comfortable.
20. Whose umbrella did you borrow?

SPEAKING APPLICATION

With a partner, take turns asking each other questions about your favorite movie, television show, and song. The person asking the questions should use interrogative adjectives.

WRITING APPLICATION

Use sentences 11, 12, and 18 in Practice 15.1I as models, and write three sentences in which you use demonstrative, interrogative, and indefinite adjectives. Circle and label the adjectives.

PRACTICE 15.1H

1. interrogative
2. demonstrative
3. interrogative
4. indefinite
5. interrogative
6. indefinite
7. indefinite
8. demonstrative
9. demonstrative
10. interrogative

PRACTICE 15.1I

11. Several—indefinite
12. What—interrogative
13. this—demonstrative
14. Which—interrogative
15. some—indefinite
16. That—demonstrative
17. Most—indefinite
18. that—demonstrative
19. These—demonstrative
20. Whose—interrogative

SPEAKING APPLICATION

Have students explain how they identified the interrogative adjectives and distinguished them from demonstrative and indefinite adjectives.

WRITING APPLICATION

Have students share one of their sentences with the class, pointing out what type of adjective is used and what question it answers. (What kind? Which one?)

Test Warm-Up

1. **B** Change ***their*** to **our**
2. **F** Change ***Saturday*** to **Saturday's**
3. **D** which
4. **H** At the end of the sale, there weren't any items left.

Reteach

If students have not mastered these skills, review the content in Section 15.1 Adjectives.

1. Using Possessive Nouns and Pronouns as Adjectives 15.1.5
2. Using Possessive Nouns and Pronouns as Adjectives 15.1.5
3. Using Pronouns as Adjectives 15.1.5
4. Using Pronouns as Adjectives 15.1.5

Test Tip

Test questions about the meaning of a word or the grammatical function of a word in a sentence often require a student to understand the context of the sentence. Suggest to students that, if a test question asks about the meaning or function of a word in a sentence, they should reread both the target sentence and the sentence before it. For example, if a question asks for the antecedent of the pronoun *it,* students should reread the prior sentence as well as the target sentence to make sure that the antecedent wasn't introduced earlier in the passage.

Test Warm-Up

DIRECTIONS
Read the introduction and the passage that follows. Then, answer the questions to show that you can use and understand the function of adjectives in reading and writing.

Jada wrote this paragraph about the school bake sale. Read the paragraph and think about the changes you would suggest as a peer editor. When you finish reading, answer the questions that follow.

The Bake Sale

(1) Our school's bake sale took place last Saturday. (2) These sales raise money for their activities—and they're fun. (3) In this case, the money was going to the art department's supplies. (4) Each student who came had a great time. (5) Students, whose contributions to Saturday sale included pies, cakes, and brownies, showed their enthusiasm for art. (6) There were so many donations; I wasn't sure that student brought what. (7) At the end of the sale, there weren't no items left. (8) That sale was our most successful to date.

1 What change should be made in sentence 2?

- **A** Change ***These*** to **Which**
- **B** Change ***their*** to **our**
- **C** Change ***their*** to **my**
- **D** Change ***These*** to **That**

2 What change should be made in sentence 5?

- **F** Change ***Saturday*** to **Saturday's**
- **G** Change ***whose*** to **which**
- **H** Change ***Students*** to **Students'**
- **J** Change ***their*** to **her**

3 The meaning of sentence 6 can be clarified by changing the word ***that*** to —

- **A** what
- **B** whose
- **C** why
- **D** which

4 How should sentence 7 be revised?

- **F** At the end of the sale, there weren't each items left.
- **G** At the end of the sale, there weren't these items left.
- **H** At the end of the sale, there weren't any items left.
- **J** At the end of the sale, there weren't much items left.

15.2 Adverbs

Adverbs can modify three different parts of speech. They make the meaning of verbs, adjectives, or other adverbs more precise.

www.phwritingcoach.com

Grammar Tutorials
Brush up on your Grammar skills with these animated videos.

Grammar Practice
Practice your grammar skills with Writing Coach Online.

Grammar Games
Test your knowledge of grammar in this fast-paced interactive video game.

An adverb modifies a verb, an adjective, or another adverb.

RULE 15.2.1

Although adverbs may modify adjectives and other adverbs, they generally modify verbs.

Using Adverbs That Modify Verbs

Adverbs that modify verbs will answer one of these four questions: *Where? When? In what way? To what extent?* These adverbs are also known as *adverbs of place, adverbs of time, adverbs of manner,* and *adverbs of degree.*

ADVERBS THAT MODIFY VERBS

WHERE?	WHEN?	IN WHAT WAY?	TO WHAT EXTENT?
push upward	will leave soon	works carefully	hardly ate
fell there	comes daily	speaks well	really surprised
stay nearby	swims often	chews noisily	almost cried
go outside	exhibits yearly	acted willingly	partly finished
is here	report later	walk quietly	nearly won
jump away	come tomorrow	smiled happily	fully agree
drove down	went yesterday	moved gracefully	totally oppose

Negative adverbs, such as *not, never,* and *nowhere,* also modify verbs.

EXAMPLES Mark **never** (adverb) **arrived** (verb) at the meeting.

She **could** (verb) **not** (adverb) **understand** (verb) the essay.

The line of questioning **led** (verb) **nowhere** (adverb).

See Practice 15.2A

Differentiated Instruction

RTI Strategy for Special Needs Students

Students may have difficulty identifying adverbs and their modifiers. Make a list of verbs. Say one verb, such as *walk,* and act it out in various ways (fast, slow, hesitantly, heavily). Then, ask students to describe the verb. Say the word *clap*. Clap loudly and excitedly. Ask students to describe your clapping. Vary your style of clapping. Write their responses on the board and tell them that each response modifies, or describes, *clap*. Vary your style of clapping and repeat the exercise. Then, work with students to use one or more of their adverbs in sentences.

Have students work with a partner to make a list of adverbs that modify another verb from the board. Then, have each pair write a sentence using the verb and one of the adverbs from their list.

Lesson Objectives

1. Use adverbs to modify verbs, adjectives, and adverbs.
2. Distinguish between adverbs and adjectives.

Using Adverbs That Modify Verbs

Explain how adverbs can add detail to and enhance the meaning of verbs, adjectives, and other adverbs.

RULE 15.2.1 Read aloud the rule and then have students repeat the line with you.

Use a Think Aloud as part of a gradual release progression.

Say: Adverbs that modify verbs answer one of these questions: *Where? When? In what way? To what extent?* To figure out which word in a sentence is an adverb, **I ask myself** questions. Consider this sentence: *Sue smiled happily.* I think *happily* is the adverb. I can check this by asking myself *In what way did Sue smile?* She smiled *happily. Happily* is an adverb that modifies the verb *smiled.*

Work with students to help them understand that negative adverbs modify verbs.

Draw attention to the chart *Adverbs That Modify Verbs.* **Have partners** create one sentence for each of the four questions.

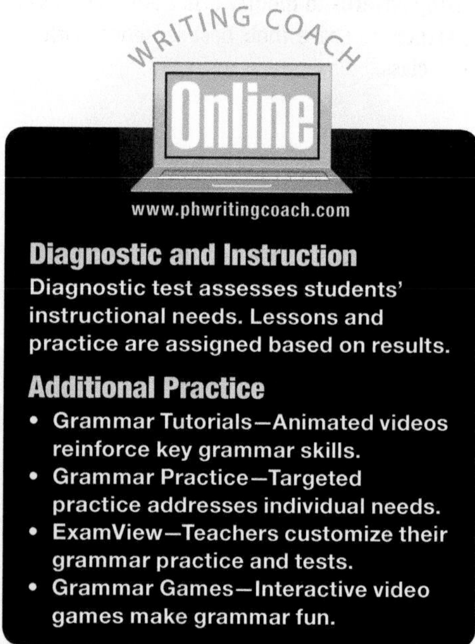

www.phwritingcoach.com

Diagnostic and Instruction
Diagnostic test assesses students' instructional needs. Lessons and practice are assigned based on results.

Additional Practice
- Grammar Tutorials—Animated videos reinforce key grammar skills.
- Grammar Practice—Targeted practice addresses individual needs.
- ExamView—Teachers customize their grammar practice and tests.
- Grammar Games—Interactive video games make grammar fun.

Using Adverbs That Modify Adjectives

Point out that adverbs that modify adjectives always answer the question *To what extent?* For example, in the sentence *I was too tired to read,* the word *too* is an adverb modifying the adjective *tired.*

RULE 15.2.2 Read aloud the rule and then have students repeat the lines with you.

Write this sentence on the board: *John was very upset.* **Then, ask:** How upset was John? In other words, to what extent was he upset? (very upset) Have students identify the adjective (upset) and the adverb (very).

Organize students into pairs. Have one student create a sentence using an adverb to modify an adjective. Have the other student ask a question using this sentence frame: *How ______ ?* Then, have the student identify the adjective and adverb.

Adverbs Modifying Other Adverbs

Discuss the distinction between an adverb and an adjective. Point out that adverbs can modify other adverbs as well as adjectives and that the adverb modifying another adverb can be identified by answering the question *To what extent?*

Have student pairs use the example sentences on page 340 as models to make sentences using adverbs to modify other adverbs. Invite partners to share their best sentence with the class.

Using Adverbs That Modify Adjectives

An adverb modifying an adjective answers only one question: *To what extent?*

When adverbs modify adjectives or adverbs, they answer the question *To what extent?*

ADVERBS THAT MODIFY ADJECTIVES	
very upset	extremely tall
definitely wrong	not hungry

EXAMPLE Beaches can be **very** **beautiful**.

The adverb *very* modifies the adjective *beautiful.*

EXAMPLE The speaker is **extremely** **tall**.

The adverb *extremely* modifies the adjective *tall.*

Adverbs Modifying Other Adverbs

When adverbs modify other adverbs, they again answer the question *To what extent?*

ADVERBS MODIFYING ADVERBS	
traveled less slowly	move very cautiously
lost too easily	lived almost happily

EXAMPLE Polar bears are **hardly** **ever** seen in this part of the park.

The adverb *hardly* modifies the adverb *ever.*

EXAMPLE When driving, I tire **too** **quickly**.

The adverb *too* modifies the adverb *quickly.*

See Practice 15.2B

Working with ELLs — ELL Sheltered Instruction: Cognitive

As students practice with adverbs on page 341, guide them to develop basic sight vocabulary used routinely in written classroom materials.

Beginning Write on the board these sight words from the Practice 15.2A directions: *where, when, what.* Read the words with students. As you use each word in an oral context sentence, call on a student to point to the word on the board. Add the words to a class list of sight words and review frequently.

Intermediate Have students read the words from the Beginning activity and review them with fluent partners. Extend by adding these sight words from the activities on page 341: *read, then, write.* Have a fluent partner write a sentence using each word, and have the Intermediate student read each sentence aloud.

Advanced Help students develop basic sight vocabulary by instructing them to use the words from the Beginning and Intermediate activities in sentences. Call on students to read their sentences aloud.

Advanced High Have students partner with Beginning or Intermediate students. Give the pairs a list of sight words to review. Remind students to coach their partners on pronunciation and provide clear context clues as needed.

PRACTICE 15.2A Identifying How Adverbs Modify Verbs

Read the sentences. Write the adverb in each sentence and list the question it answers. (*When? Where? In what way? To what extent?*)

EXAMPLE Danielle will leave tonight.

ANSWER *tonight— When?*

1. We have had good success lately.
2. Jared climbed the rock wall slowly and carefully.
3. We hardly noticed the storm brewing.
4. An unhappy customer complained loudly.
5. The coach almost tripped over the equipment on the floor.
6. Tiffany never thought it could happen to her.
7. I need your help now.
8. Ike quietly walked away from the disturbance.
9. Sophia was completely surprised by the remark.
10. Sherwin pulled ahead in the last lap.

PRACTICE 15.2B Recognizing Adverbs and Words They Modify

Read the sentences. Write the word that each underlined adverb modifies. Then, write whether that word is a *verb*, an *adjective*, or an *adverb*.

EXAMPLE The students moved very quickly out of the building during the fire drill.

ANSWER *quickly— adverb*

11. Ashley looks extremely serious.
12. Dad usually naps after working so hard.
13. Because of the weather, the traffic was moving very slowly.
14. I often walk in the park to think.
15. The mail should be coming soon.
16. Many students thought the assignment was too difficult.
17. Alex slept soundly before the exam.
18. Adam does not want to join our study group.
19. She spoke rather inappropriately.
20. Carson got an exceptionally high grade on his project.

SPEAKING APPLICATION

With a partner, take turns telling about your morning routine of preparing for school. Your partner should listen for and identify at least three adverbs and state how they modify the verbs.

WRITING APPLICATION

Write a brief paragraph in which you praise or criticize a book you've read. Use at least four adverbs. Underline each adverb and draw an arrow to the word it modifies.

PRACTICE 15.2A

1. lately—When?
2. slowly—In what way?
   carefully—In what way?
3. hardly—To what extent?
4. loudly—In what way?
5. almost— To what extent?
6. never—When?
7. now—When?
8. quietly—In what way?
   away—Where?
9. completely—To what extent?
10. ahead—Where?

PRACTICE 15.2B

11. serious—adjective
12. naps—verb
    hard—adjective
13. slowly—adverb
14. walk—verb
15. should be coming—verb
16. difficult—adjective
17. slept—verb
18. does want—verb
19. inappropriately—adverb
20. high—adjective

SPEAKING APPLICATION

Have students explain how they knew what question each adverb answered. Can they think of an adverb that answers a different question to make a new sentence? How do the new adverb and the new question change the meaning of the sentence?

WRITING APPLICATION

Have students share their paragraphs and explain how they know which words are adverbs and what words the adverbs modify.

Finding Adverbs in Sentences

Focus on the chart listing the different places where adverbs can be located in sentences. Remind students of the questions to ask when identifying an adverb: *When? Where? In what way? To what extent?*

Organize students into seven groups. Assign each group a specific adverb location. Have each group brainstorm for and construct a sentence with an adverb located in the group's specific place. Then, have students read their sentences aloud and have the other students identify the adverb, note the location, and identify the part of speech of the word the adverb modifies.

Conjunctive Adverbs

Explain that certain adverbs can serve as conjunctions, or joining words, as well as adverbs. For this reason, these words are called *conjunctive adverbs.* Three common conjunctive adverbs are *consequently, however,* and *therefore.* Write this sentence on the board: *I forgot to set my alarm; therefore, I overslept.* Ask students to point out the conjunctive adverb. Point out the two simple sentences, or independent clauses, that *therefore* is joining. Then, explain how *therefore* conveys the cause-and-effect relationship between the two sentences.

Extension

To help students synthesize and apply what they have learned, have them create an adverb thesaurus. Assign student pairs two action verbs, and have each pair list adverbs that could be used with the verbs. Students should copy or key in their lists, putting verbs in alphabetical order and alphabetized adverbs beneath each corresponding verb. Have students share lists to create a classroom reference tool.

Finding Adverbs in Sentences

Adverbs can be found in different places in sentences. The chart below shows examples of possible locations for adverbs. Arrows point to the words that the adverbs modify.

LOCATION OF ADVERBS IN SENTENCES	
LOCATION	EXAMPLE
At the beginning of a sentence	Silently, she approached the baby.
At the end of a sentence	She approached the baby silently.
Before a verb	She silently approached the baby.
After a verb	She tiptoed silently toward the baby.
Between parts of a verb phrase	She had silently approached the baby.
Before an adjective	The baby was always quiet.
Before another adverb	The baby cried rather quietly.

Conjunctive adverbs **Conjunctive adverbs** are adverbs that join independent clauses. (See Chapter 17 for more about conjunctive adverbs.)

EXAMPLES Her car broke down; **therefore**, she missed her class.
conjunctive adverb

Mike was worried that he would fail; **however**, he passed with flying colors.
conjunctive adverb

See Practice 15.2C

Adverb or Adjective?

Some words can function as adverbs or as adjectives, depending on their use in a sentence.

If a noun or pronoun is modified by a word, that modifying word is an adjective. If a verb, adjective, or adverb is modified by a word, that modifying word is an adverb.

RULE 15.2.3

An adjective will modify a noun or pronoun and will answer one of the questions *What kind? Which one? How many?* or *How much?*

An adverb will modify a verb, an adjective, or another adverb and will answer one of the questions *Where? When? In what way?* or *To what extent?*

ADVERB MODIFYING VERB

Shopkeepers **work** (verb) **hard** (adverb).

When we came to the intersection, we **turned** (verb) **left** (adverb).

ADJECTIVE MODIFYING NOUN

Shopkeepers accomplish **hard** (adjective) **tasks** (noun).

Use the **right** (adjective) **format** (noun) for your manuscript.

While most words ending in *-ly* are adverbs, some are not. Several adjectives also end in *-ly*. These adjectives are formed by adding *-ly* to nouns.

ADJECTIVES WITH *-LY* ENDINGS

a **weekly** show

a **cuddly** puppy

EXAMPLES

I like movies, but I prefer a **weekly** show.

Kodie is different because he's such a **cuddly** puppy.

See Practice 15.2D

Differentiated Instruction

RTI Strategy for Below-Level Students

Help students understand how to distinguish whether a word is functioning as an adverb or an adjective. Write these two example sentences on the board: *The snow fell softly on the ground. Soft snow covered everything*. Circle the words *softly* and *soft*. Ask students to state the word modified by *softly*, and then repeat the question with *soft*. Guide students to understand that adverbs modify verbs, adjectives, and adverbs, while adjectives modify nouns and pronouns.

Have students create their own sentences using the same or similar words as adverbs and adjectives. Invite students to share their sentences with the group.

Adverb or Adjective?

Point out that some words can be used as either adverbs or adjectives. Explain that the difference depends on which words they modify in a sentence.

RULE 15.2.3 Read aloud the rule and then have students repeat the lines with you.

Use a Think Aloud as part of a gradual release progression.

Think Aloud

Say: I know that some words can be used as either adverbs or adjectives. When I read a sentence, how can I tell whether the word is being used as an adjective or an adverb? First, I need to find the word that is modified. Then, I think about what kind of word it is. If the word being modified is a noun or a pronoun, then the modifier is an adjective. If the word being modified is a verb, adjective, or adverb, then the modifier is an adverb.

Students can ask questions to determine what kind of word is being modified. Write these questions on the board: *What kind? How many? Which one? How much? Where? When? To what extent? In what way?* Then, draw a T-chart on the board and label one column *Adjective* and the other column *Adverb*. **Work with students** to sort the questions into the correct categories.

Have student pairs brainstorm for and construct several sentences using adverbs and adjectives. Then, have pairs exchange sentences with other pairs. Partners should work together to determine whether the modifier in each sentence is an adjective or an adverb.

PRACTICE 15.2C

1. Unhappily, left
2. daily, takes
3. over, move
   comfortably, sit
4. never, have been
   so, upset
   then, was
5. brilliantly, performed
6. thoroughly, happy
7. Suddenly, went
8. not, perform
   well, perform
   yesterday, perform
9. high, aim
10. always, greets;
    cheerfully, greets

PRACTICE 15.2D

11. adverb
12. adjective
13. adverb
14. adjective
15. adjective
16. adverb
17. adjective
18. adverb
19. adverb
20. adjective

SPEAKING APPLICATION

Have students explain why they put the adverb where they did. Then, have them discuss whether moving the adverb would change the feeling and meaning of each sentence.

WRITING APPLICATION

Have students share their sentences. Let other students indicate which sentence uses *first* as an adjective and which as an adverb.

PRACTICE 15.2C Locating Adverbs

Read the sentences. Then, write each adverb and the word or words it modifies.

EXAMPLE His excuse was quite unbelievable.
ANSWER *quite, unbelievable*

1. Unhappily, the losing team left the field.
2. Camille takes a multivitamin daily.
3. Please move over, so we can all sit comfortably.
4. I have never been so upset as I was then.
5. The student actors performed brilliantly.
6. Most students were thoroughly happy with their report cards.
7. Suddenly, the room went dark!
8. Elisa did not perform well yesterday because she had a headache.
9. You must aim high to achieve success.
10. Karen always greets everyone cheerfully.

PRACTICE 15.2D Recognizing Adverbs and Adjectives

Read the sentences. Then, write whether each underlined word is an *adjective* or an *adverb*.

EXAMPLE It's been a <u>long</u> time since I've seen him.
ANSWER *adjective*

11. I arrived at school <u>early</u> this morning.
12. Dad caught the <u>early</u> train to work today.
13. Lianna speaks <u>first</u> in the debate.
14. The player easily scored his <u>first</u> goal.
15. Anna brushed her <u>straight</u> hair.
16. Stand up <u>straight</u>!
17. We had trouble planting vegetables in the <u>hard</u> ground.
18. Hassan and James worked <u>hard</u> on their project.
19. Keep your eyes <u>wide</u> open.
20. The parade route includes all of the <u>wide</u> streets in town.

SPEAKING APPLICATION

With a partner, take turns telling about an exciting event. Use at least three adverbs in different sentence locations. Your partner should identify the adverbs.

WRITING APPLICATION

Use sentences 13 and 14 as models, and write one sentence in which *first* is used as an adjective and one sentence in which *first* is used as an adverb.

Working with ELLs — ELL Sheltered Instruction: Metacognitive

Scaffold the Speaking Application, and have students respond to questions and requests to demonstrate listening comprehension of increasingly complex spoken English. Practice ways students can monitor their comprehension of spoken language during classroom instruction and interactions and seek clarification as needed.

Beginning Using adverbs, describe an exciting event. Use mime and gesture to support understanding. Help students practice asking you to repeat what you have said and requesting clarification. Repeat, and then ask: *What happened? Tell me or show me.*

Intermediate Provide a list of adverbs students might use in the Speaking Application, such as *suddenly* and *quickly*.

As students complete the activity, have listeners monitor understanding and ask partners to repeat or explain as necessary. Finally, have them answer these questions: *What happened? Why was it exciting?*

Advanced Have partners complete the Speaking Application, monitoring understanding and seeking clarification as needed. Then, have them write answers to these questions: *What happened? Why did it happen? Why was it exciting?*

Advanced High Have partners complete the Advanced activity. Then, have them suggest three other adverbs their partner might have used, explaining their choices.

CHAPTER 16 LESSON PLANNER

Prepositions

Use the Online Lesson Planner at www.phwritingcoach.com to customize your instructional plan for an integrated Language Arts curriculum.

DAY 1 16.1 Prepositions

"What Do You Notice?" **Objectives:** Identify, use, and understand prepositions, including ▪ compound prepositions	**INSTRUCTION AND PRACTICE** **Student Edition** pp. 345–348

DAY 2 16.1 Prepositions *(continued)*

Objectives: Identify, use, and understand prepositions, including ▪ prepositions used in sentences ▪ preposition or adverb?	**INSTRUCTION AND PRACTICE** **Student Edition** pp. 349–353 **Test Warm-Up** p. 354

Alternate Pacing Plans

- **Block Scheduling** Each day in the Lesson Planner represents a 40–50 minute block. Teachers using block scheduling may combine days to revise pacing to meet their classroom needs.
- **Accelerated Lesson Planning** Combine instructional days, focusing on concepts called out by students' diagnostic test results.
- **Integrated Language Arts Curriculum** Use the instruction and practice in this chapter to provide reinforcement, remediation, or extension of grammar concepts taught in your literature curriculum.

Links to Prentice Hall *LITERATURE*

Unit 3 Prepositions and Prepositional Phrases, p. 458

"To help students understand the value of prepositions and to encourage sentence variety, have students practice by writing sentences that begin with prepositional phrases ('Across the country, she waited for the phone to ring.' 'Under the weather, he stayed home.')"

—Kelly Gallagher

www.phwritingcoach.com

Grammar Assessment and Practice

Chapter diagnostic tests assess students' skills and assign instruction and practice.

DimensionL Video Games

Fast-paced interactive video games challenge students' mastery of grammar.

Grammar Assessment

Grammar Coach:	Diagnostic Assessment	End-of-Chapter Assessment	Progress Monitoring
Personalized Instruction	Students take grammar diagnostic test online and are automatically assigned instruction and practice in areas where they need support.	Teacher uses **ExamView** to administer end-of-chapter assessment and remediation. Teachers may customize **ExamView** tests or use the ones provided.	Teachers may use the **Test Warm-Ups** and the **Cumulative Reviews** in the student book or eText to check students' mastery of grammar skills. Students may also play **DimensionL** grammar video games to test their grammar skills.
Teacher-Directed Instruction	Teacher administers the diagnostic test and determines focus of instruction and practice.		

Lesson Planner continues on next page

"Have some fun with conjunctions. I love to use mnemonics to help students feel less threatened. The coordinating conjunctions become FANBOYS, helping us quickly recall for, and, nor, but, or, yet, so. *But that's just the first step—the real key to teaching conjunctions isn't memorizing them; it's learning how they function for writers and readers."*

—Jeff Anderson

Differentiated Instruction

Differentiated Instruction Boxes in this Teacher's Edition address these student populations:

- Below-Level Students
- Above-Level Students
- Gifted and Talented Students
- Special Needs Students
- English Language Learners
- Spanish Speaking Students

In addition, for further enrichment, see the **Extension** features.

Grammar Ground Rule: Keep It Clear!

Model with Students

In this chapter, keeping it clear means putting a prepositional phrase in just the right place in a sentence. Explain to students that prepositional phrases tell the relationship between a noun and some part of a sentence. To keep it clear, the prepositional phrase needs to be near that part of the sentence.

Say: I could use a prepositional phrase to help describe a noun: *the lion with the golden mane.* Or I could use one to describe a verb: *walked around his cage.* Each prepositional phrase is right next to the thing it modifiers. But what if I put those sentence parts together this way? *The lion walked around his cage with the golden mane.* One of the prepositional phrases has been moved away from the word it modifies, and the sentence doesn't make sense.

Write this sentence on the board: *The horse ran.* Ask students to think of prepositional phrases to describe either the horse or the way it ran. Have them tell you where the phrase would go in the sentence.

Small Group Activity – Finding Adjectives and Adverbs

Have students form groups to a set of directions for a simple task. Ask the groups to look for prepositional phrases in the directions. Have them discuss how moving the phrases to different places in the sentences could confuse the directions. Their discussion should answer these questions:

- What sentence part does the prepositional phrase modify?
- Is the phrase closely connected to that part?

Have a member of each group present their conclusions to the class and give one good example of prepositional phrase usage that follows this grammar ground rule: Keep it clear.

Grammar Ground Rules

1. Keep it clear.
2. Make them agree.
3. Make it specific.
4. Dot your *i*'s and cross your *t*'s.
5. Make it active.

PREPOSITIONS

Use prepositions in your writing to illustrate how words are related to each other.

WRITE GUY *Jeff Anderson, M.Ed.*

WHAT DO YOU NOTICE?

Seek out prepositions as you zoom in on this sentence from the essay "Volar: To Fly" by Judith Ortiz Cofer.

MENTOR TEXT

From up there, over the rooftops, I could see everything, even beyond the few blocks of our barrio; with my X-ray vision I could look inside the homes of people who interested me.

Now, ask yourself the following questions:

- Which prepositions help show the author's physical location as she describes what she sees?
- Which noun is part of the prepositional phrase beginning with *beyond*?

The author uses the prepositions *From* and *over* to convey her location as she observes her surroundings. The preposition *beyond* begins the prepositional phrase *beyond the few blocks*, and the noun included is *blocks*. The phrase that follows, *of our barrio*, is a separate prepositional phrase that begins with *of* and ends with the noun *barrio*.

Grammar for Writers Writers can use prepositions like markers on a map to show where events in a story take place. Prepositions also help show the timing of events.

My list of prepositions was just on my desk. Where did it go?
Let's see ... inside, outside, behind, underneath....

CHAPTER 16

345

PREPOSITIONS

As students progress in their writing skills, it will be important for them to be able to apply the rules of grammar, usage, and mechanics to their own drafts. Use the *What Do You Notice?* feature to help them see effective conventions in the work of professional writers. Encourage students to incorporate proper voice, tense, and syntax as they edit their own writing.

Read the opening sentence of the Mentor Text aloud. Discuss how prepositions are used to connect elements in a sentence. A preposition relates the noun or pronoun that follows it to another word in a sentence in order to show location, time, or direction.

WRITE GUY *Jeff Anderson, M. Ed.*

WHAT DO YOU NOTICE?

When students have read the Mentor Text, **say:** As you may already know, prepositions are words that introduce a phrase that adds some detail to the sentence. Often, prepositions tell where or when something happened. For example, a dog may have gotten a bone from his bowl. The preposition *from* introduces the phrase that tells where he got the bone.

Have students finish reading the page. Remind them that prepositions and the words that work with them may show where an event takes place.

Then, ask: How would the text you just read change if the prepositions were removed? (**Possible response:** The text would not be as descriptive because the location would be a more general one. Also, we wouldn't know about the speaker's X-ray vision.)

Invite students to name some prepositions from the text. **Ask:** Can prepositions stand alone? Guide students in understanding that prepositions begin phrases that add meaning to the text.

Grammar for Writers: Voice

Help students understand that prepositions enhance written descriptions. Carefully chosen prepositions connect words to phrases in text and can provide interesting details about where and when events happen, among other things.

16.1 Prepositions

Lesson Objectives

1. Distinguish between common and compound prepositions.
2. Identify prepositional phrases and objects of prepositions.
3. Differentiate between prepositions and adverbs.

Explain that a preposition adds detail about a noun, pronoun, verb, adjective, or adverb by relating it to a noun or pronoun.

RULE 16.1.1 Read aloud the rule and then have students repeat the lines with you.

Use a Think Aloud as part of a gradual release progression.

Say: I know a way to remember some common prepositions. I think of a box; then, I think of words that describe locations in relation to the box, like *above* the box and *near* the box.

Review the chart of 50 common prepositions with students. **Work with students** to help them apply the "box location" method of identifying prepositions. Remind them that the method does not work for all prepositions.

Then, have partners choose prepositions from the list and write sentences using them.

16.1 Prepositions

Prepositions function as connectors, relating one word to another within a sentence.

www.phwritingcoach.com

Grammar Tutorials
Brush up on your Grammar skills with these animated videos.

Grammar Practice
Practice your grammar skills with Writing Coach Online.

Grammar Games
Test your knowledge of grammar in this fast-paced interactive video game.

Prepositions help a speaker or writer express the link between separate items. They can convey information about location, time, or direction or provide details.

RULE 16.1.1

A preposition relates the noun or pronoun following it to another word in the sentence.

EXAMPLES The panda sat **on** the branch **of** the tree. (on — preposition; branch — noun; of — preposition; tree — noun; RELATES)

The child ran **across** the room and (across — preposition; room — noun; RELATES)

hid **underneath** the bed. (underneath — preposition; bed — noun; RELATES)

In the first example, the panda sat where? (on the branch) It was on what? (the tree). In the second example, the child ran where? (across the room) The child hid where? (underneath the bed)

FIFTY COMMON PREPOSITIONS				
about	behind	during	off	to
above	below	except	on	toward
across	beneath	for	onto	under
after	beside	from	opposite	underneath
against	besides	in	out	until
along	between	inside	outside	up
among	beyond	into	over	upon
around	but	like	past	with
at	by	near	since	within
before	down	of	through	without

See Practice 16.1A

www.phwritingcoach.com

Diagnostic and Instruction
Diagnostic test assesses students' instructional needs. Lessons and practice are assigned based on results.

Additional Practice

- Grammar Tutorials—Animated videos reinforce key grammar skills.
- Grammar Practice—Targeted practice addresses individual needs.
- ExamView—Teachers customize their grammar practice and tests.
- Grammar Games—Interactive video games make grammar fun.

Working with ELLs — ELL Sheltered Instruction: Cognitive

Help students speak using a variety of connecting words with increasing accuracy and ease as they learn to use prepositions to link ideas.

Beginning Show visuals illustrating the two example sentences on page 346. Read the sentences aloud to students, emphasizing the connecting words, or prepositions. Have students repeat after you. Then, guide students in using the same prepositions to describe another visual you provide.

Intermediate Have students take turns saying sentences using the connecting words *above*, *outside*, and *down*, from the table on page 346. As students speak their sentences, write them on the board. Then, have volunteers underline the prepositions in each.

Advanced Write several connecting words from the table on page 346 on index cards. Have students sit in a circle. Have the student to your left say a sentence that includes the word on the first card. Then, have the next student say a sentence with the word, and so on. Continue until all students have spoken a sentence with each word.

Advanced High Have partners develop a spoken dialogue featuring eight words from the table on page 346. Have them perform their dialogues for the class.

Compound Prepositions Prepositions consisting of more than one word are called **compound prepositions.** Some of them are listed in the chart below:

COMPOUND PREPOSITIONS		
according to	by means of	instead of
ahead of	in addition to	in view of
apart from	in back of	next to
aside from	in front of	on account of
as of	in place of	on top of
because of	in spite of	out of

Because prepositions have different meanings, using a particular preposition will affect the way other words in a sentence relate to one another. In the first sentence, for example, notice how each preposition changes the relationship between *parade* and *City Hall.*

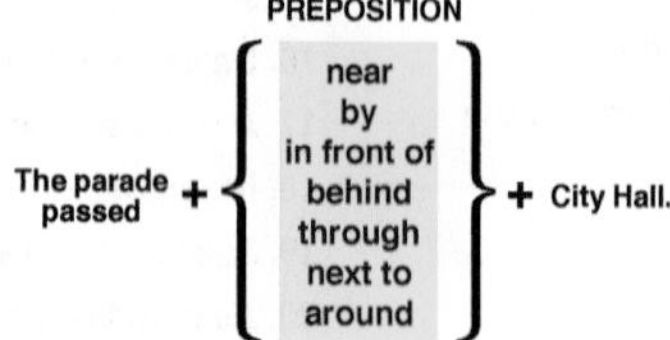

In this sentence, the preposition changes the relationship between *girls* and *gym.*

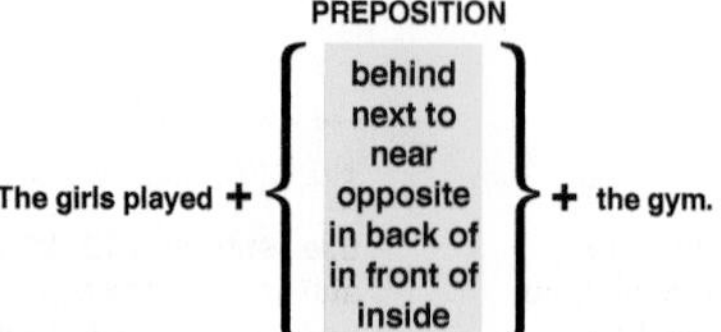

See Practice 16.1B

Compound Prepositions

Point out how compound prepositions differ from the single-word prepositions previously discussed.

Discuss the fact that some prepositions are two or three words. Remind students that these compound prepositions do the same job as a one-word preposition.

Work with students to brainstorm for sentences that include these compound prepositions: *in front of, in addition to, next to.*

Have students individually create sentences with compound prepositions. Then, have students trade their sentences with a partner. Partners should identify the compound prepositions and describe the relationship that the compound prepositions define.

Teacher Tip

If students have difficulty identifying the noun or pronoun to which a preposition relates, encourage them to ask *What?* after reading the preposition. (e.g., *Under what? Below what?*) The response to that question will be the noun or pronoun.

Differentiated Instruction

RTI Strategy for Below-Level Students Students may find it helpful to create a visual representation of some common prepositions. Have student pairs choose an object such as a football or a cell phone and draw it in the middle of a sheet of paper. Then have them write prepositions in the appropriate places, *under* the image, *over* the image, *across* the image, etc. Ask volunteers to show their illustrations to the class.

PRE-AP Enrichment for Above-Level Students Have students exercise their understanding of prepositions and their creativity by writing sentences in which both the subject and the verb are modified by prepositional phrases. Each student's first sentence should be followed by a second in which the adverb phrase in the first sentence becomes the adjective phrase. In the third sentence, the adverb phrase from the second becomes the adjective phrase.

PRACTICE 16.1A

1. of
2. In
3. outside
4. between
5. on
6. near
7. before
8. beside
9. from
10. through

PRACTICE 16.1B

11. on account of
12. in addition to
13. According to
14. because of
15. on top of
16. instead of
17. in front of
18. by means of
19. in place of
20. As of

SPEAKING APPLICATION

Have partners discuss how the prepositions helped them to clarify location. Have partners relocate and try the exercise again, discussing how the prepositions changed.

WRITING APPLICATION

Have students exchange sentences and check each other's work, explaining why it is or is not correct.

PRACTICE 16.1A Identifying Prepositions

Read the sentences. Then, write the preposition in each sentence.

EXAMPLE I will give you an answer by tomorrow.

ANSWER *by*

1. The price of the leather jacket was reduced.
2. In the mountains, the air is cooler.
3. Josh left his muddy boots outside the door.
4. Lia saw Julie between classes.
5. It appears that the train is on schedule.
6. I found a dollar near the bus stop.
7. Serena felt nervous before the concert.
8. Who is that standing beside Mike?
9. I like stories from Greek mythology.
10. Little Red Riding Hood walked through the forest.

PRACTICE 16.1B Identifying Compound Prepositions

Read the sentences. Then, write the compound preposition in each sentence.

EXAMPLE In spite of his good intentions, Rob was late.

ANSWER *In spite of*

11. School started late on account of the snow.
12. You must turn in your notes in addition to your essay.
13. According to the weather forecast, it will be sunny this week.
14. The principal wants to speak to Sam because of the incident.
15. Your dinner is staying warm on top of the stove.
16. Gayle went to the mall instead of the library.
17. A truck stopped in front of the house.
18. Ike survived by means of his wits.
19. Jessica ate a sandwich in place of a salad.
20. As of today, no one has responded to the ad.

SPEAKING APPLICATION

With a partner, take turns describing the location of another person in the room. Your partner should listen for and name three prepositions that you use.

WRITING APPLICATION

Use sentences 13, 16, and 19 as models, and write three sentences. Use the same prepositions, but change the other words.

Extension

To help students synthesize and apply what they have learned about prepositions, have them write a class poem consisting of prepositional phrases. Provide the first line of the poem: *The sun shines* . . . Then, call on volunteers to add prepositional phrases to create a poem, like this: *The sun shines / on the wet green grass, / in back of the school, / after the storm*. Students should use as many different prepositions as they can.

Prepositions Used in Sentences

A preposition is never used by itself in a sentence. Instead, it appears as part of a phrase containing one or more other words.

A preposition in a sentence always introduces a prepositional phrase.

RULE 16.1.2

Prepositional Phrases

A **prepositional phrase** is a group of words that begins with a preposition and ends with a noun or pronoun. The noun or pronoun following the preposition is the **object of the preposition.**

Some prepositional phrases contain just two words—the preposition and its object. Others are longer because they contain modifiers.

EXAMPLES **in** (preposition) **soil** (object)

from (preposition) the rain **forest** (object)

in place of (preposition) the older, cracked **phone** (object)

inside (preposition) the large, comfortable **car** (object)

with (preposition) **you** (object)

See Practice 16.1C
See Practice 16.1D
See Practice 16.1F

according to (preposition) the new **principal** (object)

Prepositional phrases convey information about location, time, or direction or provide details. (See Chapter 23 to learn about prepositional phrases and their influence on subject–verb agreement.)

Working with ELLs ELL Sheltered Instruction: Cognitive

To help students internalize and build proficiency with new grade-level academic vocabulary, have them use and reuse the vocabulary in a speaking activity. Focus on these key academic words from the lesson: *preposition* and *prepositional phrase*.

Beginning Write the sentence, *We found the money buried in the dirt*. Read the sentence aloud and have students repeat. Explain the meaning of the sentence. Then, point to the preposition *in* and say *preposition*. Have students repeat. Next, underline the prepositional phrase *in the dirt,* say *prepositional phrase,* and have students repeat. Repeat the activity with other simple sentences featuring prepositional phrases.

Intermediate Write several prepositions and prepositional phrases on the board. As you point to each one, have students speak a complete sentence: ______ *is a preposition.* ______ *is a prepositional phrase.*

Advanced Write several sentences featuring prepositional phrases on the board. Have volunteers orally identify the preposition and prepositional phrases in each, using these terms.

Advanced High Have students list ten prepositions and write a prepositional phrase for each. Then, have partners switch lists and orally identify each item as either a preposition or a prepositional phrase. Challenge students to use the prepositional phrases in complete sentences.

Prepositions Used in Sentences

Point out that a preposition does not stand alone. It begins a phrase made up of two or more words; for example, *at noon,* as in the sentence *We will meet at noon,* and *at your earliest convenience,* as in the sentence *We will meet at your earliest convenience.*

RULE 16.1.2 Read aloud the rule and then have students repeat the lines with you.

Prepositional Phrases

Discuss the example prepositional phrases on page 349. **Say:** A prepositional phrase is easy to identify because it always begins with a preposition and ends with a noun or a pronoun. The noun or pronoun that ends the phrase is called the object of the preposition.

Write this sentence on the board: *I want a pizza with everything on it.* Call for volunteers to identify the object of each preposition (everything, it).

Invite a student volunteer to say aloud a sentence with a prepositional phrase. Work with students to identify the preposition in the sentence. Then, guide students to name the prepositional phrase and the object of the preposition.

Have student pairs look around the classroom to find examples of locations that can be described by using prepositional phrases (e.g, under the shelf, on the desk). Have students identify the preposition and the object of the preposition.

Preposition or Adverb?

Point out that some words that are used as prepositions can also be used as adverbs. Read aloud the first two example sentences. Explain that *outside* is a preposition when it is followed by an object, but it is an adverb when it stands alone. Remind students that prepositions always begin phrases. Therefore, if a word that appears to be a preposition stands alone, the word is functioning as an adverb, not a preposition.

Tell students that they should not decide whether a word is a preposition until they see whether it begins a prepositional phrase.

Have students create sentences using the words listed in the *Preposition or Adverb* chart on page 350. Next, have students discuss whether each word is used as an adverb or a preposition in the sentences and how they know. Then, have students identify the prepositional phrase and the object of the preposition if the sentence includes a preposition.

Have student pairs create and share sentences with their partners. After identifying whether a word is being used as an adverb or a preposition, have the pairs create another sentence using the word in the other form.

Quick-Write Extension

To help students synthesize and apply what they have learned about prepositional phrases, have them use prepositional phrases to describe a picture. Provide a landscape painting or photograph, and direct students to use as many different prepositional phrases as they can to describe the landscape. Then, have students exchange paragraphs and underline all the prepositional phrases.

Preposition or Adverb?

Some words can be used either as prepositions or as adverbs. The following chart lists some examples. When the word is used as a preposition, it begins a prepositional phrase and is followed by the object of the preposition. If the word has no object, it is probably being used as an adverb.

PREPOSITION OR ADVERB		
above	inside	outside
after	nearby	past
around	opposite	underneath
before	out	within

PREPOSITION The broken shutter was **outside** the house.

ADVERB The man saw the broken shutter **outside**.

PREPOSITION He appeared **before** the class.

ADVERB He had not heard that **before**.

PREPOSITION The man drove **past** the food store.

ADVERB The car drove **past** quickly.

PREPOSITION He sat **inside** the restaurant.

ADVERB Please go **inside** now.

PREPOSITION The beautician stood **behind** her client.

ADVERB Ann waited **behind**.

PREPOSITION The children waited **nearby** the playground.

ADVERB I like that the stores are **nearby**.

See Practice 16.1E
See Practice 16.1G
See Practice 16.1H

Differentiated Instruction

RTI Strategy for Special Needs Students Students may have difficulty distinguishing whether a word is used as a preposition or as an adverb in a sentence. Have them create a mini-sentence diagram for each word that puzzles them, drawing a slanted line that turns into a horizontal line and putting the word on the slanted line. Explain that, if they cannot find another word to put on the horizontal line, the first word is used as an adverb and not as a preposition.

Enrichment for Gifted/Talented Students Have students as a group create a chart of words that can fill either role—adverb or preposition—in a sentence. Then have students exercise their understanding of sentence elements and their creativity by writing two or three sentences in which a word that can be used as either an adverb or a preposition is used in both senses. Ask volunteers to share their sentences with the class.

PRACTICE 16.1C **Recognizing Prepositional Phrases**

Read the sentences. Write the prepositional phrase in each sentence, and underline the object of the preposition.

EXAMPLE This old trunk is covered with dust.

ANSWER *with dust*

1. The woman in the black coat dropped her purse.
2. Not many people stayed until the end.
3. The golfer hit a ball into the pond.
4. Everyone except Ashley brought lunch.
5. Birds start singing at daybreak.
6. Mrs. Dominguez received a basket of fruit.
7. Keep your papers inside your notebook.
8. He handed the ball to me.
9. We sat around the table discussing the book.
10. That's my brother leaning against the wall.

PRACTICE 16.1D **Distinguishing Prepositions and Prepositional Phrases**

Read the sentences. Write the prepositional phrases. Then, underline the preposition in each phrase.

EXAMPLE Scrabble is among my favorite games.

ANSWER *among my favorite games*

11. Two ferries go across that river.
12. There is a fascinating world beneath the ocean.
13. The guests are playing croquet on the lawn.
14. There was a long line outside the theater.
15. The new student is from Alabama.
16. I have a gift for you.
17. You can come through the front door.
18. Your phone fell out of your pocket.
19. Please do not stand in front of the window.
20. We can talk about the schedule later.

SPEAKING APPLICATION

With a partner, take turns describing the location of an object in the room. Use at least two prepositional phrases. Your partner should listen for and identify the prepositional phrases and the objects of each preposition.

WRITING APPLICATION

Write directions to your home from school. Underline the prepositional phrases in your directions.

PRACTICE 16.1C

1. in the black coat
2. until the end
3. into the pond
4. except Ashley
5. at daybreak
6. of fruit
7. inside your notebook
8. to me
9. around the table
10. against the wall

PRACTICE 16.1D

11. across that river
12. beneath the ocean
13. on the lawn
14. outside the theater
15. from Alabama
16. for you
17. through the front door
18. out of your pocket
19. in front of the window
20. about the schedule

SPEAKING APPLICATION

Have partners explain how they identified each prepositional phrase and object of the preposition.

WRITING APPLICATION

Have students explain to a partner how they identified the prepositional phrases in their paragraphs.

Working with ELLs ELL Sheltered Instruction: Cognitive

As students study prepositional phrases, have them demonstrate English comprehension and expand their reading skills by employing the analytical skill of evaluating written information.

Beginning Write these two sentences on the board: *Walk down the street and turn left. Walk down the street and turn left at the second light.* Use visuals and the assistance of a fluent student who shares the same home language to ensure that all students understand. Then, guide them to evaluate which statement gives better directions.

Intermediate Provide students with the written sample sentences from the Beginning activity. Lead students in evaluating the difference between them. Then, have students complete the Writing Application, working with partners to revise their work. Finally, have students exchange papers and evaluate each other's work.

Advanced After students have completed the Writing Application, have them read their partners' directions for clarity. Direct them to make suggestions based on their evaluation, including suggestions for incorporating prepositional phrases.

Advanced High Have students complete the Advanced activity. Then, have them check the accuracy of their partner's directions using an online map or other reference.

PRACTICE 16.1E

1. adverb
2. adverb
3. preposition
4. adverb
5. preposition
6. preposition
7. adverb
8. preposition
9. preposition
10. preposition

PRACTICE 16.1F

Answers will vary. Sample answers:

11. The tree by the fire hydrant will be cut down.
12. The ball sailed over the net.
13. Our game with Brewster Middle School was postponed.
14. Malika baked banana bread for the party.
15. Everyone listened intently during the lecture.
16. Construction of the new hospital will begin soon.
17. The child in the blue jacket was crying.
18. I can't go without permission.
19. Why don't you use this pen instead of your own?
20. You need to make up your mind prior to the event.

SPEAKING APPLICATION

Have students share their sentences with the class, pointing out whether they used a preposition or an adverb.

WRITING APPLICATION

Have partners circle the prepositional phrases in each other's sentences.

PRACTICE 16.1E Distinguishing Prepositions and Adverbs

Read the sentences. Label each underlined word *preposition* or *adverb*.

EXAMPLE Evan left his bicycle <u>outside</u>.
ANSWER *adverb*

1. Let's go <u>in</u> now.
2. I have not seen Dave <u>around</u> lately.
3. The noise <u>outside</u> the apartment was distracting.
4. I've been to that deli <u>before</u>.
5. My notebook fell <u>behind</u> the desk.
6. We will have to go <u>around</u> the construction site.
7. Set your bundles <u>down</u> onto the table.
8. Dad needs to repair the hole <u>in</u> the fence.
9. We need to be home <u>before</u> 9:00 P.M.
10. Del lives just <u>down</u> the street from me.

PRACTICE 16.1F Supplying Prepositions and Prepositional Phrases

Read the sentences. Then, expand each sentence by adding a prepositional phrase that begins with the preposition in parentheses.

EXAMPLE You may do your research. (on)
ANSWER *You may do your research on the Internet.*

11. The tree will be cut down. (by)
12. The ball sailed. (over)
13. Our game was postponed. (with)
14. Malika baked banana bread. (for)
15. Everyone listened intently. (during)
16. Construction will begin soon. (of)
17. The child was crying. (in)
18. I can't go. (without)
19. Why don't you use this pen? (instead of)
20. You need to make up your mind. (prior to)

SPEAKING APPLICATION

With a partner, say a sentence using one of these words: *below, inside.* Your partner should identify whether you used the word as an adverb or a preposition.

WRITING APPLICATION

Write this sentence three times, expanding it with two different prepositional phrases each time: *A student dropped a book.*

Working with ELLs — ELL Sheltered Instruction: Cognitive

Scaffold the Writing Application on page 353, and help students understand information and implicit ideas in increasingly complex spoken language commensurate with grade-level learning expectations.

Beginning Using prepositions, list positive features of your neighborhood. Use mime and visuals as needed to ensure understanding. Then, ask *What is in the neighborhood?* To gauge students' understanding of implicit ideas, ask, *Is it a nice neighborhood? Is it a good neighborhood to live in? Why?*

Intermediate Using prepositions, describe positive features of your neighborhood to small groups. Monitor their understanding of information and implicit ideas by asking these questions: *What is in the neighborhood? Is it a good neighborhood to live in?* Then, invite group members to discuss their neighborhoods.

Advanced Have partners complete the Writing Application. Monitor their understanding of information and implicit ideas by having them answer these questions: *What is in the neighborhood? Where is it located? What does your partner like about it? How can you tell?*

Advanced High Have partners complete the Advanced activity. To extend the activity, have partners describe the changes they would make to their neighborhoods to improve them.

PRACTICE 16.1G Distinguishing Prepositions and Adverbs

Read the sentences. Then, label each underlined word *preposition* or *adverb*.

EXAMPLE The dog chased the squirrel around the yard.

ANSWER *preposition*

1. Did you remember to put the garbage out?
2. We went out the door quickly.
3. The school is nearby the library.
4. My best friend lives in a house nearby.
5. I had never seen that movie before.
6. We bought our tickets before the movie started.
7. Melinda went inside the house to get her books.
8. Melinda forgot her books inside.
9. I waited for her outside the school.
10. The rain was soaking the flowers outside.

PRACTICE 16.1H Supplying Prepositions and Adverbs

For each word below, write two sentences. In the first sentence, use the word as a preposition. In the second sentence, use the word as an adverb.

EXAMPLE above

ANSWER *I placed my suitcase in the bin above my seat.* [preposition]

Look at the helicopter hovering above. [adverb]

11. after
12. around
13. before
14. inside
15. nearby
16. out
17. outside
18. past
19. underneath
20. within

SPEAKING APPLICATION

Take turns with a partner. Choose five of the words in Practice 16.1H. For each word, read aloud one of the sentences you wrote. Your partner should identify whether you used the word as an adverb or as a preposition.

WRITING APPLICATION

Write a paragraph that describes your home or your neighborhood. Use at least three of the following words: *nearby, past, before, after, inside, outside.* Then, underline the word and above it write (p) for preposition or (a) for adverb.

SPEAKING APPLICATION

Have partners explain how they differentiated between adverbs and prepositions.

WRITING APPLICATION

Have students exchange paragraphs and check each other's work, explaining why it is or is not correct.

PRACTICE 16.1G

1. adverb
2. preposition
3. preposition
4. adverb
5. adverb
6. preposition
7. preposition
8. adverb
9. preposition
10. adverb

PRACTICE 16.1H

Answers will vary. Sample answers:

11. Thunder came after the lightning. [preposition]; The old history book did not say what came after. [adverb]
12. The bees hovered around the hive. [preposition]; The dog always sat around. [adverb]
13. Birds flew south before the winter. [preposition]; James worried about what happened before. [adverb]
14. The elevator was inside the lobby. [preposition]; Coughing made his chest hurt inside. [adverb]
15. The store opened nearby my house. [preposition]; There were flowers nearby. [adverb]
16. Robert looked out the window. [preposition]; The security guard threw him out. [adverb]
17. The business operated outside the law. [preposition]; Snow fell on the street outside. [adverb]
18. The library book was past the due date. [preposition]; The cars waited until the train went past. [adverb]
19. The water pipes ran underneath the floor. [preposition]; Imagine all the fish in the water underneath. [adverb]
20. The pit grows within the fruit. [preposition]; Job seekers should inquire within. [adverb]

Test Warm-Up

1. **C** Add the prepositional phrase **in your mouth** after ***melt***
2. **J** Put three drops of peppermint oil on the marble.
3. **A** Replace the adverb ***over*** with the prepositional phrase **over the marble**
4. **J** After ***it***

Reteach

If students have not mastered these skills, review the content in Section 16.1 Prepositions.

1. Prepositions Used in Sentences 16.1.2
2. Prepositions Used in Sentences 16.1.2
3. Preposition or Adverb? 16.1.2
4. Preposition or Adverb? 16.1.2

Test Tip

Tell students that, for many grammar questions, they can choose the correct answer by simply plugging the answer choices into a sentence and saying the sentence in their heads. If it sounds right it usually, but not always, is right. If students have had a difficult time with a particular grammar topic, like subjective and objective pronouns, they should not trust this test. In those cases, they should recall the rules that they have learned and apply them to the problem.

Test Warm-Up

DIRECTIONS
Read the introduction and the passage that follows. Then, answer the questions to show that you can use and understand the function of prepositions and prepositions used as adverbs in reading and writing.

The following paragraph gives directions for making peppermint pull candy. Read the paragraph and think about the changes you would suggest as a peer editor. When you finish reading, answer the questions that follow.

Peppermint Pull Candy

(1) When correctly made, peppermint pull candy will melt. (2) Rub a piece of marble with unsalted butter. (3) Put three drops of peppermint oil on. (4) Boil a mixture of sugar and water on the stove. (5) Use a candy thermometer so you know when the sugar reaches the correct temperature. (6) Once the sugar is ready, pour it over. (7) Let it sit for a few minutes to cool. (8) Then, with both hands, pull the candy. (9) Dip it in food coloring and keep pulling. (10) Finally, stretch it and cut it with scissors.

1 What change should be made in sentence 1?

- **A** Add the adverb **inside** after ***made***
- **B** Add the prepositional phrase **in the comfort of home** after ***made***
- **C** Add the prepositional phrase **in your mouth** after ***melt***
- **D** Add the adverb **before** after ***melt***

2 What is the BEST way to rewrite the ideas in sentence 3?

- **F** Put on three drops of peppermint oil on.
- **G** Put three drops of peppermint oil.
- **H** Put three drops of peppermint oil around on.
- **J** Put three drops of peppermint oil on the marble.

3 What change should be made in sentence 6?

- **A** Replace the adverb ***over*** with the prepositional phrase **over the marble**
- **B** Replace the adverb ***over*** with the adverb **outside**
- **C** Replace the adverb ***over*** with the prepositional phrase **over the floor**
- **D** Replace the adverb ***over*** with the adverb **within**

4 The meaning of sentence 10 can be clarified by inserting the adverb **out** —

- **F** After ***stretch***
- **G** Before ***with***
- **H** Before ***stretch***
- **J** After ***it***

CHAPTER 17 LESSON PLANNER
Conjunctions and Interjections

Use the Online Lesson Planner at www.phwritingcoach.com to customize your instructional plan for an integrated Language Arts curriculum.

DAY 1 17.1 Conjunctions

"What Do You Notice?" **Objectives:** Identify, use, and understand conjunctions, including ▪ coordinating conjunctions ▪ correlative conjunctions ▪ subordinating conjunctions ▪ conjunctive adverbs ▪ punctuation with conjunctive adverbs ▪ interjections	**INSTRUCTION AND PRACTICE** **Student Edition** pp. 355–361 **Test Warm-Up** p. 362

DAY 2 17.2 Interjections

Objectives: Identify, use, and understand interjections.	**INSTRUCTION AND PRACTICE** **Student Edition** pp. 363–364

DAY 3 Cumulative Review

Objectives: Identify, use, and understand the parts of speech, including ▪ nouns, pronouns, and verbs ▪ the other parts of speech	**INSTRUCTION AND PRACTICE** **Student Edition** pp.365–366

Alternate Pacing Plans

- **Block Scheduling** Each day in the Lesson Planner represents a 40–50 minute block. Teachers using block scheduling may combine days to revise pacing to meet their classroom needs.
- **Accelerated Lesson Planning** Combine instructional days, focusing on concepts called out by students' diagnostic test results.
- **Integrated Language Arts Curriculum** Use the instruction and practice in this chapter to provide reinforcement, remediation, or extension of grammar concepts taught in your literature curriculum.

Links to Prentice Hall *LITERATURE*

Unit 3 Conjunctions, p. 438; Writing Workshop: Revising to Combine Sentences Using Conjunctions, p. 487

"Have students practice using short interjections as a way of adding power to their writing. Do it! Now! Okay?"

—Kelly Gallagher

Grammar Assessment

Grammar Coach:	Diagnostic Assessment	End-of-Chapter Assessment	Progress Monitoring
Personalized Instruction	Students take grammar diagnostic test online and are automatically assigned instruction and practice in areas where they need support.	Teacher uses **ExamView** to administer end-of-chapter assessment and remediation. Teachers may customize **ExamView** tests or use the ones provided.	Teachers may use the **Test Warm-Ups** and the **Cumulative Reviews** in the student book or eText to check students' mastery of grammar skills. Students may also play **DimensionL** grammar video games to test their grammar skills.
Teacher-Directed Instruction	Teacher administers the diagnostic test and determines focus of instruction and practice.		

www.phwritingcoach.com

Grammar Assessment and Practice

Chapter diagnostic tests assess students' skills and assign instruction and practice.

DimensionL Video Games

Fast-paced interactive video games challenge students' mastery of grammar.

Lesson Planner continues on next page

"Have some fun with conjunctions. I love to use mnemonics to help students feel less threatened. The coordinating conjunctions become FANBOYS, helping us quickly recall for, and, nor, but, or, yet, so. *But that's just the first step— the real key to teaching conjunctions isn't memorizing them; it's learning how they function for writers and readers."*

—Jeff Anderson

Differentiated Instruction

Differentiated Instruction Boxes in this Teacher's Edition address these student populations:

- Below-Level Students
- Above-Level Students
- Gifted and Talented Students
- Special Needs Students
- English Language Learners
- Spanish Speaking Students

In addition, for further enrichment, see the **Extension** features.

Grammar Ground Rule: Make It Specific!

Model with Students

In this chapter, making it specific means using conjunctions to say what you really mean. Explain to students that two clauses always have some kind of relationship with each other. If they don't, they shouldn't be in the same sentence. Conjunctions make that relationship clear.

> **Say:** I could say, *I lost my pen and I can't write.* Using the conjunction *and* indicates that the two things are of equal importance and just happened together. But that's not really what I mean. I mean, *Because I lost my pen, I can't write.* One thing (losing the pen) made the other thing (not being able to write) happen. Using the specific conjunction *Because* makes the sentence communicate that relationship.

Write this sentence on the board: *The boy ate his breakfast and he went to school.* Ask students to think of a conjunction that could tell the time relationship between the boy eating his breakfast and his going to school (*before, when*).

Small Group Activity – Looking at Conjunctions

Have students form groups to find a recipe for a simple meal. If it is written in paragraph form, have students identify the subordinating conjunctions and discuss how they relate the clauses. If it is written in numbered steps, have the students turn it into a paragraph by using subordinating conjunctions, then have them discuss why they used particular conjunctions. Have a member of each group present their conclusions to the class and give one good example of conjunction usage that follows this grammar ground rule: Make it specific.

Grammar Ground Rules

1. Keep it clear.
2. Make them agree.
3. Make it specific.
4. Dot your *i*'s and cross your *t*'s.
5. Make it active.

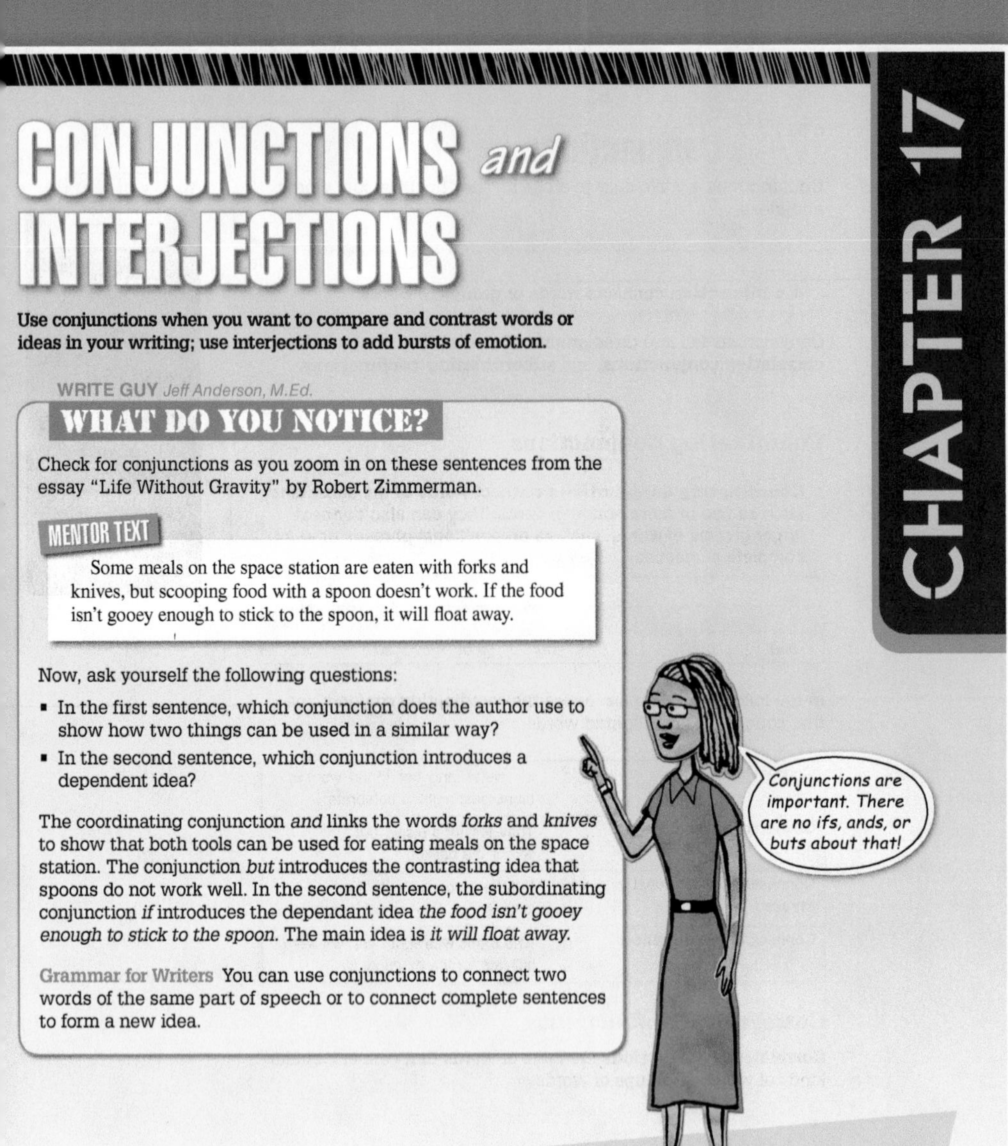

CONJUNCTIONS *and* INTERJECTIONS

Use conjunctions when you want to compare and contrast words or ideas in your writing; use interjections to add bursts of emotion.

CHAPTER 17

WRITE GUY *Jeff Anderson, M.Ed.*

WHAT DO YOU NOTICE?

Check for conjunctions as you zoom in on these sentences from the essay "Life Without Gravity" by Robert Zimmerman.

MENTOR TEXT

> Some meals on the space station are eaten with forks and knives, but scooping food with a spoon doesn't work. If the food isn't gooey enough to stick to the spoon, it will float away.

Now, ask yourself the following questions:

- In the first sentence, which conjunction does the author use to show how two things can be used in a similar way?
- In the second sentence, which conjunction introduces a dependent idea?

The coordinating conjunction *and* links the words *forks* and *knives* to show that both tools can be used for eating meals on the space station. The conjunction *but* introduces the contrasting idea that spoons do not work well. In the second sentence, the subordinating conjunction *if* introduces the dependant idea *the food isn't gooey enough to stick to the spoon.* The main idea is *it will float away.*

Grammar for Writers You can use conjunctions to connect two words of the same part of speech or to connect complete sentences to form a new idea.

Conjunctions are important. There are no ifs, ands, or buts about that!

355

CONJUNCTIONS *and* INTERJECTIONS

As students progress in their writing skills, it will be important for them to be able to apply the rules of grammar, usage, and mechanics to their own drafts. Use the *What Do You Notice?* feature to help them see effective conventions in the work of professional writers. Encourage students to incorporate proper voice, tense, and syntax as they edit their own writing.

Read the opening sentence aloud. Discuss how we use conjunctions to relate multiple ideas to one another or group ideas together. For example, in the phrase *forks and knives,* the conjunction *and* groups *forks* with *knives* so that they can be discussed together. Explain that conjunctions are common and found in all kinds of text. Point out that interjections are not common in writing but are frequently used in spoken language.

WRITE GUY *Jeff Anderson, M. Ed.*

WHAT DO YOU NOTICE?

When students have read the Mentor Text, **say:** As you may already know, conjunctions are used when combining words or ideas in a sentence. A conjunction is the word or words that connect words or ideas of the same type.

Have students finish reading the page. Explain that the words *and, if,* and *but* are some examples of conjunctions. Then, **ask:** How do conjunctions make a writer's job easier? (**Possible response:** The writer can compare two ideas in the same sentence.)

Grammar for Writers: Syntax

Help students understand that instead of writing two or more sentences, conjunctions can be used to compare words or ideas within one sentence. Good writing often means being less wordy and condensing ideas.

17.1 Conjunctions

Lesson Objectives

1. Identify and distinguish between the three types of conjunctions.
2. Identify, use, and understand the function of subordinating conjunctions and conjunctive adverbs.
3. Identify, use, and understand the function of transitions within and between sentences and paragraphs in reading, writing, and speaking.

Tell students that conjunctions join words and ideas.

RULE 17.1.1 Read aloud the rule and then have students repeat the line with you.

Coordinating Conjunctions

Point out that coordinating conjunctions include *and*, *or*, *but*, *nor*, *for*, *so*, and *yet*. Discuss the meaning of each.

RULE 17.1.2 Read aloud the rule and then have students repeat the lines with you.

Use a Think Aloud as part of a gradual release progression.

Say: When I read the coordinating conjunctions in the word chart on page 356, I recognize them as words I use often. They are used to connect two words or groups of words of roughly the same importance. Point out that coordinating conjunctions always connect two or more of the same things—for example, two words, two phrases, or two sentences.

Work with students to understand the functions of conjunctions by discussing what the conjunction does in each example sentence.

Have student pairs list three activities they have done today and use their lists and coordinating conjunctions to write sentences.

Correlative Conjunctions

Explain that correlative conjunctions are pairs of connecting words.

17.1 Conjunctions

Conjunctions are like links in a chain: They help you join words and ideas.

A conjunction connects words or groups of words.

Conjunctions fall into three groups: **Coordinating conjunctions, correlative conjunctions,** and **subordinating conjunctions.**

Coordinating Conjunctions

Coordinating conjunctions connect words of the same kind, such as two or more nouns or verbs. They can also connect larger groups of words, such as prepositional phrases or even complete sentences.

COORDINATING CONJUNCTIONS						
and	but	for	nor	or	so	yet

In the following examples, notice the coordinating conjunctions that connect the highlighted words.

Connecting Nouns	My sister and her friend went to dinner last night to celebrate.
Connecting Verbs	They left for a picnic but forgot the basket.
Connecting Prepositional Phrases	Put the groceries onto the counter or into the refrigerator.
Connecting Two Sentences	The traffic was light, yet we were still late for the meeting.

See Practice 17.1A

Correlative Conjunctions

Correlative conjunctions are *pairs* of words that connect similar kinds of words or groups of words.

Grammar Tutorials
Brush up on your Grammar skills with these animated videos.

Grammar Practice
Practice your grammar skills with Writing Coach Online.

Grammar Games
Test your knowledge of grammar in this fast-paced interactive video game.

Diagnostic and Instruction
Diagnostic test assesses students' instructional needs. Lessons and practice are assigned based on results.

Additional Practice
- Grammar Tutorials—Animated videos reinforce key grammar skills.
- Grammar Practice—Targeted practice is based on individual needs.
- ExamView—Grammar practice and tests teachers can customize.
- Grammar Games—Interactive video games make grammar fun.

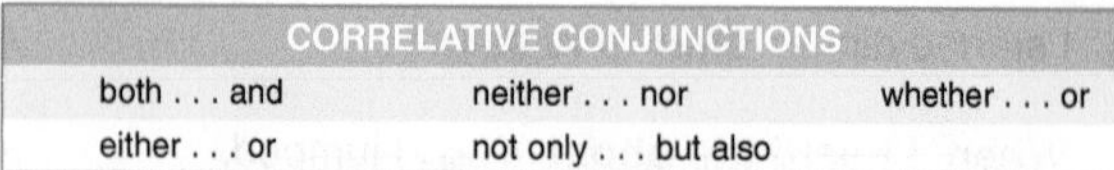

CORRELATIVE CONJUNCTIONS		
both . . . and	neither . . . nor	whether . . . or
either . . . or	not only . . . but also	

Notice the correlative conjunctions in the following examples.

Connecting Nouns	Either the train or the bus will take us there.
Connecting Pronouns	Neither they nor I are at fault.
Connecting Verbs	Every night, she both works out and reads.
Connecting Prepositional Phrases	They'll be here—whether on time or late, I can't say.
Connecting Two Clauses	Not only does he cook, but also he cleans!

See Practice 17.1B

Subordinating Conjunctions

Subordinating conjunctions connect two ideas by making one idea dependent on the other.

17.1.3 RULE

FREQUENTLY USED SUBORDINATING CONJUNCTIONS				
after	as soon as	if	though	whenever
although	as though	in order that	till	where
as	because	since	unless	wherever
as if	before	so that	until	while
as long as	even though	than	when	

Working with ELLs

ELL Sheltered Instruction: Cognitive

Help students speak using a variety of connecting words with increasing accuracy and ease as they learn to use conjunctions.

Beginning Show visuals illustrating the example sentences on page 356. Read the sentences aloud, emphasizing the connecting words, or conjunctions. Have students repeat after you. Then, guide students in using one or more of the same conjunctions to describe another visual.

Intermediate Have students take turns using the connecting words *and*, *or*, and *but*, from the table on page 356, in sentences. As students speak their sentences, write them on the board. Have volunteers underline the conjunction in each.

Advanced Write the coordinating conjunctions from the table on page 356 on index cards. Have the students sit in a circle. Have the student to your left say a sentence that includes the word on the first card. Then, have the next student say a sentence with the word, and so on. Continue until all students have spoken a sentence with each word.

Advanced High Have partners develop a skit with dialogue featuring all of the coordinating conjunctions. Have them perform their skits for the class.

Point out that correlative conjunctions are always separated by one or more words in a sentence, though these conjunctions work together to link two words or word groups of the same type, such as two subjects, two verbs, or two prepositional phrases.

Read aloud the correlative conjunctions in the chart at the top of page 357. Work with students to create a sentence that uses each pair of conjunctions correctly. Write the sentences on the board and analyze together what the conjunctions are connecting.

Have student pairs create sentences using correlative conjunctions and tell whether they are connecting nouns, pronouns, verbs, prepositional phrases, or clauses.

Subordinating Conjunctions

Explain that a subordinating conjunction always introduces a subordinate clause and links that clause to an independent clause.

RULE 17.1.3 Read aloud the rule and then have students repeat the lines with you.

Remind students that a subordinate clause contains a subject and a verb but cannot stand alone as a sentence. Write these sentences on the board: *Adara played basketball outside until it started to rain. Julian was late to class because he missed the bus.*

Have students work with a partner to identify the subordinating conjunction in each sentence. Have them discuss the dependent idea each conjunction introduces.

The Dependent Idea

Explain that every dependent idea begins with a subordinating conjunction, so locating the conjunction is a good way to identify which idea is dependent and which is independent.

Conjunctive Adverbs

Explain that conjunctive adverbs always connect two independent clauses. They provide transitions between the clauses by indicating how the clauses are related. Read aloud the example on page 358. Then, discuss how *however* provides a transition between the two clauses.

Help students to identify, use, and understand the functions of conjunctive adverbs and transitions by writing these sentences on the board: *Akim wanted to practice; otherwise, he would have been on time. Maria is here; therefore, we'll begin. John brought pizza; consequently, we didn't order lunch. Glynnis made the sculpture; furthermore, she drew all of the pictures.*

Have students identify the conjunctive adverbs and explain how these words provide transitions between different ideas. Then, have students write four sentences using four different conjunctive adverbs to provide transitions. Have students read their sentences to partners, identifying each conjunctive adverb. Have the partners explain how these words provided transitions.

The Dependent Idea The subordinating conjunction always introduces the dependent idea. The subordinating conjunction connects the dependent idea to the main idea.

EXAMPLES I started dinner **after** **she called**.

When **I heard the phone ring**, I jumped.

The examples show that the main idea can come at the beginning or at the end of the sentence. When the dependent idea comes first, it must be separated from the main idea with a comma. If the dependent idea comes second, no comma is necessary.

See Practice 17.1C
See Practice 17.1D

Conjunctive Adverbs

Conjunctive adverbs are used as conjunctions to connect complete ideas. They are often used as transitions, connecting different ideas by showing comparisons, contrasts, or results. **Transitions** are used in writing to improve the coherence from sentence to sentence and paragraph to paragraph and make your writing smoother.

CONJUNCTIVE ADVERBS			
accordingly	consequently	indeed	otherwise
again	finally	instead	then
also	furthermore	moreover	therefore
besides	however	nevertheless	thus

Notice the punctuation that is used before and after the conjunctive adverb in the following example. (See Chapter 25 for more about punctuation with conjunctive adverbs.)

EXAMPLE That movie was great; **however**, I still prefer the book.

See Practice 17.1E
See Practice 17.1F

Differentiated Instruction

RTI Strategy for Below-Level Students Remind students that all adverb clauses are introduced by subordinating conjunctions. Review the four **W**'s of adverbs: **W**hen, **W**here, **W**hy, and in **W**hat way. Make four columns on the board and label them with the **W**'s. Go over the most common subordinating conjunctions with students and have them help you put those conjunctions in the columns where they belong. Then, have students use the subordinating conjunctions in sentences, identifying what **W** each conjunction answers.

PRE-AP Enrichment for Above-Level Students Write these conjunctive adverbs on sticky notes: *as a result, consequently, furthermore, however, moreover, nevertheless, on the other hand, otherwise, therefore, thus.* Have a small group of students write each of these headings on a large sheet of paper: *And, But, Or, So.* Then, ask group members to place each sticky note beneath the coordinating conjunction with which it is roughly synonymous. For example, *furthermore* should be placed under *And.* Have students write a compound sentence for each conjunctive adverb.

PRACTICE 17.1A Supplying Coordinating Conjunctions

Read the sentences. Then, write each sentence, replacing the blank with a coordinating conjunction that makes sense in the sentence.

EXAMPLE Cats ____ dogs are the most popular house pets.

ANSWER *Cats and dogs are the most popular house pets.*

1. My sister ____ I do chores after school.
2. The lunch choices are pizza, soup, ____ sandwiches.
3. Billy swept ____ washed the floor.
4. I like science, ____ I prefer math.
5. Chris is inexperienced ____ eager to learn.
6. Mel did not do the assignment, ____ did he come to class.
7. He was late for the bus, ____ he started to run.
8. This tennis racket is light ____ sturdy.
9. We should hurry, ____ the show is about to begin.
10. Laurie has several extracurricular activities, ____ she keeps up her grades.

PRACTICE 17.1B Writing Sentences With Correlative Conjunctions

Write ten sentences, using each of the correlative conjunctions below.

EXAMPLE whether . . . or

ANSWER *Ellie could not decide whether to go to the movies or to the mall.*

The game will be played whether it rains or not.

11. both . . . and
12. either . . . or
13. neither . . . nor
14. whether . . . or
15. not only . . . but also
16. both . . . and
17. either . . . or
18. neither . . . nor
19. whether . . . or
20. not only . . . but also

SPEAKING APPLICATION

With a partner, take turns telling about something you saw yesterday or today. Use two coordinating conjunctions in your sentences. Your partner should listen for and name the conjunctions.

WRITING APPLICATION

Write a brief paragraph using two of the correlative conjunction pairs listed above.

Working with ELLs

ELL Sheltered Instruction: Cognitive

To build and reinforce student attainment of the concept of conjunctions, provide opportunities for them to listen to, derive meaning from, and respond orally to information presented in a wide variety of print, electronic, and audiovisual media.

Beginning Write *and, but,* and *or* and read them aloud with students. Play a recording of a familiar story as students follow along. Ask them to listen for *and*, *but*, and *or*. Discuss the ideas that each conjunction joins.

Intermediate Meet with groups to conduct the Beginning activity. Extend by having students discuss story elements. Guide them with sentence frames featuring conjunctions, such as ____ *and* ____ *are characters in the story.*

Advanced Instruct students to take notes while listening to an advertisement on TV or on the radio. Have them record conjunctions used, noting the ideas the conjunctions join. Then, have them meet with partners to discuss how the conjunctions reinforce the persuasive message.

Advanced High Modify the Advanced activity to have students listen to two advertisements. Have them take notes in a **Venn Diagram**, comparing the use of conjunctions in each advertisement. Have them discuss their observations with partners.

PRACTICE 17.1A

1. and; or
2. or
3. and
4. but; yet
5. but; yet
6. nor
7. so; and
8. yet; but
9. for
10. yet; but

PRACTICE 17.1B

Answers will vary. Sample answers:

11. Both Anne and Megan will help.
12. I will complete my essay either this afternoon or this evening.
13. Neither Elliot nor Sean was able to find the ball.
14. I could not tell whether the animal was a chipmunk or a squirrel.
15. Dan will bring not only snacks but also games.
16. She is in both choir and band.
17. Either a raccoon or a skunk ate the bird seed.
18. I have neither the interest nor the ability to play sports.
19. I forgot whether you wanted to go Saturday or Sunday.
20. Not only was the crew ill, but also two of them were missing.

SPEAKING APPLICATION

Have partners identify the kinds of words or word groups the coordinating conjunctions connect.

WRITING APPLICATION

Have students exchange paragraphs and identify each other's correlative conjunctions.

PRACTICE 17.1C

Answers will vary. Sample answers:

1. I went ahead and made dinner while you were upstairs.
2. Before you choose a computer, consider all the options.
3. Jasmine hasn't missed a piano lesson since last year.
4. Whenever we go on vacation, Mike brings a good book.
5. They'll celebrate their anniversary tomorrow even though they have to work.
6. Unless there is a problem, Eugene catches the five o'clock train.
7. I can't go to the movies because I do not have enough money.
8. Mr. Higgins put up a fence so that his dog would stay in the yard.
9. Joan's parents let her play computer games as long as she got good grades.
10. Until the vacuuming is done, the cat will be hiding in the closet.

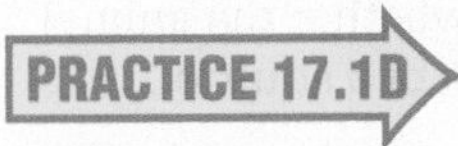

Answers will vary. Sample answers:

11. If you give me money, I will buy the tickets.
12. The doctor is there whenever I am sick.
13. Since we were late, we missed the show.
14. I read a book when there is nothing to do.
15. Because of the snow, it was hard to drive safely.
16. This is the plan unless you have a better idea.
17. As soon as we began, I knew he could not play soccer.
18. The wallet was gone before we knew what happened.
19. Although it looks flat, the world is round.
20. I bought two shirts while I was shopping.

Using Subordinating Conjunctions

Use the main ideas and subordinating conjunctions below to write complete sentences. With a partner, read your sentences and explain how the subordinating conjunction functions.

EXAMPLE We will make it to the playoffs (if)

ANSWER *If we win against the Tigers,* we will make it to the playoffs.

1. I went ahead and made dinner (while)
2. Consider all the options (before)
3. Jasmine hasn't missed a piano lesson (since)
4. Mike brings a good book (whenever)
5. They'll celebrate their anniversary tomorrow (even though)
6. Eugene catches the five o'clock train (unless)
7. I can't go to the movies (because)
8. Mr. Higgins put up a fence (so that)
9. Joan's parents let her play computer games (as long as)
10. The cat will be hiding in the closet (until)

PRACTICE 17.1D Writing With Subordinating Conjunctions

Write complete sentences using the subordinating conjunctions listed. With a partner, read the sentences aloud and explain how the subordinating conjunction functions in each.

EXAMPLE because

ANSWER *I'll walk down to the market because we're out of milk.*

11. if
12. whenever
13. since
14. when
15. because
16. unless
17. as soon as
18. before
19. although
20. while

SPEAKING APPLICATION

With a partner, take turns choosing three subordinating conjunctions and using them to talk about your after-school schedules. Your partner should listen for and identify the subordinating conjunctions you use.

WRITING APPLICATION

Write a paragraph about a favorite activity. Use at least three subordinating conjunctions. Read your paragraph to a partner, explaining how the different subordinating conjunctions function.

SPEAKING APPLICATION

Students' answers should demonstrate that they can use, identify, and understand the function of conjunctions.

WRITING APPLICATION

Students' answers should demonstrate that they can use, identify, and understand the function of subordinating conjunctions in writing.

Extension

To help students synthesize and apply what they have learned about conjunctions, have them make a conjunction bookmark. Direct students to write these headings on a strip of paper: *Coordinating, Correlative, Conjunctive, Subordinating.* Under each heading, students should list conjunctions that exemplify the words in the category. Students should then use the bookmark as a reference when they write.

PRACTICE 17.1E Using Conjunctive Adverbs in Sentences

Read the sentences. Then, rewrite each sentence, filling in the blank with a conjunctive adverb. Read each sentence to a partner and explain the function of the conjunctive adverb.

EXAMPLE I started reading that book; _____, I soon lost interest.

ANSWER *I started reading that book; however, I soon lost interest.*

1. Doctors want people to exercise; _____, many people jog or play sports.
2. Jennifer scored the winning goal in the game; _____, the coach praised her ability.
3. We wanted to play outside after school; _____, it was warm and sunny.
4. I don't want to see that movie; _____, you already saw it last week.
5. Donnie must find his textbook before the test; _____, he will not be prepared.
6. My dad reminds me to turn off the lights; _____, I still forget to do it.
7. Cory thought his jacket was in the car; _____, we did not find it there.
8. Jane ran; _____, she boarded the bus in time.
9. My mom's speech took her all day to write; _____, she worked on it at night.
10. Joaquin likes to write stories; _____, he shares them.

PRACTICE 17.1F Using and Writing Conjunctive Adverbs and Transitions

Read the pairs of sentences. Then, use conjunctive adverbs and transitions to write one new sentence. Read each new sentence to a partner and explain the function of the conjunctive adverbs and the transitions.

EXAMPLE I have to remind Betsy. She might forget to pick me up.

ANSWER *I have to remind Betsy; otherwise, she might forget to pick me up.*

11. I studied hard. I got an A this semester.
12. Maria babysat five times. She has enough money to buy her mom a present.
13. I enjoyed the first book. I bought the second book.
14. There is a new girl in our lab group. I am no longer the only one.
15. Houston is usually hot in the summer. You should pack light clothing.
16. I practiced basketball a lot. I made the team.
17. We were excited to go to the concert. We were going to see our favorite band.
18. The traffic on the way to the airport was heavy. We missed our flight.
19. Three players on the team were injured in the game. We lost the championship.
20. The play begins in 10 minutes. We ran to our seats.

SPEAKING APPLICATION

With a partner, take turns talking about a book you are reading. Use at least two conjunctive adverbs and one transition. Have your partner identify which ones you used.

WRITING APPLICATION

Write a paragraph about what you did last weekend. Use subordinating conjunctions, conjunctive adverbs, and transitions. Explain to a partner the function of each conjunction.

Working with ELLs  Sheltered Instruction: Cognitive

As students practice using subordinating conjunctions on page 360, guide them to demonstrate English comprehension by employing and expanding basic reading skills, including summarizing, distinguishing main idea from supporting details, and comparing and contrasting.

Beginning Write sentences featuring subordinating conjunctions about an after-school activity. Read the sentences aloud as students follow along. Repeat, instructing students to take notes in a cluster diagram. Then, have them use the diagram to orally summarize what they read.

Intermediate Pair students with fluent speakers to complete the Writing Application as a shared writing activity. Then, have them exchange paragraphs with another pair. Have students identify subordinating conjunctions in the written paragraph. Then, have them write a sentence expressing the main idea.

Advanced Have students complete the Writing Application and exchange paragraphs with a partner. Have them read their partners' writing silently and then write a sentence expressing the main idea.

Advanced High Have students complete the Advanced activity. To extend the activity, have them use a **Venn Diagram** to compare and contrast their paragraphs with their partners'. Invite them to share their findings.

PRACTICE 17.1E

1.	consequently	6.	nevertheless
2.	accordingly	7.	however
3.	indeed	8.	moreover
4.	besides	9.	then
5.	otherwise	10.	also

PRACTICE 17.1F

Answers will vary. Sample answers:

11. I studied hard; accordingly, I got an A this semester.
12. Maria babysat five times; thus, she has enough money to buy her mom a present.
13. I enjoyed the first book; therefore, I bought the second book.
14. There is a new girl in our lab group; finally, I am no longer the only one.
15. Houston is usually hot in the summer; therefore, you should pack light clothing.
16. I practiced basketball a lot; finally, I made the team.
17. We were excited to go to the concert; indeed, we were going to see our favorite band.
18. The traffic on the way to the airport was heavy; consequently, we missed our flight.
19. Three players on the team were injured in the game; moreover, we lost the championship.
20. The play begins in 10 minutes; thus, we ran to our seats.

SPEAKING APPLICATION

Students' responses should show that they can identify, use, and understand the function of conjunctive adverbs and transitions.

WRITING APPLICATION

Students' explanations should show that they can identify, use, and understand the function of conjunctive adverbs and transitions.

Test Warm-Up

1. **C** Add a comma after ***Tuesday***
2. **H** I overslept by 40 minutes; therefore, I had to rush to get ready for school.
3. **B** Change the comma after ***shower*** to a semicolon
4. **F** Suddenly, the smoke detectors in the entire house were going off because my toast had burned.

Reteach

If students have not mastered these skills, review the content in Section 17.1 Conjunctions.

1. Subordinating Conjunctions 17.1.3
2. Conjunctive Adverbs 17.1
3. Conjunctive Adverbs 17.1
4. Subordinating Conjunctions 17.1.3

Test Tip

Students may look for a pattern as they answer questions in a multiple-choice test. Point out to students that the questions on a single page might have several different formats. Students should approach each question individually, rather than expecting a question to require the same type of answer as the question before it. For example, one question might require students to consider a change in word choice, while the next sentence requires them to revise the structure of a sentence.

Test Warm-Up

DIRECTIONS
Read the passage that follows. Then, answer the questions to show that you can identify, use, and understand the function of subordinating conjunctions, conjunctive adverbs, and transitions in reading and writing.

One of Those Days

(1) When I woke up last Tuesday I had a funny feeling it was going to be a bad day. (2) I overslept by 40 minutes. (3) I had to rush to get ready for school. (4) I jumped in the shower, then, I discovered there was no hot water. (5) I put two pieces of bread in the toaster. (6) After that, I went back to my room to make my bed. (7) Suddenly, the smoke detectors in the entire house were going off, my toast had burned. (8) I grabbed a granola bar and ran for the bus. (9) I was five minutes late; however, the bus had just arrived. (10) The driver said, "I'm sorry I'm late. It's one of those days." (11) I answered, "I know what you mean."

1 What change, if any, should be made in sentence 1?

- **A** Add a comma after ***feeling***
- **B** Add a semicolon after ***feeling***
- **C** Add a comma after ***Tuesday***
- **D** Make no change

2 What is the BEST way to combine sentences 2 and 3?

- **F** I overslept by 40 minutes; otherwise, I had to rush to get ready for school.
- **G** I overslept by 40 minutes; nevertheless, I had to rush to get ready for school.
- **H** I overslept by 40 minutes; therefore, I had to rush to get ready for school.
- **J** I had to rush to get ready for school; because I overslept by 40 minutes.

3 What change, if any, should be made in sentence 4?

- **A** Delete the comma after ***shower***
- **B** Change the comma after ***shower*** to a semicolon
- **C** Delete the comma after ***then***
- **D** Make no change

4 What is the BEST way to revise sentence 7?

- **F** Suddenly, the smoke detectors in the entire house were going off because my toast had burned.
- **G** Suddenly, the smoke detectors in the entire house were going off; consequently, my toast had burned.
- **H** Suddenly, the smoke detectors in the entire house were going off before my toast had burned.
- **J** Suddenly, the smoke detectors in the entire house were going off; however, my toast had burned.

17.2 Interjections

The **interjection** is the part of speech that is used the least. Its only use is to express feelings or emotions.

WRITING COACH Online
www.phwritingcoach.com

Grammar Tutorials
Brush up on your Grammar skills with these animated videos.

Grammar Practice
Practice your grammar skills with Writing Coach Online.

Grammar Games
Test your knowledge of grammar in this fast-paced interactive video game.

An interjection expresses feeling or emotion and functions independently from the rest of a sentence. RULE 17.2.1

An interjection has no grammatical relationship to any other word in a sentence. It is, therefore, set off from the rest of the sentence with a comma or an exclamation mark.

Interjections can express different feelings or emotions.

JOY **Wow!** I can't believe you paid so little.

SURPRISE **Oh,** I just made plans before you called.

PAIN **Ouch!** That curling iron is hot.

IMPATIENCE **Hey!** When are we leaving?

HESITATION I, **uh,** thought you already knew.

Interjections are used more in speech than in writing. They are informal, rather than formal, expressions. When you do see them in writing, they are often included in dialogue. The following chart lists words often used as interjections.

See Practice 17.2A
See Practice 17.2B

INTERJECTIONS			
ah	gosh	nonsense	ugh
aha	great	oh	uh
alas	heavens	oops	um
boy	hey	ouch	well
darn	huh	psst	what
eureka	hurray	shh	whew
fine	my	terrible	wonderful
golly	never	terrific	wow

Lesson Objectives

1. Use and understand interjections.
2. Recognize and use punctuation marks including commas after introductory words, phrases, and clauses.

Explain that interjections are individual words that express strong emotions that are related to the main idea of a sentence, but they are not related grammatically to the sentence.

RULE 17.2.1 Read aloud the rule and then have students repeat the lines with you.

Point out that interjections have to be separated from the rest of the sentence, usually by a comma or an exclamation mark.

Work with students to generate several sentences about an exciting current event without using interjections. Discuss the emotions evoked by each event. Have students add an interjection to each sentence. Make sure students punctuate the interjections correctly.

Have student pairs write a short skit using as many interjections as they can.

www.phwritingcoach.com

Diagnostic and Instruction
Diagnostic test assesses students' instructional needs. Lessons and practice are assigned based on results.

Additional Practice
- Grammar Tutorials—Animated videos reinforce key grammar skills.
- Grammar Practice—Targeted practice is based on individual needs.
- ExamView—Grammar practice and tests teachers can customize.
- Grammar Games—Interactive video games make grammar fun.

Working with ELLs — ELL Sheltered Instruction: Cognitive

Help students speak using a variety of connecting words with increasing accuracy and ease as they learn about interjections.

Beginning Provide simple sentence strips, half with simple sentences, such as *That was fun*, and others with interjections, such as *Wow!* Have students work with fluent partners to orally join sentences with interjections. Pairs should evaluate which results make sense.

Intermediate Have partners work together to create and say sentences of their own using three interjections from the chart. Have them discuss their results as a group.

Advanced Have partners complete the Intermediate activity. Then, have them rewrite their sentences with different interjections that also make sense.

Advanced High Have partners complete the Advanced activity. Then, have them discuss if and how the tone of their sentences changed when they changed the interjections.

PRACTICE 17.2A

1. Gosh—surprise
2. Whew!—relief
3. Hey!—surprise
4. Oh, no!—disappointment
5. Ouch!—pain
6. uh—hesitation
7. Oh, brother—impatience
8. Hurray!—joy
9. Oops!—disappointment
10. Terrific!—excitement

PRACTICE 17.2B

Answers will vary. Sample answers:

11. Oh, I just don't believe that.
12. Alas, she is always late.
13. Ouch! A bee stung me!
14. Great! I'm so glad you're home safe.
15. Wow! That is a great poster.
16. Gosh, I thought we would never finish.
17. Hey, is that all you brought?
18. Oh, I beg your pardon.
19. Well, when did you think it was due?
20. Ugh! I have never seen such ugly colors.

SPEAKING APPLICATION

Partners should explain how commas would be used after introductory words to show that they can recognize and use commas after introductory words.

WRITING APPLICATION

Students' sentences should show that they can recognize and use commas after introductory words, phrases, and clauses.

PRACTICE 17.2A Identifying Interjections

Read the sentences. Write the interjection in each sentence. Then, write what emotion the interjection conveys.

EXAMPLE Wow! Did you see that catch?

ANSWER *Wow! — surprise*

1. Gosh, I didn't know that.
2. Whew! That was a long walk.
3. Hey! Why did you do that?
4. Oh, no! I can't find my key.
5. Ouch! I stubbed my toe!
6. I, uh, don't really know the answer.
7. Oh, brother, here were go again.
8. Hurray! I knew we would win.
9. Oops! I dropped it again.
10. Terrific! That's great news.

PRACTICE 17.2B Supplying Interjections

Read the sentences. Rewrite each sentence, using an appropriate interjection in place of the feeling shown in parentheses. Use a comma or an exclamation mark after each interjection.

EXAMPLE I forgot my umbrella. (disappointment)

ANSWER *Darn, I forgot my umbrella.*

11. I just don't believe that. (surprise)
12. She is always late. (impatience)
13. A bee stung me! (pain)
14. I'm so glad you're home safe. (joy)
15. That is a great poster. (surprise)
16. I thought we would never finish. (impatience)
17. Is that all you brought? (impatience)
18. I beg your pardon. (surprise)
19. When did you think it was due? (impatience)
20. I have never seen such ugly colors. (disappointment)

SPEAKING APPLICATION

With a partner, take turns role-playing someone who has just received some news, good or bad. Say your response to the news using an interjection. Your partner should listen for and identify the interjection.

WRITING APPLICATION

Write three sentences, each containing a different interjection. Use a comma or an exclamation mark after each interjection.

Working with ELLs — ELL Sheltered Instruction: Cognitive

As students begin using interjections, help students enhance and confirm their understanding of the increasingly complex spoken language by providing visual support.

Beginning Write the example sentence from Practice 17.2A on the board: *Wow! Did you see that catch?* Read the sentence aloud, providing visual support by adopting a look of extreme surprise or by showing a photograph of a clearly surprised person. Point to each part of the sentence as you say it, emphasizing the interjection. Have students repeat after you.

Intermediate Provide visual support for Practice 17.2B by creating sentence strips of the items as well as strips featuring various interjections. Have partners identify which interjections might go with which sentences. Then, speak the correct completed sentences aloud as students use their sentence strips to match your completed sentences.

Advanced Have students complete the Intermediate activity. Then, have them create alternative answers for each item and say them to their partner. Partners should replicate the answers using the sentence strips.

Advanced High Have students complete the Intermediate activity. Extend as in the Advanced activity. Then, challenge students to write a brief dialogue featuring five interjections.

Cumulative Review Chapters 13–17

PRACTICE 1 Writing Sentences With Nouns

Write five sentences, each using one of the following kinds of nouns. Circle those nouns, and underline any other nouns you use.

1. a common noun that names a place
2. a proper noun that names a person
3. a concrete noun
4. a hyphenated compound noun
5. a non-count noun

PRACTICE 2 Identifying Pronouns

Read the sentences. Then, write the pronouns that each sentence contains. Label each pronoun *personal, reflexive, intensive, demonstrative, relative, interrogative,* or *indefinite*.

1. Tony, who carves wood, made me a spoon.
2. Whose is that?
3. The lifeguard himself said that the pool is open.
4. Everybody enjoyed your fruit salad.
5. Her cat can take care of itself.
6. Has anyone seen this before?
7. Who knows anything about nutrition?
8. Toby, who studied hard, deserved his *A*.
9. My mom sometimes goes to the movies by herself.
10. I myself could never stay up so late.

PRACTICE 3 Using Action and Linking Verbs

Write two sentences for each word below. In the first sentence, use the word as an action verb; in the second sentence, use it as a linking verb.

1. smell
2. look
3. taste
4. feel
5. turn

PRACTICE 4 Identifying Helping Verbs and Main Verbs in Verb Phrases

Read the sentences. Write the complete verb phrase in each sentence. Then, label the parts of each verb phrase *helping* or *main*.

1. The boys have completed all their chores.
2. Betsy's flight will leave at noon.
3. I do not like some of those vegetables.
4. The extra study time has helped me.
5. The task must be finished in one hour.
6. No one can ever remember those song lyrics.
7. I will never again make that mistake.
8. The party has been over since ten o'clock.
9. Did you go to the playground on Monday?
10. She should have dressed in warmer clothing.

Continued on next page ▶

PRACTICE 1

Answers will vary. Sample answers:

1. The city is hectic but exciting.
2. Hugh Jackman is a popular actor.
3. My suitcase is very heavy.
4. Harriet had dinner with her sister-in-law.
5. Please pass the sugar.

PRACTICE 2

1. who—relative
   me—personal
2. Whose—interrogative
   that—demonstrative
3. himself—intensive
   that—relative
4. Everybody—indefinite
   your—personal
5. Her—personal
   itself—reflexive
6. anyone—indefinite
   this—demonstrative
7. Who—interrogative
   anything—indefinite
8. who—relative
   his—personal
9. My—personal
   herself—reflexive
10. I—personal
    myself—intensive

PRACTICE 3

Answers will vary. Sample answers:

1. (action) Some dogs smell everything.
   (linking) Some dogs smell awful.
2. (action) I always look carefully at the small print.
   (linking) Those flowers look beautiful!
3. (action) Did you taste the carrots?
   (linking) The carrots taste delicious.
4. (action) I feel a lump in the mattress.
   (linking) Some mattresses feel lumpy.
5. (action) Will you turn the sheets of music as I play the piano?
   (linking) My mom will turn forty this year.

PRACTICE 4

1. have completed
   have—helping
   completed—main
2. will leave
   will—helping
   leave—main
3. do like
   do—helping
   like—main
4. has helped
   has—helping
   helped—main
5. must be finished
   must be—helping
   finished—main
6. can remember
   can—helping
   remember—main
7. will make
   will—helping
   make—main
8. has been
   has—helping
   been—main
9. Did go
   Did—helping
   go—main
10. should have dressed
    should have—helping
    dressed—main

PRACTICE 5

Answers will vary. Sample answers:

1. Wendy found her white sweater.
2. The new girl takes a bus to school daily.
3. Grandfather snores quite loudly.
4. A lovely butterfly landed gracefully on the big, red flower.
5. The weather was rather nasty all day.
6. The boat raced rapidly through the water.
7. Cows sat contentedly in the grassy meadow.
8. She shouted loudly to me from the hallway.
9. The colorful silk shimmered like a rainbow.
10. Have you ever read a good detective story?

PRACTICE 6

Answers will vary. Sample answers:

1. He parked under the tree branch.
2. There was a swing set outside the house.
3. To get an early start, Pam awoke just before sunrise.
4. The dog snarled behind the fence.
5. A bird flew down the chimney.
6. The waves may pull him under.
7. Many trees are growing outside.
8. You probably saw a house like this before.
9. Some of us went for a walk, but I fell behind.
10. Some of the children have fallen down.

PRACTICE 7

1. coordinating conjunction
2. subordinating conjunction
3. correlative conjunctions
4. conjunctive adverb
5. coordinating conjunction

Cumulative Review Chapters 13–17

PRACTICE 5 Revising Sentences With Adjectives and Adverbs

Read the sentences. Then, rewrite each sentence by adding at least one adjective to modify a noun or a pronoun or one adverb to modify a verb, an adjective, or another adverb.

1. Wendy found her sweater.
2. The girl takes a bus to school.
3. Grandfather snores loudly.
4. A lovely butterfly landed on the flower.
5. The weather was nasty all day.
6. The boat raced through the water.
7. Cows sat in the meadow.
8. She shouted to me from the hallway.
9. The silk shimmered like a rainbow.
10. Have you read a detective story?

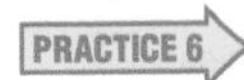

PRACTICE 6 Writing Sentences With Prepositions and Adverbs

Write ten sentences describing different scenes. In your first five sentences, use the prepositional phrases in items 1–5. In your next five sentences, use the words in items 6–10 as adverbs.

1. under the tree branch
2. outside the house
3. before sunrise
4. behind the fence
5. down the chimney
6. under
7. outside
8. before
9. behind
10. down

PRACTICE 7 Identifying Conjunctions

Read the sentences. Then, identify each underlined word or pair of words as a *coordinating conjunction*, a *subordinating conjunction*, *correlative conjunctions*, or a *conjunctive adverb*.

1. It rained a lot, but we still enjoyed the trip.
2. I laughed because the clown looked so silly.
3. Neither Joshua nor Eric is going to the party.
4. I skipped lunch; nevertheless, I'm not hungry.
5. Alicia and Ellie have joined the Girl Scouts.

PRACTICE 8 Revising to Include Interjections

Rewrite the following dialogue, adding interjections to help show the speakers' emotions. Use either a comma or an exclamation mark after each interjection.

ELIOT: Did you see the eclipse yesterday?

JANA: I guess I missed it because I had to study.

ELIOT: My brother let me observe the sky through his telescope. It was pretty fantastic.

JANA: I wish I had seen it. I've never seen an eclipse.

ELIOT: I think it will be a long time before there is another eclipse.

JANA: I am so disappointed.

ELIOT: I know. We can research when the next eclipse is expected.

JANA: What a great idea.

366 **Parts of Speech**

PRACTICE 8

Answers will vary. Sample answers:

ELIOT: Hey, did you see the eclipse yesterday?

JANA: Gosh, I guess I missed it because I had to study.

ELIOT: My brother let me observe the sky through his telescope. Wow! It was pretty fantastic.

JANA: Oh, I wish I had seen it. I've never seen an eclipse.

ELIOT: Well, I think it will be a long time before there is another eclipse.

JANA: Ugh! I am so disappointed.

ELIOT: Hey! I know. We can research when the next eclipse is expected.

JANA: Wow! What a great idea.

CHAPTER 18 LESSON PLANNER
Basic Sentence Parts

Use the Online Lesson Planner at www.phwritingcoach.com to customize your instructional plan for an integrated Language Arts curriculum.

DAY 1 18.1 The Basic Sentence; 18.2 Complete Subjects and Predicates

"What Do You Notice?" **Objectives:** Identify, use, and understand basic sentence parts, including subjects and verbs to express complete thoughts. Identify, use, and understand compound subjects and verbs.	**INSTRUCTION AND PRACTICE** **Student Edition** pp. 367–373

DAY 2 18.2 Complete Subjects and Predicates *(continued)*; 18.3 Compound Subjects and Compound Verbs

Objectives: Identify, use, and understand complete subjects and predicates. Identify, use, and understand compound subjects and verbs.	**INSTRUCTION AND PRACTICE** **Student Edition** pp. 371–376

DAY 3 18.4 Hard-to-Find Subjects

Objectives: Identify and understand hard-to-find subjects, including ▪ subject of a command or request ▪ subjects in questions ▪ subjects in sentences beginning with *here* or *there* ▪ subjects in sentences inverted for emphasis	**INSTRUCTION AND PRACTICE** **Student Edition** pp. 377–382

DAY 4 18.5 Complements

Objectives: Identify, use, and understand complements, including ▪ direct objects ▪ distinguishing between direct objects, adverbs, and objects of prepositions ▪ direct objects in questions	**INSTRUCTION AND PRACTICE** **Student Edition** pp. 383–388

Grammar Assessment

Grammar Coach:	Diagnostic Assessment	End-of-Chapter Assessment	Progress Monitoring
Personalized Instruction	Students take grammar diagnostic test online and are automatically assigned instruction and practice in areas where they need support.	Teacher uses **ExamView** to administer end-of-chapter assessment and remediation. Teachers may customize **ExamView** tests or use the ones provided.	Teachers may use the **Test Warm-Ups** and the **Cumulative Reviews** in the student book or eText to check students' mastery of grammar skills. Students may also play **DimensionL** grammar video games to test their grammar skills.
Teacher-Directed Instruction	Teacher administers the diagnostic test and determines focus of instruction and practice.		

Alternate Pacing Plans

- **Block Scheduling** Each day in the Lesson Planner represents a 40–50 minute block. Teachers using block scheduling may combine days to revise pacing to meet their classroom needs.
- **Accelerated Lesson Planning** Combine instructional days, focusing on concepts called out by students' diagnostic test results.
- **Integrated Language Arts Curriculum** Use the instruction and practice in this chapter to provide reinforcement, remediation, or extension of grammar concepts taught in your literature curriculum.

Links to Prentice Hall *LITERATURE*

Unit 3 Subjects and Predicates, p. 504; Compound Subjects and Predicates, p. 526

www.phwritingcoach.com

Grammar Assessment and Practice

Chapter diagnostic tests assess students' skills and assign instruction and practice.

DimensionL Video Games

Fast-paced interactive video games challenge students' mastery of grammar.

Lesson Planner continues on next page

DAY 5 18.5 Complements *(continued)*

Objectives	INSTRUCTION AND PRACTICE
Objectives: Identify, use, and understand complements, including ▪ indirect objects ▪ distinguishing between indirect objects and objects of prepositions	**Student Edition** pp. 389–391

DAY 6 18.5 Complements *(continued)*

Objectives	INSTRUCTION AND PRACTICE
Objectives: Identify, use, and understand subject complements	**Student Edition** pp. 392–395 **Test Warm-Up** p. 396

“If students are to edit with skill, they have to have a strong notion of what it takes to make a sentence. Though most students can write a sentence, they may not have truly internalized the successful patterns that go into good sentences. Without these essential tools, they can't perform the drafting acrobatics evolving writers require.”

—Jeff Anderson

“Fragment and run-on problems will disappear only when students are able to accurately identify the subject and the predicate. We should not take for granted that students—even those in high school—are able to make this distinction.”

—Kelly Gallagher

Differentiated Instruction

Differentiated Instruction Boxes in this Teacher's Edition address these student populations:

- Below-Level Students
- Above-Level Students
- Gifted and Talented Students
- Special Needs Students
- English Language Learners
- Spanish Speaking Students

In addition, for further enrichment, see the **Extension** features.

BASIC SENTENCE PARTS

Form well-crafted sentences in your writing by pairing carefully chosen subjects and verbs.

WRITE GUY *Jeff Anderson, M.Ed.*

WHAT DO YOU NOTICE?

Zero in on subjects and verbs as you zoom in on these sentences from the essay "The Eternal Frontier" by Louis L'Amour.

MENTOR TEXT

The question I am most often asked is, "Where is the frontier now?" The answer should be obvious. Our frontier lies in outer space.

Now, ask yourself the following questions:

- In the second and third sentences, what are the simple subjects and simple predicates?
- What are the complete subjects and complete predicates in the second and third sentences?

The simple subject in the second sentence is *answer*, and the simple predicate is *should be*. In the third sentence, the simple subject is *frontier*, and the simple predicate is *lies*. The complete subject in the second sentence is *the answer*, and the complete predicate is *should be obvious*. In the third sentence, the complete subject is *our frontier*, and the complete predicate is *lies in outer space*.

Grammar for Writers Make your sentences shorter or longer by working with your subjects and predicates. Think of your simple subject and simple predicate as the starting points of your sentences and build from there.

In the sentence "History is my favorite subject," history is the simple subject.
Well, it might be simple for you, but it's complex for me!

CHAPTER 18

367

Grammar for Writers: Syntax

Help students understand that all sentences are made up of the same basic parts. The rules in this chapter will help students recognize and use sentence parts more effectively so that they can express their ideas clearly.

BASIC SENTENCE PARTS

As students progress in their writing skills, it will be important for them to be able to apply the rules of grammar, usage, and mechanics to their own drafts. Use the *What Do You Notice?* feature to help them see effective conventions in the work of professional writers. Encourage students to incorporate proper voice, tense, and syntax as they edit their own writing.

Read aloud the opening sentence. Point out that words are the building blocks of writing, but they must be arranged into sentences in order to express ideas. Use the words *dog, cat, the,* and *chased* to show that the same words arranged differently can mean different things.

WRITE GUY *Jeff Anderson, M. Ed.*

WHAT DO YOU NOTICE?

When students have read the Mentor Text, **say:** You may recall that verbs are words that tell you the action, or what is happening, in the sentence. Subjects are the persons, places, or things about which something is being said in the sentence. Sometimes it is useful to think that the subject is doing the verb. For example, in *Ralph is talking,* Ralph (the subject) is doing the talking (verb). What are some examples of subjects and verbs in the Mentor Text? (Accept all correct responses.)

Have students read the remainder of the page. Explain that the complete subject of a sentence is the subject and all the words that directly modify it. The complete predicate is the verb plus all of the helping verbs, modifiers, and complements that complete the verb's meaning. Point out that the complete subject and complete predicate combine to make up the whole sentence.

18.1 The Basic Sentence

Lesson Objectives

1. Identify and distinguish between the subject and predicate of a sentence.
2. Recognize that every sentence must have a subject and a verb.
3. Recognize that the goal of writing a sentence is to express a complete thought.

The Two Basic Parts of a Sentence

Explain that the two most important parts of a sentence are the subject and the verb.

RULE 18.1.1 Read aloud the rule and then have students repeat the lines with you.

Write a combination of simple sentences and sentence fragments (capitalized and punctuated like sentences) on the board. Draw students' attention to one of the complete sentences you have written. Identify it as a complete sentence; then, explain that it expresses a complete thought and contains a subject and a verb. Have students identify which of the remaining examples are sentences and which are not.

The Subject

Remind students that the subject of a sentence is usually the person, place, thing, or idea on which the sentence mainly focuses.

RULE 18.1.2 Read aloud the rule and then have students repeat the lines with you.

Say: The way **I find the subject** is to think of the subject and verb together. I find the verb—the word that identifies the action or condition in the sentence—and then I put the words *Who?* or *What?* in front of it. Use the example sentences on page 368 to demonstrate.

Work with students to identify the subject of this sentence: *The wind blew the leaves.*

Have each student write three sentences. Then, have students trade sentences with a partner. Partners should identify the nouns and then identify the subject of each sentence.

18.1 The Basic Sentence

There are many kinds of sentences. Some are short; others are long. Some are simple, and others are more complex. In order to be considered complete, a sentence must have two things: a subject and a verb.

WRITING COACH Online
www.phwritingcoach.com

Grammar Practice
Practice your grammar skills with Writing Coach Online.

Grammar Games
Test your knowledge of grammar in this fast-paced interactive video game.

The Two Basic Parts of a Sentence

Every sentence, regardless of its length, must have a subject and a verb.

A complete sentence contains a subject and a verb and expresses a complete thought.

The Subject

A sentence must have a **subject.** Most subjects are nouns or pronouns. The subject is usually, but not always, found near the beginning of the sentence.

The subject of a sentence is the word or group of words that names the person, place, thing, or idea that performs the action or is described. It answers the question *Who?* or *What?* before the verb.

EXAMPLES The **keys** are lost.

Mr. Levy lost his keys.

He has lost his keys before.

The **keys** are in his pockets.

The noun *keys* is the subject in the first sentence. It tells *what* is lost. In the next sentence, the proper noun *Mr. Levy* tells *who* lost his keys. The pronoun *he* in the third sentence tells *who* lost his keys before. In the last sentence, the noun *keys* tells what are in his pockets.

368 Basic Sentence Parts

www.phwritingcoach.com

Diagnostic and Instruction
Diagnostic test assesses students' instructional needs. Lessons and practice are assigned based on results.

Additional Practice
- Grammar Practice—Targeted practice addresses individual needs.
- ExamView—Teachers customize their grammar practice and tests.
- Grammar Games—Interactive video games make grammar fun.

The Verb

As one of the basic parts of a sentence, the **verb** tells something about the subject.

The verb in a sentence tells what the subject does, what is done to the subject, or what the condition of the subject is.

EXAMPLES My dog **won** first place.
The ribbon **was given** at a ceremony.
He **seems** sleepy now.

Won tells what *my dog* did. *Was given* explains what was done with *the ribbon*. *Seems*, a linking verb, tells something about the condition of *he* by linking the subject to *sleepy*.

See Practice 18.1A

Using Subjects and Verbs to Express Complete Thoughts

Every basic sentence must express a complete thought.

A sentence is a group of words with a subject and a verb that expresses a complete thought and can stand by itself and still make sense.

18.1.4 RULE

INCOMPLETE THOUGHT in the closet in the hall
(This group of words cannot stand by itself as a sentence.)

This incomplete thought contains two prepositional phrases. The phrases can become a sentence only after *both* a subject and a verb are added to them.

COMPLETE THOUGHT The **towels** (subject) **are** (verb) in the closet in the hall.
(This group of words can stand by itself as a sentence.)

See Practice 18.1B

In grammar, incomplete thoughts are often called **fragments.**

Working with ELLs — ELL Sheltered Instruction: Cognitive

Help students read linguistically accommodated text silently with increasing comprehension and ease for increasingly long periods and with a decreasing need for accommodation. Ensure that students are able to recognize directionality of English reading, left to right, top to bottom. Make copies of page 368. Provide linguistic accommodations by circling difficult words such as *complex, noun,* and *performs* and giving simple synonyms, home language equivalents, or examples for each.

Beginning Read the first half of the page aloud slowly, word by word, as students follow along. As you read, demonstrate how to use linguistic accommodations. Then, have students reread this portion of the page silently. Afterward, discuss what they have learned.

Intermediate Model the use of linguistic accommodations, and then have students read the adapted page silently. Afterward, discuss what they have learned.

Advanced Have partners read the adapted page silently. Have them continue by reading page 369 in the Student Edition. Have them discuss the text in pairs.

Advanced High Have students read the adapted page, continuing by reading pages 369 and 370 in the Student Edition. Have them write a summary of the text.

The Verb

Explain to students that the second essential part of a sentence is the verb.

RULE 18.1.3 Read aloud the rule and then have students repeat the lines with you.

Use a Think Aloud as part of a gradual release progression.

Think Aloud **Say:** I know that the subject of the sentence tells *who* or *what* the sentence is about. So the verb tells me something more about what the subject does or is. In the sentence *My dog won first place,* the subject is *dog.* The verb tells what my dog did, which is *won.*

Read aloud the example sentences and explanation. **Guide students to understand** that verbs can be one word, as in sentences 1 and 3, or multiple words, as in sentence 2. Have students focus on sentence 2. Explain that some forms of verbs express what happened or was done to the subject. For example, in the sentence *The ribbon was given at the ceremony,* the words *was given* make up the verb.

Explain that verbs can also link the subject to a noun, pronoun, or, as in sentence 3, an adjective.

Using Subjects and Verbs to Express Complete Thoughts

RULE 18.1.4 Read aloud the rule and then have students repeat the lines with you.

Discuss with students why the first example is not a complete thought. Read aloud the second example, and have students explain why the thought is now complete. To provide practice putting incomplete thoughts together to make complete thoughts, make index cards on which incomplete thoughts are written. Have students arrange the cards to make complete sentences.

PRACTICE 18.1A

1. we, enjoyed
2. Winston, has
3. skunk, wandered
4. trucks, haul
5. Jane, knows
6. Kendra, has done
7. door, banged
8. I, miss
9. you, did get
10. Marcus, fixed

PRACTICE 18.1B

11. incomplete
12. complete
13. incomplete
14. complete
15. incomplete
16. complete
17. incomplete
18. complete
19. incomplete
20. complete

SPEAKING APPLICATION

Have partners explain to the class how they distinguished subjects from verbs.

WRITING APPLICATION

Have students explain to a partner why each sentence was incomplete and how they changed each into a complete sentence.

PRACTICE 18.1A Finding Subject and Verb

Read the sentences. Write the subject and verb of each sentence.

EXAMPLE The passengers boarded the plane.

ANSWER *passengers, boarded*

1. We enjoyed a picnic in the park.
2. Winston has two paintings in the exhibit.
3. A skunk wandered through the yard.
4. Huge trucks haul goods across the country.
5. Jane knows who left the note.
6. Kendra has not done her homework yet.
7. The door banged shut behind him.
8. I miss my old neighborhood and school.
9. Where did you get that hat?
10. Marcus fixed the flat tire.

PRACTICE 18.1B Recognizing Complete Sentences

Read the following groups of words. If a group of words expresses a complete thought, write *complete*. If a group of words expresses an incomplete thought, write *incomplete*.

EXAMPLE The new store in the mall.

ANSWER *incomplete*

11. Along a bumpy road.
12. Gloria asked them to be quiet.
13. My new MP3 player on the table.
14. Chloe has never been to Chicago.
15. Destroyed in a wildfire.
16. Randall sings in a band.
17. Finally arrived an hour late.
18. You look happy today.
19. Since I last saw you.
20. Please turn out the lights.

SPEAKING APPLICATION

With a partner, take turns talking about today's weather. Your partner should listen for and name three subjects and three verbs in your sentences.

WRITING APPLICATION

Choose three of the incomplete sentences in Practice 18.1B and write them as complete sentences.

18.2 Complete Subjects and Predicates

Have you ever seen tiles laid on a floor? First, a line is drawn in the center of the room. One tile is placed to the left of the line, and another is placed to the right. Then, more tiles are added in the same way: one to the left and one to the right.

www.phwritingcoach.com

Grammar Tutorials
Brush up on your Grammar skills with these animated videos.

Grammar Practice
Practice your grammar skills with Writing Coach Online.

Grammar Games
Test your knowledge of grammar in this fast-paced interactive video game.

Imagine that the first tile on the left is a subject and the first tile on the right is a verb. You would then have a subject and a verb separated by a vertical line, as shown in the example.

EXAMPLE **Water** | **flowed**.

Now, in the same way that you would add a few more tiles if you were tiling a floor, add a few more words.

EXAMPLE Cold **water** | **flowed** into the sink.

At this point, you could add still more words.

EXAMPLE Icy cold **water** | **flowed** into the old metal sink in a steady stream.

The centerline is important in laying tiles. It is just as important in dividing these sentences into two parts. All the words to the left of the line in the preceding examples are part of the **complete subject.** The main noun in the complete subject, *water*, is often called the **simple subject.**

The complete subject of a sentence consists of the subject and any words related to it.

RULE 18.2.1

As in the examples above, the complete subject may be just one word—*water*—or several words—*icy cold water.*

Lesson Objectives

1. Recognize the complete subject and complete predicate of a sentence.
2. Differentiate between complete and simple subjects and complete and simple predicates.
3. Identify the subject and predicate in a variety of sentence structures.

RULE 18.2.1 Read aloud the rule and then have students repeat the lines with you.

Use a Think Aloud as part of a gradual release progression.

Think Aloud **Say:** I know that the simple subject of a sentence is the noun—the person, place, or thing—that the sentence is about. But sometimes there are other words in the sentence that describe the simple subject in some way. I can see that in the third example sentence, *icy* and *cold* are words that describe the water. So *Icy cold water* is the complete subject.

Write these simple sentences on the board: *The boy read. The girl walked. Rain fell. The doorbell rang.* **Work with students** to add words to each subject to expand it.

Then, have students use the simple sentences as a basis for writing their own expanded-subject sentences.

(continued)

Differentiated Instruction

RTI Strategy for Below-Level Students

Students may be having difficulty identifying basic parts of speech, such as nouns, pronouns, verbs, adverbs, and adjectives. Have these students use an index card to cover up each of the example sentences, then move the index card to reveal one word at a time. Students should identify the part of speech before revealing the next word.

Enrichment for Gifted/Talented Students

Have students use simple two- or three-word sentences to write a skit or dramatic scene. Students should make sure that these short sentences have subjects and verbs. Then, have students rewrite the scene by adding details to the simple subjects and predicates. Compare the two versions of each student's scenes as a class. Discuss the differences in rhythm, emphasis, and emotional impact of each one.

www.phwritingcoach.com

Diagnostic and Instruction
Diagnostic test assesses students' instructional needs. Lessons and practice are assigned based on results.

Additional Practice

- Grammar Tutorials—Animated videos reinforce key grammar skills.
- Grammar Practice—Targeted practice addresses individual needs.
- ExamView—Teachers customize their grammar practice and tests.
- Grammar Games—Interactive video games make grammar fun.

RULE 18.2.2 Read aloud the rule and then have students repeat the lines with you.

Explain that the complete predicate includes the verb and all the words that modify it or complete it. These words might be adverbs or prepositional phrases or objects that receive the action of the verb.

Say: Just the way a complete subject includes the simple subject and the words related to it, the complete predicate contains the simple predicate and the words related to it. Because the simple predicate is the main verb of the sentence, I can identify the complete predicate of a sentence by first finding the verb. Then, I look for the words that modify it or complete it. For example, in the sentence *Joe climbed quickly up the hill,* I know that *climbed* is the verb. But I think that *quickly* tells how he climbed, so that is part of the complete predicate. And *up the hill* tells where he climbed, so that must also be part of the complete predicate.

Brainstrom for a variety of nouns and verbs with the class, and write them on slips of paper. Play a game in which students choose one noun and one verb and use them to create a simple sentence. Classmates can identify the subject and predicate. Then, have them add details to the subjects and predicates to create fuller, more interesting complete subjects and predicates. Challenge students to create sentences in which part of the predicate comes before the subject.

Have students create their own more detailed sentences using the expanded-subject sentences they wrote as they learned about complete subjects. Have them add words that relate to the verb to expand the predicates. Ask students to share their completed sentences.

Teacher Tip

If students are having difficulty identifying the subject when it is not near the beginning of the sentence, teach them to mentally rearrange the sentence: *After the game, our family went out to eat* can become *Our family went out to eat after the game.* Once rewritten, the subject is easier to identify.

Look at the example sentences again, plus one with new words added.

EXAMPLES Cold **water** | **flowed** into the sink.

The icy cold **water** | **flowed** into the old metal sink.

Icy cold **water** | **had flowed** into the old metal sink in a steady stream.

All the words to the right of the line in the preceding examples are part of the **complete predicate.** The verb *flowed,* or a verb phrase such as *had flowed,* on the other hand, is often called the **simple predicate.**

See Practice 18.2A

The complete predicate of a sentence consists of the verb and any words related to it.

As the examples show, a complete predicate may be just the verb itself or the verb and several other words.

Many sentences do not divide so neatly into subject and predicate. Look at the subjects and predicates in the following sentences.

EXAMPLES **After the game**, our **family** **went out to eat**.

With the snow falling, the **ski team** **began to practice**.

In these sentences, part of the predicate comes *before* the subject, and the rest of the predicate follows the subject.

As you have seen, a complete simple sentence contains a simple subject and a simple predicate. In addition, a complete simple sentence expresses a complete thought.

See Practice 18.2B

Working with ELLs — ELL Sheltered Instruction: Cognitive

Scaffold the Writing Application on page 373, and have students demonstrate their comprehension of increasingly complex English through retelling and summarizing.

Beginning Write simple statements about an animal on the board, using pictures to aid understanding. Draw a line between each complete subject and predicate. Read the statements aloud, having students echo as they follow along. Help students write key words in word webs to retell what they read. Then, guide students in writing and diagramming three sentences of their own.

Intermediate Provide partners with simple sentences about an animal. Have them read the sentences and draw a line between the complete subject and predicate in each. Then, have them complete the Writing Application and exchange papers. Have them retell their partners' work using cloze prompts such as, *The animal lives* ____.

Advanced Have students write three sentences about an animal. Then, have partners exchange sentences and draw a line between the complete subject and predicate in each. Partners should then summarize what they learned about their partners' animal.

Advanced High Have students complete the Advanced activity. Then, have them conduct research and add one sentence about the animal to their partner's work.

PRACTICE 18.2A Identifying Complete Subjects and Predicates

Read the sentences. Rewrite each sentence, and draw a vertical line between the complete subject and the complete predicate. Then, underline the subject once and the verb twice.

EXAMPLE The Larsons took a train to Washington, D.C.

ANSWER *The Larsons | took a train to Washington,* D.C.

1. Our new television has a very clear picture.
2. Coyotes roam this area at night.
3. The children enjoyed the skateboard ramp in the park.
4. Aidan delivers newspapers every day.
5. Laurie Halse Anderson wrote the novel *Speak*.
6. Reggie is looking for a job after school.
7. Nat and Roseanne did not hear about the changed schedule.
8. The hockey players usually practice early in the morning.
9. My aunt from New York has been visiting us this week.
10. Summer vacation will be here soon.

PRACTICE 18.2B Writing Complete Sentences

Read the items. Each item contains either a complete subject or a complete predicate. Rewrite each item along with the missing part to create complete sentences.

EXAMPLE _____ are coming with us.

ANSWER *My cousins from California* are *coming with us.*

11. _____ spread through the forest.
12. The governor of our state _____.
13. Skills in computer science _____.
14. _____ rolled off the counter and broke.
15. Three teenage athletes _____.
16. _____ toppled over.
17. _____ can be prevented.
18. A beautiful rainbow _____.
19. That car with the dent in its fender _____.
20. _____ occurs in the summer.

SPEAKING APPLICATION

With a partner, take turns describing one of your hobbies or pastimes using simple sentences. Your partner should listen for and identify the complete subject and predicate in your sentences.

WRITING APPLICATION

Write three sentences about any kind of animal. Draw a vertical line between the complete subject and complete predicate of each sentence.

Quick-Write Extension

To help students synthesize and apply what they have learned about complete subjects and predicates, have them write imaginary weather reports. Suggest that the weather can be as absurd as they want. Direct students to use subjects and predicates that include more than one word. Then, have students exchange paragraphs and underline all the complete subjects once and the complete predicates twice.

SPEAKING APPLICATION

Have partners explain how they identified complete subjects and predicates.

WRITING APPLICATION

Have students explain how they identified the complete subject and complete predicate.

PRACTICE 18.2A

1. Our new television | has a very clear picture.
2. Coyotes | roam this area at night.
3. The children | enjoyed the skateboard ramp in the park.
4. Aidan | delivers newspapers every day.
5. Laurie Halse Anderson | wrote the novel *Speak*.
6. Reggie | is looking for a job after school.
7. Nat, Roseanne | did not hear about the changed schedule.
8. The hockey players | usually practice early in the morning.
9. My aunt from New York | has been visiting us this week.
10. Summer vacation | will be here soon.

PRACTICE 18.2B

Answers will vary. Sample answers:

11. A wildfire spread through the forest.
12. The governor of our state spoke.
13. Skills in computer science will always be in demand.
14. Eggs rolled off the counter and broke.
15. Three teenage athletes from our school received awards.
16. The bookcase toppled over.
17. Measles can be prevented.
18. A beautiful rainbow appeared.
19. That car with the dent in its fender has been there for two days.
20. Vacation occurs in the summer.

18.3 Compound Subjects and Compound Verbs

Lesson Objectives

1. Recognize compound subjects and compound verbs in a variety of sentences.

Recognizing Compound Subjects

Explain that sometimes there are two or more nouns or pronouns that function as the subjects of the same verb in one sentence.

RULE 18.3.1 Read aloud the rule and then have students repeat the lines with you.

Say: Consider this sentence: *Birds, rabbits, and other animals will make nests to live in.* How many subjects are in this sentence? **(three)** What is the compound subject? **(Birds, rabbits, and other animals)**

Recognizing Compound Verbs

Explain that there are times when one subject has two or more verbs.

RULE 18.3.2 Read aloud the rule and then have students repeat the lines with you.

Use a Think Aloud as part of a gradual release progression.

Say: **I can see** that in the first example sentence there are two verbs: *win* and *lose.*

Point out that sentences often have both compound subjects and compound verbs. **Work with students** to help them find the compound subject and compound verb in the last example sentence.

Have student pairs work together to write sentences with both a compound subject and a compound verb.

18.3 Compound Subjects and Compound Verbs

Some sentences have more than one subject. Some have more than one verb.

WRITING COACH Online
www.phwritingcoach.com

Grammar Tutorials
Brush up on your Grammar skills with these animated videos.

Grammar Practice
Practice your grammar skills with Writing Coach Online.

Grammar Games
Test your knowledge of grammar in this fast-paced interactive video game.

Recognizing Compound Subjects

A sentence containing more than one subject is said to have a **compound subject.**

A compound subject is two or more subjects that have the same verb and are joined by a conjunction such as *and* or *or.*

EXAMPLES **Isabella and Michael** (compound subject) **are** (verb) popular baby names.

Birds, rabbits, and other animals (compound subject) **will make** (verb) nests to live in.

Recognizing Compound Verbs

A sentence with two or more verbs is said to have a **compound verb.**

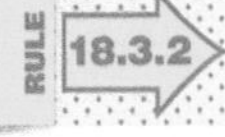

A compound verb is two or more verbs that have the same subject and are joined by a conjunction such as *and* or *or.*

EXAMPLES The **team** (subject) **may win or lose** (compound verb).

She (subject) **reads, edits, and writes** (compound verb) her books.

Sometimes a sentence will have both a compound subject and a compound verb.

EXAMPLE **Liz and Josh** (compound subject) **sang and danced** (compound verb) in the play.

See Practice 18.3A
See Practice 18.3B

Quick-Write Extension

To help students synthesize and apply what they have learned about compound subjects and verbs, have them write a description of a character in a folk tale or a superhero in a graphic novel, explaining what the character is like. Direct students to use compound subjects and verbs in their paragraphs. Then, have students exchange paragraphs and label all the compound subjects and verbs.

Diagnostic and Instruction
Diagnostic test assesses students' instructional needs. Lessons and practice are assigned based on results.

Additional Practice
- Grammar Tutorials—Animated videos reinforce key grammar skills.
- Grammar Practice—Targeted practice addresses individual needs.
- ExamView—Teachers customize their grammar practice and tests.
- Grammar Games—Interactive video games make grammar fun.

PRACTICE 18.3A **Recognizing Compound Subjects and Compound Verbs**

Read the sentences. Write the compound subject and/or the compound verb in each sentence.

EXAMPLE Brad and Tony work for the Recreation Department.
ANSWER *Brad and Tony*

1. Yolanda designs and sews her own clothes.
2. Oranges, grapefruits, and lemons are citrus fruits.
3. Nina sat in the shade and sipped a cool drink.
4. Either Ollie or Oscar left his sweatshirt here.
5. Nikki wrote a story and posted it on her Web site.
6. Canada, the United States, and Mexico are countries in North America.
7. You may climb the stairs or ride the escalator.
8. Several people in the room coughed and sneezed.
9. We looked for wild strawberries but didn't find any.
10. My friends and I sometimes go to the track and run several laps.

SPEAKING APPLICATION

With a partner, take turns describing a crowd that you saw somewhere. Your partner should listen for and identify at least one compound subject and one compound verb in your description.

WRITING APPLICATION

Use sentences 4, 7, and 10 as models, and write three sentences that have compound subjects and/or compound verbs.

PRACTICE 18.3A

1. designs and sews
2. oranges, grapefruits, and lemons
3. sat and sipped
4. Ollie or Oscar
5. wrote and posted
6. Canada, the United States, and Mexico
7. may climb or (may) ride
8. coughed and sneezed
9. looked but did (not) find
10. friends and I; go and run

SPEAKING APPLICATION

Have partners explain how they identified compound subjects and verbs.

WRITING APPLICATION

Have students identify their compound subjects and/or verbs.

Differentiated Instruction

PRE-AP Enrichment for Above-Level Students Have pairs or small groups collaborate to create stories using the skills learned in this section. Set rules for student writing, such as these:

- At least half of all sentences in the story or skit must have either a compound subject or a compound verb.
- There must be one example of a sentence in which there is a compound subject and a compound verb.

After they have finished writing their story, pairs or small groups should present it to the class. This could take a variety of formats, such as a short video or animation, a comic strip, or a skit.

Emphasize to students that good writing uses a variety of sentence types—short and long, simple and complex, normal word order and inverted word order.

PRACTICE 18.3B

1. This street and sidewalk need repairs.
2. Jonathan tried out for the team and made it.
3. I drank a glass of juice and ran for the school bus.
4. Oil paintings and pottery were on sale at the craft fair.
5. Renee wrote a long letter and sent it to the editor of the newspaper.
6. Nick mowed the grass and raked the lawn.
7. The teacher and students were happy about the test scores.
8. Wind and water are renewable energy sources.
9. A police officer examined the accident site and questioned all the witnesses.
10. Tulips and daffodils grew along the path.

SPEAKING APPLICATION

Have partners explain how they identified the compound.

WRITING APPLICATION

Have partners exchange sentences and identify the compound subject and/or compound verb.

PRACTICE 18.3B Combining Sentences With Compound Subjects and Compound Verbs

Read the sentences. Combine each pair of sentences by using compound subjects or compound verbs.

EXAMPLE Sylvia aimed the ball carefully. She made a basket.

ANSWER *Sylvia aimed the ball carefully and made a basket.*

1. This street needs repair. The sidewalk does, too.
2. Jonathan tried out for the team. He made it.
3. I drank a glass of juice. Then, I ran for the school bus.
4. Oil paintings were on sale at the craft fair. Pottery was also on sale.
5. Renee wrote a long letter. She sent it to the editor of the newspaper.
6. Nick mowed the grass. He raked the lawn.
7. The teacher was happy about the test scores. The students were, too.
8. Wind is a renewable energy source. Water is as well.
9. A police officer examined the accident site. She questioned all the witnesses.
10. Tulips grew along the path. Daffodils grew there also.

SPEAKING APPLICATION

With a partner, take turns describing something in your schoolyard. Use a compound subject or a compound verb in one of your sentences. Your partner should listen for and identify the compound.

WRITING APPLICATION

Write two short sentences about what you like to do after school. Then, combine the two short sentences into one longer sentence that has a compound subject and/or compound verb.

Working with ELLs

ELL **Sheltered Instruction:** Cognitive

Scaffold the Writing Application and provide opportunities for students to write using a variety of grade-appropriate sentence patterns. Monitor their abilities to write in increasingly accurate ways as more English is acquired.

Beginning Have students help you write simple sentences about after-school activities. Use students' prior knowledge to generate sentences: for example, *I meet my friends. I play soccer.* Model how to combine sentences using compound subjects and verbs: for example, *I meet my friends and play soccer.*

Intermediate Instruct students to write sentences about after-school activities with a fluent partner. Then, have them combine short, related sentences using compound subjects or verbs. Provide a model, such as *I play soccer. My friends do, too. My friends and I play soccer.* Have them read their sentences aloud to the class.

Advanced Have students complete the Writing Application. Then, have them exchange papers with partners and identify compound subjects and compound verbs.

Advanced High After partners complete the Advanced activity, have them repeat the activity with a new topic. If they combined subjects the first time, have them practice combining verbs the next time, and vice versa.

18.4 Hard-to-Find Subjects

It can be difficult to identify simple subjects in certain sentences. These sentences do not follow **normal word order** in which the subject comes before the verb. Sometimes the subject will follow the verb or part of a verb phrase. This is called **inverted word order.** Questions are often presented in inverted word order.

www.phwritingcoach.com

Grammar Practice
Practice your grammar skills with Writing Coach Online.

Grammar Games
Test your knowledge of grammar in this fast-paced interactive video game.

NORMAL WORD ORDER — The **meeting** (subject) **will begin** (verb) at 9:00 A.M. sharp!

INVERTED WORD ORDER — When **will** (verb) the **meeting** (subject) **begin** (verb)?

Sometimes the subject will not actually be stated in the sentence. It will be understood to be the pronoun *you.* This is often true in sentences that express commands or requests.

The Subject of a Command or Request

When a sentence commands or requests someone to do something, the subject is often unstated.

The subject of a command or request is understood to be the pronoun *you*.

COMMANDS OR REQUESTS	HOW THE SENTENCES ARE UNDERSTOOD
Go!	You go!
Start at once.	You start at once.
Please get up.	You get up.
Heather, write it down.	Heather, you write it down.
Tara, get the confirmation number.	Tara, you get the confirmation number.

See Practice 18.4A

Even though a command or request may begin with the name of the person spoken to, the subject is still understood to be *you.*

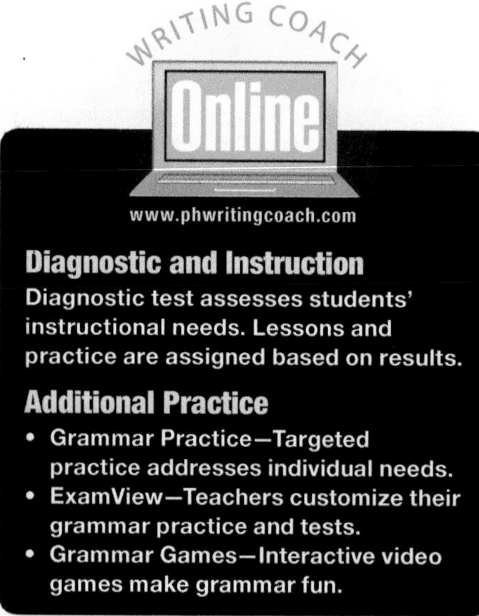

www.phwritingcoach.com

Diagnostic and Instruction
Diagnostic test assesses students' instructional needs. Lessons and practice are assigned based on results.

Additional Practice
- Grammar Practice—Targeted practice addresses individual needs.
- ExamView—Teachers customize their grammar practice and tests.
- Grammar Games—Interactive video games make grammar fun.

Lesson Objectives

1. Identify the subject in sentences that do not follow normal subject-verb word order.

The Subject of a Command or Request

Write on the board the sentence *Turn off the light.* Point out that this sentence does not seem to have a subject. Explain that some sentences have a subject that is difficult to identify.

RULE 18.4.1 Read aloud the rule and then have students repeat the lines with you.

Use a Think Aloud as part of a gradual release progression.

Think Aloud **Say:** When **I give** a command or make a request, I am usually telling or asking another person to do something. If I say *Turn off the light*, it is as if I am saying *You turn off the light. You* is the subject of the sentence even though it is not stated.

With students, read through the examples in the chart on page 377. Make sure students notice that even if the sentence starts with the person's name, the subject is still understood to be *you.*

Have students make a two-column graphic organizer of sentences similar to the chart. First, students should write several sentences that are commands or requests and that have understood subjects. Then, students should enter their sentences in the first column. Have students describe how the sentences are understood in the second column. Suggest using the sentences *Stop!* and *Please get out of the pool!* to begin their graphic organizers.

Finding Subjects in Questions

Remind students that certain types of sentences use an inverted, or reversed, word order. Questions are a good example. Often, with a question, the subject of a sentence will be in the middle or near the end of a sentence.

RULE 18.4.2 Read aloud the rule and then have students repeat the line with you.

Say: If I say *Kiko is feeling fine today*, that statement answers the question *How is Kiko feeling today?* **Then, ask:** What is the simple subject of the first sentence, *Kiko is feeling fine today?* (Kiko) What is the simple subject of the second sentence, *How is Kiko feeling today?* (Kiko) **Then, say:** Yes, in both sentences, *Kiko* is the simple subject. But you can see that in the question, the subject came after the verb.

Using the example sentences on page 378 as a guide, work with students to generate questions that begin with the words *what, which, whom, who, whose, when, where, why,* and *how.*

Have volunteers identify the subject of each sentence. Discuss whether each sentence uses inverted word order (verb-subject) or normal word order (subject-verb).

Teacher Tip

If students are having difficulty identifying the subject of a sentence, review rule 18.1.2: *The subject of a sentence is the word or group of words that names the person, place, thing, or idea that performs the action or is described. It answers the question Who? or What? before the verb.* Students can find the verb in the sentence, then think about who or what is performing that action or being described.

Finding Subjects in Questions

Questions are often presented in inverted word order. You will usually find the subject in the middle of the sentence.

In questions, the subject often follows the verb.

Some questions in inverted word order begin with the words *what, whom, when, where, why,* and *how.* Others begin with the verb itself or with a helping verb.

EXAMPLES How **are** the **muffins** today?

Did you make them fresh this morning?

Have you found a basket for them yet?

If you ever have trouble finding the subject in a question, use this trick: Change the question into a statement. The subject will then appear in normal word order before the verb.

QUESTIONS	REWORDED AS STATEMENTS
How are you feeling today?	You are feeling how today.
What did the nurse say?	The nurse did say what.
Were the newspapers delivered?	The newspapers were delivered.
Did she bring the newspaper with her?	She did bring the newspaper with her.

Not every question is in inverted word order. Some are in normal word order, with the subject before the verb. Questions beginning with *who, whose,* or *which* often follow normal word order.

EXAMPLES **Who has** the new car?

Whose new **car was** right here?

Which **driver should look** at the car?

See Practice 18.4B

PRACTICE 18.4A **Identifying Subjects in Commands or Requests**

Read the sentences. Write the subject of each sentence.

EXAMPLE Please bring your own lunch.
ANSWER *you*

1. Open your books now.
2. Reese, please show me your photos.
3. Pass the ball to Lonnie.
4. Hand me that towel, please.
5. Take the first left after the stoplight.
6. Recharge the battery when it runs down.
7. Do not leave yet.
8. Lou, work with Robert today.
9. Please call me when you get home.
10. Do not forget your gloves.

PRACTICE 18.4B **Identifying Subjects in Questions**

Read the questions. Write the subject of each question. If you have trouble finding the subject in a question, change the question into a statement.

EXAMPLE Have you seen Jack today?
ANSWER *You*

11. Is the report due tomorrow?
12. Did Rosemary enjoy the show?
13. Do you know what prize you won?
14. Does Kerri have an extra pen?
15. Did you bring water for everyone?
16. Would you like me to arrange these chairs?
17. Did Sarah put my folder on my desk?
18. Will we take a field trip?
19. Is she worried about her father?
20. Has everyone had a chance to respond?

SPEAKING APPLICATION

With a partner, take turns explaining how to do a simple task. Your partner should identify the subjects of your sentences.

WRITING APPLICATION

Use sentences 15, 16, and 20 as models and write three sentences of your own. Circle the subjects in your sentences.

PRACTICE 18.4A

1. you
2. you
3. you
4. you
5. you
6. you
7. you
8. you
9. you
10. you

PRACTICE 18.4B

11. report
12. Rosemary
13. you
14. Kerri
15. you
16. you
17. Sarah
18. we
19. she
20. everyone

SPEAKING APPLICATION

Students' responses should demonstrate that they can identify the subjects of their partners' sentences.

WRITING APPLICATION

Have students explain how they identified the subjects in their sentences.

Working with ELLs ELL Sheltered Instruction: Cognitive

To build and reinforce student attainment of the concept of a subject, help them listen, derive meaning from, and respond orally to information presented in a wide variety of print, electronic, audio, and visual media.

Beginning Display a printout from a simple how-to Web site or magazine article. Read the directions aloud with students, incorporating gestures. Review that directions are often written as commands, and that the subject of a command is understood as *you*. Lead students in restating the commands, saying: *You …*

Intermediate Have groups of students complete the Beginning activity. Call on volunteers to restate the commands using the word *you*.

Advanced Distribute a magazine or newspaper article containing questions and commands to pairs of students. Have them read and discuss the article, listing any commands or questions and identifying the subject of each. Have them present their findings to the class and respond orally to questions.

Advanced High Have students complete the Advanced activity individually. Then, have them meet in groups to discuss their examples of print media. Ensure that students identify the subjects in their media.

Finding the Subject in Sentences Beginning With *There* or *Here*

Explain that in addition to many questions, sentences that begin with *there* or *here* often use an inverted word order.

RULE 18.4.3 Read aloud the rule and then have students repeat the line with you.

Use a Think Aloud as part of a gradual release progression.

Say: When **I see that** a sentence begins with *here* or *there,* it is a clue that the subject might come after the verb. In these cases, I know that finding the verb can help me identify the subject of the sentence. In the first example sentence, I can see that *teaching* is the verb. Then, I can see that it is the professors who are teaching, so *professors* must be the simple subject.

Write this sentence on the board: *There are two children at the door.* **Work with students** to reword the sentence so that the subject, *two children*, is before the verb, *are*. (Two children are at the door.) Point out that the subject in the second sentence is the same as the subject in the first sentence.

Have students each write five sentences that begin with either *here* or *there*. Then, have them exchange sentences with a partner. Partners should change the order of words in the sentences so that the subject precedes the verb.

Teacher Tip

Students should usually locate the verb in a sentence before they look for the subject. Students may have difficulty, however, realizing that forms of the verb *to be* are part of many verbs. You may want to review these forms of the verb: Present tense: *I am; You are; He/she/it is; We are; You are; They are.* Past tense: *I was; You were; He/she/it was; We were; You were; They were.* Have students practice using each of these verb forms in a sentence.

Finding the Subject in Sentences Beginning With *There* or *Here*

Sentences beginning with *there* or *here* are usually in inverted word order.

RULE 18.4.3 ***There* or *here* is never the subject of a sentence.**

There can be used to start a sentence.

SENTENCE STARTER **There** are two professors from Harvard teaching today.

There and *here* can be used as adverbs at the beginning of sentences. As adverbs, these two words point out *where* and modify the verbs.

ADVERB **There** goes the town mayor.

Here are the cards from the ceremony.

Be alert to sentences beginning with *there* and *here.* They are probably in inverted word order, with the verb appearing before the subject. If you cannot find the subject, reword the sentence in normal word order. If *there* is just a sentence starter, you can drop it from your reworded sentence.

SENTENCES BEGINNING WITH *THERE* OR *HERE*	REWORDED WITH SUBJECT BEFORE VERB
There is a mistake on the dinner order.	A mistake is on the dinner order.
Here is the correct list of orders.	The correct list of orders is here.

See Practice 18.4C

Finding the Subject in Sentences Inverted for Emphasis

Sometimes a subject is intentionally put after its verb to draw attention to the subject.

In some sentences, the subject follows the verb in order to emphasize the subject, or make it stand out.

RULE 18.4.4

In the following examples, notice how the order of the words builds suspense by leading up to the subject.

EXAMPLES In the midst of the crowd outside the restaurant **stood** (verb) my **parents** (subject).

Flying (verb) above the yard **was** (verb) a large red-tailed **hawk** (subject).

Hiding (verb) under the warm blanket **was** (verb) my little black **puppy** (subject).

You can reword sentences such as these in normal word order to make it easier to find the subject.

INVERTED WORD ORDER	REWORDED WITH SUBJECT BEFORE VERB
In the midst of the crowd outside the restaurant stood my parents.	My parents stood in the midst of the crowd outside the restaurant.
Flying above the yard was a large red-tailed hawk.	A large red-tailed hawk was flying above the yard.
Hiding under the warm blanket was my little black puppy.	My little black puppy was hiding under the blanket.

See Practice 18.4D

Finding the Subject in Sentences Inverted for Emphasis

Explain that writers often vary the normal word order of a sentence to create a specific effect. Placing the subject at the end of a sentence can sometimes draw attention to the it. For example, *Standing pitifully at the gate was a small, mud-spattered puppy.*

RULE 18.4.4 Read aloud the rule and then have students repeat the lines with you.

Point out that the goal of the example sentences is to keep the reader in suspense until the very end. Read the first example sentence aloud, pausing and using your voice to emphasize the suspense before arriving at the subject.

Ask students to do the same with the other two examples. Encourage students to use dramatic intonation and pauses to emphasize the subject.

Remind students that these sentences all have inverted word order. If students have difficulty locating the subject, reversing the order of the major parts of the sentence will usually make the subject easier to find.

Discuss the example sentences in the chart on page 381. Then, have students use the examples as a guide in writing their own sentences. Ask them to share their sentences with a small group. Have other group members identify the subject of each sentence.

Differentiated Instruction

RTI Strategy for Below-Level Students Students may need to review nouns and verbs before continuing with the chapter. Briefly go over the definitions of nouns and verbs with students and have them say several examples. Then, have students write the words *Noun* and *Verb* on index cards. Read aloud a passage from a story or an article. Have students raise the appropriate card every time you read a noun or a verb.

PRE-AP Enrichment for Above-Level Students Explain that, when inverted word order is used for emphasis, the predicate often presents a situation that elicits a strong emotional reaction in order to make readers wonder who or what is involved. Then, challenge students to write a paragraph or a poem that uses inverted word order at least twice to achieve a dramatic effect and draw attention to the subject.

PRACTICE 18.4C

1. messages
2. coach
3. tree
4. bus
5. players
6. answer
7. farms
8. writer
9. stars
10. map

PRACTICE 18.4D

11. portrait
12. parent
13. you
14. kittens
15. shop
16. he
17. branches
18. settlers
19. water
20. you

SPEAKING APPLICATION

Have students demonstrate how they were able to identify the subjects in their partner's sentences.

WRITING APPLICATION

Have students explain how they identified the subjects in their sentences.

PRACTICE 18.4C Identifying Subjects in Sentences Beginning With *Here* or *There*

Read the sentences. Write the subject of each sentence.

EXAMPLE Here are the materials you need.
ANSWER *materials*

1. There are two unread messages in my e-mail.
2. Here comes the coach now.
3. There stood a solitary tree in the field.
4. There goes the last bus without us.
5. Here are a few more players.
6. There is only one right answer.
7. There had been dairy farms in this area.
8. Here lives a famous writer.
9. There are only a few stars out tonight.
10. Here is a map you can follow.

PRACTICE 18.4D Identifying Subjects in Sentences Inverted for Emphasis

Read the sentences. Write the subject of each sentence.

EXAMPLE Overhead flew a flock of geese.
ANSWER *flock*

11. In the middle of the hall hung Grandfather's portrait.
12. Into the office stormed an angry parent.
13. Nowhere will you find better merchandise.
14. Under the porch were two stray kittens.
15. Two blocks from here is the ice cream shop.
16. His good looks he got from his father.
17. All over the yard were broken branches.
18. On these shores landed the first settlers.
19. Down the drain swirled the muddy water.
20. Under no circumstances are you to disturb me!

SPEAKING APPLICATION

With a partner, take turns pointing out two or three things in your classroom using sentences that begin with *Here* or *There*. Your partner should identify the subjects of your sentences.

WRITING APPLICATION

Use sentences 11, 13, and 20 as models, and write three sentences with inverted order of subjects and verbs. Circle the subjects.

Working with ELLs — ELL Sheltered Instruction: Cognitive

As students learn how to identify subjects, practice using a variety of grade-appropriate connecting words to combine phrases, clauses, and sentences in increasingly accurate ways.

Beginning Use gestures and simple words to identify things in the classroom. Incorporate the words *here* and *there* from Practice 18.4C, as in these examples: *Here are pencils. There are chairs.* Write the sentences on the board, and then combine them using the connecting word *and*. Students should copy your sentences.

Intermediate Pair students with fluent speakers. Have them write the sentences they generated during the Speaking Application. Then, have them use those sentences to write longer sentences, incorporating the connecting word *and*. Provide a model: *There is the window, and here is the door.*

Advanced Have students complete the Writing Application. Then, have them rewrite their sentences by adding a connecting word and a clause to each. Provide this example: *In the middle of the hall hung Grandfather's portrait, but it was crooked.*

Advanced High Have students complete the Advanced activity. Then, have them exchange sentences with partners and circle the connecting words in each other's sentences.

18.5 Complements

Often, a subject and verb alone can express a complete thought. For example, *Birds fly* can stand by itself as a sentence, even though it contains only two words, a subject and a verb. Other times, however, the thought begun by a subject and its verb must be completed with other words. For example, *Jacob bought, The waiter told, Our waiter was, Isabella felt,* and *Carolyn won* all contain a subject and verb, but none expresses a complete thought. All these ideas need **complements.**

www.phwritingcoach.com

Grammar Practice
Practice your grammar skills with Writing Coach Online.

Grammar Games
Test your knowledge of grammar in this fast-paced interactive video game.

A complement is a word or group of words that completes the meaning of a sentence.

Complements are usually nouns, pronouns, or adjectives. They are located right after or very close to the verb. The complements are shown below in blue. The complements answer questions about the subject or verb in order to complete the sentence.

DIFFERENT KINDS OF COMPLEMENTS

Jacob (subject) **bought** (verb) **dinner** (complement).

The **waiter** (subject) **told** (verb) **us** the **specials** (complements).

Our **waiter** (subject) **was** (verb) **impatient** (complement).

Isabella (subject) **felt** (verb) **happy** (complement).

Carolyn (subject) **won** (verb) the **game** (complement).

This section will describe three types of complements: **direct objects, indirect objects,** and **subject complements.** All complements add information about the subjects or verbs in the sentence. They paint a clearer picture that helps the reader understand the writer's thoughts.

www.phwritingcoach.com

Diagnostic and Instruction
Diagnostic test assesses students' instructional needs. Lessons and practice are assigned based on results.

Additional Practice
- Grammar Practice—Targeted practice addresses individual needs.
- ExamView—Teachers customize their grammar practice and tests.
- Grammar Games—Interactive video games make grammar fun.

Lesson Objectives

1. Identify the complements used in sentences.
2. Describe the effect of complements on the meaning of the sentence.
3. Distinguish between the various types of complements.

Explain to students that, while a sentence always has a subject and a verb, these basic parts alone are not always enough to create a sentence that makes sense.

RULE 18.5.1 Read aloud the rule and then have students repeat the lines with you.

Use a Think Aloud as part of a gradual release progression.

Think Aloud **Say:** I can see that a sentence like *Our waiter was* does not make any sense, even though it has a subject and a verb. As a reader, I ask, *Our waiter was what?* Was the waiter cold, funny, late, tall, or something else?

The sentence needs more words to complete the thought. Read aloud the other example sentences, but leave out the complement(s) in each one. **Work with** students to ask the question that the complement answers. **Say:** *Jacob bought* and pause to let students ask *What did Jacob buy?* Explain that these questions can be answered and complete sentences can be formed by adding complements.

Have the class brainstorm for a list of verbs that often need complements, such as *is, was, wants, wrote,* and *like.* Begin sentences that use these verbs, and have volunteers finish the sentences by adding a complement.

Have each student generate four sentences using verbs from the list. Ask students to compare their sentences with a partner's.

Teacher Tip

To help students remember the function of a complement in a sentence, point out that *complement* is from the same root as *complete.* Both are related to the Latin root *complēre,* which means *to complete* or *to fill.* Make sure that students are not confusing *complement* with *compliment.*

Recognizing Direct Objects

Remind students that many verbs indicate action. The noun or pronoun that receives this action is called a direct object. Direct objects are a type of complement.

RULE 18.5.2 Read aloud the rule and then have students repeat the lines with you.

Say: In a sentence with a direct object, there will usually be at least two nouns: the subject and the direct object. Listen to this sentence: *My dog chews toys.* What is the simple subject? (dog) What is another noun in this sentence? (toys) Is this noun receiving the action of the verb *chews*? (Yes, the toys are getting chewed.) What question does the word *toys* answer? (What does my dog chew?)

Explain that questions and sentences with unstated subjects can also have direct objects. Write these sentences on the board and work with students to find the direct objects and the subjects.

Who threw the ball?

Eat your food!

Please put away your clothes.

Compound Direct Objects

Explain that there may be more than one noun or pronoun that receives the action of the verb.

Write these sentences on the board: *The students studied math. The students studied history. The students studied science.* **Ask:** How could I rewrite these sentences as one sentence with a compound direct object? (The students studied math, history, and science.)

Teacher Tip

Explain that only certain action verbs can take a direct object. If students are confused about what an action verb is, remind them that there are action verbs and linking verbs. Linking verbs link the subject to additional information about the subject. Action verbs describe an action. If students need to review these verb forms, make a list of several verbs and have students use a T-chart with the headings *Action Verbs* and *Linking Verbs* to classify them.

Recognizing Direct Objects

Direct objects follow action verbs.

A direct object is a noun or pronoun that receives the action of a verb.

You can find a direct object by asking *What?* or *Whom?* after an action verb.

EXAMPLES My younger **sister** (subject) **found** (verb) the hidden **presents** (direct object).

I (subject) **called** (verb) **Christina** (direct object) later that day.

My dog **Tinker** (subject) **likes** (verb) a long **run** (direct object) in the yard.

Presents, Christina, and *run* are the direct objects of the verbs in the examples. In the first sentence, *presents* answers the question *Found what?* In the second sentence, *Christina* answers the question *Called whom?* In the third sentence, *run* answers the question *Likes what?*

Compound Direct Objects

Like subjects and verbs, direct objects can be compound. That is, one verb can have two or more direct objects.

EXAMPLES The **baby** (subject) **eats** (verb) **peas** (direct object) and other **food** (direct object).

The **PTA** (subject) **chose** (verb) **Mrs. Dorf** (direct object), **Mrs. Malia** (direct object), and **Mrs. Niles** (direct object) to plan the next formal.

See Practice 18.5A
See Practice 18.5B

PRACTICE 18.5A Recognizing Direct Objects

Read the sentences. Write the direct object or the compound direct object in each sentence.

EXAMPLE Walter Dean Myers has won many awards for his books.

ANSWER *awards*

1. I usually buy my lunch in the cafeteria.
2. The troop hiked ten miles last week.
3. The rain soaked my jacket.
4. Our teacher showed a film in class.
5. Samantha washed the pots and pans after dinner.
6. Come see the view from here.
7. Tammy saved her money for six months.
8. We brought grapes and apples for snacks.
9. Carole plays both the piano and the flute.
10. Ben asked Joel and me for help.

PRACTICE 18.5B Adding Complements

Read the sentences. Rewrite the sentences, and fill in the blanks with appropriate direct objects. Use both nouns and pronouns.

EXAMPLE We are reading ____ in English class.

ANSWER We are reading *Where the Red Fern Grows* in English class.

11. Nadia saved ____ to buy a camera.
12. My family will visit ____ this summer.
13. I asked ____ for a ride home.
14. Our teacher instructed ____ and ____ to hand out the books.
15. We saw ____, ____, and a ____ at the fair.
16. Dan met ____ that day.
17. On a clear night, he watches the ____.
18. Nick designs ____ for a living.
19. I've seen that ____, but I don't know ____.
20. Brian put the ____ into the trash can.

SPEAKING APPLICATION

With a partner, take turns telling how a particular sport is played. Your partner should listen for and name at least two direct objects.

WRITING APPLICATION

Use sentences 14 and 15 as models, and write two more sentences with direct objects.

PRACTICE 18.5A

1. lunch
2. miles
3. jacket
4. film
5. pots and pans
6. view
7. money
8. grapes and apples
9. piano and flute
10. Joel and me

PRACTICE 18.5B

Answers will vary. Sample answers:

11. Nadia saved one hundred dollars to buy a camera.
12. My family will visit Orlando this summer.
13. I asked him for a ride home.
14. Our teacher instructed Tonia and me to hand out the books.
15. We saw acrobats, musicians, and a magician at the fair.
16. Dan met a new friend that day.
17. On a clear night, he watches the stars.
18. Nick designs Web sites for a living.
19. I've seen that girl, but I don't know her name.
20. Brian put the papers into the trash can.

SPEAKING APPLICATION

Have partners explain how they were able to identify the direct objects.

WRITING APPLICATION

Have students exchange sentences and identify the direct objects.

Working with ELLs

ELL Sheltered Instruction: Cognitive

As students learn about direct objects, help them demonstrate comprehension of increasingly complex English by responding to your questions about a text.

Beginning After students complete the Speaking Application, distribute simple sentences about a familiar sport. Include direct objects. Read the sentences with students, using mime as needed. Then, ask questions about the text requiring brief responses, such as *Is this sport played with a ball?*

Intermediate After students complete the Speaking Application, distribute the simple sentences from the Beginning activity to small groups. Have them read the sentences and identify the direct object in each. Monitor comprehension by asking questions, such as, *How many players are there on a team? How does a team win?*

Advanced Distribute copies of an encyclopedia article about a sport. Have pairs read the sentences and circle the direct objects. Then, ask questions to monitor their comprehension, such as *When did the sport begin? How was it different in the past?*

Advanced High Direct students to complete the Advanced activity. Then, challenge students to list techniques for finding direct objects in sentences. Provide this example: *Does the word answer* What? *or* Whom? *after an action verb?*

Distinguishing Between Direct Objects, Adverbs, and Objects of Prepositions

Point out that other words may follow the verb in a sentence, but not all of these words are direct objects.

RULE 18.5.3 Read aloud the rule and then have students repeat the lines with you.

Use a Think Aloud as part of a gradual release progression.

Think Aloud **Say:** Rule 18.5.3 explains two things a direct object is *not*. It tells me that a direct object can't be an adverb. **I remember that** an adverb tells how, when, or where an action was done. So if a word tells me *how, when*, or *where* the action was done, I know it is *not* a direct object. A direct object is always a noun or a pronoun. The rule also tells me that if a noun is part of a prepositional phrase, it can't be a direct object. So if I find a noun that closely follows a preposition and seems to relate to that preposition, I know it can't be a direct object. For example, in the sentence *I swam in the river,* it looks as if *river* is a direct object at first. But I know that *in* is a preposition, and *river* relates to *in*, so *river* can't be a direct object. In the sentence *I swam the river,* on the other hand, there is no preposition, so I can tell that *river* is the direct object.

Read aloud the example sentences with students and discuss why *quickly* and *through town* are not direct objects. Then, **say:** Dan rode on his bike. Explain that *bike* is not a direct object here because it is at the end of a prepositional phrase.

Then, display the sentence starter *Jo paddled* ______________. **Work with students** to use the example sentences to complete the sentence three ways: with a direct object, with an adverb, and with a prepositional phrase.

Display the sentence starter *Martin climbed* __________. **Have pairs work together** to complete the sentence three ways: with a direct object, with an adverb, and with a prepositional phrase.

Ask pairs to read their sentences aloud to the class. Classmates may then identify whether the sentence contains a direct object. You may wish to have students combine sentences as in the final example on page 386.

Distinguishing Between Direct Objects, Adverbs, and Objects of Prepositions

Not all action verbs have direct objects. Be careful not to confuse a direct object with an adverb or with the object of a preposition. If you are unsure if a word or phrase is a direct object, ask yourself who or what is receiving the action of the verb.

A direct object is never an adverb or the noun or pronoun at the end of a prepositional phrase.

Compare the following examples. Notice that the action verb *rode* has a direct object in only the first sentence.

EXAMPLES **Dan** (subject) **rode** (verb) his **bike** (direct object).

Dan (subject) **rode** (verb) **quickly** (adverb).

Dan (subject) **rode** (verb) **through town** (prepositional phrase).

Each example shows a very common sentence type. The first consists of a subject, a verb, and a direct object. The noun *bike* is the direct object of the verb *rode.*

The second example consists of a subject, a verb, and an adverb. Nothing after the verb in the sentence answers the question *What?* so there is no direct object. *Quickly* modifies the verb and tells *how* Dan rode.

The third example consists of a subject, a verb, and a prepositional phrase. Again, no noun or pronoun answers the question *What?* after the verb. The prepositional phrase tells *where* Dan rode.

Notice also that a single sentence can contain more than one of these three parts.

EXAMPLE Dan rode his **bike** (direct object) **quickly** (adverb) **through town** (prepositional phrase).

See Practice 18.5C

Differentiated Instruction

RTI Strategy for Special Needs Students Before discussing how to find direct objects in questions, play a game of charades to review the function of a direct object in a sentence. First, show students these sentence frames:

I love ______.

I gave a ______ *to my friend.*

I drove the ______.

Explain that the subject of each sentence is *I*. Students will take turns writing a sentence using one of the frames and acting it out. Their classmates must identify the sentence frame, then try to guess what the "missing word" is. Explain that the missing word is the direct object.

Finding Direct Objects in Questions

In normal word order, a direct object follows a verb. In questions that are in inverted word order, however, the direct object often appears before the verb and subject.

A direct object in a question will sometimes be found before the verb.

RULE 18.5.4

In the following chart, questions are paired with sentences reworded in normal word order. Direct objects are highlighted in pink, subjects are highlighted in yellow, and verbs are highlighted in orange. Compare the positions of the direct objects in each.

QUESTIONS	REWORDED IN NORMAL WORD ORDER
What recipes does your grandmother make?	Your grandmother does make what recipes.
What does the baby eat?	The baby does eat what.
Which shoes do you like, the cute flat ones or the fancy boots?	You do like which shoes, the cute flat ones or the fancy boots.
Whom did you meet at the nursery?	You did meet whom at the nursery.

In each of the five questions, the direct object appears before, rather than after, the verb. To locate the direct object in a question, put the sentence into normal word order with the subject appearing before the verb. Then, the direct object will be found in its usual position after the verb.

See Practice 18.5D

Finding Direct Objects in Questions

Remind students that the word order in questions is often inverted, that is, the verb comes before the subject. This can make it difficult to identify a direct object in a question.

RULE 18.5.4 Read aloud the rule and then have students repeat the lines with you.

Read the questions and reworded sentences in the chart on page 387 with students. Make sure that students understand that the subject in each reworded sentence is the same as the subject in the associated question. Then, ask students what they need to remember about the word order of questions. (It is often inverted.) Display this sentence for students: *Charlotte ate five pancakes.* Ask a volunteer to tell you the direct object of the sentence (pancakes). Ask another volunteer to tell you what question this statement answers (How many pancakes did Charlotte eat?). Have a third volunteer tell you the direct object of the question (pancakes).

Have each student write on a slip of paper a statement with a direct object. These statements should use normal word order. Have students fold the papers and pass them to you. Mix the papers and redistribute to students, ensuring that no one receives the same one he or she wrote. Each student should then write a question based on the statement received. Ask students to read both the statement and the related question aloud. As a class, identify the direct object in each.

Extension

To help students synthesize and apply what they have learned about finding direct objects, have students work in teams on a trivia quiz. Direct each team to write four trivia questions, researching in the library or on the Internet for interesting facts. Each question must have a direct object; for example, *Whom did President George W. Bush appoint as his first Secretary of State?* Then, have students present their questions to the other teams. Teams score two points for naming the direct object in a question and one point for answering the question correctly.

PRACTICE 18.5C

1. OP
2. ADV
3. DO
4. OP
5. ADV
6. ADV
7. DO
8. OP
9. DO
10. OP

PRACTICE 18.5D

11. answer
12. points
13. whom
14. program
15. phone
16. shoes
17. sources
18. books
19. what
20. whom

SPEAKING APPLICATION

Have students explain how they distinguished the direct objects from the adverbs and objects of prepositions.

WRITING APPLICATION

Have students exchange sentences and check each other's work, explaining why the underlining is or is not correct.

PRACTICE 18.5C Distinguishing Direct Object, Adverb, and Object of a Preposition

Read the sentences. Label each underlined word *DO* for direct object, *ADV* for adverb, and *OP* for object of a preposition.

EXAMPLE Melissa keeps a parrot in a cage.
ANSWER *OP*

1. Brad noticed two eggs in the bird's nest.
2. The firefighters responded immediately to the alarm.
3. The art students learned the basics of oil painting.
4. Morgan made a mistake on her math problem.
5. The students sat quietly through the assembly.
6. Phoebe will take Spanish next.
7. Daniel revised and edited his essay.
8. A skater glided smoothly across the ice.
9. Workers removed litter from the roadside.
10. From the top of that hill, you can see for miles.

PRACTICE 18.5D Finding Direct Objects in Questions

Read the questions. Write the direct object in each question.

EXAMPLE Which bus do you take?
ANSWER *bus*

11. What answer did you give to Lucy?
12. How many points did Kevin score?
13. Whom did the team choose as captain?
14. What program should we watch tonight?
15. Whose phone did you borrow?
16. Which shoes do you prefer?
17. What sources did you use for your project?
18. How many books did Tim read?
19. What will you do about your missing keys?
20. Whom did you see there?

SPEAKING APPLICATION

With a partner, take turns talking about something you did yesterday. Your partner should listen for and identify at least one direct object, one adverb, and one object of a preposition.

WRITING APPLICATION

Use sentences 13, 16, and 19 as models, and write three questions. Underline the direct object in each question.

Working with ELLs — ELL Sheltered Instruction: Cognitive

Have students read aloud the sentences in Practice 18.5C to give them practice speaking with increasing accuracy and ease using a variety of sentence lengths.

Beginning Read sentences 1, 8, and 9 aloud to students, having them repeat after you. Praise their efforts to speak with increased accuracy and ease. Then, use yes/no questions to help them label each underlined word as a direct object, adverb, or object of a preposition.

Intermediate Have students read the even sentences from 1–10 aloud with you several times. Coach them in speaking the sentences accurately and with ease. Work as a group to identify each underlined word as a direct object, adverb, or object of a preposition.

Advanced Have partners read sentences 1–10 aloud, coaching each other in accuracy and ease of speech. Have them work cooperatively to identify each underlined word as a direct object, adverb, or object of a preposition. Call on pairs to share their answers.

Advanced High Have students pair with Beginning students. Instruct them to read several sentences from 1–10 with their partners, providing assistance as needed. Then, have the Advanced High students work independently to identify each underlined word as a direct object, adverb, or object of a preposition. They should explain their answers to the Beginning students.

Recognizing Indirect Objects

Sentences with a direct object may also contain another kind of complement, called an **indirect object.** A sentence cannot have an indirect object unless it has a direct object.

An indirect object is a noun or pronoun that comes after an action verb and before a direct object. It names the person or thing to which something is given or for which something is done.

An indirect object answers the questions *To* or *for whom?* or *To* or *for what?* after an action verb. To find an indirect object, find the direct object first. Then, ask the appropriate question.

EXAMPLE Tovah's **dad** (subject) **told** (verb) **us** (indirect object) the **story** (direct object).

(Told *what?* [*story*])
(Told the story *to whom?* [*us*])

Keep in mind the following pattern: *Subject + Verb + Indirect Object + Direct Object.* An indirect object will almost always come between the verb and the direct object in a sentence.

Compound Indirect Objects

Like a subject, verb, or direct object, an indirect object can be compound.

EXAMPLES **Joe** (subject) **gave** (verb) each **flower and bush** (compound indirect object) a **trim** (direct object).

(Gave *what?* [*trim*])
(Gave a trim *to what?* [*each flower and bush*])

Dad (subject) **offered** (verb) **Hannah and me** (compound indirect object) **dinner and a movie** (compound direct object).

(Offered *what?* [*dinner and a movie*])
(Offered dinner and a movie *to whom?* [*Hannah and me*])

See Practice 18.5E

Recognizing Indirect Objects

Explain that another type of complement is called an indirect object. Clarify that a sentence can have an indirect object only if it also has a direct object.

RULE 18.5.5 Read aloud the rule and then have students repeat the lines with you.

Say: Consider these sentences: *Annette threw me the ball. I gave my teacher an apple.* In each case, there is a subject, a verb, a direct object that receives the action of the verb, and an indirect object that answers the question *To or for whom did Annette throw the ball?* Repeat the first sentence. **Ask:** Which word answers the question *To or for whom? did Annette throw the ball?* (me) Repeat the second sentence. **Ask:** Which word answers the question *To whom did I give an apple?* (teacher) *The answers to these questions are the indirect objects in the sentences.*

Explain that you can often identify an indirect object by placing the preposition *to* in front of it and then moving the prepositional phrase to follow the verb. If the meaning of the sentence doesn't change, the word is an indirect object. Have the class brainstorm for a variety of nouns and verbs. Work with students to use these words to write sentences that contain both direct and indirect objects.

Have pairs of students write their own sentences with indirect objects. Then, have volunteers share their sentences and identify the subject, verb, direct object, and indirect object.

Compound Indirect Objects

Remind students that subjects, verbs, and direct objects can all be compound, or contain more than one. Indirect objects can also be compound.

Have students choose one of their sentences and rewrite it so that it has a compound indirect object.

Distinguishing Between Indirect Objects and Objects of Prepositions

Remind students that an indirect object answers the questions *To* or *for whom?* or *To* or *for what?* after an action verb. Tell students an object of a preposition also answers these questions, but it always follows a preposition.

RULE 18.5.6 Read aloud the rule and then have students repeat the lines with you.

Emphasize that indirect objects and objects of prepositions often answer the same questions. The difference is in the wording.

Use a Think Aloud as part of a gradual release progression.

Say: I know that indirect objects and objects of prepositions can answer the same questions in a sentence. If I say *The girl gave her horse a treat,* I am using the indirect object *horse* to tell to whom or what the girl gave a treat. But if I say *The girl gave a treat to her horse,* I am using *horse* as the object of a preposition. This is because *to* is a preposition.

Display these sentences on the board: *My grandmother gave Robbie a sweater. She gave a book to me.* **Guide students** to distinguish between the sentence that uses an indirect object and the one that uses an object of a preposition. Point out that the difference is word order and the use of the preposition *to*.

Have each student write one sentence that uses an object of a preposition. Have them switch sentences with a partner. Partners should reword the sentence into the Subject + Verb + Indirect Object + Direct Object pattern.

Teacher Tip

If students have difficulty distinguishing between direct and indirect objects, suggest they write the pattern Subject + Verb + Indirect Object + Direct Object on an index card. Have them create a mnemonic device to help remember the pattern, such as Sugarless Valentines Impress Dentists.

Distinguishing Between Indirect Objects and Objects of Prepositions

Do not confuse an indirect object with the object of a preposition.

An indirect object never follows the preposition *to* or *for* in a sentence.

Compare the following examples.

EXAMPLES Grandpa bought **her** (indirect object) a **television** (direct object).

Grandpa bought a **television** (direct object) for **her** (object of preposition).

In the first example above, *her* is an indirect object. It comes after the verb *bought* and before the direct object *television.* In the second example, *her* is the object of the preposition *for* and follows the direct object *television.*

EXAMPLES Heather gave **Tara** (indirect object) a **book** (direct object).

Heather gave a **book** (direct object) to **Tara** (object of preposition).

To find the indirect object in the first example above, you must first find the direct object. Ask yourself what Heather gave. She gave a book, so *book* is the direct object. Then, ask yourself to whom Heather gave the book. She gave it to *Tara*, so *Tara* is the indirect object.

Use the same questions in the second example. Again, *book* is the direct object of *gave*; however, *Tara* is no longer the indirect object. Instead, it is the object of the preposition *to*.

See Practice 18.5F

Differentiated Instruction

Strategy for Spanish Speakers

Students whose home language is Spanish may overuse the preposition *to* with direct and indirect objects, as Spanish indirect objects are often accompanied by a prepositional phrase in the same sentence *(Le di el libro a él).* Spanish speakers will often insert the preposition *to* before the indirect object. For example, they may say *He gave to her the book. They brought to her the keys.* Explain that in English, when a pronoun is an indirect object it never has a preposition added to it. Only when a pronoun comes after the direct object can it be the object of a preposition and be used with *to.* On the board, write a sentence that has a direct and an indirect object: *He gave her the book.* Have students rewrite the sentence, but with the prepositional phrase: *He gave the book to her.* Then write a similar type of sentence with a prepositional phrase and have students rewrite it using an indirect object instead.

PRACTICE 18.5E Recognizing Indirect Objects

Read the sentences. Write the indirect object in each sentence.

EXAMPLE The principal asked Tad some questions.

ANSWER *Tad*

1. I've already sent her two messages.
2. Carrie fed her cats tuna.
3. Seth made his mother a solemn promise.
4. Please show me your new video game.
5. The boys gave each other a high-five.
6. The baby sitter told the children bedtime stories.
7. Will you lend him a pencil?
8. The business gave the school a donation for new equipment.
9. Our class wrote the author a letter.
10. Many people gave the hurricane victims food and shelter.

PRACTICE 18.5F Distinguishing Indirect Object and Object of a Preposition

Read the sentences. Write whether the underlined word is an *indirect object* or an *object of a preposition*.

EXAMPLE Mr. Murphy teaches us social studies.

ANSWER *indirect object*

11. Phil told Mario the answer.
12. Vanessa wrote her aunt a thank-you note.
13. Do you have any news for us?
14. Let's make ourselves a snack.
15. The teacher explained the assignment to Veronica.
16. Ivy did her research in the library.
17. David passed Brett the ball.
18. Cecilia wanted time for herself.
19. The Chamber of Commerce gives one worthy student a scholarship.
20. Tara whispered a secret to Jocelyn.

SPEAKING APPLICATION

With a partner, tell about a birthday or holiday celebration. Your partner should listen for and name two indirect objects that you use.

WRITING APPLICATION

Rewrite sentences 11, 14, and 19 to include a prepositional phrase.

PRACTICE 18.5E

1. her
2. cats
3. mother
4. me
5. each other
6. children
7. him
8. school
9. author
10. victims

PRACTICE 18.5F

11. indirect object
12. indirect object
13. object of a preposition
14. indirect object
15. object of a preposition
16. object of a preposition
17. indirect object
18. object of a preposition
19. indirect object
20. object of a preposition

SPEAKING APPLICATION

Have partners use each other's indirect objects as objects of prepositions in new sentences.

WRITING APPLICATION

Have students exchange sentences and identify the prepositional phrases.

Subject Complements

Remind students that linking verbs connect the subject of a sentence to information about the subject. When linking verbs have a complement, it is known as a subject complement.

RULE 18.5.7 Read aloud the rule and then have students repeat the lines with you.

Point out that a complement completes the thought of a sentence by giving additional information. So it makes sense that a subject complement gives information about the subject. Explain that subject complements can be nouns, pronouns, or adjectives.

Predicate Nouns and Pronouns

Confirm that students can understand and give examples of common nouns, proper nouns, and pronouns.

RULE 18.5.8 Read aloud the rule and then have students repeat the lines with you.

Read aloud the paragraph under rule 18.5.8 on page 392. Explain that a predicate pronoun or noun renames or identifies the subject. Help students use the technique of substituting an equal sign for a linking verb to determine whether a word is a predicate noun or pronoun. Then, discuss the example sentences with students. Tell them that *Bonnie will be the head of our committee* could be expressed *Bonnie* = head. *Head* renames the subject *Bonnie*, so *head* is a predicate noun.

Work with students to repeat this exercise for the remaining example sentences.

Have students write their own sentences with predicate nouns and pronouns and then express the sentences as *subject = predicate noun* or *pronoun.*

Subject Complements

Both direct objects and indirect objects are complements used with action verbs. Linking verbs, however, have a different kind of complement called a **subject complement.** Like direct and indirect objects, subject complements add information to a sentence. However, subject complements give readers more information about the subject of the sentence, not the verb.

A subject complement is a noun, pronoun, or adjective that follows a linking verb and provides important details about the subject.

Predicate Nouns and Pronouns

Both nouns and pronouns are sometimes used as subject complements after linking verbs.

A predicate noun or predicate pronoun follows a linking verb and renames or identifies the subject of the sentence.

It is easy to recognize predicate nouns and predicate pronouns. The linking verb acts much like an equal sign between the subject and the noun or pronoun that follows the verb. Both the subject and the predicate noun or pronoun refer to the same person or thing.

EXAMPLES **Bonnie** (subject) **will be** (verb) the **head** (predicate noun) of our committee.

(The predicate noun *head* renames the subject *Bonnie.*)

My first **car** (subject) **was** (verb) a white **convertible** (predicate noun).

(The predicate noun *convertible* identifies the subject *car.*)

The two **winners** (subject) **are** (verb) **we** (predicate pronoun).

(The predicate pronoun *we* identifies the subject *winners.*)

See Practice 18.5G

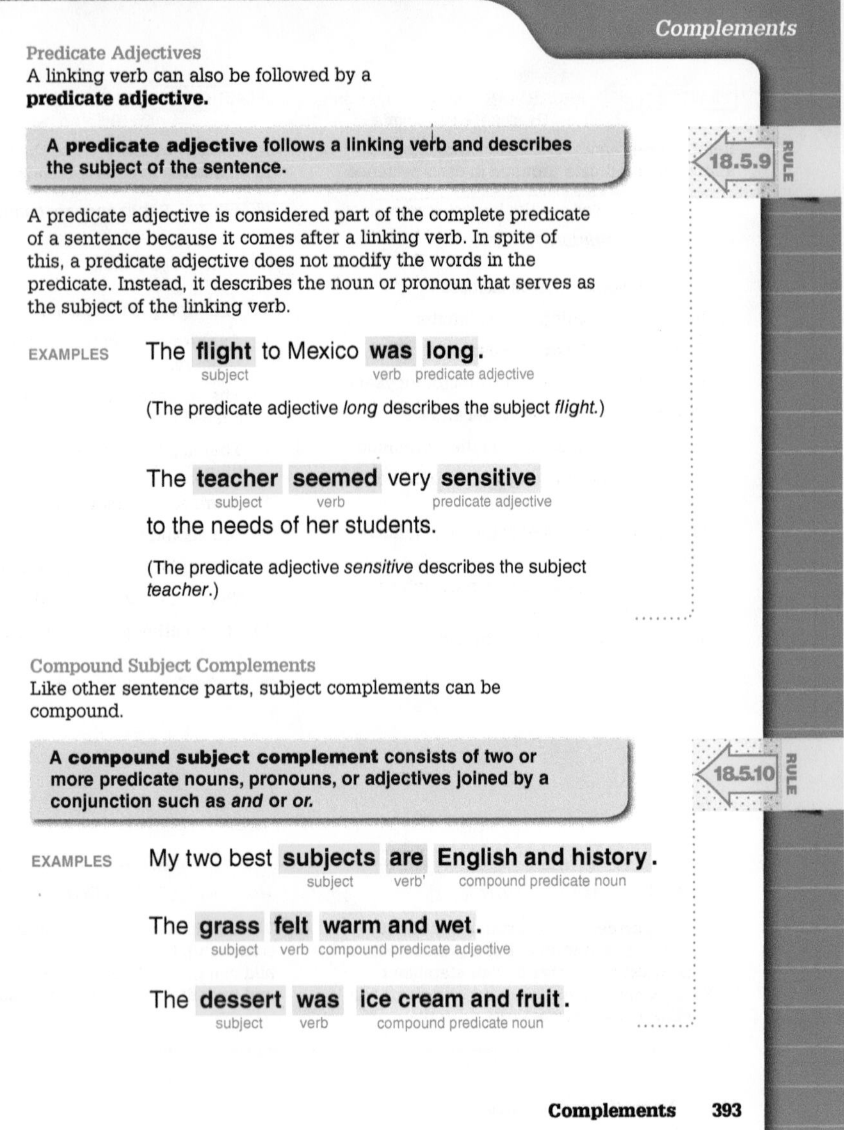

Predicate Adjectives

A linking verb can also be followed by a **predicate adjective.**

> **A predicate adjective** follows a linking verb and describes the subject of the sentence.

RULE 18.5.9

A predicate adjective is considered part of the complete predicate of a sentence because it comes after a linking verb. In spite of this, a predicate adjective does not modify the words in the predicate. Instead, it describes the noun or pronoun that serves as the subject of the linking verb.

EXAMPLES The **flight** (subject) to Mexico **was** (verb) **long** (predicate adjective).

(The predicate adjective *long* describes the subject *flight.*)

The **teacher** (subject) **seemed** (verb) very **sensitive** (predicate adjective) to the needs of her students.

(The predicate adjective *sensitive* describes the subject *teacher.*)

Compound Subject Complements

Like other sentence parts, subject complements can be compound.

> **A compound subject complement** consists of two or more predicate nouns, pronouns, or adjectives joined by a conjunction such as *and* or *or.*

RULE 18.5.10

EXAMPLES My two best **subjects** (subject) **are** (verb) **English and history** (compound predicate noun).

The **grass** (subject) **felt** (verb) **warm and wet** (compound predicate adjective).

The **dessert** (subject) **was** (verb) **ice cream and fruit** (compound predicate noun).

See Practice 18.5H
See Practice 18.5I
See Practice 18.5J

Predicate Adjectives

Explain that a predicate adjective is a subject complement that describes, but does not rename, a noun or pronoun.

RULE 18.5.9 Read aloud the rule and then have students repeat the lines with you.

Say: I use predicate adjectives all the time in my daily life. If I'm warning someone not to touch a hot stove, I'll say, *Be careful! The stove is hot!* The word *hot* is an adjective. When it follows the linking verb *is*, it is called a predicate adjective. Or, I might say, *Adrian seems tired.* The verb *seems* is acting as a linking verb, so the adjective *tired* is a predicate adjective modifying the subject *Adrian.*

On the board, write this sentence: *The music was loud.* Guide students to identify *was* as the linking verb and *loud* as the predicate adjective.

Write these sentences on the board:

The loud music made my ears ring.

Cassidy was sleepy after the long walk.

The huge campfire smelled great.

The large refrigerator looked funny.

Have students work in pairs to identify all the adjectives used in these sentences (loud, sleepy, long, huge, great, large, funny) and then decide which ones are predicate adjectives (sleepy, great, funny).

Compound Subject Complements

RULE 18.5.10 Read aloud the rule and then have students repeat the lines with you.

Explain that a clause can contain multiple predicate nouns or multiple predicate adjectives. A clause should never contain both a predicate noun or pronoun and a predicate adjective. For example, *John is tall and my cousin,* is not a correct sentence.

Read this sentence to students: *The stars were bright and small.* **Say:** This sentence includes a compound predicate adjective. **Ask:** What is the compound predicate adjective? (bright and small)

Guide students in writing their own sentences using compound predicate nouns, pronouns, and adjectives.

Differentiated Instruction

RTI Strategy for Below-Level Students If students are having difficulty distinguishing between predicate nouns and predicate adjectives, check to make sure they can distinguish between nouns and adjectives. Have students define *noun* and *adjective* and give examples of each. Then, explain that if a noun follows a linking verb and means the same as the subject, the noun is a predicate noun. If an adjective follows a linking verb and describes the subject, it is a predicate adjective. Point out that common linking verbs are *is, was,* and *are.*

PRE-AP Enrichment for Above-Level Students Point out to students that sentences may contain both an adjective and a predicate adjective. The sentence *The large refrigerator looked funny* is one example. Another is *The summer day was hot and humid.* Both adjectives and predicate adjectives describe the subject. However, often more emphasis is placed on the predicate adjective because of its position in the sentence. Encourage students to try writing sentences with both multiple adjectives and a predicate adjective.

PRACTICE 18.5G

1. lacrosse
2. painter
3. Austin
4. director
5. Isabel and she
6. swimming
7. representative
8. playwright
9. friend
10. hybrid

PRACTICE 18.5H

11. valuable
12. slippery
13. suspicious
14. delicious, filling
15. joyful
16. thankful
17. taller
18. good
19. breezy, warm
20. better

SPEAKING APPLICATION

Have partners explain how they identified the predicate noun or predicate adjective in each other's statement.

WRITING APPLICATION

Have students rewrite their sentences by changing the predicate adjectives to conventional adjectives. Then, have students explain which sentence is more effective.

PRACTICE 18.5G Identifying Predicate Nouns and Predicate Pronouns

Read the sentences. Write the predicate noun and/or the predicate pronoun in each sentence.

EXAMPLE Whales are the largest mammals.

ANSWER *mammals*

1. Gabe's favorite sport is lacrosse.
2. Regina is becoming a good painter.
3. The capital of Texas is Austin.
4. Mr. Hughes has been the director for years.
5. The group leaders are Isabel and she.
6. The best part of camp was the swimming.
7. Jordan will be our representative in the debate.
8. Shakespeare is probably the most famous playwright ever.
9. Amy remains my friend even though she moved away.
10. Your new car should be a hybrid.

PRACTICE 18.5H Identifying Predicate Adjectives

Read the sentences. Write the predicate adjective or adjectives in each sentence.

EXAMPLE Robin appears confident about her chances.

ANSWER *confident*

11. That antique table seems valuable.
12. As the storm continued, the roads became slippery.
13. The character in the black shirt looks suspicious.
14. Thanksgiving dinner was delicious and filling.
15. Laura sounded joyful about the news.
16. You should be thankful for your good health.
17. These plants grow taller every day.
18. This soup tastes so good.
19. The weather for our outing was breezy and warm.
20. Stefan felt better after a break.

SPEAKING APPLICATION

With a partner, make a statement about someone or something. Use a predicate noun or predicate adjective in your statement. Your partner should listen for and name the predicate noun or predicate adjective.

WRITING APPLICATION

Write a short paragraph describing someone or something. Use at least one predicate adjective and one predicate noun or predicate pronoun, and underline them in your paragraph.

PRACTICE 18.5I **Writing With Predicate Nouns, Predicate Pronouns, and Predicate Adjectives**

Read the sentence starters. Then, as indicated in parentheses, write a complete sentence using a predicate noun, predicate pronoun, or predicate adjective.

EXAMPLE (predicate noun) Mr. Sloan might become

ANSWER *Mr. Sloan might become the basketball coach.*

1. (predicate noun) The O'Reillys are our
2. (predicate adjective) Sunning themselves on the beach, my parents seemed
3. (predicate noun) Ms. Long could be the best
4. (predicate pronoun) The last person on the bus was
5. (predicate adjective) After dance class, she looked
6. (predicate noun) Last September, Kali became
7. (predicate pronoun) The big winner was
8. (predicate adjective) This chili tastes
9. (predicate adjective) The student council members are
10. (predicate adjective) After the game the team seemed

PRACTICE 18.5J **Writing With Compound Subject Complements**

Read the sentence starters. Then, add a compound subject complement to create a complete sentence.

EXAMPLE Ice cream, when left out too long, becomes

ANSWER *Ice cream, when left out too long, becomes warm and runny.*

11. Your speech sounded
12. My grandfather was a
13. To his friends, José seemed
14. Just how I like it, the sandwich is
15. The last two contestants were
16. Her best friend from kindergarten is now
17. After a day of exercising, Darnell is
18. The water looks
19. My two favorite foods are
20. His flight delayed again, Ted grew

SPEAKING APPLICATION

With a partner, take turns discussing sports. Use at least one predicate noun, one predicate pronoun, and one predicate adjective. Your partner should listen for and name the types of subject complements you used.

WRITING APPLICATION

Write a letter recommending a friend for a babysitting job. Use predicate nouns, predicate pronouns, and predicate adjectives. Include at least one compound subject complement.

SPEAKING APPLICATION

Have partners explain how they identified the predicate nouns, predicate pronouns, and predicate adjectives.

WRITING APPLICATION

Have students exchange letters and identify the complements, explaining how to tell the difference between compound complements and other complements.

PRACTICE 18.5I

Answers will vary. Sample answers:

1. The O'Reillys are our neighbors.
2. Sunning themselves on the beach, my parents seemed relaxed.
3. Ms. Long could be the best math teacher.
4. The last person on the bus was I.
5. After dance class, she looked exhausted.
6. Last September, Kali became a middle school student.
7. The big winner was she.
8. This chili tastes spicy.
9. The student council members are very studious.
10. After the game the team seemed happy.

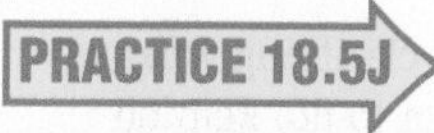

Answers will vary. Sample answers:

11. Your speech sounded clear and intelligent.
12. My grandfather was a soldier and a businessman.
13. To his friends, José seemed quiet and reserved.
14. Just how I like it, the sandwich is crunchy and thick.
15. The last two contestants were lost and confused.
16. Her best friend from kindergarten is now grown-up and tall.
17. After a day of exercising, Darnell is hungry and sleepy.
18. The water looks cold and deep.
19. My two favorite foods are pasta and seafood.
20. His flight delayed again, Ted grew angry and worried.

Test Warm-Up

1. **A** Change ***were*** to **is**
2. **H** Union Bay Band was amazing and the best.
3. **D** Make no change
4. **J** Make no change

Reteach

If students have not mastered these skills, review the content in Section 18.5 Complements.

1. Subject Complements 18.5.7
2. Compound Subject Complements 18.5.10
3. Subject Complements 18.5.7
4. Compound Subject Complements 18.5.10

Test Tip

Students may have trouble clarifying what a test or a test item asks them to do. Remind them to read all the directions carefully. Suggest that then, as they read each question stem, they mentally paraphrase the question to make sure they understand what it is asking. Students can check their understanding of a question by making sure that the answer choices make sense with their paraphrased version of the question.

Test Warm-Up

DIRECTIONS
Read the introduction and the passage that follows. Then, answer the questions to show that you can use and understand the function of subject complements in reading and writing.

Sasha wrote this paragraph about a school event called Battle of the Bands. Read the paragraph and think about the changes you would suggest as a peer editor. When you finish reading, answer the questions that follow.

Battle of the Bands

(1) The Battle of the Bands competition were hosted by my school. (2) It is my favorite school event. (3) This year, the four bands were Union Bay Band, Tim and Cat, Sushi Rocks, and Candyband. (4) Union Bay Band was amazing. (5) Union Bay Band was the best. (6) The members were very talented and energetic. (7) Candyband was the runner-up. (8) I thought their second song was much better than their first. (9) My favorites were Union Bay Band and Sushi Rocks. (10) Overall, it was a great show.

1 What change, if any, should be made in sentence 1?

A Change ***were*** to **is**
B Add a comma after ***competition***
C Add an apostrophe after the ***d*** in ***Bands***
D Make no change

2 What is the BEST way to combine sentences 4 and 5 to create a compound subject complement?

F Union Bay Band was amazing.
G Union Bay Band was the best.
H Union Bay Band was amazing and the best.
J Union Bay Band was the best, and Union Bay Band was amazing.

3 What change, if any, should be made in sentence 6?

A Change ***were*** to **was**
B Change ***and*** to **or**
C Add a comma after ***were***
D Make no change

4 What change, if any, should be made to sentence 9?

F Change ***favorites*** to **favorite**
G Change ***were*** to **was**
H Change ***favorites were*** to **favorite is**
J Make no change

CHAPTER 19 LESSON PLANNER
Phrases and Clauses

Use the Online Lesson Planner at www.phwritingcoach.com to customize your instructional plan for an integrated Language Arts curriculum.

DAY 1 19.1 Phrases

"What Do You Notice?"	INSTRUCTION AND PRACTICE
Objectives: Identify, use, and understand phrases, including ▪ prepositional phrases ▪ appositives and appositive phrases	**Student Edition** pp. 397–406 **Test Warm-Up** p. 404

DAY 2 19.1 Phrases *(continued)*

	INSTRUCTION AND PRACTICE
Objectives: Identify, use, and understand verbals and verbal phrases (participles)	**Student Edition** pp. 407–410

DAY 3 19.1 Phrases *(continued)*

	INSTRUCTION AND PRACTICE
Objectives: Identify, use, and understand verbals and verbal phrases (gerunds, infinitives).	**Student Edition** pp. 411–414

DAY 4 19.2 Clauses

	INSTRUCTION AND PRACTICE
Objectives: Identify, use, and understand adjectival clauses.	**Student Edition** pp. 415–420

Grammar Assessment

Grammar Coach:	Diagnostic Assessment	End-of-Chapter Assessment	Progress Monitoring
Personalized Instruction	Students take grammar diagnostic test online and are automatically assigned instruction and practice in areas where they need support.	Teacher uses **ExamView** to administer end-of-chapter assessment and remediation. Teachers may customize **ExamView** tests or use the ones provided.	Teachers may use the **Test Warm-Ups** and the **Cumulative Reviews** in the student book or eText to check students' mastery of grammar skills. Students may also play **DimensionL** grammar video games to test their grammar skills.
Teacher-Directed Instruction	Teacher administers the diagnostic test and determines focus of instruction and practice.		

Alternate Pacing Plans

- **Block Scheduling** Each day in the Lesson Planner represents a 40–50 minute block. Teachers using block scheduling may combine days to revise pacing to meet their classroom needs.
- **Accelerated Lesson Planning** Combine instructional days, focusing on concepts called out by students' diagnostic test results.
- **Integrated Language Arts Curriculum** Use the instruction and practice in this chapter to provide reinforcement, remediation, or extension of grammar concepts taught in your literature curriculum.

Links to Prentice Hall *LITERATURE*

- **Unit 3** Prepositions and Prepositional Phrases, p. 458
- **Unit 4** Infinitives and Infinitive Phrases, p. 598; Appositives and Appositive Phrases, p. 618; Writing Workshop: Revising Sentences Using Participles, p. 643; Independent and Subordinate Clauses, p. 662; Sentence Structures, p. 682

www.phwritingcoach.com

Grammar Assessment and Practice

Chapter diagnostic tests assess students' skills and assign instruction and practice.

DimensionL Video Games

Fast-paced interactive video games challenge students' mastery of grammar.

Lesson Planner continues on next page

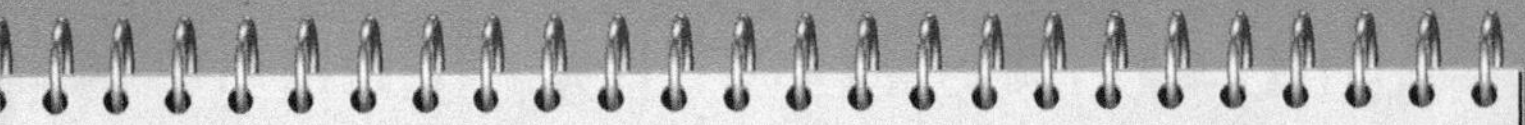

DAY 5 19.2 Clauses *(continued)*

Objectives: Identify, use, and understand adverbial clauses	**INSTRUCTION AND PRACTICE** **Student Edition** pp. 421–423

DAY 6 19.3 Classifying Sentences by Structure

Objectives: Identify, use, and understand the four structures of sentences, including ▪ simple sentences ▪ compound sentences ▪ complex sentences ▪ compound-complex sentences	**INSTRUCTION AND PRACTICE** **Student Edition** pp. 424–429 **Test Warm-Up** p. 430

"Students like to write simple sentences, usually in the 6–10 word range. It is not until we teach them how to add branches (phrases and clauses) to their sentences that we begin to see their writing flourish. We want to move our students' sentencing past the 'palm tree' stage and into writing that exhibits multiple branching."

—Kelly Gallagher

"Powerful writing has a lot to do with the artful use of phrases and clauses. In these sentence parts are the potential of powerful detail. These grammatical structures, more than any other, help students paint clear pictures and establish rhythms and patterns in their writing."

—Jeff Anderson

Differentiated Instruction

Differentiated Instruction Boxes in this Teacher's Edition address these student populations:

- Below-Level Students
- Above-Level Students
- Gifted and Talented Students
- Special Needs Students
- English Language Learners
- Spanish Speaking Students

In addition, for further enrichment, see the **Extension** features.

PHRASES and CLAUSES

Knowing how to construct phrases and clauses will help you add information to your sentences and make them more interesting.

WRITE GUY *Jeff Anderson, M.Ed.*

WHAT DO YOU NOTICE?

Search for phrases and clauses as you zoom in on lines from the poem "The Rider" by Naomi Shihab Nye.

MENTOR TEXT

A boy told me
if he rollerskated fast enough
his loneliness couldn't catch up to him,
the best reason I ever heard
for trying to be a champion.

Now, ask yourself the following questions:

- What makes the entire second line a clause?
- In the third line, what makes the words *to him* a phrase?

The second line is a clause because it is a group of words that has its own subject and verb. The subject is *he* and the verb is *rollerskated*. In the third line, *to him* is a phrase because a phrase is a group of words that does not contain a subject and verb. Phrases are used to add more information to a sentence.

Grammar for Writers Phrases and clauses are an important part of a writer's toolbox. Use them to tell more about the main nouns and verbs in your sentences.

You added some interesting information to your sentences.
It must be a phrase I'm going through.

397

CHAPTER 19

PHRASES and CLAUSES

As students progress in their writing skills, it will be important for them to be able to apply the rules of grammar, usage, and mechanics to their own drafts. Use the *What Do You Notice?* feature to help them see effective conventions in the work of professional writers. Encourage students to incorporate proper voice, tense, and syntax as they edit their own writing.

Read aloud the opening sentence. Point out that phrases and clauses are the building blocks of sentences. All sentences, whether short or long, simple or sophisticated, are made up of phrases and clauses.

WRITE GUY *Jeff Anderson, M. Ed.*

WHAT DO YOU NOTICE?

When students have read the Mentor Text, say: You may notice that the lines break in unusual ways. Poems don't always follow the rules of grammar we use when writing prose, but you can usually find basic sentence parts in their lines. Think about the first line of this poem. It has a subject—*boy.* It has a verb—*told.* It has a direct object—*me.* What other sentence parts do you see in the other lines? **(Accept all correct responses.)**

Point out that if a group of words within a sentence could be made into its own stand-alone sentence, that is, with a subject and a verb, the group is called a *clause.* Phrases are groups of words that cannot stand alone as a sentence because they do not have a subject or a verb. Then, have students finish reading the page.

Ask: Is the last line of this poem a clause or a phrase? (a phrase) Why? **(Possible response: It cannot stand alone as a complete sentence because it has no subject.)**

Grammar for Writers: Syntax

Help students understand that good writers use a variety of sentence types to keep their writing interesting. Clauses and phrases add complexity and information to writing. Not every sentence needs to have several phrases and clauses, but writers should be able to use these components correctly to express their ideas. In the lessons in this chapter, students will learn about the different types of phrases and clauses they can use to make their writing interesting and creative.

Lesson Objectives

1. Use and understand the function of adjectival phrases in reading, writing, and speaking.
2. Use and understand the function of adverbial phrases in reading, writing, and speaking.
3. Use and understand the function of appositive, participial, gerund, and infinitive phrases.

Prepositional Phrases

Discuss with students that one very common type of phrase is the prepositional phrase. As the name suggests, this type of phrase begins with a preposition.

RULE 19.1.1 Read aloud the rule and then have students repeat the lines with you.

Use a Think Aloud as part of a gradual release progression.

Say: **I remember** that a preposition shows the relationship between a noun and another word in the sentence. So if I say, *The carrots are in the refrigerator*, I am using the preposition *in* to show the relationship between the carrots and the refrigerator. In this case, the prepositional phrase is *in the refrigerator*.

Explain that a prepositional phrase begins with a preposition and ends with a noun or a pronoun called the object of the preposition. Have students name prepositions with which they are familiar, such as *in, out, above, near,* and *around*. **Work with students** to generate prepositional phrases using these prepositions or others they suggest.

Have pairs of students use these prepositional phrases to generate five original sentences. Ask pairs to share their sentences with the class.

19.1 Phrases

Sentences are usually built with more than just a subject and a predicate. **Phrases** play an important role in sentences by adding more information.

RULE 19.1.1

A phrase is a group of words that functions in a sentence as a single part of speech. Phrases do not contain a subject and a verb.

Prepositional Phrases

A **prepositional phrase** has at least two parts, a preposition and a noun or pronoun that is the object of the preposition.

EXAMPLES near **beaches**
prep object

around **palm trees**
prep object

The object of the preposition may be modified by one or more adjectives.

EXAMPLES near warm sandy **beaches**
prep adj adj object

around beautiful tall **palm trees**
prep adj adj object

The object may also be a compound, consisting of two or more objects connected by a conjunction such as *and* or *nor*.

EXAMPLES near warm sandy **beaches** and **lakes**
prep adj adj object object

around beautiful tall **palm trees** and **cacti**
prep adj adj object object

In a sentence, some prepositional phrases can act as adjectives that modify a noun or pronoun. Other prepositional phrases can act as adverbs that modify a verb, adjective, or adverb.

www.phwritingcoach.com

Grammar Tutorials
Brush up on your Grammar skills with these animated videos.

Grammar Practice
Practice your grammar skills with Writing Coach Online.

Grammar Games
Test your knowledge of grammar in this fast-paced interactive video game.

See Practice 19.1A

www.phwritingcoach.com

Diagnostic and Instruction
Diagnostic test assesses students' instructional needs. Lessons and practice are assigned based on results.

Additional Practice
- Grammar Tutorials—Animated videos reinforce key grammar skills.
- Grammar Practice—Targeted practice addresses individual needs.
- ExamView—Teachers customize their grammar practice and tests.
- Grammar Games—Interactive video games make grammar fun.

Using Prepositional Phrases That Act as Adjectives

A prepositional phrase that acts as an adjective in a sentence is called an **adjective phrase** or **adjectival phrase.**

RULE 19.1.2

An adjective phrase or adjectival phrase is a prepositional phrase that modifies a noun or pronoun by telling *what kind* or *which one.*

Unlike one-word adjectives, which usually come before the nouns or pronouns they modify, adjectival phrases usually come after the nouns or pronouns they modify.

ONE-WORD ADJECTIVES	ADJECTIVAL PHRASES
The sandy beach began there.	The beach with two lighthouses began there.
The anxious lifeguard stopped us.	The lifeguard with the anxious face stopped us.

Adjectival phrases answer the same questions as one-word adjectives do. *What kind* of beach began there? *Which* lifeguard stopped us?

USES OF ADJECTIVAL PHRASES	
Modifying a Subject	The sound of the rain scared us.
Modifying a Direct Object	It pounded the roof of the house.

When two adjectival phrases appear in a row, the second phrase may modify the object of the preposition in the first phrase or both phrases may modify the same noun or pronoun.

See Practice 19.1B
See Practice 19.1C

ADJECTIVAL PHRASES IN A ROW	
Modifying the Object of a Preposition	The gutters on the house in the field filled rapidly.
Modifying the Same Noun	There was a smell of roses in the house.

Using Prepositional Phrases That Act as Adjectives

Explain that a prepositional phrase can be used in a variety of ways in a sentence. When it is used as an adjective, it is called an adjective phrase or an adjectival phrase.

RULE 19.1.2 Read aloud the rule and then have students repeat the lines with you.

Say: Consider the sentence *The gift in the shiny wrapping paper seemed very large.* What is the prepositional phrase? **(in the shiny wrapping paper)** Does this phrase give you more information about the verb *seemed* or about the subject *gift*? **(gift)** When the phrase modifies, or gives more information about, a noun, it is acting as an adjective. This is an adjectival phrase.

On the board, write a few sentences that contain adjectival phrases. Have students identify the prepositional phrase, then decide if it modifies a noun in the sentence. Read aloud one of the sentences. Then, demonstrate how to identify the prepositional phrase. Remind students that it will always begin with a preposition and end with its object. Underline the prepositional phrase in the first sentence. Then, guide students in identifying and circling the noun the phrase modifies. You can use the questions *What kind?* and *Which one?* to help.

Working with ELLs

ELL Sheltered Instruction: Cognitive

Help students understand the general meaning, main points, and important details in spoken language in situations in which language ranges from familiar to unfamiliar. Describe a scene at a beach incorporating two of the example sentences from the first chart on page 399.

Beginning Use visuals and mime to help students understand your description. Lead students in identifying the general meaning, main points, and important details for your description. Help them use more familiar language, such as *worry,* to understand less familiar language, such as *anxious.*

Intermediate Have students restate the general meaning, main points, and important details of your description to a partner. Guide them in using familiar language in your description, such as *beach,* to understand less familiar language, such as *tide.*

Advanced Have students restate the general meaning, main points, and important details of your description by writing sentences using adjectival phrases. Have them identify unfamiliar words in your description and give definitions based on familiar context clues.

Advanced High Have students complete the Advanced activity. Extend by having them present their own descriptions of a beach scene as partners take notes on general meaning, main points, and important details.

Using Prepositional Phrases That Act as Adverbs

Tell students that they will now focus on another way prepositional phrases can be used in a sentence.

RULE 19.1.3 Read aloud the rule and then have students repeat the lines with you.

Use a Think Aloud as part of a gradual release progression.

Think Aloud **Say:** Because an adjectival phrase is a prepositional phrase that acts as an adjective, it makes sense that an adverbial phrase is a prepositional phrase that acts as an adverb. To identify adverbial phrases, **I remember** that an adverb often gives information about the verb in a sentence. It can also tell more about adjectives and other adverbs.

Write on the board *The roads were slippery after the blizzard.* **Guide students** to identify the prepositional phrase. Then, show them that the phrase points out *when* the roads were slippery.

Have students read and discuss the examples of adverbial phrases on page 400 with a partner. Have students write two complete sentences using adverbial phrases and speak them aloud to a partner. Partners should identify the adbverbial phrases.

Using Prepositional Phrases That Act as Adverbs

A prepositional phrase that acts as an adverb modifies the same parts of speech as a one-word adverb does.

An adverbial phrase or adverb phrase is a prepositional phrase that modifies a verb, an adjective, or an adverb. Adverbial phrases point out *where, when, in what way,* or *to what extent.*

Adverbial phrases are used in the same way as one-word adverbs, but they sometimes provide more precise details.

ONE-WORD ADVERBS	ADVERBIAL PHRASES
Bring your shoes here.	Bring your shoes into the garage.
The concert began early.	The concert began at exactly 6:00 P.M.

Adverbial phrases can modify verbs, adjectives, and adverbs.

USES OF ADVERBIAL PHRASES	
Modifying a Verb	Snow fell in heavy clumps. (Fell *in what way?*)
Modifying an Adjective	The day was cold for May. (Cold *in what way?*)
Modifying an Adverb	The snow fell heavily for that time of year. (Heavily *in what way?*)

See Practice 19.1D
See Practice 19.1E
See Practice 19.1F

Adverbial phrases, unlike adjectival phrases, are not always located near the words they modify in a sentence.

EXAMPLE **During the storm**, people closed up their shops. (MODIFIES)

Two or more adverbial phrases can also be located in different parts of the sentence and still modify the same word.

EXAMPLE **During the night**, the cold was felt **throughout the house**. (MODIFIES, MODIFIES)

Differentiated Instruction

RTI Strategy for Below-Level Students

Students may be having difficulty identifying prepositional phrases. Post a list of common prepositions in a prominent place where students may refer to it. Also, give students a "test" phrase as one way to identify a preposition. Phrases such as ___ *the house* or ____ *the school* can be completed with prepositions: *in the house, around the house, under the house.*

Enrichment for Gifted/Talented Students

Have students generate a list of interesting concrete nouns. Show students that each noun can be used in a prepositional phrase. Brainstorm for these phrases and list them on the board. Using the list as a starting place, have students write poems or song lyrics in which each line uses an adjectival phrase. Musical students may want to compose a melody to go with their lyrics.

PRACTICE 19.1A **Identifying Prepositional Phrases**

Read the sentences. Then, write the prepositional phrase in each sentence, and underline the object of the preposition.

EXAMPLE That story about wolves was fascinating.

ANSWER *about wolves*

1. The sound of a harp is very soothing.
2. Please take your feet off the chair.
3. Were you able to find Quentin and Stewart in the crowd?
4. Justin likes to browse through magazines.
5. Rebecca will finish her project by Monday.
6. Elizabeth II is the queen of England.
7. Everyone reads the notices on the board.
8. The train to Chicago was late.
9. Valentina likes all vegetables except eggplant.
10. I do not watch television during the week.

PRACTICE 19.1B **Identifying Adjectival Phrases**

Read the sentences. Then, write the adjectival phrase in each sentence. One sentence has two adjectival phrases.

EXAMPLE The leaves on the trees are turning brown.

ANSWER *on the trees*

11. The head of the committee read the report.
12. The plant near the window is a bamboo.
13. The singer with the deep voice stole the show.
14. Ramona delivered an excellent presentation on colonial cooking.
15. Brandon is wearing a shirt with a school logo.
16. Do you have the solution to this problem?
17. The trail up the mountain is well marked.
18. The photo in the newspaper was not very clear.
19. The girl beside Carla is her sister.
20. The first room on the left in that corridor is the nurse's office.

SPEAKING APPLICATION

With a partner, tell about your neighborhood. Your partner should listen for and name at least one adjectival phrase, one prepositional phrase, and the object of the preposition.

WRITING APPLICATION

Write this sentence twice, adding two different adjectival phrases each time: *Two girls walked into the store.* Explain to a partner how the phrase functions in the sentence.

PRACTICE 19.1A

1. of a harp
2. off the chair
3. in the crowd
4. through magazines
5. by Monday
6. of England
7. on the board
8. to Chicago
9. except eggplant
10. during the week

PRACTICE 19.1B

11. of the committee
12. near the window
13. with the deep voice
14. on colonial cooking
15. with a school logo
16. to this problem
17. up the mountain
18. in the newspaper
19. beside Carla
20. on the left, in that corridor

Quick-Write Extension

To help students synthesize and apply what they have learned in this lesson, have them use prepositional phrases to write directions from their home to a location of their choice. Directions might be realistic or playful, such as directions to Mars. Challenge students to use a variety of prepositions. Have students exchange their writing and highlight each prepositional phrase in their partner's directions. For an additional challenge, have students label each phrase as adjectival or adverbial and draw an arrow to the word it describes.

SPEAKING APPLICATION

Students should demonstrate that they can identify, use, and understand the function of adjectival phrases in speaking by describing aloud what each adjectival phrase modifies and justifying their answer.

WRITING APPLICATION

Students can show they can identify, use, and understand the function of adjectival phrases by writing new sentences containing the phrases and explaining how they function in the sentence.

PRACTICE 19.1C

Answers will vary. Sample answers:

1. The fountain in the square is a good place to make wishes.
2. Cindy bought the sparkling earrings in the store.
3. The waiter arrived with our food.
4. The audience of the play fell silent.
5. Arkee sensed something wrong with the car's suspension.
6. The get-well-soon cards piled up on the table in the hall.
7. My family is planning a vacation with my neighbors.
8. The flowers on the porch look thirsty.
9. Lin's broken collarbone healed with complications.
10. The first bite of chocolate mousse cake tasted delicious.

PRACTICE 19.1D

11. in a minute
12. at chess
13. during the recital
14. in her report
15. by the hydrant
16. onto the platform
17. across the lake
18. around her neck
19. from his nap with a start
20. without further delay

SPEAKING APPLICATION

When students say sentences, they should demonstrate that they can identify, use, and understand the function of adjectival and adverbial phrases.

WRITING APPLICATION

Students' paragraphs should show they can identify, use, and understand the function of adjectival and adverbial phrases in writing.

PRACTICE 19.1C Writing Adjectival Phrases

Read each sentence. Rewrite each sentence adding one or more adjectival phrases. Then, read the sentences to a partner who identifies the adjectival phrase.

EXAMPLE The book was dusty.

ANSWER *The book on the top shelf was dusty.*

1. The fountain is a good place to make wishes.
2. Cindy bought the sparkling earrings.
3. The waiter has arrived.
4. The audience fell silent.
5. Arkee sensed something wrong.
6. The get-well-soon cards piled up.
7. My family is planning a vacation.
8. The flowers look thirsty.
9. Lin's broken collarbone healed.
10. The first bite tasted delicious.

PRACTICE 19.1D Identifying Adverbial Phrases

Read the sentences. Then, write the adverbial phrase in each sentence. One sentence has two adverbial phrases.

EXAMPLE A hawk dived from the tree.

ANSWER *from the tree*

11. I can help you in a minute.
12. Oliver is very good at chess.
13. Franklin was bored during the recital.
14. Olivia included two graphs in her report.
15. That car parked by the hydrant was ticketed.
16. The winner stepped onto the platform.
17. The kayaker moved steadily across the lake.
18. Lily fastened the necklace around her neck.
19. The dog woke up from his nap with a start.
20. Let's go without further delay.

SPEAKING APPLICATION

With a partner, take turns talking about your favorite pastimes. Use three adjectival and three adverbial phrases. Have your partner listen for and identify the phrases you used.

WRITING APPLICATION

Write a brief description of a movie you have seen or would like to see. Use three adjectival and three adverbial phrases. Read your description to a partner, and discuss the function of each phrase.

Working with ELLs

ELL **Sheltered Instruction:** Cognitive

Using Practice 19.1E on page 403, help students use visual and contextual support to enhance and confirm understanding as they read and to develop vocabulary needed to comprehend increasingly challenging language.

Beginning Read item 1 in Practice 19.1E aloud as students track in their books. Using pictures to support your explanations, point out that *Hernando* is a boy's name and review the meaning of *read*. Then, help students use context to determine that a novel is something to *read*. Clarify by providing an example.

Intermediate List these words from Practice 19.1E: *novels, executives, essay, pounce, marching band*. Provide an image illustrating each, and have students work in small groups to match images with the words, using the context of the exercise items in which the words appear. Confirm results.

Advanced Provide an image illustrating each of these words from Practice 19.1E: *proposal, pounce, inspires, penetrated.* Have partners match images with the words, using the context of the exercise items in which the words appear. Have them confirm their conclusions in a dictionary.

Advanced High Have students complete the Advanced activity. Then, have them write a brief paragraph featuring each of the vocabulary words.

PRACTICE 19.1E Writing Adverbial Phrases

Read the sentences. Then, rewrite the sentences adding an adverbial phrase. Read your new sentences to a partner, who should identify the adverbial phrase.

EXAMPLE The janitor locked the door.

ANSWER *The janitor locked the door at night.*

1. Hernando read ten novels.
2. The executives presented the proposal.
3. Mr. Trigg checks the mail.
4. I have to write a two-page essay.
5. The tiger waited to pounce.
6. The marching band played.
7. Violet must finish cleaning her room.
8. Principal Caprio inspires trust.
9. The heat penetrated the car.
10. Tony brought donuts.

PRACTICE 19.1F Writing Adjectival and Adverbial Phrases

Read the sentences. Then, rewrite the sentences by adding adjectival or adverbial phrases, as directed in parentheses.

EXAMPLE I found your book. (adverbial phrase)

ANSWER *I found your book under the desk.*

11. A lifeguard dived. (adverbial phrase)
12. The cat yawned and walked away. (adjectival phrase)
13. The statue attracts many visitors. (adjectival phrase)
14. Scientists study the moon. (adverbial phrase)
15. Everyone admired Jana's new haircut. (adjectival phrase)
16. The jacket was extremely uncomfortable. (adjectival phrase)
17. We waited. (adverbial phrase)
18. She gave me a bowl. (adjectival phrase)
19. You will find everything you need. (adverbial phrase)
20. Four men moved furniture. (adjectival phrase, adverbial phrase)

SPEAKING APPLICATION

With a partner, take turns describing the location of something. Your partner should listen for and identify at least three adverbial phrases. Together, discuss the function, or purpose, of these phrases in the sentences.

WRITING APPLICATION

Write a paragraph about a television program. Use at least one adjectival and one adverbial phrase. Underline the prepositional phrases, and label them *adjectival* or *adverbial*. Then, explain the purpose of these phrases in your writing.

Practice 403

SPEAKING APPLICATION

Students' discussion of the functions of the phrases should demonstrate that they can identify, use, and understand the function of adverbial phrases.

WRITING APPLICATION

Students should demonstrate that they can identify, use, and understand the function of adjectival and adverbial phrases by identifying the words they modify.

PRACTICE 19.1E

Answers will vary. Sample answers:

1. Hernando read ten novels in a row.
2. At the board meeting, the executives presented the proposal.
3. Mr. Trigg checks the mail throughout the morning.
4. Without warning, I have to write a two-page essay.
5. The tiger waited with patience to pounce.
6. The marching band played during the football game.
7. Violet must finish cleaning her room without any excuses.
8. Principal Caprio inspires trust during school assemblies.
9. The heat penetrated the car at noon.
10. Tony brought donuts to the meeting.

PRACTICE 19.1F

Answers will vary. Sample answers:

11. A lifeguard dived with grace.
12. The cat from next door yawned and walked away.
13. The statue in front of the building attracts many visitors.
14. The scientists study the moon with a telescope.
15. Everyone in the class admired Jana's new haircut.
16. The jacket with the wool lining was extremely uncomfortable.
17. We waited during the intermission.
18. She gave me a bowl of chicken soup.
19. You will find everything you need in the instruction booklet.
20. Four men from the moving company moved furniture with loud grunts.

Test Warm-Up

1. **B** The small club was packed with eager listeners.
2. **J** The rhythm of the bass seemed to guide the rest of the group.
3. **B** During his solo, the piano player rearranged the melody to the delight of everyone.
4. **F** At the break, there was a sense of excitement in the room.

Reteach

If students have not mastered these skills, review the content in Section 19.1 Phrases.

1. Using Prepositional Phrases That Act as Adverbs 19.1.3
2. Using Prepositional Phrases That Act as Adjectives 19.1.2
3. Using Prepositional Phrases That Act as Adverbs 19.1.3
4. Using Prepositional Phrases That Act as Adjectives 19.1.2

Test Tip

Even though most test instructions tell students to read a passage first and then answer the questions about it, this strategy may not always be effective. Tell students that sometimes it is more effective to read the question stems (not the answer choices) before reading a passage. Then, they can search for the answers to the questions while they read the passage.

Test Warm-Up

DIRECTIONS
Read the introduction and the passage that follows. Then, answer the questions to show that you can use and understand the function of adjectival phrases and adverbial phrases in reading and writing.

Sonya wrote the following paragraph about a jazz band called the Hot Five. Read the paragraph and think about the changes you would suggest as a peer editor. When you finish reading, answer the questions that follow.

The Hot Five

(1) My dad took me to see his favorite jazz band, the Hot Five, on Friday night. (2) The small club was packed. (3) The band started with *Nights in Tunisia.* (4) The rhythm seemed to guide the rest of the group. (5) The bass set the rhythm. (6) While his solo, the piano player rearranged the melody to delight. (7) When the trumpet played by itself, the room was quiet. (8) At the break, there was a sense. (9) No one could wait to hear what they would play next.

1 How should sentence 2 be revised?

- **A** The small was packed.
- **B** The small club was packed with eager listeners.
- **C** The small in the club was packed.
- **D** The small club was with the packed.

2 What is the BEST way to combine sentences 4 and 5?

- **F** The rhythm seemed to guide the rest of the group and the bass.
- **G** The rhythm, seemed to guide the rest of the group.
- **H** The rhythm seemed to guide the bass.
- **J** The rhythm of the bass seemed to guide the rest of the group.

3 What is the BEST way to rewrite the ideas in sentence 6?

- **A** On his solo, the piano player rearranged the melody to delight.
- **B** During his solo, the piano player rearranged the melody to the delight of everyone.
- **C** His solo rearranged the melody to delight.
- **D** After his solo, the piano player rearranged the melody to delight me.

4 What is the BEST way to revise sentence 8?

- **F** At the break, there was a sense of excitement in the room.
- **G** At the break, there was a sense the night was over.
- **H** At the break, there was a sense of finality.
- **J** At the break, there was a sense to hear more.

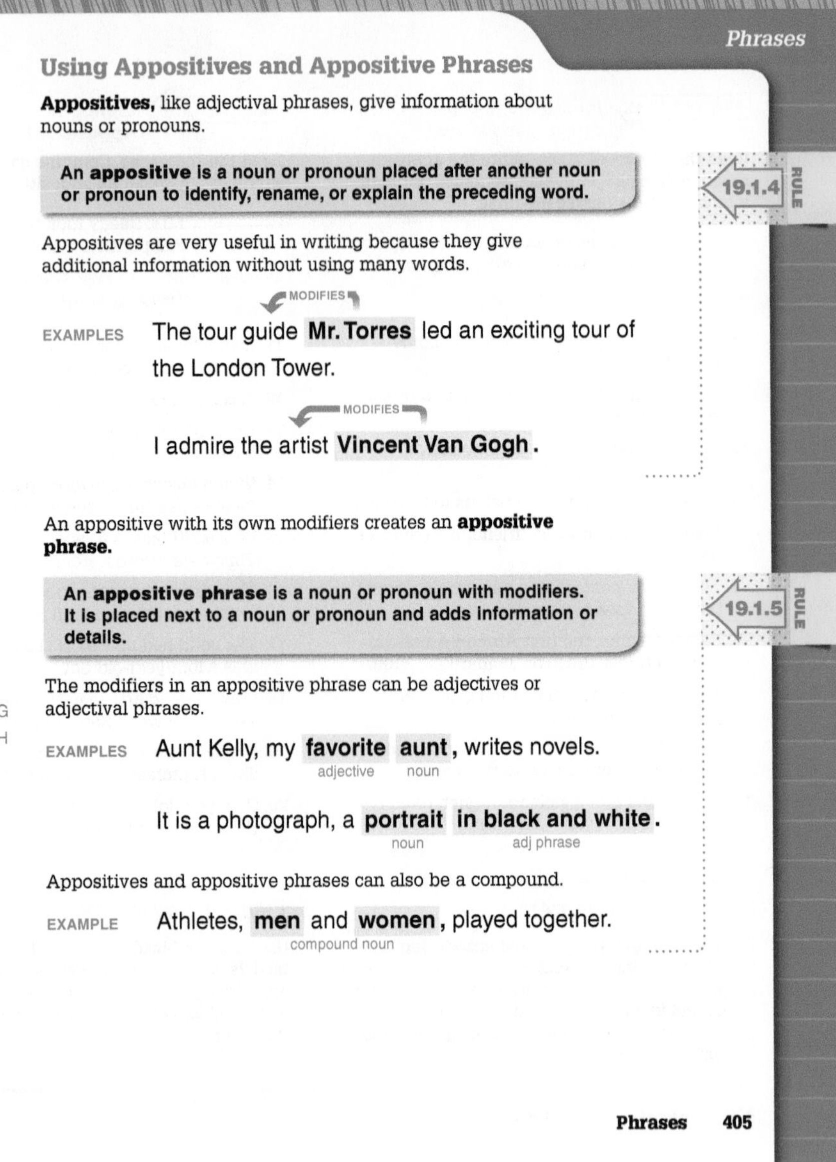

Using Appositives and Appositive Phrases

Appositives, like adjectival phrases, give information about nouns or pronouns.

An appositive is a noun or pronoun placed after another noun or pronoun to identify, rename, or explain the preceding word. RULE 19.1.4

Appositives are very useful in writing because they give additional information without using many words.

EXAMPLES The tour guide **Mr. Torres** (MODIFIES) led an exciting tour of the London Tower.

I admire the artist **Vincent Van Gogh** (MODIFIES).

An appositive with its own modifiers creates an **appositive phrase.**

An appositive phrase is a noun or pronoun with modifiers. It is placed next to a noun or pronoun and adds information or details. RULE 19.1.5

See Practice 19.1G
See Practice 19.1H

The modifiers in an appositive phrase can be adjectives or adjectival phrases.

EXAMPLES Aunt Kelly, my **favorite** (adjective) **aunt** (noun), writes novels.

It is a photograph, a **portrait** (noun) **in black and white** (adj phrase).

Appositives and appositive phrases can also be a compound.

EXAMPLE Athletes, **men** and **women** (compound noun), played together.

Using Appositives and Appositive Phrases

Explain that appositives provide information about a noun or pronoun by renaming, identifying, or explaining the noun or pronoun.

RULES 19.1.4, 19.1.5 Read aloud the rules and then have students repeat the lines with you.

Say: In the first example sentence on page 405, the name *Mr. Torres* is an appositive that gives us more information about the tour guide by telling us his name. An appositive comes immediately after a noun or pronoun that it modifies.

Say: You may recall that adjectives and adjectival phrases modify nouns. So an appositive, which is a noun, may be modified by an adjective or adjectival phrase. If so, the appositive and its adjective or adjectival phrase is called an appositive phrase. Consider the sentence *My cat loves to chase birds.* How can I add an appositive to the sentence? (My cat Stripes loves to chase birds.) How can I add an appositive phrase to the sentence? (**Possible response:** My cat, a striped furball named Stripes, loves to chase birds.)

Working with ELLs — ELL Sheltered Instruction: Cognitive

Help students understand implicit ideas and information in increasingly complex spoken language. Read the first half of page 405 aloud.

Beginning Guide students in restating the information about appositives that you have read. Use simple, familiar examples from the classroom, such as *Roberto, my student, is here*. Then, help them understand the implicit idea in the second paragraph: It is often better not to use too many words in writing.

Intermediate Have students working in small groups restate the information that you have read. Then, guide them to understand the implicit idea in the second paragraph by asking, *Why are appositives useful in writing? What does this show about good writing?*

Advanced Have partners restate the information you have read. Then, have them draw a conclusion about the qualities of good writing, based on the idea that appositives are useful in giving additional information without using many words.

Advanced High Have students complete the Advanced activity. Extend by having them write three sentences featuring appositives.

PRACTICE 19.1G

1. *Holes* by Louis Sachar (novel)
2. John (brother)
3. the first ones to arrive (She and Molly)
4. a sports fan (Owen)
5. my best friend (Bianca Wilson)
6. a panoramic view of the valley
7. the first African-American president (Barack Obama)
8. a local singing group (The Notables)
9. yellow and white roses (bouquet)
10. the group's photographer (Janelle)

PRACTICE 19.1H

11. Isabel finished her assignment, a report on animal behavior, early.
12. A car, a white sedan, was wrecked.
13. Harry's brothers, Ron and Sam, went with him to play basketball.
14. Vivian enjoys her favorite pastime, solving puzzles. *or* Vivian enjoys solving puzzles, her favorite pastime.
15. Warren Wilkes, a reporter for *The Daily Times*, wrote a story on the trial.
16. Elvis Presley, the king of rock-and-roll, lived in a mansion in Memphis.
17. The child, a four-year-old boy, had no fear of the dog.
18. I read a good article, "Eating Well for Health," in this magazine.
19. Consuela Carter, a professor of earth science, presented a talk on ecology.
20. Give your job application to Mr. Haynes, the hiring manager.

PRACTICE 19.1G Identifying Appositives and Appositive Phrases

Read the sentences. Then, write the appositive or appositive phrase in each sentence. Explain which word the phrase modifies.

EXAMPLE My science teacher, Mr. Rodriguez, directed our lab experiments.

ANSWER *Mr. Rodriguez*

1. We are reading a novel, *Holes* by Louis Sachar, for English class.
2. My brother John has been accepted by the state college.
3. She and Molly, the first ones to arrive, organized the activities.
4. Owen, a sports fan, won tickets to the game.
5. Bianca Wilson, my best friend, is in most of my classes.
6. The magnificent sight, a panoramic view of the valley, took our breath away.
7. Barack Obama, the first African American president, took office on January 20, 2009.
8. The Notables, a local singing group, will perform at the assembly.
9. A member of the audience threw a bouquet, yellow and white roses, to the singer.
10. Janelle, the group's photographer, took pictures everywhere they went.

PRACTICE 19.1H Combining Sentences With Appositive Phrases

Read the sentences. Combine each pair of sentences by using an appositive phrase.

EXAMPLE Mrs. Reedy took the band to a competition. She is the director.

ANSWER *Mrs. Reedy, the director, took the band to a competition.*

11. Isabel finished her assignment early. Her assignment was a report on animal behavior.
12. A car was wrecked. It was a white sedan.
13. Harry's brothers went with him to play basketball. Ron and Sam are his brothers.
14. Vivian enjoys her favorite pastime. Her favorite pastime is solving puzzles.
15. Warren Wilkes is a reporter for *The Daily Times.* He wrote a story on the trial.
16. Elvis Presley was the king of rock-and-roll. He lived in a mansion in Memphis.
17. The child had no fear of the dog. The child was a four-year-old boy.
18. I read a good article in this magazine. The article was "Eating Well for Health."
19. Consuela Carter presented a talk on ecology. She is a professor of earth science.
20. Give your job application to Mr. Haynes. He is the hiring manager.

SPEAKING APPLICATION

In a small group, take turns introducing one another, using one sentence with an appositive phrase in it. The group members should listen for and identify the appositive phrase. As a group, discuss the function or purpose of these appositive phrases.

WRITING APPLICATION

Use your combined sentences 13 and 20 as models, and write two new sentences with appositive phrases. Then, read each sentence aloud and explain the function, or purpose, of these appositive phrases.

SPEAKING APPLICATION

Have students demonstrate they can identify, use, and understand the function of appositive phrases in speaking by identifying the nouns to which the appositive phrases refer.

WRITING APPLICATION

Students' writing and explanation should demonstrate they can identify, use, and understand the function of appositive phrases in writing.

Quick-Write Extension

To help students synthesize and apply what they have learned in this lesson, have them use appositives to describe a cast of characters for a screenplay. Students should write a brief plot summary introduced by a descriptive list of at least five characters. Provide an example description: *Rafael, the fifteen-year-old main character of the movie, is a famous skateboarder.* Have students exchange writing and identify the appositive in each character description. For an additional challenge, have students use their descriptions and plot summaries to role play a movie pitch to a "studio executive" who asks questions about each character.

Using Verbals and Verbal Phrases

A **verbal** is any verb form that is used in a sentence not as a verb but as another part of speech.

Like verbs, verbals can be modified by an adverb or adverbial phrase. They can also be followed by a complement. A verbal used with a modifier or a complement is called a **verbal phrase.**

Participles

Participles are verb forms with two basic uses. When they are used with helping verbs, they are verbs. When they are used alone to modify nouns or pronouns, they become adjectives.

A participle is a form of a verb that is often used as an adjective.

RULE

There are two kinds of participles, **present participles** and **past participles.** Each kind can be recognized by its ending.

All present participles end in *-ing.*

EXAMPLES talking doing eating wanting

See Practice 19.1I
See Practice 19.1J

Most past participles end either in *-ed* or in *-d.*

EXAMPLES opened jumped played moved

Other past participles end in *-n, -t, -en,* or another irregular ending.

EXAMPLES grown felt bought eaten held

Both present and past participles can be used in sentences as adjectives. They tell *what kind* or *which one.*

PRESENT PARTICIPLES	PAST PARTICIPLES
She led a walking tour.	Chilled fruit juice is refreshing.
Speaking slowly, he gave us directions.	She was, by then, a grown woman.

Using Verbals and Verbal Phrases

Explain that verbs can be used as other parts of speech sometimes. When that is the case, they are called *verbals.* A verbal can be modified by an adverb, just like a regular verb, and it can have a complement.

Participles

Tell students that participles are a type of verbal.

RULE 19.1.6 Read aloud the rule and then have students repeat the lines with you.

Use a Think Aloud as part of a gradual release progression.

Think Aloud

Say: I use verbs as adjectives all the time, such as when I say *The barking dogs kept me up all night!* or *I'm not going to finish your half-eaten apple. Barking* and *eaten* are verb forms used to modify the nouns *dogs* and *apple.*

Write this sentence on the board: *The laughing baby made the mother smile.* **Say:** Consider this sentence. What is the participle in the sentence? (laughing) What noun does it modify? (baby) How can you use laughing as a verb? (**Possible response:** I was laughing.)

Explain that participles can take either the present participle form of a verb (usually ending in *-ing*) or the past participle form (often ending in *-ed*).

Work with students to write two sentences: one using *talking* as a verb, the other using it as a verbal. **Then, have students write their own sentences independently** using the participle *winning.* Have students share their sentences with the class, explaining how they used participles.

Working with ELLs — ELL Sheltered Instruction: Social/Affective

Help students use the sentences in Practice 19.1G on page 406 to enhance and confirm their understanding of the nouns and the appositive phrases in the sentences. Students should use support from peers and from you to read and to develop background knowledge needed to comprehend increasingly challenging language.

Beginning Prompt students to share their background knowledge about concepts such as *audience, white, yellow,* and *roses* in sentence 9. Have students read the words aloud with you. Then, use gestures and illustrations to act out the sentence and confirm their understanding.

Intermediate Have students read sentence 10 aloud. Then, act out taking photographs. Elicit background knowledge by asking questions such as *What is a person who takes pictures called?* Encourage partners to share what they know about the subject.

Advanced Assign partners specific items from the Practice exercises. Have them read the sentences aloud and work together to determine meaning by sharing background knowledge. Partners can use a dictionary to confirm understanding.

Advanced High Have students complete the Advanced activity. Extend by having them create background notes for each item they worked on.

Participle or Verb?

Tell students that sometimes it is hard to tell the difference between a participle and a verb phrase.

Have students consider again the sentences *The laughing baby made the mother smile* and *I was laughing.* **Then, say:** Notice that in the first sentence, *laughing* describes the baby, so it functions as an adjective to modify the noun *baby*. In the second sentence, the subject of the sentence *I* is actually doing the laughing, so it is part of the verb phrase *was laughing*. To determine whether a verb form is used as a participle or verb, look at how it functions in the sentence.

Participial Phrases

Explain that a participle may be modified by other words. A participle with all of its modifiers is known as a participial phrase.

RULE 19.1.7 Read aloud the rule and then have students repeat the lines with you.

Write several participles on the board. Have students use them to generate sentences that include participles and participial phrases.

Participle or Verb?

Sometimes, verb phrases (verbs with helping verbs) are confused with participles. A verb phrase always begins with a helping verb. A participle used as an adjective stands by itself and modifies a noun or pronoun.

VERB PHRASES	PARTICIPLES
The bicyclist **was racing** around the corner.	The **racing** bicyclist crashed into the tree.
Explorers **may have traveled** down this road.	The **traveled** road led to the finish line.

Participial Phrases

A participle can be expanded into a participial phrase by adding a complement or modifier.

RULE 19.1.7

A participial phrase is a present or past participle and its modifiers. The entire phrase acts as an adjective in a sentence.

Participial phrases can be formed by adding an adverb, an adverbial phrase, or a complement to a participle.

EXAMPLES The teacher, **speaking slowly**, explained the essay requirements.

The well-known instructor, **honored by the award**, began his speech.

The first participial phrase contains the adverb *slowly* added to the participle *speaking*. The second includes the adverbial phrase *by the award* added to the participle *honored*.

A participial phrase can also be placed at the beginning of a sentence. The phrase is usually followed by a comma.

EXAMPLE **Honored by the award**, the well-known instructor began his speech.

See Practice 19.1K
See Practice 19.1L

Differentiated Instruction

RTI Strategy for Below-Level Students Students may need extra practice distinguishing between verbs and participles. Write several common participles (e.g., breaking, shining, falling, talking, running) on index cards. Have students pick a card and make up a sentence that uses that word as either a verb or a participle. See if other students can identify whether the word was used as a verb or a participle in the sentence.

PRE-AP Enrichment for Above-Level Students One test students might use to help distinguish between verbs and participles is to identify another verb in the sentence. If there is a verb to go with the subject, the word is likely to be a participle. On the board, write the sentence *The growling dog warned us not to come inside.* Have students first identify the subject and verb. (dog, warned) This makes it easier to see that *growling* is a participle.

This is a good opportunity to remind students that a word's part of speech doesn't depend on the word itself, but how it functions in the sentence.

PRACTICE 19.1I Identifying Present and Past Participles

Read the sentences. Then, write the participle in each sentence, and label it *present participle* or *past participle*.

EXAMPLE We just watched an exciting match.

ANSWER *exciting — present participle*

1. Mel separated the good pieces of furniture from the damaged ones.
2. Sherlock Holmes solved many baffling mysteries.
3. Lucy put a frozen dinner into the microwave.
4. The gathering clouds made the picnickers finish quickly and leave.
5. Elroy made a running dive for the football.
6. A hushed audience waited for the curtain to rise.
7. The campers ate toasted sandwiches around the fire.
8. A soldier knelt by his fallen comrade.
9. Keep in mind the intended audience for your essay.
10. The rising noise level indicated that everyone was having a good time.

PRACTICE 19.1J Distinguishing Verbs and Participles

Read the sentences. Then, write *verb* or *participle* for the underlined word in each sentence. Explain how each participle or verb functions in the sentence.

EXAMPLE No one noticed him walking away.

ANSWER *participle*

11. We had not expected such a large turnout.
12. Coming closer, Fiona grabbed my hand.
13. An unhappy customer was muttering to himself.
14. We avoided the dogs snarling behind the fence.
15. Determined to get a good grade, Jane has been studying hard every night.
16. Has anyone ever stolen your lunch?
17. Stunned by the headlights, the deer just stood in the road.
18. Let's review the vocabulary we studied last week.
19. The river is rising from all the rain.
20. I must have broken it unintentionally.

SPEAKING APPLICATION

With a partner, take turns making up two sentences using these words as participles: *swinging* and *broken*. Take turns telling your sentences to your partner, who should identify what the words modify.

WRITING APPLICATION

Write two sentences using both of these words in each sentence: *dangling* and *crowded*. Use each word once as a participle and once as a verb. Read your sentences aloud to a partner. Have your partner identify which word is a participle and which is a verb.

PRACTICE 19.1I

1. damaged—past participle
2. baffling—present participle
3. frozen—past participle
4. gathering—present participle
5. running—present participle
6. hushed—past participle
7. toasted—past participle
8. fallen—past participle
9. intended—past participle
10. rising—present participle

PRACTICE 19.1J

11. verb
12. participle
13. verb
14. participle
15. verb
16. verb
17. participle
18. verb
19. verb
20. verb

Working with ELLs ELL Sheltered Instruction: Cognitive

Point out these content-based academic words from the Practice: *identify, distinguish,* and *explain*. Help students internalize new academic language by using and reusing this content-based grade-level academic vocabulary in writing activities.

Beginning Write the word *identify* and a simple sentence on the board. Circle the subject and say *I identified the subject*. Have students write *identify* on a card and draw a picture that illustrates its meaning. Then, guide them as they use and reuse the word in two written sentences of their own.

Intermediate Have students write the three terms on cards. Then, work through examples of each. On the back of each card, have students write two example sentences using each word.

Advanced Have students use the **KIM Strategy** to internalize, use, and reuse the academic terms. In a three-column chart, they should write *Key Word*, *Information*, and *Memory Cue* and write the word, a definition, and an example or illustration. Then, have them write two sentences using the words.

Advanced High Have students complete the Advanced activity. Then, have them complete the Practice and write sentences using the words to explain what they did.

SPEAKING APPLICATION

Students should demonstrate they can identify, use, and understand the function of participles by explaining how they know each word functions as a participle.

WRITING APPLICATION

Have students discuss the difference between a participle and a verb. Students' responses should show that they can identify, use, and understand the function of participles in writing.

PRACTICE 19.1K

1. wondering what to do
2. Cramming her papers into her notebook
3. closed for the day
4. Smiling sweetly
5. sitting on its nest
6. Waving his arms and shouting
7. tired after the game
8. written by Mark Twain
9. reading it aloud several times
10. found on the sidewalk

PRACTICE 19.1L

11. Mia, speaking very softly, explained what happened. *or* Speaking very softly, Mia explained what happened.
12. Trained by professionals, the gymnasts performed like ballet dancers. *or* The gymnasts, trained by professionals, performed like ballet dancers.
13. Squealing excitedly, the children played games in the yard. *or* The children, squealing excitedly, played games in the yard.
14. The dog, restrained on a leash, was unable to chase other dogs. *or* Restrained on a leash, the dog was unable to chase other dogs.
15. A fire truck, blasting its siren, sped down the street. *or* Blasting its siren, a fire truck sped down the street.
16. Thrilled by her victory, Pam jumped up and down. *or* Pam, thrilled by her victory, jumped up and down.
17. Kent finally found his homework paper tucked between the pages of his book.
18. The old letter, creased at its folds, was difficult to read.
19. Startled by the noise, Jed sat upright. *or* Jed, startled by the noise, sat upright.
20. Eli went over to speak to the girl smiling at him.

PRACTICE 19.1K Identifying Participial Phrases

Read the sentences. Then, write the participial phrase in each sentence. Underline the participle.

EXAMPLE Everyone was out enjoying the lovely day.

ANSWER *enjoying the lovely day*

1. Jeffrey sat there, wondering what to do.
2. Cramming her papers into her notebook, Vicki hurried out of the room.
3. The shop, closed for the day, was dark and quiet.
4. Smiling sweetly, the little ballerina danced her part.
5. You can see an osprey sitting on its nest in the bird sanctuary.
6. Waving his arms and shouting, Clay ran after the bus.
7. Pedro, tired after the game, relaxed on the couch.
8. *The Adventures of Huckleberry Finn,* written by Mark Twain, is a classic American novel.
9. Lola rehearsed her oral report, reading it aloud several times.
10. The glove found on the sidewalk was muddy and torn.

PRACTICE 19.1L Combining Sentences Using Participial Phrases

Read the sentences. Combine each pair of sentences by using a participial phrase. Read the new sentences to a partner. Discuss how the participles function in each sentence.

EXAMPLE Felicia did not hear the teacher's question. She was lost in a daydream.

ANSWER *Lost in a daydream, Felicia did not hear the teacher's question.*

11. Mia was speaking very softly. She explained what happened.
12. The gymnasts performed like ballet dancers. They were trained by professionals.
13. The children were squealing excitedly. They played games in the yard.
14. The dog was restrained on a leash. It was unable to chase other dogs.
15. A fire truck sped down the street. Its siren was blasting.
16. Pam was thrilled by her victory. She jumped up and down.
17. Kent finally found his homework paper. It was tucked between the pages of his book.
18. The old letter was difficult to read. It was creased at its folds.
19. Jed was startled by the noise. He sat upright.
20. Eli went over to speak to the girl. The girl was smiling at him.

SPEAKING APPLICATION

With a partner, use one of the sentences in Practice 19.1K as a model, and describe an item. Use at least one participial phrase. Your partner should listen for and identify the participial phrase.

WRITING APPLICATION

Use your combined sentences 12, 15, and 20 as models, and write two new sentences with participial phrases. Read your sentences to a partner. Have your partner identify each participle and explain how it is used in the sentence.

SPEAKING APPLICATION

Students should demonstrate they can identify, use, and understand the function of participles by identifying the participles in their sentences as past participles or present participles, and naming the words that the participles modify.

WRITING APPLICATION

Students should demonstrate they can identify, use, and understand the function of participles by identifying the participles in their partners' sentences as past or present and naming the word the participles modify.

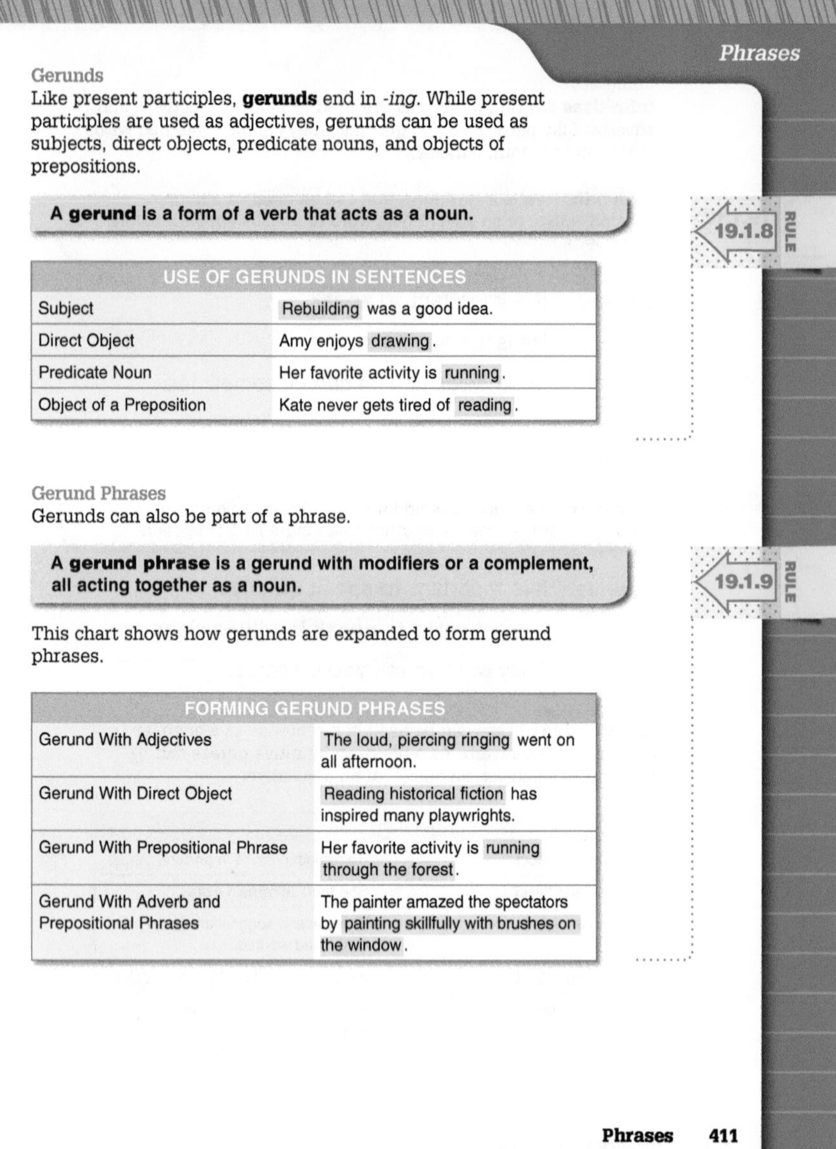

Gerunds

Like present participles, **gerunds** end in *-ing*. While present participles are used as adjectives, gerunds can be used as subjects, direct objects, predicate nouns, and objects of prepositions.

A gerund is a form of a verb that acts as a noun. RULE 19.1.8

USE OF GERUNDS IN SENTENCES	
Subject	Rebuilding was a good idea.
Direct Object	Amy enjoys drawing.
Predicate Noun	Her favorite activity is running.
Object of a Preposition	Kate never gets tired of reading.

Gerund Phrases

Gerunds can also be part of a phrase.

A gerund phrase is a gerund with modifiers or a complement, all acting together as a noun. RULE 19.1.9

This chart shows how gerunds are expanded to form gerund phrases.

FORMING GERUND PHRASES	
Gerund With Adjectives	The loud, piercing ringing went on all afternoon.
Gerund With Direct Object	Reading historical fiction has inspired many playwrights.
Gerund With Prepositional Phrase	Her favorite activity is running through the forest.
Gerund With Adverb and Prepositional Phrases	The painter amazed the spectators by painting skillfully with brushes on the window.

See Practice 19.1M
See Practice 19.1N

Gerunds

Explain that verbs can also be used as nouns. When these verbs end in *-ing*, they are called gerunds. For example, in the sentence *Sleeping is enjoyable,* the word *Sleeping* is a gerund that functions as the subject of the sentence.

RULE 19.1.8 Read aloud the rule and then have students repeat the line with you.

Read aloud and discuss each example sentence. Point out that gerunds, like nouns, can function as the subject of a sentence, a direct object, a predicate noun, and the object of a preposition.

Gerund Phrases

Explain that gerunds can also be part of a phrase.

RULE 19.1.9 Read aloud the rule and then have students repeat the lines with you.

Use a Think Aloud as part of a gradual release progression.

Say: *Like other nouns, gerunds can be modified by adjectives and can become part of a prepositional phrase.* **I can use** *the gerund* beeping *with the adjective* shrill *in the sentence* The shrill beeping of my alarm clock woke me up.

Using the example sentences as a guide, **work with students to generate** sentences that include the gerunds *swimming, playing, touching,* and *talking.*

Have pairs of students work together to use each of these gerunds as part of a gerund phrase in a sentence: *staying, going, writing, thinking, sleeping.* Have students share their sentences with the class.

Teacher Tip

If students have trouble distinguishing gerunds from participles, have students start by eliminating the word as a participle. Give students this example: *Typing is difficult for me.* Have them examine the *-ing* word to see if it modifies a noun or pronoun. If it doesn't, then have them check to see if the word is part of the verb. If it is not part of the verb in the sentence, it is most likely a gerund.

Working with ELLs — ELL Sheltered Instruction: Cognitive

Use Practice 19.1K on page 410 to allow students to practice speaking using a variety of sentence types, including sentences featuring participial phrases. Ensure that students speak with increasing accuracy and ease.

Beginning Read a sentence from Practice 19.1K. Then, have students echo you. Ask students to suggest an additional detail about a person or object in the sentence. Add this detail to the original sentence, and say the new sentence aloud. Have students repeat.

Intermediate Have partners read aloud the sentences in items 8–10 from Practice 19.1K. Then, challenge students to change the information in one sentence, such as the title and author of the book or the participle in sentence 8. Have students say their revised sentence to their partner while the partner identifies the participial phrase.

Advanced Have partners each choose three items from Practice 19.1K and say a new sentence describing a person or object in each. Direct them to use participial phrases. For example, for sentence 10 a student might say: *I see a glove lying on the sidewalk.*

Advanced High Have students complete the Advanced activity. Then, have them orally describe three objects in the classroom using participial phrases.

Infinitives

Explain that some verb forms can be used as nouns, adjectives, and adverbs. These verb forms, known as infinitives, usually begin with the word *to.*

RULE 19.1.10 Read aloud the rule and then have students repeat the lines with you.

Have students brainstorm for a list of verb forms that begin with *to* such as *to go, to run, to play, to be,* and *to drive.* Point out that these forms are very common and that their function as nouns is extremely versatile. Write this sentence on the board: *I love to ski.* Explain that in this sentence *to ski* is an infinitive that functions as a noun—the direct object of the verb *love.* Discuss the examples for rule 19.1.10 with students, discussing how each infinitive works in its sentence. Clarify that *to* can also be used as a preposition meaning "toward," but that is not its meaning when used as part of an infinitive. Have students brainstorm for sentences using the verbs listed above as infinitives.

Infinitive Phrases

Explain that, like gerunds, infinitives can be part of a phrase.

RULE 19.1.11 Read aloud the rule and then have students repeat the lines with you.

Have pairs of students work together to generate sentences with infinitives and infinitive phrases. Students can write three to four sentences that use an infinitive, then switch sentences with a partner. Partners will add modifiers or a complement to the infinitive to make it an infinitive phrase. Example: *It was my plan to stay* can become *It was my plan to stay out of the way.*

Infinitives

Infinitives are verb forms that are used as nouns, adjectives, and adverbs. Like participles and gerunds, they can be combined with other words to form phrases.

An infinitive is a verb form that can be used as a noun, an adjective, or an adverb. The word *to* usually appears before the verb.

EXAMPLES It is important **to speak**.

He is the one **to see**.

To answer can be difficult sometimes.

Infinitive Phrases

An infinitive phrase is an infinitive with modifiers or a complement, all acting together as a single part of speech.

EXAMPLES It is important **to speak quietly**.

It is not polite **to speak loudly in class**.

They want **to tell you a secret**.

An **infinitive phrase** can be used in a sentence as a noun, an adjective, or an adverb. As a noun, an infinitive phrase can function as a subject, an object, or an appositive.

USES OF INFINITIVES	
Used as a Subject	To remain calm is important.
Used as an Object	She tried to remain calm.
Used as an Appositive	The officer's suggestion, to remain calm, had worked.
Used as an Adjective	It was her intention to remain calm.
Used as an Adverb	It isn't always easy to remain calm when you're upset.

See Practice 19.1O
See Practice 19.1P

Differentiated Instruction

RTI Strategy for Special Needs Students
Before discussing infinitives, show students several simple present- and future-tense sentences, such as *I run. You see the waterfall. She will tell a story. He will remember that day for a long time!* Read the sentences aloud and identify the verb in each. Have a student volunteer underline the verb in each sentence as you identify it. Write a large *To* on a sheet of paper. Read each sentence again, and then hold up the *To* sign. Rephrase the sentence using *to.* For example, *I want to run. You walk across the bridge to see the waterfall. She would like to tell a story. He is going to remember that day for a long time!*

Tell students that when they see *to* before a verb, it is called an **infinitive.**

PRACTICE 19.1M Identifying Gerund Phrases

Read the sentences. Then, write the gerund phrase from each sentence, and underline the gerund. Remember to include all modifiers with the phrase.

EXAMPLE Listening to music relaxes me.
ANSWER *Listening to music*

1. Naomi likes reading historical novels.
2. Forecasting the weather can be a challenge.
3. You might be able to gain an advantage by using strategy.
4. Silas recently tried skateboarding on a ramp.
5. The first step in the assignment is locating appropriate sources.
6. Veronica could not stop laughing at the joke.
7. Annabel and Diana were exhausted from working all afternoon.
8. Winning the match is not everything.
9. The mayor opposed raising the speed limit through town.
10. Playing the drums is Neil's only interest.

PRACTICE 19.1N Writing Gerunds and Gerund Phrases

Read the sentences. Then, rewrite each sentence, completing it with a gerund or gerund phrase.

EXAMPLE The team celebrated by ____.
ANSWER *The team celebrated by singing the school song.*

11. ____ motivates Zelda to earn money after school.
12. Eva's family enjoyed ____ last summer.
13. Duncan sends text messages while ____.
14. Henry Ford is famous for ____.
15. ____ is the way Selena memorizes her lines for the play.
16. A fox escaped its pursuer by ____.
17. ____ builds strength and flexibility.
18. Jason thought he might give ____ a try.
19. ____ was easier than Amy expected.
20. Alonzo's job is ____.

SPEAKING APPLICATION

With a partner, take turns telling about something you like to do. Your partner should listen for and identify a gerund or gerund phrase that you use.

WRITING APPLICATION

Use sentences 12, 13, and 19 as models, and write three sentences with gerunds or gerund phrases.

Quick-Write Extension

To help students synthesize and apply what they have learned about gerunds, have them write poems beginning with "I like." Direct students to write a list of gerund phrases naming things they like to do. Explain that each phrase should begin a new line in the poem; for example, *I like walking in the rain, / sleeping outside, / talking with my friends.* For an extra challenge, have students use gerunds as subjects in alternating lines of the poem: *I like walking in the rain, / Walking in the rain is peaceful.* Ask volunteers to read their poems aloud, explaining which gerunds are subjects and which are objects.

SPEAKING APPLICATION

Students' sentences should correctly use gerunds and should be part of a phrase with modifiers.

WRITING APPLICATION

Have students write three additional sentences describing what they will do this weekend, without using any gerunds or gerund phrases. Then, have the students rewrite the sentences using gerunds.

PRACTICE 19.1M

1. reading historical novels
2. Forecasting the weather
3. using strategy
4. skateboarding on a ramp
5. locating appropriate sources
6. laughing at the joke
7. working all afternoon
8. Winning the match
9. raising the speed limit through town
10. Playing the drums

PRACTICE 19.1N

Answers will vary. Sample answers:

11. Getting a new computer motivates Zelda to earn money after school.
12. Eva's family enjoyed traveling in Alaska last summer.
13. Duncan sends text messages while waiting for dinner.
14. Henry Ford is famous for making automobiles.
15. Repeating them over and over is the way Selena memorizes her lines for the play.
16. A fox escaped its pursuer by slipping under the fence.
17. Practicing yoga builds strength and flexibility.
18. Jason thought he might give speaking Spanish a try.
19. Skating was easier than Amy expected.
20. Alonzo's job is feeding the animals.

PRACTICE 19.1O

1. to swim in the lake—noun
2. to visit the museum—noun
3. To break that record—noun
4. to go fishing—adjective
5. to understand—adverb
6. to hide in the closet—noun
7. to leave for school—adjective
8. to sell their house—noun
9. to avoid the puddle—adverb
10. to be a singer in a band—noun

PRACTICE 19.1P

Answers will vary. Sample answers:

11. The teacher raised her hands to quiet the class.
12. To meet new people is Martha's plan for this year.
13. Your next book to read is *Dragonwings*.
14. Judy's role is to coach the actors.
15. An assembly to discuss new procedures will start at 9 o'clock.
16. To disagree with the authorities may not be wise.
17. The best way to improve your skills is to practice regularly.
18. I think it is best to say nothing right now.
19. The first person to call in will win a ticket.
20. Ariana got into position to serve the ball.

SPEAKING APPLICATION

Have students explain how they were able to identify the infinitive phrases.

WRITING APPLICATION

Have partners explain how they were able to identify the infinitives.

PRACTICE 19.1O Identifying Infinitives and Infinitive Phrases

Read the sentences. Then, write the infinitive phrase from each sentence, and underline the infinitive. Also write *noun*, *adjective*, or *adverb* to describe each infinitive phrase.

EXAMPLE We stopped by the roadside to admire the view.

ANSWER *to admire the view* — adverb

1. Wade likes to swim in the lake.
2. Mrs. Manning planned to visit the museum.
3. To break that record will be a challenge.
4. That is the best place to go fishing.
5. This poem is easy to understand.
6. The child tried to hide in the closet.
7. It's time to leave for school now.
8. The Wilsons plan to sell their house.
9. The driver swerved to avoid the puddle.
10. Justin's goal is to be a singer in a band.

PRACTICE 19.1P Writing Infinitives and Infinitive Phrases

Read the sentences. Then, rewrite each sentence, completing it with an infinitive or an infinitive phrase.

EXAMPLE Kirk still has plenty of work _____.

ANSWER *Kirk still has plenty of work to finish by tomorrow.*

11. The teacher raised her hands _____.
12. _____ is Martha's plan for this year.
13. Your next book _____ is *Dragonwings*.
14. Judy's role is _____.
15. An assembly _____ will start at 9:00 o'clock.
16. _____ may not be wise.
17. The best way _____ is _____.
18. I think it is best _____.
19. The first person _____ will win a ticket.
20. Ariana got into position _____.

SPEAKING APPLICATION

In a small group, take turns "selling" each other a simple item, such as a pencil or paper clip. The group members should listen for and identify the infinitive phrases you use.

WRITING APPLICATION

Write a short paragraph explaining the purpose of the item you "sold" in the Speaking Application. Use at least two infinitive phrases and underline them.

Working with ELLs — ELL Sheltered Instruction: Cognitive

Adapt the Writing Application by having students write sentences with infinitives about the purpose of a simple object. Guide students to use sentences of a variety of grade-appropriate lengths in increasingly accurate ways.

Beginning Show a pencil. Ask: *What is this? What can I use it for?* Act out using the object. Then, provide the cloze sentence *I use ____ to write.* Have students complete the sentence by writing words such as *pens, pencils,* or *chalk.* Have students increase sentence length by adding words such as *sometimes* or *always*.

Intermediate Have student pairs write sentences describing the purposes of a simple object using the sentence frame *You can use _____ to _____.* Have them increase the length of their sentences by adding alternatives: *You can use _____ or _____ to _____.*

Advanced Have partners work together on a paragraph describing different uses for a simple object, using infinitives. Have them increase sentence length by adding details.

Advanced High Have students write a paragraph that describes the uses of a simple item using at least two infinitives. Students should check their sentences for accuracy. Then, have them combine sentences to create a variety of sentence lengths.

19.2 Clauses

Clauses are the basic structural unit of a sentence.

www.phwritingcoach.com

Grammar Tutorials
Brush up on your Grammar skills with these animated videos.

Grammar Practice
Practice your grammar skills with Writing Coach Online.

Grammar Games
Test your knowledge of grammar in this fast-paced interactive video game.

RULE 19.2.1 A **clause** is a group of words with its own subject and verb.

There are two basic kinds of clauses, **main** or **independent clauses** and **subordinate clauses.**

RULE 19.2.2 A **main** or **independent clause** has a subject and a verb and can stand by itself as a complete sentence.

As you can see in the examples below, a main clause can be long or short. All main clauses express a complete thought and can stand by themselves as complete sentences.

EXAMPLES The **girl** (subject) **skipped** (verb).

Later that night, **he** (subject) **began** (verb) reading his book.

RULE 19.2.3 A **subordinate clause,** also known as a dependent clause, has a subject and a verb but cannot stand by itself as a complete sentence. It is only part of a sentence.

SUBORDINATE CLAUSES after **she** (subject) **presented** (verb) her paper

while the **group** (subject) **studied** (verb)

After reading a subordinate clause, you will still need more information to have a complete sentence.

www.phwritingcoach.com

Diagnostic and Instruction
Diagnostic test assesses students' instructional needs. Lessons and practice are assigned based on results.

Additional Practice

- Grammar Tutorials—Animated videos reinforce key grammar skills.
- Grammar Practice—Targeted practice addresses individual needs.
- ExamView—Teachers customize their grammar practice and tests.
- Grammar Games—Interactive video games make grammar fun.

19.2 Clauses

Lesson Objectives

1. Differentiate between main and subordinate clauses.
2. Identify, use, and understand the function of adjectival clauses in reading, writing, and speaking.
3. Identify, use, and understand the function of adverbial clauses and subordinating conjunctions in reading, writing, and speaking.

Have students recall that the basic parts of a sentence are the subject and the verb. Unlike phrases, clauses contain both of these parts.

RULE 19.2.1 Read aloud the rule and then have students repeat the line with you.

Clarify that terms *main clause* and *independent clause* are used interchangeably.

RULE 19.2.2 Read aloud the rule and then have students repeat the lines with you.

Use a Think Aloud as part of a gradual release progression.

Say: I know that *independent* means that something or someone can work on its own without help. So independent clauses do not need help. They can stand alone as sentences.

Write several sentences on the board and **guide students** in identifying the main clause in one or two of these.

Have students work independently to identify the main clause in the remaining sentences.

RULE 19.2.3 Read aloud the rule and then have students repeat the lines with you.

Discuss why the subordinate clauses on page 415 cannot stand alone as sentences.

RULE 19.2.4 Read aloud the rule and then have students repeat the lines with you.

Explain to students that page 416 gives them several clues for identifying a subordinate, or dependent, clause. One clue is that these clauses may begin with a subordinating conjunction. Another clue is that they may begin with a relative pronoun. Review examples of subordinating conjunctions and relative pronouns.

Read aloud the example sentences and discuss why each clause is either a main clause or a subordinate clause.

Teacher Tip

If students are having trouble keeping the terms *independent clause*, *dependent clause*, *main clause*, and *subordinate clause* straight, clarify by drawing on their prior knowledge. For example, **say:** A subordinate is someone who works under the authority of someone else. The person is not independent. He or she is dependent on an employer, commanding officer, or other authority figure. Encourage students to make similar connections and share them with the class.

Subordinate clauses begin with subordinating conjunctions or relative pronouns.

Some subordinate clauses begin with **subordinating conjunctions,** such as *if, since, when, although, after, because,* and *while.* Others begin with **relative pronouns,** such as *who, which,* or *that.* These words are clues that the clause may not be able to stand alone. Notice how the addition of subordinating words changes the meaning of the main clauses in the examples below.

COMPARING TWO KINDS OF CLAUSES	
MAIN	SUBORDINATE
She speaks this afternoon.	*when* she speaks this afternoon
The garden has green tomatoes.	*because* the garden has green tomatoes
I planted the cucumbers.	the cucumbers *that* I planted

In order to form a complete thought, a subordinate clause must be combined with a main clause.

EXAMPLES **After she presented her paper** (subordinate clause), Rachael felt relaxed. (main clause)

The board applauded (main clause) **after Rachael presented her paper** (subordinate clause).

It was Rachael (main clause) **who was asked to present last** (subordinate clause).

When they arrive tonight (subordinate clause), the Woods will eat. (main clause)

See Practice 19.2A
See Practice 19.2B

Working with ELLs — ELL Sheltered Instruction: Cognitive

Have students use visual and contextual support as they read the student page to enhance and confirm understanding and to develop a grasp of language structures needed to comprehend increasingly challenging language.

Beginning Read aloud the first set of examples in the chart on page 416 while students track the print in their books. Have students repeat each clause after you. Emphasize that both main and subordinate clauses have a subject and verb—called out by highlighting—but that only the main clause is a complete idea—indicated by the use of capital letters and periods.

Intermediate Have partners take turns reading the chart examples. Prompt them to discuss the similarities and differences between main and subordinate clauses, using visual support such as the highlighting and the italicized words.

Advanced Have partners review the chart and use the visual support to discuss similarities and differences between main and subordinate clauses. Then, have them read the examples and explain how they can distinguish subordinate from main clauses.

Advanced High Have students complete the Advanced activity. Then, challenge them to create their own sentences with main and subordinate clauses.

PRACTICE 19.2A Identifying Main and Subordinate Clauses

Read the sentences. Then, write the main and subordinate clauses in each sentence, and label them *main clause* or *subordinate clause*.

EXAMPLE After you left, Maria opened her presents.

ANSWER *After you left — subordinate clause Maria opened her presents — main clause*

1. Although they do not always agree, Jake and Chris are best friends.
2. Dino thought about baseball practice as he walked home.
3. Please take out the garbage before you leave.
4. Because my dog is afraid of thunder, he hides under the bed during storms.
5. If you want to come with me, make sure you bring an umbrella.
6. Let's wait here until Stephen arrives.
7. We eat outside when the weather is nice.
8. Let's discuss the plans as we'll be traveling together.
9. Ethan and Grace are ready to leave as soon as the bus arrives.
10. The painting that you bought is hanging in the hallway.

PRACTICE 19.2B Identifying and Using Main and Subordinate Clauses

Read the clauses. Write *main clause* or *subordinate clause* for each clause. Then, expand each subordinate clause into a complete complex sentence by adding a main clause.

EXAMPLE Unless we find the shovel.

ANSWER *subordinate clause We cannot clear away the snow unless we find the shovel.*

11. Here is a picture of my cousin.
12. That my mother bought for me.
13. Robots are used in many factories.
14. Although my brother is a talented musician.
15. Our show did not make a profit.
16. When you make up your mind.
17. Two other people waited in the office.
18. As soon as Elizabeth gets home.
19. I just can't decide.
20. Who found Hal's wallet.

SPEAKING APPLICATION

With a partner, take turns selecting two subordinate clauses from the sentences in Practice 19.2A. Add a main clause to each, and then say the sentence.

WRITING APPLICATION

Write two complex sentences that contain both main and subordinate clauses. Underline the subordinate clauses. Explain to a partner how the main and subordinate clauses function in the sentence together.

PRACTICE 19.2A

1. Although they do not always agree—subordinate clause
   Jake and Chris are best friends—main clause
2. Dino thought about baseball practice—main clause
   as he walked home—subordinate clause
3. Please take out the garbage—main clause
   before you leave—subordinate clause
4. Because my dog is afraid of thunder—subordinate clause
   he hides under the bed during storms—main clause
5. If you want to come with me—subordinate clause
   make sure you bring an umbrella—main clause
6. Let's wait here—main clause
   until Stephen arrives—subordinate clause
7. We eat outside—main clause
   when the weather is nice—subordinate clause
8. Let's discuss the plans—main clause
   as we'll be traveling together —subordinate clause
9. Ethan and Grace are ready to leave—main clause
   as soon as the bus arrives—subordinate clause
10. The painting is hanging in the hallway—main clause
    that you bought—subordinate clause

PRACTICE 19.2B

11. main clause
12. subordinate clause
    Sample answer: This is the belt that my mother bought for me.
13. main clause
14. subordinate clause
    Sample answer: Although my brother is a talented musician, he does not like to play for people.
15. main clause
16. subordinate clause
    Sample answer: When you make up your mind, let us know your plans.
17. main clause
18. subordinate clause
    Sample answer: As soon as Elizabeth gets home, she changes her clothes.
19. main clause
20. subordinate clause
    Sample answer: The woman who found Hal's wallet returned it to him.

SPEAKING APPLICATION

Have partners explain how they identified the main and subordinate clauses in each other's sentences. Explanations should demonstrate that students can differentiate between main versus subordinate clauses in speaking.

WRITING APPLICATION

Students' sentences and explanations should demonstrate that they can differentiate between main versus subordinate clauses in writing.

Adjectival Clauses

Remind students that we classify words and groups of words based on their function in a sentence. So a clause that is functioning as an adjective in a sentence is called an adjectival clause.

RULE 19.2.5 Read aloud the rule and then have students repeat the lines with you.

Say: Adjectives, such as *warm, red,* and *fuzzy*, modify nouns, such as *sweater.* When a subordinate clause modifies a noun, it is called an adjectival clause. You can use the questions *What kind?* and *Which one?* to help decide if a subordinate, or dependent, clause is adjectival.

Recognizing Adjectival Clauses

Post the clue words *that, which, who, whom, whose, since, where,* and *when* where students can easily refer to them.

Say: Consider the sentence *The kitten, which had found a ball of yarn, was playing happily.* What is the clue word that indicates the presence of an adjectival clause? (which) Repeat with other examples.

Adjectival Clauses

A subordinate clause will sometimes act as an adjective in a sentence. An adjectival clause or adjective clause is a dependent clause and cannot stand on its own.

An adjectival clause or adjective clause is a subordinate clause that modifies a noun or a pronoun.

Like one-word adjectives and adjectival phrases, **adjectival clauses** tell *what kind* or *which one.*

EXAMPLES stars **that are bright and glowing** (WHAT KIND?)

the country **where I was born** (WHICH ONE?)

Recognizing Adjectival Clauses

Most adjectival clauses begin with the words *that, which, who, whom,* and *whose.* Sometimes an adjectival clause begins with a subordinating conjunction, such as *since, where,* or *when.* In the chart below, the adjectival clauses are hightlighted in pink.

ADJECTIVAL CLAUSES
The professor **whom I had asked for help** met with me before class. (*Which* professor?)
The charity auction, **which was advertised in the local paper**, is Friday. (*Which* charity auction?)
In the months **since she started working**, Anne has become an accomplished teacher. (*Which* months?)
I hid my jewelry box in the hall closet **on which there is a lock**. (*Which* closet?)
We visited the theme park **that honors cultures around the world**. (*Which* park?)
The theme park **whose rides include teacups** is located in Florida. (*Which* park?)

See Practice 19.2C

Working with ELLs — ELL Sheltered Instruction: Cognitive

Help students learn the academic vocabulary term *adjectival clauses* using prior knowledge. Draw a Venn diagram with circles labeled *adjectives* and *clauses*, with the area of overlap labeled *adjectival clauses*. Then:

Beginning Review the meaning of *adjectives* and *clauses* with students, using simple definitions and examples. Then, have students identify the *adjectives*, *clauses*, and *adjectival clauses* sections of the **Venn Diagram**. Discuss the meaning of the new term drawing on their prior knowledge of the other terms.

Intermediate Review the **Venn Diagram**. Have students working in groups draw their own version and give examples of adjectives and clauses based on prior knowledge. Then, help them define *adjectival clauses*.

Advanced Direct pairs to draw their own **Venn Diagram** and add examples of adjectives and of clauses. Have students use prior academic knowledge to explain what traits of adjectives and clauses adjectival clauses share.

Advanced High Have students complete the Advanced activity and then generate sentences that include adjectival clauses.

Combining Sentences With Adjectival Clauses

Two sentences can be combined into one sentence by changing one of them into an adjectival clause. Sometimes you will need to add a relative pronoun or subordinating conjunction to make the sentence read correctly. In the sentences below, the adjectival clauses are highlighted in pink.

TWO SENTENCES	COMBINED WITH AN ADJECTIVAL CLAUSE
My English professor has written novels based on fictional stories. My professor is a famous author.	My English professor, who has written novels based on fictional stories, is a famous author.
We visited the Air and Space Museum. The Air and Space Museum is my favorite museum.	We visited the Air and Space Museum, which is my favorite.
We decided to shop at the outlet mall. We usually get the best deals there.	We decided to shop at the outlet mall where we usually get the best deals.
Emma visited her grandparents. Emma's grandparents live in an apartment in New York.	Emma visited her grandparents, who live in an apartment in New York.
Carolyn goes to dance class. Her class is in a ballet studio.	Carolyn goes to dance class that is in a ballet studio.

See Practice 19.2C
See Practice 19.2D

Combining Sentences With Adjectival Clauses

Tell students that combining two sentences into one sentence is a way to make writing flow more gracefully. Combining can also clearly show the relationship between two thoughts.

Say: I know that when two sentences are related in some way, it can be helpful to show how they are related. The sentences *The musicians are having dinner* and *Joan hired the musicians* can be combined into *The musicians whom Joan hired are having dinner.* The subordinating conjunction *whom* shows the relationship between the two thoughts.

Read aloud the example sentences with students and guide them in identifying which ones use a relative pronoun and which use a subordinating conjunction.

Help students understand that they can identify, use, and understand adjectival clauses by writing these sentences on the board:

Natasha was running late.

Natasha ate quickly.

Have students combine the sentences using an adjectival clause. Then, ask students to compare their sentences with a partner's sentences.

Differentiated Instruction

RTI Strategy for Below-Level Students Support students who are finding it difficult to combine sentences using adjectival clauses. Have students use a two-column chart modeled after the one on page 419. Students write two sentences in each cell in the first column labeled *Two Sentences*. Both sentences in a cell must *either* have the same subject *or* the second sentence must give information about the direct object of the first sentence. Partners combine the sentences to complete the second column.

PRE-AP Enrichment for Above-Level Students Have students look in books, magazines, and newspapers to find pairs of sentences that could be combined using an adjectival clause. Have students rewrite the sentences using adjectival clauses. Encourage students to improve the quality of the sentences by adding additional detail or by revising the language in the sentences. You may want to keep a running total of the "improved" sentences that each student has submitted.

PRACTICE 19.2C

1. who came in a jeep
2. when people take vacations
3. which will take you right to the campground
4. who is responsible for the Louisiana Purchase
5. that belonged to my grandmother
6. where we had to turn around
7. which is part of Los Angeles
8. who will stock the shelves
9. whom you met earlier
10. that my uncle fixed up

PRACTICE 19.2D

11. The rain, which fell for two days, kept the farmers from planting their crops.
12. I need to write two more sentences that will support my topic sentence.
13. Many adventurers have climbed Mt. Everest, which is the highest peak in the world.
14. The train that leaves at 7:00 arrives in Washington, D.C., at 11:30.
15. I like to look up information on the Internet, where you can find everything.
16. The woman, whose purse was lost, was upset. *or* The woman, who lost her purse, was upset.
17. Here are some sponges that you can use to wash the car.
18. A mechanic tuned up the car, which had not been running well.
19. David told a story that made everyone laugh.
20. Alexa is my friend who made this playlist for me. *or* Alexa, who is my friend, made this playlist for me.

PRACTICE 19.2C Identifying Adjectival Clauses

Read the sentences. Then, write the adjectival clause in each sentence.

EXAMPLE This is a movie that I will never forget.

ANSWER *that I will never forget*

1. The men who came in a jeep are repairing the fence now.
2. This is the time of year when people take vacations.
3. Follow these directions, which will take you right to the campground.
4. Thomas Jefferson is the president who is responsible for the Louisiana Purchase.
5. I have a pearl necklace that belonged to my grandmother.
6. The road came to an end, where we had to turn around.
7. Hollywood, which is part of Los Angeles, is a tourist destination.
8. The manager needs someone who will stock the shelves.
9. Christa, whom you met earlier, will also be on the committee.
10. This is the house that my uncle fixed up.

PRACTICE 19.2D Combining Sentences Using Adjectival Clauses

Read the sentences. Combine the pairs of sentences by changing one of them into an adjectival clause. Read the new sentences and discuss how the adjectival clause functions.

EXAMPLE The runner is being congratulated. She won the race.

ANSWER *The runner who won the race is being congratulated.*

11. The rain fell for two days. It kept the farmers from planting their crops.
12. I need to write two more sentences. These sentences will support my topic sentence.
13. Many adventurers have climbed Mt. Everest. Mt. Everest is the highest peak in the world.
14. The train leaves at 7:00. It arrives in Washington, D.C., at 11:30.
15. I like to look up information on the Internet. You can find everything there.
16. The woman was upset. Her purse was lost.
17. Here are some sponges. You can use these to wash the car.
18. A mechanic tuned up the car. It had not been running well.
19. David told a story. It made everyone laugh.
20. Alexa is my friend. She made this playlist for me.

SPEAKING APPLICATION

With a partner, summarize a mystery story that you have read or seen on television. Use at least one sentence with an adjectival clause. Your partner should listen for and identify the adjectival clause. Together, discuss the function, or purpose, of the adjectival clause.

WRITING APPLICATION

Use your combined sentences 11, 16, and 19 as models, and write three new sentences with adjectival clauses. Read the sentences and explain how the adjectival clauses function in the sentences.

SPEAKING APPLICATION

Students' summaries should demonstrate that they can identify, use, and understand the function of adjectival clauses in speaking.

WRITING APPLICATION

Students' sentences should demonstrate that they can identify, use, and understand the function of adjectival clauses in writing.

Extension

To help students synthesize and apply what they have learned, have them use adjectival clauses to play a game of twenty questions. Students should work in pairs, with one student thinking of a person, place, or thing and the other student asking questions to identify whom or what the student has in mind. The student answering questions must speak in complete sentences that contain adjectival clauses. For example, *I'm thinking of a character on a TV show. Is the character male or female? I'm thinking of a character who is a man.*

Adverbial Clauses

Subordinate clauses can also be used as adverbs. Adverbial clauses or adverb clauses are dependent clauses.

> An **adverbial clause** or **adverb clause** is a subordinate clause that modifies a verb, an adjective, or an adverb.

RULE 19.2.6

Adverbial clauses can answer any of the following questions about the words they modify: *Where? When? In what manner? To what extent? Under what conditions?* or *Why?*

ADVERBIAL CLAUSES	
Modifying Verbs	Put the luggage wherever you find an empty closet. (Put *where?*) The game will begin after we sing the National Anthem. (Will begin *when?*) Amy spoke as if she were very serious. (Spoke *in what manner?*) I will go to Greece if you do too. (Will go *under what conditions?*)
Modifying an Adjective	I am tired because I have been working all day. (Tired *why?*)
Modifying an Adverb	She knows more than other teachers do. (More *to what extent?*)

Recognizing Adverbial Clauses

> A **subordinating conjunction** introduces an adverbial clause.

RULE 19.2.7

A **subordinating conjunction** always introduces an adverbial clause. In a sentence, the conjunction will usually appear in one of two places—either at the beginning, when the adverbial clause begins the sentence, or in the middle, connecting the independent clause to the subordinate clause. In the examples on the next page, the subordinating conjunctions are highlighted in purple.

Adverbial Clauses

Explain that subordinate clauses that modify verbs, adjectives, and adverbs are called adverbial clauses.

RULE 19.2.6 Read aloud the rule and then have students repeat the lines with you.

Ask: What is the function of an adverb in a sentence? (It modifies a verb, an adjective, or an adverb.) **Then, ask:** How is the function of an adverb related to the function of an adverbial clause? (They are the same.)

Explain that adverbial clauses answer questions such as *Where? When? In what manner? To what extent? Under what conditions?* and *Why?* Review the example questions. Draw students' attention to the first word of each adverbial clause.

Recognizing Adverbial Clauses

RULE 19.2.7 Read aloud the rule and then have students repeat the line with you.

Point out that an adverbial clause *always* begins with a subordinating conjunction. Have students look back at the examples and identify the subordinating conjunctions.

Write these sentences on the board: *Hang your wet clothing in the bathroom after you come in. I am frustrated because I did not make the team.*

Work with students to identify which question is being answered in each sentence. (*Hang when?* and *Frustrated why?*) Then, have students demonstrate their understanding of adverbial clauses by explaining how each adverbial clause functions in the sentence.

Differentiated Instruction

RTI Strategy for Below-Level Students
Play a version of a fill-in-the-blank game with students. Divide students into small groups. Have each group write a short story or news article that uses a variety of adjectival and adverbial clauses.

Next, have students identify the adverbial and adjectival clauses and rewrite the story, replacing the identified clauses with blanks.

Make sure students know if each blank should be filled with an adjectival clause or an adverbial clause. (They may want to note this directly under each blank.)

Then, have them ask other students to supply adverbial and adjectival clauses *without* reading aloud the story. Have students fill these in, then read aloud the resulting story.

Common Subordinating Conjunctions

Discuss the list of common subordinating conjunctions with students. Work with students to create sentences with adverbial clauses that are introduced by these subordinating conjunctions. For example, *After I ate lunch, I went to the game. After I ate lunch* is an adverbial clauses that answers the question: When?

Elliptical Adverbial Clauses

Remind students that an elliptical sentence is one in which some words have been left out. They are "understood" by the listener or reader. In an elliptical adverbial clause, the verb or the subject and verb have been omitted.

RULE 19.2.8 Read aloud the rule and then have students repeat the lines with you.

Point out that we encounter elliptical clauses often and automatically fill in the missing words. For example, in the sentence *Albert was faster than Jake,* the words *was fast* have been left out.

Teacher Tip

Explain that the word *ellipsis* often refers to the three dots (...) that indicate missing text from a quotation. An ellipsis is often used in articles when only the significant portion of a long quotation is published.

EXAMPLES **Because** you slept late, I will prepare breakfast.

I will prepare breakfast **because** you slept late.

Whenever you have a test, I expect you to study.

I expect you to study **whenever** you have a test.

Common Subordinating Conjunctions
Here are the most common subordinating conjunctions. Knowing them can help you recognize adverbial clauses.

COMMON SUBORDINATING CONJUNCTIONS		
after	even though	unless
although	if	until
as	in order that	when
as if	since	whenever
as long as	so that	where
because	than	wherever
before	though	while

Elliptical Adverbial Clauses
In certain adverbial clauses, words are left out. These clauses are said to be elliptical.

In an elliptical adverbial clause, the verb or the subject and verb are understood rather than stated.

Many elliptical adverbial clauses are introduced by one of two subordinating conjunctions, *as* or *than*. In the following examples, the understood words have been added in parentheses. The first elliptical adverbial clause is missing a verb; the second is missing a subject and a verb.

EXAMPLES My sister can eat as much **as I** (can eat).

I like this movie more **than** (I liked) **that one**.

See Practice 19.2E
See Practice 19.2F

Working with ELLs — ELL Sheltered Instruction: Social/Affective

As students read the student page, provide support from peers and from you to enhance and confirm understanding and to develop their grasp of the language structure of subordination needed to comprehend increasingly challenging language.

Beginning Read aloud the first pair of examples as students read with you. Act out the sentences. Explain that the word *because* tells a reason. Explain that the word *because* is called a subordinating conjunction.

Intermediate Discuss subordinating conjunctions, pointing out the highlighted examples and the chart. Then, guide students as they read the page. Ask partners to restate the ideas in their own words to confirm understanding.

Advanced Have partners work together using the **KIM Strategy**, writing a key word, information, and a memory clue about the terms *adverbial clause* and *subordinating conjunction*. After they have read the page, have them write sentences with adverbial clauses using subordinating conjunctions.

Advanced High Have partners read the page together. Ask them to discuss the meaning of each conjunction on the chart, consulting a dictionary as necessary. Then, have students make a copy of a newspaper article, highlighting adverbial clauses and circling subordinating conjunctions.

PRACTICE 19.2E **Identifying Adverbial Clauses and Recognizing Elliptical Adverbial Clauses**

Read the sentences. Then, write the adverbial clauses. For any of the adverbial clauses that are elliptical, add the understood words in parentheses.

EXAMPLE Isabel likes reading mysteries more than biographies.

ANSWER *than (she likes reading) biographies*

1. After we took a walk, we stopped for ice cream.
2. Kurt did not give his oral report today because he has laryngitis.
3. Although Maria is not especially tall, she plans to try out for basketball.
4. Driving can be unpleasant when there is a lot of traffic.
5. Brett waited while Alan collected his equipment.
6. You have grown since we last saw you.
7. We can leave as long as you are ready.
8. If you are really interested, talk to Miss Knox.
9. This computer is older than that one.
10. I am not allowed to watch television unless my homework is finished.

PRACTICE 19.2F **Combining Sentences With Adverbial Clauses**

Read the sentences. Combine each pair of sentences by changing one of them into an adverbial clause. Use an appropriate subordinating conjunction, and drop or change words as necessary.

EXAMPLE Gabe stayed in the car. I ran into the store.

ANSWER *Gabe stayed in the car while I ran into the store.*

11. Veronica took notes. We made our plans.
12. Jude was not nervous. He stepped onstage.
13. Laura did very well on her science test. She had studied.
14. I will tell you. You must keep it a secret.
15. Robin will rehearse carefully. She will give her presentation.
16. Keith feels much more energetic. He has started jogging.
17. Volunteers put sandbags on the banks. The river overflowed its banks.
18. The garden will dry up. It rains.
19. We worked hard all week. We wanted to have the weekend free.
20. I will call you. I need help.

SPEAKING APPLICATION

With a partner, make up an excuse for being late or for not doing something, using two adverbial clauses. Your partner should listen for and identify the adverbial clauses.

WRITING APPLICATION

Write a few sentences about something you learned in your social studies class. Use at least two adverbial clauses and appropriate subordinating conjunctions. Read your sentences to a partner. Discuss how the adverbial clause and subordinating conjunction function in each sentence.

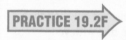

PRACTICE 19.2E

1. After we took a walk
2. because he has laryngitis
3. Although Maria is not especially tall
4. when there is a lot of traffic
5. while Alan collected his equipment
6. since we last saw you
7. as long as you are ready
8. If you are really interested
9. than that one (is)
10. unless my homework is finished

PRACTICE 19.2F

Answers will vary. Sample answers:

11. Veronica took notes as we made our plans.
12. Jude was not nervous as he stepped onstage.
13. Laura did very well on her science test because she had studied.
14. I will tell you if you keep it a secret.
15. Robin will rehearse carefully before she gives her presentation.
16. Keith feels much more energetic since he has started jogging.
17. Even though volunteers put sandbags on the banks, the river overflowed its banks.
18. The garden will dry up unless it rains.
19. We worked hard all week because we wanted to have the weekend free.
20. I will call you if I need help.

SPEAKING APPLICATION

Students' verbalizations should demonstrate that they can use, identify, and understand adverbial clauses in speaking.

WRITING APPLICATION

Students' sentences should demonstrate they can use, identify, and understand adverbial clauses and subordinating conjunctions in writing.

19.3 Classifying Sentences by Structure

Lesson Objectives

1. Recognize simple, compound, complex, and compound-complex sentence structures.
2. Write complex sentences and differentiate between main and subordinate clauses.

The Simple Sentence

Remind students that an independent clause is a clause that can stand alone as a sentence. Explain that a simple sentence is composed of one and only one independent clause.

RULE 19.3.1 Read aloud the rule and then have students repeat the line with you.

Discuss the types of simple sentences and the examples with students. Point out that some examples are very long, but classifying a sentence as a simple sentence has to do with structure, not length.

Work with students to brainstorm for one of each type of sentence shown in the chart on page 424. Write the sentences on the board, and identify the subjects and verbs. Then, have students work in pairs to write their own simple sentences.

19.3 Classifying Sentences by Structure

All sentences can be classified according to the number and kinds of clauses they contain.

www.phwritingcoach.com

Grammar Tutorials
Brush up on your Grammar skills with these animated videos.

Grammar Practice
Practice your grammar skills with Writing Coach Online.

Grammar Games
Test your knowledge of grammar in this fast-paced interactive video game.

The Simple Sentence

The **simple sentence** is the most common type of sentence structure.

RULE 19.3.1 **A simple sentence consists of a single independent clause.**

Simple sentences vary in length. Some are quite short; others can be several lines long. All simple sentences, however, contain just one subject and one verb. They may also contain adjectives, adverbs, complements, and phrases in different combinations.

Simple sentences can also have various compound parts. They can have a compound subject, a compound verb, or both. Sometimes, they will also have other compound elements, such as a compound direct object or a compound phrase.

All of the following sentences are simple sentences.

TYPES OF SIMPLE SENTENCES	
With One Subject and Verb	The snow fell.
With a Compound Subject	Snow and ice are common.
With a Compound Verb	The window squeaked and shook.
With a Compound Subject and Compound Verb	My brother and sister brought bagels and made coffee for brunch.
With a Compound Direct Object	She opened the flower box (direct object) and the card (direct object).
With a Compound Prepositional Phrase	You can drive from the east coast (prep phrase) or from the west (prep phrase).

A simple sentence never has a subordinate clause, and it never has more than one main or independent clause.

www.phwritingcoach.com

Diagnostic and Instruction
Diagnostic test assesses students' instructional needs. Lessons and practice are assigned based on results.

Additional Practice
- Grammar Tutorials—Animated videos reinforce key grammar skills.
- Grammar Practice—Targeted practice addresses individual needs.
- ExamView—Teachers customize their grammar practice and tests.
- Grammar Games—Interactive video games make grammar fun.

Working with ELLs — ELL Sheltered Instruction: Cognitive

Help students learn new language structures heard during classroom instruction by providing examples of different types of simple sentences.

Beginning Remind students that a simple sentence has one main clause. Say a simple sentence as you reinforce the meaning with actions: *I wrote a letter*. Have students repeat. If students are ready, add more elements to your simple sentence, reinforcing that it is still a simple sentence.

Intermediate Read aloud the examples of simple sentences in the chart on page 424. For each example, ask students to tell you the targeted sentence part, such as a compound subject. Then, have partners say their own simple sentences using the first three types.

Advanced Have partners take turns reading aloud the examples in the chart. Then, have each partner write an example of three different types. Have students read aloud their sentences while partners identify the type of each.

Advanced High Read aloud the examples in the chart, pointing out how the parts add different kinds of detail. Then, have students write a paragraph with four different types of simple sentences. Have students read their paragraph to a partner, who should listen for and identify the type of each simple sentence.

The Compound Sentence

A **compound sentence** is made up of more than one simple sentence.

A compound sentence consists of two or more main or independent clauses.

RULE 19.3.2

In most compound sentences, the main or independent clauses are joined by a comma and a coordinating conjunction (*and, but, for, nor, or, so,* or *yet*). They may also be connected with a semicolon (;) or a colon (:).

EXAMPLES **Jamie ran** a two-day athletic clinic**, and** four professional **athletes donated** their time.

All of the athletes **spoke** on the first day**; one was missing** the second day.

Notice in both of the preceding examples that there are two separate and complete main clauses, each with its own subject and verb. Like simple sentences, compound sentences never contain subordinate clauses.

See Practice 19.3A
See Practice 19.3B

The Complex Sentence

Complex sentences contain subordinate clauses, which can be either adjectival clauses or adverbial clauses.

A complex sentence consists of one main or independent clause and one or more subordinate clauses.

RULE 19.3.3

In a complex sentence, the independent clause is often called the **main clause.** The main clause has its own subject and verb, as does each subordinate clause.

In a complex sentence, the main clause can stand alone as a simple sentence. The subordinate clause cannot stand alone as a sentence.

The Compound Sentence

Tell students that the second type of sentence they will learn about is the compound sentence. **Say:** You have encountered this word *compound* before as you learned about sentences. What have you learned about that was compound? (compound subjects; compound verbs) What did *compound* mean in those cases? (It meant there was more than one. A compound subject had more than one subject; a compound verb had more than one verb.) This is also true of compound sentences. A compound sentence is made up of more than one simple sentence. It has two or more independent clauses.

RULE 19.3.2 Read aloud the rule and then have students repeat the lines with you.

Explain that compound sentences are usually formed by combining two simple sentences with a comma and a coordinating conjunction like *and, but, or,* or *so.*

The Complex Sentence

Point out that both simple sentences and compound sentences only contain independent clauses. In contrast, a complex sentence has both an independent (main) clause and one or more subordinate clauses.

RULE 19.3.3 Read aloud the rule and then have students repeat the lines with you.

Review the way students can determine if a sentence contains a subordinate clause. Remind students that a subordinate clause cannot stand on its own, but it does have a subject and a verb.

(continued)

Teacher Tip

Students may want to classify all short sentences as simple sentences. Show students that many short sentences can be compound or complex: *I ate, and then I played. Will he sink or will he swim? I like bread when it is warm. The dog will sleep when it is dark.*

Differentiated Instruction

Strategy for Spanish Speakers
Students whose home language is Spanish might omit subject pronouns in clauses and sentences, because in Spanish certain verb endings give enough information to identify a subject. Review the structure of clauses by writing a compound sentence on the board. Have students identify the subject and verb in each clause. Then have students practice writing their own compound sentences. Have students exchange their sentences with a partner and check each other's sentences to make sure each clause has a subject and a verb. Have students underline the subject and circle the verb in each clause and check each other's subject-verb agreement.

The Complex Sentence *(continued)*

Review the examples with students. Point out that, in a complex sentence, the subordinate clause can appear at the beginning, end, or middle of the sentence.

Have students write two complex sentences with one main and one subordinate clause. Then, have students share their sentences with the class.

The Compound-Complex Sentence

Before reading about the compound-complex sentence, have students predict the sentence structure of these example sentences based on what they have learned. Then, read the definition.

RULE 19.3.4 Read aloud the rule and then have students repeat the lines with you.

Discuss the examples with students. Ask them how they can identify which clauses are the main clauses and which are the subordinate clauses.

Work together with students to write a compound-complex sentence. Use the example sentence as a model. For example, have student volunteers fill in the blanks:

As she was ______________,
Samantha remembered ______________,
but she forgot ______________
that ______________.

Have students brainstorm for several independent and dependent clauses and write them on index cards. Distribute these to small groups of students. Have groups work together to assemble complex sentences using the cards. Then, have them differentiate between the main clause and the subordinate clause in each complex sentence.

EXAMPLES **May 14, 1948, is the day** (main clause) **that Israel became a state** (subordinate clause).

Because this day is so important, (subordinate clause) **celebrations of all kinds take place** (main clause).

In some complex sentences, the main clause is split by a subordinate clause that acts as an adjective.

EXAMPLE **Citizens**, **who have the day off**, **participate in exciting activities**.

The two parts of the main clause form one main clause: *Citizens participate in exciting activities.*

See Practice 19.3C
See Practice 19.3D
See Practice 19.3E
See Practice 19.3F

The Compound-Complex Sentence

A **compound-complex sentence,** as the name indicates, contains the elements of both a compound sentence and a complex sentence.

A compound-complex sentence consists of two or more main or independent clauses and one or more subordinate clauses.

EXAMPLE **As he was leaving for work**, (subordinate clause) **Andy remembered to take his glasses**, (main clause) but **he forgot the presentation** (main clause) **that he had worked on the night before** (subordinate clause).

Working with ELLs — ELL Sheltered Instruction: Cognitive

Have students use visual and contextual support to enhance and confirm understanding as they read and to develop a grasp of the language structure of complex sentences needed to comprehend increasingly challenging language.

Beginning Write this complex sentence on the board. Read it aloud while acting it out: After he finished reading, Jim closed his book. Repeat the sentence as students read with you. Explain that it is a complex sentence. Point out the visual and contextual clues *after* and the comma, which help to signal that the sentence is complex.

Intermediate Read aloud the examples at the top of the page while students follow along. Point out how the highlighting and the labels help students understand the structure of a complex sentence. Then, have students identify the main and subordinate clause in the sentence from the Beginning activity.

Advanced Have students read the examples of compound and compound-complex sentences. Ask partners to describe the differences between the two, using the text highlighting to aid them. Challenge them to create their own complex sentences.

Advanced High Have students complete the Advanced activity. Then, challenge them to write three compound-complex sentences.

PRACTICE 19.3A **Distinguishing Simple and Compound Sentences**

Read the sentences. Then, write *simple* or *compound* for each sentence.

EXAMPLE Many people now drive fuel-efficient cars.

ANSWER *simple*

1. Laurel discovered a box of old photos in the back of the closet.
2. Marissa watered the plants and fertilized them.
3. Calcium and vitamin D are important for strong bones, so I drink milk.
4. Evan sent a text message to his girlfriend.
5. Please follow the ushers to your seat, for the show will start soon.
6. This may be your lucky day.
7. Tourists throw coins into the fountain for good luck.
8. George thanked the presenters and sat down.
9. Martin tried to share his ideas with Eugene, but Eugene was not listening.
10. The library hired a new assistant, but I have not met him yet.

PRACTICE 19.3B **Combining Simple Sentences to Form Compound Sentences**

Read the sentences. Combine the pairs of simple sentences to form compound sentences.

EXAMPLE The newspaper was delivered this morning. I have not read it yet.

ANSWER *The newspaper was delivered this morning, but I have not read it yet.*

11. The lilacs will bloom in May. The roses and lilies bloom later.
12. No one answered the phone. I left a voice message.
13. The rain had left puddles. The children splashed through them.
14. A tornado roared through the edge of town. No one was injured.
15. Celeste stepped inside. The room became quiet.
16. Some people have good fortune. Others always struggle with hardships.
17. Martha lowered her head. Tears fell from her eyes.
18. We should hurry. The show will start soon.
19. Bea had a headache. She did not complain.
20. Rosa forgot to turn off the lights. They stayed on all night.

SPEAKING APPLICATION

With a partner, take turns describing an action. Use only simple sentences.

WRITING APPLICATION

Use your compound sentences 11, 12, and 15 as models, and write three new compound sentences.

SPEAKING APPLICATION

Have partners evaluate each other's descriptions to determine if only simple sentences were used. Then, have partners describe to each other the same action, using only compound sentences.

WRITING APPLICATION

Students should underline the independent clauses in the compound sentences. Then, have students rewrite their compound sentences into simple sentences.

PRACTICE 19.3A

1. simple
2. simple
3. compound
4. simple
5. compound
6. simple
7. simple
8. simple
9. compound
10. compound

PRACTICE 19.3B

11. The lilacs will bloom in May, but the roses and lilies bloom later.
12. No one answered the phone, so I left a voice message.
13. The rain had left puddles, and the children splashed through them. *or* The rain had left puddles; the children splashed through them.
14. A tornado roared through the edge of town, but no one was injured. *or* A tornado roared through the edge of town, yet no one was injured.
15. Celeste stepped inside, and the room became quiet. *or* Celeste stepped inside; the room became quiet.
16. Some people have good fortune, but others always struggle with hardships. *or* Some people have good fortune; others always struggle with hardships.
17. Martha lowered her head, and tears fell from her eyes.
18. We should hurry, for the show will start soon. *or* We should hurry; the show will start soon.
19. Bea had a headache, yet she did not complain. *or* Bea had a headache, but she did not complain.
20. Rosa forgot to turn off the lights, so they stayed on all night.

C = Complex,
NC = Not Complex

1. C 2. NC 3. NC 4. C 5. C
6. C 7. NC 8. NC 9. C 10. C

PRACTICE 19.3D

Answers will vary. Sample answers:

11. We should pick up Kayla at her house since it is on the left side of the street.

12. My grandparents live in Austin although it is 350 miles away.

13. The car stopped suddenly because it ran out of gas.

14. On Saturday, when the temperature reached 102 degrees, it was the third day of the heat wave.

15. I finished the math test before everyone else since it was so easy.

16. Pedro walks his dog three times a day because he is fond of animals.

17. The volleyball players were exhausted after they practiced for four hours.

18. The car accident caused the traffic to come to a complete stop although it started to move again soon.

19. I might vote for Carla since she is both smart and fair.

20. I cannot seem to finish this book because it is long and complicated.

PRACTICE 19.3C **Recognizing Complex Sentences**

Read the sentences. Then, label each sentence *complex* or *not complex*.

EXAMPLE A wave destroyed the sand castle, so the children were sad.

ANSWER *not complex*

1. If you give me the seeds, I will plant them.
2. National park rangers lead natural history tours through the parks.
3. Emily tore the paper in half and gave half to Sue.
4. Our dog was waiting as we pulled into the driveway.
5. Wendy, who has been taking art lessons, showed us a pencil sketch.
6. After she spoke with a counselor, Amber changed her mind.
7. Only the finest musicians play in the symphony orchestra.
8. On a clear night, you can see satellites moving through the sky.
9. Mimi was wearing pants that were too long.
10. The crowd roared when the designated hitter struck out.

PRACTICE 19.3D **Writing Complex Sentences**

Read the sentences. Combine each pair of sentences by changing one of them into a subordinating clause. Add or drop words and punctuation as necessary.

EXAMPLE I will cook dinner. Buy some vegetables at the store.

ANSWER *I will cook dinner if you buy some vegetables at the store.*

11. We should pick up Kayla at her house. It is on the left side of the street.
12. My grandparents live in Austin. It is 350 miles away.
13. The car stopped suddenly. It ran out of gas.
14. On Saturday, the temperature reached 102 degrees. It was the third day of the heat wave.
15. I finished the math test before everyone else. It was so easy.
16. Pedro walks his dog three times a day. Pedro is fond of animals.
17. The volleyball players were exhausted. They practiced for four hours.
18. The car accident caused the traffic to come to a complete stop. It started to move again soon.
19. I might vote for Carla. Carla is both smart and fair.
20. I cannot seem to finish this book. This book is long and complicated.

SPEAKING APPLICATION

With a partner, take turns telling about a program you watch on television. Your partner should listen for and identify at least one complex sentence.

WRITING APPLICATION

Write three complex sentences about your favorite holiday. Share your sentences with a partner, and have your partner label the main and subordinate clauses.

SPEAKING APPLICATION

Students should demonstrate that they can form complex sentences and differentiate between main and subordinate clauses in the sentences they say.

WRITING APPLICATION

Students should demonstrate that they can form complex sentences and differentiate between main and subordinate clauses in their sentences.

Working with ELLs ELL Sheltered Instruction: Cognitive

Use the prompt for the Writing Application to have students demonstrate that they understand the general meaning, main points, and important details in spoken language on topics ranging from the familiar to the unfamiliar. Describe an American holiday, discussing topics familiar to students, such as holiday celebrations, and linking them to less familiar ones, such as how a holiday becomes official.

Beginning Ask simple questions to elicit the general meaning, main points, and important details of your description. Allow students to use illustrations or gestures to demonstrate understanding.

Intermediate Provide small groups with a main idea web. Have them record your general meaning in the center circle and add main points and important details in the outer circles. Invite groups to discuss their webs, linking familiar to unfamiliar topics.

Advanced Provide pairs with a cluster diagram in which they can record the general meaning, main points, and important details of your description. Encourage students to make connections to a familiar holiday.

Advanced High Have students complete the Advanced activity. Then, have them use your holiday description as a model to describe a holiday to a partner.

PRACTICE 19.3E **Writing Complex Sentences**

Read each subordinate clause. Then, write a main clause and unite the main and subordinate clauses into a complex sentence.

EXAMPLE because his birthday is in July

ANSWER *Because his birthday is in July, Diego will have his party at a water park.*

1. if you can leave a little earlier
2. who learn a second language at an early age
3. although pet fish need feeding only once a day
4. when my alarm went off
5. that the librarian recommended
6. unless the temperature drops below 50 degrees
7. which will probably win an award
8. while Toby was away at summer camp
9. whose jewelry designs are popular
10. before she left for school

PRACTICE 19.3F **Distinguishing Compound and Complex Sentences**

Read the sentences. Then, label each sentence *compound* or *complex*.

EXAMPLE When Tanya lost her phone, she was very upset.

ANSWER *complex*

11. The hikers, who had not yet had lunch, were getting hungry.
12. The fog rolled in, and everyone felt cold.
13. Summer will be here before you know it.
14. William likes horror stories, so he has been reading Edgar Allan Poe's short stories.
15. Dorie read about the discovery in the newspaper, where there was a full-page article.
16. Seals and dolphins are sometimes stranded on beaches when the tide goes out.
17. Arlo is very well-informed, so I trust his judgment.
18. Even after we stopped shouting, we could hear the echoes in the mountains.
19. Naomi has agreed to participate, but Luanne is still thinking about it.
20. Nick is so good at chess that no one can beat him.

SPEAKING APPLICATION

With a partner, take turns explaining a process. The process could be directions for how to make something. Your partner should listen for and identify at least two complex sentences. Together discuss the function of the main clause and the subordinate clause in each sentence.

WRITING APPLICATION

Write one compound and one complex sentence. Use these words as the subject and verb in one of the clauses in each sentence: *James rode.*

Extension

To help students synthesize and apply what they have learned about complex sentences, have students work in teams to create a sentence match game. Direct teams to write six or more complex sentences, using two cards for each sentence—one for the independent clause and one for the dependent clause. Have students mix up the cards and place them face down. Have the other teams turn the cards over, two at a time, removing the ones that form a comprehensible sentence. Students should then discuss the placement of the dependent clause in the sentence and the punctuation of sentences with introductory dependent clauses. When all the cards have been removed, the game is over.

SPEAKING APPLICATION

Students should demonstrate they can use and understand complex sentences by saying aloud some complex sentences and then differentiating between the main clauses and subordinate clauses in these sentences.

WRITING APPLICATION

Students should demonstrate they can use and understand main clauses and subordinate clauses in complex sentences by writing some complex sentences. Then, students should underline the main clauses and subordinate clauses in each sentence.

PRACTICE 19.3E

1. If you can leave a little earlier, we can still make the show.
2. Many immigrants, who learn a second language at an early age, speak both languages easily.
3. Although pet fish need feeding only once a day, James worried his fish was hungry.
4. It was time to wake up when my alarm went off.
5. This was the book that the librarian recommended.
6. The machine works fine unless the temperature drops below 50 degrees.
7. It is a great new album, which will probably win an award.
8. The bicycle sat unused while Toby was away at summer camp.
9. Janet is a great artist whose jewelry designs are popular.
10. Sonia made sure everything was in her bag before she left for school.

PRACTICE 19.3F

11. complex
12. compound
13. complex
14. compound
15. complex
16. complex
17. compound
18. complex
19. compound
20. complex

Test Warm-Up

1. **B** I love my mom's mashed potatoes, which are the best I have ever tasted.
2. **H** Change ***that*** to **which** and add a comma before **which**
3. **B** Cut the potatoes that are peeled.
4. **F** Strain them and add them to a large bowl, which should contain 1/4 cup of lowfat milk and two tablespoons of butter.

Reteach

If students have not mastered these skills, review the content in Section 19.3 Classifying Sentences by Structure.

1. The Complex Sentence 19.3.3
2. The Complex Sentence 19.3.3
3. The Complex Sentence 19.3.3
4. The Complex Sentence 19.3.3

Test Tip

Students may have difficulty with the meaning of grammatical terms in a question. Explain to students that they can use key words to help them. For example, if a question requires students to identify a direct object in a sentence, students can use the key word object as a clue. They know that an object is a thing. Then, because they know a noun is the name of a person place, or thing, students can deduce that the word they are looking for is a noun or pronoun.

Test Warm-Up

DIRECTIONS
Read the introduction and the passage that follows. Then, answer the questions to show that you can write complex sentences and differentiate between main versus subordinate clauses in reading and writing.

Hernando wrote this paragraph about his favorite side dish, mashed potatoes. Read the paragraph and think about the changes you would suggest as a peer editor. When you finish reading, answer the questions that follow.

The Best Mashed Potatoes

(1) I love my mom's mashed potatoes. (2) My mom makes the best mashed potatoes I have ever tasted. (3) First, take four large red potatoes that are easy to find in the supermarket. (4) Peel the potatoes. (5) Cut, the potatoes, they are already peeled. (6) Place the potatoes in boiling water for 8 minutes. (7) Strain them and add them to a large bowl. (8) Place ¼ cup of lowfat milk and two tablespoons of butter in the large bowl first. (9) Mix the potatoes, milk, and butter with a hand mixer until smooth. (10) Add salt as needed and serve immediately.

1 What is the BEST way to combine sentences 1 and 2?

A I love my mom's mashed potatoes, she makes the best mashed potatoes I have ever tasted.

B I love my mom's mashed potatoes, which are the best I have ever tasted.

C The best mashed potatoes are my mom's, which I have ever tasted.

D The best mashed potatoes which I love are my mom's.

2 What change, if any, should be made in sentence 3?

F Delete the comma after ***First***

G Change ***that*** to **which**

H Change ***that*** to **which** and add a comma before **which**

J Make no change

3 What is the BEST way to revise sentence 5?

A Peel the potatoes, which have already been cut.

B Cut the potatoes that are peeled.

C Peel the cut potatoes.

D Cut the potatoes, already.

4 What is the BEST way to combine sentences 7 and 8?

F Strain them and add them to a large bowl, which should contain ¼ cup of lowfat milk and two tablespoons of butter.

G Strain them and add them first to a large bowl of ¼ cup of lowfat milk and two tablespoons of butter.

H Strain them and place ¼ cup of lowfat milk and two tablespoons of butter.

J Strain them and add them to a large bowl, place ¼ cup of lowfat milk and two tablespoons of butter in the large bowl first.

CHAPTER 20 LESSON PLANNER
Effective Sentences

Use the Online Lesson Planner at www.phwritingcoach.com to customize your instructional plan for an integrated Language Arts curriculum.

DAY 1 20.1 Classifying the Four Functions of a Sentence

"What Do You Notice?" **Objectives:** Identify, use, and understand the four functions of a sentence	**INSTRUCTION AND PRACTICE** **Student Edition** pp. 431–435

DAY 2 20.2 Combining Sentences

Objectives: Identify, use, and understand sentence-combining methods, including ▪ combining sentence parts ▪ joining clauses	**INSTRUCTION AND PRACTICE** **Student Edition** pp. 436–440

DAY 3 20.3 Varying Sentences

Objectives: Identify, use, and understand aspects of varying sentences, including ▪ varying sentence length ▪ varying sentence beginnings	**INSTRUCTION AND PRACTICE** **Student Edition** pp. 441–443

DAY 4 20.4 Avoiding Sentence Problems

Objectives: Identify, use, and understand methods for avoiding sentence problems, including ▪ correcting sentence fragments ▪ correcting clause fragments ▪ recognizing run-on sentences ▪ correcting run-on sentences	**INSTRUCTION AND PRACTICE** **Student Edition** pp. 444–452

Grammar Assessment

Grammar Coach:	Diagnostic Assessment	End-of-Chapter Assessment	Progress Monitoring
Personalized Instruction	Students take grammar diagnostic test online and are automatically assigned instruction and practice in areas where they need support.	Teacher uses **ExamView** to administer end-of-chapter assessment and remediation. Teachers may customize **ExamView** tests or use the ones provided.	Teachers may use the **Test Warm-Ups** and the **Cumulative Reviews** in the student book or eText to check students' mastery of grammar skills. Students may also play **DimensionL** grammar video games to test their grammar skills.
Teacher-Directed Instruction	Teacher administers the diagnostic test and determines focus of instruction and practice.		

Alternate Pacing Plans

- **Block Scheduling** Each day in the Lesson Planner represents a 40–50 minute block. Teachers using block scheduling may combine days to revise pacing to meet their classroom needs.
- **Accelerated Lesson Planning** Combine instructional days, focusing on concepts called out by students' diagnostic test results.
- **Integrated Language Arts Curriculum** Use the instruction and practice in this chapter to provide reinforcement, remediation, or extension of grammar concepts taught in your literature curriculum.

Links to Prentice Hall *LITERATURE*

- **Unit 3** Writing Workshop: Revising Errors in Adjective and Adverb Usage, p. 553
- **Unit 4** Writing Workshop: Revising Sentences Using Participles, p. 643; Writing Workshop: Revising Fragments and Run-on Sentences, p. 703
- **Unit 5** Double Negatives, p. 808; Writing Workshop: Revising to Avoid Common Usage Problems, p. 827; Sentence Functions and Endmarks, p. 858

Grammar Assessment and Practice

Chapter diagnostic tests assess students' skills and assign instruction and practice.

DimensionL Video Games

Fast-paced interactive video games challenge students' mastery of grammar.

Lesson Planner continues on next page

DAY 5 20.4 Avoiding Sentence Problems *(continued)*

Objectives: Identify, use, and understand methods for avoiding sentence problems, including ▪ properly placing modifiers ▪ avoiding double negatives.	**INSTRUCTION AND PRACTICE** **Student Edition** pp. 453–456

DAY 6 20.4 Avoiding Sentence Problems *(continued)*

Objectives: Identify, use, and understand methods for avoiding common usage problems	**INSTRUCTION AND PRACTICE** **Student Edition** pp. 457–461

DAY 7 20.4 Avoiding Sentence Problems *(continued)*

Objectives: Identify, use, and understand methods for avoiding sentence problems, including ▪ using parallel structure ▪ using consistent tenses	**INSTRUCTION AND PRACTICE** **Student Edition** pp. 462–467 **Test Warm-Up** p. 465

DAY 8 Cumulative Review

Objectives: Identify, use, and understand sentence structure and style, including ▪ subjects and predicates ▪ complements ▪ phrases and clauses ▪ combining and varying sentences ▪ avoiding sentence problems	**INSTRUCTION AND PRACTICE** **Student Edition** pp. 468–470

"Sentences should be clear, to the point, and easy to read. Often students get the idea that the harder writing is to understand, the better it is. Teaching effective sentences is the perfect opportunity to bang the drum of clarity, simplicity, and precision."

—Jeff Anderson

Differentiated Instruction

Differentiated Instruction Boxes in this Teacher's Edition address these student populations:

- Below-Level Students
- Above-Level Students
- Gifted and Talented Students
- Special Needs Students
- English Language Learners
- Spanish Speaking Students

In addition, for further enrichment, see the **Extension** features.

EFFECTIVE SENTENCES

CHAPTER 20

Knowing how different types of sentences function will help you construct clear, meaningful ideas in your writing.

WRITE GUY *Jeff Anderson, M.Ed.*

WHAT DO YOU NOTICE?

Keep an eye out for different types of sentences as you zoom in on these sentences from the screenplay *The Monsters Are Due on Maple Street* by Rod Serling.

MENTOR TEXT

So I've got a car that starts by itself—well, that's a freak thing, I admit it. But does that make me some kind of a criminal or something? I don't know why the car works—it just does!

Now, ask yourself the following questions:

- Which sentence is interrogative? How can you tell?
- What does the end punctuation tell you about the last sentence?

The second sentence is interrogative because it asks a question. You can tell the second sentence is interrogative because there is a question mark at the end of it. The exclamation mark at the end of the last sentence tells you that it is exclamatory. The purpose of an exclamatory sentence is to convey strong emotion.

Grammar for Writers Using a variety of sentences allows writers to make their writing sound lively. Think carefully about which end punctuation mark is most appropriate in each of your sentences. Try not to overuse exclamation marks or they will lose their effect.

How can I tell if a sentence is imperative?

When it's a command. Now, raise your hand before asking a question.

Grammar for Writers: Voice

Ask students how they could change the punctuation in the right-hand balloon to make the teacher's command more emphatic. Explain that learning how to use and punctuate different types of sentences will give their writing variety and help them emphasize important ideas.

EFFECTIVE SENTENCES

As students progress in their writing skills, it will be important for them to be able to apply the rules of grammar, usage, and mechanics to their own drafts. Use the *What Do You Notice?* feature to help them see effective conventions in the work of professional writers. Encourage students to incorporate proper voice, tense, and syntax as they edit their own writing.

Point out that it is important to understand the structures of different sentence types in order to write clearly and smoothly.

WRITE GUY *Jeff Anderson, M. Ed.*

WHAT DO YOU NOTICE?

When students have read the Mentor Text, discuss how the author uses different sentence types to create a sense of the narrator's personality. Then, **ask:** Would this passage be as interesting if it read like this? *A car that starts by itself is a freak thing. But that doesn't make me a criminal. I don't know why the car works that way.* (Accept all reasonable responses.)

Have students finish reading the page. Then, write these sentences on the board and ask volunteers to read them aloud: ***That's a cougar. THAT's a cougar? That's a cougar!*** Ask why each sentence sounds different from the others. Point out that punctuation marks (and a creative use of capitalization) suggest how different types of sentences should sound. Spoken questions in English end with a rising inflection. Exclamation marks add emphasis.

20.1 Classifying the Four Functions of a Sentence

Lesson Objectives

1. Identify and distinguish between the four types of sentences.
2. Punctuate each type of sentence according to its purpose.

Introduce the four types of sentences—declarative, interrogative, imperative, and exclamatory—and explain that the most common type—declarative sentences—states or declares something. Discuss why writers use declarative sentences.

RULE 20.1.1 Read aloud the rule and then have students repeat the lines with you.

Say: Look at the example sentences. Notice that they all end with the same punctuation mark. **Ask:** How do sentences ending with a period sound when they are read aloud? (**Possible response:** English speakers typically drop their voice and pause at the end of a sentence.)

Point out that the examples are all different lengths. **Ask:** What makes all of these declarative sentences? (**Possible responses:** They all have the same purpose: to state facts, declare ideas, or share information; they all end with a period.)

Have students make up and share original declarative sentences about objects in the room or a person in the news.

www.phwritingcoach.com

Diagnostic and Instruction

Diagnostic test assesses students' instructional needs. Lessons and practice are assigned based on results.

Additional Practice

- Grammar Tutorials—Animated videos reinforce key grammar skills.
- Grammar Practice—Targeted practice addresses individual needs.
- ExamView—Teachers customize their grammar practice and tests.
- Grammar Games—Interactive video games make grammar fun.

20.1 Classifying the Four Functions of a Sentence

Sentences can be classified according to what they do. Some sentences present facts or information in a direct way, while others pose questions to the reader or listener. Still others present orders or directions. A fourth type of sentence expresses strong emotion.

www.phwritingcoach.com

Grammar Tutorials
Brush up on your Grammar skills with these animated videos.

Grammar Practice
Practice your grammar skills with Writing Coach Online.

Grammar Games
Test your knowledge of grammar in this fast-paced interactive video game.

These four types of sentences are called **declarative, interrogative, imperative,** and **exclamatory.** As well as having a different purpose, each type of sentence is constructed in a different way.

The type of sentence you are writing determines the punctuation mark you use to end the sentence. The three end marks are the **period (.)**, the **question mark (?)**, and the **exclamation mark (!)**.

The **declarative sentence** is the most common type of sentence. It is used to state, or "declare," ideas.

RULE 20.1.1 **A declarative sentence** states, or declares, an idea and ends with a period.

DECLARATIVE The cellphone rang.

Cellphones help us keep in touch with our friends and family.

Although cellphones are useful in emergencies, used too often, they can lead people to waste a lot of time.

Interrogative means "asking." An **interrogative sentence** is a question. Interrogative sentences often begin with *who, what, when, why, how,* or *how many.* They end with a question mark.

Working with ELLs — ELL Sheltered Instruction: Cognitive

Give students practice speaking using a variety of sentence types by having them make statements and exclamations, give commands, and ask questions. Students should speak with increasing accuracy and ease.

Beginning Speak simple examples of each type and have students repeat, using appropriate expression and intonation. Encourage students to speak their own examples, such as asking *What is your name?* or giving a command like *Open the book.*

Intermediate List the names of each sentence type and their end marks on the board and model examples. Have partners read the example sentences from pages 432–433. Coach them to speak with appropriate expression and intonation as partners identify the sentence type.

Advanced Have students write an example sentence using one of the four types and say it to a partner, speaking with appropriate expression and intonation. Have partners listen and identify the sentence type.

Advanced High Challenge each student to write an example of each of the four sentence types, using correct punctuation. Then, have students read their sentences to a partner using appropriate expression. The partner should listen for and identify the sentence type. Have students explain how they knew which sentence type they heard.

RULE 20.1.2

An interrogative sentence asks a question and ends with a question mark.

INTERROGATIVE	When is band practice going to start?
	Where will the concert be held?
	What songs are we going to play?

RULE 20.1.3

An imperative sentence gives an order, or command, or a direction and ends with either a period or an exclamation mark.

The word *imperative* comes from the Latin word that means "commanding." **Imperative sentences** are commands or directions. Most imperative sentences start with a verb. In this type of sentence, the subject is understood to be *you.*

IMPERATIVE	Take the stairs, not the elevator.
	Walk, don't run!

Notice the punctuation at the end of these examples. In the first sentence, the period suggests that a mild command is being given in an ordinary tone of voice. The exclamation mark at the end of the second sentence suggests a strong command, one given in a loud voice.

RULE 20.1.4

An exclamatory sentence conveys strong emotion and ends with an exclamation mark.

See Practice 20.1A
See Practice 20.1B
See Practice 20.1C
See Practice 20.1D

Exclaim means "to shout out." **Exclamatory sentences** are used to "shout out" emotions such as happiness, fear, delight, or anger.

EXCLAMATORY	He isn't watching where he's going!
	The glass is going to tip over!

Quick-Write Extension

To help students synthesize and apply what they have learned about sentence types, have them write an advertisement for a favorite product, real or imaginary. Direct students to use each type of sentence at least once to create varied sentence patterns that make their advertisements appealing. Ask students to exchange advertisements and identify the sentence types used.

Teacher Tip

Tell students that the name of each type of sentence gives a clue about its purpose. Ask them to identify the clues: declarative (*declare*), interrogative (*interrogate*), imperative (*imperial* from the Latin *imperativus*, meaning "pertaining to a command"), and exclamatory (*exclaim*).

RULE 20.1.2 Read aloud the rule and then have students repeat the lines with you.

Discuss how interrogative sentences are used to find out information.

Ask volunteers to read the interrogative examples aloud. Have students listen for and explain what happens to their voices at the end of the sentence. (**Possible response:** English speakers' voices typically rise at the end of a question.)

Have students make up *What, When, Where, Who, Why,* and *How* questions about band practice or another school activity. Point out that the five W's and one H can help students gather information for reports or from interviews.

RULE 20.1.3 Read aloud the rule and then have students repeat the lines with you.

Point out that imperative sentences give commands. Explain that even polite commands that include *please* are imperative. For example, *Please let me know when you finish* is an imperative sentence.

Explain that the subject of an imperative is always *you,* even though *you* is neither written nor spoken.

RULE 20.1.4 Read aloud the rule and then have students repeat the lines with you.

Discuss why a writer might end a sentence with an exclamation mark. Explain that exclamatory sentences should be used sparingly. If they are overused, they lose their effect.

Write these sentences on the board: *A shepherd boy was bored! He cried, "A wolf is coming!" The villagers ran to save the sheep! The boy did this again! Soon the villagers stopped coming! Then, a wolf attacked! When the boy cried "Wolf!" no one believed him.* **Ask:** Why do exclamatory sentences lose their effect if they are used too often? (**Possible response:** Any special emphasis is lost.)

Work with students to decide where exclamation marks would be effective in the story of the boy who cried wolf.

PRACTICE 20.1A

1. interrogative
2. declarative
3. imperative
4. exclamatory
5. interrogative
6. declarative
7. declarative
8. exclamatory
9. imperative
10. interrogative

PRACTICE 20.1B

11. My subscription to this magazine is about to expire.
12. Explain how you arrived at that solution.
13. What are you studying in social studies?
14. Who is that lurking in the hall?
15. Come quickly!
16. Cynthia Rylant is a writer whose books I enjoy.
17. You look so happy!
18. Tell us about your trip.
19. What movie did you see last weekend?
20. I can't find my notes!

SPEAKING APPLICATION

Have students explain to the class how they identified each of the four types of sentences.

WRITING APPLICATION

Have students share their paragraphs with the class, identifying the four different types of sentences.

PRACTICE 20.1A Identifying Four Types of Sentences

Read the sentences. Then, identify each type of sentence by writing *declarative, interrogative, imperative,* or *exclamatory.*

EXAMPLE Read the instructions before you begin.

ANSWER *imperative*

1. Who brought those delicious cookies?
2. Both generals signed the treaty.
3. Ted, take your feet off the chair.
4. We all had such a good time!
5. Do you know where Erin is?
6. Ricardo is interested in entomology, the study of insects.
7. Presidents' Day celebrates the birthdays of Presidents Washington and Lincoln.
8. I forgot my money!
9. Please leave now.
10. Why are you laughing?

PRACTICE 20.1B Punctuating Four Types of Sentences

Read the sentences. Then, rewrite each sentence, adding the correct end punctuation.

EXAMPLE What time does practice start

ANSWER *What time does practice start?*

11. My subscription to this magazine is about to expire
12. Explain how you arrived at that solution
13. What are you studying in social studies
14. Who is that lurking in the hall
15. Come quickly
16. Cynthia Rylant is a writer whose books I enjoy
17. You look so happy
18. Tell us about your trip
19. What movie did you see last weekend
20. I can't find my notes

SPEAKING APPLICATION

With a small group, carry on a brief dialogue. One person will begin with a question. Each person in the group will continue with a different type of sentence until you have used all types of sentences at least once.

WRITING APPLICATION

Write a brief paragraph in which you use all four types of sentences at least once.

Working with ELLs — ELL Sheltered Instruction: Cognitive

Working from the Writing Application, have students demonstrate comprehension of increasingly complex English by responding to questions.

Beginning Provide students with a brief paragraph featuring simple sentences on a subject of your choice. Preteach vocabulary, and then read the paragraph as students track. Discuss the paragraph, supporting comprehension with visuals and mime. Then, have students respond to questions about the paragraph, such as *What is the paragraph about?*

Intermediate Have partners collaborate in completing the Writing Application. Then, have pairs exchange papers and respond to these questions: *What is the paragraph about? How does the writer feel about the topic?*

Advanced Have students complete the Writing Application individually. Have them exchange papers and respond to these questions: *What is the paragraph about? How does the writer feel about the topic? What additional information might be included? Why?*

Advanced High Have students complete the Advanced activity. Then, challenge them to offer two suggestions to improve their partner's paragraph.

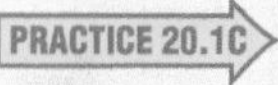

PRACTICE 20.1C Writing Four Types of Sentences

Read the topics. For each topic, write the type of sentence specified in parentheses. Be sure to use the appropriate end punctuation.

EXAMPLE this door (interrogative)
ANSWER *Why is this door locked?*

1. the bicycle trail (declarative)
2. the comedian (exclamatory)
3. you (interrogative)
4. you (imperative)
5. the kitchen in our apartment (declarative)
6. a dump truck (declarative)
7. Sam (interrogative)
8. Selena (exclamatory)
9. you (imperative)
10. who (interrogative)

PRACTICE 20.1D Revising Four Types of Sentences

Read the sentences. Rewrite each sentence, changing it to the type of sentence specified in parentheses. Be sure to use the appropriate end punctuation.

EXAMPLE The rain stopped late in the day. (exclamatory)
ANSWER *The rain finally stopped!*

11. Audrey is a very talented musician. (exclamatory)
12. Spencer had to wait for two hours. (interrogative)
13. Where will the meeting be held? (declarative)
14. Is Fiona planning to swim today? (declarative)
15. This water is cold. (exclamatory)
16. Will you take this list to the office? (imperative)
17. The fire was started by a careless camper. (interrogative)
18. What has Lisa broken? (declarative)
19. She will walk the dog. (interrogative)
20. I would like you to pay attention. (imperative)

SPEAKING APPLICATION

With a partner, name a type of sentence. Your partner will say that type of sentence and then name a different type for you to say.

WRITING APPLICATION

Write a short conversation between two people. Use each type of sentence at least once in the conversation.

PRACTICE 20.1C

Answers will vary. Sample answers:

1. The bicycle trail extends for ten miles through two towns.
2. The comedian told hilarious stories!
3. Where are you going this afternoon?
4. Jump as high as you can!
5. The kitchen in our apartment is small.
6. A dump truck delivered a load of sand to the work site.
7. Is Sam going with you?
8. Selena is such a good sport!
9. Find out what you need to bring.
10. Who wants to play miniature golf?

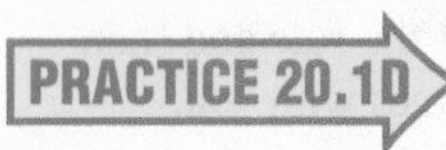

PRACTICE 20.1D

Answers will vary. Sample answers:

11. What a talented musician Audrey is!
12. Did Spencer have to wait for two hours?
13. The meeting will be held in the library.
14. Fiona is planning to swim today.
15. This water is cold!
16. Take this list to the office.
17. Was the fire started by a camper?
18. Lisa has broken her ankle.
19. Will she walk the dog?
20. Please pay attention.

SPEAKING APPLICATION

Have partners present their sentences to the class. The class should listen for and identify the different sentence types.

WRITING APPLICATION

Have students check each other's work and explain why it is or is not correct.

Lesson Objectives

1. Create sentence variety by combining sentences.
2. Use conjunctions to join two main clauses.
3. Differentiate between main and subordinate clauses.
4. Combine sentences by changing one into a phrase.

Combining Sentence Parts

Discuss why skilled writers try to vary their sentences.

RULE 20.2.1 Read aloud the rule and then have students repeat the lines with you.

Use a Think Aloud as part of a gradual release progression.

Say: I see that subjects, verbs, and objects can all be connected by the word *and.* So if I have two related sentences that I want to combine, I should try to connect similar parts using *and* to see if that works.

Work with students to identify the steps to follow in creating sentences with compound subjects, objects, or verbs. Write these sentences on the board: *Anne Marie enjoys watching mysteries. Susan enjoys watching mysteries.* Cross out the words repeated in the second sentence (*enjoys watching mysteries*) and insert *and Susan* after *Anne Marie* in the first sentence to create a compound subject. Point out that this compound subject takes a plural verb, so *enjoys* becomes *enjoy.*

Then, **have students** explain how the remaining examples on page 436 were combined to form sentences with compound verbs and objects.

20.2 Combining Sentences

Good writing should include sentences of varying lengths and complexity to create a flow of ideas. One way to achieve sentence variety is to combine sentences to express two or more related ideas or pieces of information in a single sentence.

www.phwritingcoach.com

Grammar Practice

Practice your grammar skills with Writing Coach Online.

Grammar Games

Test your knowledge of grammar in this fast-paced interactive video game.

Look at the example below. Then, look at how the ideas are combined in different ways.

EXAMPLE I went to the movies. I saw an adventure film.

COMBINED I went to the movies and saw an adventure film.
I saw an adventure film when I went to the movies.

Combining Sentence Parts

Sentences can be combined by using a compound subject, a compound verb, or a compound object.

EXAMPLE Anne Marie enjoys watching mysteries.
Susan enjoys watching mysteries.

COMPOUND SUBJECT **Anne Marie** and **Susan** enjoy watching mysteries.

EXAMPLE Ken sells movie tickets in the evening.
Ken sweeps the theater after the last show.

COMPOUND VERB Ken **sells** movie tickets in the evening and **sweeps** the theater after the last show.

EXAMPLE Marta loves romantic comedies.
Marta loves adventure films.

COMPOUND OBJECT Marta loves romantic **comedies** and adventure **films**.

See Practice 20.2A

www.phwritingcoach.com

Diagnostic and Instruction

Diagnostic test assesses students' instructional needs. Lessons and practice are assigned based on results.

Additional Practice

- Grammar Practice—Targeted practice addresses individual needs.
- ExamView—Teachers customize their grammar practice and tests.
- Grammar Games—Interactive video games make grammar fun.

Joining Clauses

A **compound sentence** consists of two or more main or independent clauses. (See Chapter 19 for more information about clauses.) Use a compound sentence when combining related ideas of equal weight.

To create a compound sentence, join two main clauses with a comma and a coordinating conjunction. Common conjunctions include *and, but, nor, for, so, or,* and *yet.* You can also link the two sentences with a semicolon (;) if they are closely related.

Sentences can be combined by joining two main clauses to create a compound sentence. RULE 20.2.2

EXAMPLE Janice went to a dance recital.
She saw several different styles of dance.

COMPOUND SENTENCE Janice went to a dance recital, and she saw several different styles of dance.

EXAMPLE Janice enjoyed watching jazz and tap dancing.
She particularly liked watching ballet.

COMPOUND SENTENCE Janice enjoyed watching jazz and tap dancing, but she particularly liked watching ballet.

EXAMPLE Janice wanted to learn to dance.
She asked the teacher for lessons.

COMPOUND SENTENCE Janice wanted to learn to dance, so she asked the teacher for lessons.

EXAMPLE Janice goes to dance class.
She studies both jazz and tap dancing.

COMPOUND SENTENCE Janice goes to dance class; she studies both jazz and tap dancing.

See Practice 20.2B

Joining Clauses

Discuss how readers react when they read writing that contains nothing but short, simple sentences. Explain that joining clauses to create compound sentences can add variety by changing the rhythm of a piece of writing.

RULE 20.2.2 Read aloud the rule and then have students repeat the lines with you.

Direct students' attention to the examples. Point out that the ideas in a compound sentence are of equal importance. Work with students to identify the coordinating conjunctions in the first three compound sentences (*and, but, so*). Discuss the purpose of each of these conjunctions. (**Possible responses:** ***And*** **joins two similar things or ideas;** ***but*** **shows contrast;** ***so*** **shows consequences.)**

Have student pairs find examples of compound sentences in a textbook, newspaper article, or reading assignment and present those examples to the class. Students should explain how the clauses have been combined.

(continued)

Teacher Tip

You can give students additional practice by taking a well-written paragraph and breaking it down into simple sentences. Then, have students use sentence combining to create an improved version of the paragraph, working individually or in pairs. Ask students to compare their version to the original. Remind them that the point is not to match the original exactly, but to experiment with different ways of putting sentences together.

Working with ELLs — ELL Sheltered Instruction: Cognitive

As students learn about combining sentences, help them use visual support—a Venn Diagram—to enhance and confirm understanding of increasingly complex spoken language.

Beginning Say *I like cats. I like dogs.* Provide pictures as support. Draw a **Venn Diagram** on the board, writing the two sentences in the outer circles. Then, write *I like cats and dogs* in the center section and say it aloud. Discuss the meaning of the new sentence.

Intermediate Say a pair of simple sentences. Have partners record the sentences in the outer circles of a **Venn Diagram.** Then, combine the sentences. Say the new sentence aloud, and have the students enter it in the center section. Help them understand the new sentence, referring to their diagrams.

Advanced Read the uncombined example sentences from page 436 to students. Have them record the parts of the sentences that are different in the outer circles of a **Venn Diagram,** writing common elements in the center. Then, say the combined sentences. Discuss their meaning as students refer to their diagrams.

Advanced High Have partners complete the Advanced activity, with each taking a turn in providing and combining sentences as the other listens and records.

Joining Clauses *(continued)*

RULE 20.2.3 Read aloud the rule and then have students repeat the lines with you.

Remind students of the definition of a subordinate clause. Review common subordinating conjunctions such as *because, after, although,* and *since.*

Say: Another way to combine sentences is to create a complex sentence. You can do this by changing one of the sentences into a subordinate clause. In the combined example on the page, the second sentence was changed to the subordinate clause *because the storm clouds blew in*; this clause is dependent on the first part of the sentence: *The sky grew dark.*

Work with students to write a sentence using one of the subordinating conjunctions mentioned in the first paragraph: *after, although, because, before, since,* and *unless.*

Then, have student pairs write sentences for each of the remaining subordinating conjunctions.

RULE 20.2.4 Read aloud the rule and then have students repeat the lines with you.

Direct students' attention to the examples for Rule 20.2.4. Work with students to identify how sentences are combined; for example, repeated words are left out and connecting words are added when needed.

On the board, write one of the combined examples, such as *The Capitol Building in Washington, D.C., is interesting to visit.* Work with students to show how embedded phrases can be moved to other places in a sentence without changing meaning; for example, *In Washington, D.C., the Capitol Building is interesting to visit.*

Teacher Tip

On the board, write these sentences: *After he visited the Alamo, Jacob wanted to learn more about Texas history. Jacob wanted to learn more about Texas history after he visited the Alamo.* Have students work in groups to create a poster explaining when a comma is needed in a complex sentence. Have them refer to page 438 and Chapter 25 for examples and explanations.

Sentences can be combined by changing one of them into a subordinate clause.

A **complex sentence** consists of one **main** or **independent clause** and one or more **subordinate clauses.** (See Chapter 19 for more information about clauses.) Combine sentences into a complex sentence to emphasize that one of the ideas in the sentence depends on the other. A subordinating conjunction will help readers understand the relationship. Common subordinating conjunctions are *after, although, because, before, since,* and *unless.* Generally no punctuation is required when a main and a subordinate clause are combined. When the subordinate clause comes first, a comma is needed. (See Chapter 25 for more information on punctuation.)

EXAMPLE The sky grew dark. The storm clouds blew in.

COMBINED The sky grew dark because the storm clouds blew in.

See Practice 20.2C

Sentences can be combined by changing one of them into a phrase.

When combining sentences in which one of the sentences simply adds details, change one of the sentences into a **phrase.**

EXAMPLE The Capitol Building is interesting to visit. It is in Washington, D.C.

COMBINED The Capitol Building in Washington, D.C. is interesting to visit.

EXAMPLE The White House is in Washington, D.C. The president and his family live there.

COMBINED The White House, where the president and his family live, is in Washington, D.C.

See Practice 20.2D

Working with ELLs — ELL Sheltered Instruction: Cognitive

As students learn about using clauses and phrases to combine sentences, help them use contextual support to enhance and confirm their understanding of increasingly complex spoken language.

Beginning Read aloud the paired sentences in the first example on page 438. Provide context by pointing and gesturing to show the sentences are about the sky and weather. Read aloud the combined sentences, and confirm understanding by asking, *Why did the sky grow dark?*

Intermediate Read aloud the paired sentences in the first example on page 438. Provide context by discussing what happens before a storm. Read the combined sentence, pointing out how the ideas connect. Repeat with other examples, providing context for each.

Advanced Provide context for each pair of uncombined example sentences. Have partners take turns speaking the pairs. The partner should listen and describe how the two sentences are related. Have partners suggest a way to combine the sentences, speaking the new sentence aloud.

Advanced High Challenge students to create three sentences about the same topic and speak these sentences to a partner. Partners should use context to identify connections and suggest how two of the sentences can be combined, speaking the new sentence aloud.

PRACTICE 20.2A **Combining Sentences Using Compound Subjects, Verbs, and Objects**

Read the sentences. Combine the sentences in each group into a single sentence. Identify each combination as *compound subject, compound verb,* or *compound object.*

EXAMPLE Leo opened the box. He took out the contents.

ANSWER *Leo opened the box and took out the contents. — compound verb*

1. Cars filled the lot. Pickup trucks were there.
2. Lia vacuumed the floor. She dusted furniture.
3. The rescue squad was at the accident site in a few minutes. Firefighters were there, too.
4. Quentin delivered two pizzas. He also delivered a large salad.
5. We often see a movie on the weekend. We often go to the mall on the weekend.
6. Hannah found some old letters in the attic. She also found some documents.
7. Mr. Pierce studied law. He also studied math.
8. Lee participated in the swim meet. I did, too.
9. The audience applauded. The audience cheered wildly.
10. We donated blankets to the shelter. We also donated food.

PRACTICE 20.2B **Combining Sentences Using Main Clauses**

Read the sentences. Combine each pair into a compound sentence, using the coordinating conjunction in parentheses. Be sure to use the correct punctuation for compound sentences.

EXAMPLE I spent an hour on the crossword puzzle. I did not finish it. (but)

ANSWER *I spent an hour on the crossword puzzle, but I did not finish it.*

11. José likes to cook. He prepares meals. (so)
12. Becky stopped searching. She no longer expected to find her lost bracelet. (for)
13. You could borrow the book from the library. You could buy it. (or)
14. Emily takes piano lessons. She practices an hour a day. (and)
15. Henry VIII was Queen Elizabeth's father. Her mother was Anne Boleyn. (;)
16. Soccer used to be Ryan's favorite sport. Now he prefers basketball. (but)
17. Patrick did not come to the meeting. He did not send in his report. (and)
18. Nelson had hoped to be the first in line for tickets. He did not arrive in time. (but)
19. Miners found gold in California in 1848. Fortune seekers soon flocked there. (and)
20. You can visit Abby in the hospital. You can wait until she comes home. (or)

SPEAKING APPLICATION

With a partner, tell about two people who did something and two things that they did. Use a compound subject and a compound verb. Your partner should listen for and identify them.

WRITING APPLICATION

Use the sentences you wrote for 11, 13, and 18 as models, and write three new compound sentences with the connectors shown in parentheses.

PRACTICE 20.2A

1. Cars and pickup trucks filled the lot.—compound subject
2. Lia vacuumed the floor and dusted furniture.—compound verb
3. The rescue squad and firefighters were at the accident site in a few minutes.—compound subject
4. Quentin delivered two pizzas and a large salad.—compound object
5. We often see a movie or go to the mall on the weekend.—compound verb
6. Hannah found some old letters and documents in the attic.—compound object
7. Mr. Pierce studied law and math.—compound object
8. Lee and I participated in the swim meet.—compound subject
9. The audience applauded and cheered wildly.—compound verb
10. We donated blankets and food to the shelter.—compound object

PRACTICE 20.2B

11. José likes to cook, so he prepares meals.
12. Becky stopped searching, for she no longer expected to find her lost bracelet.
13. You could borrow the book from the library, or you could buy it.
14. Emily takes piano lessons, and she practices an hour a day.
15. Henry VIII was Queen Elizabeth's father; her mother was Anne Boleyn.
16. Soccer used to be Ryan's favorite sport, but now he prefers basketball.
17. Patrick did not come to the meeting, and he did not send in his report.
18. Nelson had hoped to be the first in line for tickets, but he did not arrive in time.
19. Miners found gold in California in 1848, and fortune seekers soon flocked there.
20. You can visit Abby in the hospital, or you can wait until she comes home.

SPEAKING APPLICATION

Have students explain to the class how they identified the compound subject and the compound verb.

WRITING APPLICATION

Have students exchange sentences and check each other's work, explaining why it is or is not correct.

PRACTICE 20.2C

Answers will vary. Sample answers:

1. When the fog clears, the plane will take off. 2. Caleb did his chores early in the day because it would be too hot to work later. 3. Until her fracture is healed, Lara cannot play field hockey. 4. Although Central has some good players, our team has better guards. 5. As Morgan entered the room, the lights went out. 6. Since Dennis cast his fishing line into the stream, he has caught five fish. 7. If you must leave now, I'll walk with you. 8. Though he worked hard, he did not succeed. 9. When the tire blew out, the driver pulled to the side of the road. 10. People do not believe everything Dawn says because she always exaggerates.

PRACTICE 20.2D

Answers will vary as students decide which sentences to convert to phrases. Students should rewrite sentences with these suggested revisions:

11. . . . from Central to South Station.
12. The book, an exciting thriller, . . .
13. . . . in the fountain in the park.
14. Tossed around by the waves, . . .
15. . . . snarled and barked at the intruder.
16. . . . this article about the new school.
17. Walking through a dark room . . .
18. . . . by eating turkey.
19. . . . for transportation.
20. . . . were formed by glaciers.

SPEAKING APPLICATION

Students should demonstrate that they can correctly identify conjunctions.

WRITING APPLICATION

Students should exchange sentences and check each other's work, explaining why it is or is not correct.

PRACTICE 20.2C Combining Sentences Using Subordinate Clauses

Read the sentences. Combine each pair by changing one sentence into a subordinate clause, using the subordinating conjunction in parentheses. Be sure to use the correct punctuation for complex sentences.

EXAMPLE Dave paced back and forth. He rehearsed his speech. (as)

ANSWER *Dave paced back and forth as he rehearsed his speech.*

1. The fog clears. The plane will take off. (when)
2. Caleb did his chores early in the day. It would be too hot to work later. (because)
3. Lara cannot play field hockey. Her fracture is healed. (until)
4. Our team has better guards. Central has some good players. (although)
5. Morgan entered the room. The lights went out. (as)
6. Dennis cast his fishing line into the stream. He has caught five fish. (since)
7. You must leave now. I'll walk with you. (if)
8. He worked hard. He did not succeed. (though)
9. The driver pulled to the side of the road. The tire blew out. (when)
10. People do not believe everything Dawn says. Dawn always exaggerates. (because)

PRACTICE 20.2D Combining Sentences Using Phrases

Read the sentences. Combine each pair of sentences by changing one into a phrase.

EXAMPLE Olivia sells pottery. She attends craft fairs.

ANSWER *Olivia sells pottery at craft fairs.*

11. You can take the subway. It goes from Central to South Station.
12. The book sold out quickly. It was an exciting thriller.
13. Children splashed in the fountain. It was in the park.
14. The rock was very smooth. It had been tossed around by the waves.
15. The watchdog snarled and barked. It barked at the intruder.
16. I found this article. It is about the new school.
17. Alan walked through a dark room. He tripped over some shoes on the floor.
18. People celebrate Thanksgiving. They eat turkey.
19. In some countries, people use camels. Camels are their transportation.
20. Many ponds and valleys were formed. They were formed by glaciers.

SPEAKING APPLICATION

With a partner, take turns talking about something you agree or disagree with. Use subordinating conjunctions. Your partner should listen for and name the conjunctions.

WRITING APPLICATION

Use the sentences you wrote for 11, 12, and 14 as models, and write three new combined sentences. Include phrases in different locations in the sentences.

Working with ELLs — ELL Sheltered Instruction: Cognitive

Help students learn new language structures heard during classroom instruction by having them listen to and produce sentences with subordinate clauses and phrases.

Beginning Say and act out this sentence: *When I look outside, I see [a tree].* Have students repeat your sentence. Then, invite them to complete the sentence with something they see. Allow them to point or illustrate if necessary.

Intermediate Write this sentence on the board and read it aloud: *When I go home today, I will [read a book].* Point out the subordinate clause and the main clause. Then, have students supply a new main clause for the sentence.

Advanced Have partners alternate reading their completed sentences from Practice 20.2C on page 440 to each other. The listener should identify the subordinate clause in each sentence.

Advanced High Challenge partners to use their sentences from Practice 20.2C on page 440 to produce new sentences. Have students keep the subordinate clause but replace the main clause. Then, have them read the new sentences aloud to a partner. The partner should listen for and identify the new main clause.

20.3 Varying Sentences

When you vary the length and form of the sentences you write, you are able to create a rhythm, achieve an effect, or emphasize the connections between ideas.

Grammar Practice
Practice your grammar skills with Writing Coach Online.

Grammar Games
Test your knowledge of grammar in this fast-paced interactive video game.

There are several ways you can introduce variety into the sentences you write.

Varying the length of sentences makes writing lively and interesting to read. (RULE 20.3.1)

Varying Sentence Length

Reading too many long sentences in a row can be just as uninteresting as reading too many short sentences in a row. When you want to emphasize a point or surprise a reader, insert a short, direct sentence to interrupt the flow of several long sentences.

EXAMPLE Veteran's Day is a holiday that is observed in the United States to honor all of those who served in the armed forces in times of war. The holiday has not always been called Veteran's Day. **It was first called Armistice Day.** It is celebrated in most states on November 11.

You can also break some longer sentences into shorter sentences. If the longer sentence contains two or more ideas, you can break up the ideas into separate sentences. However, if a longer sentence contains only one main idea, you should not break it apart.

LONGER SENTENCE Veteran's Day was proclaimed in 1919 by President Wilson to commemorate the ending of World War I.

TWO SENTENCES Veteran's Day was proclaimed in 1919 by President Wilson. It commemorated the ending of World War I.

See Practice 20.3A

Lesson Objectives

1. Compose sentences of varying lengths.
2. Begin sentences in a variety of different ways.

Varying Sentence Length

Discuss the monotonous effect of repetitious sentence lengths.

RULE 20.3.1 Read aloud the rule and then have students repeat the lines with you.

Say: The boldfaced sentence in the example is a short sentence to emphasize the first name given to the veteran's holiday. **Ask:** How does the short sentence create emphasis? **(Possible responses:** It contrasts with the longer sentences; it highlights one key idea.)

On the board, write these sentences: *Goldilocks visited the home of three bears. She tasted their porridge. She sat in their chairs. She wanted to sleep. One bed was just right. Then, the three bears came home. Goldilocks ran away.*

Work with students to create a paragraph that tells this story with more variety in sentence lengths.

Have student pairs write their own paragraph with varied sentence lengths.

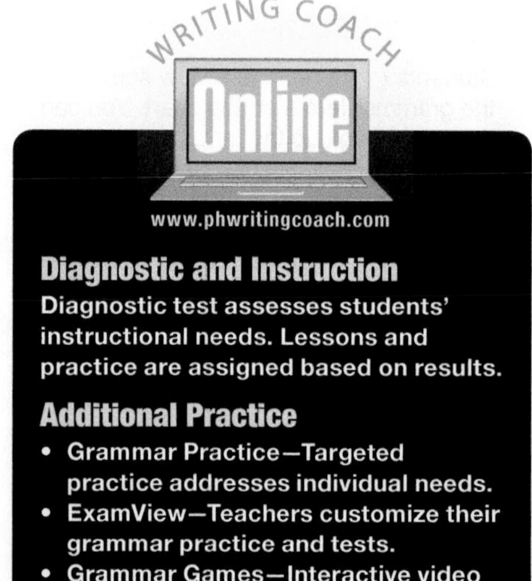

Diagnostic and Instruction
Diagnostic test assesses students' instructional needs. Lessons and practice are assigned based on results.

Additional Practice
- Grammar Practice—Targeted practice addresses individual needs.
- ExamView—Teachers customize their grammar practice and tests.
- Grammar Games—Interactive video games make grammar fun.

Varying Sentence Beginnings

To introduce inverted sentences as a sentence-variety technique, point out that writers sometimes change the normal order of English sentences from subject-verb to verb-subject. Give these examples: *Ed* walked into the room. Into the room walked *Ed*.

RULE 20.3.2 Read aloud the rule and then have students repeat the lines with you.

Point to the *Ways To Vary Sentence Beginnings* chart on page 442. It shows the same sentence with five different beginnings. **Say:** All the sentences follow normal subject-verb order, but each sentence begins in a different way. Help students identify the part of speech of the word or phrase at the beginning of each sentence by examining its function or structure.

On the board, write a sentence beginning with a noun, such as *Gymnasts usually have to be strong to succeed.* Work with students to create four sentence variations using the sentence beginnings listed in the chart. (Usually, gymnasts have to be strong to succeed. To succeed, gymnasts usually have to be strong. Being strong is usually necessary for gymnasts to succeed. For gymnasts to succeed, they usually have to be strong.)

Have student pairs create original examples that show the five ways to begin a sentence. Tell them that each sentence can be about a different subject.

Teacher Tip

Students might need to review some of the grammar terms on the chart. You can have them look up the terms or point out structural cues: adverbs often end in *-ly*; infinitives begin with *to;* gerunds end in *-ing*. You may need to remind students that gerund phrases such as *Knitting sweaters* appear to be verbs but actually function as nouns.

Varying Sentence Beginnings

Another way to create variety is by changing from the usual subject–verb order in a sentence.

Sentence beginnings can also be varied by reversing the traditional subject–verb order or starting the sentence with an adverb or a phrase.

EXAMPLES

The **team** (subject) **is** (verb) **here** (adverb).

Here (adverb) **is** (verb) the **team** (subject).

The **fullback** (subject) **dove** (verb) **into the end zone** (prepositional phrase).

Into the end zone (prepositional phrase) **dove** (verb) the **fullback** (subject).

The **referee** (subject) **called** (verb) the **play** (direct object) **quickly** (adverb).

Quickly (adverb), the **referee** (subject) **called** (verb) the **play** (direct object).

Another way to vary your sentences is to begin them in different ways. For instance, you can start sentences with different parts of speech.

See Practice 20.3B

WAYS TO VARY SENTENCE BEGINNINGS	
Start with a noun.	Sweaters, surprisingly, are not difficult to knit.
Start with an adverb.	Surprisingly, sweaters are not difficult to knit.
Start with an infinitive.	To knit sweaters is, surprisingly, not difficult.
Start with a gerund.	Knitting sweaters is, surprisingly, not difficult.
Start with a prepositional phrase.	For an accomplished knitter, sweaters are not difficult to make.

Working with ELLs — ELL Sheltered Instruction: Cognitive

As students learn about varying sentence beginnings, help them use visual support to enhance and confirm understanding of increasingly complex spoken language.

Beginning Speak a sentence using gestures for support, such as: *I ate quickly.* Write it on the board. Then, say your sentence with a different beginning: *Quickly, I ate,* using the same gestures. Write the new version on the board, using arrows to show how the word order changed.

Intermediate Speak a sentence featuring an adverb. Give students a flow chart and have them record your sentence in the top box. Have small groups change the sentence beginning and share their new sentences as listeners record them in their charts. Help students refer to the charts to confirm understanding.

Advanced Say a sentence with an adverb, prepositional phrase, or adverbial clause. Direct students to record it in the center of a cluster diagram. Have each student alter the beginning of the sentence and say it to a partner. Have partners record the different sentence beginnings in outer circles and discuss them.

Advanced High Challenge students to create sentences with adverbs, prepositional phrases, and adverbial clauses. Have them complete the Advanced activity using their sentences.

PRACTICE 20.3A **Varying Sentence Length**

Read the sentences. Rewrite each long compound sentence as two or more shorter sentences.

EXAMPLE Ivan thought he should do the yard work he had agreed to do or his homework, but instead he decided to spend his Saturday morning riding his bike.

ANSWER *Ivan thought he should do the yard work he had agreed to do or his homework. Instead, he decided to spend his Saturday morning riding his bike.*

1. If you want to take really good photographs, you could practice a lot or you could take a course or you could learn how to fix up your pictures using a computer program.
2. The doorbell rang, and Erin ran to answer it, and the dog slipped out the open door, so she ran after him.
3. Canada is a very large country with a relatively small population and only a few big cities, but these cities are close to the United States, so American tourists often visit them.
4. It was drizzling, but it was a warm rain, so people were not uncomfortable standing under big umbrellas watching a track meet.
5. Mimi had gone with her mother to an appointment, and then she went shopping with her, but she really wanted to stay home and read her book.

PRACTICE 20.3B **Varying Sentence Beginnings**

Read the sentences. Rewrite each sentence, changing the beginning as specified in parentheses. If there are two sentences, combine them, using one of the sentences to help you create the specified beginning.

EXAMPLE We stopped to get sandwiches on our way home. (Begin with a prepositional phrase.)

ANSWER *On our way home,* we stopped to get sandwiches.

6. Wendy smiled to herself, remembering the good time she had. (Begin with a participial phrase.)
7. The ice melted slowly. (Begin with an adverb.)
8. The chorus came next onto the stage. (Reverse the subject-verb order.)
9. Rob dropped his notes. It was in the middle of his speech. (Begin with a prepositional phrase.)
10. Mrs. Kane is a bird-watcher. She travels around the country to see different birds. (Begin with an appositive phrase.)

SPEAKING APPLICATION

With a partner, discuss your reasons for dividing one of the long compound sentences in Practice 20.3A into shorter sentences.

WRITING APPLICATION

Use your revised sentences 6–10 as models and write five sentences with varied beginnings.

SPEAKING APPLICATION

Have one student create a long compound sentence. Have the student's partner restate the sentence in two or more short sentences. Partners should discuss the sentences and decide which approach is more effective.

WRITING APPLICATION

Have students share their sentences with the class, pointing out the different parts of speech they used to begin their sentences.

PRACTICE 20.3A

1. If you want to take really good photographs, you could practice a lot or you could take a course. You could learn how to fix up your pictures using a computer program. *or* If you want to take really good photographs, you could practice a lot. You could take a course or learn how to fix up your pictures using a computer program.
2. The doorbell rang, and Erin ran to answer it. The dog slipped out the open door, so she ran after him. *or* The doorbell rang. Erin ran to answer it, and the dog slipped out the open door. She ran after him.
3. Canada is a very large country with a relatively small population and only a few big cities. These cities are close to the United States, so American tourists often visit them.
4. It was drizzling, but it was a warm rain. People were not uncomfortable standing under big umbrellas watching a track meet.
5. Mimi had gone with her mother to an appointment. Then, she went shopping with her, but she really wanted to stay home and read her book. *or* Mimi had gone with her mother to an appointment, and then she went shopping with her. She really wanted to stay home and read her book.

PRACTICE 20.3B

6. Remembering the good time she had, Wendy smiled to herself.
7. Slowly, the ice melted.
8. Next onto the stage came the chorus.
9. In the middle of his speech, Rob dropped his notes.
10. A bird-watcher, Mrs. Kane travels around the country to see different birds.

20.4 Avoiding Sentence Problems

Lesson Objectives

1. Recognize and correct sentence fragments and run-on sentences.
2. Use a variety of complete sentences that include properly placed modifiers.
3. Compose a variety of complete sentences that include parallel structures.
4. Compose a variety of complete sentences that include consistent tenses.

Correcting Fragments

Focus on fragments as incomplete sentences that can confuse readers.

RULE 20.4.1 Read aloud the rule and then have students repeat the lines with you.

Ask: How can you tell the difference between a fragment and a sentence? **(Possible responses:** A sentence can stand alone, has a subject and a verb, and expresses a complete thought.)

Correcting Phrase Fragments

RULE 20.4.2 Read aloud the rule and then have students repeat the lines with you.

Grammar Game Plan

20.4 Avoiding Sentence Problems

Recognizing problems with sentences will help you avoid and fix any problems in your writing.

www.phwritingcoach.com

Grammar Tutorials
Brush up on your Grammar skills with these animated videos.

Grammar Practice
Practice your grammar skills with Writing Coach Online.

Grammar Games
Test your knowledge of grammar in this fast-paced interactive video game.

Correcting Fragments

Some groups of words—even though they have a capital letter at the beginning and a period at the end—are not complete sentences. They are **fragments.**

A fragment is a group of words that does not express a complete thought.

A fragment can be a group of words that includes a possible subject but no verb. A fragment could also be a group of words that includes a possible verb but no subject. It can even be a group of words that contains no subject and no verb. Fragments can be turned into complete sentences by adding a subject, a verb, or both.

FRAGMENTS	COMPLETE SENTENCES
was ready for bed	I was ready for bed. (A subject is added.)
the clock on the wall	The clock on the wall needs to be reset. (A verb is added.)
in my room	My jeans are in my room. (A subject and verb are added.)

See Practice 20.4A

Correcting Phrase Fragments A **phrase fragment** cannot stand alone because it does not have both a subject and a verb.

A phrase fragment should not be capitalized and punctuated as if it were a sentence.

A phrase fragment can be corrected in one of two ways: (1) by adding it to a nearby sentence or (2) by adding whatever is needed to make it a complete sentence.

WRITING COACH Online

www.phwritingcoach.com

Diagnostic and Instruction
Diagnostic test assesses students' instructional needs. Lessons and practice are assigned based on results.

Additional Practice
- Grammar Tutorials—Animated videos reinforce key grammar skills.
- Grammar Practice—Targeted practice addresses individual needs.
- ExamView—Teachers customize their grammar practice and tests.
- Grammar Games—Interactive video games make grammar fun.

Working with ELLs ELL Sheltered Instruction: Cognitive

As students learn about correcting fragments, support them in speaking using a variety of grammatical structures with increasing accuracy and ease. Focus on the idea that phrases cannot stand alone.

Beginning Ask students a simple question to elicit a phrase as an answer, such as *Where is the book?* (on the desk). Write their responses on the board. Then, model changing the phrase into a simple sentence: *It is on the desk.* Say the fragment and the complete sentence and have students echo you.

Intermediate Have students read aloud the fragments and simple sentences in the chart. Coach them to say the sentences accurately and with correct intonation. Repeat with examples on page 444, using the grammatical structure of subordination.

Advanced Ask students questions to elicit phrases as a response, such as *What do you like to do on weekends? Why?* Record student responses on the board. Then, have them respond orally using complete sentences. Prompt students to use subordinate clauses as appropriate.

Advanced High Have students complete the Advanced activity using simple, compound, and complex sentences.

PHRASE FRAGMENT	The circus will begin at 8:00 on Sunday. **in the arena**
ADDED TO OTHER SENTENCE	The circus will begin at 8:00 on Sunday **in the arena**.
PHRASE FRAGMENT	There will be lions and elephants. **and tightrope walkers**
COMPLETE SENTENCES	There will be lions and elephants. There will also be **tightrope walkers**.

CHANGING PHRASE FRAGMENTS INTO SENTENCES	
PHRASE FRAGMENT	COMPLETE SENTENCE
into the center ring	The horses galloped **into the center ring**.
cheering the acrobats	The crowd was **cheering the acrobats**.
to see the clowns	The children waited **to see the clowns**.

See Practice 20.4B

Correcting Clause Fragments

All clauses have subjects and verbs, but some cannot stand alone as sentences.

A subordinate clause should not be capitalized and punctuated as if it were a sentence.

RULE 20.4.3

Subordinate clauses do not express complete thoughts. Although a subordinate adjective or adverb clause has a subject and a verb, it cannot stand by itself as a sentence. (See Chapter 19 for more information about subordinate clauses and the words that begin them.)

Like phrase fragments, **clause fragments** can usually be corrected in either of two ways: (1) by attaching the fragment to a nearby sentence or (2) by adding whatever words are needed to turn the fragment into a sentence.

Direct students' attention to the words highlighted in purple at the top of page 445. Point out that *in the arena* is a fragment because it lacks a subject and a verb, *and tightrope walkers* lacks a verb. Direct students' attention to the examples in the chart in the middle of the page. Ask students to identify what's missing in the fragments in the chart. (*Into the center ring* is a prepositional phrase, so it has neither a subject nor verb; *cheering the acrobats* is missing a subject and a helping verb; *to see the clowns* is an infinitive phrase and is therefore missing a subject and a verb.)

Correcting Clause Fragments

Focus on subordinate, or dependent, clause fragments, which begin with subordinating conjunctions.

RULE 20.4.3 Read aloud the rule and then have students repeat the lines with you.

Point out that, unlike phrase fragments, clause fragments have a subject and a verb. However, clause fragments cannot stand on their own because they begin with a subordinating conjunction or a relative pronoun.

On the board, write several clause fragments: *after the game ends, if you like Mexican food, even though it's raining, when the climbers reached the top.* Have students add an independent, or main, clause to each dependent clause to correct the fragment.

(continued)

Differentiated Instruction

RTI Strategy for Below-Level Students Explain to students that one way to test whether a group of words can stand alone is to try turning it into a yes/no question. For example, *My jeans are in my room* can become a question—*Are my jeans in my room?* However the fragment *in my room* cannot be turned into a question without adding a subject and a verb. Give students other examples of complete sentences and of phrases and have volunteers apply the question test.

PRE-AP Enrichment for Above-Level Students Explain to students that advertising slogans are often sentence fragments. Have them look through magazines and on the Internet, or brainstorm for slogans that are fragments. Ask students to decide whether the fragments are missing a subject or verb or whether they are subordinate clauses that need a main clause. Then ask them to turn the slogans into complete sentences by adding missing parts.

Correcting Clause Fragments *(continued)*

Ask: How can you tell that the clauses highlighted in green are fragments? (**Possible responses:** They begin with a subordinating conjunction, but they aren't connected to a sentence; they don't express a complete thought.) **Ask:** How were the clause fragments in the chart corrected? (**Possible response:** The subordinate clauses were connected to an independent clause.) Have students use the clause fragments on the page to write new complete sentences.

CLAUSE FRAGMENT — I saw the show. **that you described in your last letter**

COMPLETE SENTENCE — I saw the show **that you described in your last letter**.

CLAUSE FRAGMENT — I bought tickets as soon as they went on sale. **because I wanted good seats**

COMPLETE SENTENCE — I bought tickets as soon as they went on sale **because I wanted good seats**.

CLAUSE FRAGMENT — I wanted to sit in the first row. **so I could see everything**

COMPLETE SENTENCE — I wanted to sit in the first row **so I could see everything**.

To change a clause fragment into a sentence by the second method, you must add an independent clause to the fragment.

CHANGING CLAUSE FRAGMENTS INTO SENTENCES	
CLAUSE FRAGMENT	COMPLETE SENTENCE
that was ringing	Everyone heard the bell **that was ringing**. The bell **that was ringing** was heard by everyone.
when we got home	Dinner was ready **when we got home**. **When we got home**, dinner was ready.
what we were seeing	I could not believe **what we were seeing**.

See Practice 20.4C
See Practice 20.4D

Differentiated Instruction

RTI Strategy for Below-Level Students
Remind students that complete sentences can be turned into yes/no questions but that fragments cannot. Work with them to turn the complete sentences in the chart into questions. For example, *Everyone heard the bell that was ringing* becomes *Did everyone hear the bell that was ringing?* Have students apply this test to other sentences on the page and discuss their answers. Then, have students apply this test to their own writing for this or another class.

RTI Strategy for Special Needs Students
Ask students to act out the complete sentences in the chart at the bottom of page 446. Then, ask them if they can act out the fragments. Explain that, generally, the fragments will be more difficult or impossible to act out because they don't express a complete thought. On the board, copy the chart on page 446. Work with students to color code the subjects and verbs in the Complete Sentence column.

PRACTICE 20.4A **Recognizing Fragments**

Read the groups of words. Then, write whether each group of words is a *sentence* or a *fragment*.

EXAMPLE Searching for a lost ship.

ANSWER *fragment*

1. When Rodney went to Curtis Middle School.
2. Today will be a very important day.
3. Under extreme pressure.
4. Which is a very good deal.
5. A television news reporter on the scene.
6. Walking on an icy pavement can be dangerous.
7. Torn at the edges.
8. By today at noon.
9. Val was not able to take notes because the speaker talked too fast.
10. He did.

PRACTICE 20.4B **Changing Phrase Fragments Into Sentences**

Read the phrase fragments. Then, use each fragment in a sentence.

EXAMPLE during the week

ANSWER *Danielle sometimes babysits during the week.*

11. on the computer for two hours
12. aside from that
13. walking by the shore
14. a children's doctor
15. hidden from sight
16. in the waiting room of the hospital
17. the guidance counselor
18. to answer all the questions on the test
19. not on weekends
20. in the sunshine by the window

SPEAKING APPLICATION

With a partner, take turns turning three of the fragments in Practice 20.4A into sentences.

WRITING APPLICATION

Choose two of the fragments in Practice 20.4B, and write two more sentences for each of them.

PRACTICE 20.4A

1. fragment
2. sentence
3. fragment
4. fragment
5. fragment
6. sentence
7. fragment
8. fragment
9. sentence
10. sentence

PRACTICE 20.4B

Answers will vary. Sample answers:

11. Cyrus has been on the computer for two hours.
12. Aside from that, the show was excellent.
13. Walking by the shore, the girls picked up stones and shells.
14. Mrs. Simpson took her baby to a pediatrician, a children's doctor.
15. Hidden from sight, the toolshed is in the back.
16. The sick child and his mother sat in the waiting room of the hospital.
17. Mrs. Hart, the guidance counselor, helped me find a job.
18. There was not enough time to answer all the questions on the test.
19. The deli is open only on weekdays, not on weekends.
20. A cat was napping in the sunshine by the window.

SPEAKING APPLICATION

Have students explain to the class how they turned the fragments into sentences.

WRITING APPLICATION

Have students share their sentences with the class and discuss how they created their sentences. Students should demonstrate that they understand how to change fragments into sentences.

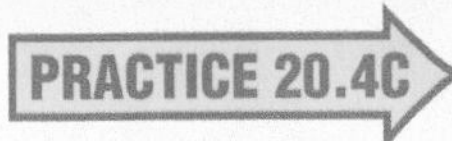

Answers will vary. Sample answers:

1. I did not know until you told me.
2. The grass looked as if it had been trampled by a herd of horses.
3. The patient was asleep when the nurse left the room.
4. You can take your cell phone with you wherever you go.
5. Because the race ended in a tie, there were two winners.
6. Cinderella's coach turned into a pumpkin as the clock struck midnight.
7. You must put your things away before the bell rings.
8. As you probably know, the time of the meeting has been changed.
9. Though the motor was running, the car would not move forward.
10. Many things have changed since we last met.

PRACTICE 20.4D

11. Sample answer: The hats and gloves are on the top shelf in the closet.
12. Sample answer: We need to find renewable sources of energy before it's too late.
13. Sample answer: Roxanne, who did all the artwork, is very skilled.
14. sentence
15. Sample answer: Diving from the rocks into the lake, the boys seemed to be having a good time.
16. Sample answer: Born on Valentine's Day, the baby girl was named Valentina.
17. sentence
18. Sample answer: Thinking about the problem, Jasper was determined to find a solution.
19. Sample answer: Ramon wrote a report on his favorite author, Walter Dean Myers.
20. Sample answer: Although it was very cold out, we decided to go skating.

PRACTICE 20.4C Changing Clause Fragments Into Sentences

Read the clause fragments. Then, use each fragment in a sentence.

EXAMPLE after the book was published

ANSWER *After the book was published, the author was famous.*

1. until you told me
2. as if it had been trampled
3. when the nurse left the room
4. wherever you go
5. because the race ended in a tie
6. as the clock struck midnight
7. before the bell rings
8. as you probably know
9. though the motor was running
10. since we last met

PRACTICE 20.4D Changing Fragments Into Sentences

Read the groups of words. If a group of words is a fragment, use it in a sentence. If a group of words is already a sentence, write *sentence*.

EXAMPLE As Olivia waited.

ANSWER *As Olivia waited, she thought about what she would say.*

11. On the top shelf in the closet.
12. Before it's too late.
13. Who did all the artwork.
14. An e-mail message came with five attachments.
15. Diving from the rocks.
16. Born on Valentine's Day.
17. Meet me in front of the entrance.
18. Thinking about the problem.
19. His favorite author, Walter Dean Myers.
20. Although it was very cold out.

SPEAKING APPLICATION

With a partner, choose one of the fragments in Practice 20.4C, and use it again in two new sentences. Take turns saying these sentences.

WRITING APPLICATION

Write two more sentences for two fragments in Practice 20.4D.

SPEAKING APPLICATION

Encourage partners to create new sentences by having one student say a clause fragment and the other student use it in a new sentence. Students should be able to demonstrate that they can correct sentence fragments.

WRITING APPLICATION

Have students share their sentences with the class, identifying independent clauses.

Run-on Sentences

A fragment is an incomplete sentence. A **run-on,** on the other hand, is two or more complete sentences that are punctuated as though they were one sentence.

Find It/FIX IT 15 Grammar Game Plan

A run-on is two or more complete sentences that are not properly joined or separated.

RULE 20.4.4

Run-ons are usually the result of carelessness. Check your sentences carefully to see where one sentence ends and the next one begins.

Find It/FIX IT 16 Grammar Game Plan

Two Kinds of Run-ons

There are two kinds of run-ons. The first one is made up of two sentences that are run together without any punctuation between them. This is called a **fused sentence.**

The second type of run-on consists of two or more sentences separated by only a comma. This type of run-on is called a **comma splice.**

FUSED SENTENCES

I go to the fair every year I like the crafts.

Jake practices hard he wants to make the team.

COMMA SPLICE

There will be fireworks on July 4, I like the parade, too.

Keisha is a great dancer, I love it when she shows me new steps.

See Practice 20.4E

A good way to distinguish between a run-on and a sentence is to read the words aloud. Your ear will tell you whether you have one or two complete thoughts and whether you need to make a complete break between the thoughts.

Run-on Sentences

Focus on what run-on sentences are and why they can be confusing to readers.

RULE 20.4.4 Read aloud the rule and then have students repeat the lines with you.

Use a Think Aloud as part of a gradual release progression.

Think Aloud **Say:** If a sentence seems to go on and on without a pause, **I might** have to take a closer look at it to judge if it is a run-on sentence. Once I notice this signal, I try to study the sentence to see if it is actually two sentences joined as one. Then, I can take the proper steps to correct it.

Write on the board *I go to the fair every year I like the crafts.* **Work with students** to determine the correct placement of punctuation. **Ask:** Is *I go to the fair* a complete thought? (yes) **Ask:** Does it make sense to put a period there? **(Possible response:** no; *Every year I like the crafts* doesn't make as much sense as *I go to the fair every year. I like the crafts).* Point out that a run-on sentence is incorrect because it is unclear where one thought ends and the other begins.

Have pairs of students write three run-on sentences. Then, have them trade sentences with another pair. Pairs should correct the run-on sentences.

Two Kinds of Run-ons

Point out that there are two kinds of run-ons: fused sentences and comma splices. **Say:** So far, you have been focusing on fused sentences, or complete sentences run together. In comma splices, complete sentences are separated only by a comma.

A comma does not signal a strong enough pause to separate two complete sentences. A comma is used to indicate a pause within a sentence. It does not, on its own, signal a break between sentences.

Discuss the comma splices on page 449. Call for volunteers to explain ways that the comma splices might be corrected.

Working with ELLs ELL Sheltered Instruction: Social/Affective

As students learn about recognizing run-on sentences, help them express themselves in contexts ranging from communicating with single words to participating in extended discussions. If students lack the exact English words, help them use learning strategies, such as requesting assistance or using non-verbal cues.

Beginning Show students pictures of the four seasons. Name and describe each one, using gestures. Elicit students' opinions, ideas, and feelings about the seasons by asking *Which seasons do you like?* Help students use non-verbal cues as necessary. Write responses on the board to illustrate complete sentences.

Intermediate List the four seasons on the board. Have students express opinions, ideas, and feelings about things they associate with each season. Help students use learning strategies, like using synonyms, when necessary. Have them use phrases and complete sentences.

Advanced Prompt groups to discuss the four seasons, expressing their opinions, ideas, and feelings. Have students ask peers for help when they don't know a word. Listeners should pay attention for run-on sentences.

Advanced High Have partners share their opinions, ideas, and feelings about the four seasons. Ensure students use correct intonation to avoid run-on sentences and request assistance as needed.

Three Ways to Correct Run-ons

Point out the three ways to correct run-ons.

Using End Marks

RULE 20.4.5 Read aloud the rule and then have students repeat the lines with you.

Say: Skilled writers make sure that the punctuation on the page matches the way they expect a sentence to sound when read aloud. Read the first run-on example on page 450 as punctuated. Then, ask a volunteer to read the correct version. Do the same for all the examples. **Ask:** How did using correct punctuation help the reader? **(Possible responses:** It showed how the sentence was supposed to sound; it let readers know how long to pause and whether their voice was supposed to go up or down; it broke the run-ons into chunks that made sense.)

On the board, write run-ons such as these: *Run-ons are punctuated as one sentence, they are really two. One way to correct run-ons is to use a comma with a coordinating conjunction, these conjunctions include* and, but, or, for, yet, *and* nor. Have students read each group of words with you as punctuated. Then, work with students to correct the run-ons.

Ask students to write a short paragraph summarizing what they have learned about punctuating sentences. Have them read the paragraph aloud to a partner, who should check that end punctuation matches pauses and vocal inflections. Students should then correct any run-ons in their paragraphs.

Using Commas and Coordinating Conjunctions

Explain that you can sometimes fix run-on sentences by clarifying how the two clauses are related.

Teacher Tip

Tell students that one way to proof for run-ons is to read their paper aloud, pausing briefly for commas and periods. Another is to find all the commas in their paper and check to see if an end mark should be used instead.

Three Ways to Correct Run-ons

There are three ways to correct run-on sentences. You can use end marks, commas and coordinating conjunctions, or semicolons.

Using End Marks

Periods, question marks, and exclamation marks are useful to fix run-on sentences.

Use an end mark to separate a run-on sentence into two sentences.

Sometimes the best way to correct a run-on is to use an end mark to split the run-on into two shorter but complete sentences. End marks help your reader pause and group your ideas more effectively.

RUN-ON I have to babysit on the weekends, my brother goes to practice.

CORRECTED I have to babysit on the weekends. My brother goes to practice.

RUN-ON Watch out the ball is coming toward you.

CORRECTED Watch out! The ball is coming toward you.

RUN-ON Have you bought your tickets I have mine.

CORRECTED Have you bought your tickets? I have mine.

RUN-ON What's going on, I can't figure out where I'm supposed to stand.

CORRECTED What's going on? I can't figure out where I'm supposed to stand.

Using Commas and Coordinating Conjunctions

Sometimes the two parts of a run-on are related and should be combined into a compound sentence.

Working with ELLs

ELL Sheltered Instruction: Cognitive

Have students learn new language structures heard in classroom instruction, including compound sentences.

Beginning On the board, write a run-on sentence such as *I like soccer I like baseball.* Then, say the sentences as a compound sentence. Explain that this new sentence is correct; it is a compound sentence. Write it on the board, pointing out the punctuation.

Intermediate Have students work to correct the examples of run-ons under Rule 20.4.6 on page 451, using a sheet of paper to cover the answer while they work. Have students read aloud the run-on and the correction, as listeners discuss the differences.

Advanced Write run-on sentences on the board and have students correct the sentences using compound as well as simple sentences. Students should read their answers to a partner. Partners should listen for correct intonation to ensure the sentences are correct.

Advanced High Have students create their own run-on sentences. Have partners trade sentences and rewrite the run-ons as compound sentences. Students should read their answers to a partner as partners listen for correct intonation to ensure the sentences are correct.

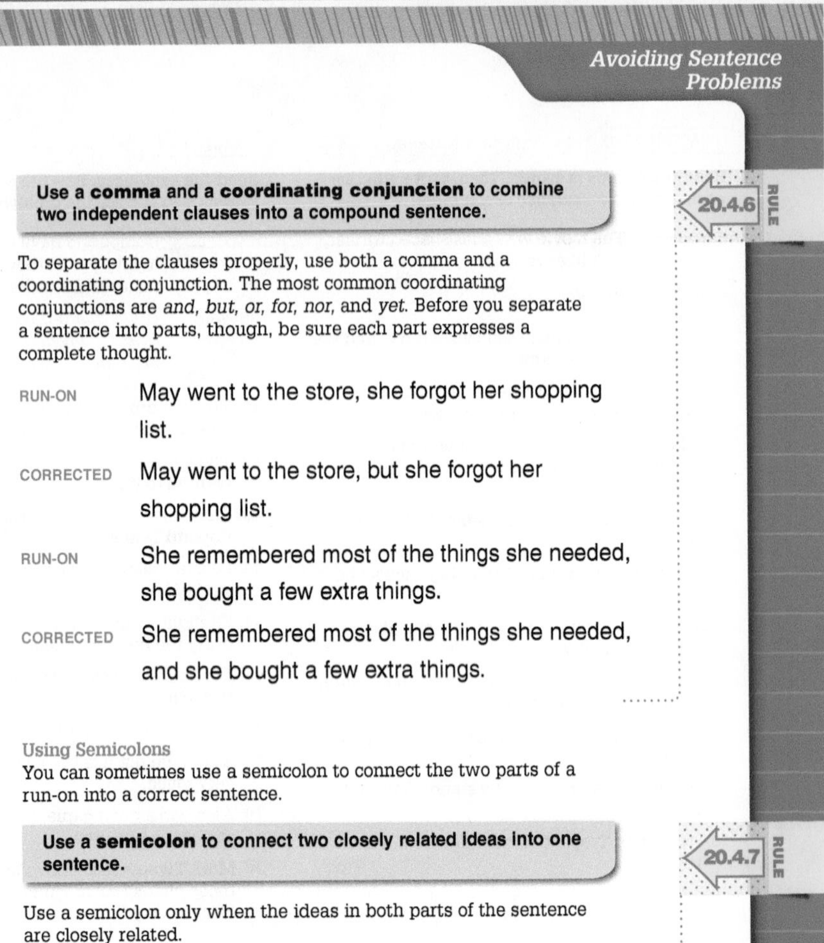

Avoiding Sentence Problems

RULE 20.4.6

Use a comma and a coordinating conjunction to combine two independent clauses into a compound sentence.

To separate the clauses properly, use both a comma and a coordinating conjunction. The most common coordinating conjunctions are *and, but, or, for, nor,* and *yet.* Before you separate a sentence into parts, though, be sure each part expresses a complete thought.

RUN-ON — May went to the store, she forgot her shopping list.

CORRECTED — May went to the store, but she forgot her shopping list.

RUN-ON — She remembered most of the things she needed, she bought a few extra things.

CORRECTED — She remembered most of the things she needed, and she bought a few extra things.

Using Semicolons

You can sometimes use a semicolon to connect the two parts of a run-on into a correct sentence.

RULE 20.4.7

Use a semicolon to connect two closely related ideas into one sentence.

Use a semicolon only when the ideas in both parts of the sentence are closely related.

RUN-ON — My first class next year starts at 8:00, my last class ends at 3:00.

CORRECTED — My first class next year starts at 8:00; my last class ends at 3:00.

See Practice 20.4F

Using Commas and Coordinating Conjunctions

RULE 20.4.6 Read aloud the rule and then have students repeat the lines with you.

Review the purpose of the common coordinating conjunctions:

and means that something is added
but, nor show contrast
or presents alternatives
for shows reason or purpose
so shows consequences
yet connects contrary ideas (People often believe. . ., yet the truth is. . .)

Have student pairs create original sentences using each of the coordinating conjunctions. Ensure that students have used the correct punctuation in their sentences.

Using Semicolons

RULE 20.4.7 Read aloud the rule and then have students repeat the lines with you.

Point out that a semicolon can be used to connect two sentences, provided that the sentences are very closely related. **Say:** One way that I can tell whether sentences are closely enough related is to see whether they are similar in structure. For example, the example sentences are closely related because they have the same subject, *class,* and similar verbs: *starts* and *ends.*

Extension

To help students synthesize and apply what they have learned about correcting run-on sentences, have them challenge each other to a punctuation showdown. Direct students to select a passage of about 50 words from a favorite story or book. Students should then copy or key in the passage, deleting all end marks of punctuation and making the capital letter at the beginning of each sentence lower case. Each student should then select a partner and challenge him or her to correct all the run-on sentences by inserting the correct punctuation and capitalization. Students should then check each other's work against the original passage.

Teacher Tip

Tell students that one way to remember the coordinating conjunctions is the acronym FANBOYS: *for, and, nor, but, or, yet, so.*

PRACTICE 20.4E

1. sentence
2. run-on
3. run-on
4. sentence
5. run-on
6. sentence
7. sentence
8. run-on
9. run-on
10. run-on

PRACTICE 20.4F

Answers will vary. Sample answers:

11. The sun dropped behind the horizon over the lake. We watched the spectacular sunset.
12. The lobby was filled with teenagers. They wanted to buy tickets to the concert.
13. Caleb likes to read limericks; he read some in Edward Lear's *A Book of Nonsense.*
14. Lola graduated from college, and then she took a job in New York.
15. Firefighters quickly arrived; they were able to bring the fire under control.
16. Rock climbing can be exciting but dangerous. Rock climbers need to be cautious.
17. First, boil the water. Then, add the rice.
18. Ethan did not like the movie, but Erica enjoyed it very much.
19. Alec had a good game. He scored two runs and made two outs.
20. Mark Twain created two famous characters. These characters are Tom Sawyer and Huckleberry Finn.

PRACTICE 20.4E Recognizing Run-ons

Read the groups of words. Then, write whether each group is a *sentence* or a *run-on*.

EXAMPLE The movie was a fast-paced thriller, Kirk likes thrillers.

ANSWER *run-on*

1. My cousin from San Diego visited me, and we talked until midnight.
2. Callie writes children's stories, she reads them during the library story hour.
3. Mark picked up the newspaper and read the headlines, then he scanned the sports section.
4. In some areas, trees are being destroyed by insects.
5. He wanted to graduate from high school he did.
6. Warren, a careful person, is serious about whatever he does.
7. Benjamin Franklin was a printer, an inventor, a diplomat, and a convention delegate.
8. Some people like to play sports, others prefer to be spectators.
9. Roy waved at me from the stands, I waved back.
10. Abby sent Troy a text message he did not reply.

PRACTICE 20.4F Correcting Run-ons

Read the sentences. Rewrite each run-on sentence to correct the problem.

EXAMPLE Computers have changed drastically in fifty years, they have become faster and smaller.

ANSWER *Computers have changed drastically in fifty years. They have become faster and smaller.*

11. The sun dropped behind the horizon over the lake, we watched the spectacular sunset.
12. The lobby was filled with teenagers, they wanted to buy tickets to the concert.
13. Caleb likes to read limericks he read some in Edward Lear's *A Book of Nonsense.*
14. Lola graduated from college then she took a job in New York.
15. Firefighters quickly arrived they were able to bring the fire under control.
16. Rock climbing can be exciting but dangerous, rock climbers need to be cautious.
17. First, boil the water then add the rice.
18. Ethan did not like the movie Erica enjoyed it very much.
19. Alec had a good game, he scored two runs and made two outs.
20. Mark Twain created two famous characters these characters are Tom Sawyer and Huckleberry Finn.

SPEAKING APPLICATION

With a partner, identify one sentence and one run-on in Practice 20.4E. Explain why the sentence is correct and the run-on is not.

WRITING APPLICATION

Use sentences 17 and 18 as models, and write a new sentence for each in the same way you corrected them.

SPEAKING APPLICATION

Have students write either a run-on or a correct sentence. Then, have students share their sentences with the class, explaining why their group of words is either a run-on or a correct sentence.

WRITING APPLICATION

Have students explain how they corrected the run-on sentences in Practice 20.4F.

Properly Placing Modifiers

If a phrase or clause acting as an adjective or adverb is not placed near the word it modifies, it may seem to modify a different word. Then the sentence may seem unclear or odd.

A modifier should be placed as close as possible to the word it describes.

RULE 20.4.8

A modifier placed too far away from the word it describes is called a **misplaced modifier.**

MISPLACED MODIFIER — Mark went scuba diving in the lake **with his flippers**.

The misplaced phrase *with his flippers* makes it seem as though the lake has flippers.

See Practice 20.4G
See Practice 20.4H

PROPERLY PLACED MODIFIER — **With his flippers,** Mark went scuba diving in the lake.

Below is a different type of misplaced modifier that is sometimes called a **dangling modifier.** A dangling modifier at the beginning of a sentence causes the sentence to be unclear.

DANGLING MODIFIER — **Sitting on the boat**, the sun felt hot.

In this sentence, *sitting on the boat* should modify a person or people. Instead, it incorrectly modifies *sun.*

CORRECTED — **Sitting on the boat**, we felt the hot sun.

Properly Placing Modifiers

Discuss the importance of properly placed modifiers in complete sentences.

RULE 20.4.8 Read aloud the rule and then have students repeat the lines with you.

Say: If a modifier is misplaced, the meaning of a sentence can change, often with amusing results. What image does this sentence bring to mind? *Jack watched the dog chasing butterflies hopping around with flapping ears.* **(Possible response:** The butterflies were hopping around with ears flopping.**)** To create the correct image, the sentence should read *Jack watched the dog hopping around with its ears flopping, chasing butterflies.*

Work with students to review the examples on page 453 so that they understand how to recognize and correct misplaced or dangling modifiers.

Have pairs of students write sentences with misplaced or dangling modifiers. Then, have the partners rewrite the sentences so that the errors are corrected.

Working with ELLs — ELL Sheltered Instruction: Cognitive

As students complete the Practice activities on page 452, guide them to spell familiar words and employ English spelling rules with increasing accuracy. Teach students the spelling rule of changing *y* to *i* in words ending with a consonant +*y* before adding a suffix.

Beginning Write the word *fly* on the board. Point to the *y* and explain that to make the word plural, you need to change the *y* to *i* and add *-es*. Write *flies* next to *fly*. Have students copy the words. Repeat with the word *pony*.

Intermediate Provide students with these words from the Practice activities: *library, story, lobby*. Have students apply the rule to spell the plural of each noun.

Advanced Provide a list of verbs ending in *y*, such as *identify,* and have students add the *-ed* ending. Supply a list of adjectives ending in *y*, such as *happy,* and have students add the *-er* ending.

Advanced High Provide partners with lists of words from the Advanced activity as well as the *-es, -ed, -er,* and *-est* endings. One partner chooses a word and its ending while the other must spell the word correctly.

Teacher Tip

You can find funny examples of misplaced modifiers by checking books by grammarians like Richard Lederer or Patricia T. O'Conner. You can also search the Web using the key words *"dangling modifiers" funny.* Have students correct the funny examples.

PRACTICE 20.4G

1. Hillary has a cat with stripes named Tiger. 2. Glen searched with a GPS system for the hidden clues. 3. While I was working on my computer, the power went out. 4. Standing on the shore, we watched seals diving for fish. 5. Sitting in the backyard, Victoria reviewed the speech that she would give. 6. Eating my lunch in the park, I watched the squirrels and pigeons. 7. The crowd cheered as the president, accompanied by the First Lady, arrived. 8. Listening to my MP3 player, I get the work done quickly. 9. A student found a black jacket with red sleeves. 10. With your book closed, please summarize what you just read.

PRACTICE 20.4H

Answers will vary. Sample answers:

11. Evan, still in his pajamas, got up early and turned on the television. 12. Rosa waited with her friends for the bus. 13. correct 14. A man jumped into the pond with all his clothes on to rescue the dog. 15. correct 16. Because of the rain, Claire took an umbrella when she walked her dog. 17. correct 18. Looking through my binoculars, I saw a red-tailed hawk. 19. correct 20. correct

PRACTICE 20.4G Revising to Correct Misplaced Modifiers

Read the sentences. Then, rewrite each sentence to correct the underlined misplaced modifier.

EXAMPLE Simon found a twenty-dollar bill walking home from school.

ANSWER *Walking home from school, Simon found a twenty-dollar bill.*

1. Hillary has a cat named Tiger with stripes.
2. Glen searched for the hidden clues with a GPS system.
3. Working on my computer, the power went out.
4. We watched seals diving for fish standing on the shore.
5. Victoria reviewed the speech that she would give sitting in the backyard.
6. I watched the squirrels and pigeons eating my lunch in the park.
7. Accompanied by the First Lady, the crowd cheered as the president arrived.
8. Listening to my MP3 player, the work gets done quickly.
9. A black jacket was found by a student with red sleeves.
10. Please summarize what you just read with your book closed.

PRACTICE 20.4H Recognizing and Correcting Misplaced Modifiers

Read the sentences. If a sentence has a misplaced modifier, rewrite the sentence so the modifier is properly placed. If a sentence is correct, write *correct*.

EXAMPLE With her tail twitching, Audra watched her cat stalk a squirrel.

ANSWER *Audra watched her cat twitching its tail and stalking a squirrel.*

11. Evan got up early and turned on the television still in his pajamas.
12. Rosa waited for the bus with her friends.
13. Putting on her best clothes, Kate prepared for an interview.
14. A man jumped into the pond to rescue the dog with all his clothes on.
15. Remembering his promise, Luis left early.
16. Because of the rain, Claire walked her dog with an umbrella.
17. On her way home, Victoria stopped at the library.
18. I saw a red-tailed hawk looking through my binoculars.
19. Gil stomped out, slamming the door.
20. I saw my friend Pedro talking to his brother in the hall.

SPEAKING APPLICATION

With a partner, take turns describing your favorite season of the year. Be sure to use a combination of simple, compound, and complex sentences with modifiers. Your partner should identify the modifiers and correct any misplaced modifiers.

WRITING APPLICATION

Write a brief description of one of your favorite meals. Include one simple sentence, one compound sentence, and one complex sentence. Then, discuss your sentences with a partner. Your partner should identify the modifiers and correct any misplaced modifiers.

SPEAKING APPLICATION

Students' descriptions should show that they can use a variety of complete sentences that include properly placed modifiers.

WRITING APPLICATION

Students' descriptions and corrections should show they can use a variety of complete sentences that include properly placed modifiers.

Working with ELLs ELL Sheltered Instruction: Cognitive

Help students use increasingly complex grammatical structures in their writing by using possessive case (apostrophe s) correctly. Use Item 1 from Practice 20.4G on page 454 to model creating a possessive. Write *Hillary has a cat. It is Hillary's cat.* Point out the apostrophe and the s. Then:

Beginning Point to an object on a student's desk. Say: *The pen belongs to [Ana]. It is [Ana]'s pen.* Write the possessive *[Ana]'s pen* on the board. Have students repeat. Point to a pen on another student's desk and have students write the possessive as you write it on the board.

Intermediate On separate note cards, write students' names and an apostrophe plus *s*. Have students use the cards to form the possessive. Then, have them write simple sentences using the possessives they formed.

Advanced Have partners identify three singular nouns in their corrected sentences from Practice 20.4G, form the possessive case of each, and use it in a new sentence.

Advanced High Have students complete the Advanced activity. Then, review the rules for forming possessives of plurals ending in *s* (add an apostrophe at the end), and have them revise their sentences by replacing singular with plural possessives.

Avoiding Double Negatives

Negative words, such as *nothing* and *not*, are used to deny or to say *no*. Some people mistakenly use **double negatives**—two negative words—when only one is needed.

Avoid writing sentences that contain double negatives.

RULE 20.4.9

In the following examples, negative words are highlighted. The first sentence in each example contains double negatives. The corrected sentences show two ways to correct each double-negative sentence.

DOUBLE NEGATIVES	Maggie **didn't** invite **nobody**.
CORRECTED SENTENCES	Maggie **didn't** invite anybody. Maggie invited **nobody**.
DOUBLE NEGATIVES	I **haven't no** more money.
CORRECTED SENTENCES	I have **no** more money. I **haven't** any more money.
DOUBLE NEGATIVES	Jack and Phil **didn't** go **nowhere**.
CORRECTED SENTENCES	Jack and Phil **didn't** go anywhere. Jack and Phil went **nowhere**.
DOUBLE NEGATIVES	It seems the sun **doesn't** shine **no** more.
CORRECTED SENTENCES	It seems the sun **doesn't** shine any more. It seems the sun shines **no** more.
DOUBLE NEGATIVES	A few rainy days **didn't** bother **no one**.
CORRECTED SENTENCES	A few rainy days **didn't** bother anyone. A few rainy days bothered **no one**.

See Practice 20.4I
See Practice 20.4J

Avoiding Double Negatives

Discuss how using two negative words or phrases in a sentence affects the meaning of an independent clause in English.

RULE 20.4.9 Read aloud the rule and then have students repeat the line with you.

Direct students' attention to the first example on page 455. Point out that the negative words or phrases are highlighted in blue. Ask students to count the number of negative words or phrases in *Maggie didn't invite nobody.* (two) Have students count the number of negative words or phrases in the two corrected sentences. (one) Have students skim the remaining examples. **Then, ask:** How were the examples on page 455 corrected? (**Possible response:** One of the two negative words or phrases was dropped; only one negative was used in each clause.)

Work with students to make a list of negative words or phrases, such as *no, not, cannot, none, nor, nothing, no one, nowhere, hardly, never,* and *not only.* Also consider words beginning with the prefix *un-* or *in-*, meaning "no" or "not."

Have student pairs write sentences containing double negatives. Then, have students trade sentences with a second pair. The second pair should correct the double negatives and then explain what they did to make the corrections.

Differentiated Instruction

Strategy for Spanish Speakers

Students whose home language is Spanish may mistakenly employ a double negative in English when intending a negative meaning, as this is a common structure in Spanish *(No voy nunca al cine,* literally *I am not going never to the movies).* Elicit from students words that are considered negative such as *nobody, not, nothing, never,* etc. On the board, write examples of sentences that show both correct use of negatives and incorrect use of double negatives. For example, write *Sara didn't see anything* and *We didn't do nothing last night.* Remind students that to convey negative meaning in a sentence, only one negative word is needed. Have students circle the negative words in each sentence to help them identify the sentences that are incorrect. Then, work with students to revise the sentences with double negatives by choosing alternative words or by changing the verb.

PRACTICE 20.4I

1. anywhere
2. any
3. any
4. can
5. anything
6. any
7. anywhere
8. anyone
9. any
10. anything

PRACTICE 20.4J

11. There wasn't anywhere to hang up the coats. *or* There was nowhere to hang up the coats.
12. I didn't get any text message from Liz. *or* I got no text message from Liz.
13. Isn't there anyone here who can give me directions? *or* Is there no one here who can give me directions?
14. The sweatshirt didn't have any hood. *or* The sweatshirt had no hood.
15. I can't find anything in this closet. *or* I can find nothing in this closet.
16. That old house hasn't had any paint for years. *or* That old house has had no paint for years.
17. There isn't anyone at the ticket window. *or* There is no one at the ticket window.
18. Tony didn't remember anything about the accident. *or* Tony remembered nothing about the accident.
19. Amber never said anything to anyone. *or* Amber said nothing to no one.
20. Tonia didn't see anything in the store that she liked. *or* Tonia saw nothing in the store that she liked.

PRACTICE 20.4I Using Negatives Correctly

Read the sentences. Then, write the word in parentheses that makes each sentence negative without creating a double negative.

EXAMPLE The teacher didn't hear (no one, anyone) answer.

ANSWER *anyone*

1. Sue doesn't go (anywhere, nowhere) without her phone.
2. Christa said she didn't want (any, no) bread.
3. Jon didn't bring (any, no) money with him.
4. Ollie (can, can't) never remember his locker combination.
5. Nadine didn't bring (anything, nothing) to the party.
6. He never has (no, any) time to help me.
7. Claudia couldn't find her ring (anywhere, nowhere).
8. Tabitha doesn't know (anyone, no one) in that class.
9. By the time we were ready for dessert, there wasn't (any, none) left.
10. Zach claims he didn't do (anything, nothing).

PRACTICE 20.4J Revising to Correct Double Negatives

Read the sentences. Then, rewrite each sentence to correct the double negative.

EXAMPLE He didn't want no help with the cleanup.

ANSWER *He didn't want any help with the cleanup.*

11. There wasn't nowhere to hang up the coats.
12. I didn't get no text message from Liz.
13. Isn't there no one here who can give me directions?
14. The sweatshirt didn't have no hood.
15. I can't find nothing in this closet.
16. That old house hasn't had no paint for years.
17. There isn't no one at the ticket window.
18. Tony didn't remember nothing about the accident.
19. Amber never said nothing to no one.
20. Tonia didn't see nothing in the store that she liked.

SPEAKING APPLICATION

With a partner or small group, take turns telling each other a very brief narrative in which you use the words *no one, nothing,* and *nowhere.* Be sure not to use double negatives.

WRITING APPLICATION

Write three sentences in which you use three of these negative words without creating a double negative: *never, no,* and *none.*

SPEAKING APPLICATION

As one student narrates, the student who is listening should identify and orally correct any double negatives.

WRITING APPLICATION

Have students share their sentences with the class, explaining why they are correct.

Avoiding Common Usage Problems

Find It/FIX IT 5 Grammar Game Plan

This section contains fifteen common usage problems in alphabetical order. Some are expressions that you should avoid in both your speaking and your writing. Others are words that are often confused because of similar spellings or meanings.

(1) accept, except Do not confuse the spelling of these words. *Accept*, a verb, means "to take what is offered" or "to agree to." *Except*, a preposition, means "leaving out" or "other than."

VERB	Meg **accepted** her award.
PREPOSITION	Everyone was given a raise **except** me.

(2) advice, advise Do not confuse the spelling of these related words. *Advice*, a noun, means "an opinion." *Advise*, a verb, means "to give an opinion."

NOUN	What **advice** can you give me about studying?
VERB	I **advise** you to study every night.

(3) affect, effect *Affect*, a verb, means "to influence" or "to cause a change in." *Effect*, usually a noun, means "result."

VERB	The hurricane **affected** the dunes on the beach.
NOUN	The **effects** of hurricanes may be seen for years.

(4) at Do not use *at* after *where*.

INCORRECT	Does your mother know **where** you're **at**?
CORRECT	Does your mother know **where** you are?

(5) because Do not use *because* after *the reason*. Eliminate one or the other.

INCORRECT	**The reason** I'm happy is **because** I won the race.
CORRECT	I'm happy **because** I won the race.
	The **reason** I'm happy is **that** I won the race.

Avoiding Common Usage Problems

Discuss reasons that usage errors should be avoided in writing.

Use a Think Aloud as part of a gradual release progression.

Say: When **I look** at this list, it seems long. So the way to handle this list is to focus on the few items that give me trouble. One thing I need to review is the difference between *affect* and *effect*. The explanation tells me that I should use *affect* when I mean "to influence." *Effect* is most often used as a noun and means "result." Even though it's rare, *effect* might be used as a verb to mean "to come into being."

Work with students to complete this sentence frame: *Seeing someone else cry always ______ me, though the ______ may not last long.* (affects, effect)

Assign student pairs one usage problem on this page. Ask them to develop a hint or memory aid to help classmates remember the rule for correct usage. Have students share their rules.

(continued)

Teacher Tip

Have students read examples of correct usage aloud to reinforce their sense of how correct usage sounds.

Working with ELLs — ELL Sheltered Instruction: Cognitive

Help students recognize and distinguish sounds in new vocabulary with increasing ease. Have them practice producing the sounds to pronounce words in an increasingly comprehensible manner and learn the relationship between the sounds and letters as they write.

Beginning Write *paint* (page 456, Practice 20.4J, item 16) on the board and have students write it as you sound it out. Explain that the vowels *ai* together usually make the long *a* sound. Then write *rain/ran* on the board. Model the difference between long and short *a*, having students repeat.

Intermediate Create note cards of words with consonant clusters from the activities, like *want*. Have partners sound out words and write them in sentences, then practice saying a new word featuring a consonant cluster.

Advanced Provide students with words from the activities and similar words with different vowel sounds, like *time/tame*. Have partners write the words in sentences and then pronounce them correctly. Have them find and pronounce a new word sharing a vowel sound with one of the activity words.

Advanced High Have students complete the Advanced activity. Challenge them to find and pronounce three new words sharing a vowel sound with one of the activity words.

Avoiding Common Usage Problems *(continued)*

Write these sentences on the board: *I am writing in reply to your ad for a student intern. The reason I would do a good job for you is because I have a great work ethic. Beside that, I work well in groups or on my own. Some day I would like to work into this field.*

Ask: What impression do you get of this person? (**Possible response:** The person seems eager and self-confident, but the number of usage errors might suggest carelessness or lack of education.)

Work with students to correct the errors: (**Possible correction:** *I am writing in reply to your ad for a student intern. One reason I would do a good job for you is that I have a great work ethic. Besides that, I work well in groups or on my own. Some day I would like to work in this field.*)

Assign student pairs one or two of the usage errors on these page. Have them make up original examples to illustrate correct usage for each error they are assigned.

Teacher Tip

Share this proofreading tip with students. They can use their word processor's Find command to check for errors they commonly make with words like *their*, *there*, and *they're*. For example, if they often use *there* when they mean *their*, they can search for *there*. Each time *there* is found, they can decide whether they need an adverb or the possessive pronoun.

(6) beside, besides These two prepositions have different meanings and cannot be interchanged. *Beside* means "at the side of" or "close to." *Besides* means "in addition to."

EXAMPLES My classroom is **beside** hers on this floor.
No one **besides** us is here in the afternoon.

(7) different from, different than *Different from* is preferred over *different than.*

EXAMPLE The new buses are **different from** last year's buses.

(8) farther, further *Farther* is used to refer to distance. *Further* means "additional" or "to a greater degree or extent."

EXAMPLES His house was **farther** than mine.
I will have no **further** communication with you.

(9) in, into *In* refers to position. *Into* suggests motion.

POSITION My books are **in** my backpack.
MOTION I put my backpack **into** my locker.

(10) kind of, sort of Do not use *kind of* or *sort of* to mean "rather" or "somewhat."

INCORRECT I'm **sort of** good at swimming.
CORRECT I'm **rather** good at swimming.

(11) like *Like*, a preposition, means "similar to" or "in the same way as." It should be followed by an object. Do not use *like* before a subject and a verb. Use *as* or *that* instead.

PREPOSITION My sister looks **like** our dad.
INCORRECT This apple doesn't taste **like** it should.
CORRECT This apple doesn't taste **as** it should.

Differentiated Instruction

RTI Strategy for Below-Level Students Have students work in small groups to make posters of some of the usage rules in this section, such as "Do not use *at* after *where.*" If appropriate, the student groups can illustrate their posters. Otherwise, simply have them letter the rule they have chosen on the poster. Then, put the posters in a prominent place in the classroom in order to remind students of the common usage problems.

PRE-AP Enrichment for Above-Level Students Divide students into two groups. Have each member of the first group write a letter asking for advice for a simple problem. Then have them give their letters to members of the second group to respond. Each member of the second group should write an answer to the letter he or she has received. In both sets of letters, students should use correctly several of the problem words in this section.

(12) that, which, who *That* and *which* refer to things. *Who* refers only to people.

THINGS	People liked the music **that** I played.
PEOPLE	The man **who** played the trumpet is my dad.

(13) their, there, they're Do not confuse the spelling of these three words. *Their,* a possessive adjective, always modifies a noun. *There* is usually used as a sentence starter or as an adverb. *They're* is a contraction of *they are.*

POSSESSIVE ADJECTIVE	The students lined up for **their** buses.
SENTENCE STARTER	**There** is the Broadway bus.
ADVERB	The bus stop is over **there**.
CONTRACTION	**They're** waiting in the rain.

(14) to, too, two Do not confuse the spelling of these words. *To* plus a noun creates a prepositional phrase. *To* plus a verb creates an infinitive. *Too* is an adverb and modifies verbs, adjectives, and other adverbs. *Two* is a number.

PREPOSITION	**to** the store	**to** Texas
INFINITIVE	**to** stand	**to** run
ADVERB	**too** cloudy	**too** badly
NUMBER	**two** shoes	**two** shirts

(15) when, where, why Do not use *when, where,* or *why* directly after a linking verb such as *is.* Reword the sentence.

INCORRECT	To explore the ruins is **why** we went to Mexico.
CORRECT	We went to Mexico to explore the ruins.
INCORRECT	In the evening is **when** I do my homework.
CORRECT	I do my homework in the evening.

See Practice 20.4K
See Practice 20.4L
See Practice 20.4M
See Practice 20.4N

Have student pairs make up examples to illustrate correct usage of these commonly misused words: ***that, which,*** and ***who; their, they're,*** and ***there;*** and ***to, too,*** and ***two.*** Have them read their examples aloud to the class without letting other students see what they have written. Students who listen to the examples should write the correct form of the commonly misused word in the example. After students have written their answers, write the correct answer on the board. Repeat until all students have had a chance to share an example or until you are confident that students know the usage rules.

Teacher Tip

Tell students that they will find it easier to check for usage errors if they check for one error at a time. Encourage them to pick two or three errors from the list. When they revise a paper, have them look for just one of those errors at a time. Although it sounds as if looking through the paper three times might take longer, it actually goes more quickly because students are looking for just one thing. The results are also more accurate when students focus on just one error at a time.

Working with ELLs — ELL Sheltered Instruction: Cognitive

Help students recognize and distinguish sounds in English with increasing ease as they learn about usage. Have students identify spoken sounds and practice producing and pronouncing sounds with increasing comprehensibility. Help students learn the relationship between sounds and letters as they write.

Beginning Write the word *like* (page 458) on the board. Have students copy as you sound it out and read it with you. Say that the *e* is silent and makes a long *i* sound. Model long and short *i* sounds, having students repeat.

Intermediate Write *different* (page 458) on the board and have students copy, then choral read it. Point out the double consonant *f*. Explain that we pronounce the consonant only once, with a short vowel before it. Have students decode double consonants and long and short vowels in new vocabulary (e.g., *later/latter*) using flash cards.

Advanced Have partners write word pairs from page 458 in sentences and read them aloud. Students should distinguish between sounds in similar words, like *farther/further*. Have them find a new word that shares a vowel sound with an activity word.

Advanced High Have partners complete the Advanced activity, finding three new words sharing a vowel sound with an activity word.

PRACTICE 20.4K

1. their
2. into
3. effects
4. except
5. advice
6. who
7. too
8. further
9. beside
10. from

PRACTICE 20.4L

11. correct
12. who
13. into
14. their
15. correct
16. from
17. correct
18. advice
19. accept
20. correct

SPEAKING APPLICATION

Have partners explain to the class the differences between *affect* and *effect* and *advice* and *advise*, presenting their sentences to the class as examples of correct usage.

WRITING APPLICATION

Students should exchange sentences and correct any errors, explaining what the errors are.

PRACTICE 20.4K Choosing the Correct Usage

Read the sentences. Then, write the word in parentheses that best completes each sentence.

EXAMPLE The hikers went (farther, further) than they had planned.

ANSWER *farther*

1. The judges have made (there, their) decision.
2. Toby took his equipment (in, into) the locker room.
3. The (affects, effects) of the hurricane are still evident.
4. Everyone has had a turn (accept, except) Lindsay.
5. I could use some (advice, advise) on how to run this machine.
6. Steve introduced his grandfather (that, who) had been a general in the army.
7. Abe's brother wanted (to, too) much money for the bike.
8. Laura needed (farther, further) encouragement to audition for the play.
9. You can place your backpack (beside, besides) the others.
10. Julian is different (from, than) his brother.

PRACTICE 20.4L Recognizing and Correcting Usage Problems

Read the sentences. If the underlined word is used correctly, write *correct*. If the word is incorrect, write the correct word.

EXAMPLE Rick is standing besides Cassie in the picture.

ANSWER *beside*

11. Poor nutrition can affect your ability in school.
12. Grace is a person that is always willing to help.
13. Jeff walked in the classroom.
14. Eve and Tara worked on they're project after school.
15. I have no further information for you at this time.
16. Gwen's idea is different than Rebecca's.
17. The students who made the banner are seventh graders.
18. Jocelyn offers advise, even if you don't want it.
19. Mark was honored to except the award.
20. Brian wants a game like Leo's.

SPEAKING APPLICATION

With a partner, use the words *advice* and *effect* to tell an observation you have made about people in general. Your partner should check that you have used the words correctly.

WRITING APPLICATION

Write two or three related sentences using all of these words correctly: *accept, advice, their,* and *too.*

Working with ELLs

ELL Sheltered Instruction: Cognitive

Help students recognize and distinguish sounds in new vocabulary with increasing ease. Have them practice producing the sounds to pronounce words in an increasingly comprehensible manner and learn the relationship between the sounds and letters as they write.

Beginning Write *beside* on the board, sound it out, and have students copy. Say that the first *e* is long, while the *e* at the end is silent. Explain that a silent *e* makes the vowel before it long. Model long and short *e* and *i*, having students repeat.

Intermediate Create flash cards of commonly misused words. Have partners decode the words, deciding if the vowel is short, long, or silent, then practice saying a new vocabulary word featuring one of the vowel sounds.

Advanced Have partners read aloud their answers from Practice 20.4K, distinguishing between the sounds in similar words. Have listeners write the word they hear to check their work. Have them find and pronounce two new words that share a sound with an activity word.

Advanced High Have students complete the Advanced activity. Challenge them to find and pronounce three new words with a sound spelled as in one of the activity words.

PRACTICE 20.4M **Recognizing and Correcting Usage Problems**

Read the sentences. Then, if a sentence has a usage problem, rewrite it to correct the problem. If a sentence is correct, write *correct*.

EXAMPLE Robin wondered where the meeting was at.

ANSWER *Robin wondered where the meeting was.*

1. The person who can help you is not here today.
2. A late paper could effect your grade.
3. Luke's goals are different from mine.
4. The Mancinos took there dog with them on vacation.
5. The reason I am late is because the bus broke down.
6. The best time is when everyone else has left and it's quiet.
7. We sat besides the Owens family.
8. People that want respect should give respect.
9. I don't know why you always say that.
10. Archie refused to accept payment for helping Mrs. Holden shovel her walk.

PRACTICE 20.4N **Avoiding Usage Problems**

Read the pairs of words. For each pair of words, write two sentences that are related in meaning.

EXAMPLE accept, except

ANSWER *The teacher accepted the papers early. Everyone except Crystal had finished.*

11. besides, beside
12. into, in
13. as, like
14. who, that
15. too, to
16. advice, advise
17. farther, further
18. their, there
19. except, accept
20. effect, affect

SPEAKING APPLICATION

With a partner, choose two of the incorrect sentences in Practice 20.4M, and explain why the usage is incorrect.

WRITING APPLICATION

Write a short paragraph in which you use all of these words correctly: *beside, affect, except,* and *there.*

PRACTICE 20.4M

1. correct
2. A late paper could affect your grade.
3. correct
4. The Mancinos took their dog with them on vacation.
5. The reason I am late is that the bus broke down. *or* I am late because the bus broke down.
6. I like the time when everyone else has left and it's quiet. *or* The time when everyone else has left and it's quiet is the best time.
7. We sat beside the Owens family.
8. People who want respect should give respect.
9. correct
10. correct

PRACTICE 20.4N

Answers will vary. Sample answers:

11. Besides visiting Central Park, we went to the Museum of Natural History. There, we stood beside a dinosaur skeleton.
12. Yolanda and Alison went into the theater. They sat in the back row.
13. We cleaned the tables as we always do. They shined like mirrors.
14. We met a photographer who takes pictures of animals. The pictures that I liked the most are the ones of the pandas and polar bears.
15. It's just too hot. We decided not to do anything today.
16. I asked my dad for advice. He advised me to talk to the coach.
17. Nat ran farther than Sam. Further, he wasn't even tired.
18. Ken and Franklin rode their bicycles to the game. They met some friends there.
19. I've finished all my homework except math. I'd be glad to accept your help with it.
20. Sunshine has a good effect on everyone's mood. Rainy days affect some people differently.

SPEAKING APPLICATION

Have partners choose two other incorrect sentences and explain why they are incorrect.

WRITING APPLICATION

Have students exchange sentences and check each other's work, explaining and correcting any errors they find.

Using Parallel Structures

Explain that parallel grammatical structures in a work make it easier to read and understand.

Recognizing the Correct Use of Parallelism

Discuss what makes Abraham Lincoln's description of American democracy as "government of the people, by the people, and for the people" such a memorable example of parallel structure.

RULE 20.4.10 Read aloud the rule and then have students repeat the lines with you.

Direct students' attention to the examples under Rule 20.4.10. **Say:** The parallel words highlighted in the first example are all adjectives. The parallel phrases in the second example all begin with verbs. **Ask:** What makes the clauses in the third example parallel? (**Possible responses:** Both are subordinate clauses; both begin with *that.*) **Ask:** What makes the sentences in the fourth example parallel? (**Possible response:** Both begin with *We have to.*)

Work with students to create another example of parallel structure. You might ask them to complete this frame: *We are not here to find fault. ________ make things better.* Then, explain that *We are here to make things better* is parallel to the first sentence. This parallelism makes the sentence more powerful than saying *We all just want to make things better.*

Have student pairs write original sentences with parallel phrases, clauses, and sentences.

Correcting Faulty Parallelism

RULE 20.4.11 Read aloud the rule and then have students repeat the lines with you.

Point out to students that coordinating conjunctions such as *and* and *but* are used to join sentence parts of equal weight, or importance. Those sentence parts must also be parallel, or similar, in form.

Using Parallel Structures

Good writers try to present a series of ideas in similar grammatical structures. This way, the ideas read smoothly. If one element in a series is not parallel with the others, the result may be confusing. Parallel structures are important in simple, compound, and complex sentences.

Recognizing the Correct Use of Parallelism

To present a series of ideas of equal importance, you should use parallel grammatical structures.

Parallelism involves presenting equal ideas in words, phrases, clauses, or sentences of similar types.

PARALLEL WORDS — The lost dog looked **scared, dirty,** and **hungry**.

PARALLEL PHRASES — I wanted more than anything to **take him home, give him a bath,** and **feed him**.

PARALLEL CLAUSES — The dog **that you found** and **that you want to bring home** belongs to someone else.

PARALLEL SENTENCES — **We have to find his owner. We have to do the right thing.**

Correcting Faulty Parallelism

Faulty parallelism occurs when a writer uses unequal grammatical structures to express related ideas. This can cause sentences to sound unbalanced.

Correct a sentence with faulty parallelism by rewriting it so that each parallel idea is expressed in the same grammatical structure.

Faulty parallelism can involve words, phrases, and clauses in a series or in comparisons.

Working with ELLs — ELL Sheltered Instruction: Cognitive

Help students spell familiar English words using English spelling patterns with increasing accuracy. Explain that the /k/ sound at the beginning of a word can be spelled with *k* or *c*. If the next letter in the word is the vowel *i* or *e*, the word is usually spelled with a *k*. If it is not, the word usually begins with *c*. Ensure students apply the spelling pattern when writing.

Beginning Write *cat* and *kitten* on the board. Have students copy, then pronounce and spell, the words with you. Speak the words in a sentence with parallel structure.

Intermediate Write *can* and *keep* on the board. Provide sentence frames with parallel structure and have students apply the spelling pattern to *cup* and *kite* (e.g., *The* cup *was cracked, chipped, and dirty*).

Advanced Read aloud words that begin with /k/ (e.g., *confuse, cause, keep, kettle*) and have students spell them correctly in sentences using parallel structure.

Advanced High Have students brainstorm for a list of words that begin with the /k/ sound. Have partners dictate their words. Partners should spell the words, paying close attention to the first letter, and write them in sentences with parallel structure.

Nonparallel Words, Phrases, and Clauses in a Series

Always check for parallelism when your writing contains items in a series.

Correcting Faulty Parallelism in a Series

NONPARALLEL STRUCTURES — Three steps in the writing process are **drafting** (gerund), **revision** (noun), and **editing** (gerund).

CORRECTION — Three steps in the writing process are **drafting** (gerund), **revising** (gerund), and **editing** (gerund).

Nonparallel Words, Phrases, and Clauses in Comparison

In writing comparisons, you generally should compare a phrase with the same type of phrase. Similarly, you should compare a clause with the same type of clause.

Correcting Faulty Parallelism in Comparisons

NONPARALLEL STRUCTURES — I think **that drafting is the easiest step** (noun clause), but **the most patience is required for revising** (independent clause).

CORRECTION — I think **that drafting is the easiest step** (noun clause) but **that revising requires the most patience** (noun clause).

NONPARALLEL STRUCTURES — **Jocelyn** (subject) prefers swimming **in cold water** (prepositional phrase) while the warm **water** (subject) delights her **friends** (direct object).

CORRECTION — **Jocelyn** (subject) prefers swimming **in cold water** (prepositional phrase) while her **friends** (subject) prefer swimming **in warm water** (prepositional phrase).

See Practice 20.4O
See Practice 20.4P

Nonparallel Words, Phrases, and Clauses in a Series

Remind students a series series consists of three or more similar words, phrases, or clauses in a row.

Correcting Faulty Parallelism in a Series

Direct students' attention to the example at the top of page 463. Remind students that gerunds end in *-ing*. Point out the labels under the words highlighted in yellow. Then, ask students to explain why *revision* was changed to *revising*. Ensure students notice that the parallel structure is used in a series.

Nonparallel Words, Phrases, and Clauses in Comparison

Read aloud the second example of nonparallel structures under Correcting Faulty Parallelism in Comparisons; then, read the correction. Ask students to listen for the two things that are being compared (cold and warm water). Then, ask how the parallel structures made it easier to identify the things being compared.

Correcting Faulty Parallelism in Comparisons

Draw a T-chart on the board. Brainstorm with students for a list of things they might compare. Then, work with them to develop comparisons that use parallel structure. For example, if *drum* was listed in the first column and *flute* in the second, a parallel comparison might be *Drums are percussion instruments; flutes are wind instruments.*

Have student pairs write complete sentences that include parallel structures. First, ask them to write two simple sentences that have parallel structures. Then, have students write compound and complex sentences that include parallel structures. Finally, have students share their sentences with another pair of students.

PRACTICE 20.4O

1. I bought two bags of potatoes, three ripe tomatoes, and one head of lettuce.
2. I could not wait to use my new surfboard and to visit my friend, Kelly.
3. The teacher is assigning a book report and is giving us a test tomorrow.
4. My hobbies are going to the movies and playing chess.
5. For your birthday, we can go bowling, but we can't go swimming.
6. correct
7. Pat likes diving, swimming, and surfing.
8. correct
9. I like to paint, sketch, and draw.
10. I am good at English, and I am not bad at math and science.

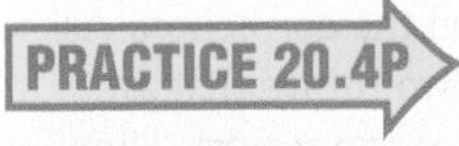

Answers will vary. Sample answers:

11. Most people work during the day, not at night.
12. Shane does the dishes while Joanna cooks.
13. I enjoyed my meal more than Christopher enjoyed his.
14. I am as fond of dogs as I am of cats.
15. Pia is as good a softball player as Shania is a basketball player.
16. Because of traffic, my mother arrived at 7:00 P.M. instead of at 5:30 P.M.
17. Juan enjoyed the nonfiction book as much as his brother enjoyed the science fiction story.
18. I prefer waking up late while my sister prefers rising early.
19. My sister prefers eating apples to eating oranges.
20. Geraldo enjoys playing the clarinet as much as his brother enjoys playing the guitar.

PRACTICE 20.4O Using Parallel Structures With Items in a Series

Read each sentence. Then, rewrite the sentences to correct the faulty parallelism. If the item is correct, then write *correct*. Read your new sentences to a partner. Your partner should identify the parallelism.

EXAMPLE My mother is an excellent dentist, a great cook, and plays the piano well.

ANSWER *My mother is an excellent dentist, a great cook, and a good pianist.*

1. I bought two bags of potatoes, three tomatoes that were ripe, and one head of lettuce.
2. I could not wait to use my new surfboard, and visiting my friend, Kelly.
3. The teacher assigned one book report and is giving us a test tomorrow.
4. My hobbies are going to the movies and chess.
5. For your birthday, we can go bowling but no swimming is allowed.
6. Some of my friends think that ping pong is not a sport, and that it shouldn't be in the Olympics.
7. Pat likes diving, swimming, and to surf.
8. We will miss the bus and be late for the play.
9. I like to paint, sketch and drawing.
10. My best subject is English, and I am not bad at math and science.

PRACTICE 20.4P Using Parallel Structures in Comparisons

Read each sentence. Then, rewrite the sentences to correct the faulty parallelism in comparisons. Read your new sentences to a partner. Your partner should identify the parallel structures.

EXAMPLE I left school at 4:30 P.M. rather than going home at 3:00 P.M.

ANSWER *I left school at 4:30 P.M. rather than at 3:00 P.M.*

11. Most people work during the day not night.
12. Shane did the dishes while Joanna cooks.
13. I enjoyed my meal more than Christopher.
14. I am as fond of dogs as much as I like cats.
15. Pia is as good a softball player as basketball is Shania's strength.
16. Because of traffic, my mother arrived at 7:00 P.M. instead of coming home at 5:30 P.M.
17. Juan enjoyed the nonfiction book as much as the science fiction story is his brother's favorite.
18. I prefer waking up late while my sister is an early riser.
19. My sister prefers apples to eating oranges.
20. Geraldo enjoys playing the clarinet as much as guitar appeals to his brother.

SPEAKING APPLICATION

With a partner, take turns talking about your favorite foods. Include at least one simple sentence, one compound sentence, and one complex sentence and use parallel structures. You partner should identify where you have used parallel structures.

WRITING APPLICATION

Write a paragraph about your school subjects. Include one simple, one compound, and one complex sentence. Show parallel structures in a series and in comparison. Read your paragraph. Your partner should identify where you have used parallel structures.

SPEAKING APPLICATION

Have partners show that they can use a variety of complete sentences that include parallel structures by saying simple, compound, and complex sentences.

WRITING APPLICATION

Have students demonstrate they can use a variety of complete sentences that include parallel structure by writing one simple, one compound, and one complex sentence that include incorrect uses of parallel structure and then correcting the errors.

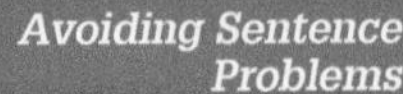

Test Warm-Up

DIRECTIONS
Read the introduction and the passage that follows. Then, answer the questions to show that you can use a variety of complete sentences (e.g., simple, compound, complex) that include parallel structures in reading and writing.

Fiona wrote this paragraph about her summer vacation. Read the paragraph and think about the changes you would suggest as a peer editor. When you finish reading, answer the questions that follow.

Summer Fun

(1) This summer, I did many different things and went to lots of places. (2) The first two weeks of the summer break, I went to the swim club, my grandma's house, and the mall was somewhere I spent time, as well. (3) The last two weeks in July, I went away to camp. (4) My favorite camp activities were tennis, arts and crafts, and of course, going to swim. (5) The last Saturday at camp is visiting day, which means that parents come to visit. (6) Friends can also come.

1 What change, if any, should be made in sentence 1?

- A Change ***did*** to **went**
- B Change ***went*** to **did**
- C Change ***lots of*** to **many different**
- D Make no change

2 What would be the BEST way to rewrite the ideas in sentence 2?

- F The first two weeks of the summer break, I went to the swim club, my grandma's house, and the mall was somewhere I spent time.
- G The first two weeks of the summer break, I went to the swim club, to my grandma's house, and to the mall.
- H The first two weeks of the summer break, the swim club, my grandma's house, and the mall were somewhere I spent time.
- J I went to the swim club and my grandma's house, as well as the mall the first two weeks of summer.

3 What change, if any, should be made in sentence 4?

- A Change ***going to swim*** to **swimming**
- B Insert **playing** after ***were***
- C Insert **making** before ***arts***
- D Make no change

4 What is the BEST way to combine sentences 5 and 6?

- F The last Saturday at camp is visiting day, which means that parents come to visit and that friends can also come.
- G The last Saturday at camp is visiting day, which means that parents and friends can come to visit.
- H The last Saturday at camp is visiting day, which means that parents come and friends also come to visit.
- J The last Saturday at camp, parents and friends come to visit on visiting day.

Test Warm-Up

1. **C** Change ***lots of*** to **many different**
2. **G** The first two weeks of the summer break, I went to the swim club, to my grandma's house, and to the mall.
3. **A** Change ***going to swim*** to **swimming**
4. **G** The last Saturday at camp is visiting day, which means that parents and friends can come to visit.

Reteach

If students have not mastered these skills, review the content in Section 20.4 Avoiding Sentence Problems.

1. Recognizing the Correct Use of Parallelism 20.4.10
2. Correcting Faulty Parallelism 20.4.11
3. Correcting Faulty Parallelism 20.4.11
4. Correcting Faulty Parallelism 20.4.11

Test Tip

Remind students that they should check over their answers if they finish a test early. Explain that, even when a test seems easy, people often make mistakes in reading a question or answer choices. Rechecking their answers can help them find and correct those mistakes.

Working with ELLs — ELL Sheltered Instruction: Metacognitive

Use the Speaking Application on page 464 to have students demonstrate listening comprehension of increasingly complex spoken English by taking notes. Guide students to monitor comprehension while listening and seek clarification of spoken language as needed.

Beginning Model the Speaking Application by talking about your favorite foods. Use simple language and provide pictures and illustrations to support student comprehension. Invite students to raise their hands when they hear something they do not understand. Then, repeat your discussion, asking students to jot down notes using **Drawings** as necessary.

Intermediate Provide students with a main idea web to take notes as you discuss your favorite foods. Ask students if there were ideas or information they didn't understand. Have students discuss the notes they wrote on their **Graphic Organizers.**

Advanced Have partners complete the Speaking Application. While one student talks, the other should take notes. Have each student monitor comprehension and ask one question to seek clarification, such as *What did you say about X?*

Advanced High Have students complete the Advanced activity. Then, have them use their notes to retell the main points of their partner's presentation.

Using Consistent Tenses

Focus on ways that writers use tense to indicate when actions or events take place.

RULE 20.4.12 Read aloud the rule and then have students repeat the lines with you.

Say: Listening for inconsistent tenses is one way to recognize them. The sentence *I make breakfast and then I ate it* doesn't sound correct. It would sound better if I said *I make breakfast and then I eat it.*

Write these sentences on the board: *The source of the Rio Grande is in Colorado. The Pueblo Indians give the river its first name: Posoge, or* big river. *In 1582, a Spanish explorer was calling it Río Turbio, or* turbulent river. *Today, it was once again known as the* big river, *or Rio Grande.*

Ask: Why is there a problem with the verb tenses in this paragraph? **(Possible response:** Inconsistent tenses make it hard to keep track of when things happen.)

Work with students to make the tenses consistent, changing *give* to *gave*, *was calling* to *called*, and *was* to *is*. Point out that *first* and *today* signal shifts in time.

Have student pairs write a short paragraph using inconsistent tenses. Then, have them exchange paragraphs with another pair. The second pair should correct the tenses so that tense is consistent throughout the paragraph.

Using Inconsistent Tenses Correctly

Ask students to write a paragraph about a single childhood memory, such as a family celebration or favorite toy, or about an event from history. Instruct them to use a variety of types of complete sentences including simple, compound, and complex. When students are finished, have them underline all the verbs. Then, have them exchange paragraphs with a partner, who checks that all tenses are consistent and that time indicators like *then, after that,* or *now* are used if a shift in tense is necessary.

Grammar Game Plan

Using Consistent Tenses

Verbs have a number of different tenses that tell when actions happen. For example, past tense is used for actions that happened in the past. Present tense shows actions that happen in the present or that happen regularly. Future tense is used to show actions that will take place in the future. Switching from one tense to another can be confusing in any type of sentence: simple, compound, and complex.

Use consistent verb tenses to show actions that occur during the same period of time.

INCONSISTENT TENSES
I **went** (past) to the movies, and
I **see** (present) my friend waiting for me.

CONSISTENT TENSES
I **went** (past) to the movies, and
I **saw** (past) my friend waiting for me.

The verb *went* sets the action in the past. The other action also occurred in the past.

Using Inconsistent Tenses Correctly

Sometimes, actions take place at different times. In these instances, you may switch from one tense to another. Sometimes you may use a time word or phrase to explain the switch in tense.

EXAMPLE
I **stayed** (past) up really late last night, so now
I **am** (present) very sleepy.

See Practice 20.4Q
See Practice 20.4R

Differentiated Instruction

RTI Strategy for Below-Level Students

Have students make a chart like the one shown here that shows three tenses used of English verbs: past, present, and future. Tell students that they will expand the chart as they work on Chapter 21.

Tense	Verb
Past	traveled
Present	travel
Future	will travel

PRACTICE 20.4Q **Writing Sentences With Consistent Verb Tenses**

Read each sentence. Then, rewrite the sentences to correct inconsistent verb tenses. Read your new sentences to a partner. Your partner should identify the consistent verb tenses.

EXAMPLE Helene goes to the mall and bought a new pair of shoes.

ANSWER *Helene went to the mall and bought a new pair of shoes.*

1. After I finished my homework, I go outside to shoot baskets with Jamie.
2. Every morning, my mom drops me off at school and then went to work.
3. Ms. Jones taught us about the scientific method and then gives a pop quiz.
4. Even though she apologized before, I was still mad at Kaitlin now.
5. Yesterday, I woke up early so that I have time to finish my report.
6. Did you go to the football game or did you went straight home?
7. The bus driver gets mad when we screamed.
8. I like when my dad came home early and plays baseball with me.
9. I am a good chess player but I was even better at checkers.
10. Lydia was mad at Amy for the mean things Amy says about Mia.

PRACTICE 20.4R **Writing Sentences With Consistent Verb Tenses**

Read the verb pairs. Then, write a sentence using each pair in the present, past, or future tense. Read your sentences to a partner. Your partner should identify the consistent tenses.

EXAMPLE leave, wait

ANSWER *Because I left my house before my sister, I waited for her on the corner.*

11. study, take
12. remember, be
13. work, play
14. cook, clean
15. enjoy, dislike
16. tell, laugh
17. win, celebrate
18. arrive, depart
19. become, dream
20. sleep, forget

SPEAKING APPLICATION

With a partner, take turns discussing your favorite weekend activities. Include at least one simple sentence, one compound sentence, and one complex sentence. Use consistent tenses in your sentences. Your partner should identify the consistent tenses.

WRITING APPLICATION

Write a paragraph about a recent event in sports, at school, or in your community. Include at least one simple, one compound, and one complex sentence. Use consistent tenses. Read your paragraph to a partner, who should identify the tenses.

PRACTICE 20.4Q

1. After I finished my homework, I went outside to shoot baskets with Jamie.
2. Every morning, my mom drops me off at school and then goes to work.
3. Ms. Jones taught us about the scientific method and then gave a pop quiz.
4. Even though she apologized before, I am still mad at Kaitlin now.
5. Yesterday, I woke up early so that I had time to finish my report.
6. Did you go to the football game or did you go straight home?
7. The bus driver gets mad when we scream.
8. I like when my dad comes home early and plays baseball with me.
9. I am a good chess player but I am even better at checkers.
10. Lydia was mad at Amy for the mean things Amy said about Mia.

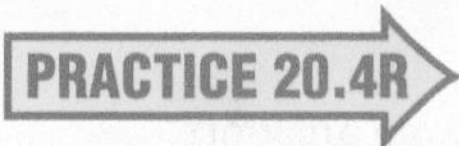

Answers will vary. Sample answers:

11. Robert studied all night then took the test the next morning.
12. Anna remembers the long car trip even though it is over.
13. Many people work during the week and play during the weekend.
14. My dad cooks dinner and cleans the dishes.
15. Either you will enjoy asparagus or you will dislike it.
16. The comedian told a joke and the audience laughed.
17. Sarah's debate team won and celebrated the victory.
18. The plane arrived on time even though it departed late.
19. I become scared when I dream a nightmare.
20. Tired people sleep and forget the day's problems.

SPEAKING APPLICATION

Students should demonstrate that they can use a variety of complete sentences that include consistent tenses when speaking. Students should use consistent tenses and at least one simple sentence, one compound sentence, and one complex sentence. Have partners correct each other's mistakes.

WRITING APPLICATION

Have partners demonstrate they can use consistent tenses in a variety of complete sentences in writing by having them revise each other's paragraphs to change the tense.

PRACTICE 1

Answers will vary. Sample answers:

1. The supermarket cashier scanned our groceries.
2. The children enjoyed the performance.
3. The television weather forecaster told a silly joke about the weather.
4. Was the science homework difficult to do?
5. The roller coaster moved up and down.
6. The frightened cat raced across the room.
7. The new community center opened last Thursday.
8. The explosion made a huge hole.
9. The boy and his parents are going to the beach.
10. The art student entered another contest.

PRACTICE 2

Answers will vary. Sample answers:

1. Dogs need attention.
2. The children are making puppets.
3. In the school office, I saw my gym teacher.
4. Janice paints furniture for a living.
5. Barry left his book bag on the table.
6. He asked the cashier for change for a dollar.
7. I enjoyed the floats at the parade.
8. Last week, Diane met Kristin in the park.
9. The pilot showed us the cockpit.
10. What caused those craters on the moon?

Cumulative Review Chapters 18–20

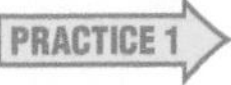

PRACTICE 1 Using Complete Subjects and Predicates

Each item below contains only a complete subject or a complete predicate. Rewrite each item, making a sentence by adding the missing part indicated in parentheses.

1. The supermarket cashier (add a predicate).
2. (add a subject) enjoyed the performance.
3. The television weather forecaster (add a predicate).
4. Was (add a subject) difficult to do?
5. The roller coaster (add a predicate).
6. (add a subject) raced across the room.
7. The new community center (add a predicate).
8. (add a subject) made a huge hole.
9. The boy and his parents (add a predicate).
10. (add a subject) entered another contest.

PRACTICE 2 Using Direct Objects

Rewrite each incomplete sentence, supplying a direct object where indicated in parentheses. You may also include the article *a*, *an*, or *the* or another modifier along with the direct object.

1. Dogs need (direct object).
2. The children are making (direct object).
3. In the school office, I saw (direct object).
4. Janice paints (direct object) for a living.
5. Barry left (direct object) on the table.
6. He asked (direct object) for change for a dollar.
7. I enjoyed (direct object) at the parade.
8. Last week, Diane met (direct object) in the park.
9. The pilot showed us (direct object).
10. What caused (direct object) on the moon?

PRACTICE 3 Identifying Indirect Objects

Read the sentences. Then, write the indirect object in each sentence. If there is no indirect object, write *none*.

1. The nurse gave the patient an injection.
2. Eddie told us a very funny joke.
3. My mom bought herself a lovely silk blouse.
4. Craig clips coupons for supermarket savings.
5. Don't hand her the scissors the wrong way.
6. The rodeo performer showed us a rope trick.
7. Amy offered her seat to a lady with a baby.
8. We wish you a happy holiday.
9. The police officer asked the driver for her license.
10. Who will give the dog a bath?

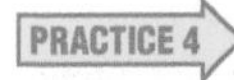

PRACTICE 4 Identifying Subject Complements

Read the sentences. Then, write the subject complement in each sentence. Also indicate whether it is a *predicate noun*, *predicate pronoun*, or *predicate adjective*.

1. The student with the best grades is you.
2. Jack London was a popular adventure writer.
3. The cousins looked happy to see each other.
4. Trina will be the next class president.
5. The drive to Springfield seemed very scenic.
6. Lucia has been the manager for ten years.
7. Of all the skaters, the most graceful one is you.
8. Please do not be late to the concert.
9. That magic show was really something.
10. Are we being careful enough?

PRACTICE 3

1. patient
2. us
3. herself
4. none
5. her
6. us
7. none
8. you
9. none
10. dog

PRACTICE 4

1. you—predicate pronoun
2. writer—predicate noun
3. happy—predicate adjective
4. president—predicate noun
5. scenic—predicate adjective
6. manager—predicate noun
7. you—predicate pronoun
8. late—predicate adjective
9. something—predicate pronoun
10. careful—predicate adjective

PRACTICE 5 Using Prepositional Phrases

Read the sentences. Then, rewrite each sentence, supplying the type of prepositional phrase indicated in parentheses.

1. Paco joined the club. (Add an adjectival phrase.)
2. Lillian tossed a Frisbee. (Add an adverbial phrase.)
3. The noise was loud. (Add an adjectival phrase.)
4. Dad grilled chicken. (Add an adverbial phrase.)
5. Dina rang the bell. (Add an adjectival phrase.)

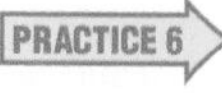

PRACTICE 6 Identifying Appositive, Participial, Gerund, and Infinitive Phrases

Read the sentences. Then, write whether the underlined phrase in each sentence is an *appositive phrase*, a *participial phrase*, a *gerund phrase*, or an *infinitive phrase*.

1. We need to buy light bulbs.
2. Alex plans on running the marathon.
3. Scared by the cat, the mouse scampered off.
4. We looked through binoculars to see the spotted owl.
5. The thesaurus, a book of synonyms, is also available online.
6. The figure dashing through the trees seemed like an owl in the fog.
7. An enthusiastic fisherman, Ernest Hemingway lived for a time in Key West.
8. Knitting woolen sweaters is one of my sister's special skills.
9. Packing her suitcase, Audra broke a fingernail.
10. Max plans to become a skiing instructor.

PRACTICE 7 Recognizing Main and Subordinate Clauses

Read the sentences. Then, write and label the *main clause* and the *subordinate clause* in each sentence.

1. The school bus was late because the traffic on Manning Boulevard was terrible.
2. When the bus neared his stop, Martin rang the bell at the rear door.
3. The state senator, who was first elected more than ten years ago, is running for office again.
4. We will visit Montana in two weeks unless a blizzard prevents the trip.
5. I watched the first episode, which I had seen before.

PRACTICE 8 Combining Sentences With Subordinate Clauses

Read the sentences. Combine each pair of sentences by turning one into a subordinate clause. Then, underline the subordinate clause, and indicate whether it is an *adjectival clause* or an *adverbial clause*.

1. My cousin is wearing a cast. She broke her leg skating on the ice last week.
2. My brother will be applying to several colleges. He is a junior in high school.
3. I hunted in every closet. I finally found that old family photo album.
4. The department store will open earlier than usual. It has a big sale today.
5. We walked nearly five miles today. My feet are very sore.

Continued on next page ▶

PRACTICE 5

Answers will vary. Sample answers:

1. Paco joined the club for birdwatchers.
2. Lillian tossed a Frisbee in the air.
3. The noise from the jackhammer was loud.
4. Dad grilled chicken in the broiler.
5. Dina rang the bell at the front door.

PRACTICE 6

1. infinitive phrase
2. gerund phrase
3. participial phrase
4. infinitive phrase
5. appositive phrase
6. participial phrase
7. appositive phrase
8. gerund phrase
9. participial phrase
10. infinitive phrase

PRACTICE 7

1. The school bus was late—main clause
   because the traffic on Manning Boulevard was terrible—subordinate clause
2. When the bus neared his stop—subordinate clause
   Martin rang the bell at the rear door—main clause
3. The state senator is running for office again—main clause
   who was first elected more than ten years ago—subordinate clause
4. We will visit Montana in two weeks—main clause
   unless a blizzard prevents the trip—subordinate clause
5. I watched the first episode—main clause
   which I had seen before—subordinate clause

PRACTICE 8

Answers will vary. Sample answers:

1. My cousin is wearing a cast because she broke her leg skating on the ice last week.—adverbial clause
2. My brother, who is a junior in high school, will be applying to several colleges.—adjectival clause
3. I hunted in every closet until I finally found that old family photo album.—adverbial clause
4. The department store, which has a big sale today, will open earlier than usual.—adjectival clause
5. After we walked nearly five miles today, my feet are very sore.—adverbial clause

PRACTICE 9

Answers will vary. Sample answers:

1. The inventor showed the students his invention, and the students asked him many questions.
2. The elevator broke last week.
3. She is running because a dog is chasing her.
4. How marvelous you look!
5. Please unlock the door for me.

PRACTICE 10

1. Geraldo and Frederica waited in the ticket line.—compound subject
2. Jacques ordered a turkey sandwich and a salad for lunch.—compound object
3. The designer selected and matched the fabrics carefully.—compound verb
4. Fern may have left her keys on the kitchen counter and her scarf in the car.—compound object
5. They were hoping for an experienced baker, but the person they finally hired has little experience.—compound sentence

PRACTICE 11

Answers will vary. Sample answers:

1. The groom was waiting at the altar.
2. correct
3. I was reading in bed; my eyes were closing.
4. When you arrive for the picnic, please choose a spot on the grass to spread your blanket.
5. The movie was awful, but I sat through it anyway.

Cumulative Review Chapters 18–20

PRACTICE 9 Writing Sentences

For each item, write the indicated type of sentence, using the words provided.

1. Write a compound sentence using *the inventor* as one of the subjects.
2. Write a declarative sentence using *the elevator* as the subject.
3. Write a complex sentence using *is running* as one of the verbs.
4. Write an exclamatory sentence using the word *marvelous.*
5. Write an imperative sentence using *unlock* as the verb.

PRACTICE 10 Combining Sentences

Read the sentences. Combine each pair of sentences by using compound structures. Indicate whether your sentence contains a *compound subject*, a *compound verb*, or a *compound object*, or whether it is a *compound sentence.*

1. Geraldo waited in the ticket line. Frederica waited there, too.
2. Jacques ordered a turkey sandwich for lunch. He also ordered a salad.
3. The designer selected the fabrics carefully. She also matched them carefully.
4. Fern may have left her keys on the kitchen counter. She may have left her scarf in the car.
5. They were hoping for an experienced baker. The person they finally hired has little experience.

PRACTICE 11 Revising to Correct Fragments and Run-ons

Read each group of words. If it is a fragment, use it in a sentence. If it is a run-on, correct the run-on. If a sentence needs no correction, write *correct.*

1. The groom waiting at the altar.
2. The child was riding on the merry-go-round.
3. I was reading in bed my eyes were closing.
4. When you arrive for the picnic.
5. The movie was awful, I sat through it anyway.

PRACTICE 12 Revising to Correct Common Usage Problems

Read the sentences. Then, rewrite each sentence to correct misplaced modifiers, double negatives, and other usage problems.

1. What does the financial planner advice your family to do?
2. Lack of sufficient daylight during the short winter days effects the mood of some people.
3. Coughing so much, she could speak no farther.
4. Wearing a warm coat, the cold weather did not bother me.
5. I like every vegetable accept cabbage.
6. Madeline didn't see none of her friends at the block party.
7. The reason I left is because I have another appointment.
8. The girls were to tired to do they're homework.
9. Phyllis wore new boots that were apparently too big on her feet.
10. Meteorology is where you study the weather.

PRACTICE 12

Answers will vary. Sample answers:

1. What does the financial planner advise your family to do?
2. Lack of sufficient daylight during the short winter days affects the mood of some people.
3. Coughing so much, she could speak no further.
4. Wearing a warm coat, I did not mind the cold weather. *or* Wearing a warm coat, I was not bothered by the cold weather.
5. I like every vegetable except cabbage.
6. Madeline didn't see any of her friends at the block party. *or* Madeline saw none of her friends at the block party.
7. The reason I left is that I have another appointment. *or* I left because I have another appointment.
8. The girls were too tired to do their homework.
9. On her feet, Phyllis wore new boots that were apparently too big. *or* Phyllis wore new boots, which were apparently too big, on her feet.
10. Meteorology is the study of the weather.

CHAPTER 21 LESSON PLANNER
Using Verbs

Use the Online Lesson Planner at www.phwritingcoach.com to customize your instructional plan for an integrated Language Arts curriculum.

DAY 1 21.1 Four Principal Parts of Verbs

"What Do You Notice?" **Objectives:** Identify, use, and understand the four principal parts of regular verbs	**INSTRUCTION AND PRACTICE** **Student Edition** pp. 471–474

DAY 2 21.1 Four Principal Parts of Verbs *(continued)*

Objectives: Identify, use, and understand the four principal parts of irregular verbs	**INSTRUCTION AND PRACTICE** **Student Edition** pp. 475–479

DAY 3 21.2 The Six Verb Tenses

Objectives: Identify, use, and understand aspects of verb tenses, including ▪ the six verb tenses ▪ conjugating the basic forms ▪ conjugating *be*	**INSTRUCTION AND PRACTICE** **Student Edition** pp. 480–485 **Test Warm-Up** p. 486

DAY 4 21.2 The Six Verb Tenses *(continued)*

Objectives: Identify, use, and understand aspects of verb tenses, including ▪ the progressive tenses of verbs ▪ the progressive tenses of *write*	**INSTRUCTION AND PRACTICE** **Student Edition** pp. 487–489

Alternate Pacing Plans

- **Block Scheduling** Each day in the Lesson Planner represents a 40–50 minute block. Teachers using block scheduling may combine days to revise pacing to meet their classroom needs.
- **Accelerated Lesson Planning** Combine instructional days, focusing on concepts called out by students' diagnostic test results.
- **Integrated Language Arts Curriculum** Use the instruction and practice in this chapter to provide reinforcement, remediation, or extension of grammar concepts taught in your literature curriculum.

Links to Prentice Hall *LITERATURE*

Unit 2 The Principal Parts of Verbs, p. 278; Writing Workshop: Revising for Correct Verb Tense, p. 305

Grammar Assessment

Grammar Coach:	Diagnostic Assessment	End-of-Chapter Assessment	Progress Monitoring
Personalized Instruction	Students take grammar diagnostic test online and are automatically assigned instruction and practice in areas where they need support.	Teacher uses **ExamView** to administer end-of-chapter assessment and remediation. Teachers may customize **ExamView** tests or use the ones provided.	Teachers may use the **Test Warm-Ups** and the **Cumulative Reviews** in the student book or eText to check students' mastery of grammar skills. Students may also play **DimensionL** grammar video games to test their grammar skills.
Teacher-Directed Instruction	Teacher administers the diagnostic test and determines focus of instruction and practice.		

www.phwritingcoach.com

Grammar Assessment and Practice

Chapter diagnostic tests assess students' skills and assign instruction and practice.

DimensionL Video Games

Fast-paced interactive video games challenge students' mastery of grammar.

Lesson Planner continues on next page

DAY 5 21.2 The Six Verb Tenses *(continued)*

Objectives: Identify, use, and understand aspects of verb tenses, including ▪ active and passive voice ▪ moods of verbs	**INSTRUCTION AND PRACTICE** **Student Edition** pp. 490–495

DAY 6 21.3 Troublesome Verbs

Objectives: Identify, use, and understand troublesome verbs	**INSTRUCTION AND PRACTICE** **Student Edition** pp. 496–500

*“*Re *means 'again.'* Vision *means 'to see.'* Revision *means the paper needs to be seen again in a different light. It must move somewhere. One simple way to improve writing is to replace weak verbs with stronger verbs. Strong verbs drive strong sentences.”*

—Kelly Gallagher

“Since strong verbs make writing vivid, it is important that we show students how much their writing pivots on crafting the right verb. Verbs place the reader in time—past, present, or future. However, when verbs don't agree in number or person or follow the patterns of standard English, clear writing grinds to a halt.”

—Jeff Anderson

Differentiated Instruction

Differentiated Instruction Boxes in this Teacher's Edition address these student populations:

- Below-Level Students
- Above-Level Students
- Gifted and Talented Students
- Special Needs Students
- English Language Learners
- Spanish Speaking Students

In addition, for further enrichment, see the **Extension** features.

USING VERBS

Understanding the different tenses of regular and irregular verbs will help you clearly convey actions in your writing.

CHAPTER 21

WRITE GUY *Jeff Anderson, M.Ed.*

WHAT DO YOU NOTICE?

Lock onto the verbs as you zoom in on these sentences from "Two Kinds," an excerpt from *The Joy Luck Club* by Amy Tan.

MENTOR TEXT

"No!" I said, and I now felt stronger, as if my true self had finally emerged. So this was what had been inside me all along.

Now, ask yourself the following questions:

- What principal part of the verb *emerge* is used in the first sentence?
- What forms of irregular verbs are used in both sentences?

In the first sentence, the principal part of the verb *emerge* is the past participle *had emerged.* The verb phrase is formed by combining the past participle *emerged* with the helping verb *had.* The forms of irregular verbs used in these sentences are *said, felt, had, was,* and *been,* which are past or past participial forms of *say, feel, have,* and *be.* They are irregular because their principal parts do not follow the pattern of adding *-ed* or *-d* to the present form to create the past and past participial forms.

Grammar for Writers Knowing how to use the principal parts of a verb correctly allows writers to communicate a time of action or state of being. Watch out for irregular verbs, and be prepared to check that you are using the correct tenses.

How do you keep from getting stuck in the past?
That's easy. Stop using the past tense!

471

Grammar for Writers: Tense

Explain to students that learning about verb forms will help them show clearly when the events that they are writing about take place. Moreover, as the Mentor Text shows, mastery of verb tenses will enable them to think about the effects that verb tenses produce on readers.

USING VERBS

As students progress in their writing skills, it will be important for them to be able to apply the rules of grammar, usage, and mechanics to their own drafts. Use the *What Do You Notice?* feature to help them see effective conventions in the work of professional writers. Encourage students to incorporate proper voice, tense, and syntax as they edit their own writing.

Read the opening sentence aloud. Tell students that verb tenses tell us not only what action has taken place, but when that action has taken place. In short, verb tenses tell us about *time.*

WRITE GUY *Jeff Anderson, M. Ed.*

WHAT DO YOU NOTICE?

When students have read the Mentor Text, **ask:** What do you notice about the speaker? For example, how is she feeling, and why? **(Possible responses:** The speaker seems angry. The exclamation mark after "No!" makes me think she said that in an angry voice. But I also think she feels good about saying "No!" because she says she felt stronger.) **Ask:** So do you think feelings had been building up in her for a long time? (**Possible response:** Yes, because it says, "This is what had been inside me all along.")

Have students finish reading the page. **Ask:** How would the passage change if the verbs were all in the present tense? Read the passage as follows: *"No!" I say, and I now feel stronger, as my true self emerges. So this is what is inside me.* Students may comment that the action seems more immediate but that they lose the sense that feelings had been building up. Point out that different verb tenses produce different effects.

21.1 The Four Principal Parts of Verbs

Lesson Objectives

1. Identify the four principal parts of verbs.
2. Distinguish between regular and irregular verbs.
3. Use the correct forms of regular and irregular verbs.

To introduce the topic of verb tense, ask a student volunteer to describe an activity (for example, lunch in the cafeteria) using only present tense verbs. Then, discuss difficulties writers would face if their language had only one tense.

RULE 21.1.1 Read aloud the rule and then have students repeat the lines with you.

Say: The four principal parts of verbs shown in the chart on page 472 are used to form all the different verb tenses. The present and past forms are probably familiar, but there are two other forms which use helping verbs. The present participle always uses a helping verb and adds *-ing* to the end of the verb, and the past participle always uses a helping verb and usually adds *-d* or *-ed* to the end of the verb.

Guide students in generating several sentences using each principal part of common regular verbs, such as *walk* or *stop*.

Have student pairs make up original sentences for each principal part of a regular verb, such as *study* or *talk*.

www.phwritingcoach.com

Diagnostic and Instruction

Diagnostic test assesses students' instructional needs. Lessons and practice are assigned based on results.

Additional Practice

- Grammar Tutorials—Animated videos reinforce key grammar skills.
- Grammar Practice—Targeted practice addresses individual needs.
- ExamView—Teachers customize their grammar practice and tests.
- Grammar Games—Interactive video games make grammar fun.

21.1 The Four Principal Parts of Verbs

Verbs have different tenses to express time. The tense of the verb *walk* in the sentence "They *walk* very fast" expresses action in the present. In "They *walked* too far from home," the tense of the verb shows that the action happened in the past. In "They *will walk* home from school," the verb expresses action in the future. These forms of verbs are known as **tenses.**

www.phwritingcoach.com

Grammar Tutorials
Brush up on your Grammar skills with these animated videos.

Grammar Practice
Practice your grammar skills with Writing Coach Online.

Grammar Games
Test your knowledge of grammar in this fast-paced interactive video game.

A verb's **tense** shows the time of the action or state of being that is being described. To use the tenses of a verb correctly, you must know the **principal parts** of the verb.

RULE 21.1.1

A verb has four principal parts: the present, the present participle, the past, and the past participle.

THE FOUR PRINCIPAL PARTS OF *VISIT*

PRESENT	PRESENT PARTICIPLE	PAST	PAST PARTICIPLE
visit	(am) visiting	visited	(have) visited

The first principal part, called the present, is the form of a verb that is listed in a dictionary. The present participle and the past participle must be combined with helping verbs before they can be used as verbs in sentences. The result will always be a verb phrase.

EXAMPLES He **visits** the library every day.

Jake **was visiting** the library yesterday.

They **visited** the library.

We **have visited** the library in the last three weeks.

The way the past and past participle of a verb are formed shows whether the verb is **regular** or **irregular.**

Differentiated Instruction

RTI Strategy for Below-Level Students
Give students additional practice in using different verb forms by having them make up sentences based on the four principal parts of a regular verb. Have one student make up a sentence using the present form *call* and share it orally. The next student would speak a sentence using the present participle with a helping verb—*am calling*. The third student should create and say a sentence using the past tense—*called*. The fourth student should create and say aloud a sentence using a helping verb and the past participle—*have called*.

Enrichment for Gifted/Talented Students
Challenge students to write and perform a song or a rhyme to teach the four principal parts of verbs. Student compositions should define or describe each verb form and give at least one example of each form. Have volunteers perform their pieces for the class as students listen to ensure that the rules are taught correctly.

Using Regular Verbs

Most verbs are **regular**, which means that their past and past participle forms follow a standard, predictable pattern.

The past and past participle of a regular verb are formed by adding *-ed* or *-d* to the present form.

21.1.2 RULE

To form the past and past participle of a regular verb such as *chirp* or *hover*, you simply add *-ed* to the present. With regular verbs that already end in *e*—verbs such as *move* and *charge*—you simply add *-d* to the present.

PRINCIPAL PARTS OF REGULAR VERBS			
PRESENT	PRESENT PARTICIPLE	PAST	PAST PARTICIPLE
call	(am) calling	called	(have) called
change	(am) changing	changed	(have) changed
charge	(am) charging	charged	(have) charged
chirp	(am) chirping	chirped	(have) chirped
contain	(am) containing	contained	(have) contained
describe	(am) describing	described	(have) described
fix	(am) fixing	fixed	(have) fixed
hover	(am) hovering	hovered	(have) hovered
jump	(am) jumping	jumped	(have) jumped
lift	(am) lifting	lifted	(have) lifted
look	(am) looking	looked	(have) looked
move	(am) moving	moved	(have) moved
play	(am) playing	played	(have) played
save	(am) saving	saved	(have) saved
serve	(am) serving	served	(have) served
ski	(am) skiing	skied	(have) skied
talk	(am) talking	talked	(have) talked
type	(am) typing	typed	(have) typed
visit	(am) visiting	visited	(have) visited
walk	(am) walking	walked	(have) walked

See Practice 21.1A
See Practice 21.1B

Using Regular Verbs

Point out that it is easy to create the principal parts of regular verbs because their past, past participle, and present participle forms follow a simple pattern.

RULE 21.1.2 Read aloud the rule and then have students repeat the lines with you.

Direct students to read the paragraph above the chart on page 473. Then, ask them to find other verbs on the chart that form the past and past participle by adding *-ed*. After students have shared several examples, ask them to find examples of verbs that form the past or past participle by adding *-d*.

Assign each student a regular verb. Have each student write four sentences using each of the principal parts of his or her assigned verb. Students should exchange sentences with a partner and have the partner read the sentences to check that the verbs are used correctly.

Challenge students to think of regular verbs that are not listed in the chart on page 473. Write those verbs on the board and have a volunteer use the verb in a sentence and identify which principal part of the verb he or she used.

Working with ELLs — ELL Sheltered Instruction: Social/Affective

As students read the student page, provide opportunities to use support from peers and from you to enhance and confirm understanding and to develop vocabulary needed to comprehend increasingly challenging language.

Beginning Choose a familiar verb and point to it in the chart. Then, read the words across each column as students echo you. Act out the verb, and then use its various forms in sentences. Repeat with another verb, and guide students to understand that both follow a *regular,* or repeated, pattern.

Intermediate Guide students as they read the page. Have small groups use context and prior knowledge to discuss and define these words from the page: *regular* and *pattern.* Have groups present their definitions. Clarify meanings as necessary.

Advanced Present these words from the page: *regular, standard, predictable, pattern*. Have partners discuss the meaning of each, consulting a dictionary and confirming understanding with you as necessary. Then, have them work together using the KIM strategy, writing a key word, information, and a memory clue for each word. Have partners read the page.

Advanced High Have partners complete the Advanced activity. Then, have them collaborate on a brief paragraph using all four words.

1. past
2. past
3. present
4. present participle
5. past participle
6. past participle
7. present participle
8. present
9. past participle
10. present participle, past

PRACTICE 21.1B

Helping verbs may vary. Parts should not.

11. watch, present; is watching, present participle; watched, past; has watched, past participle
12. burn, present; is burning, present participle; burned, past; has burned, past participle
13. complete, present; is completing, present participle; completed, past; has completed, past participle
14. suggest, present; is suggesting, present participle; suggested, past; has suggested, past participle
15. ski, present; is skiing, present participle; skied, past; has skied, past participle
16. carry, present; is carrying, present participle; carried, past; has carried, past participle
17. work, present; is working, present participle; worked, past; has worked, past participle
18. try, present; is trying, present participle; tried, past; has tried, past participle
19. stop, present; is stopping, present participle; stopped, past; has stopped, past participle
20. continue, present; is continuing, present participle; continued, past; has continued, past participle

PRACTICE 21.1A **Identifying Principal Parts of Regular Verbs**

Read the sentences. Then, label each underlined verb *present, present participle, past,* or *past participle.*

EXAMPLE Angie has invited twenty people to her party.

ANSWER *past participle*

1. The boss ordered all work to stop at once.
2. We missed you at the group meeting today.
3. I presume this is the right place.
4. Alicia was laughing at Joel's joke.
5. No one had noticed that Del was not there.
6. Hugo has attended every rehearsal.
7. Kim is wondering why you said that.
8. Alex did not continue his speech.
9. Tamara has not submitted her report yet.
10. It was raining, but the soccer team practiced anyway.

PRACTICE 21.1B **Supplying the Principal Parts of Regular Verbs**

Read the verbs. Then, write and label the four principal parts of each verb. Use a form of the helping verb *be* with the present participle and a form of the helping verb *have* with the past participle.

EXAMPLE talk

ANSWER *talk* — present
is talking — present participle
talked — past
has talked — past participle

11. watch
12. burn
13. complete
14. suggest
15. ski
16. carry
17. work
18. try
19. stop
20. continue

SPEAKING APPLICATION

With a partner, take turns making a statement in which you use two principal parts of one of the verbs in Practice 21.1B. Your partner should identify which principal parts you use.

WRITING APPLICATION

Write several sentences or a brief paragraph in which you use three principal parts of one of these verbs: *disappear, return,* and *discuss.*

SPEAKING APPLICATION

Have students explain to the class how they identified the principal parts that were used.

WRITING APPLICATION

Have students share their sentences with their partners, pointing out which principal parts were used and where they were used.

Using Irregular Verbs

While most verbs are regular, many very common verbs are **irregular**—their past and past participle forms do not follow a predictable pattern.

The past and past participle of an irregular verb are not formed by adding *-ed* or *-d* to the present tense form.

RULE 21.1.3

IRREGULAR VERBS WITH THE SAME PAST AND PAST PARTICIPLE			
PRESENT	PRESENT PARTICIPLE	PAST	PAST PARTICIPLE
bring	(am) bringing	brought	(have) brought
build	(am) building	built	(have) built
buy	(am) buying	bought	(have) bought
catch	(am) catching	caught	(have) caught
fight	(am) fighting	fought	(have) fought
find	(am) finding	found	(have) found
get	(am) getting	got	(have) got *or* (have) gotten
hold	(am) holding	held	(have) held
lay	(am) laying	laid	(have) laid
lead	(am) leading	led	(have) led
lose	(am) losing	lost	(have) lost
pay	(am) paying	paid	(have) paid
say	(am) saying	said	(have) said
sit	(am) sitting	sat	(have) sat
sleep	(am) sleeping	slept	(have) slept
spin	(am) spinning	spun	(have) spun
stand	(am) standing	stood	(have) stood
stick	(am) sticking	stuck	(have) stuck
swing	(am) swinging	swung	(have) swung
teach	(am) teaching	taught	(have) taught
win	(am) winning	won	(have) won

Check a dictionary whenever you are in doubt about the correct form of an irregular verb.

Using Irregular Verbs

Point out that the past and past participle forms of irregular verbs do not follow a predictable pattern.

RULE 21.1.3 Read aloud the rule and then have students repeat the lines with you.

Ask: What is the difference between a regular and an irregular verb? **(Possible responses:** Regular verbs follow rules for forming the past tense, past participle, and present participle; irregular verbs follow no predictable pattern.)

Ask: What do the verbs in this chart have in common? (They are all irregular verbs.)

Have students close their books and, as a class, review all of the the principal parts of the irregular verbs listed in the chart on page 475. Then, challenge students to add to the list with other irregular verbs not on the list. Make sure students know the principal parts of the irregular verbs *to be, to do, to feel, to have,* and *to say.*

Have student pairs choose three verbs from the chart and use them in at least two different forms in a narrative. They may retell a familiar story, tell a true story, or make up a story. After they finish writing their narratives, have them write the three verbs they used at the end. Then, have them exchange their story with another pair. As the second pair reads the story, have them underline the three verbs and label the forms used.

(continued)

Working with ELLs — ELL Sheltered Instruction: Cognitive

Help students comprehend vocabulary used routinely in written classroom materials. Read aloud the directions for the Practice activities on page 474. Then:

Beginning Point out these routine words from the directions, and write them on the board: *read, write, label,* and *underline*. Read them aloud with students, acting out each. Then, write a word, and have students act it out to show comprehension.

Intermediate Write vocabulary words such as *read, write, label,* and *underline* on one set of note cards. Write the names of the four principal parts of regular verbs, along with examples, on another set. Provide a page of sentences featuring each principal part. Have partners take turns choosing a card from each set, reading the instructions, and then performing the action named with the page of sentences.

Advanced Provide partners with these terms from the student page: *identify, label, supply,* and *brief paragraph*. Have partners find the words in the directions and read them aloud in context. Then, have them work together to write a brief explanation of each word, using a dictionary for support as necessary.

Advanced High Have partners complete the Advanced activity. Then, have them write instructions of their own for a grammar activity.

Teacher Tip

Students may struggle with the idea that past and past participle forms of irregular verbs do not follow a predictable pattern. Help students create flash cards for the past and past participle forms of the most common irregular verbs, such as *be, have, can, do, say, go,* and *get.* Routinely have student partners use the flash cards to quiz each other on the verb forms.

Using Irregular Verbs *(continued)*

Ask: What do the verbs on the top chart on page 476 have in common? **(For every one of them, the present form is the same as the past and past participle form.)**

Say: When very young children first learn to speak English, they often say things like, "I hurted myself." When the child does that, he or she is actually following a rule for forming a past tense, but the rule doesn't work with irregular verbs. **Ask:** What is the correct way to say this sentence? **(I hurt myself.) Say:** You most likely already know the principal parts of many irregular verbs. In the above example, you knew the past of *hurt* is also *hurt*, rather than *hurted*. Study the verbs in the first chart on page 476. **Then, ask:** Can you think of any other irregular verbs that have the same present, past, and past participle? **(Possible responses:** fit, cast, let)

Ask: What do the verbs on the bottom chart on page 476 have in common? **(Possible responses:** none of their forms are the same; they change in other ways than the irregular verbs in the first two charts.)

Write these incomplete sentences on the board:

This morning I ______. (past)

Now I am ______. (present participle)

Before __________, I had __________.
(past event; past participle)

Model how to fill in the sentence frames using an irregular verb: *This morning I ate. Now I am eating. Before the bus got to school, I had eaten all of my lunch.*

Work with students to fill in the blanks with other irregular verbs from the second chart on page 476.

IRREGULAR VERBS WITH THE SAME PRESENT, PAST, AND PAST PARTICIPLE

PRESENT	PRESENT PARTICIPLE	PAST	PAST PARTICIPLE
bid	(am) bidding	bid	(have) bid
burst	(am) bursting	burst	(have) burst
cost	(am) costing	cost	(have) cost
hurt	(am) hurting	hurt	(have) hurt
put	(am) putting	put	(have) put
set	(am) setting	set	(have) set

IRREGULAR VERBS THAT CHANGE IN OTHER WAYS

PRESENT	PRESENT PARTICIPLE	PAST	PAST PARTICIPLE
arise	(am) arising	arose	(have) arisen
be	(am) being	was	(have) been
bear	(am) bearing	bore	(have) borne
beat	(am) beating	beat	(have) beaten
begin	(am) beginning	began	(have) begun
blow	(am) blowing	blew	(have) blown
break	(am) breaking	broke	(have) broken
choose	(am) choosing	chose	(have) chosen
come	(am) coming	came	(have) come
do	(am) doing	did	(have) done
draw	(am) drawing	drew	(have) drawn
drink	(am) drinking	drank	(have) drunk
drive	(am) driving	drove	(have) driven
eat	(am) eating	ate	(have) eaten
fall	(am) falling	fell	(have) fallen
fly	(am) flying	flew	(have) flown
forget	(am) forgetting	forgot	(have) forgotten
freeze	(am) freezing	froze	(have) frozen

Differentiated Instruction

RTI Strategy for Below-Level Students
Many students might continue to have difficulty remembering the four basic forms of irregular verbs. In this case it will be important to give students additional practice. Create a Bingo game to give these students the additional practice they need. To make cards, you can create a table with five columns and five rows. Ask students to fill in the cards with past participles of their choice from the charts on pages 475–477.

To play, read present participles of verbs from the charts and have students check off or place markers over any matching past participles on their card. Students may win by connecting five spaces in a row vertically, diagonally, or horizontally.

As students become more proficient, call out the present participles more quickly and begin to call out simple present and simple past forms as well. Challenge winners to create a paragraph using the irregular verbs from their winning row.

IRREGULAR VERBS THAT CHANGE IN OTHER WAYS (CONTINUED)			
PRESENT	PRESENT PARTICIPLE	PAST	PAST PARTICIPLE
give	(am) giving	gave	(have) given
go	(am) going	went	(have) gone
grow	(am) growing	grew	(have) grown
know	(am) knowing	knew	(have) known
lie	(am) lying	lay	(have) lain
ride	(am) riding	rode	(have) ridden
ring	(am) ringing	rang	(have) rung
rise	(am) rising	rose	(have) risen
run	(am) running	ran	(have) run
see	(am) seeing	saw	(have) seen
shake	(am) shaking	shook	(have) shaken
sing	(am) singing	sang	(have) sung
sink	(am) sinking	sank	(have) sunk
speak	(am) speaking	spoke	(have) spoken
spring	(am) springing	sprang	(have) sprung
strive	(am) striving	strove	(have) striven
swear	(am) swearing	swore	(have) sworn
swim	(am) swimming	swam	(have) swum
take	(am) taking	took	(have) taken
tear	(am) tearing	tore	(have) torn
throw	(am) throwing	threw	(have) thrown
wear	(am) wearing	wore	(have) worn
weave	(am) weaving	wove	(have) woven
write	(am) writing	wrote	(have) written

See Practice 21.1C
See Practice 21.1D
See Practice 21.1E
See Practice 21.1F

As you can see, there are many irregular verbs. For most of these verbs, you should memorize the different forms. Whenever you are not sure of which form of an irregular verb to use, check a dictionary.

Ask students to skim the charts of irregular verbs on pages 475–477. Have them pick three verbs and use them in a paragraph. Ask students to deliberately include errors in forming past tenses. Then, have them exchange papers with a partner and correct the errors they find in verb forms. If students are not sure about the correct verb form, remind them to use the chart or a dictionary.

Challenge students to think of other irregular verbs that change in unpredictable ways when forming the past and past participle. Examples might be *become, bite, deal, fight, flee, forgive, hear, lend, light, mean, pay, read, seek, shed,* and *wring.* If students are having difficulty thinking of new irregular verbs, play a challenge game instead. Call out the present form of each of the verbs listed and have students provide you with the correct present participle, past, and past participle forms.

Teacher Tip

To help students memorize irregular verb forms, review the charts on this page as you work through the chapter. You may want to quiz students on the principal parts of irregular verbs. Read aloud a present form of an irregular verb and have three students work together to tell you the present participle, past, and past participle forms of the verb. Ask students to use these verb forms in sentences.

Extension

To help students synthesize and apply what they have learned about irregular verbs, have students play a verb game. Give student pairs a few note cards on which to draw four boxes labeled *Present, Present Participle, Past, Past Participle.* Explain that each student should take one card and write one of the principal parts of an irregular verb in the appropriate box. He or she should then exchange cards with his or her partner, who fills in any other box. When a student pair has completed a card, one of the students should read it to a small group, whose members check the accuracy of the verb forms.

PRACTICE 21.1C

Helping verbs may vary. Parts should not.

1. go, present; is going, present participle; went, past; has gone, past participle
2. ride, present; is riding, present participle; rode, past; has ridden, past participle
3. tear, present; is tearing, present participle; tore, past; has torn, past participle
4. ring, present; is ringing, present participle; rang, past; has rung, past participle
5. choose, present; is choosing, present participle; chose, past; has chosen, past participle
6. draw, present; is drawing, present participle; drew, past; has drawn, past participle
7. eat, present; is eating, present participle; ate, past; has eaten, past participle
8. arise, present; is arising, present participle; arose, past; has arisen, past participle
9. hurt, present; is hurting, present participle; hurt, past; has hurt, past participle
10. wear, present; is wearing, present participle; wore, past; has worn, past participle

PRACTICE 21.1D

11. burst
12. brought
13. shook
14. grown
15. taken
16. blew
17. built
18. caught
19. written
20. led

PRACTICE 21.1C Supplying the Principal Parts of Irregular Verbs

Read the verbs. Then, write and label the four principal parts of each verb. Use a form of the helping verb *be* with the present participle, and a form of the helping verb *have* with the past participle.

EXAMPLE fly

ANSWER *fly* — present
is flying — present participle
flew — past
has flown — past participle

1. go
2. ride
3. tear
4. ring
5. choose
6. draw
7. eat
8. arise
9. hurt
10. wear

PRACTICE 21.1D Choosing the Correct Form of Irregular Verbs

Read the sentences. Then, choose and write the form of the verb in parentheses that correctly completes each sentence.

EXAMPLE We had (drove, driven) all day.

ANSWER *driven*

11. The balloon (burst, bursted).
12. Aunt Lucy (bring, brought) us a gift.
13. My grandfather (shook, shaked) the apples off the tree.
14. Some of those trees in the back have (grew, grown) too tall.
15. Diana has (took, taken) piano lessons.
16. The wind (blowed, blew) fiercely all night.
17. The construction workers have already (builded, built) the foundation.
18. Ken (caught, catched) three fish during his fishing expedition.
19. Have you (wrote, written) a thank-you note to your grandmother?
20. Rhondella has (led, leaded) her team to victory.

SPEAKING APPLICATION

With a partner, take turns making a statement in which you use two principal parts of one of the verbs listed in Practice 21.1C. Your partner should identify which principal parts you use.

WRITING APPLICATION

Write three sentences, using different principal parts of these verbs: *know, choose,* and *tell*. You may use any of the sentences in Practice 21.1D as models.

SPEAKING APPLICATION

Have partners take turns naming an irregular verb and saying the principal parts of the verb.

WRITING APPLICATION

Have students share their sentences with a partner, pointing out what principal type they used for each verb.

PRACTICE 21.1E Using Irregular Verbs

Read the sentences. Rewrite each sentence, using the form of the verb in parentheses that correctly completes the sentence.

EXAMPLE Daniel (sing) the lead in last year's musical.

ANSWER *Daniel sang the lead in last year's musical.*

1. Marty has not (speak) to anyone about her plan.
2. Alexa has (choose) a new ring tone for her phone.
3. The little child has (put) his shoes on the wrong feet.
4. Curtis (pay) the bill for our meal.
5. Who (see) the shooting stars last night?
6. In the 1770s and 1780s, American colonists (fight) for independence.
7. Marya (stand) staring at her feet, trying to think of an answer.
8. The chorus (rise) together when the director (give) the signal.
9. Gary's socks (shrink) in the wash.
10. Ryan (bring) some video games for us to play.

PRACTICE 21.1F Revising for Irregular Verbs

Read the sentences. Then, if the underlined verb is in the correct form, write *correct*. If it is not, rewrite the sentence with the correct verb form.

EXAMPLE The water in the birdbath had froze.

ANSWER *The water in the birdbath had frozen.*

11. Abby blowed out the candle before she left the room.
12. Anthony's uncle taught him to play the banjo.
13. Maggie and Jennifer brung sandwiches for the group.
14. We have sat here too long.
15. Colin drank the water.
16. The *Titanic* sunk after hitting an iceberg.
17. That window has been broken twice this year.
18. The boots costed too much, so I did not buy them.
19. Sophie swum across the pond and back today.
20. I seen that movie before.

SPEAKING APPLICATION

With a partner, take turns telling about an event you have observed. Use the past and past participle forms of three of these verbs: *come, see, stand,* and *speak*.

WRITING APPLICATION

Write three sentences using the past or past participle forms of these verbs: *begin, drive,* and *write*. You may use the sentences in Practices 21.1E and 21.1F as models.

Working with ELLs — ELL Sheltered Instruction: Cognitive

Have students write using grade-appropriate connecting words to combine phrases, clauses, and sentences in increasingly accurate ways. Provide students with these connecting words: *and, but, for, nor, or, so, yet, after, before, although, when,* and *while*. (See Chapter 17.)

Beginning On the board, write: *I see a pen, but I need a pencil*. As you read the sentence aloud, hold up each object. Point out that the word *but* joins two groups of words that could stand as sentences on their own. Guide students in writing additional completions for the cloze sentence *I see a _____, but I need a _____*.

Intermediate Provide small groups with three sentences using verbs from Practice 21.1C on page 478. For each sentence, have them collaborate on an additional sentence on the same topic. Then, have them write using the connecting words to combine sentence pairs.

Advanced Have partners write simple sentences on a single topic using the verbs in Practice 21.1C on page 478. Then, have them write using the connecting words to combine sentences.

Advanced High Have individuals complete the Advanced activity. Then, direct them to exchange papers and evaluate each other's work for the appropriate choice of conjunctions, suggesting replacements as warranted.

PRACTICE 21.1E

1. Marty has not spoken to anyone about her plan.
2. Alexa has chosen a new ring tone for her phone.
3. The little child has put his shoes on the wrong feet.
4. Curtis paid the bill for our meal.
5. Who saw the shooting stars last night?
6. In the 1770s and 1780s, American colonists fought for independence.
7. Marya stood staring at her feet, trying to think of an answer.
8. The chorus rose together when the director gave the signal.
9. Gary's socks shrank in the wash.
10. Ryan brought some video games for us to play.

PRACTICE 21.1F

11. Abby blew out the candle before she left the room.
12. correct
13. Maggie and Jennifer brought sandwiches for the group.
14. correct
15. correct
16. The Titanic sank after hitting an iceberg.
17. correct
18. The boots cost too much, so I did not buy them.
19. Sophie swam across the pond and back today.
20. I saw that movie before.

SPEAKING APPLICATION

Have partners identify the forms of the verbs used in each other's stories.

WRITING APPLICATION

Have students explain how the past participle form differs from the past form for the verbs they used.

21.2 The Six Tenses of Verbs

Lesson Objectives

1. Identify the basic forms of the six tenses.
2. Use and understand the function of perfect tense and progressive tense verbs in the context of reading, writing, and speaking.
3. Use active and passive voice appropriately.

Identifying the Basic Forms of the Six Tenses

Discuss the difference between basic forms and progessive forms.

RULE 21.2.1 Read aloud the rule and then have students repeat the lines with you.

Use a Think Aloud as part of a gradual release progression.

Say: The perfect tenses shown in the chart on page 480 focus on the completion of actions. **I know** that the present perfect shows actions that were done any time right up to now. It can also show change over time: *You have grown so much!* The past perfect shows that one action happened before another: *He had spoken before he thought.* The future perfect shows that one action will be completed before another event.

Draw a chart like the one on page 480 showing the six tenses of *speak* on the board. **Work with students** to complete the chart with a regular verb, such as *finish.*

To challenge students, **have student pairs** work together to chart the six tenses of an irregular verb.

21.2 The Six Tenses of Verbs

In English, verbs have six **tenses:** the **present,** the **past,** the **future,** the **present perfect,** the **past perfect,** and the **future perfect.**

The tense of a verb shows the time of the action or state of being.

Every tense has both **basic** forms and **progressive** forms.

Identifying the Basic Forms of the Six Tenses

The chart below shows the **basic** forms of the six tenses, using *speak* as an example. The first column gives the name of each tense. The second column gives the basic form of *speak* in all six tenses. The third column gives the principal part needed to form each tense. Only three of the four principal parts are used in the basic forms: the present, the past, and the past participle.

BASIC FORMS OF THE SIX TENSES OF *SPEAK*

TENSE	BASIC FORM	PRINCIPAL PART USED
Present	I speak.	Present
Past	I spoke.	Past
Future	I will speak.	Present
Present Perfect	I have spoken.	Past Participle
Past Perfect	I had spoken.	Past Participle
Future Perfect	I will have spoken.	Past Participle

Study the chart carefully. First, learn the names of the tenses. Then, learn the principal parts needed to form them. Notice also that the last four tenses need helping verbs.

As you have already learned, some verbs form their tenses in a regular, predictable pattern. Other verbs use an irregular pattern. *Speak* is an example of an irregular verb.

Grammar Practice

Practice your grammar skills with Writing Coach Online.

Grammar Games

Test your knowledge of grammar in this fast-paced interactive video game.

See Practice 21.2A

www.phwritingcoach.com

Diagnostic and Instruction

Diagnostic test assesses students' instructional needs. Lessons and practice are assigned based on results.

Additional Practice

- Grammar Practice—Targeted practice addresses individual needs.
- ExamView—Teachers customize their grammar practice and tests.
- Grammar Games—Interactive video games make grammar fun.

Conjugating the Basic Forms of Verbs

A helpful way to become familiar with all the forms of a verb is by **conjugating** it.

A conjugation is a list of the singular and plural forms of a verb in a particular tense.

RULE 21.2.2

Each tense in a conjugation has six forms that fit with first-, second-, and third-person forms of the personal pronouns. These forms may change for each personal pronoun, and they may change for each tense.

To conjugate any verb, begin by listing its principal parts. For example, the principal parts of the verb *go* are *go, going, went,* and *gone*. The following chart shows the conjugation of all the basic forms of *go* in all six tenses. The forms of the helping verbs may also change for each personal pronoun and tense.

See Practice 21.2B

CONJUGATION OF THE BASIC FORMS OF GO

TENSE	SINGULAR	PLURAL
Present	I go. You go. He, she, or it goes.	We go. You go. They go.
Past	I went. You went. He, she, or it went.	We went. You went. They went.
Future	I will go. You will go. He, she, or it will go.	We will go. You will go. They will go.
Present Perfect	I have gone. You have gone. He, she, or it has gone.	We have gone. You have gone. They have gone.
Past Perfect	I had gone. You had gone. He, she, or it had gone.	We had gone. You had gone. They had gone.
Future Perfect	I will have gone. You will have gone. He, she, or it will have gone.	We will have gone. You will have gone. They will have gone.

Conjugating the Basic Forms of Verbs

Point out that conjugating verbs is a helpful way for students to learn verb forms. When we conjugate a verb, we list all of the tenses for the verb and the form used with first, second, and third person singular and plural pronouns.

RULE 21.2.2 Read aloud the rule and then have students repeat the lines with you.

Help students understand how verbs are conjugated. Work with students to convert the directions on page 481 for conjugating verbs into a series of numbered steps. For example, 1. List the principal parts of the verb; 2. List the singular forms for the present tense (*I; you; he, she, it*); 3. List the plural forms for the present tense (*we, you, they*); 4. Complete the remaining tenses: past, future, present perfect, past perfect, future perfect.

Use the directions to conjugate a regular verb, such as *vote.*

Write these sentences: *I sail. She spoke. You ran.* Have students rewrite the sentences in the past perfect, present perfect, and future perfect tenses. Have volunteers read their new sentences aloud while the class determines the tense of the verb in each sentence.

Differentiated Instruction

RTI Strategy for Below-Level Students

Have students make a chart that shows the basic forms of the six tenses of English verbs. Have students use the chart to write the forms of additional verbs in the second column. Then, have students create a wide third column in which they write short sample sentences for each tense.

Tense	Verb
Past	traveled
Present	travel
Future	will travel
Past Perfect	had traveled
Present Perfect	have traveled
Future Perfect	will have traveled

Conjugating *Be*

Point out that students will need to know how to conjugate *be* when they work with progressive tenses.

Assign student pairs one tense shown on the Conjugation of the Basic Forms of *Be* chart. Have them create original complete sentences that show how to use the singular and plural forms of *be* in that tense. Students' sentences should contain a predicate nominative or a predicate adjective.

Have partners work together to write three sentences that use the three perfect tenses of the verb *be*. At least one of the sentences should use the plural form. Ask partners to share their sentences with the class.

Challenge students to memorize the full conjugation of the verb *be*. Have student pairs test each other on their memorization.

Conjugating *Be*

The verb *be* is an important verb to know how to conjugate. It is both the most common and the most irregular verb in the English language. You have already seen how to use forms of *be* with the perfect tenses. You will also use the basic forms of *be* when you conjugate the progressive forms of verbs later in this section.

PRINCIPAL PARTS OF *BE*			
PRESENT	PRESENT PARTICIPLE	PAST	PAST PARTICIPLE
be	being	was	been

Once you know the principal parts of *be*, you can conjugate all of the basic forms of *be*.

CONJUGATION OF THE BASIC FORMS OF *BE*		
TENSE	SINGULAR	PLURAL
Present	I am. You are. He, she, or it is.	We are. You are. They are.
Past	I was. You were. He, she, or it was.	We were. You were. They were.
Future	I will be. You will be. He, she, or it will be.	We will be. You will be. They will be.
Present Perfect	I have been. You have been. He, she, or it has been.	We have been. You have been. They have been.
Past Perfect	I had been. You had been. He, she, or it had been.	We had been. You had been. They had been.
Future Perfect	I will have been. You will have been. He, she, or it will have been.	We will have been. You will have been. They will have been.

See Practice 21.2C
See Practice 21.2D
See Practice 21.2E
See Practice 21.2F

PRACTICE 21.2A **Identifying Present, Past, and Future Tenses of Verbs**

Read the sentences. Then, label each underlined verb *present, past,* or *future*.

EXAMPLE I will give you an answer later.
ANSWER *future*

1. May I interrupt you for a moment?
2. Judith squeezed the lemon into her tea.
3. You will enjoy the performance tomorrow.
4. Betsy saves the bottles to recycle.
5. We will remember this day forever.
6. Shyly, Neal smiled at Lizzie.
7. The team hopes for a victory tonight.
8. Kirsten attended a different school last year.
9. Felicia quickly brushed her teeth and left for school.
10. After you read the chapter, you will discuss it in groups.

PRACTICE 21.2B **Identifying Perfect Tenses of Verbs**

Read the sentences. Then, write the verb in each sentence, and label it *present perfect, past perfect,* or *future perfect*.

EXAMPLE The group has chosen James as its spokesperson.
ANSWER *has chosen — present perfect*

11. Everyone had left the cafeteria by 1:00 P.M.
12. I have not seen Will since yesterday.
13. By December, the birds will have migrated south for the winter.
14. Brandon had left his book in the gym after practice.
15. The rain has delayed the opening of the game.
16. By this time tomorrow, I will have completed my research project.
17. Mandy has seen three of the five home games.
18. I have worn my favorite red sweatshirt many times.
19. Beth had thoughtfully marked her draft for revision.
20. How long have you known her?

SPEAKING APPLICATION

With a partner, use the verbs in sentences 4, 5, and 6 to make three statements in which you use present, past, and future tenses. Your partner should identify the verb tense in each statement.

WRITING APPLICATION

Use the perfect verb tenses in sentences 11, 16, and 18, and write three sentences with other verbs in the perfect tense.

PRACTICE 21.2A

1. present
2. past
3. future
4. present
5. future
6. past
7. present
8. past
9. past, past
10. future

PRACTICE 21.2B

11. had left—past perfect
12. have seen—present perfect
13. will have migrated—future perfect
14. had left—past perfect
15. has delayed—present perfect
16. will have completed—future perfect
17. has seen—present perfect
18. have worn—present perfect
19. had marked—past perfect
20. have known—present perfect

SPEAKING APPLICATION

Students should demonstrate they can use and understand the function of present, past, and future tenses by identifying the verb tense correctly in each of their partner's statements.

WRITING APPLICATION

Students should demonstrate they can use and understand the function of perfect tense verbs in writing by writing three sentences that use the different verbs in the perfect tense and reading these sentences to the group.

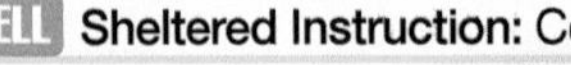

Working with ELLs ELL Sheltered Instruction: Cognitive

Help students comprehend vocabulary used routinely in written classroom materials. Read aloud the directions, examples, and sample answers on the student page. Write these words on the board: *practice, example, answer,* and *application.* Then:

Beginning Point out the words *practice, example,* and *answer* on the student page. Say the words, using gestures to indicate what each refers to, and have students repeat. Explain each word using visuals, such as images of musicians *practicing;* enactment, such as choosing an *example* from a group of similar objects; and (as available) the help of a fluent speaker who shares the same home language.

Intermediate Point out the vocabulary words as they appear on the student page. Have students work in small groups to explain each term. Have groups present their explanations, and offer clarification as needed.

Advanced Have partners write definitions of each vocabulary word, consulting a dictionary as needed. Then, have them explain the purpose of the items on the student page that are labeled with the terms. Offer clarification as needed.

Advanced High Have partners complete the Advanced activity. Then, have them discuss why a textbook might provide example practice items with answers.

PRACTICE 21.2C

Answers will vary. Sample answers:

1. My family has been healthy all year.
2. The principal will have given many awards by the end of his career.
3. I had allowed Catherine to borrow the book.
4. Jason has remembered he is late for work.
5. Brian will have scored at least one point by the end of the soccer game.
6. Grandma had spoken of her childhood many times.
7. They have forgotten why they like Lizzie's parties.
8. You will have gone by the end of the night.
9. The athletes had skated for ten years before the Olympics.
10. People have cooked for as long as we can remember.

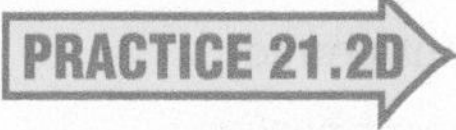

PRACTICE 21.2D

Answers will vary. Sample answers:

11. She will have run the marathon twice.
12. My mother had gone a little crazy with knitting.
13. The dog has slept in the same place for years.
14. The cat will have played enough for two cats.
15. I had studied the best way I knew how.
16. Juana has forgotten her homework.
17. Michael will have remembered to close the garage door.
18. My father had arrived early enough to see the movie previews.
19. I have enjoyed the beach this summer.
20. I had preferred the second book until I read the third.

PRACTICE 21.2C Writing Sentences Using the Perfect Tenses of Verbs

Read each present tense verb. Then, write a sentence using the perfect tense indicated in parentheses. Read your sentences to a partner, who should listen for and name the perfect tense verbs.

EXAMPLE leave (past perfect)

ANSWER *I had left the house when I realized that I forgot my backpack.*

1. be (present perfect)
2. give (future perfect)
3. allow (past perfect)
4. remember (present perfect)
5. score (future perfect)
6. speak (past perfect)
7. forget (present perfect)
8. go (future perfect)
9. skate (past perfect)
10. cook (present perfect)

PRACTICE 21.2D Writing Sentences Using the Perfect Tenses of Verbs

Read the sentences. Then, use the subjects and verbs provided to write new sentences using the perfect tense indicated in parentheses. Read your sentences to a partner, who should listen for and name the perfect tense verbs.

EXAMPLE I am. (present perfect)

ANSWER *I have been* to Sharon's house many times.

11. She runs. (future perfect)
12. My mother goes. (past perfect)
13. The dog sleeps. (present perfect)
14. The cat plays. (future perfect)
15. I study. (past perfect)
16. Juana forgets. (present perfect)
17. Michael remembers. (future perfect)
18. My father arrives. (past perfect)
19. I enjoy. (present perfect)
20. I prefer. (past perfect)

SPEAKING APPLICATION

With a partner, take turns talking about the actions of a dog or cat. Use perfect tense verbs in at least three sentences. Your partner should listen for and name the perfect tense verbs.

WRITING APPLICATION

Write six sentences about a topic of your choice. In each sentence, use a perfect tense verb. Then, underline and identify the perfect tense verb in each sentence.

484 Using Verbs

SPEAKING APPLICATION

Have students demonstrate they can use and understand the function of perfect tense verbs in speaking by explaining the function of the perfect tense verbs in their partner's sentences.

WRITING APPLICATION

Have students demonstrate they can use and understand the function of perfect tense verbs in writing by rewriting each other's sentences, using different verbs in a perfect tense correctly.

PRACTICE 21.2E **Forming Verb Tenses**

Read the sentences, which are all in the present tense. Then, rewrite each sentence, changing it to the tense indicated in parentheses.

EXAMPLE The teacher repeats the directions. (future)

ANSWER *The teacher will repeat the directions.*

1. Tina confides her plan to Rhonda. (past)
2. Ashley hints about a party. (present perfect)
3. Dom insists on paying for my lunch. (past)
4. By 9:00 P.M., the store closes. (future perfect)
5. Karen proposes a solution to the dilemma. (past perfect)
6. No one believes your excuse. (future)
7. Nick works on his project in the library. (past)
8. Hailey sketches the scene on her drawing pad. (future)
9. Noah thinks about the consequences. (past perfect)
10. Amanda performs in the talent show. (present perfect)

PRACTICE 21.2F **Using Verb Tenses Correctly**

Read the sentences. Then, write the verb in parentheses that correctly completes each sentence.

EXAMPLE Starting next week, stores (are, will be) open later for the holidays.

ANSWER *will be*

11. Joanna (eats, ate) salmon for dinner yesterday.
12. Tony never (imagined, will imagine) that he could win the spelling bee.
13. By next week, the play (has completed, will have completed) its run.
14. I (will meet, have met) you at 5:00 P.M.
15. David (shouts, shouted) with glee when he heard the news.
16. The committee (will discuss, has discussed) your proposal when it meets later this week.
17. Did you get the message I (sent, have sent) this morning?
18. I (will give, have given) you my answer already.
19. Until today, Mark (has, had) perfect attendance.
20. The ticket office (is, was) closed when we went to buy tickets.

SPEAKING APPLICATION

With a partner, take turns talking about jobs or careers that might interest you. In your sentences, use at least three perfect tense verbs. Your partner should listen for and name the perfect tense verbs.

WRITING APPLICATION

Write a paragraph about how you spent your time last summer. Use at least three perfect tense verbs. Read your paragraph to a partner. Your partner should listen for and name the perfect tense verbs.

PRACTICE 21.2E

1. Tina confided her plan to Rhonda.
2. Ashley has hinted about a party.
3. Dom insisted on paying for my lunch.
4. By 9:00 P.M., the store will have closed.
5. Karen had proposed a solution to the dilemma.
6. No one will believe your excuse.
7. Nick worked on his project in the library.
8. Hailey will sketch the scene on her drawing pad.
9. Noah had thought about the consequences.
10. Amanda has performed in the talent show.

PRACTICE 21.2F

11. ate
12. imagined *or* will imagine
13. will have completed
14. will meet *or* have met
15. shouted
16. will discuss
17. sent
18. have given
19. had
20. was

SPEAKING APPLICATION

Have students demonstrate they can use and understand the function of the perfect tense of verbs in speaking by responding to each other's career plans. Students should use three perfect tense verbs in their responses.

WRITING APPLICATION

Have students demonstrate they can use and understand the function of perfect tense verbs by writing a paragraph without perfect tense verbs. Then, have partners replace the verbs with perfect tense verbs, discussing how the perfect tense verbs change the story.

Test Warm-Up

1. **A** Change ***had ate*** to **had eaten**
2. **G** Change ***had know*** to **had known**
3. **D** He must have slipped out after I had left the room to make my bed.
4. **G** searched

Reteach

If students have not mastered these skills, review the content in Section 21.2.1, Identifying the Basic Forms of the Six Tenses of Verbs.

Test Tip

Encourage students to take note of the finish time of a test before they begin, and estimate how long they should spend on each question. If they feel one question is taking them too much time, they should move on to the next one. Tell students that, even though clock-watching is not helpful, they should check the clock once or twice during a test to determine whether they are working at the proper pace.

Test Warm-Up

DIRECTIONS
Read the introduction and the passage that follows. Then, answer the questions to show that you can use and understand the function of perfect tense verbs in reading and writing.

Nate wrote this paragraph about his dog, Jake. Read the paragraph and think about the changes you would suggest as a peer editor. When you finish reading, answer the questions that follow.

Where Had Jake Gone?

(1) My dog, Jake, had ate breakfast and wanted to go out. (2) I had opened the back door before breakfast because I had know he was going to scratch at the door. (3) I had left the room to make my bed. (4) He must have slipped out. (5) I heard my sister shouting, "Jake, where are you? Come, boy!" (6) Where had Jake gone? (7) After we had searching for 20 minutes, my mom said that we had to go to school, and that she would find him. (8) We reluctantly opened the front door, and there was Jake, wagging his little tail. (9) He had run around the yard to the front door!

1 What change, if any, should be made in sentence 1?

- **A** Change ***had ate*** to **had eaten**
- **B** Change ***had ate*** to **has eaten**
- **C** Change ***wanted*** to **has want**
- **D** Make no change

2 What change, if any, should be made in sentence 2?

- **F** Change ***had opened*** to **have opened**
- **G** Change ***had know*** to **had known**
- **H** Change ***had know*** to **have known**
- **J** Make no change

3 What is the BEST way to combine sentences 3 and 4?

- **A** I had left the room to make my bed; he must have slipped out.
- **B** He must have slipped out; I had left the room to make my bed.
- **C** Before I leave the room to make my bed, he must slip out.
- **D** He must have slipped out after I had left the room to make my bed.

4 The meaning of sentence 7 can be clarified by changing the word ***searching*** to —

- **F** search
- **G** searched
- **H** looking
- **J** look

Recognizing the Progressive Tense of Verbs

The six tenses of *go* and *be* in their basic forms were shown in the charts earlier in this section. Each of these tenses also has a progressive tense or form. The progressive form describes an event that is in progress. In contrast, the basic forms of a verb describe events that have a definite beginning and end.

The progressive tense, or form, of a verb shows an action or condition that is ongoing.

21.2.3 RULE

All six of the progressive tenses of a verb are made using just one principal part: the present participle. This is the principal part that ends in *-ing*. Then, the correct form of *be* is added to create the progressive tense or form.

Progressive Tenses of *Write*

PROGRESSIVE TENSE = **be** + **present participle**

PRESENT	I **am** (*be*) **writing** (present participle) in the class.
PAST	I **was** (*be*) **writing** (present participle) in class all day.
FUTURE	I **will be** (*be*) **writing** (present participle) in class this week.
PRESENT PERFECT	I **have been** (*be*) **writing** (present participle) since I was young.
PAST PERFECT	I **had been** (*be*) **writing** (present participle) only in class, but now I also write at home.
FUTURE PERFECT	I **will have been** (*be*) **writing** (present participle) in class for twelve years by the time I graduate high school.

Recognizing the Progressive Tense of Verbs

Write *progressive tense* on the board. Point out that the basic tenses that students have been working with generally show action that has a recognizable start and finish. Underline *progress* as you say: Progressive tenses, on the other hand, describe events that continue over a long period of time, or are still in progress.

RULE 21.2.3 Read aloud the rule and then have students repeat the lines with you.

Progressive Tenses of *Write*

Direct students' attention to the examples showing progressive tenses of *write*. **Ask:** What do you notice about the words labeled *present participle*? (They all end in *-ing*.) Have them look at the forms of *be* in the examples. **Ask:** What does change in these examples? (The forms of the verb *be*.)

Work with students to form the progressive tense for the verbs *play* and *think*. Write the conjugations on the board. Have student pairs choose a progressive conjugation and use it in a sentence. Ask pairs to share their sentences with the class.

Working with ELLs — ELL Sheltered Instruction: Cognitive

As students learn about progressive tense, support them in learning the relationship between English sounds and letters and in decoding words. Write the word *talking* on the board. Underline the *-ing* ending, explaining that it is commonly added to verbs. Then, point to the letters *ng* and explain that in English, these two letters work together to make one sound, /ng/. Model correct pronunciation, and have students echo. Then:

Beginning Write a sentence using the word *reading* on the board. Have students read the word aloud. Repeat with *writing*.

Intermediate Have partners scan the student page for words that end in *-ing*, writing them on note cards. Then, have them take turns decoding the words on the cards. Monitor to ensure that students pronounce the *ng* digraph correctly.

Advanced Have partners use *-ing* words from the student page in sentences. Have them read one another's sentences aloud, decoding words that end in *-ing*.

Advanced High Have students write verbs on note cards. Have partners choose a card, add *-ing* to the verb on the card, and write a sentence featuring the new word. Partners should read each other's sentences aloud.

Conjugating Progressive Tenses

Explain to students that, when they conjugate progressive forms of a verb, they must know the basic forms of the verb *be*.

RULE 21.2.4 Read aloud the rule and then have students repeat the lines with you.

Direct students' attention to the chart of the progressive forms of *see*. Ask them to skim the chart and notice what changes. Point out that the form of the main verb—*see*—does not change. Only the form of the helping verb *to be* changes. Then, have students read the paragraph directly above the chart.

Work with students to conjugate the progressive forms of *work*. Use the present participle *working*.

Use the verb *run* to guide students in using and understanding the progressive tense. **Say:** A sentence using *run* in the present tense would be *I run*. What is a sentence that uses *run* in the present progressive tense? (I am running.) Work with students to create more complex sentences using a progressive tense of *run*. Work through several other examples until students are comfortable using and explaining the function of progressive tense verbs.

Have student pairs work together to choose a verb and write six sentences, one for each of the progressive tenses. Ask pairs to share their sentences with the class.

Conjugating Progressive Tenses

To create the progressive tenses or forms of a verb, you must know the basic forms of *be*.

RULE 21.2.4

To conjugate the progressive forms of a verb, add the present participle of the verb to a conjugation of the basic forms of *be*.

A conjugation of the basic forms of *be* is shown earlier in this section. Compare that conjugation with the following conjugation of the progressive forms of *see*. Notice that, even though the present participle form of the verb does not change, the form of the helping verb does change. It is the form of *be* that tells you whether the action or condition is taking place in the past, present, or future.

CONJUGATION OF THE PROGRESSIVE FORMS OF *SEE*

TENSE	SINGULAR	PLURAL
Present Progressive	I am seeing. You are seeing. He, she, or it is seeing.	We are seeing. You are seeing. They are seeing.
Past Progressive	I was seeing. You were seeing. He, she, or it was seeing.	We were seeing. You were seeing. They were seeing.
Future Progressive	I will be seeing. You will be seeing. He, she, or it will be seeing.	We will be seeing. You will be seeing. They will be seeing.
Present Perfect Progressive	I have been seeing. You have been seeing. He, she, or it has been seeing.	We have been seeing. You have been seeing. They have been seeing.
Past Perfect Progressive	I had been seeing. You had been seeing. He, she, or it had been seeing.	We had been seeing. You had been seeing. They had been seeing.
Future Perfect Progressive	I will have been seeing. You will have been seeing. He, she, or it will have been seeing.	We will have been seeing. You will have been seeing. They will have been seeing.

See Practice 21.2G
See Practice 21.2H

Quick-Write Extension

To help students synthesize and apply what they have learned about progressive verbs, have them write, in the first person, a brief description of a familiar process, such as walking to school or making a sandwich. Direct them to use present progressive verbs to give the sense that the process is happening as the reader reads the description. Ask students to exchange descriptions and underline the progressive verbs.

PRACTICE 21.2G Identifying the Progressive Tenses of Verbs

Read the sentences. Then, write whether the underlined verb tense in each sentence is *present progressive, past progressive, future progressive, present perfect progressive, past perfect progressive,* or *future perfect progressive.*

EXAMPLE The group was singing on the bus.

ANSWER *past progressive*

1. Lisa is sitting next to Michael.
2. I had been planning to clean my room today.
3. We have been hoping to see the exhibit at the library.
4. Our guests will be arriving any minute now.
5. By the time we finish, we will have been painting the porch for two days.
6. He was nodding his head in agreement.
7. I had been thinking about you before you called.
8. They are preparing to leave now.
9. Our science class will be studying the solar system soon.
10. I have been spending my money foolishly.

PRACTICE 21.2H Using Progressive Tenses of Verbs

Read the sentences. Then, rewrite each sentence using the tense of the verb in parentheses.

EXAMPLE Eric _____ for a summer job. (*look*, present progressive)

ANSWER *Eric is looking for a summer job.*

11. I _____ to ask you something. (*mean*, present perfect progressive)
12. The leaves _____ faster than we could rake them. (*fall*, past perfect progressive)
13. I _____ for two hours. (*study*, present perfect progressive)
14. Will you _____ the drama club? (*join*, future progressive)
15. Carson _____ to go to the Grand Canyon. (*plan*, present perfect progressive)
16. Lou and Tom _____ at Todd's silly pun. (*laugh*, past progressive)
17. The track team _____ every day after school. (*run*, present perfect progressive)
18. Your flight _____ soon. (*depart*, future progressive)
19. We _____ to rehearse for the play. (*continue*, present progressive)
20. Vanessa _____ to use the computer. (*wait*, past progressive)

SPEAKING APPLICATION

With a partner, take turns talking about school events. Your partner should listen for and identify two verbs you use in a progressive tense.

WRITING APPLICATION

Write a paragraph about a current event. Use a variety of sentences with progressive tense verbs. Then, exchange papers with a partner. Read your sentences aloud and discuss the purpose of the progressive tense verbs.

PRACTICE 21.2G

1. present progressive
2. past perfect progressive
3. present perfect progressive
4. future progressive
5. future perfect progressive
6. past progressive
7. past perfect progressive
8. present progressive
9. future progressive
10. present perfect progressive

PRACTICE 21.2H

11. have been meaning
12. had been falling
13. have been studying
14. be joining
15. has been planning
16. were laughing
17. has been running
18. will be departing
19. are continuing
20. was waiting

SPEAKING APPLICATION

Have students demonstrate they can use and understand the function of progressive tense verbs in speaking by explaining how they identified the progressive tense verbs.

WRITING APPLICATION

Have students demonstrate they can use and understand the function of progressive tense verbs by explaining how the meaning of the sentences would change if simple present, past, and future tenses had been used.

Working with ELLs — ELL Sheltered Instruction: Social/Affective

Adapt the Speaking Application, and have students take turns asking for and giving information in situations ranging from basic communication to extended speaking assignments. Students should use both high-frequency and content-based words. Have them monitor their speech and practice self-corrective techniques. For example, if listeners appear uncertain, have speakers ask *Was I being clear?* and clarify pronunciation or word choice as needed.

Beginning Have students talk with a fluent partner, asking and answering questions such as *What is your name? Where are you from?* Have them use self-corrective techniques, and support them in responding.

Intermediate Provide students with sample prompts for asking about school, such as *Where is the cafeteria?* Have partners take turns asking and answering the questions, monitoring speech and using self-corrective techniques.

Advanced Have partners ask for and give information about school events using progressive tenses. Speakers should monitor their own speech and use self-corrective techniques. Listeners should identify two uses of a progressive tense.

Advanced High Challenge partners to complete the Speaking Application by enacting an interview about school events using progressive tenses. Have students provide thorough and extended responses to the questions. Students should monitor their speech and use self-corrective techniques.

Identifying Active and Passive Voice

Tell students that verbs can change their form to show whether or not the subject of a verb is performing an action. Write *George is being taken care of by the doctor.* **Say:** The subject is George, but George is not the one performing the action of "taking care." The doctor is the one performing the action. This sentence is in the passive voice. To change this sentence into the active voice, rewrite the sentence so it reads, *The doctor is taking care of George.* Now, the subject of the sentence is performing the action. Point out that sentences in the active voice are often shorter and livelier than those in passive voice. However, passive voice is useful when we know the result of an action, but not who or what did it: *Fish in the lake were killed.*

RULE 21.2.5 Read aloud the rule and then have students repeat the lines with you.

Ask: What determines whether a sentence is in active or passive voice? **(Possible response:** whether or not the subject performs the action)

RULE 21.2.6 Read aloud the rule and then have students repeat the lines with you.

Ask: Why are the sentences about Mike and Sandra in active voice? **(Possible response:** Because *Mike* and *Sandra* are the subjects of the sentences, and they are performing the action in the sentences.)

Work with students to create additional examples in the active voice.

RULE 21.2.7 Read aloud the rule and then have students repeat the lines with you.

Ask: Why are these sentences about Mike and Sandra in passive voice? **(Possible response:** Because *guitar* and *song* are the subjects of the sentences, but neither of them is performing the action of the sentences. Mike and Sandra are performing the action.)

Work with students to create additional examples of sentences in both the active and the passive voices.

Identifying Active and Passive Voice

Just as verbs change tense to show time, they may also change form to show whether or not the subject of the verb is performing an action.

The voice of a verb shows whether or not the subject is performing the action.

In English, most verbs have two **voices: active,** to show that the subject is performing an action, and **passive,** to show that the subject is having an action performed on it.

A verb is in the active voice when its subject performs the action.

ACTIVE VOICE
Mike **plays** the guitar.
Sandra **sang** the song.

In each example above, the subject performs the action, so the verb is said to be in the active voice.

A verb is in the passive voice when its subject does not perform the action.

PASSIVE VOICE
The guitar **is being played** by Mike.
The song **was sung** by Sandra.

In each example above, the person doing the action becomes the object of the preposition *by* and is no longer the subject. Both subjects—*guitar* and *song*—are receivers rather than performers of the action. When the subject is acted upon, the verb is said to be in the passive voice.

See Practice 21.2I

Forming the Tenses of Passive Verbs

A passive verb always has two parts.

A passive verb is always a verb phrase made from a form of *be* plus a past participle.

21.2.8 RULE

The following chart shows a conjugation of the passive forms of the verb *present* with the pronoun *it*.

CONJUGATION OF THE PASSIVE FORMS OF *PRESENT*	
TENSE	PASSIVE FORM
Present	It is presented.
Past	It was presented.
Future	It will be presented.
Present Perfect	It has been presented.
Past Perfect	It had been presented.
Future Perfect	It will have been presented.

While there are uses for the passive voice, most writing is more lively when it is in the active voice. Think about how to change each sentence below to the active voice. Follow the pattern in the first two examples.

PASSIVE It **is marked** on the board.
ACTIVE We **have marked** it on the board.

PASSIVE It **was marked** on the board.
ACTIVE We **marked** it on the board.

PASSIVE It **will be marked** on the board for the class.
It **has been marked** on the board.
It **had been marked** on the board.
It **will have been marked** on the board.

Forming the Tenses of Passive Verbs

Point out that when students conjugate passive verbs, they will need to include two parts.

RULE 21.2.8 Read aloud the rule and then have students repeat the lines with you.

Direct students' attention to the chart showing Conjugation of the Passive Forms of *Present*. Ask them to identify the forms of *be* in the second column (*is, was, will be, has been, had been, will have been*). Have them conjugate the passive forms of *tell.*

Write on the board this sentence from page 491: ***It is marked on the board.*** **Say:** When we don't know who performs the action of a sentence, the sentence is probably passive. Who is the "marker" in this sentence? **(We don't know.)** Cross out ***It is*** and write ***We have*** at the beginning of the sentence. **Say:** Now, we know who marked on the board. This sentence is in the active voice.

Point out to students that the passive sentence is less lively than the active sentence. Write this sentence on the board: *The game is being played by fierce competitors.* Show students how the passive voice is used in the sentence, and have them revise the sentence to make it active voice.

Have students write one energetic active sentence. Then, have them exchange sentences with a partner. Have them rewrite their partner's sentence in the passive voice. Partners should discuss the effect this has on the meaning of their sentences.

Differentiated Instruction

Strategy for Spanish Speakers
Students whose home language is Spanish may have difficulty forming the passive in English due to the multiple parts of passive sentences. Remind students that in the passive voice, the tense and person of the verb *to be* changes, but the main verb is always the past participle. Prepare one set of cards with the names of the six tenses listed on page 491. Elicit from students several transitive verbs and write them on the board. Have students write the past participle of each verb. For each verb, draw a card, for example *future*. Then have students write a passive sentence with the transitive verb, using an appropriate subject. For example, for the verb *build* students may write a sentence such as *The road will be built next summer*. Call on volunteers to share their sentences. Have students circle the form of the verb *to be* and underline the past participle in each sentence.

Teacher Tip

To provide students with more practice with active and passive voice, write a paragraph in the passive voice and distribute copies to students. Have partners work together to rewrite the paragraph in the active voice. Encourage students to discuss which paragraph they enjoy reading more and why.

Using Active and Passive Voices

Discuss with students various situations in which it might be beneficial to use the passive voice, for example, to persuade. The passive voice might also be used when the receiver of an action is more important than the performer, or when the performer of an action is unknown.

RULE 21.2.9 Read aloud the rule and then have students repeat the line with you.

Work with students to create two additional examples, using *saw/was seen* and *explore/ was explored*.

RULE 21.2.10 Read aloud the rule and then have students repeat the lines with you.

Ask: How does the emphasis change when the example is put into active voice? *The team supported the coach.* (**Possible response:** The emphasis is now on the team, which is performing the action.)

RULE 21.2.11 Read aloud the rule and then have students repeat the lines with you.

Point out that people sometimes use the passive voice to avoid taking responsibility. For example, they might say *It was decided* instead of *I decided.*

Have student pairs write two active sentences and two passive sentences. One passive sentence should be an example of the type in which the receiver of the action is more important than the performer of the action. The second passive sentence should have an unknown or unnamed performer of the action. Ask pairs to share their sentences with the class.

Using Active and Passive Voices

Each of the two voices has its proper use in English.

Use the active voice whenever possible.

Sentences with active verbs are less wordy and more forceful than those with passive verbs. Compare, for example, the following sentences. Notice the different number of words each sentence needs to report the same information.

ACTIVE — Students **studied** an exam guide.

PASSIVE — An exam guide **was studied** by students.

Although you should aim to use the active voice in most of your writing, there will be times when you will need to use the passive voice.

Use the passive voice to emphasize the receiver of an action rather than the performer of an action.

In the following example, the receiver of the action is the subject *coach.* It is the *team* (the direct object) that is actually performing the action.

EMPHASIS ON RECEIVER — The coach **was supported** by the team.

The passive voice should also be used when there is no performer of the action.

Use the passive voice to point out the receiver of an action when the performer is unknown or not named in the sentence.

PERFORMER UNKNOWN — The new book **was written** sometime last year.

See Practice 21.2J

Differentiated Instruction

PRE-AP Enrichment for Above-Level Students Sometimes, laws, rules, and other regulations are written in the passive voice, which can make the sentences harder to understand. Ask students to research state or city laws and find sentences that are written in the passive voice. Encourage students to rewrite the text in active voice for clarity.

RTI Strategy for Special Needs Students Remind students that most English sentences follow the pattern in which the subject performs the action of the verb and comes before the verb. Work with students to identify and practice the steps in converting a passive sentence to an active one: 1: Identify the doer of the action. 2. Drop helping verbs such as *was*. 3. Begin with the subject. 4. Continue with the action verb, revising the form when necessary. 5. End with the direct object, or the receiver of the action.

PRACTICE 21.2I Distinguishing Active and Passive Voice

Read the sentences. Then, write *AV* if the underlined verb is in active voice or *PV* if the verb is in passive voice.

EXAMPLE The injured player was carried off the field.

ANSWER *PV*

1. A new delegate was appointed by the governor.
2. A meter maid ticketed the illegally parked car.
3. The principal brought the matter to our attention.
4. The halls of the building had been swept during the night.
5. The new city hall was designed by a local architect.
6. Undoubtedly, the audience will be persuaded by your speech.
7. Deer have eaten the bark on these trees.
8. The contract had been signed by both parties.
9. The chef presented an appetizing meal.
10. The fence had been painted white.

PRACTICE 21.2J Revising to Use Active Voice

Read the sentences. Then, rewrite each sentence that is in passive voice so that it is in active voice. If the sentence is already in active voice, write *active*.

EXAMPLE The fallen tree has been removed by the landscaper.

ANSWER *The landscaper removed the fallen tree.*

11. The clerk is wrapping the package.
12. After the performance, the tents were taken down by the circus crew.
13. The principal has not yet told the students about the early dismissal.
14. The dog was walked by Thalia.
15. The coaches are planning next year's schedules.
16. These flowers were arranged by the garden committee.
17. New computers have been purchased by the school.
18. Anne has given an excellent oral report.
19. My seat was taken by someone during intermission.
20. We have been assigned two chapters by Miss Romero.

SPEAKING APPLICATION

With a partner, choose a sentence from Practice 21.2I or 21.2J and say it aloud. If the sentence is in active voice, say it again in passive voice. If it is passive, change it to active. Your partner should do the same for another sentence.

WRITING APPLICATION

Write three sentences about a performance you have seen. Use only active voice.

PRACTICE 21.2I

1. PV
2. AV
3. AV
4. PV
5. PV
6. PV
7. AV
8. PV
9. AV
10. PV

PRACTICE 21.2J

11. active
12. After the performance, the circus crew took down the tents.
13. active
14. Thalia walked the dog.
15. active
16. The garden committee arranged these flowers.
17. The school has purchased new computers.
18. active
19. Someone took my seat during intermission.
20. Miss Romero assigned us two chapters.

SPEAKING APPLICATION

Have students explain to their partners how they can identify sentences in active voice and how they can identify sentences in passive voice.

WRITING APPLICATION

Have students rewrite sentences using passive voice. Then, have students discuss which sentences are more effective.

Moods of Verbs

The word *mood* often describes feelings. With verbs, however, it means the way in which an action takes place, or the manner of the action.

RULE 21.2.12 Read aloud the rule and then have students repeat the lines with you.

Write on the board the three moods: *indicative, subjunctive, imperative.* Have students skim page 494 to find out when each mood is used.

Ask: When is the indicative mood used? (to state something or ask questions) **Ask:** When is the subjunctive mood used? (to express a wish or state something contrary to fact)

Ask: What does *contrary to fact* mean? Here's an example: *If I were better at basketball, I would have made the team.* The subjunctive mood is used in this sentence to indicate that I am not good at basketball, so it is not possible for me to make the team. The plural verb *were* is used in this sentence because the clause begins with *if.*

Ask: When is the imperative mood used? (to state a request or give a command) **Ask:** What do you notice about the tense of the verbs in the imperative examples? (All are in present tense.)

Help students understand and differentiate between the three types of sentences. Write three sentences on the board: one indicative, one subjunctive, and one imperative. Have students identify each type of sentence.

Have each student write two examples of each type of sentence and speak them aloud to a partner. Partners should identify the type of sentence.

Teacher Tip

Give students additional practice in using the subjunctive mood by asking them to complete sentences beginning with this prompt: *If I were able to do anything I wanted. . . .*

Moods of Verbs

Verbs in English also use **mood** to describe the status of an action.

There are three moods for English verbs: the indicative mood, the subjunctive mood, and the imperative mood.

The **indicative mood** indicates, or states, something. It is also used to ask questions. The **subjunctive mood** describes a wish or a condition that may be contrary to fact.

INDICATIVE MOOD	SUBJUNCTIVE MOOD
Tim **is** on my team.	I wish Bill **were** on my team too.
Kate **has** a new DVD.	If Susan **had brought** the DVD over, we could have watched it together.
I **would** like to be captain of the team.	If I **were** captain of the hockey team, I would be fair to everyone.

The subjunctive mood can be used to describe situations that are unlikely to happen or not possible. It is often used in clauses that begin with *if* or *that.* In these cases, use the plural form of the verb.

EXAMPLES If I **were** you, I would run to the store before the snow.
(I am not you, so the situation is not possible.)

John wished that he **were going** to the game this week.
(He is not going until next month, so the situation is not possible.)

The **imperative** mood states a request or command and always uses the present tense. A mild imperative is followed by a period; a strong imperative is followed by an exclamation point.

EXAMPLES **Call** me when you get home.
Watch out!

Notice that the subject, *you,* is understood but omitted.

See Practice 21.2K
See Practice 21.2L

494 **Using Verbs**

Working with ELLs — ELL Sheltered Instruction: Cognitive

Have students use the short indicative and the longer subjunctive sentences in the examples on page 494 to practice speaking using a variety of sentence lengths with increasing accuracy and ease.

Beginning Read the sentences in the top row of the chart aloud to students, having them repeat after you. Emphasize that the first sentence says what is, and the second says what the speaker wishes for.

Intermediate Have students choral read the sentences in the second and third rows of the chart. Ask why the subjunctive sentences are longer. (They contain two ideas: a condition and its consequence.) Coach them in speaking the sentences accurately and with correct intonation.

Advanced Have partners say example sentences from the chart. Then, have students write simple indicative sentences on cards. Have partners takes turns choosing a card, saying the sentence, and then saying a longer subjunctive sentence based on the sentence. Have them correct each other as needed.

Advanced High Have students complete the Advanced activity. Extend by having them also say imperative sentences based on the sentences on the cards.

PRACTICE 21.2K Identifying Moods of Verbs

Read the sentences. Then, write *indicative*, *subjunctive*, or *imperative* for the mood of the underlined verb in each sentence.

EXAMPLE If John were here now, what would he think?

ANSWER *subjunctive*

1. Tell your mother where you are going.
2. Ben went to the soccer game.
3. Listen to this lovely music!
4. I wish I had heard about this earlier.
5. Wade sat next to me at the play.
6. If I were you, I'd study for the quiz.
7. Please stay here for a little while.
8. We went out for a pizza last night.
9. If Jaime were captain, he would be fair.
10. Katherine has an appointment with her orthodontist today.

PRACTICE 21.2L Writing Sentences to Express Mood

Read the verbs. Write sentences using the different moods of verbs as indicated below.

EXAMPLE were (subjunctive)

ANSWER *If I were a contestant, I'd win the prize.*

11. turn (imperative)
12. disturbs (indicative)
13. had finished (subjunctive)
14. wanted (indicative)
15. answer (imperative)
16. had been (subjunctive)
17. stop (imperative)
18. were (subjunctive)
19. delivers (indicative)
20. take (imperative)

SPEAKING APPLICATION

Use sentences 1, 5, and 6 as models, and make up sentences of your own using the same moods. Take turns saying your sentences to a partner, who will identify the mood of each sentence.

WRITING APPLICATION

Use sentences 2, 3, and 9 as models, and write three sentences in which you use the same mood as in the model sentences.

PRACTICE 21.2K

1. imperative
2. indicative
3. imperative
4. subjunctive
5. indicative
6. subjunctive
7. imperative
8. indicative
9. subjunctive
10. indicative

PRACTICE 21.2L

Answers will vary. Sample answers:

11. Turn to page 192 in your book.
12. The noise disturbs my concentration.
13. If Shawn had finished his project on time, he would have received a better grade.
14. Tyler wanted to go along with his older brother.
15. Please answer the door.
16. If I had been more careful, I wouldn't have slipped on the ice.
17. Stop complaining.
18. If I were you, I'd hurry to class.
19. The mail carrier delivers our mail in the morning.
20. Take an umbrella with you.

SPEAKING APPLICATION

Have students explain how they identified the mood of the verb in each sentence.

WRITING APPLICATION

Have students rewrite their sentences using different moods from those originally used.

Lesson Objectives

1. Correctly use principal parts of verbs.
2. Distinguish between meanings of confusing verb pairs.
3. Avoid common mistakes in using verbs.

Discuss reasons students should master troublesome verbs.

Use a Think Aloud as part of a gradual release progression.

Say: When I look at this list, it seems overwhelming. However, not all of these verbs give me trouble. So the best thing for me to do is to focus on the few verbs that I don't always use correctly. I can add them to my list of things to check when I revise my writing. **One thing I need to review** is the difference between *did* and *done*. The explanation tells me that I should use *done* only with a helping verb.

Ask: How can I remember to use this rule when I'm writing and speaking? (Accept all reasonable responses.)

Work with students to list strategies for improving their use of troublesome verbs. For example, students might listen for how people use these verbs, find models of good usage to imitate, and identify proofing strategies they can use to check their usage of this verb in their writing (such as highlighting places they have used *done* or using their word processor's Find command).

Assign student pairs one usage problem on this page. Ask them to develop a hint or memory aid to help classmates remember the rule for correct usage. Have students share their rules.

21.3 Troublesome Verbs

The following verbs cause problems for many speakers and writers of English. Some of the problems involve using the principal parts of certain verbs. Others involve learning to distinguish between the meanings of certain confusing pairs of verbs.

WRITING COACH Online
www.phwritingcoach.com

Grammar Practice
Practice your grammar skills with Writing Coach Online.

Grammar Games
Test your knowledge of grammar in this fast-paced interactive video game.

(1) *ain't* *Ain't* is not considered standard English. Avoid using it in speaking and in writing.

INCORRECT He **ain't** the first to reach the mountain top.

CORRECT He **isn't** the first to reach the mountain top.

(2) *did, done* Remember that *done* is a past participle and can be used as a verb only with a helping verb such as *have* or *has*. Instead of using *done* without a helping verb, use *did*.

INCORRECT I already **done** my English homework.

CORRECT I already **did** my English homework.
I **have** already **done** my English homework.

See Practice 21.3A

(3) *dragged, drug* *Drag* is a regular verb. Its principal parts are *drag, dragging, dragged,* and *dragged*. *Drug* is never correct as the past or past participle of *drag*.

INCORRECT The dog **drug** the ball across the yard.

CORRECT The dog **dragged** the ball across the yard.

(4) *gone, went* *Gone* is the past participle of *go* and can be used as a verb only with a helping verb such as *have* or *has*. *Went* is the past of *go* and is never used with a helping verb.

INCORRECT James and Alice **gone** to the beach.
We **should have went** along with them.

CORRECT James and Alice **went** (or **have gone**) to the beach.
We **should have gone** along with them.

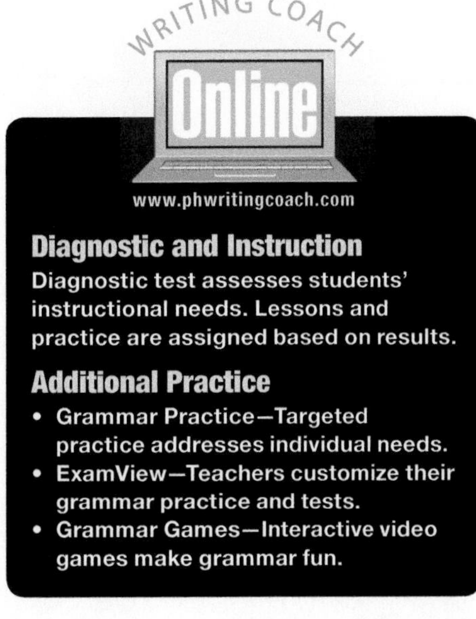

Diagnostic and Instruction
Diagnostic test assesses students' instructional needs. Lessons and practice are assigned based on results.

Additional Practice
- Grammar Practice—Targeted practice addresses individual needs.
- ExamView—Teachers customize their grammar practice and tests.
- Grammar Games—Interactive video games make grammar fun.

(5) *have, of* The words *have* and *of* often sound very similar. Be careful not to write *of* when you mean the helping verb *have* or its contraction *'ve*.

INCORRECT	We should **of** waited for Tim.
CORRECT	We should **have** (or **should've**) waited for Tim.

(6) *lay, lie* These verbs look and sound almost alike and have similar meanings. The first step in distinguishing between *lay* and *lie* is to memorize the principal parts of both verbs.

PRINCIPAL PARTS				
	lay	laying	laid	laid
	lie	lying	lay	lain

Lay usually means "to put (something) down" or "to place (something)." It is almost always followed by a direct object. *Lie* means "to rest in a reclining position" or "to be situated." This verb is used to show the position of a person, place, or thing. *Lie* is never followed by a direct object.

EXAMPLES	The teacher **lays** her chalk on the desk.
	The doctor must **lie** down to rest.

Pay special attention to the past tense of *lay* and *lie*. *Lay* is the past tense of *lie*. The past tense of *lay* is *laid*.

PRESENT TENSE OF *LAY*	I **lay** the mug on the counter.
PAST TENSE OF *LAY*	The painter **laid** his brush on the easel.
PAST TENSE OF *LIE*	The dog **lay** down in his bed.

See Practice 21.3B

(7) *leave, let* *Leave* means "to allow to remain." *Let* means "to permit." Do not reverse the meanings.

INCORRECT	**Leave** me to review the exam.
	Let the answer sheet alone.
CORRECT	**Let** me review the exam.
	Leave the answer sheet alone.

have, of **Say:** I should've gotten up earlier this morning. **Have students tell you whether the *uv* sound is *of* or the short form of *have*. Say:** I thought of you today. **Have students tell you whether the *uv* sound is *of* or the short form of *have*.**

lay, lie Write these sentences on the board:

He lays the ________ on the table.
He was laying the ________ on the table.
She laid the ________ on the table.
She had laid the ________ on the table.

Invite students to provide nouns to fill in the blanks. Then, **ask:** What kind of word goes in the blank? If students need a review of direct objects, direct their attention to the explanation of *lie/lay* and remind them that a direct object receives the action of a verb.

Have students compare the sentences on the board to the examples for *lay* on page 497. Point out that *lie* never takes a direct object.

Assign student pairs to write one or more rules for using *lie/lay* correctly.

leave, let Write these sentences on the board: *Let the dog out. Leave me the paper when you're finished. Let me alone. Leave me be.* Have students identify which sentences use the words *let* and *leave* correctly.

Differentiated Instruction

RTI Strategy for Below-Level Students Encourage students to create a personal proofing checklist to use every time they revise their writing. Have them choose three or four verbs from those listed on pages 496–498 to add to the list.

PRE-AP Enrichment for Above-Level Students Encourage students to create and perform a skit that demonstrates how to use one of the troublesome verbs correctly. They might show comic misunderstandings that arise because of usage errors or present an interaction between a teacher and student(s), or act out situations that illustrate correct usage.

Have student pairs read the explanation and examples for the troublesome verbs discussed on page 498.

Use a Think Aloud as part of a gradual release progression.

Say: Of the troublesome verbs on this list, **I think** that I have had the most trouble with *sit* and *set*. The words sound very similar. I'll need to review the meanings of each word to better understand how to use them correctly.

Lead a class discussion about the verbs listed on this page (or in this section) that students feel are the most difficult to master. Make a list on the board. **Then, guide students** in creating sentences that use each verb correctly.

Have students work in pairs to write additional examples of correct usage, using the examples on page 498 as a model. Finally, ask them to work together to write one or more rules that will help them use these troublesome verbs correctly.

(8) *raise, rise* *Raise* can mean "to lift (something) upward," "to build (something)," or "to increase (something)." It is usually followed by a direct object. *Rise* is not usually followed by a direct object. This verb means "to get up," "to go up," or "to be increased."

EXAMPLES	**Raise** the blinds so we can see the sun.
	The runners must **rise** early to train.

(9) *saw, seen* *Seen* is a past participle and can be used as a verb only with a helping verb such as *have* or *has.*

INCORRECT	I **seen** the painting last month.
CORRECT	I **saw** the painting last month.

(10) *says, said* A common mistake in reporting what someone said is to use *says* (present tense) rather than *said* (past tense).

INCORRECT	The doctor **says**, "It is urgent."
CORRECT	The doctor **said**, "It is urgent."

(11) *set, sit* The first step in learning to distinguish between *set* and *sit* is to become thoroughly familiar with their principal parts.

PRINCIPAL PARTS	set	setting	set	set
	sit	sitting	sat	sat

Set means "to put (something) in a certain place or position." It is usually followed by a direct object. *Sit* usually means "to be seated" or "to rest." It is usually not followed by a direct object.

EXAMPLES	She **set** the plate on the table.
	We **have set** the china safely in the cabinet.
	Tyler **sat** in the reclining chair.
	The eagle **has sat** on the branch since morning.

See Practice 21.3C
See Practice 21.3D

PRACTICE 21.3A Using *Did* and *Done*

Read the sentences. Then, for each sentence, if *did* or *done* is used correctly, write *correct*. If it is not, write *incorrect*.

EXAMPLE We done a group activity in class today.

ANSWER *incorrect*

1. Jeremy has done an excellent job on his science fair project.
2. We did our work quietly in study hall.
3. I done everything you asked.
4. The artist did a sketch before he began to paint.
5. We done a good job.
6. Rolanda did her homework every day.
7. Charles has done his share of the work already.
8. That red car done a U-turn in the middle of the road.
9. Lynn did ten laps in the pool today.
10. Jane and Judie have already done the grocery shopping.

PRACTICE 21.3B Using *Lay* and *Lie*

Read the sentences. Then, choose and write the correct form of the verb from the pair in parentheses.

EXAMPLE The note (lay, lie) unread on the table.

ANSWER *lay*

11. I would like to (lie, lay) down for a nap.
12. Those magazines have been (lying, laying) on the floor for a week.
13. Isabella was so tired that she (laid, lay) down right after dinner.
14. The cat has (laid, lain) in the sun all afternoon.
15. Mia (laid, lie) out two place settings at the table.
16. Natalie and Kelly (lay, lie) down in the snow and made snow angels.
17. The workers had (laid, lain) the foundation before starting on the wall.
18. (Lay, Lie) out all your notecards on your desk so you can rearrange them.
19. Earlier today, the children (laid, lay) the blocks in a circle.
20. Hal likes to (lie, lay) on the floor and read.

SPEAKING APPLICATION

With a partner, take turns using *did* and *done* in sentences.

WRITING APPLICATION

Write three sentences in which you correctly use different forms of *lay* and *lie*. You may use sentences from Practice 21.3B as models.

PRACTICE 21.3A

1. correct
2. correct
3. incorrect
4. correct
5. incorrect
6. correct
7. correct
8. incorrect
9. correct
10. correct

PRACTICE 21.3B

11. lie
12. lying
13. lay
14. lain
15. laid
16. lay
17. laid
18. Lay
19. laid
20. lie

SPEAKING APPLICATION

Have partners correct each other's sentences. Then, have them take turns using *gone* and *went* in sentences.

WRITING APPLICATION

Students should explain how they determined when to use *lay* and when to use *lie*. Then, have students write a paragraph in which they correctly use the words *raise* and *rise* in at least two different tenses.

Working with ELLs — ELL Sheltered Instruction: Social/Affective

Have students discuss and share information with one another, demonstrating listening comprehension of increasingly complex spoken English by collaborating with peers. Prepare a paragraph, based on the Speaking Application, describing three things you did in the past year. Read the paragraph aloud while all students listen.

Beginning Pair Beginning students with more proficient English speakers. Read your paragraph again, providing explanations. Have the paired students share what they understood and collaborate in writing a one-sentence summary of your presentation.

Intermediate Give each student an outline graphic organizer with three points. Reread your paragraph and have students record the main points on their outlines. Then, have them work in groups to write a summary of your presentation.

Advanced Reread your paragraph. Have students complete an outline graphic organizer. Have partners share their outlines and collaborate on a summary of your presentation.

Advanced High Have students use your presentation as a model for a short presentation about two things they did or have done. Students should give their presentation to a small group while others listen and take notes. Then, have students share what they understood from each presentation and collaborate on writing a summary.

PRACTICE 21.3C

1. set
2. sat
3. set
4. sit
5. set
6. set
7. sitting
8. sit
9. set
10. sit

PRACTICE 21.3D

11. Leave your jacket on the bench while you mow the lawn.
12. correct
13. I saw Rich at the baseball field yesterday.
14. We probably should have asked for directions.
15. correct
16. Joey said, "Help me make a spreadsheet."
17. correct
18. correct
19. correct
20. The temperature rose 10 degrees in the last hour.

SPEAKING APPLICATION

Have partners explain why the verb is being used correctly or incorrectly.

WRITING APPLICATION

Have students share their sentences with a partner and explain why *raise, seen,* and *should have* are the correct words in the context of their sentences.

PRACTICE 21.3C Using *Set* and *Sit*

Read the sentences. Then, choose and write the correct form of the verb from the pair in parentheses.

EXAMPLE Please (sit, set) your bags on the table.

ANSWER *set*

1. Rebecca (set, sat) the money on her dresser.
2. We had (set, sat) in the waiting room for almost an hour.
3. Sasha (sat, set) all the chairs in rows.
4. Will you stay and (sit, set) with me for a while?
5. Ray (set, sat) his GPS device on the table.
6. Grandfather (set, sat) his feet on a stool.
7. You can read a book while you're (sitting, setting) on the train.
8. Please (set, sit) down over there.
9. When you put the cookies in the oven, (set, sit) the timer for 10 minutes.
10. Let's (sit, set) in the shade under those trees.

PRACTICE 21.3D Using Troublesome Verbs

Read the sentences. If the underlined verb is used correctly, write *correct*. If it is not, rewrite the sentence using the correct verb.

EXAMPLE The girls have <u>went</u> for a walk.

ANSWER *The girls have gone for a walk.*

11. <u>Let</u> your jacket on the bench while you mow the lawn.
12. Alicia <u>went</u> to basketball camp for a week.
13. I <u>seen</u> Rich at the baseball field yesterday.
14. We probably should <u>of</u> asked for directions.
15. In some yoga positions, you <u>raise</u> your arms above your head.
16. I saw Joey in the hall, and he <u>says</u>, "Help me make a spreadsheet."
17. Kelsey <u>dragged</u> the cursor down the menu to choose the file she wanted.
18. Wyatt <u>isn't</u> here yet.
19. <u>Let</u> the soup cool before you eat it.
20. The temperature <u>raised</u> 10 degrees in the last hour.

SPEAKING APPLICATION

With a partner, take turns describing a favorite activity. Use at least two of the troublesome verbs in Practices 21.3C and 21.3D. Your partner should confirm that you are using the verbs correctly.

WRITING APPLICATION

Write three sentences in which you use these verbs correctly: *raise, seen,* and *should have.*

CHAPTER 22 LESSON PLANNER
Using Pronouns

Use the Online Lesson Planner at www.phwritingcoach.com to customize your instructional plan for an integrated Language Arts curriculum.

DAY 1 22.1 Case

"What Do You Notice?" **Objectives:** Recognize cases of personal pronouns	**INSTRUCTION AND PRACTICE** **Student Edition** pp. 501–503

DAY 2 22.1 Case *(continued)*

Objectives: Identify, use, and understand pronoun cases, including ▪ the nominative case ▪ the objective case	**INSTRUCTION AND PRACTICE** **Student Edition** pp. 504–505, 507–508 **Test Warm-Up** p. 510

DAY 3 22.1 Case *(continued)*

Objectives: Identify, use, and understand pronouns, including ▪ the possessive case ▪ *who* and *whom*	**INSTRUCTION AND PRACTICE** **Student Edition** pp. 506, 509, 511–512 **Test Warm-Up** p. 510

Alternate Pacing Plans

- **Block Scheduling** Each day in the Lesson Planner represents a 40–50 minute block. Teachers using block scheduling may combine days to revise pacing to meet their classroom needs.
- **Accelerated Lesson Planning** Combine instructional days, focusing on concepts called out by students' diagnostic test results.
- **Integrated Language Arts Curriculum** Use the instruction and practice in this chapter to provide reinforcement, remediation, or extension of grammar concepts taught in your literature curriculum.

Links to Prentice Hall *LITERATURE*

- **Unit 1** Personal Pronouns, p. 126; Possessive Pronouns, p. 150
- **Unit 6** Writing Workshop: Revising to Correct Use of Pronoun Case, p. 1045

> *"Students should be taught the different cases of pronouns (nominative, objective, possessive), but they will only internalize them when they begin using them in their own writing."*
>
> **—Kelly Gallagher**

Grammar Assessment

Grammar Coach:	Diagnostic Assessment	End-of-Chapter Assessment	Progress Monitoring
Personalized Instruction	Students take grammar diagnostic test online and are automatically assigned instruction and practice in areas where they need support.	Teacher uses **ExamView** to administer end-of-chapter assessment and remediation. Teachers may customize **ExamView** tests or use the ones provided.	Teachers may use the **Test Warm-Ups** and the **Cumulative Reviews** in the student book or eText to check students' mastery of grammar skills. Students may also play **DimensionL** grammar video games to test their grammar skills.
Teacher-Directed Instruction	Teacher administers the diagnostic test and determines focus of instruction and practice.		

www.phwritingcoach.com

Grammar Assessment and Practice

Chapter diagnostic tests assess students' skills and assign instruction and practice.

DimensionL Video Games

Fast-paced interactive video games challenge students' mastery of grammar.

Lesson Planner continues on next page

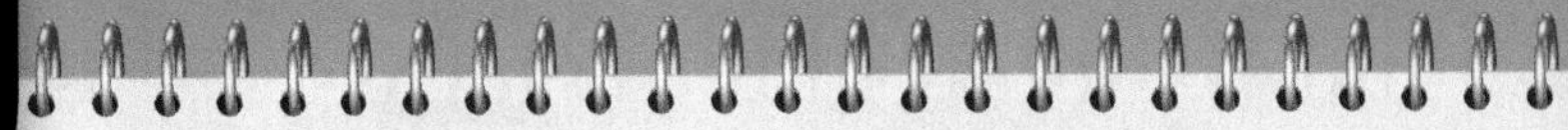

> "*Help your students see how critical pronoun placement is. Remind writers that when pronouns drift too far from the nouns they rename, connections become lost in a sea of words where no one can tell to whom* he, she, *or* it *belong. Encourage students to keep nouns and pronouns close to avoid trouble.*"
>
> **—Jeff Anderson**

Differentiated Instruction

Differentiated Instruction Boxes in this Teacher's Edition address these student populations:

- Below-Level Students
- Above-Level Students
- Gifted and Talented Students
- Special Needs Students
- English Language Learners
- Spanish Speaking Students

In addition, for further enrichment, see the **Extension** features.

Grammar Ground Rule: Keep It Simple!

Model with Students

In this chapter, keeping it simple means using **pronouns**, especially **possessive pronouns**. Explain to students that a possessive pronoun such as *his* can take the place of four or five words. That makes a sentence simpler and easier to read.

Say: Suppose I want to talk about a zebra's stripes. I could say, *A zebra never changes the stripes that belong to the zebra*. Or I could say, *A zebra never changes its stripes*. The second sentence is a simpler, better sentence because of the pronoun *its*. Or consider this sentence: *Marlie is wearing the sweater of the sister of Marlie*. It's simpler and easier to say, *Marlie is wearing her sister's sweater.*

Explain that students can use possessive pronouns to make their writing simpler and clearer, but they need to be careful. **Say:** We make a noun possessive by adding an apostrophe and an *–s*, but you should never add that to a possessive pronoun. *Steve's hat* means "the hat of Steve." *His hat* means "the hat of him." If you add an apostrophe and an *–s*, you get "the hat of him of him."

Small Group Activity – Finding Pronouns

Have students form groups and find a paragraph from a short story. Have one student read the paragraph, stopping at each pronoun. The other students should then say the words that the pronoun has replaced, if they can. Sometimes an antecedent will not be in the selection. Have students discuss how the use of pronouns makes the sentences simpler and clearer. Their discussion should answer these questions:

- What kinds of words do pronouns replace?
- How do they make sentences simpler?

Have a member of each group present their conclusions to the class and give one good example of pronoun usage that follows this grammar ground rule: Keep it simple.

Grammar Ground Rules

1. Keep it clear.
2. Make them agree.
3. Make it specific.
4. Dot your *i*'s and cross your *t*'s.
5. Make it active.

USING PRONOUNS

Make your writing easy for readers to follow by using pronouns correctly.

WRITE GUY *Jeff Anderson, M.Ed.*

WHAT DO YOU NOTICE?

Focus on the pronouns as you zoom in on these sentences from the book *Angela's Ashes* by Frank McCourt.

MENTOR TEXT

Patricia says she has two books by her bed. One is a poetry book and that's the one she loves.

Now, ask yourself the following questions:

- In the first sentence, which pronoun shows possession?
- What purpose does the pronoun *she* serve in these sentences?

In the first sentence, the pronoun *her* is possessive because it shows that the bed belongs to Patricia. The pronoun *she*, used in both sentences, refers to *Patricia*. Using *she* helps the author avoid repeating Patricia's name.

Grammar for Writers A writer can use pronouns to create sentences that flow smoothly. Keep an eye out for areas of your writing that could benefit from replacing nouns with pronouns.

Ms. Green is a great teacher. Ms. Green always knows the answer. Ms. Green plays the piano. Ms. Green ...
I get the idea. She can do anything.

501

USING PRONOUNS

As students progress in their writing skills, it will be important for them to be able to apply the rules of grammar, usage, and mechanics to their own drafts. Use the *What Do You Notice?* feature to help them see effective conventions in the work of professional writers. Encourage students to incorporate proper voice, tense, and syntax as they edit their own writing.

Read the opening sentence aloud. Remind students that pronouns are words that take the place of nouns. Some common pronouns are *I, you, he, she, we,* and *they.* Point out that using pronouns effectively can make writing flow more smoothly.

WRITE GUY *Jeff Anderson, M. Ed.*

WHAT DO YOU NOTICE?

When students have read the Mentor Text, **say:** Notice that the Mentor Text uses the pronoun *she* to take the place of the proper noun *Patricia* after the author made it clear that he was talking about *Patricia. She* replaces *Patricia.*

Have students finish reading the page. Remind them that pronouns can be subjects—who or what sentences are about, or objects—receivers of actions. Pronouns can also show possession.

Then, ask: What do you think would happen if a writer used only nouns? (**Possible response:** The writing would sound repetitive and boring.)

Invite students to name some pronouns in the text. **Ask students:** Can you find the noun that each pronoun replaces? Guide students in understanding that readers will be confused if they cannot easily understand to which noun a pronoun refers.

Grammar for Writers: Voice

Help students understand that using pronouns makes their writing flow smoothly by allowing them to avoid the unnecessary repetition of nouns. The rules in this chapter will help them use pronouns effectively in their writing and speaking.

22.1 Recognizing Cases of Personal Pronouns

Lesson Objectives

1. Identify and distinguish between various types and cases of pronouns.
2. Use and understand the difference between *who* and *whom*.

Explain that a pronoun can take different forms, such as *I* and *me,* depending on its function, or *case.*

RULE 22.1.1 Read aloud the rule and then have students repeat the lines with you.

Write these sentences on the board: *(I, Me) need help with math. You should help (I, me). I need (you, your) expertise.* **Say:** How can I figure out which pronoun form is right? I ask myself how the pronoun functions in the sentence. In the first sentence, I see that the pronoun is doing the action of needing. That makes the pronoun a subject. Subject pronouns are in the nominative case. By looking at the nominative case pronouns listed in the pronouns chart, I can choose the right form. **Read aloud the first row of the chart. Say:** I see that *I* is the correct form.

Work with students to help them figure out which pronouns to use in the other two sentences on the board.

Have pairs of students write original sentences using pronouns from each case.

22.1 Recognizing Cases of Personal Pronouns

In Chapter 13, you learned that personal pronouns can be arranged in three groups: first person, second person, and third person. Pronouns can also be grouped by their **cases.**

www.phwritingcoach.com

Grammar Practice

Practice your grammar skills with Writing Coach Online.

Grammar Games

Test your knowledge of grammar in this fast-paced interactive video game.

English has three cases: nominative, objective, and possessive.

The chart below shows the personal pronouns grouped according to the three cases. The case shows whether a pronoun is being used as a subject, an object, or a possessive.

THE THREE CASES OF PERSONAL PRONOUNS	
NOMINATIVE CASE	USE IN A SENTENCE
I, we, you, he, she, it, they	subject of a verb predicate pronoun
OBJECTIVE CASE	USE IN A SENTENCE
me, us, you, him, her, it, them	indirect object object of a preposition direct object
POSSESSIVE CASE	USE IN A SENTENCE
my, mine, our, ours, your, yours, his, her, hers, its, their, theirs	to show ownership

SUBJECT OF A VERB	**We** wanted badly to see the movie.
PREDICATE PRONOUN	The oldest is **she**.
INDIRECT OBJECT	Please give **me** the notebook.
OBJECT OF A PREPOSITION	Please show the diploma to **me**.
DIRECT OBJECT	A soccer ball hit **her** on the head.
TO SHOW OWNERSHIP	That is **my** sweater, not **yours**.

See Practice 22.1A
See Practice 22.1B

Differentiated Instruction

RTI Strategy for Below-Level Students

Some students may need a review of grammar terms such as *direct object, first person,* or *preposition.* Give students a list of terms you want them to review. Have them write a definition for each term. Collect the definitions. Then, read them aloud one at a time, asking students to name the term that matches the definition.

Enrichment for Gifted/Talented Students

Challenge students to develop a skit or multimedia presentation that might be used on a children's television program to introduce the three cases of pronouns. Ensure students write and use several examples of sentences with the correct cases of personal pronouns.

WRITING COACH Online

www.phwritingcoach.com

Diagnostic and Instruction

Diagnostic test assesses students' instructional needs. Lessons and practice are assigned based on results.

Additional Practice

- Grammar Practice—Targeted practice addresses individual needs.
- ExamView—Teachers customize their grammar practice and tests.
- Grammar Games—Interactive video games make grammar fun.

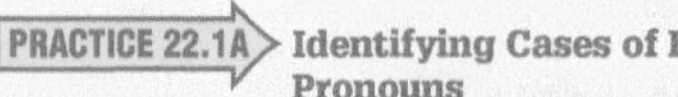

PRACTICE 22.1A **Identifying Cases of Personal Pronouns**

Read the sentences. Then, identify the case of each underlined personal pronoun by writing *nominative*, *objective*, or *possessive*.

EXAMPLE They used to live on this street.
ANSWER *nominative*

1. A reporter asked him some questions.
2. Do you know her?
3. She and I are best friends.
4. We try hard to be on time.
5. That sweatshirt on the floor is his.
6. Kerrie watched them through the window.
7. He and Glen are in the computer lab.
8. The manager thanked us for our help.
9. That seat is yours.
10. Kara brought it for me.

PRACTICE 22.1B **Identifying Pronoun Cases and Uses**

Read the sentences. Write the case of each underlined pronoun. Then, label it *subject of a verb*, *predicate pronoun*, *direct object*, *indirect object*, or *object of a preposition*.

EXAMPLE She and Tonia led the march.
ANSWER *nominative, subject of a verb*

11. Please come to the pool with me.
12. They held a bake sale to raise money.
13. Selena waved to them from the window.
14. She did not answer my message.
15. Can you give us some information?
16. The first person to sign up was he.
17. Jay dribbled the ball and passed it to Boyd.
18. We went to the airport in a taxi.
19. Can you lend her your bicycle helmet?
20. The winner was I.

SPEAKING APPLICATION

With a partner, take turns describing one of your friends and telling something about him or her. Your partner should listen for and name the personal pronouns you use.

WRITING APPLICATION

Write a short paragraph about an event in which you participated. Underline your pronouns and identify the case of each.

Practice 503

PRACTICE 22.1A

1. objective
2. objective
3. nominative, nominative
4. nominative
5. possessive
6. objective
7. nominative
8. objective, possessive
9. possessive
10. objective, objective

PRACTICE 22.1B

11. objective, object of a preposition
12. nominative, subject of a verb
13. objective, object of a preposition
14. nominative, subject of a verb
15. objective, indirect object
16. nominative, predicate pronoun
17. objective, direct object
18. nominative, subject of a verb
19. objective, indirect object
20. nominative, predicate pronoun

SPEAKING APPLICATION

Have partners identify the case of each personal pronoun and explain whether the proper case was used.

WRITING APPLICATION

Have students exchange paragraphs and check each other's work, explaining why it is or is not correct.

Working with ELLs

ELL Sheltered Instruction: Cognitive

As students learn about personal pronouns, have them write using newly acquired basic vocabulary, internalizing it by using and reusing it.

Beginning Hand a book to a student. Say and write on the board *I gave the book to [him/her]. Now [he/she] has it.* Use gestures to reinforce the meaning of the basic words in the sentences, including *gave, book, has,* and the pronouns. Then, have students write completions of the cloze sentence frame ____ *gave the book to* ____ . Repeat the activity with other frames, such as *I* ____ *the book to* ____, so that students may reuse the words.

Intermediate Review these basic words from page 502: *arranged, groups, notebook,* and *sweater*. Have partners write sentences for each word. Then, have them reuse the words in new sentences featuring pronouns.

Advanced Have students write definitions with example sentences for each of the basic words in the Intermediate activity, consulting a dictionary as necessary. Then, have them reuse the words in written sentences featuring pronouns.

Advanced High Have students complete the Advanced activity. Then, have them find synonyms for each of the basic words and use and reuse the synonyms correctly in written sentences.

The Nominative Case

Remind students that nominative case pronouns such as *I, he, she, we,* and *they* serve as subjects and predicate pronouns.

RULE 22.1.2 Read aloud the rule and then have students repeat the lines with you.

Check to see whether students need to review the definition of a predicate pronoun. Remind them that a pronoun that renames a subject and is linked to it with a linking verb such as *is* should be in the nominative case. Write this example on the board: *May I speak to Mary? This is (she, her).* **Say:** I see that the pronoun follows the linking verb *is*. Therefore, the pronoun is a predicate pronoun. That means I should use the nominative case pronoun *she*.

Checking for Errors in the Nominative Case

Students often use the incorrect pronoun form in compounds such as *between you and me.* Point out that isolating pronouns in compound subjects and objects can help students decide which case to use. Write these sentences on the board: *My friends and me can't wait for the sequel. Him and the coach made a new game plan.*

Underline the compound subjects: *my friends and me* and *him and the coach*. Have students identify the pronouns in each subject (*me, him*). Then, cross out everything in the compound subjects but the pronouns, and ask volunteers to read the sentences (*Me can't wait. . .; Him made. . .*). Ask students how the pronouns sound; then, have students identify the correct pronouns (I, He).

The Nominative Case

Personal pronouns in the nominative case have two uses.

Use the nominative case for (1) the subject of a verb and (2) a predicate pronoun.

Note that predicate pronouns follow linking verbs. Pronouns that follow linking verbs should be in the nominative case. The linking verbs are highlighted in orange in the examples below.

SUBJECTS	**She** hopes to be in the chorus.
	Excitedly, **they** prepared for the show.
PREDICATE PRONOUNS	It **was I** who suggested a hike.
	The best players **are she** and Frank.

Checking for Errors in the Nominative Case

People seldom forget to use the nominative case for a pronoun that is used by itself as a subject. Problems sometimes arise, however, when the pronoun is part of a compound subject.

INCORRECT	Chris and **me** played chess.
CORRECT	Chris and **I** played chess.

To make sure you are using the correct case of the pronoun in a compound subject, isolate the pronoun and the verb in the sentence. *Me played chess* is obviously wrong, so the nominative case *I* should be used instead.

If the sentence is in verb–subject order, rearrange it into subject–verb order, and then isolate the pronoun and verb.

INCORRECT	Are you and **her** going to the park?
REARRANGED	You and **?** are going to the park.
CORRECT	Are you and **she** going to the park?

See Practice 22.1.C
See Practice 22.1.D

Working with ELLs ELL Sheltered Instruction: Cognitive

As students learn about pronouns, call on them to demonstrate their reading comprehension of increasingly complex English using retelling and summarizing techniques.

Beginning Preteach the words *wants* and *chorus*. Write the example *She wants to be in the chorus* on the board. Read it aloud as students follow along. Help students demonstrate their comprehension by asking questions leading them to retell the sentence: for example, *What does she want to do?* Write students' responses on the board as they answer your questions.

Intermediate Guide students as they read page 504. Then, give them cloze prompts that they can complete to summarize the content. For example: *Predicate pronouns follow ____. Pronouns that follow linking verbs should be in the ____ case.* Coach students in summarizing, as needed.

Advanced Have partners reread the lesson on page 504. Have one student retell the portion of the lesson on the uses of the nominative case. Have the other retell the portion of the lesson on errors with compound subjects. Have partners correct one another's summaries.

Advanced High Have students work independently to write a summary of the page using original, creative sentences as examples. Then, have them read their summaries to the class.

The Objective Case

Personal pronouns in the objective case have three uses.

Use the objective case for (1) a direct object, (2) an indirect object, and (3) the object of a preposition.

22.1.3 RULE

DIRECT OBJECT	Joe's comment on the play upset **me**.
	The coach lectured **her**.
INDIRECT OBJECT	Tell **her** the plan.
	My friend gave **me** instructions to follow.
OBJECT OF PREPOSITION	Our class president voted for **him**.
	The bees swarmed around **me**.

Checking for Errors in the Objective Case

As with the nominative case, people seldom forget to use the objective case for a pronoun that is used by itself as a direct object, indirect object, or object of a preposition. Problems may arise, however, when the pronoun is part of a compound object.

INCORRECT	The bees swarmed around Patty and **I**.
CORRECT	The bees swarmed around Patty and **me**.

To make sure you are using the correct case of the pronoun in a compound object, use only the pronoun with the rest of the sentence. *The bees swarmed around I* is obviously wrong, so the objective case *me* should be used instead.

If the sentence is in verb–subject order, rearrange it into subject–verb order.

INCORRECT	Did my mother give Alice and **she** an apple?
REARRANGED	My mother gave Alice and **?** an apple.
CORRECT	Did my mother give Alice and **her** an apple?

See Practice 22.1E
See Practice 22.1F

The Objective Case

Point out that the objective case is used when a pronoun functions as a direct object, indirect object, or object of a preposition.

RULE 22.1.3 Read aloud the rule and then have students repeat the lines with you.

Look at the sentence that shows an objective case pronoun used as the direct object of the sentence. **Say:** I see that *me* receives the action of the verb *upset*. Therefore, *me* is a direct object, and the objective case is correct. Likewise, *me* is correct in the fourth example sentence because *me* receives the instructions. Since *instructions* is the direct object, *me* is the indirect object and in the objective case. In the fifth example sentence, the objective case *him* is correct because *him* is functioning as the object of the preposition *for*. I know that direct objects receive the action of the verb, so the pronoun following *upset* must be a direct object. I need to use an objective case pronoun as a direct object, so the correct pronoun must be *me*, which is objective case.

Checking for Errors in the Objective Case

Explain that people often mistakenly think that nominative case pronouns sound more "proper" than objective case pronouns. This misconception results in errors like these: *Please call Patty and I. Just between you and I, Patty would like you to call.* Write this sentence on the board: *The bees swarmed around Patty and I.* Point out that the sentence contains a compound object.

Isolate the pronouns in the sentence and replace the nominative pronoun (*I*) with the correct objective case pronouns (*me*).

Differentiated Instruction

Strategy for Spanish Speakers
Students whose home language is Spanish may have difficulty using personal pronouns in the objective case because of the different pronoun types in Spanish. Remind students that in English, the pronouns *me, you, her, him, it, us,* and *them* are used as direct objects, indirect objects, or objects of a preposition. Write an example of each type on the board, such as *Sally invited me to the party. Adam brought her a birthday present. Charlie gave the cake to them.* Invite volunteers to approach the board and identify each pronoun and how it is used in the sentence. Elicit additional examples of each usage from the students and invite volunteers to write the sentences on the board. Have students identify each pronoun and explain its usage in the sentence.

Teacher Tip

If students have trouble recognizing prepositions in order to identify the object of a preposition, have them use the "squirrel test." Words that fit into the frame are probably prepositions:

The squirrel ran ____________ the swing. (over, under, around, through, behind, across...)

The Possessive Case

Remind students that possessive pronouns express ownership. Discuss the advantages of using pronouns such as *his*, *hers*, and *ours* instead of phrases such as *the book that belongs to Joan*.

RULE 22.1.4 Read aloud the rule and then have students repeat the lines with you.

Say: The first example shows how possessive pronouns are usually used. Words like *its* and *my* usually show possession of nouns. In the first sentence, *its* shows possession of *race*. In the second sentence, *my* shows possession of *baseball*. Some possessive pronouns, such as *mine, yours, his, hers,* and *theirs,* can stand alone without modifying a noun. In the third sentence, *yours* and *mine* are not followed by a noun. They stand alone.

Work with students to make a list of possessive pronouns as well as a list of possessive nouns; for example, *John's, Mary's, John and Mary's,* Write the list on the board. Help students understand that possessive pronouns replace possessive nouns.

Have pairs of students write sentences using the possessive pronouns and nouns. Have students identify the possessive noun related to each possessive pronoun.

Checking for Errors in the Possessive Case

Write these words on the board: *our's, their's, it's*. Point out that these words are spelled incorrectly because possessive pronouns do not take apostrophes.

Teacher Tip

If students have access to computers, point out that they can use their word processor's Find feature to search for apostrophes. This makes it easy to correct mistakes such as using *it's* instead of the possessive pronoun *its*.

Grammar Game Plan

The Possessive Case

Personal pronouns in the possessive case show ownership of one sort or another.

RULE 22.1.4

Use the possessive case of personal pronouns before nouns to show possession. In addition, certain personal pronouns may also be used by themselves to indicate possession.

BEFORE NOUNS	The team won **its** race.
	Chris held **my** baseball.
BY THEMSELVES	Is this ruler **yours** or **mine**?
	Hers was the best essay.

Checking for Errors in the Possessive Case

Personal pronouns in the possessive case are never written with an apostrophe because they already show ownership. Keep this in mind, especially with possessive pronouns that end in *s*.

INCORRECT	This table is **our's**, not **their's**.
CORRECT	This table is **ours**, not **theirs**.

When the pronoun *it* is followed by an apostrophe and an *s*, the word becomes *it's*, which is a contraction of *it is*. The possessive pronoun *its* does not have an apostrophe.

CONTRACTION	**It's** going to snow today.
POSSESSIVE PRONOUN	The team loves **its** stadium.

To check if you need the contraction *it's* or the possessive pronoun *its*, substitute *it is* and reread the sentence.

INCORRECT	My jacket has lost **it's** button.
CORRECT	My jacket has lost **its** button.

See Practice 22.1G
See Practice 22.1H

Differentiated Instruction

RTI Strategy for Below-Level Students
When students edit their writing, have them highlight or circle every *it's*. Ask them if the sentence would still make sense if they substituted *it is*. If not, they should remove the apostrophe.

RTI Strategy for Special Needs Students
Have students make a four-column chart with four rows. The first column should be labeled *Person*. The rows should be labeled *first*, *second*, and *third*. The remaining columns should be labeled *Nominative*, *Objective*, and *Possessive*. Have students work with a partner to add examples of each type of pronoun to the chart.

PRACTICE 22.1C **Identifying Nominative Case Pronouns**

Read the sentences. Write the correct pronoun from the choices in parentheses. Then, label the pronoun *subject of a verb* or *predicate pronoun*.

EXAMPLE (She, Her) and I went together.

ANSWER *She — subject of a verb*

1. (They, Them) and the others left early.
2. Have you and (she, her) finished your project?
3. You and (me, I) should start a band.
4. (He, Him) and (me, I) both read the same book.
5. The second- and third-place winners were Ramon and (he, him).
6. The last person to leave was (she, her).
7. (She, Her) and Hugh offered to decorate the gym for the dance.
8. The Bulldogs and (we, us) made it to the finals.
9. The person who called you was (he, him).
10. The culprits in the case were (they, them).

PRACTICE 22.1D **Writing Sentences Using Nominative Case Pronouns**

Read the sentences. Then, rewrite each sentence, filling in the blank with a nominative case pronoun. Label the pronoun *subject of a verb* or *predicate pronoun*.

EXAMPLE It was ____ who called Kelly last night.

ANSWER *It was I who called Kelly last night. — predicate pronoun*

11. Max and ____ are the stars of the play.
12. ____ kids want to see them perform.
13. She and ____ are going to the dress rehearsal.
14. The best character in the play is ____.
15. Do you and ____ want to come with us tonight?
16. It is ____ who has to take care of the younger kids.
17. ____ and Veronica are well behaved.
18. He and ____ also go to bed very early.
19. It was ____ who wanted me to eat dinner at their house.
20. You and ____ have much in common.

SPEAKING APPLICATION

Tell a partner about something you and a friend did. Your partner should identify two pronouns in the nominative case.

WRITING APPLICATION

Write three sentences about a type of physical exercise you enjoy. Include a nominative case pronoun in each sentence. Then, underline each nominative case pronoun.

PRACTICE 22.1C

1. They—subject of a verb
2. she—subject of a verb
3. I—subject of a verb
4. He—subject of a verb; I—subject of a verb
5. he—predicate pronoun
6. she—predicate pronoun
7. She—subject of a verb
8. we—subject of a verb
9. he—predicate pronoun
10. they—predicate pronoun

PRACTICE 22.1D

Answers will vary. Sample answers:

11. I—subject of a verb
12. We—subject of a verb
13. I—subject of a verb
14. he—predicate pronoun
15. she—subject of a verb
16. she—predicate pronoun
17. She—subject of a verb
18. I—subject of a verb
19. they—predicate pronoun
20. he—subject of a verb

SPEAKING APPLICATION

Have partners retell the story using third-person pronouns. Then, have partners add one sentence with a predicate pronoun.

WRITING APPLICATION

Have students read their sentences to the group, and have the group identify the nominative case pronouns.

PRACTICE 22.1E

Answers will vary. Sample answers:

1. her—indirect object
2. me—object of a preposition
3. them—direct object
4. me—object of a preposition
5. us—object of a preposition
6. him—object of a preposition
7. me—indirect object
8. them—direct object
9. him—indirect object
10. you—object of a preposition

Answers will vary. Sample answers:

11. John made lunch and fed me.
12. The doctor gave her the shot.
13. The show began without him and her.
14. The hot sun beat down on him and me.
15. We gave them a chance.
16. The soccer player kicked him.
17. Sophie and Isabel took the test and the teacher passed them.
18. Lend me a pencil.
19. The ketchup sprayed onto him.
20. Music has a calming effect on her and me.

SPEAKING APPLICATION

Have partners tell each other stories using objective case pronouns and identify and correct any errors.

WRITING APPLICATION

Have students share their paragraphs with a partner, and have partners rewrite the paragraphs to change at least two objects into compound objects.

PRACTICE 22.1E Using Objective Case Pronouns

Read the sentences. Write an objective case pronoun to complete each sentence. Then, label each pronoun *direct object, indirect object,* or *object of a preposition.*

EXAMPLE I asked ____ for directions.
ANSWER *him — direct object*

1. Wayne told ____ his latest joke.
2. Between you and ____, I'd rather not go.
3. You can probably find ____ on the tennis court.
4. Meredith made dinner for Julian and ____.
5. Go with Colleen and ____ to the show.
6. I have some good news for you and ____.
7. Give ____ a turn at bat.
8. A puppy followed ____ to the bus stop.
9. The coach gave Manny and ____ some extra pointers.
10. There was a disagreement between Traci and ____.

PRACTICE 22.1F Writing Sentences Using Objective Case Pronouns

Read each objective case pronoun. Then, write a complete sentence using the objective case pronoun. The pronoun should function as a direct object, an indirect object, or an object of a preposition, as indicated in parentheses.

EXAMPLE Her (object of a preposition)
ANSWER Her mother spoke to *her* about her behavior.

11. me (direct object)
12. her (indirect object)
13. him and her (object of a preposition)
14. him and me (object of a preposition)
15. them (indirect object)
16. him (direct object)
17. them (direct object)
18. me (indirect object)
19. him (object of a preposition)
20. her and me (object of a preposition)

SPEAKING APPLICATION

With a partner, take turns describing a recent gathering with family or friends. Use at least three objective case pronouns. Your partner should identify and check for correct usage of the objective case pronouns in your statements.

WRITING APPLICATION

Write a brief paragraph about pets. Use at least three objective case pronouns in your paragraph. Then, underline the objective case pronouns and label them *direct object, indirect object,* or *object of a preposition.*

508 Using Pronouns

Working with ELLs — ELL Sheltered Instruction: Cognitive

Have Advanced High or native English speakers present responses to the Speaking Application prompt. As other students listen, help listeners use contextual support to enhance and confirm their understanding of increasingly complex spoken language.

Beginning Speak the sentence *I ate spaghetti* to students, miming the words *I ate*. Then, model the process of using context to confirm that *spaghetti* must be a food. Guide them in applying this process to the presentations, interrupting presenters as needed.

Intermediate Review the context in the presentations: a recent gathering of family and friends. As students present, have Intermediate students raise their hand when they have difficulty understanding. Have presenters repeat, and work with students to use context to enhance and confirm understanding.

Advanced Have students take notes on each presentation, including notes about parts they have difficulty understanding Have them meet with partners between presentations to review their notes. Direct them to use context from the presentation to enhance and confirm understanding, writing their interpretation of difficult parts.

Advanced High Have students complete the Advanced activity. Extend by having them give presentations themselves. Coach them in including context clues in their presentations that will help other students.

PRACTICE 22.1G Using Possessive Case Pronouns

Read the sentences. Write the correct pronoun from the choices in parentheses.

EXAMPLE That equipment is (their's, theirs).
ANSWER *theirs*

1. (My, Mine) is the green bag.
2. Caleb's notebook is on the table with (your, yours).
3. The choice will be (hers, her's) alone.
4. My shirt is missing one of (its, it's) buttons.
5. If this is Gillian's sweater, then that one is (yours, your's).
6. (Ours, Our's) is the best float in the parade.
7. This car has had (its, it's) problems.
8. Dr. Swenson is (their, theirs) dentist.
9. The large sculpture on the corner table is (her, hers).
10. Here is (my, mine) mother now.

PRACTICE 22.1H Supplying Possessive Case Pronouns

Read each possessive case pronoun. Then, write a complete sentence using the possessive case pronoun.

EXAMPLE its
ANSWER *The dog chewed on its toy bone.*

11. our
12. my
13. her
14. its
15. their
16. our
17. your
18. their
19. his
20. yours

SPEAKING APPLICATION

With a partner, take turns making statements about the ownership of items in your classroom. Your partner should identify the possessive case pronouns in your statements and make sure that they were used correctly.

WRITING APPLICATION

Write a brief paragraph about your most prized possession, such as a piece of jewelry or clothing, a book, or a photograph of someone special. Describe the object, using at least three possessive case pronouns.

Quick-Write Extension

To help students synthesize and apply what they have learned about the possessive case, have them write dialogues about who owns a particular object, such as a soccer ball or a cell phone. Direct students to work in pairs. One student should begin the dialogue, then give the paper to his or her partner. The partner should write a response to the first line of dialogue and give the paper back to the first student. Have students repeat the process for at least six lines. Ask students to use at least one personal pronoun in each line of dialogue. For an extra challenge, have pairs exchange dialogues and identify the cases of the pronouns.

PRACTICE 22.1G

1. Mine
2. yours
3. hers
4. its
5. yours
6. Ours
7. its
8. their
9. hers
10. my

PRACTICE 22.1H

Answers will vary. Sample answers:

11. There is grass in our backyard.
12. I like my new shoes.
13. Her problem is she does not like public speaking.
14. The car made its way down the street.
15. Picking a restaurant was not their strong point.
16. It is none of our business.
17. Which of these is your cat?
18. The weather did not delay their flight.
19. He read his new book.
20. Which one of these sweaters is yours?

SPEAKING APPLICATION

Have students explain how they identified the possessive case pronouns and determined when they were used correctly.

WRITING APPLICATION

Have students read their paragraphs to the group, pointing out the possessive nouns.

Test Warm-Up

1. **A** Change ***There*** to **Their**
2. **G** Change ***Them*** to **They**
3. **A** Assuming it was Jack, our uncle handed him a dollar as well.
4. **J** me

Reteach

If students have not mastered these skills, review the content in Section 22.1 Recognizing Cases of Personal Pronouns.

1. The Possessive Case 22.1.4
2. The Nominative Case 22.1.2
3. The Objective Case 22.1.3
4. The Objective Case 22.1.3

Test Tip

Some students waste time, and become needlessly upset, by trying to keep score for themselves during a test. Encourage students to not think about the end results of the test, but to focus on one question at a time.

Test Warm-Up

DIRECTIONS
Read the introduction and the passage that follows. Then, answer the questions to show that you can use and understand the function of nominative, objective, and possessive case pronouns in reading and writing.

Chloe wrote this paragraph about her younger brothers, who are twins. Read the paragraph and think about the changes you would suggest as a peer editor. When you finish reading, answer the questions that follow.

Seeing Double

(1) My younger brothers are identical twins. (2) There names are Zach and Jack. (3) Them and I get along just fine. (4) However, sometimes they work together or alone to play tricks on people. (5) One day, Zach, wearing a blue shirt, asked our uncle for money. (6) He gave Zach a dollar, and Zach walked out. (7) Five minutes later, a boy in a red shirt came in and asked for money. (8) Assuming it was Jack, our uncle handed he a dollar as well. (9) Just then, the real Jack walked into the room. (10) "Hey, I must be seeing double, Zach, give us one dollar back!" exclaimed our uncle.

1 What change, if any, should be made in sentence 2?

- **A** Change ***There*** to **Their**
- **B** Change ***are*** to **were**
- **C** Change ***and*** to **or**
- **D** Make no change

2 What change, if any, should be made in sentence 3?

- **F** Change ***I*** to **me**
- **G** Change ***Them*** to **They**
- **H** Change ***Them and I*** to **Us all**
- **J** Make no change

3 What is the BEST way to revise sentence 8?

- **A** Assuming it was Jack, our uncle handed him a dollar as well.
- **B** Assuming it was Jack, our uncle handed Jack a dollar as well.
- **C** Assuming it was him, our uncle handed Jack a dollar as well.
- **D** Assuming it was him, our uncle handed him a dollar as well.

4 The meaning of sentence 10 can be clarified by changing the word ***us*** to —

- **F** my
- **G** our
- **H** him
- **J** me

Cases of *Who* and *Whom* The pronouns *who* and *whom* are often confused. *Who* is a nominative case pronoun, and *whom* is an objective case pronoun. *Who* and *whom* have two common uses in sentences: They can be used in questions or to begin subordinate clauses in complex sentences.

Use *who* for the subject of a verb. Use *whom* for (1) the direct object of a verb and (2) the object of a preposition.

You will often find *who* used as the subject of a question. *Who* may also be used as the subject of a subordinate clause in a complex sentence.

SUBJECT OF A QUESTION	**Who** scored the most goals?
SUBJECT OF A SUBORDINATE CLAUSE	I admire the player **who** scored the most goals.

The following examples show *whom* used in questions.

DIRECT OBJECT	**Whom** did you see at the dinner?
OBJECT OF PREPOSITION	From **whom** is he getting a new puppy?

Questions that include *whom* are generally in inverted word order, with the verb appearing before the subject. If you reword the first example in subject–verb word order, you will see that *whom* is the direct object of the verb *did see: You did see whom?* In the second example, *whom* is the object of the preposition *from*: *He is getting the new puppy from whom?*

Subordinate clauses that begin with *whom* can be rearranged to show that the pronoun is a direct object.

EXAMPLE	The substitute teacher was not **whom** I expected.
REARRANGED SUBORDINATE CLAUSE	I expected **whom**?

See Practice 22.1I
See Practice 22.1J

Cases of *Who* and *Whom*

Explain that *whom* is the objective case form of the nominative case *who.*

RULE 22.1.5 Read aloud the rule and then have students repeat the lines with you.

Use a Think Aloud as part of a gradual release progression.

Think Aloud **Say:** To see whether I should use *who* or *whom,* I use my ear. **I try** substituting *he* or *him* in the sentence and listen to how it sounds. If *he* or another appropriate nominative case pronoun makes sense, I use *who.* If *him* or another appropriate objective case pronoun makes sense, I use *whom.* For example, suppose I have to decide whether to say, *Who shall I say is calling?* or *Whom shall I say is calling?* I know that questions are usually in inverted order—verb before subject—so I put the sentence in the usual subject-verb order: *I shall say who or whom is calling.* Then, I try inserting *he* or *him* into the sentence: *I shall say he is calling; I shall say him is calling.* I hear that *him is calling* sounds wrong, and *he is calling* sounds right. So I use the nominative case pronoun *who.*

Write these example sentences on the board: *Whom did you see at the dinner? From whom is he getting a new puppy?* **Work with students** to reorder the sentences and substitute *he* or *him* for *whom*: *You did see (he, him) at the dinner. He is getting a new puppy from (he, him).*

Have pairs of students write a sentence using *who* and a sentence using *whom.* Have them check to see that they have used the correct form by rewording the sentence and substituting *he* or *him.*

Differentiated Instruction

PRE-AP Enrichment for Above-Level Students Encourage students to develop a quiz to review personal pronoun cases using a game show format such as *Jeopardy*. Question categories might define terms, list pronouns, and complete rules from the chapter.

Have small groups of students write questions and answers for each category. Pool together all of the questions and answers, and then play the game as a class.

Possible answers and questions for each category include: category 1—Answer: a pronoun that shows possession/Question: What is a possessive pronoun?; category 2—Answer: *he*, *she*, or *I*/Question: What are nominative case pronouns?; category 3—Answer: The three cases of personal pronouns. Question: What are nominative, objective, and possessive?

PRACTICE 22.1I

1. who
2. Who
3. Whom
4. whom
5. Who
6. whom
7. who
8. whom
9. Whom
10. Whom

PRACTICE 22.1J

11. Do you know who is the fastest runner on the team?
12. correct
13. correct
14. This is my friend Madelyn, whom I told you about.
15. correct
16. Whom are you looking for?
17. correct
18. Luther is someone whom you can always count on.
19. Whom is that gift for?
20. Please see who is at the door.

SPEAKING APPLICATION

Have students say two sentences that use *who* and *whom* correctly and two sentences that use the pronouns incorrectly. Then, have partners identify which sentences are correct.

WRITING APPLICATION

Have students read their sentences to the class and justify their use of *who* and *whom*.

Recognizing Cases of Personal Pronouns

PRACTICE 22.1I Using *Who* and *Whom*

Read the sentences. Write the pronoun in parentheses that correctly completes each sentence.

EXAMPLE (Who, Whom) did you tell first?

ANSWER *Whom*

1. We wanted to know (who, whom) was there.
2. (Whom, Who) taught you to play a guitar?
3. (Who, Whom) do you think we should nominate?
4. To (whom, who) should I address the letter?
5. (Who, Whom) could possibly want that old thing?
6. I do not know (whom, who) you're referring to.
7. The one (who, whom) gave me this locket is my Aunt Cecile.
8. I don't know (who, whom) I can ask for advice.
9. (Whom, Who) did you hear that from?
10. (Who, Whom) did he pick for the team?

PRACTICE 22.1J Revising to Correct *Who* and *Whom*

Read the sentences. Then, if a sentence uses *who* or *whom* incorrectly, rewrite the sentence with the correct pronoun form. If a sentence has no pronoun error, write *correct*.

EXAMPLE Who did you vote for?

ANSWER *Whom did you vote for?*

11. Do you know whom is the fastest runner on the team?
12. Portia goes to Dr. Shah, who is an orthodontist.
13. Whom did you sit with at the game?
14. This is my friend Madelyn, who I told you about.
15. Did you see who that was?
16. Who are you looking for?
17. Who forgot to put the lid back onto the jar?
18. Luther is someone who you can always count on.
19. Who is that gift for?
20. Please see whom is at the door.

SPEAKING APPLICATION

With a partner, take turns asking two questions: one beginning with *who* and one beginning with *whom*. Your partner should identify how these pronouns are used in your sentences.

WRITING APPLICATION

Use sentences 2 and 3 as models, and write two questions using *who* and *whom* correctly.

Working with ELLs — ELL Sheltered Instruction: Cognitive

Use the Writing Application to give students practice with English sentence patterns. Have them write using a variety of grade-appropriate sentence patterns, including the pattern of *who/whom* questions, in increasingly accurate ways.

Beginning Read aloud the correct responses to Practice 22.1I, items 1 and 2, having students echo you. Write the sentences on the board and have students copy. Continue modeling the sentence pattern with other examples, such as *Whom did you meet?* or *Who threw the ball?* Then, guide students in writing their own *who* or *whom* questions.

Intermediate Have partners complete the Writing Application. Coach them in locating the subject and the verb in each of their sentences to enhance their understanding of this sentence pattern.

Advanced Have students complete the Writing Application, writing two questions in the *who/whom* question pattern, and then exchange papers with a partner. Then, have students write answers to their partner's questions. Have partners compare the sentence patterns of questions with the patterns of answers, noting the placement of subject and verb.

Advanced High Have students complete the Advanced activity. Challenge them to write their answers to the questions using compound and complex sentence patterns.

CHAPTER 23 LESSON PLANNER
Making Words Agree

Use the Online Lesson Planner at www.phwritingcoach.com to customize your instructional plan for an integrated Language Arts curriculum.

DAY 1 23.1 Subject-Verb Agreement

"What Do You Notice?"

Objectives: Identify, use, and understand aspects of subject-verb agreement, including

- singular and plural subjects
- singular and plural verbs
- making verbs agree with singular and plural subjects
- making verbs agree with collective nouns

INSTRUCTION AND PRACTICE

Student Edition pp. 513–519

DAY 2 23.1 Subject-Verb Agreement *(continued)*

Objectives: Identify, use, and understand aspects of subject-verb agreement, including

- making verbs agree with compound subjects
- inverted sentences

INSTRUCTION AND PRACTICE

Student Edition pp. 520–523

DAY 3 23.1 Subject-Verb Agreement *(continued)*

Objectives: Identify, use, and understand aspects of subject-verb agreement, including

- indefinite pronouns

INSTRUCTION AND PRACTICE

Student Edition pp. 524–526

DAY 4 23.2 Pronoun-Antecedent Agreement

Objectives: Identify, use, and understand aspects of pronoun-antecedent agreement, including

- personal pronouns
- avoiding problems with number and gender
- agreement between personal and indefinite pronouns

INSTRUCTION AND PRACTICE

Student Edition pp. 527–531

Test Warm-Up p. 532

Grammar Assessment

Grammar Coach:	Diagnostic Assessment	End-of-Chapter Assessment	Progress Monitoring
Personalized Instruction	Students take grammar diagnostic test online and are automatically assigned instruction and practice in areas where they need support.	Teacher uses **ExamView** to administer end-of-chapter assessment and remediation. Teachers may customize **ExamView** tests or use the ones provided.	Teachers may use the **Test Warm-Ups** and the **Cumulative Reviews** in the student book or eText to check students' mastery of grammar skills. Students may also play **DimensionL** grammar video games to test their grammar skills.
Teacher-Directed Instruction	Teacher administers the diagnostic test and determines focus of instruction and practice.		

Alternate Pacing Plans

- **Block Scheduling** Each day in the Lesson Planner represents a 40–50 minute block. Teachers using block scheduling may combine days to revise pacing to meet their classroom needs.
- **Accelerated Lesson Planning** Combine instructional days, focusing on concepts called out by students' diagnostic test results.
- **Integrated Language Arts Curriculum** Use the instruction and practice in this chapter to provide reinforcement, remediation, or extension of grammar concepts taught in your literature curriculum.

Links to Prentice Hall *LITERATURE*

- **Unit 1** Writing Workshop: Revising Incorrect Forms of Plural Nouns, p. 95; Writing Workshop: Checking Pronoun-Antecedent Agreement, p. 181
- **Unit 3** Compound Subjects and Predicates, p. 526
- **Unit 5** Writing Workshop: Correcting Subject-Verb Agreement with Compound Subjects, p. 883

www.phwritingcoach.com

Grammar Assessment and Practice

Chapter diagnostic tests assess students' skills and assign instruction and practice.

DimensionL Video Games

Fast-paced interactive video games challenge students' mastery of grammar.

Lesson Planner continues on next page

"Subject-verb agreement is one of those editing bugaboos that separate skilled writers from unskilled writers. If our students' writing skills are to excel in both school and in the workforce, the teaching of subject-verb agreement deserves extra attention."

—Kelly Gallagher

Differentiated Instruction

Differentiated Instruction Boxes in this Teacher's Edition address these student populations:

- Below-Level Students
- Above-Level Students
- Gifted and Talented Students
- Special Needs Students
- English Language Learners
- Spanish Speaking Students

In addition, for further enrichment, see the **Extension** features.

Grammar Ground Rule: Make Them Agree!

Model with Students

In this chapter, everything is about making them agree—pronouns and their antecedents, verbs and their subjects. Explain to students that, when it comes to agreement, nouns rule. Everything else must agree with them.

> **Say:** A noun that is the subject of a sentence or a clause can be singular or it can be plural. Whatever it is, the verb must agree with it. If I want to talk about one cat, any verb I use must be singular. *The cat sits. The cat runs. The cat walks across my computer keyboard.* If I'm talking about several cats, any verb I use must be plural. *The cats sit. The cats run. The cats knock over all my plants.*

Explain that the same thing is true for nouns and pronouns. If the noun antecedent is singular, the pronoun must be singular. Write on the board this sentence: *The cats ran for ______ food bowls.* Ask what pronoun belongs in the blank.

Small Group Activity – Finding and Describing Verbs

Have students form groups and find a simple science article. Have one student read the article, stopping at each verb. The other students should then tell whether the verb is singular or plural. Have students discuss helping verbs and the question of agreement. The discussion should answer these questions:

- In a verb phrase, does the helping verb need to agree with the subject?
- In a verb phrase, does the main verb change to agree with the subject?

Have a member of each group present their conclusions to the class and give one good example of verb usage that follows this grammar ground rule: Make them agree!

Grammar Ground Rules

1. Keep it clear.
2. Make them agree.
3. Make it specific.
4. Dot your *i*'s and cross your *t*'s.
5. Make it active.

MAKING WORDS AGREE

CHAPTER 23

Making subjects agree with verbs and pronouns agree with the words to which they refer will help your writing flow smoothly.

WRITE GUY *Jeff Anderson, M.Ed.*

WHAT DO YOU NOTICE?

Focus on agreement as you zoom in on these sentences from the essay "Rattlesnake Hunt" by Marjorie Kinnan Rawlings.

MENTOR TEXT

"It is a slow and heavy snake," Ross said. "It lies in wait on a small game trail and strikes the rat or rabbit passing by."

Now, ask yourself the following questions:

- What does the pronoun *it* refer to in these sentences?
- What are the verbs in the second sentence? How can you tell that these verbs agree with the subject?

The pronoun *it* refers to the noun *snake. It* agrees with *snake* because both are third person and singular. The second sentence includes a compound verb made of the verbs *lies* and *strikes.* The *-s* ending on both verbs shows they are singular and, therefore, agree with the singular subject *it.*

Grammar for Writers As writers craft sentences, they note whether their subjects are singular, plural, or compound, and choose verbs that match the subjects. As you write sentences, think about the number of each subject before choosing a verb that matches it.

My aunt say I never call her.
Hmm ... my aunt says that, too.

513

MAKING WORDS AGREE

As students progress in their writing skills, it will be important for them to be able to apply the rules of grammar, usage, and mechanics to their own drafts. Use the *What Do You Notice?* feature to help them see effective conventions in the work of professional writers. Encourage students to incorporate proper voice, tense, and syntax as they edit their own writing.

Read the opening sentence aloud. Remind students that subjects must agree with verbs and pronouns must agree with the words to which they refer. Provide students with a few examples.

WRITE GUY *Jeff Anderson, M. Ed.*

WHAT DO YOU NOTICE?

When students have read the Mentor Text, **say:** The first sentence begins with *it. It* is a pronoun. What does the pronoun *it* refer to in the first sentence? (a snake) Look at the second sentence. What is the subject of the second sentence? (it) Do the verbs in the second sentence agree with the subject? (**Possible response:** Yes. The subject is singular, and the *-s* endings on both verbs show that they are singular, too. The subject and verbs agree.)

Have students finish reading the page. **Ask:** How would the Mentor Text have to be changed if the subject of the first sentence and second sentence were *they* instead of *it*? (**Possible response:** The verbs *is, lies,* and *strikes* would have to be changed to plural forms, and *snake* in the first sentence would have to be changed to *snakes.* You might also want to change *trail, rat,* and *rabbit* to plural forms since different snakes would lie on different trails.)

Grammar for Writers: Syntax

Explain to students that writers choose verbs that match the subjects of their sentences. When students write, they should think about the number of each subject—whether the subject is singular, plural, or compound—when they choose a verb.

Lesson Objectives

1. Understand and recognize subject-verb agreement in sentences.
2. Identify, use, and understand the function of prepositions and prepositional phrases and their influence on subject-verb agreement.
3. Demonstrate subject-verb agreement in speaking and writing.

Singular and Plural Subjects

Tell students that the *number* of a noun, pronoun, or verb does not refer to a specific number. It means only *singular* or *plural.*

Discuss with students the importance of subject-verb agreement in their writing and speaking. Explain that the subject and verb in a sentence must agree in number.

RULE 23.1.1 Read aloud the rule and then have students repeat the lines with you.

Use a Think Aloud as part of a gradual release progression.

Say: In grammar, the concept of number is simple. Words can be either singular or plural. **I think** of the word *singular* as referring to a *single* one. A plural word refers to more than one item or idea. Only nouns, pronouns, and verbs have number. Most nouns are made plural by adding *-s* or *-es* to the singular form.

For example, if I read *dogs* in a sentence, I know it is plural because *-s* has been added to the singular form, *dog*. Some nouns have irregular plural forms. The plural form of *leaf*, for example, is *leaves*. If I am unsure about whether a word is singular or plural, or how to make a word plural, I can look it up in a dictionary.

Work with students to determine whether the nouns and pronouns in this group are singular or plural: *cats, cup, men, toys, girl, I, they, she, this*. Ask students to explain their thinking.

Have student pairs brainstorm for one sentence with a singular subject and one sentence with a plural subject. Invite partners to share their sentences with the group.

23.1 Subject-Verb Agreement

For a sentence to be correct, its subject and verb must match each other, or agree. Subject–verb agreement has one main rule.

Grammar Practice
Practice your grammar skills with Writing Coach Online.

Grammar Games
Test your knowledge of grammar in this fast-paced interactive video game.

The subject and verb in a sentence must agree in number.

In grammar, the concept of **number** is simple. The number of a word can be either **singular** or **plural.** A singular word indicates *one.* A plural word indicates *more than one.* In English, only nouns, pronouns, and verbs have number.

Singular and Plural Subjects

Most of the time, it is easy to tell whether a simple subject, such as a noun or pronoun, is singular or plural. That is because most nouns are made plural by adding *-s* or *-es* to their singular form.

EXAMPLES canyon canyon**s**
year year**s**
bus bus**es**
lunch lunch**es**

Some nouns form plurals in irregular ways.

EXAMPLES woman **women**
ox **oxen**
leaf **leaves**
knife **knives**

Pronouns also have different forms to indicate singular and plural. For example, the pronouns *I, he, she, it,* and *this* are singular. *We, they,* and *these* are plural. *You, who,* and *some* can be either singular or plural.

WRITING COACH Online
www.phwritingcoach.com

Diagnostic and Instruction
Diagnostic test assesses students' instructional needs. Lessons and practice are assigned based on results.

Additional Practice
- Grammar Practice—Targeted practice addresses individual needs.
- ExamView—Teachers customize their grammar practice and tests.
- Grammar Games—Interactive video games make grammar fun.

Singular and Plural Verbs

Like nouns, verbs have singular and plural forms. Problems involving number in verbs normally involve the third-person forms in the present tense (*she wants, they want*) and certain forms of the verb *be* (*I am, he is* or *was, we are* or *were*).

The chart shows all the basic forms of several different verbs in the present tense.

SINGULAR AND PLURAL VERBS IN THE PRESENT TENSE		
SINGULAR		PLURAL
First and Second Person	**Third Person**	**First, Second, and Third Person**
(I, you) send	(he, she, it) sends	(we, you, they) send
(I, you) go	(he, she, it) goes	(we, you, they) go
(I, you) look	(he, she, it) looks	(we, you, they) look
(I, you) dance	(he, she, it) dances	(we, you, they) dance
(I, you) visit	(he, she, it) visits	(we, you, they) visit
(I, you) work	(he, she, it) works	(we, you, they) work
(I, you) run	(he, she, it) runs	(we, you, they) run
(I, you) discuss	(he, she, it) discusses	(we, you, they) discuss
(I, you) vote	(he, she, it) votes	(we, you, they) vote
(I, you) choose	(he, she, it) chooses	(we, you, they) choose
(I, you) learn	(he, she, it) learns	(we, you, they) learn

Notice that the form of the verb changes only in the third-person singular, when an *-s* or *-es* is added to the verb. Unlike nouns, which usually become plural when *-s* or *-es* is added, verbs with *-s* or *-es* added to them are singular.

The helping verb *be* may also indicate whether a verb is singular or plural. The following chart shows only those forms of the verb *be* that are always singular.

FORMS OF THE HELPING VERB *BE* THAT ARE ALWAYS SINGULAR			
am	is	was	has been

Singular and Plural Verbs

Draw attention to the text describing singular and plural verbs. Point out that many problems distinguishing singular and plural verbs concern the third person forms.

Say: When I try to remember how to make subjects and verbs agree, I remind myself that they are usually opposite. If the subject has an *-s* or an *-es,* then the opposite is true of the verb. For example, in the sentence, *The foxes jump on the roof,* the word *foxes* has an *-es,* so I know the opposite must be true for the verb *jump.* It should not have an *-s.*

Have students pairs review the sentences they crafted with their partner for page 514. The sentences with singular subjects should also have singular verbs. Similarly, the sentences with plural subjects should have plural verbs. Have students use the chart on page 515 to confirm that they have used the correct verb forms.

If necessary, review the conjugation of linking verbs, page 317. Have student pairs write two additional sentences using the helping verb *to be.* One sentence should use a singular form of the verb and the other a plural.

Then, have students revise all the sentences that they wrote to make the singular subjects and verbs plural, and the plural subjects and verbs singular. Invite students to share their revised sentences with the group.

Working with ELLs — ELL Sheltered Instruction: Cognitive

Orally present the instruction on pages 514–515, and guide students to demonstrate comprehension of general meaning, main points, and important details in contexts ranging from familiar to unfamiliar. First, introduce singular and plural subjects and verbs in a familiar context—social life. A friend who says, "We will have fun," sounds friendly—plural *we* includes both friends. A friend who says, "I have to leave now" sounds less friendly—singular *I* includes only the speaker. Then, read aloud the grammar lesson. Finally, relate the discussion to an unfamiliar context: Linguistics compares languages with many verb forms to those with fewer, such as English.

Beginning Repeat portions of your presentation. Aid comprehension with the help of an English-proficient speaker of students' home language. Guide students in restating the general meaning, main points, and important details using sentence frames such as *Nouns and verbs have ____ and ____ forms. ____ means "just one." English has [many/few] verb forms.*

Intermediate Have groups complete sentence frames summarizing the general meaning, main points, and important details.

Advanced Have partners create an outline summarizing general meaning, main points, and important details.

Advanced High Have partners complete the Advanced activity and then write a brief comparison of verb forms in English and in their home language.

Teacher Tip

Sometimes, distinguishing plural nouns and verbs from singular nouns and verbs can be confusing for students. Plural nouns frequently end in *-s* or *-es*, while third person singular verbs often end in *-s* or *-es*. Have students write an example sentence on a notecard. For example, *A year passes; years pass. A bird flies; birds fly.* Students can remember this formula as an aid to distinguish plural nouns and verbs from singular nouns and verbs.

Making Verbs Agree With Singular and Plural Subjects

Explain that subject-verb agreement is determined by checking the number of the subject and making sure that the verb is in the same number.

Have students read aloud one of the sentences they crafted earlier for pages 514 and 515. Students should listen to the sentence and then state the number of the subject. They should then determine whether the verb has the same number.

RULE 23.1.2 Read aloud the rule and then have students repeat the lines with you.

Say: Sometimes, in a longer sentence it's possible to confuse the object of a prepositional phrase with the subject of the sentence. Consider this sentence: *The cheering of the boys create much noise.* What is the subject of this sentence? **(cheering)** What is the verb? **(create)** Is there subject-verb agreement? **(no)** What mistake do you think this writer made? **(Possible response:** The writer thought *boys* was the subject of the sentence. *Boys* is part of a prepositional phrase.) What advice would you give the writer for making a revision? **(Possible response:** Change the verb from a plural form to a singular form. Then, the subject and verb will agree.)

Making Verbs Agree With Singular and Plural Subjects

To check subject–verb agreement, determine the number of the subject. Then, make sure the verb has the same number.

SINGULAR SUBJECT AND VERB	**Jeff** **enjoys** swimming.
	She **was** at the park earlier today.
PLURAL SUBJECT AND VERB	**They** **enjoy** swimming.
	Joggers **were** at the park earlier today.

A prepositional phrase that comes between a subject and its verb does not affect subject–verb agreement.

Often, a subject is separated from its verb by a prepositional phrase. In these cases, it is important to remember that the object of a preposition is never the subject of a sentence.

INCORRECT	The **arrival** of the fire trucks **have caused** much excitement at the parade.
CORRECT	The **arrival** of the fire trucks **has caused** much excitement at the parade.
INCORRECT	The **cheers** of the crowd **was heard** outside.
CORRECT	The **cheers** of the crowd **were heard** outside.

See Practice 23.1A
See Practice 23.1B

In the first example, the subject is *arrival,* not *fire trucks* which is the object of the preposition *of.* Because *arrival* is singular, the singular verb *has caused* must be used. In the second example, the subject is the plural *cheers*, not *crowd*; therefore, it takes the plural verb *were heard*.

Working with ELLs — ELL Sheltered Instruction: Social/Affective

As students read page 516, provide support or have them use support from peers to enhance and confirm comprehension and to develop the vocabulary needed to comprehend increasingly challenging language.

Beginning Preteach these words from page 516: *check, agreement, number, enjoy(s), swimming, joggers,* and *park.* Then, read aloud the first part of the page (up to Rule 23.1.2) as students track in their textbooks. Review, and then guide students as they confirm comprehension by correctly completing this sentence frame: *I [enjoy/ enjoys] ______.*

Intermediate Preteach these words from page 516: *check, agreement, number, enjoy(s), separated, arrival, caused, excitement, parade,* and *cheers.* Review the concept of a prepositional phrase. Then, have students working in groups take turns reading the page aloud as others follow along. Have them discuss the lesson and then confirm understanding by presenting summaries to you.

Advanced Have partners read the page, noting unfamiliar words. Have them determine the meaning of each, consulting each other, a dictionary, and you as warranted. Then, have them reread the page and collaborate on a summary of the lesson.

Advanced High Have partners complete the Advanced activity. Then, have them use each new vocabulary word in a sentence.

PRACTICE 23.1A Making Subjects and Verbs Agree

Read the sentences. Write the verb in parentheses that agrees with the subject. Then, label the subject *singular, plural* or *both*. Be sure to think about prepositional phrases and their influence on subject-verb agreement.

EXAMPLE Usually, ducks (swim, swims) in this pond.

ANSWER *swim — plural*

1. You (was, were) early today!
2. Lisa (recognize, recognizes) the backpack as her own.
3. The computers in the lab (is, are) available for use.
4. Where (is, are) my keys?
5. One of these machines (is, are) not working.
6. My teeth (chatter, chatters) in the cold.
7. These boots (cost, costs) too much.
8. Some word problems in math (is, are) challenging.
9. There (is, are) twenty-five students in this room.
10. That bag of pretzels (is, are) not enough.

PRACTICE 23.1B Revising for Subject-Verb Agreement

Read the sentences. Then, if a sentence has an error in subject-verb agreement, rewrite the sentence correctly. Read your corrected sentences to your partner and have your partner confirm that the subject-verb agreement is correct. If a sentence has no error, write *correct*.

EXAMPLE Craters on the moon is visible through telescopes.

ANSWER *Craters on the moon are visible through telescopes.*

11. The pictures hanging on the wall is dusty.
12. Was you able to find what you needed?
13. Members of the committee are wearing nametags.
14. There's already five people waiting for the door to open.
15. The benches in the garden are wet.
16. The list of winners are posted on the bulletin board.
17. The decision of the judges is final.
18. Here is the groceries you wanted.
19. Where was the playoffs held?
20. One of the guides are able to help you.

SPEAKING APPLICATION

With a partner, take turns summarizing a story or book you read, using the present tense of the verbs and making sure the verbs agree with your subjects. Include a prepositional phrase in at least one of your sentences, and have your partner identify the phrase.

WRITING APPLICATION

Use sentences 4 and 5 as models, and write two sentences, making sure the verbs agree with the subjects. Be sure to think about prepositional phrases and their influence on subject-verb agreement.

PRACTICE 23.1A

1. were—both
2. recognizes—singular
3. are—plural
4. are—plural
5. is—singular
6. chatter—plural
7. cost—plural
8. are—plural
9. are—plural
10. is—singular

PRACTICE 23.1B

11. The pictures hanging on the wall are dusty.
12. Were you able to find what you needed?
13. correct
14. There are already five people waiting for the door to open.
15. correct
16. The list of winners is posted on the bulletin board.
17. correct
18. Here are the groceries you wanted.
19. Where were the playoffs held?
20. One of the guides is able to help you.

SPEAKING APPLICATION

Students should demonstrate they can understand the influence of prepositions and prepositional phrases on subject-verb agreement by confirming orally that the verbs in their sentences agree with the subjects of the sentences rather than the objects of prepositions.

WRITING APPLICATION

Have partners show that they understand the influence of prepositional phrases on subject-verb agreement by identifying the noun the verb agrees with, and verifying that the noun is not an object of the preposition in partners' sentences.

Making Verbs Agree With Collective Nouns

Point out to students that collective nouns name groups of people or things. Collective nouns can be tricky as subjects because they can take either singular or plural verbs. The number of the verb depends on the meaning of the collective noun in the sentence.

RULE 23.1.3 Read aloud the rule and then have students repeat the lines with you.

Use a Think Aloud as part of a gradual release progression.

Say: Sometimes, subject-verb agreement with collective nouns can be difficult because collective nouns can be used with either singular or plural verbs. **When I want to determine** what kind of verb to use with a collective noun, I think about whether the collective noun refers to the group as a whole or to individuals. For example, if I were thinking about this sentence, *The class has decided to organize an art show,* I would think to myself that *class* is a collective noun. In this sentence, the class as a single unit made a decision to organize an art show, so *class* would use a singular verb—*has decided.* Consider another sentence: *The class draw pictures for the show.* In this sentence, *class* refers to the individual members of the class. Each member of the class is drawing his or her own picture for the show. So in this second sentence the collective noun *class* uses a plural verb because the members of the class acted individually.

Work with students to brainstorm for several collective nouns. Write these words on the board. Then, ask students to describe situations in which the groups identified by the nouns might act together as a group, and separately as individuals.

Have student pairs write three sentences using the collective nouns the students listed. Invite students to read them aloud. Have students state whether the collective noun refers to a single unit or individual members, and explain their thinking.

Making Verbs Agree With Collective Nouns

Collective nouns—such as *assembly, audience, class, club,* and *committee*—name groups of people or things. Collective nouns are challenging as subjects because they can take either singular or plural verbs. The number of the verb depends on the meaning of the collective noun in the sentence.

Use a singular verb with a collective noun acting as a single unit. Use a plural verb when the individual members of the group are acting individually.

SINGULAR The **committee votes** on the topics.

PLURAL The **committee have split** the responsibilities.

SINGULAR The dance **class plans** a recital.

PLURAL The dance **class were pleased** with their individual performances.

SINGULAR The garden **club grows** vegetables and flowers.

PLURAL The garden **club have chosen** to plant their favorite vegetables and flowers.

SINGULAR The scout **troop marches** on Main Street.

PLURAL The scout **troop have prepared** different sandwiches for lunch.

SINGULAR The **team cheers** after the game.

PLURAL The **team scatter** across the playing field.

See Practice 23.1C
See Practice 23.1D

Teacher Tip

Making the distinction between singular and plural collective nouns can be difficult for students. Tell students that if they are having difficulty deciding whether a collective noun is singular or plural, they should ask themselves *Who or what is acting?* Is a group acting together as a unit, or are individuals who are part of a group acting separately? Explain that sometimes it can be helpful to talk with a partner in order to make this distinction.

Extension

To help students synthesize and apply what they have learned about making verbs agree with collective nouns, have students challenge each other to write sentences using collective nouns. Explain that the first student will call out a collective noun and either the word *singular* or the word *plural.* The other student will write a sentence that uses the noun, in the number indicated, as its subject. For example, if a student calls out "Committee, Singular," a student could answer, "The committee meets at four o'clock." Have students alternate calling words and writing sentences.

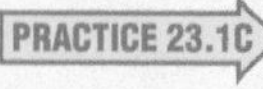

PRACTICE 23.1C **Making Verbs Agree With Collective Nouns**

Read the sentences. Then, write the verb in parentheses that agrees with the subject.

EXAMPLE The audience (is, are) waiting for the concert to begin.

ANSWER *is*

1. The team (arrive, arrives) separately before the game.
2. Our family (try, tries) to eat dinner together every evening.
3. A flock of geese (land, lands) near the river every day.
4. The jury (find, finds) the defendant guilty.
5. The board of directors (don't, doesn't) always agree among themselves.
6. The computer club (discuss, discusses) new applications.
7. A group of older kids (hang, hangs) out in the pizza parlor.
8. The army (need, needs) more volunteers.
9. The flight crew (is, are) attentive to the passengers.
10. The choir (sing, sings) every Sunday.

PRACTICE 23.1D **Revising for Agreement Between Verbs and Collective Nouns**

Read the sentences. Then, if a sentence has an error in subject-verb agreement, rewrite the sentence correctly. If a sentence has no error, write *correct*.

EXAMPLE The orchestra give a free concert every year.

ANSWER *The orchestra gives a free concert every year.*

11. The herd are waiting to be fed.
12. This bunch of radishes look wilted.
13. The navy sail around the world.
14. The faculty has a meeting at 2:30 P.M.
15. The band are rehearsing in separate rooms.
16. The crowd are eager for the candidate to appear.
17. At summer camp, the scout troop learns survival skills.
18. The staff at the fitness center are very helpful.
19. The committee don't always follow the agenda at meetings.
20. The cheerleading squad practices twice a week.

SPEAKING APPLICATION

With a partner, tell about the activities of a group you belong to or know about. Use at least two collective nouns, such as *group*, *team*, and *club*, as subjects in your sentences, and be sure your verbs agree.

WRITING APPLICATION

Write three sentences in the present tense, using these collective nouns as subjects: *crew*, *band*, and *crowd*.

PRACTICE 23.1C

1. arrive
2. tries
3. lands
4. finds
5. don't
6. discusses
7. hangs
8. needs
9. are
10. sings

PRACTICE 23.1D

11. The herd is waiting to be fed.
12. This bunch of radishes looks wilted.
13. The navy sails around the world.
14. correct
15. correct
16. The crowd is eager for the candidate to appear.
17. At summer camp, the scout troop learn survival skills.
18. correct
19. The committee doesn't always follow the agenda at meetings.
20. correct

SPEAKING APPLICATION

Have partners explain why their subject-verb agreement is correct.

WRITING APPLICATION

Students should explain why they used singular or plural verbs in their sentences.

Working with ELLs

ELL Sheltered Instruction: Cognitive

Help students develop basic sight vocabulary used routinely in written classroom materials. Write these words from the directions on page 519 on the board: *use, about,* and *tell.*

Beginning Read each basic sight word aloud as students follow along. Reread, and have students echo you. Reinforce meaning by writing each word in a simple sentence on the board, such as *Cars use gas. I tell a story. The story is about a man and a dog.* Then, read the sentences in which the words appear on the student page as students follow along. Explain the meaning of the directions.

Intermediate Read the words chorally with students. Guide students in defining or explaining them. Then, have students chorally read the sentences in which the words appear on the student page. Clarify meaning as necessary.

Advanced Have partners read the directions on page 519, locating the basic sight words. Have them write original sentences using the words and then read each other's sentences aloud. Then, have them repeat the activity for these routine words from the directions: *correct, error,* and *rewrite.*

Advanced High Have students complete the Advanced activity. Then, have them write explanations of each word in the activity.

Making Verbs Agree With Compound Subjects

Remind the class that compound subjects refer to two or more subjects that share a verb.

Say: A compound subject refers to two or more subjects that share a verb. Look at the first example sentence at the top of the page. What is the subject? **(museums and historical sites)** Notice the word *and*. Compound subjects are connected by conjunctions such as *and*, *or*, and *nor*.

Guide students in understanding how to make verbs agree with compound subjects. **Say:** Look at the example sentences. What are some differences between the three sentences? **(Possible response:** The compound subjects are joined by different conjunctions. Some compound subjects use a plural verb, while others use a singular verb.) **Ask:** Is there a difference between what verb form is used depending upon which conjunction is used? **(Possible response:** Yes, the verbs in the sentences with *or* and *nor* are singular. The verb in the sentence with *and* is plural.)

Have students write three sentences that have a compound subject.

Compound Subjects Joined by *And*

Explain that when compound subjects are connected by *and*, the verb that follows is usually plural.

RULE 23.1.4 Read aloud the rule and then have students repeat the lines with you.

Point out the exception to this rule at the bottom of the page.

Have student pairs brainstorm for and write three compound subjects connected by *and*. Have them use one of these compound subjects in a sentence using a plural verb. Ask students to share their sentences with the class.

Making Verbs Agree With Compound Subjects

A **compound subject** refers to two or more subjects that share a verb. Compound subjects are connected by conjunctions such as *and, or,* or *nor.*

EXAMPLES The **museums** and **historical sites** (compound subject) in New York City **attract** (plural verb) many visitors.

Either **Jamal** or **Catherine** (compound subject) **knows** (singular verb) the way to the train station.

Neither the **Statue of Liberty** nor **Ellis Island** (compound subject) **disappoints** (singular verb) tourists.

A number of rules can help you choose the right verb to use with a compound subject.

Compound Subjects Joined by *And*

When a compound subject is connected by *and*, the verb that follows is usually plural.

EXAMPLE **Dallas** and **Houston** (compound subject) **are** (plural verb) my favorite Texas cities.

There is an exception to this rule: If the parts of a compound subject are thought of as one person or thing, the subject is singular and takes a singular verb.

EXAMPLES **Bacon and eggs** (compound subject) **is** (singular verb) my favorite breakfast.

Cream and sugar (compound subject) **is** (singular verb) in the kitchen.

Compound Subjects Joined by *Or* or *Nor*

When two singular subjects are joined by *or* or *nor*, use a singular verb. When two plural subjects are joined by *or* or *nor*, use a plural verb.

RULE 23.1.5

SINGULAR — A **bus** or a **subway** (compound subject) **provides** (singular verb) good transportation to the city.

PLURAL — Neither **children** nor **adults** (compound subject) **like** (plural verb) to be told what to do.

In the first example, *or* joins two singular subjects. Although two vehicles make up the compound subject, the subject does not take a plural verb. Either a bus or a subway provides good transportation, not both of them.

When a compound subject is made up of one singular and one plural subject joined by *or* or *nor*, the verb agrees with the subject closer to it.

RULE 23.1.6

EXAMPLES — Either the **monuments** (plural subject) or the **White House** (singular subject) **is** (singular verb) closed to visitors today.

Either the **White House** (singular subject) or the **monuments** (plural subject) **are** (plural verb) closed to visitors today.

See Practice 23.1E

Agreement in Inverted Sentences

In most sentences, the subject comes before the verb. Sometimes, however, this order is turned around, or **inverted.** In other sentences, the helping verb comes before the subject even though the main verb follows the subject.

Compound Subjects Joined by *Or* or *Nor*

Explain that when two singular subjects are connected by *or* or *nor*, the verb that follows is usually singular. When two plural subjects are joined by *or* or *nor*, the verb that follows is usually plural. Explain the logic of this rule by pointing out that, in the first example sentence on page 521, only one of the subjects in the sentence provides good transportation. Therefore, the verb should be singular.

RULE 23.1.5 Read aloud the rule and then have students repeat the lines with you.

Have student pairs brainstorm for several singular and plural subjects joined by *or* and several singular and plural subjects joined by *nor*. Partners should then use these compound subjects in sentences. Ask students to share their sentences with the class. Students listening should say whether the two subjects are singular or plural.

RULE 23.1.6 Read aloud the rule and then have students repeat the lines with you.

Explain to students that when a compound subject is made up of one singular and one plural subject joined by *or* or *nor*, the verb agrees with the subject closer to it.

Draw students' attention to the examples on page 521. Have students create and say aloud a sentence with a compound subject made up of one singular and one plural noun joined by *or*. Then, ask another student to reverse the position of the singular and plural nouns and say the new sentence correctly.

Agreement in Inverted Sentences

Remind students that an inverted sentence is one in which the verb comes before the subject. Also, verb phrases are sometimes split up so that a helping verb comes before a subject and the main verb comes after the subject.

(continued)

Differentiated Instruction

RTI Strategy for Below-Level Students Students may have difficulty remembering the different rules regulating the use of compound subjects. Have students create a two-column compound subject chart. Explain that they should list the different rules they have learned about compound subjects and verbs in the left column. In the right column, they should illustrate their chart with example sentences and drawings. Encourage students to keep their charts handy and use them as needed.

PRE-AP Enrichment for Above-Level Students Tell students that they should imagine themselves as language mentors for new students. Their job is to create a role play explaining the different rules affecting the agreement between compound subjects and verbs. Encourage students to be creative, have fun, and be informative in their role plays.

Agreement in Inverted Sentences *(continued)*

RULE 23.1.7 Read aloud the rule and then have students repeat the lines with you.

Use a Think Aloud as part of a gradual release progression.

Say: In English we are used to seeing and hearing the subject come before the verb. But not all sentences follow this pattern. Sometimes, sentences are inverted. The verb comes before the subject. Look at the sentence at the top of page 522. The verb *do* comes before the subject *sites*. Questions often have inverted order. Also, sentences beginning with a prepositional phrase or the words *there* or *here* are often in inverted order.

To determine the subject of an inverted sentence, **I change** the order of the sentence so that it is not inverted, then look for the word or words that perform the verb. For example, I might change the first example sentence to *The historical sites in Philadelphia do sound exciting to you.* Then, I look for the nouns that sound exciting. That noun is *sites,* so *sites* must be the subject. Regardless of whether the subject comes before or after the verb, the subject and verb must *always* agree in number. This is a rule that doesn't change.

Write this sentence on the board: *Along both sides of the streets were parked cars.* **Work with students** to find the subject and verb and evaluate subject-verb agreement. Repeat the activity, using as examples a question and a sentence beginning with *there* or *here*.

Have student pairs create examples of inverted sentences. Direct them to begin one sentence with a prepositional phrase, one sentence with *there* or *here*, and one with a question. Invite pairs to read their sentences aloud. Challenge students to identify the subject of each sentence and state whether the subject and verb agree.

When a subject comes after the verb, the subject and verb still must agree with each other in number.

EXAMPLE **Do** (plural verb) the historical **sites** (plural subject) in Philadelphia sound exciting to you?

Sentences Beginning With a Prepositional Phrase

In sentences that begin with a prepositional phrase, the object of the preposition may look like a subject, even though it is not.

EXAMPLE Along the shore **were** (plural verb) many gray **seagulls** (plural subject).

In this example, the plural verb *were* agrees with the plural subject *seagulls.* The singular noun *shore* is the object of the preposition *along.*

Sentences Beginning With *There* or *Here*

Sentences beginning with *there* or *here* are almost always in inverted word order.

EXAMPLES There **were** (plural verb) several **books** (plural subject) about the economy.

Here **is** (singular verb) the latest **book** (singular subject) about the economy.

The contractions *there's* and *here's* both contain the singular verb *is*: *there is* and *here is.* Do not use these contractions as plural subjects.

INCORRECT Here**'s** the **books** for the library.

CORRECT Here **are** the **books** for the library.

Questions With Inverted Word Order

Many questions are also written in inverted word order.

EXAMPLE Where **are** (plural verb) the **books** (plural subject) for the library?

See Practice 23.1F

Quick-Write Extension

To help students synthesize and apply what they have learned about subject-verb agreement, challenge students to use compound subjects of different types in inverted sentences. Have students work in small groups, and direct the groups to list at least five compound subjects, such as *a letter and a package, Mara and James,* and so on. Then, direct groups to use each compound subject in a sentence that begins with *here* or *there* and in an inverted-order question. Call for volunteers to read their sentences to the class, and check the subject-verb agreement in each.

PRACTICE 23.1E Making Verbs Agree With Compound Subjects

Read the sentences. Then, write the verb in parentheses that agrees with the subject.

EXAMPLE A book and an apple (is, are) lying on the table.

ANSWER *are*

1. Either Dad or Mom (make, makes) breakfast every morning.
2. English and math (is, are) my favorite subjects.
3. Neither the baseball bats nor the gloves (was, were) put away.
4. Sarah or her sister (take, takes) the dog for a walk every day.
5. The book and papers (stay, stays) in the locker.
6. Neither the jacket nor the shoes (fit, fits) well.
7. Carrie, Gillian, or Hugh (write, writes) the blog each day.
8. Mrs. Carter and her daughters often (dress, dresses) alike.
9. The chairs and the table (has, have) not been moved in yet.
10. E-mail and text messaging (make, makes) communication almost instantaneous.

PRACTICE 23.1F Revising for Agreement Between Verbs and Compound Subjects

Read the sentences. Then, if a sentence has an error in subject-verb agreement, rewrite the sentence correctly. If a sentence has no error, write *correct*.

EXAMPLE Neither Billy nor John have arrived yet.

ANSWER *Neither Billy nor John has arrived yet.*

11. Joe and Ted always comes early.
12. Either Jake or Sophia collects the papers today.
13. Jeff or the dog have tracked mud onto the floor.
14. Milk or lemon is used with tea.
15. Either my watch or that clock are fast.
16. In the center of the park is a playground and a basketball court.
17. Either Regina or Zoe own that scarf.
18. Neither the plumber nor the electrician is here.
19. Eva's positive outlook and her willingness to help wins her many friends.
20. That old barn and farmhouse seems deserted.

SPEAKING APPLICATION

With a partner, take turns discussing things in the classroom, using sentence 3 as a model. Your partner should check for subject-verb agreement in your sentences.

WRITING APPLICATION

Use sentences 17, 18, and 19 as models, and write three sentences with correct subject-verb agreement.

PRACTICE 23.1E

1. makes
2. are
3. were
4. takes
5. stay
6. fit
7. writes
8. dress
9. have
10. make

PRACTICE 23.1F

11. Joe and Ted always come early.
12. correct
13. Jeff or the dog has tracked mud onto the floor.
14. correct
15. Either my watch or that clock is fast.
16. In the center of the park are a playground and a basketball court.
17. Either Regina or Zoe owns that scarf.
18. correct
19. Eva's positive outlook and her willingness to help win her many friends.
20. That old barn and farmhouse seem deserted.

SPEAKING APPLICATION

Students should justify their choice of singular or plural verbs to agree with their compound subjects.

WRITING APPLICATION

Students' writing should demonstrate that students can compose sentences in which verbs agree with compound subjects.

Working with ELLs

ELL Sheltered Instruction: Cognitive

Using the Practice activities, have students use visual and contextual support as they read to enhance and confirm their understanding of grade-appropriate content-area text and to develop the grasp of language structures needed to comprehend increasingly challenging language.

Beginning Read the corrected version of Item 3 as students follow along. On the board, draw a picture of a baseball bat and a picture of a glove. Use these drawings as visual and contextual support to help students enhance and confirm their understanding of compound subjects.

Intermediate Have students read the corrected version of Item 7 chorally. (Guide them in the pronunciation of names.) Then, coach them to use context to determine what nouns are included in the compound subject: Because the verb is *writes*, the subject must consist of writers, such as the people named.

Advanced Have partners read completed Item 10. Then, have them discuss how they used the context of the sentence to determine if the compound subject was singular or plural.

Advanced High Have students complete the Advanced activity. Then, have them help less fluent students complete the practice by creating illustrations for them to use as visual and contextual support.

Verb Agreement With Indefinite Pronouns

Discuss the fact that indefinite pronouns refer to people, places, or things in a general way. When indefinite pronouns are the subject of a sentence, the verb must agree in number with the pronoun.

RULE 23.1.8 Read aloud the rule and then have students repeat the lines with you.

Say: Consider these sentences: *Everyone has a textbook. Many have textbooks.* What are the verbs in these sentences? **(has, have)** What are the subjects? **(everyone, many)** What kinds of words are *everyone* and *many*? **(singular indefinite pronoun, plural indefinite pronoun)**

Say: When an indefinite pronoun is the subject of a sentence, the verb must agree with the pronoun in number.

Indefinite Pronouns That Are Always Singular

Draw attention to the text stating that some indefinite pronouns are always singular. Help students understand why these indefinite pronouns are singular by pointing out that *body, one,* and *thing* are all singular nouns; therefore, the indefinite pronouns that contain those singular nouns should also be singular.

Have student pairs make sentences using one of the singular indefinite pronouns from the chart on page 524 as the subject of the sentences. Tell students to make sure they use a singular verb to match their singular indefinite pronouns. Invite partners to read their sentences aloud. Ask students whether the subject and verb agree.

Teacher Tip

If identifying indefinite pronouns is difficult for students, explain that they can ask themselves three questions: 1. Does this word refer to people in a general way instead of a specific person or specific people? 2. Does this word refer to a place in a general way? 3. Does this word refer to a thing in a general way? If the answer is yes to one of those questions, then the word is an indefinite pronoun.

Verb Agreement With Indefinite Pronouns

Indefinite pronouns refer to people, places, or things in a general way.

When an indefinite pronoun is the subject of a sentence, the verb must agree in number with the pronoun.

INDEFINITE PRONOUNS				
SINGULAR			PLURAL	SINGULAR OR PLURAL
anybody	everyone	nothing	both	all
anyone	everything	one	few	any
anything	much	other	many	more
each	neither	somebody	several	most
either	nobody	someone	others	none
everybody	no one	something		some

Indefinite Pronouns That Are Always Singular
Indefinite pronouns that are always singular take singular verbs. Do not be misled by a prepositional phrase that follows an indefinite pronoun. The singular verb agrees with the indefinite pronoun, not with the object of the preposition.

EXAMPLES

Each (singular subject) of the soccer team uniforms **is** (singular verb) red and gold.

Either (singular subject) of the sweaters on the bed **is** (singular verb) warm.

Everyone (singular subject) in the theater **was** (singular verb) delighted by the play.

Each (singular subject) of the boys **takes** (singular verb) guitar lessons.

Quick-Write Extension

To help students synthesize and apply what they have learned about verb agreement with indefinite pronouns, have students write brief news reports describing a crowd of people at a sporting event. Direct students to use indefinite pronouns to tell how the parts of the crowd are alike and different in behavior, clothing, ages, attitudes, and so forth. Ask students to exchange their reports to check subject-verb agreement.

Indefinite Pronouns That Are Always Plural

Indefinite pronouns that are always plural are used with plural verbs.

EXAMPLE **Both** of my sisters **are going** to the concert.
plural subject — plural verb

Many of my friends **are coming** to cheer for me at my first track meet.
plural subject — plural verb

Several **have started** to research their reports.
plural subject — plural verb

Few **are happy** with the new uniforms.
plural subject — plural verb

Indefinite Pronouns That May Be Either Singular or Plural

Many indefinite pronouns can take either a singular or a plural verb.

The number of the indefinite pronoun is the same as the number of its referent, or the noun to which it refers.

RULE 23.1.9

The indefinite pronoun is singular if the referent is singular. If the referent is plural, the indefinite pronoun is plural.

SINGULAR **Some** of the **juice** **is** frozen.

PLURAL **Some** of the **oranges** **are** frozen, too.

In the examples above, *some* is singular when it refers to *juice*, but plural when it refers to *oranges*.

SINGULAR **All** of my **spaghetti** **is** gone.

PLURAL **All** of these **meatballs** **are** for you.

See Practice 23.1G
See Practice 23.1H

In these examples, *all* is singular when it refers to *spaghetti*, but plural when it refers to *meatballs*.

Indefinite Pronouns That Are Always Plural

Draw attention to the text stating that *both, many, several,* and *few* are indefinite pronouns that are always plural. Have students review these pronouns in the chart on page 524. When these words are used as pronouns, they always take a plural verb. Remind students that these words can also be used as adjectives. When they are used as adjectives, the nouns they modify are always plural. Point out the second example sentence on page 525. Work with students to turn the indefinite pronoun in the sentence into an indefinite adjective by removing the words *of my*.

Have student pairs revise the sentences, they created on page 524 so that they use a plural indefinite pronoun. Invite pairs to read their sentences aloud. Ask students whether the subject and verb agree.

Indefinite Pronouns That May Be Either Singular or Plural

Explain that some indefinite pronouns can take either a singular or a plural verb. To determine whether an indefinite pronoun requires a singular or plural verb, look at the word to which the pronoun refers. If that word is plural, then the pronoun is plural. If the word is singular, then the pronoun requires a singular verb.

RULE 23.1.9 Read aloud the rule and then have students repeat the lines with you.

Review the list of indefinite pronouns that may be singular or plural, on page 524. Then, have student pairs write two sentences using those indefinite pronouns. Have partners read their sentences aloud. Ask students if the subjects and verbs agree.

Differentiated Instruction

RTI Strategy for Special Needs Students
Students may have difficulty understanding the difference in number between singular and plural indefinite pronouns. Model these sentences using common classroom items: *There are many paperclips in the box. One pencil is long. Several pencils are short. Some of the students are boys.* As students repeat the sentences, have them gesture or refer to the appropriate items. **Ask:** *Is this a single item or more than one?*

Teacher Tip

Some students may have difficulty remembering the number of indefinite pronouns. To help students, provide them with a Venn diagram with the large circles labeled *Singular* and *Plural* and the center section labeled *Singular or Plural.* Work with students to fill in the Venn diagram with indefinite pronouns. Encourage students to refer to their diagrams as they complete exercises using indefinite pronouns.

PRACTICE 23.1G

1. wants
2. are
3. sing
4. is
5. is
6. are
7. have
8. answers
9. has
10. requires

PRACTICE 23.1H

11. Several of the batteries have to be replaced.
12. Nobody likes to be on the losing side.
13. Either is a good title for your story.
14. correct
15. correct
16. All of the grapes have been eaten.
17. A few of my friends go to a different school.
18. Most of the jewelry on display was quite expensive.
19. correct
20. correct

SPEAKING APPLICATION

Have partners explain how they know whether the verbs agree with the subjects of their sentences.

WRITING APPLICATION

Have students share their sentences with a partner. Have partners confirm that the subject-verb agreement is correct.

PRACTICE 23.1G Making Verbs Agree With Indefinite Pronouns

Read the sentences. Then, write the verb in parentheses that agrees with the subject.

EXAMPLE Each of the students (was, were) eager to begin.

ANSWER *was*

1. Nobody (want, wants) to take responsibility.
2. Some of these sandwiches (is, are) vegetarian.
3. Both of my sisters (sing, sings) in the chorus.
4. Everyone in the class (is, are) present today.
5. Anyone (is, are) able to solve that problem.
6. All of the computers (is, are) being used right now.
7. Many of the contestants (has, have) excellent qualifications.
8. If someone (answer, answers) the ad, let me know.
9. Most of the money (has, have) been spent.
10. Neither of the jobs (require, requires) much experience.

PRACTICE 23.1H Revising for Agreement Between Verbs and Indefinite Pronouns

Read the sentences. Then, if a sentence has an error in subject-verb agreement, rewrite the sentence correctly. If a sentence has no error, write *correct*.

EXAMPLE Neither were willing to concede defeat.

ANSWER *Neither was willing to concede defeat.*

11. Several of the batteries has to be replaced.
12. Nobody like to be on the losing side.
13. Either are a good title for your story.
14. Many of these used books are in good condition.
15. Some of these poems are pretty good.
16. All of the grapes has been eaten.
17. A few of my friends goes to a different school.
18. Most of the jewelry on display were quite expensive.
19. None of these games are much fun.
20. Any of your drawings are good enough to be exhibited.

SPEAKING APPLICATION

With a partner, tell about something in your class, using sentence 4 as a model. Your partner should listen for and confirm that your verb agrees with your subject.

WRITING APPLICATION

Use sentences 10, 13, and 19 as models, and write three sentences of your own with correct subject-verb agreement.

Working with ELLs — ELL Sheltered Instruction: Cognitive

Using the Practice items, help students learn the relationships between English sounds and letters and practice decoding words using a combination of skills.

Beginning Write *take* on the board (item 1). Review the sounds commonly represented by *t* and *k*. Point out the silent *-e*, and explain that it indicates that the *a* is long. Model the long *a* sound and have students echo. Then, lead students in decoding the word.

Intermediate Write *concede* on the board (Practice 23.1H, Example). Guide students in identifying and pronouncing the prefix *con-*. Then, review the sound *c* often makes before *e* (/s/). Guide students in decoding the word. Discuss its meaning.

Advanced Point out the word *vegetarian* (item 2). Review the sound represented by *g* followed by *e* (/j/), and guide students in identifying the suffix *-ian*. Then, prompt students to sound out the word. If students have difficulty, ask them what word would make sense in context.

Advanced High Have partners collaborate in decoding the words *chorus* (item 3), *qualifications* (item 7), *jewelry* (item 18), and *exhibited* (item 20). Provide assistance as needed. Have them contrast the sound of *ch* in *chorus* with its sound in *child*.

23.2 Agreement Between Pronouns and Antecedents

An **antecedent** is the word or words for which a pronoun stands. A pronoun's antecedent may be a noun, a group of words acting as a noun, or even another pronoun. As with subjects and verbs, pronouns should agree with their antecedents.

Grammar Game Plan

www.phwritingcoach.com

Grammar Practice
Practice your grammar skills with Writing Coach Online.

Grammar Games
Test your knowledge of grammar in this fast-paced interactive video game.

Making Personal Pronouns and Antecedents Agree

Person tells whether a pronoun refers to the person speaking (first person), the person spoken to (second person), or the person, place, or thing spoken about (third person). **Number** tells whether the pronoun is singular or plural. **Gender** tells whether a third-person-singular antecedent is masculine or feminine.

A personal pronoun must agree with its antecedent in person, number, and gender. RULE 23.2.1

EXAMPLE I told **Betsy** to bring a sweater with **her**.

In this example, the pronoun *her* is third person and singular. It agrees with its feminine antecedent, *Betsy.*

Avoiding Shifts in Person

A personal pronoun must have the same person as its antecedent. Otherwise, the meaning of the sentence is unclear.

INCORRECT The **drivers** know **we** must check the speed limit on local streets.
(Who must check the speed limit? *We* must.)

CORRECT The **drivers** know **they** must check the speed limit on local streets.
(Who must check the speed limit? *The drivers* must.)

As you can see, a shift in the person of the personal pronoun can make it unclear who is going to check the speed limit.

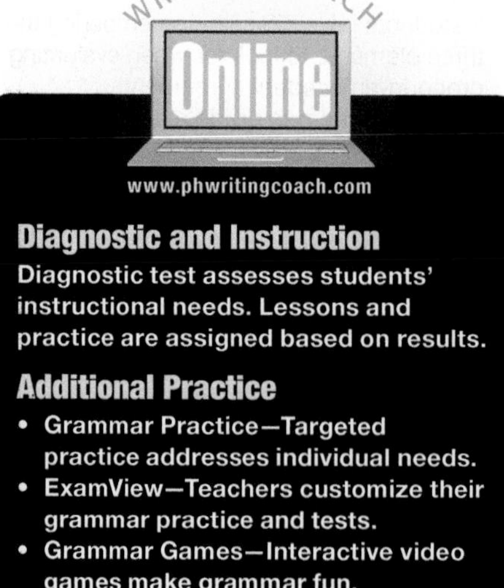

www.phwritingcoach.com

Diagnostic and Instruction
Diagnostic test assesses students' instructional needs. Lessons and practice are assigned based on results.

Additional Practice
- Grammar Practice—Targeted practice addresses individual needs.
- ExamView—Teachers customize their grammar practice and tests.
- Grammar Games—Interactive video games make grammar fun.

Lesson Objectives

1. Define and identify antecedents.
2. Maintain agreement between antecedents and pronouns in sentences.
3. Use a variety of complete sentences (e.g., simple, compound, complex) that include correctly identified antecedents.

Making Personal Pronouns and Antecedents Agree

Help students understand the meaning and function of antecedents. Tell them that an antecedent is a word for which a pronoun stands. For example, in the sentence *When Angie called, I gave her the news,* the word *her* stands for *Angie.* So *Angie* is the antecedent of *her.* Pronouns must agree with their antecedents in person, number, and gender. Disagreement between an antecedent and a pronoun makes writing very confusing.

RULE 23.2.1 Read aloud the rule and then have students repeat the lines with you.

Avoiding Shifts in Person

Direct attention to the text warning against shifts in person. Discuss how shifts in person change the meanings of sentences.

Write this sentence on the board: *Aggie and Joe gave their dog a present.*

Work with students to analyze the use of the pronoun *their.* (The dog belongs to Aggie and Joe, so it is their dog.) Discuss how a shift in person of the personal pronoun would change the meaning of the sentence.

Avoiding Problems With Number and Gender

Draw students' attention to the text, explaining how problems with number and gender arise with collective nouns, compound nouns, and unknown antecedents.

Making Pronouns Agree in Number With Collective Nouns

Explain that collective nouns can take either singular or plural pronouns. The number of the pronoun depends on the meaning of the collective noun in the sentence.

RULE 23.2.2 Read aloud the rule and then have students repeat the lines with you.

On the board, write these two sentences: *The team played its last game on Friday. The team played badly because they did not communicate well.* Refer students to each sentence and ask whether the team is acting as one unit or as many individuals. Then, point out the pronoun in each sentence.

Have student pairs write one sentence with a singular pronoun referring to a collective noun and one sentence with a plural pronoun referring to a collective noun. Invite students to read their sentences aloud. Have student volunteers explain why the pronoun and noun agree (or don't agree).

Making Pronouns Agree in Number With Compound Nouns

Say: Gabe, Letrice, or Jose won. How many people won? (**Response:** only one) Explain that, when a subject consists of two or more singular nouns joined by *or* or *nor,* a pronoun that refers to the subject is referring to only one of the nouns. Therefore, the subject must have a singular pronoun, just as it must have a singular verb.

RULE 23.2.3 Read aloud the rule and then have students repeat the lines with you.

Have student pairs write one sentence using a compound noun joined by *or* or *nor* and one sentence with a compound noun joined by *and.* Both sentences should use a pronoun. Invite students to read their sentences aloud. Ask if the pronoun and antecedent agree.

Avoiding Problems With Number and Gender

Making pronouns and antecedents agree in number and gender can be difficult. Problems may arise when the antecedent is a collective noun, when the antecedent is a compound joined by *or* or *nor,* or when the gender of the antecedent is not known.

Making Pronouns Agree in Number With Collective Nouns

Collective nouns are challenging because they can take either singular or plural pronouns. The number of the pronoun depends on the meaning of the collective noun in the sentence.

Use a singular pronoun to refer to a collective noun that names a group that is acting as a single unit. Use a plural pronoun to refer to a collective noun when the members or parts of a group are acting individually.

SINGULAR The **class** **showed** **its** appreciation with applause.

PLURAL The **class** **voted** for **their** favorite books.

In the first example above, the class is acting as a single unit when it applauds, so the singular pronoun, *its,* refers to *class.* In the second example, each member of the class is voting individually, so the plural pronoun, *their,* refers to *class.*

Making Pronouns Agree in Number With Compound Nouns

Use a singular personal pronoun to refer to two or more singular antecedents joined by *or* or *nor.* Use a plural pronoun with two or more singular antecedents joined by *and.*

Two or more singular antecedents joined by *or* or *nor* must have a singular pronoun, just as they must have a singular verb.

INCORRECT **Andrew** or **Jeff** will take **their** basketball.

CORRECT **Andrew** or **Jeff** will take **his** basketball.

CORRECT **Andrew** and **Jeff** will take **their** basketballs.

Teacher Tip

If students have difficulty remembering the three elements to look for when evaluating pronoun-antecedent agreement, encourage them to divide a sheet of paper into three equal areas. They should label one area *person*, the second area *number*, and the third area *gender*. Have students write a brief definition of each term in their own words and then provide example sentences. Instead of writing their own examples, they might find examples in books, magazines, or Web sites.

Avoiding Problems With Gender

When the gender of a third-person-singular antecedent is not known, you can make the pronoun agree with its antecedent in one of three ways:

(1) Use *he or she, him or her,* or *his or hers.*

(2) Rewrite the sentence so that the antecedent and pronoun are both plural.

(3) Rewrite the sentence to eliminate the pronoun.

Traditionally, the masculine pronouns *he* and *his* have been used to stand for both males and females. Today, using *he or she* and *him or her* is preferred. If any of these corrections seem awkward to you, rewrite the sentence.

Making Personal Pronouns and Indefinite Pronouns Agree

Indefinite pronouns are words such as *each, everybody, either,* and *one.* Pay special attention to the number of a personal pronoun when the antecedent is a singular indefinite pronoun.

Use a singular personal pronoun when its antecedent is a singular indefinite pronoun.

23.2.4 RULE

Do not be misled by a prepositional phrase that follows an indefinite pronoun. The personal pronoun agrees with the indefinite pronoun, not with the object of the preposition.

INCORRECT **One** of the dogs has lost **their** bone.

CORRECT **One** of the dogs has lost **its** bone.

INCORRECT **Everyone** in the history class wanted to tell about **their** idea.

CORRECT **Everyone** in the history class wanted to tell about **his or her** idea.

CORRECT **All** of the students in the history class told about **their** ideas.

See Practice 23.2A
See Practice 23.2B
See Practice 23.2C
See Practice 23.2D

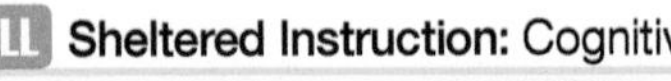

Working with ELLs — ELL Sheltered Instruction: Cognitive

As students read the section on indefinite pronouns on page 529, have them demonstrate comprehension by employing basic reading skills. Expand their skills with strategies for recording and analyzing main ideas and details.

Beginning Read the first example sentence as students follow along. Use visuals to ensure comprehension. Explain the difference between the correct and incorrect versions. Then, offer a paraphrase of the rule, such as "How many? One needs one." Have them record your paraphrase as the main idea and the examples as details in a main idea and details chart.

Intermediate Guide students as they read the example sentences aloud. Discuss the concept they illustrate. Then, read aloud the text in the green box as students follow along. Explain terms, referring to the examples. Finally, have students work in groups to record the main idea and details in a chart.

Advanced Have partners read the section and discuss its meaning. Then, have them paraphrase the main idea and list supporting details in an outline.

Advanced High Have students read the section and record main ideas and details on cards. Have them compare results with a partner's. Then, have them explain the connection between the details and the main idea. (Details support the main idea.)

Avoiding Problems With Gender

Discuss with students how to avoid problems with gender using the three strategies listed.

Write this sentence on the board: *An author takes great pride in his writing.* Have students revise the sentence using one of the strategies.

Making Personal Pronouns and Indefinite Pronouns Agree

Remind students to pay special attention to the number of a personal pronoun when the antecedent is a singular indefinite pronoun.

RULE 23.2.4 Read aloud the rule and then have students repeat the lines with you.

Say: Indefinite pronouns are words such as *each, everybody, either,* and *one.* Indefinite pronouns are no different from any other kind of pronoun. I need to use a singular personal pronoun when its antecedent is a singular indefinite pronoun.

Work with students to review the example sentences at the bottom of page 529. Have students explain why the incorrect examples are incorrect.

Have student pairs use a variety of complete sentences (e.g., simple, compound, complex) that include correctly identified antecedents. Instruct partners to write six sentences—two simple, two compound, and two complex. Students should include indefinite pronouns in at least two of their sentences. Invite students to share their sentences with the group. Have students draw an arrow from each pronoun to its antecedent and check for pronoun-antecedent agreement.

PRACTICE 23.2A

1. Alex lent us his car that was about to run out of gas.
2. Erin wanted us to meet her friend, who is about to enter our class.
3. After the movie ended, everyone told his or her impressions.
4. No one wanted to give up his or her Saturday, so we rescheduled the meeting.
5. *The* kitten curled up its little body and slept in front of the fire.
6. I lost her CD, so I had to buy her a replacement.
7. Since it stopped raining, we can ride our bikes.
8. Laslo offered to help, but the team preferred to work on its own.
9. Did you forget to bring me my scarf?
10. The students know they must study, and they form their own study groups.

PRACTICE 23.2B

Answers will vary. Sample answers:

11. The teachers enjoy their work.
12. Each has food he or she can share.
13. The musicians travel, and their instruments are heavy.
14. Billy slept since he was tired.
15. Everyone has his or her opinion, so no one agrees.
16. The dog barked because it was hungry.
17. One misses his brother, who is away.
18. Lisa and Margot relaxed now that their school day was over.
19. All wondered what to do, and they talked out a plan.
20. The orchestra plays its best pieces tonight.

PRACTICE 23.2A Using Correct Antecedents

Read these simple, compound, and complex sentences. Then, rewrite the sentences to correct pronoun-antecedent agreement. Circle the pronoun and underline the antecedent.

EXAMPLE When we went to the beach, she lent me our sunscreen.

ANSWER *When we went to the beach, she lent me her sunscreen.*

1. Alex lent us their car that was about to run out of gas.
2. Erin wanted us to meet their friend, who is about to enter our class.
3. After the movie ended, everyone told their impressions.
4. No one wanted to give up their Saturday, so we rescheduled the meeting.
5. The kitten curled up their little body and slept in front of the fire.
6. I lost its CD, so I had to buy her a replacement.
7. Since it stopped raining, we can ride its bikes.
8. Laslo offered to help, but the team preferred to work on their own.
9. Did you forget to bring me our scarf?
10. The students know they must study, and they form our own study groups.

PRACTICE 23.2B Writing Sentences With Pronoun-Antecedent Agreement

Write complete sentences with pronoun-antecedent agreement. Use each subject provided and add the correct pronoun. Write the type of sentence that is indicated in parentheses.

EXAMPLE Everyone (compound sentence)

ANSWER *Everyone offered his or her suggestion, and we decided to vote.*

11. The teachers (simple sentence)
12. Each (simple sentence)
13. The musicians (compound sentence)
14. Billy (complex sentence)
15. Everyone (compound sentence)
16. The dog (complex sentence)
17. One (complex sentence)
18. Lisa and Margot (complex sentence)
19. All (compound sentence)
20. The orchestra (simple sentence)

SPEAKING APPLICATION

Use the sentences on this page as models. With a partner, make up one simple, one compound, and one complex sentence. Your partner should check that your pronouns and antecedents agree and then tell you a sentence.

WRITING APPLICATION

Write one simple, one compound, and one complex sentence about your favorite type of music. Read your sentences aloud to a partner. Work with your partner to correct any sentences that have incorrectly identified antecedents.

SPEAKING APPLICATION

Have partners share their sentences with other groups. Students' sentences should show that they can use a variety of complete sentences that include correctly identified antecedents.

WRITING APPLICATION

Students should correctly identify the antecedents of pronouns in the simple, compound, and complex sentences they write.

PRACTICE 23.2C **Revising for Pronoun-Antecedent Agreement**

Read the sentences. Rewrite each sentence choosing the correct pronoun in parentheses. Circle the pronoun and underline the antecedent.

EXAMPLE Neither Janie nor Maria has returned (their, her) books to the library.

ANSWER *Neither Janie nor Maria has returned her books to the library.*

1. Each boy paid for (their, his) own lunch, and each boy bought a sandwich.
2. If a person asks for directions, please try to help (them, him or her).
3. Everyone should fasten (their, his or her) seat belt.
4. All students choose (their, our) classes.
5. Has Marco or Dina given (their, his or her) oral report yet?
6. If there is time, some of the students may read (their, our) poems aloud.
7. Both Andrew and Arnold were wearing (their, his) new team caps.
8. None of these pencils have (their, his) erasers, and all of them are red.
9. Everyone should cast (his or her, their) vote.
10. Each student has (his or her, their) own goals.

PRACTICE 23.2D **Writing Sentences With Pronoun-Antecedent Agreement**

Write complete sentences with pronoun-antecedent agreement. Use each subject provided and add the correct pronoun. Write the type of sentence that is indicated in parentheses.

EXAMPLE The class (complex sentence)

ANSWER *While the class wrote their reports, the teacher graded test papers.*

11. The group (simple sentence)
12. All (compound sentence)
13. Each (complex sentence)
14. Esther or Briana (simple sentence)
15. Tanya and Victor (complex sentence)
16. Everyone (complex sentence)
17. The community (simple sentence)
18. The voters (compound sentence)
19. The police department (complex sentence)
20. The police officers (simple sentence)

SPEAKING APPLICATION

With a partner, take turns discussing advantages and disadvantages of pets. Using correct pronoun-antecedent agreement, speak in a variety of simple, compound, and complex sentences. Your partner should listen for pronoun-antecedent agreement.

WRITING APPLICATION

Write one simple, one compound, and one complex sentence about a person or group you admire. Be sure to use correct pronoun-antecedent agreement. Have a partner read your sentences aloud and check for agreement.

Working with ELLs  Sheltered Instruction: Cognitive

Have students listen to, derive meaning from, and respond orally to information presented from a wide variety of print, electronic, and audiovisual media to build and reinforce language attainment. Make a recording of yourself responding to the Speaking Application prompt, and play it for students.

Beginning Pause the recording frequently and clarify as necessary. To build and reinforce language attainment, provide a small bank of words such as *pets, love, furry, mess,* and *food.* Review the words, and have students use them in responding orally to questions about the recording. For example, ask, *What word tells how I feel about my pet?*

Intermediate During playback, have students raise their hand if they have difficulty understanding. Pause to clarify. Afterward, have students respond orally to the presentation. To build language attainment, provide them with sentence frames to guide responses: for example, *One reason people like pets is that they are* _______.

Advanced Have groups discuss the presentation, offering their own views. Have them use sentence frames such as: *I agree with the point that* _______ *because* _______. *While I agree that* _______, *I also think that* _______.

Advanced High Have students complete the Advanced activity. Challenge them to use at least one compound sentence in the discussion.

PRACTICE 23.2C

1. boy, his
2. person, him or her
3. Everyone, his or her
4. students, their
5. Marco, Dina, his or her
6. students, their
7. Andrew, Arnold, their
8. pencils, their
9. Everyone, his or her
10. student, his or her

PRACTICE 23.2D

Answers will vary. Sample answers:

11. The group decided to keep its name.
12. All of the geese landed, and they ate.
13. Because it is important, each of the students writes in his or her journal daily.
14. Esther or Briana forgot her jacket.
15. Even though Tanya and Victor are siblings, they never argue.
16. Everyone brought his or her lunch, which saved money.
17. The community held its parade.
18. The voters tried, but they lost.
19. While the police department is large, it is set up to be user-friendly.
20. The police officers won their game.

SPEAKING APPLICATION

Have students explain why their partners' pronoun-antecedent agreement was either correct or incorrect.

WRITING APPLICATION

Students' writing should include simple, compound, and complex sentences with correctly identified antecedents.

Test Warm-Up

1. **B** Change ***their*** to **its**
2. **F** Change ***their*** to **his or her**
3. **C** For example, when the new words in a chapter are hard, Mr. Fernandez draws pictures to help us remember them.
4. **H** our

Reteach

If students have not mastered these skills, review the content in Section 23.2 Agreement Between Pronouns and Antecedents.

1. Making Personal Pronouns and Indefinite Pronouns Agree 23.2.4
2. Making Personal Pronouns and Indefinite Pronouns Agree 23.2.4
3. Avoiding Shifts in Person 23.2
4. Making Personal Pronouns and Indefinite Pronouns Agree 23.2.4

Test Tip

If students have tried all other strategies to answer a question and are still unsure about the correct answer, they should try to eliminate any answer choices that they know or suspect are not correct. They can then make a guess at a correct answer from the remaining answer choices.

Test Warm-Up

DIRECTIONS
Read the introduction and the passage that follows. Then, answer the questions to show that you can use a variety of complete sentences (e.g., simple, compound, complex) that include correctly identified antecedents in reading and writing.

Mario wrote this paragraph about his favorite teacher. Read the paragraph and think about the changes you would suggest as a peer editor. When you finish reading, answer the questions that follow.

Teacher of the Year

(1) This year, the school will vote for their Teacher of the Year. (2) Everyone in the school is allowed to give their opinion. (3) Most of us believe that Mr. Fernandez, who teaches Spanish and Latin, is the best because he is patient and fun. (4) For example, when the new words in a chapter is hard, Mr. Fernandez draws pictures to help us remember it. (5) Those strategies really work, and they make learning fun. (6) We hope Mr. Fernandez wins the award. (7) Our class agrees that Mr. Fernandez is its Teacher of the Year.

1 What change, if any, should be made in sentence 1?

- **A** Change ***their*** to **his or her**
- **B** Change ***their*** to **its**
- **C** Change ***their*** to **your**
- **D** Make no change

2 What change, if any, should be made in sentence 2?

- **F** Change ***their*** to **his or her**
- **G** Change ***their*** to **its**
- **H** Change ***their*** to **your**
- **J** Make no change

3 What is the BEST way to revise sentence 4?

- **A** For example, when the new words in a chapter are hard, Mr. Fernandez draws pictures to help us remember it.
- **B** For example, when the new words in a chapter is hard, Mr. Fernandez draws pictures to help us remember them.
- **C** For example, when the new words in a chapter are hard, Mr. Fernandez draws pictures to help us remember them.
- **D** For example, when the new words in a chapter is hard, Mr. Fernandez draws a picture to help us remember him.

4 The meaning of sentence 7 can be clarified by changing the word ***its*** to —

- **F** his or her
- **G** their
- **H** our
- **J** your

CHAPTER 24 LESSON PLANNER
Using Modifiers

Use the Online Lesson Planner at www.phwritingcoach.com to customize your instructional plan for an integrated Language Arts curriculum.

DAY 1 24.1 Comparisons Using Adjectives and Adverbs

"What Do You Notice?" **Objectives:** Identify, use, and understand aspects of comparison, including ▪ three forms of comparison ▪ regular modifiers with one or two syllables ▪ regular modifiers with three or more syllables ▪ adverbs ending in *–ly* ▪ *less* and *least*	**INSTRUCTION AND PRACTICE** **Student Edition** pp. 533–537

DAY 2 24.1 Comparisons Using Adjectives and Adverbs *(continued)*

Objectives: Identify, use, and understand aspects of comparison, including ▪ irregular adjective and adverb forms ▪ comparative and superlative degrees	**INSTRUCTION AND PRACTICE** **Student Edition** pp. 538–540

DAY 3 24.1 Comparisons Using Adjectives and Adverbs *(continued)*

Objectives: Identify, use, and understand aspects of making logical comparisons	**INSTRUCTION AND PRACTICE** **Student Edition** pp. 541–543

DAY 4 24.2 Troublesome Adjectives and Adverbs

Objectives: Identify, use, and understand making clear comparisons, including using troublesome adjectives and adverbs	**INSTRUCTION AND PRACTICE** **Student Edition** pp. 544–547 **Test Warm-Up** p. 548

Grammar Assessment

Grammar Coach:	Diagnostic Assessment	End-of-Chapter Assessment	Progress Monitoring
Personalized Instruction	Students take grammar diagnostic test online and are automatically assigned instruction and practice in areas where they need support.	Teacher uses **ExamView** to administer end-of-chapter assessment and remediation. Teachers may customize **ExamView** tests or use the ones provided.	Teachers may use the **Test Warm-Ups** and the **Cumulative Reviews** in the student book or eText to check students' mastery of grammar skills. Students may also play **DimensionL** grammar video games to test their grammar skills.
Teacher-Directed Instruction	Teacher administers the diagnostic test and determines focus of instruction and practice.		

Alternate Pacing Plans

- **Block Scheduling** Each day in the Lesson Planner represents a 40–50 minute block. Teachers using block scheduling may combine days to revise pacing to meet their classroom needs.
- **Accelerated Lesson Planning** Combine instructional days, focusing on concepts called out by students' diagnostic test results.
- **Integrated Language Arts Curriculum** Use the instruction and practice in this chapter to provide reinforcement, remediation, or extension of grammar concepts taught in your literature curriculum.

Links to Prentice Hall *LITERATURE*

- **Unit 2** Writing Workshop: Comparison of Adjectives and Adverbs, p. 389
- **Unit 3** Writing Workshop: Revising Errors in Adjective and Adverb Usage, p. 553

www.phwritingcoach.com

Grammar Assessment and Practice

Chapter diagnostic tests assess students' skills and assign instruction and practice.

DimensionL Video Games

Fast-paced interactive video games challenge students' mastery of grammar.

Lesson Planner continues on next page

DAY 5 Cumulative Review

Objectives: Identify, use, and understand word usage, including	**INSTRUCTION AND PRACTICE**
▪ verb tenses and forms ▪ pronouns ▪ subject-verb and pronoun-antecedent agreement ▪ modifiers	**Student Edition** pp. 549–550

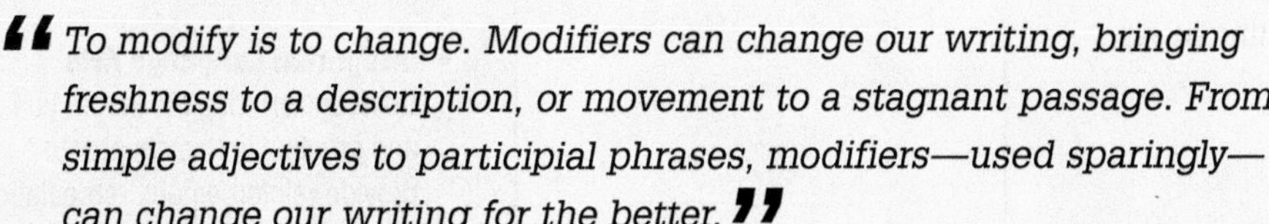

"To modify is to change. Modifiers can change our writing, bringing freshness to a description, or movement to a stagnant passage. From simple adjectives to participial phrases, modifiers—used sparingly—can change our writing for the better."

—Jeff Anderson

Differentiated Instruction

Differentiated Instruction Boxes in this Teacher's Edition address these student populations:

- Below-Level Students
- Above-Level Students
- Gifted and Talented Students
- Special Needs Students
- English Language Learners
- Spanish Speaking Students

In addition, for further enrichment, see the **Extension** features.

Grammar Ground Rule:

Model with Students

In this chapter, keeping it clear means making your comparisons logical and balanced. Explain to students that comparisons are important in many different kinds of writing, but comparisons that don't really make sense will just confuse your reader.

> **Say:** Suppose I want to compare two activities, to tell you which one I like better. I might say, *I like sewing my own clothes better than the piano.* But that's just confusing. You can't sew a piano, and that's what the sentences suggests. You can't compare an activity, like sewing, with a musical instrument, like the piano. It's much better to say, *I like sewing my own clothes better than playing the piano.* Compare things that can be compared.

Write this sentence on the board. *Riding a boogie board is easier than a surfboard*. Have students tell you what two things are being compared. (riding, surfboard) **Ask:** Does it make sense to compare these two things? How could you change the sentence so that the comparison makes sense? *(Riding a boogie board is easier than riding a surfboard.*)

Small Group Activity – Finding and Making Comparisons

Have students form groups and research or imagine two products. Have the students write a paragraph comparing the products and how they work. Have students discuss the comparisons they use in the paragraph. The discussion should answer these questions:

- What are the two things being compared?
- Does it make sense to compare these two things?

Have a member of each group present their conclusions to the class and give one good example of a comparison that follows this grammar ground rule: Keep it clear.

Grammar Ground Rules

1. Keep it clear.
2. Make them agree.
3. Make it specific.
4. Dot your *i*'s and cross your *t*'s.
5. Make it active.

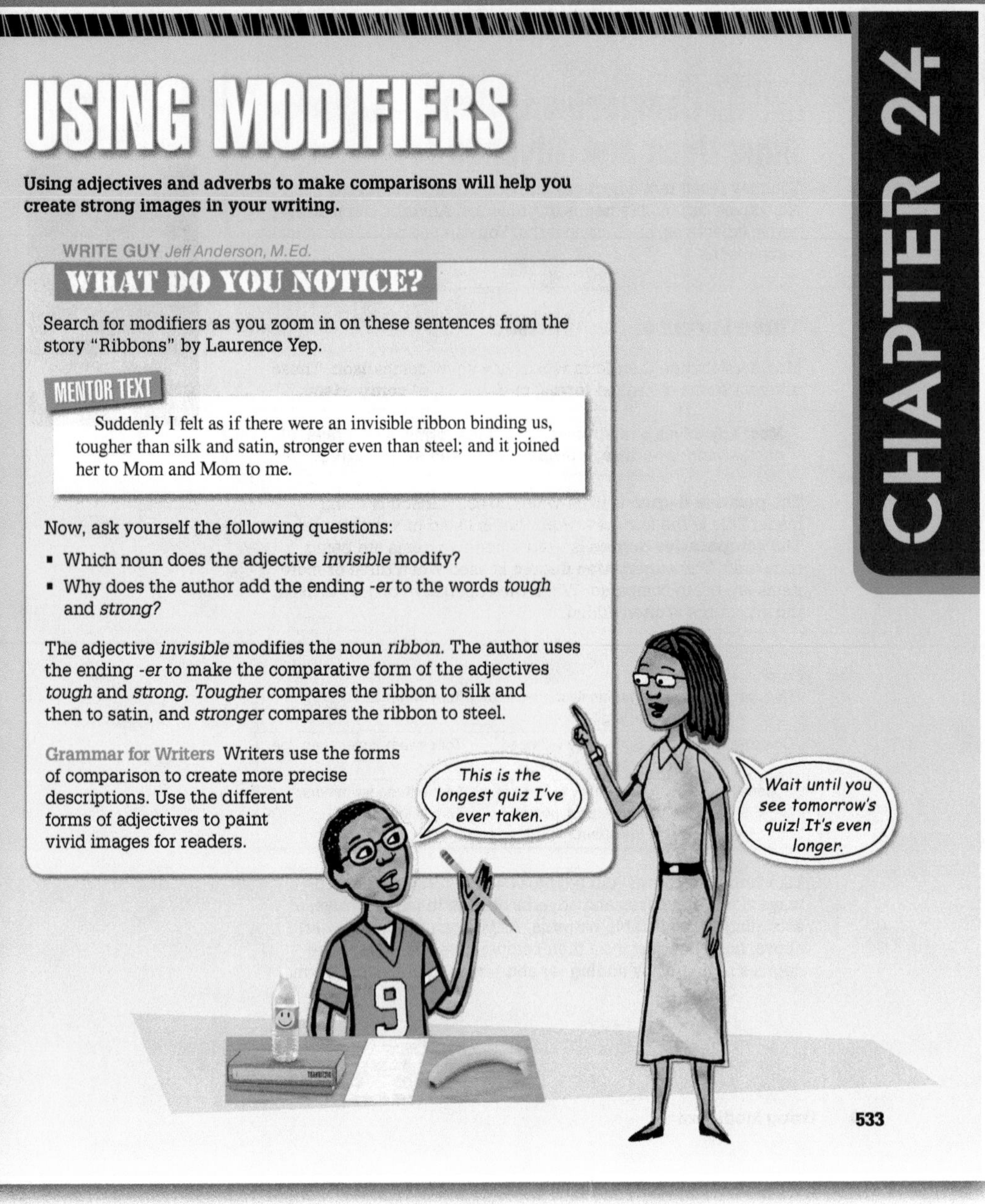

USING MODIFIERS

Using adjectives and adverbs to make comparisons will help you create strong images in your writing.

WRITE GUY *Jeff Anderson, M.Ed.*

WHAT DO YOU NOTICE?

Search for modifiers as you zoom in on these sentences from the story "Ribbons" by Laurence Yep.

MENTOR TEXT

Suddenly I felt as if there were an invisible ribbon binding us, tougher than silk and satin, stronger even than steel; and it joined her to Mom and Mom to me.

Now, ask yourself the following questions:

- Which noun does the adjective *invisible* modify?
- Why does the author add the ending *-er* to the words *tough* and *strong?*

The adjective *invisible* modifies the noun *ribbon.* The author uses the ending *-er* to make the comparative form of the adjectives *tough* and *strong. Tougher* compares the ribbon to silk and then to satin, and *stronger* compares the ribbon to steel.

Grammar for Writers Writers use the forms of comparison to create more precise descriptions. Use the different forms of adjectives to paint vivid images for readers.

CHAPTER 24

This is the longest quiz I've ever taken.
Wait until you see tomorrow's quiz! It's even longer.
9

USING MODIFIERS

As students progress in their writing skills, it will be important for them to be able to apply the rules of grammar, usage, and mechanics to their own drafts. Use the *What Do You Notice?* feature to help them see effective conventions in the work of professional writers. Encourage students to incorporate proper voice, tense, and syntax as they edit their own writing.

Read aloud the opening sentence. Remind students that adjectives modify nouns and pronouns, while adverbs modify verbs, adjectives, and other adverbs. Give examples of comparisons that contain adjectives: *My sister is taller than I am, but my best friend is the tallest of all three of us.* Then, give examples of adverb comparisons: *My dog barks louder than his. Her dog barks the loudest of all of the dogs.*

WRITE GUY *Jeff Anderson, M. Ed.*

WHAT DO YOU NOTICE?

When students have read the Mentor Text, **ask:** What do you notice about the relationship between the characters in the Mentor Text? (**Possible response:** The characters seem to be close.) **Ask:** How can you tell? (**Possible response:** It says that an invisible ribbon binds the characters together.)

Have students finish reading the page. **Ask:** How do the comparisons in the Mentor Text help you picture the ribbon? (**Possible responses:** They describe how strong the ribbon is. They are kind of unusual, in that ribbon is not usually compared to steel.) Point out that comparisons can help make descriptions more vivid.

Grammar for Writers: Voice

Help students understand that modifiers help writers compose clear descriptions. As students learn how to use adjectives and adverbs by applying the rules in the lessons, they should think about how they will use these modifiers to strengthen their writing.

24.1 Comparisons Using Adjectives and Adverbs

Lesson Objectives

1. Recognize and use positive, comparative, and superlative forms of adjectives and adverbs.
2. Correctly use comparative and superlative forms of regular and irregular modifiers.
3. Create logical, balanced comparisons.

Three Forms of Comparison

Discuss how modifiers change form when they are used to compare things or ideas.

RULE 24.1.1 Read aloud the rule and then have students repeat the lines with you.

Review the explanation of positive degree, comparative degree, and superlative degree with students, and discuss the examples in the chart on page 534.

Use a Think Aloud as part of a gradual release progression.

Say: Keeping these modifiers straight is easy, as long as I keep just one example in mind: *large, larger,* and *largest.* **I can remember** that the adjective or adverb in its plain or *positive* form—*large*—is the positive degree by thinking *P for plain form, P for positive form.* Then, I can think about the *-er* form—*larger*—as being the comparative degree—when only two things are being compared. For example, this apple is *larger* than that apple. The "super" degree is needed to compare three or more items, so I can remember that it is called the superlative degree.

Guide students in classifying modifiers as positive, comparative, or superlative. Draw three-cluster diagrams on the board. Write a modifier degree in the center of each: *Positive, Comparative, Superlative.*

Write these words on the board: *small, smallest, taller, heavier, slickest, tallest, calm, heaviest, calmer, calmest, smaller, slick, tall, slicker, heavy.* Have students tell where the modifiers should be placed on each diagram. Then, discuss how they know where to place the modifiers.

Have partners use one word from each diagram in sentences and share their sentences with the class.

24.1 Comparisons Using Adjectives and Adverbs

You may recall that adjectives and adverbs are **modifiers.** Adjectives can modify nouns or pronouns. Adverbs can modify verbs, adjectives, or other adverbs. You can use modifiers to make comparisons.

www.phwritingcoach.com

Grammar Practice
Practice your grammar skills with Writing Coach Online.

Grammar Games
Test your knowledge of grammar in this fast-paced interactive video game.

Three Forms of Comparison

Modifiers change their form when they show comparison. These different forms are called **forms,** or **degrees, of comparison.**

RULE 24.1.1

Most adjectives and adverbs have three forms, or degrees, of comparison: positive, comparative, and superlative.

The **positive degree** is used when no comparison is being made. This is the form of a word that is listed in a dictionary. The **comparative degree** is used when two items are being compared. The **superlative degree** is used when three or more items are being compared. When the superlative degree is used, the article *the* is often added.

DEGREE	ADJECTIVE	ADVERB
Positive	The family moved into a large home.	Tom swam fast.
Comparative	Soon, they will need a larger home.	Tom swam faster than Joe.
Superlative	The family is living in the largest home on the street.	Of the three swimmers, Tom is the fastest.

Like verbs, adjectives and adverbs change forms in different ways. Some adjectives and adverbs change in regular ways, or according to predictable patterns. As you can see in the chart above, *large* and *fast* form their comparative and superlative degrees regularly, by adding *-er* and *-est* to their positive form.

Teacher Tip

Some students may not have a clear understanding of what *modify* means. Explain to students that in this context, *modify* means to describe or add information to another word.

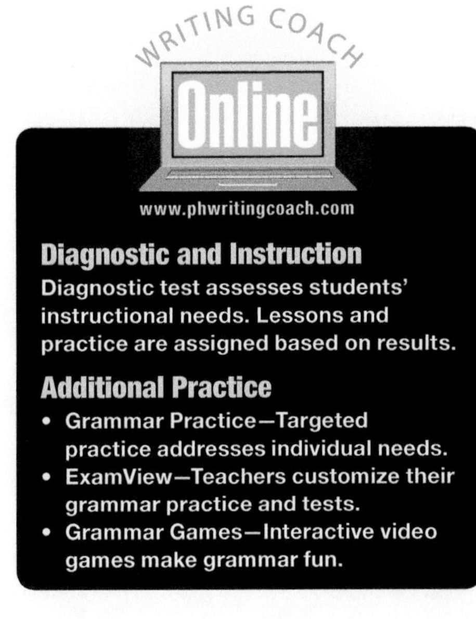

www.phwritingcoach.com

Diagnostic and Instruction
Diagnostic test assesses students' instructional needs. Lessons and practice are assigned based on results.

Additional Practice
- Grammar Practice—Targeted practice addresses individual needs.
- ExamView—Teachers customize their grammar practice and tests.
- Grammar Games—Interactive video games make grammar fun.

Regular Modifiers With One or Two Syllables

Most modifiers are **regular**—their degrees of comparison are formed in predictable ways.

Use *-er* or *more* to form the comparative degree and use *-est* or *most* to form the superlative degree of most one- and two-syllable modifiers.

24.1.2 RULE

COMPARATIVE AND SUPERLATIVE DEGREES FORMED WITH *-ER* AND *-EST*		
POSITIVE	COMPARATIVE	SUPERLATIVE
deep	deeper	deepest
fast	faster	fastest
friendly	friendlier	friendliest
narrow	narrower	narrowest
sunny	sunnier	sunniest

Use *more* to form a modifier's comparative degree when adding *-er* sounds awkward. Use *most* to form a modifier's superlative degree when adding *-est* sounds awkward.

COMPARATIVE AND SUPERLATIVE DEGREES FORMED WITH *MORE* AND *MOST*		
POSITIVE	COMPARATIVE	SUPERLATIVE
careful	more careful	most careful
complete	more complete	most complete
handsome	more handsome	most handsome
often	more often	most often
quietly	more quietly	most quietly

More and *most* should not be used when the result sounds awkward, however. If you are not sure which form to use, check a dictionary. Most dictionaries list modifiers formed with *-er* and *-est.*

See Practice 24.1A

Regular Modifiers With One or Two Syllables

Explain that it's not difficult to put most one- or two-syllable adjectives and adverbs in their comparative forms. You just apply a simple rule.

RULE 24.1.2 Read aloud the rule and then have students repeat the lines with you.

Review the first chart with students. Point out that most of the comparative degrees are formed by adding *-er* to the end of the modifier. The superlative degrees are formed by adding *-est*. Ask students what they notice about adding these endings to the adjectives and adverbs that end in *y*. (The *y* has to be changed to an *i* before adding the *-er* or *-est* ending.)

Explain that some other adjectives and adverbs don't sound right with an *-er* or *-est* ending. For these modifiers, they usually need to add *more* or *most* to create the comparative and superlative forms. Review the second chart with students.

Teacher Tip

If a student is unsure whether a particular adjective or adverb takes an ending or the word *more* or *most,* have him or her refer to a dictionary. Show the student how the word *fast* becomes *faster* and *fastest.* Display the dictionary page with these degrees listed in the word's definition.

Working with ELLs — ELL Sheltered Instruction: Social/Affective

Help students demonstrate comprehension of increasingly complex English by participating in a shared reading of page 535.

Beginning Have fluent speakers read the first two sentences on the page as Beginning students follow along. Then, have fluent speakers choose a word from the first chart and read its degrees aloud. Pointing to the word, have the fluent speaker ask, *What was added to this word to make it comparative?* Have students complete this frame: ______ *was added.*

Intermediate Have students read the page in groups of three. Have them take turns reading the words in the first chart aloud, with one student saying the word in the positive degree, one in the comparative, and one in the superlative, and review how the words change in each column.

Advanced Have partners read the page together. Have them choose a word from the first chart and write three sentences, one with each degree. Next, have students read their three sentences to each other, correcting each other as necessary.

Advanced High Have partners complete the Advanced activity. Then, challenge students to write a paragraph using one degree of each word in the first chart.

Regular Modifiers With Three or More Syllables

Explain that words with more than two syllables use *more* and *most* to form the comparative and superlative.

RULE 24.1.3 Read aloud the rule and then have students repeat the lines with you.

Use a Think Aloud as part of a gradual release progression.

Say: I know that it is sometimes automatic for me to just add an *-er* or an *-est* to form these comparative words when I am speaking. But I also know that, sometimes, doing so results in a mistake. To make sure I get these forms right, I count the number of syllables a modifier has and make sure I add *more* and *most* if the modifier has more than two syllables.

Work with students to help them realize the importance of using the grammatically correct form of these words. Invite students to pronounce the three-syllable words with an incorrect *-er* and *-est* to illustrate why these are not used.

Have partners brainstorm for additional three-syllable modifiers and write sentences using the comparative and superlative forms. Have partners share their sentences with the class.

Adverbs Ending in *-ly*

RULE 24.1.4 Read aloud the rule and then have students repeat the lines with you.

Challenge the students to think of additional adverbs ending in *-ly*. (calmly, warmly) Make a list. Ask volunteers to use each of the adverbs on the list in a sentence; then, have other students write sentences using the comparative and superlative forms of the adverbs.

Using *Less* and *Least*

RULE 24.1.5 Read aloud the rule and then have students repeat the lines with you.

Explain that *less* and *least* are opposite in meaning from *more* and *most.* Have students work with a partner to write five sentences that use *less* and *least*. Have students switch sentences with other pairs and replace *less* and *least* with *more* and *most*. Discuss the difference in meaning.

Regular Modifiers With Three or More Syllables

Modifiers for words with three or more syllables follow the same rules.

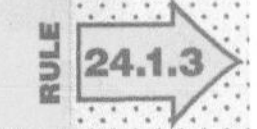

Use *more* and *most* to form the comparative and superlative degrees of all modifiers of three or more syllables. Do not use *-er* or *-est* with modifiers of more than two syllables.

DEGREES OF MODIFIERS WITH THREE OR MORE SYLLABLES		
POSTIVE	COMPARATIVE	SUPERLATIVE
expensive	more expensive	most expensive
flexible	more flexible	most flexible

Adverbs Ending in *-ly*

To modify most adverbs ending in *-ly*, use *more* or *most.*

Use *more* to form the comparative degree and *most* to form the superlative degree of most adverbs ending in *-ly*.

EXAMPLES slowly, more slowly, most slowly
quietly, more quietly, most quietly

Using *Less* and *Least*

Less and *least* can show decreasing comparisons.

Use *less* with a modifier to form the decreasing comparative degree and *least* to form the decreasing superlative degree.

EXAMPLES friendly, less friendly, least friendly
quickly, less quickly, least quickly

See Practice 24.1B

Differentiated Instruction

PRE-AP Enrichment for Above-Level Students Review the lesson material. Invite students to explain why each sentence is incorrect:

He is the tallest of the two boys.
(The comparative degree should be used to compare two things.) *That toy is the cheaper of the dozens offered.*
(The superlative degree should be used to compare more than two things.) Challenge students to write incorrect sentences and ask a partner to explain why they are wrong.

RTI Strategy for Below-Level Students Students may find it helpful to circle the ending of each comparative and superlative modifier. Guide students to see that the positive degree is the word in its base word form. Discuss how the comparative ending, *-er*, is used to compare two items. The superlative ending, *-est*, is used to compare three or more items. Have students write example sentences using all three degrees of these common adjectives: *small, beautiful.*

PRACTICE 24.1A **Forming Comparatives and Superlatives of One- and Two-Syllable Modifiers**

Read the modifiers. Write the comparative and superlative forms of each modifier.

EXAMPLE quiet
ANSWER *quieter, quietest*

1. slim
2. rich
3. happy
4. shy
5. helpful
6. soon
7. polite
8. late
9. evenly
10. dirty

PRACTICE 24.1B **Using Forms of Modifiers**

Read the sentences. Then, write each sentence, using the form of the modifier in parentheses.

EXAMPLE Today is the _____ day of the year! (*hot*, superlative)
ANSWER *Today is the hottest day of the year!*

11. Damian's _____ brother is starting college in the fall. (*old*, superlative)
12. I thought this book was _____ than the other one I read. (*funny*, comparative)
13. Celia is the _____ of the two skaters. (*graceful*, comparative)
14. Curtis felt _____ after his snack than before. (*energetic*, comparative)
15. Morgan is the _____ reader in our class. (*fast*, superlative)
16. Of all the speakers, Kara gave the _____ presentation. (*thorough*, superlative)
17. The play was _____ than we had expected. (*exciting*, comparative)
18. The sidewalk is _____ on this side of the street. (*safe*, comparative)
19. January and February are usually the _____ months. (*cold*, superlative)
20. This cereal is _____ than I like. (*sweet*, comparative)

SPEAKING APPLICATION

Tell a partner about a trait or quality of several people you know. Use a comparative and a superlative form of an adjective in this structure: Jack is taller than Kim. Dane is the tallest of all my friends.

WRITING APPLICATION

Write a paragraph comparing different versions of a game or song or several episodes of a television program. Use at least one comparative form and one superlative form of each modifier.

SPEAKING APPLICATION

Have partners identify the comparatives and superlatives in each other's sentences and check them for correctness.

WRITING APPLICATION

Have students share their paragraphs with the group, pointing out the comparative and superlative modifiers.

PRACTICE 24.1A

1. slimmer, slimmest
2. richer, richest
3. happier, happiest
4. shyer, shyest
5. more helpful, most helpful
6. sooner, soonest
7. more polite, most polite
8. later, latest
9. more evenly, most evenly
10. dirtier, dirtiest

PRACTICE 24.1B

11. Damian's oldest brother is starting college in the fall.
12. I thought this book was funnier than the other one I read.
13. Celia is the more graceful of the two skaters.
14. Curtis felt more energetic after his snack than before.
15. Morgan is the fastest reader in our class.
16. Of all the speakers, Kara gave the most thorough presentation.
17. The play was more exciting than we had expected.
18. The sidewalk is safer on this side of the street.
19. January and February are usually the coldest months.
20. This cereal is sweeter than I like.

Irregular Adjectives and Adverbs

Tell students that there are some irregular adjectives and adverbs that do not follow the rules previously discussed.

RULE 24.1.6 Read aloud the rule and then have students repeat the lines with you.

Say: I know that not everyone uses correct grammar all the time, so I have to think of the rules as I speak and write. I know that in some cases, I have heard words said incorrectly for so long—my sister always says *more prettier*—that they almost seem correct by now. So I really have to think about these rules, sometimes, to make sure I don't make the same error over and over again.

Work with students to help them realize that even though some modifiers are used incorrectly by some speakers, these uses are not correct grammar.

Have student pairs draw a three-panel illustration to visually represent the three comparative degrees of one of the irregular modifiers (for example: *good, better, best*). Tell students not to write the words they are illustrating. Have other pairs try to guess what has been illustrated.

Using Comparative and Superlative Degrees

RULE 24.1.7 Read aloud the rule and then have students repeat the lines with you.

Teacher Tip

Although students probably know the difference between adverbs and adjectives, the irregular forms may still be confusing. Display sentences using each degree of the irregular adjectives and adverbs so that students can refer to them as they strive to learn these forms.

Irregular Adjectives and Adverbs

A few adjectives and adverbs are irregular.

Memorize the comparative and superlative forms of adjectives and adverbs that have irregular spellings.

The chart lists the most common irregular modifiers.

DEGREES OF IRREGULAR ADJECTIVES AND ADVERBS		
POSITIVE	COMPARATIVE	SUPERLATIVE
bad (adjective) badly (adverb)	worse worse	worst worst
far (distance) far (extent)	farther further	farthest furthest
good (adjective) well (adverb)	better better	best best
many much	more more	most most

When you are unsure about how a modifier forms its degrees of comparison, check a dictionary.

See Practice 24.1C

Using Comparative and Superlative Degrees

Keep these rules in mind when you use the comparative and superlative degrees.

Use the comparative degree to compare *two* people, places, or things. Use the superlative degree to compare *three or more* people, places, or things.

Usually, you do not need to mention specific numbers when you are making a comparison. Other words in the sentence should help make the meaning clear whether you are comparing two items or three or more items.

Working with ELLs — ELL Sheltered Instruction: Cognitive

Help students use prereading supports to enhance comprehension of written text. Draw a concept web on the board, and model its use by writing "degrees of adjectives" in the center and writing related ideas elicited from students in the outer circles. Provide blank copies. Then:

Beginning Preteach the words *irregular, memorize, common, unsure,* and *dictionary.* Read the first section on page 538 with students, clarifying meaning. Then, have students write *irregular adjectives and adverbs* in the center of their concept webs, and guide them in filling in related ideas.

Intermediate Preteach the words *irregular, memorize,* and *modifier.* Have groups read the first section on page 538 and then collaborate in filling in a concept web for the section. Review their webs with them.

Advanced Have partners read pages 538 and 539 and fill out two concept webs, one for each section. Review their webs with them.

Advanced High Have partners read pages 538 and 539 and fill out two concept webs, one for each section. Then, have them enter their notes in an outline to summarize the sections.

EXAMPLES The coach felt **better** once all the swimmers were in the locker room on time.

The swim team completed the practice session in its **best** time this week.

Pay particular attention to the modifiers you use when you are comparing just two items. Do not use the superlative degree with fewer than three items.

INCORRECT Of their two relay races, that one was the **best**.

CORRECT Of their two relay races, that one was **better**.

INCORRECT Mark's car was the **fastest** of the two cars.

CORRECT Mark's car was the **faster** of the two cars.

Do not make double comparisons. Do not use both *-er* and *more* to form the comparative degree or both *-est* and *most* to form the superlative degree. Also, be sure not to use *-er, more,* and *most* with an irregular modifier.

RULE 24.1.8

INCORRECT She read the story the **most fastest**.

CORRECT She read the story the **fastest**.

INCORRECT The snowstorm was **more worse** than any they had seen in years.

CORRECT The snowstorm was **worse** than any they had seen in years.

See Practice 24.1D

Read aloud the incorrect and correct example sentences in the middle of the page and explain why each incorrect sentence is wrong. **Say:** At first, this sentence may sound okay: *Of their two relay races, that one was the best.* However, if I analyze the sentence, I see that the adjective is in the wrong form. Only two things are compared, so I should use the comparative form *better,* not the superlative form *best.* Similarly, in the sentence *Mark's car was the fastest of the two cars,* I should use the comparative *faster,* not the superlative *fastest,* because only two things are compared. Have students brainstorm for additional examples of sentences with comparative and superlative modifiers, and discuss whether each modifier is presented correctly or incorrectly and why.

Examples:
That puppy is the bigger of the large litter. (biggest)
This is the better day of the week. (best)
Of the four sisters, she sings better. (best)
He feels worst today than yesterday. (worse)

Remind students that double comparisons, such as *more better* and *most prettiest,* are illogical because they say the same thing twice. *More* and the suffix *-er* mean the same thing. So do *most* and *-est.* It is repetitious and incorrect to use both.

RULE 24.1.8 Read aloud the rule and then have students repeat the lines with you.

Read the examples together. Explain why *most fastest,* in the first sentence, is wrong. Invite students to tell why modifiers are not enhanced by *more* and *most* in the other incorrect sentences shown.

Differentiated Instruction

RTI Strategy for Below-Level Students Review the problem of double comparisons with students. Explain that there are three different ways to make a comparison and that they should always use only one. The three ways are to add *-er,* use *more,* or use a comparative form of an irregular verb. Say or write on the board several sentences that combine two of the forms, such as *Jorge feels worser today* and *Sheila is more faster than Jane.* Ask students to remove one of the comparison elements and read the new, correct sentence.

Enrichment for Gifted/Talented Students Have students write song lyrics to the tune of "Oh, Susannah." Have them use a series of the basic form of an adjective, the comparative, and the superlative. Example: "Fred is friendly, but Cho is friendlier. Nita is the friendliest, and so I'll work with her." Students may use other tunes or create their own. Challenge students to use interesting adjectives and adjectives with irregular comparative forms.

Teacher Tip

Some students may have difficulty correctly using standard irregular forms because they are used to hearing and using nonstandard forms. Have these students practice using the correct forms orally by answering questions. For example, ask, "Are you feeling better today?" Direct the student to use the correct form of *bad* to answer: "No, I'm feeling worse." Help students "hear" their errors and correct them.

PRACTICE 24.1C

1. further, furthest
2. worse, worst
3. more, most
4. worse, worst
5. farther, farthest
6. better, best
7. more, most

PRACTICE 24.1D

8. This book is better than the author's previous one.
9. This is the most fun I have had all week!
10. Peter and Matthew had to travel farthest to get here.
11. The storm was worse than expected.
12. I have no further interest in this subject.
13. Quentin usually does better on tests than I do.
14. Who is the best artist in the class?
15. Marcus has more songs on his playlist than Nelson does.
16. Are you feeling better today?
17. The comic performed better than the singer.

SPEAKING APPLICATION

Have students identify the comparative and superlative modifiers they have used and explain why they chose those forms for their modifiers.

WRITING APPLICATION

Have students exchange paragraphs with a partner and correct any errors, paying special attention to the comparative and superlative forms of modifiers.

Comparisons Using Adjectives and Adverbs

PRACTICE 24.1C Forming Comparatives and Superlatives of Irregular Adjectives and Adverbs

Read the modifiers. Write the comparative and superlative forms of each modifier.

EXAMPLE well (adverb)

ANSWER *better, best*

1. far (extent)
2. badly (adverb)
3. much
4. bad (adjective)
5. far (distance)
6. good (adjective)
7. many

PRACTICE 24.1D Using Comparatives and Superlatives of Irregular Adjectives and Adverbs

Read the sentences. Then, write each sentence, using the form of the modifier in parentheses.

EXAMPLE That was the _____ meal I have ever eaten. (*bad*, superlative)

ANSWER *That was the worst meal I have ever eaten.*

8. This book is _____ than the author's previous one. (*good*, comparative)
9. This is the _____ fun I have had all week! (*much*, superlative)
10. Peter and Matthew had to travel _____ to get here. (*far*, superlative)
11. The storm was _____ than expected. (*bad*, comparative)
12. I have no _____ interest in this subject. (*far*, comparative)
13. Quentin usually does _____ on tests than I do. (*well*, comparative)
14. Who is the _____ artist in the class? (*good*, superlative)
15. Marcus has _____ songs on his playlist than Nelson does. (*many*, comparative)
16. Are you feeling _____ today? (*well*, comparative)
17. The comic performed _____ than the singer. (*good*, comparative)

SPEAKING APPLICATION

Tell a partner about an event. You may exaggerate the details. Use comparative and superlative forms of any of the modifiers above.

WRITING APPLICATION

Write a short paragraph comparing several versions or brands of an item. Use at least one comparative form and one superlative form.

Working with ELLs ELL Sheltered Instruction: Cognitive

Using the activities on the page, have students speak using a variety of sentence types with increasing accuracy and ease.

Beginning Model correct intonation as you read the answers to Practice 24.1D, items 8, 9, and 14 (a statement, an exclamation, and a question) aloud. Have students repeat chorally after you. Correct their intonation as necessary to foster increasing accuracy.

Intermediate Read the answers to Practice 24.1D, items 8, 9, and 14 to students, filling in the blanks and modeling correct intonation. Have them repeat after you. Then, have students say a statement and exclamation and ask a question of their own. Correct word order and intonation as necessary for increasing accuracy.

Advanced Review complex sentences with students. Then, have partners complete the Speaking Application. Direct them to use at least two complex sentences in their spoken accounts, as well as comparative and superlative degrees of modifiers.

Advanced High Review complex sentences and prepositional phrases with students. Then, have partners complete the Speaking Application. Direct them to use at least two complex sentences and one sentence beginning with a prepositional phrase, as well as comparative and superlative degrees of modifiers.

Making Logical Comparisons

In most situations, you will have no problem forming the degrees of modifiers and using them correctly in sentences. Sometimes, however, you may find that the way you have phrased a sentence makes your comparison unclear. You will then need to think about the words you have chosen and revise your sentence, making sure that your comparison is logical.

When you make a comparison, be sure you are comparing things that have clear similarities. RULE 24.1.9

Balanced Comparisons

Most comparisons make a statement or ask a question about the way in which similar things are either alike or different.

EXAMPLE Is the **Atlantic Ocean** **deeper** than the **Pacific Ocean**?
(Both bodies of water have depths that can be measured and compared.)

Because the sentence compares depth to depth, the comparison is balanced. Problems can occur, however, when a sentence compares dissimilar things. For example, it would be illogical to compare the depth of one ocean to the shape of another ocean. Depth and shape are not similar things and cannot be compared meaningfully.

ILLOGICAL The stories in my book are longer than your book.
(*Stories* and *book* cannot be logically compared.)

LOGICAL The stories in my book are longer than the stories in your book.
(Two sets of stories can be logically compared.)

Make sure that your sentences compare only similar items. RULE 24.1.10

An unbalanced comparison is usually the result of carelessness. The writer may have simply left something out. Read the following incorrect sentences carefully.

Making Logical Comparisons

Remind students that the goal of using correct grammar in writing is to make writing clear and understandable. When a sentence is unclear, it needs to be revised. One common error is comparing two things that should not be compared. This is sometimes called comparing apples to oranges.

RULE 24.1.9 Read aloud the rule and then have students repeat the lines with you.

Work through the explanation of the first example with students. Then, read aloud the second example.

Say: At first, this sentence may sound okay: *The stories in my book are longer than your book.* When I analyze the comparison, however, I see that it is illogical. It is not logical to compare the length of stories to the length of a book. To make the comparison logical, I should compare the length of stories. To do that, I say: *The stories in my book are longer than the stories in your book.*

Balanced Comparisons

RULE 24.1.10 Read aloud the rule and then have students repeat the line with you.

Write incorrect sentences on the board and have students revise them so that each is correct: *Making cookies is quicker than a cake.* (than making a cake) *The number of students is fewer than desks.* (than the number of desks)

(continued)

Teacher Tip

If students are not able to see the weakness in the incorrect sentences, invite them to first identify and underline the complete subject. Then, have them underline what is being compared. Have them look at each underlined sentence part and ask themselves if the two parts of the sentences are aligned.

Balanced Comparisons *(continued)*

Read aloud the example sentences. Explain that students should ask themselves *What is being compared?* whenever they see a comparative or superlative form. In the first example on the page, *planting grass* (an action) is being compared to *garden*, a noun. You can't compare an action with a thing, so the sentence should be revised.

Other and *Else* in Comparisons

Explain that another kind of illogical comparison is to compare something to itself.

RULE 24.1.11 Read aloud the rule and then have students repeat the lines with you.

Use a Think Aloud as part of a gradual release progression.

Say: I am going to make sure that when I compare part of a group with the rest of the group, I use the word *other* or the word *else* to make sure that I don't compare something to itself. I will reread the comparison sentences that I write and think about what I am comparing. Then, I will make sure I add the important word to make the sentence complete.

Work with students to ensure they can identify the group in each sentence and then the individual part of the group. Write these pairs of words on the board: *pitcher – team member; student – class member; Houston – city; hamburger – food.* Have students brainstorm for sentences in which some aspect of the individual is compared with the same aspect of the group. Then, have students identify the individual and group by underlining the group and circling the individual. Call for volunteers to explain whether each comparison sentence is correct.

Have student pairs each write two sentences comparing an individual with the rest of the people or items in its group. Have students exchange papers and proofread them to ensure that the comparisons are correct.

INCORRECT **Planting grass** is **easier** than a **garden**.
The **number of inlets** on the East Coast is **larger** than the **West Coast**.

In the first sentence, planting grass is mistakenly compared to a garden. In the second sentence, the number of inlets are compared to the West Coast. Both sentences can easily be corrected to make the comparisons balanced.

CORRECT **Planting grass** is **easier** than **planting a garden**.
The **number of inlets** on the East Coast is **larger** than the **number** on the West Coast.

See Practice 24.1E

Other and *Else* in Comparisons

Another common error in writing comparisons is to compare something to itself.

RULE 

When comparing one of a group to the rest of the group, make sure your sentence contains the word *other* or *else*.

Adding *other* or *else* can make a comparison clear. For example, in the second sentence below, because *Edward* is himself a student, he cannot logically be compared to *all students.* He must be compared to *all other students.*

PROBLEM SENTENCES	CORRECTED SENTENCES
At the track meet, my brother sprinted to the finish line before anyone.	At the track meet, my brother sprinted to the finish line before anyone else.
Edward collected more kinds of shells than any student did.	Edward collected more kinds of shells than any other student did.

See Practice 24.1F

Working with ELLs — ELL Sheltered Instruction: Cognitive

Help students write using a variety of grade-appropriate sentence patterns, including balanced comparisons, in increasingly accurate ways. Review with students how to make comparisons. Then:

Beginning Read the first correct example on page 542 to students, clarifying meaning. Then, provide them with a small word bank: *writing, words, sentences, playing, soccer, easier, harder.* Review the meaning of each word, and have students use them to write a balanced comparison by completing this sentence frame: ______ *is* ______ *than* ______.

Intermediate Read the first correct example on page 542 to students. Then, have partners write a new sentence that makes a similar comparison. Coach students in identifying the subject and the verb in this simple sentence pattern.

Advanced Have partners read the correct examples on the page and identify the comparisons. Then, have each partner write five additional balanced comparisons.

Advanced High Have students complete the Advanced activity. Then, challenge them to write a compound sentence featuring two balanced comparisons.

PRACTICE 24.1E **Making Balanced Comparisons**

Read the sentences. Rewrite each sentence, correcting the unbalanced comparison.

EXAMPLE My grade on the second test was better than the first.

ANSWER *My grade on the second test was better than my grade on the first.*

1. The information on this Web site is more detailed than that one.
2. Ben's scoring record is better than Jason.
3. I like the details in this painting better than Vanessa's.
4. The weather here is as cold as Alaska.
5. There are fewer berries in my basket than yours.
6. The service at Mario's Restaurant is better than Lucky's.
7. I think the articles in this magazine are more interesting than that magazine.
8. Josie's dog is not as obedient as Ingrid.
9. Eddie's video game has better features than Manny.
10. The toddler got more food on the floor than his mouth.

PRACTICE 24.1F **Using *Other* and *Else* to Make Comparisons**

Read the sentences. Rewrite each sentence, adding *other* or *else* to make the comparisons logical.

EXAMPLE Gabby is faster than anyone on the team.

ANSWER *Gabby is faster than anyone else on the team.*

11. Dion plays his drum louder than anyone in the band.
12. Jan's outfit is more colorful than anyone's.
13. Tom uses better strategy than any player.
14. Our school has a better debate team than any school in the league.
15. Greg sings better than anyone in the group.
16. Joanne helps out as much as anyone in her family.
17. Maddie's argument is more logical than anyone's.
18. That movie was more exciting than any I have seen lately.
19. Ollie gave a better demonstration than anyone.
20. Alison was more tired than anyone in the group after the long practice.

SPEAKING APPLICATION

With a partner, use your corrected sentence 1 as a model, and make a logical comparison between two items. Your partner should check that your comparison is correct.

WRITING APPLICATION

Use sentences 12, 13, and 14 as models, and write three new sentences making logical comparisons.

Quick-Write Extension

To help students synthesize and apply what they have learned about making balanced comparisons, have them write a brief review comparing different brands of a similar product, such as two shampoos or two video games. Direct students to make each sentence in the review a comparison between the two products. Ask students to exchange their reviews with student partners to check for balance in the comparisons.

SPEAKING APPLICATION

Have partners identify the things being compared in each other's sentences and explain whether the comparison is balanced or unbalanced.

WRITING APPLICATION

Have students explain why they used *other* or *else* in each of their sentences.

PRACTICE 24.1E

1. The information on this Web site is more detailed than the information on that one.
2. Ben's scoring record is better than Jason's.
3. I like the details in this painting better than the ones in Vanessa's.
4. The weather here is as cold as the weather in Alaska.
5. There are fewer berries in my basket than in yours.
6. The service at Mario's Restaurant is better than at Lucky's.
7. I think the articles in this magazine are more interesting than the ones in that magazine.
8. Josie's dog is not as obedient as Ingrid's.
9. Eddie's video game has better features than Manny's.
10. The toddler got more food on the floor than in his mouth.

PRACTICE 24.1F

11. Dion plays his drum louder than anyone else in the band.
12. Jan's outfit is more colorful than anyone else's.
13. Tom uses better strategy than any other player.
14. Our school has a better debate team than any other school in the league.
15. Greg sings better than anyone else in the group.
16. Joanne helps out as much as anyone else in her family.
17. Maddie's argument is more logical than anyone else's.
18. That movie was more exciting than any other I have seen lately.
19. Ollie gave a better demonstration than anyone else.
20. Alison was more tired than anyone else in the group after the long practice.

24.2 Troublesome Adjectives and Adverbs

Lesson Objectives

1. Identify commonly misused adjectives and adverbs.
2. Use commonly misused adjectives and adverbs correctly in both speaking and writing.

Ensure that students understand that certain verbs—*appear, feel, look,* and *sound*—can be used as either action verbs or linking verbs. Explain that when these verbs are used to tell something about the condition of the subject, they require an adjective modifier, not an adverb. Give this example: *She appeared happy.* The adjective form *happy* is correct because *appeared* is not an action verb. The subject *She* is not doing an action. In this sentence, however, *appear* is an action: *The bus suddenly appeared.* The subject, *bus,* is doing the appearing. Because *suddenly* is modifying an action verb, it's correct to use the adverb form *suddenly.*

Discuss the example sentences that illustrate when to use *bad* and when to use *badly.* Then, have students create sentences using *appear, feel, look,* and *sound* as linking verbs modified by adjectives. Discuss the sentences and identify any sentences in which students have mistakenly used adverbs instead of adjectives.

24.2 Troublesome Adjectives and Adverbs

The common adjectives and adverbs listed below often cause problems in both speaking and writing.

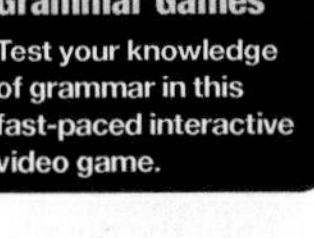

Grammar Practice
Practice your grammar skills with Writing Coach Online.

Grammar Games
Test your knowledge of grammar in this fast-paced interactive video game.

(1) *bad and badly* *Bad* is an adjective. Use it after linking verbs, such as *are, appear, feel, look,* and *sound*. *Badly* is an adverb. Use it after action verbs, such as *act, behave, do,* and *perform.*

INCORRECT Marco looked **badly** after the game.
CORRECT Marco looked **bad** after the game.

INCORRECT My sister did **bad** on the test.
CORRECT My sister did **badly** on the test.

(2) *good and well* *Good* is an adjective. *Well* can be either an adjective or an adverb, depending on its meaning. A common mistake is the use of *good* after an action verb. Use the adverb *well* instead.

INCORRECT The puppy behaved **good** all day.
The book is **well**.

CORRECT The puppy behaved **well** all day.
The book is **good**.

As adjectives, *good* and *well* have slightly different meanings, which are often confused. *Well* usually refers simply to health.

EXAMPLES Charlie felt **good** after hockey practice.
The spaghetti smells **good**.
That kitten is not **well**.

Diagnostic and Instruction
Diagnostic test assesses students' instructional needs. Lessons and practice are assigned based on results.

Additional Practice
- Grammar Practice—Targeted practice addresses individual needs.
- ExamView—Teachers customize their grammar practice and tests.
- Grammar Games—Interactive video games make grammar fun.

Differentiated Instruction

PRE-AP Enrichment for Above-Level Students Remind students that adverbs often modify verbs, and adjectives modify nouns and pronouns. Then, remind students that linking verbs link the subject to other information about the subject. Have students use the Internet or another resource to create a full list of verbs that can be used as either action verbs or linking verbs. (Most resources will list at least 10 linking verbs, including *appear, become, feel, grow, look, remain, seem, smell, sound, stay, taste.*)

Challenge small groups to create skits in which they use several different verbs as both action verbs and linking verbs. Have volunteers perform their skits for the class. Afterward, students should list each verb they used and explain when they used it as an action and when they used it as a linking verb.

(3) *fewer and less* Use the adjective *fewer* to answer the question, "How many?" Use the adjective *less* to answer the question, "How much?"

HOW MANY	**fewer** dollars	**fewer** children
HOW MUCH	**less** money	**less** water

(4) *just* When used as an adverb, *just* often means "no more than." When *just* has this meaning, place it right before the word it logically modifies.

INCORRECT Does he **just** want **one bottle of water**?

CORRECT Does he want **just** **one bottle of water**?

(5) *only* The position of *only* in a sentence sometimes affects the sentence's entire meaning. Consider the meaning of these sentences.

EXAMPLES **Only** he went to the baseball game.
(Nobody else went to the game.)

He **only** went to the baseball game.
(He did nothing else except go to the game.)

He went **only** to the baseball game.
(He went to the baseball game and nowhere else.)

Mistakes involving *only* usually occur when its placement in a sentence makes the meaning unclear.

UNCLEAR **Only** follow directions from me.

BETTER Follow directions **only** from me.
(not from anyone else)

Follow **only** directions from me.
(nothing but directions)

See Practice 24.2A
See Practice 24.2B
See Practice 24.2C
See Practice 24.2D

Read and discuss the sections on *fewer and less, just,* and *only.* Explain that *fewer* should be used with count nouns, while *less* should be used with noncount nouns. Review the definitions of count and noncount nouns as necessary. (Count nouns refer to things that can be counted, such as *three kinds of spices* and *two bottles of water.* Noncount nouns refer to things that cannot be enumerated, such as *salt* and *milk.*) Invite students to write sentences using *fewer* with count nouns and *less* with noncount nouns.

Use a Think Aloud as part of a gradual release progression for the study of *only.*

Say: *Only* is another word that can cause some confusion in our speaking and writing. When **I write** a sentence using *only,* I like to ask *What?* or *Who?* after the word *only* appears in the sentence. The response to that question tells me whether I have placed *only* correctly in the sentence. For example, *I have only one pencil.* When I ask *What do I have?* the response is *one pencil.* For the sentence *Only I have one pencil*, I ask *Who has one pencil?* The response to my question is *only I.* This is how I check to make sure my sentence is written correctly.

Work with students to ask *What?* and *Who?* questions after the word *only* in each sample sentence. Discuss how its placement affects the meaning of the sentence.

Have student pairs write three new *only* sentences and ask the *What?* and *Who?* questions. Then, have students present their sentences to the class.

Extension

To help students synthesize and apply what they have learned about the use of the word *only,* have students discuss how moving *only* to different positions in a sentence changes the sentence's meaning. Write these sentences on the board: *Only Colin and I know the answer to that question. Colin and I only know the answer to that question. Colin and I know only the answer to that question. Colin and I know the answer to only that question.* Challenge students to contrast the meaning of the sentences.

Teacher Tip

Have students who have difficulty with troublesome adjectives and adverbs write hints and tips on note cards. Encourage students to refer to the cards as they review the chapter pages.

PRACTICE 24.2A

1. good
2. well
3. badly
4. well
5. badly
6. good
7. bad
8. good
9. bad
10. good, well

PRACTICE 24.2B

11. The patient is feeling well today.
12. The plants looked bad because they had not been watered.
13. correct
14. correct
15. Nicole and Arianna danced well in the show.
16. correct
17. That flutist plays well.
18. correct
19. Joshua draws really well.
20. correct

SPEAKING APPLICATION

Have partners explain why they used *bad, badly, good,* or *well* in each of their sentences.

WRITING APPLICATION

Have students share their paragraphs with the group, explaining why their use of *bad, badly, good,* and *well* is correct.

PRACTICE 24.2A Using *Bad* and *Badly*, *Good* and *Well*

Read the sentences. Write the word in parentheses that correctly completes each sentence.

EXAMPLE My little brother behaves (bad, badly) when he is upset.

ANSWER *badly*

1. Marissa is a (good, well) swimmer.
2. Lee's new job is working out (good, well).
3. Unfortunately, the repair work was done (bad, badly).
4. Casey did (good, well) on his project.
5. This old car is running (bad, badly).
6. Charlotte looks (good, well) in her prom dress.
7. Walt looked (bad, badly) after the race.
8. The weather is looking (good, well) for the picnic.
9. Rosemary is feeling (bad, badly) today.
10. It seemed like a (good, well) idea, but it did not turn out (good, well).

PRACTICE 24.2B Revising for Troublesome Modifiers

Read the sentences. Rewrite the sentences that contain errors in the use of modifiers. If a sentence has no error, write *correct*.

EXAMPLE Jorge feels well about his decision.

ANSWER *Jorge feels good about his decision.*

11. The patient is feeling good today.
12. The plants looked badly because they had not been watered.
13. Chloe felt bad about her mistake.
14. We all look good in those pictures.
15. Nicole and Arianna danced good in the show.
16. Olivia and Sue work well together.
17. That flutist plays good.
18. Because the event was badly planned, it was not successful.
19. Joshua draws really good.
20. Rachel's intentions were good, but she did not follow through.

SPEAKING APPLICATION

Tell a partner two sentences using *bad* and *badly*. Your partner should say two sentences using *good* and *well*.

WRITING APPLICATION

Write a short paragraph evaluating a movie or television show you have recently seen. Use *bad, badly, good,* and *well* to describe the plot, the characters, or any other details of the movie or show.

Working with ELLs — ELL Sheltered Instruction: Metacognitive

Adapt the Speaking Application to have students demonstrate listening comprehension of increasingly complex spoken English by orally responding to questions and requests. Instruct them to monitor comprehension and seek clarification as needed.

Beginning Have students respond to two questions about a food they have tasted that they didn't like. Request that they use the words *bad* or *badly* in their answers. Provide a model: *The pie tasted bad.* Direct students to raise their hands to seek clarification if they do not understand something in the questions.

Intermediate Write *good, well, bad,* and *badly* on the board. Have students say each word aloud. Request that they use one of the words in answering the questions you are about to ask. Then, have students respond to two questions about a project they completed in class, directing them to ask for clarification as needed.

Advanced Have partners complete the Speaking Application. Then, have partners ask each other questions based on their respective Speaking Application responses. Have partners answer the questions, seeking clarification as needed.

Advanced High Have students complete the Advanced activity. Then, have them share with the class a tip on seeking clarification.

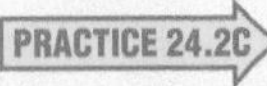

PRACTICE 24.2C Writing Sentences Using *Fewer* or *Less*

Read the sentences. If the underlined word in the sentence is incorrect, rewrite the sentence correctly. If the underlined word in the sentence is correct, write *correct*.

EXAMPLE I have less quarters than dimes.

ANSWER *I have fewer quarters than dimes.*

1. Do you have less money than you had last week?
2. There are less students in my math class than in my science class.
3. We have fewer time left to spend at the pool than I thought.
4. My mother thought the recipe called for fewer eggs than four.
5. The car had less gallons of gas than we needed to get there.
6. The car had less gas than we needed to get there.
7. Is 90 greater than or less than 900?
8. There are less grapes in this bowl than in that one.
9. I bought a small popcorn instead of a large because I wanted fewer popcorn.
10. It is healthier to eat less salty snacks and more fruit each day.

PRACTICE 24.2D Writing Sentences Using *Just* and *Only*

Read the sentences below. For each one, write a new sentence using the word *just* or *only* to match the meaning of the sentence given.

EXAMPLE We are going to this specific movie tonight. (only)

ANSWER *We are going to only this movie tonight.*

11. We have the exact amount of milk needed for the recipe. (just)
12. The person from our school at the skating rink was Brian. (only)
13. The teacher said, "Follow instructions from nobody else but me."(only)
14. Zach wants a sandwich for lunch and nothing else. (just)
15. Arlene is the one person who brought a present. (just)
16. Cindy bought oatmeal at the store and nothing else. (only)
17. Cindy was the one person who bought oatmeal at the store. (only)
18. The parents gave the babysitter their cell phone number and no other information. (just)
19. The babysitter was the one person who had the parents' cell phone number. (just)
20. Remember to do the odd-numbered math problems, not the even-numbered ones. (just)

SPEAKING APPLICATION

With a partner, take turns discussing homework or other school projects. Use *fewer, less, just,* and *only* at least once. Your partner should listen for proper use of the words and correct any errors.

WRITING APPLICATION

Write a brief paragraph about a shopping trip you plan to take. Use *fewer, less, just,* and *only* at least once. Exchange paragraphs with a partner. Check for and correct any errors in the paragraph.

SPEAKING APPLICATION

Have students explain how they determined when to use *fewer, less, just,* and *only* in their sentences.

WRITING APPLICATION

Students' sentences should demonstrate that students can use *just* and *only* correctly in their writing.

PRACTICE 24.2C

1. correct
2. There are fewer students in my math class than in my science class.
3. We have less time left to spend at the pool than I thought.
4. correct
5. The car had fewer gallons of gas than we needed to get there.
6. correct
7. correct
8. There are fewer grapes in this bowl than in that one.
9. I bought a small popcorn instead of a large because I wanted less popcorn.
10. It is healthier to eat fewer salty snacks and more fruit each day.

PRACTICE 24.2D

11. We have just the amount of milk needed for the recipe.
12. The only person from our school at the skating rink was Brian.
13. The teacher said, "Follow instructions only from me."
14. Zach wants just a sandwich for lunch.
15. Just Arlene brought a present.
16. Cindy only bought oatmeal at the store.
17. Cindy was the only person who bought oatmeal at the store.
18. The parents gave the babysitter just their cell phone number.
19. Just the babysitter had the parents' cell phone number.
20. Remember to do just the odd-numbered math problems.

Test Warm-Up

1. **B** Change ***good*** to **well**
2. **H** My neighbor said that she needed me only from 4:00 P.M. until 7:00 P.M.
3. **C** Change ***bad*** to **badly**
4. **G** Change ***less*** to **fewer**

Reteach

If students have not mastered these skills, review the content in Section 24.2 Troublesome Adjectives and Adverbs.

Test Tip

Students may feel frustrated that they don't know all the answers. Remind them that tests are designed to challenge them. They are not expected to get every answer right. Encourage students to approach each question individually without worrying about their overall score.

Test Warm-Up

DIRECTIONS
Read the introduction and the passage that follows. Then, answer the questions to show that you can use troublesome adjectives and adverbs (e.g., *bad/badly; good/well; fewer/less; just/only*) correctly in reading and writing.

Shanequa wrote this paragraph about her first job as a babysitter. Read the paragraph and think about the changes you would suggest as a peer editor. When you finish reading, answer the questions that follow.

Fewer Than Five

(1) I just completed a course in babysitting, and I think I did pretty good. (2) So, when my neighbor asked me to watch her five children on Friday, I agreed. (3) My neighbor said that she needed only me from 4:00 P.M. until 7:00 P.M. (4) She also said that if she finished her errands in less time, she'd be home earlier. (5) I wish I could say that my first babysitting experience went well, but it went bad. (6) The five kids fought the entire time. (7) I think next time I'll babysit for a family with less children.

1 What change, if any, should be made in sentence 1?

- **A** Change ***good*** to **bad**
- **B** Change ***good*** to **well**
- **C** Delete ***pretty***
- **D** Make no change

2 How should sentence 3 be revised?

- **F** Only my neighbor said that she needed me from 4:00 P.M. until 7:00 P.M.
- **G** My neighbor said only that she needed only me from 4:00 P.M. until 7:00 P.M.
- **H** My neighbor said that she needed me only from 4:00 P.M. until 7:00 P.M.
- **J** My only neighbor said that she needed me from 4:00 P.M. until 7:00 P.M.

3 What change, if any, should be made in sentence 5?

- **A** Change ***well*** to **good**
- **B** Change ***well*** to **better**
- **C** Change ***bad*** to **badly**
- **D** Make no change

4 What change, if any, should be made in sentence 7?

- **F** Change ***less*** to **lesser**
- **G** Change ***less*** to **fewer**
- **H** Change ***less*** to **just**
- **J** Make no change

Cumulative Review Chapters 21–24

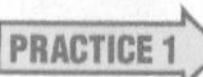

PRACTICE 1 Identifying Verb Tenses

Read the sentences. For each sentence, write whether the verb tense is *present, past, future, present perfect, past perfect,* or *future perfect.* Also indicate if the verb is *progressive.*

1. Ms. Paloma has worked at the bank for years.
2. My mother is preparing a huge meal for the holidays.
3. The committee will meet tomorrow morning.
4. On June 1, Troy will have been living in San Antonio for exactly five years.
5. Penelope has been designing her own clothing for some time.
6. Restaurants generally throw away their leftovers.
7. My father studied to be a chemical engineer.
8. The standardized test for seventh graders will be starting in half an hour.
9. A dozen swans were floating in the pond.
10. No one else had ever grown anything like Mr. Marshall's hybrid lily.

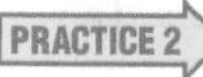

PRACTICE 2 Revising to Use Active Voice

Read the sentences. Then, rewrite each passive voice sentence so that it is in active voice. If a sentence is already in active voice, write *active.*

1. The story was written by Shirley Jackson.
2. The best guacamole is prepared by Suzie.
3. The treehouse is in the maple tree by the creek.
4. Mr. Levinson's generous gift to the town was accepted by the mayor in a special ceremony.
5. Anita is flying to Minneapolis tomorrow.

PRACTICE 3 Using Verbs Correctly

Read the sentences. Then, rewrite the sentences to correct any incorrect verb forms. If a sentence has no errors, write *correct.*

1. Last evening, I drunk a mug of cocoa.
2. I have never flew on that airline.
3. Yesterday morning, Portia lay this funny mouse pad in front of my computer.
4. You should not set in the sun for so many hours.
5. Yesterday at the movies, Peggy says to me, "Popcorn is low in calories."
6. Dad finally done his tax return.
7. The voters have chose a new person to become our state's governor.
8. I seen my cousins from the Philippines for the first time last August.
9. The bucket has apparently sprang a leak.
10. This past winter, the pipes in the old house froze and burst.

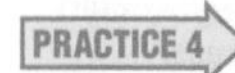

PRACTICE 4 Identifying Pronoun Cases and Uses

Read the sentences. Write whether each underlined pronoun is in the *nominative, objective,* or *possessive* case. Then, write whether it is used as a *subject,* a *predicate pronoun,* a *direct object,* an *indirect object,* or the *object of a preposition.*

1. The babysitter sang to <u>her</u> until she fell asleep.
2. The driving instructor gave <u>him</u> a lesson.
3. <u>Hers</u> is the bright blue coat.
4. The quiet music calmed <u>me</u>.
5. The best athletes on the team were Jasper and <u>I</u>.

Continued on next page ▶

PRACTICE 1

1. present perfect
2. present progressive
3. future
4. future perfect progressive
5. present perfect progressive
6. present
7. past
8. future progressive
9. past progressive
10. past perfect

PRACTICE 2

1. Shirley Jackson wrote the story.
2. Suzie prepares the best guacamole.
3. active
4. In a special ceremony, the mayor accepted Mr. Levinson's generous gift to the town.
5. active

PRACTICE 3

1. Last evening, I drank a mug of cocoa.
2. I have never flown on that airline.
3. Yesterday morning, Portia laid this funny mouse pad in front of my computer.
4. You should not sit in the sun for so many hours.
5. Yesterday at the movies, Peggy said to me, "Popcorn is low in calories."
6. Dad finally did his tax return.
7. The voters have chosen a new person to become our state's governor.
8. I saw my cousins from the Philippines for the first time last August.
9. The bucket has apparently sprung a leak.
10. correct

PRACTICE 4

1. objective, object of a preposition
2. objective, indirect object
3. possessive, subject
4. objective, direct object
5. nominative, predicate pronoun

Cumulative Review Chapters 21–24

PRACTICE 5 Using Pronouns Correctly

Read the sentences. Then, rewrite the sentences to correct any incorrect pronouns. If a sentence has no errors, write *correct.*

1. Claudia and him exchanged papers.
2. The coyote howled it's long and lonesome cry.
3. Whom did the artist portray in the painting?
4. The best swimmers are Drew and me.
5. The bus driver gave Bridget and I change.
6. Share the dessert between you and he.
7. Viv is the one who the class chose as president.
8. Their's is the last truck on the left.
9. Don't discourage Sonny and she.
10. I have no idea whom that politician is.

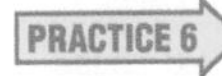

PRACTICE 6 Revising for Subject–Verb Agreement

Read the sentences. Then, rewrite the sentences to correct any errors in subject–verb agreement. If a sentence has no errors, write *correct.*

1. Each of the pianists practice for hours.
2. Neither Abe nor he see many movies.
3. A box of mints always sit atop her dresser.
4. The committee quarrels about choosing new members.
5. None of those golfers ride in the cart.
6. Deirdre and Lex enjoy line dancing.
7. Ham and eggs are my favorite breakfast.
8. The lawyer or her associates argues in court.
9. Do the mayor or the governor know the facts?
10. The class has been dismissed for the day.

PRACTICE 7 Revising for Pronoun–Antecedent Agreement

Read the sentences. Then, rewrite the sentences to correct any errors in pronoun–antecedent agreement. If a sentence has no errors, write *correct.*

1. None of the computers lost its memory.
2. Either the cat or the dog lost its collar.
3. Each of the chairs had their upholstery replaced.
4. Natasha has a job at which you input data.
5. In the past, everyone kept their hats in hatboxes.
6. Amelia and Leah wore ribbons in her hair.
7. Neither George nor Pete did their chores.
8. Several of the birds had damage to its wings.
9. Some of the beauticians did his or her own hair.
10. Did everybody know his or her state senator?

PRACTICE 8 Using Modifiers Correctly

Read the sentences. Then, rewrite the sentences to correct any errors involving modifiers. If a sentence has no errors, write *correct.*

1. The stagnant pond smells really badly.
2. I can do nothing farther for you.
3. I am feeling more well than I felt before.
4. Less customers shop here on weekends.
5. Of their three bad songs, this is the baddest.
6. The tour boats only sail in the summer.
7. Tammy is kinder than I am.
8. Beau performed good on the test.
9. In my opinion, robins are prettier than any bird.
10. Is there a guitarist more good than he is?

PRACTICE 5

1. Claudia and he exchanged papers.
2. The coyote howled its long and lonesome cry.
3. correct
4. The best swimmers are Drew and I.
5. The bus driver gave Bridget and me change.
6. Share the dessert between you and him.
7. Viv is the one whom the class chose as president.
8. Theirs is the last truck on the left.
9. Don't discourage Sonny and her.
10. I have no idea who that politician is.

PRACTICE 6

1. Each of the pianists practices for hours.
2. Neither Abe nor he sees many movies.
3. A box of mints always sits atop her dresser.
4. The committee quarrel about choosing new members.
5. correct
6. correct
7. Ham and eggs is my favorite breakfast.
8. The lawyer or her associates argue in court.
9. Does the mayor or the governor know the facts?
10. correct

PRACTICE 7

1. correct
2. correct
3. Each of the chairs had its upholstery replaced.
4. Natasha has a job at which she inputs data.
5. In the past, everyone kept his or her hats in hatboxes.
6. Amelia and Leah wore ribbons in their hair.
7. Neither George nor Pete did his chores.
8. Several of the birds had damage to their wings.
9. Some of the beauticians did their own hair.
10. correct

PRACTICE 8

1. The stagnant pond smells really bad.
2. I can do nothing further for you.
3. I am feeling better than I felt before.
4. Fewer customers shop here on weekends.
5. Of their three bad songs, this is the worst.
6. The tour boats sail only in the summer.
7. correct
8. Beau performed well on the test.
9. In my opinion, robins are prettier than any other bird.
10. Is there a guitarist better than he is?

CHAPTER 25 LESSON PLANNER
Punctuation

Use the Online Lesson Planner at www.phwritingcoach.com to customize your instructional plan for an integrated Language Arts curriculum.

DAY 1 25.1 End Marks

"What Do You Notice?" **Objectives:** Identify, use, and understand end marks, including ▪ periods ▪ question marks ▪ exclamation marks	**INSTRUCTION AND PRACTICE** **Student Edition** pp. 551–555

DAYS 2–4 25.2 Commas

Objectives: Identify and understand aspects of using commas, including ▪ in compound sentences ▪ avoiding comma splices ▪ in a series ▪ between adjectives ▪ after introductory material ▪ with parenthetical expressions ▪ with nonessential expressions ▪ with dates and geographical names ▪ in numbers ▪ with addresses and in letters ▪ with direct quotations	**INSTRUCTION AND PRACTICE** **Student Edition** pp. 556–570

DAY 5 25.3 Semicolons and Colons

Objectives: Identify and understand aspects of using semicolons and colons, including ▪ to join independent clauses ▪ to avoid confusion	**INSTRUCTION AND PRACTICE** **Student Edition** pp. 571–575 **Test Warm-Up** p. 576

Grammar Assessment

Grammar Coach:	Diagnostic Assessment	End-of-Chapter Assessment	Progress Monitoring
Personalized Instruction	Students take grammar diagnostic test online and are automatically assigned instruction and practice in areas where they need support.	Teacher uses **ExamView** to administer end-of-chapter assessment and remediation. Teachers may customize **ExamView** tests or use the ones provided.	Teachers may use the **Test Warm-Ups** and the **Cumulative Reviews** in the student book or eText to check students' mastery of grammar skills. Students may also play **DimensionL** grammar video games to test their grammar skills.
Teacher-Directed Instruction	Teacher administers the diagnostic test and determines focus of instruction and practice.		

Alternate Pacing Plans

- **Block Scheduling** Each day in the Lesson Planner represents a 40–50 minute block. Teachers using block scheduling may combine days to revise pacing to meet their classroom needs.
- **Accelerated Lesson Planning** Combine instructional days, focusing on concepts called out by students' diagnostic test results.
- **Integrated Language Arts Curriculum** Use the instruction and practice in this chapter to provide reinforcement, remediation, or extension of grammar concepts taught in your literature curriculum.

Links to Prentice Hall *LITERATURE*

- **Unit 1** Possessive Nouns, p. 68; Writing Workshop: Editing and Proofreading (Focus on the Dialogue), p. 183
- **Unit 2** Writing Workshop: Editing and Proofreading (Focus on Dialogue), p. 391
- **Unit 5** Sentence Functions and Endmarks, p. 858
- **Unit 6** Punctuation Marks, p. 932; Commas, p. 956; Writing Workshop: Revising Incorrect Use of Commas, p. 985; Abbreviations, p. 1024

WRITING COACH Online

www.phwritingcoach.com

Grammar Assessment and Practice

Chapter diagnostic tests assess students' skills and assign instruction and practice.

DimensionL Video Games

Fast-paced interactive video games challenge students' mastery of grammar.

Lesson Planner continues on next page

DAYS 6–8 25.4 Quotation Marks, Underlining, and Italics

Objectives	INSTRUCTION AND PRACTICE
Objectives: Identify and understand aspects of using quotation marks with quotations. ▪ with quotations. ▪ quotations within quotations ▪ explanatory material within quotations ▪ with other punctuation marks ▪ in titles and other special words ▪ for dialogue	**Student Edition** pp. 577–588

DAY 9 25.5 Hyphens

Objectives	INSTRUCTION AND PRACTICE
Objectives: Identify and understand aspects of using hyphens, including ▪ in numbers ▪ with prefixes and suffixes ▪ in compound words ▪ with compound modifiers ▪ at the ends of lines ▪ to divide words	**Student Edition** pp. 589–594

DAY 10 25.6 Apostrophes

Objectives	INSTRUCTION AND PRACTICE
Objectives: Identify and understand aspects of using apostrophes, including ▪ with possessive nouns ▪ with pronouns ▪ with contractions ▪ to create plurals	**Student Edition** pp. 595–599

DAY 11 25.7 Parentheses and Brackets

Objectives	INSTRUCTION AND PRACTICE
Objectives: Identify and understand aspects of using parentheses and brackets.	**Student Edition** pp. 600–602

DAY 12 25.8 Ellipses and Dashes

Objectives	INSTRUCTION AND PRACTICE
Objectives: Identify and understand aspects of using ellipses and dashes.	**Student Edition** pp. 603–606

Differentiated Instruction

Differentiated Instruction Boxes in this Teacher's Edition address these student populations:

- Below-Level Students
- Gifted and Talented Students
- English Language Learners
- Above-Level Students
- Special Needs Students
- Spanish Speaking Students

In addition, for further enrichment, see the **Extension** features.

CHAPTER 25

PUNCTUATION

Using punctuation correctly in your writing will help you present ideas clearly.

WRITE GUY *Jeff Anderson, M.Ed.*

WHAT DO YOU NOTICE?

Look out for punctuation marks as you zoom in on these sentences from "Icarus and Daedalus" by Josephine Preston Peabody.

MENTOR TEXT

> The heat of the sun had melted the wax from his wings; the feathers were falling, one by one, like snowflakes; and there was none to help.

Now, ask yourself the following questions:

- What is the purpose of the commas in this sentence?
- Why does the author use semicolons in this sentence?

The author uses commas to set off the phrase *one by one* from the rest of the sentence. Commas are used because it is a nonessential phrase; if the phrase is taken away, the sentence still makes sense. The author uses semicolons to separate the three main or independent clauses because they are closely related ideas.

Grammar for Writers A writer can use a semicolon to connect closely linked main or independent clauses. Think of a sentence as a chain and the semicolon as a link that joins equal parts into a strong whole.

My favorite fruits are apples and pears and bananas and mangos.
Have you ever tried them with a sprinkling of commas?

551

Grammar for Writers: Syntax

Explain to students that knowing when to use punctuation marks helps writers communicate more effectively. The rules in the lessons will help students to use punctuation correctly in their writing.

PUNCTUATION

As students progress in their writing skills, it will be important for them to be able to apply the rules of grammar, usage, and mechanics to their own drafts. Use the *What Do You Notice?* feature to help them see effective conventions in the work of professional writers. Encourage students to incorporate proper voice, tense, and syntax as they edit their own writing.

Remind students that it is important to use punctuation correctly in their writing. Misplaced punctuation can alter the meaning of a sentence and confuse readers. Point out that end marks, commas, semicolons, and other punctuation marks help writers present their ideas clearly.

WRITE GUY *Jeff Anderson, M. Ed.*

WHAT DO YOU NOTICE?

When students have read the Mentor Text, **say:** You probably know that punctuation clarifies meaning by signaling when a sentence ends, when to pause before and after words, whether a group of words is a quotation, and so on. What punctuation marks do you notice in the Mentor Text? (commas, semicolons, and a period)

On the board, write the Mentor Text sentence without any punctuation. Have students read the sentence to themselves. **Then, ask:** What was it like to read this sentence without punctuation? (**Possible response:** It was confusing because the ideas ran together and I couldn't tell where to pause as I read.)

Incorrectly punctuate the sentence on the board. For example, *The heat of the sun had melted; the wax from his wings; the feathers were falling, one by one like snowflakes and there was none to help?* **Then, ask:** What effect does the incorrect punctuation have on your understanding of the sentence? (Accept all reasonable responses.)

Lesson Objectives

1. Recognize and identify end marks.
2. Correctly use and understand end marks.

Using Periods

Point out that periods are used to end sentences or abbreviations. Remind students that many types of sentences require periods. Review these types as you discuss the rules.

RULES 25.1.1, 25.1.2, 25.1.3, 25.1.4 Read aloud the rules and then have students repeat the lines with you.

Use a Think Aloud as part of a gradual release progression.

Say: I keep a few simple rules in mind when I use a period to end sentences. If the sentence makes a statement or gives a command, I end it with a period. If a sentence asks an indirect question, such as *Ed asked me how he should punctuate the sentence,* I end that sentence with a period, too.

Write these sentences on the board, and **work with students to** identify why a period is (or is not) used in each case. *I like the beach.* (A period ends a declarative statement.) *She asked me if I like the beach.* (A period ends a sentence that contains an indirect question.) *Go to the beach.* (A period ends a command.) Remind students that a period follows most abbreviations and initials. Give a few examples: *Mr.* (Use a period after an abbreviation.) *J.K. Rowling* (Use a period after initials.)

Have partners brainstorm for examples of the types of sentences described. Have partners share their examples with the class.

25.1 End Marks

End marks signal the end or conclusion of a sentence, word, or phrase. There are three end marks: the **period** (.), the **question mark** (?), and the **exclamation mark** (!).

Using Periods

A **period** indicates the end of a sentence or an abbreviation.

Use a period to end a declarative sentence—a statement of fact, idea, or opinion.

DECLARATIVE SENTENCE This is a beautiful painting.

Use a period to end most imperative sentences—sentences that give directions or commands.

IMPERATIVE SENTENCE Finish doing your homework.

RULE 25.1.3

Use a period to end a sentence that contains an indirect question.

An **indirect question** restates a question in a declarative sentence. It does not give the speaker's exact words.

INDIRECT QUESTION Mike asked me if I would go.

RULE 25.1.4

Use a period after most abbreviations and initials.

ABBREVIATIONS Mr. St. Sen. in. Sr.

INITIALS John F. Kennedy T. S. Eliot

Note: The abbreviation for *inch, in.,* is the only measurement abbreviation that uses a period after it.

Grammar Tutorials
Brush up on your Grammar skills with these animated videos.

Grammar Practice
Practice your grammar skills with Writing Coach Online.

Grammar Games
Test your knowledge of grammar in this fast-paced interactive video game.

Quick-Write Extension

To help students synthesize and apply what they have learned about using periods, have them write short paragraphs recruiting other students to join imaginary clubs or organizations. Working in pairs, students should make up a club or organization and create an acronym for it; for example, *Musicians in Middle School, or MIMS.* One student in each pair should be the president, and the other student should be the vice-president. Pairs should then write a short paragraph describing the club and asking other students to join. When they write, students should refer to themselves by their initials, for example, *G. L. Jones,* for *Gregory Lawrence Jones.*

Diagnostic and Instruction
Diagnostic test assesses students' instructional needs. Lessons and practice are assigned based on results.

Additional Practice
- Grammar Practice—Targeted practice addresses individual needs.
- ExamView—Teachers customize their grammar practice and tests.
- Grammar Games—Interactive video games make grammar fun.

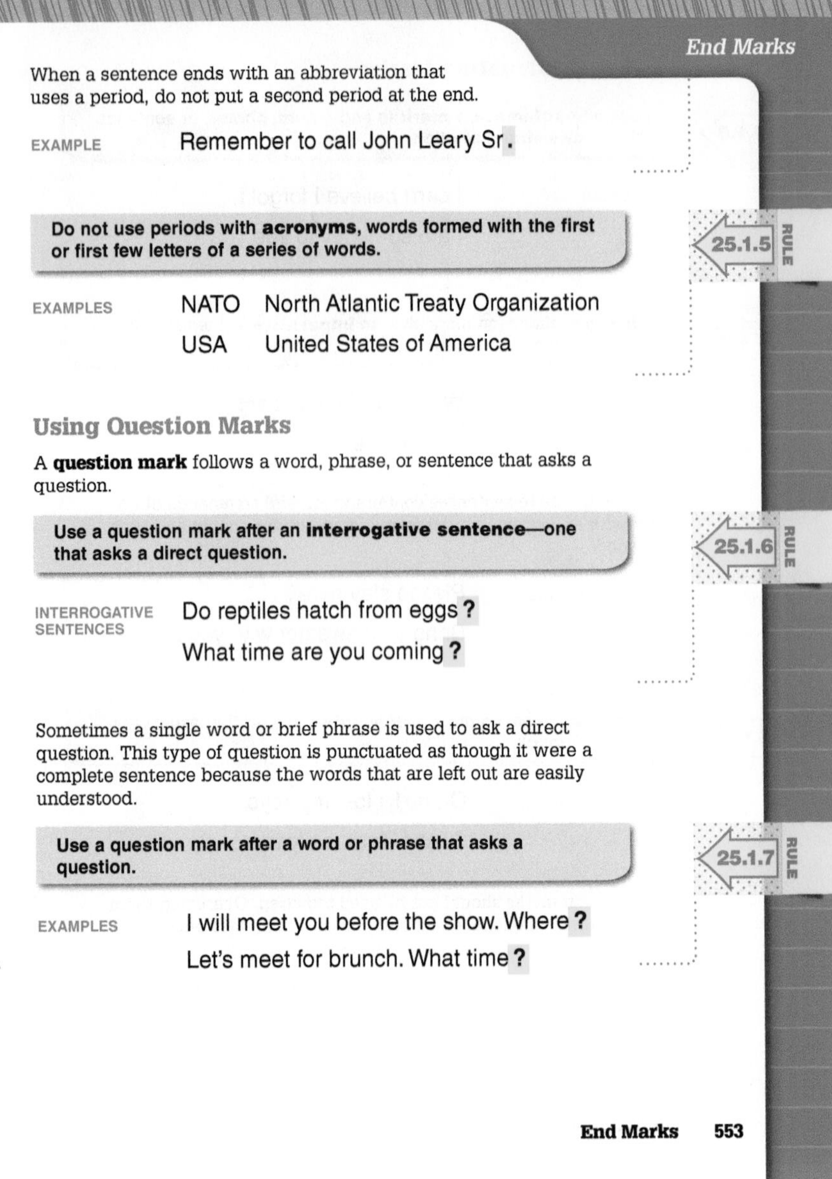

When a sentence ends with an abbreviation that uses a period, do not put a second period at the end.

EXAMPLE Remember to call John Leary Sr.

Do not use periods with acronyms, words formed with the first or first few letters of a series of words. RULE 25.1.5

EXAMPLES
NATO North Atlantic Treaty Organization
USA United States of America

Using Question Marks

A **question mark** follows a word, phrase, or sentence that asks a question.

Use a question mark after an interrogative sentence—one that asks a direct question. RULE 25.1.6

INTERROGATIVE SENTENCES
Do reptiles hatch from eggs?
What time are you coming?

Sometimes a single word or brief phrase is used to ask a direct question. This type of question is punctuated as though it were a complete sentence because the words that are left out are easily understood.

Use a question mark after a word or phrase that asks a question. RULE 25.1.7

EXAMPLES
I will meet you before the show. Where?
Let's meet for brunch. What time?

See Practice 25.1A

Remind students that it is generally incorrect to have two of the same marks of punctuation in a row. Thus, when a sentence ends with an abbreviation that uses a period, it is not necessary to add a second period to end the sentence. Study the example on page 553.

RULE 25.1.5 Read aloud the rule and then have students repeat the lines with you.

Remind students that acronyms—short expressions consisting of capital letters that stand for a phrase—do not have periods. Remind students that if they are unsure whether a group of letters is an acronym or what an acronym stands for, they can find the answer in an unabridged dictionary.

Using Question Marks

Point out that a question mark is used at the end of a sentence that asks a question.

RULES 25.1.6, 25.1.7 Read aloud the rules and then have students repeat the lines with you.

Work with students to identify which of these sentences and phrases require a question mark: *We went to the movies.* (This sentence requires a period. It is a statement of fact, not a question.) *When did you go to the movies.* (This sentence requires a question mark. It asks a direct question.) *I asked Mom if I could go.* (This sentence asks an indirect question. Therefore, it does not require a question mark.) *Why not.* (This phrase requires a question mark. The phrase asks a question.) *How so.* (This phrase requires a question mark. The phrase asks a question.)

Working with ELLs — ELL Sheltered Instruction: Cognitive

Help students identify the difference between declarative, imperative, and interrogative sentences by distinguishing intonation patterns of English with increasing ease.

Beginning Write a declarative sentence, an imperative sentence, and an interrogative sentence on the board, and then read them aloud to students, emphasizing correct intonation (e.g., raising your pitch at the end of a yes/no question). Have students repeat the sentences after you, mimicking your intonation.

Intermediate Model correct intonation as in the Beginning activity. Then, have partners find examples of declarative, imperative, and interrogative sentences in a familiar selection. Have them read the sentences aloud, correcting each other's intonation as needed.

Advanced Have students work individually to find examples of declarative, imperative, and interrogative sentences in a familiar selection. Then, have students read their sentences aloud to their partner without identifying the type of sentence. Ask listeners to tell the sentence type and the correct end mark, based on the partner's intonation.

Advanced High Challenge students to write their own declarative, imperative, and interrogative sentences. Have them speak these sentences to their partners, using correct intonation. Partners should copy the sentences down, using correct end punctuation.

Teacher Tip

If students need practice identifying questions, have student pairs take turns interviewing each other about their favorite activity. For example, *What is your favorite activity? Why do you like it?* Encourage students to pepper their interviews with single-word follow-up questions, such as *Why? How? When?*

Using Exclamation Marks

Point out that exclamation marks indicate strong emotion and forceful or urgent commands.

RULE 25.1.8 Read aloud the rule and then have students repeat the lines with you.

Explain that sentences that express surprise, anger, or other strong emotions end with an exclamation mark. Give these examples: *Yipes! I cut myself! I am furious! That's terrific!* Call for a student volunteer to read aloud each example with feeling.

RULE 25.1.9 Read aloud the rule and then have students repeat the lines with you.

Remind students that imperative sentences give commands. Point out that in some languages, it is customary to end all or most imperative sentences with an exclamation mark. In English, however, the exclamation mark is used to end only those imperatives that give forceful or urgent commands. Discuss the examples on page 554.

RULE 25.1.10 Read aloud the rule and then have students repeat the lines with you.

Say: Overusing exclamation marks reduces their effectiveness and can even have a comic effect. Write this on the board: *Oh, no! We are out of bananas! Not again! Last time I made banana bread I ran out of bananas! I used banana extract instead! Yuck! It tasted terrible!* **Ask:** What is the effect of so many exclamation marks? (Using so many exclamation marks detracts from the sentences that really are exclamations.) Replace all of the exclamation marks except *Oh, no!* and *Yuck!* with periods. Read the paragraph aloud, using your voice to emphasize the exclamatory statements. **Ask:** How does using fewer exclamation marks make the writing more effective? **(Possible responses:** It allows the real exclamations to stand out; it gives the writing more variety.)

Using Exclamation Marks

Use an exclamation mark to end a word, phrase, or sentence that shows strong emotion.

EXAMPLES I can't believe I forgot!

I am so happy to see you!

Use an exclamation mark after an imperative sentence that gives a forceful or urgent command.

IMPERATIVE SENTENCE Watch out for that car!

Don't move!

While imperative sentences containing forceful commands often end with an exclamation mark, mild imperatives should end with a period.

MILD IMPERATIVES Please stay here.

Bring your sweater with you.

Use an exclamation mark after an interjection that expresses strong emotion.

INTERJECTIONS Oh no! I lost my keys.

Ouch! That really hurts.

Exclamation marks should not be used too often. Overusing them reduces their emotional effect and makes writing less effective.

See Practice 25.1B

Working with ELLs — ELL Sheltered Instruction: Cognitive

Help students use visual and contextual support to read, to enhance and confirm understanding, and to develop vocabulary needed to comprehend increasingly challenging language.

Beginning Write the word *emotion* from rules 25.1.8 on the board. Read it aloud as students echo. Then, use facial expressions, mime, and other visual support to portray various emotions. Work with students to name each emotion. After your presentation of each, repeat the word *emotion* and guide students to understand that it names feelings generally. Then, read and discuss rule 25.1.8.

Intermediate Obtain images illustrating each of these words from page 554: *emotion, forceful, urgent, mild.* Write each word on the board. Read each aloud as students echo, and use facial expressions, mime, and the images you have provided to illustrate its meaning. Then, guide students in reading the page.

Advanced Introduce the words *emotion, forceful, urgent,* and *mild* from page 554, using visual support as in the Intermediate activity. Have students use each word in a sentence. Then, have partners read the page together, referring to the visual support to enhance and confirm meaning.

Advanced High Have students complete the Advanced activity, reading the page independently.

PRACTICE 25.1A Using Question Marks and Periods

Read the sentences. Rewrite each sentence, adding missing question marks and periods.

EXAMPLE Mr Moroney is the substitute math teacher today

ANSWER *Mr. Moroney is the substitute math teacher today.*

1. When will you return my video game
2. Proofread your final draft carefully
3. Did you watch the inauguration of the president
4. Marci asked if I would go with her to the mall
5. Will Prof J D Snow give another lecture
6. Sgt Sanchez spoke about her experiences overseas
7. Please handle that DVD carefully
8. What exactly does *digital* mean
9. Dr Angela Preston is a veterinarian
10. That old mansion has some furniture from the 1800s

PRACTICE 25.1B Using Exclamation Marks and Periods

Read the sentences. Rewrite each sentence, adding missing exclamation marks and periods.

EXAMPLE Wow What a great shot

ANSWER *Wow! What a great shot!*

11. Watch your step there
12. Boy, was she angry
13. I thought I would never finish
14. Oh, I forgot my password
15. That is the most beautiful rose I have ever seen
16. Julio has been calling me all afternoon
17. Keep your eye on the ball
18. Please close the door
19. What a brilliant idea
20. We picked up enough trash to fill three bags

SPEAKING APPLICATION

Ask a partner a question. Your partner should answer and ask you a question. Use your voices to indicate the end punctuation.

WRITING APPLICATION

Write a paragraph as if you were giving a play-by-play description of a game or other exciting event. Use appropriate end punctuation.

SPEAKING APPLICATION

Have students explain to the class how they assess appropriate punctuation through voice inflections in their speaking application exercise.

WRITING APPLICATION

Have students exchange paragraphs and check each other's work, explaining why it is or is not correct.

PRACTICE 25.1A

1. When will you return my video game?
2. Proofread your final draft carefully.
3. Did you watch the inauguration of the president?
4. Marci asked if I would go with her to the mall.
5. Will Prof. J. D. Snow give another lecture?
6. Sgt. Sanchez spoke about her experiences overseas.
7. Please handle that DVD carefully.
8. What exactly does *digital* mean?
9. Dr. Angela Preston is a veterinarian.
10. That old mansion has some furniture from the 1800s.

PRACTICE 25.1B

Answers will vary. Sample answers:

11. Watch your step there.
12. Boy, was she angry!
13. I thought I would never finish.
14. Oh, I forgot my password.
15. That is the most beautiful rose I have ever seen!
16. Julio has been calling me all afternoon.
17. Keep your eye on the ball!
18. Please close the door.
19. What a brilliant idea!
20. We picked up enough trash to fill three bags.

Lesson Objectives

1. Use punctuation marks including commas after introductory words, phrases, and clauses.
2. Use commas correctly in writing.

Using Commas in Compound Sentences

Point out that, because misused commas can obscure meaning, it is important to learn how to use commas correctly.

RULE 25.2.1 Read aloud the rule and then have students repeat the lines with you.

Use a Think Aloud as part of a gradual release progression.

Say: I know that compound sentences consist of two or more independent clauses, or simple sentences, joined by a coordinating conjunction: *and, but, for, nor, or, so,* or *yet.* Once I identify a coordinating conjunction, I look to see if it joins two independent clauses. If it does, I put a comma before the conjunction.

Work with students to identify conjunctions. For each sentence, **ask:** Does this conjunction join two independent clauses? Is the comma necessary? (The comma is necessary. The conjunction, *but,* joins two independent clauses.) Repeat the technique for all the example sentences. Students should see that in each case, the coordinating conjunction does not join independent clauses. Therefore, a comma is not necessary.

Have student pairs brainstorm for compound sentences and discuss how to punctuate them.

Avoiding Comma Splices

Explain that a comma splice occurs when two sentences are joined by a comma.

Grammar Game Plan

25.2 Commas

End marks signal a full stop. **Commas** signal a brief pause. A comma may be used to separate elements in a sentence or to set off part of a sentence. Include a comma in your writing when you want your reader to group information in your sentence.

www.phwritingcoach.com

Grammar Tutorials
Brush up on your Grammar skills with these animated videos.

Grammar Practice
Practice your grammar skills with Writing Coach Online.

Grammar Games
Test your knowledge of grammar in this fast-paced interactive video game.

Using Commas in Compound Sentences

A **compound sentence** consists of two or more main or independent clauses that are joined by a coordinating conjunction, such as *and, but, for, nor, or, so,* or *yet.*

Use a comma before the conjunction to separate two main or independent clauses in a compound sentence.

COMPOUND SENTENCE — Children have learned many things by age five, but they still may need help getting dressed.

Use a comma before a conjunction only when there are complete sentences on both sides of the conjunction. If the conjunction joins single words, phrases, or subordinate clauses, do not use a comma.

SINGLE WORDS — We saw chimpanzees and gorillas.

PHRASES — Edie likes drawing pictures and taking photos.

SUBORDINATE CLAUSES — Choose someone who has experience but who can also follow directions.

In some compound sentences, the main or independent clauses are very brief, and the meaning is clear. When this occurs, the comma before the conjunction may be omitted.

EXAMPLE — Christie tried hard but she was unsuccessful.

See Practice 25.2A

Grammar Game Plan

Avoiding Comma Splices

A **comma splice** occurs when two or more sentences have been joined with only a comma between them.

www.phwritingcoach.com

Diagnostic and Instruction
Diagnostic test assesses students' instructional needs. Lessons and practice are assigned based on results.

Additional Practice
- Grammar Practice—Targeted practice addresses individual needs.
- ExamView—Teachers customize their grammar practice and tests.
- Grammar Games—Interactive video games make grammar fun.

Avoid comma splices by making sure all of your ideas are properly linked.

RULE 25.2.2

INCORRECT The sun was shining brightly, he forgot to bring his sunglasses.

CORRECT The sun was shining brightly. He forgot to bring his sunglasses.

Using Commas in a Series

Sometimes, a sentence lists a number of single words or groups of words. When three or more of these items are listed, the list is called a **series.** Separate the items in a series with commas.

Use commas to separate three or more words, phrases, or clauses in a series.

RULE 25.2.3

A comma follows each of the items except the last one in a series. The conjunction *and* or *or* is added after the last comma.

SERIES OF WORDS The forest animals included deer, squirrels, skunks, and rabbits.

SERIES OF PHRASES Her directions sent us across the field, through the woods, and past the farmhouse.

There are two exceptions to this rule. If each item except the last one in a series is followed by a conjunction, do not use commas. Also, do not use a comma to separate groups of words that are considered to be one item.

EXAMPLES Hana brought apples and peaches and cherries.

The caterer supplied oil and vinegar, salt and pepper, and bread and butter.

See Practice 25.2B

Differentiated Instruction

RTI Strategy for Below-Level Students Help students who are having difficulty understanding when to use commas in compound sentences. Have student pairs write several independent clauses. Work with students to identify the subject and verb in each clause. Remind students that a compound sentence is two clauses joined by a coordinating conjunction (*and, but, for, nor, or, so, yet*). Challenge student pairs to create compound sentences from their independent clauses.

PRE-AP Enrichment for Above-Level Students Remind students that a subordinate clause is not a complete sentence even though it contains a subject and a verb. A comma is not used before a subordinating conjunction, such as *after, although, until, because,* or *when.* Write this example on the board: *We left the restaurant after Clarence got sick.* Have students identify the subordinate clause. Challenge student pairs to learn five additional subordinating conjunctions and to use these words to make five sentences.

RULE 25.2.2 Read aloud the rule and then have students repeat the lines with you.

Discuss the example sentences at the top of page 557. Then, work with students to identify the comma splice in this sentence: *We went to the zoo, we visited the panda bears.* Ask students how they can correct the comma splice. (Replace the comma with a period.) Then, ask them how they can turn the sentence into a compound sentence. (Insert the conjunction *and* after the comma.)

Using Commas in a Series

Explain that commas are used to separate three or more items in a row, or a series. The items may be words, phrases, or clauses.

RULE 25.2.3 Read aloud the rule and then have students repeat the lines with you.

Write this sentence on the board: *I like reading books watching movies and listening to CDs.* **Say:** When I punctuate a series, I check to see whether I have three or more similar items in a row. In this sentence, I see that I do. Underline each item in the series, saying it aloud as you do. Then, **say:** The purpose of using commas in a series is to separate the items. Therefore, I will put a comma after *reading books* to separate it from *watching movies.* Insert the comma into the sentence. **Say:** I still need to separate *watching movies* from *listening to CDs.* Therefore, I will put another comma after *watching movies.* Insert the comma. **Say:** Notice that the series has three items and two commas. There is always one comma fewer than the number of items in the series.

Review the first and second example sentences under RULE 25.2.3. Then, review the exceptions to the rule for using commas to separate items in a series. On the board, write these sentences, omitting the commas: *We took a blanket, food, and a ball to the park. Jen and Ivan and Luis went for a walk. I like bacon and eggs, peanut butter and jelly, and milk and cookies.* Work with students to insert series commas where they belong.

Using Commas Between Adjectives

Point out that commas are sometimes used between two or more adjectives in a sentence.

RULES 25.2.4, 25.2.5, 25.2.6 Read aloud the rules and then have students repeat the lines with you.

Use a Think Aloud as part of a gradual release progression.

Say: **I will use** a comma between adjectives if the adjectives are of equal rank; that is, if I can place *and* between them or change their order and have the sentence still make sense. Otherwise, I will not use a comma.

Write these sentences on the board, omitting the commas: *Frank bought a shiny, red guitar. Many loud cheers followed the performance. We wrapped the present with long, silky, yellow ribbons.* **Work with students to** determine where to place commas in the sentences.

Have student pairs brainstorm for and write sentences with coordinate adjectives. Students should use the example that illustrates Rule 25.2.4 as a model. Invite students to read their sentences aloud to the group. As students listen, they should identify where the commas should be placed.

Teacher Tip

If students need more practice using commas between adjectives, have student pairs create a sentence that uses two or more adjectives to describe an item in the classroom. For example, *I am sitting on a hard, orange chair.* Use student sentences to review the rules for using commas between adjectives.

Using Commas Between Adjectives

Sometimes, two or more adjectives are placed before the noun they describe.

Use commas to separate adjectives of equal rank.

There are two ways to tell whether adjectives in a sentence are of equal rank:

- If the word *and* can be placed between the adjectives without changing the meaning, the adjectives are of equal rank.
- If the order of the adjectives can be changed, they are of equal rank.

EXAMPLE Bianca made a simple, polite request.
(*A simple and polite request* does not change the sentence's meaning. *A polite, simple request* also does not change the meaning.)

Do not use commas to separate adjectives that must appear in a specific order.

Do not use a comma if adding *and* or changing the order of the adjectives would result in a sentence that makes no sense.

INCORRECT Some and colorful birds perched on the roof.

INCORRECT Colorful some birds perched on the roof.

CORRECT Some colorful birds perched on the roof.

Do not use a comma to separate the last adjective in a series from the noun it modifies.

INCORRECT We walked on a long, twisting, scenic, road. See Practice 25.2C

CORRECT We walked on a long, twisting, scenic road. See Practice 25.2D

Working with ELLs — ELL Sheltered Instruction: Cognitive

As students read page 558, enhance comprehension of written text by having them use prereading supports. Introduce the topic of adjectives of equal rank by having students generate examples in a word web. First, have students choose a favorite movie. Then:

Beginning Write on the board adjectives that might describe the movie. Guide students in filling out a word web with the adjectives. Then, have them select pairs of adjectives. For each pair, write a sentence on the board in which you use the adjectives before a noun. Then, read page 558 with students, referring to their examples.

Intermediate Guide small groups in filling out a word web with adjectives for the movie. Then, have them write sentences about the movie in which they use pairs of adjectives before a noun. Read page 558 with students, drawing on their examples.

Advanced Have partners fill out a word web with adjectives for the movie. Then, have them write sentences about the movie in which they use pairs of adjectives before a noun. Have them read the lesson and correct their sentences as needed.

Advanced High Have students complete the Advanced activity, using adjectives in a series in their sentences as well as pairs of adjectives.

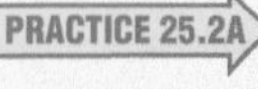

PRACTICE 25.2A **Using Commas in Compound Sentences**

Read the sentences. Rewrite each sentence, adding commas where they are needed.

EXAMPLE Our team played their best yet they still lost the game.

ANSWER *Our team played their best, yet they still lost the game.*

1. Emma wanted a cat or dog but her mother is allergic to them.
2. Brad searched diligently yet he could not find the socks for his uniform.
3. This pocket watch is valuable to me for it belonged to my grandfather.
4. We needed to earn some money for the club trip so we had a bake sale.
5. Ryan will come here later and he will bring his games.
6. Jessica and Gavin have been working on that puzzle for nearly two hours but they are not finished.
7. The referee blew the whistle and the game stopped.
8. Trina likes yogurt for breakfast but her sister likes toast and juice.
9. The tune kept running through my head yet I could not think of the title.
10. Put the milk back in the refrigerator or it will turn sour.

PRACTICE 25.2B **Using Commas in a Series**

Read the sentences. Rewrite each sentence, adding commas as needed.

EXAMPLE My grandmother knits scarves sweaters and mittens.

ANSWER *My grandmother knits scarves, sweaters, and mittens.*

11. For lunch, you can choose soup pizza or salad.
12. The hikers tramped over rocks across a stream and into a dark forest.
13. I would like a dog that wags its tail comes when I call and doesn't jump on people.
14. The actors dancers and musicians all came on stage for a bow after the performance.
15. Mrs. Wong bought carrots onions and potatoes for a stew.
16. The parts of a business letter are the date the inside address the greeting the body the closing and the signature.
17. Del grabbed his jacket rushed out the door and ran down the sidewalk.
18. My courses this year are English math science social studies and Spanish.
19. Evan looked on the floor under the table and behind the couch for the remote control.
20. Mercury Venus Mars and Jupiter are the closest planets to Earth.

WRITING APPLICATION

Use sentences 8, 9, and 10 as models and write three compound sentences. Place a comma correctly in each sentence.

WRITING APPLICATION

Complete this sentence with a series: *I have only ten dollars to spend on ______.* Punctuate the series correctly.

PRACTICE 25.2A

1. Emma wanted a cat or a dog, but her mother is allergic to them.
2. Brad searched diligently, yet he could not find the socks for his uniform.
3. This pocket watch is valuable to me, for it belonged to my grandfather.
4. We needed to earn some money for the club trip, so we had a bake sale.
5. Ryan will come here later, and he will bring his games.
6. Jessica and Gavin have been working on that puzzle for nearly two hours, but they are not finished.
7. The referee blew the whistle, and the game stopped.
8. Trina likes yogurt for breakfast, but her sister likes toast and juice.
9. The tune kept running through my head, yet I could not think of the title.
10. Put the milk back in the refrigerator, or it will turn sour.

PRACTICE 25.2B

11. For lunch, you can choose soup, pizza, or salad.
12. The hikers tramped over rocks, across a stream, and into a dark forest.
13. I would like a dog that wags its tail, comes when I call, and doesn't jump on people.
14. The actors, dancers, and musicians all came on stage for a bow after the performance.
15. Mrs. Wong bought carrots, onions, and potatoes for a stew.
16. The parts of a business letter are the date, the inside address, the greeting, the body, the closing, and the signature.
17. Del grabbed his jacket, rushed out the door, and ran down the sidewalk.
18. My courses this year are English, math, science, social studies, and Spanish.
19. Evan looked on the floor, under the table, and behind the couch for the remote control.
20. Mercury, Venus, Mars, and Jupiter are the closest planets to Earth.

WRITING APPLICATION

Have partners check each other's work to determine if commas have been correctly placed.

WRITING APPLICATION

Using the writing application question, have students identify why the commas are needed and explain their function.

PRACTICE 25.2C

1. correct
2. A rude, angry customer complained to the manager.
3. correct
4. The hot, humid air made us feel listless.
5. That cheese has a strong, unpleasant odor.
6. correct
7. correct
8. An enthusiastic, kind grandfather was telling stories to the children.
9. Charles prefers his sturdy, old bicycle to his brother's shiny, new one.
10. correct

PRACTICE 25.2D

11. A tall, elegant model walked across the stage.
12. Emily created the design for the poster, and Roger wrote the text.
13. We wondered who the woman was, where she came from, and what she wanted.
14. Sherman usually wears baggy, faded jeans, but today he is wearing shorts.
15. The children built a great big snowman, and they put a hat on its head.
16. You can take a sandwich, or you can buy lunch there.
17. Vernon eats only fruits, vegetables, beans, and whole grains.
18. Our dog chased a rabbit across the grass, through the flowers, and under a fence.
19. I tried to watch that documentary, but I didn't enjoy it, so I turned it off.
20. Leslie did not like the hot, spicy dip.

PRACTICE 25.2C Using Commas Between Adjectives

Read the sentences. Rewrite the sentences, adding commas where necessary. If no comma is needed, write *correct*.

EXAMPLE Giselle is a graceful talented gymnast.

ANSWER *Giselle is a graceful, talented gymnast.*

1. I have two large apples to share.
2. A rude angry customer complained to the manager.
3. Wild animals have many clever ways of surviving.
4. The hot humid air made us feel listless.
5. That cheese has a strong unpleasant odor.
6. We live in a red brick apartment building.
7. My parents listen to the great old songs by the Beatles.
8. An enthusiastic kind grandfather was telling stories to the children.
9. Charles prefers his sturdy old bicycle to his brother's shiny new one.
10. There were three rotten apples at the bottom of the basket.

PRACTICE 25.2D Proofreading Sentences for Commas

Read the sentences. Rewrite each sentence, adding commas where they are needed.

EXAMPLE Anna bought cheese crackers and dips.

ANSWER *Anna bought cheese, crackers, and dips.*

11. A tall elegant model walked across the stage.
12. Emily created the design for the poster and Roger wrote the text.
13. We wondered who the woman was where she came from, and what she wanted.
14. Sherman usually wears baggy faded jeans but today he is wearing shorts.
15. The children built a great big snowman and they put a hat on its head.
16. You can take a sandwich or you can buy lunch there.
17. Vernon eats only fruits vegetables beans and whole grains.
18. Our dog chased a rabbit across the grass through the flowers and under a fence.
19. I tried to watch that documentary but I didn't enjoy it so I turned it off.
20. Leslie did not like the hot spicy dip.

WRITING APPLICATION

Use the sentences in Practice 25.2C as models and write three sentences. Include two or more adjectives in each to describe something. Use a comma to separate the adjectives, if necessary.

WRITING APPLICATION

Use sentences 13 and 14 as models and write two sentences. Use commas correctly to indicate a series, a compound sentence, and equal adjectives.

WRITING APPLICATION

Have students share their sentences with the class, explaining how they decided where the commas should be placed.

WRITING APPLICATION

Have students explain how the three different uses for commas function in their sentences.

Find It/FIX IT 2 Grammar Game Plan

Using Commas After Introductory Words, Phrases, and Clauses

When a sentence begins with an introductory word, phrase, or other structures, that word or phrase is usually separated from the rest of the sentence by a comma.

RULE 25.2.7

Use a comma after most introductory words, phrases, or dependent clauses.

See Practice 25.2E

KINDS OF INTRODUCTORY MATERIAL	
Introductory Word	Hey, give me your binoculars quickly before the bear moves. Dwayne, please bring me my boots and jacket. Well, I certainly wasn't prepared for that. Shani, where did you go?
Introductory Phrase	To conserve energy, we are lowering the heat. With Jaime sick, Ana didn't know how she would finish the poster. In the morning, the highway to the city is jammed with cars. To visit Sweden, you will need a passport.
Introductory Adverbial Clause	Although it was early, my sister was dressed and waiting for the bus. When the raccoons got into the garbage, they made a mess. When the dancers took a bow, the audience applauded wildly.

When a prepositional phrase of only two words begins a sentence, a comma is not absolutely necessary.

EXAMPLES At dawn I slowly opened my eyes.

In June we plan to visit my aunt.

Using Commas After Introductory Words, Phrases, and Clauses

Point out that when a sentence begins with an introductory word or phrase, that word or phrase is usually followed by a comma.

RULE 25.2.7 Read aloud the rule and then have students repeat the lines with you.

Discuss the examples of introductory material in the chart on page 561. Then, help students apply the rule to a new example sentence. Write this sentence on the board: *After Juan was hurt the other team scored two goals.* Read the sentence aloud, pausing for a moment after the introductory clause *After Juan was hurt.* **Say:** When a sentence begins with an introductory word, phrase, or clause, that word, phrase, or clause is separated from the rest of the sentence by a comma. This sentence begins with an adverbial clause. I can tell because the group of words begins with a subordinating conjunction, *After,* and contains a subject, *Juan,* and a verb, *was hurt.* Underline the adverbial clause and insert a comma after *hurt.*

Ask students to write three sentences that use correct punctuation marks. The first sentence should begin with an introductory word, the second with an introductory phrase, and the third with an adverbial clause. Work with students to write the first sentence, and then have students write the other sentences independently. Students should then read their sentences to a partner and discuss the effect of correct punctuation in each sentence.

Working with ELLs ELL Sheltered Instruction: Cognitive

Build and reinforce student attainment of concepts of comma use by having students listen to, derive meaning from, and respond orally to information presented in a wide variety of print, electronic, and audiovisual media. Make a recording of yourself reading the sentences in Practice 25.2D on page 560, pausing where commas should appear. Then:

Beginning Play the first two sentences. Repeat, having students raise their hands when they hear a pause. Explain that in writing, the pauses are represented by commas. Help students identify the words separated by pauses. Then, guide students in restating the meaning of the sentences.

Intermediate Play the first four sentences. Repeat, having students raise their hands when they hear a pause corresponding to a comma. Discuss how the pauses help listeners follow the ideas expressed. Then, guide students in paraphrasing the sentences.

Advanced Play the recording. Repeat, having students raise their hands when they hear a pause corresponding to a comma. Discuss how the pauses help listeners follow the ideas. Then, have partners work to paraphrase the sentences.

Advanced High Have students complete the Advanced activity. Then, have students review a short video segment, noting how pauses help the speaker convey meaning.

Using Commas With Parenthetical Expressions

Remind students to use commas to set off parenthetical expressions, which are words or phrases not essential to the meaning of a sentence.

RULE 25.2.8 Read aloud the rule and then have students repeat the lines with you.

Use a Think Aloud as part of a gradual release progression.

Say: Identifying a parenthetical expression in a sentence is easy. **I look for** additional information that is not essential to the meaning of the sentence. If I read aloud a sentence with a parenthetical expression, I can usually hear the pauses before and after the expression. Write this sentence on the board: *I wonder Juan if you realize how much I miss you.* Read the sentence aloud, pausing before and after *Juan.* **Say:** I know that I paused before and after *Juan.* Let me check to see whether the sentence would make sense if I omitted the word *Juan.* Read the sentence without *Juan.* **Say:** Yes, it does make sense. That means *Juan* is parenthetical in this sentence, and I need to set off the name with commas. Insert the commas.

Work with students to review and understand the kinds of parenthetical expressions listed on the page.

Have student pairs generate sentences with parenthetical expressions and share their sentences with the class.

Using Commas With Nonessential Expressions

Remind students to use commas to set off words or phrases that are not essential to the meaning of a sentence.

Grammar Game Plan

Using Commas With Parenthetical Expressions

A **parenthetical expression** is a word or phrase that is not essential to the meaning of the sentence. These words or phrases generally add extra information to the basic sentence.

Use commas to set off parenthetical expressions from the rest of the sentence.

Grammar Game Plan

A parenthetical expression in the middle of a sentence needs two commas. A parenthetical expression at the end of a sentence needs only one.

KINDS OF PARENTHETICAL EXPRESSIONS	
Names of People Being Addressed	Listen carefully, Ava, while I tell you how to do it. Please sit down, Brian.
Certain Adverbs	The suitcase, therefore, is quite a bit heavier. I arrived too late to help, however.
Common Expressions	They know she did her best, of course. He is not the best one for the job, in my opinion.
Contrasting Expressions	The award should be theirs, not yours. These shirts, not those, are ready to be packed.

See Practice 25.2F
See Practice 25.2G

Using Commas With Nonessential Expressions

To determine when a phrase or clause should be set off with commas, decide whether the phrase or clause is **essential** or **nonessential** to the meaning of the sentence. Nonessential expressions can be left out without changing the meaning of the sentence.

Punctuation Verb Grammar

562 Punctuation

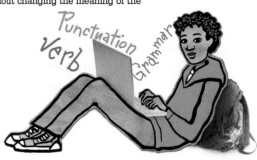

Working with ELLs ELL Sheltered Instruction: Cognitive

As you work through the lesson on page 562, have students speak using a variety of grammatical structures, including parenthetical expressions, with increasing accuracy and ease.

Beginning Read aloud two example sentences from page 562 to students, noting where the commas appear. Have students say the sentences after you. Discuss where you paused and how your pitch shifted.

Intermediate Read aloud two example sentences from page 562 to students, noting where the commas appear. Have students say the sentences after you. Discuss where you paused and how your pitch shifted. Then, have students work with more fluent partners to say aloud the other examples on the page, correcting each other's intonation.

Advanced Model correct intonation for parenthetical expressions. Have partners take turns saying aloud the examples on page 562, correcting each other's intonation.

Advanced High Have students complete the Advanced activity. Then, have students write five sentences of their own that feature parenthetical expressions. Direct partners to take turns saying each other's sentences aloud.

Use commas to set off nonessential expressions from the main clause. Do not set off essential material with commas.

RULE 25.2.9

Appositives and Appositive Phrases

Appositives are often set off with commas, but only when their meaning is not essential to the sentence. In the first example below, the appositive *West Side Story* is not set off with commas because it clarifies which movie is being discussed.

ESSENTIAL The award-winning movie *West Side Story* takes place in New York City.

NONESSENTIAL *West Side Story*, an award-winning movie, takes place in New York City.

Participial Phrases

Like appositives, participial phrases are set off with commas when their meaning is nonessential. In the first example below, *sitting on the bench* is essential because it tells which woman is the aunt.

ESSENTIAL The woman sitting on the bench is my aunt.

NONESSENTIAL Aunt Jane, sitting on the bench, visited us today.

Adjectival Clauses

Adjectival clauses, too, are set off with commas only if they are nonessential. In the second example below, *a new player who could score goals* is nonessential because it adds information about Derek. The main clause in the sentence is about the team welcoming Derek, not about what Derek can do.

ESSENTIAL The team needed a player who could score goals.

NONESSENTIAL The team welcomed Derek, who could score goals.

See Practice 25.2H

RULE 25.2.9 Read aloud the rule and then have students repeat the lines with you.

Review the difference between essential and nonessential expressions and the different kinds of clauses and phrases (appositive, participial, adjectival) on the page. Remind students that phrases and clauses are essential when they are needed to identify the noun they describe. If they do not identify the noun, they are nonessential and are set off with commas. Write this example on the board: *The man wearing the green plaid jacket stole my purse!* Ask students whether the underlined participial phrase identifies which man stole the purse. Students should see that the phrase does, indeed, identify which man. Point out that since the phrase is needed, it is essential and therefore not set off with commas.

Have student pairs generate examples of sentences with nonessential expressions. Challenge the class to identify the appositives, participial phrases, and adjectival clauses in each sentence.

Teacher Tip

If students need additional practice with nonessential expressions, write a simple sentence on the board. For example, *My brother walked to the store.* Challenge students to add a nonessential expression to the sentence. For example, *My brother, who loves to exercise, walked to the store.*

PRACTICE 25.2E

1. Oh, I forgot to tell you about the assignment.
2. Without a moment's hesitation, he agreed to help.
3. When Tiffany wants to think about something, she takes a long walk.
4. No, that's not what I meant.
5. Before you go, talk to Mr. Cortez.
6. In case of an emergency, exit the building at once.
7. As soon as I saw the situation, I knew what I had to do.
8. Suddenly, a clap of thunder startled everyone.
9. If we do not sell enough tickets, we may have to cancel the show.
10. Dad, thanks for getting me the concert tickets for my birthday.

PRACTICE 25.2F

Last week, Sylvia helped her family prepare to move, so they would be ready on moving day. First, they went through the closets, pulled out clothes they did not wear, and put them in large plastic bags so they could donate them. Then, they emptied drawers, cupboards, and bookcases. Before packing, they wrapped glasses, dishes, and other breakable things in paper. Finally, everything was neatly packed, and the movers loaded their belongings onto a truck. Off they went to their new home.

PRACTICE 25.2E Using Commas After Introductory Words, Phrases, or Clauses

Read the sentences. Rewrite each sentence, adding the comma needed after the introductory word, phrase, or clause.

EXAMPLE Actually there's no correct answer to that problem.

ANSWER *Actually, there's no correct answer to that problem.*

1. Oh I forgot to tell you about the assignment.
2. Without a moment's hesitation he agreed to help.
3. When Tiffany wants to think about something she takes a long walk.
4. No that's not what I meant.
5. Before you go talk to Mr. Cortez.
6. In case of an emergency exit the building at once.
7. As soon as I saw the situation I knew what I had to do.
8. Suddenly a clap of thunder startled everyone.
9. If we do not sell enough tickets we may have to cancel the show.
10. Dad thanks for getting me the concert tickets for my birthday.

PRACTICE 25.2F Proofreading a Passage for Commas

Read the paragraph. Rewrite the paragraph, adding commas where they are needed.

EXAMPLE When Avery wanted to take courses at the museum school he had to submit an application go to an interview and show his three best works. It was a lot to do but he thought it was worth it.

ANSWER *When Avery wanted to take courses at the museum school, he had to submit an application, go to an interview, and show his three best works. It was a lot to do, but he thought it was worth it.*

Last week Sylvia helped her family prepare to move so they would be ready on moving day. First they went through the closets pulled out clothes they did not wear and put them in large plastic bags so they could donate them. Then they emptied drawers cupboards and bookcases. Before packing they wrapped glasses dishes and other breakable things in paper. Finally everything was neatly packed and the movers loaded their belongings onto a truck. Off they went to their new home.

SPEAKING APPLICATION

Find three sentences in a newspaper or magazine that have introductory words, phrases, and clauses. Read the sentences aloud to a partner, without the commas. Discuss how the commas make the meaning clear.

WRITING APPLICATION

Write a brief narrative paragraph about an event in which you participated. Include introductory words, phrases, and clauses. Use commas correctly in your sentences. Discuss the purpose of the commas with a partner.

SPEAKING APPLICATION

Students should demonstrate that they can use commas after introductory words, phrases, and clauses by working with partners to identify the reasons that the commas have been used in the sentences.

WRITING APPLICATION

Partners should demonstrate that they can use commas after introductory words, phrases, and clauses, by checking each other's work, explaining why it is or is not correct.

PRACTICE 25.2G Using Commas With Parenthetical Expressions

Read the sentences. Rewrite each sentence, adding commas as needed to set off parenthetical expressions.

EXAMPLE I hope to see you there Jess.

ANSWER *I hope to see you there, Jess.*

1. Jasmine in my opinion is a very good artist.
2. You can of course change your mind later.
3. I think you should wear your blue shirt not this one.
4. I forgot his birthday however.
5. This is the last envelope thank goodness that I will have to lick.
6. Do you know Gil who won the award?
7. Snakes contrary to popular opinion are not slimy.
8. I really like our new principal don't you?
9. It's only been a week I think since we've been back.
10. These running shoes on the other hand will give you more support.

PRACTICE 25.2H Using Commas With Nonessential Expressions

Read the sentences. Rewrite the sentences, adding commas where necessary. If a sentence is punctuated correctly, write *correct*.

EXAMPLE This old plate which was just found dates from colonial times.

ANSWER *This old plate, which was just found, dates from colonial times.*

11. Edward Bloor the author of *Tangerine* lives in Florida.
12. That quotation is from Confucius who was a great Chinese philosopher.
13. George delivered the argument that convinced the listeners.
14. Tara's little brother a persistent troublemaker annoyed us all afternoon.
15. An athlete who practices will perform well.
16. The town hall built in 1920 needs repairing.
17. Any member missing three rehearsals will be dropped from the cast.
18. The Statue of Liberty a gift from France stands on Liberty Island in New York Harbor.
19. Yo-Yo Ma the popular cellist encourages young musicians of all types.
20. Judd the lifeguard teaches swimming.

SPEAKING APPLICATION

Take turns reading sentence 6 aloud with a partner. Explain how it can be misinterpreted without the correct punctuation.

WRITING APPLICATION

Write two sentences, one with a nonessential expression and one with an expression that is essential. Use commas correctly with the nonessential expression.

SPEAKING APPLICATION

Have students explain how to determine whether a parenthetical expression needs one comma or two.

WRITING APPLICATION

Have students explain how they decided where to use commas in their sentences.

PRACTICE 25.2G

1. Jasmine, in my opinion, is a very good artist.
2. You can, of course, change your mind later.
3. I think you should wear your blue shirt, not this one.
4. I forgot his birthday, however.
5. This is the last envelope, thank goodness, that I will have to lick.
6. Do you know, Gil, who won the award?
7. Snakes, contrary to popular opinion, are not slimy.
8. I really like our new principal, don't you?
9. It's only been a week, I think, since we've been back.
10. These running shoes, on the other hand, will give you more support.

PRACTICE 25.2H

11. Edward Bloor, the author of *Tangerine*, lives in Florida.
12. That quotation is from Confucius, who was a great Chinese philosopher.
13. correct
14. Tara's little brother, a persistent troublemaker, annoyed us all afternoon.
15. correct
16. The old town hall, built in 1920, needs repairing.
17. correct
18. The Statue of Liberty, a gift from France, stands on Liberty Island in New York Harbor.
19. Yo-Yo Ma, the popular cellist, encourages young musicians of all types.
20. Judd, the lifeguard, teaches swimming.

Using Commas With Dates and Geographical Names

Explain to students that commas are used to separate the parts of dates that are made up of two or more parts and geographical names that are made up of two or more parts.

RULE 25.2.10 Read aloud the rule and then have students repeat the lines with you.

Use a Think Aloud as part of a gradual release progression.

Say: When **I am writing** a date, I check to see if it has two or more parts. If the month and day come first, I put a comma before and after the year; for example, *June 1, 1945, is her birthdate.*

Write this sentence on the board, omitting the commas: *We will be moving from Kansas City Kansas to St. Louis Missouri on Monday October 5 2011.* **Help students to** determine where they should insert the commas.

Then, have students write sentences using dates with two and three parts. Have students exchange sentences with a partner and have the partner check for the correct use of commas.

RULE 25.2.11 Read aloud the rule and then have students repeat the lines with you.

Have each student use his or her address, including the name of the city and state, in a sentence. Check to make sure students have used commas correctly.

Using Commas With Dates and Geographical Names

Dates usually have several parts, including months, days, and years. Commas prevent dates from being unclear.

RULE 25.2.10 **When a date is made up of three parts, use a comma after each item, except in the case of a month followed by a day.**

Notice in the examples that commas are not used to set off a month followed by a numeral standing for a day. Commas are used when both the month and the date are used as an appositive to rename a day of the week.

EXAMPLES On March 12, 1945, my grandfather came to the United States with one small suitcase.

Friday, April 12, was an important date for Marco and his family.

When a date contains only a month and a year, commas are unnecessary.

EXAMPLES He will visit us in June 2015.

Most of the places we visited in July 2005 were in the Midwest.

RULE 25.2.11 **When a geographical name is made up of a city and a state, use a comma after each item except when the state ends a sentence.**

EXAMPLES She lived in Dallas, Texas, for several years and then moved to Atlanta, Georgia.

Amma went to Chicago, Illinois, to visit the many museums in the area.

See Practice 25.2I

Working with ELLs — ELL Sheltered Instruction: Cognitive

Help students demonstrate comprehension of increasingly complex English by taking notes about what they read.

Beginning Preteach these words from the student page, writing them on the board: *date, parts, item, month, year, day.* Read Rule 25.2.10 aloud as students follow along. Then, read the examples for the rule with them, clarifying meaning. Read the text again, this time asking students to jot down single words and brief phrases to record the main ideas. Encourage them also to include labeled examples.

Intermediate Guide volunteers in reading aloud from the first half of page 566. Have students request clarification of unfamiliar terms or concepts. Then, have students in small groups reread the selection, taking notes. Have students compare notes, adding to or correcting them as warranted.

Advanced Have partners read page 566 together, taking notes and asking for clarification as needed. Then, have them write sentences that tell when and where they were born, referring to their notes to ensure correct comma placement. Have partners check each other's work.

Advanced High Have students complete the Advanced activity. Then, have them write three sentences illustrating each concept on the page, referring to their notes.

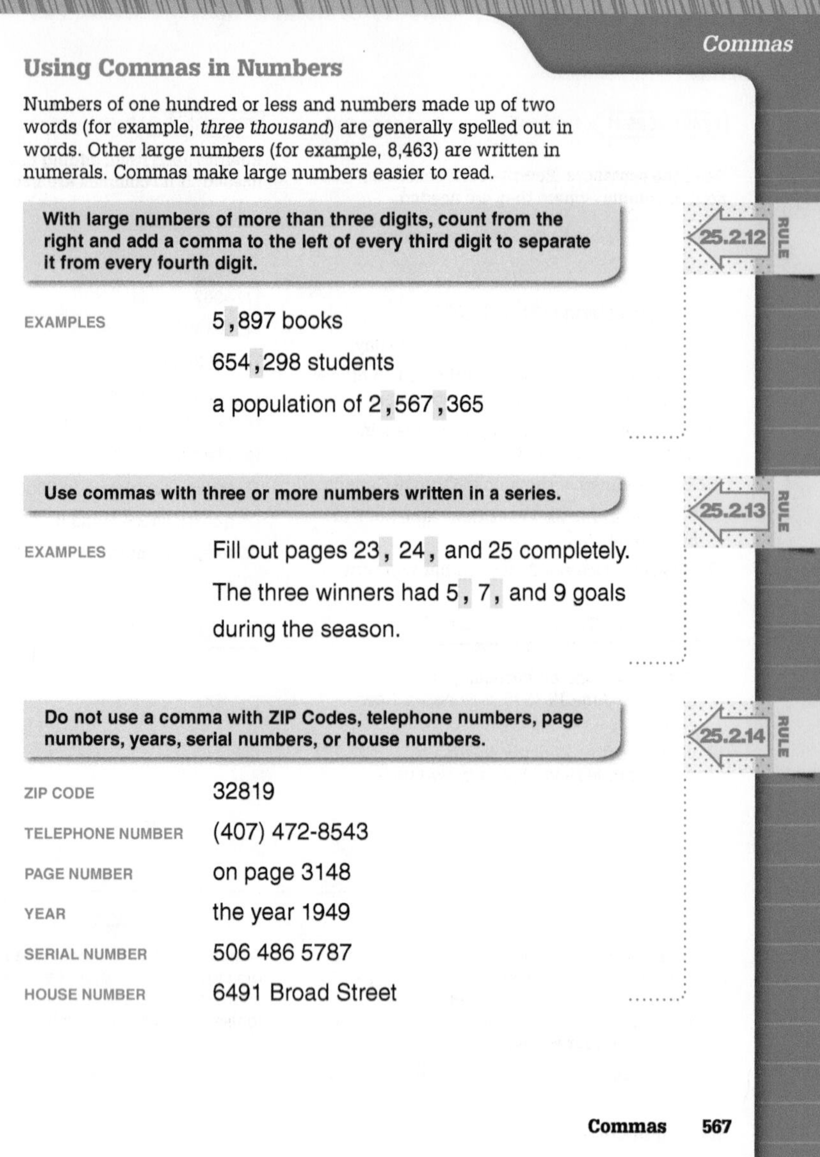

Using Commas in Numbers

Numbers of one hundred or less and numbers made up of two words (for example, *three thousand*) are generally spelled out in words. Other large numbers (for example, 8,463) are written in numerals. Commas make large numbers easier to read.

With large numbers of more than three digits, count from the right and add a comma to the left of every third digit to separate it from every fourth digit. RULE 25.2.12

EXAMPLES
5,897 books
654,298 students
a population of 2,567,365

Use commas with three or more numbers written in a series. RULE 25.2.13

EXAMPLES
Fill out pages 23, 24, and 25 completely.
The three winners had 5, 7, and 9 goals during the season.

Do not use a comma with ZIP Codes, telephone numbers, page numbers, years, serial numbers, or house numbers. RULE 25.2.14

ZIP CODE	32819
TELEPHONE NUMBER	(407) 472-8543
PAGE NUMBER	on page 3148
YEAR	the year 1949
SERIAL NUMBER	506 486 5787
HOUSE NUMBER	6491 Broad Street

See Practice 25.2J

Using Commas in Numbers

Point out that commas make large numbers easier to read, though some large numbers, such as zip codes and serial numbers, do not require commas.

RULES 25.2.12, 25.2.13, 25.2.14 Read aloud the rules and then have students repeat the lines with you.

Help the class multiply the number of students in the class by 100,000. Write this number on the board, and ask the class where to insert a comma.

Have student pairs multiply the number of students in the school by 1,000. Check to make sure they have inserted the comma(s) in the correct place. Estimate the number of students in the class, the grade, and the school. Then, write this sentence on the board, filling in the numbers that you estimated: *The number of students in the class, grade, and school is xx xx and xx.* Have students determine where the commas belong.

Review with students the types of numbers that do not require commas.

Teacher Tip

Challenge student pairs to generate a sentence that contains three or more large numbers of more than three digits each. For an extra challenge, encourage students to include at least one zip code, telephone number, page number, year, serial number, or house number in their sentence. Invite pairs to share their sentences with the class.

Differentiated Instruction

Strategy for Spanish Speakers

Students whose home language is Spanish may not know about the use of the comma in writing large numbers in English. In many Spanish-speaking countries, periods are used instead of commas. Remind students that in English, the comma is used to separate the hundreds from the thousands, the hundred thousands from the millions, and the hundred millions from the billions, and so on. Have students practice placing commas in numbers. Have volunteers write large numbers on the board as they would write them in Spanish. Then, help students understand why they should change the periods to commas. Have the rest of the students copy the number from the board. Then, on the board write a series of large numbers without the commas. Have students copy the numbers on their own paper and insert commas where they belong.

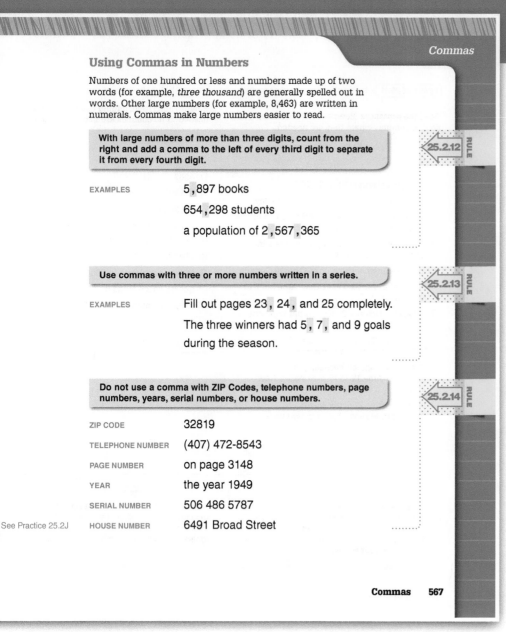

PRACTICE 25.2I

1. My date of birth is May 25, 2000.
2. I hope to visit Honolulu, Hawaii, some day.
3. The company my mother works for has offices in Atlanta, Georgia, and Chicago, Illinois.
4. President John F. Kennedy was assassinated on November 22, 1963.
5. My grandmother grew up in Ottawa, Canada.
6. We lived in Austin, Texas, from June 2002 to September 2008.
7. On Friday, October 21, my brother will turn fifteen.
8. On July 4, 1776, the Declaration of Independence was approved.
9. The first organized baseball game was played on June 19, 1846, in Hoboken, New Jersey.
10. We drove from Phoenix, Arizona, to Albuquerque, New Mexico, in two days.

PRACTICE 25.2J

11. 4,067
12. 103,000
13. 2,982,525
14. correct
15. correct
16. correct
17. India's population in 2008: 1,147,995,900
18. questions 2, 4, 5, and 6
19. correct
20. correct

PRACTICE 25.2I Using Commas in Dates and Geographical Names

Read the sentences. Rewrite each sentence, adding commas where they are needed.

EXAMPLE Dallas Texas is my hometown.

ANSWER *Dallas, Texas, is my hometown.*

1. My date of birth is May 25 2000.
2. I hope to visit Honolulu Hawaii some day.
3. The company my mother works for has offices in Atlanta Georgia and Chicago Illinois.
4. President John F. Kennedy was assassinated on November 22 1963.
5. My grandmother grew up in Ottawa Canada.
6. We lived in Austin Texas from June 2002 to September 2008.
7. On Friday October 21 my brother will turn fifteen.
8. On July 4 1776 the Declaration of Independence was approved.
9. The first organized baseball game was played on June 19 1846 in Hoboken New Jersey.
10. We drove from Phoenix Arizona to Albuquerque New Mexico in two days.

PRACTICE 25.2J Using Commas in Numbers

Rewrite each item, adding commas where needed. If no commas are needed, write *correct*.

EXAMPLE 1250717

ANSWER *1,250,717*

11. 4067
12. 103000
13. 2982525
14. the year 1950
15. 1600 Pennsylvania Avenue
16. ZIP Code 61620
17. India's population in 2008: 1147995900
18. questions 2 4 5 and 6
19. telephone number (818) 555-8888
20. page 1032

WRITING APPLICATION

Write a sentence in which you give your date of birth. In another sentence, tell the city and state in which you live. If you have also lived somewhere else, write that too. Use commas correctly in your sentences.

WRITING APPLICATION

Search online or in a reference book to find the current population of your state. Use that number in a sentence about your state. Be sure to use commas correctly in the number.

WRITING APPLICATION

Have students exchange papers and check each other's sentences for correct comma placement.

WRITING APPLICATION

Have students exchange sentences and check the comma placement in the number, explaining why it is or is not correct.

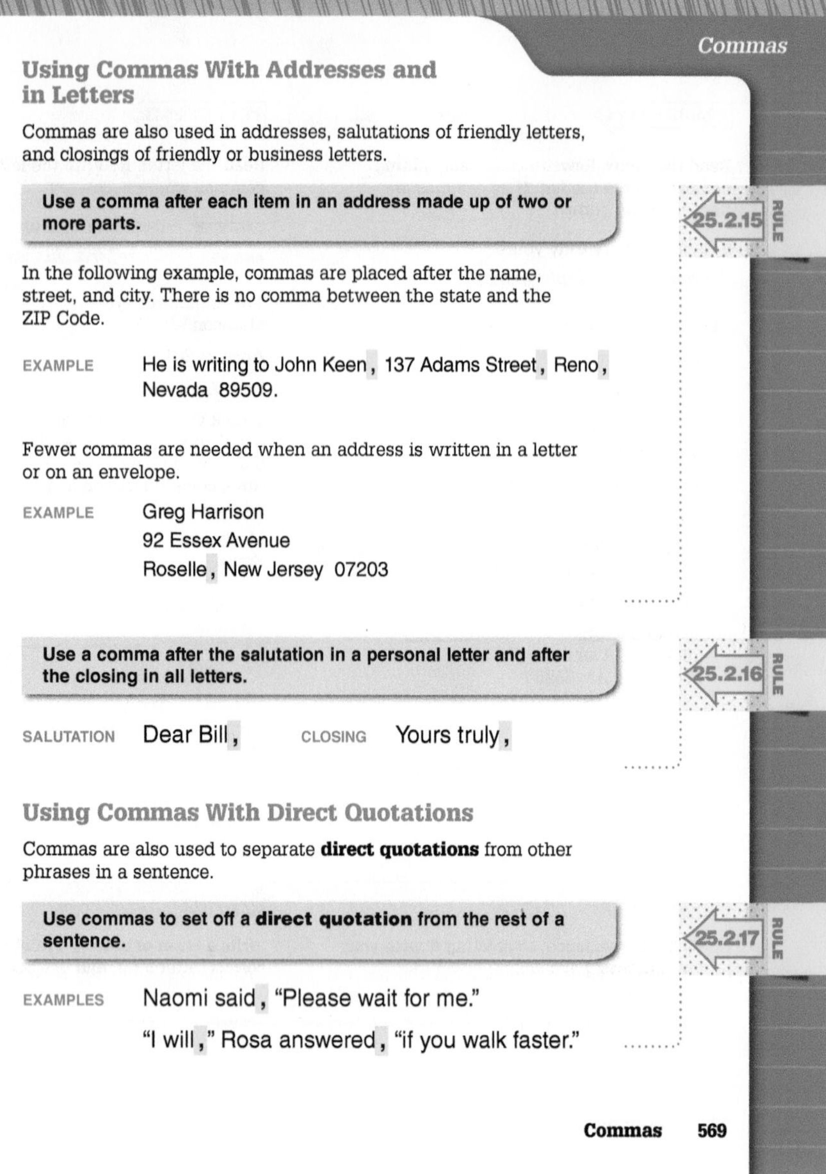

Using Commas With Addresses and in Letters

Commas are also used in addresses, salutations of friendly letters, and closings of friendly or business letters.

Use a comma after each item in an address made up of two or more parts. RULE 25.2.15

In the following example, commas are placed after the name, street, and city. There is no comma between the state and the ZIP Code.

EXAMPLE He is writing to John Keen, 137 Adams Street, Reno, Nevada 89509.

Fewer commas are needed when an address is written in a letter or on an envelope.

EXAMPLE Greg Harrison
92 Essex Avenue
Roselle, New Jersey 07203

Use a comma after the salutation in a personal letter and after the closing in all letters. RULE 25.2.16

See Practice 25.2K
See Practice 25.2L

SALUTATION Dear Bill, CLOSING Yours truly,

Using Commas With Direct Quotations

Commas are also used to separate **direct quotations** from other phrases in a sentence.

Use commas to set off a direct quotation from the rest of a sentence. RULE 25.2.17

EXAMPLES Naomi said, "Please wait for me."
"I will," Rosa answered, "if you walk faster."

Working with ELLs

ELL Sheltered Instruction: Cognitive

Help students comprehend English vocabulary used routinely in written classroom materials. On the board, write these routine words from the directions on page 568: *sentences, adding, needed, if,* and *correct.* Then:

Beginning Read each word aloud as students follow along and echo. Use gestures and visuals to explain each. For example, you might draw branching paths labeled *Yes* and *No* to illustrate *if.* Then, direct students to reread each word chorally and mime its meaning or point to the correct visual. Finally, **Echo Read** the sentence in which each word appears on the student page and clarify meaning.

Intermediate Present and explain each word as in the Beginning activity. Then, have small groups read and discuss the directions. Meet with groups, and have them share their understanding of the directions as well as their questions.

Advanced Present the words, and ask volunteers to explain the meaning of each. Then, have partners read and discuss the directions. Have them present their interpretations and questions.

Advanced High Have students complete the Advanced activity. Then, challenge students to rewrite the directions for Practice 25.2I and have their partner complete the first item following the revised directions.

Using Commas With Addresses and in Letters

Point out that commas are used in addresses, some salutations, and the closings of letters.

RULES 25.2.15, 25.2.16 Read aloud the rules and then have students repeat the lines with you.

Say: When I write a friendly letter, I put a comma after the salutation, which is the greeting at the beginning of the letter, such as *Dear Mom,* and after the closing. When I address the letter, I put a comma between the city and state.

Discuss the examples on page 569. Then, work with students to demonstrate inserting a comma after a salutation, such as *Dear Jack,* and a closing, such as *Sincerely, Ethan.*

Have student pairs write and address a letter to each other. Check to make sure the commas are correctly placed.

Using Commas With Direct Quotations

Explain that commas are used with direct quotations in a sentence to separate someone's exact words from the rest of the sentence.

RULE 25.2.17 Read aloud the rule and then have students repeat the lines with you.

Write these sentences on the board, omitting the commas: *He said, "We had 15 inches of snow in five hours." "On Thursday," she said, "I will paint the house."* Work with students to insert the commas.

Teacher Tip

Some students may feel overwhelmed by the number of comma rules they have learned by the end of the chapter. Provide students with a Cluster Diagram with *Comma Uses* written in the center circle. Work with students to fill in the outer circles with reasons to use commas (e.g., in compound sentences, in a series, between equal adjectives). Students may create more circles as needed. Encourage students to include an example of each rule. Students should refer to this diagram as needed.

PRACTICE 25.2K

1. Longview, TX 75603
2. Dear Mr. Knox,
3. correct
4. With best regards,
5. correct
6. correct
7. Yours sincerely,
8. Molly's address is 442 Ocean Avenue, 3rd floor, Tallahassee, Florida 32306.
9. Dear Grandma,
10. The Holloways
    16 Sunset Avenue
    Scottsdale, AZ 85250

PRACTICE 25.2L

1421 Mountain Drive
Madison, WI 53716

April 21, 2010

Dear Aunt Glenda,

Thank you very much for the sweater you sent for my birthday. It fits perfectly, and you know I love blue! I've already worn it to school, and I received three compliments on it. You are so thoughtful to remember me.

Much love,
Emily

WRITING APPLICATION

Have students exchange sentences and check the comma placement, explaining why it is or is not correct.

WRITING APPLICATION

Have students exchange writing and check the comma placement, explaining why it is or is not correct.

PRACTICE 25.2K Using Commas in Addresses and Letters

Read the items. Rewrite each item, adding commas where needed. If no commas are needed, write *correct*.

EXAMPLE Very truly yours
ANSWER *Very truly yours,*

1. Longview TX 75603
2. Dear Mr. Knox
3. 2662 Steele Road
4. With best regards
5. 5109 Greenway Boulevard
6. 25 Prospect Street, Apt. 3
7. Yours sincerely
8. Molly's address is 442 Ocean Avenue 3rd floor Tallahassee Florida 32306.
9. Dear Grandma
10. The Holloways
    16 Sunset Avenue
    Scottsdale AZ 85250

PRACTICE 25.2L Revising a Letter by Adding Commas

Read the letter. Rewrite the letter, adding commas where necessary.

EXAMPLE Dear Mrs. Juarez
ANSWER *Dear Mrs. Juarez,*

1421 Mountain Drive
Madison WI 53716

April 21 2010

Dear Aunt Glenda

Thank you very much for the sweater you sent for my birthday. It fits perfectly and you know I love blue! I've already worn it to school and I received three compliments on it. You are so thoughtful to remember me.

Much love
Emily

WRITING APPLICATION

Write this sentence, completing it with your own address: *I live at* _____.

WRITING APPLICATION

Write a letter or note to a relative or friend. Use correct letter form, and use commas as needed.

Working with ELLs — ELL Sheltered Instruction: Cognitive

Help students use linguistic support to enhance and confirm their understanding of increasingly complex spoken language. Present a text orally, reading aloud the letter in Practice 25.2L or a letter of your choosing. Provide linguistic support as follows.

Beginning Read each sentence aloud. Provide linguistic support by explaining unfamiliar words in simple terms. Then, repeat your reading, and guide students to summarize it.

Intermediate Provide students with vocabulary cards explaining words in the letter. Review each card. Then, read the letter aloud, pausing after each sentence featuring a vocabulary word. Ask students which word they have heard. Have them review the appropriate card, and discuss the meaning of the sentence. Then, read the letter a second time, and guide students in summarizing it.

Advanced Read the letter aloud to students, directing them to write down parts they do not understand. Discuss, identifying unfamiliar words. Have partners use the linguistic support of a dictionary to determine the meaning of each. Then, reread the letter, and have students summarize.

Advanced High Have students complete the Advanced activity. Then, have partners write and read aloud brief letters of their own. Partners should summarize.

25.3 Semicolons and Colons

The **semicolon** (;) joins related **independent clauses** and signals a longer pause than a comma. The **colon** (:) is used to introduce lists of items and in other special situations.

www.phwritingcoach.com

Grammar Tutorials
Brush up on your Grammar skills with these animated videos.

Grammar Practice
Practice your grammar skills with Writing Coach Online.

Grammar Games
Test your knowledge of grammar in this fast-paced interactive video game.

Using Semicolons to Join Independent Clauses

Sometimes two **independent clauses** are so closely connected in meaning that they make up a single sentence, rather than two separate sentences.

Use a semicolon to join related independent clauses that are not joined by the conjunctions *and, or, nor, for, but, so,* or *yet.*

INDEPENDENT CLAUSES	Bill enjoys exploring jungle areas. His sister is more interested in deserts.
CLAUSES JOINED BY SEMICOLONS	Bill enjoys exploring jungle areas; his sister is more interested in deserts.

A semicolon should be used only when there is a close relationship between the two independent clauses. If the clauses are not very closely related, they should be written as separate sentences with a period or another end mark to separate them or joined with a coordinating conjunction.

Note that when a sentence contains three or more related independent clauses, they may still be separated with semicolons.

EXAMPLES	Dark clouds rolled in; the ocean became rough; the sand began to blow.
	Bea wrote about insects; Nat wrote about spiders; Frank wrote about insects and spiders.

www.phwritingcoach.com

Diagnostic and Instruction
Diagnostic test assesses students' instructional needs. Lessons and practice are assigned based on results.

Additional Practice
- Grammar Tutorials—Animated videos reinforce key grammar skills.
- Grammar Practice—Targeted practice addresses individual needs.
- ExamView—Teachers customize their grammar practice and tests.
- Grammar Games—Interactive video games make grammar fun.

Teacher Tip

Clip a number of individual sentences out of a magazine, snipping off the end marks. Organize students into pairs, and distribute several sentences to each pair. Have student pairs work together to brainstorm for a related independent clause for each sentence and to rewrite the independent clauses as one sentence. Have student pairs share their new sentences with the class. For each sentence, ask students to identify the independent clauses and insert the semicolon in the correct place.

Lesson Objectives

1. Use punctuation marks, including semicolons and colons, correctly in writing.

Using Semicolons to Join Independent Clauses

Point out that a semicolon looks like a comma with a period on top of it because it signals a longer pause than a comma. One use of a semicolon is to connect independent clauses when the clauses are closely related.

RULE 25.3.1 Read aloud the rule and then have students repeat the lines with you.

Discuss the example sentences at the top of page 571. Then, use a Think Aloud as part of a gradual release progression.

Say: I use a semicolon to join independent clauses, or simple sentences, that are closely related. For example, *Sarah brought punch to the party; John brought cider.* These independent clauses are closely related because they are about the same topic—what Sarah brought to a party and what John brought. It is important to remember that independent clauses that are not closely related should be separated by a period. For example, *John brought cider to the party. Jesse went bowling.* These independent clauses are not closely related because they are about two different topics—what John brought to a party and what Jesse, who did not go to the party, did.

Write these two independent clauses on the board: *Juan loves the mountains Isabel loves the beach.* **Work with students** to use a semicolon to join these two independent clauses.

Have student pairs generate sentences that contain closely related independent clauses and correctly use semicolons to join the clauses. Invite students to share their sentences with the class.

Using Semicolons to Join Clauses Separated by Conjunctive Adverbs or Transitional Expressions

Explain to students that semicolons help writers show how their ideas connect.

RULE 25.3.2 Read aloud the rule and then have students repeat the lines with you.

Read aloud the lists of conjunctive adverbs and transitional expressions at the top of page 572. Help students understand that both sets of words are used to show the logical relationship between ideas. Then, write this on the board: *Sue forgot to set her alarm clock last night; as a result, she overslept and missed the bus this morning.*

Ask: What is the relationship between the two independent clauses? (**Response:** There is a cause-and-effect relationship. Sue overslept and missed the bus because she forgot to set her alarm.) **Say:** The transitional expression *as a result* connects descriptions of two events and informs us that the events have a cause-and-effect relationship. A semicolon is used before transitional expressions that show the relationship between independent clauses.

Using Semicolons to Avoid Confusion

Explain that semicolons are used to separate items in a series in order to avoid confusion.

RULE 25.3.3 Read aloud the rule and then have students repeat the lines with you.

Have student pairs use semicolons to separate items in a series that already contains commas. Students should be able to explain their reasons for using punctuation marks.

Using Semicolons to Join Clauses Separated by Conjunctive Adverbs or Transitional Expressions

Semicolons help writers show how their ideas connect.

Use a semicolon to join independent clauses separated by either a conjunctive adverb or a transitional expression.

CONJUNCTIVE ADVERBS	*also, besides, consequently, first, furthermore, however, indeed, instead, moreover, nevertheless, otherwise, second, then, therefore, thus*
TRANSITIONAL EXPRESSIONS	*as a result, at this time, for instance, in fact, on the other hand, that is*
EXAMPLE	We met Tomas at the concession stand; **otherwise**, we would never have found him at the theater.

Remember to place a comma after the conjunctive adverb or transitional expression. The comma sets off the conjunctive adverb or transitional expression, which acts as an introductory expression to the second clause.

Using Semicolons to Avoid Confusion

Sometimes, to avoid confusion, semicolons are used to separate items in a series.

Consider the use of semicolons to avoid confusion when items in a series already contain commas.

See Practice 25.3A
See Practice 25.3B

Place a semicolon after all but the last complete item in a series.

EXAMPLES	The dark, country road; the still, silent forest; and the sky, black and moonless, encouraged them to head toward home.
	Three important dates for my family are January 1, 2001; April 5, 2003; and May 28, 2000.

Working with ELLs — ELL Sheltered Instruction: Cognitive

Help students use contextual support to enhance and confirm their understanding of increasingly complex spoken language, including compound sentences and elaborated series.

Beginning Preteach the words *concession stand* and *theater*. Provide contextual support by talking to students about arranging to meet a friend in a crowded place. Then, read the Example sentence for Practice 25.3.2 aloud. Guide students in using the context you have given to understand and restate the sentence.

Intermediate Present context about meeting a friend in a crowded public place. Have volunteers describe related experiences. Then, read aloud the Example sentence for Rule 25.3.2, and have students work in groups to restate its meaning, applying the context.

Advanced Have students complete the Intermediate activity. Then, provide context for the first example under Rule 25.3.3 by discussing how people might feel at night on a country road. Read the example aloud, and have partners draw on context to restate its meaning.

Advanced High Have students complete the Advanced activity. Then, have them write three sentences using series in which items contain commas. Have partners read sentences to each other. Listeners should use the context in the sentence to restate its meaning.

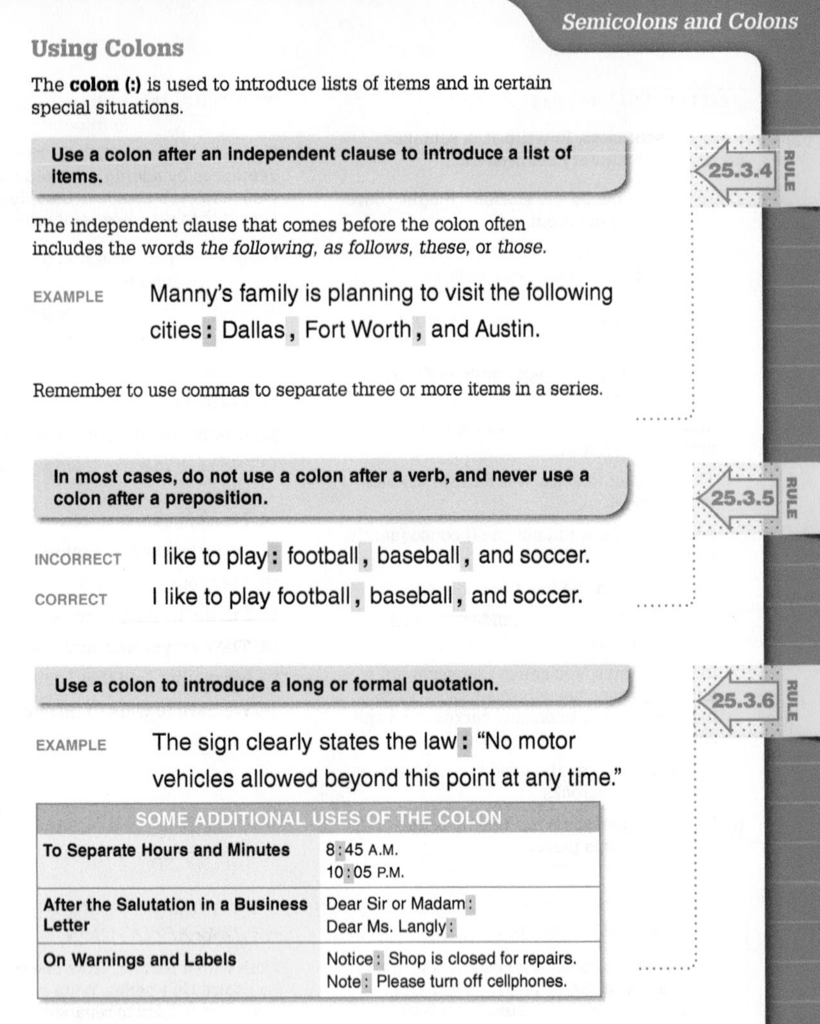

Using Colons

The **colon (:)** is used to introduce lists of items and in certain special situations.

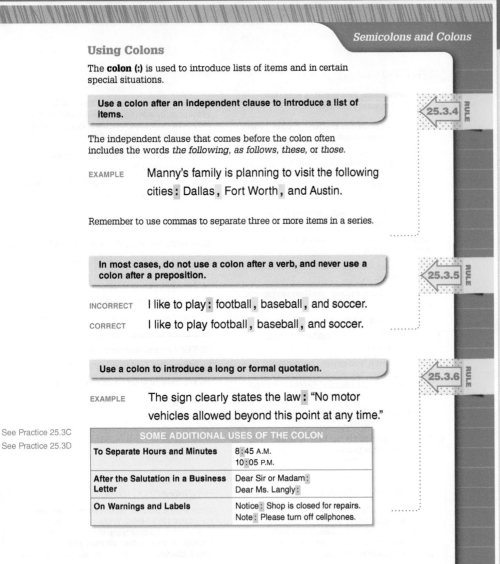

Use a colon after an independent clause to introduce a list of items. RULE 25.3.4

The independent clause that comes before the colon often includes the words *the following, as follows, these,* or *those.*

EXAMPLE Manny's family is planning to visit the following cities: Dallas, Fort Worth, and Austin.

Remember to use commas to separate three or more items in a series.

In most cases, do not use a colon after a verb, and never use a colon after a preposition. RULE 25.3.5

INCORRECT I like to play: football, baseball, and soccer.

CORRECT I like to play football, baseball, and soccer.

Use a colon to introduce a long or formal quotation. RULE 25.3.6

EXAMPLE The sign clearly states the law: "No motor vehicles allowed beyond this point at any time."

See Practice 25.3C
See Practice 25.3D

SOME ADDITIONAL USES OF THE COLON	
To Separate Hours and Minutes	8:45 A.M. 10:05 P.M.
After the Salutation in a Business Letter	Dear Sir or Madam: Dear Ms. Langly:
On Warnings and Labels	Notice: Shop is closed for repairs. Note: Please turn off cellphones.

Using Colons

Explain that a colon looks like a period on top of a period. It signals a longer pause than a comma. Discuss how colons are used to introduce lists of items and to signal a longer pause to separate certain parts of a sentence.

RULES 25.3.4, 25.3.5, 25.3.6 Read aloud the rules and then have students repeat the lines with you.

Discuss the example sentences on page 573. Then, write these sentences on the board, omitting the colons: *A sign was posted at the water's edge: "No swimming allowed." We left at 5:30.* Work with students to help them decide where to insert colons.

Have students write three sentences demonstrating that they can use colons correctly. Each sentence should use a colon in one of the ways described on page 573. Ask students to read their sentences aloud to a partner and then discuss the purpose of the colons in each sentence.

PRACTICE 25.3A

1. dinner;
2. puzzles;
3. hair; [and] feathers;
4. rain;
5. off;
6. fan;
7. confident;
8. magazines; [and] cleaners;
9. gray; [and] blew;
10. tips;

PRACTICE 25.3B

Answers will vary. Sample answers:

11. I wish I could go to camp this summer; however, I forgot to apply.
12. Charlie found a part-time job mowing lawns; as a result, he'll have more money.
13. We have to hurry if we are going to catch the bus; otherwise, we'll be late to school.
14. I prefer pears to apples; nevertheless, I eat both.
15. Emily brought an umbrella to school today; however, it never rained.
16. We should make stir-fry for dinner tonight; on the other hand, we could always make tacos.
17. Put the laundry in the dresser; then, do the dishes.
18. The election was very close; indeed, it was the closest.
19. My mother said that I could go to your house; in fact, I'm on my way over now.
20. We have to walk three more blocks; however, exercise is good.

WRITING APPLICATION

Partners should demonstrate that they can use semicolons correctly by discussing how they determined where semicolons should be placed.

WRITING APPLICATION

Students should demonstrate the correct use of semicolons by explaining the functions of the semicolons in their sentences.

PRACTICE 25.3A Using Semicolons

Read the sentences. Rewrite each sentence, adding any necessary semicolons.

EXAMPLE I opened the shades sunlight poured into the room.

ANSWER *I opened the shades; sunlight poured into the room.*

1. I'll prepare dinner meanwhile, you set the table.
2. Suzanne likes crossword puzzles Kevin prefers chess.
3. Mammals have hair birds have feathers amphibians have neither.
4. The weather forecast was for rain instead, we had sleet.
5. Andrew's alarm did not go off consequently, he was late for school.
6. Please turn on the fan we need some air.
7. Some people are very confident at least, they act that way.
8. In some stores, you can get newspapers and magazines household supplies, such as batteries and cleaners and sandwiches and soups to go.
9. The sky was gray the wind blew the waves crashed on the rocks.
10. Peter can give you some tips he is an excellent tennis player.

PRACTICE 25.3B Writing Sentences Using Semicolons

Read the sentences below. Then, write new sentences by adding a related independent clause to each sentence provided. Use semicolons correctly in your new sentences.

EXAMPLE The class was going to end in four minutes.

ANSWER *The class was going to end in four minutes; therefore, we had only enough time to finish one problem.*

11. I wish I could go to camp this summer.
12. Charlie found a part-time job mowing lawns.
13. We have to hurry if we are going to catch the bus.
14. I prefer pears to apples.
15. Emily brought an umbrella to school today.
16. We should make stir-fry for dinner tonight.
17. Put the laundry in the dresser.
18. The election was very close.
19. My mother said that I could go to your house.
20. We have to walk three more blocks.

WRITING APPLICATION

Work with a partner. Use sentences 2, 3, and 5 in Practice 25.3A as models. Write three sentences of your own. Then, read your sentences to your partner and explain the purpose of each semicolon.

WRITING APPLICATION

Work with a partner. Write one sentence using semicolons in a series. Write one sentence using a semicolon to separate two independent clauses. Have your partner read your sentences aloud, checking for the correct use of semicolons.

Working with ELLs ELL Sheltered Instruction: Cognitive

To help students write using a variety of grade-appropriate connecting words to combine sentences in increasingly accurate ways, have them use conjunctive adverbs to combine sentences in Practice 25.3B. First, review with students the conjunctive adverbs on page 572. Then:

Beginning Have students copy item 11 from the Practice. Clarify meaning. Then, use yes/no questions to elicit related ideas from them, such as *Could this person go to camp next year? Could this person be traveling with family?* List ideas on the board, writing in independent clauses. Then, list conjunctive adverbs, and work with students to choose the appropriate word to combine item 11 with each of the new clauses. Have students write each new sentence.

Intermediate Guide partners in completing the Practice activity, combining sentences with conjunctive adverbs. Then, have pairs exchange papers and underline the conjunctive adverb in each other's sentences.

Advanced Have students independently complete the Practice activity, combining sentences with conjunctive adverbs. Have students exchange papers and identify the conjunctive adverbs in each other's work.

Advanced High Have students complete the Advanced activity. Then, have them write five simple sentences about an activity and combine them with conjunctive adverbs.

PRACTICE 25.3C Using Colons

Read the sentences. Rewrite each sentence, adding any necessary colons. If no colon is needed, write *correct*.

EXAMPLE Your appointment is at 915 A.M.

ANSWER *Your appointment is at 9:15 A.M.*

1. This is what you should do apologize and give her flowers.
2. You must be ready by 6:30 P.M.
3. Warning Hard hats required at this site.
4. Microchips are found in hundreds of common devices telephones, GPS systems, and MP3 players, for example.
5. Margo packed only three things pajamas, a toothbrush, and a change of clothes.
6. So far, I have found only one good source for my report: the author's official Web site.
7. This evening's program is as follows opening remarks at 700, presentations from 715 to 800, closing remarks at 815.
8. Caution Bridge is slippery when wet.
9. Dear Sir or Madam:
10. Put the following ingredients into your salad lettuce, spinach, sliced apples, and dried cranberries.

PRACTICE 25.3D Writing Sentences Using Colons

Read the rules for using colons below. Write a sentence using a colon for each rule. Then, have a partner read your sentences aloud to check for the correct use of colons.

EXAMPLE to introduce a list of items

ANSWER *You will need the following supplies for the camping trip: a sleeping bag, a water bottle, a flashlight, and a warm jacket.*

11. to introduce a long or formal quotation
12. to separate hours and minutes
13. after the salutation in a business letter
14. on a warning
15. to introduce a list of items
16. to introduce a long or formal quotation
17. to separate hours and minutes
18. after the salutation in a business letter
19. on a label
20. to introduce a list of items

SPEAKING APPLICATION

With a partner, take turns reading aloud the sentences created in Practice 25.3D. Read the word *colon* whenever there is a colon. Then, discuss which usages of colons are most common.

WRITING APPLICATION

Write three sentences about school. In your sentences, use colons in three different ways. Exchange papers with your partner. Your partner should read your sentences aloud and explain the use of each colon.

PRACTICE 25.3C

1. This is what you should do: apologize and give her flowers.
2. correct
3. Warning: Hard hats required at this site.
4. Microchips are found in hundreds of common devices: telephones, GPS systems, and MP3 players, for example.
5. Margo packed only three things: pajamas, a toothbrush, and a change of clothes.
6. correct
7. This evening's program is as follows: opening remarks at 7:00, presentations from 7:15 to 8:00, closing remarks at 8:15.
8. Caution: Bridge is slippery when wet.
9. correct
10. Put the following ingredients into your salad: lettuce, spinach, sliced apples, and dried cranberries.

PRACTICE 25.3D

Answers will vary. Sample answers:

11. I will always remember these words from Patrick Henry: "Give me liberty or give me death."
12. My bus comes at 7:45.
13. To whom it may concern:
14. Caution: Contents are hot.
15. My list contains the following: milk, eggs, and bread.
16. Amy finished her speech with a simple, yet sincere sentence: "I am so grateful to have this chance, and I promise to make all of you proud."
17. That movie's show times are 6:10 and 8:30.
18. Dear Mr. Bridges:
19. May contain the following: nuts, milk, or milk by-products.
20. I need the following ingredients: flour, sugar, baking soda, and salt.

SPEAKING APPLICATION

Students should demonstrate that they can use colons correctly by taking turns with a partner to explain why each colon is necessary and which uses of the colon are the most common.

WRITING APPLICATION

Students should demonstrate that they can use correct punctuation marks, including colons, by checking the placement of colons in each other's sentences and explaining why it is or is not correct.

Test Warm-Up

1. **A** Change the semicolon to a colon
2. **G** Change the colon to a semicolon
3. **B** Change the comma after ***others*** to a semicolon
4. **J** Make no change

Reteach

If students have not mastered these skills, review the content in Section 25.3 Semicolons and Colons.

1. Using Colons 25.3.4
2. Using Semicolons to Join Independent Clauses 25.3.1
3. Using Semicolons to Avoid Confusion 25.3.3
4. Using Semicolons to Join Clauses Separated by Conjunctive Adverbs or Transitional Expressions 25.3.2

Test Tip

Tell students that most standardized tests have no penalty for wrong answers. Explain that, in those cases, if students can eliminate even one possible answer from a multiple choice question, they should make a guess from the remaining answers rather than skip the question. Often the test administrator will include this recommendation as part of the directions. If students are unsure whether they will be penalized for wrong answers, they should ask the test administrator before beginning the test.

Test Warm-Up

DIRECTIONS
Read the introduction and the passage that follows. Then, answer the questions to show that you can use correct punctuation, including semicolons and colons, in reading and writing.

Vince wrote this business letter to a potential employer, the owner of a convenience store. Read the letter and think about the changes you would suggest as a peer editor. When you finish reading, answer the questions that follow.

(1) Dear Mrs. Gonzalez;

(2) I am writing to express my interest in working in your store: I would like to own a convenience store some day myself. (3) I work well with others, I am friendly, helpful, and good at working with money. (4) I am also responsible; in fact, people say I'm mature for my age. (5) Please note that I can be flexible about my hours. (6) I will look forward to hearing from you.

(7) Sincerely,
(8) Vince Bradford

1 What change, if any, should be made in sentence 1?

A Change the semicolon to a colon
B Delete the semicolon
C Change the semicolon to a comma
D Make no change

2 What change, if any, should be made in sentence 2?

F Change the colon to a comma
G Change the colon to a semicolon
H Change the period to an exclamation point
J Make no change

3 What change, if any, should be made in sentence 3?

A Delete the comma after ***others***
B Change the comma after ***others*** to a semicolon
C Change the comma after ***others*** to a colon
D Make no change

4 What change, if any, should be made in sentence 4?

F Change the semicolon to a comma
G Change the semicolon to a colon
H Delete the semicolon
J Make no change

25.4 Quotation Marks, Underlining, and Italics

Quotation marks (" ") set off direct quotations, dialogue, and certain types of titles. Other types of titles may be underlined or set in *italics*, a slanted type style.

Find It/FIX IT 6 Grammar Game Plan

www.phwritingcoach.com

Grammar Practice
Practice your grammar skills with Writing Coach Online.

Grammar Games
Test your knowledge of grammar in this fast-paced interactive video game.

Using Quotation Marks With Quotations

Quotation marks identify the spoken or written words of others. A **direct quotation** represents a person's exact speech or thoughts. An **indirect quotation** reports the general meaning of what a person said or thought.

Both types of quotations are acceptable when you write. Direct quotations, however, generally result in a livelier writing style.

Direct quotations should be enclosed in quotation marks.

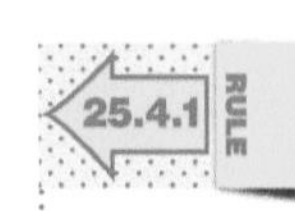

RULE 25.4.1

EXAMPLE Janine said, "Tomorrow we are going hiking."
"Does anyone know the way?" asked Ted.

Indirect quotations do not require quotation marks.

RULE 25.4.2

EXAMPLES John said that he would feed the fish.
Scott wondered why the coach hadn't called him about rescheduling the game.

Using Direct Quotations With Introductory, Concluding, and Interrupting Expressions

Commas help you set off introductory information so that your reader understands who is speaking. Writers usually identify a speaker by using words such as *he asked* or *she said* with a quotation. These expressions can introduce, conclude, or interrupt a quotation.

Find It/FIX IT 18 Grammar Game Plan

Differentiated Instruction

RTI Strategy for Special Needs Students Students may have difficulty understanding the difference between direct and indirect quotations. Organize students into pairs. Give one student several index cards. On the cards write sentences such as *Maria called out, "Hey, wait for me," to her friends. Max said, "I'm going now." "Leave it alone," my dad said.* Give the second student several index cards. On these cards write sentences with indirect quotations that match the content of the first cards. For example: *Maria called to her friends to wait for her. Max said that he is going now. My dad told me to leave it alone.* Have students discuss which set of sentences sounds as if someone's exact words are reported. Then, explain that the sentences with quotation marks contained direct quotations.

Lesson Objectives

1. Recognize and use quotation marks correctly in sentences and dialogue.
2. Use quotation marks, underlining, and italics correctly in writing.

Using Quotation Marks With Quotations

Discuss the difference between direct quotations and indirect quotations.

RULES 25.4.1, 25.4.2 Read aloud the rules and then have students repeat the lines with you.

Say: When I write, I can use direct or indirect quotations. However, direct quotations usually result in more lively writing.

Work with students to create a direct quotation set off by quotation marks in a sentence. For example, *Jazelle said, "Marilyn, may I borrow your snow shovel?"* Then, turn the direct quotation into an indirect quotation: *Jazelle asked Marilyn if she could borrow the snow shovel.* **Ask:** What is the difference between these two sentences? (The direct quotation brings Jazelle to life; the indirect quotation does not.)

Using Direct Quotations With Introductory, Concluding, and Interrupting Expressions

Discuss the function of expressions that name who is speaking, such as *she said.*

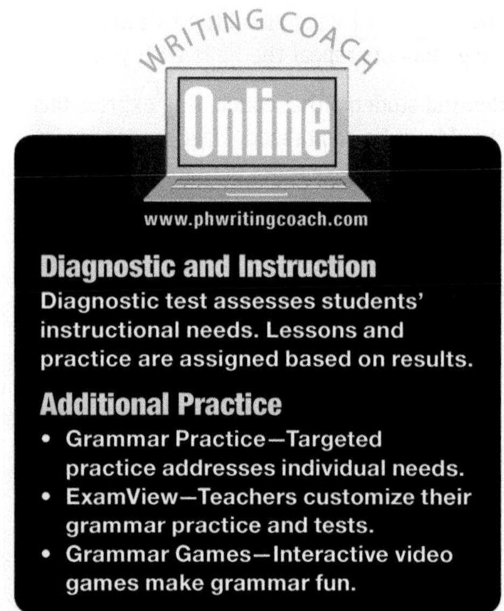

www.phwritingcoach.com

Diagnostic and Instruction
Diagnostic test assesses students' instructional needs. Lessons and practice are assigned based on results.

Additional Practice
- Grammar Practice—Targeted practice addresses individual needs.
- ExamView—Teachers customize their grammar practice and tests.
- Grammar Games—Interactive video games make grammar fun.

Direct Quotations With Introductory Expressions

Draw students' attention to the text stating that introductory expressions often precede direct quotations and are set off by a comma.

RULE 25.4.3 Read aloud the rule and then have students repeat the lines with you.

Review the examples on the page, pointing out that introductory expressions are, in general, followed by a comma, unless the expressions are very long. In that case, a colon follows the expression. Point out the relationship between the long introductory clause and the quotation that follows it in the third example sentence on page 578. The clause sums up what the quotation is about, that is, Miguel's goals. Note also that the long introductory clause can stand alone as a complete sentence. Have students compare the clause to the introductory phrases that are punctuated with a comma rather than a semicolon.

Have students brainstorm for sentences with short introductory expressions and direct quotations. Write their sentences on the board. Then, have students use commas and quotation marks to punctuate the sentences.

Direct Quotations With Concluding Expressions

Explain that direct quotations can sometimes end with a concluding expression that identifies the speaker. Concluding expressions are not complete sentences.

RULE 25.4.4 Read aloud the rule and then have students repeat the lines with you.

Remind students that concluding expressions should not be capitalized. Have student pairs brainstorm for examples of direct quotations with concluding expressions. Have pairs share their examples with the group.

Teacher Tip

For extra practice, have student pairs work together to identify direct quotations with introductory expressions and concluding expressions in a text with which they are familiar. Invite pairs to share their findings with the group. Point out the usa of commas, quotation marks, and capitalization in each example.

Direct Quotations With Introductory Expressions

Commas are also used to indicate where **introductory expressions** end.

When an introductory expression precedes a direct quotation, place a comma after the introductory expression, and write the quotation as a full sentence.

EXAMPLES Barney asked the tour guide, "Is it difficult to identify artifacts?"

Dorothy wondered, "What play will the drama club choose to present this year?"

If an introductory expression is very long, set it off with a colon instead of a comma.

EXAMPLE At the end of the practice, Miguel outlined his goals for the future: "I would like to increase my speed by the end of the year."

Direct Quotations With Concluding Expressions

Direct quotations may sometimes end with **concluding expressions.**

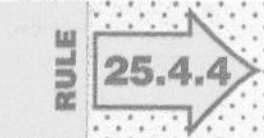

When a concluding expression follows a direct quotation, write the quotation as a full sentence ending with a comma, question mark, or exclamation mark inside the quotation mark. Then, write the concluding expression. Be sure to use end punctuation to close the sentence.

Concluding expressions are not complete sentences; therefore, they do not begin with capital letters. Notice also that the closing quotation marks are always placed outside the punctuation at the end of direct quotations followed by concluding expressions.

EXAMPLE "I think you would have fun at our camp!" said Timothy excitedly.

Working with ELLs — ELL Sheltered Instruction: Cognitive

Help students demonstrate comprehension of increasingly complex English by taking notes.

Beginning Have students follow along as a fluent partner reads Rule 25.4.3 and the first examples on page 578. Have them discuss meaning, referring to the highlighted punctuation. Then, have them repeat the reading. Students should take notes by writing important terms from the page. Then, clarify meaning by reviewing notes with students and explaining the terms.

Intermediate Assign each student in a group of three a section of page 578. Have group members take turns reading from the page aloud in round-robin style. As each student is reading, others should follow along and take notes. Have groups discuss their notes. Provide additional clarification as needed.

Advanced Have partners take turns reading from page 578. As each partner reads, the other should follow along and take notes. Have partners discuss their notes. Provide additional clarification as needed.

Advanced High Have students complete the Advanced activity. Then, have them read a newspaper article featuring direct quotations and take notes on the introductory or concluding expressions that accompany them.

Direct Quotations With Interrupting Expressions

You may use an interrupting expression in a direct quotation, which is also called a **divided quotation.** Interrupting expressions help writers clarify who is speaking and can also break up a long quotation.

When the direct quotation of one sentence is interrupted, end the first part of the direct quotation with a comma and a quotation mark. Place a comma after the interrupting expression, and then use a new set of quotation marks to enclose the rest of the quotation.

RULE 25.4.5

EXAMPLES "Because the camp is located on a lake," explained Ginnie, "we can go swimming and boating."

"Do you think," interrupted Juana, "that I could learn to water ski?"

Do not capitalize the first word of the second part of the sentence.

When two sentences in a direct quotation are separated by an interrupting expression, end the first quoted sentence with a comma, question mark, or exclamation mark and a quotation mark. Place a period after the interrupter, and then write the second quoted sentence as a full quotation.

RULE 25.4.6

EXAMPLES "We came face to face with a grizzly bear on one of our hikes," said Juan. "It was scary."

"That must have been amazing!" exclaimed Jenna. "How close did you get to the bear?"

See Practice 25.4A
See Practice 25.4B

Direct Quotations With Interrupting Expressions

Explain that writers sometimes use interrupting expressions to divide long quotations. Interrupting expressions can divide a single sentence or can be used between two sentences in a direct quotation.

RULES 25.4.5, 25.4.6 Read aloud the rules and then have students repeat the lines with you.

Use a Think Aloud as part of a gradual release progression.

Think Aloud

Say: I use Interrupting expressions to add variety to my writing by dividing direct quotations. Using interrupting expressions is easy if I remember a few simple rules. When I use an interrupting expression, such as *he said*, to divide a single sentence, I end the first part of the quotation with a comma and a quotation mark. Then, I place a comma after the interrupting expression and use a new set of quotation marks around the remainder of the sentence. When I divide two sentences with an interrupting expression, I end the first sentence with a comma, question mark, or exclamation mark, and I place a period after the expression. Then, I write the second sentence as a full quotation.

Work with students to create a short narrative about something that happened recently. Include examples of direct quotations divided by interrupting expressions. Help students write and punctuate the quotations on the board.

Have partners create their own dramatic narratives using extensive direct quotations. Encourage students to use interrupting expressions within single sentences and between related quotations. Invite pairs to share their examples with the group.

PRACTICE 25.4A

1. D; "When you come home from school," Mother said, "please do your laundry."
2. I
3. D; "I wonder," mused Catherine, "whatever happened to our former neighbors."
4. D; Jamie announced, "I feel confident about this test."
5. I
6. D; "When is this project due?" Jordan asked.
7. I
8. D; "May I see your tickets?" the usher asked.
9. I
10. D; "No," Clayton replied, "I don't think that's a good idea."

PRACTICE 25.4B

11. "Please let me see that magazine," said Dane.
12. Gregory said, "I will teach you how to play this game."
13. Juan groaned, "I think I've misplaced my phone."
14. "I would be happy to be your partner!" Elisa exclaimed.
15. "Let's call Randall," Mac suggested. "He always has some good ideas."
16. "I'm not sure," Rick said hesitantly, "where to go from here."
17. "We can park here for an hour," Carl noted. "Then, we'll have to add more money to the parking meter."
18. "I want you to notice," Steven declared, "that I have arrived on time today!"
19. Maya's text message read, "See you at lunch."
20. "I have just printed my final draft," Vinny declared. "After I proofread it, I'll hand it in."

PRACTICE 25.4A Using Quotation Marks With Direct Quotations

Read the sentences. If the sentence contains a direct quotation, write *D*. If it contains an indirect quotation, write *I*. Then, rewrite each sentence that contains a direct quotation, adding the quotation marks where needed.

EXAMPLE Jenna reported that no one was injured during the game.

ANSWER *I*

1. When you come home from school, Mother said, please do your laundry.
2. Martha wanted to know what I did yesterday.
3. I wonder, mused Catherine, whatever happened to our former neighbors.
4. Jamie announced, I feel confident about this test.
5. Abby thought that something was wrong.
6. When is this project due? Jordan asked.
7. Brian told us that he joined the drama club.
8. May I see your tickets? the usher asked.
9. Wendy said that she would join us later.
10. No, Clayton replied, I don't think that's a good idea.

PRACTICE 25.4B Punctuating With Expressions

Read the sentences. Rewrite each sentence, adding commas and quotation marks where needed.

EXAMPLE Where should we begin? Kristen asked.

ANSWER *"Where should we begin?" Kristen asked.*

11. Please let me see that magazine said Dane.
12. Gregory said I will teach you how to play this game.
13. Juan groaned I think I've misplaced my phone.
14. I would be happy to be your partner! Elisa exclaimed.
15. Let's call Randall Mac suggested. He always has some good ideas.
16. I'm not sure Rick said hesitantly where to go from here.
17. We can park here for an hour Carl noted. Then we'll have to add more money to the parking meter.
18. I want you to notice Steven declared that I have arrived on time today!
19. Maya's text message read See you at lunch.
20. I have just printed my final draft Vinny declared. After I proofread it, I'll hand it in.

SPEAKING APPLICATION

With a partner, take turns reporting direct and indirect conversational remarks. Your partner should tell whether each remark is a direct or an indirect quotation. You may use the examples in Practice 25.4A as models.

WRITING APPLICATION

Write three statements reporting something that you have said or that you have heard someone else say in the last few days. Use expressions (for example, *she said*), and put the speaker's words in quotation marks.

SPEAKING APPLICATION

Students should explain how they differentiated between direct and indirect quotations.

WRITING APPLICATION

Have students revise one of their statements to demonstrate a divided quotation using proper punctuation.

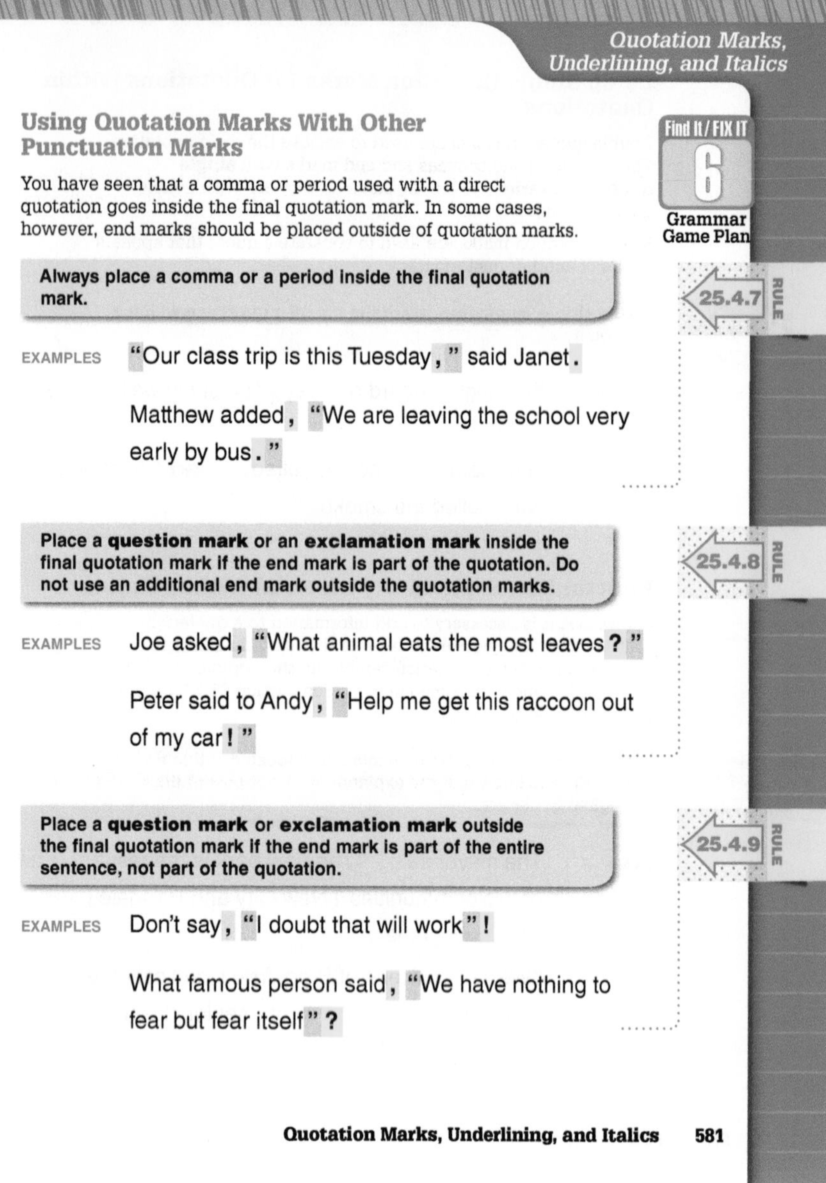

Using Quotation Marks With Other Punctuation Marks

Find It/FIX IT 6 Grammar Game Plan

You have seen that a comma or period used with a direct quotation goes inside the final quotation mark. In some cases, however, end marks should be placed outside of quotation marks.

Always place a comma or a period inside the final quotation mark. RULE 25.4.7

EXAMPLES "Our class trip is this Tuesday," said Janet.

Matthew added, "We are leaving the school very early by bus."

Place a question mark or an exclamation mark inside the final quotation mark if the end mark is part of the quotation. Do not use an additional end mark outside the quotation marks. RULE 25.4.8

EXAMPLES Joe asked, "What animal eats the most leaves?"

Peter said to Andy, "Help me get this raccoon out of my car!"

Place a question mark or exclamation mark outside the final quotation mark if the end mark is part of the entire sentence, not part of the quotation. RULE 25.4.9

EXAMPLES Don't say, "I doubt that will work"!

What famous person said, "We have nothing to fear but fear itself"?

See Practice 25.4C

Using Quotation Marks With Other Punctuation Marks

Explain that other punctuation marks, such as periods or question marks, often appear inside the final quotation marks. Sometimes, however, other punctuation marks appear outside the final quotation mark.

RULES 25.4.7, 25.4.8, 25.4.9 Read aloud the rules and then have students repeat the lines with you.

Use a Think Aloud as part of a gradual release progression.

Say: Because **I know** how to use quotation marks with other punctuation, I am able to punctuate my writing correctly. As you know, sometimes end marks appear inside quotation marks, and sometimes they appear outside quotation marks. Discuss the example sentences at the top of page 581 as well as in the middle of the page. **Ask:** When would I place an end mark inside a quotation mark? (when the end mark is part of the quotation) **Ask:** When would I place an end mark outside a quotation mark? (when the end mark is part of the entire sentence that contains the quotation, but not part of the quotation itself)

Work with students to generate examples of sentences with end marks inside of quotation marks and examples of sentences for which the end marks belong outside of the quotation marks.

Have student pairs write and punctuate two or three sentences with quotation marks and other punctuation. Invite students to read their sentences to the group.

Working with ELLs — ELL Sheltered Instruction: Social/Affective

Using a selection featuring dialogue, such as an excerpt from a short story or a feature article, have students demonstrate comprehension of increasingly complex English by participating in Shared Reading. To facilitate, project the selection on an overhead or whiteboard.

Beginning Read the selection with students, asking simple questions and clarifying meaning as needed. Point out the punctuation of dialogue. Then, have students work in small groups with more fluent peers to write a brief summary.

Intermediate Read the selection with students, encouraging volunteers to read sections. Ask comprehension questions and clarify meaning as needed. Point out the punctuation of dialogue. Then, have students partner with more fluent peers to write summaries.

Advanced Have students take turns reading from the selection. Ask comprehension questions and clarify meaning as needed. Then, have students write summaries. Finally, have them select an example of dialogue from the selection and explain how they can tell it is properly punctuated.

Advanced High Have students complete the Advanced activity. Then, have them write their own scenes featuring dialogue and conduct shared readings of them.

Using Single Quotation Marks for Quotations Within Quotations

Explain that single quotation marks are used for the inside quotation when a quotation appears within another quotation. Point out that the rules for using commas and end marks with single quotations are the same as for double quotations.

RULE 25.4.10 Read aloud the rule and then have students repeat the lines with you.

Review the examples at the top of page 582. **Ask:** When does a quotation occur within another quotation? (when the speaker reports another person's speech, word for word) Work with students to create three examples of quotations within quotations. Write the sentences on the board, and have students punctuate them.

Punctuating Explanatory Material Within Quotes

Point out that students can use brackets to insert additional explanatory information into a quotation. Discuss situations in which students may have seen brackets used in writing.

RULE 25.4.11 Read aloud the rule and then have students repeat the lines with you.

Work with students to generate examples of explanations set off by brackets within a quotation.

Using Single Quotation Marks for Quotations Within Quotations

Double quotation marks are used to enclose the main quotation. The rules for using commas and end marks with **single quotation marks (' ')** are the same as they are with double quotation marks.

Single quotation marks are used to separate a quote that appears inside of another quotation.

Use single quotation marks to set off a quotation within a quotation.

EXAMPLES "I thought I heard him say, 'I lost my wallet!' as he ran off," said Neil.

Nate said, "Someone yelled, 'Fire!' right before we smelled the smoke."

Punctuating Explanatory Material Within Quotes

Sometimes it is necessary to add information to a quotation that explains the quote more fully. In that case, brackets tell your reader which information came from the original speaker and which came from someone else. (See Section 25.7 for more information on brackets.)

Use brackets to enclose an explanation located within a quotation to show that the explanation is not part of the original quotation.

EXAMPLE The mayor said, "The new park is the result of two communities [New City and Hillsdale] working together."

"We [the citizens of Brookfield] dedicate the new community center to our senior citizens."

See Practice 25.4D

Differentiated Instruction

RTI Strategy for Below-Level Students Review the rules for using quotation marks. Remind students that single quotation marks follow the same rules as double quotation marks. Distribute unpunctuated dialogue that contains quotations within quotations. Have student pairs work together to insert punctuation into the passage. Invite students to share their work with the group. Challenge student partners to generate a dialogue that contains quotations within quotations.

PRE-AP Enrichment for Above-Level Students Organize students into pairs. Have students write a two-person dialogue. Encourage students to punctuate their dialogues correctly using quotation marks and single quotation marks, and enclosing any explanatory material within brackets. Invite students to read their dialogues aloud and then discuss the purpose of correct punctuation with their partner.

PRACTICE 25.4C **Using Quotation Marks With Other Punctuation Marks**

Read the sentences. Decide whether the missing punctuation goes inside or outside the quotation marks. Then, rewrite the sentences, adding the proper punctuation for quotations.

EXAMPLE Who wrote, "Hold fast to dreams"

ANSWER *Who wrote, "Hold fast to dreams"?*

1. Did I hear someone say, "Let's have ice cream"
2. "Who gave permission to leave" asked the assistant principal.
3. Someone shouted, "Time out"
4. Did she answer, "Not right now, thank you"
5. A new student asked, "Can you direct me to the nurse's office"
6. Did your mother really say, "I'll give you the money if you need it"
7. Milton asked, "Is it too late to apply"
8. "I knew you could do it" my dad exclaimed.
9. Dee wondered, "Where did everyone go"
10. The boating instructor shouted, "Put on your lifejackets"

PRACTICE 25.4D **Punctuating Quotations Within Quotations and Explanatory Material**

Read the sentences. Rewrite each sentence, adding single quotation marks or brackets where needed.

EXAMPLE Jon said, "I enjoyed reading The Treasure of Lemon Brown."

ANSWER *Jon said, "I enjoyed reading 'The Treasure of Lemon Brown.'"*

11. "For tomorrow," Mrs. May said, "please read the story Amigo Brothers."
12. Jan asked, "Did he say, I'll help?"
13. Paula asked, "Can anyone recite the poem Sarah Cynthia Sylvia Stout?"
14. "Did she say, I lost my hat?" Mom asked.
15. Lori wondered, "What does Longfellow mean by Each burning deed and thought?"
16. Mr. Metzger said, "I will now recite the poem Casey at the Bat."
17. "Did you hear him say, I've had it?" asked Liz.
18. The music director announced, "Miss Amory will sing Greensleeves, an old folk song."
19. Ron said, "When did you ever hear him Mr. Shah say, I don't want pizza?"
20. Sheila asked, "Does anyone know the words to the second verse of America?"

WRITING APPLICATION

Write three sentences in which you correctly use punctuation inside and outside quotation marks.

WRITING APPLICATION

Write two sentences with quotations within quotations. In your sentences, use single and double quotation marks correctly.

PRACTICE 25.4C

1. Did I hear someone say, "Let's have ice cream"?
2. "Who gave permission to leave?" asked the assistant principal.
3. Someone shouted, "Time out!"
4. Did she answer, "Not right now, thank you"?
5. A new student asked, "Can you direct me to the nurse's office?"
6. Did your mother really say, "I'll give you the money if you need it"?
7. Milton asked, "Is it too late to apply?"
8. "I knew you could do it!" my dad exclaimed.
9. Dee wondered, "Where did everyone go?"
10. The boating instructor shouted, "Put on your lifejackets!"

PRACTICE 25.4D

11. "For tomorrow," Mrs. May said, "please read the story 'Amigo Brothers.'"
12. Jan asked, "Did he say, 'I'll help'?"
13. Paula asked, "Can anyone recite the poem 'Sarah Cynthia Sylvia Stout'?"
14. "Did she say, 'I lost my hat'?" Mom asked.
15. Lori wondered, "What does Longfellow mean by 'Each burning deed and thought'?"
16. Mr. Metzger said, "I will now recite the poem 'Casey at the Bat.'"
17. "Did you hear him say, 'I've had it'?" asked Liz.
18. The music director announced, "Miss Amory will sing 'Greensleeves,' an old folk song."
19. Ron said, "When did you ever hear him [Mr. Shah] say, 'I don't want pizza'?"
20. Sheila asked, "Does anyone know the words to the second verse of 'America'?"

WRITING APPLICATION

Have students explain to the class how they determined when punctuation should be inside or outside the quotation marks.

WRITING APPLICATION

Have students exchange sentences and check the placement of quotation marks and end marks in each, explaining why it is or is not correct.

Using Quotation Marks for Dialogue

Explain that dialogue is a conversation between two or more people.

RULE 25.4.12 Read aloud the rule and then have students repeat the lines with you.

Use a Think Aloud as part of a gradual release progression.

Say: I use dialogue to bring characters to life in my writing and help my readers to experience the scene I am creating. Starting a new paragraph for each change of speaker helps my readers keep track of who is speaking.

Have two students read aloud the example dialogue on page 584, changing readers each time a paragraph ends. At the end of the example, have the class name which character each reader represented. Discuss the use of paragraph indentations, quotation marks, and information that identifies the new speaker. **Ask:** How many speakers are represented in this dialogue? (two) **Ask:** How does the writer identify the speakers? (by stating their names) **Have students create** a short oral dialogue. Then, work with students to write the dialogue on the board, using correct paragraph structure, punctuation, and speaker identification.

Have small groups of students write short narratives with extensive dialogue between two to four characters. Students should break their paragraphs as speakers change, and use correct punctuation and speaker attribution.

Teacher Tip

For more practice using quotation marks with dialogue, have groups of four create a passage of dialogue that includes three speakers, each of whom speaks at least twice. Distribute copies of the dialogue to the class. Have three group members assume the role of a speaker and one the role of the narrator. Invite groups to perform their passage for the class. After each performance, **ask:** *How were the speakers in this passage identified? How would you describe their points of view?* Invite groups to share the rules they used when punctuating the dialogue.

Using Quotation Marks for Dialogue

A conversation between two or more people is called a **dialogue.** Adding dialogue makes your writing lively because it brings different points of view into your work. It makes your work sound like speech, so dialogue makes your reader feel involved in the scene you describe.

RULE 25.4.12

When you are writing a dialogue, indent to begin a new paragraph with each change of speaker. Also be sure to add quotation marks around a speaker's words. When a new speaker is quoted, be sure to indicate the change to your reader by adding information that identifies the new speaker.

EXAMPLE

"Will you be going with us on the family trip again this summer?" Noreen asked her cousin.

Gwen hesitated before answering. "I'm afraid so. My parents think I enjoy the experience of traveling with our whole family."

"You fooled me, too," Noreen replied. "Maybe the trip will be better this year. I think we're going to places that have large parks. If we're lucky, we might even be able to go on a few rides."

"Well, at least it can't be any worse," sighed Gwen. "On the last trip, we waited in line for one hour at three different historic homes in one day!"

"I remember those lines," said Noreen. "Didn't you get sunburned while we were waiting?"

Notice that each sentence is punctuated according to the rules discussed earlier in this section.

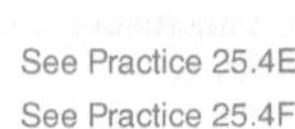

See Practice 25.4E
See Practice 25.4F

Working with ELLs — ELL Sheltered Instruction: Cognitive

Have students read linguistically accommodated text silently with increasing comprehension and ease for increasingly long periods and with a decreasing need for accommodation. Review the fact that English is read from left to right, top to bottom, and observe if students recognize the directionality of English reading.

Beginning Prepare linguistically accommodated, properly punctuated copies of the paragraph in Practice 25.4E on page 585, adding simple synonyms or explanations for words such as *fascinating* and pictures illustrating terms such as *crime show.* Have students read the first sentence silently to themselves. Discuss, referring to the accommodations. Repeat with subsequent sentences.

Intermediate Provide students with the text used in the Beginning activity. Have students read the entire paragraph silently. Then, discuss, referring to the accommodations.

Advanced Obtain an accommodated selection, such as a short story, that features dialogue. Have students silently read a section. Then, discuss, referring to the accommodations for support. Repeat with the remaining sections.

Advanced High Obtain an accommodated selection, such as a short story, that features dialogue. Have students silently read the selection. Then, discuss, referring to the accommodations for support.

PRACTICE 25.4E **Using Quotation Marks in Dialogue**

Read the dialogue. Then, rewrite the dialogue. Use proper spacing for quotations and create additional paragraphs where needed. Be sure to use quotation marks and other punctuation correctly.

EXAMPLE Can I ask you something? Matt asked Angelo. Sure Angelo answered. What?

ANSWER *"Can I ask you something?" Matt asked Angelo.*

"Sure," Angelo answered. "What?"

I would like to learn about forensic science Rose commented. You've been watching too many crime shows laughed Tim. Really Rose said it's fascinating, and I would even consider it as a career. Well there are many colleges that offer courses, but I think they're tough courses. There's a lot of science involved, Tim said. That's all right, I like science Rose replied. You could probably look online to find the requirements and places that offer courses Tim suggested. That's what I'll do Rose concluded.

PRACTICE 25.4F **Revising Dialogue for Punctuation and Paragraphs**

Read the dialogue. Then, rewrite the dialogue. Add quotation marks and other punctuation, and begin new paragraphs where needed.

EXAMPLE Hello, my name is Gwendolyn, the new girl said. What's your name? I'm Elizabeth. Nice to meet you.

ANSWER *"Hello, my name is Gwendolyn," the new girl said. "What's your name?"*

"I'm Elizabeth. Nice to meet you."

Justin and Marina walked into the sandwich shop for lunch. When they were seated at a table, a waiter came to take their order. What can I get you the waiter asked. I'll have the tuna salad sandwich with pickles Justin said. I'll have the vegetarian special Marina added. What would you like to drink with that asked the waiter. We'll both have water Marina responded. The waiter said Thank you. I'll bring your orders shortly. Then, he walked away.

SPEAKING APPLICATION

Read the dialogue in Practice 25.4E with a partner, each of you taking the part of one speaker. Read it again after you have revised it. Discuss why the original dialogue is confusing to read and your revised dialogue is easy to read.

WRITING APPLICATION

Write a dialogue in which you have participated, or you can make up a conversation. Use expressions (for example, *he said, she replied*), quotation marks, and correct paragraphing.

PRACTICE 25.4E

"I would like to learn about forensic science," Rose commented.

"You've been watching too many crime shows," laughed Tim.

"Really," Rose said, "it's fascinating, and I would even consider it as a career."

"Well, there are many colleges that offer courses, but I think they're tough courses. There's a lot of science involved," Tim said.

"That's all right, I like science," Rose replied.

"You could probably look online to find the requirements and places that offer courses," Tim suggested.

"That's what I'll do," Rose concluded.

PRACTICE 25.4F

Justin and Marina walked into the sandwich shop for lunch. When they were seated at a table, a waiter came to take their order.

"What can I get you?" the waiter asked.

"I'll have the tuna salad sandwich with pickles," Justin said.

"I'll have the vegetarian special," Marina added.

"What would you like to drink with that?" asked the waiter.

"We'll both have water," Marina responded.

The waiter said, "Thank you. I'll bring your orders shortly." Then, he walked away.

SPEAKING APPLICATION

Have students present their explanations to the class. The class should comment on whether or not the students correctly followed the rules.

WRITING APPLICATION

Have students exchange dialogues and check each other's work, explaining why it is or is not correct.

Using Quotation Marks in Titles

Point out that quotation marks are used to identify titles of short works, such as short stories, chapters, poems, television episodes, and songs.

RULES 25.4.13, 25.4.14 Read aloud the rules and then have students repeat the lines with you.

Review with students the examples of written works and artistic works listed in the charts on page 586. For each category of work, brainstorm for a new example of a work with which students are familiar that fits into that category. Use a Think Aloud as part of a gradual release progression.

Say: When **I refer** to a short work in my writing, I put the title of the work in quotes. For example, if I were to write an article about Charles Dickens's book *David Copperfield*, I would set the title of Chapter 1, "I Am Born," in quotation marks. If you were to write an article that quoted my article, you would put its title, "Discovering David Copperfield," in quotation marks.

Work with students to generate a list of short works with which they are familiar. Create and speak aloud two or three sentences that contain the names of works on the list. Then, write the sentences on the board, using quotation marks correctly.

Have partners brainstorm for several sentences that include these short works. Have partners write their example sentences, using quotation marks correctly to enclose the titles. Then, have students share their examples, including their use of quotation marks, with the class.

Using Underlining and Italics in Titles

Point out that many types of titles and special names are called out with italics or underlining when they appear in writing.

Using Quotation Marks in Titles

Quotation marks are generally used to set off the titles of shorter works.

RULE 25.4.13

Use quotation marks to enclose the titles of short written works and around the title of a work that is mentioned as part of a collection.

WRITTEN WORKS THAT USE QUOTATION MARKS	
Title of a Short Story	"The Gift of the Magi"
Chapter From a Book	"The Test Is in the Tasting" from *No-Work Garden Book*
Title of a Short Poem	"Lucy"
Title of an Article	"How to Build a Birdhouse"
Title Mentioned as Part of a Collection	"Uncle Vanya" in *Eight Great Comedies*

RULE 25.4.14

Use quotation marks around the titles of episodes in a television or radio series, songs, and parts of a long musical composition.

ARTISTIC WORKS THAT USE QUOTATION MARKS	
Title of an Episode	"The Nile" from *Cousteau Odyssey*
Title of a Song	"The Best Things in Life Are Free"
Title of a Part of a Long Musical Work	"The Storm" from the *William Tell Overture*

Using Underlining and Italics in Titles

Underlining and **italics** help make titles and other special words and names stand out in your writing. Underlining is used only in handwritten or typewritten material. In printed material, italic (slanted) print is used instead of underlining.

UNDERLINING The Secret Garden ITALICS *The Secret Garden*

Working with ELLs ELL **Sheltered Instruction:** Cognitive

Have students spell familiar English words by employing spelling patterns with increasing accuracy. Point out the familiar word *title* on page 586. Explain this spelling pattern to students: in many English words ending with a consonant followed by the /əl/ or /'l/ sound, the sound is spelled *le*. Give them the additional examples of *table, battle,* and *apple*.

Beginning Review the model words with students. Have students copy them correctly. Then, say the words *little, able,* and *cattle.* Guide students to apply the pattern as they spell each. Review results.

Intermediate Review the model words with students. Then, have them apply the spelling pattern to spell familiar words, such as *little, able,* and *gentle,* as well as unfamiliar words, such as *cattle* and *trifle.* Review results.

Advanced Provide each partner in a pair with two different lists of familiar and unfamiliar words that follow the pattern. Then, have partners take turns reading words as the listener writes each correctly.

Advanced High Have students complete the Advanced activity. Then, have them use a dictionary to find three new words that follow the pattern and spell them correctly in sentences.

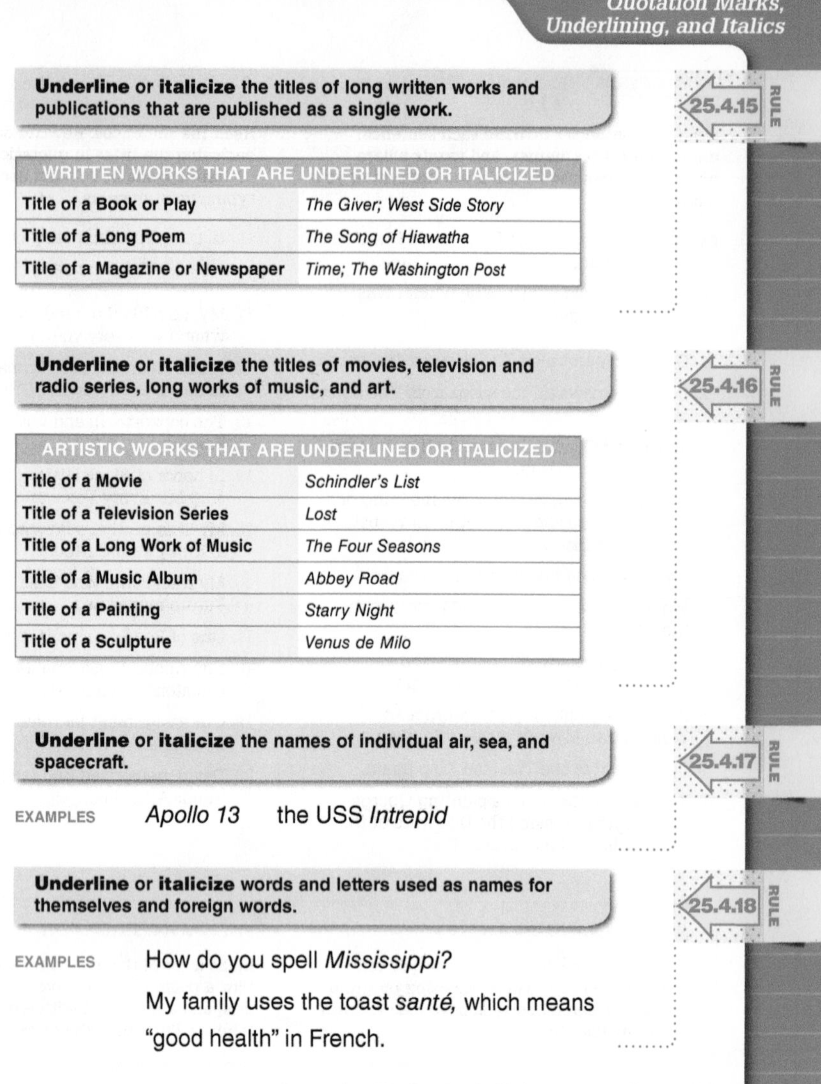

Underline or **italicize** the titles of long written works and publications that are published as a single work.

RULE 25.4.15

WRITTEN WORKS THAT ARE UNDERLINED OR ITALICIZED	
Title of a Book or Play	*The Giver; West Side Story*
Title of a Long Poem	*The Song of Hiawatha*
Title of a Magazine or Newspaper	*Time; The Washington Post*

Underline or **italicize** the titles of movies, television and radio series, long works of music, and art.

RULE 25.4.16

ARTISTIC WORKS THAT ARE UNDERLINED OR ITALICIZED	
Title of a Movie	*Schindler's List*
Title of a Television Series	*Lost*
Title of a Long Work of Music	*The Four Seasons*
Title of a Music Album	*Abbey Road*
Title of a Painting	*Starry Night*
Title of a Sculpture	*Venus de Milo*

Underline or **italicize** the names of individual air, sea, and spacecraft.

RULE 25.4.17

EXAMPLES *Apollo 13* the USS *Intrepid*

Underline or **italicize** words and letters used as names for themselves and foreign words.

RULE 25.4.18

EXAMPLES How do you spell *Mississippi*?

My family uses the toast *santé*, which means "good health" in French.

See Practice 25.4G
See Practice 25.4H

Explain that underlining is used to identify certain types of works when one is hand writing the titles or using a typewriter to write them. Italic print is used for printed material or writing generated on a computer.

RULES 25.4.15, 25.4.16, 25.4.17 Read aloud the rules and then have students repeat the lines with you.

Discuss the examples on the charts that list written works and artistic works that are underlined or italicized. Have students create their own two-column charts that list each type of work that is underlined or italicized. Have students replace the examples in the charts with examples with which they are familiar.

Have students add one additional category to their charts: names of individual ships, planes, and spacecraft.

RULE 25.4.18 Read aloud the rule and then have students repeat the lines with you.

Explain that when you refer directly to a word as a name for itself, it should be underlined or italicized. **Say:** For example, if I want to write "My favorite word is *curmudgeon*," I should underline or italicize *curmudgeon*.

Have students write a paragraph in which they define several words they have made up. Remind students to italicize the words they define and to set off the definitions with quotation marks.

Differentiated Instruction

RTI Strategy for Below-Level Students

Help students understand the rules regarding the use of italics and quotation marks. Gather together a variety of different books, magazines, and DVDs that are in the classroom. Direct attention to the title of a book. **Ask:** *If you were writing about this book, would you underline or italicize this, or would you put it in quotation marks?*

Have students raise their hands and answer the question. Ask a volunteer to write on the board a sentence containing the book title. Then, direct attention to a magazine. Open the magazine and point to the title of an article. **Ask:** *If you were writing about this article, would you underline or italicize it, or would you put it in quotation marks?*

Continue the question and answer session until students have a better understanding of the rules regarding italics and quotation marks.

PRACTICE 25.4G

1. The Phantom Tollbooth
2. The Sound of Music
3. Goodnight Moon
4. amorphous, Webster's New World Dictionary
5. The Houston Chronicle
6. High School Musical
7. Titanic
8. Bad Boy
9. The Lion King
10. George Washington Crossing the Delaware

PRACTICE 25.4H

11. Pat the Bunny
12. Now, "How to Survive a Computer Crash"
13. "America the Beautiful"
14. "Lift Every Voice and Sing"
15. Krazy Kats Cartoons
16. Future
17. The Thinker
18. Apollo 13
19. "Ribbons"
20. "The Raven"

WRITING APPLICATION

Have students explain what types of works would have required quotation marks rather than underlining.

WRITING APPLICATION

Have students justify the way they represented the titles.

PRACTICE 25.4G Underlining Titles, Names and Words

Read the sentences. Rewrite each sentence, underlining titles, names, and words where needed. You can use italics if you are typing your answers.

EXAMPLE I loved Stuart Little when I was younger.

ANSWER I loved Stuart Little when I was younger.

1. Our class performed The Phantom Tollbooth.
2. Caroline knows all the songs from The Sound of Music.
3. Suzie read Goodnight Moon to the children she was babysitting.
4. Amanda was uncertain of the meaning of amorphous, so she looked it up in Webster's New World Dictionary.
5. My mom reads The Houston Chronicle.
6. We plan to see High School Musical at the theater next month.
7. Chloe really enjoyed the RMS Titanic exhibition at the children's museum.
8. For his biography report, Jethro read Walter Dean Myers's memoir Bad Boy.
9. I can't wait to see The Lion King again.
10. You can see the famous painting George Washington Crossing the Delaware at the Metropolitan Museum of Art.

PRACTICE 25.4H Using Underlining and Quotation Marks

Read the sentences. Rewrite each sentence, enclosing the titles in quotation marks or underlining them. You can use italics if you are typing your answers.

EXAMPLE The choir sang Oh Shenandoah.

ANSWER The choir sang "Oh Shenandoah."

11. My mom liked to read Pat the Bunny to me when I was very young.
12. I read an article in Now magazine titled How to Survive a Computer Crash.
13. The concert will end with America the Beautiful.
14. In honor of Black History Month, LaVerne will sing Lift Every Voice and Sing.
15. My little brother's favorite television program is Krazy Kats Cartoons.
16. My friend Jim, who likes technology, reads Future magazine.
17. One of Rodin's famous statues is The Thinker.
18. The Apollo 13 astronauts faced life-threatening challenges in space.
19. Our assignment for tomorrow is to read Laurence Yep's story Ribbons.
20. David memorized and recited The Raven by Edgar Allan Poe.

WRITING APPLICATION

Write several sentences in which you refer to a movie you have seen, a television program you watch, and a book you have read recently. Underline the titles.

WRITING APPLICATION

Make a list of the following: a song that you like, a poem that you have read in language arts, and a magazine with which you are familiar. Punctuate the titles correctly.

Working with ELLs — ELL Sheltered Instruction: Cognitive

Use the language in the directions for the Practice activities to help students develop basic sight vocabulary used routinely in written classroom materials. Ensure that students understand how this vocabulary will assist them as they respond to the activity. Write the words *where, answer, list,* and *your* on the board.

Beginning Read each word aloud as students read with you, and discuss its meaning. Then, locate each word in the directions. Read the directions with students, clarifying meaning. Then, guide them in completing the first items in Practice 25.4G.

Intermediate Say the words aloud, and discuss their meaning. Then, direct students to read the Practice activity directions to a partner. To ensure students understand the directions, have them summarize each set. Then, have them work in a group to complete the Practice activities.

Advanced Introduce the words, and have students locate them in the directions. Then, review these routine words: *underlining, titles, quotation marks.* Have students read the directions aloud, restating their meaning. Then, have them complete the activities.

Advanced High Have students complete the Advanced activity. Then, have them write definitions or explanations of each word discussed.

25.5 Hyphens

Hyphens (-) are used to combine words and to show a connection between the syllables of words that are broken at the ends of lines.

Grammar Game Plan

www.phwritingcoach.com

Grammar Practice
Practice your grammar skills with Writing Coach Online.

Grammar Games
Test your knowledge of grammar in this fast-paced interactive video game.

Using Hyphens in Numbers

Hyphens are used to join compound numbers and fractions.

RULE 25.5.1 Use a **hyphen** when you write two-word numbers from twenty-one through ninety-nine.

EXAMPLES twenty-four fifty-one

RULE 25.5.2 Use a **hyphen** when you use a fraction as an adjective but not when you use a fraction as a noun.

ADJECTIVE The class is three-fourths full.

NOUN Two thirds of the students attended.

Using Hyphens for Prefixes and Suffixes

Many words with common prefixes are no longer hyphenated. The following prefixes are often used before proper nouns: *ante-*, *anti-*, *post-*, *pre-*, *pro-*, and *un-*. Check a dictionary when you are unsure about using a hyphen.

RULE 25.5.3 Use a **hyphen** after a prefix that is followed by a proper noun or adjective.

EXAMPLES post-Revolutionary mid-April

RULE 25.5.4 Use a **hyphen** in words with the prefixes *all-*, *ex-*, and *self-* and the suffix *-elect.*

EXAMPLES all-powerful ex-leader

www.phwritingcoach.com

Diagnostic and Instruction
Diagnostic test assesses students' instructional needs. Lessons and practice are assigned based on results.

Additional Practice
- Grammar Practice—Targeted practice addresses individual needs.
- ExamView—Teachers customize their grammar practice and tests.
- Grammar Games—Interactive video games make grammar fun.

Lesson Objectives

1. Use punctuation marks, including hyphens, correctly.
2. Use hyphens correctly in writing to divide words and to form compound words.

Using Hyphens in Numbers

Point out that hyphens have many uses. They are used to represent two-word numbers, to divide a word between syllables at the end of a line, and to form compound words and compound modifiers. Hyphens signal that numbers or words are joined or divided.

RULES 25.5.1, 25.5.2 Read aloud the rules and then have students repeat the lines with you.

Discuss the example sentences on page 589. Then, say several two-word numbers to students. Have them write the numbers, using hyphens correctly. Say these two sentences aloud: One-half credit is better than none. I got nine tenths of the answers right. Ask students to explain which sentences should have hyphens, and why.

Using Hyphens for Prefixes and Suffixes

Point out that, in general, hyphens are no longer used with most prefixes. Explain that there are times, however, when hyphens should be used with certain prefixes and suffixes. It is a good idea to consult a dictionary to verify whether to use a hyphen.

RULES 25.5.3, 25.5.4 Read aloud the rules and then have students repeat the lines with you.

Discuss the examples on page 589. Then, **say:** A few simple rules help me decide when to hyphenate prefixes and suffixes. If I keep in mind that many words with common prefixes are no longer hyphenated, that narrows it down a bit. But when should I use a hyphen? Review the rules for using hyphens with prefixes and suffixes.

Work with students to brainstorm for examples of words with prefixes or suffixes that require a hyphen. **Say:** Now, let's consult the dictionary to see if we've hyphenated our words correctly.

Have student pairs look up the words and share their findings with the class.

Using Hyphens in Compound Words

Discuss how hyphens are used to create compound words.

RULE 25.5.5 Read aloud the rule and then have students repeat the lines with you.

Discuss the examples on page 590. Then, write *great-grandfather* on the board. **Say:** A compound word is two words joined together with a hyphen to represent a single idea. Who knows what a great-grandfather is? (the father of one's grandfather) *Great-grandfather* is a compound word. It is made up by the words *great* and *grandfather.*

Write these words on the board: *daughter in law, great grandfather, uncle, step sister, mother.* Work with students to pick out compound words that require hyphens.

Have student pairs write the words correctly using hyphens. Repeat the exercise if necessary, using different words.

Using Hyphens With Compound Modifiers

Point out to students that hyphens help readers group information properly. Students can use a hyphen to connect a compound modifier that comes before a noun.

RULE 25.5.6 Read aloud the rule and then have students repeat the lines with you.

Discuss with students the importance of using hyphens correctly. Review the examples of compound modifiers provided on page 590.

Using Hyphens in Compound Words

Compound words are two or more words that must be read together to create a single idea.

Use a hyphen to connect two or more nouns that are used as one compound word, unless a dictionary gives a different spelling.

EXAMPLES son-in-law great-grandmother

Using Hyphens With Compound Modifiers

Hyphens help your reader group information properly.

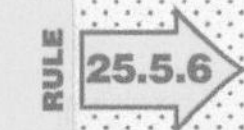

Use a hyphen to connect a compound modifier that comes before a noun. Do not use a hyphen with a compound modifier that includes a word ending in *-ly* or in a compound proper adjective.

EXAMPLE	The team used a full-court press.	
INCORRECT	poorly-written text	South-Asian tourist
CORRECT	poorly written text	South Asian tourist

A hyphen is not necessary when a compound modifier follows the noun it describes.

See Practice 25.5A
See Practice 25.5B

MODIFIER BEFORE NOUN The storm moved in an east-to-west direction.

MODIFIER AFTER NOUN The storm moved in the direction east to west.

However, if a dictionary spells a word with a hyphen, the word must always be hyphenated, even when it follows a noun.

EXAMPLE The goalie is happy-go-lucky.

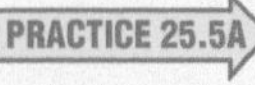

PRACTICE 25.5A **Using Hyphens in Numbers and Words**

Read the following items. Write each item, adding hyphens where needed. If an item is already correct, write *correct*.

EXAMPLE a world famous star

ANSWER *a world-famous star*

1. mid January temperature
2. sixty six pencils
3. a bench that is well built
4. self respect
5. one third of a cup
6. one hundred people
7. two thirds of the students
8. well known actor
9. post Civil War
10. president elect

PRACTICE 25.5B **Proofreading for Hyphens**

Read the sentences. Rewrite each sentence, adding hyphens where needed.

EXAMPLE At the half, our team was ahead by twenty two points.

ANSWER *At the half, our team was ahead by twenty-two points.*

11. Success builds self confidence.
12. Red hot embers glowed in the fireplace.
13. The recipe calls for one half teaspoon of cinnamon.
14. In London, we rode on the top level of a double decker bus.
15. My brother in law took me to the movies yesterday.
16. Sometimes, Beau's friends are annoyed by his all knowing attitude.
17. Rubble from a torn down building was strewn over the lot.
18. The ex governor stood on the platform beside the governor elect.
19. Fifty five people attended the fund raiser last night.
20. The adventurers will need an off road vehicle to get to that remote campsite.

SPEAKING APPLICATION

With a partner, brainstorm and list five terms that you use or have seen that are written with a hyphen. Take turns using these terms in phrases or sentences.

WRITING APPLICATION

Write two sentences in which you use words with *self-* or *ex-* as prefixes.

PRACTICE 25.5A

1. mid-January temperature
2. sixty-six pencils
3. correct
4. self-respect
5. correct
6. correct
7. correct
8. well-known actor
9. post-Civil War
10. president-elect

PRACTICE 25.5B

11. self-confidence
12. Red-hot
13. one-half
14. double-decker
15. brother-in-law
16. all-knowing
17. torn-down
18. ex-governor, governor-elect
19. Fifty-five, fund-raiser
20. off-road

Working with ELLs

ELL Sheltered Instruction: Cognitive

Have students listen to, derive meaning from, and respond orally to information presented in a wide variety of print, electronic, and audiovisual media to build attainment of the concept of hyphenated words. Provide students with a print article that includes hyphenated words.

Beginning Read the article aloud as students follow along. Have students raise their hands whenever you read a hyphenated term. Discuss the reason for the use of the hyphen in each case. Ask students simple questions about the meaning of hyphenated and nonhyphenated modifiers in the article, such as, *What kind of person is the article about? How many people were at the event?*

Intermediate Have students read the article in small groups. Then, ask students comprehension questions, such as *Where did this happen?* Finally, have them identify hyphenated words, explain the function of the hyphens, and discuss what each word contributes to the article.

Advanced Have partners read the article and discuss the text. Next, have them identify hyphenated words, explain the function of the hyphens, and explain what each word contributes to the reader's understanding or impressions.

Advanced High Have students complete the Advanced activity. Then, have them use several of the hyphenated words correctly in a paragraph of their own.

SPEAKING APPLICATION

Have students show that they can use hyphens correctly by explaining their rationales for using or not using hyphens.

WRITING APPLICATION

Have students show that they can use hyphens correctly by exchanging sentences and checking the placement of hyphens, explaining why it is or is not correct.

Using Hyphens at the End of Lines

Explain that hyphens are used to divide a word between syllables at the end of a line if the entire word will not fit within the margins.

RULES 25.5.7, 25.5.8 Read aloud the rules and then have students repeat the lines with you.

Use a Think Aloud as part of a gradual release progression.

Say: While hyphens are a useful way to divide words at the end of a line, too many hyphens can make my writing choppy. If I cannot avoid dividing a word, I will divide it between syllables, and I will make sure the hyphen appears at the end of the first line, not at the beginning of the second line. **I will also consult a dictionary** to make sure I have correctly divided the word between syllables.

Work with students to find examples of hyphens used at the ends of lines in a text with which they are familiar and to share their findings with the class.

Have students write short paragraphs, correctly dividing words that don't fit on one line.

Using Hyphens Correctly to Divide Words

Explain that one-syllable words can never be divided at the end of a line.

RULE 25.5.9 Read aloud the rule and then have students repeat the lines with you.

Using Hyphens at the Ends of Lines

Hyphens serve a useful purpose when they are used to divide words at the ends of lines. They should not, however, be used more often than is necessary because they can make reading feel choppy.

Avoid dividing words at the end of a line whenever possible. If a word must be divided, always divide it between syllables.

EXAMPLE Marcia seems to have taken my advice most seriously and is doing better.

Check a dictionary if you are unsure how a word is divided into syllables. Looking up the word *seriously*, for example, you would find that its syllables are *se-ri-ous-ly*.

A hyphen used to divide a word should never be placed at the beginning of the second line. It must be placed at the end of the first line.

INCORRECT Julio has taken many photo
-graphs of animals.

CORRECT Julio has taken many photographs of animals.

Using Hyphens Correctly to Divide Words

One-syllable words cannot be divided.

Do *not* divide one-syllable words even if they seem long or sound like words with two syllables.

INCORRECT	fif-th	brow-se	stra-ight
CORRECT	fifth	browse	straight

Working with ELLs — ELL Sheltered Instruction: Cognitive

Have students spell familiar English words with increasing accuracy by employing spelling rules. Point out the example word *seriously* on page 592. Explain that the word is made by adding *-ly* to *serious.* Then, review familar *-ly* words such as *quickly, tamely, happily,* and *gently.* Explain these spelling rules: When adding *-ly* or another suffix beginning with a consonant to a word ending in a consonant or silent *e,* you usually do not change the spelling of the base word. When adding *-ly* or another suffix to a word ending consonant + *y*, you usually change the *-y* to *-i.* When adding *-ly* to a word ending *-le,* such as *gentle,* you drop the *-le.*

Beginning Have students write each example word, spelling it correctly. Then, guide students as they add *-ly* to these adjectives: *kind, late, cozy, noble.*

Intermediate Provide groups with lists of familiar and unfamiliar adjectives, and have them add *-ly* to each, spelling it correctly.

Advanced Provide partners with a list of familiar and unfamiliar adjectives. Have them add *-ly* to each, following the rules.

Advanced High Have students complete the Advanced activity. Then, have them use a dictionary to find three new words that illustrate the rules.

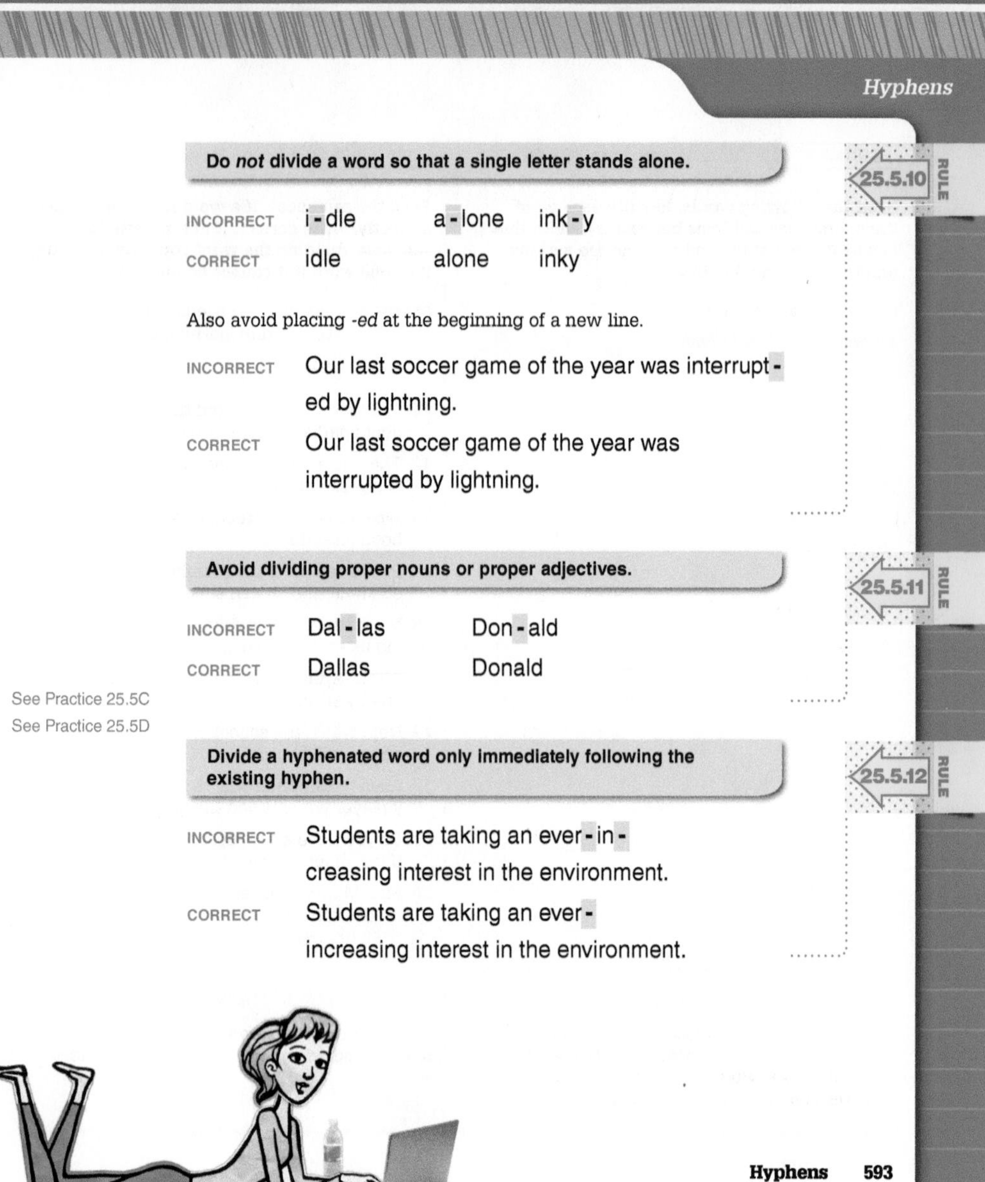

Do *not* divide a word so that a single letter stands alone.

RULE 25.5.10

INCORRECT	i-dle	a-lone	ink-y
CORRECT	idle	alone	inky

Also avoid placing *-ed* at the beginning of a new line.

INCORRECT Our last soccer game of the year was interrupt-ed by lightning.

CORRECT Our last soccer game of the year was interrupted by lightning.

Avoid dividing proper nouns or proper adjectives.

RULE 25.5.11

INCORRECT	Dal-las	Don-ald
CORRECT	Dallas	Donald

See Practice 25.5C
See Practice 25.5D

Divide a hyphenated word only immediately following the existing hyphen.

RULE 25.5.12

INCORRECT Students are taking an ever-in-creasing interest in the environment.

CORRECT Students are taking an ever-increasing interest in the environment.

Explain to students that hyphens help correctly divide words between syllables.

RULES 25.5.10, 25.5.11, 25.5.12 Read aloud the rules and then have students repeat the lines with you.

Explain that proper names and proper adjectives should never be divided with a hyphen at the end of a line.

Occasionally, students may need to divide a compound word at the end of a line. If the compound word has already been hyphenated, it should be divided at the existing hyphen.

Have students brainstorm for three words with three or more syllables. They should mark the syllables by drawing vertical lines. Then, have students write three sentences using the words. Each sentence should require that one of the three-syllable words be divided at the end of the line. Students should demonstrate that they can use correct punctuation, including hyphens, by correctly hyphenating the words at the line breaks. Have students exchange papers with a partner. Partners should proofread sentences to check for correct punctuation marks.

Teacher Tip

If students are having difficulty dividing words into syllables, have them say the words aloud and clap the syllables. Model this using the word *telescope.* Then, have students speak and clap in unison. Finally, have students speak and clap with a partner. Provide a list of multisyllabic words for additional practice.

PRACTICE 25.5C

1. tor | na | do
2. warned
3. sac | ri | fice
4. spe | cial
5. pre | dic | tion
6. ques | tion
7. re | ad | just
8. in | ves | ti | gate
9. for | get | ful
10. col | lapse

PRACTICE 25.5D

11. correct
12. The university students par-ticipated in a rally.
13. correct
14. Please tell me if the plumber has called about our broken sink.
15. correct
16. correct
17. Next week, the school-wide tour-nament will begin.
18. I believe Stephen was the only player who missed the game.
19. correct
20. correct

WRITING APPLICATION

Have students demonstrate that they can correctly use hyphens by taking turns dividing words by pausing between syllables to indicate hyphens.

WRITING APPLICATION

Students should demonstrate that they can correctly use hyphens by exchanging sentences, checking each other's work, and explaining why it is or is not correct.

Hyphens

PRACTICE 25.5C Using Hyphens to Divide Words

Read the following words. Rewrite each word. Then, draw vertical lines between syllables that can be divided at the end of a line. Do nothing to words that cannot be divided.

EXAMPLE vocabulary
ANSWER *vo|cab|u|lar|y*

1. tornado
2. warned
3. sacrifice
4. special
5. prediction
6. question
7. readjust
8. investigate
9. forgetful
10. collapse

PRACTICE 25.5D Using Hyphens in Words in Sentences

Read the sentences. If a word has been divided correctly, write *correct*. If not, rewrite the sentence, dividing the word correctly or writing it as one word if it cannot be divided.

EXAMPLE Many of my friends are in-terested in learning Spanish.
ANSWER *correct*

11. The water was blue and the sun-light sparkled on the waves.
12. The university students pa-rticipated in a rally.
13. We strolled the streets of our neighbor-hood after dinner.
14. Please tell me if the plumber has call-ed about our broken sink.
15. My mother will be driv-ing us to the concert.
16. A mid-April snowstorm took every-one by surprise.
17. Next week, the school-wide tourn-ament will begin.
18. I believe Stephen was the onl-y player who missed the game.
19. Do you have any specific ques-tions about the quiz instructions?
20. Mrs. Marquez asked us to cir-cle the correct answer.

WRITING APPLICATION

Look at a draft of a piece of writing you have done. Select three words and write them in syllables, showing how you would break them at the end of a line using a hyphen.

WRITING APPLICATION

Use three sentences from Practice 25.5D as models, and write sentences with hyphenated words.

Working with ELLs ELL Sheltered Instruction: Cognitive

Use Practice 25.5D to help students write using increasingly complex grammatical structures, such as correct verbs and tenses. Review the past, present, and future tense, as well as the concept of correct tense.

Beginning Pair beginners with more fluent speakers. Have them complete an item from the Practice activity and then identify the verb in the sentence and its tense. Then, have them rewrite the sentence in another tense, explaining what context is appropriate for each sentence.

Intermediate Have students complete the Practice. Then, have students work in small groups to identify the verb in each sentence and its tense. Have them rewrite the sentence in another tense, explaining what context is appropriate for each sentence.

Advanced Have students complete the Practice. Then, have partners identify the verb in each sentence and its tense. Have them rewrite the sentence twice, each time in a different tense, explaining what context is appropriate for each sentence.

Advanced High Have students complete the Practice. Then, have individuals identify the verb in each sentence and its tense. Have them rewrite the sentence twice, each time in a different tense, explaining what context is appropriate for each sentence. Finally, have them exchange papers and check each other's work.

25.6 Apostrophes

The **apostrophe (')** is used to show possession or ownership. It is also used in shortened forms of words called contractions. In a contraction, the apostrophe marks the place where letters have been omitted.

Grammar Game Plan

www.phwritingcoach.com

Grammar Practice
Practice your grammar skills with Writing Coach Online.

Grammar Games
Test your knowledge of grammar in this fast-paced interactive video game.

Using Apostrophes With Possessive Nouns

Apostrophes are used with nouns to show ownership or possession.

Add an apostrophe and -s to show the possessive case of most singular nouns and plural nouns that do not end in -s or -es. RULE 25.6.1

EXAMPLES The doctor's advice included plenty of rest.

The men's store in town is having a huge sale.

Even when a singular noun already ends in *-s*, you can usually add an apostrophe and *-s* to show possession.

EXAMPLE It was her boss's idea to work longer hours.

In classical or ancient names that end in *-s*, it is common to omit the final *-s* to make pronunciation easier.

EXAMPLE Ulysses' wisdom was well known.

Add an apostrophe to show the possessive case of plural nouns ending in -s or -es. Do not add an -s. RULE 25.6.2

EXAMPLE The bees' buzzing was all I could hear.

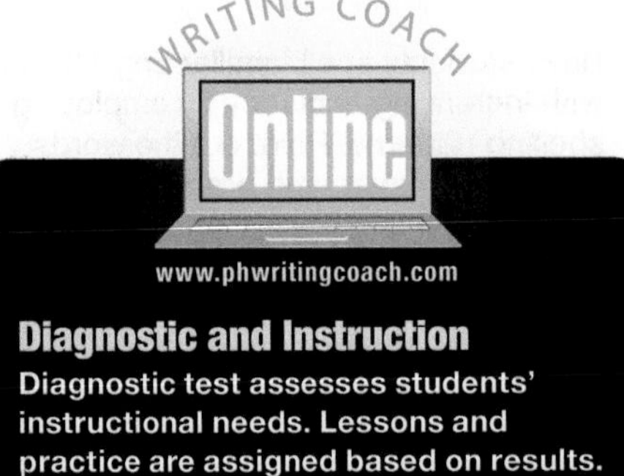

www.phwritingcoach.com

Diagnostic and Instruction
Diagnostic test assesses students' instructional needs. Lessons and practice are assigned based on results.

Additional Practice
- Grammar Practice—Targeted practice addresses individual needs.
- ExamView—Teachers customize their grammar practice and tests.
- Grammar Games—Interactive video games make grammar fun.

Lesson Objectives

1. Use apostrophes to show ownership, make contractions, and create plural forms.
2. Use apostrophes correctly in writing.

Using Apostrophes With Possessive Nouns

Point out that apostrophes are used with nouns to show ownership or possession.

RULES 25.6.1, 25.6.2 Read aloud the rules and then have students repeat the lines with you.

Use a Think Aloud as part of a gradual release progression.

Say: When **I want** to make a noun possessive in my writing, I use an apostrophe. But I keep in mind that the position of the apostrophe varies depending on whether the noun is singular or plural and whether it already ends in -s.

Write the words *children*, *father*, *girls*, *vice president*, and *class* on the board. **Work with students to** form the possessive case of each word. Remind students that most nouns that don't end in *-s* or *-es* can be made possessive simply by adding *'s*. Have students form possessive nouns of *children*, *father*, and *vice president*, using this rule. For each word, **ask:** Is this a plural or singular noun?

Explain that plural nouns that end in *-s* or *-es* can be made possessive by adding an apostrophe to the end of the word. Ask students how they would form the possessive of the plural noun *girls*.

Have pairs of students make a list of eight additional nouns including at least two plural nouns and two nouns that end in *-s*. Have students write the possessive form of each noun.

Using Apostrophes With Possessive Nouns (continued)

RULES 25.6.3 Read aloud the rule and then have students repeat the lines with you.

Discuss the examples with students, and have them brainstorm for other compound nouns that would form plurals in this manner.

Using Apostrophes With Pronouns

Point out that both indefinite and personal pronouns can show possession.

RULES 25.6.4, 25.6.5 Read aloud the rules and then have students repeat the lines with you.

Review the examples on the page. Write these words on the board: *someone, their, our, your, everyone.* Work with students to form the possessive of each word. Prompt students to name whether each word is an indefinite or personal pronoun.

Teacher Tip

For extra practice using apostrophes with pronouns, have students write a passage describing the ownership of one or more items in their home. For example, *My mother's favorite table is in the front hallway. Our neighbor put it out on the curb, so it became ours. The junk on top of the table is my sister's. She leaves her stuff all over the place.* Have students share their passages with the class. Have the class identify the indefinite and personal pronouns in each passage.

Add an apostrophe and -s (or just an apostrophe if the word is a plural ending in -s) to the last word of a compound noun to form the possessive.

EXAMPLES the Boy Scouts' camping trip

my grandfather's house

See Practice 25.6A

Using Apostrophes With Pronouns

Both indefinite and personal pronouns can show possession.

Use an apostrophe and -s with indefinite pronouns to show possession.

EXAMPLES anyone's seat everyone else's name

Do not use an apostrophe with possessive personal pronouns.

POSSESSIVE PERSONAL PRONOUNS		
	SINGULAR	PLURAL
First Person	I, me, my, mine	we, us, our, ours
Second Person	you, your, yours	you, your, yours
Third Person	he, him, his; she, her, hers; it, its	they, them; their, theirs

Some of these pronouns act as adjectives.

EXAMPLES The dog carried a ball in its mouth.

Their house is for sale.

Others act as subjects, objects, and subject complements.

EXAMPLES Mine is the blue jacket.

The red jacket is hers.

See Practice 25.6B

Working with ELLs — ELL Sheltered Instruction: Cognitive

Have students spell familiar English words with increasing accuracy by employing spelling patterns. Point out the words *compound, noun,* and *pronoun* on page 596. Explain that they illustrate a pattern of English spelling: the /ow/ sound is often spelled *ou*. Give these familiar examples: *cloud, loud, round.*

Beginning Review the pattern using the familiar example words. Write them on the board, and have students copy, spelling each correctly. Have students apply the pattern by writing the words again as you dictate them.

Intermediate Review the pattern and the example words. Then, say familiar words, such as *sound, proud,* and *found.* Have students apply the pattern to spell each correctly. Repeat with unfamiliar words, such as *rebound* and *astound.*

Advanced Have partners list words that follow the pattern, spelling each correctly. Then, have them list words in which the /ow/ sound is spelled *ow.* Finally, have them check their work in a dictionary and then use each word in a sentence.

Advanced High Have students complete the Advanced activity. Then, have partners quiz each other on the spelling of each word they have listed.

Using Apostrophes With Contractions

Contractions are used in informal speech and writing, especially in dialogue because they create the sound of speech.

Use an apostrophe in a contraction to show where one or more letters have been omitted. RULE 25.6.6

COMMON CONTRACTIONS		
Verb + *not*	is not = isn't	cannot = can't
Noun or Pronoun + *will*	I will = I'll	we will = we'll
Noun or Pronoun + *be*	you are = you're	Andy is = Andy's
Noun or Pronoun + *would*	she would = she'd	who would = who'd

Avoid using contractions in formal speech and writing. RULE 25.6.7

Contractions may be used in dialogue and in informal speech and writing, but they should be avoided in formal usage.

INFORMAL WRITING What's the latest news?

FORMAL WRITING What is the latest news?

Using Apostrophes to Create Plurals

Do not use an apostrophe to form plurals, except in specific instances.

Use an apostrophe and -s to create the plural form of a letter, numeral, or a word used as a name for itself. RULE 25.6.8

See Practice 25.6C
See Practice 25.6D

EXAMPLES Remember your *thank you's.*

Your *b's* and *d's* look alike.

Using Apostrophes With Contractions

Remind students that contractions are shortened words. Apostrophes indicate that letters have been omitted. Point out that writers should use contractions sparingly in formal writing.

RULES 25.6.6, 25.6.7 Read aloud the rules and then have students repeat the lines with you.

Review the example contractions on page 597 with the class. Have student partners generate a sentence for each common contraction on the chart. Invite pairs to share their examples with the group.

Using Apostrophes to Create Plurals

Explain that apostrophes are not always used to form plurals.

RULE 25.6.8 Read aloud the rule and then have students repeat the lines with you.

Discuss the examples on the page and work with students to brainstorm for other examples.

Teacher Tip

For extra practice using apostrophes with contractions, have students write a friendly letter to a relative or friend. Encourage students to use contractions whenever possible in their letter. Invite students to share their letters with the class. Remind students that if they were writing a formal letter, they would want to avoid contractions.

PRACTICE 25.6A

1. the painter's work
2. Nina's hat
3. the Maldonados' apartment
4. a cat's eyes
5. Atlas' strength
6. Mario's pizzeria
7. a week's vacation
8. girls' soccer team
9. the catcher's mitt
10. Ollie's brother's idea

PRACTICE 25.6B

11. This is someone else's scarf, not mine.
12. correct
13. No one's ideas will be ignored.
14. correct
15. Everyone's support is necessary.
16. The seats in the first row are ours.
17. Someone's equipment was left in the gym.
18. The choice will be yours alone.
19. correct
20. Our writing group shared papers with another group; we read theirs and they read ours.

WRITING APPLICATION

Have students exchange work and check it, explaining why it is or is not correct.

WRITING APPLICATION

Have students exchange sentences and check them, explaining why the use of possession is or is not correct.

PRACTICE 25.6A Using Apostrophes to Show Ownership

Read each phrase. Write the possessive form of each item.

EXAMPLE clothing store for men

ANSWER *men's clothing store*

1. work of the painter
2. hat belonging to Nina
3. apartment where the Maldonados live
4. eyes of a cat
5. the strength of Atlas
6. pizzeria owned by Mario
7. a vacation for a week
8. the soccer team for girls
9. the mitt belonging to the catcher
10. an idea from the brother of Ollie

PRACTICE 25.6B Using Apostrophes With Pronouns

Read the sentences. If all pronouns in a sentence are used correctly, write *correct*. If one or more pronouns are used incorrectly, rewrite the sentence correctly.

EXAMPLE Her's is the best drawing.

ANSWER *Hers is the best drawing.*

11. This is someone elses scarf, not mine.
12. We found everyone else's folder but not his.
13. No ones ideas will be ignored.
14. The dog was favoring its left front paw.
15. Everyones support is necessary.
16. The seats in the first row are our's.
17. Someones equipment was left in the gym.
18. The choice will be your's alone.
19. After you read your poem aloud, Julie will read hers.
20. Our writing group shared papers with another group; we read their's and they read ours.

WRITING APPLICATION

Look around the classroom. List five items or characteristics that you see and the possessor of each.

WRITING APPLICATION

Write two or three sentences in which you use *our, ours,* and the possessive form of *someone*.

598 **Punctuation**

Working with ELLs ELL Sheltered Instruction: Cognitive

To help students spell familiar words with increasing accuracy, introduce this rule: *If a word ends in a silent* e*, you usually drop the* e *if you add a suffix that begins with a vowel. You usually keep the* e *if you add a suffix that begins with a consonant.*

Beginning Model the rule with the familiar word *use*, adding the suffixes *-ful* and *-ing* and writing *useful* and *using* on the board. Discuss meaning. Then, write a sentence for each of the words. Have students copy the sentences.

Intermediate Write the familiar words *use, waste,* and *hope* on the board, along with an unfamiliar word such as *force.* Then, write the suffixes *-ful, -ing,* and *-ed*. Have students use the words and the suffixes to complete the Writing Application, applying the spelling rule.

Advanced Provide students with a list of familiar and unfamiliar silent *-e* words. Have students complete the Writing Application, using words formed by adding suffixes to the words on the list. Direct students to apply the rule as they form the words.

Advanced High Have students complete the Writing Application. Direct them to include at least three words that follow the spelling rule, including two unfamiliar words from a dictionary.

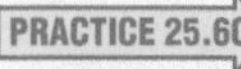

PRACTICE 25.6C **Using Apostrophes in Contractions**

Read the sentences. Each sentence contains a word group that can be written as a contraction. Write the contractions.

EXAMPLE That is a very good question.

ANSWER *That's*

1. I cannot eat another bite!
2. We are planning to go in a group.
3. Kyle will not be here today.
4. Who is still in need of help?
5. I have been working for two days on this essay.
6. It does not matter what you say now.
7. We do not have the resources we need for this job.
8. It is too early to predict the outcome.
9. What will we do next?
10. I would be glad to help you with that.

PRACTICE 25.6D **Proofreading for Apostrophes**

Read the sentences. Rewrite each sentence, adding apostrophes where needed.

EXAMPLE Mike said he couldnt go to the park today.

ANSWER *Mike said he couldn't go to the park today.*

11. Its a difficult situation to be in.
12. Why dont you come also?
13. Hes been spending time with a new crowd.
14. I wouldve been here earlier if I had not been stuck in traffic.
15. Shell be right with you.
16. Arent you finished yet?
17. We shouldve thought of that sooner.
18. Alans on his way now.
19. Youre going to need a warm jacket.
20. Wed better hurry if we want to get there on time.

WRITING APPLICATION

Use your rewritten sentences 3, 4, and 5 as models, and write three new sentences with the same subjects and contractions.

WRITING APPLICATION

Use the contractions you wrote for sentences 11, 14, and 16, and write three sentences of your own.

PRACTICE 25.6C

1. can't
2. We're
3. won't
4. Who's
5. I've
6. doesn't
7. don't
8. It's
9. What'll
10. I'd

PRACTICE 25.6D

11. It's a difficult situation to be in.
12. Why don't you come also?
13. He's been spending time with a new crowd.
14. I would've been here earlier if I hadn't been stuck in traffic.
15. She'll be right with you.
16. Aren't you finished yet?
17. We should've thought of that sooner.
18. Alan's on his way now.
19. You're going to need a warm jacket.
20. We'd better hurry if we want to get there on time.

WRITING APPLICATION

Have students exchange sentences and check each other's work, explaining why it is or is not correct.

WRITING APPLICATION

Have students exchange sentences and check each other's work, explaining why it is or is not correct.

25.7 Parentheses and Brackets

Lesson Objectives

1. Recognize and identify parentheses and brackets.
2. Use parentheses and brackets correctly in writing.

Parentheses

Explain that writers use parentheses to separate information from the rest of a sentence or paragraph.

RULES 25.7.1, 25.7.2, 25.7.3 Read aloud the rules and then have students repeat the lines with you.

Discuss the examples on page 600. Then, use a Think Aloud as part of a gradual release progression.

Think Aloud **Say:** Sometimes, when I'm reading I come across parentheses. **I know** parentheses set off explanations or other information that is related to the rest of the sentence. There are a few rules I should follow when using parentheses. A parenthetical sentence within another sentence should not begin with a capital letter. Also, a parenthetical sentence within another sentence can use a question mark or an exclamation mark, but not a period.

Work with students to find examples of parentheses in books, magazines, and Web sites. Discuss the examples and have students determine whether they follow rules 25.7.1, 25.7.2, and 25.7.3.

Have student pairs write three sentences, one simple, one compound, and one complex. Students should include a parenthetical sentence within each sentence, but not mark the parentheses. Student pairs should then exchange sentences with other pairs and correctly punctuate the sentences. Invite students to read selected sentences aloud.

25.7 Parentheses and Brackets

Parentheses and **brackets** enclose explanations or other information that may be omitted from the rest of the sentence without changing its basic meaning or construction.

WRITING COACH Online
www.phwritingcoach.com

Grammar Practice
Practice your grammar skills with Writing Coach Online.

Grammar Games
Test your knowledge of grammar in this fast-paced interactive video game.

Parentheses

Parentheses are used to separate information from the rest of a sentence or paragraph.

RULE 25.7.1 **Use parentheses to set off explanations or other information that is loosely related to the rest of the sentence.**

EXAMPLE James Fenimore Cooper (1789–1851) was well known for his historical novels.

RULE 25.7.2 **A parenthetical sentence within another sentence should not begin with a capital letter unless the parenthetical sentence begins with a word that should be capitalized.**

EXAMPLE New puppies (my family just bought one) require a lot of care and patience.

RULE 25.7.3 **A parenthetical sentence within another sentence may end with a question mark or exclamation mark if applicable, but it should not end with a period.**

INCORRECT The playoff schedule (the league is working on it.) will be available soon.

CORRECT The playoff schedule (the league is still working on it!) will be available soon.

Extension

To help students synthesize and apply what they have learned about using parentheses, have students work in teams to research and write time lines. Each team should choose a historical event or movement and use library sources or the Internet to find information. In each entry on the time line, students should use parentheses to add information. Example: *May 16, 1975, Junko Tabei (of Japan) was the first woman to reach the peak of Mount Everest.* Challenge students by having them write introductory paragraphs to their timelines, using a variety of sentence types and end punctuation.

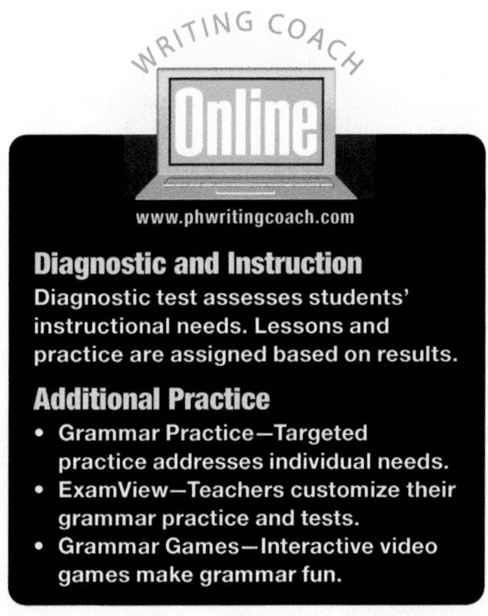

Diagnostic and Instruction

Diagnostic test assesses students' instructional needs. Lessons and practice are assigned based on results.

Additional Practice

- Grammar Practice—Targeted practice addresses individual needs.
- ExamView—Teachers customize their grammar practice and tests.
- Grammar Games—Interactive video games make grammar fun.

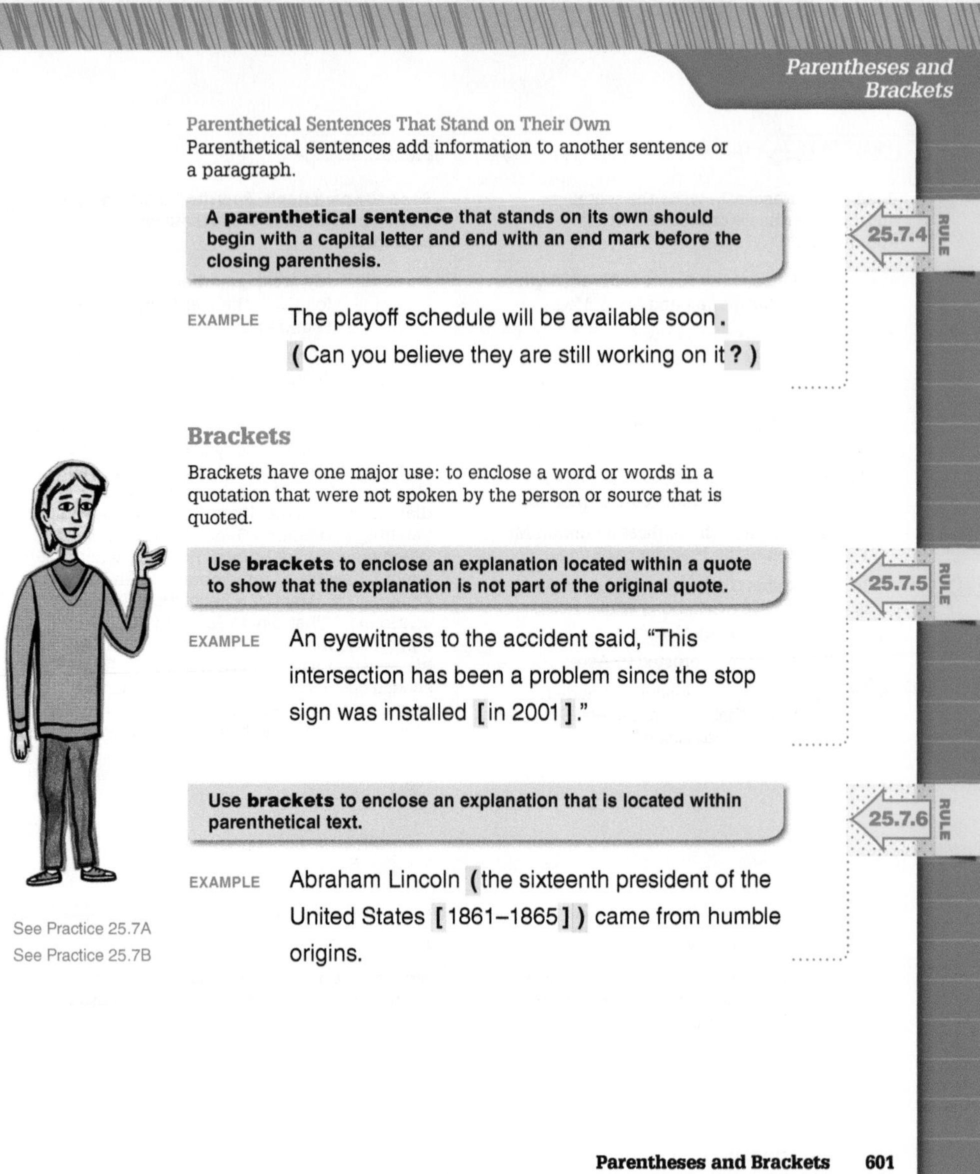

Parentheses and Brackets

Parenthetical Sentences That Stand on Their Own

Parenthetical sentences add information to another sentence or a paragraph.

A parenthetical sentence that stands on its own should begin with a capital letter and end with an end mark before the closing parenthesis. RULE 25.7.4

EXAMPLE The playoff schedule will be available soon. (Can you believe they are still working on it?)

Brackets

Brackets have one major use: to enclose a word or words in a quotation that were not spoken by the person or source that is quoted.

Use brackets to enclose an explanation located within a quote to show that the explanation is not part of the original quote. RULE 25.7.5

EXAMPLE An eyewitness to the accident said, "This intersection has been a problem since the stop sign was installed [in 2001]."

Use brackets to enclose an explanation that is located within parenthetical text. RULE 25.7.6

EXAMPLE Abraham Lincoln (the sixteenth president of the United States [1861–1865]) came from humble origins.

See Practice 25.7A
See Practice 25.7B

Parentheses and Brackets 601

Parenthetical Sentences That Stand on Their Own

Tell students that writers use parenthetical sentences to add information to another sentence or a paragraph. Parenthetical sentences are treated like other sentences—they begin with a capital letter and end with an end mark.

RULE 25.7.4 Read aloud the rule and then have students repeat the lines with you.

Have student pairs write two sentences. The second sentence should be a parenthetical sentence that adds information to the first sentence. Invite students to share their sentences with the group.

Brackets

Discuss the one major function of brackets: to show, in a quotation, that a word or words were not spoken or written by the person or source indicated. Writers use brackets to clarify quotations.

RULES 25.7.5, 25.7.6 Read aloud the rules and then have students repeat the lines with you.

Point out in the first example that the phrase *in 2001* is additional information about the installation of the stop sign not provided by the eyewitness.

In the second example, the years *1861–1865* provide more explanation for the parenthetical text (when Abraham Lincoln was president of the United States).

Working with ELLs — ELL Sheltered Instruction: Cognitive

Help students distinguish intonation patterns of English with increasing ease. Read the example for Rule 25.7.2 on page 600 aloud, modeling proper intonation for parenthetical sentences within another sentence (pausing before and after each parenthesis and, often, lowering pitch for the parenthetical sentence). Then:

Beginning Read the example sentence aloud several times, first without the embedded parenthetical sentence, then with. Have students repeat each version after you.

Intermediate Provide partners with three sentences with embedded parenthetical sentences. Have each student read the sentences aloud, using correct intonation. Have the listener explain how the intonation in his or her partner's voice changed when reading the text in parentheses.

Advanced Provide each partner with a different set of sentences with embedded parenthetical sentences. Then, have students read their sentences aloud. Ask listeners to write each sentence, following intonation to decide where to place the parentheses.

Advanced High Challenge students to write three sentences with embedded parenthetical sentences. Have them speak these sentences to their partners, using correct intonation. Partners should copy the sentences, following their partner's intonation to decide where to place the parentheses.

Teacher Tip

If students are having difficulty distinguishing proper use of parentheses and brackets, give them this tip: brackets are used only with quotations or inside of parentheses. Parentheses are used with regular text. Provide students with additional sentences to proofread and correct for proper use of parentheses and brackets.

PRACTICE 25.7A

1. Being late for a movie (something I can't stand) doesn't seem to bother some of my friends.
2. The coach finally dismissed the players. (They'd put in three long hours of practice.)
3. We hope to climb the highest mountain (Mt. Washington) in the Presidential Range.
4. In some states (Connecticut, for example), it is illegal to use a cellphone while driving.
5. After Jennifer's trip to Mexico (June 15–25), she became very interested in Aztec culture.
6. During the solo, someone in the audience commented, "That student [Phoebe Robinson] is a very talented musician."

PRACTICE 25.7B

My great-grandfather's diary read, "That was the year [1917] we entered the war." I had studied that war (World War I) in school, so the diary interested me. He wrote, "We were under Pershing's command [General John J. Pershing]. When we got here [France], Pershing wanted to honor Lafayette." (I remembered Lafayette from studying the American Revolution.) The diary continued, "That day in July [July 4, 1917], we had a parade to his [Lafayette's] tomb. Pershing's aide [his assistant] said, 'Lafayette, we are here!' That speech cheered up our friends [the French]." So many Americans died (about 120,000). I'm glad my great-grandfather (he lived to age 85) wasn't one of them.

WRITING APPLICATION

Have students explain how the parentheses add to the sentence.

WRITING APPLICATION

Have students review each other's sentences.

PRACTICE 25.7A Using Parentheses and Brackets

Read the sentences. Rewrite the sentences, adding parentheses or brackets where appropriate.

EXAMPLE Louisa May Alcott 1832–1888 wrote *Little Women* and *Little Men.*

ANSWER *Louisa May Alcott (1832–1888) wrote Little Women and Little Men.*

1. Being late for a movie something I can't stand doesn't seem to bother some of my friends.
2. The coach finally dismissed the players. They'd put in three long hours of practice.
3. We hope to climb the highest mountain Mt. Washington in the Presidential Range.
4. In some states Connecticut, for example, it is illegal to use a cellphone while driving.
5. After Jennifer's trip to Mexico June 15–25, she became very interested in Aztec culture.
6. During the solo, someone in the audience commented, "That student Phoebe Robinson is a very talented musician."

PRACTICE 25.7B Proofreading for Parentheses and Brackets

Read the paragraph. Rewrite the paragraph, adding parentheses or brackets where appropriate.

EXAMPLE My great-grandfather wrote, "I fought in the war World War I as a young man."

ANSWER *My great-grandfather wrote, "I fought in the war [World War I] as a young man."*

My great-grandfather's diary read, "That was the year 1917 we entered the war." I had studied that war World War I in school, so the diary interested me. He wrote, "We were under Pershing's command General John J. Pershing. When we got here France, Pershing wanted to honor Lafayette." I remembered Lafayette from studying the American Revolution. The diary continued, "That day in July July 4, 1917, we had a parade to his Lafayette's tomb. Pershing's aide his assistant said, 'Lafayette, we are here!' That speech cheered up our friends the French." So many Americans died about 120,000. I'm glad my great-grandfather he lived to age 85 wasn't one of them.

WRITING APPLICATION

Use sentences 1 and 4 as models, and write two new sentences into which you insert parenthetical information.

WRITING APPLICATION

Write a sentence that includes a quotation with a comment inserted into the quotation using brackets.

25.8 Ellipses and Dashes

An **ellipsis** (. . .) shows where words have been omitted from a quoted passage. It can also mark a pause in dialogue. A **dash** (—) shows a strong, sudden break in thought or speech.

Grammar Practice
Practice your grammar skills with Writing Coach Online.

Grammar Games
Test your knowledge of grammar in this fast-paced interactive video game.

Using the Ellipsis

An **ellipsis** consists of three evenly spaced periods, or ellipsis points, in a row. There is a space before the first ellipsis point, between ellipsis points, and after the last ellipsis point. The plural form of the word *ellipsis* is *ellipses.*

Use an ellipsis to show where words have been omitted from a quoted passage. Including an ellipsis shows the reader that the writer has chosen to omit some information.

QUOTED PASSAGE	"Four score and seven years ago our fathers brought forth on this continent a new nation conceived in liberty and dedicated to the proposition that all men are created equal." –Abraham Lincoln, *The Gettysburg Address,* November 19, 1863
QUOTED PASSAGE WITH WORDS OMITTED	"Fourscore and seven years ago our fathers brought forth . . . a new nation . . . dedicated to the proposition that all men are created equal."

Ellipses in Advertising

Ellipses are commonly used in ads for movies and other media. When you see an ellipsis in an ad, think about what might have been omitted. You might want to find the original review because the ad might be giving a different impression from what the reviewer intended.

ORIGINAL REVIEW	"I am amazed that anyone would think this movie is exciting or even worth seeing."
AD WORDING	" . . . exciting . . . worth seeing"

Diagnostic and Instruction
Diagnostic test assesses students' instructional needs. Lessons and practice are assigned based on results.

Additional Practice
- Grammar Practice—Targeted practice addresses individual needs.
- ExamView—Teachers customize their grammar practice and tests.
- Grammar Games—Interactive video games make grammar fun.

Lesson Objectives

1. Recognize and identify ellipses in sentences.
2. Recognize and identify dashes in sentences.
3. Use ellipses and dashes correctly in writing.

Using the Ellipsis

Relate to students that an ellipsis consists of three evenly spaced periods in a row.

RULE 25.8.1 Read aloud the rule and then have students repeat the lines with you.

Discuss the examples of quoted passages on page 603. Point out that writers should not overuse ellipses. The material into which ellipses have been inserted must be able to stand on its own. In other words, it must make sense to readers who do not have the complete version.

Ellipses in Advertising

Use a Think Aloud as part of a gradual release progression.

Say: When I am reading and I come across an ellipsis, **I know** that the writer has omitted some words from a quoted passage. Writers use ellipses to show that information has been omitted from the quoted passage. In regular writing, writers use ellipses to omit unnecessary words and information. In advertising, however, sometimes ellipses can be used in tricky ways. Look at the example sentences at the bottom of page 603. If I read only the ad wording, I would think this movie was a good one to see. But when I read the original review, I learned that the reviewer had a very different impression.

Distribute magazines and newspapers. Have students access the Internet, if possible. **Work with students** to find examples of ellipses in advertising. Lead a discussion about the uses of ellipses in advertising.

Have student pairs take one of the examples of ellipses in advertising. Students should rewrite the example by removing the ellipses and use their imaginations to fill in the missing words and information. Invite students to share their sentences aloud.

(continued)

Using the Ellipsis *(continued)*

Several rules guide the use of ellipses.

RULES 25.8.2, 25.8.3, 25.8.4, 25.8.5 Read aloud the rules and then have students repeat the lines with you.

Discuss the examples on page 604. Then, distribute a brief quotation from a book or an article with which students are already familiar. Have students use ellipses to remove unnecessary words and information. Tell students that ellipses can be used to mark a pause in a dialogue or speech. Ask students to indicate whether their ellipses are omitting information or marking a pause. Invite students to read aloud their quotations.

Use an ellipsis to mark a pause in a dialogue or speech.

EXAMPLE "But, in a larger sense, we can not dedicate ... we can not consecrate ... we can not hallow ... this ground."

It is not necessary to use an ellipsis to show an omission at the beginning of material you are quoting. However, if you choose to omit any words *within* material you quote, you must use an ellipsis to show where information has been omitted.

UNNECESSARY " ... Now we are engaged in a great civil war, testing whether that nation, or any nation, so conceived and so dedicated, can long endure."

CORRECT "Now we are engaged in a great civil war, testing whether that nation, or any nation so conceived and so dedicated, can long endure."

Use an ellipsis to show an omission, pause, or interruption in the middle of a sentence.

EXAMPLE "But, in a larger sense, we cannot dedicate ... this ground."

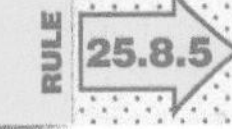

Use an ellipsis and an end mark to show an omission or a pause at the end of a sentence.

EXAMPLE "I don't know how we are going to get this mess cleaned up. Maybe we could. ..."

If you omit words from a source you are quoting, omit the punctuation that accompanies the words unless it is correct in your sentence.

See Practice 25.8A

Working with ELLs — ELL Sheltered Instruction: Cognitive

Help students use linguistic support to enhance and confirm their understanding of increasingly complex spoken language.

Beginning Provide linguistic support by writing these words on the board: *ellipsis, pause, speech, interruption*. Say each aloud, and review its meaning. Then, read aloud Rules 25.8.2 and 25.8.4 as students listen. Repeat, and then guide students in confirming understanding by reviewing the examples on the student page.

Intermediate Provide linguistic support by writing these words on the board: *ellipsis, pause, speech, omission, omit, quoting, interruption*. Say each aloud, and review its meaning. Then, read aloud each of the rules as students listen. Repeat your reading. Then, have students meet in small groups to summarize what they have learned, drawing on the linguistic support you have provided.

Advanced Have students use the linguistic support of a dictionary to look up each of the words listed for the Intermediate activity. Read aloud each of the rules, and have partners discuss what they have learned.

Advanced High Have students complete the Advanced activity. Then, have them apply what they have learned by writing three sentences with ellipses.

Dashes

Like commas and parentheses, **dashes** separate certain words, phrases, or clauses from the rest of the sentence or paragraph. Dashes, however, signal a stronger, more sudden interruption in thought or speech than commas or parentheses. A dash may also take the place of certain words before an explanation.

Use a dash to show a strong, sudden break in thought or speech. (RULE 25.8.6)

EXAMPLE I can't believe how quickly we arrived—hey, where are you going?

If the interrupting expression is in the middle of the sentence, use a dash on either side of it to set it off from the rest of the sentence.

EXAMPLE I read a book—it's in the library—about dinosaurs that have been newly discovered.

Use a dash in place of *in other words, namely,* or *that is* before an explanation. (RULE 25.8.7)

EXAMPLES Dario reads books for one purpose—to learn.

To come in first in the relay race—this was the team's hope.

Dashes can also be used to set off nonessential appositives or modifiers.

EXAMPLE A team player—someone who will make sacrifices for the good of the team—is what we need.

See Practice 25.8B

Dashes

Explain that dashes are similar to commas and parentheses. All three types of punctuation separate words, phrases, or clauses from the rest of the sentence or paragraph. Dashes are distinctive because they signal a stronger, more sudden interruption in thought or speech. Writers use dashes to show a strong, sudden break in thought or speech.

RULES 25.8.6, 25.8.7 Read aloud the rules and then have students repeat the lines with you.

Use a Think Aloud as part of a gradual release progression.

Think Aloud

Say: When **I see** dashes in a book or article, I know the writer is showing a sudden, strong break in thought or speech. Dashes can also be used in place of certain words, such as *namely, that is*, or *in other words*. When I am writing, sometimes I might use dashes. Dashes can make writing energetic. However, overusing dashes can make writing seem disconnected and hard to understand.

Work with students to find examples of dashes in books, articles, or Web sites.

Have student pairs write three sentences using dashes. Students should not include the dashes in the sentences. Then, partners should exchange sentences with another pair. Student pairs should then insert dashes in the correct places in the sentences. Invite students to read selected sentences aloud to the group.

Differentiated Instruction

Enrichment for Gifted/Talented Students
Remind students that correct use of ellipses requires understanding of the quoted text. Ellipses remove unnecessary words and information, leaving only the main points and the words to communicate those points. Distribute copies of a historical text (such as the preamble to the U.S. Constitution). Have students read the text and then use ellipses to remove everything except the main points and the words to communicate those points. Ask students to explain why they removed certain words and information.

Teacher Tip

If students find ellipses and dashes confusing, remind them that ellipses are used with quoted material. Ellipses indicate omitted information. Dashes, on the other hand, show stronger, sudden interruptions in thought or speech. Read aloud several sentences. Some sentences should use commas, others should use ellipses, and still others should use dashes. Indicate with your phrasing the differences between pauses for commas, ellipses, and dashes. Have students read with you, and then have students read aloud to a partner.

PRACTICE 25.8A

1. pause
2. omission
3. pause
4. omission
5. pause
6. omission
7. pause
8. omission
9. pause
10. omission

PRACTICE 25.8B

11. There's only one thing I still need to pack for my trip—sunscreen.
12. All of the preparations for the dance—including the decorations—have been made.
13. I would like to present the winner—Hector Rodriguez.
14. I already have all of the ingredients for this recipe—even the walnuts.
15. Head east on the trail—wait, you forgot the map!
16. The money—thirty dollars—is on the table.
17. The committee announced what they need to get the job done—more money, more time, more people.
18. Jonah had only one goal—to be the fastest sprinter on the team.
19. My favorite restaurant—The Corner Diner—is closed for renovations.
20. An Academy Award—an Oscar—recognizes outstanding work in a motion picture.

SPEAKING APPLICATION

Have students check each other's work, explaining why it is or is not correct.

WRITING APPLICATION

Have students check each other's passages, explaining whether the use of ellipses creates a passage that is or is not clear.

Ellipses and Dashes

PRACTICE 25.8A Using Ellipses

Read the sentences. For each sentence, tell whether ellipses (or ellipsis points) are used to indicate a *pause* or an *omission*.

EXAMPLE "Well . . . I'm not sure about this," said Luis.

ANSWER *pause*

1. Wow . . . I don't know how to thank you.
2. In her review, Kate wrote, "This exciting movie kept me on the edge of my seat . . . I can't wait to see it again."
3. Of course, we could always . . . uh . . . try a different tactic.
4. John F. Kennedy said, "Ask not what your country can do for you . . . ."
5. Mom . . . are you sure I can't go to Max's house after I finish my homework?
6. The Preamble to the Constitution reads, "We the people of the United States . . . do ordain and establish this Constitution for the United States of America."
7. Well . . . um . . . let me think about it.
8. The words of Dr. Martin Luther King Jr., "Let freedom ring . . . From every mountainside, let freedom ring," still move us today.
9. Keena . . . are you still there . . . or did you hang up?
10. The last line of "All Summer in a Day" reads, "They unlocked the door . . . and let Margot out."

PRACTICE 25.8B Using Dashes

Read the sentences. Rewrite each sentence, adding dashes where they are needed.

EXAMPLE Bernard plays several instruments guitar, banjo, and drums.

ANSWER *Bernard plays several instruments —guitar, banjo, and drums.*

11. There's only one thing I still need to pack for my trip sunscreen.
12. All of the preparations for the dance including the decorations have been made.
13. I would like to present the winner Hector Rodriguez.
14. I already have all of the ingredients for this recipe even the walnuts.
15. Head east on the trail wait, you forgot the map!
16. The money thirty dollars is on the table.
17. The committee announced what they need to get the job done more money, more time, more people.
18. Jonah had only one goal to be the fastest sprinter on the team.
19. My favorite restaurant The Corner Diner is closed for renovations.
20. An Academy Award an Oscar recognizes outstanding work in a motion picture.

SPEAKING APPLICATION

With a partner, read aloud Sentences 7 and 9. Then, together, write a sentence that uses ellipsis points for the same purpose.

WRITING APPLICATION

Copy a passage from a selection in your literature textbook. Leave out a part of the passage, either in the middle or at the end, and use ellipses to show where the omission occurs.

606 Punctuation

Working with ELLs

ELL Sheltered Instruction: Cognitive

Using the long and short sentences in Practice 25.8B, have students speak using a variety of sentence lengths with increasing accuracy and ease.

Beginning Pair fluent speakers with Beginning students. Have fluent partners read aloud sentence 16, pausing to indicate the dashes in the sentence. Have the Beginning students echo their partners. Repeat with other short sentences in the exercise. Finally, provide practice with longer sentences by having partners repeat the exercise, adding *he said* or *she said* to the beginning of each sentence.

Intermediate Have partners take turns reading each sentence in Practice 25.8B aloud, indicating with pauses where the dashes appear. Coach students as they encounter sentences with increasing lengths.

Advanced Have partners read the sentences in Practice 25.8B aloud, pausing to indicate dashes. Have each partner choose three sentences to copy, adding information to increase the length of the sentence. Partners should exchange papers and read the sentences aloud.

Advanced High Have partners complete the Advanced activity. As they create longer sentences, challenge them to use compound and complex sentences.

CHAPTER 26 LESSON PLANNER
Capitalization

Use the Online Lesson Planner at www.phwritingcoach.com to customize your instructional plan for an integrated Language Arts curriculum.

DAY 1 26.1 Capitalization

	INSTRUCTION AND PRACTICE
"What Do You Notice?" **Objectives:** Identify, use, and understand capitalization, including ▪ with the word *I* ▪ in sentences ▪ in quotations ▪ for proper nouns	**Student Edition** pp. 607–611, 613–620 **Test Warm-Up** p. 612

DAY 2 26.1 Capitalization

	INSTRUCTION AND PRACTICE
Objectives: Identify, use, and understand capitalization, including ▪ for proper adjectives ▪ for titles of people ▪ for titles of works ▪ in letters ▪ in abbreviations, acronyms, and initials	**Student Edition** pp. 621–628

DAY 3 Cumulative Review

	INSTRUCTION AND PRACTICE
Objectives: Identify, use, and understand mechanics, including ▪ punctuation ▪ capitalization	**Student Edition** pp. 629–630

> *"With apologies to e.e. cummings, capitalization needs to be addressed more vigorously in our classrooms. This is especially true in the age of text-messaging, instant messaging, and social Web site posts."*
>
> **—Kelly Gallagher**

Grammar Assessment

Grammar Coach:	Diagnostic Assessment	End-of-Chapter Assessment	Progress Monitoring
Personalized Instruction	Students take grammar diagnostic test online and are automatically assigned instruction and practice in areas where they need support.	Teacher uses **ExamView** to administer end-of-chapter assessment and remediation. Teachers may customize **ExamView** tests or use the ones provided.	Teachers may use the **Test Warm-Ups** and the **Cumulative Reviews** in the student book or eText to check students' mastery of grammar skills. Students may also play **DimensionL** grammar video games to test their grammar skills.
Teacher-Directed Instruction	Teacher administers the diagnostic test and determines focus of instruction and practice.		

Alternate Pacing Plans

- **Block Scheduling** Each day in the Lesson Planner represents a 40–50 minute block. Teachers using block scheduling may combine days to revise pacing to meet their classroom needs.
- **Accelerated Lesson Planning** Combine instructional days, focusing on concepts called out by students' diagnostic test results.
- **Integrated Language Arts Curriculum** Use the instruction and practice in this chapter to provide reinforcement, remediation, or extension of grammar concepts taught in your literature curriculum.

Links to Prentice Hall *LITERATURE*

- **Unit 1** Common and Proper Nouns, p. 46
- **Unit 6** Capitalization, p. 1004

Grammar Assessment and Practice

Chapter diagnostic tests assess students' skills and assign instruction and practice.

DimensionL Video Games

Fast-paced interactive video games challenge students' mastery of grammar.

Lesson Planner continues on next page

"Teach capitalization by asking students to look at a book they are reading and list all the words that are capitalized on five pages, excluding the first words of sentences or repeated words. In groups, invite them to combine and categorize the words. Next, have them label their categories, share in groups. From there, your class can construct the list of rules."

—Jeff Anderson

Differentiated Instruction

Differentiated Instruction Boxes in this Teacher's Edition address these student populations:

- Below-Level Students
- Above-Level Students
- Gifted and Talented Students
- Special Needs Students
- English Language Learners
- Spanish Speaking Students

In addition, for further enrichment, see the **Extension** features.

Grammar Ground Rule: Dot Your *i*'s and Cross Your *t*'s!

Model with Students

In this chapter, dotting your *i*'s and crossing your *t*'s means being careful to use the right capitalization. Explain to students that, when almost everything was written by hand, dotting your *i*'s and crossing your *t*'s was very important.

> **Say:** An undotted *i* could look like an *e*, and an uncrossed *t* could look like an *i*. So the last thing a writer did was to go over what he or she had written to make sure that these letters were dotted and crossed. Today, we use this phrase to mean "make sure you've got the details right." In other words, you need to edit your writing. I don't like to worry about all the details of capitalization when I'm writing my first draft. I like to let the ideas flow. That's why I make sure that I always edit what I've written.

Write this sentence on the board, incorrect capitalization and all: *when mr. thomas went to houston, he took the Train*. Have students work with you to edit and revise the sentence. As they make suggestions for capitalizing, have them explain why they think the word in question should be capitalized or lower case.

Small Group Activity – Editing and Revising

Have students form groups to find an article about a vacation area. Have the students rewrite a paragraph from the article, changing the capitalization so that it is incorrect. Then have the groups exchange articles and edit the paragraphs. As they do their revisions, have the groups discuss the changes they are making. The discussions should answer these questions:

- Why should this particular word be capitalized?
- Why should this other word *not* be capitalized?

Have a member of each group present their conclusions to the class and give one good example of a sentence that follows this grammar ground rule: Dot your *i*'s and cross your *t*'s.

Grammar Ground Rules

1. Keep it clear.
2. Make them agree.
3. Make it specific.
4. Dot your *i*'s and cross your *t*'s.
5. Make it active.

CAPITALIZATION

Understanding the rules of capitalization will help you to craft clear sentences.

WRITE GUY *Jeff Anderson, M.Ed.*

WHAT DO YOU NOTICE?

Locate capital letters as you zoom in on sentences from the folktale "Sun and Moon in a Box," retold by Alfonso Ortiz and Richard Erdoes.

MENTOR TEXT

> "Let us steal the box," said Coyote.
> "No, that would be wrong," said Eagle. "Let us just borrow it."
> When the Kachinas were not looking, Eagle grabbed the box and flew off. Coyote ran after him on the ground.

Now, ask yourself the following questions:

- Why are the words *eagle* and *coyote* capitalized?
- In Eagle's quotation, why are the words *no* and *let* capitalized?

The words *eagle* and *coyote* are usually common nouns, but here they are the names of characters, so they are capitalized as proper nouns. Because Eagle's quotation includes two complete sentences, the first word of each sentence begins with a capital letter.

Grammar for Writers A capital letter not only signals the start of a sentence, but it can also show the beginning of a quotation. When writing dialogue, be sure to follow capitalization rules, so readers can hear your character's words clearly.

What word should be capitalized in this sentence?
What? The word what!

CHAPTER 26

CAPITALIZATION

As students progress in their writing skills, it will be important for them to be able to apply the rules of grammar, usage, and mechanics to their own drafts. Use the *What Do You Notice?* feature to help them see effective conventions in the work of professional writers. Encourage students to incorporate proper voice, tense, and syntax as they edit their own writing.

Read the opening sentence aloud. Remind students that capitalization plays a role in crafting well-written sentences. Used correctly, it tells the reader which words are proper nouns or when a new sentence or dialogue begins.

WRITE GUY *Jeff Anderson, M. Ed.*

WHAT DO YOU NOTICE?

When students have read the Mentor Text, **ask:** What do you notice about the names of the characters in the text? **(Possible responses:** Some of them are animal names.) **Ask:** What if the word *Coyote* were changed to *the coyote* in the first sentence? Would the reader receive the same information? **(Possible response:** No. When *coyote* is capitalized, it tells the reader that the word is a character's name. Without capitalization, there's just a coyote speaking.) **Say:** Why is it important that *Eagle* is capitalized in the text? **(Possible response:** It tells the reader that *Eagle* is also a specific character, like *Coyote*. The reader needs to know this to understand the text.) **Say:** Why do you think the word *Kachinas* is capitalized, even though it is preceded by the word *the*? Doesn't the word *the* suggest that *Kachinas* is a common noun? **(Possible response:** No. *Kachina* must be the name of a specific group or family, so it would be capitalized just like any other family name.)

Explain that capitalization is one important way writers relay information to readers. Without it, ideas would not be accurately expressed. Capitalization helps writers be precise.

Grammar for Writers

Explain that correct capitalization helps readers understand whether a group of words is a title; when a new sentence begins; and whether a word refers to a specific person, place, or thing or a general one. The rules in this chapter will help students understand and apply the major capitalization rules that all writers should know.

Lesson Objectives

1. Use conventions of capitalization correctly.
2. Proofread for capitalization.

The Word *I*

Tell students that the pronoun *I* always represents a specific person. For that reason, it is always capitalized.

RULE 26.1.1 Read aloud the rule and then have students repeat the lines with you.

Write on the board several sentences using the pronoun *I*, but do not capitalize *I*. Ask students to come to the board and correct the errors in capitalization.

Sentences

Give students a strategy for remembering to capitalize the beginning of every sentence. Tell them that all sentences should "introduce" themselves. Explain that a capital letter introduces the words and ideas that make up a sentence.

RULE 26.1.2 Read aloud the rule and then have students repeat the lines with you.

Write on the board these scrambled sentences. Have students unscramble each and then apply the capitalization rules for sentences.

1. is knitting activity my favorite. (Knitting is my favorite activity).
2. morning it's snowing since been yesterday! (It's been snowing since yesterday morning!)
3. outside wash dishes the before you go. (Wash the dishes before you go outside.)
4. ready who's for? dinner (Who's ready for dinner?)

Have students brainstorm for and write four sentences (declarative, interrogative, imperative, exclamatory) that apply the rules of capitalization. Tell students to include one sentence in which the missing parts are understood. Make sure that students begin each sentence with a capital letter.

Grammar Game Plan

26.1 Using Capitalization

Capital letters are used for the first words in all sentences and in many quotations. They are also used for the word *I*, whatever its position in a sentence.

The Word *I*

The pronoun *I* is always capitalized.

EXAMPLE **I** worked for two years as an assistant before **I** received a promotion.

Sentences

One of the most common uses of a capital letter is to signal the beginning of a sentence. The first word in a sentence must begin with a capital letter.

Capitalize the first word in declarative, interrogative, imperative, and exclamatory sentences.

DECLARATIVE **S**trong gusts of wind made it very difficult to golf on the course.

INTERROGATIVE **W**ho found the answer to that very difficult question?

IMPERATIVE **T**hink carefully before you answer.

EXCLAMATORY **W**hat an amazing situation this is!

Sometimes only part of a sentence is written. The rest of the sentence is understood. In these cases, a capital is still needed for the first word.

EXAMPLES **W**here? **W**ho said? **S**urely!

Grammar Tutorials
Brush up on your Grammar skills with these animated videos.

Grammar Practice
Practice your grammar skills with Writing Coach Online.

Grammar Games
Test your knowledge of grammar in this fast-paced interactive video game.

See Practice 26.1A

See Practice 26.1B

www.phwritingcoach.com

Diagnostic and Instruction
Diagnostic test assesses students' instructional needs. Lessons and practice are assigned based on results.

Additional Practice
- Grammar Tutorials—Animated videos reinforce key grammar skills.
- Grammar Practice—Targeted practice addresses individual needs.
- ExamView—Teachers customize their grammar practice and tests.
- Grammar Games—Interactive video games make grammar fun.

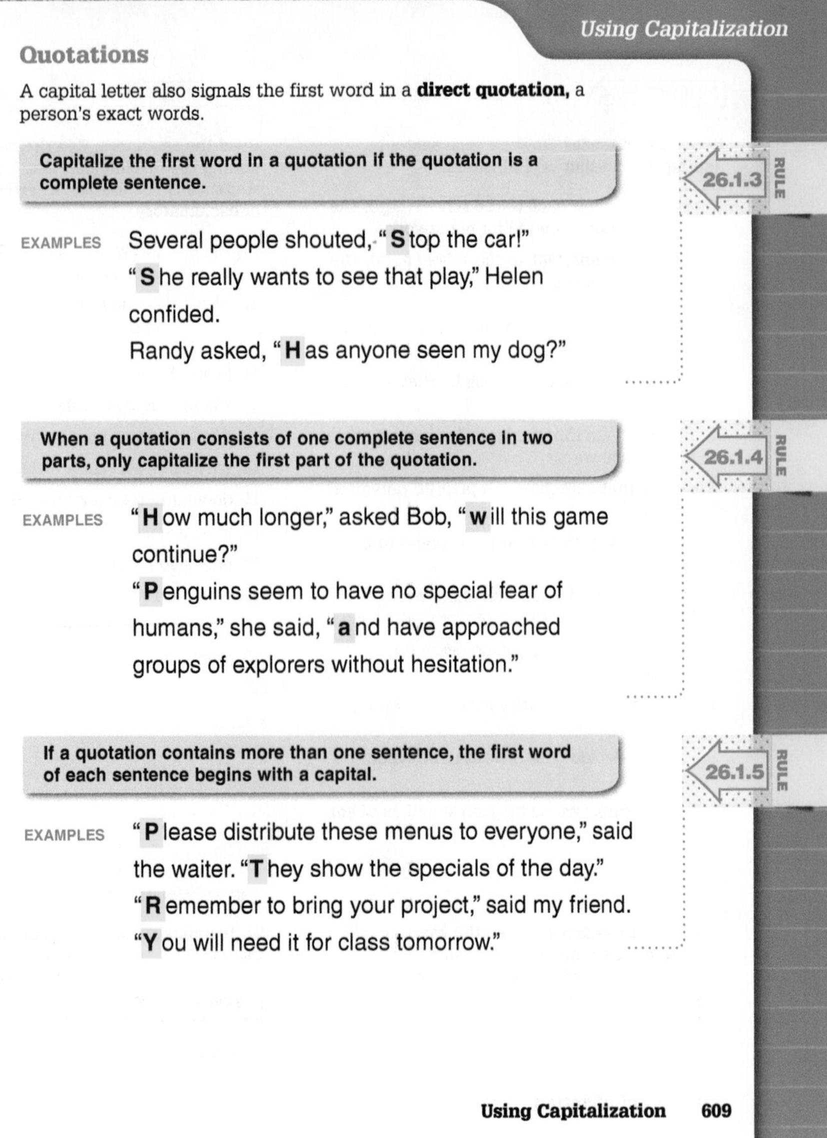

Quotations

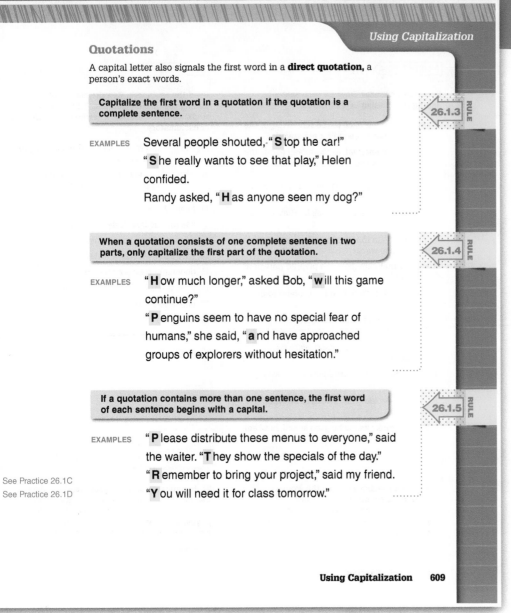

A capital letter also signals the first word in a **direct quotation,** a person's exact words.

Capitalize the first word in a quotation if the quotation is a complete sentence. 26.1.3 RULE

EXAMPLES Several people shouted, "**S**top the car!"
"**S**he really wants to see that play," Helen confided.
Randy asked, "**H**as anyone seen my dog?"

When a quotation consists of one complete sentence in two parts, only capitalize the first part of the quotation. 26.1.4 RULE

EXAMPLES "**H**ow much longer," asked Bob, "**w**ill this game continue?"
"**P**enguins seem to have no special fear of humans," she said, "**a**nd have approached groups of explorers without hesitation."

If a quotation contains more than one sentence, the first word of each sentence begins with a capital. 26.1.5 RULE

EXAMPLES "**P**lease distribute these menus to everyone," said the waiter. "**T**hey show the specials of the day."
"**R**emember to bring your project," said my friend. "**Y**ou will need it for class tomorrow."

See Practice 26.1C
See Practice 26.1D

Quotations

Remind students that, when we use a direct quotation, we repeat the exact words of another person. One convention of capitalization is to place a capital letter right after a quotation mark if the quoted sentence is complete.

RULES 26.1.3, 26.1.4, 26.1.5 Read aloud the rules and then have students repeat the lines with you.

Say: Writers often split direct quotations. They may interrupt a quotation to clarify who is speaking or to make a comment. If a sentence in a quotation is split apart by a phrase like *she said,* or *Aaron replied,* capitalize only the first word of each complete sentence in the quotation.

When a direct quotation consists of several complete sentences, the first word of each sentence begins with a capital letter.

Distribute magazines to student pairs. Have them identify an example of a direct quotation that consists of a single sentence that is not split, a direct quotation that is split, and a direct quotation that consists of two or more sentences. They should copy each quotation, underline the first word of each complete sentence, and note whether the quotation is a complete sentence, a split quotation, or more than one complete sentence.

Working with ELLs — ELL Sheltered Instruction: Cognitive

Have students demonstrate reading comprehension and expand reading skills by employing inferential skills, such as making predictions. Choose a selection that students are reading. Review the portion of the selection that students have already read. Then:

Beginning Guide students in mapping possible outcomes based on what they have read so far. Then, with students, preview the illustrations for the next part. Guide students in using simple terms and, if needed, drawings to express predictions about what will happen next.

Intermediate Have students work in small groups to map possible outcomes based on what they have read so far. Have them preview illustrations for the next part. Then, have groups make a prediction about what will happen next. Have them record part of their discussion using this frame: _____ *said, "* _______*."*

Advanced Have partners review what they have read, preview the next part, and predict what will happen next. Have them record predictions, stating one as a direct quotation.

Advanced High Have partners complete the Advanced activity. Then, have them write a dialogue based on their discussion using direct quotations.

PRACTICE 26.1A

1. I; I
2. I; I
3. I; I
4. I; I
5. I; I; I
6. I; I
7. I; I
8. I; I
9. I; I; I
10. I; I; I

PRACTICE 26.1B

11. I—exclamatory
12. Ask—imperative
13. It—declarative
14. Why—interrogative
15. Do—imperative
16. Todd—declarative
17. I—exclamatory
18. When—interrogative
19. I—exclamatory
20. Aren't—interrogative

WRITING APPLICATION

Students' sentences should demonstrate correct use of conventions of capitalization.

WRITING APPLICATION

Students should demonstrate the correct use of conventions of capitalization in the paragraphs they write.

PRACTICE 26.1A Writing Sentences Using Capitalization

Read the sentences. Rewrite each sentence, adding the missing capitalization.

EXAMPLE i went back to the school to get the book i needed for homework.

ANSWER *I went back to the school to get the book I needed for homework.*

1. My mother said i could buy the shoes that i saw in the magazine.
2. i want to read another book by that author i like.
3. Because i am the youngest, i often get chores no one else wants.
4. i know that i am my dog's favorite person in the family.
5. i thought i told you that i was going to be late.
6. i played football after i finished my homework.
7. i have to practice the piano every day if i want to improve.
8. i tried out for the school play, and i was chosen for a part.
9. i cannot decide what i want to be when i grow up.
10. i didn't think i would be good at golf, but i am.

PRACTICE 26.1B Writing Sentences Using Capitalization

Read the sentences. Rewrite each sentence, adding the missing capitals. Then, write if the sentence is declarative, interrogative, imperative, or exclamatory.

EXAMPLE did you really get the highest grade in the class?

ANSWER *Did you really get the highest grade in the class? — interrogative*

11. i can't believe it either!
12. ask me the next time you borrow my sweater.
13. it is time to go home now.
14. why can't we stay a little longer?
15. do your homework after dinner.
16. todd wasn't able to fix the computer.
17. i miss you, too!
18. when are you going on your fishing trip?
19. i love your new shoes!
20. aren't they great?

WRITING APPLICATION

Write four sentences using the word *I*. Remember to capitalize each sentence correctly. Exchange sentences with a partner. Check each other's work for correct capitalization.

WRITING APPLICATION

Write a paragraph about your favorite holiday. Use at least one declarative, one interrogative, one imperative, and one exclamatory sentence in your paragraph. Exchange paragraphs with a partner and check for correct capitalization.

Working with ELLs

ELL Sheltered Instruction: Metacognitive

Using the Writing Application for Practice 26.1D on page 611, have students demonstrate listening comprehension of increasingly complex spoken English by taking notes. Instruct students to monitor comprehension and seek clarification as needed.

Beginning Write a conversation, and read the conversation aloud, sharing roles with a fluent speaker. Remind students to monitor understanding, asking for clarification as needed. Then, ask students comprehension questions such as *Who was I speaking to? What were we talking about?* Write their responses on the board, and have students copy the responses as notes.

Intermediate Read aloud a model conversation as students take notes. Have students monitor understanding by using their notes to retell the conversation, asking for clarification as needed.

Advanced Have partners complete the Writing Application and then take turns reading their conversations aloud as the listening partner takes notes. Have students monitor understanding and seek clarification by asking their partner questions based on their notes.

Advanced High Have partners complete the Writing Application and then take turns reading their conversations aloud as the listening partner takes notes. Have students write a summary based on their notes, asking for clarification as needed.

PRACTICE 26.1C **Supplying Capitalization**

Read the sentences. Rewrite each sentence, adding the missing capitals.

EXAMPLE she and i became good friends.
ANSWER *She and I became good friends.*

1. my teacher thinks i have a good chance to get the role i want in the play.
2. spencer asked, "where did you get that hat?"
3. what should we do first?
4. will you come with us? why not?
5. who said, "i have but one life to give for my country"?
6. "my favorite color," said kerrie, "is blue."
7. are you going to the rodeo? when?
8. what a great idea that is!
9. "start your research in the library," our teacher told us. "the media specialist will help you find sources."
10. jen asked, "do you have a pencil i may borrow?"

PRACTICE 26.1D **Proofreading for Capitalization**

Read the sentences. Rewrite each sentence, correcting any capitalization errors.

EXAMPLE Which book should i read for my report?
ANSWER *Which book should I read for my report?*

11. I don't know what i'll wear to the dance.
12. Gail called and said, "i need some help with my math homework. Will you come over soon?"
13. "where," wondered Mrs. Getz, "is my measuring cup?"
14. let me see your artwork.
15. Perry quoted this line from *Hamlet*: "to be, or not to be: that is the question."
16. did you ask Jackie to distribute some of these flyers?
17. "I'll be finished by six o'clock," Dorie said. She added, "may I meet you then?"
18. if you wait a minute, i'll walk with you.
19. Wow! did you see that home run?
20. wait for the signal before you begin.

WRITING APPLICATION

Using sentences 6 and 9 in Practice 26.1C as models, write two new sentences with correct capitalization in quotations.

WRITING APPLICATION

Write a short conversation you had with someone yesterday or today. Check that you have used correct capitalization.

WRITING APPLICATION

Students' sentences should demonstrate that they can use the conventions of capitalization correctly in writing.

WRITING APPLICATION

Students should demonstrate they can use and understand the function of conventions of capitalization in the conversations that they write.

PRACTICE 26.1C

1. My teacher thinks I have a good chance to get the role I want in the play.
2. Spencer asked, "Where did you get that hat?"
3. What should we do first?
4. Will you come with us? Why not?
5. Who said, "I have but one life to give for my country"?
6. "My favorite color, " said Kerrie, "is blue."
7. Are you going to the rodeo? When?
8. What a great idea that is!
9. "Start your research in the library," our teacher told us. "The media specialist will help you find sources."
10. Jen asked, "Do you have a pencil I may borrow?"

PRACTICE 26.1D

11. I don't know what I'll wear to the dance.
12. Gail called and said, "I need some help with my math homework. Will you come over soon?"
13. "Where," wondered Mrs. Getz, "is my measuring cup?"
14. Let me see your artwork.
15. Perry quoted this line from *Hamlet*: "To be, or not to be: That is the question."
16. Did you ask Jackie to distribute some of these flyers?
17. "I'll be finished by six o'clock," Dorie said. She added, "May I meet you then?"
18. If you wait a minute, I'll walk with you.
19. Wow! Did you see that home run?
20. Wait for the signal before you begin.

Test Warm-Up

1. **C** Change ***robyn and i*** to **Robyn and I**
2. **H** "It's hard to believe," Robyn exclaimed when she saw me, "how tall you've gotten!"
3. **B** Change ***mexican*** to **Mexican**
4. **J** Make no change

Reteach

If students have not mastered these skills, review the content in Section 26.1 Using Capitalization.

Test Tip

Explain to students that sometimes they will be asked to choose the "best answer," or they will encounter a question for which no answer seems to be completely right. In those cases, they should try to compose a correct answer in their head, then choose the answer that is closest to the answer they have composed.

Test Warm-Up

DIRECTIONS
Read the introduction and the passage that follows. Then, answer the questions to show that you can use and understand the function of conventions of capitalization in reading and writing.

Carmen wrote this paragraph about a weekend trip to her cousin's house. Read the paragraph and think about the changes you would suggest as a peer editor. When you finish reading, answer the questions that follow.

My Cousin Robyn

(1) My cousin robyn and i are close, but we live many miles apart. (2) Robyn lives in Austin, and I live in Houston. (3) I was excited to visit her over a long weekend. (4) "It's hard to believe, Robyn exclaimed when she saw me, "How tall you've gotten." (5) She was right; I have grown over four inches this year. (6) We enjoyed our time together, shopping and eating at a fabulous mexican restaurant. (7) It was sad saying goodbye. (8) "Do you promise," Robyn asked, "to e-mail me the pictures you took?" (9) I sent Robyn the pictures the next day!

1 What change, if any, should be made in sentence 1?

- **A** Change ***cousin*** to **Cousin**
- **B** Change ***are*** to **is**
- **C** Change ***robyn and i*** to **Robyn and I**
- **D** Make no change

2 What is the BEST way to edit sentence 4?

- **F** "It's hard to believe, Robyn exclaimed when she saw me, "how tall you've gotten."
- **G** "It's hard to believe," Robyn exclaimed when she saw me, "How tall you've gotten!"
- **H** "It's hard to believe," Robyn exclaimed when she saw me, "how tall you've gotten!"
- **J** "It's hard to believe, Robyn exclaimed when she saw me, "how tall you've gotten?"

3 What change, if any, should be made in sentence 6?

- **A** Change ***restaurant*** to **Restaurant**
- **B** Change ***mexican*** to **Mexican**
- **C** Change ***shopping*** to **Shopping**
- **D** Make no change

4 What change, if any, should be made in sentence 8?

- **F** Change ***to*** to **To**
- **G** Delete the comma after asked
- **H** Change the question mark to an exclamation mark
- **J** Make no change

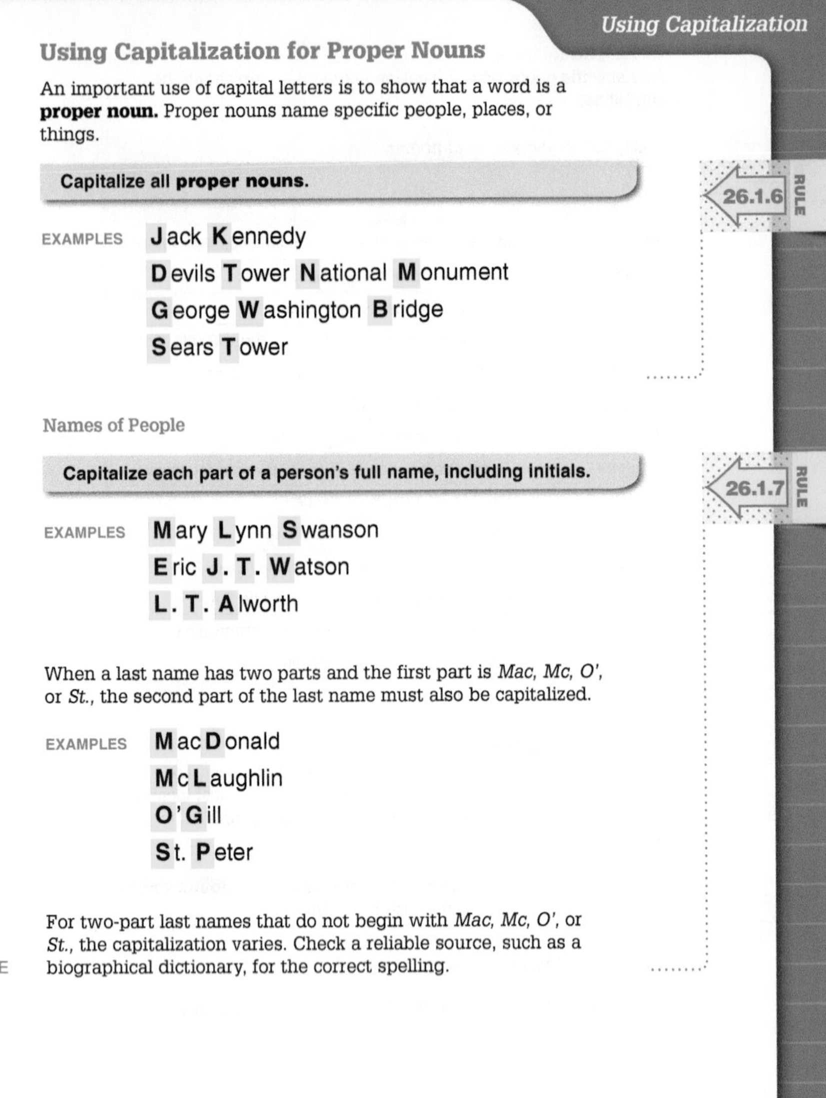

Using Capitalization for Proper Nouns

An important use of capital letters is to show that a word is a **proper noun.** Proper nouns name specific people, places, or things.

Capitalize all proper nouns. RULE 26.1.6

EXAMPLES **J**ack **K**ennedy
Devils **T**ower **N**ational **M**onument
George **W**ashington **B**ridge
Sears **T**ower

Names of People

Capitalize each part of a person's full name, including initials. RULE 26.1.7

EXAMPLES **M**ary **L**ynn **S**wanson
Eric **J**. **T**. **W**atson
L. **T**. **A**lworth

When a last name has two parts and the first part is *Mac, Mc, O',* or *St.,* the second part of the last name must also be capitalized.

EXAMPLES **M**ac**D**onald
Mc**L**aughlin
O'Gill
St. **P**eter

See Practice 26.1E

For two-part last names that do not begin with *Mac, Mc, O',* or *St.,* the capitalization varies. Check a reliable source, such as a biographical dictionary, for the correct spelling.

Using Capitalization for Proper Nouns

Explain to students that one function of capitalization is to distinguish proper nouns from common nouns. Specific persons, places, and things are easily identified when they're capitalized. Say the names of a student, the school, and the state as examples of proper nouns.

RULE 26.1.6 Read aloud the rule and then have students repeat the line with you.

Have students brainstorm for a list of proper nouns. Then, direct students to capitalize and use each proper noun correctly in a sentence.

Names of People

Clarify for students the importance of capitalizing each part of a person's full name. Because an initial stands in place of a name, it is also capitalized.

RULE 26.1.7 Read aloud the rule and then have students repeat the line with you.

Use a Think Aloud as part of a gradual release progression.

Say: I know that nouns that refer to general types of persons, places, or things should not be capitalized. Recite this sentence: *The White House is one of our nation's most important buildings.* **Ask:** In that sentence, which words refer to the White House? (***White House*** and ***buildings***) And which of those words are capitalized? (White House) Why? (because they name a specific building) Why isn't the word *buildings* capitalized? (It names a general thing.)

Work with students to use conventions of capitalization to capitalize the names of several students and teachers.

Have student pairs brainstorm for and write the names of five family members and friends. Remind students that the names must use conventions of capitalization. Have students post their names around the room. Then, have students walk around and critique the capitalization of their classmates' names.

Differentiated Instruction

RTI Strategy for Below-Level Students

In order for students to apply the conventions of capitalization to proper nouns, they must understand what distinguishes proper nouns from common nouns. Provide practice in distinguishing between the two. Give students several pairs of related words written on small slips of paper. In each pair, there should be a common and a proper noun. Do not capitalize either word. Some examples include *woman, mrs. washington; state, maryland; store, mel's mart.*

Have students use the conventions of capitalization to write the correctly capitalized words in a T-chart labeled *Common Nouns* and *Proper Nouns.* (**Answers:** Common Nouns: woman, state, store. Proper Nouns: Mrs. Washington, Maryland, Mel's Mart.)

Geographical Places

Remind students that the names of geographical places often include words that can function as common nouns. For example, the name *Rocky Mountains* includes the common noun *mountain.* Because *Mountains* is a part of the mountain range's name, it is capitalized.

RULE 26.1.8 Read aloud the rule and then have students repeat the line with you.

Remind students that names of specific geographical places, such as those that would be found on a map, are always capitalized. Have students write a sentence correctly capitalizing the name of a place they would like to visit.

Regions and Map Directions

To help students differentiate between regions and directions, tell them that a region can be visited but a map direction cannot be visited. It indicates a direction, not a specific place.

RULE 26.1.9 Read aloud the rule and then have students repeat the lines with you.

Say: Specific geographic places are just like all other specific places—they must be capitalized. What should be capitalized in these sentences? *We drove south to West Virginia. I grew up in the East.* (**Response:** *West Virginia* and *East.* The word *south* is not capitalized because it is used as a direction.)

As a class, discuss specific geographic locations students have visited or read about. Work with students to help them understand the difference between proper and common nouns.

Have students write a paragraph about a specific geographic place. Tell students to include these elements: 1. the name of the particular geographic place; 2. the name of a geographic region; 3. at least one map direction.

Teacher Tip

Have a wall map or globe handy for students unable to think of a specific geographic place. Allow students to use the map in order to brainstorm for ideas. It may also be helpful to draw and post the compass points.

Geographical Places

Any specific geographical location listed on a map should be capitalized.

Capitalize geographical names.

GEOGRAPHICAL NAMES	
Streets	Warren Street, Carlton Avenue, Interstate 10
Cities	Baltimore, London, Memphis, Tokyo
States	Arizona, Florida, Hawaii, Idaho
Nations	Italy, Canada, Kenya, France, Peru, South Korea
Continents	North America, Asia, Africa, Antarctica
Deserts	Sahara, Negev, Mojave
Mountains	Mount Everest, Rocky Mountains
Regions	Great Plains, Appalachian Highlands, Northwest
Islands	Canary Islands, Fiji Islands
Rivers	Mississippi River, Amazon River
Lakes	Lake Michigan, Great Salt Lake, Lake Erie
Bays	Hudson Bay, Baffin Bay, Biscayne Bay
Seas	Black Sea, Mediterranean Sea, North Sea
Oceans	Atlantic Ocean, Arctic Ocean

Regions and Map Directions

Names of regions, such as the South and the Northeast, are capitalized because they refer to a specific geographical location. Map directions that do not refer to a specific geographical location are not capitalized.

Do not capitalize compass points, such as north, southwest, or east, when they simply refer to direction.

REGION My uncle lives in the Southeast.

DIRECTION Our car headed south on River Street.

Working with ELLs ELL **Sheltered Instruction:** Cognitive

Help students comprehend language structures used routinely in written classroom materials, including correctly capitalized geographical names and other proper nouns. Provide students with a copy of a simple historical map labeled with names of places, people, and events. Then:

Beginning Review entries on the map. Guide students in identifying words spelled with capital letters. Clarify the meaning of each, identifying the language structure it represents (personal name, place name, and so on).

Intermediate Have students work in groups to list terms on the map that are capitalized and to identify the language structure that each represents (personal name, place name, and so on). Have them seek clarification as needed. Then, guide them to restate in writing two facts that they learn from the map, capitalizing terms correctly.

Advanced Have partners list capitalized terms on the map and identify the language structure that each represents. Have them list four facts represented on the map and draw a conclusion about geography or history based on those facts.

Advanced High Have partners complete the Advanced activity. Then, have them compare the map to a current map of the region and write a brief comparison.

Specific Events and Time Periods

Capitalize the names of specific events, periods of time, and documents.

RULE 26.1.10

The following chart contains examples of events, periods of time, and documents that require capitalization.

SPECIFIC EVENTS AND TIMES	
Historical Periods	Age of Enlightenment, Middle Ages, the Renaissance
Historical Events	World War II, Boston Tea Party, Battle of Lexington
Documents	Bill of Rights, Treaty of Paris, Declaration of Independence
Days	Wednesday, Saturday
Months	December, October
Holidays	Thanksgiving, Labor Day
Religious Days	Christmas, Passover, Ramadan
Special Events	Fiddlers' Convention, Boston Marathon, Super Bowl

Names of Seasons

The names of the seasons are an exception to this rule. Even though they name a specific period of time, the seasons of the year are not capitalized unless they are part of a title or an event name.

SEASONS A popular activity this winter is skiing.
The students traveled in the fall.

TITLE During a hot spring, I read *The Long Winter.*

EVENT It was so hot at the Spring Festival it felt like summer.

See Practice 26.1F

Specific Events and Time Periods

Explain to students that specific events, time periods, and documents are capitalized as a way to express their importance.

RULE 26.1.10 Read aloud the rule and then have students repeat the lines with you.

Discuss the chart of specific events and times with students. Explain that the names of historical periods, events, and documents are capitalized only if many different people would recognize the specific event, time period, or document from the name. If the name could mean different things to different people, it is probably not capitalized. Then, have students identify specific events and time periods in a newspaper. Encourage students to identify specific documents that are named in the newspaper as well. Don't forget to point out that the newspaper itself is a specific document.

Names of Seasons

Have students practice distinguishing between seasons used as names of time periods that reoccur every year and seasons that are used as part of an event name or a title. Say aloud the names of the four seasons (winter, autumn or fall, summer, spring) and two event titles (Summer Festival, Autumn Extravaganza). Ask students to write one sentence using each. Tell students they must use conventions of capitalization in their sentences.

Differentiated Instruction

Strategy for Spanish Speakers

Students whose home language is Spanish may find capitalization in English confusing. Remind students that capitalization is used much more frequently in English than in Spanish. Review the table on page 615. Put students in pairs or small groups. Provide each group with a blank copy of the table with enough space to write in each category. Tell students they will have three minutes to write examples for each category. Remind them to capitalize where necessary. Time the students and then see which group came up with the most examples. Have students share their answers and fill in a master chart on the board for the whole class to see.

PRACTICE 26.1E

1. McMullens
2. Edgar Allan Poe
3. T. J. Gonzales
4. Gina DeAngelo, Paul O'Connor
5. Pete, Scottie
6. Mom
7. Louis L'Amour
8. Susan B. Anthony
9. Grandma's
10. Julianna Claire Maria Lugo, Juli

PRACTICE 26.1F

11. Tokyo, Japan
12. Panama Canal, Caribbean Sea, Pacific Ocean
13. July, Warsaw, Poland
14. Mississippi River
15. Middle East
16. Kenya
17. New England, Maine, New Hampshire, Vermont
18. New York City Marathon
19. Middle Ages, Europe
20. Pennsylvania

PRACTICE 26.1E Using Capitalization for Names of People

Read the sentences. Write each name, adding the missing capitals.

EXAMPLE ina and ivy are twins.

ANSWER *Ina, Ivy*

1. The mcmullens live next door to us.
2. Our class read a story by edgar allan poe.
3. t. j. gonzales will be the speaker at the assembly.
4. gina deangelo and paul o'connor are both in my social studies class.
5. pete named his dog scottie.
6. May I have a piece of cake, mom?
7. louis l'amour wrote stories and essays about the West.
8. susan b. anthony was an American civil rights leader.
9. Today is grandma's birthday.
10. My full name is julianna claire maria lugo, but my friends call me juli.

PRACTICE 26.1F Using Capitalization for Geographical Places, Specific Events, and Time Periods

Read the sentences. Write the name of each geographical place, specific event, and time period, adding the missing capitals.

EXAMPLE The colorado river flows through the grand canyon.

ANSWER *Colorado River, Grand Canyon*

11. My brother lives in tokyo, japan.
12. The panama canal links the caribbean sea with the pacific ocean.
13. Last july, my family visited warsaw, poland.
14. Huck Finn and Jim floated down the mississippi river on a raft.
15. World leaders are trying to resolve the conflicts in the middle east.
16. The Morrisons gave a slide show of their safari in kenya.
17. We visited three new england states: maine, new hampshire, and vermont.
18. My cousin plans to run in the new york city marathon next year.
19. During the middle ages in europe, many towns and cities grew as trade developed.
20. My grandparents sold their house in pennsylvania and moved south.

WRITING APPLICATION

Write your full name and the names of your siblings if you have any. Then, write the names of your teachers and your principal.

WRITING APPLICATION

Write your address, including your city and state. Then, list any bodies of water or mountains in your region.

WRITING APPLICATION

Students' responses should demonstrate they can correctly use the conventions of capitalization.

WRITING APPLICATION

Students' responses should demonstrate that they can use and understand the functions and conventions of capitalization.

Working with ELLs — ELL Sheltered Instruction: Social/Affective

As students work through Practice 26.1F, have them use support from peers and from you to read, to enhance and confirm understanding, and to develop background knowledge needed to comprehend increasingly challenging language.

Beginning Choose a sentence from Practice 26.1F, and have students read it with you. Help students share their background knowledge about geography to enhance understanding, and develop background by locating the places named on a map or by sharing their history. Then, guide students in completing the item.

Intermediate Have groups read the items in the Practice, sharing geographical and historical background knowledge to enhance and confirm understanding. Circulate, and provide additional background as needed. Have groups complete the Practice.

Advanced Have partners read and discuss the items in the Practice, sharing geographical and historical background knowledge to enhance and confirm understanding and asking for additional background from you as needed. Then, partners should complete the Practice.

Advanced High Have partners complete the Advanced activity. Then, have them use library or Internet resources to acquire additional background about three of the places named in the Practice. Have them share their findings with the class.

Specific Groups

Proper nouns that name specific groups also require capitalization.

Capitalize the names of various organizations, government bodies, political parties, and nationalities, as well as the languages spoken by different groups.

26.1.11 RULE

EXAMPLES We made a very generous donation to the Red Cross.

My friend Shirley, who speaks Chinese fluently, works as a translator.

The Department of Transportation often issues travel alerts.

The proper nouns shown in the chart are groups with which many people are familiar. All specific groups, however, must be capitalized, even if they are not well known.

SPECIFIC GROUPS	
Clubs	Kiwanis Club Rotary Club
Organizations	National Governors Association National Organization for Women
Institutions	Massachusetts Institute of Technology Smithsonian Institution
Businesses	Simon Chemical Corporation Fido's Favorite Pet Foods
Government Bodies	United States Congress Supreme Court
Political Parties	Democrats Republican Party
Nationalities	Chinese, German Nigerian, Iranian
Languages	English, Spanish Korean, Swahili

See Practice 26.1G

Specific Groups

The names of specific groups are capitalized because they represent a particular body of people. Remind students that each part of a group's name must be capitalized.

RULE 26.1.11 Read aloud the rule and then have students repeat the lines with you.

With students, read through and discuss the examples for Rule 26.1.11 and the examples in the chart on page 617.

Say: What are some of the clubs to which you or your family and friends belong? How should they be capitalized? (Accept all correct answers.) What are the names of some businesses you saw on your way to school today? List a few examples that you know of if students can't think of any. (Accept all correct answers.) And what did you notice about the names of the businesses? Were they capitalized? Discuss the appearances of the names, noting the conventions of capitalization.

Work with students to list the names of familiar institutions, government bodies, nationalities, languages, and other specific groups using conventions of capitalization. As students identify groups, write the names of the groups on the board. Define and discuss the groups if necessary. **Say:** When you write, always be sure to capitalize the names of specific groups.

Have students select five of the specific groups you've listed. Pair students and have them write a paragraph using the group names. Tell students they can write about anything they'd like. Remind students to use the conventions of capitalization.

Teacher Tip

It may be helpful to give students visual examples of specific groups. Photographs of signs that show a business's name written using the conventions of capitalization or a pamphlet with the name of a college or neighborhood club may help them understand how a specific group's name is written.

Religious References

Discuss the importance of capitalizing the names of religions, deities, and religious scriptures. Note that religious references are proper nouns because they name specific people, places, and things.

RULE 26.1.12 Read aloud the rule and then have students repeat the lines with you.

Say: Religions and religious references are always capitalized. It may be helpful for you to think of religions in the same way you do abstract nouns—those nouns that you can't access through the senses. Though you can't see, hear, taste, touch, or smell a religion, you can think and write about it. Allow students to ask any questions they may have.

With students, discuss the chart of specific religious references that are capitalized. Remind students the words *god* and *goddess* are not capitalized when they refer to deities in Greek or Roman mythology. The individual names of ancient Greek and Roman gods and goddesses, however, are proper nouns and should always be capitalized.

Write on the board these sentence pairs. Have students select and copy the sentences that use the conventions of capitalization. Discuss students' answers.

1. The Torah contains Jewish laws and scripture.
2. The torah contains jewish laws and scripture.
3. christianity's holy book is called the bible and islam's holy book is called the qur'an.
4. Christianity's holy book is called the Bible and Islam's holy book is called the Qur'an.

(Correct answers: 1 and 4).

Religious References

Use capitals for the names of the religions of the world and certain other words related to religion.

RULE 26.1.12 **Capitalize references to religions, deities, and religious scriptures.**

The following chart presents words related to five of the world's major religions. Next to each religion are examples of some of the related religious words that must be capitalized. Note that the name of each religion is also capitalized.

RELIGIOUS REFERENCES	
Christianity	God, Lord, Father, Holy Spirit, Bible, books of the Bible (Genesis, Deuteronomy, Psalms, and so on)
Judaism	Lord, Father, Prophets, Torah, Talmud, Midrash
Islam	Allah, Prophet, Mohammed, Quran
Hinduism	Brahma, Bhagavad Gita, Vedas
Buddhism	Buddha, Mahayana, Hinayana

Note in the following examples, however, that the words *god* and *goddess* in references to mythology are not capitalized. A god's or goddess's name, however, is capitalized.

EXAMPLES In Greek mythology, the supreme god was Zeus.
The goddess Hera was the wife of Zeus and was the goddess of women.

Differentiated Instruction

RTI Strategy for Below-Level Students
In order to apply the conventions of capitalization to religious references, students must understand what qualifies as a religious reference. Students may fail to capitalize religious references because they don't recognize them. To help students avoid making errors, teach them how to find information about unfamiliar words using printed reference works and online sources. Show students how to use reputable online references to define unfamiliar words. Once students know a word's part of speech and definition, they can correctly apply capitalization conventions.

Enrichment for Gifted/Talented Students
Have students use reliable online sources to research a world religion of their choice. Students should create a chart of common religious references used in the religion. Have students explain their charts to the class.

Specific Places and Items

Monuments, memorials, buildings, celestial bodies, awards, the names of specific vehicles, and trademarked products should be capitalized.

Capitalize the names of specific places and items. RULE 26.1.13

OTHER SPECIAL PLACES AND ITEMS	
Monuments	Statue of Liberty Washington Monument
Memorials	Winston Churchill Memorial Vietnam Veterans Memorial
Buildings	Houston Museum of Fine Arts Empire State Building the Capitol Building (in Washington, D.C.)
Celestial Bodies (except the moon and sun)	Earth, Milky Way Jupiter, Aries
Awards	Newbery Medal Nobel Peace Prize
Air, Sea, and Space Craft	*Spirit of St. Louis* *Monitor* *Voyager 2* *Metroliner*
Trademarked Brands	Krazy Korn Eco-Friendly Cleanser
Names	Zenox Kermit the Frog the Great Houdini

Capitalize the names of awards. RULE 26.1.14

Notice that *the* is not capitalized in these examples.

EXAMPLES the Emmy Awards
the Rhodes Scholarship
the Most Valuable Player Award
the Purple Heart

See Practice 26.1H

Specific Places and Items

Explain that certain types of places, items, and awards require capitalization.

RULES 26.1.13, 26.1.14 Read aloud the rules and then have students repeat the lines with you.

Read aloud the examples of names that are capitalized in the chart on page 619. With students, discuss why each name is capitalized.

Provide students with a copy of this paragraph. Have students correct capitalization errors.

Last summer, my family took a road trip. My dad thought we should see some of the nation's most important sights. We visited the statue of liberty in New York, the lincoln memorial in Washington D.C., and the grand canyon in Arizona. Throughout our journey, my sisters and I constantly asked my dad to stop at restaurants such as burger way or pizza time, but he said that we should eat healthful snacks such as vegetables and fruit. We would nominate him for a healthy life medal. (Correct answers: Statue of Liberty, Lincoln Memorial, Grand Canyon, Burger Way, Pizza Time, Healthy Life Medal)

Teacher Tip

Point out context clues in the paragraph to help students identify each specific place or item. *We visited* and *restaurants such as* may signal proper nouns.

PRACTICE 26.1G

1. Green Valley Cyclers
2. International Red Cross
3. College Board
4. Supreme Court
5. Howard University
6. Girl Scouts
7. Chamber of Commerce
8. Sammy's Sporting Goods
9. City Council
10. Northern Community College

PRACTICE 26.1H

11. Mars
12. Seder, Passover
13. Vietnam Veterans Memorial, Capitol
14. Muslims, Hajj
15. *Air Force One*
16. Oscars
17. *Acela*
18. Yogi's Yogurt Yummies
19. Bible, Torah, Qur'an
20. USS *John F. Kennedy*

WRITING APPLICATION

Students' responses should demonstrate they can use conventions of capitalization correctly for names of organizations.

WRITING APPLICATION

Students' responses should demonstrate that they can use the conventions of capitalization for names of events, planets, brand names, and names of specific places.

PRACTICE 26.1G Using Capitalization for Groups and Organizations

Read the sentences. Write each group or organization, adding the missing capitals.

EXAMPLE My little brother just joined the cub scouts.

ANSWER *Cub Scouts*

1. The green valley cyclers go on biking trips every weekend.
2. The international red cross provides local assistance after disasters.
3. The college board sponsors college entrance exams.
4. That case went all the way to the supreme court.
5. Our superintendent graduated from howard university.
6. The girl scouts sell cookies every year.
7. I found local information at the chamber of commerce.
8. You can get new running shoes at sammy's sporting goods.
9. The city council meets every Wednesday.
10. You can take some interesting and unusual courses at northern community college.

PRACTICE 26.1H Using Capitalization for Religious References and Specific Items and Places

Read the sentences. Write each term that should be capitalized, adding the missing capitals.

EXAMPLE Author Toni Morrison won a nobel prize in literature.

ANSWER *Nobel Prize in Literature*

11. The planet mars has always fascinated scientists.
12. The Goldbergs host a seder dinner during passover.
13. In Washington, D.C., we visited the vietnam veterans memorial and the capitol.
14. Many muslims make an annual pilgrimage to Mecca, called the hajj.
15. The president travels on *air force one*.
16. I enjoy watching the oscars ceremony.
17. My father took the *acela* train from Providence to New York.
18. yogi's yogurt yummies are my new favorite snack.
19. The bible, the torah, and the qur'an are three major religious texts.
20. The USS *john f. kennedy* aircraft carrier is no longer in operation.

WRITING APPLICATION

Write the names of five organizations or groups in your school and community. Capitalize the names correctly.

WRITING APPLICATION

Write the names of the following:

- **a religious event or holiday**
- **a planet**
- **your favorite cereal**
- **a building in your town or city**

Working with ELLs — ELL Sheltered Instruction: Cognitive

Have students read linguistically accommodated text silently with increasing ease and comprehension for longer periods of time and with a decreasing need for accommodation. Monitor to ensure all students are able to recognize directionality of English reading, reading left to right. Create a handout of Practice 26.1H, simplifying the language as much as possible and providing explanatory glosses of vocabulary. Then:

Beginning Have students silently read the directions on your handout. Then, read the directions aloud as they follow along. Clarify meaning, and repeat with the Example.

Intermediate Have students silently read the directions, Example, and first two items on your handout. Then, discuss the text, clarifying meaning. Repeat with the next four items, and then with the final four.

Advanced Have partners silently read the handout. Discuss their questions about the text. Then, have them complete the Practice.

Advanced High Have partners silently read the handout. Discuss their questions about the text. Then, have them turn back to the student page and complete the original Practice.

Using Capitalization for Proper Adjectives

When a proper noun or a form of a proper noun is used to describe another noun, it is called a **proper adjective.** Proper adjectives usually need a capital letter.

Capitalize most proper adjectives.

RULE 26.1.15

In the following examples, notice that both proper nouns and proper adjectives are capitalized. Common nouns that are modified by proper adjectives, however, are not capitalized.

PROPER NOUNS	World War II
	Mexico
PROPER ADJECTIVES	a World War II battleship
	a Mexican hat

The names of some countries and states must be modified to be used as proper adjectives. For example, something from Kenya is Kenyan, someone from Texas is Texan, a chair from Spain is a Spanish chair, and a building in France is a French building.

Brand Names as Adjectives

Trademarked brand names are considered to be proper nouns. If you use a brand name to describe a common noun, the brand name becomes a proper adjective. In this case, capitalize only the proper adjective and not the common noun.

Capitalize brand names used as adjectives.

RULE 26.1.16

PROPER NOUN	Fruit Grains
PROPER ADJECTIVE	Fruit Grains cereal

Notice that only the proper adjective *Fruit Grains* is capitalized. The word *cereal* is not capitalized because it is a common noun; it is not part of the trademarked name.

See Practice 26.1I

Using Capitalization for Proper Adjectives

Remind students that proper adjectives are formed from proper nouns. For example, in the sentence *I like Irish music,* the word *Irish* is a proper adjective that is formed from the proper noun *Ireland.*

RULE 26.1.15 Read aloud the rule and then have students repeat the line with you.

Discuss the examples of proper nouns and proper adjectives listed for rule 26.1.15 on page 621. Focus on the fact that proper adjectives should be capitalized. Have students use these proper nouns in five original sentences: *Texas, North America, Earth, World Series, Tuesday.* Students should convert these words into proper adjectives and write sentences using the proper adjectives with correct capitalization.

Brand Names as Adjectives

Explain that a *brand name* is the name of a specific product or group of products that is sold or made by a specific company. Other companies might make or sell a similar product, but their products would have different brand names. As a class, list and discuss several brand names.

RULE 26.1.16 Read aloud the rule and then have students repeat the line with you.

Play a game with students to strengthen their capitalization skills. Tell students that they will have 60 seconds to write as many brand names beginning with the capital letter *T* as they can. The student who writes the longest list of brand names that are accurately capitalized is the winner. Write on the board the brand names students listed. Then brainstorm with students for sentences that use the brand names as proper adjectives. Write several of the sentences on the board, capitalizing the proper adjectives correctly.

Using Capitalization for Titles of People

Point out that whether a person's title is capitalized depends upon how it is used in a sentence.

Social and Professional Titles

RULE 26.1.17 Read aloud the rule and then have students repeat the lines with you.

Review the examples for rule 26.1.17 with students. Explain that *Reverend* and *Doctor* are capitalized because they are directly followed by the person's name. *Lieutenant* is capitalized because it is a title used as a noun of direct address.

Use a Think Aloud as part of a gradual release progression.

Say: **I know** that a title that is immediately followed by a person's name should be capitalized. Also, I know that if a person's name can be substituted for a title, the title should be capitalized. If the person's name cannot be substituted, the title should not be capitalized. I can use this rule to determine whether to capitalize *nurse* in the sentence *Thank you for the advice, Nurse.* The title *nurse* takes the place of the nurse's name, so it must be capitalized.

On the board, write several titles followed by specific names. Some examples include *Governor Brown* and *Miss Langley.* Have students generate a few examples of their own.

On the board, write these examples and **work with students** to capitalize titles:

1. I tell you, reverend, I've been worrying all night. (Point out that if *Reverend* were replaced with *David* the sentence would still make sense, so *Reverend* should be capitalized.)
2. The doctor was very professional. (Point out that if *doctor* were replaced with *Rebecca,* the sentence would not make sense, so *doctor* should not be capitalized.)

On the board, write these sentences. **Have students work in pairs to** fill in the blanks using the conventions of capitalization.

1. The (title) will be in shortly.
2. (title) (proper name) never arrived

(**Possible answers:** 1. doctor; 2. Mr. Richards)

Using Capitalization for Titles of People

A person's title shows his or her or relationship to other people. Whether a title is capitalized often depends on how it is used in a sentence.

Social and Professional Titles

Social and professional titles may be written before a person's name or used alone in place of a person's name.

RULE 26.1.17

Capitalize the title of a person when the title is followed by the person's name or when it is used in place of a person's name in direct address.

BEFORE A NAME — **R**everend O'Connor and **D**octor Brennan have arrived.

IN DIRECT ADDRESS — Look, **L**ieutenant, here is the missing clue!

TITLES OF PEOPLE	
Social	Mister, Madam or Madame, Miss, Ms., Sir
Business	Doctor, Professor, Superintendent, Attorney
Religious	Reverend, Father, Rabbi, Bishop, Sister
Military	Private, Ensign, Captain, General, Admiral
Government	President, Senator, Representative, Governor, Mayor, Prince, Queen, King

In most cases, do not capitalize titles that are used alone or that follow a person's name—especially if the title is preceded by the articles *a, an,* or *the.*

EXAMPLES — Roger Simmons, the **d**etective assigned to the case, will call you.

Tell your **state representative** how you feel about the issue.

My brother George, who is a **p**rivate in the army, will be home on leave soon.

Differentiated Instruction

RTI Strategy for Special Needs Students Students will benefit from repetition of instruction. Each time they review a concept, they gain a bit more confidence. Over the course of a few days, review the rules for capitalizing the titles of people. Each time, allow students to exercise more independence. During the first review, use specific sentence starters to provide students with structured practice.

For example: *I'm waiting for my (lowercase title of person who helps people) to assist me.*

During the second review, delete sentence starters and allow students to rely on their knowledge: *I'm waiting for my _______ to assist me.*

Government Officials

Capitalize the titles of government officials when they immediately precede the name of specific officials. If no person is named, these titles should be written in lower case.

RULE 26.1.18

EXAMPLES

Vice President Biden will preside at the meeting.

The club vice president will preside at the meeting.

Superintendent Waller will speak to the students about the quality of education.

The superintendent of schools is responsible for the quality of education.

Note: Certain honorary titles are always capitalized, even if the title is not used with a proper name or direct address. These titles include the First Lady of the United States, Speaker of the House of Representatives, Queen Mother of England, and the Prince of Wales.

Titles for Family Relationships

Capitalize titles showing family relationships when the title is used with the person's name or as the person's name—except when the title comes after a possessive noun or pronoun.

RULE 26.1.19

BEFORE A NAME	We respect Aunt Betsy's opinion.
IN PLACE OF A NAME	Is Grandfather going?
AFTER POSSESSIVES	Jeff's father is the team doctor.

Notice that the family title *father* used in the last example is not capitalized because it is used after the possessive word *Jeff's*.

See Practice 26.1J

Teacher Tip

Provide a word bank of common government titles so that students focus on using capitalization conventions rather than on identifying titles.

Government Officials

Point out that the capitalization conventions for titles of government officials are similar to the capitalization conventions for the titles of other people.

RULE 26.1.18 Read aloud the rule and then have students repeat the lines with you.

Review the examples for rule 26.1.18 with students. For each example, have students explain why the title is capitalized or is not capitalized.

Titles for Family Relationships

Explain that the way in which a family title is used in a sentence determines whether or not it is capitalized.

RULE 26.1.19 Read aloud the rule and then have students repeat the lines with you.

On the board, write these sentences, omitting the capitalization. For each, ask students to highlight the title and/or proper name and then explain why the title is capitalized or not capitalized.

1. My uncle will be in California later this week.
2. Every Friday, Aunt Deidre makes the best salmon!
3. Last week, Grandmother King moved to New Orleans.
4. Rick's mother has been watching football all afternoon.

(1. The word *uncle* is not used with the person's name or as the person's name, so it is not capitalized. 2. The word *Aunt* is used with the person's name, so it must be capitalized. 3. Because *Grandmother* is immediately followed by the person's proper name, it should be capitalized. 4. Because *mother* comes after a possessive noun or pronoun, it should not be capitalized.)

PRACTICE 26.1I

1. Egyptian
2. Japanese
3. Gothic
4. Irish
5. German
6. Thai
7. Caribbean
8. American, English
9. Florida
10. Spanish

PRACTICE 26.1J

11. correct
12. Judge
13. Governor
14. Lieutenant
15. correct
16. Uncle
17. Senator
18. correct
19. correct
20. Professor

WRITING APPLICATION

Students' sentences should correctly use conventions of capitalization with proper adjectives.

WRITING APPLICATION

Students' responses should demonstrate that they can correctly use conventions of capitalization.

PRACTICE 26.1I Using Capitalization for Proper Adjectives

Read the sentences. Write the proper adjectives, adding the correct capitalization.

EXAMPLE The canadian winters can be quite severe.

ANSWER *Canadian*

1. The egyptian pyramids are one of the wonders of the world.
2. I saw an exhibit of japanese woodblock prints at the museum.
3. Mary Shelley wrote *Frankenstein*, an early gothic novel.
4. My mother enjoys irish breakfast tea.
5. Ivan was interested in the german sports cars at the auto show.
6. We went to a restaurant for thai food.
7. Bill and Cindy Duquette are dreaming about a caribbean vacation.
8. In 1776, american colonists declared independence from their english rulers.
9. We drink florida orange juice every day.
10. Will you help me study for the spanish test?

PRACTICE 26.1J Using Capitalization for Titles of People

Read the sentences. If the title in each sentence is correctly capitalized, write *correct*. If it is not, rewrite the title correctly.

EXAMPLE My mother took me to doctor Perez when I had the flu.

ANSWER *Doctor*

11. In the opening ceremony, Mayor Massey will cut the ribbon and give a speech.
12. All in the court rose as judge Saris entered.
13. The evening news featured an interview with governor Chase.
14. An army recruiter, lieutenant Carson, will be here next week.
15. The ceremony was performed by Reverend Walker.
16. I went on a camping trip with uncle Stan.
17. Perhaps you should write a letter to senator Olson.
18. General Colin Powell later became Secretary of State.
19. My grandma Ginny loves to cook.
20. The library will present a lecture by professor Watkins on green energy.

WRITING APPLICATION

Write three proper adjectives and the nouns they modify. You may use the proper adjectives in the sentences above as models. Capitalize the proper adjectives.

WRITING APPLICATION

Write the title and name of one of your town or city officials, the governor of your state, and one senator and representative from your state.

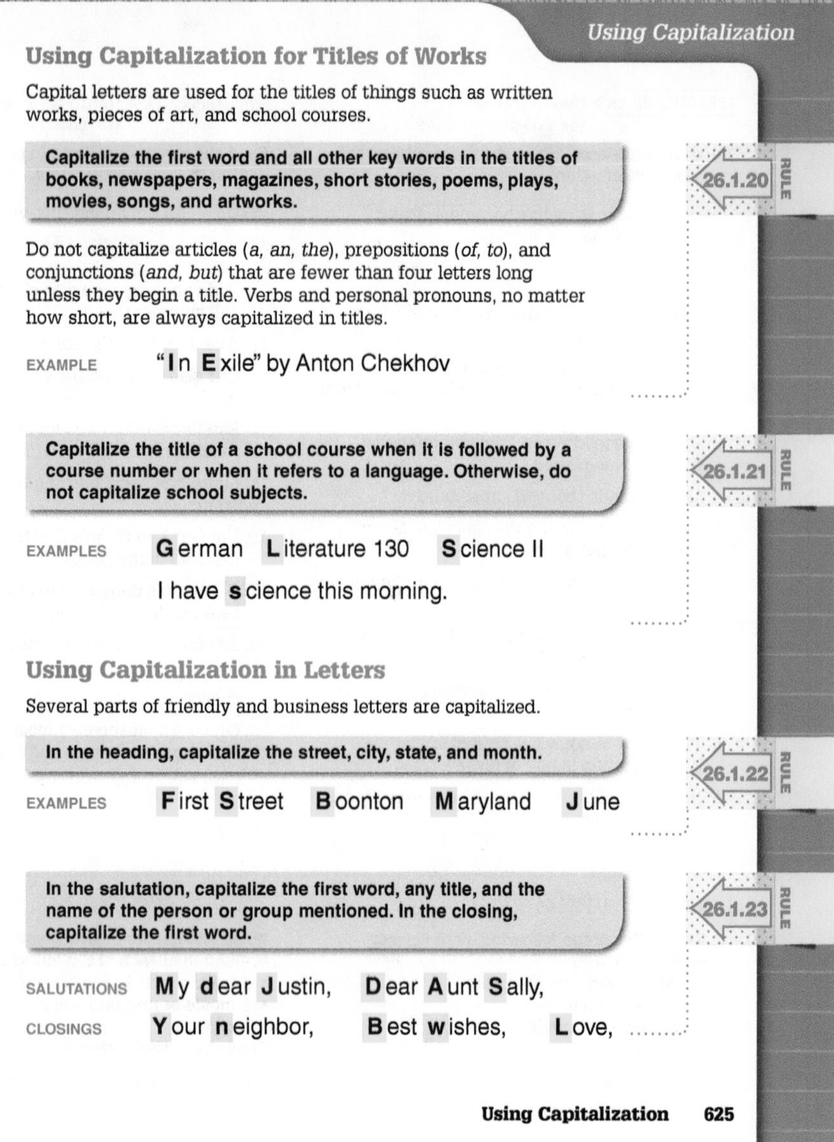

Using Capitalization for Titles of Works

Capital letters are used for the titles of things such as written works, pieces of art, and school courses.

Capitalize the first word and all other key words in the titles of books, newspapers, magazines, short stories, poems, plays, movies, songs, and artworks. RULE 26.1.20

Do not capitalize articles (*a, an, the*), prepositions (*of, to*), and conjunctions (*and, but*) that are fewer than four letters long unless they begin a title. Verbs and personal pronouns, no matter how short, are always capitalized in titles.

EXAMPLE "In Exile" by Anton Chekhov

Capitalize the title of a school course when it is followed by a course number or when it refers to a language. Otherwise, do not capitalize school subjects. RULE 26.1.21

EXAMPLES German Literature 130 Science II

I have science this morning.

Using Capitalization in Letters

Several parts of friendly and business letters are capitalized.

In the heading, capitalize the street, city, state, and month. RULE 26.1.22

EXAMPLES First Street Boonton Maryland June

In the salutation, capitalize the first word, any title, and the name of the person or group mentioned. In the closing, capitalize the first word. RULE 26.1.23

See Practice 26.1K
See Practice 26.1L

SALUTATIONS My dear Justin, Dear Aunt Sally,

CLOSINGS Your neighbor, Best wishes, Love,

Working with ELLs

ELL Sheltered Instruction: Social/Affective

As students learn about capitalization, help them demonstrate comprehension of increasingly complex English by participating in a Shared Reading. Write a sample letter in which the writer names works she is reading for her classes. Provide students with a copy.

Beginning Pair students with fluent speakers, and have the fluent speaker read as the Beginning student follows along. Then, have pairs repeat the reading, stopping after each sentence or item that contains capital letters and discussing its meaning, as well as the reasons for capitalizing the terms.

Intermediate Have students working in small groups read the letter, with each student taking a turn reading aloud as the others follow along. Then, have groups repeat the reading, pausing to discuss the meaning of each section and the capitalization rules it illustrates.

Advanced Have students complete the Intermediate activity. Then, have them write their own letters modeled on yours.

Advanced High Have students write their own letters based on your model, mentioning titles of works and courses and following proper letter format. Have them conduct shared readings of one another's letters, correcting capitalization as needed.

Using Capitalization for Titles of Works

Explain that the formal titles of publications and published works are capitalized.

RULES 26.1.20, 26.1.21 Read aloud the rules and then have students repeat the lines with you.

Ask students to create a chart with these headings: *Books, Poems, Movies, Songs.*

Have students write two of their favorite works in each column. Remind students that articles, prepositions, and short conjunctions are not capitalized unless they begin the title. Once students have completed their charts, have them share them with a partner. Ask partners to check the charts for their correct use of capitalization. Allow students to discuss their favorite works with their partners.

Write on the board a list of courses offered by your school. Omit all capitalization. Have students copy the course names correcting their capitalization.

Using Capitalization in Letters

Identify the parts of a letter that are commonly capitalized, and discuss how capitalization rules are applied to salutations and closings.

RULES 26.1.22, 26.1.23 Read aloud the rules and then have students repeat the lines with you.

Have students write a friendly letter to a friend or relative. Students may write about anything they like, but in their letters they should correctly apply conventions of capitalization.

PRACTICE 26.1K

Italicized answers may be underlined instead.

1. "The Highwayman"
2. *The Adventures of Tom Sawyer*
3. "The Star-Spangled Banner"
4. *The Wall Street Journal*
5. *Charlie and the Chocolate Factory*
6. *Mona Lisa*
7. "Twinkle, Twinkle, Little Star"
8. *Newsweek*
9. "A Noiseless Patient Spider"
10. Mayflower

PRACTICE 26.1L

Italicized answers may be underlined instead.

11. "All Summer in a Day"
12. *The Lion King*
13. "Seventh Grade"
14. *Kira-Kira*
15. "Minuet in G"
16. *Starry Night*
17. Algebra I, Algebra II
18. *Sports Illustrated*
19. Chemistry 101
20. *The Tragedy of Romeo and Juliet*

WRITING APPLICATION

Students' responses should correctly use conventions of capitalization for titles of works.

WRITING APPLICATION

Students' responses should demonstrate that they can correctly use conventions of capitalization.

PRACTICE 26.1K Using Capitalization for Titles of Things

Read the sentences. Write the titles, adding the correct capitalization.

EXAMPLE *star wars* has become a classic movie.

ANSWER *Star Wars*

1. Our teacher gave a dramatic reading of the poem "the highwayman" by Alfred Noyes.
2. Do you know how Tom got people to whitewash the fence in *the adventures of tom sawyer*?
3. Everyone stood when "the star-spangled banner" was played.
4. My dad reads *the wall street journal.*
5. The book *charlie and the chocolate factory* was made into a film.
6. I would like to see the *mona lisa* in the Louvre Museum in Paris.
7. The children in nursery school sang "twinkle, twinkle, little star."
8. Andy used *newsweek* magazine as one of his sources for his report.
9. The poem "a noiseless patient spider" by Walt Whitman is one of my favorites.
10. In 1620, the Pilgrims crossed the Atlantic on the *mayflower.*

PRACTICE 26.1L Using Capitalization for Titles of Things

Read the sentences. Rewrite each sentence, adding the missing capitals.

EXAMPLE I am taking first-year spanish.

ANSWER *I am taking first-year Spanish.*

11. Today in language arts class, we discussed "all summer in a day."
12. Allie has seen *the lion king* six times.
13. Our class enjoyed Gary Soto's story "seventh grade."
14. Estelle read *kira-kira* for her independent reading report.
15. Laura has been learning to play J. S. Bach's "minuet in g."
16. Vincent Van Gogh's painting *starry night* has inspired many people.
17. Caitlin has done well in algebra I, so next year she'll take algebra II.
18. Jeff faithfully reads *sports illustrated.*
19. My sister is taking chemistry 101 at her college.
20. One of Shakespeare's most popular plays is *the tragedy of romeo and juliet.*

WRITING APPLICATION

Write titles of the following, with correct capitalization:

- **a short story you have read**
- **a book you like**
- **your favorite movie**
- **a television program**

WRITING APPLICATION

Write statements in which you make an evaluation of each of the following:

- **a book or article you have read recently**
- **a movie or program you have viewed recently**

Capitalize titles correctly.

Working with ELLs ELL Sheltered Instruction: Cognitive

The Writing Application for 26.1L on page 626 provides students an opportunity to write using a variety of grade-appropriate sentence lengths in increasingly accurate ways. Read the directions aloud. Then:

Beginning Pair students with more fluent speakers. Have partners brainstorm for a movie, book, or television program they have enjoyed, with fluent speakers prompting Beginning students by asking simple questions. Then, have partners choose adjectives to describe the work. Next, have the fluent speaker compose a sentence about the work using one of the adjectives. Have the Beginning student copy the sentence. Finally, have partners write a longer sentence by adding another adjective to their original.

Intermediate Have partners complete the Writing Application for 26.1L. Then, have them write longer sentences by adding descriptive words or phrases to their sentences.

Advanced Have students complete the Writing Application for 26.1L. Then, have them write longer sentences by adding clauses to their statements, forming compound or complex sentences.

Advanced High Have students write a one-paragraph review of a book, article, movie, or television program, capitalizing titles correctly. Have them reread their drafts and revise to ensure that they have used a variety of sentence lengths.

Using Capitalization in Abbreviations, Acronyms, and Initials

An **abbreviation** is a shortened form of a word or phrase. An **acronym** is an abbreviation of a phrase that takes one or more letters from each word in the phrase being abbreviated.

In general, capitalize abbreviations, acronyms, and initials if the words or names they stand for are capitalized. RULE 26.1.24

INITIALS	A. C. Black
TITLES	Dr. Samuel Green Sr.
ACADEMIC DEGREES	Samuel Green, M.D., Ben Queen, Ph.D.
ACRONYMS	UNICEF, ROTC

Abbreviations for most units of measurement are not capitalized.

EXAMPLES in. (inches) tbsp. (tablespoon)

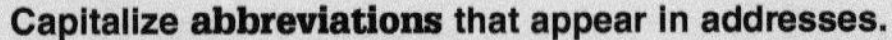

Capitalize abbreviations that appear in addresses. RULE 26.1.25

Use a two-letter state abbreviation without periods when the abbreviation is followed by a ZIP code in an address. Capitalize both letters of the state abbreviation.

EXAMPLE Trenton, NJ 08629

Capitalize acronyms that stand for proper nouns, such as businesses, government bodies, and organizations. RULE 26.1.26

Spell out the name of an organization and include its acronym in parentheses the first time you use it. Use only the acronym in later references.

EXAMPLE Have you heard of the Food and Drug Administration (FDA)? The FDA is responsible for protecting the public health.

See Practice 26.1M
See Practice 26.1N

Using Capitalization in Abbreviations, Acronyms, and Initials

Point out to students that conventions of capitalization apply to abbreviations, acronyms, and initials because they often stand for words that are capitalized.

RULES 26.1.24, 26.1.25, 26.1.26 Read aloud the rules and then have students repeat the lines with you.

Use a Think Aloud as part of a gradual release progression.

Say: Even when **I abbreviate** a word or write an acronym or set of initials, I must use conventions of capitalization. To remember the importance of capitalizing in these cases, I remind myself that abbreviations, acronyms, and initials may represent proper nouns or academic degrees. Tell students to write their names and their initials using conventions of capitalization.

Write the following on the board:

1. The initials of someone famous
2. Doctor Paul Moore
3. Bachelor of Arts degree
4. Federal Bureau of Investigation
5. 11 feet
6. Buffalo, New York

Work with students to use the conventions of capitalization to write the abbreviation, acronym, or initial for number 1. Then, **have students** complete the rest of the list on their own.

Responses:

1. Accept all answers that correctly represent a person's initials.
2. Dr. Paul Moore
3. B. A.
4. FBI
5. 11 ft.
6. Buffalo, NY

PRACTICE 26.1M

1. correct
2. Dr. Suarez
3. Atlanta, GA 30301
4. USS *Constitution*
5. Richard Smith Jr.
6. correct
7. correct
8. Maj. Armstrong
9. 146 Lake St.
10. correct

PRACTICE 26.1N

11. NASA's
12. D.V.M.
13. correct
14. correct
15. NCAA
16. correct
17. NAACP
18. CJ
19. ASPCA
20. T. F., R.I.

SPEAKING APPLICATION

Have students demonstrate the correct use of conventions of capitalization by explaining how their acronyms should be written.

WRITING APPLICATION

Students' addresses should demonstrate the correct use of conventions of capitalization.

PRACTICE 26.1M Using Capitalization for Abbreviations

Read the items. Rewrite each item, adding capitals as needed. If the item is already correct, write *correct*.

EXAMPLE Columbia rd.

ANSWER *Columbia Rd.*

1. Gov. Brown
2. dr. Suarez
3. Atlanta, ga 30301
4. uss *Constitution*
5. Richard Smith jr.
6. one tsp. salt
7. Sixth Ave.
8. maj. Armstrong
9. 146 lake st.
10. 5 ft 2 in.

PRACTICE 26.1N Using Capitalization for Initials and Acronyms

Read the sentences. Write the initials and acronyms, adding capitals as needed. If the sentence is correct, write *correct*.

EXAMPLE Have you read *The Lord of the Rings* trilogy by j.r.r. Tolkien?

ANSWER *J.R.R.*

11. We visited nasa's Johnson Space Center when we were in Houston.
12. Arthur Kelly, d.v.m., works at the veterinary hospital where we take our dog.
13. The John F. Kennedy Presidential Library and Museum in Boston opened in 1979.
14. Check the SPF before you buy that sunscreen.
15. The ncaa basketball tournament is a popular event every spring.
16. The speed limit on this street is 25 mph.
17. The naacp played an active role in the civil rights movement in the 1960s.
18. My brother's name is Christopher John, but he likes to be called cj.
19. Because she loves animals, Heather volunteers for the aspca.
20. We flew into t. f. Green Airport in Providence, r.i.

SPEAKING APPLICATION

Make up an acronym and use it in a sentence. Share your sentence with a partner, who will guess what the acronym stands for. Explain the acronym if necessary.

WRITING APPLICATION

Address a letter envelope to a relative or acquaintance. Use the person's title and full name, including middle initial. Use abbreviations for the street and state.

Quick-Write Extension

To help students synthesize and apply what they have learned about using capitalization in abbreviations, acronyms, and initials, have them write brief entries for an encyclopedia of not-for-profit organizations. Direct students to choose familiar organizations and write everything they know or can quickly research. Have students exercise care in the capitalization of their entries and exchange the entries with their partners to be checked for correctness.

Cumulative Review Chapters 25–26

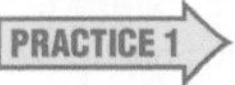

PRACTICE 1 Using Periods, Question Marks, and Exclamation Marks

Read the sentences. Then, rewrite the sentences, adding periods, question marks, and exclamation marks where needed.

1. Ana lives on St Charles Ave in New Orleans
2. Is he coming to the picnic
3. She asked if she left her umbrella here
4. Please set the table for dinner
5. What a brilliant student he is
6. Watch out for the monster
7. On what street is the office located
8. Yikes Did I forget your birthday
9. The stranger knocked on every door Why
10. How excited I am about the concert

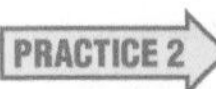

PRACTICE 2 Using Commas Correctly

Read the sentences. Then, rewrite the sentences, adding commas where needed. If a sentence is correct as is, write *correct*.

1. To get enough calcium drink plenty of milk.
2. A pencil would work but a pen would be better.
3. The gerbil a small rodent resembles a hamster.
4. Josie said "So Agnes where are you going?"
5. His scarred rugged face showed character.
6. The news is in the paper on television and online.
7. They got those two black dogs in May 2008.
8. We served precisely 1211 meals on July 4 2009.
9. "You did well on the test of course" said Lee.
10. It's at 77 East Adams Street Chicago Illinois 60603.

PRACTICE 3 Using Colons, Semicolons, and Quotation Marks

Read the sentences. Then, rewrite the sentences, using colons, semicolons, and quotation marks where needed. If a sentence is correct as is, write *correct*.

1. Dad likes tennis, however, he likes golf more.
2. Please buy the following milk, eggs, and bread.
3. Who said, Whatever you are, be a good one?
4. Yes, said Mrs. Ross, the class ends at 330.
5. The artist has a new exhibit, I love her work.
6. Caution Do not walk between the subway cars.
7. Marla asked, Did you see my hat anywhere?
8. How I enjoyed the poem The Highwayman!
9. Tomas asked that we turn off our cellphones.
10. Originating in Africa are okra, a plant, gumbo, a stew, and the banjo, a musical instrument.

PRACTICE 4 Using Apostrophes Correctly

Read the sentences. Then, rewrite the sentences, adding or removing apostrophes as needed. If a sentence is correct as is, write *correct*.

1. This is clearly Lucas's work and nobody elses.
2. Jans not here and cant help with Als homework.
3. The dog gnaws on it's bone when its hungry.
4. Most students' grades are A's or B's.
5. The Greek myth described Zeus's anger.
6. My sister Sarahs photo is in the yearbook.
7. I'm shocked that you dont tell her shes right.
8. Hers is the nicest shop on Main Street.
9. Randy would'nt go anywhere on Friday's.
10. Please indicate whats theirs and whats yours.

Continued on next page ▶

PRACTICE 1

1. Ana lives on St. Charles Ave. in New Orleans.
2. Is he coming to the picnic?
3. She asked if she left her umbrella here.
4. Please set the table for dinner.
5. What a brilliant student he is!
6. Watch out for the monster!
7. On what street is the office located?
8. Yikes! Did I forget your birthday?
9. The stranger knocked on every door. Why?
10. How excited I am about the concert!

PRACTICE 2

1. To get enough calcium, drink plenty of milk.
2. A pencil would work, but a pen would be better.
3. The gerbil, a small rodent, resembles a hamster.
4. Josie said, "So, Agnes, where are you going?"
5. His scarred, rugged face showed character.
6. The news is in the paper, on television, and online.
7. correct
8. We served precisely 1,211 meals on July 4, 2009.
9. "You did well on the test, of course," said Lee.
10. It's at 77 East Adams Street, Chicago, Illinois 60603.

PRACTICE 3

1. Dad likes tennis; however, he likes golf more.
2. Please buy the following: milk, eggs, and bread.
3. Who said, "Whatever you are, be a good one"?
4. "Yes," said Mrs. Ross, "the class ends at 3:30."
5. The artist has a new exhibit; I love her work.
6. Caution: Do not walk between the subway cars.
7. Marla asked, "Did you see my hat anywhere?"
8. How I enjoyed the poem "The Highwayman"!
9. correct
10. Originating in Africa are okra, a plant; gumbo, a stew; and the banjo, a musical instrument.

PRACTICE 4

1. This is clearly Lucas's work and nobody else's.
2. Jan's not here and can't help with Al's homework.
3. The dog gnaws on its bone when it's hungry.
4. correct
5. The Greek myth described Zeus' anger.
6. My sister Sarah's photo is in the yearbook.
7. I'm shocked that you don't tell her she's right.
8. correct
9. Randy wouldn't go anywhere on Fridays.
10. Please indicate what's theirs and what's yours.

Cumulative Review Chapters 25–26

Using Underlining (or Italics), Hyphens, Dashes, Parentheses, Brackets, and Ellipses

Read the sentences. Then, rewrite the sentences, adding underlining (or italics if you type your answers on the computer), hyphens, dashes, brackets, parentheses, and ellipses. If a sentence is correct as is, write *correct*.

1. My brother in law is a self taught tennis player.
2. Who wrote the novel To Kill a Mockingbird?
3. The book is set during World War I 1914–1918.
4. We invited Gretchen she is a new student to come to the tryouts for the school play.
5. The paper published her nicely written letter.
6. In her speech, the mayor said, "He Mr. Rodriguez did a great service for our city."
7. Our founders accepted as "unalienable rights . . . Life, Liberty, and the Pursuit of Happiness."
8. The legislature voted on the bill. See page 3 for a list of members' votes column 1.
9. The ship on which Columbus himself sailed was the Santa Maria.
10. Sandra's goal an Olympic medal seemed as distant as ever.

Using Correct Capitalization

Read the sentences. Then, rewrite each sentence, using capital letters where needed.

1. the american revolution formally ended with the signing of the treaty of paris.
2. t. s. eliot, a british author born in america, wrote the poem "the love song of j. alfred prufrock."
3. each spring, grandpa buys good guys fertilizer.
4. author toni morrison has won the nobel prize in literature.
5. visiting the northwest, we saw mount hood.
6. the planet venus is named for the roman goddess venus, whom the greeks called aphrodite.
7. "the last time doctor abis left the usa for a vacation," ingrid said, "was in june of 2007."
8. the high museum of art is just east of interstate 85 at 1280 peachtree street in atlanta, georgia.
9. metro networks monitors traffic conditions in the new york area from atop the empire state building.
10. the current president of the united states belongs to the democratic party.
11. is aunt margie a member of the aarp?
12. We spoke with reverend graves last sunday.
13. "i met ms. lee," said ian, "last summer in iowa."
14. my cousin takes biology 101 at duke university.
15. the vedas are sacred scriptures of hinduism.

Writing Sentences With Correct Capitalization

Read the following items. Then, write a sentence about each item. Be sure to use correct capitalization.

1. a local politician
2. a famous or local zoo
3. your favorite beach or park
4. your favorite movie
5. a novel that you really liked or really disliked

PRACTICE 5

1. My brother-in-law is a self-taught tennis player.
2. Who wrote the novel <u>To Kill a Mockingbird</u>? *or* Who wrote the novel *To Kill a Mockingbird*?
3. The book is set during World War I (1914–1918).
4. We invited Gretchen—she is a new student—to come to the tryouts for the school play.
5. correct
6. In her speech, the mayor said, "He [Mr. Rodriguez] did a great service for our city."
7. correct
8. The legislature voted on the bill. (See page 3 for a list of members' votes [column 1].)
9. The ship on which Columbus himself sailed was the <u>Santa Maria</u>. *or* The ship on which Columbus himself sailed was the *Santa Maria*.
10. Sandra's goal—an Olympic medal—seemed as distant as ever.

PRACTICE 6

1. The American Revolution formally ended with the signing of the Treaty of Paris.
2. T. S. Eliot, a British author born in America, wrote the poem "The Love Song of J. Alfred Prufrock."
3. Each spring, Grandpa buys Good Guys fertilizer.
4. Author Toni Morrison has won the Nobel Prize in Literature.
5. Visiting the Northwest, we saw Mount Hood.
6. The planet Venus is named for the Roman goddess Venus, whom the Greeks called Aphrodite.
7. "The last time Doctor Abis left the USA for a vacation," Ingrid said, "was in June of 2007."
8. The High Museum of Art is just east of Interstate 85 at 1280 Peachtree Street in Atlanta, Georgia.
9. Metro Networks monitors traffic conditions in the New York area from atop the Empire State Building.
10. The current president of the United States belongs to the Democratic Party.
11. Is Aunt Margie a member of the AARP?
12. We spoke with Reverend Graves last Sunday.
13. "I met Ms. Lee," said Ian, "last summer in Iowa."
14. My cousin takes Biology 101 at Duke University.
15. The Vedas are sacred scriptures of Hinduism.

PRACTICE 7

Answers will vary. Sample answers:

1. Mayor Daley was in Grant Park on Sunday.
2. An amazing children's clock chimes outside the Central Park Zoo in New York City.
3. I love the shell-strewn beach in Key West, Florida.
4. My favorite movie is <u>The Dark Knight</u>. *or* My favorite movie is *The Dark Knight*.
5. I loved the humor in <u>The Adventures of Huckleberry Finn</u> by Mark Twain. *or* I loved the humor in *The Adventures of Huckleberry Finn* by Mark Twain.

RESOURCES FOR Writing COACH

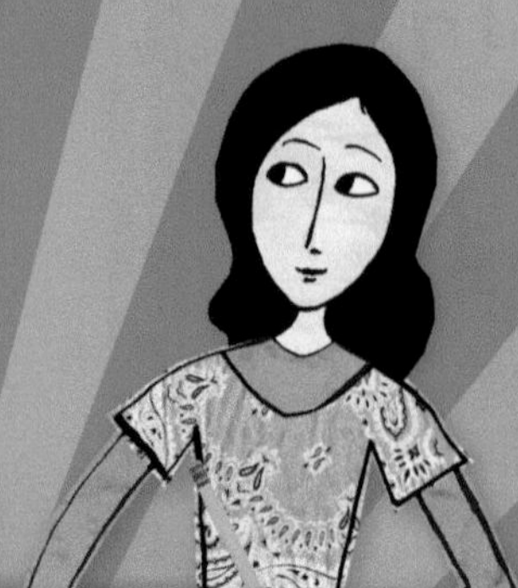

WRITING IN THE *Content Areas*

Writing in the content areas—math, social studies, science, the arts, and various career and technical studies—is an important tool for learning. The following pages give examples of content area writing along with strategies.

FORMS OF MATH WRITING

Written Estimate An estimate, or informed idea, of the size, cost, time, or other measure of a thing, based on given information.

Analysis of a Problem A description of a problem, such as figuring out how long a trip will take, along with an explanation of the mathematical formulas or equations you can use to solve the problem.

Response to an Open-Ended Math Prompt A response to a question or writing assignment involving math, such as a word problem or a question about a graph or a mathematical concept.

Writing in Math

Prewriting

- **Choosing a Topic** If you have a choice of topics, review your textbook and class notes for ideas, and choose one that interests you.
- **Responding to a Prompt** If you are responding to a prompt, read and then reread the instructions, ensuring that you understand all of the requirements of the assignment.

Drafting

- **State Problems Clearly** Be clear, complete, and accurate in your description of the problem you are analyzing or reporting on. Make sure that you have used technical terms, such as *ratio*, *area*, and *factor*, accurately.
- **Explain Your Solution** Tell readers exactly which mathematical rules or formulas you use in your analysis and why they apply. Clearly spell out each step you take in your reasoning.
- **Use Graphics** By presenting quantitative information in a graph, table, or chart, you make it easier for readers to absorb information. Choose the format appropriate to the material, as follows:
  - ✔ **Line Graphs** Use a line graph to show the relationship between two variables, such as time and speed in a problem about a moving object. Clearly label the x- and y-axis with the variable each represents and with the units you are using. Choose units appropriately to make the graph manageable. For example, do not try to represent time in years if you are plotting changes for an entire century; instead, use units of ten years each.
  - ✔ **Other Graphs** Use a pie chart to analyze facts about a group, such as the percentage of students who walk to school, the percentage who drive, and the percentage who take the bus. Use a bar graph to compare two or more things at different times or in different categories. Assign a single color to each thing, and use that color consistently for all the bars representing data about that thing.
  - ✔ **Tables** Use a table to help readers look up specific values quickly, such as the time the sun sets in each month of the year. Label each column and row with terms that clearly identify the data you are presenting, including the units you are using.

Revising

- **Ensure Accuracy** For accuracy, double-check the formulas you use and the calculations you make.
- **Revise for Traits of Good Writing** Ask yourself the following questions: *How well have I applied mathematical ideas? Does my organizational plan help readers follow my reasoning? Is my voice suitable to my audience and purpose? Have I chosen precise words and used mathematical terms accurately? Are my sentences well constructed and varied? Have I made any errors in grammar, usage, mechanics, and spelling?* Use your answers to help you revise and edit your work.

Writing in Science

Prewriting

- **Choosing a Topic** If you have a choice of topics, look through class notes and your textbook, or conduct a "media flip-through," browsing online articles, or watching television news and documentaries to find a science-related topic.
- **Responding to a Prompt** If you are responding to a prompt, read the instructions carefully, analyzing the requirements and parts of the assignment. Identify key direction words in the prompt or assignment, such as *explain* and *predict*.
- **Gathering Details**
  - ✔ If your assignment requires you to conduct research, search for credible and current sources. Examples of strong sources may include articles in recent issues of science magazines or recently published books. Confirm key facts in more than one source.
  - ✔ If your assignment requires you to conduct an experiment, make sure you follow the guidelines for the experiment accurately. Carefully record the steps you take and the observations you make, and date your notes. Repeat the experiment to confirm results.

Drafting

- **Focus and Elaborate** In your introduction, clearly state your topic. Make sure you tell readers why your topic matters. As you draft, give sufficient details, including background, facts, and examples, to help your readers understand your topic. Summarize your findings and insights in your conclusion.
- **Organize** As you draft, follow a suitable organizational pattern. If you are telling the story of an important scientific breakthrough, consider telling events in chronological order. If you are explaining a natural process, consider discussing causes and the effects that follow from them. If you are defending a solution to a problem, you might give pros and cons, answering each counterargument in turn.
- **Present Data Visually** Consider presenting quantitative information, such as statistics or measurements, in a graph, table, or chart. Choose the format appropriate to the material. (Consult the guidance on visual displays of data under "Use Graphics" on page R2.)

Revising

- **Meet Your Audience's Needs** Identify places in your draft where your audience may need more information, such as additional background, more explanation, or the definition of a technical term. Add the information required.
- **Revise for Traits of Good Writing** Ask yourself the following questions: *How clearly have I presented scientific ideas? Will my organization help a reader see the connections I am making? Is my voice suitable to my audience and purpose? Have I chosen precise words and used technical terms accurately? Are my sentences well constructed and varied? Have I made any errors in grammar, usage, mechanics, and spelling?* Use your answers to revise and edit your work.

FORMS OF SCIENCE WRITING

Lab Report A firsthand report of a scientific experiment, following an appropriate format. A standard lab report includes a statement of the hypothesis, or prediction, that the experiment is designed to test; a list of the materials used; an account of the steps performed; a report of the results observed; and the experimenter's conclusions.

Cause-and-Effect Essay A scientific explanation of the causes and effects involved in natural or technical phenomena, such as solar flares, the digestion of food, or the response of metal to stress.

Technical Procedure Document A step-by-step guide to performing a scientific experiment or performing a technical task involving science. A well-written technical procedure document presents the steps of the procedure in clear order. It breaks steps into substeps and prepares readers by explaining what materials they will need and the time they can expect each step to take.

Response to an Open-Ended Science Prompt A response to a question or writing assignment about science.

Summary of a Science-Related Article A retelling of the main ideas in an article that concerns science or technology, such as an article on a new medical procedure.

Writing in Social Studies

FORMS OF SOCIAL STUDIES WRITING

Social Studies Research Report An informative paper, based on research, about a historical period or event or about a specific place or culture. A well-written research report draws on a variety of sources to develop and support a thoughtful point of view on the topic. It cites those sources accurately, following an accepted format.

Biographical Essay An overview of the life of a historically important person. A well-written biographical essay reports the life of its subject accurately and clearly explains the importance of his or her contributions.

Historical Overview A survey, or general picture, of a historical period or development, such as the struggle for women's right to vote. A successful historical overview presents the "big picture," covering major events and important aspects of the topic without getting lost in details.

Historical Cause-and-Effect Essay An analysis of the causes and effects of a historical event. A well-written historical explanation makes clear connections between events to help readers follow the explanation.

Prewriting

- **Choosing a Topic** If you have a choice of topics, find a suitable topic by looking through class notes and your textbook. Make a quick list of topics in history, politics, or geography that interest you and choose a topic based on your list.
- **Responding to a Prompt** If you are responding to a prompt, read the instructions carefully, analyzing the requirements and parts of the assignment. Identify key direction words in the prompt or assignment, such as *compare*, *describe*, and *argue*.
- **Gathering Details** If your assignment requires you to conduct research, consult a variety of credible sources. For in-depth research, review both primary sources (documents from the time you are investigating) and secondary sources (accounts by those who analyze or report on the information). If you find contradictions, evaluate the likely reasons for the differences.

Drafting

- **Establish a Thesis or Theme** If you are writing a research report or other informative piece, state your main point about your topic in a thesis statement. Include your thesis statement in your introduction. If you are writing a creative piece, such as a historical skit or short story, identify the theme, or main message, you wish to convey.
- **Support Your Thesis or Theme** Organize your work around your main idea.
  - ✔ In a research report, support and develop your thesis with well-chosen, relevant details. First, provide background information your readers will need, and then discuss different subtopics in different sections of the body of your report. Clearly connect each subtopic to your main thesis.
  - ✔ In a creative work, develop your theme through the conflict between characters. For example, a conflict between two brothers during the Civil War over which side to fight on might dramatize the theme of divided loyalties. Organize events to build to a climax, or point of greatest excitement, that clearly conveys your message.

Revising

- **Sharpen Your Focus** Review your draft for sections that do not clearly support your thesis or theme, and consider eliminating them. Revise unnecessary repetition of ideas. Ensure that the sequence of ideas or events will help reader comprehension.
- **Revise for Traits of Good Writing** Ask yourself the following questions: *How clearly have I developed my thesis or my theme? Will my organization help a reader follow my development of my thesis or theme? Is my voice suitable to my audience and purpose? Have I chosen precise and vivid words, accurately using terms from the period or place about which I am writing? Are my sentences well constructed and varied? Have I made any errors in grammar, usage, mechanics, and spelling?* Use your answers to revise and edit your work.

Writing About the Arts

Prewriting

Experience the Work Take notes on the subject of each work you will discuss. Consider its mood, or general feeling, and its theme, or insight into life.

- ✔ For visual arts, consider the use of color, light, line (sharp or smooth, smudged or definite), mass (heavy or light), and composition (the arrangement and balance of forms).
- ✔ For music, consider the use of melody, rhythm, harmony, and instrumentation. Also, consider the performers' interpretation of the work.

Drafting

Develop Your Ideas As you draft, support your main ideas, including your insights into or feelings about a work, with relevant details.

Revising

Revise for Traits of Good Writing Ask yourself the following questions: *How clearly do I present my ideas? Will my organization help a reader follow my points? Is my voice suitable to my audience and purpose? Have I chosen precise and vivid words, to describe the works? Are my sentences varied? Have I made any errors in grammar, usage, and mechanics?* Use your answers to revise and edit your work.

FORMS OF WRITING ABOUT THE ARTS

Research Report on a Trend or Style in Art An informative paper, based on research, about a specific group of artists or trend in the arts.

Biographical Essay An overview of the life of an artist or performer.

Analysis of a Work A detailed description of a work offering insights into its meaning and importance.

Review of a Performance or Exhibit An evaluation of an artistic performance or exhibit.

Writing in Career and Technical Studies

Prewriting

Choosing a Topic If you have a choice of topics, find a suitable one by looking through class notes and your textbook or by listing your own related projects or experiences.

Drafting

Organize Information As you draft, follow a logical organization. If you are explaining a procedure, list steps in the order that your readers should follow. If they need information about the materials and preparation required, provide that information first. Use formatting (such as headings, numbered steps, and bullet points), graphics (such as diagrams), and transitional words and phrases (such as *first*, *next*, and *if… then*).

Revising

Revise for Traits of Good Writing Ask yourself the following questions: *Have I given readers all the information they will need? Will my organization help a reader follow my points? Is my voice suitable to my audience and purpose? Have I chosen precise words, using technical terms accurately? Are my sentences well constructed? Have I made errors in grammar, usage, and mechanics?* Use your answers to revise and edit your work.

FORMS OF CAREER AND TECHNICAL WRITING

Technical Procedure Document A step-by-step guide to performing a specialized task, such as wiring a circuit or providing first aid.

Response to an Open-Ended Practical Studies Prompt A response to a question or writing assignment about a task or concept in a specialized field.

Technical Research Report An informative paper, based on research, about a specific topic in a practical field, such as a report on balanced diet in the field of health.

Analysis of a Career An informative paper explaining the requirements for a particular job, along with the responsibilities, salary, benefits, and job opportunities.

WRITING FOR *Media*

New technology has created many new ways to communicate. Today, it is easy to contribute information to the Internet and send a variety of messages to friends far and near. You can also share your ideas through photos, illustrations, video, and sound recordings.

Writing for Media gives you an overview of some ways you can use today's technology to create, share, and find information. **Here are the topics you will find in this section:**

- **Blogs**
- **Social Networking**
- **Widgets and Feeds**
- **Multimedia Elements**
- **Podcasts**
- **Wikis**

Blogs

A **blog** is a common form of online writing. The word *blog* is a contraction of *Web log*. Most blogs include a series of entries known as posts. The posts appear in a single column and are displayed in reverse chronological order. That means that the most recent post is at the top of the page. As you scroll down, you will find earlier posts.

Blogs have become increasingly popular. Researchers estimate that 75,000 new blogs are launched every day. Blog authors are often called bloggers. They can use their personal sites to share ideas, songs, videos, photos, and other media. People who read blogs can often post their responses with a comments feature found in each new post.

Because blogs are designed so that they are easy to update, bloggers can post new messages as often as they like, often daily. For some people blogs become a public journal or diary in which they share their thoughts about daily events.

Types of Blogs

Not all blogs are the same. Many blogs have a single author, but others are group projects. These are some common types of blog:

- **Personal blogs** often have a general focus. Bloggers post their thoughts on any topic they find interesting in their daily lives.
- **Topical blogs** focus on a specific theme, such as movie reviews, political news, class assignments, or health-care opportunities.

WEB
SAFETY

Using the Internet safely means keeping personal information personal. Never include your address (e-mail or physical), last name, or telephone numbers. Avoid mentioning places you go to often.

Never give out passwords you use to access other Web sites and do not respond to e-mails from people you do not know.

Anatomy of a Blog

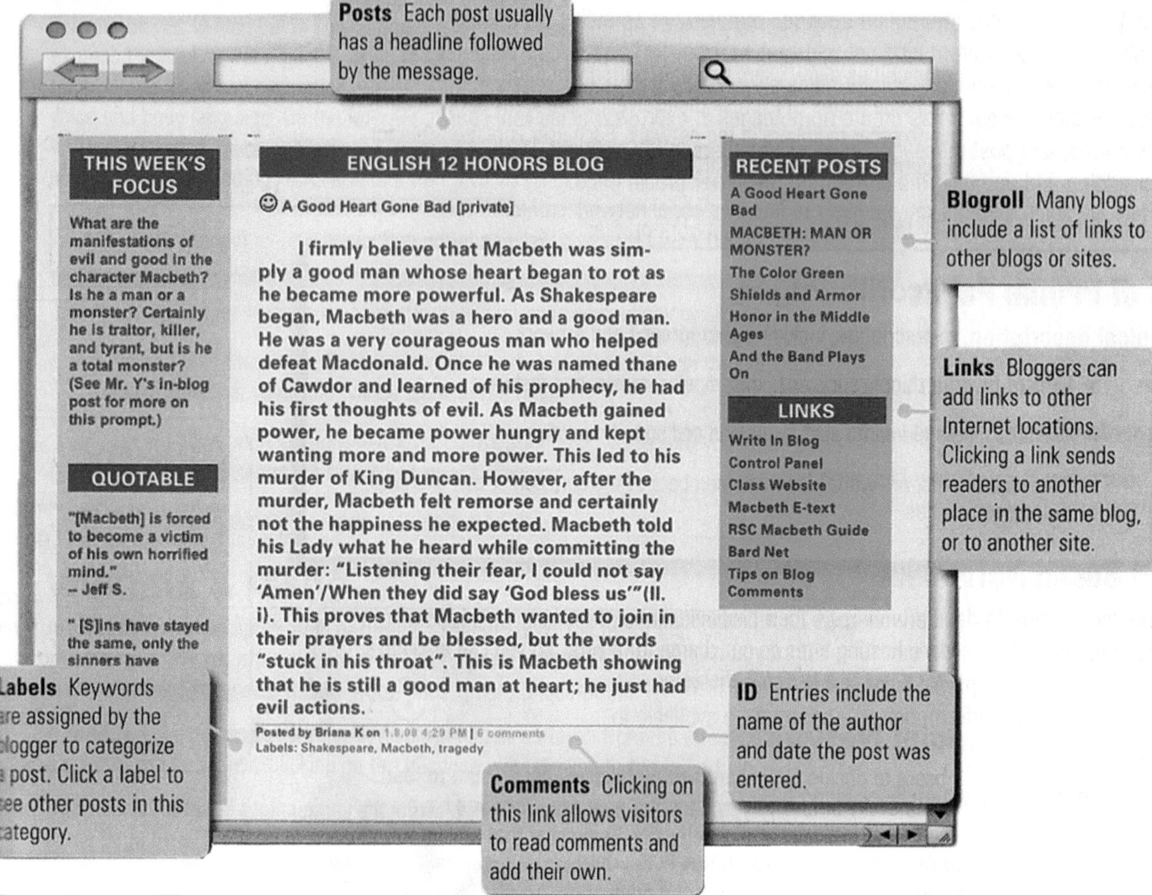

Posts Each post usually has a headline followed by the message.
THIS WEEK'S FOCUS
What are the manifestations of evil and good in the character Macbeth? Is he a man or a monster? Certainly he is traitor, killer, and tyrant, but is he a total monster? (See Mr. Y's in-blog post for more on this prompt.)
QUOTABLE
"[Macbeth] is forced to become a victim of his own horrified mind." – Jeff S.
" [S]ins have stayed the same, only the sinners have
ENGLISH 12 HONORS BLOG
A Good Heart Gone Bad [private]
I firmly believe that Macbeth was simply a good man whose heart began to rot as he became more powerful. As Shakespeare began, Macbeth was a hero and a good man. He was a very courageous man who helped defeat Macdonald. Once he was named thane of Cawdor and learned of his prophecy, he had his first thoughts of evil. As Macbeth gained power, he became power hungry and kept wanting more and more power. This led to his murder of King Duncan. However, after the murder, Macbeth felt remorse and certainly not the happiness he expected. Macbeth told his Lady what he heard while committing the murder: "Listening their fear, I could not say 'Amen'/When they did say 'God bless us'"(II. i). This proves that Macbeth wanted to join in their prayers and be blessed, but the words "stuck in his throat". This is Macbeth showing that he is still a good man at heart; he just had evil actions.
Posted by Briana K on
Labels: Shakespeare, Macbeth, tragedy
RECENT POSTS
A Good Heart Gone Bad
MACBETH: MAN OR MONSTER?
The Color Green
Shields and Armor
Honor in the Middle Ages
And the Band Plays On
LINKS
Write In Blog
Control Panel
Class Website
Macbeth E-text
RSC Macbeth Guide
Bard Net
Tips on Blog Comments
Blogroll Many blogs include a list of links to other blogs or sites.
Links Bloggers can add links to other Internet locations. Clicking a link sends readers to another place in the same blog, or to another site.
Labels Keywords are assigned by the blogger to categorize a post. Click a label to see other posts in this category.
ID Entries include the name of the author and date the post was entered.
Comments Clicking on this link allows visitors to read comments and add their own.

Creating a Blog

Keep these hints and strategies in mind to help you create an interesting and fair blog:

- Focus each blog entry on a single topic.
- Vary the length of your posts. Sometimes, all you need is a line or two to share a quick thought. Other posts will be much longer.
- Choose font colors and styles that can be read easily.
- Many people scan blogs rather than read them closely. You can make your main ideas pop out by using clear or clever headlines and boldfacing key terms.
- Give credit to other people's work and ideas. State the names of people whose ideas you are quoting or add a link to take readers to that person's blog or site.
- If you post comments, try to make them brief and polite.

Social Networking

Social networking means any interaction between members of an online community. People can exchange many different kinds of information, from text and voice messages to video images. Many social network communities allow users to create permanent pages that describe themselves. Users create home pages to express themselves, share ideas about their lives, and post messages to other members in the network. Each user is responsible for adding and updating the content on his or her profile page.

Here are some features you are likely to find on a social network profile:

Features of Profile Pages

- A **biographical description**, including photographs and artwork
- **Lists of favorite things**, such as books, movies, music, and fashions
- **Playable media** elements such as videos and sound recordings
- **Message boards**, or "walls," on which members of the community can exchange messages

Privacy in Social Networks

Social networks allow users to decide how open their profiles will be. Be sure to read introductory information carefully before you register at a new site. Once you have a personal profile page, monitor your privacy settings regularly. Remember that any information you post will be available to anyone in your network.

Users often post messages anonymously or using false names, or pseudonyms. People can also post using someone else's name. Judge all information on the net critically. Do not assume that you know who posted some information simply because you recognize the name of the post author. The rapid speed of communication on the Internet can make it easy to jump to conclusions—be careful to avoid this trap.

You can create a social network page for an individual or a group, such as a school or special interest club. Many hosting sites do not charge to register, so you can also have fun by creating a page for a pet or a fictional character.

Tips for Sending Effective Messages

Technology makes it easy to share ideas quickly, but writing for the Internet poses some special challenges. The writing style for blogs and social networks is often very conversational. In blog posts and comments, instant messages, and e-mails, writers often express themselves very quickly, using relaxed language, short sentences, and abbreviations. However in a face-to-face conversation, we get a lot of information from a speaker's tone of voice and body language. On the Internet, those clues are missing. As a result, Internet writers often use italics or bracketed labels to indicate emotions. Another alternative is using emoticons—strings of characters that give visual clues to indicate emotion.

:-) **smile** *(happy)* :-(**frown** *(unhappy)* ;-) **wink** *(light sarcasm)*

Use these strategies to communicate effectively when using technology:

- ✓ *Before you click Send,* ***reread your message*** *to make sure that your tone is clear.*
- ✓ ***Do not jump to conclusions****—ask for clarification first. Make sure you really understand what someone is saying before you respond.*
- ✓ ***Use abbreviations*** *your reader will understand.*

Widgets and Feeds

A **widget** is a small application that performs a specific task. You might find widgets that give weather predictions, offer dictionary definitions or translations, provide entertainment such as games, or present a daily word, photograph, or quotation.

A **feed** is a special kind of widget. It displays headlines taken from the latest content on a specific media source. Clicking on the headline will take you to the full article. Many social network communities and other Web sites allow you to personalize your home page by adding widgets and feeds.

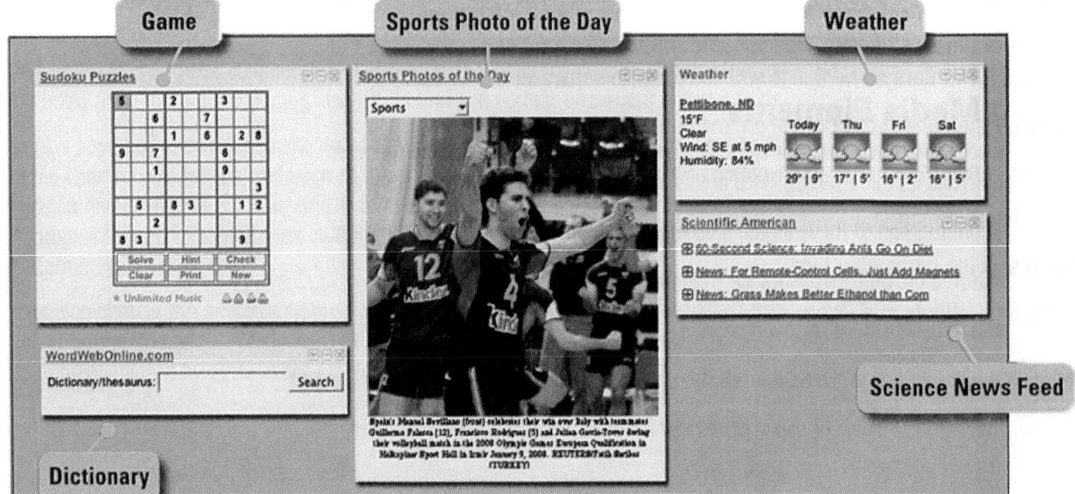

Multimedia Elements

One of the great advantages of communicating on the Internet is that you are not limited to using text only. When you create a Web profile or blog, you can share your ideas using a wide variety of media. In addition to widgets and feeds (see page R9), these media elements can make your Internet communication more entertaining and useful.

GRAPHICS	
Photographs	You can post photographs taken by digital cameras or scanned as files.
Illustrations	Artwork can be created using computer software. You can also use a scanner to post a digital image of a drawing or sketch.
Charts, Graphs, and Maps	Charts and graphs can make statistical information clear. Use spreadsheet software to create these elements. Use Internet sites to find maps of specific places.

VIDEO	
Live Action	Digital video can be recorded by a camera or recorded from another media source.
Animation	Animated videos can also be created using software.

AUDIO	
Music	Many social network communities make it easy to share your favorite music with people who visit your page.
Voice	Use a microphone to add your own voice to your Web page.

Editing Media Elements

You can use software to customize media elements. Open source software is free and available to anyone on the Internet. Here are some things you can do with software:

- **Crop** a photograph to focus on the subject or brighten an image that is too dark.
- **Transform** a drawing's appearance from flat to three-dimensional.
- **Insert** a "You Are Here" arrow on a map.
- **Edit** a video or sound file to shorten its running time.
- **Add** background music or sound effects to a video.

Podcasts

A **podcast** is a digital audio or video recording of a program that is made available on the Internet. Users can replay the podcast on a computer, or download it and replay it on a personal audio player. You might think of podcasts as radio or television programs that you create yourself. They can be embedded on a Web site or fed to a Web page through a podcast widget.

Creating an Effective Podcast

To make a podcast, you will need a recording device, such as a microphone or digital video camera, as well as editing software. Open source editing software is widely available and free of charge. Most audio podcasts are converted into the MP3 format. Here are some tips for creating a podcast that is clear and entertaining:

- **Listen to several podcasts by different authors** to get a feeling for the medium.
- **Make a list** of features and styles you like and also those you want to avoid.
- **Test your microphone** to find the best recording distance. Stand close enough to the microphone so that your voice sounds full, but not so close that you create an echo.
- **Create an outline** that shows your estimated timing for each element.
- **Be prepared** before you record. Rehearse, but do not create a script. Podcasts are best when they have a natural, easy flow.
- **Talk directly to your listeners**. Slow down enough so they can understand you.
- Use software to **edit your podcast before publishing it**. You can edit out mistakes or add additional elements.

Wikis

A **wiki** is a collaborative Web site that lets visitors create, add, remove, and edit content. The term comes from the Hawaiian phrase *wikiwiki*, which means "quick." Web users of a wiki are both the readers and the writers of the site. Some wikis are open to contributions from anyone. Others require visitors to register before they can edit the content. All of the text in these collaborative Web sites was written by people who use the site. Articles are constantly changing, as visitors find and correct errors and improve texts.

Wikis have both advantages and disadvantages as sources of information. They are valuable open forums for the exchange of ideas. The unique collaborative writing process allows entries to change over time. However, entries can also be modified incorrectly. Careless or malicious users can delete good content and add inappropriate or inaccurate information. Wikis may be useful for gathering background information, but should not be used as research resources.

You can change the information on a wiki, but be sure your information is correct and clear before you add it. Wikis keep track of all changes, so your work will be recorded and can be evaluated by other users.

WRITING FOR THE *Workplace*

Writing is something many people do every day at work, school, or home. They write letters and reports, do research, plan meetings, and keep track of information in notes.

Writing for the Workplace shows you some models of the following forms of writing:

- **Note Cards**
- **Meeting Agenda**
- **Business Letter**
- **Friendly Letter**

Creating Note Cards

Whether you are working on a research report or gathering information for another purpose, it is helpful to keep your notes on individual cards or in note files on a computer. You will need to make sure that you note your sources on your cards. You can organize information many different ways, but it is most helpful to keep notes of one kind together.

You can name the **source**, as shown here, or refer to the source by number (e.g., Source 3) if you are using source cards.

The **topic** is the main focus of the notes.

Topic: Octopus

Source: PBS Web site Accessed 10/15/2010

http://www.pbs.org/wnet/nature/episodes/ the-octopus-show/ a-legend-of-the-deep/2014/

- Acrobatic and shy animals
- Can squeeze into very small spaces to hide or catch food
- Talented swimmers
- Can change color
- Live in all kinds of environments

In the notes section focus on the ideas that are most important to your research. Note that these ideas may not always be the main ideas of the selection you are reading. You do not need to write in full sentences. However, you may want to use bullets to make your notes easier to read.

Writing a Meeting Agenda

When you have a meeting, it is helpful to use an agenda. An agenda tells what will be discussed in the meeting. It tells who is responsible for which topic. It also provides a guide for the amount of time to be spent on each topic.

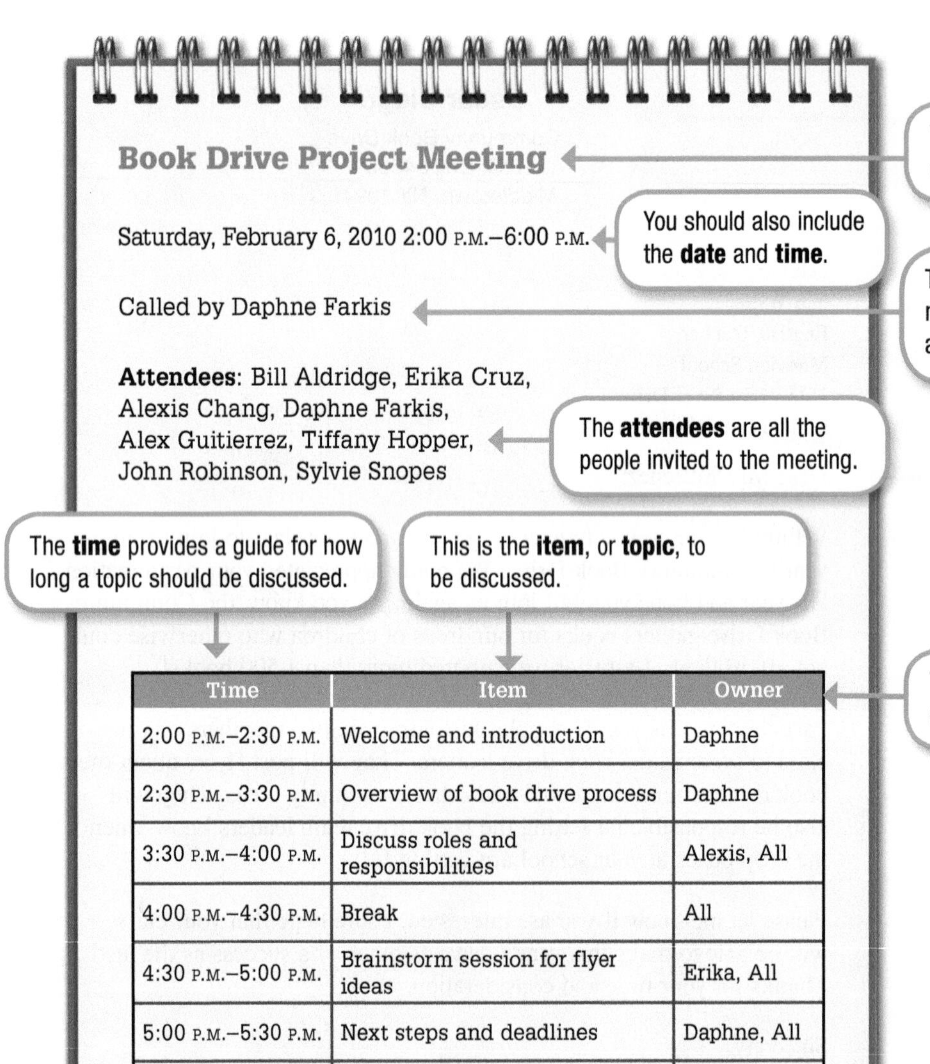
Book Drive Project Meeting
Your meeting will need a **title** that explains the purpose of the meeting.
Saturday, February 6, 2010 2:00 P.M.–6:00 P.M.
You should also include the **date** and **time**.
Called by Daphne Farkis
This is the person who **called** the meeting. The person often, but not always, leads parts of the meeting.
Attendees: Bill Aldridge, Erika Cruz, Alexis Chang, Daphne Farkis, Alex Guitierrez, Tiffany Hopper, John Robinson, Sylvie Snopes
The **attendees** are all the people invited to the meeting.
The **time** provides a guide for how long a topic should be discussed.
This is the **item**, or **topic**, to be discussed.
The **owner** is the person who will lead each section of the meeting.

Time	Item	Owner
2:00 P.M.–2:30 P.M.	Welcome and introduction	Daphne
2:30 P.M.–3:30 P.M.	Overview of book drive process	Daphne
3:30 P.M.–4:00 P.M.	Discuss roles and responsibilities	Alexis, All
4:00 P.M.–4:30 P.M.	Break	All
4:30 P.M.–5:00 P.M.	Brainstorm session for flyer ideas	Erika, All
5:00 P.M.–5:30 P.M.	Next steps and deadlines	Daphne, All
5:30 P.M.–6:00 P.M.	Recap and adjournment	Daphne

Writing Business Letters

Business letters are often formal in tone and written for a specific business purpose. They generally follow one of several acceptable formats. In block format, all parts of the letter are at the left margin. All business letters, however, have the same parts: heading, inside address, salutation, body, closing, and signature.

The **heading** shows the writer's address and organization (if any).

Oscar Diego
Community Book Drive
P.O. Box 34535
Middletown, NY 10941

The **inside address** indicates where the letter will be sent and the date.

February 10, 2010
Yin Wallenez
English Teacher
Marsden School
1515 Main River Drive
Middletown, NY 10940

A **salutation**, or **greeting,** is punctuated by a colon. When the specific addressee is not known, use a general greeting such as "To Whom It May Concern."

Dear Ms. Wallenez:

The **body** of the letter states the writer's purpose. In this case, the writer requests that the class participate in the book drive.

We are writing to you to encourage you and your class to join in this year's Community Book Drive. We really appreciated your participation last year and hope you will join us again. As you know, the Community Book Drive gathers books for hundreds of children who otherwise could not afford them. Last year we gathered more than 1,500 books!

Participating this year is simple. Just nominate two members of your class to serve as the book drive leaders. They will post flyers about the book drive around the school and other community areas. They will also be responsible for letting the book drive team leaders know when the drop boxes at your school are getting full.

Please let me know if you are interested. I sure hope that your class will be able to make this year's drive as much of a success as the last! Thanks for your time and consideration.

The **closing**, "Sincerely," is common, as are "Best regards," "Yours truly," and "Respectfully yours."

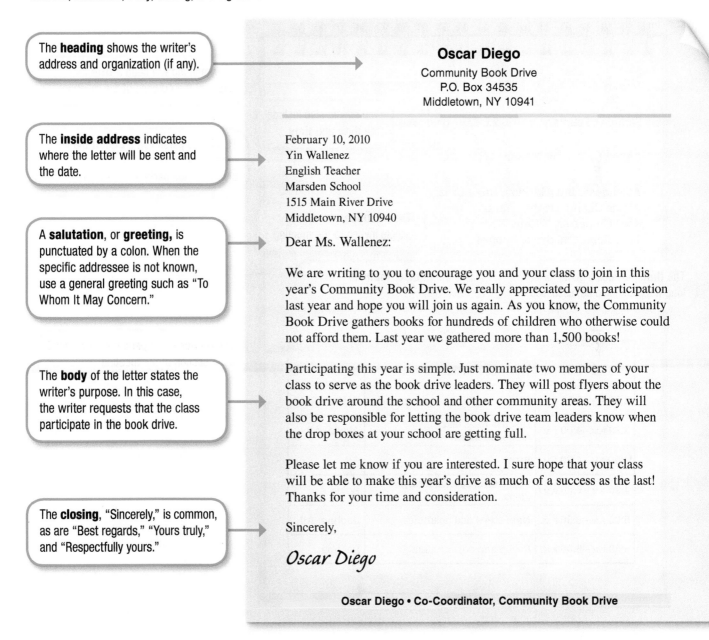

Sincerely,

Oscar Diego

Oscar Diego • Co-Coordinator, Community Book Drive

Writing Friendly Letters

Friendly letters are less formal than business letters. You can use this form to write to a friend, a family member, or anyone with whom you'd like to communicate in a personal, friendly way. Like business letters, friendly letters have the following parts: heading, inside address, salutation, body, closing, and signature. The purpose of a friendly letter might be:

- to share news and feelings
- to send or answer an invitation
- to express thanks

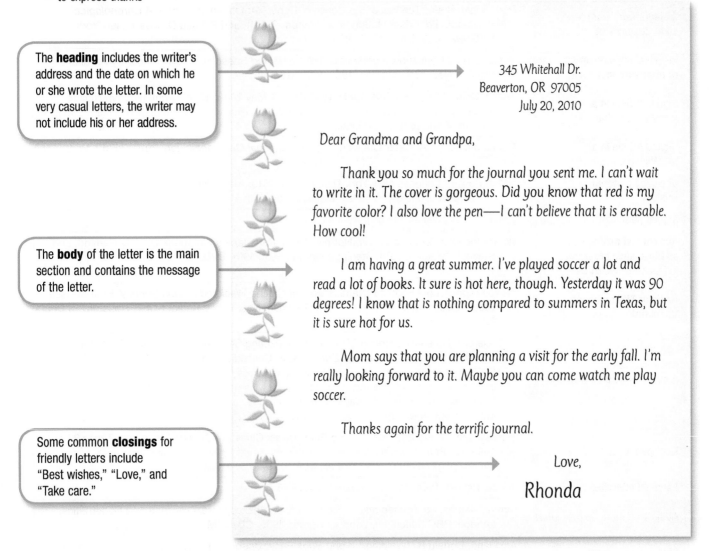

The **heading** includes the writer's address and the date on which he or she wrote the letter. In some very casual letters, the writer may not include his or her address.

345 Whitehall Dr.
Beaverton, OR 97005
July 20, 2010

Dear Grandma and Grandpa,

Thank you so much for the journal you sent me. I can't wait to write in it. The cover is gorgeous. Did you know that red is my favorite color? I also love the pen—I can't believe that it is erasable. How cool!

The **body** of the letter is the main section and contains the message of the letter.

I am having a great summer. I've played soccer a lot and read a lot of books. It sure is hot here, though. Yesterday it was 90 degrees! I know that is nothing compared to summers in Texas, but it is sure hot for us.

Mom says that you are planning a visit for the early fall. I'm really looking forward to it. Maybe you can come watch me play soccer.

Thanks again for the terrific journal.

Some common **closings** for friendly letters include "Best wishes," "Love," and "Take care."

Love,
Rhonda

MLA Style for Listing Sources

Book with one author	London, Jack. *White Fang.* Clayton: Prestwick, 2007. Print.
Book with two or three authors	Veit, Richard, and Christopher Gould. *Writing, Reading, and Research.* 8th ed. Boston: Wadsworth-Cengage Learning, 2009. Print.
Book prepared by an editor	Twain, Mark. *The Complete Essays of Mark Twain.* Ed. Charles Neider. New York: Da Capo, 2000. Print.
Book with more than three authors or editors	Donald, Robert B., et al. *Writing Clear Essays.* 3rd ed. Upper Saddle River: Prentice, 1996. Print.
A single work from an anthology	Poe, Edgar Allan. "The Fall of the House of Usher." *American Literature: A Chronological Approach.* Ed. Edgar H. Schuster, Anthony Tovatt, and Patricia O. Tovatt. New York: McGraw, 1985. 233–247. Print. [Indicate pages for the entire selection.]
Introduction, foreward, preface, or afterward in a book	Vidal, Gore. Introduction. *Abraham Lincoln: Selected Speeches and Writings.* By Abraham Lincoln. New York: Vintage, 1992. xxi–xxvii. Print.
Signed article in a weekly magazine	Walsh, Brian. "Greening This Old House." *Time* 4 May 2009: 45–47. Print. [For a multipage article that does not appear on consecutive pages, write only the first page number on which it appears, followed by a plus sign.]
Signed article in a monthly magazine	Fischman, Josh. "A Better Life with Bionics." *National Geographic* Jan. 2010: 34–53. Print.
Unsigned editorial or story	"Wind Power." Editorial. *New York Times* 9 Jan. 2010: A18. Print. [If the editorial or story is signed, begin with the author's name.]
Signed pamphlet	[Treat the pamphlet as though it were a book.]
Audiovisual media, such as films, slide programs, videocassettes, DVDs	*Where the Red Fern Grows.* Dir. Norman Toker. Perf. James Whitmore, Beverly Garland, and Stewart Peterson. 1974. Sterling Entertainment, 1997. DVD.
Radio or TV broadcast transcript	"Texas High School Football Titans Ready for Clash." *Weekend Edition Sunday.* Host Melissa Block. Guests Mike Pesca and Tom Goldman. Natl. Public Radio. KUHF, Houston, 18 Dec. 2009. Print. Transcript.
A single page on a Web site	U.S. Census Bureau: Customer Liaison and Marketing Services Office. "State Facts for Students: Texas." *U.S. Census Bureau.* U.S. Census Bureau, 15 Oct. 2009. Web. 1 Nov. 2009. [Indicate the date of last update if known or use "n.d." if not known. After the medium of publication, include the date you accessed the information. You do not need the URL unless it is the only way to find the page. If needed, include it in angled brackets at the end, i.e. <http://www.census.gov/schools/facts/texas.html >.]
Newspaper	Yardley, Jim. "Hurricane Sweeps into Rural Texas; Cities Are Spared." *New York Times* 23 Aug. 1999: A1. Print. [For a multipage article that does not appear on consecutive pages, write only the first page number on which it appears, followed by a plus sign.]
Personal interview	Jones, Robert. Personal interview. 4 Sept. 2006.
Audio with multiple publishers	Simms, James, ed. *Romeo and Juliet.* By William Shakespeare. Oxford: Attica Cybernetics; London: BBC Education; London: Harper, 1995. CD-ROM.
Signed article from an encyclopedia	Askeland, Donald R. "Welding." *World Book Encyclopedia.* 1991 ed. Print. [For a well-known reference, you do not need to include the publisher information, only the edition and year, followed by the medium used.]

Commonly Misspelled Words

The list on this page presents words that cause problems for many people. Some of these words are spelled according to set rules, but others follow no specific rules. As you review this list, check to see how many of the words give you trouble in your own writing.

absence
absolutely
accidentally
accurate
achievement
affect
agreeable
aisle
all right
allowance
analysis
analyze
ancient
anniversary
answer
anticipate
anxiety
apologize
appearance
appreciate
appropriate
argument
athletic
attendance
awkward
bargain
battery
beautiful
beginning
believe
benefit
bicycle
bought
brief
brilliant
bulletin
bury
buses
business
cafeteria
calendar
campaign
canceled
candidate
capital
capitol
career
cashier
category
ceiling
certain
changeable
characteristic
clothes
colonel
column
commercial
commitment
condemn
congratulate
conscience
conscientious
conscious
continuous
convenience
coolly
cooperate
correspondence
courageous
courteous
criticism
curiosity
deceive
decision
defendant
definitely
dependent
description
desert
dessert
dining
disappointed
distinguish
effect
eighth
embarrass
enthusiastic
envelope
environment
especially
excellent
exercise
experience
explanation
extension
extraordinary
familiar
fascinating
February
fiery
financial
foreign
fourth
generally
genuine
government
grammar
guidance
height
humorous
immediately
immigrant
independence
independent
individual
intelligence
judgment
knowledge
lawyer
legible
library
license
lightning
likable
literature
mathematics
maximum
minimum
misspell
naturally
necessary
neighbor
niece
ninety
noticeable
occasion
occasionally
occur
occurred
occurrence
opinion
opportunity
parallel
particularly
personally
persuade
physician
possibility
precede
preferable
prejudice
previous
probably
procedure
proceed
pronunciation
realize
really
receipt
receive
recognize
recommend
rehearse
repetition
restaurant
rhythm
sandwich
schedule
scissors
theater
truly
usage
valuable
various
vegetable
weight
weird
whale
yield

English Glossary

A

action (ak′shən) *n.* in a story or play, the events which are part of the plot

advantage (ad vant′ij) *n.* something that puts a person in a better position than others; a way in which one thing is better than another

analysis (ə nal′ə sis) *n.* the process of looking at something closely to understand its meaning, structure, or parts

analyze (an′ə līz) *v.* to look at something carefully to understand its meaning or structure

anticipate (an tis′ə pāt′) *v.* to expect or predict; to foresee and then be ready to deal with

argument (är′gyü mənt) *n.* a discussion (written or spoken) which aims to persuade; a set of statements putting forward and backing up an idea or position

audience (ô′dē əns) *n.* the readers of a book or other piece of writing; a group of listeners or viewers

authority (ə thôr′ə tē) *n.* a person or written work that is accepted as a source of reliable or expert information

C

cause (kôz) *n.* a person, object, or event that makes something happen

character (kar′ik tər) *n.* a person (or animal) who plays a part in the action of a story, play, or movie

chronological (krän′ə läj′i kəl) *adj.* described or arranged in the order of time, starting with what happened first

coherence (kō hir′ənts) *n.* the state of having ideas that are clear and logical

coherent (kō hir′ənt) *adj.* well-planned, clear, logical; holding together well

compare (kəm par′) *v.* to examine the differences and similarities between things

comparison (kəm par′ə sən) *n.* the act of comparing, examining the differences and similarities between two or more things

conclusions (kən klü′zhənz) *n.* opinions and ideas formed about something after careful study or thought

conflict (kän′flikt′) *n.* the struggle between people or opposing forces which creates the dramatic action in a play or story

connection (kə nek′shən) *n.* an event or thing that brings together people or ideas; a relationship between people and/or ideas

consequence (kän′si kwens′) *n.* the result, or outcome, of a previous action

consider (kən sid′ər) *v.* to take into account; to think about with care

contradict (kän′trə dikt′) *v.* to say something is wrong or not true

contrast (kən trast′) *v.* to compare in a way that shows differences

controversial (kän′trə vur′shəl) *adj.* something which is likely to stir up strong disagreement

convey (kən vā′) *v.* to make something (for example, an idea or a feeling) known to someone; to communicate

counter-argument (kount′ər är′gyü mənt) *n.* a reason against the original argument

D

demonstrate (dem′ən strāt′) *v.* to make a fact clear by giving proof or evidence

detail (dē′tāl′) *n.* a specific fact or piece of information about something

develop (di vel′əp) *v.* to explain or build an idea or example bit by bit

device (di vīs′) *n.* the use of words to gain a particular effect in a piece of writing

dialogue (dī′ə lôg′) *n.* a conversation between two or more people in a book, play, or movie

differentiate (dif′ər en′shē āt′) *v.* to notice differences in information

documentation (däk′yü mən tā′shən) *n.* the noting of sources to back up an idea or opinion

E

effect (e fekt′) *n.* the way that something changes because of a separate action

effective (e fekt´iv) *adj.* successful in getting the desired results

emotion (ē mō´shən) *n.* a feeling, such as love or joy; feelings and automatic responses, as opposed to logical thoughts and conclusions

evidence (ev´ə dəns) *n.* anything that gives proof or shows something to be true

external (ek stûr´nəl) *adj.* on the outside

extraneous (ek strā´nē əs) *adj.* not relevant, unnecessary; unrelated to the subject being discussed

F

factor (fak´tər) *n.* something that is one of the reasons for a particular result or outcome

fact (fakt) *n.* a piece of information that can be shown to be true

focus (fō´kəs) *n.* the main topic or most important point; the center of attention

formal (fôr´məl) *adj.* reflecting language that is traditional and correct, not casual

formatting (fôr´mat´ing) *adj.* related to the arrangement of text, images, and graphics on a page

G

genre (zhän´rə) *n.* a type of writing that contains certain features

H

hyperbole (hī pur´bə lē) *n.* over-the-top exaggeration

I

idiom (id´ē əm) *n.* an expression, made up of a group of words, where the meaning as a whole is different from what the words mean individually

image (im´ij) *n.* a word or phrase in a poem or other kind of writing which appeals to one or more of the five senses

imagery (im´ij rē) *n.* descriptive language that paints pictures in the mind or appeals to the senses

inconsistencies (in´kən sis´tən sēz) *n.* things that contradict each other

information (in´fər mā´shən) *n.* facts about a subject or topic

insight (in´sīt´) *n.* a useful, important, and deep understanding about a topic

internal (in tûr´nəl) *adj.* on the inside

introduce (in´trə düs) *v.* to present a person or information to another for the first time

introduction (in´trə duk´shən) *n.* the part at the beginning of a piece of writing which often tells what the rest will be about

J

judgment (juj´mənt) *n.* an opinion or conclusion formed after careful thought and evaluation

L

letter (let´ər) *n.* a written or printed message

line (līn) *n.* the direction of the action in a plot or story ("plot line" and "story line"); one row of words in a poem; one set of words spoken by an actor in a play or movie

literary (lit´ər ar´ē) *adj.* of or relating to books or other written material

logical (läj´i kəl) *adj.* clear and reasonable; based on logic

M

meter (mēt´ər) *n.* a poem's rhythmic pattern, made by the number of beats in each line

N

narrative (nar´ə tiv) *n.* a story, either fiction or nonfiction

note (nōt) *v.* to observe and/or mention

O

offensive (ə fens´iv) *adj.* upsetting, embarrassing, rude, hurtful or angering; aggressive, attacking

opinion (ə pin´yən) *n.* a belief or view that is not necessarily based on facts

oppose (ə pōz´) *v.* go against, disagree

organized (ôr´gə nīzd´) *adj.* the state of being in order

P

paraphrase (par´ə frāz´) *v.* to reword information into one's own words

personal (pūr´sən əl) *adj.* individual, relating to a particular person

personification (pər sän´ə fə kā´shən) *n.* a type of figurative language where animals or other non-humans are given human characteristics

plausible (plô´zə bəl) *adj.* likely to be true or valid

point of view (point uv vyü) *n.* the perspective from which a story is told; an attitude, position, standpoint, or way of looking at a situation; an opinion

position (pə zish´ən) *n.* a point of view or attitude toward something

profound (prō found´) *adj.* very deep, intense, or strong; full of insight

Q

quality (kwôl´ə tē) *n.* the degree of excellence of something

quotation (kwō tā´shən) *n.* a group of words copied exactly from a speech or piece of writing

R

reader-friendly (rēd´ər frend´lē) *adj.* easy for an audience to read and understand

research (rē´surch´) *v.* to carefully study information on a topic; *n.* the careful study of information on a topic

reasoning (rē´zən ing) *n.* the process of reaching a conclusion by looking at the facts

reflect (ri flekt´) *v.* to show, make apparent

resolution (rez´ə lü´shən) *n.* what happens to resolve the conflict in the plot of a story

rhetorical devices (ri tôr´i kəl di vī´səz) *n.* strategies and techniques, for example metaphor and hyperbole, used by writers to draw in or persuade readers

S

scheme (skēm) *n.* (for a poem) a design or ordered structure

sensory (sen´sər ē) *adj.* of or relating to the five senses

sequence (sē´kwəns) *n.* when the items in a group follow each other in a particular order

setting (set´ing) *n.* the time and place of the action in a story or other piece of writing

stanza (stan´zə) *n.* a group of lines of poetry, usually with a similar length and pattern, separated from other lines with spaces

strategy (strat´ə jē) *n.* in a piece of writing, a literary tactic or method (such as flashback or foreshadowing) used by the writer to achieve a certain goal or effect

structure (struk´chər) *n.* the way something is organized and put together; *v.* to put together according to a pattern or plan

style (stīl) *n.* a way of doing something; a way of writing

subject (sub´jekt) *n.* something that is discussed or studied; a topic

support (sə pôrt´) *v.* to hold up, to back

suspense (sə spens´) *n.* a feeling of anxiety and uncertainty about what will happen in a story or other piece of writing

sustain (sə stān´) *v.* to keep up, hold up; to affirm or support as true

symbol (sim´bəl) *n.* anything that stands for or represents something else

synthesize (sin´thə sīz´) *v.* to combine, to bring different parts together into a whole

T

technique (tek nēk´) *n.* a special way of doing something

theme (thēm) *n.* a central message, concern, or purpose in a literary work

thesis (thē´sis) *n.* an idea or theory that is stated and then discussed in a logical way

tone (tōn) *n.* a writer's attitude toward his or her subject

topic (täp´ik) *n.* a subject that is written about or discussed

transition (tran zish´ən) *n.* the change from one part, place, or idea to another; in writing, the change between sentences, paragraphs, and ideas

V

verse (vūrs) *n.* a group of lines that make a unit in a poem, a stanza; writing, such as poetry, that has a meter

viewpoint (vyü´point´) *n.* an attitude, position, standpoint, or way of looking at a situation

Spanish Glossary

A

action / acción *s.* en una historia u obra de teatro, los eventos que son parte del argumento

advantage / ventaja *s.* algo que le pone a alguien en una mejor posición que a otros; la forma en la que una cosa es mejor que otra

analysis / análisis *s.* el proceso de examinar algo detenidamente para entender su significado, su estructura o sus partes

analyze / analizar *v.* examinar algo detenidamente para entender su significado o estructura

anticipate / anticipar *v.* esperar o predecir; prever y estar preparado para tratar con algo

argument / argumento *s.* razonamiento (escrito o hablado) con el fin de persuadir; una serie de declaraciones que proponen o apoyan una idea o postura

audience / audiencia, público *s.* los lectores de un libro u otra obra escrita; un grupo de oyentes o espectadores

authority / autoridad *s.* una persona u obra escrita que es aceptada como una fuente de información fiable o experta

C

cause / causa *s.* una persona, objeto, o evento que hace que ocurra algo

character / personaje *s.* un individuo (humano o animal) que tiene un papel en la acción de un cuento, una obra de teatro o una película

chronological / cronológico *adj.* descrito o arreglado en el orden temporal, empezando con el evento que ocurrió primero

coherence / coherencia *s.* el estado de tener ideas claras y lógicas

coherent / coherente *adj.* bien planeado, claro, lógico; congruente

compare / comparar *v.* examinar las diferencias y semejanzas entre cosas

comparison / comparación *s.* el acto de comparar, examinar las diferencias y semejanzas entre dos más cosas

conclusions / conclusiónes *s.* opioniones o ideas sobre una materia o deducción a que se ha llegado tras su estudio o análisi

conflict / conflicto *s.* la lucha entre personas o fuerzas opuestas que crea la acción dramática en una obra de teatro o un cuento

connection / conexión *s.* un evento o una cosa que une a las personas o ideas; una relación entre personas y/o ideas

consequence / consecuencia *s.* el resultado de una acción previa

consider / considerar *v.* tomar en cuenta; meditar sobre algo

contradict / contradecir *v.* decir algo que no es correcto o que no es verdad

contrast / contrastar *v.* comparar dos o más cosas para señalar las diferencias entre ellas

controversial / controvertido *adj.* algo que tiende a levantar diferencias de opiniones

convey / expresar *v.* darse a entender algo a alguien (por ejemplo una idea o sentimiento); comunicar

counter-argument / contraargumento *s.* una razón contra el argumento original

D

demonstrate / demostrar *v.* aclarar un hecho por dar pruebas o evidencia

detail / detalle *s.* un dato específico o información específica de algo

develop / desarrollar *v.* explicar o exponer poco a poco una idea o ejemplo

device / técnica (literaria) *s.* el uso de palabras para tener un efecto específico en una obra escrita

dialogue / diálogo *s.* una conversación entre dos personajes o más en un libro, obra de teatro o película

differentiate / diferenciar *v.* notar las diferencias

documentation / documentación *s.* la anotación de fuentes para apoyar una idea u opinión

E

effect / efecto *s.* la manera en la que algo cambia a causa de una acción separada

effective / efectivo, eficaz *adj.* exitoso en producir los resultados deseados

emotion / sentimiento *s.* una sensación emotiva como el amor o la alegría; sensaciones y respuestas automáticas, en contraste a los pensamientos y conclusiones lógicos

evidence / pruebas *s.* cualquier cosa que demuestre o indique que algo es cierto

external / externo *adj.* afuera de

extraneous / superfluo *adj.* irrelevante, innecesario, no relacionado al tema tratado

F

factor / factor *s.* algo que es una de las razones de un resultado determinado

fact / hecho *s.* un dato que se puede verificar

focus / foco, idea central *s.* el tema principal o la idea más importante; el centro de atención

formal / formal *adj.* que refleja lenguaje tradicional y correcto, no informal

formatting / formateo *s.* la colocación de texto, imágenes y gráficos en una página

G

genre / género *s.* una clase de escritura que tiene características específicas

H

hyperbole / hipérbole *s.* exageración excesiva

I

idiom / modismo *s.* una expresión compuesta de un grupo de palabras cuyo significado en conjunto es diferente de lo que significan las palabras individuales

image / imagen *s.* una palabra o frase en un poema u otra clase de escritura que atrae uno o más de los cinco sentidos

imagery / imágenes *s.* lenguaje descriptivo que crea dibujos en la mente o que atrae los sentidos

inconsistencies / inconsecuencias *s.* cosas que se contradicen

information / información *s.* datos sobre un asunto o tema

insight / perspicacia *s.* el profundo entendimiento útil e importante de un tema

internal / interno *adj.* dentro de

introduce / presentar *v.* dar a conocer a una persona o información por primera vez

introduction / introducción *s.* la parte inicial de una obra escrita que muchas veces cuenta de qué se trata el resto de la obra

J

judgment / juicio *s.* una opinión o conclusión formada después de una consideración y evaluación cuidadosa

L

letter /carta *s.* un mensaje escrito o impreso

line / línea, verso *s.* la dirección de la acción en un argumento o historia (por ejemplo, “plot line” y “story line” en inglés); una línea de palabras en un poema; un grupo de palabras habladas por un actor en una obra de teatro o película

literary / literario *adj.* perteneciente o relativo a los libros u otra materia escrita

logical / lógico *adj.* claro y razonable; basado en la lógica

M

meter / métrica *s.* el patrón rítmico de un poema, marcado por el tiempo y ritmo de cada verso

N

narrative / narrativa *s.* un cuento de ficción o no ficción

note / notar *v.* observar y/o mencionar

O

offensive / ofensivo *adj.* que provoca disgusto, vergüenza, daño o enfado; grosero, agresivo, combativo

opinion / opinión *s.* una creencia o perspectiva que no es necesariamente basada en los hechos

oppose / oponerse *v.* estar en contra, no estar de acuerdo

organized / organizado *adj.* que está ordenado

P

paraphrase / parafrasear *v.* formular información utilizando sus propias palabras

personal / personal *adj.* individual, relativo a una persona particular

personification / personificación *n.* un tipo de lenguaje figurado en el que los animales u otros seres no humanos tienen características humanas

plausible / creíble *adj.* con buena probabilidad de ser verdadero o válido

point of view / punto de vista *n.* la perspectiva de la cual se cuenta una historia; una actitud, postura, o manera de ver una situación; una opinión

position / postura *n.* el punto de vista o la actitud hacia algo

profound / profundo *adj.* muy intenso o fuerte; lleno de perspicacia

Q

quality / calidad *s.* el grado de excelencia de algo

quotation / cita *s.* un grupo de palabras copiadas exactamente de un discurso o texto

R

reasoning / razonamiento *s.* el proceso de llegar a una conclusión por examinar los hechos

reflect / reflejar *v.* mostrar, hacer aparente

research / investigar *v.* estudiar cuidadosamente la información sobre un tema; investigación s. el estudio cuidadoso de la información sobre un tema

resolution / resolución *s.* lo que ocurre para resolver el conflicto en el argumento de una historia

rhetorical devices / técnicas retóricas *s.* estrategias y técnicas, por ejemplo la metáfora y la hipérbole, utilizadas por los escritores para atraer o persuadir a los lectores

S

scheme / esquema *s.* (para un poema) un diseño o estructura ordenada

sensory / sensoriai *adj.* perteneciente o relativo a los cinco sentidos

sequence / secuencia *s.* cuando una serie de eventos ocurre en un orden determinado

setting / escenario *s.* el lugar y el momento de la acción en un cuento u otra obra escrita

stanza / estrofa *s.* un grupo de líneas de poesía, normalmente con un patrón y extensión similar, separado por espacios de otras líneas

strategy / estrategia *s.* en un texto, una táctica o método literario (como el flashback o el presagio) empleado por el autor para lograr un objetivo o efecto específico

structure / estructura *s.* la manera en la que algo está organizado o compuesto; estructurar v. organizar o componer según un patrón o plan

style / estilo *s.* una manera de hacer algo; una forma de escribir

subject / tema *s.* algo de que se habla o que se estudia; un tema

support / apoyar *v.* sostener, respaldar

suspense / suspenso *s.* una sensación de ansiedad e incertidumbre sobre lo que va a pasar en una historia u otra obra escrita

sustain / sostener *v.* mantener, apoyar; afirmar o confirmar como verdadero

symbol / símbolo *s.* algo que representa o significa otra cosa

synthesize / sintetizar *v.* combinar, unir diferentes partes para formar una totalidad

T

technique / técnica *s.* una manera especial de hacer algo

theme / tema *s.* una idea, asunto, o propósito principal de una obra literaria

thesis / tesis *s.* una idea o teoría que se expone y que se discute de una manera lógica

tone / tono *s.* la actitud del autor hacia su tema o materia

topic / tema *s.* una idea de la cual se escribe y que se discute

transition / transición *s.* el cambio entre partes, lugares y conceptos; en la escritura, el cambio entre oraciones, párrafos e ideas

V

verse / verso *s.* un grupo de líneas que componen una unidad en un poema, una estrofa; texto, como la poesía, que tiene una métrica

viewpoint / punto de vista *s.* una actitud, postura, o manera de interpretar una situación

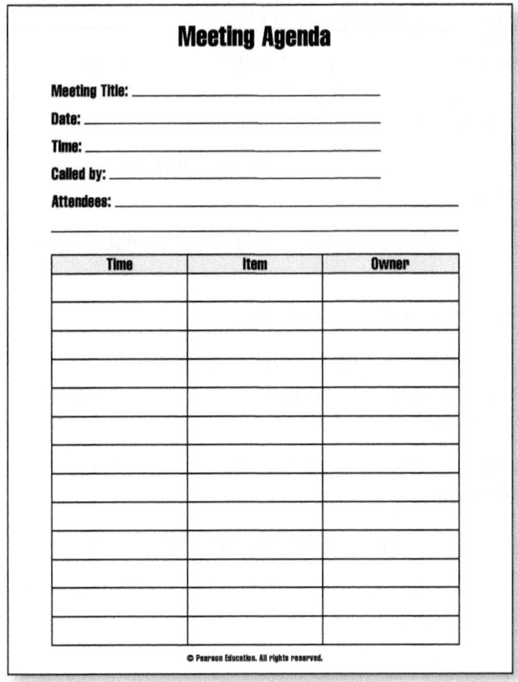

Meeting Agenda

Meeting Title: ______________________

Date: ______________________

Time: ______________________

Called by: ______________________

Attendees: ______________________

Time	Item	Owner

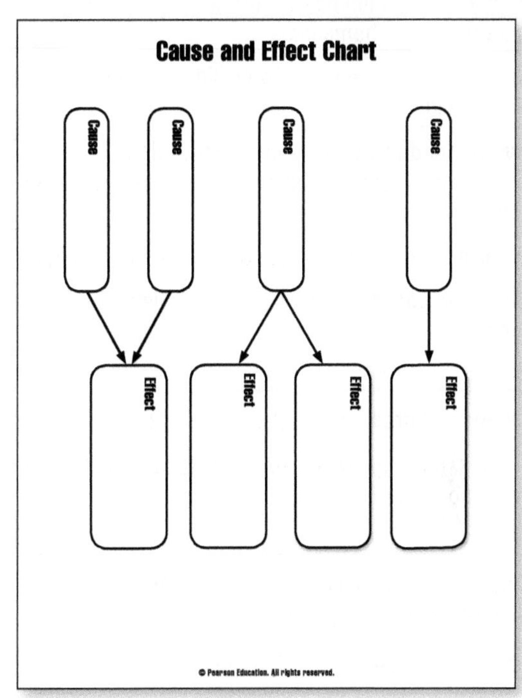

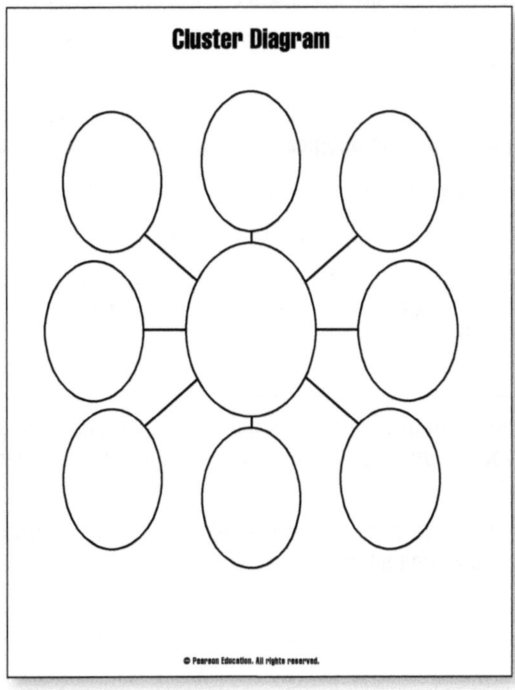

Five Ws Chart

Use these questions as you read, and write important details. Remember, you may not need to answer every question.

Who?
What?
When?
Where?
Why?

Writing Coach Online  **Resource** Go online for printable versions of these graphic organizers.

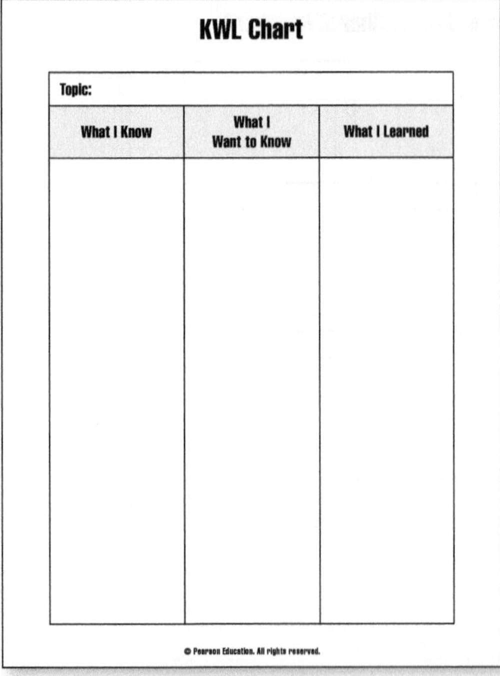
KWL Chart

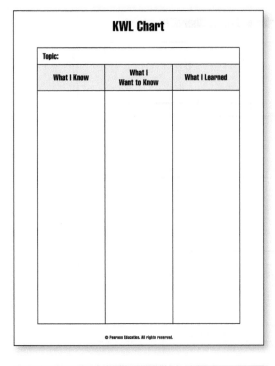

Topic:		
What I Know	What I Want to Know	What I Learned

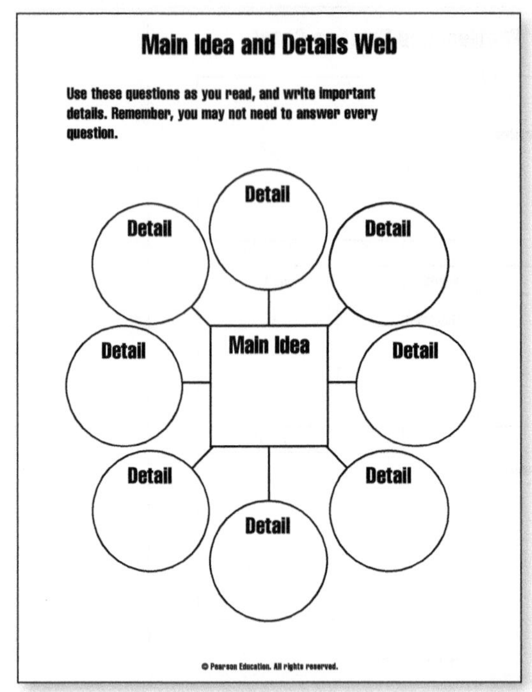

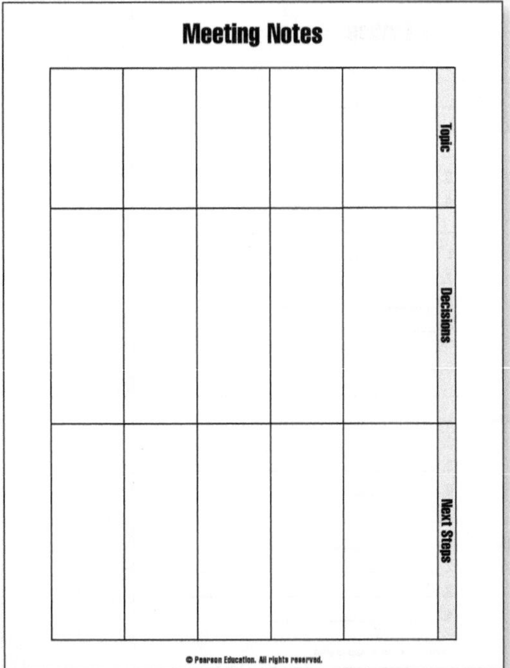

Note Card

Topic:

Source:

-
-
-

Topic:

Source:

-
-
-

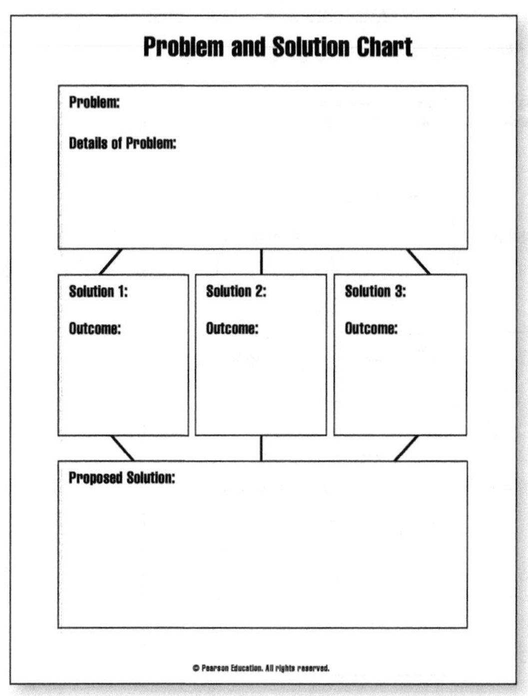

Problem and Solution Chart

Problem:

Details of Problem:

Solution 1:

Outcome:

Solution 2:

Outcome:

Solution 3:

Outcome:

Proposed Solution:

Series of Events Chart/Flowchart

Source Card

Source Number: ____________

Source Name: ____________

Kind of Source: ____________

Author(s): ____________

Editor (when applicable): ____________

Publisher: ____________

Publication Date: ____________

Publication Location: ____________

Other Information ____________

Source Number: ____________

Source Name: ____________

Kind of Source: ____________

Author(s): ____________

Editor (when applicable): ____________

Publisher: ____________

Publication Date: ____________

Publication Location: ____________

Other Information ____________

Outline

Topic I. ____________

Subtopic A. ____________

Supporting details 1. ____________
2. ____________
3. ____________
4. ____________

Subtopic B. ____________

Supporting details 1. ____________
2. ____________
3. ____________
4. ____________

Topic II. ____________

Subtopic A. ____________

Supporting details 1. ____________
2. ____________
3. ____________
4. ____________

Subtopic B. ____________

Supporting details 1. ____________
2. ____________
3. ____________
4. ____________

Steps in a Process Chart

Steps	Details
Step 1:	
Step 2:	
Step 3:	
Step 4:	
Step 5:	

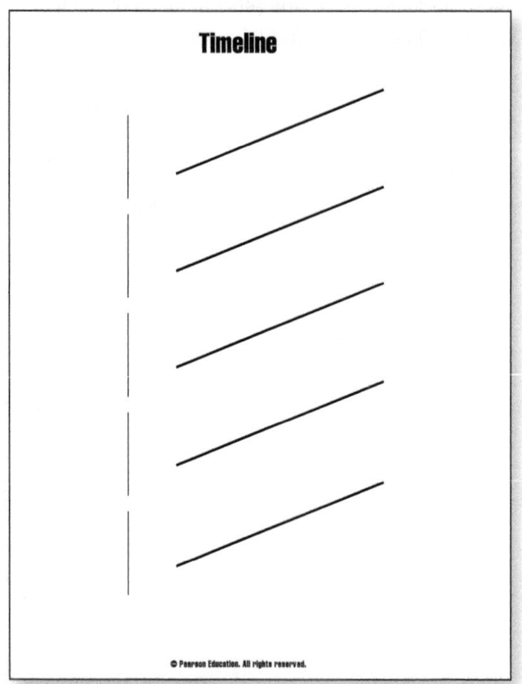

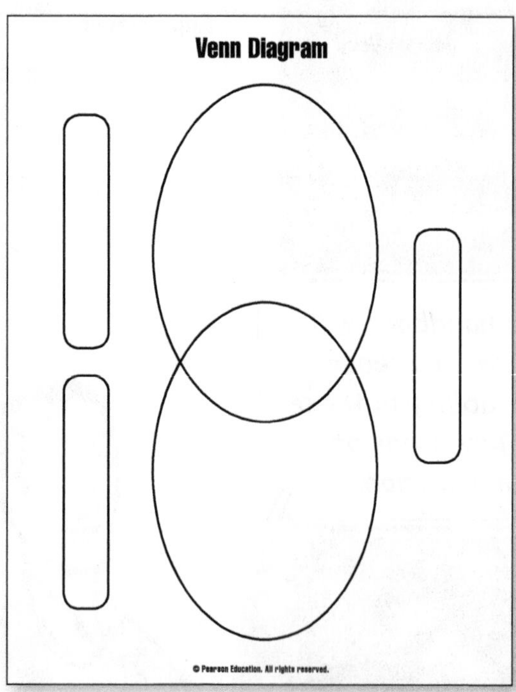

Listening and Speaking Handbook

Communication travels between people in many forms. You receive information by listening to others, and you convey information through speaking. The more developed these skills are, the more you will be able to communicate your ideas, as well as to comprehend the ideas of others.

If you improve your listening skills, it will become easier to focus your attention on classroom discussions and to identify important information more accurately. If you develop good speaking skills, you will be better prepared to contribute effectively in group discussions, to give formal presentations with more confidence, and to communicate your feelings and ideas to others more easily.

Listening

Different situations call for different types of listening. Learn more about the four main types of listening—critical, empathic, appreciative, and reflective—in the chart below.

Types of Listening

Type	How to Listen	Situations
Critical	Listen for facts and supporting details to understand and evaluate the speaker's message.	Informative or persuasive speeches, class discussions, announcements
Empathic	Imagine yourself in the other person's position, and try to understand what he or she is thinking.	Conversations with friends or family
Appreciative	Identify and analyze aesthetic or artistic elements, such as character development, rhyme, imagery, and descriptive language.	Oral presentations of a poem, dramatic performances
Reflective	Ask questions to get information, and use the speaker's responses to form new questions.	Class or group discussions

This handbook will help you increase your ability in these two key areas of communication.

Using Different Types of Questions

A speaker's ideas may not always be clear to you. You may need to ask questions to clarify your understanding. If you understand the different types of questions, you will be able to get the information you need.

- An **open-ended question** does not lead to a single, specific response. Use this question to open up a discussion: "What did you think of the piano recital?"
- A **closed question** leads to a specific response and must be answered with a yes or no: "Did you play a piece by Chopin at your recital?"
- A **factual question** is aimed at getting a particular piece of information and must be answered with facts: "How many years have you been playing the piano?"

Participating in a Group Discussion

In a group discussion, you openly discuss ideas and topics in an informal setting. The group discussions in which you participate will involve, for the most part, your classmates and focus on the subjects you are studying. To get the most out of a group discussion, you need to participate in it.

Use group discussions to express and to listen to ideas in an informal setting.

Communicate Effectively Think about the points you want to make, the order in which you want to make them, the words you will use to express them, and the examples that will support these points before you speak.

Ask Questions Asking questions can help you improve your comprehension of another speaker's ideas. It may also call attention to possible errors in another speaker's points.

Make Relevant Contributions Stay focused on the topic being discussed. Relate comments to your own experience and knowledge, and clearly connect them to your topic. It is important to listen to the points others make so you can build off their ideas. Work to share the connections you see. For example, say whether you agree or disagree, or tell the goup how your ideas connect.

Speaking

Giving a presentation or speech before an audience is generally recognized as public speaking. Effective speakers are well prepared and deliver speeches smoothly and with confidence.

Recognizing Different Kinds of Speeches

There are four main kinds of speeches: informative speeches, persuasive speeches, entertaining speeches, and extemporaneous speeches.

Consider the purpose and audience of your speech before deciding what kind of speech you will give.

- Give an **informative speech** to explain an idea, a process, an object, or an event.
- Give a **persuasive speech** to get your listeners to agree with your position or to take some action. Use formal English when speaking.
- Give an **entertaining speech** to offer your listeners something to enjoy or to amuse them. Use both informal and formal language.
- Give an **extemporaneous speech** when an impromptu occasion arises. It is an informal speech because you do not have a prepared manuscript.

Preparing and Presenting a Speech

If you are asked to deliver a speech, begin choosing a topic that you like or know well. Then, prepare your speech for your audience.

To prepare your speech, research your topic. Make an outline, and use numbered note cards.

Gather Information Use the library and other resources to gather reliable information and to find examples to support your ideas.

Organizing Information Organize your information by writing an outline of main ideas and major details. Then, when you deliver your speech, write the main ideas, major details, quotations, and facts on note cards.

When presenting your speech, use rhetorical forms of language and verbal and nonverbal strategies.

Use Rhetorical Language Repeat key words and phrases to identify your key points. Use active verbs and colorful adjectives to keep your speech interesting. Use parallel phrases to insert a sense of rhythm.

Use Verbal and Nonverbal Strategies Vary the pitch and tone of your voice, and the rate at which you speak. Speak loudly and emphasize key words or phrases. Avoid consistently reading your speech from your notes. Work to maintain eye contact with the audience. As you speak, connect with the audience by using gestures and facial expressions to emphasize key points.

Evaluating a Speech

Evaluating a speech gives you the chance to judge another speaker's skills. It also gives you the opportunity to review and improve your own methods for preparing and presenting a speech.

When you evaluate a speech, you help the speaker and yourself to learn from experience. Listed below are some questions you might ask yourself while evaluating another person's speech or one of your own speeches.

- Did the speaker introduce the topic clearly, develop it well, and conclude it effectively?
- Did the speaker support each main idea with appropriate details?
- Did the speaker approach the platform confidently and establish eye contact with the audience?
- Did the speaker's facial expressions, gestures, and movements appropriately reinforce the words spoken?
- Did the speaker vary the pitch of his or her voice and the rate of his or her speaking?
- Did the speaker enunciate all words clearly?

Listening Critically to a Speech

Hearing happens naturally as sounds reach your ears. Listening, or critical listening, requires that you understand and interpret these sounds.

Critical listening requires preparation, active involvement, and self-evaluation from the listener.

Learning the Listening Process Listening is interactive; the more you involve yourself in the listening process, the more you will understand.

Focus Your Attention Focus your attention on the speaker and block out all distractions—people, noises, and objects. Find out more about the subject that will be discussed beforehand.

Interpret the Information To interpret a speaker's message successfully, you need to identify and understand important information. You might consider listening for repeated words or phrases, pausing momentarily to memorize and/or write key statements, watching non-verbal signals, and combining this new information with what you already know.

Respond to the Speaker's Message Respond to the information you have heard by identifying the larger message of the speech, its most useful points, and your position on the topic.

Index

Note: Page numbers in **boldface** refer to pages where terms are defined; *italicized* page numbers refer to writing applications.

Index of Authors and Titles

Acknowledgments

Grateful acknowledgment is made to the following for copyrighted material:

Carole Berglie, Literary Estate of May Swenson

"Southbound on the Freeway" by May Swenson from *Imaginary Gardens: American Poetry and Art for Young People.* Copyright © 1978 by May Swenson. Used by permission of The Literary Estate of May Swenson. All rights reserved.

Enslow Publishers, Inc.

From *Sandra Cisneros: Latina Writer and Activist* by Caryn Mirriam-Goldberg. Copyright © 1998 by Caryn Mirriam-Goldberg. Published by Enslow Publishers, Inc., Berkeley Heights, NJ. All rights reserved. Used by permission.

National Council of Teachers of English (NCTE)

"Mistakes are a fact of Life: A National Comparative Study" by Andrea A. Lunsford and Karen J. Lunsford translated from *bcs.bedfordstmartins.com/lunsford/PDF/Lunsford_article_Mistakes.pdf.* Copyright © NCTE. Used by permission of National Council of Teachers of English (NCTE).

Naomi Shihab Nye

"The Rider" by Naomi Shihab Nye from *Invisible.* Copyright © 1998 by Naomi Shihab Nye. All rights reserved. Used by permission of the author.

Marian Reiner, Literary Agent

"December Leaves" by Kaye Starbird from *Don't Ever Cross A Crocodile.* Copyright © 1963, Copyright renewed © 1991 Kaye Starbird. Used by permission of Marian Reiner, Literary Agent.

Science News for Kids / Society for Science & the Public

"Brainy Bees Know Two from Three" by Liz Savage from *http://www.sciencenewsforkids.org/articles/20090218/note3.asp.* Copyright © 2009 Society for Science & the Public. Used by permission of Science News.

Paul Zindel Revocable Trust c/o Curtis Brown, Ltd.

"My First Fistfight" by Paul Zindel. First published in *The Pigman and Me*, published by HarperCollins. Copyright © 1992 by Paul Zindel. Used by permission of Curtis Brown, Ltd.

Note: Every effort has been made to locate the copyright owner of material reproduced in this component. Omissions brought to our attention will be corrected in subsequent editions.

Image Credits

Illustrations
Robert Chouinard

All interior photos provided by Jupiter Images. Except

64: © Barry Austin/age fotostock; 90: © Inti St Clair/age fotostock; 118: © Louis Brawley Louisey/age fotostock; 170: © Blend Images / SuperStock; 226, 228: Courtesy of The Library of Congress; 256: © Alistair Berg/ age fotostock.

Sentence Diagraming Workshop

Sentence diagraming is one of many useful tools for teaching the elements of English grammar. Sentence diagrams are particularly helpful to visual learners, but they can encourage all students to build their knowledge of sentence structure, placing each new concept logically on those that precede it. As you use this workshop, point out to students how diagraming clearly illustrates the relationship of one word to another in a sentence.

> *"Every English poet should master the rules of grammar before he attempts to bend or break them."*
>
> **—Robert Graves**

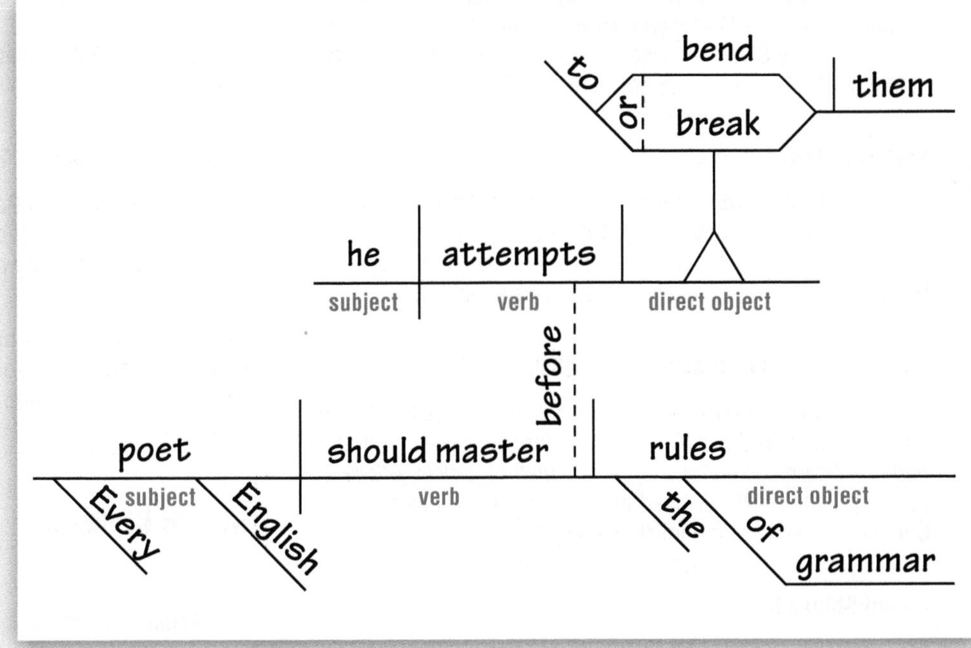

The Basics of Diagraming

This Sentence Diagraming workshop provides instruction that you can use with the downloadable practice pages you will find online, covering the basics of diagraming step by step.

- Sentence Forms and Modifiers
- Compound Sentence Elements
- Complements
- Prepositional Phrases and Appositive Phrases
- Participles and Participial Phrases
- Gerund Phrases
- Infinitives and Infinitive Phrases
- Compound Sentences
- Complex Sentences
- Compound-Complex Sentences

Each step of the process is accompanied by example sentences for you to use in the classroom, with diagrams and, in some cases, italics that will help you identify sentence parts. The practice pages allow you to give your students further diagraming work to hone their skills. You can download copies of the Practice pages in the Teacher Center at www.phwritingcoach.com and distribute them to students. Practice page answers are included in this workshop.

Sentence Forms and Modifiers

Have students look at the most basic skeleton of a sentence by diagraming sentences with a variety of subject/verb orders. Emphasize these points.

Declarative Sentences

The basic diagram is a horizontal line, intersected by a vertical line.

- Place the simple subject to the left of the vertical line.
- Place the simple verb to the right of the vertical line.

EXAMPLE: Kathleen laughed.

Kathleen | laughed

Adding Modifiers

Explain that, to show how the words relate, place modifiers on slanted lines *directly below* the words they modify.

EXAMPLE: Quite hesitant, my sister did not answer quickly.

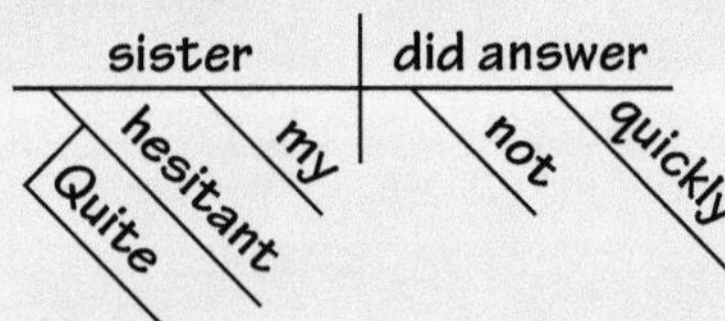

Imperative Sentences

The subject of an imperative sentence is understood to be *you*. To show this, place *(you)* in the usual place for the subject.

EXAMPLE: Stand up.

(you) | Stand
up

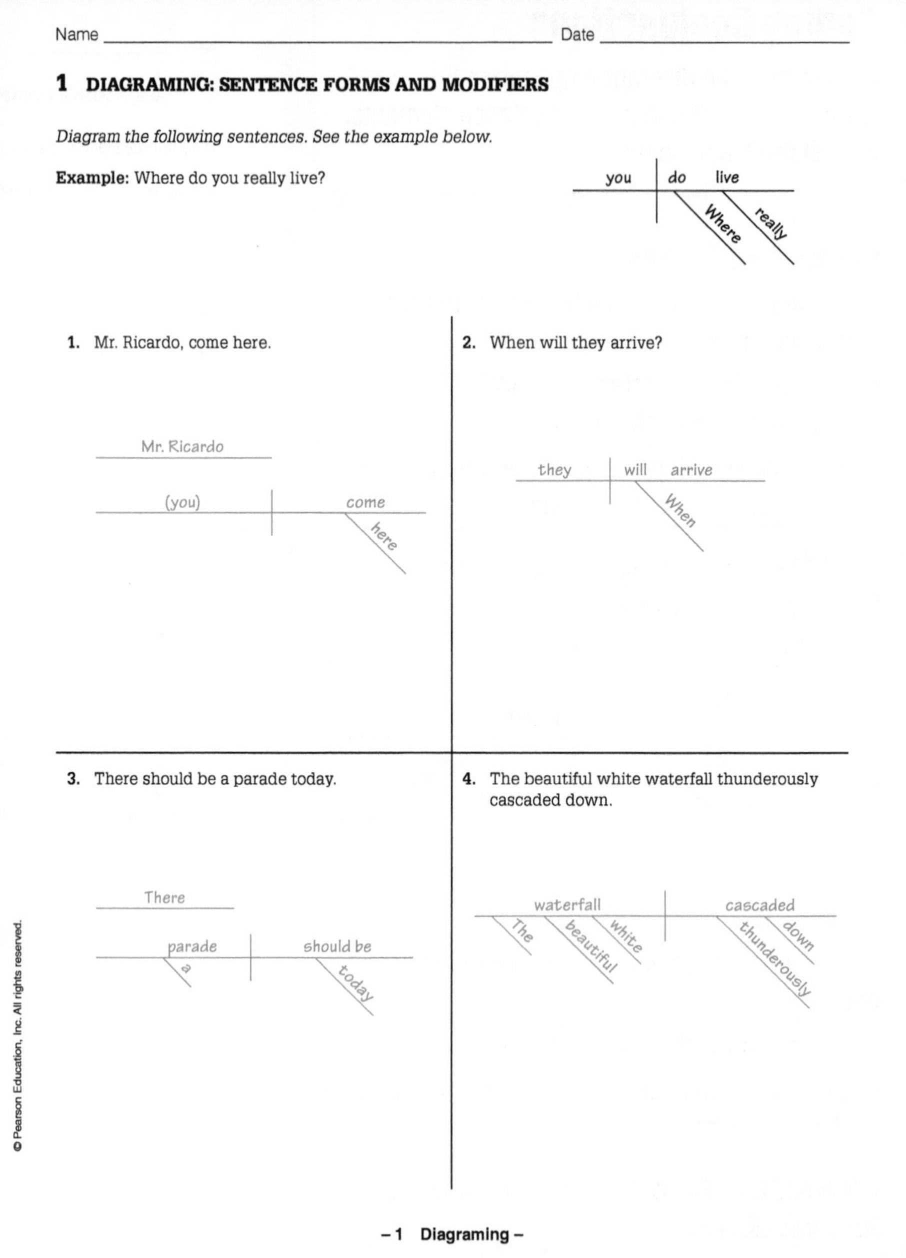
Name ______________________ Date ______________

1 DIAGRAMING: SENTENCE FORMS AND MODIFIERS

Diagram the following sentences. See the example below.

Example: Where do you really live?

you | do live
Where
really

1. Mr. Ricardo, come here.

Mr. Ricardo
(you) | come
here

2. When will they arrive?

they | will arrive
When

3. There should be a parade today.

There
parade | should be
a
today

4. The beautiful white waterfall thunderously cascaded down.

waterfall | cascaded
The
beautiful
white
down
thunderously

– 1 Diagraming –

Interrogative Sentences

Inverted sentences follow the usual subject-verb order in a diagram. This is useful for locating the subject and verb in a sentence.

EXAMPLE: How are you?

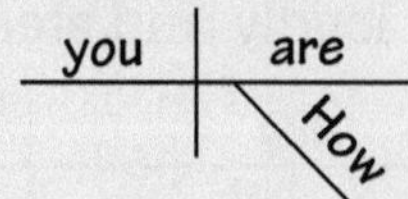

Diagraming Practice

You can download copies of the Practice pages in the Teacher Center at www.phwritingcoach.com and distribute them to students.

Adding Conjunctions

Explain how the diagram emphasizes the parallel nature of compound sentence elements. Emphasize these points.

Compound Subjects

Split the horizontal line to the left of the diagram and place one subject on each line.

- Connect the subjects with a dotted line and write the conjunction next to it.
- Place two-word correlative conjunctions on either side of the dotted line.

EXAMPLE: Neither Amanda nor Lisa lived near the school.

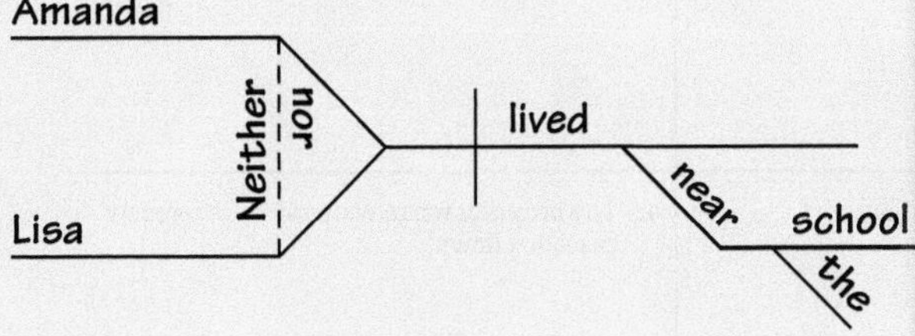

Compound Predicates

Split the horizontal line on the right side of the diagram.

- Place each verb on its own line.
- Place the conjunction on a dotted line between the two verbs.

EXAMPLE: Felicia walked into the room and sat down.

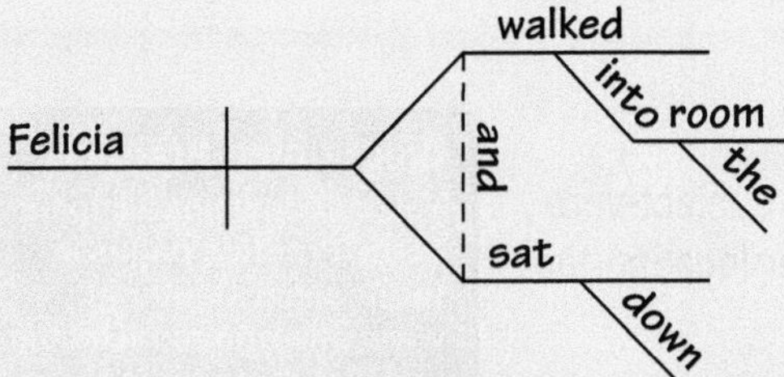

Note: When an adjective or adverb modifies both parts of a compound sentence element, place it on the main line.

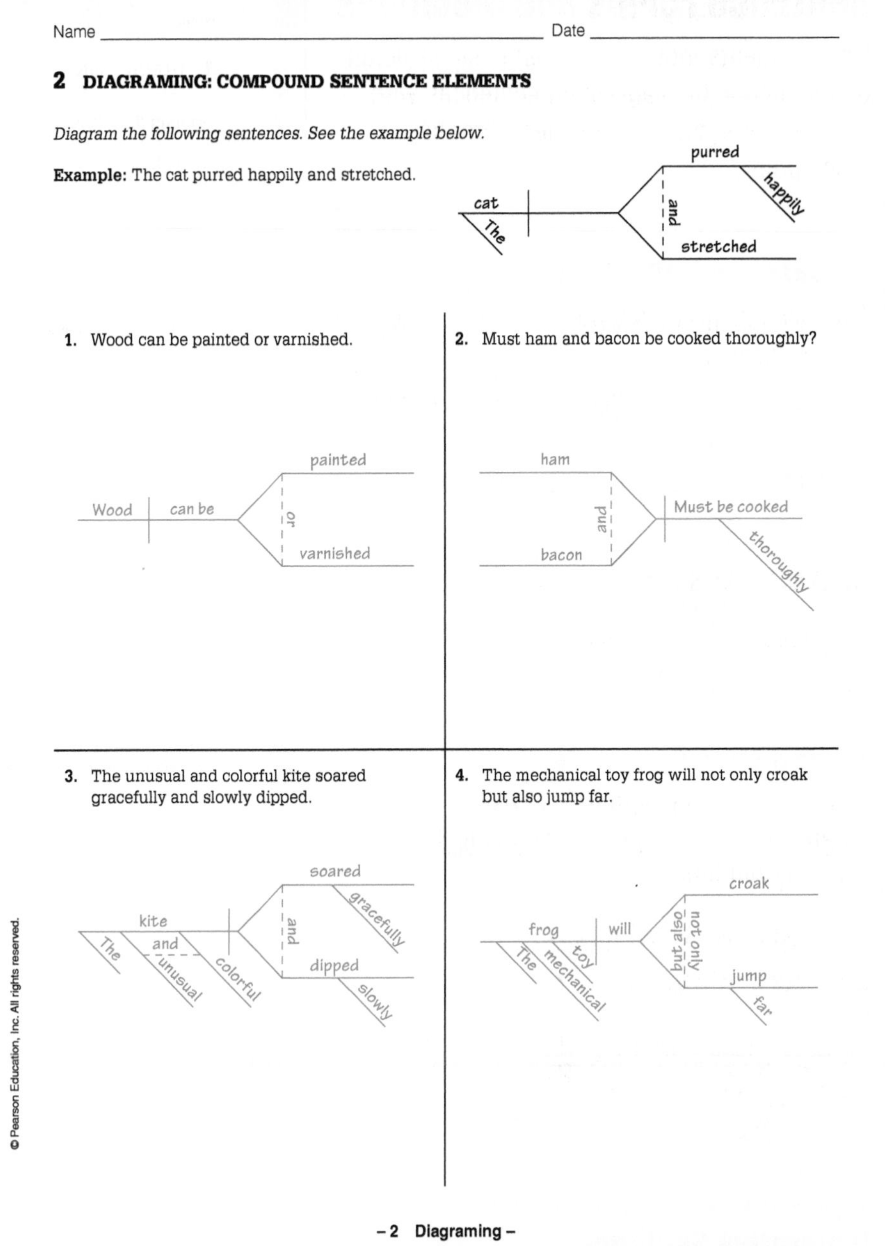

Name
Date
2 DIAGRAMING: COMPOUND SENTENCE ELEMENTS
Diagram the following sentences. See the example below.
Example: The cat purred happily and stretched.
cat
The
and
purred
happily
stretched
1. Wood can be painted or varnished.
Wood
can be
or
painted
varnished
2. Must ham and bacon be cooked thoroughly?
ham
and
bacon
Must be cooked
thoroughly
3. The unusual and colorful kite soared gracefully and slowly dipped.
kite
The
and
unusual
colorful
and
soared
gracefully
dipped
slowly
4. The mechanical toy frog will not only croak but also jump far.
frog
The
mechanical
toy
will
not only
but also
croak
jump
far
© Pearson Education, Inc. All rights reserved.
– 2 Diagraming –

Compound Modifiers

Draw a dotted line between modifiers that a conjunction connects and write the conjunction on that line.

EXAMPLE: The small but fierce dog barked loudly and steadily.

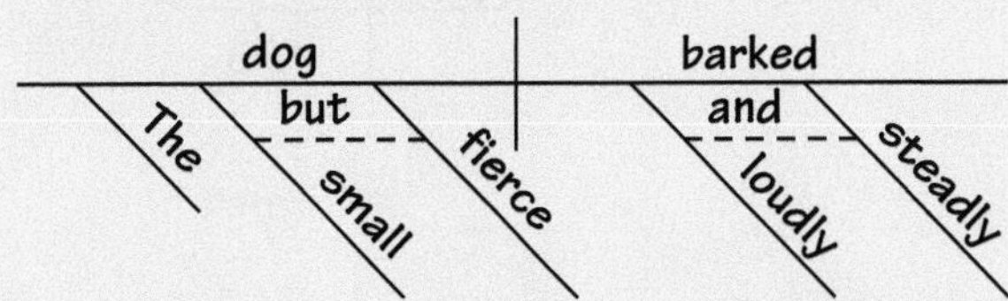

Diagraming Practice

You can download copies of the Practice pages in the Teacher Center at www.phwritingcoach.com and distribute them to students.

Complements

Help students recognize the relationship of a complement to the word it works with in the diagram. Emphasize these points.

Direct Objects and Indirect Objects

When diagraming a direct object, draw a vertical, upright line after the verb.

- Place the direct object to the right of that line.
- Place the indirect object, if any, on a horizontal line extended from a slanted line directly below the verb.

EXAMPLE: I gave Ted advice.

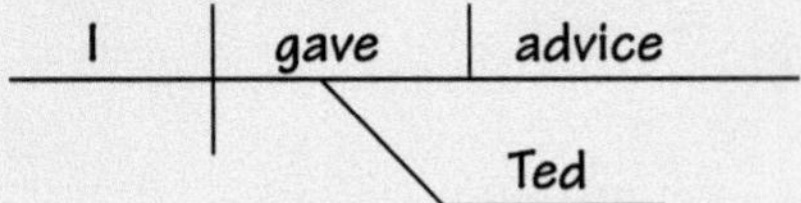

Objective Complement

Draw a line that slants to the left after the direct object and place the objective complement to the right of that line.

EXAMPLE: The President named him Chief of Staff.

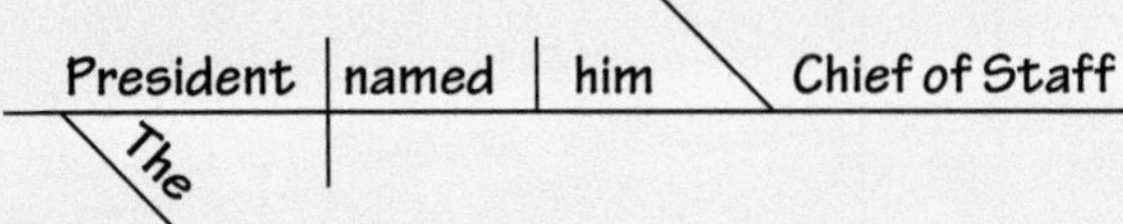

Predicate Nominatives and Predicate Adjectives

Draw a line that slants to the left after the verb and place the predicate nominative or the predicate adjective to the right of the line.

EXAMPLE: My dog is a spaniel.

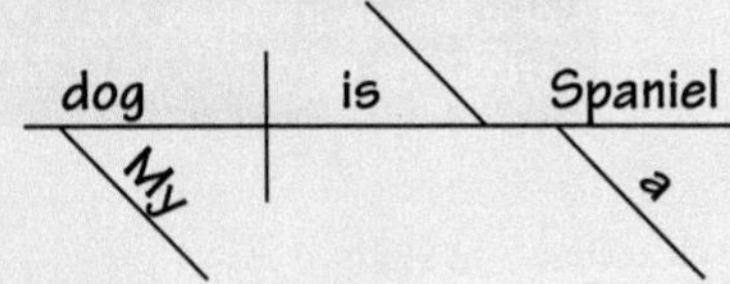

EXAMPLE: We felt grouchy.

We | felt \ grouchy

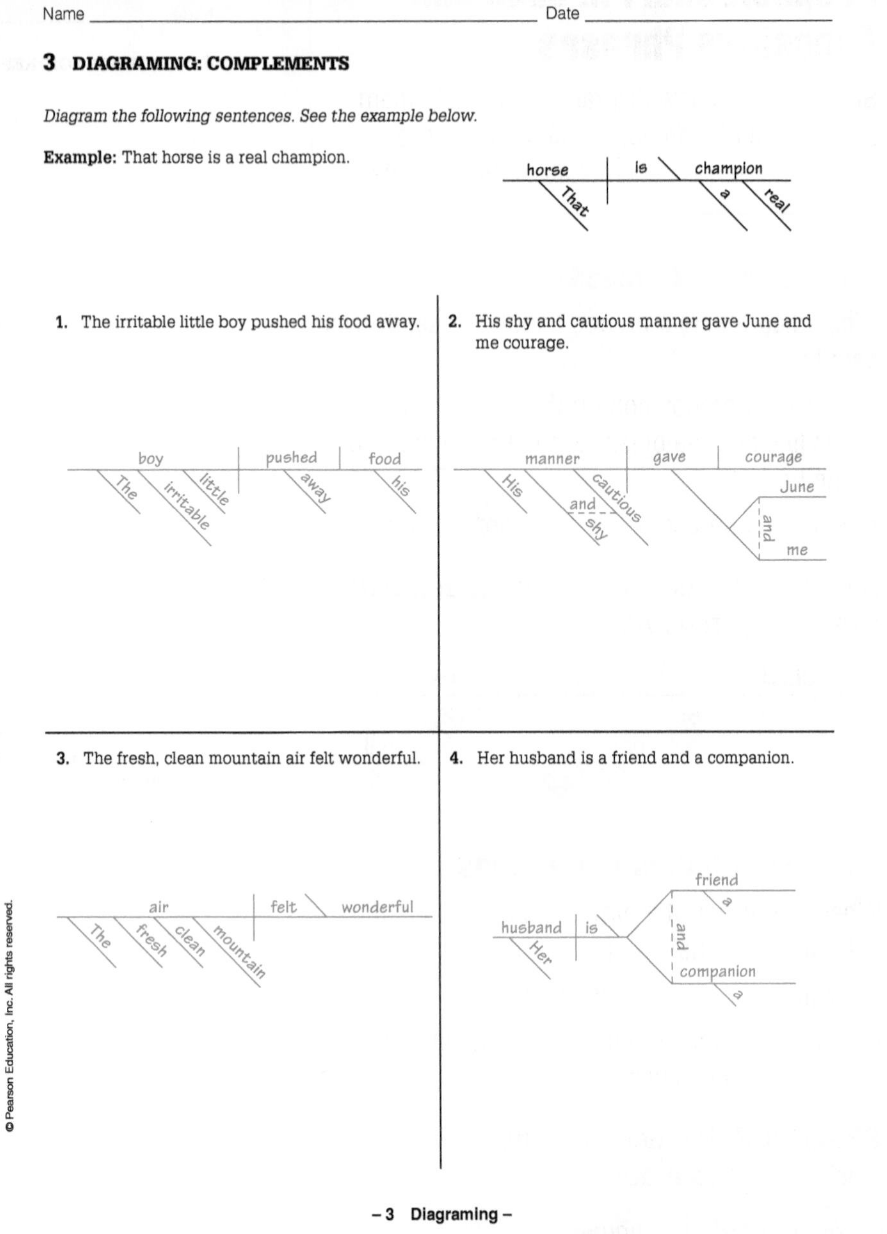

Diagraming Practice

You can download copies of the Practice pages in the Teacher Center at www.phwritingcoach.com and distribute them to students.

Prepositional Phrases and Appositive Phrases

Show students how diagraming can help them see the role of a prepositional or appositive phrase in a sentence. Emphasize these points.

Prepositional Phrases

When diagraming a prepositional phrase, draw a bent line.

- Place the preposition on the slanted part of the line and the object of the preposition on the horizontal part.
- Place the phrase below the word modified.

EXAMPLE: The child *with the red ball* skipped *up the hill.*

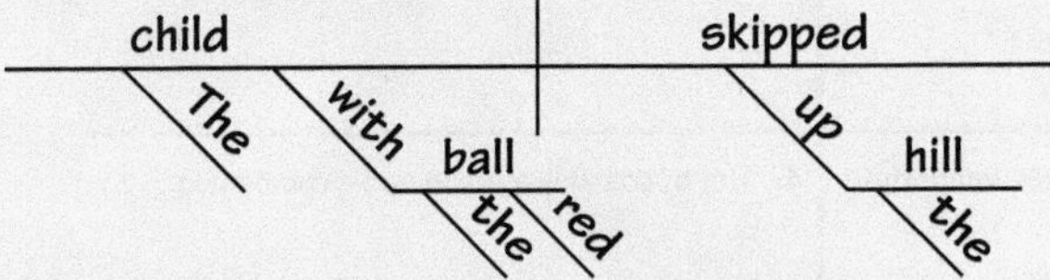

Compound Object of a Preposition

When the object of a preposition is compound, split the horizontal line for the object.

- Write each object on its own line.
- Place the conjunction on a dotted line between the two object lines.

EXAMPLE: We need a house *with three bedrooms and a den.*

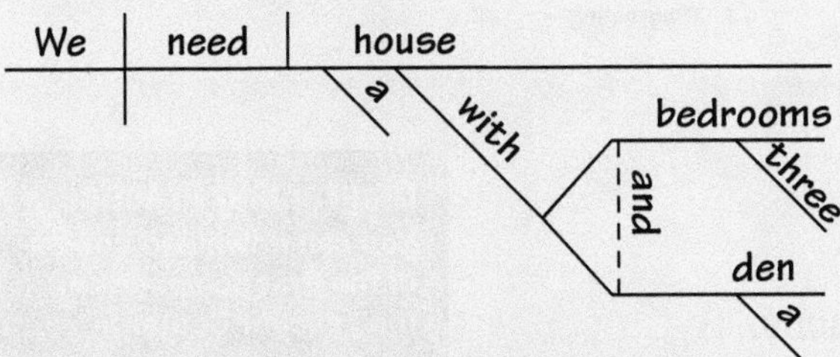

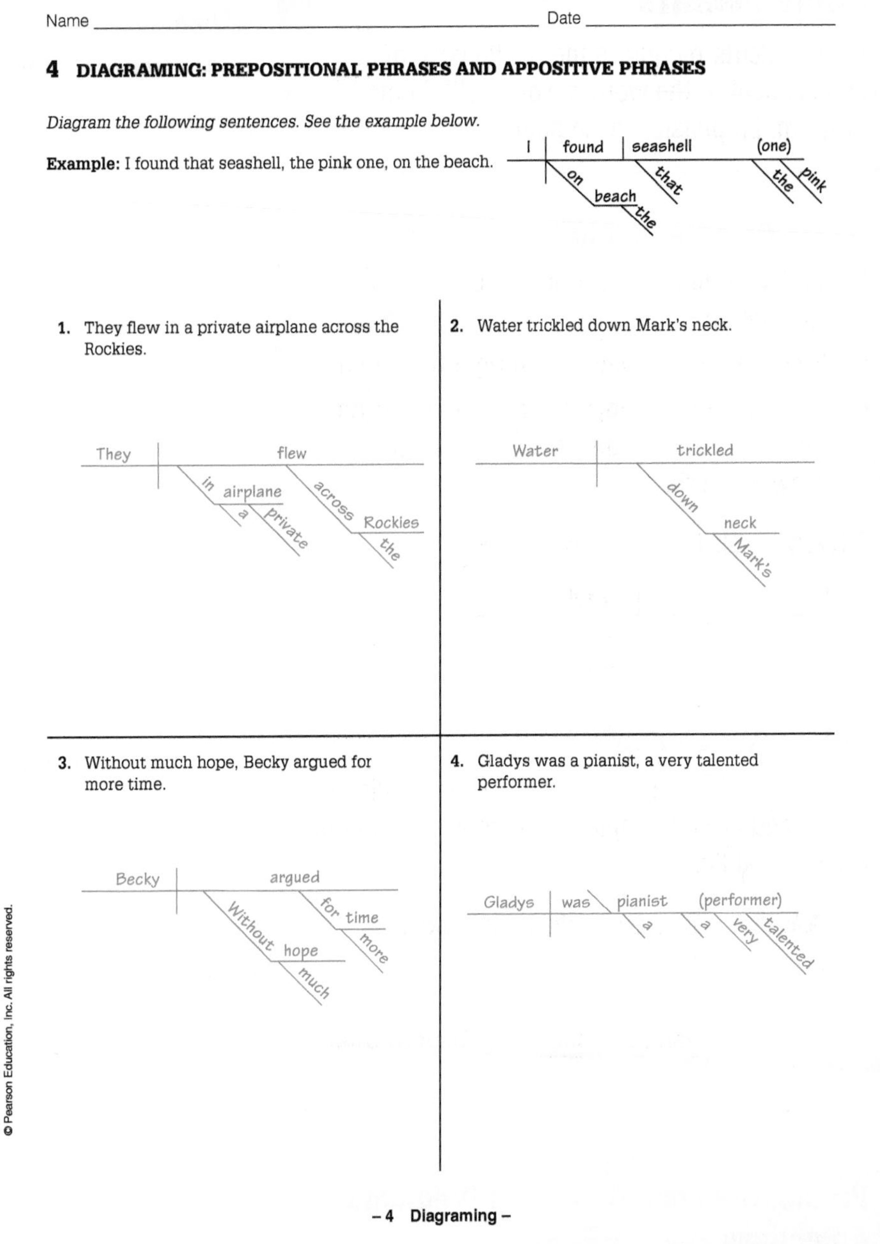

Name ______________________ Date ______________

4 DIAGRAMING: PREPOSITIONAL PHRASES AND APPOSITIVE PHRASES

Diagram the following sentences. See the example below.

Example: I found that seashell, the pink one, on the beach.

1. They flew in a private airplane across the Rockies.

2. Water trickled down Mark's neck.

3. Without much hope, Becky argued for more time.

4. Gladys was a pianist, a very talented performer.

– 4 Diagraming –

Diagraming Practice
You can download copies of the Practice pages in the Teacher Center at www.phwritingcoach.com and distribute them to students.

Appositives and Appositive Phrases

Place an appositive in parentheses just to the right of the noun or pronoun it identifies, renames, or explains. Place any modifiers of the appositive directly below it.

EXAMPLE: Harriet Danby, *her friend,* is a lawyer.

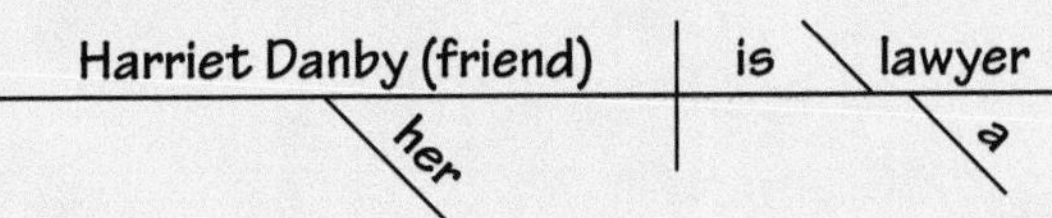

Participles and Participial Phrases

Help students see how a diagram helps them understand the role a participle plays in a sentence. Emphasize these points.

Participial Phrase

Place a participial phrase on a bent line, like that of a prepositional phrase. Explain that the form of the diagram helps us see that the phrase is a modifier.

- Write the participle in a curve along the line.
- As an adjective, a participle or participial phrase is placed directly below the noun or pronoun it modifies.

EXAMPLE: *Stopping suddenly*, I almost fell.

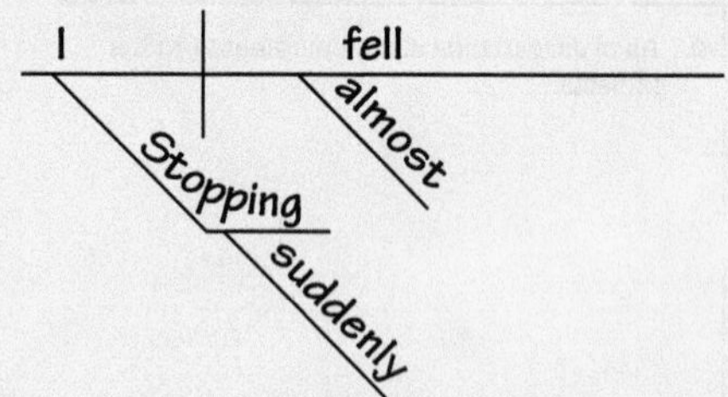

Participle With a Complement

A participial phrase may have a complement, just like a sentence or a prepositional phrase, and it is diagramed in a similar way.

- When a participle has a direct object, place the object after a vertical line.
- When a participle has a predicate adjective or predicate nominative, place that complement after a line that slants to the left.

EXAMPLE: *Carefully reviewing books for children*, Russell stays busy.

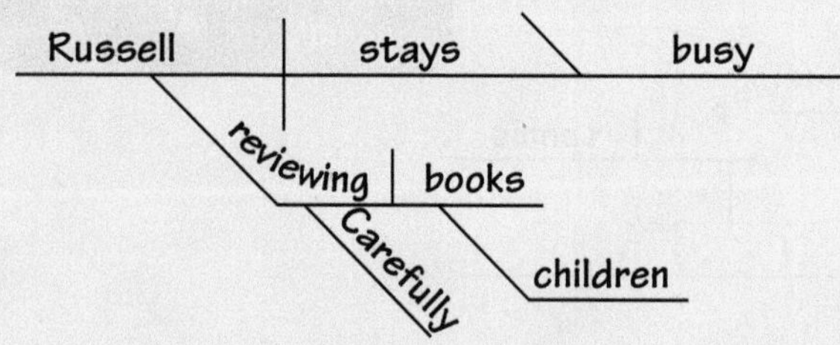

Name ______________________ Date ______________

5 DIAGRAMING: PARTICIPLES AND PARTICIPIAL PHRASES

Diagram the following sentences. See the example below.

Example: Turning away, the exhausted runner cried.

1. He held a basket brimming with fruit.
2. Going without sleep, many volunteers worked into the night.
3. This deserted island offers peace and tranquility.
4. From the beehive came a loud buzzing noise.

Diagraming Practice
You can download copies of the Practice pages in the Teacher Center at www.phwritingcoach.com and distribute them to students.

Gerund Phrases

Explain to students that, because gerunds always act as nouns, they are placed where a noun would be placed in a diagram. Emphasize these points.

Gerund Phrases

The basic diagram for a gerund phrase is a line similar to that of a prepositional phrase or participle.

- However, draw a stairstep, rather than a slanted line, at the left side.
- Curve the gerund around the stairstep.
- When a gerund acts as a subject, direct object, object of a preposition, or predicate nominative, place the stairstep on a pedestal wherever it would go if it were simply a noun.

EXAMPLE: The lease forbids *keeping any pets on the premises.*

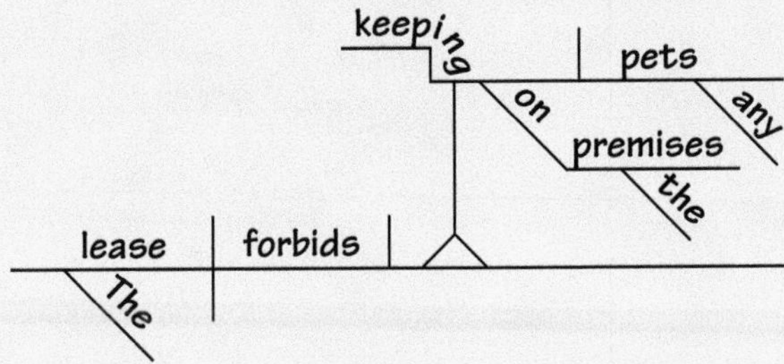

Gerund Phrases as Indirect Objects

When a gerund acts as an indirect object, place the stairstep diagram under the verb, joined to the main line by a slanted line.

EXAMPLE: His lecture gave *traveling to South America* new dimensions.

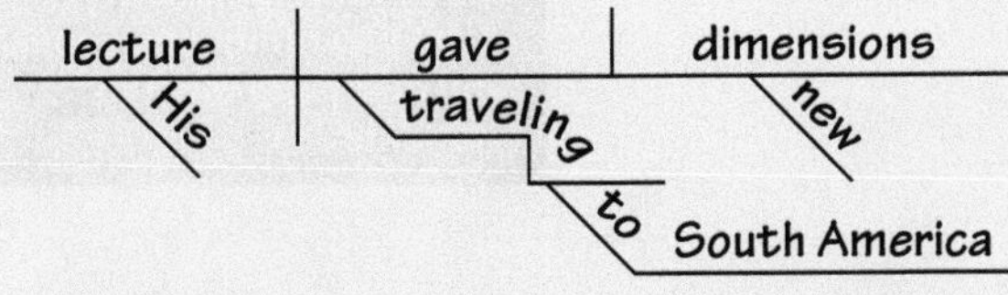

Gerund Phrases as Appositives

When a gerund or gerund phrase acts as an appositive, place it on a pedestal to the right of the noun or pronoun it identifies, renames, or explains. Place parentheses around the bottom of the pedestal.

EXAMPLE: We mastered one sport, *playing tennis.*

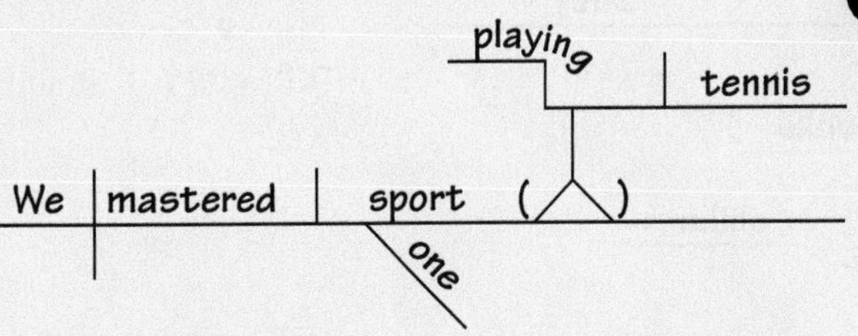

Name ______________________ Date ______________

6 DIAGRAMING: GERUND PHRASES

Diagram the following sentences. See the example below.

Example: Paul loved working in the garden.

1. His favorite activity was hiking through the woods.
2. Achieving the position of senator will be very difficult.
3. Clark's fear, injuring his elbow, kept him on the bench.
4. All of Jill's friends like helping her with her projects.

– 6 Diagraming –

Diagraming Practice

You can download copies of the Practice pages in the Teacher Center at www.phwritingcoach.com and distribute them to students.

Infinitives and Infinitive Phrases

Explain to students that diagraming can help them see how an infinitive functions in a sentence, as a noun or as a modifier. Emphasize these points.

Infinitive Phrases as Nouns

When an infinitive phrase is used as a noun, place it on a bent line, like that of a prepositional phrase.

- Place the phrase diagram on a pedestal like that of a gerund.
- Place the object of an infinitive to the right of a vertical line on the horizontal line.
- Place the pedestal wherever it would go if the phrase were simply a noun.

EXAMPLE: She wanted *to show us her stamp collection.*

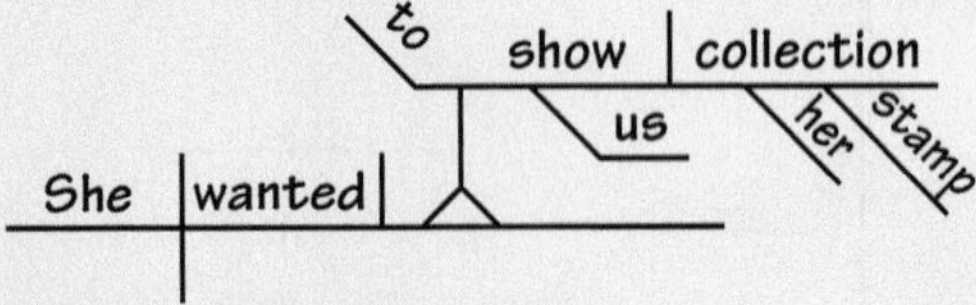

Infinitive Phrases With Subjects

When an infinitive phrase has a subject, place it on a horizontal line extending to the left from the diagram for the infinitive.

EXAMPLE: We asked *her* to stay.

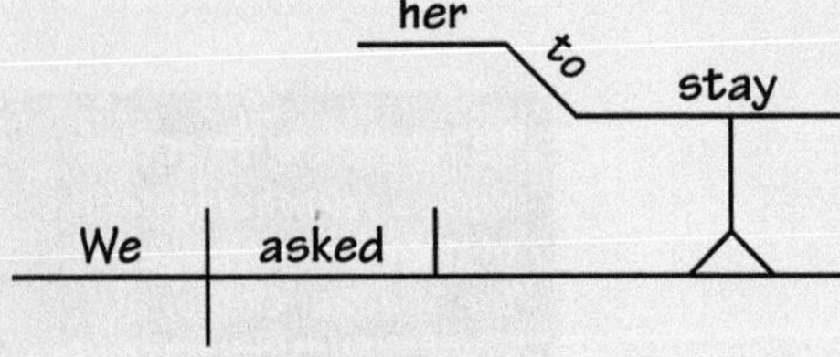

Infinitives as Modifiers

When an infinitive is used as an adjective or adverb, diagram it as you would a prepositional phrase.

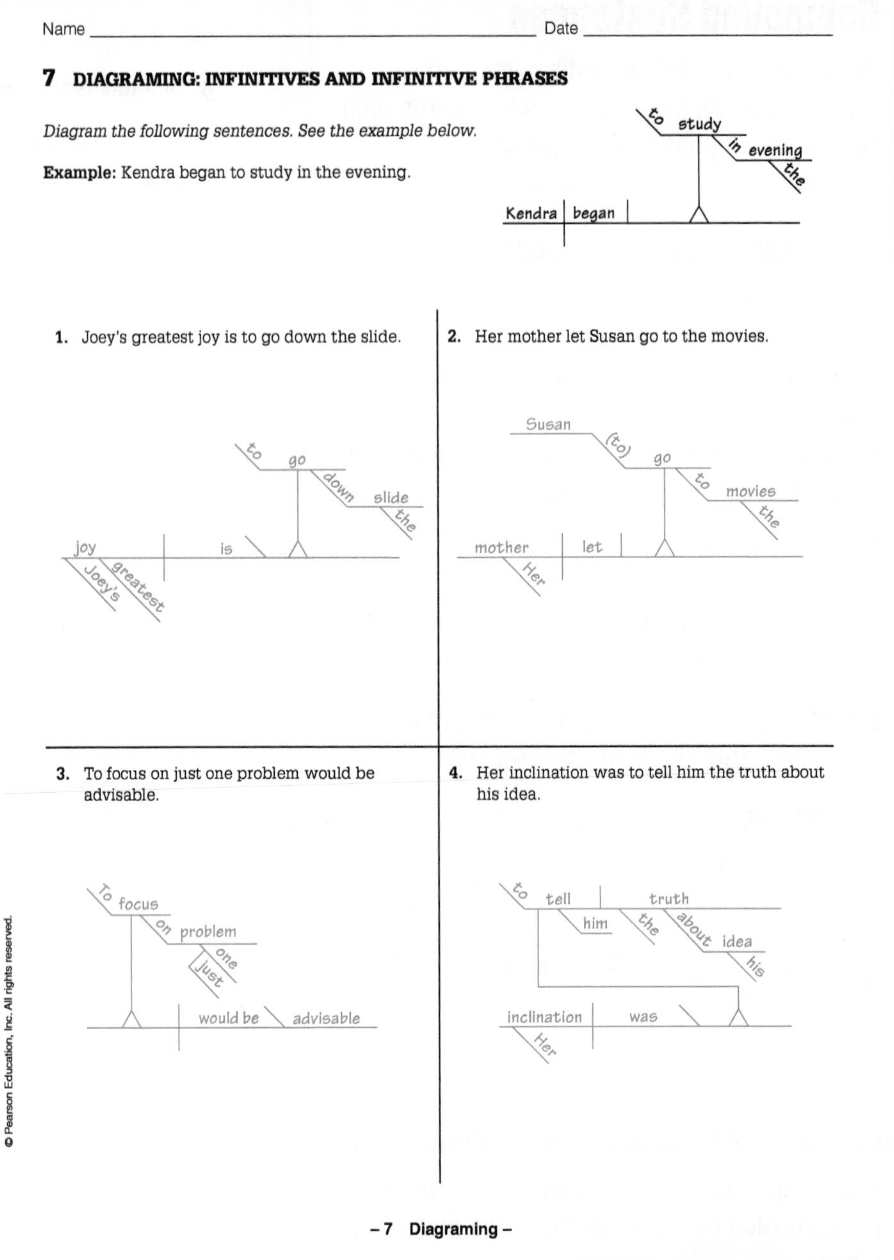

EXAMPLE: Beth was proud *to try.*

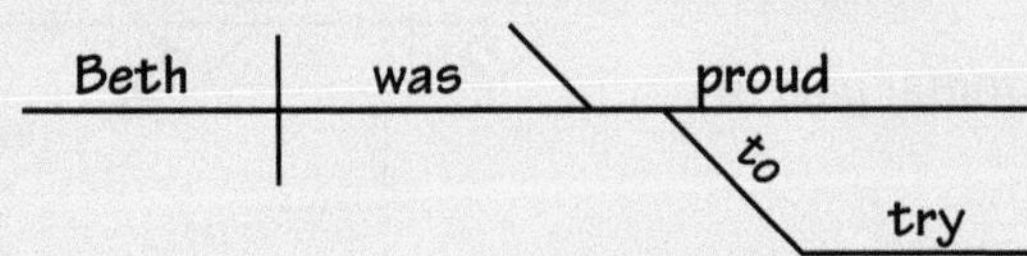

Note: When an infinitive does not include the word *to*, add that word to the diagram in parentheses.

Diagraming Practice
You can download copies of the Practice pages in the Teacher Center at www.phwritingcoach.com and distribute them to students.

Compound Sentences

Point out to students how diagraming makes clear the parallel nature of clauses in compound sentences. Emphasize these points.

Compound Sentences With Conjunctions

In a compound sentence joined by a conjunction, diagram each clause separately, one under the other.

- Join the two clauses with a stairstep dotted line between the two verbs.
- Write the conjunction on the horizontal part of the dotted line.
- Check to see whether the two clauses both have subjects and verbs.

EXAMPLE: A gentle breeze blew across the lake, and the raft floated inland.

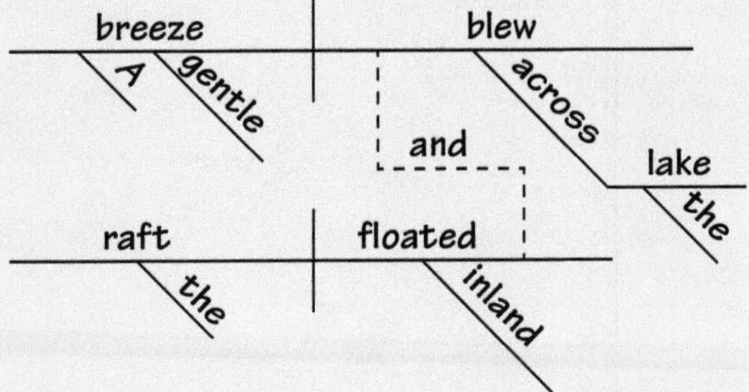

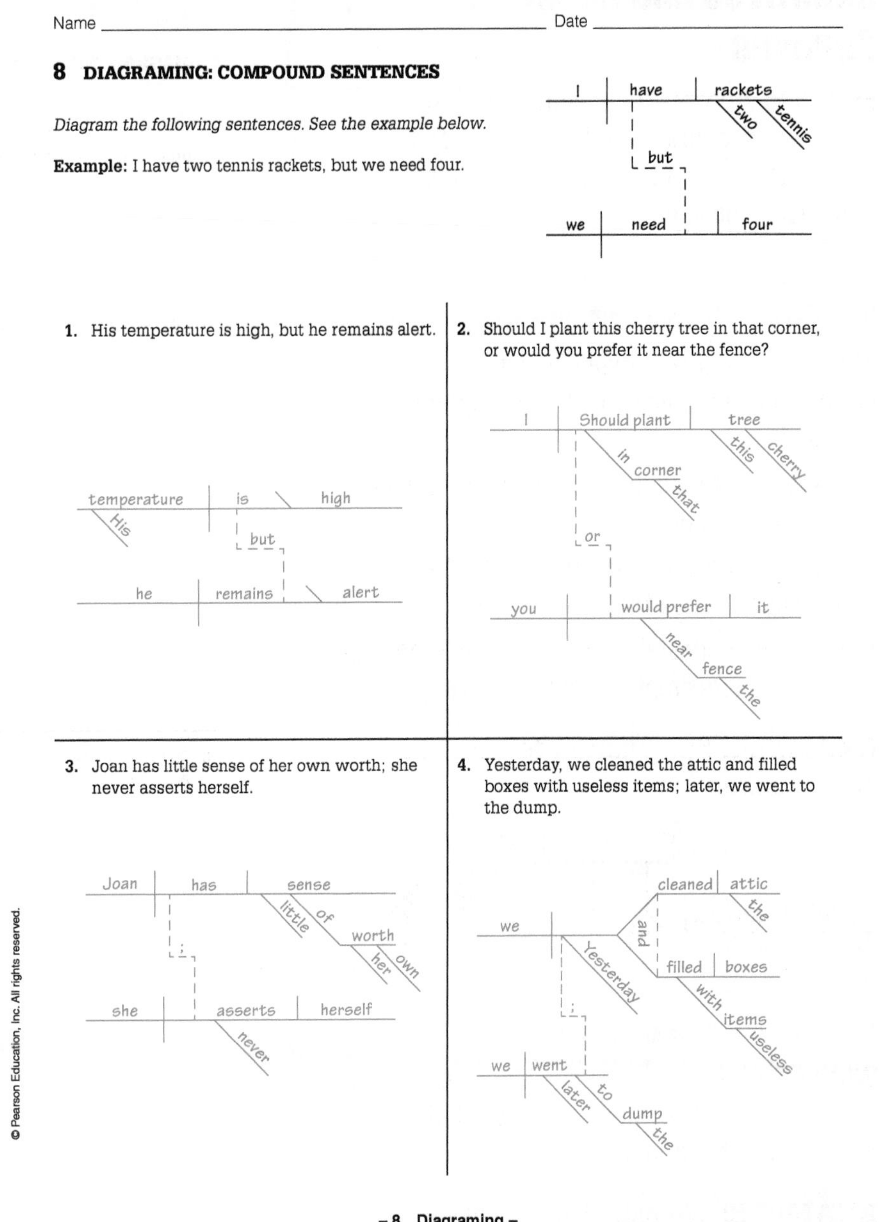

Name ______________________ Date ____________

8 DIAGRAMING: COMPOUND SENTENCES

Diagram the following sentences. See the example below.

Example: I have two tennis rackets, but we need four.

1. His temperature is high, but he remains alert.
2. Should I plant this cherry tree in that corner, or would you prefer it near the fence?
3. Joan has little sense of her own worth; she never asserts herself.
4. Yesterday, we cleaned the attic and filled boxes with useless items; later, we went to the dump.

– 8 Diagraming –

Compound Sentences With Semicolons

In a compound sentence joined by a semicolon, diagram each clause separately, one under the other.

- Join the two clauses with a stairstep dotted line between the two verbs.
- Write the semicolon on the horizontal part of the dotted line.

EXAMPLE: The book fell from the shelf; it was too close to the edge.

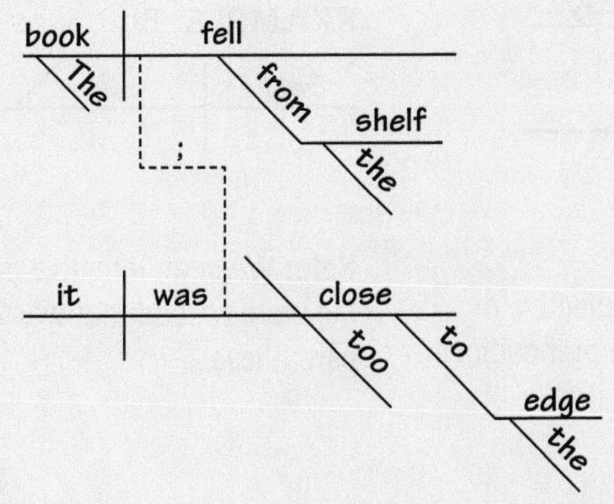

Diagraming Practice

You can download copies of the Practice pages in the Teacher Center at www.phwritingcoach.com and distribute them to students.

Complex Sentences

Explain to students how diagraming a complex sentence can help them see how a subordinate clause functions. Emphasize these points.

Adjective Clauses

When diagraming a complex sentence with an adjective clause, diagram the main clause first.

- Below it, diagram the adjective clause.
- Connect the clauses with a dotted line extending from the modified noun or pronoun to the relative pronoun in the adjective clause.

EXAMPLE: My friend *whom you met* just called.

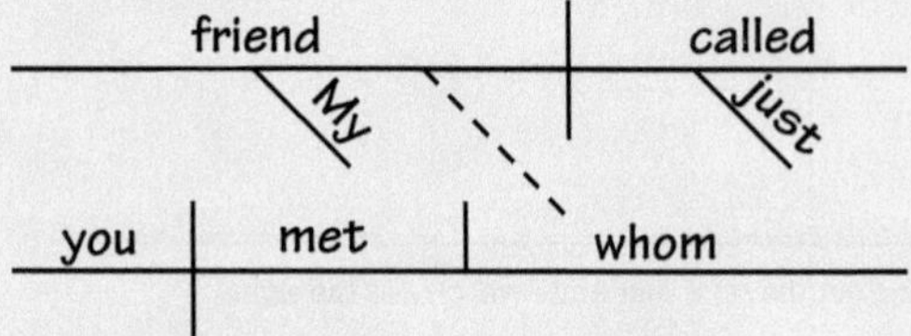

Adverb Clauses

When diagraming a complex sentence with an adverb clause, diagram the main clause first.

- Below it, diagram the adverb clause.
- Connect the clauses with a dotted line extending from the modified verb to the verb in the adverb clause.
- Write the subordinating conjunction that joins them on the dotted line.

EXAMPLE: She looks *before she leaps.*

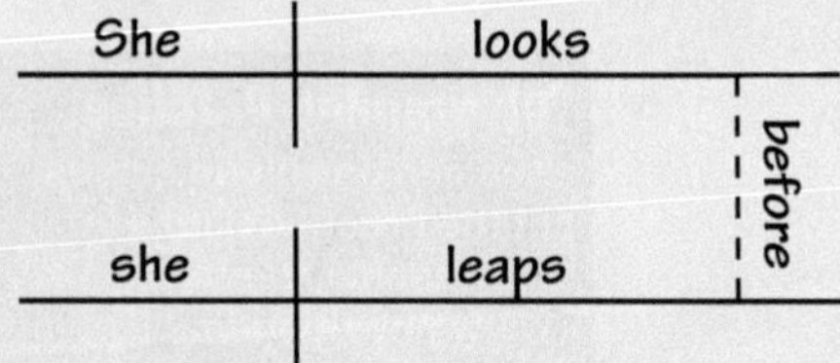

Noun Clauses

When diagraming a complex sentence with a noun clause, diagram the main clause first.

- Diagram the noun clause separately, on a pedestal that extends upward from the position the noun clause fills in the sentence.

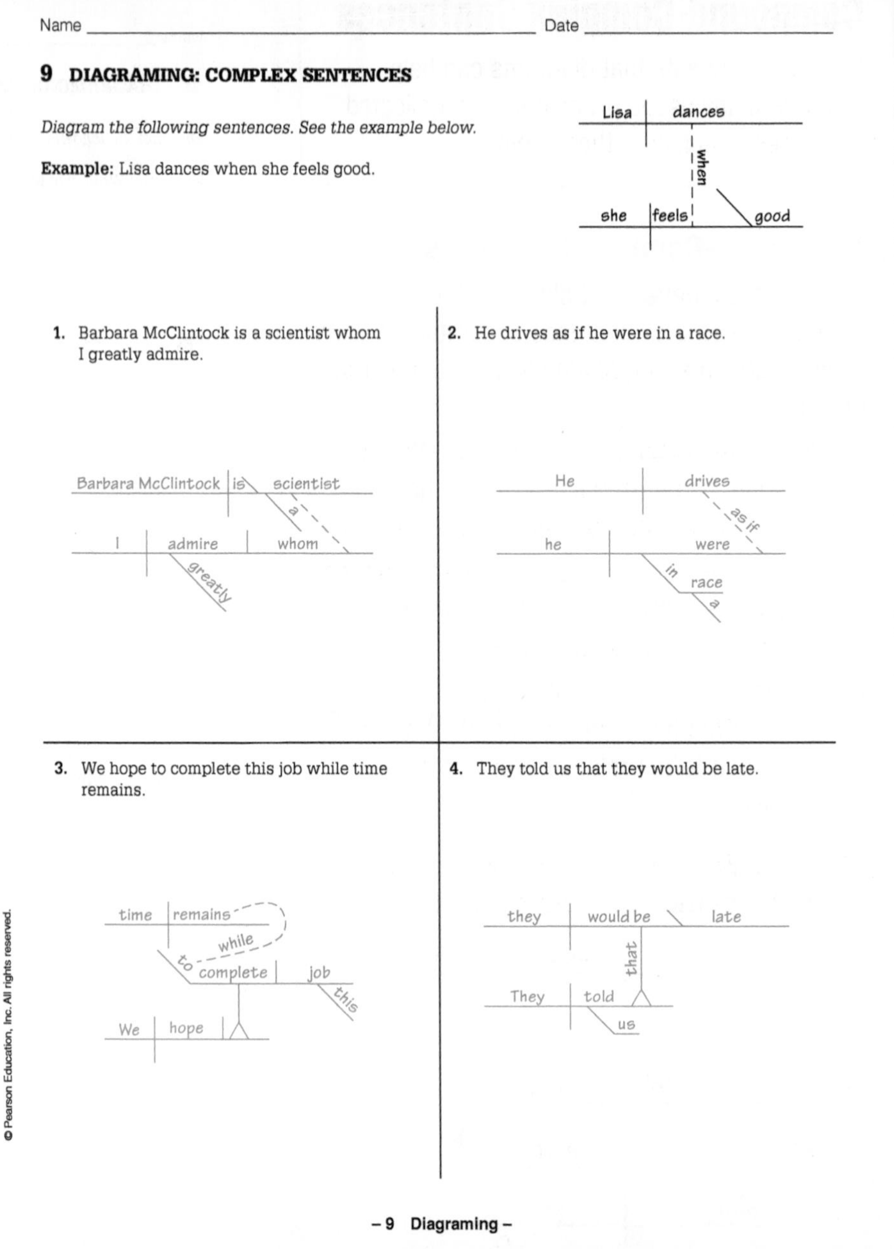
Name ______ Date ______

9 DIAGRAMING: COMPLEX SENTENCES

Diagram the following sentences. See the example below.

Example: Lisa dances when she feels good.

1. Barbara McClintock is a scientist whom I greatly admire.
2. He drives as if he were in a race.
3. We hope to complete this job while time remains.
4. They told us that they would be late.

– 9 Diagraming –

- The pedestal should meet the noun clause diagram at the verb.

EXAMPLE: *Whatever you decide* is fine.

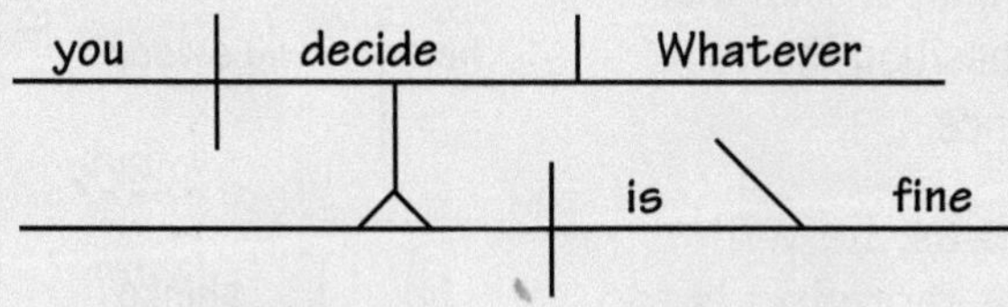

Diagraming Practice
You can download copies of the Practice pages in the Teacher Center at www.phwritingcoach.com and distribute them to students.

Compound-Complex Sentences

Explain to students that diagrams can help illustrate many usage problems in complicated sentences. Emphasize these points.

Compound-Complex Sentences

Diagram the independent clauses of a compound-complex sentence separately, leaving room to attach subordinate clauses to either and/or both.

- Connect the independent clauses with a stairstepped dotted line, placing the conjunction on the horizontal part of the line.
- Diagram the subordinate clauses and connect them at the appropriate places to their respective independent clauses.
- An adjective clause should be connected with a dotted line from the modified noun or pronoun to the relative pronoun in the adjective clause.

EXAMPLE: The musician whom we like plays the piano, and she sings, too.

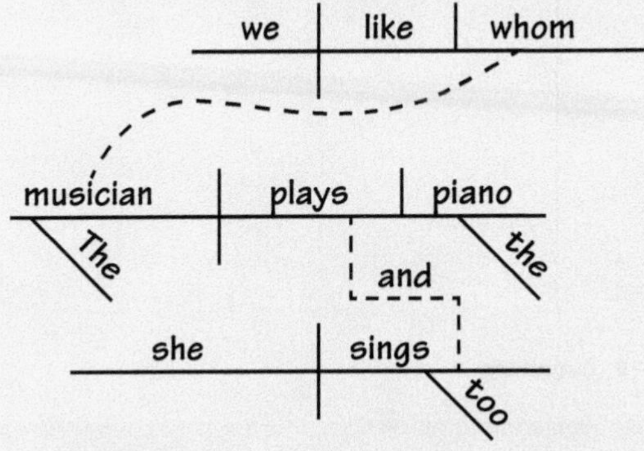

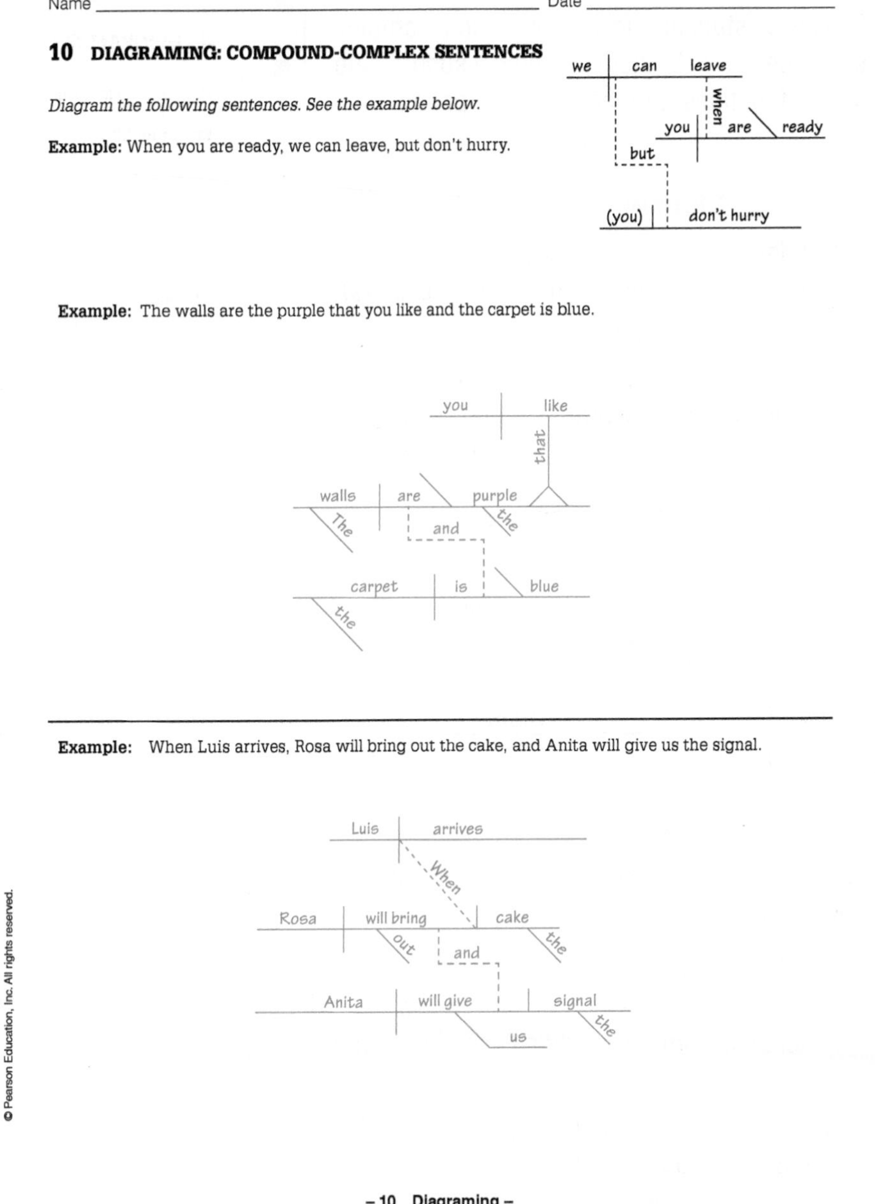
Name ______________________ Date ______________

10 DIAGRAMING: COMPOUND-COMPLEX SENTENCES

Diagram the following sentences. See the example below.

Example: When you are ready, we can leave, but don't hurry.

Example: The walls are the purple that you like and the carpet is blue.

Example: When Luis arrives, Rosa will bring out the cake, and Anita will give us the signal.

– 10 Diagraming –

- An adverb clause should be connected with a dotted line extending from the modified verb to the verb in the adverb clause.
- A noun clause should sit on a pedestal that extends upward from the position the noun would occupy in the sentence.

EXAMPLE: Before he leaves, he will sweep, but he thinks that mopping is too hard.

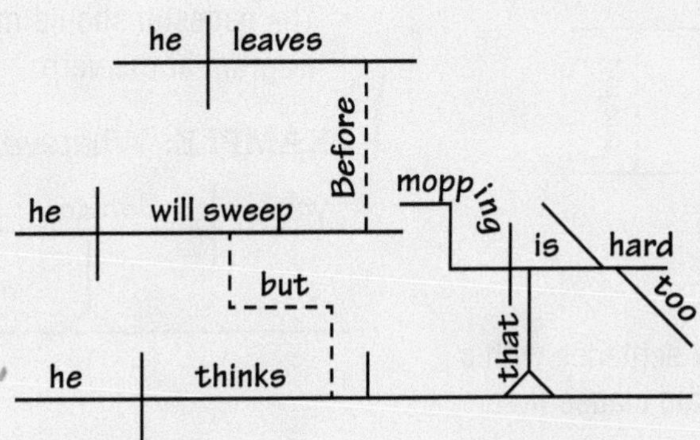

Diagraming Practice

You can download copies of the Practice pages in the Teacher Center at www.phwritingcoach.com and distribute them to students.

WELCOME TO Writing COACH

Seven Great Reasons to Learn to Write Well

> *"The bottom line is, students need to feel and experience what writing can do to enhance their lives and thinking."*
> —Jeff Anderson

1. Writing is hard, but hard is **rewarding**.
2. Writing helps you **sort things out**.
3. Writing helps you **persuade** others.
4. Writing makes you a **better reader**.
5. Writing makes you **smarter**.
6. Writing helps you get into and through **college**.
7. Writing **prepares you** for the world of work.

> *"Writing doesn't just allow you to write what you already know. Sometimes writing generates ideas you didn't know you had."*
> —Kelly Gallagher

Teacher's Edition

PRENTICE HALL WRITING COACH

Grade Seven

Acknowledgments appear on page TR53, which constitute an extension of this copyright page.

ISBN-13: 978-0-13-253721-6
ISBN-10: 0-13-253721-4
8 9 10 V092 14 13

Upper Saddle River, New Jersey | Boston, Massachusetts | Chandler, Arizona | Glenview, Illinois

S0-AAC-071